THE OXFORD HANDBOOK OF

POLITICAL

INSTITUTIONS

THE
OXFORD
HANDBOOKS
OF
POLITICAL
SCIENCE

GENERAL EDITOR: ROBERT E. GOODIN

The *Oxford Handbooks of Political Science* is a ten-volume set of reference books offering authoritative and engaging critical overviews of all the main branches of political science.

The series as a whole is under the General Editorship of Robert E. Goodin, with each volume being edited by a distinguished international group of specialists in their respective fields:

POLITICAL THEORY
John S. Dryzek, Bonnie Honig & Anne Phillips

POLITICAL INSTITUTIONS
R. A. W. Rhodes, Sarah A. Binder & Bert A. Rockman

POLITICAL BEHAVIOR
Russell J. Dalton & Hans-Dieter Klingemann

COMPARATIVE POLITICS
Carles Boix & Susan C. Stokes

LAW & POLITICS
Keith E. Whittington, R. Daniel Kelemen & Gregory A. Caldeira

PUBLIC POLICY
Michael Moran, Martin Rein & Robert E. Goodin

POLITICAL ECONOMY
Barry R. Weingast & Donald A. Wittman

INTERNATIONAL RELATIONS
Christian Reus-Smit & Duncan Snidal

CONTEXTUAL POLITICAL ANALYSIS
Robert E. Goodin & Charles Tilly

POLITICAL METHODOLOGY
Janet M. Box-Steffensmeier, Henry E. Brady & David Collier

This series aspires to shape the discipline, not just to report on it. Like the Goodin–Klingemann *New Handbook of Political Science* upon which the series builds, each of these volumes will combine critical commentaries on where the field has been together with positive suggestions as to where it ought to be heading.

THE OXFORD HANDBOOK OF

POLITICAL INSTITUTIONS

Edited by

R. A. W. RHODES

SARAH A. BINDER

and

BERT A. ROCKMAN

OXFORD
UNIVERSITY PRESS

OXFORD

UNIVERSITY PRESS

Great Clarendon Street, Oxford OX2 6DP

Oxford University Press is a department of the University of Oxford.
It furthers the University's objective of excellence in research, scholarship,
and education by publishing worldwide in

Oxford New York

Auckland Cape Town Dar es Salaam Hong Kong Karachi
Kuala Lumpur Madrid Melbourne Mexico City Nairobi
New Delhi Shanghai Taipei Toronto

With offices in

Argentina Austria Brazil Chile Czech Republic France Greece
Guatemala Hungary Italy Japan Poland Portugal Singapore
South Korea Switzerland Thailand Turkey Ukraine Vietnam

Oxford is a registered trade mark of Oxford University Press
in the UK and in certain other countries

Published in the United States
by Oxford University Press Inc., New York

British Library Cataloguing in Publication Data

Data available

Library of Congress Cataloging in Publication Data

Data available

Typeset by SPI Publisher Services, Pondicherry, India
Printed in Great Britain
on acid-free paper by
CPI Antony Rowe, Chippenham and Eastbourne

ISBN 978-0-19-927569-4 (Hbk.)   978-0-19-954846-0 (Pbk.)

5 7 9 10 8 6

Contents

PART IV OLD AND NEW

About the Contributors

John H. Aldrich is Pfizer-Pratt University Professor in the Department of Political Science, Duke University.

Christopher Ansell is Associate Professor, Department of Political Science in the University of California, Berkeley.

Samuel H. Beer is Eaton Professor of the Science of Government emeritus, Harvard University.

Sarah A. Binder is a Senior Fellow in Governance Studies at the Brookings Institution and Professor of Political Science at George Washington University.

Jean Blondel is Professorial Fellow at the European University Institute, Florence, and Visiting Professor, University of Siena.

Shaun Bowler is Professor and interim Chair in the Department of Political Science, University of California, Riverside.

John Braithwaite is an Australian Research Council Federation Fellow in RegNet, the Research School of Social Sciences, Australian National University.

Ian Budge is Professor in the Department of Government, University of Essex.

John M. Carey is Professor in the Department of Government, Dartmouth College.

Josep M. Colomer is Research Professor in Political Science in the Higher Council of Scientific Research, Barcelona.

John S. Duffield is Professor in the Department of Political Science, Georgia State University.

Ann Florini is Senior Fellow, Foreign Policy Studies, The Brookings Institution.

Brian Galligan is Professor in the Department of Political Science, University of Melbourne.

James L. Gibson is Sidney W. Souers Professor of Government at Washington University in St. Louis.

Jacob S. Hacker is Peter Strauss Family Associate Professor of Political Science at Yale University.

Jose Harris is Professor of Modern History, University of Oxford.

Colin Hay is Professor of Political Analysis in the Department of Politics and International Studies, University of Birmingham.

Hugh Heclo is Clarence J. Robinson Professor of Public Affairs, George Mason University.

Richard Higgott is Professor of Politics and International Studies at the University of Warwick.

Matthew Holden, Jr. is Emeritus Professor in the Department of Politics, University of Virginia.

William G. Howell is an Associate Professor in the Harris School of Public Policy, University of Chicago.

Bob Jessop is Director of the Institute for Advanced Studies and Professor of Sociology at Lancaster University.

Donald F. Kettl is Director of the Fels Institute of Government and Stanley I. Sheer Endowed Chair in the Social Sciences at University of Pennsylvania.

James G. March is Emeritus Professor in the Department of Political Science, Stanford University.

Lisa L. Martin is Clarence Dillon Professor of International Affairs in the Government Department at Harvard University.

Kevin T. McGuire is Associate Professor in the Department of Political Science, University of North Carolina.

Michael Moran is W. J. M. Mackenzie Professor of Government in the School of Social Sciences, University of Manchester.

Johan P. Olsen is Professor in the Centre for European Studies, University of Oslo.

R. A. W. Rhodes is Professor of Political Science and Head of Program in the Research School of Social Sciences, Australian National University.

Bert A. Rockman is Professor of Political Science and Head of the Department at Purdue University.

Elizabeth Sanders is Professor in the Department of Government, Cornell University.

Alberta M. Sbragia is Jean Monnet Chair ad personam in the Department of Political Science and the Director of the Center for West European Studies and of the European Union Center of Excellence at the University of Pittsburgh.

Peter M. Shane is Joseph S. Platt/Porter Wright Morris and Arthur Professor of Law at Ohio State University.

Kenneth A. Shepsle is George D. Markham Professor of Government in the Social Sciences at Harvard University.

Matthew Søberg Shugart is Professor of Political Science and at the Graduate School of International Relations and Pacific Studies, University of California, San Diego.

Gerry Stoker is Professor in the Institute of Political and Economic Governance, University of Manchester.

Jean-Claude Thoenig is Professor of Sociology at INSEAD, Fontainebleau, and Directeur de recherche at Dauphine Recherche en Management (DMSP), University of Paris Dauphine.

John Uhr is Reader in Politics in the Asia Pacific School of Economics and Government, Australian National University.

Eric M. Uslaner is Professor in the Department of Government and Politics, University of Maryland.

Klaus von Beyme is Professor Institutsprofil, zentrale Einrichtungen, University of Heidelberg.

Thomas Zittel is Project Director, European Political Systems and their Integration, at the University of Mannheim.

PREFACE

The study of political institutions is central to the identity of the discipline of political science. When political science emerged as a separate field, it emphasized the study of formal-legal arrangements as its exclusive subject matter (Eckstein 1963, 10–11). For a time, institutions "receded from the position they held in the earlier theories of political scientists" (March and Olsen 1984, 734). Recent decades have seen a neoinstitutionalist revival in political science—a return to the roots of political study. This *Handbook* begins in that most appropriate of places, an institutionalist call to arms by March and Olsen themselves.

While the older study of institutions is often caricatured today as having been largely descriptive and atheoretical, more nuanced accounts of the origins of the professionalized study of politics recall the profession's early focus on political institutions as prescriptive based on comparative, historical, and philosophical considerations (see especially Chapter 6). The older studies of institutions were rooted in law and legal institutions, focusing not only on how "the rules" channeled behavior, but also on how and why the rules came into being in the first place, and, above all, whether or not the rules worked on behalf of the common good.

As political science foreswore its historical, legal, and philosophical foundations, it borrowed deeply from economics, sociology, anthropology, and social and (later) cognitive psychology—the currents of knowledge that formed the bases of the "behavioral revolution" (Dahl 1961). That revolution followed from empirical observations in organizational and industrial sociology and psychology that revealed discrepancies between behaviors and organization forms noted in the 1930s (Roethlisberger and Dickson 1939). People frequently did not adhere to the rules, and informal groups of peers often became more influential than the formal organizational settings these individuals found themselves in. Moreover, the advent of the technology of mass surveys at mid-century allowed researchers to discover how remote average citizens were from the normative role of involved rationality toward and comprehension of the political environment (Campbell et al. 1960). The institutions of constitutional government seemed to operate at some distance from the cognitive limits of citizens.

The return of institutions to the mainstream of political studies arose, in part, from comparative behavioral research suggesting that differences in behavior more likely flowed from variations in political organization than in essential variability between citizenries of different political systems (Converse and Pierce 1986). But there also was a suspicion that less sophisticated versions of the behavioral revolution had run their course—that "opinions" were free-floating and unhinged from incentives to behave on them and that opinions were being treated as increasingly endogenous, that is, individuals had either more or less structure to their beliefs. What were the consequences, if any, of opinion? That question and the need to understand the nature of continuity and change were fundamental to the resurgence of institutions as a focus of analysis. Because institutions channeled the opportunities and incentives for behavior or induced powerful insulation to change, opinion distributions by themselves told us little.

Political scientists' return to the study of institutions has been explored and developed in many venues, most visibly perhaps by James March and Johan Olsen (1984, 1989, 1995). As has become clear by the numerous essays examining the institutional and historical turn of political science, no single orientation characterizes the vast scholarship that falls under the heading of neoinstitutionalism (see, among others, Hall and Taylor 1996; Pierson and Skocpol 2002). And as the chapters in Part II of this volume attest, the range of theoretical approaches underlying the contemporary study of institutions is remarkably diverse, let alone the range of empirical and methodological orientations.

Despite the incredible growth in institutional studies in recent decades, we lack a singular definition of an institution on which students of politics can find wide agreement. Indeed, if anything, we have witnessed an even greater diversity of ideas over the period as to what constitutes an institution. This range of ideas is consequential: it signals that there are also considerable differences of view about why and how we should study institutions, about the impact of institutions, and indeed about the extent to which institutions may be thought to be endogenous (independent or autonomous) or inextricably exogenous (woven into traditions, culture, norms, and preferences).

There is no doubt that institutions are said to do quite a lot. For example, they may be thought to embed history and political thought and to reflect, therefore, a set of traditions and practices, whether written or unwritten. Institutions thus can be interpreted as reflecting habits and norms, more likely to be evolved than to be created. But institutions also may be seen as architecture and as rules that determine opportunities and incentives for behavior, inclusion and exclusion of potential players, and structuring the relative ease or difficulty of inducing change, and the mechanisms through which change may be facilitated or denied.

Rational-choice institutionalists think of institutions as a system of rules and incentives. They remind us that this way of seeing institutions has traditions in law, but also in political engineering. The founders of American political science were themselves proponents of a science of political engineering to improve the common good—or at least they so justified these efforts in this way. Of course, the founders of the political science profession in the USA were themselves greatly affected by the temper of their times (the emergence of middle-class Progressivism as a political force) which emphasized the reform of political institutions as a way of weeding out both corruption and partisanship from politics—with the aim of reorganizing politics more in the form of administration. The institutional reform motif of American political science in the early twentieth century reflected not only the reform focus of its time but also the idiosyncrasies of its own political culture. Political institutions were largely seen as endogenous: rules, design, structures. It was plausible to imagine institutions in this particular way in a society that had developed a strong legalistic tradition based on written documents and that lacked a past struggle between aristocracy and commerce or a powerful working class mobilization. Thus, there was little history—or so it was perceived—to be embedded into American governing institutions other than through its colonial experience.

Defined as rules, design, and structures, institutions are a potential variable in the political process. In this view, rules that define institutions or that alter thresholds for participation in the institution are likely to be contested to the immediate political advantage of some set of actors over another. Institutions in this sense provide arenas for conflict, and efforts to alter them stimulate conflict inasmuch as they change the rules of the game in such a way as to alter the allocation of advantages and disadvantages. From this vantage point rules are never neutral, but are instead part of a struggle between challengers and holders of power.

Still, a more prevalent view of institutions as rules—derived from economic models of cooperation—suggests that institutions may be the product of agreements that are Pareto optimal—that is, one party is made better off, but no one is made worse off. Log rolls, reciprocities, mutual advantages also produce new institutional arrangements. And there is a reciprocal relationship here; that is, institutions of certain forms, particularly ones that fragment power and provide multiple veto points, are likely to induce log rolling, reciprocities, and mutual back scratching. Such conditions make coherent change or direction and central leadership less likely, all things equal, though hardly impossible.

Inevitably, institutions advantage some in the short term and disadvantage others, but the long run may be a different story. The same rules and structures may, over longer stretches of time, provide advantages or disadvantages to different interests, indeed even reversing which interests are advantaged or disadvantaged. The so-called filibuster rule of the US Senate, ironically the product of an effort to create greater institutional efficiencies by deterring tiny minorities from tying up the Senate indefinitely, clearly helps concerted and substantial minorities and frustrates majorities that are less than supermajorities. It had been used by conservatives to block liberals' civil rights agendas. Now it is being used by liberals to forestall the aims of conservatives. In this sense—what goes around comes around—institutions that strengthen the blocking power of minorities may be remarkably equitable, though perhaps only when viewed in historical, rather than immediate, terms.

Historical institutionalists see institutions as continuities. As they point out, institutions are meant to be preservative. Indeed, the emphasis on path dependence is another way of saying that the transaction costs of doing things differently is almost always prohibitively high, although dire conditions may reduce the marginal costs of change. But if institutions are about preservation, politics is about manipulation and leadership is about overturning constraints. Consequently, institutions are like dried cement. Cement can be uprooted when it has dried, but the effort to do so is substantial. It is easier to alter the substance before it hardens. Exiting leaders want to harden their preferences through institutions; new leaders often want to extirpate the past. The consequence is that institutions may be designed to fail. Given uncertainty about future political control, majorities may prefer to hedge their bets (Tsebelis 1990) or even prefer to design ineffective institutions than risk having their creations used against them (Moe 1990).

Institutions, of course, are constituted at many levels. They may be constitutional; they may be procedural; and they may be programmatic—for example, national health insurance or national pension systems. One should expect programs that have been durable and thus thought of as being institutionalized to be more responsive to exogenous shocks than changes at the constitutional level. But it is not always clear that this logic obtains in a general sense. Durable programs are partly a reflection of the real financial costs of altering them and the political costs of changing popular programs. Changing the social security system wholesale by privatizing it could be done in an authoritarian system under the Pinochet government in Chile, but it has proven to be much more complicated in democratic systems. The cumulative weight of past choices—which help to shape actors' preferences, routines, and expectations—plus the preferences of stable majorities inhibit large-scale or relatively rapid change.

Clearly, in any conception of institutions, the cost of change whether formal or non-formal and whether financial or organizational must be part of what an institution confers. Equally, the political costs of trying to disturb the status quo are far greater where the struggle involves many actors with diverse preferences rather than only a few with homogeneous preferences. So, any system that makes decision-making difficult tends toward the preservation of existing institutions. But none of this is absolute.

Sociological institutionalism sees institutions as norms and culture. It points to an alternative view, which suggests that institutions are almost wholly exogenous, by which they mean that the history and norms of a polity become embedded into institutions. We think of institutions in this perspective as exogenous, because it is hard to consider them as creations of ambitious political actors. Instead, institutions are viewed as independent entities that over time shape a polity by influencing actors' preferences, perceptions, and identities. Individuals are governed, as March and Olsen (1989, 1995) would say, by the "logic of appropriateness"—meaning that institutions can be considered as embedding rules and routines that define what constitutes appropriate action. Rather than acting out of overt rational self-interest, individuals are said to behave according to their sense of duty and obligation as structured by prevailing rules and routines. However, when preferences are sufficiently homogeneous, it may be in one's self-interest to get along rather than be seen as a deviant.

This view of institutions has implications for the character and pace of institutional change. We might say that there is a superstability to institutions because they are woven into an historical and normative fabric. In other words, there are no obvious means of altering institutions, short of significant social, cultural, or political change. The important implication is that institutions evolve in a rather indeterminate way, resembling if anything geological shifts and drift, rather than conscious design. This geological view recalls the perspective of institutional scholars of the early twentieth century, such as Edward Sait, who viewed institutions as "coral reefs" that grew by "slow accretions" (Sait 1938). The historical approach underlying this view of institutions as norms and culture should thus come as no surprise.

This brief survey of the multiple conceptions of institutions provides an apt launching point for this volume on political institutions. It may be that this book raises more questions than it answers about the origins, evolution, and impact of institutions on politics and policy alike. Our hunch is that such questions and controversies will remain central to the agendas of political scientists for some time to come. Where do institutions come from? How have they evolved and often hardened over time? How difficult or easy are the rules governing their change? What are the consequences of institutions for political behavior and policy outcomes? Can institutions resist exogenously induced pressures for change including leaders' efforts to overturn the past? These questions are at the heart of the chapters that follow—questions that we trust will continue to energize research on politics in the years to come.

Starting with a statement from the founders of the "new institutionalism," Part II builds on various attempts (Hall 1996; Lowndes 1996; Peters 1999) to characterize the diversity of institutional approaches. It surveys several theoretical approaches, including normative institutionalism, rational choice institutionalism, historical institutionalism, international institutionalism, constructed institutionalism, and network institutionalism, as well as older traditions. Part III covers the traditional concerns of political science with constitutions, federalism, executives, legislatures, courts, parties, etc. These reflect the broadening concerns of the field in recent years with chapters on international institutions and the institutions of state and civil society. Furthermore, these reflect more recent interest in theory and the constructed nature of institutions. Finally, Part IV provides four reflections on "the state of the art" by some of the master practitioners of the field.

In his *Pensées*, Joseph Joubert (1842) advised, "One of the surest ways of killing a tree is to lay bare its roots. It is the same with institutions. We must not be too ready to disinter the origins of those we wish to preserve." We disinter institutions, not to kill them, but rather to learn from them as repositories of our collective experience.

For any book on this scale, the editors need help. Rod Rhodes would like to thank Bob Goodin and Mary Hapel. Sarah Binder would like to thank Alan Murphy for research assistance. All the editors would like to thank the contributors for their patience and cooperation when asked to revise their chapters.

REFERENCES

CAMPBELL, A., CONVERSE, P. E., MILLER, W. A., and STOKES, D. 1960. *The American Voter.* New York: Wiley.

CONVERSE, P. E. and PIERCE, R. 1986. *Political Representation in France.* Cambridge, Mass.: Harvard University Press.

DAHL, R. A. 1961. The behavioral approach in political science: epitaph for a monument to a successful protest. *American Political Science Review,* 55: 763–72.

ECKSTEIN, H. 1963. A perspective on comparative politics: past and present. Pp. 3–32 in *Comparative Politics: A Reader,* ed. H. Eckstein and D. E. Apter. Glencoe, Ill.: Free Press.

HALL, P. and TAYLOR, R. 1996. Political science and the three institutionalisms. *Political Studies,* 44: 936–57.

JOUBERT, J. 1842/1928. *Pensées and Letters,* trans. H. P. Collins. New York: Brenatno's.

LOWNDES, V. 1996. Varieties of new institutionalism: a critical appraisal. *Public Administration,* 74: 181–97.

MARCH, J. G. and OLSEN, J. P. 1984. The new institutionalism: organizational factors in political life. *American Political Science Review,* 78: 734–49.

—— —— 1989. *Rediscovering Institutions.* New York: Free Press.

—— —— 1995. *Democratic Governance.* New York: Free Press.

MOE, T. 1990. Political institutions: the neglected side of the story. *Journal of Law, Economics, and Organization,* 6: 213–53.

PETERS, B. G. 1999. *Institutional Theory in Political Science: The "New Institutionalism."* London: Pinter.

PIERSON, P. and SKOCPOL, T. 2002. Historical institutionalism in contemporary political science. Pp. 693–721 in *Political Science: State of the Discipline,* ed. H. Milner and I. Katznelson. New York: Norton.

ROETHLISBERGER, F. J. and DICKSON, W. J. 1939. *Management and the Worker.* Cambridge, Mass.: Harvard University Press.

SAIT, E. M. 1938. *Political Institutions: A Preface.* New York: Appleton-Century.

TSEBELIS, G. 1990. *Nested Games.* Berkeley: University of California Press.

PART I

INTRODUCTION

CHAPTER 1

ELABORATING THE "NEW INSTITUTIONALISM"

JAMES G. MARCH *Stanford*

JOHAN P. OLSEN *University of Oslo*

1 AN INSTITUTIONAL PERSPECTIVE

An institution is a relatively enduring collection of rules and organized practices, embedded in structures of meaning and resources that are relatively invariant in the face of turnover of individuals and relatively resilient to the idiosyncratic preferences and expectations of individuals and changing external circumstances (March and Olsen 1989, 1995). There are constitutive rules and practices prescribing appropriate behavior for specific actors in specific situations. There are structures of meaning, embedded in identities and belongings: common purposes and accounts that give direction and meaning to behavior, and explain, justify, and legitimate behavioral codes. There are structures of resources that create capabilities for acting. Institutions empower and constrain actors differently and make them more or less capable of acting according to prescriptive rules of appropriateness. Institutions are also reinforced by third parties in enforcing rules and sanctioning non-compliance.*

* We thank Robert E. Goodin for constructive comments.

While the concept of institution is central to much political analysis, there is wide diversity within and across disciplines in what kinds of rules and relations are construed as "institutions" (Goodin 1996, 20). Moreover, approaches to political institutions differ when it comes to how they understand (a) the nature of institutions, as the organized setting within which modern political actors most typically act; (b) the processes that translate structures and rules into political impacts; and (c) the processes that translate human behavior into structures and rules and establish, sustain, transform, or eliminate institutions.

Institutionalism, as that term is used here, connotes a general approach to the study of political institutions, a set of theoretical ideas and hypotheses concerning the relations between institutional characteristics and political agency, performance, and change. Institutionalism emphasizes the endogenous nature and social construction of political institutions. Institutions are not simply equilibrium contracts among self-seeking, calculating individual actors or arenas for contending social forces. They are collections of structures, rules, and standard operating procedures that have a partly autonomous role in political life.

Institutionalism comes in many flavors, but they are all perspectives for understanding and improving political systems. They supplement and compete with two other broad interpretations of politics. The first alternative is a *rational actor* perspective which sees political life as organized by exchange among calculating, self-interested actors. The second alternative is a *cultural community* perspective which sees political life as organized by shared values and world-views in a community of common culture, experience, and vision. The three perspectives— institutional, rational actors, and cultural community—are not exclusive. Most political systems can be interpreted as functioning through a mix of organizing principles. Nor are the perspectives always easy to distinguish. True believers in any one of the three can reduce each of the other two to the status of a "special case" of their preferred alternative. Pragmatically, however, the three perspectives are different. They focus attention on different aspects of political life, on different explanatory factors, and on different strategies for improving political systems.

The key distinctions are the extent to which a perspective views the rules and identities defined within political institutions as epiphenomena that mirror environmental circumstances or predetermined individual preferences and initial resources; and the extent to which a perspective pictures rules and identities as reproduced with some reliability that is, at least in part, independent of environmental stability or change.

Within an institutional perspective, a core assumption is that institutions create elements of order and predictability. They fashion, enable, and constrain political actors as they act within a logic of appropriate action. Institutions are carriers of identities and roles and they are markers of a polity's character, history, and visions. They provide bonds that tie citizens together in spite of the many things that divide them. They also impact institutional change, and create elements of "historical inefficiency".

Another core assumption is that the translation of structures into political action and action into institutional continuity and change, are generated by comprehensible and routine processes. These processes produce recurring modes of action and organizational patterns. A challenge for students of institutions is to explain how such processes are stabilized or destabilized, and which factors sustain or interrupt ongoing processes.

To sketch an institutional approach, this chapter elaborates ideas presented over twenty years ago in "The New Institutionalism: Organizational Factors in Political Life" (March and Olsen 1984). The intent of the article was to suggest some theoretical ideas that might shed light on particular aspects of the role of institutions in political life. The aspiration was not to present a full-blown theory of political institutions, and no such theory is currently available. The ideas have been challenged and elaborated over the last twenty years,[1] and we continue the elaboration, without making an effort to replace more comprehensive reviews of the different institutionalisms, their comparative advantages, and the controversies in the field.[2]

2 THEORIZING POLITICAL INSTITUTIONS

The status of institutionalism in political science has changed dramatically over the last fifty years—from an invective to the claim that "we are all institutionalists now" (Pierson and Skocpol 2002, 706). The behavioral revolution represented an attack upon a tradition where government and politics were primarily understood in formal-legal institutional terms. The focus on formal government institutions, constitutional issues, and public law was seen as "unpalatably formalistic and old-fashioned" (Drewry 1996, 191), and a standard complaint was that this approach was "relatively insensitive to the nonpolitical determinants of political behavior and hence to the nonpolitical bases of governmental institutions" (Macridis 1963, 47). The aspiration was to penetrate the formal surface of governmental

---

[1] March and Olsen 1984, 1986, 1989, 1995, 1998, 2006. Some have categorized this approach as "normative" institutionalism (Lowndes 1996, 2002; Peters 1999; Thoenig 2003). "Normative" then refers to a concern with norms and values as explanatory variables, and not to normative theory in the sense of promoting particular norms (Lowndes 2002, 95).

[2] Goodin 1996; Peters 1996, 1999; Rothstein 1996; Thelen 1999; Pierson and Skocpol 2002; Weingast 2002; Thoenig 2003.

institutions and describe and explain how politics "really works" (Eulau and March 1969, 16).

Theorizing political institutions, Polsby, for example, made a distinction between seeing a legislature as an "arena" and as "transformative." The distinction reflected variation in the significance of the legislature; its independence from outside influence and its capacity to mould and transform proposals from whatever source into decisions. In an arena-legislature, external forces were decisive; and one did not need to know anything about the internal characteristics of the legislature in order to account for processes and outcomes. In a transformative-legislature, internal structural factors were decisive. Polsby also suggested factors that made it more or less likely that a legislature would end up as an arena, or as a transformative institution (Polsby 1975, 281, 291–2).

More generally, students of politics have observed a great diversity of organized settings, collectivities, and social relationships within which political actors have operated. In modern society the polity is a configuration of many formally organized institutions that define the context within which politics and governance take place. Those configurations vary substantially; and although there are dissenters from the proposition, most political scientists probably would grant that the variation in institutions accounts for at least some of the observed variation in political processes and outcomes. For several centuries, the most important setting has been the territorial state; and political science has attended to concrete political institutions, such as the legislature, executive, bureaucracy, judiciary, and the electoral system.

Our 1984 article invited a reappraisal of how political institutions could be conceptualized, to what degree they have independent and endurable implications, the kinds of political phenomena they impact, and how institutions emerge, are maintained, and change:

First, we argued for the relative autonomy and independent effects of political institutions and for the importance of their organizational properties. We argued against understanding politics solely as reflections of society (contextualism) or as the macro aggregate consequences of individual actors (reductionism).

Second, we claimed that politics was organized around the interpretation of life and the development of meaning, purpose, and direction, and not only around policy-making and the allocation of resources (instrumentalism).

Third, we took an interest in the ways in which institutionalized rules, norms, and standard operating procedures impacted political behavior, and argued against seeing political action solely as the result of calculation and self-interested behavior (utilitarianism).

Fourth, we held that history is "inefficient" and criticized standard equilibrium models assuming that institutions reach a unique form conditional on current circumstances and thus independent of their historical path (functionalism).

In this view, a political order is created by a collection of institutions that fit more or less into a coherent system. The size of the sector of institutionalized activity changes over time and institutions are structured according to different principles (Berger and Luckmann 1967; Eisenstadt 1965). The varying scopes and modes of institutionalization affect what collectivities are *motivated* to do and what they are *able to do*. Political actors organize themselves and act in accordance with rules and practices which are socially constructed, publicly known, anticipated, and accepted. By virtue of these rules and practices, political institutions define basic rights and duties, shape or regulate how advantages, burdens, and life-chances are allocated in society, and create authority to settle issues and resolve conflicts.

Institutions give order to social relations, reduce flexibility and variability in behavior, and restrict the possibilities of a one-sided pursuit of self-interest or drives (Weber 1978, 40–3). The basic logic of action is rule following—prescriptions based on a logic of appropriateness and a sense of rights and obligations derived from an identity and membership in a political community and the ethos, practices, and expectations of its institutions.[3] Rules are followed because they are seen as natural, rightful, expected, and legitimate. Members of an institution are expected to obey, and be the guardians of, its constitutive principles and standards (March and Olsen 1989, 2006).

Institutions are not static; and institutionalization is not an inevitable process; nor is it unidirectional, monotonic, or irreversible (Weaver and Rockman 1993). In general, however, because institutions are defended by insiders and validated by outsiders, and because their histories are encoded into rules and routines, their internal structures and rules cannot be changed arbitrarily (March and Olsen 1989; Offe 2001). The changes that occur are more likely to reflect local adaptation to local experience and thus be both relatively myopic and meandering, rather than optimizing, as well as "inefficient," in the sense of not reaching a uniquely optimal arrangement (March 1981). Even when history is relatively "efficient," the rate of adaptation is likely to be inconsistent with the rate of change in the environment to which the institution is adapting.

3 INSTITUTIONAL IMPACTS ON POLITICAL ACTORS AND OUTCOMES

Although it is argued that much of the "established wisdom" about the effects of political institutions is very fragile (Rothstein 1996, 155), scholars who deal with

---

[3] "Appropriateness" refers to a specific culture. There is no assumption about normative superiority. A logic of appropriateness may produce truth telling, fairness, honesty, trust, and generosity, but also blood feuds, vendettas, and ethnic conflicts in different cultures (March and Olsen 2006).

political institutions are generally less concerned with *whether* institutions matter, than to what extent, in what respects, through what processes, under what conditions, and why institutions make a difference (Weaver and Rockman 1993; Egeberg 2003, 2004; Orren and Skowronek 2004). In this tradition, institutions are imagined to organize the polity and to have an ordering effect on how authority and power is constituted, exercised, legitimated, controlled, and redistributed. They affect how political actors are enabled or constrained and the governing capacities of a political system. Institutions simplify political life by ensuring that some things are taken as given. Institutions provide codes of appropriate behavior, affective ties, and a belief in a legitimate order. Rules and practices specify what is normal, what must be expected, what can be relied upon, and what makes sense in the community; that is, what a normal, reasonable, and responsible (yet fallible) citizen, elected representative, administrator, or judge, can be expected to do in various situations.

It is commonplace to observe that the causal relation between institutional arrangements and substantive policy is complex. Usually, causal chains are indirect, long, and contingent (Weaver and Rockman 1993), so that political institutions can be expected to constrain and enable outcomes without being the immediate and direct cause of public policy. The same arrangement can have quite different consequences under different conditions. The disentanglement of institutional effects is particularly difficult in multilevel and multicentered institutional settings, characterized by interactions among multiple autonomous processes (Orren and Skowronek 2004; March and Olsen 2006).

One cluster of speculations about the effects of institutions focuses on rules and routines. The basic building blocks of institutions are rules, and rules are connected and sustained through identities, through senses of membership in groups and recognition of roles. Rules and repertoires of practices embody historical experience and stabilize norms, expectations, and resources; they provide explanations and justifications for rules and standard ways of doing things (March and Olsen 1989, 1995). Subject to available resources and capabilities, rules regulate organizational action. That regulation, however, is shaped by constructive interpretations embedded in a history of language, experience, memory, and trust (Dworkin 1986; March and Olsen 1989). The openness in interpretation means that while institutions structure politics and governance and create a certain "bias" (Schattschneider 1960), they ordinarily do not determine political behavior or outcomes in detail. Individuals may, and may not, know what rules there are and what they prescribe for specific actors in specific situations. There may be competing rules and competing interpretations of rules and situations. Indeed, the legitimacy of democratic political institutions is partly based on the expectation that they will provide open-ended processes without deterministic outcomes (Pitkin 1967).

A central theme of organization theory is that identification and habituation are fundamental mechanisms in shaping behavior. In institutionalized worlds actors are socialized into culturally defined purposes to be sought, as well as modes of appropriate procedures for pursuing the purposes (Merton 1938, 676). Members of an organization tend to become imbued not only with their identities as belonging to the organization but also with the various identities associated with different roles in the organization. Because they define themselves in terms of those identities, they act to fulfill them rather than by calculating expected consequences (Simon 1965, 115, 136).

Observing that political actors sometimes deviate from what rules prescribe, institutional scholars have distinguished between an institutional rule and its behavioral realization in a particular instance (Apter 1991). They have sought an improved understanding of the types of humans selected and formed by different types of institutions and processes, how and why different institutions achieve normative reliability (Kratochwil 1984), and under what institutional conditions political actors are likely to be motivated and capable of complying with codes of appropriate behavior. The coexistence of the logic of appropriateness and the logic of consequences, for example, also raises questions about how the two interact, which factors determine the salience of different logics, and the institutional conditions under which each logic is likely to dominate.[4]

With whom one identifies is affected by factors such as how activities are subdivided in an organization, which positions individuals have and their responsibilities. It makes a difference how interaction, attention, experience, and memory are organized, the degree to which goals are shared, and the number of individual needs satisfied by the organization. Identification is also affected by tenure and turnover, the ratio of veterans to newcomers, opportunities for promotion and average time between promotions, job offers from outside, external belongings, and the prestige of different groups (March and Simon 1958; Lægreid and Olsen 1984).

Strong identification with a specific organization, institution, or role can threaten the coherence of the larger system. It has, in particular, been asked to what degree political order is achievable in multicultural societies where it is normatively problematic and probably impossible to create common identities through the traditional nation-building techniques (Weber 1977). For example, in the European Union, national identities are dominant. Identities are, nevertheless, increasingly influenced by issues and networks that cross national boundaries and there is no single center with control over education, socialization, and indoctrination (Herrmann, Risse, and Brewer 2004; Checkel 2005). The vision of "constitutional patriotism" reflects a belief in the forming capacity of shared institutions and that political participation will fashion a post-national civic

---

[4] March and Olsen 1998, 2006; Fehr and Gächter 1998; Isaac, Mathieu, and Zajac 1991; Olsen 2001, 2005.

European identity (Habermas 1994). Still, it is difficult to balance the development of common political institutions and the protection of cultural diversity. It is argued that the EU will face deadlock if governance aims at cultural homogeneity and that the EU needs institutions that protect cultural diversity as a foundation for political unity and collective identity, without excluding the possibility of transforming current identities (Kraus 2004).

Over the last few years, students of political institutions have learned more about the potential and the limitations of institutional impacts on policy and political actors. More is known about the processes through which individuals are transformed into office holders and rule followers with an ethos of self-discipline, impartiality, and integrity; into self-interested, utility maximizing actors; or into cooperating actors oriented towards the policy networks they participate in. More is also known about the processes through which senses of civic identities and roles are learned, lost, and redefined (March and Olsen 1995; Olsen 2005). Still, accomplishments are dwarfed by the number of unanswered questions about the processes that translate structures and rules into political impacts and the factors that impinge upon them under different conditions. This is also true for how institutional order impacts the dynamics of institutional change.

These interests in describing the effects of institutions are supplemented by interests in designing them, particularly in designing them for democratic political systems. The more difficult it is to specify or follow stable rules, the more democracies must rely on institutions that encourage collective interpretation through social processes of interaction, deliberation, and reasoning. Political debates and struggles then connect institutional principles and practices and relate them to the larger issues, how society can and ought to be organized and governed. Doing so, they fashion and refashion collective identities and defining features of the polity—its long-term normative commitments and causal beliefs, its concepts of the common good, justice, and reason, and its organizing principles and power relations.

Legitimacy depends not only on showing that actions accomplish appropriate objectives, but also that actors behave in accordance with legitimate procedures ingrained in a culture (Meyer and Rowan 1977; March and Olsen 1986). There is, furthermore, no perfect positive correlation between political effectiveness and normative validity. The legitimacy of structures, processes, and substantive efficiency do not necessarily coincide. There are illegitimate but technically efficient means, as well as legitimate but inefficient means (Merton 1938). In this perspective, institutions and forms of government are assessed partly according to their ability to foster the virtue and intelligence of the community. That is, how they impact citizens' identities, character, and preferences—the kind of person they are and want to be (Mill 1962, 30–5; Rawls 1993, 269).

4 INSTITUTIONAL ORDER AND CHANGE

The dynamics of institutional change include elements of design, competitive selection, and the accidents of external shocks (Goodin 1996, 24–5). Rules, routines, norms, and identities are both instruments of stability and arenas of change. Change is a constant feature of institutions and existing arrangements impact how institutions emerge and how they are reproduced and changed. Institutional arrangements can prescribe and proscribe, speed up and delay change; and a key to understanding the dynamics of change is a clarification of the role of institutions within standard processes of change.

Most contemporary theories assume that the mix of rules, routines, norms, and identities that describe institutions change over time in response to historical experience. The changes are neither instantaneous nor reliably desirable in the sense of moving the system closer to some optimum. As a result, assumptions of historical efficiency cannot be sustained (March and Olsen 1989; March 1994). By "historical efficiency" we mean the idea that institutions become in some sense "better" adapted to their environments and quickly achieve a uniquely optimum solution to the problem of surviving and thriving. The matching of institutions, behaviors, and contexts takes time and has multiple, path-dependent equilibria. Adaptation is less automatic, less continuous, and less precise than assumed by standard equilibrium models and it does not necessarily improve efficiency and survival.

The processes of change that have been considered in the literature are primarily processes of single-actor design (in which single individual actors or collectivities that act as single actors specify designs in an effort to achieve some fairly well-specified objectives), conflict design (in which multiple actors pursue conflicting objectives and create designs that reflect the outcomes of political trading and power), learning (in which actors adapt designs as a result of feedback from experience or by borrowing from others), or competitive selection (in which unvarying rules and the other elements of institutions compete for survival and reproduction so that the mix of rules changes over time).

Each of these is better understood theoretically than it is empirically. Institutions have shown considerable robustness even when facing radical social, economic, technical, and cultural change. It has often been assumed that the environment has a limited ability to select and eliminate political institutions and it has, for example, been asked whether governmental institutions are immortal (Kaufman 1976). In democracies political debate and competition has been assigned importance as sources of change. Yet, institutions seem sometimes to encourage and sometimes to obstruct reflection, criticism, and opposition. Even party structures in competitive systems can become "frozen" (Lipset and Rokkan 1967).

The ideal that citizens and their representatives should be able to design political institutions at will, making governing through organizing and reorganizing institutions an important aspect of political agency, has been prominent in both democratic ideology and the literature. Nevertheless, historically the role of deliberate design, and the conditions under which political actors can get beyond existing structures, have been questioned (Hamilton, Jay, and Madison 1787 [1964, 1]; Mill 1861 [1962, 1]). In spite of accounts of the role of heroic founders and constitutional moments, modern democracies also seem to have limited capacity for institutional design and reform and in particular for achieving intended effects of reorganizations (March and Olsen 1983; Goodin 1996; Offe 2001). Constitutions limit the *legitimacy* of design. The *need* for major intervention may be modest because routine processes of learning and adaptation work fairly well and the *capability* may be constrained by inadequate causal understanding, authority, and power (Olsen 1997).

The standard model of punctuated equilibrium assumes discontinuous change. Long periods of institutional continuity, where institutions are reproduced, are assumed to be interrupted only at critical junctures of radical change, where political agency (re)fashions institutional structures. In this view, institutions are the legacy of path dependencies, including political compromises and victories.[5] Massive failure is an important condition for change.

The assumption, that institutional structures persist unless there are external shocks, underestimates both intra- and interinstitutional dynamics and sources of change. Usually, there is an internal aspiration level pressure for change caused by enduring gaps between institutional ideals and institutional practices (Broderick 1970). Change can also be rule-governed, institutionalized in specific units or sub-units, or be generated by the routine interpretation and implementation of rules. Typically, an institution can be threatened by realities that are meaningless in terms of the normative and causal beliefs on which it is founded, and efforts to reduce inconsistency and generate a coherent interpretation are a possible source of change (Berger and Luckmann 1967, 103). As people gradually get or lose faith in institutional arrangements, there are routine switches between institutional repertoires of standard operating procedures and structures. Reallocation of resources also impacts the capability to follow and enforce different rules and therefore the relative significance of alternative structures (March and Olsen 1995).

Thus, a focus on "critical junctures" may underestimate how incremental steps can produce transformative results (Streeck and Thelen 2005). For example, in the post-Second World War period most Western democracies moved stepwise towards an intervening welfare state and a larger public sector. The Scandinavian countries,

---

[5] Krasner 1988; Thelen 1999; Pierson and Skocpol 2002; Orren and Skowronek 2004; Pierson 2004.

in particular, saw a "revolution in slow motion" (Olsen, Roness, and Sætren 1982). Since the end of the 1970s most Western democracies have moved incrementally in a neoliberal direction, emphasizing voluntary exchange, competitive markets, and private contracts rather than political authority and democratic politics. Suleiman, for example, argues that the reforms add up to a dismantling of the state. There has been a tendency to eliminate political belongings and ties and turn citizens into customers. To be a citizen requires a commitment and a responsibility beyond the self. To be a customer requires no such commitment and a responsibility only to oneself (Suleiman 2003, 52, 56).

Institutions face what is celebrated in theories of adaptation as the problem of balancing exploitation and exploration. Exploitation involves using existing knowledge, rules, and routines that are seen as encoding the lessons of history. Exploration involves exploring knowledge, rules, and routines that might come to be known (March 1991). Rules and routines are the carriers of accumulated knowledge and generally reflect a broader and a longer experience than the experience that informs any individual actor. By virtue of their long-term adaptive character, they yield outcome distributions that are characterized by relatively high means. By virtue of their short-term stability and their shaping of individual actions, they give those distributions relatively high reliability (low variability). In general, following the rules provides a higher average return and a lower variance on returns than does a random draw from a set of deviant actions proposed by individuals. The adaptive character of rules (and thus of institutions) is, however, threatened by their stability and reliability. Although violation of the rules is unlikely to be a good idea, it sometimes is; and without experimentation with that possibility, the effectiveness of the set of rules decays with time.

It is obvious that any system that engages only in exploitation will become obsolescent in a changing world, and that any system that engages only in exploration will never realize the potential gains of its discoveries. What is less obvious, indeed is ordinarily indeterminate, is the optimal balance between the two. The indeterminacy stems from the way in which the balance depends on trade-offs across time and space that are notoriously difficult to establish. Adaptation itself tends to be biased against exploration. Since the returns to exploitation are typically more certain, sooner, and more in the immediate neighborhood than are the returns to exploration, adaptive systems often extinguish exploratory options before accumulating sufficient experience with them to assess their value. As a result, one of the primary concerns in studies of institutional change is with the sources of exploration. How is the experimentation necessary to maintain effectiveness sustained in a system infused with the stability and reliability characteristic of exploitation (March 1991)?

Most theories of institutional change or adaptation, however, seem to be exquisitely simple relative to the reality of institutions that is observed. While the concept of institution assumes some internal coherence and consistency, conflict is also endemic in institutions. It cannot be assumed that conflict is solved through the terms of some prior agreement (constitution, coalition agreement, or employment contract) and that all participants agree to be bound by institutional rules. There are tensions, "institutional irritants," and antisystems, and the basic assumptions on which an institution is constituted are never fully accepted by the entire society (Eisenstadt 1965, 41; Goodin 1996, 39). There are also competing institutional and group belongings. For instance, diplomacy as an institution involves an inherent tension between being the carrier of the interests and policies of a specific state and the carrier of transnational principles, norms, and rules maintained and enacted by the representatives of the states in mutual interaction (Bátora 2005).

Institutions, furthermore, operate in an environment populated by other institutions organized according to different principles and logics. No contemporary democracy subscribes to a single set of principles, doctrines, and structures. While the concept "political system" suggests an integrated and coherent institutional configuration, political orders are never perfectly integrated. They routinely face institutional imbalances and collisions (Pierson and Skocpol 2002; Olsen 2004; Orren and Skowronek 2004) and "politics is eternally concerned with the achievement of unity from diversity" (Wheeler 1975, 4). Therefore, we have to go beyond a focus on how a specific institution affects change and attend to how the dynamics of change can be understood in terms of the organization, interaction, and collisions among competing institutional structures, norms, rules, identities, and practices.

Within a common set of generalized values and beliefs in society, modernity involved a large-scale institutional differentiation between institutional spheres with different organizational structures, normative and causal beliefs, vocabularies, resources, histories, and dynamics. Institutional interrelations varied and changed. Institutions came to be specialized, differentiated, autonomous, and autopoietic—self-referential and self-produced with closure against influence from the environment (Teubner 1993). There are strains and tensions and at transformative points in history institutions can come in direct confrontation. In different time periods the economy, politics, organized religion, science, etc. can all lead or be led and one cannot be completely reduced either to another or to some transcendent spirit (Gerth and Mills 1970, 328–57; Weber 1978).

A distinction, then, has to be made between change within fairly stable institutional and normative frameworks and change in the frameworks themselves. For example, there are routine tensions because modern society involves several criteria of truth and truth-finding. It makes a difference whether an issue is defined as a technical, economic, legal, moral, or political question and there are clashes between, for instance, legal and scientific conceptions of reality, their starting assumptions, and methods of truth-finding and interpretation (Nelken 1993, 151).

Likewise, there are tensions between what is accepted as "rational," "just," and a "good argument" across institutional contexts. Different institutions are, for instance, based on different conceptions of both procedural fairness and outcome fairness and through their practices they generate different expectations about how interaction will be organized and different actors will be treated (Isaac, Mathieu, and Zajac 1991, 336, 339).

There are also situations where an institution has its *raison d'être*, mission, wisdom, integrity, organization, performance, moral foundation, justice, prestige, and resources questioned and it is asked whether the institution contributes to society what it is supposed to contribute. There are radical intrusions and attempts to achieve ideological hegemony and control over other institutional spheres, as well as stern defenses of institutional mandates and traditions against invasion of alien norms. An institution under serious attack is likely to reexamine its ethos, codes of behavior, primary allegiances, and pact with society (Merton 1942). There is rethinking, reorganization, refinancing, and possibly a new "constitutional" settlement, rebalancing core institutions. Typically, taken-for-granted beliefs and arrangements are challenged by new or increased contact between previously separated polities or institutional spheres based on different principles (Berger and Luckmann 1967, 107–8).

Contemporary systems cope with diversity in a variety of ways. Inconsistencies are buffered by institutional specialization, separation, autonomy, sequential attention, local rationality, and conflict avoidance (Cyert and March 1963). Inconsistencies are also debated in public and a well-functioning public sphere is seen as a prerequisite for coping with diversity (Habermas 1994). Modern citizens have lost some of the naive respect and emotional affection for traditional authorities and the legitimacy of competing principles and structures have to be based on communicative rationality and claims of validity. Their relative merits have to be tested and justified through collective reasoning, making them vulnerable to arguments, including demands for exceptions and exemptions that can restrict their scope (Kratochwil 1984, 701).

In general, the Enlightenment-inspired belief in institutional design in the name of progress is tempered by limited human capacity for understanding and control. The institutional frames within which political actors act impact their motivations and their capabilities, and reformers are often institutional gardeners more than institutional engineers (March and Olsen 1983, 1989; Olsen 2000). They can reinterpret rules and codes of behavior, impact causal and normative beliefs, foster civic and democratic identities and engagement, develop organized capabilities, and improve adaptability (March and Olsen 1995). Yet, they cannot do so arbitrarily and there is modest knowledge about the conditions under which they are likely to produce institutional changes that generate intended and desired substantive effects.

5 THE FRONTIER OF INSTITUTIONALISM

As the enthusiasm for "new institutional" approaches has flourished over the last twenty years, so also has the skepticism. It has been asked whether institutional accounts really present anything new; whether their empirical and theoretical claims can be sustained; whether their explanations are falsifiable; and whether institutional accounts can be differentiated from other accounts of politics (Jordan 1990; Peters 1999).

It has, however, turned out to be difficult to understand legislatures (Gamm and Huber 2002), public administration (Olsen 2005), courts of law (Clayton and Gillman 1999), and diplomacy (Bátora 2005) without taking into account their institutional characteristics. It has also been argued that the study of institutions in political science has been taken forward (Lowndes 2002, 97); that "there is a future for the institutional approach" (Rhodes 1995); and even that the variety of new institutionalisms have "great power to provide an integrative framework" and may represent the "next revolution" in political science (Goodin and Klingeman 1996, 25).

The "new institutionalism" tries to avoid unfeasible assumptions that require too much of political actors, in terms of normative commitments (virtue), cognitive abilities (bounded rationality), and social control (capabilities). The rules, routines, norms, and identities of an "institution," rather than micro-rational individuals or macro-social forces, are the basic units of analysis. Yet the spirit is to supplement rather than reject alternative approaches (March and Olsen 1998, 2006; Olsen 2001). Much remains, however, before the different conceptions of political institutions, action, and change can be reconciled meaningfully.

The fact that political practice in contemporary political systems now seems to precede understanding and justification may, however, permit new insights. Political science is to a large extent based upon the study of the sovereign, territorial state, and the Westphalian state-system. Yet the hierarchical role of the political center within each state and the "anarchic" relations between states are undergoing major transformations, for example in the European Union. An implication is that there is a need for new ways of describing how authority, rights, obligations, interaction, attention, experience, memory, and resources are organized, beyond hierarchies and markets (Brunsson and Olsen 1998). Network institutionalism is one candidate for understanding both intra- and interinstitutional relations (Lowndes 2002).

There is also a need to go beyond rational design and environmental dictates as the dominant logics of institutional change (Brunsson and Olsen 1998). There is a need for improved understanding of the processes that translate political action into institutional change, how an existing institutional order impacts the dynamics of change, and what other factors can be decisive. The list of questions is long, indeed (Thelen 1999; Orren and Skowronek 2004; Streeck and Thelen 2005). Which institutional characteristics favor change and which make institutions resistant to change? Which factors are likely to disrupt established patterns and processes of institutional maintenance and regeneration? What are the interrelations between change in some (parts of) institutions and continuity in others, and between incremental adaptation and periods of radical change? Under what conditions does incremental change give a consistent and discernable direction to change and how are the outcomes of critical junctures translated into lasting legacies? Which (parts of) political institutions are understood and controlled well enough to be designed and also to achieve anticipated and desired effects?

REFERENCES

APTER, D. A. 1991. Institutionalism revisited. *International Social Science Journal*, August: 463–81.

BÁTORA, J. 2005. Does the European Union transform the institution of diplomacy? *Journal of European Public Policy*, 12 (1): 1–23.

BERGER, P. L. and LUCKMANN, T. 1967. *The Social Construction of Reality*. New York: Doubleday/Anchor.

BRODERICK, A. (ed.) 1970. *The French Institutionalists. Maurice Hauriou, Georges Renard, Joseph Delos.* Cambridge, Mass.: Harvard University Press.

BRUNSSON, N. and OLSEN, J. P. 1998. Organization theory: thirty years of dismantling, and then ...? Pp. 13–43 in *Organizing Organizations*, ed. N. Brunsson and J. P. Olsen. Bergen: Fagbokforlaget.

CHECKEL, J. T. 2005. International institutions and socialization in Europe: introduction and framework. *International Organization* (Special issue), 59(5).

CLAYTON, C. W. and GILLMAN, H. (eds.) 1999. *Supreme Court Decision-Making: New Institutionalist Approaches.* Chicago: University of Chicago Press.

CYERT, R. M. and MARCH, J. G. 1963. *A Behavioral Theory of the Firm.* Englewood Cliffs, NJ: Prentice Hall (2nd edn. 1992). Oxford: Basil Blackwell.

DREWRY, G. 1996. Political institutions: legal perspectives. Pp. 191–204 in *A New Handbook of Political Science*, ed. R. E. Goodin and H.-D. Klingemann. Oxford: Oxford University Press.

DWORKIN, R. 1986. *Law's Empire.* Cambridge, Mass.: Harvard University Press.

EGEBERG, M. 2003. How bureaucratic structure matters: an organizational perspective. Pp. 116–26 in *Handbook of Public Administration*, ed. B. G. Peters and J. Pierre. London: Sage.

—— 2004. An organizational approach to European integration: outline of a complementary perspective. *European Journal of Political Research*, 43 (2): 199–219.

EISENSTADT, S. 1965. *Essays on Comparative Institutions.* New York: Wiley.

EULAU, H. and MARCH, J. G. (eds.) 1969. *Political Science.* Englewood Cliffs, NJ: Prentice Hall.

FEHR, E. and GÄCHTER, S. 1998. Reciprocity and economics: the economic implications of *Homo Reciprocans. European Economic Review*, 42: 845–59.

GAMM, G. and HUBER, J. 2002. Legislatures as political institutions: beyond the contemporary Congress. Pp. 313–43 in *Political Science: State of the Discipline*, ed. I. Katznelson and H. V. Miller. New York: Norton.

GERTH, H. H. and WRIGHT MILLS, C. (eds.) 1970. *From Max Weber: Essays in Sociology.* London: Routledge and Kegan Paul.

GOODIN, R. E. 1996. Institutions and their design. Pp. 1–53 in *The Theory of Institutional Design*, ed. R. E. Goodin. Cambridge: Cambridge University Press.

—— and KLINGEMANN, H.-D. 1996. Political science: the discipline. Pp. 3–49 in *A New Handbook of Political Science*, ed. R. E. Goodin and H.-D. Klingemann. Oxford: Oxford University Press.

HABERMAS, J. 1994. Citizenship and national identity. Pp. 20–35 in *The Condition of Citizenship*, ed. B. van Steenbergen. London: Sage.

HAMILTON, A., JAY, J., and MADISON, J. 1964 [1787]. *The Federalist Papers.* New York: Pocket Books.

HERRMANN, R. K., RISSE, T., and BREWER, M. B. (eds.) 2004. *Transnational Identities: Becoming European in the EU.* Lanham, Md.: Rowman and Littlefield.

ISAAC, R. M., MATHIEU, D., and ZAJAC, E. E. 1991. Institutional framing and perceptions of fairness. *Constitutional Political Economy*, 2 (3): 329–70.

JORDAN, A. G. 1990. Policy community realism versus "new institutionalism" ambiguity. *Political Studies*, 38: 470–84.

KAUFMAN, H. 1976. *Are Government Organizations Immortal?* Washington, DC: Brookings Institution.

KRASNER, S. 1988. Sovereignty: an institutional perspective. *Comparative Political Studies*, 21 (1): 66–94.

KRATOCHWIL, F. 1984. The force of prescription. *International Organization*, 38 (4): 685–708.

KRAUS, P. A. 2004. A union of peoples? Diversity and the predicaments of a multinational polity. Pp. 40–4 in *Political Theory and the European Constitution*, ed. L. Dobson and A. Føllesdal. London: Routledge.

LÆGREID, P. and OLSEN, J. P. 1984. Top civil servants in Norway: key players—on different teams. Pp. 206–41 in *Bureaucrats & Policy Making*, ed. E. N. Suleiman. New York: Holmes and Meyer.

LIPSET, S. M. and ROKKAN, S. 1967. Cleavage structures, party systems, and voter alignments: an introduction. Pp. 1–64 in *Party Systems and Voter Alignments: Cross-National Perspectives*, ed. S. M. Lipset and S. Rokkan. New York: Free Press.

LOWNDES, V. 1996. Varieties of new institutionalism: a critical appraisal. *Public Administration*, 74 (2): 181–97.

—— 2002. Institutionalism. Pp. 90–108 in *Theory and Methods in Political Science*, ed. D. Marsh and G. Stoker (2nd edn.). Basingstoke: Palgrave Macmillan.

MACRIDIS, R. C. 1963. A survey of the field of comparative government. Pp. 43–52 in *Comparative Politics: A Reader*, ed. H. Eckstein and D. E. Apter. New York: Free Press of Glencoe.

MARCH, J. G. 1981. Footnotes to organizational change. *Administrative Science Quarterly*, 16: 563–77.

—— 1991. Exploration and exploitation in organizational learning. *Organization Science*, 2: 71–87.

—— 1994. *A Primer on Decision Making: How Decisions Happen.* New York: Free Press.

—— and OLSEN, J. P. 1983. Organizing political life: what administrative reorganization tells us about government. *American Political Science Review*, 77: 281–97.

—— —— 1984. The new institutionalism: organizational factors in political life. *American Political Science Review*, 78 (3): 734–49.

—— —— 1986. Institutional perspectives on political institutions. *Governance*, 9 (3): 247–64.

—— —— 1989. *Rediscovering Institutions*. New York: Free Press.

—— —— 1995. *Democratic Governance*. New York: Free Press.

—— —— 1998. The institutional dynamics of international political orders. *International Organization* 52: 943–69. Reprinted pp. 303–29 in P. J. Katzenstein, R. O. Keohane, and S. D. Krasner (eds.) 1999, *Exploration and Contestation in the Study of World Politics*. Cambridge, Mass.: MIT Press.

—— —— 2006. The logic of appropriateness. In *The Oxford Handbook of Public Policy*, ed. M. Moran, M. Rein, and R. E. Goodin. Oxford: Oxford University Press.

—— and SIMON, H. A. 1958. *Organizations*. New York: Wiley.

MERTON, R. K. 1938. Social structure and anomie. *American Sociological Review*, 3: 672–82.

—— 1942. Science and technology in a democratic order. *Journal of Legal and Political Sociology*, 1: 115–26.

MEYER, J. and ROWAN, B. 1977. Institutionalized organizations: formal structure as myth and ceremony. *American Journal of Sociology*, 83: 340–63.

MILL, J. S. 1962 [1861]. *Considerations on Representative Government*. South Bend, Ind.: Gateway.

NELKEN, D. 1993. The truth about law's truth. Pp. 87–160 in *European Yearbook in the Sociology of Law*, ed. A. Febbrajo and D. Nelken. Milan: Giuffrè.

OFFE, C. 2001. Institutional design. Pp. 363–9 in *Encyclopedia of Democratic Thought*, ed. P. B. Clarke and J. Foweraker. London: Routledge.

OLSEN, J. P. 1997. Institutional Design in Democratic Contexts. *Journal of Political Philosophy*, 5 (3): 203–29.

—— 2000. How, then, does one get there? An institutionalist response to Herr Fischer's vision of a European federation. Pp. 163–79 in *What Kind of Constitution for What Kind of Polity?* ed. C. Joerges, Y. Mény, and J. H. H. Weiler. Florence: EUI.

—— 2001. Garbage cans, new institutionalism, and the study of politics. *American Political Science Review*, 95 (1): 191–8.

—— 2004. Unity, diversity and democratic institutions: lessons from the European Union. *Journal of Political Philosophy*, 12 (4): 461–95.

—— 2005. Maybe it is time to rediscover bureaucracy. *Journal of Public Administration Research and Theory*, 16: 1–24.

—— RONESS, P. G., and SÆTREN, H. 1982. Norway: still peaceful coexistence and revolution in slow motion. Pp. 47–79 in *Policy Styles in Western Europe*, ed. J. J. Richardson. London: Allen and Unwin.

ORREN, K. and SKOWRONEK, S. 2004. *The Search for American Political Development*. Cambridge: Cambridge University Press.

PETERS, B. G. 1996. Political institutions: old and new. Pp. 205–20 in *A New Handbook of Political Science*, ed. R. E. Goodin and H.-D. Klingemann. Oxford: Oxford University Press.

—— 1999. *Institutional Theory in Political Science: The "New" Institutionalism*. London: Pinter.

PIERSON, P. 2004. *Politics in Time*. Princeton, NJ: Princeton University Press.

PIERSON, P. and SKOCPOL, T. 2002. Historical institutionalism in contemporary political science. Pp. 693–721 in *Political Science: State of the Discipline*, ed. I. Katznelson and H. V. Miller. New York: Norton.

PITKIN, H. 1967. *The Concept of Representation*. Berkeley: University of California Press.

POLSBY, N. W. 1975. Legislatures. Pp. 257–319 in *Handbook of Political Science*, vol. 5, ed. F. Greenstein and N. W. Polsby. Reading, Mass.: Addison-Wesley.

RAWLS, J. 1993. The basic structure as subject. Pp. 257–88 in *Political Liberalism*. New York: Columbia University Press.

RHODES, R. 1995. The institutional approach. Pp. 42–57 in *Theory and Methods in Political Science*, ed. D. Marsh and G. Stoker. London: Macmillan.

ROTHSTEIN, B. 1996. Political institutions: an overview. Pp. 133–66 in *A New Handbook of Political Science*, ed. H. E. Goodin and H.-D. Klingemann. Oxford: Oxford University Press.

SCHATTSCHNEIDER, E. E. 1960. *The Semi-Sovereign People*. New York: Holt, Rinehart and Winston.

SIMON, H. A. 1965. *Administrative Behavior* (2nd edn.). New York: Macmillan.

STREECK, W. and THELEN, K. 2005. Introduction: institutional change in advanced political economies. Pp. 1–39 in *Beyond Continuity: Institutional Change in Advanced Political Economies*, ed. W. Streeck and K. Thelen. Oxford: Oxford University Press.

SULEIMAN, E. 2003. *Dismantling Democratic States*. Princeton, NJ: Princeton University Press.

TEUBNER, G. 1993. *Law as an Autopoietic System*. Oxford: Blackwell.

THELEN, K. 1999. Historical institutionalism in comparative politics. Pp. 369–404 in *Annual Review of Political Science*, vol. 2, ed. N. Polsby. Palo Alto, Calif.: Annual Reviews.

THOENIG, J.-C. 2003. Institutional theories and public institutions: traditions and appropriateness. Pp. 127–37 in *Handbook of Public Administration*, ed. B. G. Peters and J. Pierre. London: Sage.

WEAVER, R. K. and ROCKMAN, B. A. (eds.) 1993. *Do Institutions Matter? Government Capabilities in the United States and Abroad*. Washington, DC: Brookings.

WEBER, M. 1977. *Peasants into Frenchmen: The Modernization of Rural France*. London: Chatto and Windus.

—— 1978. *Economy and Society*. Berkeley: University of California Press.

WEINGAST, B. R. 2002. Rational-choice institutionalism. Pp. 660–92 in *Political Science: State of the Discipline*, ed. I. Katznelson and H. V. Miller. New York: Norton.

WHEELER, H. 1975. Constitutionalism. Pp. 1–91 in *Handbook of Political Science: Governmental Institutions and Processes*, vol. 5, ed. F. I. Greenstein and N. W. Polsby. Reading, Mass.: Addison-Wesley.

PART II

APPROACHES

CHAPTER 2

RATIONAL CHOICE INSTITUTIONALISM

KENNETH A. SHEPSLE *Harvard*

"An irrational passion for dispassionate rationality will take all the joy out of life," wrote the economist John Maurice Clark a century ago. Canonical rational choice theory has been a staple in political science for four decades. While it may have taken the joy out of life for many traditionalists in the field and a behavioralist or two, it has become an engine of social scientific research, producing theoretical microfoundations, an equilibrium orientation, deductively derived theorems and propositions about political activity, a comparative statics methodology yielding testable hypotheses, and an accumulation of tools and approaches that are routinely found in the curriculum of major graduate programs. We think more sophisticatedly today about optimizing political actors, the organizations of which they are a part, and most recently the role of information in retrospective assessment, systematic foresight, and strategic calculation more generally—that is, we think more sophisticatedly about political purposes, beliefs, opinions, and behavior. We also have more nuanced views about the contexts in which political activity unfolds, the way these contexts channel behavior, and the way behavior, in turn, maintains or alters contexts. These contexts are inhabited by political actors and organizations to be sure, but it is the institutions that arise and persist there

* This chapter benefited from the constructive comments of volume editors Sarah Binder, Rod Rhodes, and Bert Rockman, and series editor, Bob Goodin.

that provide scripts for political processes. These institutional arrangements and the patterns and regularities they produce are the subject of the present chapter.

This chapter is loosely organized into several themes. The first deals with defining the terrain, in particular reviewing the several theoretical ways in which institutions are interpreted by rational choice theorists. The second theme surveys the progress we have made in understanding what I call structured and unstructured institutions. The third theme looks briefly at the limitations of rational choice institutionalism, and at the ways in which some of the bright lines that formerly distinguished this flavor of institutionalism from the many others (see Hall and Taylor 1996) are becoming less discernible.[1]

1 INTERPRETATIONS OF INSTITUTIONS

Within the rational choice tradition there are two now-standard ways to think about institutions. The first takes institutions as *exogenous constraints*, or as an exogenously given *game form*. The economic historian Douglass North, for example, thinks of them as "the rules of the game in a society or, more formally, . . . the humanly devised constraints that shape human interaction" (North 1990, 3). An institution is a script that names the *actors*, their respective *behavioral repertoires* (or *strategies*), the *sequence* in which the actors choose from them, the *information* they possess when they make their selections, and the *outcome* resulting from the combination of actor choices. Once we add actor *evaluations* of outcomes to this mix—actor *preferences*—we transform the game form into a game.

---

[1] Rational choice institutionalism is a large topic and not one easily summarized in a brief essay. So the interested reader should avail him- or herself of other surveys that complement the present one. Weingast 1996, 2002 and Shepsle 2006 cover some of the recent political science literature. Accessible textbooks on rational choice political analysis include Hinich and Munger 1997, Laver 1997, and Shepsle and Boncheck 1997. A comprehensive review of the public choice literature in economics and political science is found in Mueller 2003. Systematic coverage of the work of political economics in a comparative framework is presented in Persson and Tabellini 2000. An intelligent methodological perspective is offered in Diermeier and Krehbiel 2003. And finally, the gold standard for positive political theory is the two-volume treatise by Austen-Smith and Banks 1999, 2005.

[2] An early formulation of institutions as exogenous constraints is found in Shepsle 1979, and elaborated further in North 1990. A critique of this formulation is found in Riker 1980. Schotter 1981 and Calvert 1995 develop the endogenous interpretation of institutions. Distinctions between exogenous and endogenous institutions is presented in Shepsle 1986, 2006. Weingast 2002 organizes his outstanding review of rational choice institutionalism around this distinction as well. For alternative frameworks, an excellent source is Crawford and Ostrom 1995 and Ostrom 2005.

To give an ancient example of a game form from Downs (1957), the actors are n voters and two candidates. The candidates each select a policy position represented by a point on the unit interval, [0,1]. They either do this simultaneously, or choose in a particular sequence but the candidate choosing second does not know the first candidate's choice in advance of his own choice. (While candidates do not know the choices of other candidates, they do know voter preferences as defined below.) Voters then vote for one candidate, the other candidate, or abstain. The candidate with the most votes is elected. If each candidate obtains the same number of votes (including none if all voters abstain), then a random device determines which of them is elected. This is a game form, an exogenously provided script that gives the various ways the strategic interaction can develop. If (i) candidates prefer winning to tying to losing, and (ii) each voter i has single-peaked preferences on [0,1] symmetric about his or her most preferred policy, then we have characterized actor preferences and now have a game. The well-known Median Voter Theorem applies: The candidate who locates closest to the most-preferred policy of the median voter wins the election. In game-theoretic language, the Nash equilibrium of this game is for both candidates to locate at the median ideal point and one of them to be randomly chosen as the winner.[3,4] Shepsle (1979) called this a *structure-induced equilibrium* of the institutional game.

The second interpretation of institutions is deeper and subtler. It does *not* take institutions as given exogenously. Instead of external provision, the rules of the game in this view are provided by the players themselves; they are simply the ways in which the players want to play. A group of children, for example, might take the official rules of baseball as a starting point to govern their interactions, but then adapt them to specific circumstances or tastes. A ball rolling into the creek that borders the field, as I recall from my childhood, allows the baserunner to advance only one additional base. On any particular day, however, the kid who brought the bat and ball might insist on a variation to that rule more to his liking—say, a ball in the creek is an automatic home run—and be in a position to induce the others to accept his preference. In this view of institutions, there is nothing exogenous about the rules of the game, and certainly nothing magical. They do not compel observance, but rather reflect the willingness of (nearly) everyone to engage with one another according to particular patterns and procedures (nearly all the time). The institutional arrangements are, in this view, *focal* (Schelling 1960) and may induce coordination around them. Calvert (1995), one of the intellectual architects of this perspective (see also Schotter 1981), puts it well:

---

[3] A *Nash Equilibrium* is a set of strategies, one for each player, with the property that no player can improve her or his position by changing to some other strategy (assuming other players stick to their initial strategies).

[4] If there is a cost to voting, then indifferent voters abstain. If voting is costless then indifferent voters randomize their choice (or abstain). In either case the expectation is a tie between the candidates which is broken randomly.

[T]here is, strictly speaking, no separate animal that we can identify as an institution. There is only rational behavior, conditioned on expectations about the behavior and reactions of others. When these expectations about others' behavior take on a particularly clear and concrete form across individuals, when they apply to situations that recur over a long period of time, and especially when they involve highly variegated and specific expectations about the different roles of different actors in determining what actions others should take, we often collect these expectations and strategies under the heading *institution*... (Calvert 1995, 73–4).

Institutions are simply equilibrium ways of doing things. If a decisive player wants to play according to different rules—like the kid who threatens to take his bat and ball home if the rules are not adjusted to his liking—then the rules are not in equilibrium and the "institution" is fragile.

We come to think of institutions (in the ordinary language sense) as scripts that constrain behavior—the first interpretation above—because in many political contexts "highly variegated and specific expectations about the different roles of different actors" are involved, and decisive individuals or coalitions are not pre-pared to change the way business is conducted. Calvert's point, however, is that this does not mean decisive actors are *never* inclined to push for change. Early in the last decade, for example, a newly elected Labour government in Great Britain, to the surprise of many, transformed the Bank of England from one of the most dependent central banks in the developed world into a much more independent agency. A revision of the Rules of the US Senate—particularly Rule 22 to make it easier to end filibusters—has been contemplated on many occasions (Binder and Smith 1996). Twice in the last century there were major changes in the rules to make cloture first possible, and then easier. The Republican majority in the US Senate of the 109th Congress (2005–7) has raised this issue again in the context of the confirmation of judges and justices.[5]

There is a third interpretation of institutions (indeed, there are many others) that is decidedly *not* rational choice in nature; it bears describing briefly in order to contrast it with the two interpretations just given. I associate it with Sait (1938) and his legacy in various forms is found in the work of modern historical institution-alists. For Sait, institutions *are* magical. He describes them with the wide-eyed wonderment of someone examining a coral reef for the first time.[6] They just form, and re-form, according to complex, essentially unknowable forces. Law, slavery, feudalism, language, property rights—these are the "edifices" Sait considers institutions. His emphasis differs from that of the institutions-as-constraint and institutions-as-equilibrium schools of thought described above. Institutions for him are macrosociological practices defined, and altered, by historical

---

[5] Powerful agents need not be myopic, of course. Thus, they may forgo an immediate gain for long-run reasons. Institutions, as a consequence, often have a persistence even in the face of potential windfalls for powerful agents.

[6] March and Olsen 1984 were also struck by Sait's coral-reef metaphor.

contingency. There is microanalysis neither of the patterns of behavior they induce and sustain nor of the human attempts to alter institutional properties. There is for him no architect of Roman Law, for example. An institution is an accretion, changing ever so slowly and never by identifiable human agency. Perhaps we need a different name for one of these.

2 STRUCTURED AND UNSTRUCTURED INSTITUTIONS

I think of institutions that are robust over time, and lend themselves to comparisons across settings, as *structured*. They persist in roughly the same form from year to year, and their similarities to and differences from objects sharing their label in other places also persist.[7] Thus, the US Congress, or the New York Assembly, or the Irish Dail are structured in this sense. So, too, is a parliamentary cabinet, a judicial court, an administrative bureau, a regulatory agency, a central bank, an electoral regime, even a political party, a royal court, or an army. Rational choice institutionalism has explored many of these. There is surely variation among the myriad instances of any one of these structured institutions; but there are also powerful central tendencies. This is what induces us to group them together and to think it sensible to compare them.

Other institutions are less structured. Like structured institutions, they may be described as practices and recognized by the patterns they induce, but they are more amorphous and implicit rather than formalized. Norms, coordination activity, cooperative arrangements, and collective action are instances of what I have in mind.

Senatorial courtesy, for example, is a norm of the US Senate effectively giving a senator a veto on judicial appointments in his or her state (Binder and Maltzman 2005; Jacobi 2005). *Seniority* was a norm of both chambers of the US Congress for most of the twentieth century, establishing queues or ladders in congressional committees on which basis privileged positions—committee and subcommittee chairs, the order of speaking and questioning in hearings, access to staff, etc.—were assigned.[8] Neither of these norms is a formal rule of the institutions.

---

[7] In Shepsle 2006 I examine the various endogenous mechanisms by which institutions may be changed, including amendment procedures, interpretive courts, escape clauses, nullification, suspension of the rules, and emergency powers.

[8] Each of these examples illustrates that unstructured institutional practices may exist in structured institutions, often constituting their sociological underbelly.

Various forms of patterned informal interaction, including coordinated agreements like which side of the road to travel, sharing rules like "split the difference," and understandings like "tit for tat" (Axelrod 1984) and "taking turns" (Ward 1998), also constitute unstructured institutions. These patterns emerge informally and often are not actually written down as formal rules; they simply come to be known as "the way things are done around here." They are, in short, equilibrium patterns.

Collective action—the capacity of a group of individuals to coordinate for mutual advantage—sits close to the boundary between structured and unstructured institutions. Sometimes it takes the form of well-organized and formalized arrangements; other times it looks spontaneous and idiosyncratic. Interest-group political organizations described by Olson (1965) constitute instances of the former, while intergroup ethnic relations, sometimes peaceful sometimes not, are often patterned but unstructured and implicit (Fearon and Laitin 1996).

2.1 Structured Institutions

Probably the single biggest success of the rational choice institutionalism program is the analysis of structured institutions. There are several factors that facilitate rigorous analysis and thus account for this success.

First, politicians in these settings are selected in a relatively well-defined way— election to legislatures or party offices, appointment to courts, regulatory agencies, or higher executive posts. Politicians may thus be thought of as agents of (s)electors (Bueno de Mesquita, Smith, Siverson, and Morrow 2003). Their activities while in office will be motivated in part by the objectives of the (s)electorate—see below.

Second, politician objectives can be specified with some precision, due in part to selection effects. In the literature these objectives are often grouped into *office preferences* and *policy preferences*.[9] Ideal-types holding preferences of the former category care primarily (only?) about office and the perquisites that come with incumbency—salary, influence, control of staff, generalized prestige. More recent work, under the rubric of *career concerns*, places special emphasis on selection effects.[10] The policy preferences ideal-type cares about policy outcomes. In the spirit of Downs (1957), office-oriented politicians make policy in

---

[9] In the context of the multiparty politics of Western Europe, the issue of politician objective functions is taken up in Müller and Strøm 1999. Also see Calvert 1985 and Wittman 1973.

[10] Holmstrom 1979, 1982 is the exemplar of this genre. A good survey is found in Dewatripont, Jewitt, and Tirole 1999. Recent work by Ashworth and Bueno de Mesquita 2004 applies the career concerns logic to legislative politicians.

order to win elections whereas policy-oriented politicians win elections in order to make policy.[11]

Third, politician behavioral repertoires are delineated by institutional rules and processes. A legislator on the floor of the chamber, for example, may seek recognition from the presiding officer or not. If he does, he may offer a substantive motion, a second to a motion, an amendment to an existing motion, a procedural motion (to table, to recommit, to adjourn, etc.), a point of order or information, and so on—some of which are permitted by the rules ("in order") and some of which are not ("out of order"). If a vote is called, he may vote yea, vote nay, or abstain (in whatever manner of vote expression is required). That is, the "legislation game" may be written down and the strategies available to the politicians specified.[12] In other structured institutional settings, the repertoires of judges and bureaucrats may be portrayed in clear-cut ways.

Fourth, outcomes are clearly implied by the configuration of rules in a structured institution. These rules prescribe the mechanism for aggregating behaviors into a final result. Thus, any combination of behavioral repertoires by institutional politicians maps into a specific outcome.

Fifth, payoffs may be inferred from the objective functions of politicians. Policy-oriented players will prefer the combination of behavioral repertoires that map into more desirable outcomes. Office-motivated politicians will prefer those repertoire combinations that improve their prospects with their (s)electorate. If the selection mechanism chooses politicians with policy preferences closely aligned to those of their (s)electorate, then we may not be able to distinguish between the two preference types empirically. The strategic choices of office types and policy types will be observationally equivalent.

Finally, there is the matter of (s)electorate preferences. The (s)electorate is the collective principal that chooses an institutional politician to act as its agent. With their preferences in hand, we complete the circle. (S)electorates are vulnerable to two kinds of "agency problems"—*adverse selection* and *moral hazard.* The first problem is associated with hidden information—characteristics of the prospective agent that cannot be known in advance by the principal. Is the politician of "high quality?" Does he or she share policy preferences with the (s)electorate? The second problem is associated with hidden action—strategic agent behavior that

---

[11] Some revision is required to take account of the fact that ambition, whether for policy influence or for office enjoyment, need not be static. Progressively ambitious politicians, for instance, continuously monitor their environment for opportunities to seek higher office (Schlesinger 1966). These comments pertain to judges and bureaucrats, too, though with some amendment since the terms of tenure and career advancement differ from those of legislators.

[12] The strategies can be quite sophisticated, subtle, even arcane. For example, because a motion to "reconsider" may only be offered by someone on the *winning* side of a vote, a legislator who wishes to see a bill ultimately defeated (or its supporters visibly embarrassed may support a bill against her preferences at one stage to position herself to force a second vote.

may not be discernible by the principal. Does the politician support the preferences of the (s)electorate in arenas where his or her behavior cannot be directly observed (an unrecorded vote, a secret committee meeting or party caucus, a meeting with a lobbyist)? The connection between (s)electorate and politician entails some form of *delegation* from principal to agent and is characterized by more or less *accountability* by the agent to the wishes of the principal. The rational choice literature on each of these facets of institutions is vast.[13]

2.2 Unstructured Institutions

The Archimedian lever of rational choice institutionalism is provided by the *structure* of structured institutions. This structure embeds the logic of optimization in a strategic context. The context of unstructured institutions is more fluid, providing a less firm foundation for analysis. Many more things are possible; many more contingencies need to be accounted for. However, considerable progress has been made.

The great success story in this region of the rational choice institutionalism program is the logic of collective action (Olson 1965). The foundational basis for this work is the analysis of public goods, dating back to the early work of Samuelson (1954). Collective action for a group is a public good, an outcome desired by its members but difficult to elicit costly contributions for its production. Members, according to this logic, are attracted to the *free-riding* option since non-contribution is a dominant strategy in the collective action game. Mancur Olson took this insight and demolished prevailing pluralist and Marxist views on groups by arguing that they will not of necessity form around common interests and objectives (as these more sociological arguments had taken for granted) precisely because of the logic of free-riding. Individual contributions are both personally costly and often only trivially important in achieving a group goal, especially in large groups. So individuals are tempted to abstain from contributing. This temptation is reinforced by the realization that everyone else will be tempted to free-ride.

Groups do form and not everyone free-rides all the time. Why? Answering this question has constituted something of a light industry. Olson argued that since success in inducing an individual to contribute does not come from the prospect of realizing group objectives (which will be enjoyed if the group succeeds whether she contributes or not, and whose contribution is negligible in any event), then it must

---

[13] On accountability, the *loci classicus* are Barro 1972, Ferejohn 1986, 1999, Austen-Smith and Banks 1989, Banks and Sunduram 1993, and Fearon 1999. On delegation, Kiewiet and McCubbins 1991 and Epstein and O'Halloran 1999 provide a guide to research with special emphasis on the American system.

come from some other source. Groups must be able to offer things of value to contributors *and only to contributors*—selective benefits, not collective benefits. The group objective is financed, therefore, as a *byproduct* of bribing individuals to contribute with private compensation.

One of the earliest responses to Olson's classic was a book review by Wagner (1966). There he pointed out a glaring omission in the byproduct logic of Olson's theory of collective action—namely, the role of leadership. (Also see Frohlich, Oppenheimer, and Young 1971.) Wagner suggested that even Olson's byproduct logic must have some source of implementation. Inventing the term *political entrepreneur*, he argued that particular individuals may make unusually large contributions of time and energy and financial and (especially) logistical resources not (only) because they care passionately about the group's objective but (also) because they see an opportunity to parlay this investment into something personally (read: selectively) rewarding. It is no surprise, for example, when a congressman from south Florida (home to many retirees) provides political leadership on issues benefiting the elderly—the electoral connection supplies the explanation (whether the congressman is personally passionate about these issues or not). Likewise, it is surely not entirely explained by "generosity of spirit" when a young lawyer takes on a cause—say, the lead-poisoning of inner city infants—even though there may be no immediate remuneration. Applying the career concerns logic just suggested about the congressman, this political entrepreneur takes leadership of an issue in order to advance a personal agenda (of which finding a solution to the issue at hand may be part, but only part), possibly parlaying his public spirit into a political career, a network of contacts, future remuneration for his legal practice, etc. The leadership explanation is not entirely compelling in all settings. But it invites us to scrutinize some of the less obvious motives of those who assume the mantle of leadership. (On the rational choice analysis of leadership more generally, see Fiorina and Shepsle 1989; and Shepsle and Bonchek 1997, ch. 14.)

A feature of all collective action from a purely rational perspective is that outcomes are not Pareto optimal. Everyone would be better off if there were some way to coerce contributions. Selective benefits and political entrepreneurs are two of the most important contributions of rational choice institutionalism to an appreciation of solutions to collective action phenomena. Leadership, in fact, may be interpreted as giving some agent the authority to wield carrots and sticks—that is, provide selective incentives—to induce contributions to group objectives and thus move the collectivity onto the Pareto surface. (Indeed, this is a rough approximation of arguments made centuries ago by Hobbes and Hume to justify the existence of the state. Generally, see Buchanan and Tullock 1962; Hardin 1982; Sandler 1992.)

A third "solution" to the problem of collective action is best understood in the problem writ small—the problem of *cooperation*. Axelrod (1984) paved the way to understanding how to get individuals to seize a cooperation dividend, rather than leaving it on the table, by examining repeated prisoners' dilemma (PD) situations.[14] In the PD an individual can cooperate with another and capture a benefit, exploit the cooperative inclinations of the other by non-cooperating and do even better while the other suffers a loss, or join his opposite number in non-cooperation and get nothing. A dominant strategy in the one-shot PD is for both individuals not to cooperate, producing a zero payoff and something left on the table. (What is left on the table is a positive payoff had both cooperated.) The idea exploited by Axelrod, and I count this as the third important solution to collective action problems (along with selective benefits and leadership), is *repeat play*. Axelrod noticed what game theorists had discovered even earlier—that repeat play allows for "history contingent" strategies. Thus, in the play of a PD game at any time *t*, each player may take into account the way the game was played in earlier periods, and make his or her behavior in the current interaction contingent on previous play. Today's play, therefore, determines not only today's payoff but will influence the behavioral choices of others tomorrow. This may, depending upon how much the players value tomorrow's payoff relative to today's, induce them to eschew their dominant strategies in the one-shot play of the PD and choose to cooperate instead. Indeed, unlike leadership and selective benefit solutions to collective action, repeat play is more like an *invisible hand*.

I have oversimplified this discussion, but it allows me to observe that history dependent behaviors in equilibrium—"tit for tat," "take turns," "split the difference"—come very close to the ordinary language meaning of norms and conventions.[15] The program of rational choice institutionalism thus provides analytical handles on the collective action problem writ large and writ small.

3 CONCLUSION: "LIMITATIONS" OF RATIONAL CHOICE INSTITUTIONALISM

The research program of rational choice institutionalism is founded on abstraction, simplification, analytical rigor, and an insistence on clean lines of analysis from basic axioms to analytical propositions to empirical implications. Much of the research in this program actually practices what it preaches! Self-conscious and

---

[14] Even earlier, Hardin 1971 noted the connection between Olson's collective action problem and an *n*-person version of the PD. Also see Taylor 1976 .

[15] Other types of two-person repeated interactions capture different kinds of norms. Equilibrium behavior in repeated play of the "Battle of the Sexes" game made famous by Luce and Raiffa 1954, for example, may be identified with coordination norms like "drive on the right and pass on the left (unless you live in Great Britain."

self-imposed limits are an inherent part of the program so that conclusions can be stated in the confidence that they can be traced back to their progenitors. For some (Green and Shapiro 1994) this is a fatal weakness. Limits, after all, are *limiting*.

In another sense, however, they are liberating—hence the quotation marks in the title of this concluding section. The measured relaxation of limitations is the way forward both to generalize what we already know from limited contexts and to expand the intellectual coverage of the program. Through this process the rational institutionalism program has been engaged, almost since its beginnings, in a conscious blurring of distinctions. Perhaps the most obvious of these is *bounded rationality* (Simon 1957, 1969; Cyert and March 1963). A second is the rise of *behavioral economics* and the experimental methodology closely associated with it. A third is *transaction-costs economics*. And a fourth is *analytical narratives*. I treat each of these briefly.

3.1   Bounded Rationality

Initiated in the early work of Herbert Simon, though also associated closely with the work of the social psychologist Sidney Siegel, bounded rationality takes the perspective that being rational is costly on the one hand, and is constrained by cognitive limitations on the other.[16] Consequently, real human beings, in contrast to automatons, are only approximately rational. Their behavior reveals levels of aspiration, rules of thumb, standing decisions, stopping rules, and satisficing. At times boundedly rational behavior can be shown to be identical to canonical rational behavior under uncertainty and costly decision-making, so it is not a radical departure from the canonical program. But it has loosened the strictures and thus paved the way for a second, more recent development.

3.2   Behavioral Economics

This branch of rational choice examines what happens in markets and firms when individual agents are cognitively constrained. Perhaps the most influential work in this area was stimulated by the ground-breaking research of two psychologists, Daniel Kahneman and Amos Tversky (1979, 1981). The emphasis here is on rationality qualified by psychological limitations—loss aversion, framing effects,

---

[16] A recent elaboration of this approach that brings attention to the relevance of the work of modern cognitive science for democratic theory is Lupia and McCubbins 1998. A broad interpretive essay on this same subject by Goodin 2000*a* is well worth consulting.

hyperbolic discounting. This work is only just finding its way into the rational institutionalist research program, but again is an illustration of how the bright line between canonical rationality and psychological reality is fading.[17]

3.3   Transaction-cost Economics

This work has its origins in the seminal contributions of Ronald Coase (1937, 1960) and applications of his ideas (along with those of students of bounded rationality) by Oliver Williamson (1985). In this work the fundamental unit of analysis is the transaction and the fundamental institution of transactions is the contract. Emphasis is focused on the costliness of searching for transaction partners, drafting agreements, anticipating contingencies of relevance to the agreement, devising mechanisms to interpret agreements in novel circumstances, policing and enforcing compliance, and dealing with transgressions. Exchange, in short, is neither automatic nor cost-free. It requires institutions of governance. The economic institutions of capitalism, to use Williamson's phrase, are in effect *political*. Running a firm is governing a firm. Implementing a contract requires a framework of governance. The structure of a firm provides a framework for "private politics." And economic exchange, properly understood, is political to its core. Economics segues into politics. This is no more apparent than in Weingast and Marshall's (1988) transaction cost analysis of the organization of legislatures.

3.4   Analytical Narratives

A final blurring of distinctions attacks the line between rational choice institution-alism and historical institutionalism. Separately and collectively, Robert Bates, Avner Greif, Margaret Levi, Jean-Laurent Rosenthal, and Barry Weingast, have developed the analytical narrative as a case-oriented methodology for studying institutional development in historical context (Bates et al. 1998). The object of analysis is an historical case—economic growth in medieval Italian city-states, conscription, the institutional origins of the American civil war, the coffee cartel in Latin America, the historical evolution of European absolutist regimes. What distinguishes this approach from mainstream historical institutionalism is the use of analytical models—a spatial representation, a game form, an optimization set-up—as a framework in which to embed the case. An analytical narrative *is* a

---

[17] Stimulating explorations of the Kahneman–Tversky approach for political phenomena, includ-ing public opinion and citizen competence, are found in Druckman 2001, 2004.

case study but there is an underlying model that motivates analysis and frames the empirical materials.

Rational choice institutionalism began as pure theft, lifting analytical tools from mathematics, operations research, and economics. In its focus on institutions in politics, economics, and society, it developed boundaries, a canon, and an identity. Some of this has been surveyed in this chapter. The program has prospered but is not without its critics. Many have felt, almost from the outset as the quotation from Clark that introduces this chapter suggests, that the assumption of rationality is too demanding; developments in bounded rationality and behavioral economics are responding to this. Some believed that even canonically rational actors would have trouble in the world of politics living up to the expectations of the invisible-hand standards of market exchange; explorations of transaction cost phenomena attempt to deal with some of these frictions. Still others emphasized the ahistorical quality of rational choice institutionalism; history dependent and contextualized aspects are now a part of game theory, and rich historical cases are now examined in a rigorously analytical fashion.

In defense of the early program in rational choice institutionalism, it must be acknowledged that a paradigm, as Kuhn (1970) reminded us, develops protective boundaries in order to permit normal science to progress. Rational choice institutionalists were no exception, differentiating their product and pushing its paradigmatic assumptions as far as they could. Eventually, however, some of the criticism is constructive, it begins to attract attention, the boundaries weaken, and practitioners seek ways to accommodate what they had formerly rejected. I believe this is the current state of the program in rational choice institutionalism. It is increasingly responsive, not imperialistic, and the distinctions between it and its institutionalist cousins are beginning to weaken.[18]

References

ASHWORTH, S. and BUENO DE MESQUITA, E. 2004. Electoral selection and incumbency advantage. Working paper.

AUSTEN-SMITH, D. and BANKS, J. 1989. Electoral accountability and incumbency. Pp. 121–50 in *Models of Strategic Choice in Politics*, ed. P. Ordeshook. Ann Arbor: University of Michigan Press.

—— —— 1999. *Positive Political Theory I: Collective Preferences*. Ann Arbor: University of Michigan Press.

—— —— 2005. *Positive Political Theory II: Strategy and Structure*. Ann Arbor: University of Michigan Press.

---

[18] For interesting suggestions on the shape an emerging synthesis might take, see Goodin 2000*b*.

AXELROD, R. 1984. *The Evolution of Cooperation*. New York: Basic Books.

BANKS, J. and SUNDURAM, R. 1993. Adverse selection and moral hazard in a repeated elections model. Pp. 295–313 in *Political Economy: Institutions, Competition, and Representation*, ed. W. Barnett, M. Hinich, and N. Schofield. Cambridge: Cambridge University Press.

BARRO, R. 1972. The control of politicians: an economic model. *Public Choice*, 14: 19–42.

BATES, R., GREIF, A., LEVI, M., ROSENTHAL, J.-L., and WEINGAST, B. 1998. *Analytical Narratives*. Princeton, NJ: Princeton University Press.

BINDER, S. A. and MALTZMAN, F. 2005. Congress and the politics of judicial appointments. Pp. 297–317 in *Congress Reconsidered*, 8th edn, ed. L. Dodd and B. Oppenheimer. Washington, DC: CQ Press.

BINDER, S. A. and SMITH, S. 1996. *Politics or Principle? Filibustering in the United States Senate*. Washington, DC: Brookings Press.

BUCHANAN, J. and TULLOCK, G. 1962. *The Calculus of Consent*. Ann Arbor: University of Michigan Press.

BUENO DE MESQUITA, B., SMITH, A., SIVERSON, R., and MORROW, J. 2003. *The Logic of Political Survival*. Cambridge, Mass.: MIT Press.

CALVERT, R. 1985. Robustness of the multidimensional voting model: candidates' motivations, uncertainty, and convergence. *American Journal of Political Science*, 29: 69–95.

—— 1995. Rational actors, equilibrium, and social institutions. Pp. 57–95 in *Explaining Social Institutions*, ed. J. Knight and I. Sened. Ann Arbor: University of Michigan Press.

COASE, R. 1937. The nature of the firm. *Economica*, 4: 386–405.

—— 1960. The problem of social cost. *Journal of Law and Economics*, 3: 1–44.

CRAWFORD, S. and OSTROM, E. 1995. The grammar of institutions. *American Political Science Review*, 89: 582–600.

CYERT, R. and J. MARCH. 1963. *A Behavioral Theory of the Firm*. Englewood Cliffs, NJ: Prentice Hall.

DEWATRIPONT, M., JEWITT, I., and TIROLE, J. 1999. The economics of career concerns part I: comparing information structures. *Review of Economic Studies*, 66: 183–98.

DIERMEIER, D. and KREHBIEL, K. 2003. Institutionalism as a methodology. *Journal of Theoretical Politics*, 15: 123–45.

DOWNS, A. 1957. *An Economic Theory of Democracy*. New York: Harper and Row.

DRUCKMAN, J. 2001. The implications of framing effects for citizen competence. *Political Behavior*, 23: 225–56.

—— 2004. Political preference formation: competition, deliberation, and the (ir)relevance of framing effects. *American Political Science Review*, 98: 671–86.

EPSTEIN, D. and O'HALLORAN, S. 1999. *Delegating Powers*. New York: Cambridge University Press.

FEARON, J. 1999. Electoral accountability and the control of politicians: selecting good types versus sanctioning poor performance. Pp. 55–97 in *Democracy, Accountability, and Representation*, ed. A. Przeworski, S. Stokes, and B. Manin. New York: Cambridge University Press.

—— and LAITIN, D. 1996. Explaining interethnic cooperation. *American Political Science Review*, 90: 715–35.

FEREJOHN, J. 1986. Incumbent performance and electoral control. *Public Choice*, 50: 5–25.

—— 1999. Accountability and authority: toward a theory of political accountability. Pp. 131–54 in *Democracy, Accountability, and Representation*, ed. A. Przeworski, S. Stokes, and B. Manin. New York: Cambridge University Press.

FIORINA, M. and SHEPSLE, K. 1989. Formal theories of leadership: agents, agenda setters, and entrepreneurs. Pp. 17–41 in *Leadership in Politics*, ed. B. Jones. Lawrence: University Press of Kansas.

FROHLICH, N., OPPENHEIMER, J., and YOUNG, O. 1971. *Political Leadership and Collective Goods*. Princeton, NJ: Princeton University Press.

GOODIN, R. 2000a. Institutional gaming. *Governance*, 13: 523–33.

—— 2000b. Rationality redux: reflections on Herbert Simon's vision of politics. Pp. 58–83 in *Competition and Cooperation: Conversations with Nobelists about Economics and Political Science*, ed. J. Alt, M. Levi, and E. Ostrom. New York: Russell Sage Foundation Press.

GREEN, D. and SHAPIRO, I. 1994. *Pathologies of Rational Choice*. New Haven, Conn.: Yale University Press.

HALL, P. and TAYLOR, R. 1996. Political science and the three new institutionalisms. *Political Studies*, 44: 936–57.

HARDIN, R. 1971. Collective action as an agreeable n-prisoners' dilemma. *Behavioral Science*, 16: 472–81.

—— 1982. *Collective Action*. Washington, DC: Resources for the Future.

HINICH, M. and MUNGER, M. 1997. *Analytical Politics*. New York: Cambridge University Press.

HOLMSTROM, B. 1979. Moral hazard and observability. *Bell Journal of Economics*, 10: 74–91.

—— 1982. Moral hazard in teams. *Bell Journal of Economics*, 13: 324–40.

JACOBI, T. 2005. The senatorial courtesy game: explaining the norm of informal vetoes in "advice and consent" nominations. *Legislative Studies Quarterly*, 30: 193–217.

KAHNEMAN, D. and TVERSKY, A. 1979. Prospect theory: an analysis of decision under risk. *Econometrica*, 47: 263–91.

—— —— 1981. The framing of decisions and the psychology of choice. *Science*, 211: 453–8.

KIEWIET, R. and McCUBBINS, M. 1991. *The Logic of Delegation*. Chicago: University of Chicago Press.

KUHN, T. 1970. *The Structure of Scientific Revolutions*. Chicago: University of Chicago Press.

LAVER, M. 1997. *Private Desires, Political Action*. London: Sage.

LUCE, R. and RAIFFA, H. 1954. *Games and Decisions*. New York: Wiley.

LUPIA, A. and McCUBBINS, M. 1998. *The Democratic Dilemma*. New York: Cambridge University Press.

MARCH, J. and OLSEN, J. 1984. The new institutionalism: organizational factors in political life. *American Political Science Review*, 78: 734–49.

MUELLER, D. 2003. *Public Choice III*. New York: Cambridge University Press.

MÜLLER, W. and STRØM, K. 1999. *Policy, Office, or Votes? How Political Parties in Western Europe Make Hard Decisions*. Cambridge: Cambridge University Press.

NORTH, D. 1990. *Institutions, Institutional Change, and Economic Performance*. New York: Cambridge University Press.

OLSON, M. 1965. *The Logic of Collective Action*. Cambridge, Mass.: Harvard University Press.

OSTROM, E. 2005. *Understanding Institutional Diversity*. Princeton, NJ: Princeton University Press.

PERSSON, T. and TABELLINI, G. 2000. *Political Economics*. Cambridge, Mass.: MIT Press.

RIKER, W. 1980. Implications from the disequilibrium of majority rule for the study of institutions. *American Political Science Review*, 74: 432–46.

SAIT, E. 1938. *Political Institutions: A Preface*. New York: Appleton-Century-Crofts.

Samuelson, P. 1954. The pure theory of public expenditure. *Review of Economics and Statistics*, 36: 387–90.

Sandler, T. 1992. *Collective Action: Theory and Applications*. Ann Arbor: University of Michigan Press.

Schelling, T. C. 1960. *The Strategy of Conflict*. Cambridge, Mass.: Harvard University Press.

Schlesinger, A. 1966. *Ambition and Politics*. New York: Rand-McNally.

Schotter, A. 1981. *The Economic Theory of Social Institutions*. New York: Cambridge University Press.

Shepsle, K. 1979. Institutional arrangements and equilibrium in multidimensional voting models. *American Journal of Political Science*, 23: 23–57.

—— 1986. Institutional equilibrium and equilibrium institutions. Pp. 51–82 in *Political Science: The Science of Politics*, ed. H. Weisberg. New York: Agathon.

—— 2006. Old questions and new answers about institutions: the Riker objection revisited. In *The Oxford Handbook of Political Economy*, ed. B. Weingast and D. Wittman. Oxford: Oxford University Press.

—— and Bonchek, M. 1997. *Analyzing Politics*. New York: W.W. Norton.

Simon, H. 1957. *Models of Man*. New York: John Wiley.

—— 1969. *The Sciences of the Artificial*. Cambridge, Mass.: MIT Press.

Taylor, M. 1976. *Anarchy and Cooperation*. New York: Wiley.

Wagner, R. 1966. Pressure groups and political entrepreneurs. *Papers on Non-Market Decision Making*, 1: 161–70.

Ward, H. 1998. A game theoretic analysis of the politics of taking it in turns. *British Journal of Political Science*, 28: 355–87.

Weingast, B. 1996. Political institutions: rational choice perspectives. Pp. 167–90 in *A New Handbook of Political Science*, ed. R. Goodin and H.-D. Klingemann. Oxford: Oxford University Press.

—— 2002. Rational-choice institutionalism. Pp. 660–92 in *Political Science: The State of the Discipline*, ed. I. Katznelson and H. Milner. New York: W.W. Norton.

—— and W. Marshall. 1988. The industrial organization of congress; or, why legislatures, like firms, are not organized as markets. *Journal of Political Economy*, 96: 132–63.

Williamson, O. 1985. *The Economic Institutions of Capitalism*. New York: Free Press.

Wittman, D. 1973. Parties as utility maximizers. *American Political Science Review*, 67: 490–8.

CHAPTER 3

HISTORICAL INSTITUTIONALISM

ELIZABETH SANDERS *Cornell*

The central assumption of historical institutionalism (HI) is that it is more enlightening to study human political interactions: (a) in the context of rule structures that are themselves human creations; and (b) sequentially, as life is lived, rather than to take a snapshot of those interactions at only one point in time, and in isolation from the rule structures (institutions) in which they occur.

As to the development of the behavior shaping rule structures themselves, a now conventional notion, borrowed from economics and popularized by Paul Pierson (2000), is that institutional development over time is marked by path dependence (PD). A crisis, or a serendipitous confluence of events or social pressures, produces a new way of doing things. For example, in the case of regulating railroads by independent commission, "increasing returns" accrued to the steady elaboration of this path—and not to fluctuating experimentation with *other* methods of reducing social costs occasioned by uncontrolled railroad entrepreneurship—and, for that reason, the railroad commission lasted a long time and its functional connections to society became ever more elaborate. Transportation businesses, trade unions, investor decisions, and legislative and party politics gained a stake in the "path" of railroad regulation by independent commission and calculated and defended their interests within its rules. To understand the actions of all these political players, one must take cognizance of the historical development of the institution, and the original, distinct culture and problems in which it arose. That is the central logic of HI, and to its practitioners the advantage of studying politics this way is obvious and noncontroversial.

Nevertheless, the popularity of historical analysis of institutions—their origins, development, and relationship to policy and behavior—has by no means been continuous. As historians of knowledge remind us, attention to the development of institutions has fluctuated widely across disciplines, and over time. Its popularity has waxed and waned in response to events in the social/economic/political world and to the normal intradisciplinary conflicts of ideas and career paths (Ross 1995). This chapter will examine the context in which a new attention to institutional analysis arose in the social sciences in the 1970s, the distinctions between historical institutionalism and its closest competitors (rational choice and quantitative cross-sectional analysis), and the search for agents of institutional maintenance and change that is at the core of HI. It will conclude with comments on aspects of institutional development that have received (I argue) too little attention: the pathologies that become imbedded in public institutions and constitute "moral hazards" in the performance of public officials.

1 THE WANING AND WAXING OF HISTORICAL INSTITUTIONALISM

It is true that some classic works that analyze institutions in historical perspective have enjoyed a more or less continuous life on political science syllabi. Books by Max Weber, Maurice Duverger, Alexis de Tocqueville, John Locke, Woodrow Wilson, Robert McCloskey, and Samuel Beer are prominent examples. Such work was increasingly sidelined, however, with the rise of behaviorism after the Second World War, particularly with the emergence of survey research and computer technology. With the availability of large data-sets on contemporaneous attitudes, elections, and legislative roll call votes, and with statistical analysis of those data made enormously easier by computers and statistical software, political scientists largely abandoned the study of history and institutional structures in the 1960s.

However, after a hiatus of several decades, the study of institutions in historical perspective reemerged in political science in the 1970s, took on new, more analytical, epistemological characteristics, and flowered in the 1980s and 1990s. Why this reemergence? The simplest explanation is that economic relationships were in crisis, if that is not too strong a word ("flux" would be far too mild). Largely as a result of their revealed malfunctions and vulnerabilities, post-Second World War democratic institutions based on stable economic growth were being criticized and challenged in the 1970s as they had not been since the 1940s.

Increasingly loud criticism of institutions that had long been taken for granted (particularly those concerned with regulation, money supply, and social welfare) now provoked questions that intrigued a generation of scholars: why had those institutions been created, how had they evolved to reach this point, and why were they no longer adapting successfully to changing needs? How, in other words, had the stable, adaptive path dependence of Western institutions come to experience operational crisis and undermined confidence in the ideas and processes on which they were founded? And how did the different sets of national institutions differ in the way they accommodated to the new economy of the late twentieth century? That it raised such questions should not imply that finding the answers has been easy for HI, as the approach lends itself much better to the study of incremental growth around an original path than to sudden, drastic change.

2 The Epistemology of Historical Institutionalism and its Competitors

The search for the causes and agents of institutional change has had many epistemological consequences, not least of which was a new attention to ideas. In steady state, the ideas and assumptions that institutions incorporate tend to be taken for granted. But in times of crisis, new ideas are put forward and find adherents. In economics, the ideational turn of the 1970s and 1980s discredited Keynsianism and promoted contending arguments mainly associated with the "Chicago School." The new paradigm incorporated neoclassical theories about the greater efficiency of minimally regulated markets, and new theories about money supply (Eisner 1991; Hall 1989). In political science, a revived influence of economic ideas—pioneered after the Second World War by Kenneth Arrow, Mancur Olson, and Anthony Downs—augmented the popularity of a rational choice paradigm (RC) focused on individual preferences and utility maximizing strategies. (See Shepsle, this volume.)

But, somewhat paradoxically, there was, at roughly the same time, a rebellion of social scientists and historians against the individual centered behaviorism that had dominated political science (most completely in the United States), and against its dominant paradigm, pluralism (see esp. Lowi 1969). The "normal" political science of the 1950s and 1960s, focused on contemporary (but well established) interest groups and individual attitudes (as measured by survey responses), was of little help in understanding the apparent maladaptation of institutions after long periods of stability, or the challenge to institutions posed by the new social movements of the 1960s and 1970s.

A major outcome of the 1960s–70s challenge to pluralism was the rediscovery of the importance of state institutions and their partial autonomy from civil society (that is, the perception that public institutions were much more than "black boxes" processing demands from society by turning them into policies). The attack on pluralism thus contributed importantly to the new flowering of historical institutionalism (HI).

As it turned out, rational choice practitioners and historical institutionalists were largely in agreement on one essential definition and premise: that institutions constitute the "humanly devised constraints that shape human interaction" (North 1990). But the two schools differ greatly in the object and timespan of their studies. For RC, it is the microcosmic *game*, the particular interaction of preference-holding, utility-seeking individuals *within* a set of (stable) institutional constraints (whether those are viewed as exogenous, or permeable and action-constructed) that is of interest, and RC borrowings are mainly from economics and mathematics.

For HI, what is mainly of interest is the *construction, maintenance*, and *adaptation* of institutions. HI scholars are not uninterested in individual preferences and the logic-driven, stylized way they might play out, but HI is more likely to define human motivation in terms of *goals*—which have a more public, less self-interested dimension—and in collective action, whether among executive officials, legislators, or social groups. RC (at least as perceived by HI) cares more about the abstracted game under the microscope, whereas HI is generally more concerned with the long-term evolution and *outcome* (intended or not) of a welter of interactions among goal-seeking actors, both within institutions, and with their challengers outside.

This attention to goals, collective action, outcomes, and persistence inevitably draws HI to ideas, and ideas are different from the preferences or consciousness of rules with which RC is concerned. Ideas are relational, and often embody normative a prioris. Whether or not ideas are mere abstractions from, or disguises for, individual preferences is less interesting to HI than the obvious fact that ideas serve as mobilizing forces for collective action by social groups that want to create or change institutions (Lieberman 2002, for example); and for institutional actors themselves, ideas serve as the glue that holds an administration, party, or agency together in its tasks, help to garner public support, and provide a standard to evaluate the institution's policy outcomes.

It is a short step from concern with ideas and outcomes to concern with evaluative/normative questions about the "goodness" of particular institutions, or struggles to achieve a "good state." HI scholars have a more normative, reformist bent than the studiously dispassionate and market-affirming RC group (one must interject here Polanyi's now-classic observation that the decision to let markets determine outcomes is itself a *normative* choice, and that the apparatus of the presumably "free" and "natural" market takes a lot of deliberate constructing and coercive buttressing to survive).

The analysis of the RC fraternity, in Shepsle's words, is "founded on abstraction, simplification, analytical rigor, and an insistence on clean lines of analysis from basic axioms," whereas most HI analysis is founded on dense, empirical description and inductive reasoning. A focus on interactive games draws RC to mathematics and economics, while interest in the construction, maintenance, and outcomes of institutions draws HI toward history and philosophy. The former proceed essentially through equations; the latter often count manifestations of behavior (and in fact have a stronger empirical bent than most RC exercises), but HI employs much more narrative in setting out its causal chains; and of course, its causal chains are much longer.

In sum, HI pays more attention to the long-term viability of institutions and their broad consequences; RC, to the parameters of particular moments in history that are the setting for individual self-interest maximization. As Paul Pierson (2004) has emphasized, RC takes preferences for granted, whereas HI is interested in how ideas, interests, and positions *generate* preferences, and how (and why) they evolve over time. There is no reason why the two approaches should be viewed as antithetical, however. They may well be complementary. The choice of focus between practitioners of RC and HI may be a matter of individual temperament and the assumptions and methodological affinities that go with it, but the questions they ask may well be of mutual interest. That is certainly the case for the present writer.

3 THREE VARIETIES OF HISTORICAL INSTITUTIONALISM: AGENTS OF DEVELOPMENT AND CHANGE

If institutions are humanly designed constraints on subsequent human action, then those who study them over time will inevitably be drawn to ask: *whose* design? And when institutions change, or collapse, what are the exogenous social forces or internal group dynamics that are responsible? These questions about agency-in-change receive a lot of attention in HI—more attention, it is probably fair to claim, than in RC or conventional pluralist social science. The notion of path dependence that is central to HI is compatible with diverse scholarly orientations toward agency in path *establishment*, as well as in pressures for institutional *change*. Thus the identification of agents provides one way to organize a brief discussion of the contributions of HI.

The choice of where one goes to look for prime movers in the genesis and development of institutions may again be conditioned by scholarly temperament, as well as philosophical and methodological inclinations. Some analysts have started at the top, attributing agency in the establishment and development of institutions to presidents, judges, high-level bureaucrats, and the intellectuals and business aristocracy who advise and inform them. Others have gone to the bottom, seeing the broader public, particularly social movements and groups motivated by ideas, values, and grievances, as the instigators of institutional construction, change, and destruction.

Inevitably, other scholars have come forward to argue that neither a focus on the top, nor on the bottom can, by itself, tell the whole story of institutional estab-lishment, development, and change; and so one must adopt an interactive approach that analyzes the ideas, interests, and behavior of actors in both state and society. Comparativists, in particular, prefer a multifocal (multivariate) search for the actors and conditions that produce differences in national outcomes, but even HI scholars who work on single country settings seem increasingly drawn to interactive approaches.

The choice of focus has methodological implications, because at the top there are few actors and one is likely to proceed by analyzing documents, decisions, speeches, memoirs, and press reports of actions/events. In the study of social movements, voters, and the legislators who are usually the "first responders" to their demands, the "*n*" is larger, and quantitative analysis more plausible. But a high word-to-number ratio usually characterizes HI work in all categories, and distinguishes it from both RC institutionalism and conventional, cross-sectional, quantitative, hypothesis-testing political science. Compare, for example, the work of Eric Schickler (2001) and Sarah Binder (1997)—both historical institutional works that analyze changes over time in congressional rules—to the conventional *American Political Science Review* quantitative and RC studies of congressional politics.

All this diversity—of agency, methodology, and single-country vs. comparative analysis—might be seen as a weakness in HI. It is, undeniably, a messily eclectic genre, and the lack of agreement on foci and approaches does distinguish HI from RC and conventional, cross-sectional political science. The "undisciplined" nature of HI in its late adolescence was no doubt what prompted the two founders of APD's flagship journal (*Studies in American Political Development*) to write their 2004 book, *The Search for American Political Development* (Orren and Skowronek). However, worries about lack of common definitions, methods, and parameters have not produced, as yet, much sentiment to impose order via more restrictive criteria for scholars in the American HI fold.

4 Institutional Formation and Change from the Top Down

The 1980s revival of HI among political scientists in the United States was strongly centered on actors in the national state, and its explanation for the birth and development of a modern centralized state tended to start at the top. Social scientists rediscovering history (and the state in history) were influenced by the work of the neo-Marxist and other elite focused historians with similar foci. Such was the case with Theda Skocpol's pioneering *States and Social Revolutions* (1979) and the seminal article on the differential success of innovative agricultural and industrial policies in the New Deal by Skocpol and Kenneth Finegold (1990), as well as Stephen Skowronek's *Building a New American State: The Expansion of National Administrative Capacities, 1877–1920* (1982). These scholars were pioneers in the budding 1980s sub-field of American political development, and in the creation of a new section on politics and history in the American Political Science Association (APSA). It might be noted that HI's respectability, in a discipline dominated for the previous half century by RC and ahistorical quantitative work, is evidenced by the size of the politics and history section in its parent professional organization. It ranks in the top quintile of APSA's thirty-four sections, and has been joined by a new political history section with an exclusively international focus.

As Skowronek and his co-author Karen Orren write in *The Search for American Political Development*, the historical analysis of politics assumes that political institutional development unfolds on *sites* that are defined by rule structures and their enforcers, holders of "plenary authority." It is not surprising, then, that the first wave of HI in the United States has done its process tracing with a focus on those plenary authorities in national government, the rules they promulgate and uphold, and the ideas that motivate their actions. That is in itself a tall order, and in practice leaves little space for attention to "ordinary people." The latter are seen as the *objects* of governance, not as *subjects* whose ideas and demands might shape institutional development and provoke institutional change.

Ironically, then, as historians were abandoning the study of powerful white men for the lives of ordinary people, political scientists of an historical/institutional bent were rediscovering the momentous agency of "state managers." Social movements of the poor and middling orders of society, if they were noticed at all, tended to be viewed as inconvenient obstacles to the modernizing projects of political elites, or as clients of reformist state actors. For Stephen Skowronek (1982), farmers and their representatives in the progressive era Congress, along with judges jealous of the power of the new regulatory agencies, were the main obstacles to the holistic modernization schemes of a few visionaries in the Interstate Commerce Commission (ICC) and Senate. For Skocpol and Feingold (1990), workers were important

New Deal *clients*, but not themselves *agents* of labor policy change in the New Deal. (For an opposing view that stresses labor agency, see Goldfield 1989.)

Skowronek's *Building A New American State (1982)*, one of the founding works in the 1980s revival of historical institutionalism in the United States, focused on three cases in the modernization of the American national state: the beginning of national railroad regulation, the fight for a meritocratic civil service, and the struggle for a permanent professional army. Though each case of necessity touched on Congress, the states, and parties, the prime movers in these accounts were distinctively elite. In the case of civil service reform, Mugwump intellectual reformers, with the support of important businessmen who hoped for a more efficient bureaucracy, were the activists who championed a meritocratic bureaucracy against party "spoilsmen." Of course, it was acknowledged that elites had to settle for partial loaves and halting progress, in view of the centrality of patronage resources for American parties. Skowronek's central argument is that a disjointed state "of courts and parties" could succeed only in erecting a "patchwork" rather than a fully rationalized administrative state.

In the fight for railroad legislation, according to Skowronek, well-educated intellectual reformers worked through a savvy Midwestern senator to restrain (while moderately responding to) agrarian forces in Congress. In 1887, they created the nation's first independent regulatory agency, the Interstate Commerce Commission. From the time of its founding, commissioners, judges, and ultimately presidents were the principle actors, in Skowronek's narrative.

Presidents, intellectuals, and generals were the prime movers in the struggle to create a professional army (the "continental army" of progressive era policy debate). Elite business actors were strongly supportive, since a permanent, professional military promised better protection for investment, at home and abroad, than the traditionally decentralized and part-time militia. Reflecting the power of path dependence unfolding from initial policy decisions, echoes of this debate still reverberate in the speeches of Secretary of Defense Rumsfeld, who would clearly prefer a larger professional military (and private national contractor corps) to what he sees as the reluctant amateurs in the national guard contingents raised by the states.

To a large extent, the elite-centered account of APD in Skowronek's early work was shaped by the chosen cases: the campaigns for military and civil service professionalism were not popular causes in the United States (far from it). Likewise, Daniel Carpenter (2001) has recently challenged claims of social movement responsibility for reforms in the early twentieth-century United States. His careful archival and statistical work has demonstrated that entrepreneurs in the country's early bureaucracies came up with ideas for expanded bureaucratic authority and then engineered social movements to support new postal services and food and drug regulation. However, the elite leadership in these two arenas cannot be generalized to other policy domains (Sanders 1999), and the phenomenon of bureaucratic entrepreneurship of the order reported by Carpenter may itself be time-bound, particularly marking the struggles for legitimacy of fledgling agencies.

But there are, surely, resounding cases of institution building and expansion in which elite leadership is to be expected. One is monetary policy, in which financial elites and their governmental allies pioneered the creation of central banks and stable national currencies (although the structure and powers of the resulting agencies did not follow elite designs in critical areas: Livingston 1986; Broz 1997; Sanders 1999). Another is military policy, where (as Skowronek's case study of the campaign for a national, professionalized army underlines) *expansion* of bureaucratic resources has been, in the United States, almost entirely under presidential leadership; on the other hand, major attempts at *rationalization* of military and intelligence bureaucracies (through reorganization and new mandates) has come from Congress. As the 9/11 episode revealed, presidents have been more interested in assuring that the defense and intelligence agencies support their policy preferences than in assuring that these agencies effectively serve the national security interest (Zegart 2000, 2005).

Skowronek's early HI work centered on the critical policies that initiated the rise of a modern administrative state. John Gerring, also a pioneer of HI, and of the establishment of a distinct field of qualitative methods that gained popularity in the wake of HI's emergence, shifted the focus to political party ideologies and their development over two centuries (Gerring 2001). As critical intermediary institutions linking leaders and their societal constituent groups, parties have been ambiguous institutions in HI. The early work of Skocpol and Finegold (1990, 1995) treated them as extensions of political elites—recalling Maurice Duverger's (1954) labeling of major US parties as "cadre" organizations, founded by and elaborated around competing national political figures.

Gerring follows this perspective, too, centering his narrative (and impressively rigorous counting of patterns of discourse in party platforms and official pronouncements) on the expressed ideas of party elites (mainly nominees for, and holders of, the presidency). The ideas that constitute the public philosophies, and guide the policy foci of different party regimes—in two distinct periods for the Whig/Republicans and three for the Jeffersonian/Democrats—are assumed to arise with elites, and then find favor with the masses. This is the usual assumption of scholarship focused on elites and ideas, though constructivists would argue for a broader and more socially interactive ideational provenance.

An alternative, but still elite-centered way to look at party institutions in APD is found in Richard Bensel's thick and empirically buttressed account of the rise and maintenance of the post-Civil War "party-state" constructed by leaders of the victorious Republican Party. The identifying contours of that party ideological superstructure (Bensel would say "facade") do not differ significantly from Gerring's account, but where Gerring sees a coherent national party ideology organized in the minds of national political leaders and then articulated to the masses, Bensel sees party leaders instrumentally brokering bargains among coalition factions who have very different policy interests, and then herding them into a corral that flies an ideological banner (Bensel 1991, 2000, 2004).

Bensel parses out the institutional complexity that buttressed Republican ideational and policy dominance for half a century by allowing different coalitional interests to hold sway in different institutions. He shows that different aspects of the GOP postwar program (policies concerned with the tariff, gold standard, and creation of an unfettered national market) were parceled out to Congress, the White House, and the federal courts—and *that* institutional differentiation, rather than a national consensus on ideas, held the GOP together, in his account (Bensel 2000).

5 SOCIETAL AGENTS IN INSTITUTIONAL DEVELOPMENT AND CHANGE

Political scientists, historians, and sociologists of the 1960s–80s grew uncomfortable with the implication that elites were the motor of history, even as they condemned the "naive" assumptions of dispersed power so dear to pluralism. Sociologists and historians made vital contributions to knowledge by disputing the reigning ideas about social movements of the poor and marginalized that had marked post-Second World War scholarship. American Greenbackers and Populists, once condemned as clownish or dangerously atavistic factions of an otherwise healthily modernizing polity (or worse, as proto-fascists), were subjected to new and much more rigorous analyses that revealed them to be impressively rational, inventive democratic reformers responsible for much of the social, political, and economic progress of later periods (McMath 1975; Schwartz 1976; Goodwyn 1976; Pollack 1987).

His own participation in the civil rights movement of the 1960s led Doug McAdam (1982) to undertake an analytical history of the rise of that movement that set out a whole new theory of social movement formation and interaction with the state, one that stressed grassroots organizational resources and the opportunities available to movements of the disadvantaged in times of serious elite conflict. By the end of the 1980s, the flaws in previous journalistic and literary works on populism and other "petit-bourgeois," presumably status-obsessed movements (work typified by Hofstadter 1955) were clearly revealed, and the superficial connections made between American dissidents and European fascists were no longer sustainable (Brinkley 1982).

These path-breaking movement studies exploited primary sources and (in the case of Michael Schwartz and Doug McAdam) methods indebted to rational choice and statistical political science, to suggest linkages between past and present movement struggles. William Gamson's important meta-analysis of the political achievements of "challenging groups" from 1800 to 1945 further clarified the theoretical insights that could be gained from the historical study of social movements. These studies by sociologists and historians thus contributed significantly to the revival of interest in history, and in "poor people's movements" (the title of a 1977 book by sociologists Piven and Cloward) among political scientists, but their focus was on the emergence of dissident organization and strategy in the context of political economy, *not* on the development of political institutions. It remained to link group struggles "from below" to the dynamics of institution formation and development.

Sociologists moving into the developing sub-field of politics and history made important contributions to this linkage. Theda Skocpol, a pioneer of politics and history and of American Political Development (HI's foremost vehicle in the United States), turned her attention from political elites to dissident social organizations with her 1992 book, *Protecting Soldiers and Mothers: The Political Origins of Social Policy in the United States.* Connecting a "maternalist" cultural ethic and the hard work of women's local and national movement organizations in the late nineteenth and early twentieth centuries, Skocpol traces the modestly successful efforts of voteless women to influence social policy for women and children (and, ultimately, to win suffrage). Another political sociologist, Elisabeth Clemens, published in 1997 *The People's Lobby,* an important analysis of the honing of lobbying skills and strategies by farm, labor, and women's groups targeting state legislatures in and after the 1890s. The emergence of energetic grassroots organizations, linked in state and national associations that paralleled the structure of federalism, not only produced an outpouring of new state legislation in the progressive era, but created the template for the intermediary political institutions so intimately involved in US politics from that era forward.

In 2003, Theda Skocpol took another important look at the interaction between the national state and social organizations in *Diminished Democracy,* a richly detailed account of the rise and decline (after about 1950) of voluntary civic, occupational, and fraternal organizations in the post-Civil War United States. In this book, she lays out not only the extraordinary level of group membership in (often cross-class) civic organizations, but also their diverse political agendas and contribution to reform. Then, in a fascinating twist on the presumed direction of group influence to government action, Skocpol describes the numerous instances in which national officials turned to the voluntary groups for assistance in the First and Second World Wars. The large voluntary associations became important purveyors of war-related services, and most prospered as a result of the wartime state–group cooperation (though, one may ask, at what cost in autonomy and future effectiveness?).

6 THE DYNAMICS OF STATE–SOCIETY INTERACTION IN HI

As Skocpol's focus on the "patriotic partnerships" developed in wartime suggests (Skocpol 2003; Skocpol, Munson, Karch, and Bayliss 2002), social mobilization and institutional development can be seen as interactive processes. Dissident movements often demand, or indirectly call into being, new or expanded governmental institutions. They may use independent, non-, or bipartisan strategies, or become components of existing major parties, and thereby transform the party itself (Sanders 1999, 104). Once a new policy and its implementing institutions are in place, group demands and coalitional dynamics are themselves shaped by the making and interpretation of rules by public officials.

Even the decisions of the US Supreme Court, which many earlier scholars treated as philosopher-kings constructing and disseminating the public philosophies that guided subsequent policy-making at all levels of government, can, from a more historical and developmental perspective, be viewed as reactions to social movements and party realignment (Rosenberg 1991; Gates 1992). In a more nuanced and interactive way, the doctrinal landmarks of philosophical regimes defined and promulgated by the Supreme Court have been described by Ken Kersh (2004) as the *culmination* of "a layered succession of... spirited ideological and political campaigns" in society—a process that is far from linear, but rather (borrowing a Skowronek–Orren term), one marked by "intercurrence, disharmony, and complexity" (Kersh 2004, 18).

As we have seen in the fierce ideological and religious combat of early twenty-first-century US politics, the enshrining of those "culminating" doctrines (like the liberal dicta on abortion, gay rights, and religion) become themselves the provocation around which new social movements form.

"Policy begets politics," as Theodore Lowi put it in 1969, though his focus was on the societal elaboration of clientele supports for developing state institutions—powerful groups and second-level institutions (like the congressional committee and the administrative bureau) that ultimately could "wag the dog" of national policy elaboration. Disdaining the abandonment of institutions by 1950s political science, Lowi pioneered both the "return to the state" and an early formulation of path dependence.

His definition of institutions was the legalistic one that most historical institutionalists have adopted: institutions for Lowi were not just any set of behavior constraining rules or social norms, but the *formal* rules and procedures established by the action of governments, and backed, ultimately, by the coercive power of the state. Less interested than his students would be in how and why institutions had been created in the first place, or in the reformers who pressed for new laws and institutions, Lowi urged attention to what happened *after* institutions are established, and demanding and sustaining interests become attached to, and evolve in tandem with, the agency.

Perhaps the most closely examined, mutually constitutive relationship between state institutions and social movements is the case of organized labor. Long identified as a major determinant of national differences in social policy, the strength of labor movements and their relationship with political parties and courts has been a favorite subject of HI scholars. In the United States, with its powerful, independent judiciary, the doctrines handed down by the courts shaped labor's organizational and political strategies, its language, and its very self-conception (Tomlins 1985; Forbath 1991; Hattam 1993; Robertson 2000). And yet, when and where it could manage to amass sufficient political strength, organized labor might change the law and the personnel on the courts, and even emancipate itself from ancient feudalisms embedded in the common law (Orren 1991).

Racial divisions and animosities among workers have further burdened the politics of American labor, and diminished the political support for social welfare policies. Discriminatory racial norms were frozen in 1930s labor and social policy, their mitigation dependent on presidential political and wartime manpower needs, the slow amassing of voting power in northern cities, and sometimes—in a departure from its constraining role in labor organizational rights—racial accommodation leadership from the federal courts (Mettler 1998; Lieberman 2001; Kryder 2001; Frymer 2003). In Congress, however, disfranchisement of blacks in the south and segregationists' fears that trade unions would undermine white supremacy led southern Democrats to ally with conservative Republicans and use their institutional power to build an edifice of labor law that sapped the legal foundations of worker organization in the decade of labor's greatest membership growth (Katznelson, Geiger, and Kryder 1993; Katznelson and Farhang 2005).

Those who seek to unravel the complex and interactive evolution of parties, unions, cultural norms and ideologies, and state policy are logically drawn to comparative studies of two or more nations. Among the important contributions in this field are economist Gerald Friedman's *State-Making and Labor Movements: France and the United States, 1876–1914* (1999), which analyzes and compares labor organizational and partisan strategies, and national government responses in those two countries.

Of course, the marshalling of sufficient empirical evidence to make one's case will inevitably limit the time period covered, and the fullest understanding of policy paths and policy change can probably be gained by studies that concentrate on single-country experiences, like that of Daniel Tichenor's (2002) comprehensive HI analysis of social pressures and the twists and turns of US immigration policy in the nineteenth and twentieth centuries; and Jacob Hacker's (2002) masterful, theoretically original treatise on the development of the peculiar public/private hybrid welfare state that grew up in the USA after the mid-1930s.

7 CONCLUSION

Those who ignore history, as the old adages go, are doomed to repeat it...as farce and tragedy. Reason enough to learn what we can from the history of institutions. But there are two aspects of political institutions that remain under-explored, and considering their importance, this is both a mystery and a concern. There is a perhaps inevitable modernization focus in HI. The expansion and elaboration of national states is implicitly applauded, and that may account for the minute attention given to deregulation, privatization, devolution, and the other state-shrinking processes of the post-Reagan/Thatcher era which so violate the path dependent assumption. But one area of the state has *not* shrunk in the United States: the presidency and the war-fighting bureaucracies. These agencies are now of historically gargantuan size, and the pathological consequences of such un-checked (by internal or external rivals) power are increasingly apparent.

But expanded executive power, control of news, manipulative propaganda, wars of dubious necessity, and the starving of the domestic social and regulatory state to pay for the warfare state—all these conditions have existed in the past, and may be more implicit in the incentive structure of executive power, even in (or perhaps especially in) a democracy. Stephen Skowronek's *The Politics Presidents Make* (1997) calls attention to the timeless qualities of executive behavior in a two-party democracy, but lacks a critical perspective on the pathologies that recur in regime cycles (such as the attractiveness of war-making for "articulating" presidents).

That is not a weakness of his analysis, so much as an opening to further reflection on the unanticipated, largely unacknowledged "moral hazards" entailed by the growth of executive power. Changes in the candidate recruitment process that affect the personal qualities, and group and class ties, of presidents since 1972, and the amassing of enormous military resources and extensive control of infor-mation that accompany the rise of the USA to unrivaled global power, suggest that it may be time for a critical examination of the *institution* of the presidency, quite apart from the usual attention to the individuals that inhabit it.

Historical institutionalists, then, will not be distracted by wishful thinking about different personalities occupying executive power. If HI teaches us anything, it is that the place to look for answers to big questions about class, power, war, and reform is in institutions, not personalities, and over the longer landscapes of history, not the here and now.

REFERENCES

BEER, S. H. 1982. *Modern British Politics*, 3rd edn. New York: W. W. Norton.

BENSEL, R. F. 1991. *Yankee Leviathan: The Origins of Central State Authority in America, 1859–1877*. New York: Cambridge University Press.

—— 2000. *The Political Economy of American Industrialization*. New York: Cambridge University Press.

—— 2004. *The American Ballot Box in the Mid-Nineteenth Century*. New York: Cambridge University Press.

BINDER, S. 1997. *Minority Rights, Majority Rule: Partisanship and the Development of Congress*. Cambridge: Cambridge University Press.

BRINKLEY, A. 1982. *Voices of Protest*. New York: Alfred A. Knopf.

BROZ, J. L. 1997. *The International Origins of the Federal Reserve System*. Ithaca, NY: Cornell University Press.

CARPENTER, D. 2001. *The Forging of Bureaucratic Autonomy*. Princeton, NJ: Princeton University Press.

CLEMENS, E. 1997. *The People's Lobby: Organizational Innovation and the Rise of Interest Group Politics in the United States, 1890–1925*. Chicago: University of Chicago Press.

DUVERGER, M. 1954. *Political Parties: Their Organization and Activity in the Modern State*. New York: Routledge and Kegan Paul.

EISNER, M. A. 1991. *Antitrust and the Triumph of Economics*. Chapel Hill: University of North Carolina Press.

FORBATH, W. E. 1991. *Law and the Shaping of the American Labor Movement*. Cambridge, Mass.: Harvard University Press.

FRIEDMAN, G. 1999. *State-Making and Labor Movements: France and the United States, 1876–1914*. Ithaca, NY: Cornell University Press.

FRYMER, P. 2003. Acting when elected officials won't: federal courts and civil rights enforcement in U.S. labor unions, 1935–1985. *American Political Science Review*, 97(3): 483–99.

GATES, J. B. (1992). *The Supreme Court and Partisan Realignment*. Boulder, Colo.: Westview Press.

GERRING, J. 2001. *Party Ideologies in America, 1828–1926*. New York: Cambridge University Press.

GOLDFIELD, M. 1989. Worker insurgency, radical organization, and New Deal labor organization. *American Political Science Review*, 83(4): 1257–82.

GOODWIN, L. 1976. *Democratic Promise: The Populist Movement in America*. New York: Oxford University Press.

HACKER, J. 2002. *The Divided Welfare State*. New York: Cambridge University Press.

HALL, P. (ed.) 1989. *The Political Power of Economic Ideas: Keynesianism Across Nations*. Princeton, NJ: Princeton University Press.

HATTAM, V. C. 1993. *Labor Visions and State Power*. Princeton, NJ: Princeton University Press.

HOFSTADTER, R. 1955. The age of reform: from Bryar to F. D. R. New York: Vintage.

KATZNELSON, I. and FARHANG, S. 2005. The southern imposition: Congress and labor in the New Deal and Fair Deal. *Studies in American Political Development*, 19(1): 1–30.

KATZNELSON, I., GEIGER, K., and KRYDER, D. 1993. Limiting liberalism: the southern veto in Congress, 1933–1950. *Political Science Quarterly*, 108: 283–306.

KESH, K. 2004. *Constructing Civil Liberties*. New York: Cambridge University Press.

KRYDER, D. 2001. *Race and the American State During World War II*. Cambridge: Cambridge University Press.

LIEBERMAN, R. C. 2001. *Shifting the Color Line: Race and the American Welfare State*. Cambridge, Mass.: Harvard University Press.

—— 2002. Ideas, institutions, and political order: explaining political change. *American Political Science Review*, 96(4): 697–712.

LIVINGSTON, J. 1986. *Origins of the Federal Reserve System: Money, Class, and Corporate Capitalism, 1890–1913*. Ithaca, NY: Cornell University Press.

LOCKE, J. 1690. *Two Treatises on Government*. New Haven, Conn.: Yale University Press.

LOWI, T. J. 1969. *The End of Liberalism: The Second Republic of the United States*. New York: W. W. Norton.

MCADAM, D. 1982. *Political Process and the Development of Black Insurgency, 1930–1970*. Chicago: University of Chicago Press.

MCCLOSKEY, R. G. 1994. *The American Supreme Court*, 2nd edn. Chicago: University of Chicago Press.

MCMATH, R. 1975. *Populist Vanguard: A History of the Southern Farmers' Alliance*. New York: W. W. Norton.

METTLER, S. 1998. *Divided Citizens: Gender and Federalism in New Deal Public Policy*. Ithaca, NY: Cornell University Press.

NORTH, D. C. 1990. *Institutions, Institutional Change, and Economic Performance*. New York: Cambridge University Press.

ORREN, K. 1991. *Belated Feudalism*. New York: Cambridge University Press.

—— and SKOWRONEK, S. 2004. *The Search for American Political Development*. Cambridge: Cambridge University Press.

PIERSON, P. 2000. Increasing returns, path dependence, and the study of politics. *American Political Science Review*, 94(2): 251–66.

—— 2004. *Politics in Time: History, Institutions and Social Analysis*. Princeton, NJ: Princeton University Press.

POLLACK, N. 1987. *The Just Polity: Populism, Law, and Human Welfare*. Urbana: University of Illinois Press.

ROBERTSON, D. 2000. *Capital, Labor, and the State*. New York: Rowman and Littlefield.

ROSENBERG, G. N. 1991. *The Hollow Hope*. Chicago: University of Chicago Press.

ROSS, D. 1995. The many lives of institutionalism in American social science. *Polity*, 28(1): 117–23.

SANDERS, E. 1999. *Roots of Reform: Farmers, Workers, and the American State, 1877–1917.* Chicago: University of Chicago Press.

SCHICKLER, E. 2001. *Disjointed Pluralism: Institutional Innovation and the Development of the U.S. Congress.* Princeton, NJ: Princeton University Press.

SCHWARTZ, M. 1976, 1988. *Radical Protest and Social Structure: The Southern Farmers' Alliance and Cotton Tenancy, 1880–1890.* Chicago: University of Chicago Press.

SKOCPOL, T. 1979. *States and Social Revolutions: A Comparative Analysis of France, Russia and China.* Cambridge: Cambridge University Press.

—— 1992. *Protecting Soldiers and Mothers: The Political Origins of Social Policy in the United States.* Boston: Belknap Press.

—— 2003. *Diminished Democracy: From Membership to Management in American Civic Life.* Norman: University of Oklahoma Press.

—— and FINEGOLD, K. 1990. Explaining New Deal labor policy. *American Political Science Review,* 84(4): 1297–304.

—— —— 1995. *State and Party in America's New Deal: Industry and Agriculture in America's New Deal.* Madison: University of Wisconsin Press.

SKOWRONEK, S. 1982. *Building a New American State: The Expansion of National Administrative Capacities, 1877–1920.* New York: Cambridge University Press.

—— 1997. *The Politics Presidents Make: Leadership from John Adams to Bill Clinton.* Boston: Belknap Press.

TICHENOR, D. 2002. *Dividing Lines: The Politics of Immigration Control in America.* Princeton, NJ: Princeton University Press.

DE TOCQUEVILLE, A. 1835. *Democracy in America.* New York: Signet Press.

TOMLINS, C. L. 1985. *The State and the Unions: Labor Relations, Law, and the Organized Labor Movement in America, 1880–1960.* Cambridge: Cambridge University Press.

SKOCPOL, T., MUNSON, Z., KARCH, A., and BAYLISS, C. 2002. Patriotic partnerships: why great wars novrished American civic volunteerism. Pp. 134–80 in *Shaped by War and Trade: International Influences on American Political Development,* ed. I. Katznelson and M. Shefter. Princeton, NJ: Princeton University Press.

WILSON, W. 1891. *Congressional Government: A Study in American Politics.* Boston: Houghton.

ZEGART, A. 2000. *Flawed by Design: The Evolution of the CIA, JCS, and NSC.* Stanford, Calif.: Stanford University Press.

—— 2005. September 11 and the adaptation failure of U.S. intelligence agencies. *International Security,* 29(4): 78–111.

CHAPTER 4

CONSTRUCTIVIST INSTITUTIONALISM

COLIN HAY

The proliferation of new institutionalist scholarship has, perhaps unremarkably, led to a corresponding proliferation in the adjectives used to characterize its variants. In 1984 James G. March and Johan P. Olsen spoke quite comfortably of the new institutionalism in the singular. By 1996 Peter A. Hall and Rosemary Taylor eventually settled on three new institutionalisms (having toyed, in earlier iterations of the same now classic article, with four). And by 1998 B. Guy Peters identified no less than seven new institutionalisms. Yet none of these authors made any reference to constructivism, far less to a distinctive constructivist variant of institutionalism in its own right.[1] Indeed, until very recently, there has been very little if any reference to what is now variously described as an ideational, discursive, or as here, *constructivist* institutionalism. This is for three very good reasons—constructivist institutionalism is by far the most recent addition to the family of institutionalisms, it arises out of an engagement with the limitations of the others, and, as a consequence and in contrast the others, it is still very much in its

---

* I am greatly indebted to Mark Blyth and to the editors for encouraging and perceptive comments on an earlier version of this chapter. Alas, I must bear sole responsibility for the errors of substance and interpretation.

[1] The first published references that I can discern to a discursive and/or ideational institutionalism are in John L. Campbell and Ove K. Pedersen's (2001) edited collection on *The Rise of Neoliberalism and Institutional Analysis*.

inception. It is, nonetheless, already highly distinctive (ontologically, analytically, and methodologically), and it poses a series of challenges to extant institutionalisms (see also Abdelal, Blyth, and Parsons 2006; Schmidt 2006).

My aim in this brief chapter is quite simple—to summarize the distinctiveness of constructivist institutionalism and to identify the nature of the challenge that it poses. The chapter proceeds in three sections. In the first, I consider the origins of constructivist institutionalism in an attempt to grapple with the limits of pre-existing institutionalist scholarship to deal with post-formative institutional change, particularly that associated with disequilibrium dynamics. In the second, I consider the ontological and analytical distinctiveness of constructivist institutionalism's turn to ideas and the associated nature of the challenge its poses to existing neoinstitutionalist perspectives. In the third and concluding section, I consider the contribution to the analysis of complex institutional change that constructivist institutionalism has thus far made.

1 FROM HISTORICAL TO CONSTRUCTIVIST INSTITUTIONALISM

Constructivist institutionalism, as I will label it, has its origins in attempts to grapple with questions of complex institutional change—initially from within the confines of existing neoinstitutionalist scholarship (see also Schmidt 2006).[2] In this respect, rational choice and normative/sociological institutionalism proved most obviously limiting (see Table 4.1). The reason was simple. Constructivist institutionalists were motivated by the desire to capture, describe, and interrogate

---

[2] I prefer the term constructivist institutionalism to either ideational or discursive institutionalism since the former implies a distinct ontology such as might credibly inform a distinctive approach to institutional analysis. This would seem consistent with Peter A. Hall and Rosemary C. R. Taylor's (1996) reference to rational choice institutionalism, sociological institutionalism, and historical institutionalism, each of which might lay claim to a distinctive ontology (or, in the case of historical institutionalism, perhaps, a combination of ontologies). This is a point to which we return. On the ontological differences between these four new institutionalisms, see Figure 4.1. One of the implications of labeling institutionalisms in terms of their ontological assumptions is that network institutionalism (see Chapter 5) is not further discussed in this chapter, since it is not characterized by its distinct ontology so much as by its empirical concerns. At this point, it is perhaps also important to note that the term sociological institutionalism is by no means always enthusiastically embraced by those to whom it is intended to refer. In what follows I will, then, depart slightly from Hall and Taylor's terminology by referring to normative/sociological institutionalism where they refer to sociological institutionalism.

Table 4.1 The ontological distinctiveness of constructivist institutionalism

	Rational choice institutionalism	Historical institutionalism	Normative/sociological institutionalism	Constructivist institutionalism
Theoretical approach	Context-specific theoretical modelling (where possible); qualified parsimony	To contextualize agency both historically and institutionally; to sensitize analysts to logics of path dependence	To contextualize agency culturally and institutionally; to sensitize analysts to logics of appropriate conduct within institutionalized settings	To sensitize the analyst to key moments of change and to the conditions of existence of complex institutional change
Theoretical assumptions	"Calculus" approach—actors are instrumentally rational	Actors display a combination of "cultural" and "calculus" logics	"Cultural" approach—actors follows norms and conventions	Actors are both strategic and socialized—they can behave in a variety of different ways
Analytical approach	Deductive	Deductive–inductive	Deductive–inductive	Deductive–inductive
Method	Mathematical modeling (where possible)	Theoretically-informed; historical; narrative	Often statistical (thesis testing); sometimes narrative	Theoretically-informed process tracing; discourse analysis
Conception of institutions	"The rules of the game in a society" (North)	"Formal and informal procedures, routines, norms and conventions" (Hall)	Cultural conventions, norms, cognitive frames	Institutions as codified systems of ideas and the practices they sustain
Institutional change	1 Focus on the (positive) functions an institution performs	1 Focus on institutional creation as defining the path down which subsequent	1 Focus on institutional creation as the diffusion of a pre-existing	1 Focus on the socially constructed nature of political opportunity structures

	2 Focus on rational institutional design	evolution occurs 2 "Punctuated equilibrium" yet little emphasis on post-formative institutional change	institutional template 2 Focus on the equilibrating effects of institutionalization and associated logics of appropriateness	2 Focus both on institutional creation and post-formative institutional change 3 Focus on the ideational preconditions of institutional change
Key themes	Bounded rationality	Path dependence	Diffusion of institutional templates	Discursive construction of crises; institutionalization as the normalization of policy paradigms
Weaknesses	Functionalist; static	Rather static	Rather static	Unclear about the origins of both interests and of systems of ideas; unclear about the relative significance of material and ideational factors

Common bias towards moments of institutional creation (focus on institutional genesis but not on subsequent development) institutional *disequilibrium*.[3] As such, rational choice and normative/sociological institutionalism, which rely albeit for rather different reasons on the assumption of equilibrium, were theoretical non-starters.[4] Unremarkably, then, and by a process of elimination, most routes to constructivist institutionalism can trace their origins to historical institutionalism (see, for instance, Berman 1998; Blyth 2002; Campbell 2001, 2004; Hay 2001, 2002; McNamara 1998; Schmidt 2002).

Yet if historical institutionalism has typically served as an initial source of inspiration for constructivist institutionalists, it has increasingly become a source of frustration and a point of departure. For, whilst ostensibly concerned with "process tracing" and hence with questions of institutional change over time, historical institutionalism has tended to be characterized by an emphasis upon institutional genesis at the expense of an adequate account of post-formative institutional change.[5] Moreover, in so far as post-formative institutional dynamics have been considered (for instance Hall 1993; Hall and Soskice 2001; Pierson 1994), they tend either to be seen as a consequence of path dependent lock-in effects or, where more ruptural in nature, as the product of exogenous shocks such as wars or revolutions (Hay and Wincott 1998). Historical institutionalism, it seems, is incapable of offering its own (i.e. endogenous) account of the determinants of the "punctuated equilibria" (Krasner 1984) to which it invariably points. This, at least, is the charge of many constructivist institutionalists (see, for instance, Blyth 2002, 19–23; Hay 2001, 194–5).

If one follows Peter A. Hall and Rosemary C. R. Taylor (1996) in seeing historical institutionalism as animated by actors displaying a combination of "calculus" and

---

[3] Though hardly constructivist, the work of Robert H. Bates et al. (1998) is particularly interesting in this regard. Operating from an avowedly rational choice institutionalist perspective, yet concerned with questions of social and political change under conditions of disequilibrium which they freely concede that rational choice institutionalism is poorly equipped to deal with (1998, 223), they effectively import insights from constructivist research in developing a more dynamic but still essentially rational choice theoretical model. Whilst the resulting synthesis can certainly be challenged in terms of its internal consistency—ontologically and epistemologically—it does lend further credence to the notion that constructivist insights have much to offer an analysis of institutional change under disequilibrium conditions (for a critical commentary see also Hay 2004a, 57–9).

[4] Strictly speaking, normative/sociological institutionalism does not so much assume as predict equilibrium. For the "logics of appropriateness" that constitute its principal analytical focus and that it discerns and associates with successful institutionalization are themselves seen as equilibrating. The key point, however, is that, like rational choice institutionalism, it does not offer (nor, indeed, claim to offer) much analytical purchase on the question of institutional dynamism in contexts of disequilibrium.

[5] Interestingly, this is something it seems to have inherited from the attempt to "bring the state back into" (North American) political science in the 1980s out of which it evolved (see, for instance, Evans et al. 1985). For, in the former's emphasis, in particular, upon the institutional and organizational capacity to wage war effectively upon the process of state formation, it came to identify the highly consequential and path-dependent nature of institutional genesis for post-formative institutional evolution (see Mann 1988; Tilly 1975). In Charles Tilly's characteristically incisive aphorism, "wars make states and states make war."

"cultural" logics, then it is perhaps not difficult to see why. For, as already noted, instrumental logics of calculation (calculus logics) *presume* equilibrium (at least as an initial condition)[6] and norm-driven logics of appropriateness (cultural logics) are themselves equilibrating. Accounts which see actors as driven either by utility maximization in an institutionalized game scenario (rational choice institutionalism) or by institutionalized norms and cultural conventions (normative/sociological institutionalism) or, indeed, both (historical institutionalism), are unlikely to offer much analytical purchase on questions of complex post-formative institutional change. They are far better placed to account for the *path-dependent* institutional change they tend to assume than they are to explain the periodic, if infrequent, bouts of *path-shaping* institutional change they concede.[7] In this respect, historical institutionalism is no different than its rational choice and normative/sociological counterparts. Indeed, despite its ostensible analytical concerns, historical institutionalism merely compounds and reinforces the incapacity of rational choice and normative/sociological institutionalism to deal with disequilibrium dynamics. Given that one of its core contributions is seen to be its identification of such dynamics, this is a significant failing.

This is all very well, and provides a powerful justification for a more constructivist path from historical institutionalism. It does, however, rest on the assumed accuracy of Hall and Taylor's depiction of historical institutionalism—essentially as an amalgamation of rational choice and normative/sociological institutionalist conceptions of the subject. This is by no means uncontested. It has, for instance, been suggested that historical institutionalism is in fact rather more distinctive ontologically than this implies (compare Hay and Wincott 1998 with Hall and Taylor 1998). For if one returns to the introduction to the volume which launched the term itself, and to other seminal and self-consciously defining statements of historical institutionalism, one finds not a vacillation between rationalized and socialized treatments of the human subject, but something altogether different.

Thelen and Steinmo, for instance, are quite explicit in distancing historical institutionalism from the view of the rational actor on which the calculus approach

---

[6] This is, of course, not to deny that standard rational choice/neoclassical economic models can describe/predict disequilibrium outcomes (think, for instance, of a multiplayer prisoner's dilemma game). Yet they do, assuming initial equilibrium conditions.

[7] The distinction between path-dependent and path-shaping logics and dynamics is a crucial one. New institutionalists in general have tended to place far greater emphasis on the former than the latter. This perhaps reflects the latent structuralism of the attempt to bring institutions back into contemporary political analysis (see Hay 2002, 105–7). For institutions, as structures, are invariably seen to limit, indeed delimit, the parameters of political choice. As such, they are constraints on political dynamism. This is certainly an important insight, yet there is a certain danger in tilting the stick too strongly in the direction of structure. For, under certain conditions, institutions, and the path-dependent logics they otherwise impose, are recast and redesigned through the intended and unintended consequences of political agency. Given the importance of such moments, the new institutionalism has had remarkably little to say on these bouts of path-shaping institutional change.

is premised. Actors cannot simply be assumed to have a fixed (and immutable) preference set, to be blessed with extensive (often perfect) information and foresight, or to be self-interested and self-serving utility maximizers. Rational choice and historical institutionalism are, as Thelen and Steinmo note, "premised on different assumptions that in fact reflect quite different approaches to the study of politics" (1992, 7).

Yet, if this would seem to imply a greater affinity with normative/sociological institutionalism, then further inspection reveals this not to be the case either. For, to the extent that the latter assumes conventional and norm-driven behavior thereby downplaying the significance of agency, it is equally at odds with the defining statements of historical institutionalism. As Thelen and Steinmo again suggest:

institutional analysis . . . allows us to examine the relationship between political actors as objects and *as agents of history*. The institutions that are at the centre of historical institutionalist analysis . . . can shape and constrain political strategies in important ways, *but they are themselves also the outcome (conscious or unintended) of deliberate political strategies of political conflict and of choice.* (Thelen and Steinmo 1992, 10; emphasis added)

Set in this context, the social ontology of historical institutionalism is highly distinctive, and indeed quite compatible with the constructivist institutionalism which it now more consistently seems to inform. This brings us to a most important point. Whether constructivist institutionalism is seen as a variant, further development, or rejection of historical institutionalism depends crucially on what historical institutionalism is taken to imply ontologically. If the latter is seen, as in Hall and Taylor's influential account, as a flexible combination of cultural and calculus approaches to the institutionally-embedded subject, then it is considerably at odds with constructivist institutionalism. Seen in this way, it is, moreover, incompatible with the attempt to develop an endogenous institutionalist account of the mechanisms and determinants of complex institutional change. Yet, if it is seen, as the above passages from Thelen and Steinmo might suggest, as an approach predicated upon the dynamic interplay of structure and agent (institutional context and institutional architect) and, indeed, material and ideational factors (see Hay 2002, chs. 2, 4, and 6), then the difference between historical and constructivist institutionalisms is at most one of emphasis.

Whilst the possibility still exists of a common historical and constructivist institutionalist research agenda, it might seem unnecessarily divisive to refer to constructivist institutionalism as a new addition to the family of institutionalisms. Yet this can, I think, be justified. Indeed, sad though this may well be, the prospect of such a common research agenda is perhaps not as great as the above comments might suggest. That this is so is the product of a recent "hollowing-out" of historical institutionalism. Animated, it seems, by the (laudable) desire to build bridges, many of the most prominent contemporary advocates of historical institutionalism (notably Peter Hall (with David Soskice, 2001) and Paul Pierson (2004)) seem increasingly to have resolved the calculus–cultural balance which they discern at the heart of historical institutionalism in favor of the former. The bridge which they would seem to be anxious to build, then, runs from historical institutionalism, by way of an acknowledgment of the need to incorporate micro-foundations into institutionalist analysis, to rational choice institutionalism. This is a trajectory that not only places a sizable and ever-growing wedge between cultural and calculus approaches to institutional analysis, but one which essentially also closes off the alternative path to a more dynamic historical constructivist institutionalism.

2   THE ANALYTICAL AND ONTOLOGICAL DISTINCTIVENESS OF CONSTRUCTIVIST INSTITUTIONALISM

In the context, then, of contemporary developments in new institutionalist scholarship, the analytical and ontological assumptions of constructivist institutionalism are highly distinctive. They represent a considerable advance on their rationalist and normative/sociological predecessors, at least in terms of their capacity to inform an endogenous account of complex institutional evolution, adaptation, and innovation.[8]

Actors are strategic, seeking to realize certain complex, contingent, and constantly changing goals. They do so in a context which favors certain strategies over others and must rely upon perceptions of that context which are at best incomplete and which may very often prove to have been inaccurate after the event. Moreover, ideas in the form of perceptions "matter" in a second sense— for actors are oriented normatively towards their environment. Their desires, preferences, and motivations are not a contextually given fact—a reflection of material or even social circumstance—but are irredeemably ideational, reflecting a normative (indeed moral, ethical, and political) orientation towards the context

[8] This is an important caveat. Ontologies are not contending theories that can be adjudicated empirically—since what counts as evidence in the first place is not an ontologically-neutral issue. Thus, while certain ontological assumptions can preclude a consideration, say, of disequilibrium dynamics (by essentially denying their existence), this does not in itself invalidate them. On the dangers of ontological evangelism, see Hay (2005).

in which they will have to be realized. As this suggests, for constructivists, politics is rather less about the blind pursuit of transparent material interest and rather more about both the fashioning, identification, and rendering actionable of such conceptions, and the balancing of (presumed) instrumentality and rather more affective motivations (see also Wendt 1999, 113–35).[9] Consequently, actors are not analytically substitutable (as in rational choice or normative/sociological institutionalism), just as their preference sets or logics of conduct cannot be derived from the (institutional) setting in which they are located. Interests are social constructions and cannot serve as proxies for material factors; as a consequence they are far more difficult to operationalize empirically than is conventionally assumed (at least, in a non-tautological way: see also Abdelal, Blyth, and Parsons 2005; Blyth 2003).

In common with rationalist variants of institutionalism, the context is viewed in largely institutional terms. Yet institutions are understood less as functional means of reducing uncertainty, so much as structures whose functionality or dysfunctionality is an open—empirical and historical—question. Indeed, constructivist institutionalists place considerable emphasis on the potentially ineffective and inefficient nature of social institutions; on institutions as the subject and focus of political struggle; and on the contingent nature of such struggles whose outcomes can in no sense be derived from the extant institutional context itself (see, especially, Blyth 2002).

These are the basic analytical ingredients of constructivist institutionalism's approach to institutional innovation, evolution, and transformation. Within this perspective, change is seen to reside in the relationship between actors and the context in which they find themselves, between institutional "architects," institutionalized subjects, and institutional environments. More specifically, institutional change is understood in terms of the interaction between strategic conduct and the strategic context within which it is conceived, and in the *later* unfolding of its consequences, both intended and unintended. As in historical institutionalism, such a formulation is *path dependent*: the order in which things happen affects how they happen; the trajectory of change up to a certain point itself constrains the trajectory after that point; and the strategic choices made at a particular moment

---

[9] The affinities between constructivism in international relations theory and constructivist institutionalism are, perhaps on this point especially, considerable. And, on the face of it, there is nothing terribly remarkable about that. Yet however tempting it might be to attribute the latter's view of preference/interest formation to the former, this would be mistaken. For while the still recent labeling of constructivist institutionalism as a distinctive position in its own right has clearly been influenced by the prominence of constructivism within international relations theory (Abdelal et al. 2005), the causal and constitutive role accorded to ideas by such institutionalists predates the rise of constructivism in international relations (see, for instance, Blyth 1997; Hall 1993; Hay 1996). As such, constructivism in international relations and constructivist institutionalism are perhaps best seen as parallel if initially distinct developments.

eliminate whole ranges of possibilities from later choices while serving as the very condition of existence of others (see also Tilly 1994). Yet, pointing to path dependence does not preclude the identification of moments of path-shaping institutional change, in which the institutional architecture is significantly reconfigured. Moreover, and at odds with most existing new institutionalist scholarship, such path-shaping institutional change is not merely seen as a more-or-less functional response to exogenous shocks.

Further differentiating it from new institutionalist orthodoxy, constructivist institutionalists emphasize not only institutional path dependence, but also ideational path dependence. In other words, it is not just institutions, but the very ideas on which they are predicated and which inform their design and development, that exert constraints on political autonomy. Institutions are built on ideational foundations which exert an independent path dependent effect on their subsequent development.

Constructivist institutionalism thus seeks to identify, detail, and interrogate the extent to which—through processes of normalization and institutional-embedding—established ideas become codified, serving as cognitive filters through which actors come to interpret environmental signals. Yet, crucially, they are also concerned with the conditions under which such established cognitive filters and paradigms are contested, challenged, and replaced. Moreover, they see paradigmatic shifts as heralding significant institutional change.

Such a formulation implies a dynamic understanding of the relationship between institutions on the one hand, and the individuals and groups who comprise them (and on whose experience they impinge) on the other. It emphasizes institutional innovation, dynamism, and transformation, as well as the need for a consideration of processes of change over a significant period of time. In so doing it offers the potential to overturn new institutionalism's characteristic emphasis upon institutional inertia. At the same time, however, such a schema recognizes that institutional change does indeed occur in a context which is structured (not least by institutions and ideas about institutions) in complex and constantly changing ways which facilitate certain forms of intervention whilst militating against others. Moreover, access to strategic resources, and indeed to knowledge of the institutional environment, is unevenly distributed. This in turn affects the ability of actors to transform the contexts (institutional and otherwise) in which they find themselves.

Finally, it is important to emphasize the crucial space granted to ideas within this formulation. Actors appropriate strategically a world replete with institutions and ideas about institutions. Their perceptions about what is feasible, legitimate, possible, and desirable are shaped both by the institutional environment in which they find themselves and by existing policy paradigms and world-views. It is through such cognitive filters that strategic conduct is conceptualized and ultimately assessed.

3   CONSTRUCTIVIST INSTITUTIONALISM APPLIED: CRISES, PARADIGM SHIFTS, AND UNCERTAINTY

Whilst there may well be something of a tension between the contemporary trajectory of historical institutionalism and the developing constructivist institutionalist research agenda, this should not hide the considerable indebtedness of the latter to earlier versions of the former. The work of Peter A. Hall, in particular that on policy paradigms, social learning, and institutional change (1993), has proved a crucial source of inspiration for many contemporary currents in constructivist institutionalism. Indeed, the latter's indebtedness to historical institutionalism is arguably rather greater than its indebtedness to constructivism in international relations theory. For despite the ostensible similarities between constructivist institutionalism and constructivism in international relations theory, the former has been driven to a far greater extent than the latter by the attempt to resolve particular empirical puzzles. Those puzzles, principally concerned with understanding the conditions of existence of significant path-shaping institutional change, have led institutionalists to consider the role of ideas in influencing the developmental trajectory of institutions under conditions of uncertainly and/or crisis. They were explored first by historical institutionalists, most notably Peter A. Hall.

Hall's work represents by far the most sustained, consistent, and systematic attempt within the historical institutionalist perspective to accord a key role for ideas in the determination of institutional outcomes. Like most of the constructivist institutionalist scholarship which it would come to inform, Hall's approach to ideas comes not from a prior ontological commitment (as in constructivist international relations theory), but from the observation of an empirical regularity—ideational change invariably precedes institutional change. Drawing inspiration from Kuhn, Hall argues that policy is made within the context of "policy paradigms." Such interpretative schema are internalized by politicians, state managers, policy experts, and the like. They come to define a range of legitimate policy techniques, mechanisms, and instruments, thereby delimiting the very targets and goals of policy itself. In short, they come to circumscribe the realm of the politically feasible, practical, and desirable. As Hall elaborates:

policy makers customarily work within a framework of ideas and standards that specifies not only the goals of policy and the kind of instruments that can be used to attain them, but also the very nature of the problems they are meant to be addressing.... [T]his framework is embedded in the very terminology through which policy makers communicate about their work, and it is influential precisely because so much of it is taken for granted and unamenable to scrutiny as a whole. (1993, 279)

The identification of such distinctive policy paradigms allows Hall to differentiate between: (a) periods of "normal" policy-making (and change) in which the paradigm remains largely unchallenged (at least within the confines of the policy-making arena) and in which change is largely incremental; and (b) periods of "exceptional" policy-making (and change), often associated with crises, in which the very parameters that previously circumscribed policy options are cast asunder and replaced, and in which the realm of the politically possible, feasible, and desirable is correspondingly reconfigured.

Hall concentrates on developing an abstracted, largely deductive, and theoretically-informed periodization of the policy process which might be applied in a variety of contexts. It stresses the significance of ideas (in the form of policy-making paradigms which are seen to act as cognitive filters) and leads to a periodization of institutional change in terms of the policy-making paradigms such institutions instantiate and reflect. Yet it remains largely descriptive, having little to say about the processes of change which underlie the model.

This provides the point of departure for a significant body of more recent, and more self-consciously constructivist, scholarship (see, especially, Blyth 2002; Hay 2001). This still nascent literature asks under what conditions paradigms emerge, consolidate, accumulate anomalies, and become subject to challenge and replacement. Attention has focused in particular upon the moment of crisis itself, a concept much invoked but rarely conceptualized or further explicated in the existing literature.[10]

Blyth's meticulous work on the US and Swedish cases (2002) shows well the additional analytical purchase that constructivism offers to institutionalists interested not only in institutional process tracing but in accounting for the emergence of new policy paradigms and attendant institutional logics in and through moments of crisis.[11] Indeed, his landmark study demonstrates the causal and constitutive role of ideas in shaping the developmental trajectories of advanced capitalist economies. It has rapidly become a, perhaps *the*, key referent and point of departure for the constructivist institutionalist research programme.

The analytical focus of his attentions is the moment of crisis itself, in which one policy paradigm is replaced by another. Crises, he suggests, can be viewed as moments in which actors' perceptions of their own self-interest become problematized. Consequently, the resolution of a crisis entails the restoration of a more "normal" condition in which actors' interests are once again made clear and transparent to them. As nature abhors a vacuum, so, it seems, political systems abhor uncertainty. Crises thus unleash short bouts of intense ideational contestation in which agents struggle to provide compelling and convincing diagnoses of the pathologies afflicting the old regime/policy paradigm and the reforms appropriate to the resolution of the crisis. Moreover, and crucially for his analysis, such crisis theories, arising as they do in moments of uncertainty, play a genuinely constructive

---

[10] It is perhaps again important to note that although constructivist institutionalists come to a position very similar to that of their fellow constructivists in international relations suggesting, for instance, that "crises are what states make of them" (cf. Wendt 1992), this is an empirical observation not a logical correlate of a prior ontological commitment.

[11] The following paragraphs draw on and further develop the argument first presented in Hay (2004b, 207–13).

role in establishing a new trajectory of institutional evolution. They are, in other words, not reducible to the condition they seek to describe and explain.

The implications of this are clear—if we are to understand path-shaping institutional change we must acknowledge the independent causal and constitutive role of ideas, since the developmental trajectory of a given regime or policy paradigm cannot be derived from the exhibited or latent contradictions of the old regime or policy paradigm. It is, instead, contingent upon the ideational contestation unleashed in the moment of crisis itself. Though this is not an inference that Blyth himself draws, there is, then, no hope of a predictive science of crisis resolution, capable of pointing prior to the onset of crisis to the path of institutional change—for the causal chain is incomplete until such time as the crisis has been successfully narrated.

This is an important intervention and it provides a series of correspondingly significant insights into the developmental trajectories of Swedish and US capitalism in the twentieth century. In particular, it draws attention to the role of business in proselytizing and sponsoring new and/or alternative economic theories and in setting the discursive parameters within which influential crisis narratives are likely to be framed, and to the crucial relationship between business, think tanks, and professional economists. It also reminds us, usefully, that in order to prove influential, (economic) ideas need not bear much relationship to the reality they purportedly represent. In a classically constructivist institutionalist vein, it demonstrates that, if believed and acted upon, economic ideas have a tendency to become self-fulfilling prophecies (see also Hay and Rosamond 2002).

Yet its limitations also show that constructivist institutionalism is still very much a work in progress. Blyth raises just as many theoretical, methodological, and, indeed, empirical questions as he answers. Moreover, the text is characterized by some significant and by no means unrepresentative tensions, contradictions, and silences. None of these are insurmountable impediments to the development of a more consistently constructivist institutionalism. Yet they do perhaps serve to indicate the work still required if the profound challenge that constructivism poses to more conventional approaches to institutional analysis, and the insights it offers, are both to be more widely appreciated.

In the context of contemporary neoinstitutionalism, it is Blyth's comments on the relationship between ideas and interests that are likely to prove most controversial. It is in these comments that the distinctiveness of the constructivist variant of institutionalism resides. His core claim is, in essence, that actors' conduct is not a (direct) reflection of their material interests but, rather, a reflection of particular *perceptions* of their material interests (see also Wendt 1999, 113–35). Our material circumstances do not directly determine our behavior, though our perceptions of such circumstances (and, indeed, of our stake in various conceivable outcomes), may.[12] In his own terms, it is ideas that render interests "actionable" (Blyth 2002, 39).

---

[12] The parentheses are important here. There is something of a tendency in the existing literature to treat the issue of interest-formation and representation as a question solely of the accuracy of the information actors have about their external environment. If there is a disparity between an actor's

However intuitively plausible or obvious this may seem, it is important to note that it sits in some considerable tension to almost all existing neoinstitutionalist scholarship. For, conventionally, it is actors' material interests rather than their perceptions of those interests that are assumed the key determinants of their behavior. Though convenient and parsimonious, this is unrealistic—and this is the constructivist's point. Yet, there is some ambiguity and inconsistency in the manner in which he operationalizes this important insight, which speaks to a potentially wider ambiguity within constructivist institutionalism. For, on occasions, Blyth refers to interests as "social constructs that are open to redefinition through ideological contestation" (2002, 271; see also Abdelal, Blyth, and Parsons 2006). All trace of a materialist conception of interest is eliminated at a stroke. At other points in the text, however, interests are treated as materially given and as clearly separate from perceptions of interests, as for instance when he counterposes the "ideas held by agents" and "their structurally-derived interests" (2002, 33–4). Here, like many other constructivists, Blyth seems to fall back on an essentially material conception of interests (see also Berman 1998; McNamara 1998; Wendt 1999). Obviously it makes no sense to view the latter as social constructs. To be clear, though these two formulations are mutually exclusive (interests are either social constructs or given by material circumstances, they cannot be both), neither is incompatible with Blyth's core claim (that in order to be actionable, interests have to be capable of being articulated). They are merely different ways of operationalizing that core assumption. Yet it does serve to hide a potentially more fundamental lacuna.

This only becomes fully apparent when Blyth's second core premise is recalled: crises are situations in which actors' interests (presumably here conceptualized as social constructs rather than material givens) become blurred. In itself this is far from self-evident and, given the centrality of the claim to the overall argument he presents, it is perhaps surprising that Blyth chooses not to defend the claim. It is not clear that moments of crisis do indeed lead to uncertainty about actors' interests. Indeed, whilst crises might plausibly be seen to provide focal points around which competing political narratives might serve to reorient actors' sense of their own self-interest, in the first instance are they not more likely to result in the vehement reassertion, expression, and articulation of prior conceptions of self-interest—often in the intensity of political conflict? Is it not somewhat perverse, for instance, to suggest that during the infamous Winter of Discontent of 1978–9 (as clear an instance of crisis as one might imagine), Britain's striking

---

perceived interests and those we might attribute to them given an exhaustive analysis of their material circumstances, this is assumed to be a function solely of the incompleteness of the actor's information. Arguably this is itself a gross simplification. Interests are not merely a reflection of perceived material circumstance, but relate, crucially, to the normative orientation of the actor towards her external environment. My perceived self-interest with respect to questions of environmental degradation, for instance, will reflect to a significant extent my normative sense of obligation to other individuals (living and yet to be born) and, conceivably, other species.

public sector workers were unclear about their interests in resisting enforced wage moderation? Or to see the Callaghan Government as unclear about its interests in bringing such industrial militancy to an end?

A second problem relates to the rather uneven ontology that Blyth seems to rely upon here. In situations in which actors' interests are not problematized, ideas matter less and, presumably, non-constructivist techniques will suffice; yet in conditions of crisis, in which interests are rendered problematic, and ideas "matter more," only constructivism will do (for similar formulations see Berman 1998; Campbell 2001). As I have suggested elsewhere (Hay 2002, 214–15), however tempting it may be to see ideas as somehow more significant in the uncertainty and confusion of the moment of crisis, this is a temptation we should surely resist. It is not that ideas matter *more* in times of crisis, so much that *new* ideas do and that we are particularly interested in their impact. Once the crisis is resolved and a new paradigm installed, the ideas actors hold may become internalized and unquestioned once again, but this does not mean that they cease to affect their behavior.

Yet this is not the key point at issue here. For it is only once we accept as self-evident the claim that moments of crisis problematize pre-existing conceptions of self-interest that the problems really start. If crises are moments of radical indeterminacy in which actors an incapable of articulating and hence rendering "actionable" their interests (moments of "Knightian uncertainty" in Blyth's terms), then how is it that such situation are ever resolved? Blyth, it would seem, must rely upon certain actors—notably influential opinion formers with access to significant resources for the promotion and dissemination of crisis narratives—to be rather clearer about their own interests. For the resolution of the crisis requires, in Blyth's terms, that such actors prove themselves capable of providing an ideational focus for the reconstitution of the perceived self-interests of the population at large. Whose self-interests does such a new paradigm advance? And in a situation of Knightian uncertainty, how is it that such actors are capable of rendering actionable their own interests? In short, where do such ideas come from and who, in a moment of crisis, is capable of perceiving that they have a clearly identified self-interest to the served by the promotion of such ideas? If, as Blyth consistently seems to suggest, it is organized interests with access to significant material resources (such as business) that come to seize the opportunity presented by a moment of crisis, then the role of ideas in determining outcomes would seem to have been significantly attenuated. If access to material resources is a condition of successful crisis-narration, if only organized business has access to such resources, and if neoliberalism is held to reflect the (actual or perceived) self-interest of business, then won't a materialist explanation of the rise of neoliberalism in the USA in the 1970s or Sweden in the 1980s suffice? To prevent this slippage towards a residual materialism, Blyth and other exponents of constructivist institutionalism need to be able to tell us rather more about the determinants (material and ideational), internal dynamics, and narration of the crisis itself. The overly parsimonious conception of crises as moments of Knightian uncertainty may, in this respect, obscure more than it reveals.

This is perhaps suggestive of a broader, indeed somewhat characteristic, failing of constructivist institutionalism to date—its tendency to fall back upon, or at least not to close off fully, the return to a rump materialism. Very often, as in this case, alternative and more parsimonious accounts can be offered of the very same data constructivist institutionalists present that make little or no causal reference to the role of ideas.

A second set of concerns relates to the theoretical status of constructivist institutionalist insights. Again, the issue is a more general one. For, like much work within this development tradition, although constructed as a work of explanatory/causal analysis, it is not always clear that Blyth does adequately *explain* the outcomes whose origins he details. Indeed, it would seem as though abstracted redescription and explanation are frequently conflated. In other words, an abstract and stylized sequence consistent with the empirical evidence is presented as an explanation of specific outcomes in the context being considered. While crises may well be what states make of them, it is not clear that constructivist institutionalists have explained why states make of them what they do—indeed, it is precisely in this ambiguity that the possibility of the return to a residual materialism arises.

This brings us to a further, and closely related, issue—the epistemological status of the claims Blyth makes about the US and Swedish cases, specifically, and those made by constructivists about institutional change more generally. Understandably, Blyth is keen to stress that his chosen constructivist brand of institutionalism provides us with a "better understanding of political change" than more conventional materialist modes of political analysis (2002, ix; see also Abdelal, Blyth, and Parsons 2005; Berman 1998). Yet it is not clear from the text why sceptics should accept such a view—largely because no sustained consideration is given to how one might adjudicate preferences between contending accounts (see, for instance, Bevir and Rhodes 2003). Nor is it clear that constructivists can easily claim the kind of epistemological self-confidence required to pronounce the analytical superiority of their perspective. Presumably, "better" here means more complex, more nuanced, and more able to capture the rich texture of social, political, and economic interaction—in short, the standard that Blyth seems to construct is one of correspondence to an external reality. This is all very well, but external realities, as most constructivists would concede, can be viewed differently. Moreover, whilst complexity and correspondence can plausibly be defended as providing the standards by which competing theories should be adjudicated, parsimony, analytical purchase, and predictive capacity have arguably just as much claim to provide such a standard. And by that standard, most constructivist institutionalism is likely to be found wanting.

Constructivism has much to contribute to contemporary institutional analysis, though its appeal is likely to be greatest for those who do not believe that a predictive science of politics is possible. Yet whether its clear superiority to other contending positions has already been, or is ever likely to be, established, is another matter. Blyth's concluding remarks are, in this respect, particularly problematic. The purpose of his book, he suggests, is "to demonstrate that large-scale institutional change cannot be understood from class alignments, materially given coalitions, or other structural prerequisites.... [I]nstitutional change only makes sense by reference to the ideas that inform agents' responses to moments of uncertainty and crisis" (2002, 251). This is a bold and almost certainly overstated claim. For, rather than demonstrating that structural prerequisites cannot inform a credible account of institutional change, constructivist institutionalism is perhaps better seen as demonstrating that alternative and compelling accounts can be constructed that do not restrict themselves to such material factors. Moreover, Blyth here seems to drive something of a wedge between the consideration of ideational and material factors in causal analysis. This is unfortunate, because as he at times seems quite happy to concede, there are almost certainly (some) material conditions of existence of ascendant crisis narratives and crises themselves would seem to have both material and ideational determinants. Ideational factors certainly need to be given greater attention, but surely not at the expense of all other variables.

4   CONCLUSION

As the above paragraphs hopefully suggest, whilst constructivist institutionalism has much to contribute to the analysis and, above all, the explanation of complex institutional change, it is still very much a work in progress. Its particular appeal resides in its ability to interrogate and open up the often acknowledged and yet rarely explored question of institutional dynamics under disequilibrium conditions. As a consequence of this focus, it has already gone some way to overcoming the new institutionalism's characteristic failure to deal adequately with post-formative institutional change and its tendency to find it rather easier to describe (and, even more so, to explain) path-dependent as opposed to path-shaping logics. Yet, in so doing, it has stumbled over other problems. In particular, it seems unclear whether constructivist institutionalists are prepared to abandon altogether the long association of interests and material factors in political analysis that they ostensibly challenge. Similarly, the extent to which constructivist institutionalism entails the substitution of material by ideational explanations, the development of explanations which dissolve the dualistic distinction between the two, or merely the addition of ideational variables to pre-existing material accounts remains unclear.

Finally, there is still something of a tension it seems between the assuredness and confidence with which the superiority of constructivist institutionalist insights are proclaimed and the theoretical modesty that a constructivist ontology and epistemology would seem almost naturally to entail. None of these are fundamental impediments to the development of a fourth new institutionalism alongside the others; but they do provide a sense of the debates that must, and are likely to, animate the constructivist institutionalist research programme over the next decade.

REFERENCES

ABDELAL, R., BLYTH, M., and PARSONS, C. 2006. The case for a constructivist international political economy. In *Constructivist Political Economy*, ed. R. Abdelal, M. Blyth, and C. Parsons.

BATES, R. H., DE FIGUEIREDO, R. J. P., and WEINGAST, B. R. 1998. The politics of integration: rationality, culture and transition. *Politics and Society*, 26 (2): 221–56.

BERMAN, S. 1998. *The Social Democratic Moment: Ideas and Politics in the Making of Interwar Europe*. Cambridge, Mass.: Harvard University Press.

BEVIR, M. and RHODES, R. A. W. 2003. *Interpreting British Governance*. London: Routledge.

BLYTH, M. 1997. "Any more bright ideas?" The ideational turn of comparative political economy. *Comparative Politics*, 29 (1): 229–50.

—— 2002. *The Great Transformations*. Cambridge: Cambridge University Press.

—— 2003. Structures do not come with instruction sheets: interests, ideas and progress in political science. *Perspectives on Politics*, 1 (4): 695–706.

CAMPBELL, J. L. 2001. Institutional analysis and the role of ideas in political economy. In *The Second Movement in Institutional Analysis*, ed. J. L. Campbell and O. K. Pedersen. Princeton, NJ: Princeton University Press.

—— 2004. *Institutional Change and Globalisation*. Princeton, NJ: Princeton University Press.

—— and PEDERSEN, O. K. (eds.) 2001. *The Second Movement in Institutional Analysis*. Princeton, NJ: Princeton University Press.

EVANS, P. B., RUESCHEMEYER, D., and SKOCPOL, T. (eds.) 1985. *Bringing the State Back In*. Cambridge: Cambridge University Press.

HALL, P. A. 1993. Policy paradigms, social learning and the state: the case of economic policy-making in Britain. *Comparative Politics*, 25 (3): 185–96.

—— and SOSKICE, D. (eds.) 2001. *Varieties of Capitalism*. Oxford: Oxford University Press.

—— and TAYLOR, R. C. R. 1996. Political science and the three new institutionalisms. *Political Studies*, 44 (4): 936–57.

—— —— 1998. The potential of historical institutionalism: a response to Hay and Wincott. *Political Studies*, 46 (5): 958–62.

HAY, C. 1996. Narrating crisis: the discursive construction of the Winter of Discontent. *Sociology*, 30: 253–77.

—— 2001. The "crisis" of Keynesianism and the rise of neo-liberalism in Britain: an ideational institutionalist approach. In *The Second Movement in Institutional Analysis*, ed. J. L. Campbell and O. K. Pederson. Princeton, NJ: Princeton University Press.

HAY, C. 2002. *Political Analysis*. Basingstoke: Palgrave.

—— 2004a. Theory, stylised heuristic or self-fulfilling prophecy? The status of rational choice theory in public administration. *Public Administration*, 82 (1): 39–62.

—— 2004b. Ideas, interests and institutions in the comparative political economy of great transformations. *Review of International Political Economy*, 11 (1): 204–26.

—— 2005. Making hay... or clutching at ontological straws? Notes on realism, "as-if-realism" and actualism. *Politics*, 25 (1): 39–45.

—— and ROSAMOND, B. 2002. Globalisation, European integration and the discursive construction of economic imperatives. *Journal of European Public Policy*, 9 (2): 147–67.

—— and WINCOTT, D. 1998. Structure, agency and historical institutionalism. *Political Studies*, 46 (5): 951–7.

KRASNER, S. 1984. Approaches to the state: alternative conceptions and historical dynamics. *Comparative Politics*, 16: 223–46.

MCNAMARA, K. 1998. *The Currency of Ideas: Monetary Politics in the European Union*. Ithaca, NY: Cornell University Press.

MANN, M. 1988. *States, War and Capitalism*. Oxford: Blackwell.

MARCH, J. G. and OLSEN, J. P. 1984. The new institutionalism: organisation factors in political life. *American Political Science Review*, 78: 734–49.

PETERS, B. G. 1998. *Institutional Theory in Political Science: The "New Institutionalism."* London: Pinter.

PIERSON, P. 1994. *Dismantling the Welfare State? Reagan, Thatcher and the Politics of Retrenchment*. Cambridge: Cambridge University Press.

—— 2004. *Politics in Time: History, Institutions and Social Analysis*. Princeton, NJ: Princeton University Press.

SCHMIDT, V. 2002. *The Futures of European Capitalism*. Oxford: Oxford University Press.

—— 2006. Institutionalism and the state. In *The State: Theories and Issues*, ed. C. Hay, M. Lister, and D. Marsh. Basingstoke: Palgrave.

THELEN, K. and STEINMO, S. 1992. Historical institutionalism in comparative politics. In *Structuring Politics: Historical Institutionalism in Comparative Analysis*, ed. S. Steinmo, K. Thelen, and F. Longstreth. Cambridge: Cambridge University Press.

TILLY, C. (ed.) 1975. *The Formation of National States in Western Europe*. Princeton, NJ: Princeton University Press.

—— 1994. The time of states. *Social Research*, 61 (2): 269–95.

WENDT, A. 1992. Anarchy is what states make of it: the social construction of power politics. *International Organization*, 46: 391–425.

—— 1999. *Social Theory of International Politics*. Cambridge: Cambridge University Press.

CHAPTER 5

....

NETWORK
INSTITUTIONALISM

....

CHRISTOPHER ANSELL *UC Berkeley*

1 OVERVIEW

....

In some respects, "network institutionalism" is an oxymoron. The term "network" tends to imply informality and personalism, while "institutionalism" suggests formality and impersonalism. Network perspectives also tend to be more behavioral than institutional. Nevertheless, it is reasonable to understand networks as informal institutions (though they may in some cases be formal). In this sense, a network can be thought of as an institution to the extent that it represents a *stable or recurrent pattern* of behavioral interaction or exchange between individuals or organizations. In much the same spirit as Peter Hall has described institutionalism, the network approach views networks as critical mediating variables that affect the distribution of power, the construction of interests and identities, and the dynamics of interaction (Hall 1986, 19–20).

No single network paradigm exists, but rather overlapping discussions in political science, organization theory, public administration, and economic sociology. Yet it is fair to say that four meta-principles or assumptions are shared across the various strands of network institutionalism.[1] The first and most general principle is a *relational perspective* on social, political, and economic action. Emirbayer (1997) contrasts relational with attributional approaches to social explanation. In the latter,

---

[1] Wellman (1988) provides both an intellectual history of the network approach and an important statement of its distinctiveness.

phenomena are explained in terms of the attributes of individuals, groups, or organizations. Network institutionalism, by contrast, emphasizes relationships—which are not reducible to individual attributes—as the basic unit of explanation. A second meta-principle is a presumption of *complexity*. Relationships that connect individuals, groups, and organizations are assumed to be complex, in the sense that linkages between them are overlapping and cross-cutting. Groups and organizations are not neatly bounded, certainly not unitary, and are often interpenetrating. The third meta-principle of network institutionalism is that networks are both *resources* and *constraints* on behavior. As resources, they are channels of information and aid mobilized in the pursuit of certain gains; as constraints, they are structures of social influence and control that limit action. The final meta-principle is that networks mobilize information, social influence, resources, and social capital in highly *differentiated* ways. Not only is the social world complex, but also highly biased. Networks provide variegated access to resources, information, and support.

Although this chapter aims to provide a broad interdisciplinary overview of network institutionalism, it is worth briefly describing how the network approach is congenial to political science.[2] First, political scientists have long been fascinated by the ways in which power and influence work through channels of personal connections—the proverbial "old boys network." Network institutionalism offers an approach that systematizes this fascination. Second, many problems in political science involve complex bargaining and coordinating relationships between interest groups, public agencies, or nations. While it may be sufficient to describe these relationships as "coalitions," "factions," or "alliances," network institutionalism suggests that precise patterns of connection matter for explaining political outcomes. Third, network institutionalism rejects any simple dichotomy between individualist and group-oriented explanation. It insists that individual behavior must be understood contextually, but rejects the assumption of unitary groups—a salutary perspective given the tensions in political science between individualistic and group-oriented approaches.

The remainder of the chapter clarifies the meaning of the term "network," provides a brief survey of techniques used to analyze networks, and then focuses on five substantive domains in which network institutionalism has been prominent: (a) policy networks; (b) organizations; (c) markets; (d) political mobilization and social movements; and (e) social influence, social psychology, and political culture.

2   WHAT IS A NETWORK?

A network is a set of relationships between individuals, groups, or organizations. A relationship, for example, might be a friendship between two Members of Parlia-

---

[2] See Knoke 1994 for a more comprehensive account of network approaches to politics.

ment or a cooperative exchange between two public agencies. Although conflict between two individuals or organizations could also count as a relationship, network institutionalism tends to presume positive relationships. Informed by a Durkheimian perspective on social solidarity, many network studies emphasize the *social* and *affectual* bases of relationships. However, it is not always necessary to assume that networks are solidaristic. Networks may be merely patterns of interaction or connection. For instance, two stakeholder groups may interact frequently in the context of a policy arena or the boards of two NGOs might share the same directors. Such relationships do not necessarily produce social solidarity and may be rife with conflict. But they imply the possibility that these connections are conduits, even if inadvertent, for information, ideas, or resources. Frequent interaction in a legislative committee, for example, might be the basis for the flow of critical information (regardless of whether the actors involved have any sense of mutual obligation). Interdependence offers a third way to interpret networks. For example, one lobbyist might have information that another lobbyist needs or two nations might have extensive trading relations. This interdependence may motivate them to engage in *exchange* relationships with each other. Successful exchange can, in turn, generate strong norms of *mutual obligation* and *reciprocity* (sometimes referred to as "generalized exchange"). The prominence of bargaining in political relationships makes this exchange approach to networks a natural one for political science.

Granovetter (1985) has argued that social network approaches steer a course between oversocialized (norm determined) and undersocialized (self-interest determined) understandings of social behavior. From this perspective, social networks have both a social (affectual) and instrumental (exchange) dimension. If the neoclassical market exchange takes places at "arms-length," we should expect little loyalty in such relationships and we should not expect them to provide the basis for the kind of trust or reciprocity necessary to produce exchange where goods are ill-defined or the timeframe for exchange is poorly specified. It is precisely the social character of network relationships built on loyalty and mutual obligation that allows us to think of them as *social structures*. Yet, Granovetter suggests, social actors are not mindlessly governed by these social norms. An instrumental calculus, mediated by social norms, remains at work in most social relationships.

A relationship between two actors (dyad) is the basic unit of any network. However, network approaches are typically interested in sets of interconnected dyadic relationships. The term *network* typically refers to this aggregate of interconnected relationships. The simplest network therefore actually requires at least three different actors—a triad. Much of network analysis is concerned with the global properties of a network as a single social structure—that is, as an aggregation of interconnected dyads. In network analytic terms, a typical organizational hierarchy is one kind of network. Subordinates are connected to their superordinates, who are in turn connected to their superordinates, until one reaches the top of the pyramid. However, many discussions, particularly in organization theory, suggest that networks are different from hierarchies. As pointed out by Kontopoulos (1993), the difference is that hierarchies are distinguished by "many-to-one" relationships, in which many subordinates are linked to only one superordinate. A network by contrast is an "entangled" web of relationships characterized by "many-to-many" relationships. Ansell (2000) uses this many-to-many criterion to characterize regional (subnational) policy in Europe.

Thus, a network can be distinguished both by the content of relationships (positive recurrent relations, built on mutual obligation, affection, trust, and reciprocity, etc.) and by its global structure (interconnected dyads, many-to-many relationships).

3   NETWORK ANALYSIS

One of the distinguishing features of network institutionalism is the availability of a range of quantitative techniques designed to analyze the properties of networks. The development of these techniques grew out of the use of graph theory to represent networks, though much recent network analysis also draws on algebraic methods. It is beyond the scope of this article to provide more than a cursory discussion of these methods. However, several book-length introductions are available. Scott (1998) and Degenne and Forsé (1999) provide useful surveys of social network analysis and Wasserman and Faust (1994) provide a comprehensive, but more mathematically demanding treatment. Several software programs are also available for social network analysis, of which the most popular is UCINET.

Prominent techniques of social network analysis include centrality and "sub-group" identification. Centrality is a particularly useful measure because it identifies the relative importance or prominence of individual actors in a network based on information about all the actors in the network. Various measures of centrality have been developed (degree, closeness, betweenness, etc.) that seek to capture different aspects of what it means to be a central actor. For example, betweenness centrality defines centrality in such a way as to identify actors likely to serve as important brokers. Another class of network techniques identify "sub-groups" within the network and they are particularly useful for identifying social cleavages or factions. These techniques range from those that identify sub-groups in relatively inclusive terms (e.g. component analysis) to those that are much more restrictive (e.g. clique detection).

Social network analysis also distinguishes between "cohesion" and "equivalence" as the basis for sub-groups. The cohesion approach suggests that sub-groups are based on the density of direct dyadic ties. Hence, the greater the number of ties within a group, the more cohesive it should be. By contrast, the equivalence approach argues that sub-groups will be composed of actors with equivalent ties to third parties. Marx's analysis of class formation is a classic example: workers are brought together not by their direct solidaristic ties, but by their common opposition to employers.

The distinction between cohesion and equivalence is related to a broader set of discussions in network analysis. Research on what came to be known as the "small world phenomenon" discovered that people were often connected to quite distant others through a surprisingly short number of intervening steps. As Watts (2003) has clarified, this is most surprising when networks are relatively "sparse." Watts found that small world networks have particular properties. They exhibit high local clustering combined with a limited number of "shortcuts" between clusters. Granovetter (1973) also built on the small world phenomenon in his influential argument about the "strength of weak ties." He found, for instance, that jobs were often not found directly through friends (strong ties), but through friends of friends (weak ties). The logic is that weak ties often "bridge" across clusters. Burt (1992) has further refined this logic in his work on "structural holes." He argues that information in small tightly knit clusters is redundant (everybody knows everybody's business). Moreover, clustering creates "holes" in the global network that limit the flow of information. Thus, ties that bridge across structural holes ("shortcuts" in Watt's terms, "weak ties" in Granovetter's) are powerful conduits of information.

The cohesion perspective suggests that the critical mechanism in networks operates through direct dyadic ties. An extension of this logic suggests that the stronger the tie (e.g. the more frequent, intimate, and intense the interaction), the more cohesive the relationship. At the global network level, then, a denser network is presumed to be a more cohesive one. The logic extends to multiple networks. Network analysis refers to the situation in which two actors are tied together in different types of ways—for example friendship, advice, co-work, residence—as *multiplexity*. In the cohesion logic, the more multiplex the network, the stronger it is. By contrast, the equivalence perspective emphasizes the importance of *indirect* as well as direct ties. Actors are similar not because they have strong ties to one another, but because they have similar ties to others. Actors who are structurally equivalent are therefore interpreted as having a similar position in the network. Multiple networks are important when they reinforce structural equivalence.

The difficulty of collecting network data has been one of the limits on the more widespread usefulness of social network methods. Two basic classes of network data exist. *Egocentric networks* begin with a focal actor or actors (ego) and then collect network information on relationships of ego to others (alters). A later phase of data collection collects further information on the relationships between ego's alters. The general problem with egocentric data is that it is highly selective, since by definition it reflects only ego's network. Alternatively, a *complete network* provides a more comprehensive perspective. Data for a complete network are collected by first identifying a group of actors and then collecting information on relationships between all of them. Such data can be difficult to collect for two reasons. First, identifying connections between all the actors in a network creates a large volume of data for even a small number of actors. Second, complete networks confront a problem of boundary specification. As the small world phenomenon demonstrates, everyone may be (at several removes) connected to everyone else. So where should the boundary be drawn? Network analysts generally solve this problem in one of two ways—each of which corresponds to a different technique for gathering the data. One approach is to specify the boundary at the outset on the basis of non-network criteria—for example the boundary of the organization or work unit, the policy sector, or geographical units. In such cases, it is often useful to begin with a complete list of the individuals, groups, or organizations contained within this boundary. The researcher then asks each actor on the list about their relationship with every other actor on the list. A second approach is often used when the boundary is difficult to specify ahead of time. In fact, identification of who is part of the network may be one of the main purposes for gathering data. In this case, snowball sampling is used to collect network data. Much like egocentric data, this approach starts with a few focal actors and then asks them about their relationships. It then builds outward, asking actors specified in the first round of interviewing who they are related to. Sampling may continue until the discovery of new actors drops off.

4   POLICY NETWORKS

The network analysis literature described above has mostly been developed in sociology and anthropology. In political science, a largely separate body of research has developed to study "policy networks." The policy network literature itself arose at the confluence of several streams of research. Among the earliest precursors to the policy network literature was Heclo and Wildavsky's (1974) study of the British Treasury Department, which uncovered the importance of personal networks between civil servants and politicians as an important factor shaping policy decisions. In the USA, development of the policy network concept arose out of work on "sub-governments"—the idea that policy-making and implementation were controlled by a select group of agencies, legislators, and interest groups. Working in this tradition, Heclo (1978) coined the term "issue network" to describe more diffuse forms of linkage than implied by the terms "sub-government" or "iron triangle." A closely related stream of European work on policy networks grew out of studies of corporatism and interest intermediation (Katzenstein 1978; Lembruch 1984). A second stream of research arose from an international group of researchers studying complex interorganizational relationships in government in the 1970s (e.g. Hanf and Scharpf 1979). This work emphasized that policy-making and implementation required complex coordination and negotiation among many different actors. A third stream of policy network research grew out of work on "community power studies," which essentially examined the social structure of politics in cities. Work by Lauman and Pappi (1976), in particular, advanced this into the study of policy networks.

All of these approaches combine two somewhat opposed images of political organization and process: all of them stress that political structure and process is highly differentiated, comprising the participation of a diverse range of actors; the opposing image suggests that these actors are linked together around their mutual interest or interdependence in specific policy domains. Thus, the network approach has the advantage of representing the ideas of both pluralists (empha-sizing differentiation) and elite theorists (emphasizing connectivity).

The next generation of policy network research began to clarify differences internal to networks and to articulate mechanisms by which they worked. Notably, Rhodes (1985) distinguished Heclo's concept of "issue networks" from "policy communities" in terms of the stability and restrictiveness of networks. He also articulated a "power-dependence" perspective that provided a framework for thinking about why and how networks were formed and how they operated. In a recent review of the policy network literature, Rhodes (2006) contrasts this "power-dependence" approach with the rational choice institutionalist approach to policy networks developed by Scharpf (1997).

Some of the policy network literature has drawn on the network analysis techniques described above. Laumann and Knoke's (1987) massive study of Ameri-can policy networks and Knoke, Pappi, Broadbent, and Tsujinaka's (1996) comparative study of labor policy networks offer important examples.

5   ORGANIZATIONS

The study of organizations is another area in which network institutionalism is well represented. La Porte's (1975) work on complexity, which defined organizational complexity in terms of the number of units and the number of interconnections between these units, provides an early precursor to this network institutionalism.

The shift to an open systems perspective, particularly with its increased focus on interorganizational relations, provided another impetus. Benson's (1975) political economy approach to interorganizational relations claimed "networks" of organizations were a new unit of analysis.

A decade or more later, the rising influence of institutional economics provided another context for the articulation of network ideas. The work of Oliver Williamson posed "markets" and hierarchies" as two alternative means of organizing economic transactions. The framework placed organization on a continuum between contract (market) and authority (hierarchy). In an influential article, Powell (1990) argued that "network organizations" were neither markets nor hierarchies. He argued that network organizations achieve coordination through trust and reciprocity rather than through contract or authority.

Other work on organizations points to structural aspects that made them difficult to describe either as markets or as hierarchies. For example, Faulkner (1983) applied network models to the process of forming project teams in the American film industry. At the same time, the burgeoning importance of strategic alliances and joint ventures between firms gave credence to thinking of interorganizational relations between firms in network terms. Gerlach's (1992) network analysis of Japanese intercorporate relations provides a notable example. A 1990 volume by Nohria and Eccles gave additional impetus to thinking of organizations as networks. These ideas have been used in political science to describe political parties (Schwartz 1990).

A somewhat separate line of research in public administration stressed the importance of thinking about interorganizational relationships in network terms. Fragmentation of service delivery and the complexity of implementation processes was a major concern of this literature. One common theme was how to achieve coordination among multiple public agencies with overlapping missions and authority. Chisholm's (1989) study of the role of informal networks in coordinating multiple transportation agencies and Provan and Milward's (1995) comparison of mental health networks in four American cities offer good examples of this genre. The managerial emphasis of this work is well represented in Kickert, Klijn, and Koppenjan (1997).

6   MARKETS

The fields of political economy and economic sociology have also used the idea of networks to conceptualize markets and market dynamics, and to describe the relationship between states and markets. Baker's (1984) study of social relationships on the floor of the Chicago stock exchange was among the first to call attention to social networks underpinning market exchange. He demonstrated that even in the archetypical market, actual patterns of buying and selling were shaped by social relationships. Social networks helped to manage the uncertainty that traders experienced in the stock market.

Drawing on Polanyi's description of the social embeddedness of markets, Granovetter (1985) provided a seminal statement of the network approach to markets. Much like Powell's argument that network organizations were different from either markets or hierarchies, Granovetter argued that many economic transactions were shaped by social relationships that build on norms of trust and reciprocity. His statement spawned serious research on the way in which embeddedness shaped economic decision-making and cooperation. Notable studies include Brian Uzzi's several studies of the banking, garment, and law industries and Mizruchi and Stearns' (2001) study of bank decision-making.

Another well-developed line of economic sociology research examines interlocking corporate boards. This work treats the overlapping memberships of boards of directors as a social network that connects otherwise independent firms together. Notable studies include Mizruchi's (1992) analysis of interlocking directorates to explain political campaign contributions and Davis's (1991) analysis of the diffusion of managerial strategies (the "poison pill") through interlocking directorates.

A range of other research has described the structure and dynamics of markets in network terms. Important exemplars include Powell, Koput, and Smith-Doerr's (1996) analysis of knowledge creation in the biotech industry in terms of interfirm networks, Padgett's (2001) study of networks underpinning the emergence of modern banking in Renaissance Florence, and Stark and Bruzst's (1998) description of the evolution of post-Communist East European markets in network terms. Political scientists Anno Saxenian (1996) and Richard Locke (1994) have also used network ideas to describe regional economies and the logic of state intervention in these economies.

7   POLITICAL MOBILIZATION AND SOCIAL MOVEMENTS

The network concept has also had significant impact in the study of political mobilization and social movements. Much of this work has been historical. For example, Bearman (1993) analyzed the way in which the Puritan faction in the

English Civil War emerged from networks of religious patronage and Padgett and Ansell (1993) demonstrated the way the Medicis' successful control over the Florentine state was based on the mobilization of a powerful political party constructed from economic and marriage ties. Gould (1995) demonstrated that resistance on the barricades in the Paris Commune of 1871 was based on neighborhood networks.

The social movement literature has drawn extensively on network concepts. Work by McAdam and others (e.g. McAdam and Fernandez 1990) demonstrated that social recruitment in movements often operates through social networks. Other work has demonstrated that the network concept can be used to describe and analyze broader social movement fields. For example, Diani (1995) uses the network approach to describe relationships between environmental organizations and between environmental activists in Milan. By studying overlapping memberships in underground protest organizations in Poland, Osa (2003) explains how the powerful Solidarity movement emerged to challenge the Communist regime. Diani and McAdam (2003) provide an overview of the relationship between social movements and networks. Closely related work by political scientists has been attentive to international networks of NGOs dubbed "transnational advocacy networks" (Keck and Sikkink 1998).

Network approaches have also been used to study social capital. In contrast to economic capital, social capital is conceived of as capital derived from social structure. Network approaches provide a useful representation of this social structure. While much of the best known work on social capital draws loosely on network metaphors, Lin, Cook, and Burt (2001) suggest a specific social network approach to social capital.

8   SOCIAL INFLUENCE, SOCIAL PSYCHOLOGY, AND POLITICAL CULTURE

The network approach has also been used to understand patterns of social influence, social cognition, and political culture. Krackhardt's (1990) concept of cognitive networks is among the most intriguing ideas in this genre. In studying a computer firm, Krackhardt found that more centrally located employees in actual social networks were also more accurate in their cognitive understanding of these social networks (cognitive networks). He also showed that reputational power in the firm was associated with this cognitive accuracy. Social psychologists have also used network approaches to model how social influence processes work through networks. Friedkin (1998) provides a powerful approach for modeling these influence processes. In political science, network processes are also understood as a way to model "contextual effects" precisely. Political scientists have used these network models to analyze the influence of neighbors on political attitudes towards candidates (Huckfeldt and Sprague 1987).

In addition to studying cognition and social influence, network approaches have also been applied to studying political culture. Examples include Mohr and Duquenne's (1997) network analysis of the historical evolution of social welfare categories in New York City and Ansell's (1997) study of how institutional networks and symbols interacted to produce a significant realignment of French working class institutions.

9   CRITIQUE AND PROGRESS

The work cited above is by no means exhaustive and many more specific domains of application could be reviewed. In fact, the network approach remains more a diverse set of overlapping discussions than a single unified approach to understanding institutions. Although the usefulness of the network approach has been proven across a range of disciplines, two basic types of criticism are often leveled against it. The first is that the network approach tends to produce a static and overly structural view of the world not sufficiently sensitive to process, agency, and meaning. Emirbayer and Goodwin (1994) forcefully made this critique of social network analysis and Bevir and Rhodes (2003) have made it of policy networks. These authors agree that network language tends to slip easily into the kind of structuralism that treats networks as objects. In particular, they suggest that network approaches must be more attentive to the cultural or interpretive elements of relationships. Just as network institutionalism criticizes the reification of groups, it must avoid a similar reification of networks. Padgett's (2001) recent work provides a good example of efforts to overcome the tensions between structure, culture, and agency in network institutionalism.

A second related critique is that the network approach is primarily a framework for description rather than explanation. It is good at describing economic, political, or social complexity, but less useful for deriving testable causal arguments. There is truth in this criticism: the network approach lends itself more easily to description than to explanation. The obvious retort is that a good description is the necessary foundation of a good explanation. But that response sells short the explanatory potential of network institutionalism. This chapter has featured work attentive to the ways in which networks operate as mechanisms to explain political mobilization, social influence, or interest intermediation.

This chapter concludes by returning to the current and potential value of network institutionalism for political science. One of the principal advantages of network institutionalism is that it provides an analytical framework that grasps the ever-increasing complexity of our age. As our technologies become more like networks, so must our institutions. The archetypical pattern of governance at the beginning of the twenty-first century requires political coordination across levels and between jurisdictions of government; the number of stakeholders has increased and elaborate webs of interaction and exchange between them have developed. Network institutionalism provides an unfinished, but highly promising paradigm for describing this complexity and explaining its consequences.

REFERENCES

ANSELL, C. 1997. Symbolic networks: the realignment of the French working class, 1887–1894. *American Journal of Sociology*, 103 (2): 359–90.

—— 2000. The networked polity: regional development in Western Europe. *Governance*, 13 (3): 303–33.

BAKER, W. 1984. The social structure of a national securities market. *American Journal of Sociology*, 89: 775–811.

BEARMAN, P. 1993. *Relations Into Rhetorics: Local Elite Social Structure in Norfolk, England, 1540–1640*. New Brunswick, NJ: Garland Press.

BENSON, J. K. 1975. The interorganizational network as a political economy. *Administrative Science Quarterly*, 20: 229–49.

BEVIR, M. and RHODES, R. A. W. 2003. *Interpreting British Governance*. London: Routledge.

BURT, R. 1992. *Structural Holes: The Social Structure of Competition*. Cambridge, Mass.: Harvard University Press.

CHISHOLM, D. 1989. *Coordination Without Hierarchy: Informal Structures in Multiorganizational Systems*. Berkeley: University of California Press.

DAVIS, G. 1991. Agents without principles? The spread of the poison pill through the intercorporate network. *Administrative Science Quarterly*, 36 (4): 583–613.

DEGENNE, A. and FORSÉ, M. 1999. *Introducing Social Networks*. Thousand Oaks, Calif.: Sage.

DIANI, M. 1995. *Green Networks: A Structural Analysis of the Italian Environmental Movement*. Edinburgh: Edinburgh University Press.

—— and McADAM, D. 2003. *Social Movements and Networks: Relational Approaches to Collective Action*. Oxford: Oxford University Press.

EMIRBAYER, M. 1997. Manifesto for a relational sociology. *American Journal of Sociology*, 103 (2): 281–317.

—— and GOODWIN, J. 1994. Network analysis, culture, and the problem of agency. *American Journal of Sociology*, 99: 1411–54.

FAULKNER, R. 1983. *Music on Demand: Composers and Careers in the Hollywood Film Industry*. New Brunswick, NJ: Transaction.

FRIEDKIN, N. 1998. *A Structural Theory of Social Influence*. New York: Cambridge University Press.

GERLACH, M. 1992. *Alliance Capitalism: The Social Organization of Japanese Business*. Berkeley: University of California Press.

GOULD, R. 1995. *Insurgent Identities: Class, Community, and Protest in Paris from 1848 to the Commune*. Chicago: University of Chicago Press.

GRANOVETTER, M. 1973. The strength of weak ties. *American Journal of Sociology*, 78 (5): 1360–80.

—— 1985. Economic action and social structure: the problem of embeddedness. *American Journal of Sociology*, 91 (3): 481–510.

HALL, P. 1986. *Governing the Economy: The Politics of State Intervention in Britain and France*. Oxford: Oxford University Press.

HANF, K. and SCHARPF, F. (eds.). 1979. *Interorganizational Policy-Making*. London: Sage.

HECLO, H. 1978. Issue networks and the executive establishment. In *The New American Political System*, ed. A. King. Washington, DC: American Enterprise Institute.

—— and WILDAVSKY, A. 1974. *The Private Government of Public Money*. London: Macmillan.

HUCKFELDT, R. and SPRAGUE, J. 1987. Networks in context: the social flow of information. *American Political Science Review*, 81 (4): 1197–216.

KATZENSTEIN, P. 1978. *Between Power and Plenty: Foreign Economic Policies of Advanced Industrial States*. Madison: University of Wisconsin Press.

KECK, M. and SIKKINK, K. 1998. *Activists Beyond Borders: Advocacy Networks in International Politics*. Ithaca, NY: Cornell University Press.

KICKERT, W. J. M., KLIJN, E.-H., and KOPPENJAN, J. F. M. (eds.) 1997. *Managing Complex Networks: Strategies for the Public Sector*. London: Sage.

KNOKE, D. 1994. *Political Networks: The Structural Perspective*. Cambridge: Cambridge University Press.

—— PAPPI, F., BROADBENT, J., and TSUJINAKA, Y. 1996. *Comparing Policy Networks: Labor Politics in the U.S., Germany, and Japan*. New York: Cambridge University Press.

KONTOPOULOS, K. 1993. *The Logics of Social Structure*. New York: Cambridge University Press.

KRACKHARDT, D. 1990. Assessing the political landscape: structure, cognition, and power in organizations. *Administrative Science Quarterly*, 35: 342–69.

LA PORTE, T. 1975. *Organized Social Complexity: Challenge to Politics and Policy*. Princeton, NJ: Princeton University Press.

LAUMANN, E. and KNOKE, D. 1987. *The Organizational State*. Madison: University of Wisconsin Press.

—— and PAPPI, F. 1976. *Networks of Collective Action: A Perspective on Community Influence Systems*. New York: Academic Press.

LEMBRUCH, G. 1984. Concertation and the structure of corporatist networks. In *Order and Conflict in Contemporary Capitalism: Studies in the Political Economy of Western European Nations*, ed. J. Goldthorpe. Oxford: Oxford University Press.

LIN, N., COOK, K., and BURT, R. (eds.) 2001. *Social Capital: Theory and Research.* New York: Aldine de Gruyter.

LOCKE, R. 1994. *Rebuilding the Economy: Local Politics and Industrial Change in Contemporary Italy.* Ithaca, NY: Cornell University Press.

McADAM, D. and FERNANDEZ, R. 1990. Microstructural bases of recruitment to social movements. In *Research in Social Movements, Conflict, and Change,* vol. 12, ed. L. Kriesberg. Greenwich, Conn.: JAI Press.

MIZRUCHI, M. 1992. *The Structure of Corporate Political Action: Interfirm Relations and their Consequences.* Cambridge, Mass.: Harvard University Press.

—— and STEARNS, L. B. 2001. Getting deals done: the use of social networks in bank decision-making. *American Sociological Review,* 66: 647–71.

MOHR, J. and DUQUENNE, V. 1997. The duality of culture and practice: poverty relief in New York City, 1888–1917. *Theory and Society,* 26: 305–55.

NOHRIA, N. and ECCLES, R. 1990. *Networks and Organizations: Structure, Form, and Action.* Cambridge, Mass.: Harvard Business School Press.

OSA, M. J. 2003. *Solidarity and Contention: The Networks of Polish Opposition, 1954–81.* Minneapolis: University of Minnesota Press.

PADGETT, J. 2001. Organizational genesis, identity, and control: the transformation of banking in rennaissance Florence. Pp. 211–57 in *Networks and Markets,* ed. J. Rauch and A. Casella. New York: Russell Sage Foundation.

—— and ANSELL, C. 1993. Robust action and the rise of the Medici: 1400–1434. *American Journal of Sociology,* 98 (6): 1259–319.

POWELL, W. W. 1990. Neither market nor hierarchy: network forms of organization. Pp. 296–336 in *Research in Organizational Behavior,* vol. 12, ed. B. Staw. Greenwich, Conn.: JAI Press.

—— KOPUT, K., and SMITH-DOERR, L. 1996. Interorganizational collaboration and the locus of innovation: networks of learning in biotechnology. *Administrative Science Quarterly,* 41: 116–45.

PROVAN, K. and MILWARD, H. B. 1995. A preliminary theory of interorganizational effectiveness: a comparative study of four community mental health systems. *Administrative Science Quarterly,* 10: 1–33.

RHODES, R. A. W. 1985. Power-dependence, policy communities, and intergovernmental networks. *Public Administration Bulletin,* 49: 4–20.

—— 2006. Policy network analysis. In *The Oxford Handbook of Public Policy,* ed. M. Moran, M. Rein, and R. E. Goodin. Oxford: Oxford University Press.

SAXENIAN, A. 1996. *Regional Advantage: Culture and Competition in Silicon Valley and Route 128.* Cambridge, Mass.: Harvard University Press.

SCHARPF, F. 1997. *Games Real Actors Play: Actor-Centred Institutionalism in Policy Research.* Boulder, Colo.: Westview Press.

SCHWARTZ, M. 1990. *The Party Network: The Robust Organization of the Illiniois Republicans.* Madison: University of Wisconsin Press.

SCOTT, J. 1998. *Social Network Analysis: A Handbook.* Thousand Oaks, Calif.: Sage.

STARK, D. and BRUSZT, L. 1998. *Postsocialist Pathways: Transforming Politics and Property in East Central Europe.* New York: Cambridge University Press.

WASSERMAN, S. and FAUST, K. 1994. *Social Network Analysis: Methods and Applications.* Cambridge: Cambridge University Press.

WATTS, D. 2003. *Six Degrees: The Science of a Connected Age.* New York: W. W. Norton.

WELLMAN, B. 1988. Structural analysis: From method and metaphor to theory and substance. Pp. 19–61 in *Social Structures: A Network Approach,* ed. B. Wellman and S. D. Berkowitz. Cambridge: Cambridge University Press.

CHAPTER 6

OLD INSTITUTIONALISMS

R. A. W. RHODES

1 INTRODUCTION

Over the past decade, the narrative of the "new institutionalism" has been touted as the new paradigm for political science. For example, Goodin and Klingemann (1996) claim that political science has an overarching intellectual agenda based on rational choice analysis and the new institutionalism. That is one set of approaches, one research agenda, and specific to American political science. The focus of this chapter is broader; it looks at the study of political institutions, whenever, wherever. I define and give examples of four different traditions in the study of political institutions: modernist-empiricist, formal-legal, idealist, and socialist. My aims are simple: to show there are several long-standing traditions in the study of institutions in the Anglo-American world, and to illustrate that variety worldwide.

I have a second, equally important objective. It is a taken for granted assumption that the rise of the "new institutionalism" replaced the "old institutionalism." Old institutionalism is not limited to formal-legal analysis. It encompasses all the

* I would like to thank Haleh Afsher, Mark Bevir, John Dryzek, Jenny Fleming, Bob Goodin, and John Wanna for either help, or advice, or criticism, and sometimes all three. I must record a special thank you to Robert Elgie for his thorough and detailed advice on French political science (personal correspondence, 6 June and 20 July 2005).

traditions discussed below. I argue there is life in all these old dogs. Moreover, formal-legal analysis is not dead. Rather I argue it is a defining starting point in the study of *political* institutions. The distinctive contribution of political science to the study of institutions is the analysis of *the historical evolution of formal-legal institutions and the ideas embedded in them.* The "new institutionalisms" announced the rediscovery by American modernist-empiricist political scientists of this theme, and they offer sophisticated variations on it, but it is still the starting point.

I cannot cover the many traditions of political science worldwide, so I focus on the two most similar countries—the UK and the USA. If I can show different traditions in the Anglo-Saxon world, then my argument will travel well beyond it. To show that potential, I provide brief examples of the study of political institutions in Australia, France, and the Muslim world. I offer a narrative that is just one among several of possible narratives. I set my narrative of traditions side-by-side with the narratives elsewhere in Part II. The aim is to decenter the dominant Anglo-American tradition found in many "state of the art" assessments.

2   TRADITIONS IN THE STUDY OF POLITICAL INSTITUTIONS

A tradition is a set of understandings someone receives during socialization. A certain relationship should exist between beliefs and practices if they are to make up a tradition. First, the relevant beliefs and practices should have passed from generation to generation. Second, traditions should embody appropriate conceptual links. The beliefs and practices that one generation passes on to another should display minimal consistency.

This stress on the constructed nature of traditions should make us wary of essentialists who equate traditions with fixed essences to which they credit variations. For example, Greenleaf (1983, 15–20), following Dicey (1914, 62–9), describes the British political tradition as the dialectic between libertarianism and collectivism. But Greenleaf's categories of individualism and collectivism are too ahistorical. Although they come into being in the nineteenth century, after that they remain static. They act as fixed ideal types into which individual thinkers and texts are then forced. At the heart of the notion of tradition used in this chapter is the idea of agents using their reason to modify their contingent heritage (see Bevir and Rhodes 2003, 2006). So, tradition is a starting point for a historical story. This idea of tradition differs also from that of political scientists who associate the term with

Table 6.1 Traditions in the study of political institutions

Traditions	Modernist-empiricist	Formal-legal	Idealist	Socialist
Definition of political institution	Formal rules, compliance procedures, and standard operating practices that structure relationships between individuals in various units of the polity and the economy	Public laws that concern formal governmental organizations	Institutions express...ideas about political authority...and embody a continuing approach to resolving the issues which arise in the relations between citizen and government	The specific articulation of class struggle
		Eckstein 1979: 2		Miliband 1977: 19
	Hall 1986: 19–20			
			Johnson 1975: 131, 112	
Present-day examples	USA: New institutionalisms	French constitutionalism	UK: Conservative Idealism	Pan-European post-Marxism
Examples	March and Olsen 1989	Chevallier 2002	Johnson 2004	Laclau 1990

customary, unquestioned ways of behaving or with the entrenched folklore of premodern societies (cf. Oakeshott 1962, 123, 128–9).

Table 6.1 identifies four distinct traditions in the study of political institutions: formal-legal, idealist, modernist-empiricism, and socialist. Of course, these traditions are examples. The list is not exhaustive.

3   WHERE ARE WE NOW—MODERNIST-EMPIRICISM?

For many, the study of political institutions is the story of the "new institutionalism." In outline, the story goes that the new institutionalism was a reaction against behavioralism. Thus, for Thelen and Steinmo (1992, 3–5) both historical institutionalism and rational choice are a reaction against behavioralism just as behavioralism was a reaction against the old institutionalism. This reaction comes in three main guises, each rooted in one of the main social science disciplines. So, political science gave us historical institutionalism, economics gave us rational choice institutionalism, and sociology gave us sociological institutionalism (see Goodin 1996, 2–20; Hall and Taylor 1996, 936). Approaches proliferate (Lowndes 2002; Peters 1999). The labels vary—sociological institutionalism begat ideational institutionalism begat constructivism. The several proponents squabble. For aficionados of such debates, the several approaches, the key contributions, and their differences are clearly set out in Chapters 1–5. A further summary is unnecessary.

There are important differences between the several approaches; for example, between inductive and deductive methods. However, such differences are less important than their common ground in a modernist-empiricist epistemology. Thus, institutions such as legislatures, constitutions, and civil services are treated as discrete objects that can be compared, measured, and classified. If American concern with hypothesis testing and deductive methods raises the collective skeptical eyebrow of British political science, then Bryce's claim (1929, vol. 1, 13) that "[I]t is Facts that are needed: Facts, Facts, Facts" would resonate with many. British modernist empiricism has much in common with the positivism underpinning mainstream American political science; both believe in comparison, measurement, law-like generalization, and neutral evidence.

In so labeling the new institutionalism, I do not seek to criticize it, only to locate it in a broader tradition. Adcock et al. (2006) do this job admirably. They explore the diverse roots of the new institutionalism to dismiss the conventional narrative of a shared rejection of behavioralism. They dispute there is a shared research agenda or even the prospect of convergence. The new institutionalism is composed of diverse strands, building on different and probably incompatible intellectual traditions, united only in the study of political institutions and their commitment to modernist-empiricism. The new institutionalism may be a shared label but its divergent roots in incommensurable traditions mean the several strands have little else in common. When we move further afield, the divergence is even more marked.

At first glance, British political science took to historical institutionalism like a duck to water. However, many British political scientists denied any novelty to the new institutionalism. After all, in Britain, neither the behavioral revolution nor rational choice had swept the study of institutions away. Also, the new institutionalism is such a jumble of ideas and traditions that it can be raided for the bits that easily fit with other traditions. So, British political scientists could interpret the rise of the new institutionalism in America as a vindication of British modernist empiricism, with its skepticism toward both universal theory, and the scientism characterizing American political science. Thus, Marshall (1999, 284–5) observes we do not need "more or deeper conceptual theories" because "we have already have most of what we need" for "detailed description, classification and comparison" and the "explanatory problem is simply that of describing relevant segments of the system in sufficient detail to expose what happens or happened." Case studies of institutions can be dressed up as a revitalized institutionalism and British political scientists can claim they wear the latest fashionable clothes. But, if you look closely little has changed. Barry (1999, 450–5) concludes there is no shared intellectual agenda based on the new institutionalism, no shared methodological tool kit, and no band of synthesizers of the discipline. The new institutionalism is little more than a cloak with which Whigs and modernist-empiricists can pursue the kinds of work they long have done unruffled by the pretensions of behavioralism and rational choice.

The same argument can be made for Australian political science. Aitkin (1985, 4–6) notes the discipline was shaped by the strong intellectual links with Britain and the dominance of law, history, and philosophy in the universities. Formal-legal studies were alive, even dominant, well into the 1980s (see Jinks 1985). It is hard to discern the local impact of the new institutionalism (see McAllister et al. 2003, part 2) and the impact of rational choice was even less (see the locally influential critique by Stretton and Orchard 1994).

4   WHERE DID WE COME FROM— FORMAL-LEGAL ANALYSIS?

The study of political institutions is central to the identity of the discipline of political science. Eckstein (1963, 10–11) points out, "If there is any subject matter at all which political scientists can claim exclusively for their own, a subject matter that does not require acquisition of the analytical tools of sister-fields and that sustains their claim to autonomous existence, it is, of course, formal-legal political structure." Similarly, Greenleaf (1983, 7–9) argues that constitutional law, constitutional history, and the study of institutions form the "traditional" approach to political science, and he is commenting, not criticizing. Eckstein (1979, 2) succinctly defines this approach as "the study of public laws that concern formal governmental organizations."

The formal-legal approach treats rules in two ways. First, legal rules and procedures are the basic independent variable and the functioning and fate of democracies the dependent variable. For example, Duverger (1959) criticizes electoral laws on proportional representation because they fragment party systems and undermine representative democracy. Moreover, the term "constitution" can be narrowly confined to the constitutional documentation and attendant legal judgments. This use is too narrow. Finer (1932, 181), one of the doyens of the institutional approach, defines a constitution as "the system of fundamental political institutions." In other words, the formal-legal approach covers not only the study of written constitutional documents but also extends to the associated beliefs and practices or "customs" (Lowell 1908, 1–15). The distinction between constitution and custom recurs in many ways; for example, in the distinctions between formal and informal organization. Second, rules are prescriptions; that is, behavior occurs because of a particular rule. For example, local authorities limit local spending and taxes because they know the central government (or the prefect, or a state in a federation) can impose a legal ceiling or even directly run the local authority.

Eckstein (1979, 2) is a critic of formal-legal study, objecting that its practitioners were "almost entirely silent about all of their suppositions." Nonetheless, he recognizes its importance, preferring to call it a "science of the state"—*staatswissenschaft*—which should "not to be confused with 'political science' " (Eckstein 1979, 1). And here lies a crucial contrast with my argument. *Staatswissenschaft* is not distinct from political science; it is at its heart.

The formal-legal approach is comparative, historical, and inductive (Rhodes 1995, 43–6 and for the usual caricature see Thelen and Steinmo 1992, 3). Finer (1932) is a fine exponent of the comparative approach (and see Eckstein 1963, 18–23 and Bogdanor 1999 for more examples). In sharp contrast to many of his contemporaries, Finer did not adopt a country-by-country approach but compared institution-by-institution across countries. He locates his institutional analysis in a theory of the state. For Finer (1932, 20–2), the defining characteristic of the state is its legitimate monopoly of coercive power (see also Sait 1938, ch. 5). He surveys the main political institutions "not only in their legal form, but in their operation" (Finer 1932, viii), as they evolved. Political institutions are "instrumentalities" which embody the "power-relationship between [the state's] individual and associated constituents" (Finer 1932, 181). Then and only then does he begin to compare the political institutions of America, Britain, France, and Germany. His analysis covers the elements of state organization, including: democracy, separation of powers, constitutions, central-local territorial relations, and federalism. Finally, he turns to "the principal parts of modern political machinery, namely, the Electorate, the Parties, Parliament, the Cabinet, the Chief of State, the Civil Service and the Judiciary" (1932, 949). His approach is not narrow and formal. It is grounded in a theory of the state and explores both the evolution of the institutions and their operation. The critics of the institutional approach do not do justice to his sophisticated analysis.

Formal-legal analysis is also historical. It employs the techniques of the historian and explores specific events, eras, people, and institutions. History is extolled as "the great teacher of wisdom" because it "enlarges the horizon, improves the perspective" and we "appreciate...that the roots of the present lie buried deep in the past, and...that history is past politics and politics is present history" (Sait 1938, 49). Because political institutions are "like coral reefs" which have been "erected without conscious design," and grow by "slow accretions," the historical approach is essential (Sait 1938, 16).

Finally, formal-legal analysis is inductive. The great virtue of institutions was that we could "turn to the *concreteness* of institutions, the *facts* of their existence, the character of their *actions* and the *exercise* of their power" (Landau 1979, 181; emphasis in the original). We can draw inferences from repeated observations of these objects by "letting the facts speak for themselves" (Landau 1979, 133).

In Britain and the USA, formal-legal analysis remains alive and well today in textbooks, handbooks, and encyclopedias too numerous to cite. Major works are still written in the idiom. Finer's (1997) three-volume history of government combines a sensitivity to history with a modernist-empiricist belief in comparisons across time and space, regularities, and neutral evidence. He attempts to explain how states came to be what they are with a specific emphasis on the modern European nation state. He searches for regularities across time and countries in an exercise in diachronic comparison. The *History* sets out to establish the distribution of the selected forms of government throughout history, and to compare their general character, strengths, and weaknesses using a standardized typology. It then provides a history of government from ancient monarchies (about 1700 BC) to 1875 AD. As Hayward (1999, 35) observes, Finer is either "the last trump reasserting an old institutionalism" or "the resounding affirmation of the potentialities of a new historical institutionalism within British political science." Given the lack of any variant of new institutional theory, the result has to be old institutionalism, and a fine example of an eclectic modernist-empiricism at work.

Formal-legal analysis is a dominant tradition in continental Europe. It was the dominant tradition in Germany, although challenged after 1945. The challenge is yet to succeed in, for example, Italy, France, and Spain. Here I can only give a flavor of the variety that is French political science and establish it as a distinctive endeavor that runs at times in a different direction to, and at times parallel with, Anglo-American political science.

There is a strong French tradition of constitutionalism. It is a species of the "old institutionalism" in that it is descriptive, normative, and legalistic. It focuses on the formal-legal aspects of institutions, but not on case law. It is another example of *staatswissenschaft*. For example, Chevallier (1996, 67) argues that "the growth of the French liberal state in the nineteenth century led to the predominance of the law and lawyers emphasizing the guarantee of citizen's rights and limits on state power." These jurists monopolized the field for nearly a century and it remains a major influence (see for example Chevallier 2002). So, despite various challenges, the 1980s witnessed "the resurgence" of "legal dogma" with its focus on the state's structures and functions (Chevallier 1996, 73).

Outside the tradition of constitutionalism, the French approach to the study of institutions remains distinctive and does not engage with the Anglo-American literature. An early example is Duverger (1954, 1980). Although his work on electoral systems and semi-presidentialism is probably better known outside France than inside, nonetheless it was a major challenge to the academic lawyers and influenced a younger generation of scholars. Latterly, "the strategic analysis of institutions" is an example of the new institutionalism before that term was invented. Its main proponents include, for example, Duhamel and Parodi (1985). Their heyday was the 1970s and 1980s but Parodi remains a major figure. The approach focuses on electoral systems, and core political institutions (such as the presidency), and tries to identify how institutions, singly and in combination, affect behavior (for citations see Elgie 1996). Parodi explains the changing nature of the Fifth Republic's political system by identifying how, for example, the direct election of the president with a majoritarian electoral system for the National Assembly bipolarized the party system. The approach is positivist and rigorous with some clear affinities to both rational choice and empirical institutionalism (see Peters 1999, ch. 5). However none of the proponents of the strategic analysis of institutions publish in English; none engage with the Anglo-American literature. Francophone and Anglophone traditions proceed in mutual ignorance. In short, French political science is rooted in constitutionalism or *staatswissenschaft* and, when it diverges from that tradition, it remains distinctive.

5   WHAT ARE THE COMPETING TRADITIONS—IDEALISM?

In British political science, the idealist tradition encompasses those who argue that social and political institutions do not exist apart from traditions or our theories (or ideas) of them (see Nicholson 1990). The major British idealist of recent times is Oakeshott (1991 and the citations on pp. xxiii–xvi). I concentrate on the application of his ideas to the study of political institutions.

The inheritors of idealism challenged behavioralism for its neglect of meanings, contexts, and history. Oakeshott (1962, 129–30) argued political education required the "genuine historical study" of a "political tradition, a concrete manner of behavior." The task of political science, although he would never use that label, is "to understand a tradition," which is "participation in a conversation," "initiation into an inheritance," and "an exploration of its intimations."

For Oakeshott (1962, 126–7) a tradition is a "flow of sympathy" and in any political activity we "sail a boundless and bottomless sea" and "the enterprise is to keep afloat on an even keel." This is a conservative idealism that treats tradition as a resource to which one should typically feel allegiance (cf. Taylor 1985; Skinner 1969).

For Johnson (1989, 131, 112), political institutions "express...ideas about political authority...and embody a continuing approach to resolving the issues which arise in the relations between citizen and government." Institutions are also normative, "serv[ing] as means of communicating and transmitting values." They are the expression of human purpose, so political institutions necessarily contain a normative element (Johnson 1975, 276–7). The task of "political science," a term Johnson would abhor, is to study institutions using "the methods of historical research...to establish what is particular and specific rather than to formulate statements of regularity or generalisations claiming to apply universally." History is "the source of experience" while philosophy is "the means of its critical appraisal" (Johnson 1989, 122–3). Johnson's (1977, 30; emphasis in original) analysis of the British constitution is grounded in the "extraordinary and basically unbroken continuity of conventional political habits." The British "constitution *is* these political habits and little else" and the core notion is "the complete dominance" of the idea of parliamentary government. Johnson (2004) applies this idea of the customary constitution of practices "mysteriously handed down as the intimations of a tradition" and "inarticulate major premises" (the reference is, of course, to Oakeshott) to New Labour's constitutional reforms; for example, devolution. His detailed commentary is of little concern here. Of relevance is his "bias" towards "the customary constitution" because of its "remarkable record of adaptation to changing circumstances and challenges" (Johnson 2004, 5). However, a customary constitution depends on support from a society that is sympathetic to "habit, convention and tradition." Johnson fears there is a "crumbling respect for tradition" and ponders whether the current reforms move "beyond custom and practice," and "piecemeal adaptation may have its limits." The customary supports of the constitution may well have been "eroded beyond recall." Johnson (2004) ends on this interrogatory note.

The notion of institutions as embedded ideas and practices is central to Johnson's analysis. It also lies at the heart of the Islamic study of political institutions. Al-Buraey (1985, ch. 6) identifies a distinctive Islamic approach to the institutions and processes of administrative development. Its distinctive features include: its emphasis on Islamic values and ethical standards; prayers in an Islamic organization—*salah* five times a day is a duty because it is as necessary to feed the soul as to feed the body; bureaucracies that represent the groups they serve; and *shura* or the process of continuous dialogue between ruler and ruled until a consensus emerges. Also, as Omid (1994, 4) argues, Islam can produce two contrasting views of the role of the state. The state exists "only to protect and apply the laws as stated by God." The

Saudi model means that you cannot have elections, leaders emerge by consensus and rule according to the teachings of the Koran. The Iranian model builds on the alternative view that Muslims have to abide by the rulings of Islam but that which is not prohibited is permitted. So, there can be elections, parliament, and legislation but the laws have to be subject to scrutiny by a council of guardians. I do not end on an interrogatory note, but stress the primacy of ideas in the study of political institutions (see also Blyth 2002; Campbell and Pederson 2001; Hay 2002).

6   What are the Competing Traditions—Socialism?

If historical materialism and economic determinism have been relegated to the dustbin of history, what is left? I seek to show that the tradition persists and introduce briefly the Marxist theory of the state; the post-Marxists, whose work has been influenced by "the linguistic turn;" and the non-Marxists with their predilection for social engineering.

6.1   Marxist Political Economy

The specific area of concern to the student of political institutions is their analysis of the state. The literature burgeoned (see for example Hay 1996, 1999; Jessop 1990; and Chapter 7).

Jessop is a central figure. He argues against all those approaches to state theory predicated on a distinction between structure and agency. He treats structure and agency only as an analytical distinction; they do not exist apart from one another. Rather we must look at the relationship of structure to action and action to structure. So, "structures are thereby treated analytically as strategic in their form, content and operation; and actions are thereby treated analytically as structured, more or less context sensitive, and structuring." This approach involves examining both "how a given structure may privilege some actors, some identities, some strategies...some actions over others," and "the ways...in which actors...take account of this differential privileging through 'strategic-context analysis' " (Jessop 2001, 1223). In other words, individuals intending to realize certain objectives and outcomes make a strategic assessment of the context in

which they find themselves. However that context is not neutral. It too is strategically selective in the sense that it privileges certain strategies over others. Individuals
learn from their actions and adjust their strategies. The context is changed by their
actions, so individuals have to adjust to a different context. Institutions or functions no longer define the state. It is a site of strategic selectivity; a "dialectic of
structures and strategies" (Jessop 1990, 129).

According to Hay (1999, 170), Jessop's central achievement has been to transcend
"more successfully than any other Marxist theorist past or present" the "artificial
dualism of structure and agency." I do not want to demur from that judgment or
attempt any critical assessment. For my purposes, I need to note only that Jessop's
contribution is widely noticed in Continental Europe and substantially ignored by
mainstream political science in America and Britain.

6.2   Post-Marxism

Ernesto Laclau is a leading figure in post-Marxism (Laclau 1990; Laclau and Mouffe
1985). His roots lie in Gramscian Marxism and with post-structuralist political
philosophy, not with mainstream political science. Discourse theory has grown
without engaging with mainstream political science. There is no specific critique of
political science. Rather it is subsumed within a general critique of both modernism and naturalism in the social sciences (as in for example Winch 1990).

Discourse theory analyses "all the practices and meanings shaping a particular
community of social actors." It assumes that "all objects and actions are meaningful" and that "their meaning is the product of historically specific systems of rules."
Discourse analysis refers to the analysis of linguistic and non-linguistic material as
"texts . . . that enable subjects to experience the world of objects, words and practices" (Howarth 2000, 5, 8, 10). The "overall *aim* of social and political analysis
from a discursive perspective is to describe, understand, interpret and evaluate
carefully constructed objects of investigation." So, "instead of applying theory
mechanically to empirical objects, or testing theories against empirical reality,
discourse theorists argue for the *articulation* and *modification* of concepts and
logics in each particular research context." At the heart of the approach is an
analogy with language. Just as we understand the meaning of a word from its
context, so we understand a political institution as sedimented beliefs within a
particular discourse (and for commentary see Critchley and Marchant 2005).

If Laclau's debt to post-structuralism has undermined many of the characteristic
themes of Marxist thinking—for example, his emphasis on the role of discourses
and on historical contingency leaves little room for Marxist social analysis with its
basic materialism—nonetheless he leaves us with the deconstruction of institutions
as discourse.

6.3 Non-Marxists: Fabian Social Engineering

One strand in Fabian thought espoused social and administrative engineering: "disinterested inquiries into social problems that could be utilized by the leaders of either of the major parties." This "application of the scientific method or 'systematized common sense'" stressed such topics as public ownership in the guise of nationalizing industry and extending municipal enterprise (Pierson 1979, 314, 335). Its proponents range from Sydney and Beatrice Webb at the turn of the twentieth century, through postwar advocates such as William Robson and John Stewart, to the current heirs in such New Labour thinks tanks as Demos and the Institute for Public Policy Research. British political science differs sharply from American political science because it has a strong, differentiated socialist tradition.

Robson was "one of the Olympian Fabians, worthy company to the Webbs" (Hill 1986, 12) and a founder of public administration in Britain. His approach to the study of British government and public administration was formal-legal institutionalism and analyzed the history, structure, functions, powers, and relationships of government organizations. In Robson (1939, 1960), he fought for vigorous local democracy and he was a staunch defender of the public corporation. In the *festschrift* for Robson, Griffith (1976, 216) revisited Robson's (1928) *Justice and Administrative Law*, concluding that it was "a remarkable work of academic scholarship and political perception" that "challenged some major assumptions of the system, and not merely some defects which needed remedy." To modern eyes much of his work seems overly polemical. Robson took as self-evident, truths and propositions we would challenge today; for example, the positive relationship between increasing size and efficiency. It matters not. Robson typifies that blend of institutional description and reformism so typical of the British school.

I seek not to praise or bury Caesar, simply to point out that the Fabian social and administrative engineering tradition is alive and well and advising the New Labour government (see Perri 6, Leat, Seltzer, and Stoker 2002; and on the antecedents see Bevir 2005). And this conclusion applies to the several strands of the socialist tradition. It is long-standing, durable, varied, and still with us whether it is analyzing the state, deconstructing institutions as discourse, or advocating network governance reforms.

7 CONCLUSIONS

I address two questions. Were we right all along to focus on formal institutions? Where are we going in the study of political institutions?

7.1   Were We Right all Along?

My concern has been to identify and describe some of the many distinctive traditions in the study of political institutions. I have not even remotely exhausted the variety of such traditions. I have not attempted to pass judgment on their relative merits. I am wary of treating any one theoretical perspective as the valid one from which to judge all others, preferring to probe for neglected traditions. If there is a judgment, it is that we should not overlook them. For many readers, the formal-legal tradition may seem an anachronism, but if one looks at constitution making throughout developing countries, Eastern Europe, and the former Soviet Union, one has to conclude the tradition is alive and well.

When we look beyond Anglo-American institutionalism and cover at least some of the various traditions in the study of institutions we see there is a common core of ideas. The distinctive contribution of political science to the study of institutions lies in its emphasis on: *describing the written constitutional documents and their associated beliefs and practices, drawing on history and philosophy—the founding constituent disciplines of political science—to explore the historical evolution of political institutions.* Such texts and their allied customs constitute the governmental traditions that shape the practices of citizen, politician, administrator, and political scientists alike. Even for Anglo-American institutionalism such analysis provides the basic building blocks of analysis.

Of course modernist-empiricism adds two more ingredients to the pot: some permutation of the modernist-empiricist tool kit of hypothesis testing, deductive methods, atomization, classification, and measurement; and contemporary social and political theory, under the label "the new institutionalisms." For proponents of behavioralism and the new institutionalism alike, the kiss of death for formal-legal analysis is its atheoretical approach. Behavioralism found the study of political institutions wanting because of its "hyperfactualism," or "reverence for the fact," which meant that political scientists suffered from "theoretical malnutrition" and neglected "the general framework within which these facts could acquire meaning" (Easton 1971, 75, 77, 79). New institutionalism takes it for granted that the "old institutionalism" was "atheoretical" (see Thelen and Steinmo 1992, 4; and for a survey of the various criticisms and reply see Rhodes 1995).

Viewed from the modernist-empiricist tradition, these criticisms seem like the death knell. Proponents of the formal-legal approach do not spell out their causal theory. However, many would dispute the relevance of this criterion. If you are not persuaded of the merits of present-day social science, then you do not aspire to causal theory but turn to the historical and philosophical analyses of formal-legal institutionalism. For example, Greenleaf (1983, 286) bluntly argues that although "the concept of a genuine social science has had its ups and downs, and it still survives, . . . we are as far from its achievement as we were when Spencer (or Bacon for that matter) first put pen to paper." Indeed, he opines, these "continuous attempts . . . serve only to demonstrate . . . the inherent futility of the enterprise." He holds a "determinedly old-fashioned" view of the study of politics, with its focus on history, institutions, and the interaction between ideas and institutions (Greenleaf 1983, xi). Moreover, Bogdanor (1999, 149, 150, 175, 176–7, 178) is not about to apologize for his version of "political science." He has a profound aversion to "over-arching theory" and "positivism," opting for "an indigenous British approach to politics, a definite intellectual tradition, and one that is worth preserving." This is the tradition of Dicey, "who sought to discover what it was that distinguished the British constitution from codified constitutions;" and Bagehot, "who . . . sought to understand political 'forms' through the analysis of political 'forces'." Similarly, viewed from a constructivist standpoint, the absence of the conventional battery of social science theories is also not a problem because its proponents emphasize the meanings of rules for actors seeking the explanation of their practices in the reasons they give. Null hypotheses and casual modeling play no part. Formal-legal analysis has its own distinctive rationale and, understood as the analysis of *the historical evolution of formal-legal institutions and the ideas embedded in them*, it is the defining characteristic of the political science contribution to the study of political institutions.

7.2   Where are We Going? History, Ethnography, and the Study of Political Institutions

A key concern in the formal-legal analysis of institutions, in idealism, in post-Marxism, and in various species of the new institutionalism is the interplay of ideas and institutions. In their different ways, all analyze the historical evolution of formal-legal institutions and the ideas embedded in them. So, we read constitutions as text for the beliefs they embed in institutions. We also explore the related customs by observing politicians and public servants at work because observation is the prime way of recovering ideas and their meanings. My argument for the continuing validity of old institutionalism, therefore, stresses, not the provision of "facts, facts, facts," but historical and philosophical analysis.

The focus on meanings is the defining characteristic of interpretive or constructivist approaches to the study of political institutions. So, an interpretive approach to political institutions challenges us to decenter institutions; that is, to analyze the ways in which they are produced, reproduced, and changed through the particular and contingent beliefs, preferences, and actions of individuals. Even when an institution maintains similar routines while personnel change, it does so mainly because the successive personnel pass on similar beliefs and preferences. So, interpretive theory rethinks the nature of institutions as sedimented products of contingent beliefs and preferences.

If institutions are to be understood through the beliefs and actions of individuals located in traditions, then historical analysis is the way to uncover the traditions that shape these stories and ethnographers reconstruct the meanings of social actors by recovering other people's stories (see for example Geertz 1973; Taylor 1985). The aim is "to see the world as they see it, to adopt their vantage point on politics" (Fenno 1990, 2). Ethnography encompasses many ways of collecting qualitative data about beliefs and practices. For example, Shore's (2000, 7–11) cultural analysis of how EU elites sought to build Europe uses participant observation, historical archives, textual analysis of official documents, biographies, oral histories, recorded interviews, and informal conversations as well as statistical and survey techniques. The techniques are many and varied but participant observation lies at the heart of ethnography and the aim is always to recover other people's meanings.

This "interpretive turn" is a controversial challenge to the mainstream. It is probably premature and certainly unwise to claim we are on the threshold of a postmodern political science. However, postmodernism does not refer only to debates about epistemology. It also refers to the postmodern epoch and the idea of a shift from Fordism, or a world characterized by mass production of consumer goods and large hierarchically structured business organizations, to flexible specialization, and customized production (see for example Clegg 1990, 19–22, 177–84). By extension, a postmodern political science may well be characterized by a Fordist heartland in the guise of rational choice institutionalism *and* customized political science rooted in national political traditions. And among these niches, old institutionalism will continue to thrive. Also, for the Fordist heartland, it will remain the starting point.

Pondering the aphorism "what goes around comes around," I conclude that old institutionalism has not only stayed around but that its focus on texts *and* custom and its commitment to historical and philosophical analysis make it increasingly relevant. Weighing the mounting criticism of rational choice institutionalism (as in for example Green and Shapiro 1994; Hay 2004), I expect to listen to a new generation of stories about actors and institutions. Interrogating the "interpretive turn," I conclude it is built on shifting sands because our notion of institutions is variously constructed within competing, non-commensurable traditions. So, we already live in a postmodern world with its tribes of political scientists. The key issue is whether we talk past one another or whether we have a reasoned engagement.

Bates et al. (1998) are distinguished proponents of rational choice who also argue for political anthropology and attempt to synthesize rational choice and interpretive theory. As Hay (2004, 58) argues, and Bates et al. acknowledge, "the postpositivist epistemology and post-naturalist ontology of interpretivism cannot be easily reconciled with the positivist epistemology and naturalist ontology of rational choice theory." Interpretive theory has not been assimilated to the rational choice mainstream. Rather, Bates et al. should be seen as "deploying rational choice *techniques* and *analytical strategies* in the service of an interpretivist *theory*" (Hay 2004, 58; emphasis in original). But, more important, their work is an example of reasoned engagement between the traditions.

Such engagement ought to be our future. I fear the professionalization of the political science discipline is the enemy of diversity; a case of "*vive la différence*," but not too much.

References

ADCOCK, R., BEVIR, M., and STIMSON, S. 2006. Historicizing the new institutionalisms. In *Modern Political Science: Anglo-American Exchanges since 1880*, ed. R. Adcock, M. Bevir, and S. Stimson. Princeton, NJ: Princeton University Press.

AITKIN, D. 1985. Political science in Australia: development and situation. Pp. 1–35 in *Surveys of Australian Political Science*, ed. D. Aitkin. Sydney: Allen and Unwin for the Academy of Social Sciences in Australia.

AL-BURAEY, M. A. 1985. *Administrative Development. An Islamic Perspective.* New York: Kegan Paul International.

BARRY, B. 1999. The study of politics as a vocation. Pp. 425–67 in *The British Study of Politics in the Twentieth Century*, ed. J. Hayward, B. Barry, and A. Brown. Oxford: Oxford University Press for the British Academy.

BATES, R. H., GREIF, A., LEVI, M., ROSENTHAL, J.-L., and WEINGAST, B. R. 1998. *Analytic Narratives.* Princeton, NJ: Princeton University Press.

BEVIR, M. 2005. *New Labour: A Critique.* London: Routledge.

—— and RHODES, R. A. W. 2003. *Interpreting British Governance.* London: Routledge.

—— —— 2006. *Governance Stories.* London: Routledge.

BLYTH, M. 2002. *The Great Transformations.* Cambridge: Cambridge University Press.

BOGDANOR, V. 1999. Comparative politics. Pp. 147–79 in *The British Study of Politics in the Twentieth Century*, ed. J. Hayward, B. Barry, and A. Brown. Oxford: Oxford University Press for the British Academy.

BRYCE, J. 1929. *Modern Democracies*, 2 vols. London: Macmillan.

CAMPBELL, J. L. and PEDERSEN, O. K. (eds.). 2001. *The Second Movement in Institutional Analysis.* Princeton, NJ: Princeton University Press.

CHEVALLIER, J. 1996. Public administration in statist France. *Public Administration Review*, 56 (1): 67–74.

—— 2002. *Science Administrative*, 3rd edn. Paris: PUF, Coll. Thémis.

CLEGG, S. 1990. *Modern Organizations: Organization Studies in a Postmodern World.* London: Sage.

CRITCHLEY, S. and MARCHANT, O. (eds.). 2005. *Laclau: A Critical Reader.* London: Routledge.

DICEY, A. V. 1914. *Lectures on the Relations between Law and Public Opinion During the Nineteenth Century.* London: Macmillan.

DUHAMEL, O. and PARODI, J.-L. (eds.) 1985. *La constitution de la Cinquième République.* Paris: Pressees de las FNSP.

DUVERGER, M. 1959 [1954]. *Political Parties*, 2nd rev. edn. London: Methuen.

—— 1980. A new political system model: semi-presidential government. *European Journal of Political Research*, 8: 165–87.

EASTON, D. 1971 [1953]. *The Political System. An Inquiry into the State of Political Science*, 2nd edn. New York: Alfred A Knopf.

ECKSTEIN, H. 1963. A perspective on comparative politics, past and present. Pp. 3–32 in *Comparative Politics: A Reader*, ed. H. Eckstein and D. E. Apter. London: Free Press of Glencoe.

—— 1979. On the "science" of the state. *Daedalus*, 108 (4): 1–20.

ELGIE, R. 1996. The French presidency: conceptualizing presidential power in the Fifth Republic. *Public Administration*, 74 (2): 275–91.

FARR, J., DRYZEK, J. S., and LEONARD, S. T. (eds.). 1995. *Political Science in History: Research Programs and Political Traditions*. New York: Cambridge University Press.

FENNO, R. F. 1990. *Watching Politicians: Essays on Participant Observation*. Berkeley: Institute of Governmental Studies, University of California.

FINER, H. 1932. *The Theory and Practice of Modern Government*, 2 vols. London: Methuen.

FINER, S. E. 1997. *The History of Government from the Earliest Times*, 3 vols. Oxford: Oxford University Press.

GEERTZ, C. 1973. *The Interpretation of Cultures*. New York: Basic Books.

GOODIN. R. E. 1996. Institutions and their design. Pp. 1–53 in *The Theory of Institutional Design*, ed. R. E. Goodin. Cambridge: Cambridge University Press.

—— and KLINGEMANN, H.-D. 1996. Political science: the discipline. Pp. 3–49 in *A New Handbook of Political Science*, ed. R. E. Goodin and H.-D. Klingemann. Oxford: Oxford University Press.

GREEN, D. P. and Shapiro, I. 1994. *Pathologies of Rational Choice*. New Haven, Conn.: Yale University Press.

GREENLEAF, W. H. 1983. *The British Political Tradition, Volume 1: The Rise of Collectivism*. London: Methuen.

GRIFFITH, J. A. G. 1976. Justice and administrative law revisited. Pp. 200–16 in *From Policy to Administration: Essays in Honour of William A. Robson*, ed. J. A. G. Griffith. London: Allen and Unwin.

GUNNELL, J. G. 2004. *Imagining the American Polity: Political Science and the Discourse of Democracy*. University Park: Pennsylvania State University Press.

HALL, P. 1986. *Governing the Economy: The Politics of State Intervention in Britain and France*. New York: Oxford University Press.

HALL, P. and TAYLOR, R. 1996. Political science and the three institutionalisms. *Political Studies*, 44: 936–57.

HAY, C. 1996. *Re-stating Social and Political Change*. Buckingham: Open University Press.

—— 1999. Marxism and the state. In *Marxism and Social Science*, ed. A. Gamble, D. Marsh, and T. Tant. London: Macmillan.

—— 2002. *Political Analysis*. Basingstoke: Palgrave.

—— 2004. Theory, stylised heuristic or self-fulfilling prophecy? The status of rational choice theory in public administration. *Public Administration*, 82 (1): 39–62.

HAYWARD J. 1999. British approaches to politics: The dawn of a self-deprecating discipline. Pp. 1–36 in *The British Study of Politics in the Twentieth Century*, ed. J. Hayward, B. Barry, and A. Brown. Oxford: Oxford University Press.

HILL, C. E. 1986. *A Bibliography of the Writings of W. A. Robson*. London: London School of Economics and Political Science, Greater London Paper No. 17.

HOWARTH, D. 2000. *Discourse*. Buckingham: Open University Press.

JESSOP, B. 1990. *State Theory: Putting Capitalist States in their Place*. University Park: Pennsylvania State University Press.

—— 2001. Bringing the state back in (yet again): reviews, revisions, rejections, redirections. *International Review of Sociology*, 11 (2): 149–73.

JINKS, B. 1985. Political institutions. Pp. 119–78 in *Surveys of Australian Political Science*, ed. D. Aitkin. Sydney: Allen and Unwin for the Academy of Social Sciences in Australia.

JOHNSON, N. 1975. The place of institutions in the study of politics. *Political Studies*, 25: 271–83.

—— 1977. *In Search of the Constitution*. Oxford: Perganon.

—— 1980. *In Search of the Constitution*. London: Methuen University Paperback.

—— 1989. *The Limits of Political Science*. Oxford: Clarendon Press.

—— 2004. *Reshaping the British Constitution: Essay in Political Interpretation*. Basingstoke: Palgrave Macmillan.

LACLAU, E. 1990. *New Reflections on the Revolution of Our Time*. London: Verso.

—— and MOUFFE, C. 1985. *Hegemony and Socialist Strategy: Towards a Radical Democratic Politics*. London: Verso.

LANDAU, M. 1979 [1972]. *Political Theory and Political Science: Studies in the Methodology of Political Inquiry*. Sussex: Harvester Press.

LEVI, M. 1988. *Of Rule and Revenue*. Berkeley: University of California Press.

LOWELL, A. L. (1908). *The Government of England*, 2 vols. New York: Macmillan.

LOWNDES, V. 2002. The institutional approach. Pp. 90–108 in *Theory and Methods in Political Science*, ed. D. Marsh and G. Stoker. Houndmills: Palgrave.

MCALLISTER, I., DOWRICK, S., and HASSAN, R. 2003. *The Cambridge Handbook of Social Sciences in Australia*. Melbourne: Cambridge University Press.

MARCH, J. G. and OLSEN, J. P. 1989. *Rediscovering Institutions: The Organizational Basis of Politics*. New York: Free Press.

MARSHALL, G. 1999. The analysis of British political institutions. Pp. 257–85 in *The British Study of Politics in the Twentieth Century*, ed. J. Hayward, B. Barry, and A. Brown. Oxford: Oxford University Press for the British Academy.

MILIBAND, R. 1977. *Marxism and Politics*. Oxford: Oxford University Press.

NICHOLSON, P. P. 1990. *The Political Philosophy of British Idealist: Selected Studies*. Cambridge: Cambridge University Press.

OAKESHOTT, M. 1991 [1962]. *Rationalism in Politics and Other Essays*, 2nd expanded edn. Indianapolis: Liberty Press.

OMID, H. 1994. *Islam and the Post-revolutionary State in Iran*. Basingstoke: Macmillan.

PERRI 6, LEAT, D., SELTZER, K., and STOKER, G. 2002. *Towards Holistic Governance: The New Reform Agenda*. Basingstoke: Palgrave.

PETERS, G. 1999. *Institutional Theory in Political Science: The "New Institutionalism."* London: Pinter.

PIERSON, S. 1979. *British Socialists: The Journey from Fantasy to Politics*. Cambridge, Mass.: Harvard University Press.

RHODES, R. A. W. 1995. The institutional approach. Pp. 42–57 in *Theories and Methods in Political Science*, ed. D. Marsh and G. Stoker. London: Macmillan.

RHODES, R. A. W. 1997. *Understanding Governance*. Buckingham: Open University Press.

ROBSON, W. A. 1928. *Justice and Administrative Law*, 2nd edn 1947, 3rd edn 1951. London: Macmillan.

—— 1939. *The Government and Misgovernment of London*. London: Allen and Unwin.

—— 1962 [1960]. *Nationalized Industries and Public Ownership*, 2nd edn. London: Allen and Unwin.

SAIT, E. M. 1938. *Political Institutions: A Preface*. New York: Appleton-Century.

SHORE, C. 2000. *Building Europe: The Cultural Politics of European Integration*. London: Routledge.

SKINNER, Q. 1969. Meaning and understanding in the history of ideas. *History and Theory*, 8: 199–215.

STRETTON, H. and ORCHARD, L. 1994. *Public Goods, Public Enterprise, Public Choice*. Basingstoke: Macmillan.

TAYLOR, C. 1985. *Philosophical Papers, Volume 2: Philosophy and the Human Sciences*. Cambridge: Cambridge University Press.

THELEN, K. and STEINMO, S. 1992. Historical institutionalism in comparative politics. Pp. 1–32 in *Structuring Politics: Historical Institutionalism in Comparative Analysis*, ed. S. Steinmo, K. Thelen, and F. Longstreth. New York: Cambridge University Press.

WEINGAST, B. R. 2002. Rational choice institutionalism. Pp. 660–92 in *Political Science: The State of the Discipline*, ed. I. Katznelson and H. Milner. New York: W. W. Norton.

WINCH, P. 1990 [1958]. *The Idea of a Social Science and its Relation to Philosophy*, 2nd edn. London: Routledge.

PART III

INSTITUTIONS

CHAPTER 7

THE STATE AND STATE-BUILDING

BOB JESSOP

The state has been studied from many perspectives but no single theory can fully capture and explain its complexities. States and the interstate system provide a moving target because of their complex developmental logics and because there are continuing attempts to transform them. Moreover, despite tendencies to reify the state and treat it as standing outside and above society, there can be no adequate theory of the state without a wider theory of society. For the state and political system are parts of a broader ensemble of social relations and neither state projects nor state power can be adequately understood outside their embedding in this ensemble.

1 WHAT IS THE STATE?

This innocuous-looking question challenges anyone trying to analyze states. Some theorists deny the state's very existence (see below) but most still accept that states are real and provide a valid research focus. Beyond this consensus, however, lies conceptual chaos. Key questions include: Is the state best defined by its legal form, coercive capacities, institutional composition and boundaries, internal operations and modes of calculation, declared aims, functions for the broader society, or sovereign place in the international system? Is it a thing, a subject, a social relation, or a construct that helps to orient political action? Is stateness a variable and, if so, what are its central dimensions? What is the relationship between the state and law, the state and politics, the state and civil society, the public and the private, state power and micropower relations? Is the state best studied in isolation; only as part of the political system; or, indeed, in terms of a more general social theory? Do states have institutional, decisional, or operational autonomy and, if so, what are its sources and limits?

Everyday language sometimes depicts the state as a subject—the state does, or must do, this or that; and sometimes as a thing—this economic class, social stratum, political party, or official caste uses the state to pursue its projects or interests. But how could the state act *as if* it were a unified subject and what could constitute its unity as a "thing?" Coherent answers are hard because the state's referents vary so much. It changes shape and appearance with the activities it undertakes, the scales on which it operates, the political forces acting towards it, the circumstances in which it and they act, and so on. When pressed, a common response is to list the institutions that comprise the state, usually with a core set of institutions with increasingly vague outer boundaries. From the political executive, legislature, judiciary, army, police, and public administration, the list may extend to education, trade unions, mass media, religion, and even the family. Such lists typically fail to specify what lends these institutions the quality of statehood. This is hard because, as Max Weber (1948) famously noted, there is no activity that states always perform and none that they have never performed. Moreover, what if, as some theorists argue, the state is inherently prone to fail? Are the typical forms of state failure properly part of its core definition or merely contingent, variable, and eliminable secondary features? Finally, who are the state's agents? Do they include union leaders involved in policing incomes policies, for example, or media owners who circulate propaganda on the state's behalf?

An obvious escape route is to define the state in terms of means rather than ends. This approach informs Weber's celebrated definition of the *modern* state as the "human community that successfully claims legitimate monopoly over the means of coercion in a given territorial area" as well as definitions that highlight its formal sovereignty vis-à-vis its own population and other states. This does not mean that modern states exercise power largely through direct and immediate coercion—this would be a sign of crisis or state failure—but rather that coercion is their last resort in enforcing binding decisions. For, where state power is regarded as legitimate, it can normally secure compliance without such recourse. Even then all states reserve the right—or claim the need—to suspend the constitution or specific legal provisions and many states rely heavily on force, fraud, and corruption and their subjects' inability to organize effective resistance.

Building on Weber and his contemporaries, other theorists regard the essence of the state (premodern as well as modern) as the territorialization of political authority. This involves the intersection of politically organized coercive and symbolic power, a clearly demarcated core territory, and a fixed population on which political decisions are collectively binding. Thus the key feature of the state is the historically variable ensemble of technologies and practices that produce, naturalize, and manage territorial space as a bounded container within which political power is then exercised to achieve various, more or less well integrated, and changing policy objectives. A system of formally sovereign, mutually recognizing, mutually legitimating national states exercising sovereign control over large and exclusive territorial areas is only a relatively recent institutional expression of state power. Other modes of territorializing political power have existed, some still coexist with the so-called Westphalian system (allegedly established by the Treaties of Westphalia in 1648 but realized only stepwise during the nineteenth and twentieth centuries), new expressions are emerging, and yet others can be imagined. For example, is the EU a new form of state power, a rescaled "national" state, a revival of medieval political patterns, or a post-sovereign form of authority? And is the rapid expansion of transnational regimes indicative of the emergence of global governance or even a world state?

Another influential theorist, the Italian Communist, Antonio Gramsci, defined the state as "political society + civil society;" and likewise analyzed state power in modern democratic societies as based on "hegemony armoured by coercion." He defined hegemony as the successful mobilization and reproduction of the "active consent" of dominated groups by the ruling class through the exercise of political, intellectual, and moral leadership. Force in turn involves the use of a coercive apparatus to bring the mass of the people into conformity and compliance with the requirements of a specific mode of production. This approach provides a salutary reminder that the state only exercises power by projecting and realizing state capacities beyond the narrow boundaries of state; and that domination and hegemony can be exercised on both sides of any official public–private divide (for example, state support for paramilitary groups such as the Italian *fascisti*, state education in relation to hegemony) (Gramsci 1971).

Building on Marx and Gramsci, a postwar Greek political theorist, Nicos Poulantzas (1978), developed a better solution. He claimed that the state is a social relation. This elliptical phrase implies that, whether regarded as a thing (or, better, an institutional ensemble) or as a subject (or, better, the repository of specific political capacities and resources), the state is far from a passive instrument or neutral actor. Instead it is always biased by virtue of the structural and strategic selectivity that makes state institutions, capacities, and resources more accessible to some political forces and more tractable for some purposes than others. Poulantzas interpreted this mainly in class terms and grounded it in the generic form of the capitalist state; he also argued that selectivity varies by particular political regimes.

Likewise, since it is not a subject, the capitalist state does not, and indeed cannot, exercise power. Instead its powers (plural) are activated by changing sets of politicians and state officials located in specific parts of the state in specific conjunctures. If an overall strategic line is discernible in the exercise of these powers, it is due to strategic coordination enabled through the selectivity of the state system and the role of parallel power networks that cross-cut and unify its formal structures. Such unity is improbable, according to Poulantzas, because the state is shot through with contradictions and class struggles and its political agents must always take account of (potential) mobilization by a wide range of forces beyond the state, engaged in struggles to transform it, determine its policies, or simply resist it from afar. This approach can be extended to include dimensions of social domination that are not directly rooted in class relations (for example, gender, ethnicity, "race," generation, religion, political affiliation, or regional location). This would provide a bridge to non-Marxist analyses of the state and state power (see below on the strategic-relational approach).

2   THE ORIGINS OF THE STATE AND STATE-BUILDING

State formation is not a once-and-for-all process nor did the state develop in just one place and then spread elsewhere. It has been invented many times, had its ups and downs, and seen recurrent cycles of centralization and decentralization, territorialization and deterritorialization. This is a rich field for political archeology, political anthropology, historical sociology, comparative politics, evolutionary institutional economics, historical materialism, and international relations. Although its origins have been explained in various monocausal ways, none of these provides a convincing general explanation. Marxists focus on the emergence of economic surplus to enable development of specialized, economically unproductive political apparatus concerned to secure cohesion in a (class-)divided society (see, classically, Engels' (1875) *Origins of the Family, Private Property, and the State*); military historians focus on the role of military conquest in state-building and/or the demands of defense of territorial integrity in the expansion of state capacities to penetrate and organize society (Hintze's (e.g. 1975) work is exemplary; see also Porter 1994). Others emphasize the role of a specialized priesthood and organized religion (or other forms of ideological power) in giving symbolic unity to the population governed by the state (Claessen and Skalnik 1978). Feminist theorists have examined the role of patriarchy in state formation and the state's continuing role in reproducing gender divisions. And yet other scholars focus on the "imagined political communities" around which nation states have been constructed (classically Anderson 1991).

The best approach is multicausal and recognizes that states change continually, are liable to break down, and must be rebuilt in new forms, with new capacities and functions, new scales of operation, and a predisposition to new types of failure. In this context, as Mann (1986) notes, the state is polymorphous—its organization and capacities can be primarily capitalist, military, theocratic, or democratic in character and its dominant crystallization is liable to challenge as well as conjunctural variation. There is no guarantee that the modern state will always (or ever) be primarily capitalist in character and, even where capital accumulation is deeply embedded in its organizational matrix, it typically takes account of other functional demands and civil society in order to promote institutional integration and social cohesion within its territorial boundaries. Whether it succeeds is another matter.

Modern state formation has been analyzed from four perspectives. First, the state's "historical constitution" is studied in terms of path-dependent histories or genealogies of particular parts of the modern state (such as a standing army, modern tax system, formal bureaucracy, parliament, universal suffrage, citizenship rights, and recognition by other states). Second, work on "formal constitution" explores how a state acquires, if at all, its distinctive formal features as a modern state, such as formal separation from other spheres of society, its own political rationale, modus operandi, and distinctive constitutional legitimation, based on adherence to its own political procedures rather than values such as divine right or natural law. Third, agency-centered theorizations focus on state projects that give a substantive (as opposed to formal) unity to state actions and whose succession defines different types of state, for example, liberal state, welfare state, competition state. And, fourth, configurational analyses explore the distinctive character of state–civil society relations and seek to locate state formation within wider historical developments. Eisenstadt's (1963) work on the rise and fall of bureaucratic empires, Elias's (1982) work on the state and civilization, and Rokkan's (1999) work on European state formation over the last 400–500 years are exemplary here.

3   MARXIST APPROACHES TO THE STATE

Marx's and Engels' work on the state comprises diverse philosophical, theoretical, journalistic, partisan, *ad hominem*, or purely ad hoc comments. This is reflected in the weaknesses of later Marxist state theories, both analytically and practically, and has prompted many attempts to complete *the* Marxist theory of the state based on selective interpretations of these writings. There were two main axes around which these views moved. Epiphenomenalist accounts mainly interpreted state forms and functions as more or less direct reflections of underlying economic structures and interests. These views were sometimes modified to take account of the changing stages of capitalism and the relative stability or crisis-prone nature of capitalism. Instrumentalist accounts treated the state as a simple vehicle for political class rule, moving as directed by those in charge. For some tendencies and organizations (notably in the social democratic movement) instrumentalism could justify a parliamentary democratic road to socialism based on the electoral conquest of power, state planning, or nationalization of leading industrial sectors. Others argued that parliamentary democracy was essentially bourgeois and that extra-parliamentary mobilization and a new form of state were crucial to make and consolidate a proletarian revolution. Frankfurt School critical theorists examined the interwar trends towards a strong, bureaucratic state—whether authoritarian or totalitarian in form. They argued that this corresponded to the development of organized or state capitalism, relied increasingly on the mass media for its ideological power, and had integrated the trade union movement as a political support or else smashed it as part of the consolidation of totalitarian rule.

Marxist interest revived in the 1960s and 1970s in response to the apparent ability of the Keynesian welfare national state to manage the postwar economy in advanced capitalist societies and the alleged "end of ideology" that accompanied postwar economic growth. Marxists initially sought to prove that, notwithstanding the postwar boom, contemporary states could not really suspend capital's contradictions and crisis-tendencies and that the state remained a key factor in class domination.

The relative autonomy of the state was much debated in the 1970s and 1980s. Essentially this topic concerned the relative freedom of the state (or, better, state managers) to pursue policies that conflicted with the immediate interests of the dominant economic class(es) without becoming so autonomous that they could undermine their long-term interests too. This was one of the key themes in the notoriously difficult Miliband–Poulantzas debate in the 1970s between an alleged instrumentalist and a purported determinist, respectively. This controversy generated much heat but little light because it was based as much on different presentational strategies as it was on real theoretical differences. Thus Miliband's (1969) work began by analyzing the social origins and current interests of economic and political elites and then proceeded to analyze more fundamental features of actually existing states in a capitalist society and the constraints on its autonomy. Poulantzas (1973) began with the overall institutional framework of capitalist societies, defined the ideal-typical capitalist type of state (a constitutional democratic state based on the rule of law), then explored the typical forms of political class struggle in bourgeois democracies (concerned with winning active consent for a national-popular project), and concluded with an analysis of the relative autonomy of state managers. Whilst not fully abandoning his earlier approach, Poulantzas later argued that the state is a social relation (see above).

The best work in this period formulated two key insights with a far wider relevance. First, some Marxists explored how the typical form of the capitalist state actually caused problems rather than guaranteed its overall functionality for capital accumulation and political class domination. For the state's institutional separation from the market economy, a separation that was regarded as a necessary and defining feature of capitalist societies, results in the dominance of different (and potentially contradictory) institutional logics and modes of calculation in state and economy. There is no certainty that political outcomes will serve the needs of capital—even if (and, indeed, precisely because) the state is operationally autonomous and subject to politically-mediated constraints and pressures. This conclusion fuelled work on the structural contradictions, strategic dilemmas, and historically conditioned development of specific state forms. It also prompted interest in the complex interplay of social struggles and institutions. And, second, as noted above, Marxist theorists began to analyze state power as a complex social relation. This involved studies of different states' structural selectivity and the factors that shaped their strategic capacities. Attention was paid to the variability of these capacities, their organization and exercise, and their differential impact on the state power and states' capacities to project power into social realms well beyond their own institutional boundaries. As with the first set of insights, this also led to more complex studies of struggles, institutions, and political capacities (see Barrow 1993; Jessop 2001).

4   STATE-CENTERED THEORIES

The flourishing of Marxist state theories in the 1970s prompted a counter-movement in the 1980s to "bring the state back in" as a critical explanatory variable in social analysis. This approach was especially popular in the USA and claimed that the dominant postwar approaches were too "society-centered" because they explained the state's form, functions, and impact in terms of factors rooted in the organization, needs, or interests of society. Marxism was accused of economic reductionism for its emphasis on base-superstructure relations and class struggle; pluralism was charged with limiting its account of competition for state power to interest groups and movements rooted in civil society and ignoring the distinctive role and interests of state managers; and structural-functionalism was criticized for assuming that the development and operations of the political system were determined by the functional requirements of society as a whole. "State-centered" theorists claimed this put the cart before the horse. They argued that state activities and their impact are easily explained in terms of its distinctive properties as an administrative or repressive organ and/or the equally distinctive properties of the broader political system encompassing the state. Societal factors, when not irrelevant, were certainly secondary; and their impact on state affairs was always filtered through the political system and the state itself. The classic statement of this approach is found in Evans, Rueschemeyer, and Skocpol (1985).

In its more programmatic guise the statist approach advocated a return to classic theorists such as Machiavelli, Clausewitz, de Tocqueville, Weber, or Hintze. In practice, statists showed little interest in such thinkers, with the partial exception of Weber. The real focus of state-centered work is detailed case studies of state-building, policy-making, and implementation. These emphasize six themes: (a) the geopolitical position of different states in the interstate system and its implications for the logic of state action; (b) the dynamic of military organization and the impact of warfare on the overall development of the state—reflected in Tilly's claim that, not only do states make war, but wars make states; (c) the state's distinctive administrative powers—especially those rooted in its capacities to produce and enforce collectively binding decisions within a centrally organized, territorially bounded society—and its strategic reach in relation to all other social sub-systems (including the economy), organizations (including capitalist enterprises), and forces (including classes) within its domain; (d) the state's role as a distinctive factor in shaping institutions, group formation, interest articulation, political capacities, ideas, and demands beyond the state; (e) the distinctive pathologies of government and the political system—such as bureaucratism, political corruption, government overload, or state failure; and (f) the distinctive interests and capacities of "state managers" (career officials, elected politicians, and so on). Although "state-centered" theorists emphasized different factors or combinations thereof, the main conclusions remain that there are distinctive political pressures and processes that shape the state's form and functions; give it a real and important autonomy when faced with pressures and forces emerging from the wider society; and thereby endow it with a unique and irreplaceable centrality both in national life and the international order. In short, the state is a force in its own right and does not just serve the economy or civil society (Evans, Rueschemeyer, and Skocpol 1985).

Their approach leads "state-centered" theorists to advance a distinctive interpretation of state autonomy. For most Marxists, the latter is primarily understood in terms of the state's capacity to promote the long-term, collective interests of capital even when faced with opposition—including from particular capitalist interests. Only in exceptional and typically short-lived circumstances can the state secure real freedom of action. Neostatists reject such a class- or capital-theoretical account and suggest that it is usual for the state to exercise autonomy in its own right and in pursuit of its own, quite distinctive, interests. Accordingly, they emphasize: (a) state managers' ability to exercise power independently of (and even in the face of resistance from) non-state forces—especially where a pluralistic universe of social forces opens significant scope for maneuver; and (b) the grounding of this ability in the state's distinctive political resources and its ability to use these to penetrate, control, supervise, police, and discipline modern societies. Neostatists also argue that state autonomy is not a fixed structural feature of each and every governmental system but differs across states, by policy area, and over time. This is due partly to external limits on the scope for autonomous state action and partly to variations in state managers' capacity and readiness to pursue a strategy independent of non-state actors.

The extensive body of statist empirical research has generally proved a fruitful counterweight to one-sided class- and capital-theoretical work. Nonetheless four significant lines of criticism have been advanced against neostatism. First, the rationale for neostatism is based on incomplete and misleading accounts of society-centered work. Second, neostatism itself focuses one-sidedly on state and party politics at the expense of political forces outside and beyond the state. In particular, it substitutes "politicians for social formations (such as class or gender or race), elite for mass politics, political conflict for social struggle" (Gordon 1990). Third, it allegedly has a hidden political agenda. Some critics claim that it serves to defend state managers as effective agents of economic modernization and social reform rather than highlighting the risks of authoritarianism and autocratic rule. Fourth, and most seriously, neostatism involves a fundamental theoretical fallacy. It posits clear and unambiguous boundaries between the state apparatus and society, state managers and social forces, and state power and societal power; the state can therefore be studied in isolation from society. This renders absolute what are really emergent, partial, unstable, and variable distinctions. This excludes hybrid logics such as corporatism or policy networks; divisions among state managers due to ties between state organs and other social spheres; and many other forms of overlap between state and society. If this assumption is rejected, however, the distinction between state- and society-centered approaches dissolves. This in turn invalidates, not merely the extreme claim that the state apparatus should be treated as the independent variable in explaining political and social events, but also lesser neostatist claims such as the heuristic value of bending the stick in the other direction or, alternatively, of combining state-centered and society-centered accounts to produce the complete picture.

5   FOUCAULDIAN APPROACHES

If state-centered theorists hoped to bring the state back in as an independent variable and/or an autonomous actor, Foucault aimed to undermine the analytical centrality of the state, sovereignty, or law for power relations. He advanced three key claims in this regard. First, state theory is essentialist: it tries to explain the state and state power in terms of their own inherent, pre-given properties. Instead it should try to explain the development and functioning of the state as the contingent outcome of specific practices that are not necessarily (if at all) located within, or openly oriented to, the state itself. Second, state theory retains medieval notions of a centralized, monarchical sovereignty and/or a unified, juridico-political power. But there is a tremendous dispersion and multiplicity of the institutions and practices involved in the exercise of state power and many of these are extra-juridical in nature. And, third, state theorists were preoccupied with the summits of the state apparatus, the discourses that legitimated sovereign state power, and the extent of the sovereign state's reach into society. In contrast Foucault advocated a bottom-up approach concerned with the multiple dispersed sites where power is actually exercised. He proposed a microphysics of power concerned with actual practices of subjugation rather than with macropolitical strategies. For state power is dispersed. It involves the active mobilization of individuals and not just their passive targeting, and can be colonized and articulated into quite different discourses, strategies, and institutions. In short, power is not concentrated in the state: it is ubiquitous, immanent in every social relation (see notably Foucault 1980a,b).

Nonetheless Foucault did not reject all concern with the macrophysics of state power. He came to see the state as the crucial site of statecraft and "governmentality" (or governmental rationality). What interested him was the art of government, a skilled practice in which state capacities were used reflexively to monitor the population and, with all due prudence, to make it conform to specific state projects. *Raison d'état*, an autonomous political rationality, set apart from religion and morality, was the key to the rise of the modern state. This in turn could be linked to different modes of political calculation or state projects, such as those coupled to the "police state" (*Polizeistaat*), social government, or the welfare state. It was in and through these governmental rationalities or state projects that more local or regional sites of power were colonized, articulated into ever more general mechanisms and forms of global domination, and then maintained by the entire state system. Foucault also insisted on the need to explore the connections between these forms of micropower and mechanisms for producing knowledge—whether for surveillance, the formation and accumulation of knowledge about individuals, or their constitution as specific types of subject.

Foucault never codified his work and changed his views frequently. Taking his ideas on the ubiquity of power relations, the coupling of power-knowledge, and governmentality together, however, he offers an important theoretical and empirical corrective to the more one-sided and/or essentialist analyses of Marxist state theory and to the taken-for-grantedness of the state that infuses neostatism. But his work remains vulnerable to the charge that it tends to reduce power to a set of universally applicable power technologies (whether panoptic surveillance or disciplinary normalization) and to ignore how class and patriarchal relations shape the state's deployment of these powers as well as the more general exercise of power in the wider society. It also neglects the continued importance of law, constitutionalized violence, and bureaucracy for the modern state. Moreover, whatever the merits of drawing attention to the ubiquity of power, his work provided little account of the bases of resistance (bar an alleged "plebeian" spirit of revolt). More recent Foucauldian studies have tried to overcome these limitations and to address the complex strategic and structural character of the state apparatus and statecraft and the conditions that enable the state to engage in effective action across many social domains.

6   FEMINIST APPROACHES

While feminists have elaborated distinctive theories of the gendering of social relations and provide powerful critiques of malestream political philosophy and political theory, they have generally been less interested in developing a general feminist theory of the state. In part this reflects their interest in other concepts that are more appropriate to a feminist theoretical and political agenda and their concern to break with the phallocratic concerns of malestream theory (Allen 1990; MacKinnon 1989). The main exception in the first wave of postwar state theorizing was Marxist–feminist analyses of the interaction of class and gender in structuring states, state intervention, and state power in ways that reproduce both capitalism and patriarchy. Other currents called for serious analysis of the state because of its centrality to women's lives (e.g. Brown 1992). This is reflected in various theories about different aspects of the state (Knutilla and Kubik 2001 compare feminist with classical and other state theories).

Some radical feminist theories simply argued that, whatever their apparent differences, all states are expressions of patriarchy or phallocracy. Other feminists tried to derive the necessary form and/or functions of the patriarchal state from the imperatives of reproduction (rather than production), from the changing forms of patriarchal domination, from the gendered nature of household labor in the "domestic" mode of production, and so on. Such work denies any autonomy or contingency to the state. Others again try to analyze the contingent articulation of patriarchal and capitalist forms of domination as crystallized in the state. The best work in this field shows that patriarchal and gender relations make a difference to the state but it also refuses to prejudge the form and effects of this difference. Thus, "acknowledging that gender inequality exists does not automatically imply that every capitalist state is involved in the reproduction of that inequality in the same ways or to the same extent" (Jenson 1986). An extensive literature on the complex and variable forms of articulation of class, gender, and ethnicity in particular state structures and policy areas has since revealed the limits of gender essentialism. This "intersectional" approach has been taken further by third wave feminists and queer theorists, who emphasize the instability and socially constructed arbitrariness of dominant views of sexual and gender identities and demonstrate the wide variability of masculine as well as feminine identities and interests. Thus there is growing interest in the constitution of competing, inconsistent, and even openly contradictory identities for both males and females, their grounding in discourses about masculinity and/or femininity, their explicit or implicit embedding in different institutions and material practices, and their physico-cultural materialization in human bodies. This has created the theoretical space for a revival of explicit interest in gender and the state, which has made major contributions across a broad range of issues—including how specific constructions of masculinity and femininity, their associated gender identities, interests, roles, and bodily forms, come to be privileged in the state's own discourses, institutions, and material practices. This rules out any analysis of the state as a simple expression of patriarchal domination and questions the very utility of patriarchy as an analytical category.

The best feminist scholarship challenges key assumptions of "malestream" state theories. First, whereas the modern state is commonly said to exercise a legitimate monopoly over the means of coercion, feminists argue that men can get away with violence against women within the confines of the family and, through the reality, threat, or fear of rape, also oppress women in public spaces. Such arguments have been taken further in recent work on masculinity and the state. Second, feminists critique the juridical distinction between "public" and "private." For, not only does this distinction obfuscate class relations by distinguishing the public citizen from the private individual (as Marxists have argued), it also, and more fundamentally, hides the patriarchal ordering of the state and the family. Whilst Marxists tend to equate the public sphere with the state and the private sphere with private property, exchange, and individual rights, feminists tend to equate the former with the state *and* civil society, the latter with the domestic sphere and women's alleged place in the "natural" order of reproduction. Men and women are differentially located in the public and private spheres: indeed, historically, women have been excluded from the public sphere and subordinated to men in the private. Yet men's independence as citizens and workers rests on women's role in caring for them at home. Moreover, even where women win full citizenship rights, their continuing oppression and subjugation in the private sphere hinders their exercise and enjoyment of these rights. A third area of feminist criticism focuses on the links between warfare, masculinity, and the state. In general terms, as Connell (1987) notes, "the state arms men and disarms women."

In short, feminist research reveals basic flaws in much malestream theorizing. Thus an adequate account of the state must include the key feminist insights into the gendered nature of the state's structural selectivity and capacities for action as well as its key role in reproducing specific patterns of gender relations (for attempts to develop such an approach, see Jessop 2004).

7 DISCOURSE ANALYSIS AND STATELESS STATE THEORY

Some recent discourse-analytic work suggests that the state does not exist but is, rather, an illusion—a product of political imaginaries. Thus belief in the existence of the state depends on the prevalence of state discourses. It appears on the political scene because political forces orient their actions towards the "state," acting *as if* it existed. Since there is no common discourse of the state (at most there is a dominant or hegemonic discourse) and different political forces orient their action at different times to different ideas of the state, the state is at best a polyvalent, polycontextual phenomenon which changes shape and appearance with the political forces acting towards it and the circumstances in which they do so.

This apparently heretical idea has been advanced from various theoretical or analytical viewpoints. For example, Abrams (1988) recommended abandoning the idea of the state because the institutional ensemble that comprises government can be studied without the concept of the state; and the "idea of the state" can be studied in turn as the distinctive collective *misrepresentation* of capitalist societies which serves to mask the true nature of political practice. He argues that the "state idea" has a key role in disguising political domination. This in turn requires historical analyses of the "cultural revolution" (or ideological shifts) involved when state systems are transformed. Similarly, Melossi (1990) called for a "stateless theory of the state." This regards the state as a purely juridical concept, an idea that enables people to *do* the state, to furnish themselves and others with a convenient vocabulary of motives for their own (in)actions and to account for the unity of the state in a divided and unequal civil society. Third, there is an increasing interest in specific narrative, rhetorical, or argumentative features of state power. Thus case studies of policy making suggest that state policies do not objectively represent the interests located in or beyond the state or objectively reflect "real" problems in the internal or external environments of the political system. Policies are discursively-mediated, if not wholly discursively-constituted, products of struggles to define and narrate "problems" which can be dealt with in and through state action. The impact of policy-making and implementation is therefore closely tied to their rhetorical and argumentative framing. Indeed, whatever the precise origins of the different components of the modern state (such as the army, bureaucracy, taxation, legal system, legislative assemblies), their organization as a relatively coherent institutional ensemble depends crucially on the emergence of the state idea.

Such discourse-theoretical work clearly differs from state-centered theorizing and Foucauldian analyses. On the one hand, it rejects the reification of the state; and, on the other, it highlights the critical role of narrative and rhetorical practices in creating belief in the existence of the state. This role is variously defined as mystification, self-motivation, pure narrativity, or self-description but, regardless of standpoint, discourses about the state have a key constitutive role in shaping the state as a complex ensemble of political relations linked to society as a whole.

8   The "Strategic-relational Approach"

An innovative approach to the state and state-building has been developed by Jessop and others in an attempt to overcome various forms of one-sidedness in the Marxist and state-centered traditions. His "strategic-relational approach" offers a general account of the dialectic of structure and agency and, in the case of the state, elaborates Poulantzas's claim that the state is a social relation (see above). Jessop argues that the exercise and effectiveness of state power is a contingent product of a changing balance of political forces located within and beyond the state and that this balance is conditioned by the specific institutional structures and procedures of the state apparatus as embedded in the wider political system and environing societal rela-tions. Thus a strategic-relational analysis would examine how a given state apparatus may privilege some actors, some identities, some strategies, some spatial and tem-poral horizons, and some actions over others; and the ways, if any, in which political actors (individual and/or collective) take account of this differential privileging by engaging in "strategic-context" analysis when choosing a course of action. The SRA also introduces a distinctive *evolutionary* perspective into the analysis of the state and state power in order to discover how the generic evolutionary mechanisms of selection, variation, and retention may operate in specific conditions to produce relatively coherent and durable structures and strategies. This implies that opportunities for reorganizing specific structures and for strategic reorientation are themselves subject to structurally-inscribed strategic selectivities and therefore have path-dependent as well as path-shaping aspects. For example, it may be necessary to pursue strategies over several spatial and temporal horizons of action and to mobilize different sets of social forces in different contexts to eliminate or modify specific constraints and opportunities linked to particular state structures. Moreover, as such strategies are pursued, political forces will be more or less well-equipped to learn from their experiences and to adapt their conduct to changing conjunctures.

Over time there is a tendency for reflexively reorganized structures and recursively selected strategies and tactics to co-evolve to produce a relatively stable order, but this may still collapse owing to the inherent structural contradictions, strategic dilemmas, and discursive biases characteristic of complex social formations. Moreover, because structures are strategically selective rather than absolutely constraining, there is always scope for actions to overflow or circumvent structural constraints. Likewise, because subjects are never unitary, never fully aware of the conditions of strategic action, never fully equipped to realize their preferred strategies, and may always meet opposition from actors pursuing other strategies or tactics; failure is an ever-present possibility. This approach is intended as a heuristic and many analyses of the state can be easily reinterpreted in strategic-relational terms even if they do not explicitly adopt these or equivalent terms. But the development of a strategic-relational *research programme* will also require many detailed comparative historical analyses to work out the specific selectivities that operate in types of state, state forms, political regimes, and particular conjunctures (for an illustration, see Jessop 2002).

9   NEW DIRECTIONS OF RESEARCH

Notwithstanding declining interest in the more esoteric and abstract modes of state theorizing, substantive research on states and state power exploded from the 1990s onwards. Among the main themes are: the historical variability of statehood (or stateness); the relative strength or weakness of states; the future of the national state in an era of globalization and regionalization; the changing forms and functions of the state; issues of scale, space, territoriality, and the state; and the rise of governance and its articulation with government.

First, interest in stateness arises from growing disquiet about the abstract nature of much state theory (especially its assumption of a ubiquitous, unified, sovereign state) and increasing interest in the historical variability of actual states. Thus some theorists focus on the state as a conceptual variable and examine the varied presence of the idea of the state. Others examine the state's differential presence as a distinctive political form. Thus Badie and Birnbaum (1983) usefully distinguish between the political center required in any complex social division of labor and the state as one possible institutional locus of this center. For them, the state is defined by its structural differentiation, autonomy, universalism, and institutional solidity. France is the archetypal state in a centralized society; Britain has a political center but no state; Germany has a state but no center; and Switzerland has neither. Such approaches historicize the state idea and stress its great institutional variety. These issues have been studied on all territorial scales from the local to the international with considerable concern for meso-level variation.

Second, there is growing interest in factors that make for state strength. Internally, this refers to a state's capacities to command events and exercise authority over social forces in the wider society; externally, it refers to the state's power in the interstate system. This concern is especially marked in recent theoretical and empirical work on predatory and/or developmental states. The former are essentially parasitic upon their economy and civil society, exercise largely the despotic power of command, and may eventually undermine the economy, society, and the state itself. Developmental states also have infrastructural and network power and deploy it in allegedly market-conforming ways. Unfortunately, the wide variety of interpretations of strength (and weakness) threatens coherent analysis. States have been described as strong because they have a large public sector, authoritarian rule, strong societal support, a weak and gelatinous civil society, cohesive bureaucracies, an interventionist policy, or the power to limit external interference (Lauridsen 1991). In addition, some studies run the risk of tautology insofar as strength is defined purely in terms of outcomes. A possible theoretical solution is to investigate the scope for variability in state capacities by policy area, over time, and in specific conjunctures.

Third, recent work on globalization casts fresh doubt on the future of national territorial states in general and nation states in particular. This issue is also raised by scholars interested in the proliferation of scales on which significant state activities occur, from the local, through the urban and regional, to cross-border and continental cooperation and a range of supranational entities. Nonetheless initial predictions of the imminent demise of the national territorial state and/or the nation state have been proved wrong. This reflects the adaptability of state managers and state apparatuses, the continued importance of national states in securing conditions for economic competitiveness, political legitimacy, social cohesion, and so on, and the role of national states in coordinating the state activities on other scales from the local to the triad to the international and global levels.

Fourth, following a temporary decline in Marxist theoretical work, interest has grown in the specific forms and functions of the capitalist type of state. This can be studied in terms of the state's role in: (a) securing conditions for private profit—the field of economic policy; (b) reproducing wage-labor on a daily, lifetime, and intergenerational basis—the field of social policy broadly considered; (c) managing the scalar division of labor; and (d) compensating for market failure. On this basis Jessop (2002) characterizes the typical state form of postwar advanced capitalism as a Keynesian welfare national state. Its distinctive features were an economic policy oriented to securing the conditions for full employment in a relatively closed economy, generalizing norms of mass consumption through the welfare state, the primacy of the national scale of policy-making, and the primacy of state intervention to compensate for market failure. He also describes the emerging state form in the 1980s and 1990s as a Schumpeterian workfare postnational regime. Its distinctive features are an economic policy oriented to innovation and competitiveness in relatively open economies, the subordination of social policy to economic demands, the relativization of scale with the movement of state powers downwards, upwards, and sideways, and the increased importance of various governance mechanisms in compensating for market failure. Other types of state, including developmental states, have been discussed in the same terms.

Fifth, there is interest in the changing scales of politics. While some theorists are inclined to see the crisis of the national state as displacing the primary scale of political organization and action to the global, regional, or local scale, others suggest that there has been a relativization of scale. For, whereas the national state provided the primary scale of political organization in the Fordist period of postwar European and North American boom, the current after-Fordist period is marked by the dispersion of political and policy issues across different scales of organization, with none of them clearly primary. This in turn poses problems about securing the coherence of action across different scales. This has prompted interest in the novelty of the European Union as a new state form, the re-emergence of empire as an organizing principle, and the prospects for a global state (see, for example, Beck and Grande 2005; Shaw 2000).

Finally, "governance" comprises forms of coordination that rely neither on imperative coordination by government nor on the anarchy of the market. Instead they involve self-organization. Governance operates on different scales of organization (ranging from the expansion of international and supranational regimes through national and regional public–private partnerships to more localized networks of power and decision-making). Although this trend is often taken to imply a diminution in state capacities, it could well enhance its power to secure its interests and, indeed, provide states with a new (or expanded) role in the meta-governance (or overall coordination) of different governance regimes and mechanisms (Zeitlin and Trubek 2003 on Europe; and Slaughter 2004 on the world order).

Interest in governance is sometimes linked to the question of "failed" and "rogue" states. All states fail in certain respects and normal politics is an important mechanism for learning from, and adapting to, failure. In contrast, "failed states" lack the capacity to reinvent or reorient their activities in the face of recurrent state failure in order to maintain "normal political service" in domestic policies. The discourse of "failed states" is often used to stigmatize some regimes as part of interstate as well as domestic politics. Similarly, "rogue states" is used to denigrate states whose actions are considered by hegemonic or dominant states in the interstate system to threaten the prevailing international order. According to some radical critics, however, the USA itself has been the worst rogue state for many years (e.g. Chomsky 2001).

10   AN EMERGING AGENDA?

There is a remarkable theoretical convergence concerning the contingency of the state apparatus and state power. First, most approaches have dethroned the state from its superordinate position in society and analyze it as one institutional order among others. Marxists deny it is the ideal collective capitalist; neostatists no longer treat it as a sovereign legal subject; Foucauldians have deconstructed it; feminists have stopped interpreting it as the patriarch general; and discourse analysts see it as constituted through contingent discursive or communicative practices. In short, the state is seen as an emergent, partial, and unstable system that is interdependent with other systems in a complex social order. This vast expansion in the contingency of the state and its operations requires more concrete, historically specific, institutionally sensitive, and action-oriented studies. This is reflected in substantive research into stateness and the relative strength (and weakness) of particular political regimes.

Second, its structural powers and capacities can only be understood by putting the state into a broader "strategic-relational" context. By virtue of its structural selectivity and specific strategic capacities, its powers are always conditional or relational. Their realization depends on structural ties between the state and its encompassing political system, the strategic links among state managers and other political forces, and the complex web of interdependencies and social networks linking the state and political system to its broader environment.

Finally, it is increasingly recognized that an adequate theory of the state can only be produced as part of a wider theory of society. But this is precisely where we find many of the unresolved problems of state theory. For the state is the site of a paradox. On the one hand, it is just one institutional ensemble among others within a social formation; on the other, it is peculiarly charged with overall responsibility for maintaining the cohesion of the formation of which it is a part. As both part and whole of society, it is continually asked by diverse social forces to resolve society's problems and is equally continually doomed to generate "state failure" since many problems lie well beyond its control and may even be aggravated by attempted intervention. Many differences among state theories are rooted in contrary approaches to various structural and strategic moments of this paradox. Trying to comprehend the overall logic (or, perhaps, "illogic") of this paradox could provide a productive entry point for resolving some of these differences and providing a more comprehensive analysis of the strategic-relational character of the state in a polycentric social formation.

References

ABRAMS, P. 1988. Notes on the difficulty of studying the state. *Journal of Historical Sociology*, 1: 58–89.

ALLEN, J. 1990. Does feminism need a theory of "the state?" In *Playing the State: Australian Feminist Interventions*, ed. S. Watson. London: Verso.

ANDERSON, B. 1991. *Imagined Communities: Reflections on the Origin and Spread of Nationalism*, 2nd edn. London: Verso.

BADIE, B. and BIRNBAUM, P. 1983. *The Sociology of the State*. Chicago: University of Chicago Press.

BARROW, C. W. 1993. *Critical Theories of the State: Marxist, neo-Marxist, post-Marxist*. Madison: University of Wisconsin Press.

BECK, U. and GRANDE, E. 2005. *Cosmopolitan Europe: Paths to Second Modernity*. Cambridge: Polity.

BROWN, W. 1992. Finding the man in the state. *Feminist Studies*, 18: 7–34.

CHOMSKY, N. 2001. *Rogue States: The Rule of Force in World Affairs*. London: Pluto.

CLAESSEN, H. J. M. and SKALNIK, P. (eds.) 1978. *The Early State*. The Hague: Mouton.

CONNELL, R. W. 1987. *Gender and Power: Society, the Person and Sexual Politics*. Stanford, Calif.: Stanford University Press.

EISENSTADT, S. N. 1963. *The Political Systems of Empires: The Rise and Fall of Bureaucratic Societies*. New York: Free Press of Glencoe.

ELIAS, N. 1982. *The Civilizing Process: State Formation and Civilization*. Oxford: Blackwell.

ENGELS, F. 1875/1975. *The Origins of the Family, Private Property, and the State*. Pp. 129–276 in Karl Marx and Friedrich Engels, *Collected Works*, vol. 26. London: Lawrence and Wishart.

EVANS, P. B., RUESCHEMEYER, D., and SKOCPOL, T. (eds.) 1985. *Bringing the State Back In*. Cambridge: Cambridge University Press.

Foucault, M. 1980a. *The History of Sexuality*, vol. 1. Harmondsworth: Penguin.

—— 1980b. *Power/Knowledge*. Brighton: Harvester

Gordon, L. 1990. The welfare state: towards a socialist-feminist perspective. *Socialist Register 1990*. New York: Monthly Review Press.

Gramsci, A. 1971. *Selections from the Prison Notebooks*. London: Lawrence and Wishart.

Hintze, O. 1975. *The Historical Essays of Otto Hintze*. New York: Oxford University Press.

Jenson, J. 1986. Gender and reproduction: or, babies and state. *Studies in Political Economy*, 20: 9–46.

Jessop, B. 2001. Bringing the state back in (yet again). *International Review of Sociology*, 11: 149–73.

—— 2002. *The Future of the Capitalist State*. Cambridge: Polity.

—— 2004. The gendered selectivity of the state. *Journal of Critical Realism*, 2: 207–37.

Knutilla, M. and Kubik, W. 2001. *State Theories: Classical, Global and Feminist Perspectives*. London: Zed.

Lauridsen, L. S. 1991. The debate on the developmental state. In *Development Theory and the Role of the State in Third World Countries*, ed. J. Martinussen. Roskilde: Roskilde University Centre.

MacKinnon, C. 1989. *Towards a Feminist Theory of the State*. Cambridge, Mass.: Harvard University Press.

Mann, M. 1986. *The Sources of Social Power*, vol. 1. Cambridge: Cambridge University Press.

Melossi, D. 1990. *The State and Social Control*. Cambridge: Polity.

Miliband, R. 1969. *The State in Capitalist Society*. London: Weidenfeld and Nicolson.

Porter, B. 1994. *War and the Rise of the State*. New York: Free Press.

Poulantzas, N. 1973. *Political Power and Social Classes*. London: New Left Books.

—— 1978. *State, Power, Socialism*. London: Verso.

Rokkan, S. 1999. *State Formation, Nation-Building and Mass Politics in Europe: The Theory of Stein Rokkan*. Oxford: Oxford University Press.

Shaw, M. 2000. *Theory of the Global State*. Cambridge: Cambridge University Press.

Slaughter, A.-M. 2004. *A New World Order*. Princeton, NJ: Princeton University Press.

Weber, M. 1948. Politics as a vocation. In *Essays from Max Weber*. London: Routledge and Kegan Paul.

Zeitlin, J. and Trubek, D. M. (eds.) 2003. *Governing Work and Welfare in a New Economy*. Oxford: Oxford University Press.

CHAPTER 8

DEVELOPMENT OF CIVIL SOCIETY

JOSE HARRIS

No concept in political theory and political science has had, and continues to have, a more ambiguous and elusive character than that of civil society. From the last days of the Roman republic down to the present day, both the term "civil society" and the practical arrangements that it signifies have been understood by historians, theorists, and contemporary actors in a multiplicity of ways. Some of these understandings, while differing in emphasis and detail, have nevertheless recognizably stemmed from a shared intellectual tradition. Others have been deeply and diametrically opposed to each other, to such an extent that the term sometimes seems to refer to institutions, values, analytical categories, and visions of civilization, that are not just very different but mutually exclusive. Thus, one central tradition of writing about civil society has portrayed it as virtually coterminous with government, law-enforcement, and the cluster of institutions that comprise "the state" (Model 1). A very different tradition has identified civil society with private property rights, commercial capitalism, and the various legal, institutional, and cultural support-systems that these entail (Model 2). Yet another line of thought has seen civil society as quintessentially composed of voluntaristic, non-profit-making, civic and mutual-help movements, coexisting with but nevertheless quite distinct in ethos and function from the spheres of both states and markets (Model 3). And in very recent discourse "civil society" has come to be increasingly identified with the enunciation of universal standards of democracy, fair procedures, the rule of law, and respect for human rights (preferably to be imposed by cultural permeation and persuasion, but nevertheless backed up by economic sanctions, international courts, and the threat or actuality of physical force) (Model 4).

Such extreme diversity and uncertainty in the meaning of the term might be thought to render "civil society" of little significance as a way of thinking about how political institutions actually work. Yet this has been very far from being the case. Since the 1980s this ancient but long-neglected concept has been rediscovered and redeployed by political analysts in many parts of the globe. In eastern and western Europe, in north and south America, and in Africa and Asia, promotion of the principles of "civil society" has been widely urged as a strategic remedy for perceived defects in the governance, political cultures, and community structures of many contemporary states. Unusually, such strategies have won support right across the political spectrum, in both national and international settings. From neocommunists through to free-market liberals, from radical activists through to civic conservatives, and from both proponents and critics of "globalization," there has come widespread endorsement of the goals and values deemed to be associated with "civil society."

This apparent consensus has, nevertheless, largely glossed over the very wide spectrum of diversity and uncertainty that continues to surround the precise meaning and wider resonance of the term. Indeed, some commentators who currently lay claim to the mantle of "civil society" seem quite oblivious of the fact that, in both the past and the present, the term has been applied to institutions and strategies often quite different from those which they themselves espouse. The present article will attempt to trace the historic roots and evolution of the concept of "civil society," and will then look at the variety of ways in which it has been understood in its more recent revival. It will conclude, not by adjudicating on which account of civil society is the "correct" one, but by attempting to explain why this resurgence has occurred, and by identifying what (if any) are the underlying perspectives that theorists and protagonists of the concept have held in common, across many different epochs, contexts, and cultures.

"Civil society" (*civitas* or *societas civilis*) first surfaced in the vocabulary of European politics during the dying years of republican Rome, and was subsequently to become a standard point of reference in the writings of the classic Roman jurists. Nevertheless, it is important to recall that the Latin word *societas* (not just in Rome, but through many subsequent centuries of post-Roman European history) did not have the comprehensive macrosociological meaning that it was to acquire in the nineteenth and twentieth centuries. A *societas* in Roman law was merely any contract-based "partnership" set up for a particular purpose. It was an arrangement that might range in size and function from a marriage partnership between husband and wife, through to a large-scale public or private enterprise association. The largest and most powerful "society" in Rome or any other political culture was typically that which existed to manage public affairs and to make and enforce the laws; that is, the *civitas, societas civilis,* or what later generations would come to refer to as "the state." Moreover, though state power in Rome was often notoriously run as the private fief of individual dynasties, a quite different conception was hinted at by the very adjective *civilis. Societas civilis* indicated a neutral arena of public life whose membership was in principle determined not by tribe or family, but by common citizenship or status before the law (even though, in day-to-day Roman practice, family ties and interests often heavily influenced civic ones). It was in this sense that the term had been used by Cicero and other defenders of "republican" themes; namely, to mean a system of government that routinely observed rules and procedures applying equally to all citizens, rather than being dependent on the arbitrary whims of a Pompey or a Caesar. This was to be the standard usage of the term throughout the Roman imperial era; but over the course of several centuries the notion of a *societas civilis* also came to embrace non-citizens, as continuous expansion of international trade brought large numbers of people throughout the Mediterranean world into the universalizing ambit of Roman civil law. Thus while Roman *political* thought powerfully shaped a long-lasting conception of civil society as a law-abiding *state* (Model 1), Roman *jurisprudence* and *civil law* also sowed the seeds of the what, many centuries later in European history, would become an alternative conception of civil society, as the characteristic sphere of *private property, business, and commerce* (Model 2) (Ehrenberg 1999, 19–27; Justinian 1985).

Both visions of civil society were largely eclipsed (together with any explicit reference to the term) by the quite different notions of public affairs and political authority that prevailed in Europe following the disintegration of Roman rule. Throughout western Europe exclusive and self-governing ecclesiastical, military, civic, and vocational corporations (of a kind particularly abhorrent to Roman civil law) flourished and came to dominate public, economic, and social life; while for many centuries the location and character of ultimate civil power was to be continually contested between warlords, emperors, feudal kingship, and the Catholic church. But it was no coincidence that, when in the fourteenth century some theorists began to search for a new notion of political authority that might transcend or bypass these conflicts, they turned to the earlier model of "civil society" as a neutral sphere of political association, based on free contract and consent between citizens, rather than on religious identity, ties of feudal fealty, or mere physical force. At this stage there was no suggestion that organized religion should withdraw from the public sphere, but simply that there should be a functional separation between "religious society" and "civil society," with the former enjoying political, legal, and physical protection in return for giving moral, cultural, and spiritual support to the latter (Black 1984; Ehrenberg 1999, 45–57; Figgis 1907, 31–54).

The religious and civil wars that periodically ravaged Europe in the sixteenth and seventeenth centuries might seem to suggest that, whatever may have been the visions of political theorists, the notion of "civil society" as a neutral arena of public space that transcended lesser or rival identities remained largely a dead letter. Nevertheless, the seventeenth century was to see major developments in the definition and crystalization of "civil society" as an abstract political, legal, and normative idea (and, much more sketchily, as a guide to political practice). Both the establishment of state churches headed by secular rulers, and the principle of "toleration" (permitting plurality of religious beliefs) were portrayed by some contemporaries as promoting and embodying important principles of "civil society" (Figgis 1916, 94–115). The gradual revival of interest in Roman civil law, and its insemination into contemporary political thought greatly enhanced the notion of civil authority as an impersonal sphere regulated by law, rather than—or at least in addition to—a hierarchy of interpersonal allegiances climaxing in the person of a royal ruler. And in England the writings of the contractarian school— Richard Hooker, Thomas Hobbes, and John Locke—all powerfully reinforced the notion of "civil society" as identical with settled political authority and effective law-enforcement (Hooker 1977, 95–149; Hobbes 1952, 1983; Locke 1965). For Thomas Hobbes it was "*civil* society" (i.e. a civil government able to enforce the law) that made possible the very existence of mere "society" (the latter implying, not the all-encompassing category envisaged in present-day discourse, but "sociability" or the coming together of citizens for a multiplicity of purposes in small groups) (Hobbes 1952, 1983; Locke 1965, 367–8). John Locke, unlike Hobbes, thought that "the People" (i.e. an aggregate of persons interacting outside politics) might survive even if "Civil Society" (i.e. the body politic) were to break down. But even Locke thought that such collective social survival could only be short-lived unless a new *civil* society, that is legislative and governing institutions and agencies of law enforcement, were to be rapidly re-formed (Locke 1965, 476–7). In the works of all these writers, the terms "civil society" and "political society" were not contrasted but used interchangeably. The writings of the contractarians also emphasized that an effective "civil society" did not have to be a specifically Christian one: the governments of Turkey and China, for example, were perfectly capable of constituting "civil societies," provided that they maintained the peace, acted justly, and obeyed natural laws. By contrast, the regime of Louis XIV in France (widely deemed the most "civilized" nation in Europe) was classed by English authors as "not a civil society," because its citizens could be arbitrarily imprisoned without trial and because earlier concessions to religious pluralism had been rescinded under the revocation of the Edict of Nantes (Locke 1965, 454, 459, 476–7).

This model of "civil society"—not as voluntary self-help, or community action, or a "non-governmental" public sphere, but as a cluster of institutions synonymous with the functioning of a law-making, law-enforcing, and law-abiding state—was to be a commonplace of much British, and to a lesser extent European, political thought down to the period of the late nineteenth and earlier twentieth century. Despite many recent misconceptions to the contrary, this view of civil society was shared by major theorists of the British liberal tradition, such as Locke, Adam Smith, Adam Ferguson, J. S. Mill, Lord Acton, and T. H. Green; and it was likewise what was meant by the notion of a "societé civile," that stemmed from Rousseau and was developed in France during the French Revolution and under the regime of Napoleon (Harris 2003, 23–9). Within this common discourse there were many differences of emphasis and detail. British writers mostly viewed civil society as a political framework that permitted and encouraged widespread associational diversity and autonomy, whereas French civil society theorists were much more inclined to emphasize equality and uniformity beneath the overarching umbrella of central government and the Napoleonic Code (Acton 1862, 2–25). Both British and French traditions, however, continued to identify civil society with the sphere of government and the state; while social life and voluntary association were nearly always viewed as the beneficent *outcome* of civil society, rather than as its characteristic embodiment.

Nevertheless, from the mid-eighteenth century onwards, there were spasmodic signs of various substantive and semantic shifts in this long-standing politico-legal understanding of the term. The most important of these changes took place in Germany, where some authorities began to portray "civil society" as a much grander idea, others as something much more flawed and limited, than in its classical and "early modern" formulations. A shift in the former direction was apparent in the writings of Immanuel Kant, who hinted at a conception of "civil society" as a cluster of common civic, legal, ethical, and visionary norms that potentially embraced not just the denizens of any particular kingdom or polity but the whole human race (Reiss 1970, 41–53) (Model 4). And a move in the opposite direction took the form of an increasing identification of civil society (*bürgerlich Gesellschaft*) not with kingly or princely "government" but with the quasi-public, quasi-private activities of production, commerce, banking, and finance: a shift that may have reflected the resurgence of interest within post-Napoleonic Germany in the economic doctrines of Roman civil law. It was in this latter context that an important new conception of "civil society" was to be developed by Hegel and Marx; a conception that referred—not to the disinterested, impartial, *public* sphere conjured up by Cicero and the English contract theorists—but to the self-interested, competitive, *private* sphere of the bourgeois commercial economy. In the writings of Karl Marx the very term "*bürger*" or "*bourgeois*" lost its older, "public" connotation of the disinterested citizen, and was transferred instead to the socioeconomic category of the "private" entrepreneur (Hegel 1991, 220–74; Marx 1975) (Model 2).

Similar changes were perceptible in other aspects of the language of civil society. In France the phrase *societé civile* came to be applied in some circles, not to public and legal institutions, but to what in English was often referred to as "polite society" (meaning the world of salons, culture, fashion, and good manners) (Harris 2003, 21–2). Likewise, in English, French, and German narratives, the adjectives "political" and "civil" (previously identical) began slowly to drift apart. The former came increasingly to mean "party-political" or "partisan," while the latter was used to refer (among other things) to those areas of public life that were deemed to be "outside" or "above" politics. These shifts of meaning took place in a variety of spheres: in the emergence in Britain and elsewhere of the ideal of a "civil service" that was explicitly apolitical; in the drafting of national "civil codes" of law; and in Alexis de Tocqueville's (1966) *Democracy in America*, where "political society" (meaning the political struggle to control government) was categorically contrasted with "civil association" (meaning people coming together in voluntary groups). De Tocqueville's account signaled the emergence of what was eventually to become one of the major building blocks of civil-society discourse in the later twentieth century. This was the identification of civil society as the distinctive sphere of altruism, communalism, and voluntary cooperation; themes that were often closely linked to notions of "disinterested public service," but were nevertheless quite distinct from the formal structures of government and the state (Tocqueville 1966, 232–40, 671–6) (Model 3).

Whether because of this gradual blurring of the original "statist" meaning of the term, or for some other reason, "civil society" gradually faded from mainstream writings on the theory and practice of politics during the later decades of the nineteenth century. The densely self-governing, mutualist, and voluntarist culture of late-Victorian Britain has often been identified by recent commentators as a paradigmatic example of a flourishing "civil society," but it was never thus described by the Victorians themselves (and was not what they would have understood by the term). In Germany the revisionist socialist leader Edouard Bernstein protested strongly against the Marxist conflation of "*bürgerlich Gesellschaft*" with mere "bourgeois" economic self-interest, but Bernstein's attempt to retrieve a more "public" conception of civil society (*Zivillgesellschaft*) met at the time with very limited success (Tudor and Tudor 1988). Similarly, in liberal and conservative thought, the language of "the state" came increasingly to dominate and crowd out much of the conceptual space previously occupied by traditional legalistic understandings of civil society. Even the great spate of early twentieth-century Anglo-American writings on "civics" and "good citizenship" rarely if ever linked these ideas to a civil society framework. And at the same time there was, throughout Europe and North America, an ever-growing interest in the phenom-enon of what had become known simply as "society." This latter word appeared very similar to, but in fact conveyed a range of meanings very different from, the older Latin construction of *societas*. Though always eluding precise definition, the idea of "society" in this newer sense came increasingly to resemble something like "the sum total of all human affairs." This was a mysterious entity, seemingly propelled by its own impersonal societal laws, that appeared quite distinct both from the private motivations of individuals and from the rationalist and purposive conception of politics that traditional "state-centric" notions of civil society had entailed (Durkheim 1938, lvi–viii; Wallas 1914, 3–29, 305–40). Those few theorists who continued to talk of "civil society" in the early twentieth century (mainly academic "pluralists," rooted in classical and legalistic ways of thought, such as Figgis, Maitland, Laski, and Duguit) did so in a low-key, limited, and largely negative way. They emphasized that "civil society" was merely one *societas* among many, and that its special but circumscribed function of maintaining law and order should not be allowed to obtrude upon the equally important functions of other autonomous "societies," such as churches, trade unions, universities, professional associations, and similar corporate entities. Unsurprisingly, this subtle but arcane style of argument was to have a diminishing impact in the era of mass politics, revolutionary violence, and global war.

What *is* surprising, however, is that the tradition of debate about civil society played such a minimal, almost non-existent, role in European democratic and liberal responses to the rise of totalitarianism. In political writings of the interwar era occasional reference was made to the idea of a *societas civilis* as a possible antidote to fascism. The French Catholic philosopher, Jacques Maritain, for example, drew upon the model of late medieval corporatist theorists, including Thomas Aquinas, who had portrayed civil society as a mutually-civilizing partnership between the Church and the secular state (Maritain 1938, 157–76). But such references were marginal to mainstream political debate of the period, where "civil society" more typically appeared (if invoked at all) not as an impartial public sphere, but as the institutional epitome of competitive bourgeois selfishness. Indeed for several decades the economic model of civil society appears to have largely obliterated all trace of the older "civic" model from collective political memory. From the 1920s through to the 1960s, English language textbooks on social and political science either ignored "civil society" completely, or simply assumed that its definitive meaning was that which had been employed by Hegel and Marx (Laski 1938; MacIver and Page 1950).

How and why did the notion of "civil society" recover from its mid-twentieth century eclipse? The 1960s explosion of non-Soviet versions of Marxism helped to revive familiarity with the concept, and in particular with the "cultural" portrayal of civil society as a buttress of capitalist "hegemony" advanced by Antonio Gramsci (1957). A more complex thesis was suggested by Jürgen Habermas, who welded together the classical and Marxian models of civil society by portraying each as the corollary of the other, in a world in which premodern demarcations between "public" and "private," "political" and "economic," "objectivity" and "subjectivity" no longer applied. Habermas's interpretation was to be of considerable importance in the long-term reworking of ideas about civil society (and about political thought more generally) but it was of limited immediate influence, not least because it was not to be translated into English until 1980 (Habermas 1962). More accessible was the work of Ralf Dahrendorf, who took over the Marxian and Gramscian accounts of civil society and used them *against* the goals of revolutionary socialism. In Dahrendorf's account it was precisely the growth and flourishing of non-state bourgeois economic and cultural institutions in many parts of Europe (most notably in Britain) that over the previous two centuries had made liberty, equality, prosperity, and social peace widely attainable; and it was precisely the *absence* or *under-development* of such institutions (most notably in Germany) that had led to factional violence, state tyranny, and fascist oppression (Dahrendorf 1968, 128–9, 200–20).

References to civil society gathered momentum in academic writing during the 1970s and early 1980s, most notably in the German *Sonderweg* controversy among historians, and in increasing criticism by political and social scientists of the "big government" solutions to policy problems that had been pursued throughout Europe after 1945. Not until the late 1980s, however, did "civil society" burst into the arena of international and mass media debate, as dissidents in eastern Europe, particularly Poland and Czechoslovakia, began to press for the development of autonomous public, legal, and social institutions that could act as counterweights to the overweening powers of totalitarian states (Keane 1988, 261–398). The collapse of Communism opened the way in eastern European countries to attempts to revive "civil society" in several of the senses identified above: in the establishment of "impartial" legal and governing institutions (including oppositional ones), in the removal of prohibitions and limitations on private voluntary associations (including churches and other religious bodies), and in the re-emergence of private capitalism (the latter attended by many of the evils deplored by Marx, no less than the blessings urged by economic liberals).

Although it began as a reaction against Communism, however, this explosion of interest in civil society soon began unexpectedly to manifest itself in many other contexts and channels. Indeed, just as many east European politicians were trying to address the problems of post-Communism by emulating the "civil society" institutions of Western countries, so in Britain, western Europe, the USA, and elsewhere, political theorists and civic activists began to draw on the discourse of "civil society" to explain and redress certain perceived deficiencies in their own "liberal" and "democratic" regimes. The decay of urban and inner-city communities; over-extended and inefficient welfare states; problems of social, racial, religious, and sexual exclusion; rising levels of violent crime and delinquency; and low levels of electoral turnout and involvement in public life—all came to be diagnosed in terms of a decline or shortfall in civil society, and of the need for its urgent restoration and extension. Thus in Britain over the past decade, civil society has been invoked by politicians of all major political parties, as a remedy for such diverse ills as family breakdown, welfare fraud, environmental pollution, sectarian violence in Northern Ireland, and tribal conflict in Iraq and Afghanistan (Willetts 1994; Hague 1998; Patten 2000; Blunkett 2001; Brown 2001). In Europe, and particularly in Germany, civil society discourse has more closely followed the route suggested by Habermas, of pressing for closer democratic monitoring of public institutions and sharper legal definition of rights. In North America the term has been less prominent in the pronouncements of politicians, but among academics and intellectuals it has been embraced by Kantian liberals, communitarian conservatives, and former Marxists (the latter now reinterpreting civil society as a prerequisite of, rather than a barrier to, goals of distributive justice and structural change) (Walzer 1995; Etzioni 1995; Cohen and Arato 1992). More-over, these trends have by no means been confined to the developed world. In many Third World contexts "civil society" has been identified with the work of numerous "non-governmental organizations," often partly manned by American and European expatriates, who aim to create new structures and services that supple-ment or bypass the activities of corrupt or under-resourced national governments. And the work of "NGOs" in turn has given rise to many new non-European formulations of "civil society," advanced by African, Asian, and Latin American thinkers, who have identified many of its principles and traditions (such as altruism, mediation, civility, and respect for law) as part of their own indigenous moral and historic structures (Kaviraj and Khilnani 2001; Rowse 2003, 303–10). Most ambitious of all have been the aspirations of the movement for "Global Civil Society," which since the late 1990s has campaigned on many fronts—through university research groups, activist pressure groups, NGOs, and international institutions—for the development of a common agenda for "civil society" in all conceivable cross-national settings, including conflict resolution and avoidance of wars. This agenda envisages a future when organizations speaking on behalf of voluntary, non-profit-making, and participatory movements will constitute a powerful "third sector," on a par with state governments and the international economy, in every part of the world (Barber 2001–2a,b; Keane 2003; Kaldor in Kaldor, Anheier and Glasius 2003).

That "civil society" has radically shifted its meaning many times over the course of 2,000 years in different cultures and contexts is perhaps unsurprising. What is more surprising is that this idea, dreamt up by a small handful of lawyers and intellectuals in the dying days of republican Rome, still burns and crackles with a very long fuse in the early twenty-first century. Nevertheless, the massive resur-gence of "civil society" in recent years makes it a matter of some importance to clarify what those who constantly invoke it understand by the term, both as a reformist strategy and as a model of future civilization. When different versions of civil society clash, or hurtle past each other like ships in a fog, how is the active citizen or detached political observer to know what is really on offer?

The answer to this question is no simple matter. Since the 1980s the outline of civil society envisaged by its protagonists has taken many forms, ranging over all four major models suggested above, as well as numerous lesser ones. Thus, in some quarters civil society has been seen as requiring *much more extensive* state legisla-tion, agencies of law enforcement, and monitoring of public services to ensure greater equality, "social inclusion," and mediation of conflict. But in other quarters it has been seen as pointing in quite the opposite direction, towards a revival of more microscopic, self-helping, neighborhood-based arrangements, in place of the infantilizing and regulatory support mechanisms of central government (Green 2000). For some commentators the widespread decline within many "advanced" cultures of citizen involvement in clubs, campaign groups, neighborhood schemes, and voluntary societies is the prime index of the breakdown of civil society (i.e. the "bowling-alone syndrome" diagnosed by Putnam 2000). But for others the very opposite is true: The autonomous, free-standing, ethical-choice-making individual—unencumbered by partisan community ties, and attached only to the remote even-handedness of the law—is precisely what the enterprise of twenty-first century civil society is all about (Seligman 1995, 200–19; Harris 2003, 7–9). Likewise, in the eyes of some authorities, "civil society" necessarily entails a much more comprehensive and "universalist" national culture, whereas to others it means a much more diverse and pluralistic one. (The contrast here is nicely captured in the philosophic differences between French and British approaches to questions of ethnic and religious integration.) Religion itself has a similarly ambivalent standing in many current debates, some participants portraying civil society as by definition "secular" (with religion confined to an entirely "private" sphere); whilst others stress the close correlation between religious observance of all kinds (Christian, Jewish, and Islamic) and high levels of public participation in the voluntarist, philanthropic, "not-for-profit" sectors (Ireland, Israel, Belgium, and the Netherlands being outstanding examples of this correlation) (Barber 2002b, 8). Similarly, within the Global Civil Society movement, there have been many grades of opinion about ways in which "civil society" meshes with different historic cultures. Are such attributes, for example, as democracy, gender equality, liberal marriage laws, and the leadership role of an educated middle class, absolute prerequisites, or are they matters of cultural autonomy that should be treated as variable and locally negotiable (Barber 2002b, 7–11)? The relation of "global civil society" to globalization itself—whether of an economic, cultural, linguistic, or merely "Internet" kind—remains highly contentious, with many "civil society" enthusiasts hating one kind of global interaction while relishing others. And, echoing the historic origins of the term, there have been some like Habermas and Skocpol who have strongly questioned the severing of civil society from its links with the traditional concept of a well-ordered state. This questioning seems particularly pertinent, in view of a survey of twenty-seven countries in 2001 which found that more than 42 per cent of the income of NGOs and other "non-profit-making" bodies was in fact coming from government and tax-financed sources (Habermas 1962; Skocpol 1996, 19–25; Barber 2002b, 8, 23).

Civil society therefore remains a curiously obtuse, malleable, and much contested idea, difficult to define categorically by reference to either *what it is* or *what it is not*. It is widely assumed that (whatever else may be the case) it is not compatible with fascism, feudalism, patriarchalism, totalitarianism, communal violence, or rule by a local mafia. But each of the four models mentioned above has very often incorporated at least one of these supposedly antithetical social arrangements. As one participant in a recent forum put it: "Where I come from, the Ku Klux Klan is part of civil society. It's non-governmental, non-profit, membership-based, internally democratic ... and members work passionately on a voluntary basis to advance the mission of the organization." It is equally difficult to locate it with precision on any of the conceptual axes that stretch from a command economy through to laissez-faire capitalism, from cultural universalism to cultural pluralism, from "human rights" to basic resources through to the claims of private property, or from an "interventionist" through to a "nightwatchman" model of the state. Because of the gradual build-up of diverse meanings over many centuries, it is also impossible to treat civil society simply as a Weberian "ideal type," designed to advance knowledge through sharply-defined theoretical insights, rather than with reference to exact historical facts. Current fashionable uses of the term should perhaps therefore be seen as a cluster of loosely overlapping "elective affinities," of use in conveying a wide range of moral, cultural, and social aspirations, rather than as a set of precise analytical concepts in political and social science.

REFERENCES

ACTON, LORD (J. E. E. DAHLBERG-ACTON) 1862. Nationality. *Home and Foreign Review,* 1: 2–25.

BARBER, B. et al. 2002. Conference proceedings on: (*a*) The theory and practice of civic globalism; (*b*) Measuring global civic trends. Washington, DC: Democracy Collaborative. Available at: http://www.democracycollaborative.org/programs/global.

BLACK, A. 1984. *Guilds and Civil Society in European Political Thought from the Twelfth Century to the Present.* London: Methuen.

BLUNKETT, D. 2001. *Politics and Progress: Renewing Democracy and Civil Society.* London: Politico's.

BOBBIO, N. 1988. Gramsci and the concept of civil society. Pp. 73–99 in *Civil Society and the State,* ed. J. Keane. London: Verso.

BROWN, J. G. 2001. *Civic Society in Modern Britain,* ed. J. Wilson. Amersham: Smith Institute.

CICERO, M. T. 1999. *On the Commonwealth and On the Laws.* Cambridge: Cambridge University Press (originally composed c.54–51 BC).

COHEN, J. J. and ARATO, A. 1992. *Civil Society and Political Theory.* Cambridge, Mass.: MIT Press.

DAHRENDORF, R. 1968. *Society and Democracy in Germany,* English trans. London: Weidenfeld and Nicolson (German edn. Munich: 1965).

DURKHEIM, E. 1938. *The Rules of Sociological Method.* London: Macmillan (orig. pub. 1895).

EHRENBERG, J. 1999. *Civil Society: The Critical History of an Idea.* New York: New York University Press.

ETZIONI, A. 1995. *The Spirit of Community*. New York: HarperCollins.

FIGGIS, J. N. 1907. *Studies of Political Thought from Gerson to Grotius*. Cambridge: Cambridge University Press, 2nd edn 1916.

GELLNER, E. 1994. *Conditions of Liberty: Civil Society and its Rivals*. London: Hamish Hamilton.

GRAMSCI, A. 1957. *The Modern Prince, and Other Writings*. New York: International, 2nd edn. 1967.

GREEN, D. G. 2000. *The Guiding Philosophy and Research Agenda of the Institute for the Study of Civil Society*. London: Institute for the Study of Civil Society.

HABERMAS, J. 1962. *The Structural Transformation of the Public Sphere*, trans. T. Burger and F. Lawrence. Cambridge: Polity (English edn. 1980).

HAGUE, W. 1998. Speaking with conviction. Conservative Party Forum.

HALL, J. A. 1995. *Civil Society: Theory, History, Comparison*. Cambridge. Polity Press.

—— and TRENTMANN, F. 2005. *Civil Society: A Reader in History, Theory and Global Politics*. Basingstoke: Palgrave Macmillan.

HARRIS, J. (ed.) 2003. *Civil Society in British History*. Oxford: Oxford University Press.

HEGEL, G. 1991. *Elements of the Philosophy of Right*, ed. A. W. Wood. Cambridge: Cambridge University Press.

HOBBES, T. 1952. *Leviathan*, ed. M. Oakeshott. Oxford: Blackwell (orig. pub. 1651).

—— 1983. *De Cive; or the Philosophicall Rudiments concerning Government and Society*, ed. H. Warrender. Oxford: Oxford University Press (orig. pub. 1642).

HOOKER, R. 1977. *Of the Laws of Ecclesiastical Polity, Book I*, ed. W. Speed Hill. Cambridge, Mass.: Belknap Press (orig. pub. 1593).

JUSTINIAN 1985. *The Digest of Justinian*, vols. I–IV, ed. A. Watson. Philadelphia: University of Pennsylvania Press.

KALDOR, M., ANHEIER, H., GLASIUS, M. (eds.) 2003. *Global Civil Society*. Oxford: Oxford University Press.

KAVIRAJ, S. and KHILNANI, S. (eds.) 2001. *Civil Society: History and Possibilities*. Cambridge. Cambridge University Press.

KEANE, J. (ed.) 1988. *Civil Society and the State: New European Perspectives*. London: Verso.

—— 1998. *Civil Society: Old Images, New Visions*. Cambridge: Polity.

—— 2003. *Global Civil Society?* Cambridge: Cambridge University Press.

LASKI, H. J. 1938. *A Grammar of Politics, With a New Chapter*. New Haven, Conn.: Yale University Press.

LOCKE, J. 1965. *Two Treatises of Government*, ed. P. Laslett. Cambridge: Cambridge University Press.

MACIVER, R. M. and PAGE, C. H. 1950. *Society: An Introductory Analysis*. London: Macmillan.

MARITAIN, J. 1938. *True Humanism*, trans. M. Adamson. London: Bles (orig. pub. 1936).

MARX, K. 1975. *Early Writings*, ed. L. Colletti. Harmondsworth: Penguin.

NICHOLLS, D. 1974. *Three Varieties of Pluralism*. London Macmillan.

PATTEN, C. 2000. *Respect for the Earth: Sustainable Development*. London: Profile.

PUTNAM, R. D. 2000. *Bowling Alone: the Collapse and Revival of American Community*. New York: Simon and Schuster.

REISS, H. 1970. *Kant's Political Writings*. Cambridge: Cambridge University Press.

ROWSE, T. 2003. Britons, settlers, and aborigines. Pp. 293–310 in *Civil Society in British History*, ed. J. Harris. Oxford: Oxford University Press.

SELIGMAN, A. 1995. Animadversions upon civil society and civic virtue in the last decade of the twentieth century. Pp. 200–23 in *Civil Society: Theory, History, Comparison*, ed. J. A. Hall. Cambridge: Polity Press.

SKOCPOL, T. 1996. Unravelling from above. *American Prospect*, 25: 20–5. Reprinted pp. 234–7 in *Civil Society: A Reader in History, Theory, and Global Politics*, ed. J. A. Hall and F. Trentman. Basingstoke: Palgrave Macmillan, 2005.

DE TOCQUEVILLE, A. 1966. *Democracy in America*, ed. J. P. Mayer and M. Lerner. New York: Harper and Row.

TUDOR, H. and TUDOR, J. M. 1988. *Marxism and Social Democracy: The Revisionist Debate 1896–1898*. Cambridge: Cambridge University Press.

WALLAS, G. 1914. *The Great Society*. London: Macmillan.

WALZER, M. (ed.) 1995. *Towards a Global Civil Society*. Oxford: Bergahn.

WILLETTS, D. 1994. *Civic Conservatism*. London: Social Market Foundation.

CHAPTER 9

....

ECONOMIC
INSTITUTIONS

....

MICHAEL MORAN

1 ECONOMIC INSTITUTIONS AND POLITICAL INSTITUTIONS

....

Why include a chapter on economic institutions in a handbook of *political* institutions? For brevity we can give three answers; all are illuminating about the way the political and the economic are interconnected.

The first is that the very recognition of an "economic institution" is a political act. Indeed a constructed distinction between "market" and "state" is a basic operating principle of the ideology of market capitalism: "In a *perfectly* competitive market, as idealized by neoclassical economists, there is no organization among or between buyers and sellers" (Lazonick 1991, 60). But whatever the policy arguments for operational separation, analytically the divide makes little sense: the "economy" is embedded in civil society, and the state is likewise embedded in that wider civil sphere.

This fact of "construction" reflects the second reason for the political scientist's interest in economic institutions: How well or badly "economic" institutions perform is in part a function of how they are governed. In turn, how they are governed, we shall see, is in large part shaped by state bodies and by the wider political sphere.

* I am grateful to the editors and to R. E. Goodin for comments on earlier drafts.

The interactions between "economic" and "political" institutions are complex not only because the political shapes the fate of the economic, but also because economic institutions are critical to the fate of political institutions—the third important ground for this chapter. In advanced capitalist democracies the shaping influence is at its most obvious in the link between electoral success and perceived economic performance. But this is only the most immediately visible—and possibly transient—connection. There are bigger stakes than simply the fortunes of particular governments. The fates of whole state constellations may turn on the nexus between the economic and the political.

Writing about the design of institutions, Goodin argues that different preoccupations drive inquiry in different disciplines: for instance, choice in economics, and power in politics (1996: 11, 16). The problem of choice is a driver in this chapter, but it is not the classic problem of choice in the face of scarcity: It is, rather, choice (or its absence) in the face of the constraints of history and culture. What agents can—and cannot—do with economic institutions is thus a recurrent theme of the following pages.

2   ECONOMIC INSTITUTIONS AND INSTITUTIONALISM

"In the beginning, so to speak, there were markets," says Williamson (1981, 1547). But this seems either a drastically foreshortened historical vision, or a highly normative social model. "In the beginning" there were, variously, bandit groups (Olson 2000) or social arrangements where exchange took the symbolic form of the gift (Mauss 1970). The ideologies of market liberalism constructed a line of division between different mechanisms of social allocation: in particular, between "the market" and the thing called "the state." This in turn rhetorically separated out the world of institutions from that of the market, which was "naturalized" as a supposedly automatic sphere of exchange governed by immutable laws.

This discursive separation was not only strange; it was a vulgarization of the great tradition of political economy. The founding father of the theory of the market's "invisible hand" also established a powerful tradition of analysis in classical political economy where the institutional and cultural settings of exchange were crucial to economic outcomes (Smith 1790/1976). An "old institutionalism" in economics overlapped with studies in the sociology of economic life to explore the importance of the legal framework of economic life, and the importance of the cultures of economic organizations (see Rutherford 1996). Indeed, in an obvious historical sense, states created markets, for the fundamentals of market exchange were only possible in a juridical framework of commercial law created by states. Polanyi puts it pithily: "Regulation and markets, in effect, grew up together" (1944–57, 68).

The "new institutionalism" in economics is associated with the work of North (North and Thomas 1973; North 1991). It is striking how far this new economic institutionalism parallels the concerns of the new institutionalism that swept over political science following the publication of March and Olsen's landmark works (1984, 1989). Four similarities merit emphasis.

The first is the extent to which an almost theological debate developed about the meaning of "institutions." Indeed North on institutions sounds almost mystical: "We cannot see, feel, touch, or even measure institutions; they are constructs of the human mind" (1991, 107).

In North, however, this insistence is connected to a second theme which parallels the political science new institutionalism: The importance of distinguishing institutions from organizations. The distinction is critical because: "Institutions . . . determine the opportunities in a society. Organizations are created to take advantage of those opportunities" (1991, 7).

Why do these opportunities exist? Because of a third feature which parallels one of the key elements of political science institutionalism—perhaps the most important parallel. These are the linked characteristics of feedback and lock-in. Feedback is the process by which institutions adapt in the light of messages arising from their preceding activities, and interaction with their environment. "Lock-in" is the process by which institutions are constrained into particular patterns of development and behavior by the impact of past actions and commitments (North 1991, 7). The idea is plainly central to the wider, and more familiar, notion of "path dependency." The emphasis on "path dependency" turns out to have large implications for understanding change in institutional life, and for making sense of the role of human agency in change. Of course this is to put things only in terms of the restriction that path dependency creates. The wider literature on institutionalism reminds us that the other side of the path dependency coin is beneficial: It creates routine, certainty, and trust in economic and other social exchanges (Pierson 2000).

How does institutional choice work? This is the fourth parallel theme uniting the concerns of economic and "political science" institutionalism, and it can be illustrated from a recurrent problem—that of understanding the significance of a peculiarly important organization, the firm. As Moe puts it:

The neoclassical theory of the firm is not in any meaningful sense a theory of economic organization. It centers around the entrepreneur, a hypothetical individual who, by assumption, makes all the decisions for the firm and is endowed with a range of idealized properties defining his knowledge, goals, computational skills, and transaction costs. (Moe 1984, 740)

That problematic quality has been made more acute by the development of the firm in the modern industrial economy—by the extent to which it has become, in

Chandler's (1977) famous phrase, a "visible hand," a hierarchical structure organizing the mobilization and allocation of resources. Chandler's account of this process is benign, or at least neutral. Hannah reminds us, on the other hand, that the visible hand has often displaced the market in making brutal decisions: "The harshnesses of capitalism that remain may still bear down heavily on individuals...[but]...more as a result of decisions which emanate from a managerial hierarchy which has supplemented the market as a means of co-ordinating economic activities" (Hannah 1983, 2).

The giant firm is a dominant feature in the landscape of the modern market economy, and one question takes us to the heart of the political science interest in economic institutions: How can the firm be controlled? An economical way to explore this is through the study of economic regulation.

3   Economic Institutions and Economic Regulation

The study of economic regulation strikingly illustrates our key opening theme: The inseparability of the life of conventionally labeled "political" and "economic" institutions. The theme emerges clearly in examination of three big questions about economic regulation. First, how do the institutions of economic regulation evolve and operate? Second, have the great changes in economic policy and practice associated with the end of the "long boom" of the middle decades of the twentieth century created a paradigmatic shift in the relationship between economic and political institutions—an assertion that lies behind some theories of the emergence of a "regulatory state" governing economic life. Finally, what has been the impact of the most argued over structural economic shift of recent decades—the accelerated pace of globalization—on the regulation of economic institutions?

For brevity, we can approach the first of these questions through two contrasting sets of hypotheses: the "national styles" hypothesis and the "reflexive regulation" hypothesis. The first asserts that the institutions of regulation are likely to be unique to their national setting; the second that in structure and performance they are converging on a common model.[1]

---

[1] There is another important stream in the regulation literature, derived from neoliberalism: it offers charging as an alternative to command and control. I do not discuss it here partly for reasons of space and because some of the "charging" model is accommodated within reflexivity models.

The first is exemplified in the work of Vogel (1983, 1986, 1996). Vogel's key argument is that in the regulation of economic life there are distinctive national institutional structures, and distinctive national patterns in the way those structures function. In particular, the institutions of economic regulation in the most important capitalist democracy, the United States, are exceptional: in their reliance on a network of specialized regulatory agencies; in the extent to which those agencies operate legally enforced rules; in the detail of those rules; and in the degree to which the practice of regulation involves highly adversarial relationships between the two key sets of institutions—the agencies that do the regulating and the firms in the regulated industries (see also Kelman 1981). The contrast lies between the United States and two other kinds of national model: Those that, while relying heavily on legal institutions, are strongly consensual in operation, a common pattern across mainland Western Europe; and those that substantially dispense with the law, relying instead on highly consensual forms of self-regulation, a pattern exemplified by the United Kingdom (Jordana and Levi-Faur 2004, part II).

Whence come these national contrasts? The answers take us immediately to those themes in North that stress the importance of lock-in and path dependency shaped by the constraints of history. The contrast between the USA and the UK illustrates. In the United States, on the one hand, the development of formal democracy, and the rise of populist movements hostile to modern corporate capitalism, preceded the creation of regulatory institutions. In the UK, by contrast, regulatory institutions, and regulatory styles, were laid down, notably in the middle decades of the nineteenth century, before the development of either an interventionist state or formally democratic institutions. (On this kind of national peculiarity, see Atiyah 1979; MacDonagh 1961, 1977; Moran 2003). Modes of regulatory thinking which stressed the importance of informal cooperation, naturally strong in a pre-democratic society where politics was dominated by a coalition of bourgeois and aristocratic elites, were thus well established before the emergence of formally democratic institutions. Crudely: America first got populism, then economic regulation; Britain first got economic regulation, then democracy.

Two difficulties with the national styles hypothesis are obvious. The less serious is that this can never be anything but a thesis about *modal* institutional patterns, and we still have to make sense of the distribution around the mode. But a more serious difficulty takes us directly to the competing alternative posed above, reflexive regulation. There are many different nuances in reflexive accounts, but all share this belief: that conditions of high social and economic complexity oblige the development of common institutional patterns and practices. The measures of complexity include the technological complexity of many modern industrial processes; the institutional complexity of modern firms and industries; and the intellectual complexity of modern regulatory operations. Complexity undermines institutions that rely for compliance on command, including command law. The search for effectiveness forces a secular shift to more "reflexive" forms. Practically,

ECONOMIC INSTITUTIONS   149

this means increasing reliance on "soft law" (codes over commands); on modes of self-regulation; and an emphasis precisely on "reflexivity"—on malleability, flexibility, and a willingness to adapt and learn.[2] In short, lock-in and path dependency arising from national historical experience are not determinate; paths can change—and converge.

One important consequence of this account is to reinstate *agency* as an influence on institutional design. The possibilities are well illustrated in Ayres and Braithwaite's (1992) influential model of enforced self-regulation. This attempts to develop a theory of institutional choice, departing from a straightforward universal emphasis on reflexivity: one where both choice in institutional design, and choice of particular institutional instruments in particular regulatory circumstances, once again becomes a possibility. Part of the importance of agency in their model rests on the notion that choices can be made between command and reflexivity: in their world, regulatory authorities at the top of the regulatory pyramid speak the soft language of reflexivity, but carry a big stick.

All these versions of reflexivity root institutional change in common structural conditions across industrial societies, notably high social and technical complexity. An alternative account is rooted in more contingent historical and institutional circumstances. The best-known version is encapsulated in Majone's theory of the emergence of a new regulatory state (1991, 1996, 1999). This amounts to both an empirical and a prescriptive theory of the *constitution* of economic life. Some of Majone's themes echo theorists of high complexity. This is particularly noticeable in his argument that the regulation of economic life demands a Madisonian constitution: a system that entrenches expert opinion and interested minorities in the decision-making process, at the expense of modes of majoritarian constitutions. Some of Majone's arguments also respond to the political economy of advanced capitalism after the end of the long boom, notably to the (alleged) exhaustion of command modes in economic life associated with high Keynesianism. Some respond more immediately to the problem of making sense of the institutional forms being developed by, and appropriate for, the new system of economic government developing in the European Union. All converge on the claim that institutional structures have to display two features in the new regulatory state: the state has to abstain from anything more ambitious than the promulgation of broad rules governing the behavior of institutional actors in economic life; and responsibility for the implementation of rules must be delegated to the lowest possible institutional level. The latter, in practice, commonly means institutional actors in markets—trade associations, standard setting institutes, professional bodies, and individual firms.

---

[2] The convergence on reflexivity comes from very different theoretical, and substantive, starting points: I draw heavily on the theoretical work of Teubner 1987, 1993, and 1994; Collins 1999 on contract; Gunningham, Grabosky, and Sinclair 1998 on environmental policy; and Gunningham and Johnstone 1999 on health and safety in the enterprise.

It is obvious from this account of different theoretical positions that there are powerful tensions between different ways of conceiving how the institutions of economic regulation are shaped: as an outcome of historical contingency, or as a response to secular social conditions, such as high complexity. Accounts of the changing character of regulation, which fall under the third major heading identified at the start of this section—globalization—exemplify this tension. One influential way is to think of globalization as diffusing the power of American (or Euro-American) institutions. In this account, globalization involves strengthening the hand of a raft of institutions of global economic management that are heavily under American influence, or under the influence of American-led alliances: Among the most obvious at the macro level are institutions such as the World Bank and the International Monetary Fund; at the meso level, regulatory bodies concerned with the regulation of markets and sectors, such as IOSCO, the main international federation of securities markets regulators; and at the micro level the carriers of structural power, notably the great transnational corporations.[3] On this account, we are seeing indeed a newly configured relationship between political and economic institutions, adapting to the development of an economy increasingly organized on a global scale, where the characteristic institution of globalization—the multinational corporation—routinely organizes its affairs to evade the control of national regulatory authorities. (Consider, for instance, Strange 1996; Dicken 1998.) But this new "global regulatory state" is developing a set of institutions, and economic practices which are heavily mediated by American structural power. Regulatory practice is in turn shaped by domestic American regulatory cultures. Regulatory outcomes are the result of hard bargaining governed by the contours of American structural power. The result diffuses the special institutional practices of the American regulatory state, notably its pathologies of adversarialism and juridification.

Contrast this with the picture presented in Braithwaite and Drahos's (2000) study of global business regulation. Here global change has produced a "decentered" world where state institutions are only one of a wide range of bodies concerned with economic regulation. Webs of governance join a dizzying variety of institutions in the regulatory process: bits of states, firms, trade associations, NGOs, and many more. The connections between political and economic institutions—and indeed between economic institutions—are shifting and unstable. The borders between the economic and the political, the global, the regional, the national, and the sub-national, are barely recognizable; and the conventional language of power used to describe the internal character of those institutions, and their relations to each other, is of little use. This returns us to two key general themes. The first is the uncertainty, highlighted at the very start

[3] On the evidence and debates surrounding the propositions about these levels see, respectively: Nye 2002; Lutz 1998; Strange 1996.

of the chapter, about the boundaries between "economic" and "political" institutions. The second is the importance of agency, for this unstable world of global webs of governance precisely creates spaces for the intervention of human agency.

4   ECONOMIC INSTITUTIONS AND CAPITALISM

Examining the institutions of economic regulation has reminded us of key themes in the study of institutions generally: the importance of the comparative method; the key issue of performance effectiveness; and the role or otherwise of agency in institutional life. All these now recur in examining economic institutions and capitalism.

The history of the comparative study of economic institutions, notably of the institutions of capitalism, shows that a focus on institutions did not begin with "institutionalism," old or new. The focus is as old as the political economy of the market, and is central to the "classical" traditions of political economy, from Smith to Schumpeter. It is also central to sub-fields as diverse as the anthropology of economic life and the study of economic history; indeed the most important modern institutionalist revivalist, North, began precisely with historical problems.[4] The comparative study of economic systems was prolonged in the twentieth century by the rise of alternatives to capitalism, in the form both of corporatist fascism and command Communism (Wiles 1977). But the most important form taken by the modern comparative study of economic institutions lies in the "varieties of capitalism" literature, for the straightforward reason that capitalism proved the most durable of the great twentieth-century alternatives. The comparative study of capitalist institutions is, we shall see, important for a host of practical, policy related reasons. But it is also important because it highlights the institutionally contingent character of market organization; because it links to key issues of performance, economic and political; and because the spread of capitalist organizational forms has made this comparative differentiation the key to our understanding of modern political economies.

---

[4] For instance North and Thomas 1973; and see North's discussion of his own work in North 1991, 7ff.

Themes of contingency, performance, and agency are all present in the first modern landmark study in this tradition, Shonfield's *Modern Capitalism* (1965). He puts the varying role of a classic political institution—the state—at the center of differentiation; and claims to trace a close link between institutional differentiation and economic performance. In particular, since this was the height of French economic success, a central role is ascribed to the state as a steerer of economic institutions and manager of capitalist performance under systems of indicative planning (especially pp. 151–75).

Though the details of institutional differentiation have changed in each successive wave of the "models" debates, the basic principles of differentiation have remained similar in the very different work of, for instance, Albert (1993), Coates (2000), and Hall and Soskice (2001). Different ensembles of states, firms, and unions recur in the various models: Rhineland/Anglo-Saxon capitalisms (Albert); Liberal Capitalism and Trust-Based Capitalism (Coates); Coordinated Market Economies and Liberal Market Economies (Hall and Soskice). In Shonfield, as we have seen, the state was a key actor, since it "steered" a system of indicative planning. Others, such as Coates, have put the treatment of labor, and of unions as a proxy for labor, at the center of model building. Whether unions are so placed turns critically on estimations of how far unions can be institutionally integrated in a cooperative fashion into the management of a capitalist economy: Whether a "high trust" incorporating strategy which suppresses market forces is the best way to create a labor force that cooperates flexibly in the hunt for high productivity.

In part, such differences depend on varying views of the place of the state in managing the core institution of capitalism, the firm. In Shonfield, the French state guided firms through mechanisms of indicative planning. Other models have offered different accounts of the state/firm nexus, and these differences have in turn depended heavily on the role of different institutions in the organization of industrial finance and the practice of corporate governance. They help define one of the best established classifications in the literature: between Anglo-Saxon (which predominantly means Anglo-American) capitalism, where well organized securities markets not only dominate capital markets, but also enforce a system of corporate governance which marginalizes the state and enforces a pattern of corporate governance privileging the pursuit of shareholder value over the interests of other potential stakeholders; Rhineland Capitalism, where a history of bank domination of capital markets, and elaborate systems of corporate cross-ownership, result in the coordination of firm strategies by networks that unite state and corporate elites; and East Asian capitalism, where a more recent history of spectacular economic development is attributed in part to the capacity of public bureaucratic agencies to manage firm investment and disinvestment in the light of strategic state goals. (The explicitly political roots are exposed in Roe 1994, 2003.)

As this discussion shows, model building is closely tied to a concern with the alleged connection between institutional form and policy performance. But the way this link has been traced highlights once again the problematic role of agency. In debates until the beginning of the 1990s differences in the roles of the state, and of key financial institutions, were systematically linked to the capacity to make strategic investment (and disinvestment) decisions. Perhaps the high point of this literature was a single case, Johnson's (1982) study of the role of MITI in Japanese economic performance. These arguments had a fatalistic tinge, resembling an elaboration of Gerschenkron's (1966) thesis of the economic advantages of historical backwardness. Crudely, the conclusion from the experience of the "long boom" in capitalism in the thirty glorious years after 1945 seemed to be: Don't have the bad luck to be first in economic success, or you will be stuck with an anachronistic institutional order, notably with a state unable to act strategically. The most sophisticated formulation of this is in the work of Lazonick, in its view that each successful institutional formation (British Industrial Revolution "proprietary" capitalism, American "multidivisional" and vertically integrated capitalism) has inscribed within it the conditions of its very historical obsolescence and decline (Lazonick 1991, 12–19).

The second "long boom" in the United States, and to a lesser extent in other Anglo-Saxon economies, from the early 1990s, coupled with stagnation in Japan and poor economic performance across much of what came to be known as the euro-zone, has forced reappraisals of these accounts. These reappraisals turn us back to issues of agency and institutional change—though in complicated ways. The first complication is that it is now clear that a kind of Manichean division of models of capitalism into bad and good performers is unrealistic. The comparatively "good" performance of the Anglo-Saxon models in some areas from the early 1990s onwards, such as in tackling unemployment, was accompanied by "bad" performance—at least according to some normative stances—in others, such as securing long-term security of employment or control over levels of wealth inequality. (For instance, Crouch and Streeck 1997; Coates 2000.) A simple-minded constraint on agency in institutional redesign thus might be that there are trade-offs that have to be endured: for instance, one could so weaken labor unions and the social forces associated with them that it was possible to achieve highly flexible labor markets capable of disciplining workers in the pursuit of high productivity; but that very weakness would strengthen the hand of corporate elites and lead to huge increases in inequality. A more complex version of the argument occurs in Hall and Soskice, where the familiar institutional building blocks—firms, states, unions—are held to be organized in complicated, historically shaped ensembles that govern the way they strategically interact. Intervention to reshape one of the building blocks has effects on the other blocks, and success in intervention depends on the contingent character of institutional patterns in different national systems (Hall and Soskice 2001, 1–21).

The sharp rise in income inequality in the Anglo-Saxon economies intensifies a long established debate about the connection between the economic institutions of capitalism and democratic government. It was a well established position in the "politics and markets" literature that one job of democratic government was precisely to moderate the inequalities generated by markets (Korpi 1983; Esping-Andersen 1985). But if the price of a dynamic Anglo-Saxon style capitalism is huge and rising inequality, that gives some support to radical arguments that more fundamental reform is required in the power structures of capitalist institutions (for instance Dahl 1985).

Agency and institutional change are also linked in another key issue. One possible conclusion from experiences since the early 1990s—a conclusion appealing to many policy elites—is that political leadership can be critical in reshaping institutional structures and practices. On that view a key difference was that the UK, for instance, was "lucky" enough to produce a Margaret Thatcher at the end of the 1970s, while Germany was "unlucky" enough to end up with Helmut Kohl three years later. But even setting aside one obvious objection—that a Thatcher could only function in the institutional setting offered by the UK—the links between agency, institutional change, and policy performance remain complicated by another powerful set of institutional contingencies. Even the most polemical supporters of the "agency" view rely on the argument that historical agents were effective because they embraced more impersonal structural changes—notably, the wave of globalization that, originating in a global financial services revolution, has swept over the economies of the advanced capitalist world since the early 1970s. On this view, the key role of agency consists in recognizing inevitability, and in reshaping the traditional institutional ensembles of Rhineland and East Asian capitalism to accommodate a familiar Anglo Saxon pattern of domination by highly developed, globally trading securities markets. Here is a revived institutional fatalism smuggled in by the back door of agency. And this fatalism has in turn produced the argument that pre-existing institutional legacies can be exploited to combat this fatalism. The best known version is associated with Garrett (for instance 1998a, 5; 1998b), where it is held that an active state can build institutional systems, for instance in labor markets, that promote economic competitiveness in global markets, and can coordinate those social forces to resist attacks on the institutions of developed welfare states. In this way, it is possible to create "a virtuous circle between activist government and international openness" (1998b, 789). In short, agency may involve more than recognizing the "inevitability" of globalization; it can involve shaping a social democratic response to it.

The "democracy" part of social democracy in this argument provides a natural link to the next section, where we examine the connection between economic institutions and democratic government.

5   ECONOMIC INSTITUTIONS AND DEMOCRATIC GOVERNMENT

The connection between democratic political institutions and capitalist economic institutions is troubling and complex, and has generated both a huge literature and complex policy change. In the space available here we can only examine three issues: how far democratic government can or should try to constrain the operations of economic institutions; conversely, how far economic institutions can and should try to constrain democratic politics; and finally, how far democratic government can and should model its operations on business institutions.

The first of these issues is central to something we have already discussed: the process of economic regulation. But there are wider questions and they go to the heart of the connection between democracy and the market order. Two very different sets of problems can illustrate the point: the control of trade unions and the control of business. The control of trade unions emerged as a *policy* issue in the era of full employment of the "thirty glorious years." But why would unions *as institutions* be thought to constitute a problem for democratic government? A converging stream of work offered a variety of answers: because their position in the division of labor allowed them to exploit organized social complexity to disrupt economic and social processes; because they were institutions of coercion incompatible with democratic liberties; and/or because they were veto groups that obstructed the functioning of democratic government (for instance, Brittan 1975). One of the most influential syntheses was contained in Olson (1982) where the institutional power of unions was assimilated to a wider theory of collective action—one where the incentives for organization favored the development of sectional groups intent on protecting interests, against policies that ensured economic efficiency. Long-term democratic stability obstructed economic efficiency by fostering the spread of these groups, who in turn hobbled the policy performance of democratic governments. One way out of this impasse was catastrophe—such as military defeat—which destroyed the institutions of sectionalism.[5]

There is an air of fatalism about these accounts, which sits uneasily with the policy practice, notably in the Anglo-Saxon democracies, where the 1980s and 1990s saw full frontal, and often successful, attacks on the power of sectional groups like trade unions. Something of the same fatalism attaches to those accounts which see a sharp contradiction between democratic politics and business institutions. Alongside the well known Marxist versions of this account can be

---

[5] But though Olson's was a theory of sectionalism generally his instances are strikingly biased in the direction of unions: see 1982, 77–9.

set the views crystallised in Lindblom's (1977) influential argument that only polyarchy—competitive elitism—was possible given the organization of the institutions of business in a market economy. Here, the characteristic institutions of capitalism—legally instantiated private property and its concomitant privileges—are seen as spiriting away from the democratic arena a wide range of key decisions: for instance, over investment, and via investment over employment and economic growth. A more immediate version of this, particularly pertinent in an American setting, is the capacity of the biggest firms, with their enormous resources, simply to use money to shape the democratic process: to buy influence over voters through opinion shaping, and influence over parties and legislators by campaign contributions and other donations (Jacobson 1980; Marchand 1998; Silverstein 1998).

A crude summary of the view outlined above is that capitalist institutions are the enemy of democratic government. Almost a mirror image of this is the view that democratic government is a threat to the effective working of capitalist institutions. These hesitations about majoritarian democracy run through, for instance, the work of Hayek.[6] Their full-blooded policy manifestation can be found in the management of economic policy from the 1990s onwards across the advanced capitalist world, with the rise of non-majoritarian agencies of economic management. The most important changes concerned the relations between democratic government and one key institution—the central bank. Throughout the decade, there was a consistent tendency to revise institutional/constitutional arrangements, both to strengthen generally the independence of central banks against democratic governments, and to give them power over, in particular, the control of short-term interest rates: "More countries increased the independence of their central banks during the 1990s than in any other decade since World War II" (McNamara 2002, 47).[7] In the same decade a new paradigm of central bank independence was created for the whole euro-zone, displacing a variety of arrangements within democratic national governments (Moran 2002). These changes represented the rise of new policy paradigms, and the paradigmatic shift highlights one of the opening themes of this chapter: that the division between an "economic" and a "political" institution is not settled, but is shaped precisely by paradigmatic creations. Explaining the sources of the movement to bind the discretionary power of democratic government by empowering institutions like central banks raises large and perennial explanatory problems: it could indeed be

---

[6] For instance Hayek 1960, 105–9. I am indebted to Gamble 1996, 91–7 for clarification of this argument. Some of Hayek's arguments go well beyond endowing central banks with discretionary power to marketizing the whole central banking process. But I use him as an example here both because of his rhetorical power and because he dramatizes the key point—the tension with democratic control of the market economy.

[7] The evidence that this had desired policy outcomes is another disputed matter: see Hall and Franzese 1998.

traced to the rise of distinctive ideas; or it could be seen as the response to structural changes, notably to the great wave of financial globalization originating in the 1970s that made democratic governments anxious to conciliate new footloose financial institutions.

How we think of the connection between "economic" and "political" institutions is a function of the paradigmatic world we inhabit—a point that is reinforced by the third aspect of the connection between democratic institutions and economic institutions examined here, a connection shaped by the rise of the New Public Management: the modelling of public institutions on business institutions. These effects can be summed up under three headings: The rise of contractualism in the public sector; the rise of executive agencies; and the spread of a consultancy culture.

"Contractualism" summarizes a wide range of developments—contracting out of functions and services, the development of managed "internal" markets which mimic market exchange, the full-scale privatization of services—but all have a common thread: The attempt to replace the routines and cultures of public service bureaucracy with the routines and cultures—or at least the perceived routines and cultures—of the characteristic institutions of the market place (Pollitt and Talbot 2004).

Agency creation is associated with some of these changes, but has taken a more exactly institutional form. In the case of central banking we saw that it consisted in part in a growth in the degree of control exercised by central banks over key instruments of economic policy. This growth in autonomy can be viewed as a special case of the more general process of "hiving off" agencies in a variety of forms, establishing a range of relationships again based on contract. Institutionally, this development has had a number of consequences: It has blurred the tradition-ally constructed separation between "state" and "market," thus overturning traditional "constructions" of the political and the economic; and, more concretely, it has been an important means of introducing "business" cultures into the public sector (Self 2000; Sahlin-Andersson 2002).

In this sense agency creation has also been a mechanism by which the cultures of business institutions are diffused to public sector bodies, a process reinforced by the more formal reliance on management consultancies. "Consultocracy" (Saint-Martin 1998) is a key political feature of New Public Management. Two forces are fashioning this, one supply led and one demand led. The supply is created by aggressive competition in the service sector, especially in the financial services sector, which has led, notably among the multinational accounting firms and merchant banks, to the development of consultancy arms, hunting for business across both the public and private sectors. One of the most important areas of institutional change under the New Public Management lies in the international privatization movement of the last couple of decades, where the marketing of expertise in the privatization process has been an important means by which the phenomenon of privatization itself has been diffused. On the demand side, the business of private sector consultancies has been boosted by the search for private sector exemplars and by the wish to use consultancies as a means of introducing "businesslike" practices into hitherto standardized Weberian bureaucracies. One of the most striking examples of this is provided by the huge health care sectors that dominate all the national systems of Western Europe, where a paradigm shift away from a public service model has led to the widespread creation of systems of managed markets that attempt to mimic the relations between business institutions in the market system (Saltman and von Otter 1992).

6   Conclusions: Politics, Markets, and Agents

"The subject matter of economics," Schumpeter once wrote, "is essentially a unique process in historic time" (1954, 12). This uniqueness also lies at the heart of all institutions, including economic institutions. A conclusion properly looks back and forward: to sum up what we think we know, and to sketch what we need to know more of:

- We know that the modern study of economic institutions resurrects many of the concerns of an older institutionalism, but in very different intellectual and policy environments: intellectually, it is marked by more self-consciousness and uncertainty about the meaning of "institution," and about the processes of institutional design; in policy, it is now inseparable from the landmark changes of the last three decades, notably those usually summed up by "globalization."
- We know that these features strikingly parallel the histories of "old" and "new" institutionalism in political science.
- We know that institutions *matter:* that ensembles of organizations make a difference to political outcomes (such as the viability of democracy) or to economic outcomes (such as the character of market regulation or even the wider fate of whole capitalist orders.)

What we do not know is of course limitless, and we are caught in a familiar bind: the most damaging and important areas of ignorance are those of which we are not even aware. But the most important areas of ignorance about which we are highly conscious, or should be highly conscious, are twofold:

- The connections between institutional change, institutional design, and human agency remain bafflingly complex. The history of different varieties of capitalism since the early 1990s dramatizes the puzzles: models that seemed, path dependency fashion, to be set on the road to decline, notably in the Anglo-Saxon world, experienced an unexpected revival, and in at least some instances, the most notable of which is the UK, may have done so through the unexpected intervention of decisive historical actors.

- That the divide between the "economic" and the "political" in institutional life is a constructed divide now seems a truism. But the mystery of construction, how and why it changes, runs through all the substantive areas examined in the preceding pages. The mystery brings us back to the whiff of mysticism in North: "We cannot see, feel, touch, or even measure institutions." And we cannot "see, feel or touch" because at heart an institution is an idea. Understanding economic institutions is at heart not about understanding structures, but about understanding the role of ideas in economic and political life. And as is shown in Blyth's (2002) study of "economic ideas and institutional change in the twentieth century," we have barely scratched the surface of that problem.

At the root of many of the particular issues examined in the preceding pages lies a much grander set of issues, too large for the scale of this chapter, but an important theme of Braithwaite's accompanying chapter in this volume. They can be summed up in the familiar language of the principal–agent problem. Principal–agent problems are endemic in the kinds of societies examined here— those marked by high levels of organized complexity and by a refined division of labor. They are, too, at the heart of problems of accountability under democratic *representative* government. Since the pioneering work of Berle and Means (1932/ 1968) on the separation of ownership and control they have been central to understanding power and control in the characteristic economic institution of modern capitalism—the large corporation. The study of institutions, whether conventionally "economic" or conventionally "political," reminds us that there is no escaping these problems: choosing the "market" over the "state" just involves deciding to live with one set of principal–agent problems rather than another.

References

Albert, M. 1993. *Capitalism against Capitalism*. London: Whurr.

Atiyah, P. S. 1979. *The Rise and Fall of Freedom of Contract*. Oxford: Clarendon Press.

Ayres, I. and Braithwaite, J. 1992. *Responsive Regulation: Transcending the Deregulation Debate*. Oxford: Oxford University Press.

Berle, A. and Means, G. 1932/1968. *The Modern Corporation and Private Property*, 4th edn. New York: Harcourt Brace.

Blyth, M. 2002. *Great Transformations: Economic Ideas and Institutional Change in the Twentieth Century*. Cambridge: Cambridge University Press.

BRAITHWAITE, J. and DRAHOS, P. 2000. *Global Business Regulation*. Cambridge: Cambridge University Press.

BRITTAN, S. 1975. The economic contradictions of democracy. *British Journal of Political Science,* 15: 129–59.

CHANDLER, A. 1977. *The Visible Hand: The Managerial Revolution in American Business.* Cambridge, Mass.: Belknap Press.

COATES, D. 2000. *Models of Capitalism: Growth and Stagnation in the Modern Era.* Cambridge: Polity.

COLLINS, H. 1999. *Regulating Contracts.* Oxford: Oxford University Press.

CROUCH, C. and STREECK, W. 1997. Introduction. Pp. 1–18 in *Political Economy of Modern Capitalism: Mapping Convergence and Diversity,* ed. C. Crouch and W. Streeck. London: Sage.

DAHL, R. 1985. *A Preface to Economic Democracy.* Cambridge: Polity.

DICKEN, P. 1998. *Global Shift: Transforming the World Economy,* 3rd edn. London: Chapman.

ESPING-ANDERSEN, G. 1985. *Politics against Markets: The Social Democratic Road to Power.* Princeton, NJ: Princeton University Press.

GAMBLE, A. 1996. *Hayek: The Iron Cage of Liberty.* Cambridge: Polity.

GARRETT, G. 1998a. *Partisan Politics in the Global Economy.* Cambridge: Cambridge University Press.

—— 1998b. Global markets and national politics: collision course or virtuous circle? *International Organization,* 52: 767–824.

GERSHCHENKRON, A. 1966. *Economic Backwardness in Historical Perspective.* Cambridge, Mass.: Harvard University Press.

GOODIN, R. 1996. Institutions and their design. Pp. 1–53 in *The Theory of Institutional Design,* ed. R. Goodin. Cambridge: Cambridge University Press.

GUNNINGHAM, N. and JOHNSTONE, R. 1999. *Regulating Workplace Safety: Systems and Sanctions.* Oxford: Oxford University Press.

—— GRABOSKY, P., and SINCLAIR, D. 1998. *Smart Regulation: Designing Environmental Policy.* Oxford: Clarendon Press.

HALL, P. and FRANZESE, R. 1998. Mixed signals: central bank independence, coordinated wage bargaining, and European monetary union. *International Organization,* 52: 502–36.

—— and SOSKICE, D. (eds.) 2001. *Varieties of Capitalism: The Institutional Foundations of Comparative Advantage.* Oxford: Oxford University Press.

HANNAH, L. 1983. *The Rise of the Corporate Economy,* 2nd edn. London: Methuen.

HAYEK, F. A. 1960. *The Constitution of Liberty.* London: Routledge.

JACOBSON, G. 1980. *Money in Congressional Elections.* New Haven, Conn.: Yale University Press.

JOHNSON, C. 1982. *MITI and the Japanese Miracle: The Growth of Industrial Policy 1925–1975.* Stanford, Calif.: Stanford University Press.

JORDANA, J. and LEVI-FAUR, D. (eds.) 2004. *The Politics of Regulation: Institutions and Regulatory Reforms for the Age of Governance.* Cheltenham: Edward Elgar.

KELMAN, S. 1981. *Regulating America, Regulating Sweden: A Comparative Study of Occupational Safety and Health Policy.* Cambridge, Mass.: MIT Press.

KORPI, W. 1983. *The Democratic Class Struggle.* London: Routledge.

LAZONICK, W. 1991. *Business Organization and the Myth of the Market Economy.* Cambridge: Cambridge University Press.

LINDBLOM, C. 1977. *Politics and Markets: The World's Political-economic Systems.* New York: Basic Books.

Lutz, S. 1998. The revival of the nation state? Stock exchange regulation in an era of globalized financial markets. *Journal of European Public Policy*, 5: 53–68.

MacDonagh, O. 1961. *A Pattern of Government Growth 1800–1860: The Passenger Acts and their Enforcement*. London: Macgibbon and Kee.

—— 1977. *Early Victorian Government 1830–1870*. London: Weidenfeld and Nicolson.

McNamara, K. 2002. Rational fictions: central bank independence and the social logic of delegation. *West European Politics*, 25: 47–76.

Majone, G. 1991. Cross-national sources of regulatory policymaking in Europe and the United States. *Journal of Public Policy*, 11: 79–109.

—— 1996. *Regulating Europe*. London: Routledge.

—— 1999. The regulatory state and its legitimacy problems. *West European Politics*, 22: 1–24.

March, J. and Olsen, J. 1984. The new institutionalism: organizational factors in political life. *American Political Science Review*, 78: 734–49.

—— —— 1989. *Rediscovering Institutions: The Organizational Basis of Politics*. New York: Free Press.

Marchand, R. 1998. *Creating the Corporate Soul: The Rise of Public Relations and Corporate Imagery in American Big Business*. Berkeley: University of California Press.

Mauss, M. 1970. *The Gift: Forms and Functions of Exchange in Archaic Societies*, trans. I. Cunnison. London: Cohen and West.

Moe, T. 1984. The new economics of organization. *American Journal of Political Science*, 28: 739–77.

Moran, M. 2002. Politics, banks and financial market governance in the euro-zone. Pp. 257–77 in *European States and the Euro: Europeanization, Variation and Convergence*, ed. K. Dyson. Oxford: Oxford University Press.

—— 2003. *The British Regulatory State: High Modernism and Hyper-Innovation*. Oxford: Oxford University Press.

North, D. 1991. *Institutions, Instiutional Change and Economic Performance*. Cambridge: Cambridge University Press.

—— and Thomas, R. 1973. *The Rise of the Western World: A New Economic History*. Cambridge: Cambridge University Press.

Nye, J. 2002. *The Paradox of American Power*. Oxford: Oxford University Press.

Olson, M. 1982. *The Rise and Decline of Nations: Economic Growth, Stagflation, and Social Rigidities*. New Haven, Conn.: Yale University Press.

—— 2000. *Power and Prosperity: Outgrowing Communist and Capitalist Dictatorships*. New York: Basic Books.

Pierson, P. 2000. Increasing returns, path dependence and the study of politics. *American Political Science Review*, 94: 51–68.

Polanyi, K. 1944–57. *The Great Transformation: The Political and Economic Origins of Our Time*. Boston: Beacon Hill Press.

Pollitt, C. and Talbot, C. (eds.) 2004. *Unbundled Government: A Critical Analysis of the Global Trend to Agencies, Quangos and Contractualism*. London: Routledge.

Roe, M. 1994. *Strong Managers, Weak Owners: The Political Roots of American Corporate Finance*. Princeton, NJ: Princeton University Press.

—— 2003. *Political Determinants of Corporate Governance: Political Context, Corporate Impact*. Oxford: Oxford University Press.

Rutherford, M. 1996. *Institutions in Economics: The Old and the New Institutionalism*. Cambridge: Cambridge University Press.

SAHLIN-ANDERSSON, K. 2002. National, international and transnational constructions of New Public Management. Pp. 43–72 in *New Public Management: The Transformation of Ideas and Practice*, ed. T. Christensen and P. Lægreid. Aldershot: Ashgate.

SAINT-MARTIN, D. 1998. The new managerialism and the policy influence of consultants in government: an historical institutionalist analysis of Britain, Canada and France. *Governance*, 11: 319–56.

SALTMAN, R. and VON OTTER, C. 1992. *Planned Markets and Public Competition: Strategic Reform in Northern European Health Systems*. Buckingham: Open University Press.

SCHUMPETER, J. 1954. *History of Economic Analysis*. Oxford: Oxford University Press.

SELF, P. 2000. *Rolling Back the State. Economic Dogma & Political Choice*. New York: St Martin's Press.

SHONFIELD, A. 1965. *Modern Capitalism: The Changing Balance of Public and Private Power*. Oxford: Oxford University Press.

SILVERSTEIN, K. 1998. *Washington on $10 Million a Day: How Lobbyists Plunder the Nation*. Monroe, Me.: Common Courage Press.

SMITH, A. 1790/1976. *The Theory of Moral Sentiments*, ed. D. D. Raphael and A. L. McFie. Oxford: Clarendon Press.

STRANGE, S. 1996. *The Retreat of the State: The Diffusion of Power in the World Economy*. Cambridge: Cambridge University Press.

TEUBNER, G. 1987. Juridification—concepts, aspects, limits solutions. Pp. 3–48 in *Juridification of Social Spheres: A Comparative Analysis of the Areas of Labor, Antitrust and Social Welfare Law*, ed. G. Teubner. Berlin: de Gruyter.

—— 1993. *Law as an Autopoietic System*, trans. A. Bankowska and R. Adler, ed. Z. Bankowski. Oxford: Blackwell.

—— 1994. Enterprise corporatism: new industrial policy and the "essence" of the legal person. Pp. 51–79 in *The Law of the Business Enterprise*, ed. S. Wheeler. Oxford: Oxford University Press.

VOGEL, D. 1983. The political power of business in America: a reappraisal. *British Journal of Political Science*, 13: 19–43.

—— 1986. *National Styles of Regulation: Environmental Policy in Great Britain and the United States*. Ithaca, NY: Cornell University Press.

—— 1996. *Kindred Strangers: The Uneasy Relationship Between Politics and Business in America*. Princeton, NJ: Princeton University Press.

WHEELER, S. (ed.) 1994. *The Law of the Business Enterprise*. Oxford: Oxford University Press.

WILES, P. 1977. *Economic Institutions Compared*. Oxford: Blackwell.

WILLIAMSON, O. 1981. The modern corporation: origins, evolution, attributes. *Journal of Economic Literature*, 19: 1537–68.

—— 1985. *The Economic Institutions of Capitalism: Firms, Markets, Relational Contracting*. New York: Free Press.

CHAPTER 10

EXCLUSION, INCLUSION, AND POLITICAL INSTITUTIONS

MATTHEW HOLDEN, JR.

1 THE POLITICAL ORDER

Institutions are indispensable. People cannot live together under complete randomness or Hobbesian disorder. "An institution," March and Olsen (Ch. 1) tell us, "is a relatively enduring collection of rules and organized practices, embedded in structures of meaning and resources that are relatively invariant in the face of turnover of individuals and relatively resilient to the idiosyncratic preferences of individuals and changing external circumstances."

The very meaning of "institution" is that values are settled within it (Selznick 1967). Other values that impose strain are repelled or excluded. "Inclusion-and-exclusion" is the name we give this problem. As a concept in political science, it is not well enough known to have a formal name or distinctive literature, although such a tradition does exist in sociology (Gamson 1969). But the themes of inclusion and exclusion reference several different literatures in this chapter.

Institutions are excellent at exclusion and poor at inclusion. Vast political trouble hangs upon that fact. All states are administrative, and the study of "inclusion" and "exclusion" is critically about the choices that are made by persons exercising some administrative authority or some judicial authority at a "lower" or operational level. Precisely because institutions embody "settled values," they must exclude or greatly disadvantage those who wish to unsettle the status quo.

Because institutions define "a way of life" they sometimes are deeply insulated from stimuli with which they are unfamiliar. More concretely, institutional elites often fail to accommodate change because they cannot recognize it or when cognizant of it cannot imagine an alternative state of affairs than the present one from which all of their perquisites flow. Just instrumentally, institutions often contain so many impediments to receiving and processing information that is either unfamiliar or which signals events that are accorded very low probability that disaster is unavoidable. In the case of bureaucracies, Pearl Harbor (Wohlstetter 1962), 9/11 (US National Commission 2004), and the collapse of New Orleans are decisive examples. Institutions, in sum, have tendencies toward closure from their environment and from new information. That is inherently part of what makes them institutions.

The institutional tendency toward closure is troubling, notably when conflict concerns social demand. Unless issues of that type can be resolved in civil society, they will reappear as challenges within institutions. They may be so severe that, like social hurricanes, they simply overwhelm institutions. They may be incorporated in institutions in some form. And sometimes institutions may have a momentary capacity for inclusionary decision, when driven by other intense needs. Such instances may be reflected in events in the US Congress in 1964 and 1965 when two landmark pieces of civil rights legislation were passed after seven decades of extraordinary resistance. But institutions also have the capacity, sometimes, for exclusionary decisions, to get rid of some who are present (Ranki 1999). The elimination of African-Americans from the political process in the Southern states after the reconstruction period following the civil war may serve as an example.

As a matter of time and convenience, this chapter will omit some institutions that, in principle, are worth analysis, for example, the executive and the courts.

2   GETTING TO INCLUSION: THE HYPOTHESIS OF THE COUNTER-ATTACK

Once inclusion is attained, sequential problems of institutional adaptation follow. Interesting as these issues are, my main focus is on how groups get to inclusion. For any group, the minimal condition of "inclusion" is getting to inclusion, or getting to the point at which it need not worry about being forced out altogether. I assert, subject to testing, the hypothesis of the counter-attack; that is, social change driven by, or on behalf of, groups (interests) from the outside can only be achieved by the defeat of others that are already incorporated within the institutions.

Attempts at inclusion generate two types of response: the counter-attack and entrapment. Counter-attack (or counter-mobilization) is to be expected in politics as it is in military engagement. When an initial defeat occurs, at least some members of the losing side will continue to assert their position and try to reverse the outcome. They do not recede merely because of defeat. Nor are they dissuaded because they are extreme. Some members of the losing side may go into psychological exile abandoning politics altogether. Some may go into physical exile, never to return. But others will be galvanized to continue the struggle.

Some, of course, will make pragmatic adaptations, accepting what they cannot overcome. Others may actually be converted. But there is a hardcore residue. They may chatter incessantly to the boredom or amusement of others who think them fanatics. Or they may seethe in silence, expressing their views only within circles where they are completely comfortable. If opportunity presents itself, they will re-emerge and, if possible, revert to as much of the *status quo ante* as they can. Sometimes they will be more successful than any realist a short time before would have imagined.

Another possible outcome is entrapment. Entrapment is an outcome of minimal inclusion whereby the premise of a democratic commitment to state and society is accepted (Dryzek 1996). As Dryzek notes (1996, 475–87): "Once universal adult citizenship rights have been secured in a society, democratization is mostly a matter of the more authentic political inclusion of different groups and categories, for which formal political equality can hide continued exclusion or oppression." Dryzek observes, however, that symbolic inclusion is easier to achieve than genuine inclusion. Acceptance of the former means abiding by the terms of commitment to constitutional processes which in turn means entrapment within a system hostile to a group's real inclusion.

3   CURRENT POLITICAL SCIENCE AND THE DOUBLE PROBLEM OF INCLUSION AND EXCLUSION

Two notable forms of group classification around which struggles about inclusion-and-exclusion take place are gender and ethnicity, in the broad sense to include race. In contemporary literature on political institutions, "inclusion" belongs chiefly to the political science of "democracy"(Dahl 1998; 2005, 187–97; Dryzek 1996). Dahl has specified the institutions that are essential for large-scale democracy: elected officials; free, fair, and frequent elections; freedom of expression; access to alternative sources of information; and associational autonomy. In addition to these, he specifies "inclusive citizenship" by which "no adult permanently resident in the country and subject to its laws can be denied the rights that are available to others" (Dahl 2005: 189).

3.1   What is Inclusion?

The problem of inclusion and exclusion can be understood partly in the classical democratic theoretic issue of "majorities" and "minorities." That assumes membership in the polity and is merely about the terms of decision and the terms of veto. In creating institutions, people who are going to live within them need a substantial degree of understanding as to who are accepted as members, who are acceptable aliens (some metics in ancient Athens or green card holders in the United States), and who are merely there as convenient people. Some people will have lower status than that, and may have no rights at all.

The category of persons who may potentially become officeholders (let us call it the "reservoir") must be defined, along with the recruitment rules for choosing persons from the reservoir from time to time. There must be some rules or understandings governing the decision process, if officeholders are not to be granted full and dictatorial powers to do whatever they may think is right. There must be substantive output rules (policy rules) as to what those holding office may do, may not do, and must do. And there must be some rules for changing the rules. Perfect inclusion is inclusion in every step of the process. Perfect exclusion is to be present at no step of the process.

In the formal sense, the basic right is the right to vote. But there are other rights and capacities that are important. The right to speak your piece, and thus gratify yourself and sometimes influence others, is vital. So is the right to earn some money and keep it, or to use it any legal way, and so is the capacity to participate in influencing the choices that are put before others. In declining order from the public to private, there is access to the vote, access to political roles beyond the vote, access to some social benefits, access to equality of social benefits as good as anyone else gets, and even access to treatment for special needs.

Political scientists have discussed electoral mechanisms in their full range and variety of forms as to how they affect inclusion and exclusion in terms of conferring advantage and, conversely, disadvantage. Inclusion begins with enfranchisement. But electoral mechanisms themselves have known effects. Those mechanisms that enhance the likelihood of female and minority representation are critical tools of potential inclusion. But electoral mechanisms equally can be used as tools to exclude as well.

3.2   Election Rules

As a general matter, the rules governing elections and the modalities of representation are frequently contentious and in play for "reform." To an unusual degree, and perhaps uniquely, politicians in the United States (state legislatures) have the power to define both legislative districts at the state level and those for the US House of Representatives. It is not surprising that once party politicians have the power to define districts—which because states often have divided government they do not always do—they will exercise that power to enhance their party's position. Sometimes they can do this by stacking the other party's constituents into a few districts which may facilitate, ironically, both greater minority representation and lessened minority influence over policy. Computer technology has made the art of the gerrymander into a science.

3.3   Election Types and Inclusion/Exclusion

3.3.1   *Run-off Elections*

Run-off elections force an electoral majority behind a single candidate. This electoral form typically disadvantages minorities who are seeking inclusion when that status is contested by the majority. Normally, in a single seat winner-take-all election, the requirement of a majority may be said to be more representative of voters' preferences than a pure first-past-the post plurality requirement inasmuch as it induces a delayed form of agreement voting. However, the requirement of an electoral majority also diminishes opportunities for minority candidates in majority-dominant constituencies, at least to the extent that inclusion issues remain.

3.3.2   *At-large Versus Single Member Districts*

James Madison, whom some designate "the Father of the Constitution" (Brant 1950), was surely a crucial participant in the initial shaping of American political institutions. Madison argued, in *Federalist* 10, that the broader the territorial compass the more that would be likely to engender diverse factions (or in contemporary language, diverse interests). Actual results depend upon the composition of the at-large constituency, but unless the at-large electoral unit also has proportional representation, it is more likely to represent concentrated minorities than voting by district, other things being equal.

3.3.3 *Descriptive and Substantive Representation*

What difference does it make if an elected representative is of a given gender or ethnic-racial background? This has perhaps not been settled in empirical analysis of the many countries with some kind of multiethnic or multiracial composition. It is highly contested in political science research in the United States. We should contrast the work of Carol Swain, who contends that white legislators can represent black constituents' interests as well as blacks (Swain 1995), and Kenny Whitby whose data seem to reveal a distinctiveness in what black representatives of black constituencies do (Whitby 1997).

Obviously, one answer to that question is that it depends on the characteristics of the officeholder's party and the nature of the electing or selecting constituency. The nature of the constituency, in turn, depends on the sharpness of the cleavages separating the interests of the officeholder's ethnic group from the interests of other constituencies. To put it more directly, can someone be elected from a constituency not dominated by her or his ethnic group?

Gender, in contrast to some racial and ethnic characteristics, has one essential difference. Male and female populations cannot be physically separated on a continuing basis. Nor does conflict reduce itself to the same kinds or degrees of violence that racial and ethnic conflict sometimes do. Political scientists do differ as to whether gender makes a significant substantive difference by itself, even though some issues clearly affect women more than men. The question is also posed as to whether more critical differences are intragender; that is, whether women are married and not in the workforce or single and in the workforce and, especially, their race. Issues of representation around gender appear to be largely ones of descriptive representation in that greater female representation can be added to the reservoir of officeholders.

Both gender and racial-ethnic representation, broadly speaking, may be different over time and across societies. In societies based upon large-scale and rapid incorporation of different population streams, the issues can be very severe. Whether a candidate for elected office is of Italian, Irish, Anglo, or Germanic descent is these days of little matter. But that was not always so when differences between various European descended populations were much greater. There is, however, great demand for representation directly by members of ethnic groups whose inclusion status is still in doubt, mainly people of non-European origin.

However, whether greater direct representation means equivalent substantive representation is unclear at the very least. As representation in the elite reservoir increases, it is likely that this increase will require minority ethnic representatives to represent more heterogeneous constituencies. Assuming the operation of the "electoral connection" in district based elections, minority representatives in more diverse constituencies are unlikely to afford to be minority representatives as substantively as their peers in more minority dense districts.

Redistricting, which has been mentioned, also plays a role in potentially increasing the minority elite reservoir while possibly limiting the substantive representation of minorities. Redistricting allows for stacking and concentrating minorities into safe districts (almost always the party of the left), but more districts are likely to be constituted in a way that produces more representatives who are likely to be less favorably inclined toward minorities' policy preferences. And, to some extent, these policy preferences may differ across minorities. But it is likely that when one speaks of minorities whose inclusion status is in question, one is also speaking about class. Not exclusively, of course, but nonetheless significantly. In any event, it is clear that the relationship between descriptive and substantive representation remains to be explored, particularly in the context of different electoral and representational systems.

3.3.4 Proportional Representation Systems

Proportional representation (PR) systems facilitate the representation of minorities because they encourage minorities to create their own parties if they feel underrepresented in the larger ones. (In Israel, for example, there had been a party whose constituency was almost exclusively drawn from Russian immigrants.) The costs of new party entry into the political marketplace are lower than in single member district systems. To keep groups from straying, larger parties may seek to place candidates on the party list who reflect minority party constituencies. Ultimately, though, who becomes an elected officeholder depends upon positioning on the party list. Further, given the party discipline prevalent in PR systems, representation in parliament is inevitably more descriptive or symbolic than substantive.

3.3.5 Inclusion and Coalition-building

Some literature on inclusion starts from the unspoken predicate that the newest ethnic minority will be unable to exert sufficient pressure by itself. Therefore, the question is whether it can find others with compatible interest. In the United States, the newest version of this concerns African-Americans and Latinos in American cities.

Contemporary political science takes for granted that political agreement is called for. Accordingly, it focuses upon the various means of representation, especially representation in assemblies (or legislative bodies). Canon concludes:

While the racial divide in the United States is not so severe as racial or ethnic divisions in South Africa, the former Yugoslavia, India, or many other nations, American political scientists (and citizens) who are interested in helping bridge the racial divide can learn from the competitive experience. (Canon 1999, 373)

Karen M. Kaufmann treats the problem of inclusion in the context of Latino entry into the political arena. Her focus is on mass attitudes and the propensity of blacks and Latinos to build electoral coalitions. Using recent public opinion data, Kaufmann's research explores the levels of perceived commonality between blacks and Latinos and, in particular, it studies the process by which Latinos come to feel close to African-Americans. Her findings suggest that pan-Latino affinity is a robust predictor of Latino/black commonality, but that long-term Latino political acculturation, in its current form, is unlikely to result in particularly high levels of closeness to blacks.

The conclusion of the article points to the important role that Latino leadership and political organizations play in promoting strong pan-ethnic identities and suggests that the prospects for future coalitions between African-Americans and Latinos rest, in part, on the development of these more inclusive Latino orientations.

Bickford (1999, 86–108) seeks to merge pluralist theories of unequal groups and identity politics. The objective is to analyze "the institutional representation of disadvantaged groups." Bickford says theorists can neither treat group identity as fixed, nor dismiss "identity politics." She makes reference to Guinier's (1994) model as encouraging coalitions between groups, and as having the potential to engender citizen action beyond the electoral moment. Other approaches pertinent to inclusion, in their use of pluralism, include Bohman (1995), Keller (1988), Olson (1988), Fraga (1999), Kim and Lee (2001, 631–7), McClure (1990, 361–91), and Levite and Tarrow (1983).

Laura Scalia (1998, 49–376) offers a stimulating critique of the ideological basis of racial exclusion. She does so by examining a sample of state constitutional conventions held during the first half of the nineteenth century. The author focuses on speeches therein that deal with questions of who should participate in leader selection. Debates over how far to empower freemen of African descent verify recent studies which argue that ethnocentric language rationalized political exclusions. In debates over white empowerment, however, those arguing to restrict citizen privileges unequivocally used the language of liberalism to make their case. Nineteenth-century liberalism was not just the language of greater empowerment and inclusion. It was dynamic enough to serve as the language of exclusion as well.

Haggard and Kaufman (1997, 263–83) adapt Dankwart A. Rustow's emphasis on elite bargaining to offer a "theory of democratic transitions [that] focuses on the way economic performance affects constitutional rules, political alignments, and institutions." It can be extended to explain the policy challenges facing new democratic governments and the prospects for consolidation.

Ranki (1999) is one of the few authors to combine inclusion and exclusion in one analysis. What is impressive for its clue to deep research is the demonstration that inclusion is not, in and of itself, inherently irreversible. The conditions may have been special. But the phenomenon is that the Jewish population of Hungary had moved increasingly into a condition of inclusion and acceptance, then to the reversal and being ground up in the history of a brutal exclusion, near the end of a war, when it was no longer necessary for Hungary's rulers to do what they did.

4 DIFFERENT INSTITUTIONS DEAL DIFFERENTLY WITH INCLUSION/EXCLUSION

Comparable institutions do not necessarily deal with the problem of inclusion/exclusion in the same way, although under the logic of institutional analysis there should be similar outcomes. Parties, for example, do not welcome all voters, but only those voters whose attachments will not disturb their existing internal balance (Holden 1966.)

Some institutions are almost inherently exclusionary. The police and the military are both such, unless what they are to control has no distinction between the dominant and the subordinate parts of the population. But where ethnic diversity is a part of domination and subordination, ethnic difference is immediately apparent in the results of administrative practice. (Holden 1996, ch. 8).

There can, of course be institutions that operate at least some of the time on an inclusive basis. This was true, under one set of circumstances, when the Department of Justice began to make the legal argument for the equality of black persons and white persons under the United States Constitution (McMahon 2004). The same Department of Justice, in the same period of time, would not take action, requested by the War Department, against local law officials who victimized African-American soldiers in uniform (Gibson 2005, 200–1; and Novkov, email communication, October 14, 2005).

The design of the United States executive (the presidency) in theory, is to represent "the whole people," but after a vote there is no mechanism by which any interest that wants even to be "heard" can assure that it is "heard."

We postpone until below a closer analysis of two institutions (legislature and federalism) and two significant groups with whom the problem of getting to inclusion has already been faced. The legislature is the vehicle by which, in theory, everyone has some representative, at least if the design is right. But complete exclusion is when any group (or potential interest) has no actual standing in any institution in the legislature.

Congress is the means by which one group shields itself from the demands of the other that the lesser side can only wallow in discouragement or explode in rage. In short, the legislative process may become a form of dictatorship by group A over group B.

5   DOMINANT GROUPS AND SUBORDINATE GROUPS

The logic of power is that dominant groups respond to different new interests differently. It is logically possible, therefore, for "inside" groups to look at "outside" groups from one of the following perspectives:

1.   Dominant groups can be in a position where they can decide everything that is to be decided. The "others" are vassals or slaves over whom they can exercise prerogatives as they please.
2.   They can act as if they were "fiduciaries" and the "outside" groups were "wards" in whose best interest they should act.
3.   They could act as very strong allies (or even patrons), in aid of some client.
4.   They could adopt something like the same role in relation to an outside weak ally, from whose presence they need something besides moral verification.
5.   They could act as political entrepreneurs in search of new partners.
6.   Finally, they could act as trading partners, knowing that the others also have wide freedom, but with the aim of establishing continuing "special relationship" friendships, and comradeships that are not purely utilitarian. By the time that happens, inclusion is a fact.

Correlatively, the outside party must also see what role it is to adopt. Inclusion may also mean, even if one is not an exploitable resource, being a ward or client of someone more important. There is perhaps no distinction between the ward and the client except that the former is in a dependent (and protected) status with little effort to get there, whereas the client may be the person who has made some effort. Depending on the time or place, the individual who was neither a ward nor client, even in twentieth-century America, could have trouble being accepted.

Historically, there have been at least four major points of inclusion-and-exclusion. Class/caste divisions have expressed the predicate that some groups were entitled to rule, and would rule, and that was that. Caste politics is not irrelevant, but does not preclude some kind of overt political participation in the largest democracy in the world, India (Hasan, Sridharan, and Sudarshan 2005; Jain 1997, 198–208, Lijphart 1996, 258–68).

Class, at any rate, is not irrelevant and shows up in bold divisions between those who own and those who do not (Im 1987, 231–57). Religion has been the second big identifier of those who are "in" and those who are "out." It has been, and obviously remains, a profound source of social division. But such social division, in the countries to which political science has paid close attention, is not that of preemptory exclusion, but of a variety of forms of discrimination. There have been times, even in such a country as Canada, with its reputation for moderation, when religion combined with class made representative government inert (Gunn 1966, 185–6).

The criterion that, in principle, is easy to change, but can be highly exclusionary, is religion. The question is whether A is a member of a valid religious community is not made easier by the fact that, under the United States Constitution, Congress shall make no law respecting an establishment of religion. As of 1787, the principle did not extend to the states: "Maryland and Massachusetts required a belief in the Christian religion." The same source says "Georgia, New Hampshire, New Jersey, and North Carolina had Protestant tests." Delaware required "faith in God the Father, and in Jesus Christ, His only Son, and in the Holy Ghost, One God, blessed forever more"(Stokes and Pfeffer 1964, 37). It is obvious that such tests would have been either exclusionary or negated, by non-enforcement. Even if there are no formal legal tests, it is obvious that a variety of religious tests exist in civil society, and that Muslim populations especially have become the foci of extraordinarily intense issues.

6   THE LEGISLATIVE INSTITUTION

6.1   Two Cases of Inclusion-and-Exclusion and their Handling in Congress

There are innumerable cases of inclusion-and-exclusion in human history, including a large number in the contemporary world. Wherever there are situations of high exclusion, political scientists, from their own analytical first principles, must predict that a change from "outsider" status to some degree of inclusion will only come after a protracted struggle. But we first present an historically oriented account of two situations of high exclusion (gender, the status of women, and "race," or the status of persons of African ancestry in the United States).

The cases, though historically connected, are different in crucial ways. But they are analytically similar in that the leaders of each deemed it necessary to go well beyond ordinary boundaries for tactics of public relations and self-abnegation that elicited the horror and repulsion of other public elites (Clift 2003, 113–54).

6.2   Case 1: Gender—A Case of Delay and Fitful Inclusion

Chowdbury and Nelson say that "political systems, whatever the ideology, form, and mobilization capacity, rest on the virtual exclusion of women from formal politics" (Chowdbury and Nelson 1994, 15). This subject appears, in fact, both simple and at the same time complex. For present purposes, I ground myself in the review essay by Nancy Burns (2002, 462–87) which, in turn, is crucially grounded in work by Marianne Githens (1983) almost two decades earlier and by Virginia Sapiro (1983). "Gender is a repertoire of mechanisms that provide social interpretations of sex, that enable sex to structure people's lives" (Burns 2002, 463). It is (in Burns's formulation) a "principle of social organization [or] hierarchy" (Burns 2002, 464).

In most places in the world, until about 200 years ago, women as a group were distinctively subordinate. Moreover, the finding that one is obliged to draw from Chowbury and Nelson (1994), as cited, is that they are still so. Some anthropological and historical material dealing with gender roles, however, suggests a wider variety of conditions. Political scientists may need to be sure of the bases on which they are grounding analysis. In traditional Ashanti society, for example, while no equivalent notion of "democracy" existed, there still were well defined customary roles within which people acted. Autocracy was not the norm (Busia 1951); nor was straightforward female subordination. Among the Ashanti, there were times when the consent of "female monarch," translated as "queen-mother," was essential for legitimation.

In this matrilineal society, the queen-mother performed the function of deciding which young men were eligible for chieftaincy. And the queen-mother had the duty to advise the chief, and to offer reproof even beyond the advice of the chief's councilors. In the nineteenth century, something changed. What happened and why deserves study. At present, historical analysis does not appear to be an important ingredient in the political science scholarship on the status of women, any more than it is in most other aspects of political science. There is literature on argument and doctrine, and famous figures, as in the case of Mary Wollstonecraft (Sapiro 1992).

The nineteenth-century women's suffrage movement began with a commitment to social and philosophical radicalism. In the USA, Elizabeth Cady Stanton's overt rebellion against subordination was against her own subordination to men in

Abolitionist meetings. Over time, as women suffragists picked up other support, they also broadened their appeals.

For a time, the right to vote came to be defined as the crucial women's issue (Ostrogorski [1980] 1893). Why does an apparently settled pattern, of long duration, change? Ostrogorski (1980), writing in 1893, attributes it to the diffusion of "natural right" ideas from the French Revolution (1980, xii). Diffusion of ideas, public opinion clamor, and legislation follow: "In the politics of some countries the rights of women obtain, for the sake of the party game, something like a negotiable value on 'Change, they are quoted, they are speculated upon, some with hope, by others with dread of their coming before long to rule the market" (1980, xiii).

As with other groups, the women's rights leaders calculated the costs and benefits of alliances, especially those with other excluded populations. The language of rights for women had come into American speech as early as the late nineteenth century, as the much cited correspondence between John Quincy Adams and Abigail Adams serves to show. But women's suffrage as a social movement shows the adaptation of excluded groups, in this case women, to the norms and requirements of dominant groups. The women's suffrage movement came directly out of Abolitionism, with a rebellion against women's exclusion from meetings to decide what to do about slavery.

In this rebellion, the women suffragists had the symbolic support of Frederick Douglass. But as time passed, and suffrage came into more open and acceptable political discussion, suffragists did not further attach to their own cause the weakening political causes of black citizenship. At the beginning the twentieth century, Chapman Catt did not hesitate to move away from an anti-racism stance for example. And other women's rights leaders during that era cooperated with racism in the South.

Within twenty-five years of the time when Ostrogorski wrote, women's suffrage had come to Britain. The United States had the "Susan B. Anthony Amendment" on the national agenda. The political scientist P. Orman Ray could write of the extension of women's suffrage in a number of countries in Europe, the white countries of the British Empire, and the United States." Ray was too cautious to forecast "early ratification by the requisite number of States" (Ray 1919, 238). The Nineteenth Amendment was adopted in 1919 and ratified in 1920 (Brown 1995, 2175–204; Clift 2003, 155–80).

Thereafter, the logical questions concern other issues that are logically contingent. What happened with customary barriers to office holding, even though there were no formal-legal barriers to voting, once the Nineteenth Amendment was adopted? What have been the broad changes in social customs and in expanding the elite reservoir with regard to women? What has happened regarding changes in policy content on gender specific matters, or simply on those matters where women's attitudes differ broadly from those of men?

The Burns (2002) analysis is that political science analysis has oriented itself to sex differences and how they work in institutional settings (2002, 470), and to rules in institutions and how they affect what women do. In her view, political science has, on its agenda of unfinished work, a good deal on sex segregation of institutions and role differentiation, and what this does to constrain opportunities for women.

By Burns's account the existing literature deals largely with the women's movement as a movement grounded in prior networks (2002, 473). That literature is also oriented to the study of public opinion (2002, 476), and is (in her words) "consumed" by a focus on difference in the attitudes of men and women on a variety of subjects. (Pippa Norris 1997 presents further analysis and commentary consistent with the same point. Note especially Mills, in that volume, pp. 41–55.) Burns further reports that existing research has a strong focus on participation and civic engagement (2002, 479), with a variety of explanations for a lower level of participation by women, compared to men.

Finally, she sums up a variety of studies of women as policy-makers, which she distinctly refers to as "legislators." (For still newer material in twenty cases outside the United States, see Galligan and Tremblay 2005.) Most research focuses on two issues: What do women officeholders seek and change? Do they face discrimination in their office holding roles, compared to men in those roles?

These issues belong in the arena, for the most part, of what Chowdbury and Nelson (1994) characterize as women's exclusion from "formal politics." Their report is that, "At the end of 1990, only 6 of the 159 countries represented in the United Nations had women as chief executives. In nearly 100 countries men held all the senior and deputy ministerial positions in 1987–88" (Chowbury and Nelson 1994, 14).

While the questions can be asked on a worldwide basis, it appears that actual behavior being studied differs sharply between the United States and Europe, and the rest of the world. According to the literature, wide gaps appeared between women in the USA and Western Europe and women in Central and Eastern Europe with regard to the importance of a female demographic presence in government (Montgomery 2003, 1, 3). Moreover, once this is grasped, the new research, with a great deal of technical study of election systems, is about European countries, not about Russia or the other countries that emerged from the former Soviet Union.

Social rules about marriage, divorce, childbearing, childreading, whether to work for whom and on what terms, and about the inheritance, holding, use, and transfer of property are quite fundamental. In Lasswellian terms, these encompass welfare values (well-being, wealth, skill, and enlightenment) and deference values (being taken into consideration) (Lasswell and Kaplan 1963). On some of these underlying social rules (other than the abortion controversy) it seems that little appears frequently in the political science research about the United States or Europe.

These issues, however, have a different significance elsewhere. In Nigeria, women traders have had an independent role, and at least one contemporary writer has expressed the desire that women not lose the traditional spaces for their trading roles (Amadiume 2000). Reports on some of the Nigerian peoples (the Igbo) show female political roles in far more substantive and subtle ways. Whether to work, for whom, and on what terms has reportedly been demonstrated in the Nicaraguan revolutionary underground when a woman refused to do her squad leader's laundry. He prevailed upon her to do so, as it would embarrass him and undermine his persuasive authority with peasants if they saw him doing his own washing. But he never again asked (Luciak 2001, 19).

Mounira Charrad, a sociologist, reports on changes in, or the maintenance of, traditional family law, not so much as an outgrowth of women's issues per se, but for strategies of building state power (Charrad 2001, 237–8).

From the point of view of the politics of inclusion and exclusion, and of the role of institutions, it is intellectually imperative to seek a model that incorporates a broader stretch of history. In principle, it would be desirable to incorporate a broader stretch in the study of gender and politics. The existing literature does not support such an analysis. Thus, we return to the hypothesis that the counter-attack is in principle pertinent. It is not possible, on the basis of the existing literature, fully to accept this hypothesis, and it is surely not possible to disclaim it.

6.3   Case 2: African-Americans—The Hypothesis of the Counter-attack

It is possible to do a little better on the subject of the African-American population, to which we turn now. Discussion of the African-American case is warranted for two reasons. There is no advanced industrial democracy, except perhaps Australia with the Aborigines, in which inclusion and exclusion has had a more pronounced form. Yet the experience is also more complex than is generally understood by scholars or attentive lay persons. Political science, like political journalism, focuses upon the African-American civil rights movement in a quite concentrated period. Basically, it has built an image around the ten-year career of Martin Luther King, Jr., as a public figure. That is, from the Montgomery bus boycott of 1958 until his assassination in 1968. It especially focuses upon the seven years of greatest success, ending in the adoption of the Voting Rights Act of 1965. "We Shall Overcome" has become a global hymn.

The United States did not begin with a concept that made the institutionalized racism of the twentieth century a forgone conclusion. It is doubtful to say that "not only did the Declaration of Independence not include slaves but the Constitution recognized slavery" (Ranki 243, n. 1) There is no question that the United States was a slaveholding society (1789–1861) (Holden 1994, 2). But the same slaveholding society began with a system in which free African franchise existed and, in fact, was sometimes used, in which some held the expectation that slavery had been put on "the course of ultimate extinction," and would in due course come to argue that it was unconstitutional (Mellen 1973; Henry 1914). Congress reflected these interests around slaveholding, containing members both in favor of and averse to slaveholding. The very first Congress, elected in 1788, contained at least twenty members who had been in the Philadelphia Convention (Franklin 1995). These twenty equal half the number of the final Convention delegates. This first Congress "that did so much in setting precedents and patterns for the future and that defined who could become a citizen of the United States" and "*[n]ot one* raised any objection to barring free blacks from becoming naturalized citizens" (Franklin 1995, 12).

Those averse to the African-American interest were able to launch three major counter-attacks in the span of 200 years. The overall effect was to move from a modest possibility of institutional openness, in the very first Congress, to a period of institutional closure where slavery could not be the subject of a petition. But the struggle in shifting social demand brought a new openness in Congress just after the Civil War. That, in turn, was shut down by a tight institutional closure from around 1890 until the New Deal year, when openness returned.

Counter-attack 1 was a drastic assertion of the desirability of slavery as a form of organization. Some interests averse to slaveholding adopted the fiduciary posture. The very first interest group petition to the new Congress was that of the Quakers against slavery (diGiacomantonio 1995, 169–97). They acted on the doctrine that Africans, like others in the United States, were presumed entitled to freedom. Some constitutional ratifiers had deemed slavery an unfortunate exception to be attenuated by time and law (Elliot's Debates). Congress came to a major forum in which these issues were expounded, and a major arena in which they were fought.

This was the first of a set of petitions for the abolition of slavery and/or the slave trade. The Congressional committee reported that from the nature of the matters contained in those memorials (petitions from the Quakers) they (the committee) were induced to examine the powers vested in Congress, under the present constitution (H. Doc. #13, *Abolition of Slavery*, March 5, 1790, 12) to the abolition of slavery. The report is written as if to an audience that could plausibly contemplate the abolition of slavery. The report took note that the Constitution provided that importation of slaves could not be prohibited before 1808. "Congress, by a fair construction of the constitution, are equally restrained from interfering in the emancipation of slaves who already are within any of the . . . States."

Political learning took place at once. The fiduciaries (Quakers) learned that Congress could only debate restrictions on how the slave trade was conducted. The Quakers persisted in their interest, some of them some petitioning Congress to adopt a law "prohibiting the trade carried on by citizens of the United States, for the purpose of supplying slaves to foreign nations, and to prevent foreigners from fitting out vessels of the slave trade in the ports of the United States" (US Congress, House Document 44, February 11, 1794). The fiduciary interventions were futile, except in as much as they played a similar role as theatrical shows that might influence, or even generate, public opinion. Weak interests, represented only by fiduciaries, would fall before strong interests, at least in the near term. The fiduciaries lost. Their effort anticipated the struggle over "the gag rule," which addressed whether Congress could even receive a petition on the subject of slavery. The fight against the gag rule is famous. The leading protagonist of this struggle was the former president and then member of the House of Representatives John Quincy Adams (Miller 1996).

After the Civil War, the Union-maintaining and power-seeking Republicans found it imperative to extend the franchise to the freed Africans. This set the terms for the second counter-attack.

Counter-attack 2, in the last quarter of the century, *was substantially successful in limiting the effect of the Civil War.* It led to the establishment of white supremacy as public policy that Congress would accept as fact. In the end, those who wanted to defend the freed slaves' franchise, as a means of defending both the Republican party and the Union, could not win. The Civil War Amendments were accepted as verbal formalities. Federal armed force was not used to any notable degree. Those private persons who wished by force to exclude blacks were free to do so. This implicates federalism.

The experience of these sixty-odd years was the reopening of the question of white supremacy—and the cognate question of blacks' rights in the late 1920s and early 1930s. The concept, but not the actual policy, of acceptance of white supremacy was overthrown in the 1950s. White supremacy as policy was rejected by Congress in the 1960s.

When African-Americans began to arrive in Congress, the question of their access to privileges was apparently problematic. There were but two Congresses (the 46th Congress, convening in 1881, and the 50th Congress, convening in 1889) between 1869 and 1901 when there were no African-American members at all. The question of their own access to privilege was also necessarily a question about their ability to provide effective representation.

Government was divided for most of the time between the end of the Civil War and the beginning of the twentieth century. The last notable effort directly to protect the franchise was the Federal Elections Bill of 1890, a bill similar in concept to the Voting Rights Act of 1965. The defeat of this bill should probably be accounted one of the major events of the decade. Divided government plus an

American *violencia* resulted in a victory, in Congress and outside, that could be seen by 1890. It was fully consolidated by the first decade of the twentieth century. The legislative institution was white supremacy's stronghold.

A challenge to white supremacy would be forthcoming, but not its overthrow. This would not happen for more than seventy years until the mid 1960s. Challenges began after 1934 through the imperatives of another institution, the political party. 1934 was the first year that African-Americans in the North, who could vote, began to switch to the Democrats. African-Americans in the South could generally still not vote. In 1935, evidence of these realigning effects among voting African-Americans began to be visible. A large number of anti-lynching bills were suddenly being introduced in the Congress. Northern Democrats, for the first time, sponsored bills to protect African-Americans from abuses and from persecution.

Racial exclusion began to be challenged by racial inclusion issues, restated as "civil rights." The "civil rights issue" was, by 1948, admitted to be vital in Democratic presidential politics. However, it would be another sixteen years (1964) before Congress passed the Civil Rights Act.

The absolutely predictable Southern Democratic filibuster could never be broken, except with Republican cooperation. Republican cooperation, within the convoluted world of political maneuver, was possible. But the principle of the counter-attack is always in play, unless the issues are subject to resolution in civil society. The counter-attack will make use of institutional procedures when these are both available and favorable and seek to circumvent institutions when they are not. The civil rights movement in the United States made ample use of both strategies—peaceful but extra-institutional demonstrations and sit-ins when excluded from institutional possibilities and the use of the judicial system as a way to break through the political logjam.

Counter-attack 3 emerged as civil rights issues were concerned, those issues served as a wedge between Northern Democrats who favored legislation and Southern Democrats to whom it was absolutely unacceptable. The Goldwater campaign was the vehicle by which active racism in the South expressed itself. A recent historian, in a rather full biography, refers to Goldwater's consistent advocacy of conservative principles. "Ignoring power realities in the South and remaining consistent with his states' rights stand, Goldwater deemed segregation a problem best handled at the community level" (Goldberg 1995, 140). Goldwater could not have been so far removed from reality as to know what handling at the "community level" meant in a world of violence against African-Americans and those supporting their cause.

Goldwater, more than George Wallace, who in old age recanted his earlier politics, made the Republican Party the party of the self-conscious *white* voters in the Deep South. Economic change is a powerful component, but without the racial struggle, the Republican domination of Southern politics would never have occurred.

7   THE INSTITUTION OF FEDERALISM

Institutional closure may also present itself in the case of federalism. Federalism in the United States is often discussed as if the preservation of "the states" or the protection of state authority had some obvious theoretical merit. It is also sometimes discussed as if the preservation of state authority was always among the principal aims of the writers of the 1787 Constitution. Federalism is often discussed as if there were some objective and meritorious principle of freedom that justifies it. It is also discussed if there were some efficiency principle, under which some things, inherently "appropriate" to state jurisdiction, are left to state governments. The historical evidence contradicts this view and does not serve to sustain this pristine version of principled motivation for the institutions of federalism and state prerogative.

In 1787 Virginia was the largest state. The Virginia delegation went to the 1787 Constitutional Convention with a plan for a unicameral federal legislature, with strong authority over the states (Robertson 2005, 243–67; Brant 1950). Viewed from another angle, this is not a surprise. In reality, federalism is a system of power typically predicated—as all systems of power are—on serving or accommodating particular interests—or, in other words, keeping some people in and others out (Riker 1964, 10).

There can be many results attributable to federal systems. One clear consequence of federalism in the United States, though, was that blacks were a subject population under the rule of the states. Insofar as the African-American experience is concerned, states were primarily constellations of interests based upon the exploitation of the Africans. African-Americans were always losers under the rules of that system. Federalism as a constitutional process allowed the groups within state politics to do to other groups whatever they pleased, with very little limitation. Federalism was, in practice, an institutional arrangement that made the United States safe for chattel slavery.

In the contemporary United States, there are large experiential tests to be met. What is the meaning of the election of L. Douglas Wilder, an African-American politician, as Governor of Virginia? In what sense is voting still so racially polarized that most African-American candidates would lose if most of the voters are white? A social scientist can extend this question with other questions about representation, namely African-American representation in governors' cabinets, among senior civil servants, on courts, and in local government offices.

By the 1990s African-American representation in local government had grown substantially. But the capacity of many of those governments had become problematic and are recurrently so. Where African-American politicians have risen to top political leadership positions in local politics, they are often in command of an empty vessel—cities and other local governments that are short on investment capital, weak in their tax base, and faced with problems of poverty, poor educational systems, and higher crime rates. Such problems may be local, but they can rarely be solved locally. The irony is that inclusion of African-Americans in the elite reservoir grows, especially if they do not have to seek office where constituencies are predominantly white. Persons of color may enter in other ways—appointive and bureaucratic offices, for instance—while social marginalization of African-Americans may be relatively unaffected.

8   PREMISES ABOUT THE PROCESS OF INCLUSION

What kind of claim are those seeking inclusion making? What claims are being made? One form of claim is the assertion of some legal right. The claim of legal right may be highly effective in situations where the norms of "right," both legal and moral, are generally accepted. Such claims were staked by African-Americans through the judicial system by the 1940s. These claims against the segregationist system played an increasingly large role in the articulation of claims that the civil rights movement of the 1950s and 1960s could make to white audiences.

The actor seeking inclusion can also be in the position of being a claimant of rectitude. One may perfectly well perceive that one lacks power, but seek to influence some other audience by asserting oneself as the moral conscience, thus claiming moral rectitude and embarrassing the other party on the assumption that he or she also has a public need to display evidence of a moral conscience to which an appeal is possible. Violence toward, and even murders of, African-American civil rights activists galvanized support among some whites on the basis of moral claims, making the civil rights struggle a moral as well as a legal cause.

A third claim is that attention to one's own need fits the interest of the other party, notably its financial interest, although some other political interest is also plausible. This can be connected to a kind of "fact of life" claim, such as when actor X seeks to communicate to actor Y that X's presence is a "fact of life" which it is inconvenient to ignore. The revolt against "back of the bus" segregated seating (or, more often, standing) brought the power of the purse to bear in the bus boycott in Montgomery, Alabama in 1955, an event made famous by Rosa Parks who would not concede the necessity of her standing in the back of the bus while seats were available in the front. The purpose of the boycott was to bring financial pressure against the bus company as was the objective of other commercial boycotts against those businesses that maintained patterns of segregation or discriminated in their workforce. Legality, morality, and mutual self-interest are all strategies in the struggle for inclusion.

9   INSTITUTIONS AND THE PROBLEM OF EXCLUSION

No serious empirical theory of politics can work on the assumption that what democratic liberals take as normatively desirable is what will always occur. That recognition is inherent in the hypothesis of the counter-attack. What degree of exclusion is possible and/or probable? There is prevention of entry, where the elite can say "you may not come in." In principle there can be some kind of conditional admission, with restrictions as to what kind of life can be lived, work be done, and so forth. Exclusion is, by definition, unseemly for political scientists who study "democracy," "liberalism," or "constitutionalism." Nonetheless, students of political science cannot escape the question of exclusion as an ever-present possibility.

Expulsion, too, is an ever-present possibility. Extermination is one of the forms of expulsion, and is so utterly repellent that we have no way of comprehending it. The ultimate objects may be people who have already been incorporated, and now are excluded. Extermination has been invoked verbally, and sometimes in actual practice, in the United States and in Australia, against the Native Americans and the Aborigines respectively. The folklore that "the only good Indian is a dead Indian" was not for the movies only, but was sometimes expressed in tactics of extermination.

Peter J. G. Pulzer makes the case that anti-Semitism reached its most virulent intensity after a great deal of emancipation had taken place for Jews. German Jews were a highly cultivated population. In the twentieth century, Jews had come far from old restrictions, to the point that Walther Rathenau was Foreign Minister at his assassination in 1922.

Both the Holocaust and the massive killings that took place in eastern Africa in 1994 would fit the pattern of expulsion via extermination. So would the efforts at "ethnic cleansing" in the Balkans. In parallel, the savage interethnic slaughter in Rwanda by some Hutu factions against Tutsis was one of killings amongst groups, the members of which were intermarried with each other.

In general terms, it is possible to identify the most significant criteria of exclusion. Those to be excluded from "the people" are those who are considered repulsive for what they do, have done, or would do, of their own will, which they could choose to alter if they were perceived to be morally fit to do so. Sex offenders under contemporary American criminal law are so regarded even when they return to civil society. They are, in essence, branded with a scarlet letter as morally unfit. Some expulsions and exterminations, however, are also predicated on physical differences about which nothing can be done. Moral deficiencies and other frequently fatal shortcomings are then postulated as derivative qualities of physical difference. Such was, but hardly exclusively, the basis of the virulently racist Nazi ideology.

When the American Revolutionary War occurred, a substantial share of the population remained attached to the Crown, for emotional reasons or practical ones. New York was a center of loyalism, as was South Carolina (Wertenbaker 1948). Overall, 15 per cent of the whole American population at the time refused to accept the independence movement (Elster 2004, 51). They were thus obliged to leave for Canada or other parts of the British Empire.

9.1   Looking Forward

If we begin with the Hobbesian problem as stated, and with the core concept that institutions are inherently exclusionary, our approach to institutions is somewhat that of oncologists to the human body. Analytically, we are aware of danger and seek to increase the opportunities of hope. Thus, we identify three big remaining issues which concern learning enough to improve the making and maintaining of commonwealths.

9.1.1   *Intellectual Problem 1*

The disappearance or reduction of exclusion as a general proposition is itself worthy of serious study. That disappearance or reduction in America is known by the term "melting pot." But it is virtually a cliché. It is well known that identification as a Roman Catholic was a barrier to voters' acceptance of a presidential candidate until 1960. It is hard now to make the case of serious discrimination, and surely not of exclusion, for either Catholics or Jews in the United States.

What meaning should be attached to the presence of a Jewish leader of the British Tory party (Michael Howard) is also a matter of interest as is that of a female Chancellor in Germany, a system in which women are notoriously underrepresented in the elite reservoir. From the point view of theory, how, in fact, does substantial change take place?

9.1.2 *Intellectual Problem 2*

Where do criteria of inclusion and exclusion offer big challenges to the making and maintaining of commonwealths in this, the twenty-first, century?

Consider religion. Norris and Inglehart (2004) offer a worldwide study of religion and politics filled with quantitative data. Their findings run contrary to the Huntington thesis. There were no significant differences between the publics living in the West and in Muslim religious cultures in their approval of how democracy works in practice, their support of democratic ideals, and their approval of strong leadership (Norris and Inglehart 2004, 146).

Why then is religion regarded as a centerpiece for inclusion and exclusion? It is less likely that the type of religion is at issue than the form in which any given one is practiced, probably one reason why an aggregate measure of religion at the societal level will not yield much about political cultural differences. Religion becomes a centerpiece when it is linked with other cultural or class attributes, when its practitioners are stereotyped, when it appears exotic against a host culture, and when there is theological or quasi-theological rule that does not accept religious pluralism.

The case of the rapid pace at which the barriers against women seem to be collapsing is worthy of close study, for it is not obvious why it has happened that way. At the same time, there are no factors that one can foresee that would reverse what is occurring. The significant question concerns the future of gender relations in the world.

9.1.3 *Intellectual Problem 3*

What should be anticipated, given that growing diversity of populations in the rest of the world is a most important phenomenon. Immigration in the United States—as most elsewhere—historically has been good for buyers in labor markets. It has been less good for populations disproportionately located toward the bottom of the social stratification system where most of the immigrants compete in the labor market.

While immigration involves peoples from around the world and penetrates different sectors of the labor market, a substantial change can occur in the relative proportion and historical experiences of minorities in the United States. This has happened before. As a matter of policy, in the late eighteenth century, the desire to attract European settlers was partly to offset dependence on the black slave population.

A similar dynamic was presented in the large post-Civil War European migration into the United States. It repeats itself in the movement of the Spanish-speaking people. This Hispanic population is very diverse. It sometimes racially overlapped with the African-American population. But it is already regarded as the single largest ethnic group of color.

It may be that these two groups will form alliances. It is also plausible that they may be in contest with one another, especially in jockeying for position within the elite reservoir just as earlier European-derived ethnic groups—such as the Irish and Italians—had been. Under what circumstances will institutions conduce to cooperation or to conflict? And to what extent will labor markets as well as laws and increasingly norms, encouraging diversity, allow for positive-sum or zero-sum relations between them?

Students of politics may take note that what is happening in the United States has its counterparts in other immigrant-receiving countries. Inclusion/exclusion for any group was seldom to be taken for granted, as derived from social and cultural habits only. Inclusion/exclusion was also embedded into law, politics, and institutional practice. In Europe, there appears to be a growing cultural divide between Europeans and immigrant populations, particularly those from Muslim countries. To what extent will inclusion be possible and on what terms? To what extent will exclusion and even expulsion be sought? And, if sought, will it be selective or non-selective? To what extent will communal autonomy result in the abrogation of rights, especially women in patriarchal communities, as it did people of African descent under American federalism? To what extent will homogenizing secular policies and institutions (French centralism and secularism, for example) fuel communal resentments or, alternatively, force sectarianism to come to terms with civil law and the secular state, or even force civil law and the secular state to come to terms with deviant practice that it has hitherto been able to contain?

There are no certain answers, but instead many challenges. In such a country as France, for instance, will strategies of forced assimilation or communal accommodation work best? What precisely are the boundaries between social pluralism and the sovereign authority of the state? The liberal democratic view is that negotiating civic peace and inclusion in increasingly diverse settings is the fundamental democratic challenge to which the polity should rise. Karl W. Deutsch (1957) approached the same analytical problem in a study of the historical experience of the integration of countries in the North Atlantic. As he looked at the historical data, Deutsch thought he could analytically reconstruct the conditions for failure. They included, at least, a combination of greater activity by those who had been passive, an increase in ethnic and linguistic differentiation, a reduction in capacity for timely governmental action, and closure of the existing elites. Deutsch (1957) also thought he could see some conditions that were favorable. Among these were: capabilities that allowed each to do something for the other, compatibility of expectations, and mutual predictability and reciprocity in respect.

Are institutions part of the solution or part of the problem? If the hints drawn from Deutsch (which could be restated in Lasswellian deference and welfare terms) are taken seriously, institutions are not irrelevant. The political scientist, coming into that tradition, is likely to say "How we can all get along—whether we wish to or not—is, as Thomas Hobbes observed in rather different language, the fundamental task of political authority, however that authority is imposed."

But no particular form of institution, in and of itself, guarantees reciprocal adjustment. For students of institutions, this poses the particularly difficult challenge of knowing what adaptations may be helpful. Even more, it poses the difficult challenge of learning what incentives give conflicting parties the motivation to make institutions work rather than to pile up future trouble by ignoring the realities around them. There, finally, the point with which one begins. The liberal democratic motives are not the only ones driving action, and institutions may have values built up in that call for closure rather than inclusion. It is not intellectually useful to assume that the normatively-desired conclusion will be the empirically-attainable result. Ascertaining the greater likelihood is the task of a political science.

References

AMADIUME, I. 2000. *Daughters of the Goddess, Daughters of Imperialism: African Women Struggle for Culure, Power, and Democracy.* London: Zed.

AMORETTI, U. M. 2004. Introduction. In *Federalism and Territorial Cleavages*, ed. U. M. Amoretti and N. Bermeo. Baltimore: Johns Hopkins University Press.

BICKFORD, S. 1999. Reconfiguring pluralism: identity and institutions in the inegalitarian polity. *American Journal of Political Science*, 43 (1): 86–108.

BOHMAN, J. 1995. Public reason and cultural pluralism: political liberalism and the problem of moral conflict. *Political Theory*, 23 (2): 253–79.

BOUTWELL, G. 1867. *Speeches and Papers Relating to the Rebellion and the Overthrow of Slavery.* Boston: Little, Brown.

BRANT, I. 1950. *James Madison: Father of the Constitution, 1787–1800.* Indianapolis: Bobbs-Merrill.

BROWN, T. H. 1995. Boutwell, George, S. In *The Encyclopedia of the United States Congress*, vol. 1, ed. D. C. Bacon, R. H. Davidson, and M. Keller. New York: Simon and Schuster.

BURNS, N. 2002. Gender, public opinion, and political action. In *Political Science: The State of the Discipline*, ed. I. Katznelson and H. V. Milner. New York: W. W. Norton.

BUSIA, K. A. 1951. *The Position of the Chief in the Modern Political System of Ashanti: A Study of the Influence of Contemporary Social Changes on Ashanti Political Institutions.* London: Oxford University Press for the International African Institute.

CANON, D. T. 1999. Electoral systems and the representation of minority interests in legislatures. *Legislative Studies Quarterly*, 24 (3): 331–84.

CHARRAD, M. M. 2001. *States and Women's Rights: The Making of Post-Colonial Tunisia, Algeria, and Morocco.* Berkeley: University of California Press.

CHOWDBURY, N. and NELSON, B. J., with K. A. CARVER, N. J. JOHNSON, and P. L. O'LOUGHLIN. 1994. Redefining politics: patterns of women's political engagement from a global perspective. In *Women and Politics Worldwide*, ed. B. J. Nelson and N. Chowdbury. New Haven, Conn.: Yale University Press.

CLIFT, E. 2003. *Founding Sisters and the Nineteenth Amendment.* New York: John Wiley & Sons, Inc.

COLEMAN, K. 2001. Women's electoral participation and representation in elective office. In *Women and Women's Issues in Congress: 1832–2000*, ed. J. V. Lewis. Huntington, NY: Nova Science.

DAHL, R. A. 1998. *On Democracy*. New Haven, Conn.: Yale University Press.

—— 2005. What political institutions does large-scale democracy require? *Political Science Quarterly*, 120 (1): 187–97.

DEUTSCH, K. W. 1957. *Political Community and the North Atlantic Area*. Princeton, NJ: Princeton University Press.

DIGIACOMANTONIO, W. 1995. "For the gratification of a volunteering society." Antislavery pressure group politics in the first federal Congress. *Journal of the Early Republic*, 13: 169–97.

DRYZEK, J. S. 1996. Political inclusion and the dynamics of democratization. *American Political Science Review*, 90 (3): 475–87.

ELLIOTS DEBATES. 1937. Available at: http://www.memory.loc.gov/ammem/1wed.html.

ELSTER, J. 2004. *Closing the Books: Transnational Justice in Historical Perspective*. New York: Cambridge University Press.

FOX, D. R. 1917. The negro vote in old New York. *Political Science Quarterly*, 32 (2): 252–75.

FRAGA, L. R. 1999. Review of *Morning Glories: Municipal Reform in the Southwest*, by Amy Bridges. *American Political Science Review*, 93 (3): 710.

FRANKLIN, J. H. 1995. Race and the constitution in the nineteenth century. In *African Americans and the Living Constitution*, ed. J. H. Franklin and G. R. McNeill. Washington, DC: Smithsonian Institution Press.

GALLIGAN, Y. and TREMBLAY, M. 2005. *Sharing Power*: Women, Parliament, Democracy. Aldershot, Hants: Ashgate.

GIBSON, T. K., Jr., with HUNTLEY, S. 2005. *Knocking Down Barriers: My Fight for Black America*. Evanston; Ill.: Northwestern University Press.

GITHENS, M. 1983. The elusive paradigm, gender, politics, and behavior: the state of the art. In *Political Science: The State of the Discipline*, ed. A. Finifter. Washington, DC: American Political Science Association.

GOLDBERG, R. A. 1995. *Barry Goldwater*. New Haven, Conn.: Yale University Press.

GOLDEN, M. 1986. Interest representation, party systems, and the state: Italy in comparative perspective. *Comparative Politics*, 18 (3): 279–301.

GROFMAN, B. 2005. Race and redistricting in the twenty-first century. Pp. 255–301 in *Diversity in Democracy: Minority Representation in the United States*, ed. G. M. Segura and S. Bowler. Charlottesville: University Press of Virginia.

GUINIER, L. 1994. *The Tyranny of the Majority: Fundamental Fairness in Representative Democracy*. New York: The Free Press.

GUNN, G. E. 1966. *The Political History of Newfoundland, 1832–1864*. Toronto: University of Toronto Press.

HASAN, Z., SRIDHARAN, E., and SUDARSHAN, R. (eds.) 2005. *India's Living Constitution: Ideas, Practices, Controversies*. London: Anthem Press.

HENRY, H. M. 1914. *Police Control Over the Slave in South Carolina*, Emory, Va.: n.p.

HOBBES, T. [1651] 1991. *The Leviathan*, ed. R. W. Tuck. Cambridge: Cambridge University Press.

HOLDEN, M., Jr. (ed.) 1994. *The Challenge to Racial Stratification (National Political Science Review)*, vol. 4. Somerset, NJ: Transaction.

—— 1996. *Continuity & Disruption: Essays in Public Administration*. Pittsburgh: University of Pittsburgh Press.

HOLZER, T., SCHNEIDER, G., and WIDMER, T. 2000. Discriminating decentralization: federalism and the handling of asylum applications in Switzerland, 1938–1996. *Journal of Conflict Resolution,* 44 (2): 250–76.

IM, H. B. 1987. The rise of bureaucratic authoritarianism in South Korea. *World Politics,* 39 (2): 231–57.

JAIN, R. B. 1997. Surviving the odds in the case of Indian democracy. In *Institutions and Democratic Statecraft,* ed. M. Heper, A. Kazancigil, and B. A. Rockman. Boulder, Colo.: Westview Press.

KAUFMANN, K. M. 2003. Cracks in the rainbow: group commonality as a basis for Latino and African-American political coalitions. *Political Research Quarterly,* 56 (2): 199–210.

KELLER, E. J. 1988. Review of *Black Political Mobilization: Leadership, Power, and Mass Behavior 1 Whose Votes Count? Affirmative Action and Minority Voting Rights,* by Minion K. C. Morrison. *American Political Science Review,* 82 (4): 1381–2.

KELLOGG, C. F. 1967. *NAACP.* Baltimore: Johns Hopkins University Press.

KIM, C. J. and LEE, T. 2001. Interracial politics: Asian Americans and other communities of color. *Political Science and Politics,* 34: 631–7.

LASSWELL, H. D. and KAPLAN, A. [1950] 1963. *Power and Society: A Framework for Inquiry.* New Haven, Conn.: Yale University Press.

LEVITE, A. and TARROW, S. 1983. The legitimation of excluded parties in dominant party systems: a comparison of Israel and Italy. *Comparative Politics,* 15 (3): 295–327.

LIJPHART, A. 1996. The puzzle of Indian democracy: a consociational interpretation. *American Political Science Review,* 90 (2): 252–68.

LUCIAK, I. A. 2001. *After the Revolution: Gender and Democracy in El Salvador, Nicaragua, and Guatemala.* Baltimore: Johns Hopkins University Press.

McCLURE, K. M. 1990. Difference, diversity, and the limits of toleration. *Political Theory,* 18 (3): 361–91.

MATLAND, R. E. and MONTGOMERY, K. A. 2003. *Women's Access to Political Power in Post-Communist Europe.* New York: Oxford University Press.

MELLEN, G. W. F. [1844] 1973. *An Argument on the Unconstitutionality of Slavery, Embracing an Abstract of the Proceedings of the National and State Conventions on This Subject.* New York: AMS Press.

McMAHON, K. J. 2004. *Reconsidering Roosevelt on Race: How the Presidency paved the road to Brown.* Chicago: Chicago University Press.

MILLER, W. L. 1996. *Arguing About Slavery: The Great Battles in the United States Congress.* New York: Alfred A. Knopf.

MILLS, K. 1997. What differences do women journalists make? In *Women, Media, and Politics,* ed. P. Norris. New York: Oxford University Press.

MONTGOMERY, K. A. 2003. Introduction. In *Women's Access to Political Power in Post-Communist Europe,* ed. R. E. Matland and K. A. Montgomery. New York: Oxford University Press.

NORRIS, P. (ed.) 1997. *Women, Media, and Politics.* New York: Oxford University Press.

—— and INGLEHART, R. 2004. *Sacred and Secular: Religion and Politics Worldwide.* New York: Cambridge University Press.

NOVKOV, J. 2005. Email communication with Matthew Holden, Jr., October 14, 2005, retained for evidentiary purposes in files of Matthew Holden, Jr.

OLSON, D. J. 1988. Review of *Race and Ethnicity in Chicago Politics: A Reexamination of Pluralist Theory,* by Dianne M. Pinderhughes. *American Political Science Review,* 82 (4): 1382–3.

OSTROGORSKI, M. 1980. *The Rights of Women: A Comparative Study in History and Legislation.* Philadelphia: Porcupine Press; repr. of 1893 edn.

POWER, T. J. and ROBERTS, J. T. 1995. Compulsory voting, invalid ballots, and abstention in Brazil. *Political Research Quarterly,* 48 (4): 795–826.

RANKI, V. 1999. *The Politics of Inclusion and Exclusion: Jews and Nationalism in Hungary.* New York: Harper & Row.

RAY, P. O. 1919. The world-wide woman suffrage movement. *Journal of Comparative Legislation and International Law,* 1 (3): 220–38.

RIKER, W. H. 1964. *Federalism: Origin, Operation, Significance.* Boston: Little, Brown.

ROBERTSON, D. B. 2005. Madison's opponents and constitutional design. *American Political Science Review,* 99 (2): 225–43.

SAPIRO, V. 1983. *The Political Integration of Women.* Urbana: University of Illinois Press.

—— 1992. *A Vindication of Political Virtue: The Political Theory of Mary Wollstonecraft.* Chicago: University of Chicago Press.

SCALIA, L. J. 1998. Who deserves political influence? How liberal ideals helped justify mid nineteenth century exclusionary policies. *American Journal of Political Science,* 42 (2): 339–76.

SCHLOSBERG, D. 1998. Resurrecting the pluralist universe. *Political Research Quarterly,* 51 (3): 583–615.

SELZNICK, P. 1967. *Leadership in Administration.* Evanston, Ill.: Row, Peterson.

STOKES, A. P. and PFEFFER, L. 1964. *Church and State in the United States.* Revised one-volume edn. New York: Harper & Row.

SWAIN, C. M. 1995. *Black Faces, Black Interests: The Representation of African Americans in Congress.* Cambridge, Mass.: Harvard University Press.

U. S. HOUSE OF REPRESENTATIVES 1790. 1st Congress. 2nd Session. H. Doc. 413, *Abolition of Slavery,* March ~H, 1790, 12.

—— 1794. 3rd Congress. 1st Session. H. Doc. 44, Slave Trade. Communicated to the House of Representatives, February 11.

U. S. NATIONAL COMMISSION ON TERRORIST ATTACKS UPON THE UNITED STATES 2004. *The 9/11 Commission Report: Final Report of the National Commission on Terrorist Attacks Upon the United States.* Authorized edition. New York: W. W. Norton.

WEAVER, R. K. 2004. Electoral rules and party systems in federations. In *Federalism and Territorial Cleavages,* ed. U. M. Amoretti and N. Bermeo. Baltimore: Johns Hopkins University Press.

WERTENBAKER, T. J. 1948. *Father Knickerbocker Rebels: New York City During the Revolution.* New York: Charles Scribner's Sons.

WHITBY, K. J. 1997. *The Color of Representation: Congressional Behavior and Black Interests.* Ann Arbor: University of Michigan Press.

WOHLSTETTER, R. 1962. *Pearl Harbor: Warning and Decision.* Stanford, Calif.: Stanford University Press.

CHAPTER 11

ANALYZING CONSTITUTIONS

PETER M. SHANE

Constitutions, written or unwritten, are sets of rules, practices, and customs that polities regard as their fundamental law (DeSmith and Brazier 1989, 3–4). In modern form, they typically aspire to constrain government power, assure adherence to the rule of law, and protect individual rights (Rosenfeld 1994, 3). As such, they fit Douglass North's conception of an institution as a socially imposed constraint or set of constraints upon human behavior (North 1990, 3). Of course, in their variety and significance, they pose questions of obvious interest to political scientists, sociologists, and legal scholars. Some of these questions are comparative in nature: Why do different constitutions take the different forms they do? What political or other differences do distinctions in constitutional form and substance actually make (e.g. Sartori 1994)? Other questions can be sensibly asked with regard to constitutions in general or particular constitutions as they operate in particular societies: What are the social and political functions of a constitution? Through what social and political processes are the provisions of a constitution actually translated into meaningful constraints or authorities? This chapter offers a perspective on constitutional analysis that examines these latter questions, largely through an American lens.

Because constitutions, written or unwritten, can be given operational meaning only through the workings of other political institutions, any analysis of how constitutions shape and facilitate human interaction must necessarily be complex. In the United States, it is impossible to speak sensibly of "what the Constitution does" without reference to its invocation and use by the three branches of federal and state governments, as well as by local political entities and even by the organizations of civil society. This fact, however, entails an additional complexity. The primary human activity through which constitutions are translated into operational authorizations or constraints is *interpretation*. Yet, the available research on constitutional interpretation—most of which focuses on the operation of constitutional interpretation in the United States Supreme Court—tends to fall into two very disparate perspectives on the nature of the interpretive enterprise.

The two distinct views may helpfully be referred to "internal" and "external" (Feldman 2005, 89–90). According to the "internal view," what legal materials say—that is, the history and wording of constitutions, statutes, prior judicial opinions, and so on—significantly determines how they are interpreted. Under this view, when lawyers and judges give operational meaning to constitutions, statutes, and legal precedents, they are meaningfully limited by what can logically be deduced from the rules and principles that emanate from such legal materials (Feldman 2005). Although there is probably no one who thinks that those limits offer a complete explanation for all of the behavior of all legal actors, it is a premise of most modern legal scholarship that the internal view is, to some significant degree, well-founded.

In contrast, according to the external view, what governs the behavior of legal actors are stimuli external to the legal materials themselves (Feldman 2005). Chief among them are the actors' political orientations, namely, preferences or ideologies that, depending on the model, may follow from any number of causes—economic or political self-interest being the most obvious (Segal and Spaeth 1993, 64–9). This is undoubtedly the predominant view among political scientists (Feldman 2005, 90). One meta-analysis of over eighty papers has found a robust association between judicial decisions and judicial political attitudes across legal issues, court systems, and statistical method of analysis (Pinello 1999). Thus, in the external view, what a judge decides may be rationalized in the language of law, but it is not the law that produces outcomes, but other sources of judicial attitude.

An accurate picture almost certainly requires a perspective that draws on both these views. A significant ongoing project among legal researchers is the attempt to produce an "internal" view that affords room for legal actors to involve their personal political and moral values in an appropriately channeled and therefore legitimate manner in constitutional interpretation (e.g. Feldman 2005; Dworkin 1996). Among political scientists, perhaps the most exciting new development is the "new institutionalism," an effort to show how the attitudes of legal actors, especially judges, are shaped not only by individual preference, but also by the institutions through which these actors operate and the relationship of those institutions to others. Leading writers in this vein include Cornell Clayton, Howard Gillman, Mark Graber, Rogers Smith, and Keith Whittington (Gillman 1993; Gillman and Clayton 1999; Graber 2002; Smith 1988; Whittington 2000).

These complementary lines of analysis reflect an admirable effort to get beyond reductionist models of law that either treat legal interpretation as implausibly objective and mechanical or reduce law to something merely obfuscatory or "epiphenomenal" (Feldman 2005, 92).

1   THE STATUS AND FUNCTION OF CONSTITUTIONS

In the American public law system, a constitution is invariably fundamental in the sense that a government act undertaken pursuant to a state or federal constitution is expected to conform to its requirements and limitations. Since the revolutionary period, this essential characteristic of American constitutions, both state and federal, has been regarded as flowing inexorably from their written character.[1] Other systems, most notably that of Great Britain, may feature a constitutional doctrine of parliamentary supremacy, in which the constitution imposes no more than theoretical limits on legislative acts (DeSmith and Brazier 1989, 15). Even in such systems, however, courts may presume an ordinary parliamentary intention not to depart from the constitution, written or unwritten, and may limit the reach of legislative measures through judicial interpretation designed to reconcile parliamentary acts with judicially inferred constitutional constraints (Krotoszynski 1994, 7–11).

In the American and other systems where a constitution is understood to constrain legislative action, constitutions will differ with regard to how easy they are to change and with respect to the authorities empowered to interpret whether government conformity to the constitution has been achieved. For example, state constitutions in the United States are frequently easy to amend by popular referendum (Marks and Cooper 2003, 300–14). Internationally, part of what makes the United States Constitution distinctive is that it is difficult to amend formally, and yet, from near the beginning, it has been interpreted as vesting in ordinary courts of general jurisdiction the power to determine whether government acts violate the Constitution and thus may be set aside. The easy availability of judicial review may seem yet more notable as compared to other legal systems because, at the federal level, the judges involved are presidential appointees with lifetime tenure and no direct electoral accountability.

There are at least four ways in which constitutions may be thought to shape or facilitate the actions of government institutions or of citizens themselves—

[1] Marbury vs. Madison, 1 Cranch (5 U.S.) 137, 177 (1803).

implementing the political bargains that make nation-building possible, structuring the exercise of government power, limiting the exercise of government power, and creating affirmative obligations of government to the citizenry.

2   IMPLEMENTING KEY FOUNDING BARGAINS

Americans tend to pay greatest attention to those constitutional provisions that articulate deeply-held value commitments, such a free speech or due process, or implement what we take to be enduring principles of institutional design, such as the separation of powers. Constitutions, however, typically include at least some features that do not fall into either category. That is because, when a written constitution is drafted concurrently with the formation of a new regime or nation state, it is likely that the document will be formulated, in part, to entrench particular political bargains, often messy ones, that were essential to regime formation. In the case of the United States, the subjects of the key bargains are well known. One was the fear of smaller states, especially states without good ports, that their interests would be overlooked or subordinated in a union with their more powerful neighbors. The second was slavery.

Because of the original small-state concerns, the United States Constitution continues to entrench most forcefully its most deeply anti-democratic provision, namely, the design of a federal upper legislative House with two members for every state, regardless of size. Although the United States Constitution is always difficult to amend, typically requiring two-thirds of each House of Congress to propose an amendment and ratification by three-fourths of the states, the small states' hold on the Senate is protected by the additional provision in Article V that "no state, without its consent, shall be deprived of its equal suffrage in the Senate." As a consequence, the United States seems to be stuck permanently with a Senate in which a majority of Senators routinely represent a minority of US voters (Shane 2003, 539). Furthermore, under Article I, section 10, states are not allowed, without consent of Congress, to "lay any imposts or duties on imports or exports," or to "enter into any agreement of compact with another state," thus providing small states yet further protection from predation by their larger neighbors.

Yet more ignominious bargains were struck, however, because of slavery. Although the words "slave" and "slavery" never appear in the document—a gesture to the free states' sensibilities—the Constitution prohibited Congress from stopping or even taxing the international slave trade prior to 1808 (Art. I, § 9). It credited the slave states, for purposes of legislative apportionment, with a population that included three-fifths of their slaves (Art. I, § 2). The Article on constitutional amendment protected the twenty-year slave trade "window" by prohibiting any amendments that would shorten it (Art. V). The Constitution still includes text providing that no state may enact laws purporting to discharge from "service or labor" any person who escapes to that state from another in which they are lawfully "held to service or labor" (Art. IV, § 2). Instead, any such escapee "shall be delivered up on claim of the party to whom such service or labor may be due" (Art. IV, § 2). Over the long term, these attempts to mediate the interests of free and slave states through law proved unavailing without war, and yet, it is certainly true that, without the initial bargains, no national union spanning the full east coast of the present-day United States would have been possible.

Idiosyncratic constitutional arrangements reflecting merely the political exigencies of a founding era can bedevil the enterprise of constitutional interpretation. Contemporary constitutional scholars along with numerous civil society groups often argue, for example, that the United States Constitution ought to be interpreted in light of what is taken to be a fundamental commitment in that document to the value of democracy (e.g. Ely 1980). But, given the entrenched Senate structure, the exclusion of DC residents from voting representation in Congress, and the arcane machinery of the presidential election process—each of which is a constitutional response to some eighteenth-century political anxiety that may no longer be salient—it may seem difficult to give the Constitution any coherent democratic reading. Moreover, political interests that still draw strength from these provisions are likely to prevent their change.

3   STRUCTURING THE EXERCISE OF POWER

At a more general level, it is, of course, the function of the United States Constitution, and presumably of all constitutions, to create the basic skeleton of offices and official processes through which government power shall be exercised, as well as the processes through which officeholders shall be selected. In structuring the allocation of government authority, the United States Constitution is generally described as embodying two fundamental government design principles, around which its more particularized provisions are oriented: federalism and the separation of powers. Federalism describes the allocation of power to both federal and state authorities, motivated by two general goals: a federal governmental competence adequate to address national challenges and protection for the governmental prerogatives of the states, which are regarded as closer and more accountable to the people. The separation-of-powers principle likewise aims to implement a balance of virtues: the protection against tyranny deemed to result from assuring that the power to make, implement, and interpret law is largely vested in different institutions, and the greater efficiency and effectiveness thought to follow from focusing each branch's attention on tasks especially suited to its composition and processes (Fisher 1971).

With regard to a number of these key details of organization and process, the Constitution is sufficiently explicit so that few occasions have arisen calling for further interpretation. Yet, on a host of critical issues, the provisions through which the founders articulated their designs for federalism and separation of powers have proved highly ambiguous. These ambiguities have helped to sustain over two centuries of controversy largely because the purposes underlying the design principles are themselves notably in tension.

With regard to federalism, for example, the overriding question has been whether to regard the achievement of national competence or the insulation of state sovereignty as the primary value.[2] Debates have been especially heated with regard to the scope of the clause that authorizes Congress to regulate "commerce with foreign nations, and among the several states" (Art. I, § 8). Many Supreme Court Justices, especially since the New Deal, have regarded the so-called Commerce Clause as embodying the framers' desire that Congress have sufficient authority to deal with virtually all social and economic problems of national scope. Such Justices would extend Congress's commerce power to include the direct regulation of interstate commercial activity for virtually any purpose, as well as the regulation of virtually any activity—local or not, commercial or not— that, taken in the aggregate, could have a significant effect on interstate commerce.[3] Yet other Justices are concerned that, read in this way, Congress's authority under the Commerce Clause could be expanded to obliterate what they regard as a fundamental constitutional commitment to primary state control over issues of health, safety, and public welfare and morals. For such Justices, Congress may regulate local or non-commercial activities that substantially affect interstate

---

[2] A closely related, but analytically distinct debate concerns the role of courts in enforcing whatever federalism principles are embodied in the Constitution. In a much-noted article, Herbert Wechsler argued in the 1950s that the drafters of the Constitution intended the constitutional values of federalism to be protected chiefly through the structure and operation of the federal system itself and the elected branches of the federal government (Wechsler 1954). Significant entries in the now-mountainous literature on this subject include: Calabresi 1995; Choper 1980; Kramer 2000; LaPierre 1982; McConnell 1987; Marshall 1998; Rubin and Feeley 1994; Shapiro 1995; Van Alstyne 1985; and Yoo 1997. Interestingly, debates over the substantive values underlying federalism do not fall reliably on a conservative–liberal axis. For significantly contrasting views on the value of federalism by two constitutional liberals, see Chemerinsky 1995 and Merritt 1994.

[3] For one of many strong judicial statements to this effect, see Justice Thurgood Marshall's opinion for the majority in Hodel vs. Virginia Surface Mining and Reclamation Association, 452 U.S. 254, 276–82 (1981), upholding federal strip mining standards.

commerce only if such activities relate to commerce in a sufficiently distinct way that their regulation would still leave intact the states' traditional areas of sovereignty.[4]

The search for balance between these views may prove elusive, even for a single Court. Thus, for example, in 1995, the Supreme Court held, in a 5–4 vote, that Congress overreached its authority in purporting to criminalize the knowing possession of a firearm in a so-called local "school zone."[5] Despite the obvious linkage between threats of gun violence and the quality of education, and between the quality of education and the robustness of the interstate economy, the majority found such reasoning too attenuated to support the regulation of behavior that had nothing by itself to do with commerce or economic activity.[6] By contrast, just ten years later, a different majority of six Justices held that Congress could regulate the local growth and possession of marijuana for purely medicinal purposes, on the ground that such a prohibition was integral to a comprehensive effort to eliminate the national market in marijuana.[7] A compelling jurisprudential distinction between the cases is not easy to spot.

A similar sort of debate has bedeviled the development of constitutional jurisprudence regarding the separation of powers. For proponents of what might be called a "pluralist" view of this aspect of constitutional design—prominent examples include Cynthia Farina, Martin Flaherty, Abner Greene, Thomas Sargentich, Peter Shane, and Peter Strauss—the primary goal is to restrain the exercise of government power by allowing each branch to "check" and "balance" the initiatives of the other two branches (Farina 1998; Flaherty 1996; Greene 1994; Sargentich 1993; Shane 1995). By recognizing the overlapping powers of multiple authorities, this theory emphasizes the framers' desire for a pluralist consensus in the making of public policy. The contrasting view suggests that the key to separation of powers is the right of each branch to maintain its authorities inviolate against the initiatives of the other two branches. Champions of the latter view, including Steven Calabresi, Elena Kagan, Lawrence Lessig, Geoffrey Miller, Saikrishna Prakash, and Cass Sunstein, generally advance an ambitious vision of executive power under the Constitution, and thus the modern-day version of this stance can accurately be called "presidentialist" (Calabresi and Prakash 1994; Kagan 2001; Lessig and Sunstein 1994; Miller 1986).

The United States Constitution generally erects only the most basic scaffolding for the system by which the government's public officers are chosen. Federal judges, as noted above, are appointed by the president, pursuant to the advice and consent

---

[4] United States vs. Lopez, 514 U.S. 549, 565 (1995) (invalidating federal statute prohibiting possession of guns within so-called "school zones").

[5] United States vs. Lopez, 514 U.S. 549, 565 (1995)

[6] United States vs. Lopez at 564.

[7] Gonzales vs. Raich, 125 S. Ct. 2195 (2005).

of the Senate, and hold lifetime tenure, subject only to impeachment (Shane 1993). Originally, three modes of selection were employed for the elected branches: direct popular election for members of the House of Representatives, election by state legislatures for members of the Senate, and presidential selection through an elaborate scheme of federal electors, who were themselves to be chosen through processes specified by the respective legislatures of every state. It was not until 1913 that the Constitution was amended to provide for the popular election of Senators, but the torturous process for choosing presidents remains intact, largely because it favors the smaller states, which are sufficient in number to have defeated, so far, all attempts to amend the process (Edwards 2004).

The scheme of presidential election is a poignant example of how institutional responses to founding era anxieties can outlive their salience. The decision to vest presidential election power in dispersed groups of state electors chosen under a variety of differing state rules is sometimes portrayed as a deliberate and principled attempt to further the American constitutional commitment to federalism (Best 2004). This is not so. The so-called "electoral college" system was a largely undiscussed compromise that resulted after the drafters rejected the two options they quite consciously did not want: direct popular election or selection by Congress (Rakove 2004). It was anxieties about mass democracy and about subordinating federal executive authority to federal legislative power that motivated the adoption of America's idiosyncratic system. For all the influence the United States Constitution has had on subsequent efforts, no other country has adopted the electoral college.

4   LIMITING THE EXERCISE OF GOVERNMENT POWER

Beyond its affirmative allocations of government power and specifications of offices and processes by which that power shall be exercised, the Constitution also limits the exercise of government power in the name of individual rights. Although the original 1787 document included a number of significant provisions of this kind—disallowing states from discriminating against residents of other states (Art. IV, § 2), prohibiting the imposition of any "religious test" as a qualification for federal office (Art. VI), proscribing bills of attainder and *ex post facto* laws (Art. I, § 9), and guaranteeing the right of habeas corpus except in certain cases of "rebellion or invasion" (Art. I, §9)—its drafters thought the

Constitution's primary protections for individual liberty lay in the checking and balancing structure of the national government (Brown 1991) and in the limitation of the new national government to a set of enumerated powers. Today, the best known and most enduringly controversial of the limitations on government authority are contained in the Bill of Rights and in the post-Civil War Amendments, most notably the Fourteenth.

For at least two reasons, it can hardly be surprising that the content of such rights remains the subject of heated debate. First, the key beneficiaries of these provisions may include those whose limited social status or political clout makes it difficult for them to protect their interests through electorally accountable institutions. The claims such citizens make are likely to be unpopular. Second, the rights articulated are virtually always framed in broad terms that clearly signal a potential scope of applicability way beyond any specific understanding at the time they were drafted. It has been argued—for example, by former judge Robert Bork (1989) and by current United States Supreme Court Associate Justice Antonin Scalia (1997, 47)—that courts should not limit majoritarian governance in the name of rights that were not clearly anticipated when the relevant constitutional text was adopted. Such a stance would require, however, that—to the degree that Americans remain intent on entrenching a robust understanding of individual rights in their constitution—the Constitution would have to be continually amended as changes in economic, social, and political circumstances pose unanticipated issues. For individual rights, the exercise of which is likely to challenge majority sentiment, this seems highly problematic.

A profound, but indirect consequence of the Constitution's role in protecting individual rights is that the American Constitution, virtually from the founding, has provided a focus and a shape to a host of movements for social change. These include movements to amend the Constitution, for example, to guarantee women's suffrage or to give statehood to Washington, DC, as well as movements that insist that the Constitution, properly interpreted, would advance a social cause, such as abolitionism in the nineteenth century or same-sex marriage now.[8] At the moment, the proposal of new constitutional amendments seems a preferred political organizing tactic of conservatives—amendments to prohibit same-sex marriage, forbid abortion, or authorize the criminalization of flag desecration are all of this type. There is emerging, however, a debate on the political left whether equivalent efforts ought not be mustered on behalf of stronger voting rights, guarantees of equal educational resources, and protections of such "safety net" features as publicly financed health care or housing (Jackson 2001).

The persistence of constitutional rhetoric as a leitmotif running through a such a wide array of political movements suggests the enormous power of a constitution

---

[8] The leading history of the role of the United States Constitution in American culture is Kammen 1986.

to channel political protest into largely peaceful forms and to significantly legit-imate an existing regime, even as it holds out the promise of revolutionary challenge to the status quo (Powell 1986). The implicit premises of movements either to change a constitutional text or to "improve" its interpretation are that constitutional entrenchment is an appropriate mechanism for protecting social values and that existing processes for constitutional change are worthy of pursuit. In the American system, such movements also imply the legitimating impact of judicial pronouncements concerning the constitutionality of government acts (Black 1969). Advocates of constitutional change tacitly recognize that, in the eyes of many Americans, court judgments upholding laws against constitutional challenge enhance their legitimacy. Thus, judicial interpretation is an essential target of movements to change what the Constitution says.

Although Americans are presumably inclined to believe that their freedom is enhanced by the constitutional entrenchment of individual liberties, the precise contribution of any constitution to the degree or quality of freedom that any society enjoys is not easy to assess. In the decades after the Civil War, the Fourteenth Amendment's guarantee of "equal protection of the laws" accom-plished little for the African-Americans who were the Amendment's primary intended beneficiaries (Bell 1980, 30–8). Constitutional skeptics can cite the failure of challenges to the suppression of dissident speech and political activity around the First World War or to the internment of Japanese-Americans during the Second as evidence of the Constitution's limited reliability. In an influential critique from the mid-1980s, Owen Fiss bemoaned the Supreme Court's more recent oblivious-ness in free speech disputes to the state's potential role in supporting and enriching public debate, frequently valuing the autonomy of wealthy or corporate interests over the access of individual citizens to meaningful, well-informed, politically robust discourse (Fiss 1986). Yet, it seems completely improbable that America's textual commitment to fundamental liberties is irrelevant to its success in main-taining a comparatively open society.

5   CREATING AFFIRMATIVE GOVERNMENT OBLIGATIONS

A fourth function of constitutions is to establish affirmative public welfare rights, and the United States Constitution is now among the minority that fails to acknowledge such rights explicitly. Yet, affirmative rights litigation is not unknown in American courts. Although it remains conventional wisdom that the United States Constitution does not create welfare rights that are enforceable in federal courts, many state courts have interpreted state constitutional provisions regarding public education as mandating not only a minimally adequate level of education, but also equity among school districts in the funding of public schools (Dayton and Dupree 2004).

There is some historical irony here. Those constitutions around the globe that protect social and economic rights may reflect the influence of the Weimar Constitution of 1919 or of socialist legal thought. It is also true, however, that many of the social rights provisions of post-Second World War constitutions draw their inspiration from the rights discourse of the American New Deal, including Franklin Roosevelt's call for "the four freedoms" and "a second Bill of Rights" (Sunstein 2004). More recently, American constitutional theorists, most notably Frank Michelman (1969) and William Forbath (1999, 2001), have tried to argue that the United States Constitution, properly interpreted, actually does imply some minimal set of welfare rights as a precondition to meaningful citizenship. But, although the Warren Court in the 1960s seemed to be edging towards that view, the Burger and Rehnquist Courts were notably unsympathetic.

Where constitutions do not articulate social rights expressly, it is likely to be not just—or even primarily—the absence of authorizing text, but rather anxieties about judicial enforcement of such rights that impedes their recognition. As recounted by Forbath (2004, 622–7), judges may regard social rights as too indeterminate to permit justiciability. They may entertain a related fear that the articulation and prospective enforcement of social welfare rights would tempt judges to overstep the appropriate judicial role and to implement personal policy preferences in the guise of law. Judges may regard courts as lacking the competence to engage in the sensitive allocational trade-offs that social rights remedies could entail. They may regard judicial decision-making about welfare rights, especially because of the potential budgetary impacts, as posing too great a set of constraints on the decisional authority of the elected branches of govern-ment. Relatedly, should unelected judges take too conspicuous a role in the allocation of social resources, the resulting incursion into the citizenry's role in self-governance may be seen by voters as too great a threat to overall democratic accountability.

Notwithstanding this list of objections, it is still worth noting that a number of constitutional courts around the globe have been enforcing social rights, as did, for example, the South African Constitutional Court in mandating that its government make broadly available a drug called Nevirapine, which inhibits the transmission of HIV/AIDS from pregnant women to their children (Tushnet 2004, 1906–7). It may be that such courts regard the anti-social rights arguments as resembling closely those arguments against judicial review that have generally proved unpersuasive with regard to the enforcement of "classic" or "negative" constitutional rights. In addition, rights-protective courts may believe that the anxieties about the judicial articulation of social rights can be substantially addressed by acknowledging only relatively modest powers to enforce those rights through judicial decree. Mark Tushnet, for example, has noted what may be, in some systems, a preference for combining strong articulations of social entitlements with relatively weak judicial enforcement powers (Tushnet 2004).

6   CONSTITUTIONAL INTERPRETATION AND CHANGE

Constitutions cannot fulfill their functions simply by existing; they must be implemented. The foundational task in implementing a constitution is interpretation. Researchers have differed profoundly in their views as to the nature of the interpretive enterprise, and whether legal actors, most notably judges, are guided substantially in their constitutional judgments by what the Constitution says or rather by personal preferences external to the law.

The position that legal actors are wholly unconstrained by what a constitution says seems implausible; the rules that a constitution formally embodies surely do matter. For example, if the United States Constitution permitted Congress to oust presidents on grounds more easily demonstrated than "high crimes or misdemeanors," the balance of powers between the elected branches of the federal government would surely be different than they are today. Likewise, if the text specifically stated, "Neither Congress, nor any state shall inflict a sentence of death for any crime," then the United States would have a different system of justice from the one that has developed under the more general proscription of "cruel and unusual punishment." Nonetheless, the relationship between constitutional text and the actual behavior of governments remains difficult to specify. Whether, for example, Britons enjoy materially less communicative liberty than do Americans because they lack a written Bill of Rights is debatable.[9] We may wonder whether Japanese women enjoy greater equality than do American women, notwithstanding the provision of the Japanese Constitution that "there shall be no discrimination in political, economic or social relations because of . . . sex." Indeed, because of the likely gaps that exist everywhere between constitutional text and the realities of

---

[9] The absence of a written Bill of Rights in Great Britain may be of especially tenuous significance since the United Kingdom became a signatory, in 1953, to the European Convention on Human Rights, which has been "a fruitful source of rights for the individual" (DeSmith and Brazier 1989, 426).

governance, we might wish to prefer using the term "constitution" to mean a fundamental law as it is actually given life and meaning by the operation of all relevant institutional actors, or we might allow "constitution" to refer to the formal rules of the fundamental law, but acknowledge that the institutional impacts of constitutions cannot be ascertained simply by reading them. In either case—and they amount to much the same thing—the obvious starting point for appreciating how a constitution actually plays its role in society is examining interpretation, and most especially, the role of courts in interpreting constitutions and how that role relates to other processes of constitutional change.

7   MODES OF ARGUMENT

When a legal dispute under the United States Constitution is properly presented for resolution to an American court, the process of interpreting the Constitution is a complex one. Judges face disagreement not only as to what various provisions of the Constitution mean, but even as to the methods most legitimately employed, both in general and in specific contexts, to discern such meaning. There are at least six varieties of argument that regularly appear in the written decisions of American courts interpreting the Constitution: historical arguments, textual arguments, structural arguments, ethical arguments, doctrinal arguments, and prudential arguments (Bobbitt 1984). In reviewing each category, the immediate point is not that any one method is sound, the best, or even appropriate, but rather that it is indisputably available to American courts. Thus, in facing a constitutional challenge to any executive or legislative act, an ordinary court of general jurisdiction is acting in a manner consistent with conventional judicial practice in entertaining arguments along any of these lines in resolving how the Constitution applies.

Historical arguments generally appeal to what the drafters of particular constitutional provisions had in mind when they added relevant text to the Constitution—or, with perhaps more justification, what those who ratified various proposals believed they were ratifying. Arguments of this kind—championed prominently by such scholars as Richard Kay (1988) and Michael Perry (1996)—are sometimes described as relying on "original intent." In the American system, the doctrine of judicial review is itself perhaps the most prominent example of this approach. Although the text of the Constitution is at best ambiguous on the point, there is little doubt that those who adopted the Constitution of 1787 expected that federal courts would have the power to void legislation not in conformity with the new document. It was not surprising that, in 1803, the Supreme Court formally claimed the power to set aside federal statutes it deemed to exceed Congress's constitutional authorities, even though the Constitution nowhere expressly articulates the judiciary's power to do so. Moreover, the power of judicial review was "rapidly accepted" following the Supreme Court's *Marbury* decision[10] (Nowak and Rotunda 2004, 11).

An important variation of historical argument is one that Lawrence Lessig has dubbed "fidelity as translation" (Lessig 1993). The core idea is that the modern judge should provide the constitutional text whatever contemporary reading will give the text the same meaning in its current context as it was intended to have in its original context (Lessig 1997, 1371). To take a fanciful example, consider that Art. I, section 8 of the Constitution allows Congress to create "an army" and "a navy." This would seem, linguistically, to exclude the prospect of "an air force." Imagine that we now have conclusive evidence that the founding generation had actually considered the prospect of human flight and were dead set against it as a breach of the natural order. Nonetheless, a modern judge should read the words "army" and "navy" to include "air force" because the framers intended the armed services clauses to allow for an adequate national defense and, once we are aware of their historic purpose, we should give the text a modern translation that is faithful to that purpose.

Yet another variation of historical argument may also appeal to long-standing institutional practice that may settle constitutional meaning even more definitely than any extant evidence of framer design. Thus, for example, it has been understood since the first Washington Administration that the Senate's power to give advice with regard to executive-negotiated treaties is to be rendered only after negotiations are complete, an interpretation that has prevailed chiefly because no one has since departed from this initial institutional precedent (Shane and Bruff 2005, 639).

Textual arguments appeal to the wording of constitutional text, although they may do so in different ways. An "originalist" textual argument would appeal to a proffered understanding of how the text would most likely have been understood at the time of its adoption. Thus, for example, a state might argue that the ban on "cruel and unusual punishment" should not be read in 2005 to proscribe capital punishment because, during the late eighteenth century, the death penalty would not have been understood to be "cruel and unusual." The best known proponent of this approach, both as a scholar and as a judge, is Associate Justice of the United States Supreme Court Antonin Scalia (1997).

A textual argument could also appeal, however, to the most reasonable current understanding of the text. For example, no one in the late eighteenth century could have envisioned an electronic wiretap, much less considered such a phenomenon covered by the constitutional use of the word "search." In 2005, however, anyone

---

[10] Marbury vs. Madison, 1 Cranch (5 U.S.) 137 (1803).

reading the protection against "unreasonable searches" would certainly expect the words to cover electronic forms of discovery, even without physical trespass on the subject's property. One could thus make a contemporary textual argument that the Constitution ought apply in such cases.[11]

Textual arguments of the originalist sort may seem the same as historical arguments based on original intent, but they depart when there is arguably a disjunction between what the drafters anticipated and the words actually used. For example, the text of the Constitution's Eleventh Amendment unambiguously precludes only federal lawsuits against a state that are "commenced or prosecuted" by citizens of another state or of a foreign state. Yet, the Supreme Court, in a series of sharply divided decisions, has ruled that the amendment signals a broader implicit historical understanding that states were not to be suable in state or federal court, without their consent, whether the plaintiffs are citizens of another state, of a foreign state, or of the defendant state itself (Mashaw, Merrill, and Shane 2003, 1260–8). In this context, the Court has favored the historical argument over the textual.[12]

Structural arguments make appeal to "inferences from the existence of constitutional structures and the relationships which the Constitution ordains among those structures" (Bobbitt 1984, 74). This method was given modern scholarly prominence with the work of Charles Black (1969), and is more recently exemplified in the writings of Akhil Amar (1999). A good example of the salience of structural argument arose during the impeachment trial of President Clinton. President Clinton's trial had proceeded under the conventional understanding that the Senate could try him only for "high crimes or misdemeanors," and that conviction would necessarily entail removal from office. Some of his political opponents, however, foreseeing that he would not be removed from office, argued that it would be consistent with the constitutional text to recognize Senate authority to convict the president for any offense, including forms of wrongdoing that would not amount to "high crimes or misdemeanors." Conviction of the president for something less than a "high crime or misdemeanor" would simply entail some penalty less onerous than removal.

The Senate never appeared to take this possibility seriously. One of the most telling arguments against it was presumably that the tripartite structure of the federal government into three co-equal branches intended a kind of equilibrium that would be unbalanced should one branch, the legislative, have the capacity to

---

[11] This modernist "take" on constitutional text is likely to produce results identical to Lawrence Lessig's view of "fidelity in translation," discussed above. The key difference is that Lessig's view puts interpretive emphasis on the framers' historical purposes, and a modern textualist is emphasizing the sense of the text to the modern mind. The modern sense of the text, however, is likely to resonate well with the text's broad historical purposes.

[12] And there is a strong argument that the Supreme Court got the Eleventh Amendment history wrong (Hovenkamp 1996).

discipline the head of another, the executive, on any grounds of its choosing. This inference, based on structure, likely settles the matter of proper interpretation.

Ethical argument, an approach most prominently identified with Ronald Dworkin (1996), is an argument that seeks to impute to constitutional text its most morally attractive plausible meaning. Perhaps the most celebrated Supreme Court decision seemingly based on such an argument occurred in a case called *Bolling vs. Sharpe* (347 U.S. 497, 1954), which invalidated mandatory racial segregation in the public schools in the District of Columbia. On the same day, in a series of cases consolidated as *Brown vs. Board of Education* (347 U.S. 483, 1954), the Court had held that the Fourteenth Amendment guarantee of "the equal protection of the laws" invalidated mandatory racial segregation in the public schools of states. Because the District of Columbia is not a state, however, but a federal district, the Fourteenth Amendment did not apply. The Fifth Amendment, which gives to the residents of the federal district an equivalent textual guarantee of "due process of law," does not mention equal protection. Nonetheless, the Court in *Bolling* extended the law of *Brown* to the District of Columbia. The Court said simply that there could be no legitimate justification for the legally compelled segregation of the races—seemingly, a straightforward moral argument. Implicitly, the Court was also rejecting as illegitimate the prospect that racial segregation should be legally permitted in the United States only in the national capital, which would have been a morally repugnant result.

Over the years, of course, judicial decisions based on all the categories of argument just catalogued will necessarily take on a jurisprudential life of their own (Strauss 1996). Especially in a common law system, one would thus expect that, over time, constitutional disputes will begin to be resolved in ways that seek to adduce decisional principles from decided precedents, rather than from constitutional text alone. This gives rise to a fifth mode of argument, "doctrinal." For example, no United States Supreme Court decision of recent decades has stirred more heated battle than *Roe vs. Wade* (410 U.S. 113, 1973), the decision that invalidated most state laws barring abortion in the first two trimesters of a woman's pregnancy. The opinion is written, however, chiefly as a straightforward doctrinal argument. In earlier decisions, the Court had held both that a constitutionally implicit right to privacy protects a married couple's right to acquire contraception and that the guarantee of equal protection implicitly extends that right to unmarried persons. For the *Roe* majority, it hardly seemed a stretch to extend the right of privacy to include the decision whether to terminate pregnancy. The Court likewise insisted, based also on earlier cases, that states enjoy authority to regulate for the protection of maternal and child health, as well as for the safe practice of medicine, even if there would be some resulting burden on a woman's capacity to choose abortion.

Professor Bobbitt recognizes a sixth category of argument, which he terms, "prudential," namely, "constitutional argument which is actuated by the political and economic circumstances surrounding the decision" (Bobbitt 1982, 61). It is a form of argument identified most strongly with the work of the late Alexander Bickel (1962). Among the most notable examples of prudential arguments are those, which may also be a variety of structural argument, that persuade the federal courts that certain questions are beyond their purview. For example, albeit without producing a majority opinion, the Supreme Court in *Goldwater vs. Carter* (444 U.S. 996, 1979) refused to rule whether the president was legally entitled, without either express statutory authority or Senate advice and consent, to withdraw from the Mutual Defense Treaty with the Republic of China (Taiwan), a necessary precursor to awarding diplomatic recognition to the Chinese government in Beijing. Then-Justice Rehnquist, writing for a plurality, determined that anxieties about the potential real-world consequences should federal courts interfere with the elected branches' control of US foreign policy counseled for a determination that treaty termination questions are beyond the courts' jurisdiction.

8 INTERPRETATION AND LEGITIMACY

The anxieties of opponents of judicial review are, of course, only intensified by the rich menu of interpretive possibilities that this analysis exposes. Champions of any of these forms of argument will find ample precedent for their use in the records of past constitutional decisions. It hardly requires hindsight to spot the inevitability that a constitutional law germinated through such a broad spectrum of arguments—especially arguments other than those based on "original intent" and "original meaning"—is likely to induce substantial changes in constitutional meaning over time. Because the United States Constitution, as do presumably all Constitutions, explicitly specifies processes for its amendment, the legitimacy of constitutional change effected through other means is open to question.

The various responses of constitutional theorists to this legitimacy challenge have tended to fall within one of three types. First, the legitimacy challenge seems to posit that the imposition of constitutional constraints are legitimate only if envisioned by the drafters or ratifiers of the relevent text. Yet, there is also reason to think that the original drafters or ratifiers imagined that change would occur along the lines that the country has witnessed. That is, even though earlier generations might not have specifically anticipated the results of particular challenges—for example, that the ban on cruel and unusual punishments would invalidate the death penalty for minors or that the equal protection clause would outlaw legally mandated race segregation—the ways in which these changes have occurred, through the procedurally acceptable application of conventional techniques of legal interpretation, would have themselves been acceptable to the framers (Powell 1985).

A second line of argument is pragmatist, positing that the test of legitimacy, to paraphrase Oliver Wendell Holmes, is experience, not logic. The Constitution of the United States declares a variety of purposes including the establishment of justice, the insurance of "domestic tranquility," the promotion of the "general welfare," and the securing for posterity of "the blessings of liberty." In this light, a pragmatist would argue that the legitimacy of the judicial function as it has actually been performed ought to be tested by whether that function has actually aided in the Constitution's accomplishment of those purposes. So long as the public continues to have confidence in its courts, so long as the United States continues to enjoy commendable levels of peace, security, justice, and liberty, the making of constitutional law ought to be viewed as legitimate.

A third line of argument roots the objections to both judge-led constitutional change and its defense in democratic theory. From a democratic standpoint, the defect of constitutional change wrought by unelected judges is the implicit departure from the ideal of popular sovereignty, namely, that "the people," most often through their elected representatives, should be the authors of the laws that bind them.[13] Constitutional constraints are legitimately imposed upon current political authorities only because "the people" ordained the Constitution. To permit changes to the Constitution through processes other than those "the people" themselves prescribed through the Constitution is to undermine popular self-governance.

Responses to this line of argument that are rooted in democratic theory take different forms. Bruce Ackerman, for example, accepts that some form of popular ratification is necessary to legitimate constitutional change that occurs other than through the formally prescribed constitutional amendment process. Retracing US history, he asserts that constitutional change may legitimately occur when triggered by the enactment of "transformative statutes," through which the elected branches place their imprimatur on a constitutional understanding at odds with contemporary constitutional law (Ackerman 1991, 268). Based on such statutes, a court may choose to alter its understanding of constitutional law if intervening elections signal that the people, through their civic deliberation, have demonstrated adequate public support for a de facto amendment of the Constitution. Ackerman's paradigm case is the Court's New Deal decisions greatly expanding the reach of Congress's regulatory authorities under the Commerce Clause.

Another line of theory, also resting on the premise that equates democratic legitimacy with popular sovereignty, argues that the courts nonetheless have a significant role in reinforcing democratic rule. Pursuant to this line of thought,

---

[13] The history of legal thought regarding this so called "counter-majoritarian" difficulty is exhaustively traced in Friedman 1998, 2000, 2001, 2002a,b.

forcefully argued by the late John Hart Ely (1980), a paradigm example of legitimate judicial creativity would be the reapportionment cases, in which the Supreme Court forced state legislatures to redesign electoral districts on a "one person, one vote" basis. Such a result might be hard to square with an historical reading of the Constitution, but would be legitimate, in Ely's view, because the result of the decisions was to expand the people's capacity to govern themselves fairly through their elected representatives.

There is, however, yet a third brand of democratic theory that starts by challenging both the metaphor of popular sovereignty and the practical equation of democracy with electoral accountability (Shane 2004a). Under this view, what legitimates democratic governance are really two things: the degree to which citizens enjoy opportunities to act meaningfully in choosing their political fate and the degree to which the system fosters the equal consideration of the interests of all persons in decision-making that affects the public at large. Elections are an important part of this equation; they obviously provide the focus for much of what people experience as autonomous political activity. But they cannot be everything. A system cannot be legitimate, whatever its electoral rules, if the interests of some are universally disregarded in favor of the interests of others, regardless of the equity of their claims. From this point of view, constitutional law-making in the courts functions, in part, to energize a legitimacy-enforcing dialogue with the elected branches. The function of this dialogue is to give voice to interests and to public values that, for structural reasons, the elected branches might be expected in some systemic way to overlook or underweigh.[14] The net result, echoing James Madison's theory in the famous *Federalist Papers,* No. 10, is to help insure that law is driven by the public interest, rather than by merely private interest or the passion of the moment.

Closely related to these debates over the legitimacy of judicial review is the related, but distinct question of judicial supremacy—the degree to which constitutional interpretation uttered by the courts should be deemed the "final say." There is currently in the United States a significant debate, both empirical and normative, on the role of "popular constitutionalism."[15] The questions are the degree to which institutions outside the courts are also responsible for constitutional meaning and to what degree they should be so. The debate admits of a host of positions; some scholars who believe that legislatures and executives share authority to interpret the Constitution nonetheless embrace judicial review, while others do not. This is a slippery debate because it is not clear exactly what

[14] A great deal has been written arguing that constitutional review by unelected judges can convincingly be viewed as part of a democracy-reinforcing dialogue with the elected branches of government. Important writers in this vein include Fisher 1988 and Eisgruber 2001.

[15] Major new works in this vein are pouring forth and key examples include: Johnsen 2004; Kramer 2004; Kramer et al. 2005; and Tushnet 1999.

judicial supremacy consists of. When legislatures perceive judicial pronouncements to be out of step with popular feeling, they frequently respond by enacting new statutes that can be distinguished only minimally from others already held unconstitutional. That happens with seeming frequency on the subjects of abortion and church–state relations. Whether or not this is a wise use of legislative time, it would seem hard to dismiss as illegitimate. A harder question might be whether executive or legislative authorities should be deemed to act unlawfully or illegitimately if they persist in precisely those behaviors or enactments that, as to other parties or in other forms, the courts have already ruled against. It is true enough that such defiance, at least since the desegregation of America's public schools, is exceedingly rare. But this seems less to be the result of any well-understood legal doctrine of judicial supremacy than a popular expectation that legislatures will not act defiantly to this degree.

An intriguing question is whether constitutions that are easier to amend through their formally specified processes witness less change through informal interpretation by non-judicial actors. Although there do not appear to be any rigorous attempts at a quantitative assessment, one political scientist has recently verified that what he calls "informal political construction" of constitutions does occur in the American states, even though state constitutions are notably easier to amend than is the federal (Besso 2005). Informal change processes may thus be an important subject of study with regard to all constitutions.

9   DIRECTIONS FOR FUTURE RESEARCH

It is quite unlikely that the debates of two centuries over a constitution's roles and the ways in which legal actors properly implement those roles are going to subside. Moreover, because of both intellectual trends and the press of historical events, it is likely that at least the following half dozen avenues of intellectual inquiry will engage even greater attention in the coming decades' debates over constitutional analysis.

One is the subject of comparative constitutional analysis, which is almost entirely beyond the domain of this chapter. The wave of democratic reform in the newly constituted states of the former Soviet Union, in Africa, and perhaps in the Middle East has created a significant cottage industry among legal experts seeking to identify how various extant constitutions and their various provisions for the structure of government and protection of individual rights have actually fared, and why (Horowitz 2002). There is no evidence of that trend subsiding.

Relatedly, there is likely to be exciting research done on the relationship between constitutions and the mediation of ethnic conflict. On this subject, the American lens through which this chapter has been written is concededly too narrow. The group of Americans who drafted, debated, and enjoyed authority to help ratify the United States Constitution were a relatively homogeneous bunch. Although the Constitution would prove to have profound consequences for Native Americans and for African-Americans, there was no thought given in 1787 to "power sharing" with either. By contrast, power sharing in ethnically divided states is perhaps the paramount challenge facing drafters of new constitutions in the twenty-first century. There is deep debate over the appeal of what has come to be known as "consociational democracy," namely, some form of constitutional arrangement in which different ethnic groups share executive power proportionally, enjoy substantial group autonomy, and rely on consensus for a significant portion of government decision-making (compare Lijphart 2002 with Horowitz 2002). Such decisions could be classed, if we follow the list of functions noted above, as "implementing key founding bargains," but the relationship of constitutionalism to interethnic cooperation is so complex a subject that a much more fine-grained picture of constitutional elements would be necessary to do justice to it.

A third project, fed by the first two, is likely to be an intensification of interest in the relationship between constitutionalism and democratic theory. The global proliferation of new constitutional activity, on both the national and the supranational level (consider the European Union), coincides with the rapid growth of interactive information and communications technologies that can conceivably facilitate wholly novel institutional forms and processes through which citizens may engage with one another and with the state in relation to public policy-making (Shane 2004b). Researchers are only beginning to explore the implications of these new technologies for democratic theory and practice, and it is easy enough to predict that ongoing developments in democratic theory and constitutional design will cross-pollinate significantly over the coming decades.

A fourth project of continuing interest is likely to be the effort, noted at the outset of this chapter, to synthesize internal and external accounts of constitutional interpretation to provide a more fully effective model than either can provide alone (Feldman 2005). The increasing interest among law faculties in interdisciplinary inquiry, accompanied by the increasing receptiveness among political scientists to accounts of judicial behavior more nuanced than the pure attitudinal model, should help accelerate this development.

Fifth, and related to the growth of interdisciplinary inquiry, we are likely to see a greater role for cognitive and decision psychology in exploring how legal actors fulfill their roles. Research on bias, attitudes, and stereotypes is likely to inform debates about how judges interpret the law and whether there exist structures, processes, or techniques effective in limiting the role of individual bias in legal interpretation (Ferguson, Babcock, and Shane 2005). Similarly, given the significant prominence of critical legal studies, feminism, and critical race studies in the United States, there is likely to be continuing interest in possible psychological mechanisms through which legal interpretation may operate to reinforce social hierarchies based on wealth, gender, race, or indeed, all of the above.

Finally, and as challenging as any of the other subjects, legal scholarship is paying increasing attention to the role of actors other than judges in giving meaning to the Constitution. Far more often than constitutional disputes reach the judiciary, the elected branches of federal and state governments are required, in the course of implementing their official responsibilities, to determine what the Constitution means. In many cases—perhaps most notably, at the federal level, with regard to the proper allocation of war powers between Congress and the president—the issues presented are unlikely ever to be addressed, much less resolved in judicial proceedings. The role of the Constitution in such settings, the relationship, both normative and empirical, between judicial interpretations and "extra-judicial" interpretations of the Constitution (Shane 1987), and the impacts, if any, of extra-judicial interpretations on public understanding of constitutional meaning are all subjects ripe for both empirical and theoretical investigation. These are also frontiers that, among political scientists, appear to be all but unexplored.

References

ACKERMAN, B. 1991. *We the People, I: Foundations*. Cambridge, Mass.: Harvard University Press.

AMAR, A. R. 1999. Intratextualism. *Harvard Law Review*, 112: 747–827.

BELL, D. 1980. *Race, Racism and American Law*, 2nd edn. Boston: Little, Brown.

BESSO, M. 2005. Constitutional amendment procedures and the informal political construction of constitutions. *Journal of Politics*, 67: 69–87.

BEST, J. 2004. Presidential selection: complex problems and simple solutions. *Political Science Quarterly*, 119: 39–59.

BICKEL, A. 1962. *The Least Dangerous Branch*. New Haven, Conn.: Yale University Press.

BLACK, C. L. 1969. *Structure and Relationship in Constitutional Law*. Baton Rouge: Louisiana State University Press.

BOBBITT, P. 1982. *Constitutional Fate: A Theory of the Constitution*. New York: Oxford University Press.

BORK, R. 1989. *The Tempting of America*. New York: Free Press.

BROWN, R. 1991. Separated powers and ordered liberty. *University of Pennsylvania Law Review*, 139: 1513–66.

CALABRESI, S. G. 1995. "A government of limited and enumerated powers:" in defense of *United States v. Lopez*. *Michigan Law Review*, 94: 752–831.

—— and PRAKASH, S. B. 1994. The president's power to execute the laws. *Yale Law Journal*, 104: 541–665.

CHEMERINSKY, E. 1995. The values of federalism. *Florida Law Review*, 47: 499–540.

CHOPER, J. 1980. *Judicial Review and the National Political Process.* Chicago: University of Chicago Press.

DAYTON, J. and DUPRE, A. 2004. School funding litigation: who's winning the war? *Vanderbilt Law Review,* 57: 2351–413.

DESMITH, S. and BRAZIER, R. 1989. *Constitutional and Administrative Law,* 6th edn. London: Penguin.

DWORKIN, R. 1977. *Taking Rights Seriously.* Cambridge, Mass.: Harvard University Press.

—— 1996. *Freedom's Law: The Moral Reading of the Constitution.* Cambridge, Mass.: Harvard University Press.

EDWARDS III, G. C. 2004. *Why the Electoral College is Bad for America.* New Haven, Conn.: Yale University Press.

EISGRUBER, C. L. 2001. *Constitutional Self-Government.* Cambridge, Mass.: Harvard University Press.

ELY, J. H. 1980. *Democracy and Distrust: A Theory of Judicial Review.* Cambridge, Mass.: Harvard University Press.

FARINA, C. R. 1998. Undoing the New Deal through the new presidentialism. *Harvard Journal of Law & Public Policy,* 22: 227–38.

FELDMAN, S. M. 2005. The rule of law or the rule of politics? Harmonizing the internal and external views of Supreme Court decision making. *Law and Social Inquiry,* 30: 89–135.

FERGUSON, J. R., BABCOCK, L., and SHANE, P. M. 2005. The subconscious influence of policy preferences on constitutional reasoning.

FISHER, L. 1971. The efficiency side of separated powers. *Journal of American Studies,* 5: 113–31.

—— 1988. *Constitutional Dialogues: Interpretation as Political Process.* Princeton, NJ: Princeton University Press.

FISS, O. 1986. Free speech and social structure. *Iowa Law Review,* 71: 1405–25.

FLAHERTY, M. S. 1996. The most dangerous branch. *Yale Law Journal,* 105: 1725–839.

FORBATH, W. E. 1999. Caste, class, and equal citizenship. *Michigan Law Review,* 98: 1–91.

—— 2001. The New Deal constitution in exile. *Duke Law Journal,* 51: 165–222.

—— 2004. Not so simple justice: Frank Michelman on social rights, 1969–present. *Tulsa Law Review,* 39: 597–638.

FRIEDMAN, B. 1998. The history of the countermajoritarian difficulty, part one: the road to judical supremacy. *New York University Law Review,* 73: 333–433.

—— 2000. The history of the countermajoritarian difficulty, part four: law's politics. *University of Pennsylvaina Law Review,* 148: 971–1064.

—— 2001. The history of the countermajoritarian difficulty, part three: the lesson of *Lochner. New York University Law Review,* 76: 1383–445.

—— 2002a. The birth of an academic obsession: the history of the countermajoritarian difficulty, part five. *Yale Law Journal,* 112: 153–259.

—— 2002b. The history of the countermajortarian difficulty, part II: reconstruction's political court. *Georgetown Law Journal,* 91: 1–65.

GILLMAN, H. 1993. *The Constitution Besieged: The Rise and Demise of* Lochner *Era Police Powers Jurisprudence.* Durham, NC: Duke University Press.

—— and CLAYTON, C. W. (eds.) 1999. *Supreme Court Decision-Making: New Institutionalist Approaches.* Chicago: University of Chicago Press.

GRABER, M. A. 2002. Constitutional politics and constitutional theory: a misunderstood and neglected relationship. *Law & Social Inquiry,* 27: 309–38.

GREENE, A. S. 1994. Checks and balances in an era of presidential lawmaking. *University of Chicago Law Review*, 61: 123–96.

HOROWITZ, D. 2002. Constitutional design: proposals versus processes. In *The Architecture of Democracy: Constitutional Design, Conflict Management, and Democracy*, ed. A. Reynolds. Oxford: Oxford University Press.

HOVENKAMP, H. 1996. Judicial restraint and constitutional federalism: the Supreme Court's Lopez and Seminole tribe decisions. *Columbia Law Review*, 96: 2213–47.

JACKSON, J. L., JR., 2001. *Toward a More Perfect Union: Advancing New American Rights*. New York: Welcome Rain.

JOHNSEN, D. 2004. Functional departmentalism and nonjudicial interpretation: who determines constitutional meaning? *Law and Contemporary Problems*, 67: 105–47.

KAGAN, E. 2001. Presidential administration. *Harvard Law* Review, 114: 2245–385.

KAMMEN, M. 1986. *A Machine That Would Go of Itself: The Constitution in American Culture*. New York: Vintage.

KAY, R. S. 1988. Adherence to the original intentions in constitutional adjudication: three objections and responses. *Northwestern University Law Review*, 82: 226–92.

KRAMER, L. D. 2000. Putting the politics back into the political safeguards of federalism. *Columbia Law Review*, 100: 215–93.

—— 2004. *The People Themselves: Popular Constitutionalism and Judicial Review*. New York: Oxford University Press.

—— SAGER, L. G., FLEMING, J. E., GREENE, A. S., KACZAROWSKI, R. J., SAIGER, A., and ZIPURSKY, B. C. 2005. Symposium: theories of taking the constitution seriously outside the courts. *Fordham Law Review*, 73: 1343–476.

KROTOSZYNSKI, R. J. Jr., 1994. *Brind and Rust v. Sullivan*: free speech and the limits of a written constitution. *Florida State University Law Review*, 22: 1–34.

LAPIERRE, B. 1982. The political safeguards of federalism redux: intergovernmental immunity and the states as agents of the nation. *Washington University of Law Quarterly*, 60: 779–1056.

LESSIG, L. 1993. Fidelity in translation. *Texas Law Review*, 71: 1165–268.

—— 1997. Fidelity as translation. *Fordham Law Review*, 65: 1365–433.

—— and SUNSTEIN, C R. 1994. The president and the administration. *Columbia Law Review*, 94: 1–123.

LIJPHART, A. 2002. The wave of power-sharing democracy. In *The Architecture of Democracy: Constitutional Design, Conflict Management, and Democracy*, ed. A. Reynolds. Oxford: Oxford University Press.

MCCONNELL, M. W. 1987. Federalism: evaluating the Founders' Design. *University of Chicago Law Review*, 54: 1484–512.

MARKS, T. C. JR., and COOPER, J. F. 2003. *State Constitutional Law*. St. Paul, Minn.: Thomson-West.

MARSHALL, W. 1998. American political culture and the failures of process federalism. *Harvard Journal of Law & Public Policy*, 22: 139–55.

MASHAW, J. R., MERRILL, R. A., and SHANE, P. M. 2003. *Administrative Law: The American Public Law System*. St. Paul, Minn.: Thomson-West.

MERRITT, D. J. 1994. Three faces of federalism: finding a formula for the future. *Vanderbilt Law Review*, 47: 1563–85.

MICHELMAN, F. I. 1969. Foreword: on protecting the poor through the Fourteenth Amendment. *Harvard Law Review*, 83: 7–59.

MILLER, G. P. 1986. Independent agencies. *Supreme Court Review,* 1986: 41–97.

NORTH, D. C. 1990. *Institutions, Institutional Change and Economic Performance.* New York: Cambridge University Press.

NOWAK, J. E. and ROTUNDA, R. D. 2004. *Constitutional Law,* 7th edn. St.Paul, Minn.: Thomson-West.

PERRY, M. J. 1996. *The Constitution in the Courts: Law or Politics?* New York: Oxford University Press.

PINELLO, D. 1999. Linking party to judicial ideology in American courts: a meta-analysis. *Justice System Journal,* 20: 219–54.

POWELL, H. J. 1985. The original understanding of original intent. *Harvard Law Review,* 98: 885–948.

—— 1986. Parchment matters: a meditation on the constitution as text. *Iowa Law Review,* 71: 1427–35.

RAKOVE, J. 2004. Presidential selection: electoral fallacies. *Political Science Quarterly,* 119: 21–37.

ROSENFELD, M. 1994. Modern constitutionalism as interplay between identity and diversity. In *Constitutionalism, Identity, Difference and Legitimacy,* ed. M. Rosenfeld. Durham, NC: Duke University Press.

RUBIN, E. L. and FEELEY, M. 1994. Federalism: some notes on a national neurosis. *UCLA Law Review,* 41: 903–52.

SARGENTICH, T. O. 1993. The administrative process in crisis—the example of presidential oversight of agency rulemaking. *Administrative Law Journal of the American University,* 6: 710–20.

SARTORI, G. 1994. *Comparative Constitutional Engineering: An Inquiry into Structures, Incentives and Outcomes.* New York: New York University Press.

SCALIA, A. 1997. *A Matter of Interpretation: Federal Courts and the Law.* Princeton, NJ: Princeton University Press.

SEGAL, J. A. and SPAETH, H. J. 1993. *The Supreme Court and the Attitudinal Model.* New York: Cambridge University Press.

SHANE, P. M. 1987. Legal disagreement and negotiation in a government of laws: the case of executive privilege claims against Congress. *Minnesota Law Review,* 71: 461–542.

—— 1993. Who may remove or discipline federal judges? A constitutional analysis. *University of Pennsylvania Law Review,* 142: 209–42.

—— 1995. Political accountability in a system of checks and balances: the case of presidential review of rulemaking. *Arkansas Law Review,* 48: 161–214.

—— 2000. Federalism's "old deal:" what's right and wrong with conservative judicial activism. *Villanova Law Review,* 45: 201–43.

—— 2003. When interbranch norms break down: of arms-for-hostages, "orderly shutdowns," presidential impeachments, and judicial coups. *Cornell Journal of Law & Public Policy,* 12: 503–42.

—— 2004*a*. The electronic federalist: the internet and the eclectic institutionalization of democratic legitimacy. In *Democracy Online: The Prospects for Political Renewal through the Internet,* ed. P. M. Shane. New York: Routledge.

—— (ed.) 2004*b*. *Democracy Online: The Prospects for Political Renewal through the Internet.* New York: Routledge.

—— and BRUFF, H. H. 2005. *Separation of Powers Law: Cases and Materials,* 2nd edn. Durham, NC: Carolina Academic Press.

SHAPIRO, D. L. 1995. *Federalism: A Dialogue.* Chicago: Northwestern University Press.

SMITH, R. M. 1988. Political jurisprudence, the new institutionalism, and the future of public law. *American Political Science Review*, 82: 89–108.

STRAUSS, D. A. 1996. Common law constitutional interpretation. *University of Chicago Law Review*, 63: 877–935.

STRAUSS, P. L. 1997. Presidential rulemaking. *Chicago-Kent Law Review*, 72: 965–86.

SUNSTEIN, C. R. 2004. *The Second Bill of Rights: FDR'S Unfinished Revolution and Why We Need It More than Ever.* New York: Basic Books.

TUSHNET, M. 1999. *Taking the Constitution Away from the Courts.* Princeton, NJ: Princeton University Press.

—— 2004. Social welfare rights and the forms of judicial review. *Texas Law Review*, 82: 1895–919.

VAN ALSTYNE, W. 1985. The second death of federalism. *Michigan Law Review*, 83: 1709–33.

WECHSLER, H. 1954. The political safeguards of federalism: the role of the states in the composition and selection of the national government. *Columbia Law Review*, 54: 543–60.

WHITTINGTON, K. E. 2000. Once more unto the breach: postbehavioralist approaches to judicial politics. *Law & Social Inquiry*, 25: 601–34.

YOO, J. 1997. The judicial safeguards of federalism. *Southern California Law Review*, 70: 1311–405.

CHAPTER 12

COMPARATIVE CONSTITUTIONS

JOSEP M. COLOMER

1 INTRODUCTION

Constitutions came earlier than democracy (Strong 1963). During the late Middle Ages and early modern times, constitutions were mainly devices for establishing rights and limiting powers, functions that are still emphasized in certain academic literature on constitutions (see, for example, North and Weingast 1989; North 1990; Buchanan 1990; Weingast 1995). But as the old powers to be limited were autocratic, constitutionalism advanced almost naturally, together with the expansion of suffrage rights and democratization.

A constitution is usually defined as "a set of rules" for making collective decisions (see, for example, Buchanan and Tullock 1962; Elster and Slagstad 1988; Mueller 1996). Enforceable decisions made by means of rules can solve human coordination and cooperation dilemmas (as discussed by Brennan and Buchanan 1985; Hardin 1989; Ordeshook 1992). However, different rules may favor different decisions with differently distributed benefits. Two sets of rules can be distinguished: (a) those "to regulate the allocation of functions, powers and duties among the various agencies and offices of government," and (b) those to "define the relationships between these and the public," which in democracy are based on elections (Finer 1988).

2   ORIGINS AND EVOLUTION
OF CONSTITUTIONAL MODELS

2.1   Division of Powers

The first set of constitutional rules just mentioned regulates the division of powers among different institutions. Virtually all the political regimes in world history have been based on a dual formula: a one-person office combined with multiple-person offices (as remarked by Congleton 2001). The rationale for this dualism is that, while a one-person institution may be highly effective at decision-making and implementation, a multiple-person institution may be more representative of the different interests and values in the society. In modern times, a few basic constitutional models can be compared in the light of this dualism. They include: the old, transitional model of constitutional monarchy; the modern democratic models of parliamentary regime and checks-and-balances regime; and two variants of the latter usually called presidentialism and semi-presidentialism.

The model of constitutional monarchy reunites a one-person non-elected monarch with executive powers and a multiple-person elected assembly with legislative powers. This mixed formula was formally shaped by the French constitution of 1791, which, although ephemeral in its implementation, became a reference for many constitutions in other countries during the nineteenth century, including Austria, Belgium, Brazil, Germany, Norway, Portugal, Spain, and Sweden; in more recent times, similar formulas have been adopted in some Arab monarchies, such as Jordan and Morocco. With broadening suffrage and democratization, the non-elected monarch's powers were reduced, while those of the elected assembly expanded, especially regarding the control of executive ministers, thus moving towards formulas closer to the parliamentary regime.

The parliamentary regime is one of the two democratic formulas that can result from the process of enhancing the role of the electing assembly and limiting the monarch's executive powers. According to the English or "Westminster" model developed since the late seventeenth century, the parliament became the sovereign institution, also assuming the power of appointing and dismissing ministers, while the monarch remained a ceremonial though non-accountable figure. Not until the creation of the Third French Republic in 1871 did a parliamentary republic exist. Nowadays, there are parliamentary regimes in approximately half of the democratic countries in the world, including, with the British-style monarchical variant, Australia, Belgium, Canada, Denmark, Japan, the Netherlands, New Zealand, Norway, Spain, and Sweden, and with the republican variant, Austria, Czech Republic, Estonia, Finland, Germany, Greece, Hungary, India, Ireland, Italy, Latvia, Slovakia, Slovenia, South Africa, and Switzerland.

In this framework, the development of political parties was usually interpreted as a force eroding the central role of the parliament. In old constitutional studies, the British model was provocatively labeled rather than "parliamentary," a "cabinet" regime (see, for instance, Loewenstein 1957; Jennings 1959; Crossman 1963; Wheare 1963). However, it has more recently been remarked that the growth of party was instrumental in reducing the influence of the monarch but not necessarily that of the parliament. With the reduction of the monarch to a figurehead, the prime minister has indeed become the new one-person relevant figure, but the position of the cabinet has weakened. In contrast, the role of parliament has survived, and even, in a modest way, thrived. Despite long-standing concerns regarding the balance of power, "parliament has always remained the primary institution of the British polity" (Flinders 2002; see also Bogdanor 2003; Seaward and Silk 2003).

In the other democratic formula, which originated with the 1787 constitution of the United States, it is not only the multiple-person legislative assembly that is popularly elected but also the one-person chief executive. The non-elected monarch was replaced with an elected president with executive powers. This model of political regime implies, thus, separate elections and divided powers between the chief executive and the legislative branch. It was widely imitated in Latin American republics, but with the introduction of strong biases in favor of the presidency, as will be discussed below; other variants have also been adopted in a number of Asian countries under American influence, including Indonesia, South Korea, the Philippines, and Taiwan.

In the original US version, this model is a complex system of "checks and balances" or mutual controls between separately elected or appointed institutions (presidency, house, senate, court). They include term limits for the president, limited presidential veto of congressional legislation, senate rules permitting a qualified minority to block decisions, senatorial ratification of presidential appointments, congressional appointment of officers and control of administrative agencies, congressional impeachment of the president, and judicial revision of legislation.

Recent analyses have formally shown how these counter-weighting mechanisms play in favor of power sharing between institutions and as equivalent devices to supermajority rules for decision-making. The obstacles introduced by the numerous institutional checks may stabilize socially inefficient status quo policies, but they also guarantee that most important decisions are made by broad majorities able to prevent the imposition of a small, or minority, group's will. With similar analytical insight but a different evaluation, other analyses have remarked that separate elections and divided governments create a "dual legitimacy" prone to "deadlock;" that is, legislative paralysis and interinstitutional conflict (Hammond and Miller 1987; Riggs 1988; Neustadt 1990; Linz 1990a; Cox and Kernell 1991; Riker 1992; Krehbiel 1996, 1998; Brady and Volden 1998; Cameron 2000; Dahl 2002; Colomer 2005b).

Another two variants of political regime with separate elections for the presidency and the assembly have developed. The first, usually called "presidentialism," have eventually emerged in almost all twenty republics in Latin America from the mid- or late nineteenth century, including in particular Argentina, Brazil, Chile, Colombia, Costa Rica, Mexico, Peru, Uruguay, and Venezuela. As mentioned, some founding constitution makers in these countries claimed to be imitating the United States Constitution, but, in contrast to the preventions against one-person's expedient decisions introduced in the USA, some of them looked farther back to the absolutist monarchies preceding any division of powers and mixed regimes and aimed at having "elected kings with the name of presidents" (in Simón Bolívar's words). The distinction between US-style checks-and-balances, unified government in presidential regimes, and "presidentialism," which can be referred to Madison, Jefferson, and Hamilton, respectively (according to Burns 1965), was already remarked in old constitutional studies for Latin America (García Calderón 1914; Fitzgibbon 1945; Loewenstein 1949; Stokes 1959; Lambert 1963).

Presidential dominance has been attempted through the president's veto power over legislation and his control of the army, which also exist in the USA, supplemented with long presidential terms and re-elections, unconstrained powers to appoint and remove members of the cabinet and other highly-placed officers, legislative initiative, the capacity to dictate legislative decrees, fiscal and administrative authority, discretionary emergency powers, suspension of constitutional guarantees, and, in formally federal countries, the right to intervene in state affairs. The other side of this same coin is weak congresses, which are not usually given control over the cabinet and are frequently constrained by short session periods and a lack of resources (Linz 1990a; Shugart and Carey 1992; Linz and Valenzuela 1994; Aguilar 2000; Cox and Morgenstern 2002; Morgenstern and Nacif 2002). Proposals for reform have included moves towards all the other regime types, including semi-parliamentarism (Nino 1992), Westminster features (Mainwairing and Shugart 1997), US-style checks-and-balances (Ackerman 2000), and multi-party parliamentarism (Colomer and Negretto 2005).

The second variant, usually called a "semi-presidential" regime, but also "semi-parliamentary," "premier-presidential," or "dual-executive," had been experimented with in Finland and Germany after the First World War but was more consistently shaped with the 1958 constitution of France. Similar constitutional formulas have been recently adopted in a few countries in Eastern Europe, including Lithuania, Poland, Romania, and Russia, as well as a number of others in Africa. With this formula, the presidency and the assembly are elected separately, as in a checks-and-balances regime, but it is the assembly that appoints and can dismiss a prime minister, as in a parliamentary regime. The president and the prime minister share the executive powers in a "governmental diarchy" (Duverger 1970, 1978, 1980; Duhamel and Parodi 1988).

At the beginning of the French experience it was speculated that this constitutional model would produce an alternation between presidential and parliamentary phases, respectively favoring the president and the prime minister as a one-person dominant figure. The first phase of the alternation was indeed confirmed with presidents enjoying a compact party majority in the assembly. In these situations, "the president can become more powerful than in the classical presidential regimes," as well as more powerful than the British-style prime minister because he accumulates the latter's powers plus those of the monarch (Duverger 1998). The second, parliamentary phase was, in contrast, not confirmed, since, even if the president faces a prime minister, a cabinet, and an assembly majority with a different political orientation, he usually retains significant powers, including the dissolution of the assembly, as well as partial vetoes over legislation and executive appointments, among others, depending on the specific rules in each country. This makes the president certainly more powerful than any monarch or republican president in a parliamentary regime. (A gradual acknowledgment that a significant division of powers exists in the "cohabitation" phase can be followed in more recent works in French by Duverger 1986, 1996, 1998). There can, thus, indeed be two "phases," depending on whether the president's party has a majority in the assembly and can appoint the prime minister or not; however, the two phases are not properly presidential and parliamentary, but they rather produce an even higher concentration of power than in a presidential regime and a dual executive, respectively. (See also discussion in Bahro, Bayerlein, and Veser 1998; Sartori 1994; Elgie 1999).

2.2   Electoral Rules

The second set of constitutional rules mentioned above regulates the relationships between citizens and public officers by means of elections. A long tradition of empirical studies, usually focusing on democratic regimes during the second half of the twentieth century, has assumed that elections and electoral systems could be taken as an independent variable from which the formation of political parties and other features of a political system derive (Duverger 1951; Rae 1967; Grofman and Lijphart 1986; Taagepera and Shugart 1989; Lijphart 1994; Cox 1997; Katz 1997). But an alternative point of view emphasizes that it is the governments and parties that choose constitutional rules, including electoral systems, and, thus, the role of the dependent and the independent variables in the previous analytical framework could be upside down (Grumm 1958; Lipson 1964; Särlvick 1982; Boix 1999; Colomer 2004, 2005a).

Most modern electoral rules originated as alternatives to a traditional electoral system composed of multimember districts, open ballots permitting individual candidate voting, and plurality or majority rule. This understudied type of electoral system was used very widely in local and national assemblies in pre-democratic or early democratic periods before and during the nineteenth century; it is still probably the most common procedure in small community, condominium, school, university, professional organization, corporation board, and union assemblies and elections; and it has also been adopted in a small number of new democracies in recent times. It appears indeed as almost "natural" and "spontaneous" to many communities when they have to choose a procedure for collective decision-making based on votes, especially because it permits a varied representation of the community.

But while this set of rules can produce fair representation, at the same time it creates strong incentives for the formation of "factional" candidacies or voting coalitions, which are the most primitive form of political parties. In elections in multimember districts by plurality rule, factions or parties tend to induce "voting in bloc" for a closed list of candidates, which may provoke a single-party sweep. Once partisan candidacies, partisan voting in bloc, and partisan ballots emerged within the framework of traditional assemblies and elections, political leaders, activists, and politically motivated scholars began to search for alternative electoral systems able to reduce single-party sweeps and exclusionary victories (Duverger 1951; see also LaPalombara and Weiner 1966; and the survey by Scarrow 2002).

During the nineteenth and early twentieth centuries, new electoral procedures were invented and adopted as innovative variations of the traditional system mentioned above. They can be classified into three groups, depending on whether they changed the district magnitude, the ballot, or the rule. The first group implied a change of the district magnitude from multimember to single-member districts, of course keeping both individual candidate voting and majoritarian rules. With smaller single-member districts, a candidate that would have been defeated by a party sweep in a multimember district may be elected. This system, thus, tends to produce more varied representation than multimember districts with party closed lists, although less than the old system of multimember districts with an open, individual candidate ballot. The second group of electoral rules introduced new forms of ballot favoring individual candidate voting despite the existence of party candidacies, such as limited and cumulative voting, while maintaining the other two essential elements of the traditional system: multimember districts and majoritarian rules. Finally, the third group of new electoral rules implied the introduction of proportional representation formulas, which are compatible with multimember districts and also, in some variants, with individual candidate voting, and permit the development of multipartism (Colomer 2006).

Different electoral rules and procedures create different incentives to coordinate the appropriate number of candidacies (as has been emphasized by Cox 1997). However, coordination may fail, especially under restrictive formulas based on plurality rule that may require paramount efforts to concentrate numerous potential candidates into a few broad, potentially winning candidacies. By analyzing party systems and elections over long periods and, in some studies, within each country, it has been shown that electoral systems based on plurality or majority rules tend to remain in place only to the extent that two large parties are able to attract broad electoral support and alternate in government. But when multiple parties develop in spite of and against the incentives provided by the existing majoritarian system and through coordination failures, they tend to adopt more permissive electoral rules, especially proportional representation formulas.

Generally, the choice of electoral systems follows what can be called "Micro-mega's rule," by which the large prefer the small and the small prefer the large: a few large parties tend to prefer small assemblies, small district magnitudes, and rules based on small quotas of votes for allocating seats, such as plurality rule, while multiple small parties tend to prefer large assemblies, large district magnitudes, and large quotas such as those of proportional representation. Nowadays, more than 80 percent of democratic regimes in countries with more than one million inhabitants use electoral systems with proportional representation rules (Lijphart 1994; Blais and Massicotte 1997; Colomer 2004, 2005*a*).

The relevant implication of this discussion for constitutional analysis is that electoral systems are intertwined with party systems, which in turn shape the relations between the legislature and the executive. All these elements define different types of political regime.

3 CONSTITUTIONAL REGIME TYPOLOGIES

Traditional legalistic classifications of constitutional regimes focused, in addition to the distinction between autocracy and democracy, on the difference, within the latter, between "parliamentary" and "presidential" regimes (see, for example, Duverger 1955; Verney 1959; and the compilation by Lijphart 1992). The introduction of a second dimension, the electoral system, discussed in the previous section, makes the classification of democratic regimes more complex. In particular, within parliamentary regimes one can distinguish between those using majoritarian electoral rules, which typically imply that a single party is able to win an assembly majority and appoint the prime minister, and those using proportional representation, which correspond to multiparty systems and coalition cabinets. Presidential regimes and their variants, in contrast, are less affected by the electoral system dimension since at least one of the systems, the one for the election of the president, must be majoritarian and produce a single absolute winner.

What has possibly been the most influential political regime typology in recent comparative studies is based on the two institutional dimensions mentioned and the corresponding degrees of concentration of constitutional and party powers (Lijphart 1984, 1999). Lijphart primarily analyzes the "executives–parties" dimension; that is, the relation between cabinets and parliaments and the set of party and electoral systems, as well as a number of other highly-correlated variables (while another dimension not to be discussed here regards the degree of territorial centralization). By statistical correlations and factor analysis of the empirical data, he arrives at a dual political regime typology, organized around the "majoritarian" (or Westminster) and the "consensus" models of democracy, respectively characterized by high power concentration and broad power sharing.

This simple empirical dichotomy, however, seems to be a contingent result of the sample of countries considered, since very few have checks-and-balances, presidential, or semi-presidential regimes (1 percent in the first exercise with twenty-one countries, 17 percent in the second with thirty-six). Therefore, according to this widely used typology, such a diversity of political regimes as the parliamentary-majoritarian of the United Kingdom, the checks-and-balances of the United States, and semi-presidential of France, among others, are included in the "majoritarian" type, while the consensus type refers to parliamentary-proportional regimes, mostly located in continental Europe. (For methodological critiques and alternative operational proposals, see Bogaards 2000; Taagepera 2003.)

Other approaches to the way different constitutional regimes work do not focus on a priori analysis of institutions but give primacy to the role of political parties. Some authors have promoted broad uses of the categories of "unified" and "divided" government. This new dual typology was initially applied to the analysis of the United States, where a "unified government" with the president's party having a majority in both houses of Congress has existed for only 59 percent of the time from 1832 to 2006, while "divided government," which was very frequent during the second half of the twentieth century, implies that two different political party majorities exist in the presidency and Congress. However, US congressional rules have traditionally included the ability of 40 percent of senators to block any decision by filibustering, which has almost always made the president's party unable to impose its decisions on its own. This could explain why no significant differences in legislative performances between periods of "unified" and "divided" governments have been observed (as persistently reported by King and Ragsdale 1988; Mayhew 1991; Fiorina 1992; Cox and McCubbins 1993; Peterson and Greene 1993; Edwards, Barrett, and Peake 1997; Epstein and O'Halloran 1999; but see discussion in Howell, Adler, Caneron, and Riemann 2000; Conley 2003).

Assuming that, in order to prevent deadlock, a situation of divided government (and, in the United States, almost any real situation) may lead to negotiations between the president's and other parties to form a sufficient congressional majority to make laws, it has been postulated that the absence of a single-party parliamentary majority in a parliamentary regime should also be characterized as "divided government." The integration into the same category of both the congressional minority president in a regime of separation of powers and the typical multiparty coalition or minority government in a parliamentary-proportional regime would make the USA "not exceptional" (Laver and Shepsle 1991; Elgie 2001).

A related approach also integrating institutions and parties in the same count centers on so-called "veto-players" (Tsebelis 1995, 2002). In this approach, political regimes can be analyzed for how many veto-players exist, which may have significant consequences on the degree of complexity of policy decision-making. In the analysis of parliamentary systems, the number of veto-players turns out to be equivalent to the number of parties in government, thus not taking into account whether they are pivotal or superfluous to making the coalition a winning one (a subject largely discussed, in contrast, in the literature on coalition formation, as well as that on power indices, as revised by Felsenthal and Machover 1998; Leech 2002). In checks-and-balances and similar regimes, the number of veto-players increases with the number of "chambers" (including the presidency) with different partisan control. A single veto-player situation would be equivalent to "unified government" as defined above, thus also making parliamentary and checks-and-balances and related regimes equivalent when the decision-power is highly concentrated.

In contrast to other approaches, this may result in non-dual classifications, since not only one or two, but several numbers of veto-players can exist in a political system. However, this approach pretends to analyze how political institutions work in practice, not the a priori characteristics of different constitutional formulas, which does make it less appealing for constitutional choice, advice, or design. The exclusion of the electoral stage from the analysis tends even to blur the fundamental distinction between autocracy and democracy. From the perspective provided by the veto-player approach, single-party governments would work in the same way independently of whether they were autocratic or democratic (for methodological critiques, see Moser 1996; Ganghof 2005).

Taking into account the analyses of both the relations between the executive and the legislature and the electoral rules previously reviewed, a more complex five-fold typology of democratic constitutional regimes can be derived. The relatively high number of a priori, polar types here considered does not presume that there are always significant differences in the working and proximate outcomes of all of them, but it does not preclude potentially interesting empirical findings that more simple or dualistic typologies may make impossible to observe. Empirical analyses may reduce the number of relevant types when, for the purposes of the problem under scrutiny, some of them may appear to be collapsed into a single one. But this may be a result of the analysis rather than an a priori simplifying assumption. From lower to higher degrees of concentration of power, the types of constitutional regimes previously discussed are:

1. parliamentary-proportional (e.g. Germany, the Netherlands);
2. checks and balances (e.g. United States, Indonesia);
3. semi-presidential (e.g. France, Poland);
4. presidentialist (e.g. Argentina, Mexico);
5. parliamentary-majority (e.g. United Kingdom, Canada).

Note that types 1 and 5 correspond to the classical category of "parliamentary" regime, here drastically split for different party systems and electoral systems, while types 2, 3, and 4 are variants of the classical category of "presidential" regime as discussed in the previous section. Regarding the other typologies reviewed above, the "consensus" model would correspond to type 1, while the "majoritarian" model would include types 2, 3, 4, and 5; type 1 would usually be associated with "divided government," while types 2, 3, and 4 would alternate between "divided" and "unified" governments, and type 5 would usually be associated with "unified government;" there could be multiple veto-players in types 1, 2, 3, and 4, although not always, while type 5 would tend to have a single veto-player with higher frequency. Thus, the different typologies here reviewed only agree on considering types 1 and 5 as extreme, respectively implying diffuse and concentrated power, while types 2, 3, and 4 are differently classified, either together with any of the two extreme types or as intermediate ones.

4   CONSTITUTIONAL CONSEQUENCES

It has been repeatedly postulated that different constitutional formulas have different consequences on politics, policy, and the polity. The "proximate" political consequences of different constitutional arrangements regard mainly the type, party composition, and degree of stability of governments. The rest of the consequences should be considered relatively "remote," indirect, and perhaps identifiable in terms of constraints, limits, and opportunities, rather than determining specific decisions or outcomes. They may affect economic and other public policy-making, as well as the corresponding performance, but only partially. Also, different constitutional formulas may help democracy to endure or facilitate its shortening. On all of these levels, significant and interesting empirical correlations between different constitutional formulas and outcomes have been found. But these correlations do not always go together with the specification of the mechanisms by which they may exist; in particular, how different types of governments may be linked to different policy performances, and how the latter may be related to the duration of democratic regimes.

4.1   Government Formation

In parliamentary regimes with majoritarian electoral rules, a single party, even with minority electoral support, usually finds sufficient institutional levers to form a government. This tends to make these governments more internally consistent and more durable than multiparty coalition or minority governments typical of parliamentary regimes with proportional representation, which are more vulnerable to coalition splits, censure, or confidence-lost motions, and other events and strategies provoking anticipated elections (Grofman and Roozendaal 1997; Strom and Swindle 2002; Smith 2004).

However, relatively stable single-party parliamentary governments, as well as presidential governments with a president's party majority in the assembly and fixed terms, tend to produce more changing and unstable policies than those relying upon the support of multiple parties or interinstitutional agreements. To understand this, consider that a single-party government is the institutional result of an election that becomes decisive for all the multiple policy issues that may enter the government's agenda. As the "spatial theory" of voting can illuminate, the "single-package" outcome of political competition in a policy "space" formed by multiple issues and dimensions can be highly unpredictable. The election may be won on the basis of a small set of issues that become prominent during the campaign and in voters' information driving their vote. But the subsequent single-party government may have a free hand to approve and implement its preferred policies on many issues, even if they have not been salient in the previous debate and campaign.

In contrast, in multiparty elections producing coalition cabinets, as well as in interinstitutional relations involving different political majorities, each party can focus on a different set of issues, globally enlarging the electoral agenda and the corresponding debate. In the further institutional process, certain issues (typically including major domains such as macroeconomic policy, interior, and foreign affairs) are dealt with separately on single-issue "spaces." Each of them can usually be the subject of a broad multiparty or interinstitutional agreement around a moderate position, which precludes drastic changes and induces policy stability in the medium or long term. Other issues can be negotiated in such a way that the minority with more intense preferences on each issue may see its preferred policy approved, whether through the distribution of cabinet portfolios to parties focused on different domains (such as finance for liberals, education for Christian-democrats, social or labor policy for social-democrats, etc.) or through logrolling among different groups on different issues in congress. This second mechanism creates different but enduring political supports to the decisions on each issue and also tends to produce relative policy stability. (Some ideas of this sort can be found in Blondel and Müller-Rommel 1988, 1993; Budge and Keman 1990; Laver and Schofield 1990; Strom 1990; Laver and Shepsle 1994, 1996; Deheza 1998; Müller and Strom 2000).

4.2   Policy Performance

A seminal analysis of the policy effects of different constitutional regimes and the type of governments they produce emerged from the study of British politics (see early discussion in Finer 1975). As seen from this observatory, a parliamentary-majoritarian regime creating single-party governments on the basis of a minority of popular votes is the scene of "adversary politics." This implies two major consequences: first, electorally minority governments with a social bias are more prone to be captured by minority interest groups and to implement redistributive and protectionist policies hurting broad social interests; second, frequent alternation of socially and electorally minority parties in government produces policy reversal and instability (including changes in regulations of prices, the labor market, taxes), which depress investment incentives. The bases for sustained economic growth seemed, thus, to be damaged by the likely effects of Westminster-type constitutional rules on government formation and policy-making.

This kind of argument has been tested in a number of studies basically using the (Westminster) majoritarian/consensus dual typology reviewed in the previous section. Most empirical findings show no significant differences in the performance of the two types of political regimes regarding economic growth, although some of them indicate a slightly better record for consensus democracies on inflation and unemployment. Better results for the consensus model have been found regarding electoral participation, low levels of politically motivated violence, women's representation, and social and environmental policies (Powell 1982; Baylis 1989; Lijphart 1984, 1999; Crepaz 1996; Birchfield and Crepaz 1998; Eaton 2000).

Using a different approach, it has also been held that parliamentary regimes with proportional representation tend to develop broad programs benefiting a majority of the voters, including redistribution through social security and welfare policies, in contrast to narrower targets in both parliamentary regimes with majoritarian elections and presidential regimes. The parliamentary-proportional regimes appear to be associated with better growth-promoting policies, but they also have relatively high taxes and public spending, which do not necessarily favor growth (Persson and Tabellini 2003).

The weakness of empirical relations such as those reported here might reflect a relative remoteness of the independent variable (constitutional models) from the dependent one (economic and social performance). Economic growth, in particular, has indeed many more "proximate" causes than political institutions, such as capital formation, labor productivity, entrepreneurship, trade, technology availability, and education. The opposite of "proximate," which would correspond to the role of institutions, should be "remote," since the "proximate" causes just mentioned may in turn depend on institutions but also on other non-institutional variables such as climate and natural resources, population, and human capacities. Regarding institutions, those favoring state effectiveness and an effective judiciary, as well as those regulating property rights, contracts, and finances, might be more relevant to explaining economic growth than certain variants in constitutional formulas and not necessarily closely related to them. (For recent discussions, see Hammond and Butler 2003; Alesina and Glaeser 2004; Glaeser, La Porta, and Lopez-de-Silanes 2004; Przeworski 2004; Acemoglu, Johnson, and Robinson 2005).

A new way to research could be designed by analogy to some recent studies on the relation between electoral systems and party systems reported above. In both problems (the relation between electoral systems and party systems, and the relation between constitutional formulas and economic growth), the main tradition in empirical studies is comparative statics; that is, the comparison of different supposedly independent variables established in different countries. An alternative approach would compare different supposedly independent variables within the same country. In a similar way as changes in party systems have been identified before and after the change of electoral rules in each country, the rates of economic growth or other interesting variables could be compared for periods with different constitutional formulas in each country (including democracy or dictatorship). This may require difficult collection of data for very long periods. But it would permit a better identification of the specific effects of changing political-institutional variables over the background of presumably more constant variables for each country, such as natural resources and population.

4.3   Democracy Duration

Different constitutional formulas have also been linked to different rates of success of attempts at democratization and to the duration of democratic regimes. Recent analyses of political change have emphasized that strategic choices of different constitutional formulas are driven by actors' relative bargaining strength, electoral expectations, and attitudes to risk (Przeworski 1986, 1991; Elster 1996; Elster, Offe, and Preuss 1998; Colomer 1995, 2000; Geddes 1996; Goodin 1996; Voigt 1999). A common assumption is that citizens and political leaders tend to support those formulas producing satisfactory results for themselves and reject those making them permanently excluded and defeated. As a consequence, those constitutional formulas producing widely-distributed satisfactory outcomes should be more able to develop endogenous support and endure. In general, widely representative and effective political outcomes should feed social support for the corresponding institutions, while exclusionary, biased, arbitrary, or ineffective outcomes might foster citizens' and leaders' rejection of the institutions producing such results. In this approach, support for democracy is not necessarily linked to good economic performance, as discussed above, but to a broader notion of institutional satisfaction of citizens' political preferences. This is consistent with a rational notion of legitimacy (Rogowski 1974), it can modeled as a positive relation between institutional pluralism and democratic stability (Miller 1983), and it can be refined with the concepts of behavioral and institutional equilibrium (Shepsle 1986; Colomer 2001*b*, 2205*a*; Diermeier and Krehbiel 2003).

Citizens' political satisfaction with democratic outcomes has been estimated by means of measures of congruence between citizens' preferences and policy-makers' positions and through survey polls. From the first approach, it has been found that cabinets in parliamentary regimes with proportional representation include the median voter's preference with higher frequency than those using majoritarian electoral rules, in both parliamentary and presidential regimes; proportional representation and multiparties reduce, thus, the aggregate "distance" between citizens and rulers (Huber and Powell 1994; Powell 2000). Consistent with these findings, an analysis of survey polls in Western European countries show that political satisfaction with the way democracy works is more widely and evenly distributed in pluralistic regimes than in majoritarian ones (Anderson and Guillory 1997).

In general, constitutional democracies favoring power sharing and inclusiveness should be able to obtain higher endogenous support and have greater longevity than those favoring the concentration of power. Indeed, empirical accounts show that democratic regimes are the most peaceful ones, while semi-democratic or transitional regimes are most prone to conflict, even more than exclusionary dictatorships (basically because the latter increase the costs of rebellion) (Snyder 1996; Hegre, Ellingsen, Gates, and Gleditsch 2001). Among democracies, parliamentary regimes are more resilient to crises and more able to endure than presidential ones (Linz 1990*b*; Stepan and Skach 1993; Mainwaring 1993; Linz and Valenzuela 1994; Przeworski, Alvarez, Cheibub, and Limongi 2000; but see discussion by Power and Gasiorowski 1997; Cheibub and Limogi 2002). But by using a three-fold typology that, in consistency with the discussion above, also takes electoral systems into account, parliamentary majoritarian regimes appear to be associated with a higher frequency of ethnic and civil wars than presidential regimes, while parliamentary proportional regimes are the most peaceful ones (Reynal 2002, 2005). Proportional representation systems also experience fewer transnational terrorist incidents than majoritarian ones (Li 2005).

Actually, almost no new democracy established in the world during the broad "third wave" of democratization starting in 1974 has adopted the British-style constitutional model of parliamentary regime with a two-party system and majoritarian electoral rules. This may make comparisons based on the dual typology parliamentary/presidential less reductive for this period since the former type has become, in fact, largely identified with its variant of proportional representation elections. But the three-fold typology can illuminate the pitfalls of the British constitutional model in previous periods, when most new democracies having adopted this model eventually fell and were replaced with dictatorships.

The number of constitutional democracies rose enormously during the last quarter of the twentieth century, encompassing for the first time a majority of total world population since 1996. This has been the result of a very long-term evolution, which started in the so-called first and second "waves" of democratization (basically corresponding to the aftermaths of the First and Second World Wars), and accelerated in recent times with the end of the cold war. Thus, constitutionalism has been increasingly linked to democratization, as noted at the beginning of this survey.

Among democratic constitutions, there has been a trend in favor of formulas permitting relatively high levels of social inclusiveness, political pluralism, policy stability, and democracy endurance. This reflects the relatively greater capability of pluralistic formulas to generate endogenous support. Not only may citizens obtain relatively broad satisfaction of their expectations and demands from democratic institutional formulas requiring the formation of a broad majority to make collective decisions. Power-seeking politicians may also ultimately reject or abandon institutional formulas producing absolute losers and the total exclusion of relevant actors from power. Of the democratic countries with more than one million inhabitants, nowadays only less than one-sixth use parliamentary majority constitutional formulas, while about half are checks-and-balances regimes or its presidentialist and semi-presidential variants, and more than one-third are parliamentary-proportional representation regimes (updated from Colomer 2001a).

5   CONCLUSION

A number of questions addressed in the previous pages have become key questions in the political science literature on constitutions and may guide future research. There is still some room for discussion over the conceptual and empirical adequacy of the different political regime typologies. A clear distinction should be made between a priori institutional characteristics of the different models and the actual working of the samples of cases observed, which are always unavoidably limited and can thus induce biased inferences. The important role of party systems and electoral systems in shaping the relations between parliaments and governments is nowadays generally accepted, in contrast to narrower legalistic approaches that were typical of constitutional studies a few years ago. But other questions remain open to more accurate analysis in a comparative perspective. They include the differences between the US-style "checks-and-balances" model favoring power sharing, and the "presidentialist" model, diffused in Latin America and possibly other parts of the world, favoring the concentration of power and some exclusiveness. Also, it is not clear whether the so-called "semi-presidential" model should be conceived as an alternation between different phases corresponding to alternative constitutional models rather than as an intermediate type.

The scope of direct political consequences that have been attributed to different constitutional models also deserves to be revised. Fairly direct consequences may include different degrees of policy stability and instability, which seem to be associated, perhaps counter-intuitively, with complex and simple constitutional frameworks respectively. Regarding economic performance, it would probably be wise to consider that constitutional formulas may have only an indirect role that should be put in a broader framework of non-institutional variables. While the comparative method has been mostly applied to the hypothetical consequences of different constitutional formulas used in different countries, a temporal dimension may enhance the analysis. Rates of economic growth or other relevant variables could be compared not only for different countries with different regimes, but also for periods with different constitutional formulas in each country, including democracy and dictatorship.

Finally, theoretical and comparative analyses should help to improve constitutional choice, advice, and design. The present wide spread of democracy in the world raises new demands for constitutional formulas able to produce efficient decision-making and broad social satisfaction with the outcomes of government.

REFERENCES

ACEMOGLU, D., JOHNSON, S. and ROBINSON, J. 2005. Institutions as the fundamental cause of long-run growth. In *Handbook of Economic Growth*, ed. P. Aghion and S. Durlauf. Amsterdam: North-Holland.

ACKERMAN, B. 2000. The new separation of powers. *Harvard Law Review*, 113: 633–729.

AGUILAR RIVERA, J. A. 2000. *En pos de la quimera: Reflexiones sobre el experimento constitucional atlántico.* Mexico: Fondo de Cultura Económica.

ALESINA, A. and GLAESER, E. 2004. *Fighting Poverty in the U.S. and Europe.* Oxford: Oxford University Press.

ANDERSON, C. and GUILLOY. C. 1997. Political institutions and satisfaction with democracy. *American Political Science Review*, 91 (1): 66–81.

BAHRO, H., BAYERLEIN, B., and VESER, E. 1998. Duverger's concept: semi-presidential government revisited. *European Journal of Political Research*, 34: 201–24.

BAYLIS, T. 1989. *Governing by Committee.* Albany: State University of New York Press.

BIRCHFIELD, V. and CREPAZ, M. 1998. The impact of constitutional structures and collective and competitive veto points on income inequality in industrialized democracies. *European Journal of Political Research*, 34: 175–200.

BLAIS, A. and MASSICOTTE, L. 1997. Electoral formulas: a macroscopic perspective. *European Journal of Political Research*, 32: 107–29.

BLONDEL, J. and MÜLLER-ROMMEL, F. (eds.) 1988. *Cabinets in Western Europe*. New York: St Martin's Press.

—— —— 1993. *Governing Together*. London: Macmillan.

BOGAARDS, M. 2000. The uneasy relationship between empirical and normative types in consociational theory. *Journal of Theoretical Politics*, 12 (4): 395–423.

BOGDANOR, V. (ed.) 1988. *Constitutions in Democratic Politics*. Aldershot: Gower.

—— (ed.) 2003. *The British Constitution in the Twentieth Century*. Oxford: Oxford University Press.

—— and BUTLER, D. (eds.) *Democracy and Elections*. Cambridge: Cambridge University Press.

BOIX, C. 1999. Setting the rules of the game: the choice of electoral systems in advanced democracies. *American Political Science Review*, 93: 609–24.

BRADY, D. and VOLDEN, C. 1998. *Revolving Gridlock*. Boulder, Colo.: Westview Press.

BRENNAN, G. and BUCHANAN, J. 1985. *The Reason of Rules: Constitutional Political Economy*. Cambridge: Cambridge University Press.

BUCHANAN, J. 1990. The domain of constitutional economics. *Constitutional Political Economy*, 1 (1): 1–18.

—— and TULLOCK, G. 1962. *The Calculus of Consent: Logical Foundations of Constitutional Democracy*. Ann Arbor: University of Michigan Press.

BUDGE, I. and KEMAN, H. 1990. *Parties and Democracy*. Oxford: Oxford University Press.

BURNS, J. 1965. *Presidential Government*. Boston: Houghton Mifflin.

CAMERON, C. 2000. *Veto Bargaining*. Cambridge: Cambridge University Press.

CHEIBUB, J. A. and LIMOGI, F. 2002. Modes of government formation and the survival of presidential regimes. *Annual Review of Political Science*, 5: 151–79.

COLOMER, J. M. 1995. *Game Theory and the Transition to Democracy: The Spanish Model*. Cheltenham: Edward Elgar.

—— 2000. *Strategic Transitions*. Baltimore: Johns Hopkins University Press.

—— 2001a. *Political Institutions*. Oxford: Oxford University Press.

—— 2001b. The strategy of institutional change. *Journal of Theoretical Politics*, 13 (3): 235–48.

—— (ed.) 2004. *Handbook of Electoral System Choice*. New York: Palgrave-Macmillan.

—— 2005a. It's the parties that choose electoral systems (or Duverger's laws upside down). *Political Studies*, 53 (1): 1–21.

—— 2005b. Policy making in divided government. *Public Choice*, 125: 247–69.

—— 2006. On the origins of electoral systems and political parties. *Electoral Studies*, forthcoming. Available at: http://www.econ.upf.edu/cat/faculty/onefaculty.php?id=p261.

—— and NEGRETTO, G. 2005. Can presidentialism work like parliamentarism? *Government and Opposition*, 40 (1): 60–89.

CONGLETON, R. D. 2001. On the durability of king and council. *Constitutional Political Economy*, 12 (3): 193–215.

CONLEY, R. 2003. *The Presidency, Congress, and Divided Government*. College Station: Texas A&M University Press.

COX, G. 1997. *Making Votes Count*. Cambridge: Cambridge University Press.

—— and KERNELL, S. 1991. *The Politics of Divided Government*. Boulder, Colo.: Westview.

—— and MCCUBBINS, M. 1993. *Legislative Leviathan*. Berkeley: University of California Press.

Cox, G. and Morgenstern, S. 2002. Latin America's reactive assemblies and proactive presidents. In *Legislative Politics in Latin America*, ed. S. Morgenstern and B. Nacif. Cambridge: Cambridge University Press.

Crepaz, M. 1996. Consensus vs. majoritarian democracy: political institutions and their impact on macroeconomic performance and industrial disputes. *Comparative Political Studies*, 19 (1): 4–26.

Crossman, R. H. 1963. Introduction. In Walter Bagehot, *The English Constitution*. Ithaca, NY: Cornell University Press.

Dahl, R. A. 2002. *How Democratic is the American Constitution?* New Haven, Conn.: Yale University Press.

Deheza, G. I. 1998. Gobiernos de coalición en el sistema presidencial: América del Sur. Pp. 151–69 in *El presidencialismo renovado*, ed. D. Nohlen and M. Fernández. Caracas: Nueva Sociedad.

Diermeier, D. and Krehbiel, K. 2003. Institutionalism as a methodology. *Journal of Theoretical Politics*, 15 (2): 123–44.

Duhamel, O. and Parodi, J. L. (eds.) 1988. *La Constitution de la Vè République*. Paris: Fondation Nationale des Sciences Politiques.

Duverger, M. 1951. *Les parties politiques*. Paris: Seuil (English trans. *Political Parties*. New York: Wiley, 1954).

—— [1955] 1970. *Institutions politiques et droit constitutionnel*, 11th edn. Paris: Presses Universitaires de France.

—— 1978. *Échec au roi*. Paris: Albin Michel.

—— 1980. A new political system model: semi-presidential government. *European Journal of Political Research*, 8 (2): 168–83.

—— (ed.) 1986. *Les régimes semi-présidentiels*. Paris: Presses Universitaires de France.

—— 1996. *Le système politique français*, 21st edn. Paris: Presses Universitaires de France.

—— 1998. *Les constitutions de la France*, 14th edn. Paris: Presses Universitaires de France.

Eaton, K. 2000. Parliamentarism versus presidentialism in the policy arena. *Comparative Politics*, 32: 355–76.

Edwards, G., Barrett, A., and Peake, J. 1997. Legislative impact of divided government. *American Journal of Political Science*, 41 (2): 545–63.

Elgie, R. (ed.) 1999. *Semi-presidentialism in Europe*. Oxford: Oxford University Press.

—— (ed.) 2001. *Divided Government in Comparative Perspective*. Oxford: Oxford University Press.

Elster, J. (ed.) 1996. *The Round Table Talks in Eastern Europe*. Chicago: University of Chicago Press.

—— and Slagstad, R. (eds.) 1988. *Constitutionalism and Democracy*. Cambridge: Cambridge University Press.

—— Offe, C., and Preuss, U. (eds.) 1998. *Institutional Design in Post-Communist Societies*. Cambridge: Cambridge University Press.

Epstein, D. and O'Halloran, S. 1999. *Delegating Powers*. Cambridge: Cambridge University Press.

Felsenthal, D. and Machover, M. 1998. *The Measurement of Voting Power*. Cheltenham: Edward Elgar.

Finer, S. E. 1988. Notes towards a history of constitutions. Pp. 17–32 in *Constitutions in Democratic Politics*, ed. V. Bogdanor. Aldershot: Gower.

—— (ed.) 1975. *Adversary Politics and Electoral Reform*. London: Anthony Wigram.

FIORINA, M. 1992. *Divided Government.* New York: Macmillan.

FITZGIBBON, R. 1945. Constitutional development in Latin America: a synthesis. *American Political Science Review,* 39 (3): 511–22.

FLINDERS, M. 2002. Shifting the balance? Parliament, the executive and the British constitution. *Political Studies,* 50 (1): 23–42.

GANGHOF, S. forthcoming. Veto points and veto players: a skeptical view. In *Consequences of Democratic Institutions,* ed. H. Kitschelt.

GARCÍA CALDERÓN, F. 1914. *Les démocraties latines de l'Amérique.* Paris: Flammarion.

GEDDES, B. 1996. Initiation of new democratic institutions in Eastern Europe and Latin America. Pp. 15–42 in *Institutional Design in New Democracies,* ed. A. Lijphart and C. Waisman. Berkeley: University of California Press.

GLAESER, E., LA PORTA, R., and LOPEZ-DE-SILANES, F. 2004. Do institutions cause growth? *Journal of Economic Growth,* 9 (3): 271–303.

GOODIN, R. E. (ed.) 1996. *The Theory of Institutional Design.* Cambridge: Cambridge University Press.

GROFMAN, B. (ed.) 1989. *The Federalist Papers and the New Institutionalism.* New York: Agathon.

—— and LIJPHART, A. (eds.) 1986. *Electoral Laws and their Political Consequences.* New York: Agathon.

—— and VAN ROOZENDAAL, P. 1997. Modeling cabinet durability and termination. *British Journal of Political Science,* 27: 419–51.

GRUMM, J. 1958. Theories of electoral systems. *Midwest Journal of Political Science,* 2 (4): 357–76.

HAMMOND, T. and BUTLER, C. 2003. Some complex answers to the simple question "Do institutions matter?" *Journal of Theoretical Politics,* 15 (2): 145–200.

—— and MILLER, G. 1987. The core of the constitution. *American Political Science Review,* 81: 1155–74.

HARDIN, R. 1989. Why a constitution? In *The Federalist Papers and the New Institutionalism,* ed. B. Grofman. New York: Agathon.

HEGRE, H., ELLINGSEN, T., GATES, S., and GLEDITSCH, N. 2001. Toward a democratic civil peace? *American Political Science Review,* 95 (1): 33–48.

HOWELL, W., ADLER, S., CAMERON, C., and RIEMANN, C. 2000. Divided government and the legislative productivity of Congress, 1945–94. *Legislative Studies Quarterly,* 25 (2): 285–312.

HUBER, J. and POWELL, G. B. 1994. Congruence between citizens and policymakers in two visions of liberal democracy. *World Politics,* 46 (3): 291–326.

JENNINGS, I. 1959. *Cabinet Government.* Cambridge: Cambridge University Press.

KATZ, R. 1997. *Democracy and Elections.* Oxford: Oxford University Press.

KING, G. and RAGSDALE, L. 1988. *The Elusive Executive.* Washington, DC: Congressional Quarterly.

KREHBIEL, K. 1996. Institutional and partisan sources of gridlock: a theory of divided and unified government. *Journal of Theoretical Politics,* 8: 7–40.

—— 1998. *Pivotal Politics.* Chicago: University of Chicago Press.

LAMBERT, J. 1963. *Amérique Latine: Structures sociales et institutions politiques.* Paris: Presses Universitaires de France.

LAPALOMBARA, J. and WEINER, M. (eds.) 1966. *Political Parties and Political Development.* Princeton, NJ: Princeton University Press.

LAVER, M. and SCHOFIELD, N. 1990. *Multiparty Government*. Oxford: Oxford University Press.

—— and SHEPSLE, K. 1991. Divided government: America is not exceptional. *Governance*, 4 (3): 250–69.

—— —— (eds.) 1994. *Cabinet Ministers and Parliamentary Government*. Cambridge: Cambridge University Press.

—— —— 1996. *Making and Breaking Governments*. Cambridge: Cambridge University Press.

LEECH, D. 2002. An empirical comparison of the performance of classical power indices. *Political Studies*, 50 (1): 1–22.

LI, Q. 2005. Does democracy promote or reduce transnational terrorrist incidents? *Journal of Conflict Resolution*, 49 (2): 278–97.

LIJPHART, A. 1984. *Democracies*. New Haven, Conn.: Yale University Press.

—— (ed.) 1992. *Parliamentary versus Presidential Government*. Oxford: Oxford University Press.

—— 1994. *Electoral Systems and Party Systems*. Oxford: Oxford University Press.

—— 1999. *Patterns of Democracy*. New Haven, Conn.: Yale University Press.

—— and GROFMAN, B. (eds.) 1988. *Choosing an Electoral System*. New York: Praeger.

LINZ, J. J. 1990a. The perils of presidentialism. *Journal of Democracy*, 1 (1): 51–69.

—— 1990b. The virtues of parliamentarism. *Journal of Democracy*, 1 (2): 84–91.

—— and VALENZUELA, A. (eds.) 1994. *The Failure of Presidential Democracy*. Baltimore: Johns Hopkins University Press.

LIPSON, L. 1964. *The Democratic Civilization*. Oxford: Oxford University Press.

LOEWENSTEIN, K. 1949. The presidency outside the U.S. *Journal of Politics*, 11 (3): 447–96.

—— 1957. *Political Power and the Governmental Process*. Chicago: University of Chicago Press.

MAINWARING, S. 1993. Presidentialism, multipartism, and democracy: the difficult combination. *Comparative Political Studies*, 26: 198–228.

—— and SHUGART, M. (eds.) 1997. *Presidentialism and Democracy in Latin America*. Cambridge: Cambridge University Press.

MAYHEW, D. 1991. *Divided We Govern*. New Haven, Conn.: Yale University Press.

MILLER, N. 1983. Pluralism and social choice. *American Political Science Review*, 21: 769–803.

MORGENSTERN, S. and NACIF, B. (eds.) 2002. *Legislative Politics in Latin America*. Cambridge: Cambridge University Press.

MOSER, P. 1996. The European Parliament as a conditional agenda setter. *American Political Science Review*, 90: 834–8.

MUELLER, D. 1996. *Constitutional Democracy*. Oxford: Oxford University Press.

MÜLLER, W. and STROM, K. 2000. *Coalition Governments in Western Europe*. Oxford: Oxford University Press.

NEUSTADT, R. 1990. *Presidential Powers and the Modern Presidents*. New York: Free Press.

NINO, C. 1992. *El presidencialismo puesto a prueba*. Madrid: Centro de Estudios Constitucionales.

NORTH, D. 1990. *Institutions, Institutional Change, and Economic Performance*. Cambridge: Cambridge University Press.

—— and WEINGAST, B. 1989. Constitutions and commitment. *Journal of Economic History*, 49 (4): 803–32.

ORDESHOOK, P. 1992. Constitutional stability. *Constitutional Political Economy*, 3: 137–75.

PERSSON, T. and TABELLINI, G. 2003. *The Economic Effects of Constitutions.* Cambridge, Mass.: MIT Press.

PETERSON, P. and GREENE, J. 1993. Why executive–legislative conflict in the U.S. is dwindling. *British Journal of Political Science,* 24: 33–55.

POWELL, G. B. 1982. *Contemporary Democracies.* Cambridge, Mass.: Harvard University Press.

—— 2000. *Elections as Instruments of Democracy.* New Haven, Conn.: Yale University Press.

POWER, T. and GASIOROWSKI, M. 1997. Institutional design and democratic consolidation in the Third World. *Comparative Political Studies,* 30 (2): 123–55.

PRZEWORSKI, A. 1986. Some problems in the study of transitions to democracy. Pp. 47–63 in *Transitions from Authoritarian Rule,* ed. G. O'Donnell, P. Schmitter, and L. Whitehead. Baltimore: Johns Hopkins University Press.

—— 1991. *Democracy and the Market.* Cambridge: Cambridge University Press.

—— 2004. The last instance: are institutions a deeper cause of economic development? *Archives Européennes de Sociologie,* 45: 165–88.

—— ALVAREZ, M., CHEIBUB, J. A., and LIMONGI, F. 2000. *Democracy and Development.* Cambridge: Cambridge University Press.

RAE, D. 1967. *The Political Consequences of Electoral Laws.* New Haven, Conn.: Yale University Press.

REYNAL-QUEROL, M. 2002. Ethnicity, political systems and civil wars. *Journal of Conflict Resolution,* 46 (1): 29–54.

—— 2005. Does democracy preempt civil wars? *European Journal of Political Economy,* 21 (2): 445–65.

RIGGS, F. 1988. The survival of presidentialism in America. *International Political Science Review,* 9 (4): 247–78.

RIKER, W. H. 1992. The justification of bicameralism. *International Political Science Review,* 13 (1): 101–16.

ROGOWSKI, R. 1974. *Rational Legitimacy.* Princeton, NJ: Princeton University Press.

SÄRLVIK, B. 1982. Scandinavia. Pp. 123–48 in *Democracy and Elections,* ed. V. Bogdanor and D. Butler. Cambridge: Cambridge University Press.

SARTORI, G. 1994. *Comparative Constitutional Engineering.* London: Macmillan.

SCARROW, S. (ed.) 2002. *Perspectives on Political Parties.* New York: Palgrave-Macmillan.

SEAWARD, P. and SILK, P. 2003. The House of Commons. In *The British Constitution in the Twentieth Century,* ed. V. Bogdanor. Oxford: Oxford University Press.

SHEPSLE, K. 1986. Institutional equilibrium and equilibrium institutions. Pp. 51–81 in *Political Science: The Science of Politics,* ed. H. Weisberg. New York: Agathon.

SHUGART, M. S. and CAREY, J. 1992. *Presidents and Assemblies.* Cambridge: Cambridge University Press.

SMITH, A. 2004. *Election Timing.* Cambridge: Cambridge University Press.

SNYDER, J. 1996. *From Voting to Violence.* New York: Norton.

STEPAN, A. and SKACH, C. 1993. Constitutional frameworks and democratic consolidation. *World Politics,* 44: 1–22.

STOKES, W. 1959. *Latin American Politics.* New York: Crowell.

STROM, K. 1990. *Minority Governments and Majority Rule.* Cambridge: Cambridge University Press.

—— and SWINDLE, S. 2002. Strategic parliamentary dissolution, *American Political Science Review,* 96: 579–91.

STRONG, C. F. 1963. *A History of Modern Political Constitutions.* New York: Capricorn.

TAAGEPERA, R. 2003. Arend Lijphart's dimensions of democracy. *Political Studies,* 51 (1): 1–19.

—— and SHUGART, M. S. 1989. *Seats and Votes.* New Haven, Conn.: Yale University Press.

TSEBELIS, G. 1995. Decision making in political systems. *British Journal of Political Science,* 25: 289–326.

—— 2002. *Veto Players.* Princeton, NJ: Princeton University Press.

VERNEY, D. 1959. *Analysis of Political Systems.* London: Routledge.

VOIGT, S. 1999. *Explaining Constitutional Change.* Cheltenham: Edward Elgar.

WEINGAST, B. 1995. The economic role of political institutions. *Journal of Law, Economics and Organization,* 7 (1): 1–31.

WHEARE, K. 1963. *Legislatures.* Oxford: Oxford University Press.

CHAPTER 13

....

AMERICAN FEDERALISM AND INTERGOVERNMENTAL RELATIONS

....

ALBERTA M. SBRAGIA

Although scholars have defined federalism in multiple ways, federalism as currently understood in American political and scholarly debate has to do with the role of subnational governments as both independent decision-makers and as implementors of federal legislation.[1] The use of federalism as a term typically signals a concern with the independence and political autonomy of subnational governments in policy-making or with the complex relationships which exist among levels of government as they carry out policy adopted in Washington.

To what degree should subnational governments be able to act independently? To what degree are they able to do so? How much power should Washington be able to exercise? These questions have framed the federalism discussion in the USA for many decades. Much of the literature argues that the nationalization of the

[1] The study of federalism has been multifaceted as it has incorporated works on intergovernmental relations. Key works in the post-Second World War period include Grodzins 1960; Riker 1964, 1975; Elazar 1962, 1966; Beer 1973, 1978; Wright 1988; Derthick 1970; Peterson, Rabe, and Wong 1986; Conlan 1998; Weingast 1995; Lowry 1992.

federal system since the 1970s mitigates against subnational governments being able to bring their discretionary resources to bear on their unique needs. The possibilities of significant policy diversity within the system have therefore been reduced. In that sense, the "politics of federalism" actually have to do with the politics of implementation of federally-designed policies and the politics of intergovernmental management involved in such implementation rather than with diversity within the overall federal system.

The complexities of American federalism are such that while some scholars argue the system has become highly centralized, others focus on the considerable discretion that state governments still possess. The paradox of American federalism in fact may lie in that scholars differ so widely in their analysis of—and conclusions about—the system.

While Samuel Beer views federalism as having been important only in the area of representation rather than in the recognition of territorial diversity (Beer 1978), others (Chhibber and Kollman 2004) argue that it is the centralization of authority in that system which has led to national parties. Some view the concentration of authority in Washington as a negation of a federal system while others see it as simply a change in a system which can vary from decentralization to centralization. Some view the states as counterweights to Washington while others focus on their technocratic capabilities. While some view the federal system as "coercive," others conclude that it reflects a "pragmatic" set of norms leading the federal government to be relatively sensitive to state concerns (Glendening and Reeves 1984; Elazar 1990; Kincaid 1990; Gormley 2005). While some analysts—especially those contributing to the theoretical literature on political economy—argue from a normative perspective rather than show an interest in the actual role of institutions (Rodden 2006), others carry out detailed analyses of what is actually going on in financial transfers. The literature on federalism in fact seems as disparate and confusing as the topic it is trying to analyze.

This chapter analyzes the shape of American federalism and concludes by arguing that the conflict between territorial and functional politics lies at the heart of the politics of federalism in the United States. National institutions, Congress in particular, are organized by functional areas whereas the representation of subnational governments' interest involves the insertion of territorial criteria into that functionally dominated process. Given the structural dominance of functional politics in the American national arena, and the weaknesses in the system by which states and local governments represent their own interests, it is not surprising that federalism as a value has become of secondary importance in Washington.

Whereas traditional notions of federalism viewed diversity as an intrinsic strength of a federal system, the increased nationalization of the system is caused by a desire to achieve more national uniformity and less diversity. The growth of the national regulatory state has been a major force in triggering such nationalization, especially as state and local governments have not been exempted from its reach. "Cooperative federalism,"[2] it is argued, existed when the process of nationalization was much less advanced; currently the force of mandates and the lack of clout wielded by intergovernmental groups are such that the system is one of "coercive federalism" (Kincaid 1990, 1996). Still other scholars argue that the federalism in the US "is a continuum in terms of national-state relations, ranging from nil to cooperative to coercive with the precise location of a given relationship on the continuum determined by function or component of a function concerned" (Zimmerman 2001, 28).

Constitutionally, federalism in the USA involves the relationship between Washington and state capitals. The Tenth Amendment reads, "The powers not delegated to the United States by the Constitution, nor prohibited by it to the States, are reserved to the States respectively, or to the people." States rather than "subnational" governments are the topic. Governments below the level of state governments were not included; they do not have constitutional standing. State governments could not be abolished but those below the state level did not have constitutional protection.

The constitutional protection granted to state governments by the US Constitution does anchor American federalism. Krause and Bowman argue that the "persistent tension regarding the proper balance of power between the national government and the states is an enduring feature of American federalism" (Krause and Bowman 2005, 360). Having acknowledged the role of the states, however, it is also true that federalism in the USA, when expanded beyond its constitutional/legal dimension, is characterized by the existence of tens of thousands of local governments which themselves have organized into national associations and form part of the so-called "intergovernmental lobby."

Contemporary federalism, therefore, focuses on the relationship between Washington and subnational governments. The fact that federalism in the USA is not limited to the relationship between Washington and state capitals is extremely important in understanding the political dynamics of American federalism. Counties, municipalities, public authorities, and special districts (all categorized as local governments) are, in legal terms, not only constitutionally unprotected but are "creatures of the state."

It is true that Krause and Bowman have found intriguing empirical evidence for the thesis that the partisan color of state governments influences whether Congress is willing to grant authority to state governments. They conclude that "when national level Democrats scan state institutions and find Democrats in control, they are more willing to shift power to the sub national level" (Krause and Bowman 2005, 365). The same holds for national-level Republicans when state-level Republicans are in power (Krause and Bowman 2005). Whether intergovernmental

---

[2] "Cooperative federalism," Daniel Elazar argued, was a more appropriate description of national–state relations than was "dual federalism." The latter, in the words of S. Rufus Davis, "envisaged a dual world of sovereign, coordinate, coequal, independent, autonomous, demarcated, compartmentalized, segregated, and distinct constitutional personae, the federal and state governments" (Davis 1978, 182–3 cited in Zimmerman 2001, 19; Elazar 1964).

lobbying constitutes the mechanism through which such partisan coupling is managed is unclear.

We do know that in practice, constitutional standing and partisan identity notwithstanding, state governments constantly compete with local governments for their place in the federal system. The role of state governments is far less privileged politically than it is constitutionally. Mayors and county officials as well as governors and state legislators lobby Congress. Cities and counties as well as state governments implement federal legislation. Mayors and county officials do not accept the argument that states should have privileged access to Washington. They do not accept that they should play a secondary role to governors in intergovernmental politics or in national policy-making. State and local officials are therefore constantly competing with one another for privileged access to Washington. "National–state" relations should often read "national–state and local" relations. Thus, the constitutional dimension of federalism differs very considerably from the political/policy dimension which has developed.

Access to Washington, however, has become more problematic over time. The policy-making process in Congress is structured functionally, and the policy communities which have developed are also functional. That is, they focus on specific policy areas, and the policy debate is cast in programmatic terms. Many of the major interest groups are also functionally oriented. By contrast, state and local governments, when presenting their case, necessarily are focusing on jurisdictional prerogatives. Their claim is based on territorial rather than programmatic or functional representation. The claims of territory do not fit easily into a system which is structured along very different lines.

The conflict between territorial and functional politics lies at the heart of the politics of federalism in the United States. National institutions, Congress in particular, are organized by functional areas whereas the representation of subnational governments' interests involves the insertion of territorial criteria into that functionally-dominated process. Given the structural dominance of functional politics in the American national arena, and the weaknesses in the system by which states and local governments represent their own interests, it is not surprising that federalism as a value has become of secondary importance in Washington.

1   TERRITORIAL POLITICS

Debates about federalism are very much debates about the claims of territory. They involve disagreements about the importance of the spatial dimension in governance, in public policy, and in representation. To what extent should Washington legislate in the arena of domestic policy? To what extent should the federal government pass laws which do not exempt state and local governments? To what extent should federal monies destined for state and local governments have "strings" (i.e. conditions) attached? To what extent should the elected officials of a territorial unit be given access to or be given special standing by Congress? Most fundamentally, to what extent should states be conceptualized as "polities" as opposed to "managers" in an "administrative chain of command" with Washington at its head (Elazar 1981, 71)? Should Congress treat states as it treats individuals and companies or should states be given special deference?

Some scholars have valued the autonomous role of state (and local) governments in legislative decision-making for reasons having to do with a defense against the abuse of power, as an avenue of democratic participation, or as a way to provide choice for taxpayers. Daniel Elazar and Thomas Dye both have forcefully argued that states are not simply administrative units or sub-units of the federal government. Elazar, defined states as "polities" and argued that the states were not "middle managers" (Elazar 1981). Thomas Dye argued that "state and local governments are political systems, not administrative units of the national government. Their primary function remains political, not managerial" (Dye 1990, 4). In this latter view, informed by public choice theory, one of the key political functions of state and local governments was to "compete for consumer-taxpayers by offering different packages of services and cost [so that] the closer each consumer-taxpayer can come to realizing his or her own preferences" (Dye 1990, 14). State and local governments could only compete with one another if they were free to decide for themselves on the shape of the "package of services" that would be offered to the consumer-taxpayer.

In practice, the role of the states, however, is very much shaped by the institutional structure of the federal government. The US Senate, in a comparative perspective, is extremely unusual in that each state elects two senators, regardless of the state's population (Lee and Oppenheimer 1999; Tsebelis and Money 1997). However it is electorates (constituents) from states rather than state *governments* themselves which are represented. Functional (policy) interests sometimes have a territorial dimension in the American Congress, as some policy interests are territorially concentrated (Sbragia 2004). Nonetheless, even in those cases, the representatives who speak for such interests are elected by voters; representatives are accountable to voters rather than to subnational officials. Furthermore, the very structure of the committee system in both houses of Congress is shaped around policy areas. Conflict primarily centers around the content of programs as well as the territorial distribution of programmatic benefits—and not around the role of subnational governments. Functional interests trump the interests of subnational governments.

The role of territorial governments—and the difference between functional and territorial politics—in the political arena becomes clear when examining intergovernmental lobbying. When state and local officials, organized in national associations, go to Washington to lobby, they are representing the interests of subnational governments rather than that of constituents (although the two may of course overlap).

The conflict between territorial and functional interests is key to the politics of federalism. The "institutional self-interest" of subnational elected officials has to do with maintaining as much authority and control as they possibly can over their own geographic area. By contrast, the interest of Congress lies in exercising national control in functionally defined policy areas.

2   TERRITORIAL GOVERNMENTS AND REPRESENTATION

American states, while constitutionally privileged in that they cannot be abolished by Washington, are not involved in national decision-making. They do not have a "seat at the decision-making table" in Washington. The original notion of "dual federalism" mandated a separation between the national and the state level—each would legislate in its own "spheres of action" (Kincaid 1996, 29). Thus, state officials would legislate within their own territory within many policy areas and the federal institutions would legislate for the entire country in a restricted number of policy areas. Although originally senators were selected by state legislatures, the Seventeenth Amendment led to senators being directly elected. The direct election of senators cut the tie between state-level institutions and national decision-making.

The Seventeenth Amendment has deeply altered the nature of American federalism. A comparison with the German federal system demonstrates the importance of *direct* state representation in the states' exercise of constitutional prerogatives. Whereas German federalism allows state governments to be involved in a great deal of national decision-making, American federalism views state governments as making decisions which apply only to the residents of their particular state. While the German state executive branch is represented as an institution in the national parliament's second chamber (the Bundesrat), American state governments are not represented in either the Senate or the House. Governors are only represented by their national interest groups.

Territorial politics—the representation of territorial interests as expressed through state governments—is central to the organization of the German federal system. Territorial interests can even override partisan differences. The German equivalent of governors sit in the Federal Republic's upper chamber. In the USA, by contrast, governors are not national decision-makers. Governors are lobbyists in Washington rather than decision-makers, a crucial distinction. While they can and do lobby at the national level, they are not constitutionally-designated decision-makers at the federal level as are the German Länder (Cammisa 1995; Sbragia 1992).

The lack of a "seat" for state governments in Washington means that the latter can ignore territorially-based claims. Thus, states and localities can be refused if they claim privileges or exemptions based on federal principles. States are powerless to prevent the national government from asserting its own jurisdiction in policy arenas traditionally dominated by subnational governments. This fact became particularly important as a national regulatory state developed in the postwar period and shapes the contemporary debate about federalism. Not surprisingly, therefore, the No Child Left Behind Act "federalized" public education, an area traditionally dominated by subnational governments. Claims related to federal principles are not typically found to be compelling. Some programmatic adjustments will be made and financial assistance may be provided, but the fundamental decision about whether the federal government will assert its own authority in a policy area will not typically be influenced by arguments related to federalism as such.

3   TERRITORIAL INTEREST AND PUBLIC POLICY

The issues tied to federalism in the USA are as old as the republic itself. Those, such as Alexander Hamilton, who argued for a strong national system which would allow the US to become a major commercial republic, have debated those, such as Thomas Jefferson, who feared that a strong central government would endanger the very roots of democracy and liberty. Those debates, while transformed, have not disappeared. Those who argue for diversity among the American states and argue against the imposition of federal rules and laws on states confront those who view broad national policies as the only way to ensure some kind of uniformity for all citizens regardless of their place of residence.

The rationale of such arguments has varied. The argument for national policies has been put forth by those who want to achieve equal civil rights for all citizens as well as some kind of "floor" in both economic opportunity and social protection. However, it can also be made by those who want a relatively non-interventionist government, one which is seen as "market-preserving," and who do not therefore want interventionist state governments counteracting the impact of national policies designed to build (rather than correct) markets (Weingast 1995; Sbragia 2000). As an example of the latter case, the (Republican) Reagan administration, which stressed its support of states' rights, supported business firms when they came into conflict with state-level administrative agencies (Gormley 2005). When state regulators came into conflict with businessmen, state regulators lost. Federalism was to be secondary to market forces.

The Reagan administration's rhetorical support for states rights, however, has been the norm for those wishing to limit the role of government generally. Federalism in the USA typically has been emphasized by those interested in less rather than more government. The assumption has been that many state governments, if left to their own devices, would be less interventionist than the federal government has been since the New Deal. Furthermore, such latitude would encourage competition among the states, with "competitive federalism" being favorably viewed as most supportive of those incentives conducive to economic growth and the expansion of markets (Dye 1990; Lowry 1992).

By contrast, those in favor of greater public intervention have typically argued for a stronger federal role in the belief that Washington would establish a "floor" higher than that found in many states. Such intervention has historically been tied to the expansion of the welfare and regulatory state, and thus a centralized federalism has become associated with social protection. Those interested in urban (rather than state) issues have also argued for a strong federal role in redistributive policy, concluding that only the federal government has the tools to carry out redistributive policy without harming the prospects for economic development (Peterson 1981). In this view, states, engaged in competitive federalism, are unable to redistribute resources as effectively as can the federal government (Thomas 2000).

More recently, however, those seeking more social protection have begun viewing the states rather than the federal government as possible allies (Nathan and Doolittle 1987, 357). Once conservative Republicans controlled Congress and the presidency, advocates of the welfare state and environmental protection began viewing the states as possible counterweights to the conservative policies coming out of Washington. Governors began being viewed as more pragmatic and less ideological than their party brethren in Washington, and more willing to consider policies which were viewed with hostility in Washington. The issue area of climate change was perhaps the most striking in this respect: while neither President Bush nor Congress would support legislation restricting carbon dioxide emissions, both Republican and Democratic governors began experimenting with an emissions trading scheme (Rabe 2004).

The view of states as liberal counterweights to Washington is relatively new, however. More typical has been the view that many state governments, if left to their own devices, would, in the view of liberals, begin a "race to the bottom," or in the view of conservatives, allow market forces to work as they should. The conflict between a vision based on competitive federalism with its concomitant reliance on state rather than federal power and one based on centralized federalism with Washington wielding very considerable power underlies both public policy and the scholarship—much of it with strong normative overtones—on American federalism.

Literature interested in the intersection of public authority and markets tends to make the argument for competitive federalism—the view being that competitive federalism is "market-preserving." By contrast, both activists and scholars interested in either social regulation (such as environmental protection) or social protection (such as assistance to the needy or rights for the disabled) tend to make the argument for various degrees of federal preemption of state authority. States are very engaged in economic development activities—which requires their competing with one another to keep and attract business firms as well as creating the infrastructure conducive to business activity (Fosler 1988; Thomas 2000). Many therefore fear that without the intervention of Washington, competitive federalism forces generous states to become more conservative in order not to frighten—as well as to attract—mobile capital. In a similar vein, generous states are viewed as running the risk of becoming "welfare magnets" so that only federal social policy can effectively address poverty (Peterson and Rom 1990, 8). Generous states, in fact, may support federal intervention precisely to avoid being isolated and to insulate themselves from the forces of competitive federalism.[3]

---

[3] It should be noted that there is still no scholarly consensus regarding the extent to which competitive federalism affects welfare policies. Research on competitive federalism and welfare revolves around the questions of whether more generous benefits have an impact on the location decision of the poor (namely whether generous states become "welfare magnets") and on whether states compete down with neighboring states, reducing benefits if their neighbors reduce them (the "race-to-the-bottom" hypothesis).

It should be noted that these questions may not be empirically linked, in that political incentives may induce state policy-makers to engage in a "race to the bottom" over welfare benefits even though more generous benefits do not affect, or only marginally affect, the location decisions of prospective welfare recipients (Bailey and Rom 2004, 327; Brueckner 2000, 508).

Empirical results on both hypotheses have been mixed. As regards the first hypothesis, some have found very little evidence of states acting as welfare magnets (Schram, Nitz, and Krueger 1998; Schram and Soss 1998; Levine and Zimmerman 1999; Allard and Danziger 2000; Berry, Fording, and Hanson 2003) while others do find evidence that supports the welfare magnet hypothesis, although the size of the effect of welfare benefits on location decisions tends to be small (Bailey 2005; Enchautegui 1997).

As regards the race-to-the-bottom hypothesis, most research has found statistically significant (although in most cases substantively small) effects, indicating that there is some competition to reduce welfare benefits among similar states, even though the extent of the impact of this competition on actual benefit levels is low (Figlio, Kolpin, and Reid 1999; Saavedra 2000; Rom, Peterson, and

In the real world of policy-making, however, the scene is murkier. Although Republicans have traditionally been seen as supporters of both more power to the states and deregulating market forces, it was a Republican president (George W. Bush) who engineered the No Child Left Behind Act, a piece of legislation which nationalized public elementary and secondary education in a way that was new to the United States. While the field of public education had traditionally been viewed as firmly under state and local control, it became nationalized with relatively little opposition and with support from key Democratic political leaders in Congress. In fact, President Bush, although a former governor of Texas, has not emphasized federalism as a value. In a similar vein, President George Herbert Walker Bush managed to renew far-reaching federal environmental legislation, legislation which in fact had been originally passed under the Republican President Richard Nixon. Republican presidents, therefore, have supported federal legislation which significantly erodes the power of state governments and which constrains market forces. Programmatic preferences have overridden claims regarding subnational autonomy.

Furthermore, those Republican leaders who have emphasized federalism, while agreeing that Washington is too powerful, have also differed very significantly in their proposals for change. President Nixon did not see "government as the problem" while President Reagan and Newt Gingrich, the Speaker of the House of Representatives in 1995–8, wanted to scale back all government at all levels. In Conlan's words:

Nixon viewed his federalism strategy as a means of improving and strengthening government, especially at the state and local levels. His proposals, unlike those of subsequent Republican reformers, were intended to improve government, not dismantle it. Reagan, in contrast, viewed his New Federalism proposals as part of a broader strategy to reduce the role of government in society at every level. . . . Reagan's positive vision, though heavily localistic, lacked a strong role for government of any kind. . . . Gingrich argued . . . [that] the appropriate solution would be to eliminate the national welfare state, root and branch. (Conlan 1998, 12–14)

In spite of Nixon's commitment to decentralization, perhaps best symbolized by revenue sharing, Conlan concludes that "Nixon left behind a federal system that was probably more centralized than the one he inherited. Federal expenditures for many domestic functions were increased dramatically, and an unprecedented federal intergovernmental regulatory presence was institutionalized" (Conlan 1998, 91). It is precisely that outcome which has led most scholars to argue that although a form of "devolution revolution" has been promised many times, it has not materialized (Kincaid 1998; Nathan 1996).

Scheve 1998; Berry, Fording, and Hanson 2003; Bailey and Rom 2004). However, some research has disputed these findings. In particular, Craig Volden has argued that competitive federalism affects the choices states make with regard to the benefit levels they offer, but not in the sense that they are engaged in a race to the bottom. Rather, state interaction slows down the increase in benefits, in that states increase their benefit levels only after their neighbors have also raised them (Volden 2002).

4   INTERGOVERNMENTAL RELATIONS

Although the constitutional definition of federalism in the USA privileges only state governments, scholars such as Thomas Dye (1990) invariably included local governments as components of the federal system. It was that extension of the federal system which underpinned the term "intergovernmental relations," a term which has come to be used interchangeably with federalism in a great deal of literature. Yet the replacement of federalism, with its political connotations, with intergovernmental relations, with its administrative and managerial overtones, was vehemently opposed by scholars such as Dye. And in fact the implicit assumptions of those two types of analyses are quite different. Federalism has tended to remain a normative concept subject to political and scholarly conflict while "intergovernmental relations" revolves around issues of management and administration, with administrative rather than political elites playing a key role.

Nonetheless, in much scholarly literature, the concept of federalism has become linked to the complex ways in which the system of public authority actually works in the USA—a system which includes Washington, state capitals, county governments, municipalities, and special districts as well as school districts has become entangled with the study of intergovernmental relations to such an extent that the two terms are often used together to refer to similar phenomena.[4] Federalism refers to the constitutional division of powers and authority between the federal government in Washington and the state governments of the American states. Intergovernmental relations refers to the complex set of relationships which entangle all levels of government with one another. The fact that the two terms are often used nearly interchangeably points to the fact both that power in the American system has become concentrated in Washington over the last decades and that the relationship between Washington and other governments does not focus exclusively on state governments.

The relationships between levels of government incorporated in the term "intergovernmental relations" (IGR) have increasingly involved administrative officials who play key roles in operating the system. As scholars of public administration in particular have focused on the role of such officials, the term intergovernmental management (IGM) has been introduced into the literature. Federalism, intergovernmental relations, and intergovernmental management therefore coexist uneasily in a disparate literature which is largely segmented and divided between those who argue from a normative position and those who examine the actual workings

---

[4] In many works, the terms federalism, federal system, and intergovernmental relations are used interchangeably. See for example Anton 1989; O'Toole 2000; Zimmerman 1992; Camissa 1995; Posner 1998; Wright 1990.

of an intricate system which incorporates both elected officials and administrators. Deil Wright captures well the evolution of the scholarly discussion in the field of "federalism" broadly defined:

The concept of federalism has two centuries of U.S. history, tradition, law, and practice behind it. The concept of IGR has a comparatively short half century of application to the American context, and it remains a term that falls somewhat short of either standardized or universal usage. By way of contrast, IGM appeared as a phrase on the public scene only recently—during the 1970s. (Wright 1990, 170)

The reason that intergovernmental relations have received a great deal of attention, however, is precisely because subnational governments have become so entangled in the implementation of federal programs. Such programs are adopted by Congress and the implementing regulations, which are in fact the key requirements for subnational governments, are developed by federal agencies. It is that combination of legislation and regulation which forms the structure within which subnational governments can exercise discretion and be subject to constraint. And it is that structure which maximizes the importance of management within a system of tremendous complexity.

5 NATIONALIZATION OF POLICY

It is not surprising that the term intergovernmental relations became popular in the post-Second World War period. It is in that period that state and federal functions became entangled in particularly dense ways. The concentration of power in the American system is tied to both the Sixteenth Amendment, which allowed Washington to impose a federal income tax, and the New Deal, which expanded the regulatory and social welfare functions of the federal government. The income tax gradually allowed the federal government to increase its power within the federal system because of the amounts of money that flowed into it as the economy grew. During the Second World War, Washington was able to "withhold" tax monies from salary checks so that its revenue stream became more predictable while the tax burden became politically more palatable in that tax monies were withdrawn weekly or monthly rather than being paid in lump sums at the year's end.

State and local governments retained their traditional taxing powers, but their tax policies became tied to those of Washington in complicated ways. In fact, the links became especially noticeable when the second Bush administration dramatically reduced estate and capital gains taxes, forcing states to decide whether to "couple" or "decouple" their state tax systems with the federal system.

The question of whether there has been a net centralization of power in the postwar period is not settled in the scholarly literature. Scholars who focus on periods in which Washington seems to be moving power back to the states tend to be more sanguine about the process of "devolution" than are those who examine the entire postwar period (Donahue 1997). Further, much research focuses on just one policy sector or examines one institution (the Supreme Court, for example) (Conlan and Vergniolle de Chantal 2001). Different studies use different time periods so that it is difficult to draw general conclusions. Finally, as Walker argues, "in the regulatory, judicial, program, and fiscal areas, no one tendency is consistently dominant" (Walker 2000, 2).

However, the most comprehensive quantitative study on policy centralization in the period 1947–98 (the data-set consists of public laws and executive orders but excludes the judicial arena and administrative tools such as waivers) concludes that "in terms of policymaking authority, the pulls have been far more powerful than the pushes. Elected federal officials have demonstrated less interest in restoring lost policymaking power to sub national governments than previously presumed" (Bowman and Krause 2003, 320). Another, studying the period 1981–2004, examining three policy sectors, and including legislation, lawsuits, waivers, and partnerships in his data, finds "a pattern of growing sensitivity and responsiveness by federal government to the needs and preferences of the states. Federal funding has increased, unfunded mandates have declined" (Gormley 2005, 2–26). Yet, as Gormley points out, "for every waiver that is granted, the federal government extracts some concessions that require states to make policy adjustments they would rather not make.... Thus what the federal government perceives as flexibility and responsiveness, state governments perceive as micro-management and red-tape" (Gormley 2005, 27).

The judgment about the relative balance of power between Washington and subnational governments has to do with the benchmark being used. If the benchmark is the period of cooperative federalism in which even regulatory laws exempted state and local governments in deference to the norms of federalism, there has clearly been a net centralization of power. If the benchmark, however, moves to the period when a host of laws dealing with social regulation (such as environmental policy) were being adopted with inflexible provisions leading to lawsuits (Kelemen 2004, 68), and which led to the label of "coercive federalism," Gormley's findings seem rather different. In that case, the kind of responsiveness found by Gormley seems like "pragmatic" federalism rather than the coercive federalism symbolized by that initial phase of building the American regulatory state.

6   MONEY AND REGULATION

The building blocks of intergovernmental relations are federal monies and federal regulation. Both are highly visible federal interventions. From the point of view of subnational governments, grants are positive and regulation is much more mixed.

Federal monies became increasingly important to states and localities in the 1960s. Such monies came in different forms depending on the decade and the programs involved.

Categorical grants in aid were particularly restrictive so that the advent of revenue sharing and block grants in the Nixon administration were viewed as a boon to intergovernmental flexibility. However, as federal deficits began to balloon, such monies became increasingly controversial. The Carter administration initially cut back aid, and the Reagan administration subsequently dramatically limited financial assistance to subnational governments. Revenue sharing was terminated in 1986.

The federal government became more generous under the first President Bush, under President Clinton, and in the second President Bush's first term. Nonetheless, in 1980, federal grants were 16 percent of federal outlays, and they did not reach that level of priority until 1999 (although they were 14 percent or higher between 1993 and 1999). In 2001–3, the figure rose to 17 percent and in 2004 federal grants were 18 percent of federal outlays (Gormley 2005, 32). Block grants became more prominent under both the Reagan and Clinton administrations. Even though the second President Bush proposed block grants, Congress refused to approve them and only established four new block grants during his first term (Gormley 2005, 10).

In the period between 1981 and 1995, the federal government became particularly interventionist as federal mandates became almost routine. Some mandates involved complete federal preemption while others underfunded the activities subnational governments were required to take. However, it was the so-called "unfunded mandates" which became particularly visible as governments began to quantify their cost.

The burden of mandates was not surprising as the 1980s witnessed the creation of more intergovernmental regulatory programs than did the 1970s. As Posner points out, "mandates as a term can potentially apply to a wide range of policy actions... including grant conditions, cross-cutting requirements, cross-over sanctions, partial preemptions, and total preemption" (Posner 1998, 9–11). From the point of view of state and local governments, they became ever more onerous (Posner 1998, 223; Conlan 1998, 192). Imposing costs on subnational governments through mandates was a "free" way for Congress to act without contributing to the federal deficit.

As Congress in the 1970s began to adopt new legislation in the area of social regulation (in contrast to the economic regulation imposed by the New Deal), subnational governments began to feel the "bite." Prior to that time, state and local governments had been exempt from major regulatory statutes adopted by Congress (Posner 1998, 22–3). However, as the value of federalism as traditionally defined gradually waned, state and local officials found themselves subject to the same kinds of constraints and regulations as individuals and companies. The lack of funds accompanying such restrictions only made the situation worse. In spite of President Reagan's view of government, the 99th Congress, for example, passed environmental legislation which imposed significant new costs on subnational governments (Conlan 1998, 193).

The decreasing influence of state and local government officials in Congress was at least partially due to their fading influence in their political parties. As long as they had been influential in the two political parties, they exerted informal influence in Congress. (The fact that mayors and county officials were important actors in parties helps to explain why governors were never able to become the "supreme" subnational leaders and had to compete with county and municipal elected officials for influence). Once they lost their leverage in the nomination process, their political clout in Congress declined. In fact, state and local officials competed with congressional candidates for money and visibility. Deference to the norms of federalism declined (Posner 1998, 79–80).

The Unfunded Mandates Reform Act (UMRA), adopted in 1995, was initially seen as a major force in restoring the balance between Washington and subnational governments. State and local governments were to be protected from mandates which cost them money. Yet in fact, mandates continued to be adopted (Posner 1998, 182, 190). The Personal Responsibility and Work Opportunity Reconciliation Act of 1996 reformed welfare and while providing generous block grants also imposed numerous new requirements on the states (Posner 1998, 189; Weaver 2000; Winston 2002). Although that reform was a major example of devolution, it gave states flexibility while also constraining them.

In the first term of the second Bush administration, waivers from federal requirements became particularly important in the area of Medicaid. That program, more expensive than Medicare, was consuming roughly 20 percent of state budgets by 2003. The waivers granted by the Bush administration allowed states both to improve the quality of care and to cut the number of beneficiaries. States did both, and, to critics, those states who used their waivers to cut the number of beneficiaries in an effort to control rising costs symbolized the problems created for vulnerable populations when the federal government loosened its regulatory grip. However, the need to obtain waivers is seen by many state officials as emblematic of the problems with federal controls on the states. Jeb Bush, Republican governor of Florida, argued:

States should not need waivers to establish meaningful co-payments, charge fair premiums, target care for certain populations or geographic areas. States should be able to implement managed care in its various forms, establish nursing-home diversion programs, or implement consumer-directed care, without first seeking waivers from Washington. (Serafini 2003, 1078)

7   INTERGOVERNMENTAL LOBBYING:
FUNCTIONAL VS. TERRITORIAL CLAIMS

Given that state governments are not represented in the US Senate, they, along with their local counterparts, can only make their views known through lobbying. In that sense, they are similar to other interests. In fact, state and local governments have organized governmental interest groups who represent governments rather than voters. The emphasis here is on the plural, for subnational officials do not speak with a unitary voice. County officials belong to the National Association of Counties, municipalities belong to the National League of Cities, mayors of big cities belong to the US Conference of Mayors, and state legislators belong to the National Conference of State Legislatures. Collectively, these groups are known as the "intergovernmental lobby."

Their lobby is often as—if not more—interested in who will control the process of implementation than it is in the actual programmatic contents of legislation. Subnational officials, when organized into public interest lobbies, represent a "spatial or geographic interest" above all. As Ann Commisa, drawing on work by Donald Haider, points out:

Government lobbies have a spatial interest (maintaining authority over their own geographic sphere) as well as a functional (policy) interest. While government lobbies are interested in particular policies, they . . . are also interested in the spatial dimension of any policy, that is, who will have the authority in implementation and control over the funds. . . . Subnational governments are interested in the process of policy (that is, who implements it) to a greater extent than its outcomes. (Cammisa 1995, 25; Haider 1974)

The intergovernmental lobby faces two key problems. The first is that Congress is organized by policy area. Committees are organized by functional area, and functional interest groups and policy communities have grown around each policy arena. For example, interest groups representing low-income groups were actively involved with the legislation dealing with welfare reform (Winston 2002). Beneficiaries of programs are critical to lobbying efforts (Anton 1989), and they are not interested in the intergovernmental dimensions of legislation unless it affects benefits in some fashion. There is a "mismatch" therefore between the "programmatic" structure of Congress and of policy communities and the "spatial" concerns of the intergovernmental lobby.

The dilemma is particularly acute because the lobbies representing governments, especially those representing elected officials such as the National Governors Association, at times come into conflict with lobbies representing state program officials lobbying for a particular program. In a sense, governors can come into conflict with the members of their own executive branch who are programmatically committed and who view mandates as useful in giving them leverage in budget battles back home. Lobbyists for the National Governors Association spend a good deal of time "fighting organizations of state bureaucrats" (Posner 1998, 83) "picket fence federalism" presents real problems for elected officials fighting to retain control over programs.

Secondly, the intergovernmental lobby finds it very difficult to create and sustain internal cohesion. Levels of government compete with one another. Mayors want a direct relationship with Washington, whereas governors argue that states are best equipped to allocate resources to lower levels of government. Counties for their part argue that they are the critical local units. Given that the federal system assumes that the federal government will not itself deliver services, the competition among other governments to be the key service provider in any policy area can be fierce. Furthermore, partisan divisions can also be important. For example, during the debate over welfare reform, the Republican Governors Association "played a central role with the bipartisan...NGA stymied by internal dissension...about funding formulas" (Winston 2002, 44).

The problem of cohesion is so serious that intergovernmental lobbies are far less effective than one might imagine, especially when they are confronting function-ally-based interests. Even if they can agree on general positions, they find it difficult to agree when it comes to specific proposals. Even though competition among subnational officials has been a truism, the partisan splits within those groups are multiplying the problems they face. The usual divisions based on territorial diversity are being exacerbated it seems by partisan cleavages which are deeper than they have been previously.

8 CONCLUSION

Contemporary American federalism is unsettled and so is the scholarly literature. Perhaps that is to be expected for as Anton has argued, the federal system is one "in which relationships among goverments are permanently unstable" (Anton 1989, 231). The federal system is extraordinarily complex precisely because it is so intergovernmental, involving all types of local as well as state governments. These governments compete with one another, with the federal government being able to choose the winners.

The federal system presents a clear challenge to political scientists interested in understanding how territorially-based claims, programmatic outcomes, administrative dynamics, and political parities intersect. The nationalization of policy has proceeded in spite of attempts to reverse that process, and thus the system is like an archeological dig with some programs showing the scars of attempted "devolution" coexisting with new programs which impose new requirements on subnational governments. Identifying systematic patterns across policy areas and programs and across defined time periods represents a huge methodological challenge for the discipline.

The twentieth century has been one of overall policy centralization coexisting with the fact that state and local governments have taken on new functions themselves. Federalism as a norm or as a value has in practice been downgraded. Both Republicans and Democrats, presidents and Congress members, have typically chosen to impose policy preferences on subnational governments while making concessions in terms of the conditions attached to implementation. The strategic decisions about public policy, however, have been taken in Washington without much consideration of the "federal dimension."

Such centralization has been due to multiple factors, but the difficulty of maintaining the strength of territorial politics in a system characterized by institutions dealing with functional issues and the fragmentation of the intergovernmental arena itself are two components. The fragmentation of the "subnational" government universe almost guarantees that federalism will be defined by national rather than subnational institutions. The lack of a unified "territorial" interest which can be easily mobilized and articulated has led to programmatic policy goals trumping those of territory. Functional interests consistently outweigh territorial ones; subnational elected officials are unable to defend their jurisdictional prerogatives.

Beneficiaries of federal programs, organized into coalitions, typically do not give priority to territorially-based claims unless those claims support programmatic goals. Given the role that beneficiaries play in the federal system (Anton 1989) and given the lack of cohesion of the intergovernmental lobby, it is not surprising that territorial claims often do not find a receptive audience in the United States.

It is important, however, to understand better the conditions under which territorial claims do matter. Given the current state of the field, it will be important to study systematically the dynamics of intergovernmental relations across multiple policy areas in order to move beyond the use of case studies. Data-sets need to be developed so as to allow researchers more easily to build on each other's work. Case studies, however, will continue to contribute to our understanding of the administrative politics intrinsic to making the federal system work. Issues of research design need to be more explicitly taken into account when using the case study method to study administrative politics.

Perhaps the most important intellectual step that needs to be taken in the next phase of scholarly research, however, is to integrate the study of American federalism into the emerging field of comparative federalism. Comparisons with Australia, Canada, Germany, and the European Union may well provide new research questions. The emergence of the European Union, with a policy-making system which resembles that of the American in its fragmentation, provides a particularly useful comparative case (Kelemen 2004; Sbragia forthcoming). Being able to compare the USA with a another "separated system" (Jones 1994, 2) should facilitate the development of theoretical frameworks which have heretofore been lacking.

While the study of American federalism has been viewed by many political scientists as much less theoretically interesting than the study of federal institutions such as Congress, integrating the study of such federal institutions into the study of federalism may lead to both better theory and a better understanding of the American political system as a whole. The use of comparison, when judiciously implemented, seems to be the best bet for improving the theoretical sophistication of the study of American federalism.

References

ALLARD, S. and DANZIGER, S. 2000. Welfare magnets: myth or reality? *Journal of Politics*, 62: 350–68.

ANTON, T. J. 1989. *American Federalism and Public Policy: How the System Works*. Philadelphia: Temple University Press.

BAILEY, M. A. 2005. Welfare and the multifaceted decision to move. *American Political Science Review*, 99 (1): 125–35.

—— and ROM, M. C. 2004. A wider race? Interstate competition across health and welfare programs. *Journal of Politics*, 66 (2): 326–47.

BEER, S. H. 1973. The modernization of American federalism. *Publius*, 3 (2): 49–95.

—— 1978. Federalism, nationalism, and democracy in America. *American Political Science Review*, 72 (1): 9–21.

BERRY, W. D., FORDING, R. C., and HANSON, R. L. 2003. Reassessing the "race to the bottom" thesis: a spatial dependence model of state welfare policy. *Journal of Politics*, 65: 327–49.

BOWMAN, A. O'M. and KRAUSE, G. A. 2003. Power shift: measuring policy centralization in U.S. intergovernmental relations, 1947–1998. *American Politics Research*, 31: 301–25.

BRUECKNER, J. K 2000. Welfare reform and the race to the bottom: theory and evidence. *Southern Economic Journal*, 66 (3): 505–25.

CAMMISA, A. 1995. *Governments as Interest Groups*. Westport, Conn.: Praeger.

CHHIBBER, P. K. and KOLLMAN, K. 2004. *The Formation of National Party Systems: Federalism and Party Competition in Canada, Great Britain, India, and the United States*. Princeton, NJ: Princeton University Press.

CONLAN, T. 1998. *From New Federalism to Devolution: Twenty-Five Years of Intergovernmental Reform*. Washington, DC: Brookings.

—— and VERGNIOLLE DE CHANTAL, F. 2001. The Rehnquist Court and contemporary American federalism. *Political Science Quarterly*, 116 (2): 253–75.

DAVIS, S. R. 1978. *The Federal Principle: A Journey Through Time in Quest of Meaning*. Berkeley: University of California Press.

DERTHICK, M. 1970. *The Influence of Federal Grants: Public Assistance in Massachusetts.* Cambridge, Mass.: Harvard University Press.

DONAHUE, J. D. 1997. *Disunited States.* New York: Basic Books.

DYE, T. R. 1990. *American Federalism: Competition Among Governments.* Lexington, Mass.: Lexington Books.

ELAZAR, D. J. 1962. *The American Partnership: Intergovernmental Cooperation in the Nineteenth Century United States.* Chicago: University of Chicago Press.

—— 1964. Federal–state collaboration in the nineteenth-century United States. *Political Science Quarterly,* 79: 248–81.

—— 1966. *American Federalism: A View from the States.* New York: Thomas Y. Crowell.

—— 1981. States as polities in the federal system. *National Civic Review,* 70 (2): 77–82.

—— 1990 Opening the third century of American federalism: issues and prospects. *Annals of the American Academy of Political and Social Science,* 509: 11–21.

ENCHAUTEGUI, M. E. 1997. Welfare payments and other economic determinants of female migration. *Journal of Labor Economics,* 15 (3): 529–54.

FIGLIO, D. N., KOLPIN, VAN W., and REID, W. E. 1999. Do states play welfare games? *Journal of Urban Economics,* 46: 437–54.

FOSLER, R. S. 1988. *The New Economic Role of American States: Strategies in a Competitive World Economy.* Oxford: Oxford University Press.

GLENDENING, P. N. and REEVES, M. M. 1984. *Pragmatic Federalism,* 2nd edn. Pacific Palisades, Calif.: Palisades.

GORMLEY, W. T. 2005. Pragmatic federalism: conflict, cooperation, and the quest for WA. Unpublished paper.

GRODZINS, M. 1960. The federal system in the United States, President's Commission on National Goals 1960. Available at: http://pittcat.edu.

HAIDER, D. 1974. *When Governments Come to Washington: Governors, Mayors and Intergovernmental Lobbying.* New York: Free Press.

JONES, C. O. 1994. *The Presidency in a Separated System.* Washington, DC: Brookings.

KELEMEN, D. R. 2004. *The Rules of Federalism: Institutions and Regulatory Politics in the EU and Beyond.* Cambridge, Mass.: Harvard University Press.

KINCAID, J. 1990. From cooperative to coercive federalism. *Annals of the American Academy of Political and Social Science,* 509: 139–52.

—— 1996. From dual to coercive federalism in American intergovernmental relations. Pp. 29–47 in *Globalization and Decentralization: Institutional Contexts, Policy Issues, and Intergovernmental Relations in Japan and the United States,* ed. J. S. Jun and D. S. Wright. Washington, DC: Georgetown University Press.

—— 1998. The devolution tortoise and the centralization hare. *New England Economic Review,* May/June: 13–40.

KRAUSE, G. A. and BOWMAN, A. O'M. 2005. Adverse selection, political parties, and policy delegation in the American federal system. *Journal of Law, Economics, and Organization,* 21: 359–87.

LEE, F. E. and OPPENHEIMER, B. I. 1999. *Sizing Up the Senate: The Unequal Consequences of Equal Representation.* Chicago: University of Chicago Press.

LEVINE, P. and ZIMMERMAN, D. 1999. An empirical analysis of the welfare magnet debate using the NLSY. *Journal of Population Economics,* 12: 391–409.

LOWRY, W. R. 1992. *The Dimensions of Federalism: State Governments and Pollution Control Policies.* Durham, NC: Duke University Press.

NATHAN, R. P. 1996. The devolution revolution: an overview. *Rockefeller Institute Bulletin,* 5–13.

—— and DOOLITTLE, F. C. 1987. *Reagan and the States.* Princeton, NJ: Princeton University Press.

O'TOOLE, L. J. (ed.) 2000. *American Intergovernmental Relations: Foundations, Perspectives, and Issues,* 3rd edn. Washington, DC: CQ Press.

PETERSON, P. E. 1981. *City Limits.* Chicago: University of Chicago Press.

—— and ROM, M. C. 1990. *Welfare Magnets: A New Case for a National Standard.* Washington, DC: Brookings.

—— RABE, B. G. and WONG, K. K. 1986. *When Federalism Works.* Washington, DC: Brookings.

POSNER, P. L. 1998. *The Politics of Unfunded Mandates: Whither Federalism?* Washington, DC: Georgetown University Press.

RABE, B. G. 2004. *Statehouse and Greenhouse: The Emerging Politics of American Climate Change Policy.* Washington, DC: Brookings.

RIKER, W. H. 1964. *Federalism.* Boston: Little, Brown.

—— 1975. Federalism. Pp. 93–172 in *Handbook of Political Science, Volume 5: Governmental Institutions and Processes,* ed. F. I. Greenstein and N. W. Polsby. Reading, Mass.: Addison-Wesley.

RODDEN, J. 2006. The political economy of federalism. In *The Oxford Handbook of Political Economy,* ed. B. Weingast and D. Wittman. Oxford: Oxford University Press.

ROM, M. C., PETERSON, P. E. and SCHEVE, K. F. 1998. Interstate competition and welfare policy. *Publius,* 28: 17–38.

SAAVEDRA, L. A. 2000. A model of welfare competition with evidence from AFDC. *Journal of Urban Economics,* 47: 248–79.

SBRAGIA, A. M. (ed.) 1992. *Euro-politics.* Washington, DC: Brookings Institution.

—— 2000. Governance, the state, and the market: what is going on? *Governance,* 13 (2): 243–50.

—— 2004. Territory, representation and policy outcome: the United States and European Union compared. Pp. 205–24 in *Restructuring Territoriality: Europe and the United States Compared,* ed. C. K. Ansell and G. Di Palma. Cambridge: Cambridge University Press.

—— forthcoming. The United States and the European Union: overcoming the challenge of comparing two "sui genesis" systems. In *Comparative Federalism: The United States and the European Union,* ed. A. Menon and M. Schain. Oxford: Oxford University Press.

SCHRAM, S., NITZ, L., and KRUEGER, G. 1998. Without cause or effect: reconsidering welfare migration as a policy. *American Journal of Political Science,* 42 (1): 210–30.

—— and SOSS, J. 1998. Making something out of nothing: welfare reform and a new race to the bottom. *Publius,* 28 (3): 67–88.

SERAFINI, M. W. 2003. Waiving red flags. *National Journal,* April 3: 1072–8.

THOMAS, K. P. 2000. *Competing for Capital: Europe and North America in a Global Era.* Washington, DC: Georgetown University Press.

TSEBELIS, G. and MONEY, J. 1997. *Bicameralism.* Cambridge: Cambridge University Press.

UNITED STATES, PRESIDENT'S COMMISSION ON NATIONAL GOALS 1960. *Goals for Americans.* Englewood Cliffs, NJ: Prentice Hall.

VOLDEN, C. 2002. The politics of competitive federalism: a race to the bottom in welfare benefits? *American Journal of Political Science,* 46: 352–63.

WALKER, D. B. 2000. *The Rebirth of Federalism,* 2nd edn. New York: Chatham House.

WEAVER, R. K. 2000. *Ending Welfare as We Know It*. Washington, DC: Brookings Institution Press.

WEINGAST, B. 1995. The economic role of political institutions. *Journal of Law, Economics, and Organization*, 11: 1–31.

WINSTON, P. 2002. *Welfare Policymaking in the States: The Devil in Devolution*. Washington, DC: Georgetown University Press.

WRIGHT, D. S. 1988. *Understanding Intergovernmental Relations*, 3rd edn. Pacific Grove, Calif.: Brooks/Cole.

—— 1990. Federalism, intergovernmental relations, and international management: historical reflections and conceptual comparisons. *Public Administration Review*, 50 (2): 168–78.

ZIMMERMAN, J. F. 1992. *Contemporary American Federalism: The Growth of National Power*. New York: Praeger.

—— 2001. National–state relations: cooperative federalism in the twentieth century. *Publius*, 31 (2): 15–30.

....

CHAPTER 14

COMPARATIVE FEDERALISM

....

BRIAN GALLIGAN

There is a resurgence of interest in federalism at the beginning of the twenty-first century, most notably in the institutional reconfiguration of Europe (Filippov, Ordeshook, and Shevtsova 2004) which is at the "epicenter" of a worldwide "federalizing tendency" (Russell 2005, 13). According to Imbeau (2004, 13), "we can view federal systems as historical experiments at sharing policy responsibilities and look at them as working models of a new global order." Federalism is a defining feature of many national systems of government and is spreading to others. During the last half-century, federalism has proved its resilience and flexibility in the older established federations of the United States, Switzerland, Canada, and Australia. Federal constitutions were successfully reestablished in Germany and Austria, countries with long federal traditions, after the Second World War. While there were some notable failures of postwar federations that were artificially cobbled together by military victors or retreating colonial powers (Franck 1968), federalism has taken root in a number of Asian countries, most notably India, but also Malaysia, as well as Latin America with Argentina, Brazil, Venezuela, and Mexico becoming, to some extent, federal. Within Europe, some traditionally centralist countries have become more federal, most notably Spain with autonomous regional communities, and Great Britain with devolution to Scotland, Wales, and Northern Ireland. In addition, Belgium has become effectively a federal country as a way of accommodating its distinct French- and Dutch-speaking peoples. If federalism has not fared well in Africa, it remains an essential part of the Nigerian constitution, while South Africa has adopted significant federal features in its new constitution.

The discussion of the chapter moves from consideration of the changing global environment that favors federalism to the more familiar structures of country-specific federal systems. Subsequent sections examine the robustness and flexibility of federalism that result from its particular blend of institutions and depend upon a highly developed civic and constitutional culture. But first we examine the changing international environment and historical setting of federalism and its fit with the changing global order.

1   FEDERALISM AND A CHANGING WORLD

Federalism's resurgence is in part due to its compatibility with the new world order and the jettisoning of national sovereignty orthodoxy. The world environment has changed from the twentieth century's primary focus on national sovereignty and centralized government to the twenty-first century's concern with cosmopolitanism and multiple sphere government.

One notable change is the decline of Keynesianism in favor of neoliberal economics, and the collapse of socialism and centralist planning in favor of market solutions in most domestic economies. Federalism had been considered an obstacle to managing a capitalist economy by many twentieth-century commentators. Laski (1939) pronounced "the obsolescence of federalism," and influenced a generation of postwar scholars like Gordon Greenwood (1976) from Australia who applied Laski's thesis to the supposed needs of postwar reconstruction and managing a modern economy. Such claims were always exaggerated as the established federations of the United States, Canada, and Australia flourished, and successful federal systems were reestablished in Germany and Austria. In any case, the structural forces of capitalism have changed with combined economic and technological developments, especially in communications and commerce, producing a version of globalization that has reduced the relative significance of nation states. Partly in reaction, and partly sustained by the same technological advances, local and regional communities and groupings of people are demanding greater participation, a phenomenon that Tom Courchene (1995) has called "glocalization."

Federalism is broadly compatible with the post-sovereignty world of the twenty-first century which is "characterized by shifting allegiances, new forms of identity and overlapping tiers of jurisdiction" (Camilleri and Falk 1992, 256). As Andrew Linklater pointed out, "the subnational revolt, the internationalization of decision-making and emergent transnational loyalties in Western Europe reveal that the processes which created and sustained sovereign states in this region are being reversed" (1998, 113). Hedley Bull (1977) had earlier argued that the world was moving towards a form of "neo-medievalism" of overlapping structures and cross-cutting loyalties. "Complex interdependency" (Keohane and Nye 1977) character-izes much of the modern world of international relations. In contrast, the twenti-eth-century concern was more with national sovereignty, even though for many dependent and unstable countries formal sovereignty was often little more than "organized hypocrisy" (Krasner 1999).

For many federal countries, including new world ones like Australia and Canada as well as old European ones like Germany, the post-sovereignty world of the future is in some ways a return to the past. The sweep of political history includes long periods of sprawling empire when nations became states with varying degrees of autonomy. The British Empire is a case in point, with Australia, along with Canada, South Africa, India, and many other countries, becoming nations without sovereignty through the nineteenth and twentieth centuries, (Galligan, Roberts, and Trifiletti 2001). Europe and Asia have long histories of complex state arrange-ments not characterized by sovereign nation states. Great Britain itself, once the paradigm of a unitary state with a sovereign parliament, has granted devolution to Scotland and Wales and joined the European Union.

If federalism was at risk in the mid-twentieth century world of nation building and sovereign nation states, it should thrive in the twenty-first century of complex interdependency, multiple citizenship allegiances, interdependent and overlapping jurisdictions, and multiple centers of law and policy-making. As we shall see in the next sections, federalism is a system of divided sovereignty and multiple govern-ments with partly separate and partly shared jurisdiction. Adding another inter-national sphere of governance where some norms and standards are formulated and collective decisions are made that impinge on a nation's domestic affairs complicates things (Lazar, Telford, and Watts 2003), but in ways that are broadly congenial with federalism. The "paradigm shift" that Ron Watts identifies, is "from a world of sovereign nation-states to a world of diminished state sovereignty and increased interstate linkages of a constitutionally federal character" (Watts 1999, ix).

2   FEDERALISM'S INTERPRETERS AND NATIONAL SETTINGS

Federalism is characterized by two spheres of government, national and state, operating in the one political entity according to a defined arrangement for sharing powers so that neither is sovereign over the other. According to William Riker's definition, "the activities of government are divided between regional governments and a central government in such a way that each kind of government has some activities on which it makes final decisions" (Riker 1975, 101). For Daniel Elazar, "the constituting elements in a federal arrangement share in the processes of common policy making and administration by right, while the activities of the common government are conducted in such a way as to maintain their respective integrities." Elazar summed this up in the neat epigram "*self-rule plus shared rule*" (Elazar 1987, 12; italics in original)—self-rule in regional communities and shared rule at the national level. While this has become a cliché about federalism and is consistent with Elazar's approach in *American Federalism: A View from the States* (1984), it is somewhat misleading as self-rule and shared rule are features of both spheres of government in a balanced federal system.

The notion of federalism as an association of associations is an old, and partly misleading one. The old federal form was a league or confederation of member states that agreed to share in certain matters of collective decision-making, often for strategic or trade purposes. An early theoretical exposition is found in Johannes Althusius' notion of an association of associations (Carney 1965). This was the institutional form of the earlier American Articles of Confederation that provided a weak form of national government, unsuited to raising the taxes and armies necessary to fight the War of Independence. In 1789, the American constitutional founders restructured federalism, strengthening central government through making its key offices independent of the member states and directly responsible to the people (*Federalist Papers*, Numbers 9 and 10; Diamond 1961). In his observations in *Democracy in America*, Alexis de Tocqueville affirmed that this American innovation in federal design "rests in truth upon a wholly novel theory, which may be considered as a great discovery in modern political science"—namely, making citizens rather than states or societies, members of the national union (Tocqueville [1835] 1945, 162).

This grounding of federalism on dual citizenship, that is membership of the new national union and continuing membership of the older and smaller state unions, was a major innovation not only in institutional design but also in popular government. Indeed the two are inextricably linked with the two spheres of government being independently based in popular sovereignty (Beer 1993). This helps us answer the question that is sometimes posed as to whether there can be genuine federalism without democracy. The answer is negative if we are talking about the modern American or republican form of federalism. Moreover, it is hard to envisage alternative non-democratic bases to federalism that would be sufficient to anchor both spheres of government. If this is the case, successful federalism requires robust democracy in which citizens share membership of two political communities and participate politically in both. The corollary requirement of such dual citizenship is real but moderate attachment to both spheres of government.

Federalism presupposes a sophisticated citizenry with multiple allegiances and a constitutional culture of limited government.

This is very different from the earlier sociological view that federalism was a consequence of ethnically diverse societies: as William Livingston put it (1956, 4), "Federalism was a function not of constitutions but of societies." William Riker's earlier reflections on federalism were based on a similar sociological rationale: he questioned why Australia bothered with federalism when it had no ethnically based differences (1964), and argued federalism was trivial without such differences (1970). Riker, however, was to change his mind about federalism, moving from sociological to institutional explanations, and from being a New Dealer critic to an advocate concerned with big government (1975; 1987, xii–xiii). Riker concluded his federal odyssey on a traditional note that vindicated Madison and the American founders: "Taking together all federations in the world at all times, I believe that federalism has been a significant force for limited government and hence for personal freedom" (1993, 513). This view of federalism as reinforcing a liberal pluralist system of government in America was shared by Theodore Lowi (1984), and also by Geoffrey Sawer based upon his reflections on Australian and comparative federalism (1976).

Federalism can provide an institutional basis for ethnically distinct peoples, but paradoxically that can also facilitate secession, as Donald Horowitz has pointed out: "federalism can either exacerbate or mitigate ethnic conflict" (Horowitz 1985, 603). In a recent study of federalism and secession in North America, Lawrence Anderson has a similar warning: "Federalism may actually whet a given region's appetite for secession by creating opportunities for conflict and providing the region with the opportunity and the institutions needed to mobilize support for secession" (Anderson 2004, 96). Secession of the Southern states of the United States and Canada's long-standing national crisis with Quebec separatism are illustrative cases. Studies of failed federations and attempts to deal with regions of ethnic conflict provide further evidence of this dangerous aspect of federalism (Dorff 1994). Federalism is in trouble where there is too little national sense among the people, and too sharp differences among regionally based ethnic, religious, and linguistic groups. The ongoing crisis of Canadian federalism is a consequence of both: Canadians never properly constituted themselves as a sovereign people, according to Peter Russell (2004), and there has been an ongoing struggle to head off Quebec separatism that periodically threatens the nation (Smiley 1980). Federalism failed in Yugoslavia because, as Mitja Zagar (2005, 123) explains, "The existing constitutional and political system failed to provide for the necessary cohesion of the multiethnic Yugoslav community."

Nevertheless, providing an institutional outlet for subnational distinct peoples as in Switzerland, Canada, Belgium, and India is one of a number of purposes that federalism serves. More generally, federalism facilitates government in geographically large countries such as the United States and Australia as well as Canada and

Germany. Federalism in its modern form was designed by the American founders to provide a system of decentralized and limited government for liberal and pluralist societies. This has been its main purpose in the United States, Germany, and Australia, and also a major purpose in Switzerland and Canada (Sharman 1990). Federalism thrives in polities imbued with civil virtues of moderation, toleration, and support for limited government. Rather than providing a support structure for ethnically distinct groups concentrated in subnational states, federalism works best in pluralist countries with multiple interests and geographically scrambled differences.

3   FEDERAL COUNTRIES

Federalism is a popular form of government. Watts lists twenty-four countries—twenty-three after the collapse of Yugoslavia—with about 40 percent of the world's population, although the bulk of these live in India (Watts 1999, 8–10). Watts' list includes quasi-federations or hybrids that are "predominantly federations in their constitutions and operation but which have some overriding federal government powers more typical of a unitary system." Examples are India, Pakistan, and Malaysia because of their overriding central emergency powers, and South Africa that retains some of its pre-1996 unitary features. The new federations since Elazar's earlier 1987 list (1987, 43–4) are Belgium, Spain, and South Africa, even though the latter two countries do not use the term federal in their constitutions, the two tiny island federations of St. Kitts and Nevis and Micronesia, and Ethiopia.

Federal countries are quite heterogeneous in having different political cultures and being at such different stages of development that meaningful comparison is hardly possible. Hence scholars typically group federal countries in manageable clusters of more similar countries: for example, "less developed countries" (Bahl and Linn 1994), Latin American countries, which now include Spain (Montero 2001), or more usually well-established Anglo and European federations, Australia, Austria, Canada, Germany, Switzerland, and the United States (Obinger, Leibfried, and Castles 2005). Because of its scale and history, India is unique and tends to be studied individually (Khan 1992; Verney 2003; Rao 2003).

As we might expect, federal counties score highest on Arend Lijphart's "Index of federalism" that is based on quantifying variables of federal–unitary dimensions on a scale of 1 to 5 (Lijphart 1999, appendix A, 312–13). Whereas unitary countries like Great Britain, New Zealand, and Greece score 1, the five well-established federations, Australia, Canada, Germany, Switzerland, and the United States, all score 5.

The other federal countries to score highly are Austria and India with 4.5, Venezuela with 4, Belgium with 3.2, and Spain with 3. Because they are sufficiently similar and have high federal characteristics, the developed European and Anglo federations are usually chosen for comparative study of federal institutions even though this narrows the scope of findings. Such selectivity underpins both the strength and limitations of most federalism studies.

4 INSTITUTIONS OF FEDERALISM

Federalism has been institutionally embodied in a variety of ways in different federal countries. Nevertheless there is a set of institutions that are sufficiently common to be identified as typical by writers on federalism. These are first, a written constitution that is difficult to amend; second a bicameral legislature with a strong federal chamber to represent the constituent regions; third, a supreme or constitutional court to protect the constitution though the power of judicial review; and fourth, intergovernmental institutions and processes to facilitate collaboration in areas of shared or overlapping jurisdiction (Watts 1999, 7; Lijphart 1999, 4, 187 lists only the former three). It should be noted that none of these features is exclusively federal, and all can be found in varying forms in non-federal systems. That is perhaps most obvious for a written constitution, but also applies to some extent to a system of intergovernmental relations where unitary states have decentralized arrangements of local government.

The fact that federalism has no uniquely defining institutional arrangements has led some like Iva Duchacek (1987) and Rufus Davis (1978) to conclude that federalism lacks a coherent theory. A contrary view by Filippov, Ordeshook, and Shevtsova offers "a theory of federal design that is universal and complete," based upon the political party system that channels elites' behavior to support federalism (2004, 17, 39–40). Both views are too extreme. The former skeptical view is premised upon too tight presuppositions of distinctiveness in core institutions that federalism lacks. The latter claim that political party can provide a universal and complete theory of federal design is overstated because parties in federal systems are partly shaped by them and their supporting political culture. Federalism remains a complex and messy system that takes common political institutions and uses them in federal ways. Moreover, in any particular federal country there exists a variety of institutions and practices, some federal and others non-federal, that interact in complex ways. In addition, political institutions worked by human agents have a reflexive capacity and can be worked in different ways: non-federal ones for federal ends or federal ones for unitary ends. In reviewing the set of four key "federal institutions" identified above, we need to keep these considerations in mind.

5   WRITTEN CONSTITUTION

While having a written constitution that is difficult to amend is not exclusive to federal systems—Japan has one—it does serve a crucial function in underpinning federalism by anchoring the two levels of government, national and state, and defining the division of powers between them. The essence of federalism is two spheres of government neither of which is sovereign but each of which has defined and limited powers. The written constitution is the institutional means of achieving this. The precise form varies among federal constitutions in ways that reflect their historical origins and political cultures.

The Anglo constitutions were formed from existing smaller states and provinces that had been quasi-independent colonies within the British Empire. Hence their federal constitutions serve the dual functions of creating the national institutions of government with specified powers while guaranteeing the continuing existence of subnational states or provinces with their powers. Since the latter already existed with their own establishing acts or constitutions, they receive relatively scant attention in the US and Australian constitutions that affirm the states' continuing existence and residual powers in so far as these are not modified by the constitution. Although more centralist in its original design, the Canadian constitution spells out the main powers of the provinces. Germany's Basic Law adopted in 1949 gives a more comprehensive account of the interdependent roles of federal and Länder governments (Jeffery 1999). The Swiss constitution is the most decentralized in securing the powers of the cantons in order to protect their linguistic diversity.

A key function of the written constitution is specifying the division of powers or competencies between the national and state governments. The way this is done is important in defining the character of the federal system, although judicial review and political practice may subsequently vary the way in which a federal system develops. Legal scholarship has focused on the formal division of powers, and legal scholars like K. C. Wheare (1963), an Australian professor at Oxford, dominated the Anglo study of federalism in the post-Second World War decades. A prominent difference in the basic division of powers is that between the US model of enumerating Congress' heads of power and guaranteeing the residual to the states, that Australia followed, and the Canadian model of enumerating both sets of powers. In Canada's case, however, the difference has been blurred through judicial review and federal politics with the Privy Council expanding provincial powers in sanctioning that country's evolution from a centralized to a decentralized federation. In other words, the constitutional division of powers does not necessarily tell us how a federal system has developed or operates today.

This is acknowledged in recent European scholarship that takes account of both the distribution of legislative power and practical implementation in distinguishing between *interstate* and *intrastate* federalism According to Dietmar Braun (2004, 47), in the interstate model "jurisdictional authority is separated between territorial actors and competition and bipolarity predominate," whereas in intrastate federalism "most of the decisions are taken at the federal level where subgovernments and the federal government have their say" and "implementation is almost completely in the hands of subgovernments." Canada epitomizes interstate federalism with Canadian provinces having no direct say in federal legislation or implementation, but being relatively autonomous in their own legislative powers. Germany has intrastate federalism with the Länder having a direct say in national legislation, through representation in the Bundesrat, and also the main responsibility for its implementation.

6   DIFFICULT TO AMEND

The leading federal countries all have constitutions that are hard to amend and score highly on Lijphart's (1999, 220–1) most difficult category, that requiring "supermajorities" greater than two-thirds approval of both houses of the national legislature. On a scale of 1 to 4, unitary countries such as the United Kingdom and Sweden score 1, whereas federal countries such as Australia, Canada, Germany, Switzerland, and the United States score 4. The mean index of constitutional rigidity for all countries is 2.6 and the median 3. According to Lijphart, Germany's score of 3.5 on the index is understated because its amendment procedure requires a two-thirds majority in both houses of the national legislature and these are significantly different in composition. The only unitary country to score highly is Japan, which requires a referendum in addition to two-thirds majorities in both houses of its legislature.

Among the five federal countries with constitutions that are difficult to amend, the procedures vary significantly. Australia followed Switzerland in having popular referendum procedures that are also federally weighted: majorities of voters overall, and majorities in a majority of the states and cantons. Yet the two countries are quite different in their patterns of usage and success. Switzerland uses referendums widely for policy as well as constitutional purposes, whereas Australia has a slim record of passing only eight amendments from forty-four proposals (Galligan 2001). The United States has ratification by three-quarters of the states in addition to two-thirds majorities in both houses of Congress. Canada has a weighted federal formula that takes account of both numbers of provinces and population— two-thirds of the provincial legislatures from provinces containing at least half the total population—with unanimity required for sections concerning basic language rights. Germany has the two-thirds rule for majorities in both houses, with the Bundesrat representing the Länder.

The purpose of having difficult-to-amend constitutions is to protect the higher law character of the constitution that controls the other institutions of government. As Donald Lutz puts it, constitutional amendment should be "neither too easy nor too difficult" and successful constitutions should have "a moderate amendment rate" (Lutz 1994, 357). The amendment rate is affected by a number of factors, most notably the length of the constitution and difficulty of the amendment process. Longer constitutions are more likely to require alteration of their detail; and easy amendment processes are likely to attract change proposals. The rate of amendment also depends on whether there are alternative avenues for change, such as judicial review. Australia and the United States with short constitutions, difficult amendment procedures, and active judicial review have exceptionally low rates of change and low counts on Lutz's amendment rate index (calculated by dividing the number of amendments by the total years of operation of the constitution): 0.09 and 0.13, respectively. Switzerland is higher at 0.78 and Germany with 2.91 is above the 2.54 average for thirty-two countries (Lutz 1994, 369). Canada is omitted because it continued to rely upon Britain's Westminster parliament until Trudeau's patriation of the constitution in the 1980s, replete with complex amendment procedures and a Charter of Rights. Since then Canada has been engaged in successive rounds of discussion for "mega-constitutional" change that have been overly ambitious and fruitless (Russell 2004).

7   JUDICIAL REVIEW

While federal constitutions specify in broad terms the division of powers between national and state governments, judges and courts interpret and apply those provisions in specific cases. Some federations have specialized constitutional courts for making such decisions, while others rely upon general courts (Watts 1999, 100). The United States, Australia, Canada, India, Malaysia, and Austria have general multipurpose courts, while Germany, Belgium, and Spain have specialized constitutional courts. Switzerland has a more limited Federal Tribunal to decide the validity of cantonal laws, but uses popular referendums for federal laws. The jurisprudence of courts exercising judicial review is affected by their character and staffing, with generalist courts often taking a more literalist approach. Whereas constitutional experts are appointed to constitutional courts, specialists in various branches of the law or legal generalists are required for general purpose courts where constitutional adjudication is only part of the workload. The Australian High Court is a case in point where, typically, leading barristers and judges from lower courts with only incidental constitutional experience are appointed by the Commonwealth government after consultation with the states. In contrast, the German constitutional court has specialists in constitutional law appointed equally by the Bundesrat and the Länder. Irrespective of the character of the court, federations with linguistic diversity such as Canada and Switzerland have arrangements for ensuring proportional representation of judges from those linguistic groups.

Within federations, constitutional adjudication and interpretation are important because they affect government powers as well as individual rights and group interests. In deciding particular cases involving constitutional matters, courts also determine the way constitutions are to be interpreted. While courts can make bold and innovative constitutional decisions, they rely upon cases coming to them. That requires the mobilization of support groups with the dedication and financial backing to bring test cases (Epp 1998). Courts also have to ensure their decisions are accepted by the other branches of government, so cannot get too far out of step with the mainstream political consensus. Through the appointment process, governments can shape the direction of courts over the longer term, and can often work around their decisions in the shorter term.

The significance of courts as arbiters in federal systems varies from time to time and among federations. In recent decades the expansive interpretation of powers in federations such as the United States, Canada, and Australia has reduced the role of their supreme courts as arbiters of their federal systems. As a consequence, the balance of powers between national and state or provincial governments is determined mainly by patterns of national politics and the push and pull of intergovernmental relations. National governments have become more prominent since the Second World War, although in Canada's case this has been more than offset by province building by Quebec and western Canada. Moreover, constitutional adjudication in Canada and the United States has shifted mainly to rights protection in interpreting charters and bills of rights. Lacking a constitutional bill of rights, the Australian High Court flirted with implied constitutional rights during the 1990s but is severely constrained in extending its rights jurisdiction without a bill of rights.

8   LEGISLATIVE BICAMERALISM

Legislative bicameralism is one of the institutional bastions of federalism and a standard feature of all significant federations (Watts 1999, 92). Legislative bicameralism is not peculiar to federal systems, however, and traditionally effected sectoral and class representation. Within federal systems, bicameralism has become an important institution for representing subnational governments or groupings of peoples in the national legislature in a variety of ways.

Historically, bicameralism was a key part of the Connecticut compromise between large and small states that underpinned the United States constitution. A bicameral Congress with the Senate based on equal state representation was necessary to secure small states' support for the constitution. Through representing different interests, based on state rather than local constituencies, the Senate would also be an important check on congressional power. Originally appointed by the states, the US Senate increased its legitimacy and standing when direct election by the people of the states was introduced in 1913.

Australia followed the American model with its Senate having virtually co-equal powers with the House of Representatives. While it cannot propose or amend money bills, the Australian Senate has the larger power of passing or refusing to pass them. The first restriction is common to the US constitution, and the second is to respect the monetary prerogative of the responsible government executive based in the House of Representatives. The number of senators per state is equal, originally set at six but now twelve per state plus two for each of the two territories, with the total number fixed to half the size of the House of Representatives that has been increased from time to time. The earlier 1891 draft of the Australian constitution copied the American model of having the senate elected by state legislatures, but this was changed by the 1897–98 convention to election by the people of the states. Party discipline dominates the Australian Senate, much more so than the American, but the adoption of proportional representation in 1948 has opened up the chamber to minor parties and independents that have usually held the balance of power.

Germany's bicameral arrangement has a more directly federal purpose, with the second chamber or Bundesrat comprised of delegates appointed by Länder governments and voting on their instructions. The Länder quota of members is proportional to relative population size and varies from three to six. The Bundesrat has veto power over all federal legislation that involves Länder administration, which in practice is over 50 percent. Germany's bicameral structure its highly integrative and underpins its intrastate brand of federalism. Nevertheless, German bicameralism provides a substantial check on legislative power because of the representation it gives different national and regional, as well as popular and party, interests.

Switzerland has a strong bicameral system in which the second chamber or Council of States has full legislative powers and hence a veto over all legislation. Members of the Council are chosen by direct election of the people of the cantons, with two representatives for each of the twenty larger cantons and one each for the six smaller ones.

Canada is the exception with an ineffectual bicameral system due to the appointment of senators by the national government on political and patronage grounds. This makes the Canadian Senate a tame chamber despite its considerable formal powers of having to pass, and being in theory able to reject, any bills. Ineffectual bicameralism has exacerbated problems in Canadian governance, especially the incorporation of the western provinces in national decision-making. While western reformers advocate a Triple-E Senate—elected, equal, and effective—on the Australian model, national governments dominated by the most populous central provinces, Ontario and Quebec, have been reluctant to address the issue. Alberta's attempt to legitimate its senators by selecting candidates through provincial elections has been stymied by the national government's refusal to appoint those elected to the Senate.

Apart from having different institutional structures, bicameral legislatures work differently depending on how they interact with other parts of the political system, especially political parties. While it is customary to emphasize that federal second chambers represent state or regional interests (Watts 1999, 95), this is only part of the story. Because Australian parties are dominant and well integrated across national and state spheres, senators represent party interests that are national rather than state focused. Nevertheless, senators bring state issues into parliamentary caucuses and provide disproportionate representation for smaller states. United States senators have state constituencies, but party and national concerns are typically more significant. In Germany, party provides a dynamic overlay on Länder representation through Länder governments' choosing their delegates to the Bundesrat (Sturm 1999). Similarly, in Switzerland party is significant in the regional representation role of Council of States members. Bicameralism increases the complexity of representation through bringing combinations of party and state and regional interests into the national legislature.

9   INTERGOVERNMENTAL RELATIONS

Federalism divides powers and allocates them to separate spheres of government, whereas the making and management of public policy in complex areas often requires close cooperation. Hence, intergovernmental relations are an important operational part of federal systems, and have proliferated with the expansion of modern government, especially the roles and responsibilities of national governments, and the complexity of major policy areas that attract both spheres of government. As Agranoff points out, "a steady demand for governmental services in health, education, housing, income maintenance, employment and training, and personal social services has forced governments at all levels to become more interdependent" (Agranoff 1986). So much so that in the United States, "public administration and the processes of federalism have merged to a nearly indistinguishable point" (Agranoff and McGuire 2001, 671).

The basic view of federalism underlying most political and policy studies is a concurrent one—both spheres of government sharing in major policy areas. As one of the pioneers of this view put it, federalism was more like a marble than a layered cake (Grodzins 1966), where there was a mixing and blending of federal and state government activities. Elazar formulated this more technically as a non-hierarchical policy-matrix—"polycentric by design," like "a communications network that establishes the linkages that create the whole" (1987, 13). Understanding how such a complex system works entails exploring institutions and processes of intergovernmental relations. Except among mainly constitutional lawyers, this view of federalism has largely replaced the older, classic view of federalism as a coordinate system consisting of two sets of machinery criss-crossing without ever touching or hampering one another's functioning, as Bryce put it in describing American federalism in the nineteenth century (Bryce 1888, vol. 1, 425; also Wheare 1963, 93).

Intergovernmental fiscal relations are a crucial part of federalism and of major interest to scholars of public finance and public choice economics who have attempted to incorporate political mechanisms into their abstract models (see classic papers collected in Grewal, Brennan, and Mathews 1980). One key concern has been with the relationship between federalism and the size of government. Geoffrey Brennan and James Buchanan (1980, 15) argued that decentralization of taxes and expenditures produced smaller government because people and corporations could vote with their feet, and hence governments would have to compete for mobile sources of revenue. This anti-Leviathan thesis is disputed by Jonathan Rodden (2003) who argues that expenditure decentralization is associated with faster growth in overall government spending due to "over fishing" by competing governments in the common fiscal pool. Rodden concludes that only when decentralized expenditure is funded by "own-source" taxes is there slower government growth (2003, 697–8). But this conclusion is not robust, drawing mainly on the experience of the highly decentralized federations, Canada, Switzerland, and the United States, whose tax decentralization and smaller government might well be manifestations of more basic political economy factors. As well, constraining mechanisms imposed by central government on recipient states can restrain their over fishing. Australia is not included in Rodden's analysis and is a case in point—the Australian states rely on central grants for half their revenue but are also constrained by strong central controls. Thus, whether federalism is associated with smaller or larger government depends on the mix of political and institutional factors of particular countries.

Political scientists and policy analysts have been probing other political and institutional factors that shape processes and outcomes in federal systems. A recent finding is that political-institutional variables—the proximity of elections, the ideology of incumbent governments, and the severity of formal rules limiting deficits—all have a significant effect on budgetary outcomes (Petry 2004, 222). This conclusion is based upon pooled evidence over the past couple of decades for five federations. In this and other studies, Canada and Germany stand out as high deficit countries, while Australia, Switzerland, and the United States are low deficit countries.

Different types of intergovernmental institutions affect federal fiscal policy-making in different ways, as Dietmar Braun (2003, 2004) shows using case studies of Canada, Germany, Belgium, and Switzerland. He identifies Canada and Germany as opposite federal types—"interstate" and "intrastate," respectively—and explains how their institutional differences are played out in fiscal policy processes and outcomes. Canada's national government has extensive scope for fiscal policy-making but weak implementation because provinces are independent with their own legislative powers. The federal government can gain leverage through providing incentives such as contributing to shared cost programs, or it can cut its expenditure and reign in provincial spending through withdrawing from shared programs. Whereas Canada has a competitive tax system, albeit with a shared collection arrangement for income tax, Germany has a cooperation one (Braun 2003, 118). Germany's intrastate federalism incorporates the Länder in national fiscal policy via the Bundesrat that ensures consensus but favors the status quo, and facilitates implementation because everyone has agreed (Braun 2004, 25–8).

One of the main concerns with federalism, that fuelled the opposition of many left-wing parties and commentators in the mid-twentieth century, was its conservative character in favoring the status quo and making reform and innovation difficult. A new study by Obinger, Leibfried, and Castles (2005) shows the complexity of federalism's interaction on social policy in "new world," Australia, Canada, and the United States, and European federations, Austria, Germany, and Switzerland. Using historical case studies, they find that federalism impeded social welfare policy early on, but after consolidation in mature systems other cross-national differences explain variations among countries. The ways in which federalism affects policy innovation and development are multiple and complex, variable over time, and contingent on particular institutional configurations, political actors, and pressure groups, as well as broader historical and cultural contexts. Federalism provides multiple veto-points (Tsebelis 2002) that can check national government initiatives, but of course these can be either progressive or conservative. In addition, federalism provides multiple entry points for new initiatives, and multiple sites for policy innovation.

10   CONCLUSION AND FUTURE DIRECTIONS

Federalism has proved to be a flexible and resilient form of government, and federal countries have generally prospered since the mid-twentieth century. In recent decades, the government environment has changed in ways that are congenial to federalism, with increased prominence of market solutions over government direction and planning that lessens the need for centralized and unitary govern-ment. The prominence of national independence and sovereignty has decreased with increased globalization of rule making, standard setting, communications, and business. How federal systems are affected by globalization and how particular federal countries respond require careful study of individual countries as well as comparative analysis (Lazar, Telford, and Watts 2003). Timeframes, as well as country specific and comparative studies, remain important, as the study of federalism and the welfare state shows (Obinger, Liebfried, and Castles 2005). Whether federalism produces larger or smaller government, or whether it impedes or facilitates policy change, depend on the complex interaction of multiple political as well as institutional factors at a particular time, and since these factors are dynamic there can be significant change over time. The serious study of federalism is not for the faint-hearted, and simple-minded prognostications such as Laski's (1939) "obsolescence of federalism" claim are no longer acceptable.

The study of federalism will remain central to understanding the politics of particular federal countries, so detailed country studies will remain necessary. For example, as the recent study by Bakvis and Skogstad (2002) shows, federalism is central to major political and public policy developments and challenges in Can-ada, quite apart from the ongoing constitutional issues of trying to accommodate Quebec within Canada's constitutional federalism. Comparative federal studies are also necessary to deepen the understanding of the complex working of federalism, as has been the case particularly in the study of fiscal federalism (Braun 2003).

While some countries might adopt federal systems, as Belgium and Spain and, to a lesser extent, South Africa, have recently done, the more likely future scenario is for a proliferation of quasi-federal, asymmetric, and part-federal arrangements tailored to particular purposes and needs. More typical will be cases like the close political association between Australia and New Zealand that has a blend of inter-national, federal, and asymmetric elements (Galligan and Mulgan 1999). While federal frameworks are helpful in understanding aspects of non-federal countries, for example China's fiscal decentralization (Davis 1999), it is unlikely that China will evolve into a classic federal system. The challenge for scholars will be to adapt and develop conceptual models for understanding evolving and new forms of decentralization, especially in non-Western countries like China.

Federal systems provide working models of power sharing in complex systems of multiple spheres of government. Whether this is helpful for understanding the expanding sphere of regional and global governance and the interactions between these and domestic governments, as Imbeau claims (2004, 13), is to be established. The suggestion made here is that the two are compatible. A challenge for future scholarship will be to show whether and in what ways the study of federal systems assists in the study of larger regional and global spheres of governance. The blending of international and intergovernmental relations will likely be a rich field that benefits both international and federal studies.

References

AGRANOFF, R. J. 1986. *Intergovernmental Management: Human Services Problem-Solving in Six Metropolitan Areas.* Albany: State University of New York Press.

—— and McGUIRE, M. 2001. American federalism and the search for models of management. *Public Administration Review,* 6: 671–81.

ANDERSON, L. M. 2004. Exploring the paradox of autonomy: federalism and secession in North America. *Regional and Federal Studies,* 14: 89–112.

BAHL, R. and LINN, J. 1994. Fiscal decentralization and intergovernmental transfers in less developed countries. *Publius,* 24: 1–19.

BAKVIS, H. and SKOGSTAD, G. (eds.) 2002. *Canadian Federalism: Performance, Effectiveness, and Legitimacy.* Toronto: Oxford University Press.

BEER, S. H. 1993. *To Make a Nation: The Rediscovery of American Federalism.* Cambridge, Mass.: Harvard University Press.

BRAUN, D. 2003. *Fiscal Policies in Federal States.* Aldershot: Ashgate.

—— 2004. Intergovernmental relationships and fiscal policymaking in federal countries. Pp. 21–48 in *Politics, Institutions, and Fiscal Policy: Deficits and Surpluses in Federated States,* ed. L. M. Imbeau and F. Petry. London: Lexington Books.

BRENNAN, G. and BUCHANAN, J. 1980. *The Power to Tax: Analytic Foundations of a Fiscal Constitution.* Cambridge: Cambridge University Press.

BRYCE, J. 1888. *The American Commonwealth.* London: Macmillan.

BULL, H. 1977. *The Anarchical Society: A Study of Order in World Politics.* London: Macmillan.

CAMILLERI, J. A. and FALK, J. 1992. *The End of Sovereignty? The Politics of a Shrinking and Fragmented World.* Aldershot: Edward Elgar.

CARNEY, F. S. (ed.) 1965. *The Politics of Johannes Althusius.* London: Eyre and Spottiswoode.

COURCHENE, T. 1995. Glocalization: the regional/international interface. *Canadian Journal of Regional Science*, 18: 1–20.

DAVIS, M. C. 1999. The case for Chinese federalism. *Journal of Democracy*, 10 (2): 124–37.

DAVIS, S. R. 1978. *The Federal Principle: A Journey through Time in Quest of a Meaning.* Berkeley: University of California Press.

DIAMOND, M. 1961. The federalist's view of federalism. Pp. 21–64 in *Essays in Federalism*, ed. G. C. S Benson et al. Claremont, Calif.: Institute for Studies in Federalism, Claremont Men's College.

DORFF, R. H. 1994. Federalism in Eastern Europe: part of the solution or part of the problem? *Publius*, 24 (2): 99–114.

DUCHACEK, I. D. 1987. *Comparative Federalism: The Territorial Dimension of Politics.* Lanham, Md.: University Press of America.

ELAZAR, D. J. 1984. *American Federalism: A View from the States*, 3rd edn. New York: Harper and Row.

——— 1987. *Exploring Federalism.* Tuscaloosa: University of Alabama Press.

EPP, C. 1998. *The Rights Revolution: Lawyers, Activists and Supreme Courts in Comparative Perspective.* Chicago: University of Chicago Press.

FEDERALIST PAPERS 1961. *The Federalist Papers*, ed. A. Hamilton, J. Madison, and J. Jay. New York: Mentor; orig. pub. 1787.

FILIPPOV, M., ORDESHOOK, P. C., and SHEVTSOVA, O. 2004. *Designing Federalism: A Theory of Self-Sustainable Federal Institutions.* Cambridge: Cambridge University Press.

FRANCK, T. M. (ed.) 1968. *Why Federations Fail.* New York: New York University Press.

GALLIGAN, B. 2001. Amending constitutions through the referendum device. Pp. 109–24 in *Referendum Democracy: Citizens, Elites, and Deliberation in Referendum Campaigns*, ed. M. Meldelsohn and A. Parkin. London: Palgrave.

——— and MULGAN, R. 1999. Asymmetric political association: the Australasian experiment. Pp. 57–72 in *Accommodating Diversity: Asymmetry in Federal States*, ed. R. Agranoff. Baden-Baden: Nomos Verlagsgesellschaft.

——— ROBERTS, W., and TRIFILETTI, G. 2001. *Australians and Globalisation.* Cambridge: Cambridge University Press.

GREENWOOD, G. 1976. *The Future of Australian Federalism*, 2nd edn. St. Lucia, University of Queensland Press; orig. pub. 1946.

GREWAL, B. S., BRENNAN, G., and MATHEWS, R. L. (eds.) 1980. *The Economics of Federalism.* Canberra: Australian National University Press.

GRODZINS, M. 1966. *The American System: A New View of Government in the United States*, ed. D. Elazar. New Brunswick, NJ: Transaction.

HOROWITZ, D. L. 1985. *Ethnic Groups in Conflict.* Berkeley: University of California Press.

IMBEAU, L. M. 2004. The political-economy of public deficits. Pp. 1–20 in *Politics, Institutions, and Fiscal Policy: Deficits and Surpluses in Federated States*, ed. L. M. Imbeau and F. Petry. London: Lexington Books.

JEFFERY, C. (ed.) 1999. *Recasting German Federalism: The Legacies of Unification.* London: Pinter.

KEOHANE, R. and NYE, J. S. 1977. *Power and Interdependency: World Politics in Transition.* Boston: Little, Brown.

KHAN, R. 1992. *Federal India: A Design for Change.* New Delhi: Vikas.

KRASNER, S. 1999. *Sovereignty: Organized Hypocrisy.* Princeton, NJ: Princeton University Press.

LASKI, H. J. 1939. The obsolescence of federalism. *New Republic*, 3: 367–9.

LAZAR, H., TELFORD, H., and WATTS, R. L. (eds.) 2003. *The Impact of Global and Regional Integration on Federal Systems: A Comparative Analysis.* Montreal: McGill-Queen's University Press.

LIJPHART, A. 1999. *Patterns of Democracy: Government Forms and Performance in Thirty-Six Countries.* New Haven, Conn.: Yale University Press.

LINKLATER, A. 1998. Citizenship and sovereignty in the post-Westphalian state. Pp. 113–37 in *Re-imagining Political Community: Studies in cosmopolitan democracy,* ed. D. Archibugi, D. Held, and M. Kohler. Stanford, Calif.: Stanford University Press.

LIVINGSTON, W. S. 1956. *Federalism and Constitutional Change.* Oxford: Clarendon Press.

LOWI, T. J. 1984. Why there is no socialism in the United States: a federal analysis. *International Political Science Review,* 5: 369–80.

LUTZ, D. 1994. Towards a theory of constitutional amendment. *American Political Science Review,* 88: 355–70.

MONTERO, A. P. 2001. After decentralization: patterns of intergovernmental conflict in Argentina, Brazil, Spain, and Mexico. *Publius,* 31 (4): 43–66.

OBINGER, H., LEIBFRIED, S., and CASTLES, F. C. (eds.) 2005. *Federalism and the Welfare State: New World and European Experiences.* Cambridge: Cambridge University Press.

PETRY, F. 2004. Deficits and surpluses in federal states: a pooled analysis. Pp. 203–24 in *Politics, Institutions, and Fiscal Policy: Deficits and Surpluses in Federated States,* ed. L. M. Imbeau and F. Petry. London: Lexington Books.

RAO, M. G. 2003. Incentivizing fiscal transfers in the Indian federation. *Publius,* 33 (4): 43–63.

RIKER, W. H. 1964. *Federalism: Origin, Operation, Significance.* Boston: Little, Brown.

—— 1970. The triviality of federalism. *Politics* [now the *Australian Journal of Political Science*], 5: 239–41.

—— 1975. Federalism. In *Handbook of Political Science,* vol. 5: *Governmental Institutions and Processes,* ed. F. I. Greenstein and N. W. Polsby. Reading, Mass.: Addison-Wesley.

—— 1987. *The Development of American Federalism.* Boston: Kluwer.

—— 1993. Federalism. In *A Companion to Contemporary Political Philosophy,* ed. R. E. Goodin and P. Pettit. Oxford: Basil Blackwell.

RODDEN, J. 2003. Reviving Leviathan: fiscal federalism and the growth of government. *International Organization,* 57: 695–729.

RUSSELL, P. H. 2004. *Constitutional Odyssey: Can Canadians Become a Sovereign People?* 3rd edn. Toronto: University of Toronto Press.

—— 2005. The future of Europe in an era of federalism. Pp. 4–20 in *The Changing Face of Federalism: Institutional Reconfiguration in Europe from East to West,* ed. S. Ortino, M. Zagar, and V. Mastny. Manchester: Manchester University Press.

SAWER, G. 1976. *Modern Federalism.* Melbourne: Pitman.

SHARMAN, C. 1990. Parliamentary federations and limited government: constitutional design and redesign in Australia and Canada. *Journal of Theoretical Politics,* 2: 205–30.

SMILEY, D. V. 1980. *Canada in Question: Federalism in the Eighties,* 3rd edn. Toronto: University of Toronto Press.

STURM, R. 1999. Party competition and the federal system: the Lehmbruch hypothesis revised. Pp. 107–216 in *Recasting German Federalism: The Legacies of Unification,* ed. C. Jeffery. London: Pinter.

DE TOCQUEVILLE, A. 1945. *Democracy in America.* New York: Vintage; orig. pub. 1835.

TSEBELIS, G. 2002. *Veto Players: How Political Institutions Work.* Princeton, NJ: Princeton University Press.

VERNEY, D. V. 2003. From quasi-federation to quasi-confederacy? The transformation of India's party system. *Publius*, 33 (4): 153–72.

WATTS, R. L. 1999. *Comparing Federal Systems*, 2nd edn. Montreal: McGill-Queen's University Press.

WHEARE, K. C. 1963. *Federal Government*, 4th edn. Oxford: Oxford University Press; orig. pub. 1946.

ZAGAR, M. 2005. The collapse of the Yugoslav federation and the viability of asymmetrical federalism. Pp. 107–33 in *The Changing Face of Federalism: Institutional Reconfiguration in Europe from East to West*, ed. S. Ortino, M. Zagar, and V. Mastny. Manchester: Manchester University Press.

CHAPTER 15

TERRITORIAL INSTITUTIONS

JEAN-CLAUDE THOENIG

Territorial politics as social and political constructs are major issues for government and for policy-making. Studying its properties and its dynamics shapes a domain of its own in social sciences. The present chapter presents dominant approaches that structure knowledge about center–periphery relationships. It also summarizes key findings from a comparative perspective.

1 THE TERRITORY AS A SOCIAL AND POLITICAL CONSTRUCT

Reflecting a federalist or pluralist perspective, the object of territorial politics is often called intergovernmental relationships. In centralized nation states influenced by Roman law, it is rather defined as the study of center–local relationships.

Relating territorial administration and political authority is a fundamental problem for public institutions and polities. The distribution of governmental authority by area and by function had already puzzled the founding fathers of political theory and public administration (Fesler 1949). The question still remains open today: Is it possible to define an acceptable level and size of territory for administering policies?

Common sense defines territory as a geographical factor. Nature and topography may condition economic activity, social interaction, and political jurisdiction. But physical features do not constitute the whole meaning of territory as a fundamental feature in politics, policy-making, and polity.

Social sciences define space as a dependent variable (Gottmann 1980). Territory is associated with the spatial limits within which a governmental institution has authority and legitimacy, and representation and participation are structured.

Political institutions constitute jurisdictions for public policy and for representation. But territorial politics should never be restricted to the description of legal texts and the levels that are formalized—the local or municipal, the regional, the state or national, the supranational or international. Space and its management are defined and redefined not only by lawyers and administrators but also by social contest and by changing identities and solidarities.

2   CONTEMPORARY ISSUES

Territory had been closely associated with the emergence and the triumph of the nation state throughout Europe. But, at the end of the nineteenth century, it started to be considered as a legacy of traditional society. Its decline was predicted. The reason was that massive urbanization, a new social division of labor, and the expansion of economic markets would require more functional approaches (Durkheim 1964). Differentiated localisms would be merged into a unified national system. Territorial roots and identities would be substituted by functional and economic cleavages (Paddison 1983).

Territorial politics was considered as belonging to the past. The reason was partly due to a theoretical confusion. The economy became internationally integrated. Distance was shortened in terms of time of transportation. Cultural standardization and mass markets spread around the globe. Modernization was considered as incompatible with territory.

Territorial issues, far from declining, have come back on the political agenda. Subnational levels of government absorb a greater share of governmental growth than the center (Sharpe 1988). Public monies are in shortage, the exploding costs of the welfare state model not being balanced by increasing public revenues. The state, even in the countries where it is strong and centralized, is unable to manage by itself the various facets of life (Balme, Garraud, Hoffmann-Martinot, and Ritaine 1994).

3   SOME ISSUES RELATE TO THE NATION STATES

Productivity gains and better coordination between various levels induce rationalization. Small local jurisdictions are merged. A wide redistribution of functions and policy domains is undertaken by a strong decentralization of authority, revenues, and accountability. Quasi-market principles claimed by "new public management"-style reforms relax the command and control approaches of intergovernmental relationships. They tend to separate the democratic element of government from the managerial aspects of delivering service.

Democratization and participation initiatives are said to strengthen democracy and lower civic apathy (Gabriel, Hoffmann-Martinot, and Savitch 2000). National government seems out of reach for ordinary citizens. Elections are considered an insufficient voice strategy by inhabitants and representation an unreliable accountability process to control decision-makers. To bring the people back at the subnational level without weakening national control, to co-opt stakeholders without lowering the legitimacy of elected bodies, become key concerns.

Regionalisms keep reemerging in many countries (Rokkan and Urwin 1982). Top-down regionalism refers to decentralization institutionalized from and by the national level. National governments share the funding of policy domains with subnational levels, and transfer specific functions to a level considered as more efficient (Stoltz 2001). Bottom-up regionalism expresses social mobilization within civil society around ideological references and identity claims (Keating 1998). It is less a violent revolt against an oppressive or colonialist center, aiming at setting up a totally separate nation state, and more a claim for institutional autonomy and functional devolution. It expresses the will to have ethnic or linguistic identities recognized (Moreno 1997).

Public problems undergo profound changes. Issues ignore more and more the limits of territorial jurisdictions. Their treatment may induce externalization effects. Solutions cannot be broken down in a set of simple repetitive technical solutions but imply integrated interdisciplinary approaches. Solutions become more uncertain while the problem to address becomes more complex. A clear and stable division of functions between levels is no longer possible. More horizontal coordination, ad hoc functional flexibility, and pragmatic interinstitutional cooperation are required.

4   OTHER ISSUES RELATE TO BEYOND THE NATION-STATES DYNAMICS

Supranational political configurations tend to cover most continents. A spectacular change happens with the emergence of the European Union. Neither a full state nor a mere association of free country members, it provides a fruitful ground for innovative patterns of intergovernmental relationships. To foster economic development in an open economy implies that territorial dimensions play a key role in keeping jobs located in high salary regions while attracting investments to underdeveloped areas. With the increasing role played by world public institutions, nation states lose actual control when not the monopolist of regulatory policies in many sectors.

These phenomena raise old questions in new terms and new questions in classic terms: the formation of states and their disintegration, territorial roots of governmental legitimacy, advantages and disadvantages of decentralization and recentralization, ethnic identities, spatial territories, and socioeconomic development.

5   A DOMAIN OF ITS OWN

The international community shares a common standard of scientific excellence. The time is over when distaste for theory, predilection for ideological advocacy, and social engineering were acceptable. Eclectic methodology and lack of rigor are discarded, despite the fact that some atheoretical publications have been quite influential depicting in a learned manner territorial politics in the UK (Bulpitt 1983) or in France (Chevallier 1978). The links with prescriptive approaches influenced by law, such as the French "*science administrative*," or with mere descriptions of formal institutional settings, as in the case of prebehavioral American public administration theory, have been cut.

Territorial politics borrows massively from disciplines like political science, sociology, and economics. Streams and domains like local government studies (Chisholm 1989), community studies (Aiken and Mott 1970), policy analysis (Pressman and Wildavsky 1973), urban affairs (Goldsmith 1995), not to mention electoral and party studies (Gibson 1997), international relations, and economic sociology, paved the way for the understanding of intergovernmental relationships as such.

A center–periphery paradigm has been quite influential in political science. Within society, a center has the monopoly of defining what is sacred, with the ultimate and irreducible content in the realm of beliefs, values, and symbols (Shils 1975). The periphery is taken to be in itself awkward, narrow-minded, unpolished, and unimaginative. To avoid impoverished autonomy, it accepts enriching dependence and defers to the center as providing the locus of excellence, vitality, and creativity. Centrality provides cultural salvation. The center also controls action tools such as roles and institutions that embody these cultural frameworks and propagate them. Dependency theories studying underdevelopment (Frank 1967) and world order (Wallerstein 1974) argue that conflict loaded domination relationships link core or metropolis to satellites or peripheries. The center imposes a principle of order, acts as a dominator, and structures a unitary capacity to a periphery that is fragmented, disorganized, and not cohesive.

Territorial politics has reached the status of a proper domain. It has its own research agenda. Asymmetries, cultural flows, and dependencies are considered as research questions. They no longer should be treated as postulates. It is up to inquiry to verify how far, in a given empirical context, the center also depends on the periphery, if the relationships between national, regional, and local levels really are transitive or linear, in which conditions the role of the center is stable, increasing, or losing ground, and whether more than one center may exist.

6   APPROACHES AND DEBATES

A common domain does not imply uniformity and consensus. Debates are permanent and differentiation exists.

Some forms of national insularities suggest a diversity of emphasis and agendas. Countries such as the USA, Britain, and France had entered the field quite early in the 1960s and in the 1970s. Britain and France have maintained a persistent stream of publications. In the 1990s the institutional expansion of the EU has offered a new knowledge frontier and has attracted an impressive volume of literature.

The USA had made massive contributions in the 1960s and 1970s. The irony is that American scholars carried out more in-depth field research on European countries than on their own. During the 1970s political scientists like Douglas Ashford and Sidney Tarrow made pioneering contributions on France, the UK, Italy, and Sweden (Tarrow 1977; Ashford 1982). In more recent years they have experienced a decline in academic attention to the relationships between federal, state, and local levels. Comprehensive textbooks, that remain today references, had already been published in the 1980s (Anton 1989). North American research has developed a far greater interest for policy studies dealing mainly with policy performances and who gets what, when, and how from governments. In parallel they have kept much interest for an established tradition like community power studies.

In the late 1960s French territorial politics was studied using extensive field observation and identifying in a systematic way the informal links and practices that bind local elected officials and central government bureaucrats and representatives (Thoenig 1975; Grémion 1976). Its apparently normative neutral and empirically rooted perspective, as well as the rather counterintuitive observations it collected, were a source of inspiration for many scholars in Europe and abroad.

In the UK a publicly-funded initiative was launched at the end of the 1970s on the specific topic of center–local government relationships. British political science has become a leading contributor to the advancement of agnostic knowledge in the domain (Rhodes 1981; Goldsmith 1986; Page and Goldsmith 1987; Jones 1988; Sharpe 1989).

Academic debates are still alive. Territorial politics as a domain has attracted research approaches and interpretations that may lead to opposite conclusions. The lack of consensus among scholars is reinforced by ideological competition and partisan conflicts inside civil society about the model of good government to adopt for the coming years. Several classifications of approaches have been suggested (Rhodes 1991; Stoker 1995; Pierre and Peters 2000). They can be subdivided into four main classes: political dynamics; state theories; interorganizational theory; and negotiated governance.

7 POLITICAL DYNAMICS: POLITIES MATTER

Territorial politics as a domain has marginalized traditional public administration. It postulates that a rather specific world called a polity exists with its own processes and rationalities. Institutions are a research problem, not a given. Field research makes a difference. Real practices, and not formal authority, enable an understanding of who matters more and who has less influence. Political dynamics are main causes of a consequence called territorial politics.

Centralization provided the enigma to be solved about territorial politics. All major countries on both sides of the Atlantic were experiencing a spectacular concentration of resources, issues to be handled and policy domains covered in the hands of their national authorities, in federal as well as in unitary states. Many writers adopted a way of reasoning that implied a kind of zero-sum game. The role of the center increases at the expense of the role of the periphery. The autonomy the localities lose is equal to the autonomy the center wins. In Western democracies a general rule is supposed to exist. The reason why central governments are able to impose their wills in such an easy way has mainly to do with the fact that local government is politically weak (Page and Goldsmith 1987).

The interpretation of centralization has fueled intensive debate (King 1993; Stoker 1995). A dual polity approach pushes political scientists to look not only at the national level but to consider also the local levels involved, their interests, cultures, and margins of discretion. But it also postulates that the national level acts as a unitary and strategic actor. It assumes that the national state is able to get its decisions implemented. Political science tends to overestimate the ability of political leaders, either local or national, to set the rules of the game. Alternative approaches such as organization theory give recurrent proof of such fallacies. Is the center a mere set of loosely coupled political fractions? The answer is: it depends, and strong evidence is needed to prove it (Dupuy and Thoenig 1985). The link with old institutionalism is cut when social sciences, having observed how scattered and fragmented the national level polity is when it is not the executive, adopts words that fit the complexity of the real world (Hayward and Wright 2002).

Mainstream political science favors bottom-up approaches. The emphasis is given to local political phenomena. The national level is basically described as a set of background factors such as legalistic principles and budgetary transfers. Historical evolution over more than a century is assumed to explain how the periphery is integrated, the representation models, and the national resources allocation structure to localities. Interviews with local elected officials and administrators provide a major data source. Their policy brokerage styles, their administrative activism, and their partisan commitments are compared. Inferences are made from their experience about political entrepreneurship and political conflict in central–local relationships (Tarrow 1977; Page 1991).

Money talks (Wright 1988). Financial data have to be questioned as relevant indicators. For instance, is the percentage of national grants in the revenues of local authorities a reliable indicator of their subordination to the national polity and central policy-making? Is money an effective way for the center actually to call the tune (Anton, Crawley, and Kraner 1980; Anton 1989)? A fiscal federalism perspective deals with multilevel government within the same geographical area, and policy instruments such as intergovernmental grants, fiscal decentralization, and revenue sharing (Oates 1999). Models are built with respect to the appropriate assignment of tasks and finances, in the case of EU tax harmonization and local government finance in the UK (James 2004) or about the equalizing performance of central grants to communes in France (Gilbert and Guengant 2002).

Political dynamics should test counter-intuitive hypotheses. Increasing centralization does not mechanically imply less autonomy and influence for the localities; quite the reverse. Classic political science approaches tend to assume that political variables explain most of the variance about territorial politics. Are polities really in control? To what extent should one consider political dynamics not as causes but as intended or unintended consequences of subnational affairs and their government?

8   STATE THEORIES: GLOBAL CONTEXTS MATTER

Most state theories share a paradox. They state that macro-level factors determine patterns of central–local relations. Broader political, economic, and social contexts give birth to an unending series of crises and changes preventing territorial public affairs from reaching a level of stability. Center–local relationships are considered as dependent variables, as social constructs. Independent or exogenous variables explain why and how formal as well as informal links and norms emerge and evolve.

Early social class conflict approaches assumed that local governments are mere passive servants of national and international capitalism (Castells and Godard 1974; Dunleavy 1980). Critical scholars argued that territorial politics does not really matter as a relevant knowledge domain and action arena. In the 1980s two less abrupt functional explanations were offered. The dual state thesis argues that the state keeps control of social investment policies at the national level. It leaves the management of social consumption policies in the hands of subnational authorities. Local democracy provides remedies to help the poor fighting the failures of markets, while national politics allocates, in a closed corporate manner, support, goods, and services to the profitable private sector (Saunders 1982). Social consumption being necessarily subordinate to social investment, local levels are therefore dominated by central levels.

Another model argued that the domination of the national state stems from the fact that major tensions occur between the center and the localities. Societies are divided and unevenly developed. The local state is caught in a dilemma: It represents local interests to the center but also is in charge of implementing national policies within its jurisdictions (Duncan and Goodwin 1988). A more recent line of reasoning argues that the changing nature of territorial politics at the end of the twentieth century is less the consequence of some functional imperative and more the product of social struggles in unstable international economies and societal orders (Stoker 1990, 1991; Painter 1991). Post-Fordist mass production and consumption require new regimes to support sustained economic growth. Ruling political elites may still occasionally shape intergovernmental relations according to their wills but they have lost part of their control. Established roles of localities, as set up for a Fordist welfare state, are losing ground. New institutional arrangements are still not stabilized. Local government may not necessarily remain a major player. New management thinking favors principles such as hyper-flexibility, customer-orientation, and enterprise culture.

Such a research stream, active in France and in the UK, has been influenced by neo-Marxism and by political economics such as regulationist theory (Aglietta 1979). Urban renewal, housing, employment, and fiscal-financial issues provide favorite empirical entry points. Observing local government leads many writers to interpret in a much broader way reforms of the national state. Changes in the socioeconomic stratification of the population, formal reform designs, and ideological struggles between the left and the right have inspired many writers, especially in the UK (Crouch and Marquand 1989; Rhodes 2000).

9   INTERORGANIZATIONAL ANALYSIS: SYSTEMS MATTER

A third research tradition has deep roots in the sociology of organizations. Organizations are considered as pluralist arenas for action. They are structured by and around power games. To satisfy their specific stakes and achieve their respective tasks, actors are dependent on each other. The central concern for this tradition lies in unraveling the extent to which asymmetric exchanges occur and power is distributed. Their actual inner functioning is treated as a central problem for inquiry. Center–local relations are considered as an independent variable, as a cause, and not only as a consequence, of policy-making and polities.

This perspective explores the intergovernmental black box: Dependence and power games. Central–local relationships operate like a quasi-organized system, as a configuration of interorganizational relations, and not as a centrifugal set of partitioned worlds. Despite the fact that in most countries no formal pyramidal hierarchy integrates the various levels of government, and that in federal countries states or Länder have a lot of discretionary autonomy, all stakeholders involved in the process of territorial government are linked by some common action ground. The national level acts and non-acts have direct or indirect consequences for the local level, and vice versa, even when each level does not intervene in exactly the same policy domains.

Michel Crozier and Jean-Claude Thoenig model the central–local relationships in France as a honeycomb structure linking the smallest village to Paris (Crozier and Thoenig 1976). It views relationships between subnational elected politicians such as mayors and national state field agents such as prefects as typical and repetitive mutual dependence games. Each of them takes a decisive advantage from getting access and support to a partner belonging to the other institutional side. The reason is that each side controls information, legitimacy, monies, know-how, and policies that are crucially needed by the other side. Exchanges of resources are daily practices. The model is structured around a process of cross-regulation that stabilizes the system beyond electoral hazards and partisan diversity. Its members follow informal but strongly established interaction norms. This model explains that the national level would be blind and powerless without having access to the local politicians. Local councils have much more influence on the state than one would expect in a jacobine country such as France.

Rod Rhodes (1981) suggests a similar model about British territorial politics. It too underscores dependence games between national authorities and local administrators, participants maneuvering for selfish reasons such as achieving their goals, deploying resources to increase their influence while avoiding becoming dependent on other players.

Power is defined as the ability for an actor or a coalition of actors to get from other actors acts and non-acts the latter would not deliver without being dependent on the former to succeed in their own task or turf. How some form of compatibility between different logics of action is achieved, by formal coordination or by informal cooperation, how arrangements are worked out between various players active at various levels or the same levels, which kinds of de facto rules and social norms regulate these games between elected legislators and executives, administrative agencies, interest groups, inhabitants, and even firms, allow an understanding of and an anticipation about why a system operates the way it does, therefore why it handles issues and policies in the way it does.

Interorganizational analysis relies on case studies. It brings the fieldwork back in. Information collected by observations of daily behaviors and in-depth semi-structured interviews plays an important role. It does not rule out that those who have legitimate authority at the top, whether inside specific institutions—for instance the top elected officer such as the mayor in a city—or inside the intergovernmental system—for instance the national cabinet—are also those who have real power on issues and policies. But it favors a bottom-up approach and the study of how decisions, whether small and routinely-based or highly visible and strategic, are made and actually implemented.

Center–local relationships systems are considered as meso-social orders. Their properties do not mechanically and passively reflect the interests of some dominant social class, the wills of the constitutional designers, or national folk culture. They also are not mere applications of broader institutional patterns, as institutional theory would predict. Two countries may share a similar federal constitution or may adopt identical new public management guidelines. The chances are high that, actually, the way they manage territorial affairs shall be very different. In a world of increasing globalization, local variations are kept alive across countries, regions, and even policy domains. Interorganizational approaches tend to treat intergovernmental systems as independent variables. Local orders impose appropriate issues, norms, and practices on their members that are out of their individual control and awareness.

Territorial systems address specific content issues. Several interorganizational oriented scholars add two other facets to their analysis: policy networks and policy analysis.

Power and dependence approaches take into account the impact of territorial interorganization systems on and their variation across policy networks. Such networks draw together the organizations that interact within a particular field. Rod Rhodes (1988) identifies six types for Britain in which local authorities are involved and that reflect a series of discrete policy interests. They differentiate according to their level of integration. Some are loosely knit. They are basically issue networks regrouping a large number of participants with a limited degree of interdependence such as inner city partnerships (Leach 1985). Others are closely coupled. Their access is restricted. They regroup extremely dependent and homogenous communities belonging to the same regional territory and communities that share common policy and service delivery responsibility (Ranson, Jones, and Walsh 1985). Some, called intergovernmental, are moderately integrated such as national bodies representing local government councils (Rhodes 1986).

Territorial local orders select issues to be part of governmental agendas at various levels and elaborate solutions or policies (Duran and Thoenig 1996). Their legitimacy derives to a large extent from the outcomes they deliver, and not only from law and elections. Roles, interdependence relationships, and power structure vary a lot between policy sectors even when the same parties—communes, central state agencies, regional councils—are involved. At the same time social norms are shared that allow repetitive games and predictable behaviors to last. The Thoenig model also comes close to a conclusion made by the Rhodes model. In many cases the standards defined in a rigid way by the center are not applicable or even applied, unless a lot of flexibility is given to those locally implementing national policies. In both countries the center faces a fragmentation constraint. Despite the existence of the prefect, it lacks coordinating capacity among its many own field agencies and cannot command local authorities. To discover that centralized systems such as France and Great Britain experience similar difficulties imposing a top-down approach to centrifugal territories and de facto autonomous actors, even when as in France the state formally controls an impressive web of field agencies, is one of the most valuable contributions of interorganizational approaches.

10   NEGOTIATED ORDERS: PROCESS MATTERS

Multilevel governance emerged in the 1990s. Governance remains a loose concept, ranging from another way to name government to an alternative way to govern (Rhodes 1996). When dealing with intergovernmental relationships, it focuses on the discrepancy between governance and the constitutional map of political life (Rhodes 2000). Governance is a particular form of political game. Its baseline agenda is that territorial relationships should be considered as sets of non-hierarchical linkages (Pierre and Stoker 2000; Peters and Pierre 2001; Bache and Flinders 2004). Negotiated order approaches lead their theorists to criticize for empirical reasons and on ideological grounds the center–periphery paradigm. State-centrism plays the role of a theoretical straw man.

Schools of thought such as new institutionalism, game theory (Scharpf 1988, 1997, 2001), and policy analysis stimulate multilevel governance perspectives. EU integration and the evolving relations between subnational, national, and European levels give birth to numerous publications (Marks, Hooghe, and Blank 1996; Puchala 1999). Developments propelling multilevel governance also occur within states. Cities in the USA (Peters 2001) and regions associated with metropolitan areas in EU countries (Le Galès and Harding 1998) have become laboratories for a reinvention of government. The national level has less financial incentives to provide to steer subnational government. Decentralization does not suffice. New inclusive models are developed in many countries such as those of Scandinavia, Germany, France, the UK, Spain, or Japan. The studies underscore three major facets.

National states no longer stand as the "unrivalled kings of the hill" (Peters and Pierre 2001). Transnational forms and levels of government are massively embedded in subnational politics. Therefore no more central level exists that has the monopoly on authority. More than ever central state authorities face a serious challenge. Their legitimacy to intervene is questioned. They have less money to allocate. The level of their achievements is under closer evaluation by local stake-holders and authorities. How is it still for them to remain relevant players in territorial politics? Another consequence of loosening territorial authority is that institutional relationships do not operate through intermediaries but take place directly between the local and the transnational authorities. Bypassing regions and states becomes ordinary practice and appropriate behavior when no more formal vertical orders exist.

Parties involved in territorial policy-making and politics are not stable. They may come and leave according to issues or spatial territories but also as a result of their own discretionary choice. Who sits around the same table with whom results from ad hoc opportunistic arrangements. Highly visible programs such as struc-tural funds co-funded by the EU, national states, and local authorities have been the major source for regional socioeconomic development in many members (Smith 1997). Legalistic grant allocation programs by which the center puts incen-tives to the peripheries lose importance. Local levels in their turn use financial incentives to fund projects that are part of regional interest or belong under state jurisdiction. Cross-funding patterns freely bargained between multiple parties are the main vehicles for political bodies like regional councils or communes to finance their own projects. Quasi-markets for funding projects are present in strong nation states (Gilbert and Thoenig 1999). Horizontal pooling and multilevel cooperation also include public–private partnership. Where and when publicness ends or starts is no longer easy to define.

Constitutionally defined authority or law based procedures matter less than processes of exchanges and bargaining. Order and action stem from open and ongoing negotiations. Elected officials question the meaningfulness of principles such as sovereignty and autonomy. Beside governmental authorities, public problem definition and solving also involve private firms, lobbies, moral cause groups, and inhabitants. A series of policy arenas and wide civil society partici-pation imply that political councils, bureaucracies, and parties lose the monopoly on agenda building. All major Western countries follow an identical evolution pattern, from Sweden (Bogason 1998) to Australia (Painter 2001) and Canada (Simeon and Cameron 2002). The national level allocates less money, controls less, and decentralizes more. It makes widespread use of constitutive policies to integrate new partners and negotiate their involvement. Institutionalization of policy arenas and cooptation of issue communities become ordinary tools of government.

Called *"action publique"* in French, public governance is defined by some authors as an empirical phenomenon (Thoenig 1998). It refers to the process by which various stakeholders, public and private, deal with mutual dependency, exchange resources, coordinate actions, define some common stake to handle and build goals to reach (Rhodes 1997). For other authors, governance means a new theory about politics, policy-making, and polities.

Multilevel governance approaches often favor top-down only approaches. The EU framework fascinates analysts by a continuous flow of institutional innovation in many policy domains (Marks, Hooghe, and Blank 1996). Various models of multitiered governance are identified from an action perspective. They generate differentiation and transformation across territorial systems (Hooghe 1996). Relying on North American and European research, Liesbet Hooghe and Gary Marks claim that the days of central state control are over (Hooghe and Marks 2003). They conceptualize prescriptive models and discuss their respective virtues. A first type conceives of flexible, task specific, and intersecting jurisdictions. A second type disperses authority to non-intersecting, general purpose, and durable jurisdictions. No alternative exists to liberal democracy about the way collective decisions should be made. Therefore territorial politics as a domain should focus on jurisdictional design and architecture. For whom collective decisions can and should be made matters more.

Debates are numerous about the actual relevance and the scientific rigor of multitiered governance theory. They hardly rely upon evidence about how jurisdictional designs are implemented and do not evaluate the actual outcomes they generate (Le Galès 1998). They misconceive institutional path dependencies. They discard macro- and meso-determinisms from an action as well as an interpretation angle. They misunderstand the limits of informal, consensual, and inclusive processes of decision-making. In-depth field surveys suggest that the visible growth of negotiations and governance patterns does not jeopardize democratic legitimacy and the power of politicians. Massive decentralization has made multilevel governance a routine process at all levels. Nevertheless a national political class dominated by a lasting and powerful cross-partisan coalition of elected officials cumulating local and national mandates still calls the tune when institutional reforms are considered and decided (Thoenig 2005). Decentralization, modernization, and negotiation are acceptable as long as the institutional and legalistic factors that protect their power bases are not jeopardized.

Institutions, but also interorganizational relationships inside the public sector, are not irrelevant. Therefore multilevel governance theory should escape the "Faustian bargain" model where making a deal leads the parties involved to ignore the darker effects of the deal (Peters and Pierre 2004). Do multigovernance approaches describe spatially ordered relationships or does it refer to networking? The answer is: It depends. Governance is a confusing term. Consociationalism provides tools for action taking (Skelcher 2005). They address institutional solutions for polycentric contexts at two levels: Informal norms that pattern behavior in and round them and formal organizational structures and arrangements.

11   NATIONAL AND COMPARATIVE CONTEXTS

Defining the main characteristics of territorial politics within countries and classifying national contexts into different types of families are parts of the ambitions many social scientists keep in mind.

Classic political science approaches have initially favored local government based comparisons. Comparing two states ruled by Roman law grounded centralization, Sidney Tarrow finds that in the 1970s partisan politics is the fundamental mechanism of integration between the center and the localities, and that the peripheries are governed in a scattered and bureaucratic way (Tarrow 1977; Tarrow, Katzenstein, and Graziano 1979). France is integrated by administrative interactions. Territorial representation matters more than partisan affiliation, and localities are well controlled by seasoned active and management oriented mayors. Studying the Local Government Act of 1972, Douglas Ashford argues that the British central government handles local government structure with a frontal attack, suggesting ideological dogmatism and authoritarianism. By contrast France, the ideal type of a Napoleonic centralized state, favors consensual pragmatism and incremental reforms. The reason is that its center is rather weak and cautious, the local political officials having a lot of influence on the wills and the policies of the national state. Britain has a powerful center with a lot of room for functional erratic and inadequate initiatives, local politicians being extraordinarily complacent and vulnerable (Ashford 1979, 1982, 1989).

The interpretative value of soft descriptions has been questioned. More theoretically based patterns should be applied to broader samples of countries. A secondary analysis of monographs on seven unitary European states—Norway, Sweden, Denmark, the UK, France, Italy, and Spain—takes into consideration patterns of localism and centralism (Page 1991). Legal and political localism is used as a synthetic denominator. Two types are defined: a northern European family and a southern European one. They differ according to two main indicators: legal-constitutional subordination—measured by the relative percentage of total public expenditures of local and national budgets; the proportion of local expenditures financed by grants; and by institutional proxies such as which services in various policy fields localities are mandated or just allowed to deliver—and political localism—the availability of direct and indirect accesses to the national level. A secondary analysis using identical indicators but adding federal countries suggests a third type, the middle European or Germanic class—Germany, Switzerland, Austria—as well as unitary countries being in the process of quasi-federal devolutions such as Belgium and Spain (Goldsmith 1995). Alternative classifications also distinguish three families: an Anglo type (Britain, North America, and Australia), a southern Europe type (France, Italy, Spain, Belgium, etc.), and a northern Europe type (Austria, Scandinavia, Germany, Switzerland, plus Japan) (Hesse and Sharpe 1991). US federalism suggests the existence of several types of intergovernmental phases or models over seven decades (Wright 1988). Comparisons also assess decentralization policies in Latin American states and Spain (Montero 2001).

A central control perspective adds a lot to the discussion of intergovernmental systems. The fact is that during the 1980s and 1990s the ways central governments formally design and informally handle their relationships with subnational levels have experienced major changes in many national states. With a few exceptions, processes of devolution, decentralization, regionalization, and merger of local jurisdictions have induced less direct control and operational interference, and more indirect control by regulatory procedures.

A comparative perspective of central control enables a second visit to the classifications set up by approaches relying on the autonomy or discretion of local government (Goldsmith 2002). Germanic class countries have experienced the least visible and dramatic changes. The federal level has kept developing forms of cooperation with large urban communes and intermediary tiers that are based on negotiation and bargaining. But the Länder in Germany and the cantons in Switzerland keep playing a very important role in controlling the autonomy of smaller communes. Many southern-type countries like France, Spain, and Belgium, have significantly reduced central control on subnational authorities. Intermediary tiers have increased their role vis-à-vis rural and small size communes that remain weak players. They control monies and policy domains that matter for them. But they have not been granted the possibility, as in federal countries, legally to redesign the limits, the tasks, and the constitution of municipal authorities. In France territorial administration looks more like a market than a hierarchy. The various government levels compete with each other to reinforce their local influence by the power of the purse and by adding new policy domains to their portfolios. A wide variety of interinstitutional patterns of cooperation are at work across the country.

In other unitary countries, no major changes are visible. In Greece and Portugal the center keeps a strong capacity to command and control. In the Netherlands the center remains financially strong and quite active in launching all kinds of experiments. The fact is that it also has a long established tradition of co-governance with local governments. The Nordic countries had made major reforms already before the 1980s, as Sweden did, or have regionalized but without going as far as France and Spain. Scandinavia has experienced an increasing fragmentation of local government. Reforms such as user-governed public management, particularized state grants, contracting out of services, and neighborhood councils have challenged territorial democracy, increased governance by negotiation and interorganizational links, and not reduced the influence of professionals (Bogason 1996). In the UK Whitehall has decentralized significant functions to Wales, Scotland, and Northern Ireland (Keating and Loughlin 2002). Emerging stronger intermediate ties inside national arrangements may limit, to some extent, the autonomy of localities. At the same time they may provide a tool for further decentralization. While the center has looser control over local authorities, it nevertheless keeps its hands on a number of tools allowing it to limit the autonomy of the peripheries.

The case of Western Europe suggests that to classify national states in families requires some prudence. Typologies make national states look more alike than they really are. They give the impression that the evolution of territorial politics is identical across countries. Another lesson is that the growth of transnational arrangements or even economic globalization does not imply a convergence between domestic arrangements. Western Europe is making a transition from local government to local governance (John 2001). But the emergence of the EU as an actor in territorial politics does not make its member states more similar, as reported by a study on subnational democracy and center-level relations in the fifteen member countries (Loughlin 2001). To some extent their institutional fabrics dealing with territorial politics have even become more differentiated. The EU announced that it would favor regions as partners of some of its policies. In fact, regions remain on the whole weak tiers in terms of governmental actors and governance networks (Le Galès and Lequesne 1998). Except in countries like Germany, and in a few cases in Spain and Italy, they do not really matter as politically autonomous actors. They rather remain functional frameworks and highly dependent on the national level. Power is subdivided among numerous levels and networks. A typology of regional government models is applied to twelve major Western Europe states (Keating 1998). Regionalization inside the EU has benefited less regional authorities, and more metropolitan areas and big cities. To some extent the latter have become even stronger in terms of influence and resources. Their autonomy has increased. They may even challenge regional policies.

Reforms tending to separate the democratic element of government from the managerial aspects of delivering service have dissimilar impacts between national contexts. In the US they increase the autonomy of state and local government vis-à-vis the federal authorities (Peters 2001). In Germany they have not had much impact on such relationships (Wollmann 2001).

The idea that the national states are hollowing out does not make much sense when considering the facts (Rhodes 1996). Regionalization is an ambivalent process. Transferring finances and policy domains to subnational levels, far from weakening the national center, provides a solution to increase its own power and role in territorial politics (Wright 1998). Transnational levels such as the EU or NAFTA, and international or world institutions like the World Bank or the United Nations, have not seized control and command from the central states. In some countries the national legislative and executive branches, and more generally the politicians democratically elected by the people, have not really lost control of the agenda of territorial politics.

Intergovernmental relations call for further research on most of the issues listed above. At least three aspects may benefit from closer attention. How is it possible for public institutions to exert authority and to build legitimacy in increasingly changing contexts and power based multilevel arrangements? What happens once new institutional arrangements have been set up? Longitudinal field research and in-depth surveys may provide fruitful answers. Do best models of territorial organization and organizing really exist, and if so, do they matter? Performance of public institutions still remains a subject to be studied and debated from a political perspective.

REFERENCES

AGLIETTA, M. 1979. *A Theory of Capitalist Regulation*. London: New Left Books.

AIKEN, M. and MOTT, P. E. (eds.) 1970. *The Structure of Community Power*. New York: Random House.

ANTON, T. J. 1980. *Administered Politics: Elite Political Culture in Sweden*. Boston: Martinus Nijhoff.

—— 1989. *American Federalism and Public Policy: How the System Works*. Temple: Temple University Press.

—— CRAWLEY, J. P., and KRAMER, K. L. 1980. *Moving Money*. Cambridge, Mass. Oelgeschlager, Gunn, and Hain.

ASHFORD, D. E. 1979. The limits of consensus: the reorganization of British local government and the French contrast. In *Territorial Politics in Industrial Nations*, ed. S. Tarrow, P. J. Katzenstein, and L. Graziano. New York: Praeger.

—— 1982. *British Dogmatism and French Pragmatism: Central-Local Policymaking in the Welfare State*. London: George Allen and Unwin.

—— 1989. British dogmatism and French pragmatism revisited. In *The New Centralism. Britain Out of Step in Europe?*, ed. C. Crouch and D. Marquand. London: Blackwell.

BACHE. I. and FLINDERS. M. (eds.) 2004. *Multi-level Governance*. Oxford: Oxford University Press.

BALME, R., GARRAUD, P., HOFFMANN-MARTINOT, V., and RITAINE, E. 1994. Analysing territorial policies in Western Europe: the case of France, Germany, Italy, and Spain. *European Journal of Political Research*, 25: 389–411.

BOGASON, P. 1996. Fragmentation of local government in Scandinavia. *European Journal of Political Research*, 30 (1): 65–86.

—— 1998. Changes in the Scandinavian model: from bureaucratic command to interorganisational negotiation. *Public Administration*, 76 (2): 335–54.

BULPITT, J. 1983. *Territory and Power in the United Kingdom: An Interpretation*. Manchester: Manchester University Press.

CASTELLS, M. and GODARD, F. 1974. *Monopolville: L'entreprise, l'état, l'urbain*. Paris: Mouton.

CHEVALLIER, J. (ed.) 1978. *Centre, périphérie, territoire*. Paris: Presses Universitaires de France.

CHISHOLM, D. 1989. *Coordination Without Hierarchy: Informal Structure in Multiorganizational Systems*. Berkeley: University of California Press.

CROUCH, C. and MARQUAND, D. 1989. *The New Centralism: Britain Out of Step in Europe?* London: Blackwell.

CROZIER, M. and THOENIG, J. C. 1976. The regulation of complex organized systems. *Administrative Science Quarterly*, 21: 547–70.

DUNCAN, S. and GOODWIN, M. 1988. *The Local State and Uneven Development.* Cambridge: Polity Press.

DUNLEAVY, P. 1980. *Urban Political Analysis.* London: Macmillan.

DUPUY, F. and THOENIG, J. C. 1985. *L'administration en miettes.* Paris: Fayard.

DURAN, P. and THOENIG, J. C. 1996. L'etat et la gestion publique territoriale. *Revue Française de Science Politique*, 4: 580–623.

DURKHEIM, E. 1964. *The Division of Labor in Society.* New York: Free Press.

FESLER, J. 1949. *Area and Administration.* Alabama: University of Alabama Press.

FRANK, A. G. 1967. *Capitalism and Underdevelopment in Latin America.* New York: Monthly Review Press.

GABRIEL, O. W., HOFFMANN-MARTINOT, V., and SAVITCH, H. (eds.) 2000. *Urban Democracy.* Opladen: Leske und Budrich.

GIBSON, E. L. (1997) The populist road to market reforms: policy and electoral coalitions in Mexico and Argentina. *World Politics*, 49 (3): 155–83.

GILBERT, G. and GUENGANT, A. 2002. The equalizing performance of central government grants to local authorities: the case of France. In *National Tax Association: Proceedings of the 95th Conference.* Cachan: Ecole Normale supérieure.

—— and THOENIG, J. C. 1999. Les cofinancements publics: des pratiques aux rationalités. *Revue d'Économie Financière*, 51 (1): 45–78.

GOLDSMITH, M. (ed.) 1986. *New Research in Centre–local Relations.* Aldershot: Gower.

—— 1995. Autonomy and city limits. In *Theories of Urban Politics*, ed. D. Judge, G. Stoker, and H. Wollmann. London: Sage.

—— 2002. Central control over local government—a western European comparison. *Local Government Studies*, 28 (3): 91–112.

—— and NEWTON, K. 1988. Centralisation and decentralisation: changing patterns of intergovernmental relations in advanced western societies—an introduction by the editors. *European Journal of Political Research*, 16: 359–63.

GOTTMANN, J. (ed.) 1980. *Centre and Periphery: Spatial Variation in Politics.* Beverly Hills, Calif.: Sage.

GRÉMION, P. 1976. *Le pouvoir périphérique.* Paris: Le Seuil.

HAYWARD, J. and WRIGHT, V. 2002. *Governing from the Centre: Core Executive Coordination in France.* Oxford: Oxford University Press.

HESSE, J. J. and SHARPE, L. J. 1991. Conclusions. In *Local Governement and Urban Affairs in International Perspective*, ed. J. J. Hesse. Baden-Baden: Nomos.

HOOGHE, L. 1996. *Cohesion Policy and European Integration: Building Multi-level Governance.* Oxford: Oxford University Press.

—— and MARKS, G. 2003. Unraveling the central state, but how? Types of multilevel governance. *American Political Science Review*, 97 (2): 223–43.

JAMES, S. 2004. Financing multi-level government. *Journal of Finance and Management in Public Services*, 4 (1): 17–32.

JOHN, P. 2001. *Local Governance in Western Europe.* London: Sage.

JONES, G. 1988. The crisis in British central–local relationships. *Governance*, 1 (2): 162–84.

KEATING, M. 1998. *Territorial Restructuring and Political Change.* Cheltenham: Edward Elgar.

—— 1998. *The New Regionalism in Western Europe: Territorial Restructuring and Political Change.* Aldershot: Edward Elgar.

—— and LOUGHLIN, J. 2002. *Territorial Policy Communities and Devolution in the United Kingdom.* Badia Fiesolana: European University Institute, Working Paper SPS No 1.

KING, D. 1993. Government beyond Whitehall. In *Between Centre and Locality,* ed. P. Dunleavy, A. Gamble, I. Holliday, and G. Peele. London: Allen and Unwin.

LEACH, S. 1985. Inner cities. In *Between Centre and Locality,* ed. S. Ranson, G. Jones, and K. Walsh. London: Allen and Unwin.

LE GALÈS, P. 1998. Government and governance of regions: structural weaknesses and new mobilisations. In *Regions in Europe,* ed. P. Le Galès and C. Lequesne. London: Routledge.

—— and HARDING, A. 1998. Cities and states in Europe. *West European Politics,* 21: 120–45.

—— and LEQUESNE, C. (eds.) 1998. *Regions in Europe.* London: Routledge.

LOUGHLIN, J. (ed.) 2001. *Subnational Democracy in the European Union: Challenges and Opportunities.* Oxford: Oxford University Press.

MARKS, G., HOOGHE, L., and BLANK, K. 1996. European integration from the 80s: state-centric vs multi-level governance. *Journal of Common Market Studies,* 34: 343–77.

MONTERO, A. P. 2001. After decentralization: patterns of intergovernmental conflict in Argentina, Brazil, Spain, and Mexico. *Publius,* 31 (4): 43–65.

MORENO, L. 1997. Federalization and ethnoterritorial concurrence in Spain. *Publius,* 27 (4): 65–85.

OATES, W. E. 1999. An essay on fiscal federalism. *Journal of Economic Literature,* 37: 1120–49.

PADDISON, R. 1983. *The Fragmented State: The Political Geography of Power.* Oxford: Rober Blackwell Press.

PAGE, E. and GOLDSMITH, M. (eds.) 1987. *Central and Local Government Relations: A Comparative Analysis of West European Unitary States.* Thousand Oaks, Calif.: Sage.

PAGE, E. C. 1991. *Localism and Centralism in Europe: The Political and Legal Bases of Local Self-Government.* Oxford: Oxford University Press.

PAINTER, J. 1991. Regulation theory and local governement. *Local Government Studies,* 17 (6): 23–43.

PAINTER, M. 2001. Multi-level governance and the emergence of collaborative federal institutions in Australia. *Policy and Politics,* 29 (2): 137–50.

PETERS, B. G. 2001. Administrative reform and political power in the United States. *Policy and Politics,* 29 (2): 171–80.

—— and PIERRE, J. 2001. Developments in intergovernmental relations: towards multi-level governance. *Policy and Politics,* 29: 131–65.

—— —— 2004. Multi-level governance: a Faustian bargain? In *Multi-level Governance,* ed. I. Bache and M. Flinders. London: Oxford University Press.

PIERRE, J. and PETERS, B. G. 2000. *Governance, Politics and the State.* London: Macmillan.

—— and STOKER, G. 2000. Towards multi-level governance. In *Developments in British Politics,* ed. P. Dunleavy, A. Gamble, I. Holliday, and G. Peele. London: Macmillan.

PRESSMANN, J. and WILDASKY, A. 1973. *Implementation.* Berkeley: University of California Press.

PUCHALA, D. 1999. Institutionalism, intergovernmentalism and European integration: a review article. *Journal of Common Market Studies,* 37: 317–32.

RANSON, S., JONES, G., and WALSH, K. (eds.) 1985. *Between Centre and Locality.* London: Allen and Unwin.

RHODES, R. A. W. 1981. *Control and Power in Central-local Relations.* Aldershot: Gower.

—— 1986. *The National World of Local Governement.* London: Allen and Unwin.

—— 1988. *Beyond Westminster and Whitehall: The Sub-central Governments of Britain.* London: Hyman and Unwin.

—— 1991. Theory and methods in British public administration: the view from political science. *Political Studies,* 39 (3): 533–54.

—— 1996. The new governance: governing without governance. *Political Studies,* 44: 652–67.

—— 1997. *Understanding Governance: Policy Networks, Governance, Reflexivity and Accountability.* Buckingham: Open University Press.

—— 2000. Governance and public administration. In *Debating Governance: Authority, Steering and Democracy,* ed. J. Pierre. Oxford: Oxford University Press.

—— 2000. *Transforming British Governement.* London: Macmillan.

ROKKAN, S. and URWIN, D. W. (eds.) 2002. *The Politics of Territorial Identity: Studies in European Regionalism.* London: Sage.

SAUNDERS, P. 1982. Why study central–local relations? *Local Government Studies,* 8: 55–6.

SCHARPF, F. W. 1988. The joint-decision trap: lessons from German federalism and European integration. *Public Administration,* 66 (3): 239–79.

—— 1997. The problem-solving capacity of multi-level governance. *Journal of European Public Policy,* 4: 520–38

—— 2001. Notes toward a theory of multilevel governing in Europe. *Scandinavian Political Studies,* 24 (1): 1–26.

SHARPE, L. J. 1988. The growth and decentralization of the modern democratic state. *European Journal of Political Research,* 16: 365–80.

—— 1989. Fragmentation and territoriality in the European state system. *International Political Science Review,* 10 (3): 223–39.

SHILS, E. 1975. *Center and Periphery.* Chicago: University of Chicago Press.

SIMEON, R. and CAMERON, D. 2002. Intergovernmental relations and democracy: an oxymoron if there was ever one. In *Canadian Federalism: Performance, Effectiveness and Legitimacy,* ed. H. Bakvis and G. Skogstad. Oxford: Oxford University Press.

SKELCHER, C. 2005. Juridictional integrity, polycentrism, and the design of democratic governance. *Governance,* 18 (1): 89–110.

SMITH, A. 1997. Studying multi-level governance: examples from French translations of the structural funds. *Public Administration,* 75: 711–29.

STOKER, G. 1990. Regulation theory, local government and the transition from Fordism. In *Challenges to Local Government,* ed. D. King and J. Pierre. London: Sage.

—— 1991. *The Politics of Local Government.* London: Macmillan.

—— 1995. Intergovernmental relations. *Public Administration,* 73 (1): 101–22.

STOLTZ, K. 2001. The political class and regional institution-building: a conceptual framework. *Regional and Federal Studies,* 11 (1): 80–101.

TARROW, S. 1977. *Between Center and Periphery: Grassroots Politics in Italy and France.* New Haven, Conn.: Yale University Press.

—— KATZENSTEIN, P. J., and GRAZIANO, L. (eds.) 1979. *Territorial Politics in Industrial Nations.* New York: Praeger.

THOENIG, J. C. 1975. La relation entre le centre et la périphérie en France: une analyse systémique. *Bulletin de l'Institut International d'Administration Publique*, 36: 77–123.

—— 1998. Politiques publiques et action publique. *Revue Internationale de Politique Comparée*, 5 (2): 295–314.

—— 2005. Territorial administration and political control: decentralization in France. *Public Administration*, 83: 685–708.

WALLERSTEIN, I. 1974. *The Modern World-System*. New York: Academic Press.

WOLLMANN, H. 2001. Germany's trajectory of public sector modernisation—continuities and discontinuities. *Policy and Politics*, 29 (2): 151–71.

WRIGHT, D. S. 1988. *Understanding Intergovernmental Relations*. Belmont, NY: Brooks-Cole.

WRIGHT, V. 1998. Intergovernmental relations and regional government in Europe: a sceptical view. In *Regions in Europe*, ed. P. Le Galès and C. Lequesne. London: Routledge.

CHAPTER 16

EXECUTIVES—THE AMERICAN PRESIDENCY

WILLIAM G. HOWELL

In the early 1980s, George Edwards took the presidency sub-field to task for its failure to adopt basic norms of social science. While scholars who contributed to the various other sub-fields of American politics constructed hard theory that furnished clear predictions that, in turn, were tested using original data-sets and the latest econometric techniques, too many presidency scholars, it seemed to Edwards, insisted on wading through a bog of anecdotes and poorly justified prescriptions. Unlike their would-be closest kin, congressional scholars, presidency scholars tended to prefer complexity to simplicity, nuance to generality, stories to data. Consequentially, Edwards noted, "Research on the presidency too often fails to meet the standards of contemporary political science, including the careful definition and measurement of concepts, the rigorous specification and testing of propositions, the employment of appropriate quantitative methods, and the use of empirical theory to develop hypotheses and explain findings" (Edwards 1983, 100). If the sub-field hoped to rejoin the rest of the discipline and enter the modern era of political science, it would need to nurture and reward scholars conducting quantitative research.

Edwards did not sit alone with such sentiments. In a damning report to the Ford Foundation, Hugh Heclo summarized the state of the presidency literature circa

1977 as follows: "Political observers have written excellent interpretations of the Presidency. Important questions about Presidential power have been raised. But considering the amount of such writing in relation to the base of original empirical research behind it, the field is as shallow as it is luxuriant. To a great extent, presidential studies have coasted on the reputations of a few rightfully respected classics on the presidency and on secondary literature and anecdotes produced by former participants" (Heclo 1977, 30). By recycling over and over again a handful of old chestnuts and witticisms, Heclo observed, scholars had failed to establish even the most basic empirical facts about the presidency.

In the years that followed, others delivered similar lamentations. According to Stephen Wayne, the presidency field languished for lack of clearly defined concepts and standards of measurement. As he put it, "By concentrating on personalities, on dramatic situations, and on controversial decisions and extraordinary events, students of the presidency have reduced the applicability of social science techniques" (Wayne 1983, 6). A decade later, Gary King bemoaned the fact that "Presidency research is one of the last bastions of historical, non-quantitative research in American politics" (King 1993, 388). And jumping yet another decade in time, Matthew Dickinson observed that "American presidency research is often described as the political science discipline's poor stepchild. Compared, for example, to election or congressional studies, presidency research is frequently deemed less clearly conceptualized, more qualitative and descriptive, overly focused on the personal at the expense of the institution, and too prone to prescribing reforms based on uncertain inferences" (Dickson 2004, 99).

Of course, not everyone agreed that more, and better, quantitative research constituted the solution to this dispiriting state of affairs. A variety of scholars made powerful cases for the value of legal analysis (Fisher 2002), carefully constructed case studies (Thomas 1983), and theoretically informed historical research (Skowronek 2002). And they plainly had cause to do so. Some of the best insights and most theoretically informed treatises on the American presidency come through biographical, historical, and case study research;[1] and there are many questions about the presidency that simply are not amenable to quantitative research. Hence, no one now, or then, could plausibly argue that quantitative research should wholly supplant any of the more qualitative modes of research.

Still, Edwards spoke for many when he recommended that presidency scholars direct greater investments towards more systematic data collection efforts and the development of statistical skills needed to conduct quantitative research. For the presidency sub-field to recover its rightful stature in the discipline, a genuine science of politics would need to take hold among presidency scholars; and to do

---

[1] Many of the most influential books ever written on the American presidency do not contain any quantitative analysis of any sort. Prominent examples include: Corwin 1948; Rossiter 1956; Barber 1972; Schlesinger 1973; Greenstein 1982; Neustadt 1990; Skowronek 1993.

so, clear, falsifiable theory and systematic data collection efforts would need to replace the subfield's preoccupation with personalities, case studies, reflective essays, and biographical accounts. Hence, by the early 1980s, one observer would later reflect, "observation, data collection, quantification, verification, conceptual clarification, hypothesis testing, and theory building [became] the order of the day" (Hart 1998, 383).

This chapter surveys the state of quantitative research on the presidency a quarter-century after Edwards issued his original entreaty. After briefly documenting publication trends on quantitative research on the presidency in a variety of professional journals, it reviews the substantive contributions of selected quantitative studies to long-standing debates about the centralization of presidential authority, public appeals, and presidential policy-making. Though hardly an exhaustive account of all the quantitative work being conducted, this chapter pays particular attention to the ways in which recent scholarship addresses methodological issues that regularly plague studies of the organization of political institutions, their interactions with the public, and their influence in systems of separated powers.

1   Publication Trends on the American Presidency

Though numerous scholars have complained about the arrested state of quantitative research on the American presidency, none, ironically, has actually assembled the data needed to answer some basic empirical questions: What proportion of articles in the field journal for presidency scholars is quantitative in nature? Has this proportion increased or decreased over the past several decades? Are articles published in this journal more or less likely to contain a quantitative component than are articles on the presidency that are published in the top professional journals? And how does the literature on the presidency compare to that on other political institutions, notably Congress? This section provides answers to these questions.

In a survey of publication trends during the past several decades, I identified almost 500 articles on the American presidency published in prominent, mainstream American politics journals, as well as another 800 articles published in the flagship sub-field journal for presidency scholars.[2] Among articles on the

---

[2] I counted all articles with the words "presidency," "presidential," or "president" in the title or abstract and discussing the US president somewhere in its text; articles had to be published between 1980 and 2004 in the field journal for presidency scholars, *Presidential Studies Quarterly* (*PSQ*), or

American presidency, I then identified those that were quantitative in nature.[3] The differences could not be more striking. Whereas the top journals in American politics published almost exclusively quantitative articles on the American presidency, the field journal for presidency scholars published them only sporadically. In a typical year, the proportion of presidency articles published in mainstream outlets was nine times as high as the proportion of presidency articles published in the sub-field journal. And though some over-time trends are observed in these publication rates, in every year the differences across these various journals are both substantively and statistically significant. Nor are such differences simply a function of the publication trends of mainstream and sub-field journals. When writing for their respective sub-field journals, congressional scholars were seven times more likely to write articles with a quantitative component than were presidency scholars.

Who wrote the presidency articles that appeared in these various journals? For the most part, contributors came from very different circles. A very small percentage of scholars who contributed presidency articles to the top, mainstream journals also wrote for the sub-field journal; and an even smaller percentage of scholars who contributed to the sub-field journal also wrote for the mainstream journals. The following, however, may be the most disturbing fact about recent publication trends: of the 1,155 scholars who contributed research on the presidency to one of these journals during the past twenty-five years, only 51 published articles on the presidency in both the sub-field journal and the mainstream American politics journals.

Unavoidably, such comparisons raise all kinds of questions about the appropriate standards of academic excellence, the biases of review processes, and the value of methodological pluralism. For the moment, though, let us put aside the larger epistemological issues of whether the top journals in political science are right to

one of the top three professional journals in American politics more generally: *American Political Science Review* (*APSR*), *American Journal of Political Science* (*AJPS*), and *Journal of Politics* (*JOP*). Excluded were: articles written by undergraduates, articles that were fewer than five manuscript pages (not including references) or that were submitted to symposia, transcripts of speeches, rejoinders, responses, research notes, comments, editorials, updates, corrections, and book reviews. In total, 799 articles meeting these criteria were published in *PSQ*, 155 in *APSR*, 165 in *AJPS*, and 160 in *JOP*. I gratefully acknowledge the research assistance of Ben Sedrish and Charlie Griffin.

[3] To count, an article had to subject actual data to some kind of statistical analysis, however rudimentary. Articles were identified as quantitative if they reported the results of any kind of regression, Bayesian inference, data reduction technique, natural or laboratory experiment, or even a simple statistical test of difference of means. Hence, an article that reported an occasional public opinion rating, or even one that tracked trends in public opinion in a figure or table, was excluded; however, an article that analyzed the determinants of public opinion, that tested for structural shifts in public opinion, or that decomposed measures of public opinion was appropriately counted as quantitative. Case studies, first-person narratives, and biographies, though certainly drawing upon empirical evidence, were not counted as quantitative; and neither were game theoretic models or simulations.

primarily accept quantitative articles on the presidency; whether the sub-field journal for presidency scholars is right to provide a venue for research that does not follow these methodological orientations; or whether congressional scholars are right to incorporate these basic norms into the research that fills their own sub-field's journal. I cannot possibly settle such issues here. From the vantage point of a graduate student or young professor intent on assembling a record that will secure employment and tenure at a major research university, the more practical conclusions to draw from these data could not be clearer: if you intend to publish research on the American presidency in one of the field's top journals, you would do well to assemble and analyze data. Though purely theoretical essays and case study research may gain entrée into the presidency sub-field's premier journal, they appear to offer substantially fewer rewards in the discipline more generally.

If a sub-field's alienation from the broader discipline is appropriately measured by the regularity with which its scholars publish in both top mainstream journals and their chosen sub-field journal, then we have obvious cause for concern. For most of this period, few bridges could be found between the main publication outlet designated expressly for presidency scholars and the best journals in American politics. Indeed, if contributing to a sub-field's journal constitutes a prerequisite for membership, then the vast majority of scholars assembling the literature on the presidency in the top journals cannot, themselves, be considered presidency scholars. With some notable exceptions, meanwhile, those who can lay claim to the title of presidency scholar, at least by this criterion, do not appear to be contributing very much to the most influential journals in American politics.

2   A Literature's Maturation

Not all the news is bad. For starters, a slight shift in the methodological underpinnings of presidency research can be observed. The proportion of quantitative work on the American presidency has increased rather notably of late.[4] And an increasingly wide spectrum of scholars is now contributing to the presidency sub-field's journal.[5] In both the mainstream and sub-field journals, there exists a

[4] Between 1980 and 1984, 30 percent of articles on the presidency published in the four journals examined in this chapter had a quantitative component; between 2000 and 2004, 46 percent did so. The percentage of quantitative articles published in *PSQ* alone since 2000, the first full year that George Edwards served as the journal's editor, nearly tripled.

[5] Of those scholars who wrote on the presidency in both mainstream and sub-field journals between 1980 and 2004, fully 65 percent contributed an article to *PSQ* during the first five years of Edwards' editorship.

considerably richer body of quantitative research on the American presidency than was available as little as a decade ago.

Obviously, disciplinary progress should not be measured only by reference to the number of articles amassed, no matter what their methodological tendencies might be. The mere addition of quantitative articles on the American presidency does not ensure that students today know anything more about the office than did their immediate or more distant predecessors. Fortunately, though, recent developments in the presidency literature provide additional cause for optimism. By attending to a host of standard problems of research design and causal inference, problems endemic to quantitative research throughout the social sciences, scholars have materially enhanced the quality of research conducted on the American presidency, just as they have gained fresh insights into the institution itself. This section reviews some of the ways in which scholars have grappled with a host of methodological challenges in order to make fresh contributions to ongoing debates about the political control over the bureaucracy, public appeals, and presidential power.

2.1   Political Control of the Bureaucracy

In a series of highly influential articles in the 1980s and early 1990s, Terry Moe spelled out a political rationale for presidents to politicize the appointment process and centralize authority within the Executive Office of the President (Moe 1985, 1987, 1990; Moe and Wilson 1994). Moe observed that in an increasingly volatile political world, one wherein opportunities to effect change are fleeting, power is always contested, and opposing factions stand mobilized at every turn, presidents and their immediate advisers have a strong incentive to hunker down, formulate policy themselves, and fill administrative agencies with people who can be counted on to do their bidding faithfully. Neutral competence and bureaucratic independence, Moe observed, does not always suit the president's political needs. Rather than rely upon the expertise of a distant cadre of civil servants, presidents, for reasons built into the design of a political system of separated powers, have considerable cause to surround themselves with individuals who are responsive, loyal, and like-minded.

By focusing explicitly on institutional incentives and resources, and by dispensing with the normative considerations that then pervaded much of the public administration work on bureaucratic design and oversight, Moe's research had a huge impact on the ways in which scholars thought about presidential power. The theory that Moe postulated, however, lacked the dynamic components needed to identify when, precisely, presidents would centralize or politicize authority and when they would not—that is, Moe's work did not generate any clear comparative statics. Moreover, Moe's empirical analysis resembled the existing literature's at the time. Evidence of centralization and politicization consisted of selected case studies of individual agencies and a handful of policies they helped write, and little else.

Fortunately, subsequent scholars picked up where Moe left off. Consider, for instance, Andrew Rudalevige's recent book, *Managing the President's Program* (2002).[6] Using the *Public Papers of President*, Rudalevige tabulated some 2,796 messages from the president to Congress on 6,926 proposals. He then drew a random sample of 400 proposals and examined their legislative "pre-histories." Specifically, Rudalevige identified whether each presidential proposal was the product of cabinet departments and/or executive agencies; of mixed White House/departmental origin, with department taking the lead role; of mixed White House/departmental origin, with White House taking the lead role; of centralized staff outside the White House Office, such as Office of Management and Budget or Council of Economic Advisors; or of staffers within the White House itself. So doing, Rudalevige constructed a unique data-set that allowed him systematically to investigate the regularity with which presidents centralized the policy-making process within the EOP.[7]

Notably, Rudalevige discovered that many of the proposals that presidents submit to Congress are formulated outside of the confines of his immediate control. Only 13 percent of the proposals Rudalevige examined originated in the White House itself; and just 11 percent more originated in the EOP. Cabinet departments and executive agencies drafted almost half of all the president's legislative proposals. Moreover, Rudalevige found, the occurrence of "centraliza-tion" did not appear to be increasing over time. Though the proportion of proposals that originated within the EOP fluctuated rather dramatically from year to year, the overall trend line remained basically flat for most of the postwar period. Rudalevige did not find any evidence that presidents were centralizing authority with rising frequency.

The real contribution of Rudalevige's book, however, lay in its exploration of the political forces that encouraged presidents to centralize. Positing a "contingent theory of centralization," Rudalevige identified the basic trade-off that all presidents face when constructing a legislative agenda: by relying upon their closest advisers and staff, they can be sure that policy will reflect their most important goals and principles; but when policy is especially complex, the costs of assembling the needed information to formulate policy can be astronomical. Though Moe correctly claimed that centralization can aid the president, Rudalevige cautioned that the strategy will only be employed for certain kinds of policies aimed at certain kinds of reforms.

---

[6] For other recent quantitative works that examine presidential control over the bureaucracy, see Wood and Waterman 1991; Waterman and Rouse 1999; Dickinson 2003; Lewis 2003.

[7] Testing various dimensions of Moe's claims about politicization, a growing quantitative literature also examines presidential appointments. See, for example, Cameron, Cover, et al. 1990; McCarty and Razaghian 1999; Binder and Maltzmann 2002.

To demonstrate as much, Rudalevige estimated a series of statistical models that predicted where within the executive branch presidents turned to formulate different policies. His findings are fascinating. Policies that involved multiple issues, that presented new policy innovations, and that required the reorganization of existing bureaucratic structures were more likely to be centralized; while those that involved complex issues were less likely to be. For the most part, the partisan leanings of an agency, divided government, and temporal indicators appeared unrelated to the location of policy formation. Whether presidents centralized, it would seem, varied from issue to issue, justifying Rudalevige's emphasis on "contingency."

Rudalevige's work makes two important contributions. First, and most obviously, he extends Moe's theoretical claims about the organizational structure of the executive branch. Rudalevige goes beyond recognizing that presidents have cause to centralize authority in order to explore the precise conditions under which presidents are most likely to do so. Though the microfoundations of his own theory need further refinement, and the statistical tests might better account for the fact that presidents decide where to formulate policy with a mind to whether the policy will actually be enacted, Rudalevige deftly shifts the debate onto even more productive ground from where Moe had left it.

Second, Rudalevige demonstrates how one might go about testing, using quantitative data, a theory that previously had strictly been the province of archival research. Before Rudalevige, no one had figured out how one might actually measure centralization, had determined what kinds of policies might be subject to centralization, or had identified and then collected data on the key determinants of centralization. No one, that is, had done the work needed to assemble an actual database that could be used to test Moe's claims. Plainly, future research on centralization will (and should) continue to rely upon case studies—there is much about centralization that Rudalevige's data cannot address. But residing in the background of Rudalevige's work is gentle encouragement to expand not only the number of data-sets assembled on the US presidency, but also the kind.

2.2 Public Appeals

In another influential book, *Going Public: New Strategies of Presidential Leadership*, Samuel Kernell (1997) recognized the rising propensity of presidents to bypass Congress and issue public appeals on behalf of their legislative agendas. To explain why presidents often abandon the softer, subtler tactics of negotiation and bargaining, the supposed mainstays of presidential influence during the modern era (Neustadt 1990),[8] Kernell emphasized the transformation of the nation's polity, beginning in the early 1970s, from a system of "institutionalized" to "individualized" pluralism. Under institutional pluralism, Kernell explained, "political elites, and for the most part only elites, matter[ed]" (Kernell 1997, 12). Insulated from public opinion, presidents had only to negotiate with a handful of "protocoalition" leaders in Congress. But under the new individualized pluralist system, opportunities for bargaining dwindled. The devolution of power to subcommittees, the weakening of parties, and the profusion of interest groups greatly expanded the number of political actors with whom presidents would have to negotiate; and compounded with the rise of divided government, such developments made compromise virtually impossible. Facing an increasingly volatile and divisive political terrain, Kernell argued, presidents have clear incentives to circumvent formal political channels and speak directly to the people.

But just as Moe did not posit a theory that specified when presidents would (and would not) centralize authority, Kernell did not identify the precise conditions under which presidents would issue public appeals. Kernell offered powerful reasons why presidents in the 1980s and 1990s went public more often than their predecessors in the 1950s or 1960s. But his book did not generate especially strong expectations about whether presidents holding office during either of these periods would be more or less likely to issue public appeals on one issue versus another. Additionally, Kernell did not identify the precise conditions under which such appeals augment presidential influence, and when they do not.

During the last decade a number of scholars, very much including Kernell himself, have extended the analyses and insights found in *Going Public*. Two areas of research have been especially prodigious. The first examines how changes in the media environment, especially the rise of cable television, have complicated the president's efforts to reach his constituents (Groeling and Kernell 1998; Baum and Kernell 1999). Whereas presidents once could count on the few existing television networks to broadcast their public appeals to a broad cross-section of the American public, now they must navigate a highly competitive and diffuse media environment, one that caters to the individual interests of an increasingly fickle citizenry. Hence, while structural changes to the American polity in the 1970s may have encouraged presidents to go public with greater frequency, more recent changes to the media environment have limited the president's ability to rally the public behind a chosen cause.

It should not come as much of a surprise, then, that public appeals do not always change the content of public opinion, which constitutes the second body of quantitative research spawned by Kernell's work (Cohen 1998; Edwards 2003; Barrett 2004). Though it may raise the salience of particular issues, presidential

---

[8] With over a million copies sold, Neustadt's book remains far and away the most influential treatise on presidential power. And as does any classic, Neustadt's book has attracted a fair measure of controversy. For selected critiques, see Sperlich 1969; Moe 1993; Howell 2005.

speeches typically do not materially alter citizens' views about particular policies, especially those that involve domestic issues. Either because an increasingly narrow portion of the American public actually receives presidential appeals, or because these appeals are transmitted by an increasingly critical and politicized media, or both, presidential endorsements of specific policies fail to resonate broadly.

Brandice Canes-Wrone has also examined the conditions under which presidents will issue public appeals; and given its methodological innovations, her research warrants discussing at some length (Canes-Wrone 2001, 2005; Canes-Wrone and Shotts 2004). By increasing the salience of policies that already enjoy broad-based support, Canes-Wrone argues, plebiscitary presidents can pressure members of Congress to respond to the (otherwise latent) preferences of their constituents. Further recognizing the limited attention spans of average citizens and the diminishing returns of public appeals, Canes-Wrone argues that presidents will only go public when there are clear policy rewards associated with doing so. Then, by building a unique database that links presidential appeals to budgetary outlays over the past several decades, Canes-Wrone shows how such appeals, under specified conditions, augment presidential influence over public policy.

Two methodological features of Canes-Wrone's work deserve special note, as they address fundamental problems that scholars regularly confront when conducting quantitative research on the presidency. First, by comparing presidential budget proposals with final appropriations, Canes-Wrone introduces a novel metric that defines the proximity of final legislation with presidential preferences. This is no small feat. When conducting quantitative research, scholars often have a difficult time discerning presidential preferences, and an even more difficult time figuring out the extent to which different laws reflect these preferences. The challenge, though, does not negate the need. If scholars are to gauge presidential influence over the legislative process, they need some way of identifying just how well presidents have fared in a public policy debate.

Prior solutions to the problem—focusing on presidential proposals or accounting for what presidents say or do at the end of the legislative process—have clear limitations. Just because Congress enacts a presidential initiative does not mean that the final law looks anything like the original proposal made; and just because another law is enacted over a presidential veto does not mean that every provision of the bill represents an obvious defeat for the president. Moreover, even when such ambiguities can be resolved, it often remains unclear how observers would compare the "success" observed on one policy with the "success" claimed on another.

By measuring the differences between proposed and final appropriations, Canes-Wrone secures a readily interpreted basis for comparing relative presidential successes and failures across different policy domains. Now of course, the proposals that presidents themselves issue may be endogenous—that is, they are constructed with some mind to how Congress is likely to respond—and hence not perfectly indicative of their sincere preferences. But for Canes-Wrone's analyses to yield biased results, presidents must adjust their proposals in anticipation of Congress's responses in different ways depending upon whether or not they issue public appeals. This is possible, perhaps, but the most likely scenario under which it is to occur would actually depress the probability that Canes-Wrone would find significant effects. If presidents systematically propose more extreme budgetary allotments when they plan to go public, anticipating a boost in public support from doing so, then Canes-Wrone may actually underestimate the influence garnered from public appeals.

Budgetary appropriations provide a second benefit as well. Because presidents must issue budget proposals every year, Canes-Wrone skirts many of the selection biases that often arise in quantitative studies of the legislative process. The problem is this: the sample of bills that presidents introduce and Congress subsequently votes on, which then become the focus of scholarly inquiry, are a subset of all bills that presidents might actually like to see enacted. And because presidents are unlikely to introduce bills that they know Congress will subsequently reject, the sample of roll calls that scholars analyze invariably constitutes a non-random draw from the president's legislative agenda.

Without accounting for those bills that presidents choose not to introduce, two kinds of biases emerge. First, when tracking congressional votes on presidential initiatives, scholars tend to overstate presidential success. Hence, because Congress never voted on the policy centerpiece of Bush's second term, social security reform, the president's failure to rally sufficient support to warrant formal consideration of the initiative did not count against him in the various success scores that *Congressional Quarterly* and other outlets assembled. And second, analyses of how public opinion, the state of the economy, the partisan composition of Congress, or any other factor influences presidential success may themselves be biased. Without explicitly modeling the selection process itself, estimates from regressions that posit presidential success, however measured, against a set of covariates are likely to be biased.

Unfortunately, no formal record exists of all the policies that presidents might like to enact, making it virtually impossible to diagnose, much less fix, the selection biases that emerge from most analyses of roll call votes. But because presidents must propose, and Congress must pass, a budget every year, Canes-Wrone avoids these sample selection problems. In her statistical analyses, Canes-Wrone does not need to model a selection stage because neither the president nor Congress has the option of tabling appropriations. Every year, the two branches square off against one another to settle the terms of a federal budget; and without the option to retreat, we, as observers, have a unique opportunity to call winners and losers fairly in the exchange.

2.3   Policy Influence beyond Legislation

Outside of elections and public opinion, the most common type of quantitative research conducted on the presidency has concerned the legislative process. Scholars have examined how different political alignments contributed to (or detracted from) the enactment of presidential initiatives (Wayne 1978; Edwards 1989; Bond and Fleisher 1990; Peterson 1990; Mayhew 1991; Edwards, Barrett, et al. 1997; Coleman 1999; Bond and Fleisher 2000; Howell, Adler, et al. 2000; Peake 2002). Following on from Aaron Wildavsky's famous claim that there exist two presidencies—one foreign, the other domestic—scholars have assembled a wide range of measures on presidential success in different policy domains (Wildavsky 1966; LeLoup and Shull 1979; Sigelman 1979; Edwards 1986; Fleisher and Bond 1988; Wildavsky 1989). Scholars have critically examined the president's capacity to set Congress's legislative agenda (Edwards and Wood 1999; Edwards and Barrett 2000). And a number of scholars have paid renewed attention to presidential vetoes (Cameron 1999; Gilmour 2002; Conley 2003; Cameron and McCarty 2004). Given the sheer amount of attention paid to the legislative process, one might justifiably conclude that policy influence depends almost entirely upon the president's capacity to influence affairs occurring within Congress, either by convincing members to vote on his behalf or by establishing roadblocks that halt the enactment of objectionable bills.

Recently, however, scholars have begun to take systematic account of the powers that presidents wield outside of the legislative arena. Building on the insights of legal scholars and political scientists who first recognized and wrote about the president's "unilateral" or "prerogative" powers (Cash 1963; Morgan 1970; Hebe 1972; Schlesinger 1973; Fleishman and Aufses 1976; Pious 1991), scholars recently have built well-defined theories of unilateral action and then assembled original data-sets of executive orders, executive agreements, proclamations, and other sorts of directives to test them. In the past several years, fully five books have focused exclusively on the president's unilateral powers (Mayer 2001; Cooper 2002; Howell 2003; Warber 2006; Shull forthcoming), complemented by a bevy of quantitative articles (Krause and Cohen 1997; Deering and Maltzman 1999; Mayer 1999; Krause and Cohen 2000; Howell and Lewis 2002; Mayer and Price 2002; Howell 2005; Lewis 2005; Martin 2005).

Collectively, the emerging quantitative literature on unilateral powers makes two main contributions to our substantive understanding of presidential power. First, and most obviously, it expands the scope of scholarly inquiry to account for the broader array of mechanisms that presidents utilize to influence the content of public policy. Rather than struggling to convince individual members of Congress to endorse publicly a bill and then cast sympathetic votes, presidents often can seize the initiative, issue new policies by fiat, and leave it to others to revise the new political landscape. Rather than dally at the margins of the policy-making process, presidents regularly issue directives that Congress, left to its own devices, would not enact. So doing, they manage to leave a plain, though too often ignored, imprint on the corpus of law.

Second, the literature highlights the ways in which adjoining branches of government effectively check presidential power. After all, should the president proceed without statutory or constitutional authority, the courts stand to overturn his actions, just as Congress can amend them, cut funding for their operations, or eliminate them outright. And in this regard, the president's relationship with Congress and the courts is very different from the one described in the existing quantitative literature on the legislative process. When unilateral powers are exercised, legislators, judges, and the president do not work cooperatively to effect meaningful policy change. Opportunities for change, in this instance, do not depend upon the willingness and capacity of different branches of government to coordinate with one another, as traditional models of bargaining would indicate. Instead, when presidents issue unilateral directives, they struggle to protect the integrity of orders given and to undermine the efforts of adjoining branches of government to amend or overturn actions already taken. Rather than being a potential boon to presidential success, Congress and the courts represent genuine threats. For presidents, the trick is to figure out when legislators and judges are likely to dismantle a unilateral action taken, when they are not, and then to seize upon those latter occasions to issue public policies that look quite different from those that would emerge in a purely legislative setting.

Some of the more innovative quantitative work conducted on unilateral powers highlights the differences between policies issued as laws versus executive orders. In his study of administrative design, for instance, David Lewis shows that modern agencies created through legislation tend to live longer than those created by executive decree (Lewis 2003). But what presidents lose in terms of longevity they tend to gain back in terms of control. By Lewis's calculations, between 1946 and 1997, fully 67 percent of administrative agencies created by executive order and 84 percent created by departmental order were placed either within the Executive Office of the President or the cabinet, as compared to only 57 percent of agencies created legislatively. Independent boards and commissions, which further dilute presidential control, governed only 13 percent of agencies created unilaterally, as compared to 44 percent of those created through legislation. And 40 percent of agencies created through legislation had some form of restrictions on the kinds of appointees presidents can make, as compared to only 8 percent of agencies created unilaterally.

In another study of the trade-offs between legislative and unilateral strategies, I show that the institutional configurations that promote the enactment of laws impede the production of executive orders, and vice versa (Howell 2003). Just as large and cohesive legislative majorities within Congress facilitate the enactment of legislation, they create disincentives for presidents to issue executive orders. Meanwhile, when gridlock prevails in Congress, presidents have strong incentives to deploy their unilateral powers, not least because their chance of building the coalitions needed to pass laws is relatively small. The trade-offs observed between unilateral and legislative policy-making are hardly coincidental, for ultimately, it is the checks that Congress and the courts place on the president that define his (someday her) capacity to change public policy by fiat.

Quantitative work on the president's unilateral powers is beginning to take systematic account for unilateral directives other than executive orders and departmental reorganizations—most importantly, perhaps, those regarding military operations conducted abroad. Presidency scholars have already poured considerable ink on matters involving war. Until recently, however, quantitative work on the subject resided exclusively in other fields within the discipline. Encouragingly, a number of presidency scholars have begun to test theories of unilateral powers and interbranch relations that have been developed within American politics using data-sets that were assembled within international relations (Howell and Pevehouse 2005, forthcoming; Kriner 2006; Shull forthcoming). Just as previous scholarship examined how different institutional configurations (divided government, the partisan composition of Congress) affected the number of executive orders issued in any given quarter or year, this research examines how such factors influence the number of military deployments that presidents initiate, the timing of these deployments, and their duration. Though still in its infancy, this research challenges presidency scholars to take an even more expansive view of presidential power, while also bridging long-needed connections with scholars in other fields who have much to say about how, and when, heads of state wield authority.

3   CONCLUDING THOUGHTS

This very brief survey offers mixed assessments of the quantitative literature on the US presidency. On the one hand, the publication rates of quantitative presidency research have been rather dismal. In the last twenty-five years, only one in ten research articles published in the sub-field's premier journal had a quantitative component. By contrast, in the top American politics journals, almost nine in ten articles on the presidency did so. Additionally, the scholars who wrote about the presidency in top mainstream journals almost never contributed to the presidency sub-field's premier journal, while those who contributed to the sub-field's journal almost never wrote about the presidency in the top mainstream journals. Of the 1,000 plus authors who wrote about the American presidency in the four journals surveyed in this chapter, a minuscule 4 percent contributed to both the mainstream and the sub-field outlets.

Signs, however, suggest that change is afoot. In the last several years, the presidency sub-field's journal has published a greater proportion of quantitative studies, written by a wider assortment of scholars. And the more recent quantitative work being conducted on the presidency makes a variety of substantive and methodological contributions to the sub-field. The literatures on bureaucratic control, public appeals, and unilateral policy-making have made considerable advances in the past several years in large part because of the efforts of scholars to assemble original data-sets and to test a variety of competing claims. On each of the topics considered here, quantitative analyses did considerably more than merely dress up the extant presidency literature—indeed, they stood at the core of the enterprise and constituted the key reason that learning occurred.

Moving forward, quantitative research on the US presidency confronts a number of challenges. Three, in my mind, stand out. First, much quantitative research on the presidency, as with quantitative research on political institutions generally, lacks strong theoretical footings. When conducting such research, scholars all too often proceed through the following three steps: (a) collect data on some outcome of interest, such as whether a proposal succeeds, a war is waged, an order is issued, or a public appeal is delivered; (b) haul out the standard list of covariates (public opinion, divided government, the state of the economy, etc.) that are used to predict the things that presidents say and do; and (c) estimate a statistical model that shows how well each covariate influences the outcome of interest, offering a paragraph or two on why each of the observed relationships does or does not conform to expectations. Though occasionally a useful exercise, this formulaic approach to quantitative analysis ultimately is unsustainable. Without theory, we cannot ascertain the covariates' appropriate functional forms; whether other important covariates have been omitted; whether some of the explanatory variables ought to be interacted with others; whether endogeneity is a concern, and how it might be addressed. And without theory to furnish answers to such issues, the reader has little grounds for assessing whether or not the results can actually be believed. Rote empiricism, moreover, is no substitute for theory. For when different results emerge from equally defensible statistical models, theory is ultimately needed to adjudicate the dispute.

Second, greater attention needs to be paid to the ways in which adjoining branches of government (Congress and the courts), international actors (foreign states and international governing agencies), and the public shape presidential calculations, and hence presidential actions. At one level, this claim seems obvious. Ours, after all, is hardly a system of governance that permits presidents to impose their will whenever, and however, they choose (Jones 1994). The trouble, though, lies in the difficulty of discerning institutional constraints—and here, I suggest, there is room for continued improvement. Too often, when trying to assess the extent to which Congress constrains the president, scholars take an inventory of the number of times that vetoes are overridden, investigations are mounted, hearings are held, or bills are killed, either in committee or on the floor. Such lists are helpful, if only because they convey some sense for the variety of ways in which Congress checks presidential power. The deeper constraints on presidential power, however, remain hidden, as presidents anticipate the political responses that different actions are likely to evoke and adjust accordingly.[9] To assess congressional checks on presidential war powers, for instance, it will not do to simply count the number of times that Congress has invoked the War Powers Resolution or has demanded the cessation of an ongoing military venture. One must, instead, develop a theory that identifies when Congress is especially likely to limit the presidential use of force, and then assemble data that identify when presidents delay some actions and forgo others in anticipation of congressional opposition—opposition, it is worth noting, that we may never observe. The best quantitative research on the presidency recognizes the logic of anticipated response and formulates statistical tests that account for it.

Finally, scholars too often rely exclusively on those data that are most easily acquired, which typically involves samplings of presidential orders, speeches, and proposals issued during the modern era. But as Stephen Skowronek (1993) rightly insists, much is to be learned from presidents who held office before 1945, the usual starting point for presidential time series. Early changes in political parties, the organizational structure of Congress and the courts, media coverage of the federal government, and public opinion have had huge implications for the development of the presidency. And, as Skowronek demonstrates, the similarities between modern and premodern presidents can be just as striking as the differences between presidents holding office since Roosevelt. When searching around for one's keys, it makes perfect sense to begin where the proverbial street lamp shines brightest. Eventually, though, scholars will need to hone their sights on darker corners; and, in this instance, commit the resources required to build additional data-sets of presidential activities during the nineteenth and early twentieth centuries.

It remains to be seen whether scholars can build a vibrant and robust body of quantitative scholarship on the presidency. To be sure, some trends are encouraging. Important advances have been made. But until the literature is better integrated into the discipline, and until quantitative research addresses some of the problems outlined above, there will be continued cause to revisit and reiterate the simple pleas that George Edwards issued a quarter-century ago.

---

[9] For a survey of the recent game theoretic research that accounts for these interbranch dynamics, see de Figueiredo, Jacobi, et al. 2006.

References

BARRETT, A. 2004. Gone public: the impact of going public on presidential legislative success. *American Politics Review*, 32: 332–70.

BAUM, M. and KERNELL, S. 1999. Has cable ended the golden age of presidential television? *American Political Science Review*, 93 (1): 99–114.

BINDER, S. and MALTZMANN, F. 2002. Senatorial delay in confirming federal judges, 1947–1998. *American Journal of Political Science*, 46 (1): 190–9.

BOND, J. and FLEISHER, R. 1990. *The President in the Legislative Arena*. Chicago: University of Chicago Press.

—— —— 2000. *Polarized Politics: Congress and the President in a Partisan Era*. Washington, DC: Congressional Quarterly Press.

CAMERON, C. M. 1999. *Veto Bargaining: Presidents and the Politics of Negative Power*. New York: Cambridge University Press.

—— and McCARTY, N. M. 2004. Models of vetoes and veto bargaining. *Annual Review of Political Science*, 7: 409–35.

—— and COVER, A., et al. 1990. Senate voting on Supreme Court nominees: a neoinstitutional model. *American Political Science Review*, 84: 525–34.

CANES-WRONE, B. 2001. The president's legislative influence from public appeals. *American Journal of Political Science*, 45 (2): 313–29.

—— 2005. *Who's Leading Whom?* Chicago: University of Chicago Press.

—— and SHOTTS, K. W. 2004. The conditional nature of presidential responsiveness to public opinion. *American Journal of Political Science*, 48 (4): 690–706.

CASH, R. 1963. Presidential power: use and enforcement of executive orders. *Notre Dame Lawyer*, 39 (1): 44–55.

COHEN, J. 1998. *Presidential Responsiveness and Public Policy-Making: the Public and the Policies that Presidents Choose*. Ann Arbor: University of Michigan Press.

COLEMAN, J. J. 1999. Unified government, divided government and party responsiveness. *American Political Science Review*, 93: 821–36.

CONLEY, R. 2003. George Bush and the 102nd Congress: the impact of public and private veto threats on policy outcomes. *Presidential Studies Quarterly*, 33 (4): 730–50.

COOPER, P. 2002. *By Order of the President: The Use and Abuse of Executive Direct Action*. Lawrence: University Press of Kansas.

CORWIN, E. 1948. *The President, Office and Powers, 1787–1948: History and Analysis of Practice and Opinion*. New York: New York University Press.

DE FIGUEIREDO, R., JACOBI, T., et al. 2006. The separation of powers approach to American politics. In *The Oxford Handbook of Political Economy*, ed. B. Weingast and D. Wittman. New York: Oxford University Press.

DEERING, C. and MALTZMANN, F. 1999. The politics of executive orders: legislative constraints on presidential power. *Political Research Quarterly*, 52 (4): 767–83.

DICKINSON, M. 2003. Explaining the growth of the presidential branch, 1940–2000. In *Uncertainty in American Politics*, ed. B. Burden. New York: Cambridge University Press.

DICKINSON, M. 2004. Agendas, agencies and unilateral action: new insights on presidential power? *Congress & the Presidency*, 31 (1): 99–109.

Edwards, G. 1983. Quantitative analysis. In *Studying the Presidency*, ed. G. Edwards and S. Wayne. Knoxville: University of Tennessee Press.

—— 1986. The two presidencies: a reevaluation. *American Politics Quarterly*, 14 (3): 247–63.

—— 1989. *At the Margins: Presidential Leadership of Congress*. New Haven, Conn.: Yale University Press.

—— 2003. *On Deaf Ears: The Limits of the Bully Pulpit*. New Haven, Conn.: Yale University Press.

—— and Barrett, A. 2000. Presidential agenda setting in Congress. In *Polarized Politics: Congress and the President in a Partisan Era*, ed. J. Bond and R. Fleisher. Washington, DC: Congressional Quarterly.

—— —— et al. 1997. The legislative impact of divided government. *American Journal of Political Science*, 41 (2): 545–63.

—— and Wood, B. D. 1999. Who influences whom? The president, Congress, and the media. *American Political Science Review*, 93 (2): 327–44.

Fisher, L. 2002. A dose of law and realism for presidential studies. *Presidential Studies Quarterly*, 32 (4): 672–92.

Fleisher, R. and Bond, J. 1988. Are there two presidencies? Yes, but only for Republicans. *Journal of Politics*, 50 (3): 747–67.

Fleishman, J. and Aufses, A. 1976. Law and orders: the problem of presidential legislation. *Law and Contemporary Problems*, 40: 1–45.

Gilmour, J. 2002. Institutional and individual influences of the president's veto. *Journal of Politics*, 64 (1): 198–218.

Greenstein, F. 1982. *The Hidden-Hand Presidency: Eisenhower as Leader*. New York: Basic Books.

Groeling, T. and Kernell, S. 1998. Is network news coverage of the president biased? *Journal of Politics*, 60 (4): 1063–87.

Hart, J. 1998. Neglected aspects of the study of the presidency. *Annual Review of Political Science*, 1: 379–99.

Hebe, W. 1972. Executive orders and the development of presidential powers. *Villanova Law Review*, 17: 688–712.

Heclo, H. 1977. *Studying the Presidency: A Report to the Ford Foundation*. New York: Ford Foundation.

Howell, W. G. 2003. *Power without Persuasion: The Politics of Direct Presidential Action*. Princeton, NJ: Princeton University Press.

—— 2005. Power without persuasion: rethinking foundations of executive influence. In *Presidential Politics*, ed. G. Edwards. Belmart, Calif.: Wadsworth.

—— Adler, S., et al. 2000. Divided government and the legislative productivity of Congress, 1945–1994. *Legislative Studies Quarterly*, 25: 285–312.

—— and Lewis, D. 2002. Agencies by presidential design. *Journal of Politics*, 64 (4): 1095–114.

—— and Pevehouse, J. 2005. Presidents, Congress, and the use of force. *International Organization*, 59 (1): 209–32.

—— —— 2007. *While Dangers Gather: Congressional Checks on Presidential War Powers*. Princeton, NJ: Princeton University Press.

Jones, C. 1994. *The Presidency in a Separated System*. Washington, DC: Brookings Institution.

KERNELL, S. 1997. *Going Public: New Strategies of Presidential Leadership.* Washington, DC: Congressional Quarterly Press.

KING, G. 1993. The methodology of presidential research. In *Researching the Presidency: Vital Questions, New Approaches,* ed. G. Edwards, J. Kessel, and B. Rockman. Pittsburgh: University of Pittsburgh Press.

KRAUSE, G. and COHEN, D. 1997. Presidential use of executive orders, 1953–1994. *American Politics Quarterly,* 25: 458–81.

—— and COHEN, J. 2000. Opportunity, constraints, and the development of the institutional presidency: the case of executive order issuance, 1939–1996. *Journal of Politics,* 62: 88–114.

KRINER, D. 2006. Taming the imperial presidency: Congress, presidents, and the conduct of military action. Ph.D. dissertation, Harvard University.

LeLOUP, L. T. and SHULL, S. A. 1979. Congress versus the executive: the "Two Presidencies" reconsidered. *Social Science Quarterly,* 59 (4): 704–19.

LEWIS, D. E. 2003. *Presidents and the Politics of Agency Design.* Stanford, Calif.: Stanford University Press.

—— 2005. Staffing alone: unilateral action and the politicization of the executive office of the president, 1988–2004. *Presidential Studies Quarterly,* 35 (3): 496–514.

MARTIN, L. 2005. The president and international commitments: treaties as signaling devices. *Presidential Studies Quarterly,* 35 (3): 440–65.

MAYER, K. 1999. Executive orders and presidential power. *Journal of Politics,* 61 (2): 445–66.

—— 2001. *With the Stroke of a Pen: Executive Orders and Presidential Power.* Princeton, NJ: Princeton University Press.

—— and PRICE, K. 2002. Unilateral presidential powers: Significant executive orders, 1949–99. *Presidential Studies Quarterly,* 32 (2): 367–86.

MAYHEW, D. R. 1991. *Divided We Govern: Party Control, Lawmaking, and Investigations, 1946–1990.* New Haven, Conn.: Yale University Press.

McCARTY, N. and RAZAGHIAN, R. 1999. Advice and consent: Senate response to executive branch nominations 1885–1996. *American Journal of Political Science,* 43 (3): 1122–43.

MOE, T. 1985. *The Politicized Presidency.* Washington, DC: Brookings Institution.

—— 1987. An assessment of the positive theory of "Congressional Dominance." *Legislative Studies Quarterly,* 12 (4): 475–520.

—— 1990. The politics of structural choice: toward a theory of public bureaucrcy. In *Organization Theory: From Chester Barnard to the Present and Beyond,* ed. O. E. Williamson. New York: Oxford University Press.

—— 1993. Presidents, institutions, and theory. In *Researching the Presidency: Vital Questions, New Approaches,* ed. G. Edwards, J. Kessel, and B. Rockman. Pittsburgh: University of Pittsburgh Press.

—— and WILSON, S. A. 1994. Presidents and the politics of structure. *Law and Contemporary Problems,* 57 (2): 1–44.

MORGAN, R. P. 1970. *The President and Civil Rights: Policy Making by Executive Order.* New York: St. Martin's Press.

NEUSTADT, R. E. 1990. *Presidential Power and the Modern Presidents.* New York: Free Press.

PEAKE, J. 2002. Coalition building and overcoming gridlock in foreign policy, 1947–1998. *Presidential Studies Quarterly,* 32 (1): 67–83.

PETERSON, M. 1990. *Legislating Together: The White House and Capitol Hill from Eisenhower to Reagan.* Cambridge, Mass.: Harvard University Press.

PIOUS, R. 1991. Prerogative power and the Reagan presidency. *Political Science Quarterly*, 106: 499–510.

ROSSITER, C. 1956. *The American Presidency*. New York: Harcourt, Brace and World.

RUDALEVIGE, A. 2002. *Managing the President's Program: Presidential Leadership and Legislative Policy Formation*. Princeton, NJ: Princeton University Press.

SCHLESINGER, A. 1973. *The Imperial Presidency*. Boston: Houghton Mifflin.

SHULL, S. A. 2006. *Policy by Other Means: Alternative Policymaking by Presidents*. College Station: Texas A&M University Press.

SIGELMAN, L. 1979. A reassessment of the two presidencies thesis. *Journal of Politics*, 41 (4): 1195–205.

SKOWRONEK, S. 1993. *The Politics Presidents Make*. Cambridge, Mass.: Harvard University Press.

—— 2002. Presidency and American political development: a third look. *Presidential Studies Quarterly*, 32 (4): 743–52.

SPERLICH, P. 1969. Bargaining and overload: an essay on presidential power. In *The Presidency*, ed. A. Wildavsky. Boston: Little, Brown.

THOMAS, N. C. 1983. Case studies. In *Studying the Presidency*, ed. G. Edwards and S. Wayne. Knoxville: University of Tennessee Press.

WARBER, A. 2006. *Executive Orders and the Modern Presidency: Legislating from the Oval Office*. New York: Lynne Rienner.

WATERMAN, R. W. and ROUSE, A. A. 1999. The determinants of the perceptions of political control of the bureaucracy and the venues of influence. *Journal of Public Administration Research and Theory*, 9: 527–69.

WAYNE, S. 1978. *The Legislative Presidency*. New York: Harper and Row.

—— 1983. An introduction to research on the presidency. In *Studying the Presidency*, ed. G. Edwards and S. Wayne. Knoxville: University of Tennessee Press.

WILDAVSKY, A. 1966. The two presidencies. *Trans-Action*, 4: 7–14.

—— 1989. The two presidencies thesis revisited at a time of political dissensus. *Society*, 26 (5): 53–9.

WOOD, B. D. and WATERMAN, R. W. 1991. The dynamics of political control of the bureaucracy. *American Political Science Review*, 85 (3): 801–28.

CHAPTER 17

EXECUTIVES IN PARLIAMENTARY GOVERNMENT

R. A. W. RHODES

1 INTRODUCTION: MAPPING THE FIELD

The literature on executive government in parliamentary systems can often be more fun to read because it is *not* written by political scientists. There are the popular biographies of individual prime ministers with varying degrees of lurid detail about their private lives. There are psycho-biographies probing childhood and other formative experiences. There are the journalists recording the comings and goings of our leaders, with an eye for a story that is never discomforted by an inconvenient fact. There are novels. But where are the theories, the models, and the typologies of executive government in parliamentary systems that distinguish political scientists from their more racy rivals? In fact, the academic political science literature is limited—more so than readers might expect or the importance of the subject warrants.

It is limited in part by the continuing need to break free of worn-out debates, especially in the analysis of Westminster systems. Instead of the tired debate about the power of the prime minister, the study of executives in parliamentary

* I would like to thank Sarah Binder, Bob Goodin, Bert Rockman, and John Wanna for their advice, with a special thank you to Robert Elgie for exemplifying the phrase "constructive criticism."

government would be far more vibrant if it engaged with core debates in the comparative politics literature. I try to build such bridges in this chapter. Of course, conceptual ambiguity and contestable assumptions lie at the heart of most current classifications and definitions of regimes (Elgie 1998). I adopt Shugart's (Chapter 18, 348) definition. "Pure" parliamentary democracy is defined by two basic features: "executive authority, consisting of a prime minister and cabinet, arises out of the legislative assembly;" and "the executive is at all times subject to potential dismissal via a vote of 'no confidence' by a majority of the legislative assembly".

Mapping the field is further complicated because the study of the executive is both a subset of the study of parliamentary government and related to broader concepts than parliamentary government (such as democratic effectiveness, political leadership, presidentialism, and the comparative analysis of regimes). This can both diffuse the focus on the executive and oversimplify the analysis of, for example, democratic effectiveness (which is shaped by more than the actions of the executive). I range widely despite these dangers, however, given the importance of placing the executive in its broader context.

Finally, the topic is also inextricably linked to broader trends in political science and the way we study politics. It is no coincidence that the shift from the formal-legalism of the Westminster approach to modernist-empiricism to rational choice institutionalism parallels trends in political science. My conclusions go with this flow. I counterpoise rational choice institutionalism with the interpretive turn because that is the recurring debate in present-day political science.

The first section of this chapter discusses existing approaches to executive government—Westminster, modernist-empiricism, core executive, and rational choice institutionalism. Second, I look at core debates and challenges in the study of parliamentary executives, the main examples of which are Britain, the Commonwealth, and Western Europe (see Shugart, Chapter 18, Table 18.1). For these countries, I cover: the presidentialization of prime ministers, executive coordination, policy advice and policy capacity, and the comparative analysis of parliamentary government. Finally, I look at the future research agenda, covering rational choice institutionalism's redefinition of the field as the analysis of veto-players; and the interpretive turn and the analysis of court politics and traditions.

2   APPROACHES TO EXECUTIVE GOVERNMENT

For most of the twentieth century, the *Westminster approach* was the most common framework of analysis. The notion of the "Westminster system" is remarkably diffuse. It commonly refers to a family of ideas that includes: a unitary state; parliamentary sovereignty; strong cabinet government; accountability through elections; majority party control of the executive (that is, prime minister, cabinet, and the civil service); elaborate conventions for the conduct of parliamentary business; institutionalized opposition; and the rules of debate (Gamble 1990, 407).

Lists of defining characteristics invariably include the "efficient secret" of "the closer union, the nearly complete fusion, of the executive and legislative powers" (Bagehot 1963, 65). In other words, the party or parties with a majority in parliament form the executive, defined by key positions (that is, prime minister and cabinet). The cabinet is collectively responsible for its decisions, and its members (or ministers) are individually responsible to parliament for the work of their departments. The Westminster approach also assumes that power lies with specific positions and the people who occupy those positions. The literature is dominated by such topics as the relative power of prime minister and cabinet (see below, pp. 327–9), and the relationship between the executive and parliament (see Chapter 18).

The *modernist-empiricist* or *behavioral approach* treats political executives as discrete objects that can be compared, measured, and classified. Its core beliefs are measurement, law-like generalization, and neutral evidence (see Bevir and Rhodes 2006, ch. 5). Early studies focused on political elites, especially the notion of political leadership (see Elgie 1995; Mughan and Patterson 1992). There is a plethora of country studies. The popular topics include, for example: the recruitment, tenure, and careers of prime ministers and ministers; ministerial and prime ministerial relationships with bureaucracy and other sources of policy advice; their links with political parties, the media, and the public; and the resources and personal qualities of ministers and prime ministers (see, for example, Blondel and Thiébault 1991; Jones 1991). While valuable as compendia, of information, such studies fall foul of Rudyard Kipling's (1990, 181) nostrum, "and what should they know of England who only England knows" ("The English Flag," 1891)?

Others are more ambitious. Blondel and Müller-Rommel's (1993a, 15) work on Western Europe studies the "the interplay of one major independent variable—the single-party or coalition character of the cabinet—with a number of structural and customary arrangements in governments, and of the combined effect of these factors on decision making processes" in twelve West European cabinets. It is "a fully comparative analysis" with data drawn from a survey of 410 ministers in nine countries, and an analysis of newspaper reports on cabinet conflicts in eleven countries.

The core executive approach was developed in the analysis of British government (Dunleavy and Rhodes 1990), but it has travelled well (Elgie 1997). It defines the executive in functional terms. So, instead of asking which position is important, we can ask which functions define the innermost part or heart of government. For example, the core functions of the British executive are to pull together and integrate central government policies and to act as final arbiters of conflicts between different elements of the government machine. These functions can be carried out by institutions other than prime minister and cabinet; for example, the Treasury and the Cabinet Office. By defining the core executive in functional terms, the key question becomes, "who does what?"

But power is contingent and relational; that is, it depends on the relative power of other actors and events. Ministers depend on the prime minister for support in getting funds from the Treasury. In turn, the prime minister depends on his ministers to deliver the party's electoral promises. Both ministers and prime minister depend on the health of the American economy for a stable pound and a growing economy to ensure the needed financial resources are available. This power-dependence approach focuses on the distribution of such resources as money and authority in the core executive and explores the shifting patterns of dependence between the several actors (see for example Elgie 1997; Rhodes 1995; Smith 1999).

The term "core executive" directs our attention, therefore, to two key questions: "Who does what?" and "Who has what resources?" If the answer for several policy areas and several conflicts is that the prime minister coordinates policy, resolves conflicts, and controls the main resources, we will indeed have prime ministerial government.

The *rational choice institutionalism* approach comes in many guises and increasingly focuses on the analysis of prime ministers and cabinets. One example must suffice: Strøm and his colleagues' principal–agent theory of delegation and accountability in parliamentary democracies (see also Cox 1987; Laver and Shepsle 1996; Tsebelis 2002).

Strøm, Müller, and Bergman (2003, chapters 3 and 23) conceive of parliamentary democracy as a chain of delegation from principals to agents: from voters to their elected representatives, from legislators to the chief executive, from the chief executive to ministerial heads of departments, and from ministers to civil servants. Principals and agents are in a hierarchic relationship and both act rationally to gain exogenously given preferences. No agent is perfect. So agency loss occurs because the actual consequences of delegation diverge from the principal's ideal outcome. There are two main causes of agency loss. First, there may be a conflict of interest between the principal and the agent who may, for example, have different policy objectives. Second, there may be limited information and resources and, for example, the principal may not know what the agent is doing. When principals know less than agents, two problems occur, moral hazard and adverse selection. Moral hazard arises when an agent takes actions of which a principal disapproves. Adverse selection occurs when an agent is unwilling or unable to pursue the principal's interests. A principal can use *ex ante* mechanisms, such as screening of applicants, to control adverse selection problems, and *ex post* mechanisms, such as contracts, to deal with moral hazard. This framework is then used to analyse, for example, the strengths of Westminster parliamentary systems, which are said to be coordination and efficiency.

Each of these approaches has its limitations. Westminster's formal-legal approach ignores larger debates both in the study of comparative politics and in political science. It can revel in archaism, taking its stance from Bagehot (Bogdanor 1999, 175). The sheer scale of Blondel's modernist-empiricism is impressive but it is the scale that poses problems. Dogan and Pelassy (1990, 116) comment that such comparative studies disappoint because "comparability is very low." Citing Blondel's (1980) analysis of all "heads of government in the post-war period," they ask: "what sense is there in comparing the 'regular ministerial career' in the Middle East and in the Atlantic and communist worlds? Aren't we here misled simply by verbal similarities?" Ignoring the general criticisms of rational choice (see Green and Shapiro 1994; Hay 2004), there are the specific limitations of principal–agent theory when applied to the study of executives. For example, the assumption of hierarchy does not hold. Ministers are embedded in webs of vertical and horizontal dependencies and only the former can be conceptualized as principal–agent chains. Webs or networks are conspicuous by their absence despite their centrality to both delegation and accountability.

3   DEBATES AND CHALLENGES

This section will cover the growth of prime ministerial power, referred to as the presidentialization thesis; executive coordination; policy advice and policy capacity; accountability; the effects of institutional differences; and comparative analysis.

3.1   Presidentialization of Prime Ministers

The conventional cliché is that the prime minister is no longer "first among equals" in the government but the elected "first magistrate" (Crossman 1963, 22–3; Mack-intosh 1968, 627). There is a corresponding decline in cabinet government. It is difficult to overstate the scale of this debate in the academic literature. It is the defining debate of the Westminster approach and refers to three main claims: there has been a centralization of coordination, a pluralization of advice, and the personalization of party leadership and elections.[1] The broad argument is common

---

[1] On the several definitions of the presidentialization thesis see: Foley 1993, ch. 1; Pryce 1997, 37, 67; Mughan 2000, 9–10; and Poguntke and Webb 2005a, 5, 8–11. For the key articles on prime ministerial power see Dunleavy and Rhodes 1995; King 1969, 1985.

to Westminster systems such as Australia, Britain, and Canada as well as West European parliamentary systems.[2]

Foley's (2000) analysis of "spatial leadership" has proved influential. The phrase refers to "the way in which political authority is protected and cultivated by the creation of a sense of distance, and...detachment from government." He sees Margaret Thatcher as the pioneer in Britain. From the start, she was an outsider in her own party with an unconventional political and policy agenda with populist appeal. She became distanced from her own government, respected by the public for her leadership while few supported her policies. Tony Blair dared to be Thatcher and "raised the concept and application of spatial leadership to unprecedented levels of development and sophistication" (Foley 2000, 98, 110). The key methods are "going public," or building support by appealing to the public over the heads of government and entrenched interests, and "getting personal," or using the media in all its forms to build personal rapport with the public independent of party and government. They are no longer leaders but "flagships" (Foley 2000), dominating the media coverage, waging permanent election campaigns, and exercising a major influence over election results. The party remains under tight control and the leader often reminds the party not only of their duty to the public but of his special link with them. Indeed, Foley's argument seems to be more about the changing role of parties and party leadership than about prime ministers and cabinets.

Such presidential tales are not told of all prime ministers (see Hennessy 2000, chapter 19). Of the twelve postwar British prime ministers, only three have attracted the epithet "presidential"—Harold Wilson (1964–70), Margaret Thatcher (1979–90), and Tony Blair (1997 onwards). And of these three, judgments about their presidentialism varied while they were in office. It helps to distinguish between the electoral, policy-making, and implementation arenas.

First, personalization is a prominent feature of media management and electioneering in Britain. If we must use presidential language, it is here in the electoral and party arena that it is most apt. Wilson, Thatcher, and Blair were figureheads (see for example Seymour-Ure 2003). Spatial leadership has arrived.

In the policy-making arena, there is some truth to the claim of a centralization of policy-making on the prime minister's office. However, for Australia, Canada, as well as Britain, this claim applies to selected policy areas only, with the equally important proviso that the prime minister's attention is also selective. Thus, the continuous reform of the British center speaks of the failure of coordination, not its success.

The prime minister's influence is most constrained in the policy implementation arena, so it is conspicuous for its absence in most accounts of presidentialism. Here, other senior government figures, ministers and their departments, and other

---

[2] On the comparative analysis of Westminster systems see Campbell 1998; Foley 2000; Hargrove 2001; Savoie 1999; and Weller 1985. On the small Westminster systems of the Pacific see Pattapan, Wanna, and Weller 2005. For the equivalent debate in Canada see Punnett 1977, ch. 1; and cf. Savoie 1999 with Bakvis 2000. For Australia, see Aulich and Wettenhall 2005; and Weller 1993.

agencies are key actors. There is a second story of prime ministerial power that focuses on the problems of governance and sees the prime minister as constantly involved in negotiations and diplomacy with a host of other politicians, officials, and citizens (for a summary and critique see Marinetto 2003). Prime ministers are just one actor among many interdependent ones in the networks that criss-cross Whitehall, Westminster, and beyond (and there can be no clearer example than the dependence of Blair on Gordon Brown, Chancellor of the Exchequer; see Seldon 2004).

The decline of cabinet government is the reverse side of the presidentialization coin, but what exactly has been lost? Pat Weller (2003, 74–8) distinguishes between the cabinet as the constitutional theory of ministerial and collective responsibility, as a set of rules and routines, as the forum for policy-making and coordination, as a political bargaining arena between central actors, and as a component of the core executive. Those commentators who justify talk of the demise of cabinet by treating policy-making and coordination as the defining functions of cabinet have failed to notice that these functions have been carried out by several central agencies, including but not limited to the cabinet, for over half a century. This conclusion also stands for most West European cabinets (see Blondel and Müller-Rommel 1993b). To suggest that any postwar prime minister abandoned the doctrine of collective responsibility is nonsense. Leaks are abhorred. Unity is essential to electoral success. Dissenters go. Prime ministers have a pragmatic view of individual ministerial responsibility; ministers go when the political costs of keeping them exceed the costs of a resignation.

In sum, the fortunes of "presidential" prime ministers vary markedly between arenas and during their period of office. It is misleading to focus only on the prime minister and cabinet because political power is not concentrated in them, but more widely dispersed. It is contested, so the standing of any individual—prime minister or chancellor—or institution—cabinet or Treasury—is contingent. As Helms (2005, 259) concludes from his comparison of American, British, and German core executives, "there is rather limited evidence of presidentialization," although Poguntke and Webb (2005b, 347) disagree, arguing the various shifts "generate *a greater potential for, and likelihood of,* this 'presidential' working mode" irrespective of regime (emphasis added). Fifty years have elapsed in the UK, so not there yet then! Fear not, the debate will go on, and on . . .

3.2 Executive Coordination

Problems of coordination loom large and come in two guises—the practical strand of how do we improve it, and the academic strand of what is it and when and why does it work.

Pollitt and Bouckaert's (2000, 79–83, 165–6) review of recent public sector reforms in ten countries shows that most struggle to balance specialization and coordination. The means are many and varied. The outcomes remain uncertain. In response to the prime minister of Australia's call for a "whole of government approach," the Australian Public Service (APS) produced *Connecting Government* (MAC 2004, 1), which defines the whole-of-government approach as "public service agencies working across portfolio boundaries to achieve a shared goal and an integrated government response to particular issues." Detailing the specific mechanisms is less important than noting the several problems that quickly emerged. First, how do you get ministers to buy into interdepartmental coordination? The short answer is reluctantly because they want to make a name for themselves, not their colleagues. Second, departments are competing silos. The rewards of departmentalism are known and obvious. For interdepartmental coordination, it is the costs that are known and obvious! For most managers, coordination costs time, money, and staff and is not their main concern. Third, coordination is *for* central agencies! It serves their priorities, not those necessarily of the line departments. Fourth, there is a tension between managerialism, which seeks to decentralize decision-making, and the call for better coordination, which seeks to centralize it. Fifth, in countries like Australia and Canada, federalism is a major check of Commonwealth aims. Coordination is for the Commonwealth, not state governments and other agencies. The Commonwealth does not control service delivery. It has limited reach, so it has to negotiate. Central coordination presumes agreement with the priorities of central agencies when it is the lack of such agreement that creates many of the problems—a Catch-22.

All of these problems are common to executives in parliamentary government. We know that despite strong pressures for more and proactive coordination throughout Western Europe, the coordination activities of central governments remain modest. Such coordination has four characteristics. First, it is "negative, based on persistent compartmentalization, mutual avoidance, and friction reduction between powerful bureaux or ministries." Second, it occurs "at the lower levels of the state machine and is organised by specific established networks." Third, it is "rarely strategic" and "almost all attempts to create proactive strategic capacity for long-term planning ... have failed." Finally, it is "intermittent and selective ... improvised late in the policy process, politicised, issue-oriented and reactive" (Wright and Hayward 2000, 33). In sum, coordination is the "philosopher's stone" of modern government, ever sought, but always just beyond reach, all too often because it assumes both agreement on goals and a central coordinator (Seidman 1975, 190).

3.3 Accountability

Mulgan's (2003, 113) survey of accountability documents how government accountability is "seriously impeded" by an executive branch that "remains over-dominant and too easily able to escape proper scrutiny." There are three common problems in holding the powerful to account in Westminster systems: individual and collective ministerial responsibility, public sector reform and managerial accountability, and network accountability or the problem of many hands.

3.4   Ministerial Responsibility

The doctrine of ministerial responsibility resembles "the procreation of eels" (Marshall 1986, 54). Thus, it "can be suspended or breached except in circumstances when the Prime Minister, having considered the immediate and long-term political implications, feels it to be more honoured in the observance" (Marshall 1986, 223). Similarly, on collective responsibility, "Cabinet may have a policy, if it wishes, of permitting public disagreements between Ministers even on matters of major policy without endangering constitutional principles" (Marshall 1986, 225). In short, ministers do not resign and cabinets disagree in public. Whether ministerial responsibility and collective responsibility apply depends on the political standing of the minister and the judgment of the prime minister (see also Woodhouse 2003).

This summary errs on the side of dry. It is worth noting that 43 percent of all resignations between 1945 and 1991 in the UK were for sexual or financial scandals, not personal or departmental error (Dowding 1995, 165). There is a serious point to this aside. It suggests that ministerial responsibility is alive and well, but not in its conventional formulation. It is no longer the prime minister and the political standing of the minister that decides a resignation—but the media maelstrom (see also Woodhouse 2004, 17).

The position differs little in Australia where, "if individual ministerial responsibility ever meant that ministers were expected to resign for major policy blunders or for serious errors of maladministration by a government department, it is dead." Nonetheless, collective responsibility is alive and well: "If ministers cannot publicly support a cabinet decision or the general direction of government policies, they resign" (Thompson and Tillotsen 1999, 56).

3.5   Civil Service Accountability

Sir Richard Wilson (1999), former head of the British home civil service, questioned how good top civil servants were at policy advice and how often their advice had been evaluated. It was a rhetorical question. There were no formal mechanisms for holding the civil service to account for its policy advice. In Australia, political control of the public service became the order of the day in the 1990s. The language of reform called for "responsiveness" by public servants to the needs and wishes of ministers and five-year contracts for top public servants were instituted to reinforce the message. Pollitt and Bouckaert (2000, 155) identify similar trends in Canada, France, and Sweden.

The accountability of public servants for their management work is scarcely any better. In theory, responsibility (for management) can be delegated to agency chief executives, while accountability (for policy) remains with the minister. But this distinction hinges on clear definitions of both policy and management and of the respective roles and responsibilities of ministers, senior civil servants, and chief executives. As the British Cabinet Office (1994, 24) observes, "it is not always possible to clearly separate policy and management issues." It also comments that "some Chief Executives, especially the ones from the private sector, are very conscious of being in what they consider to be a fairly precarious position." Again, similar problems occur in Australia and Canada (see Weller 2001 and Aucoin 1995). Pollitt and Bouckaert (2000, 157) dryly observe that "politicians have not been spectacularly willing to relinquish their former habits of detailed intervention." Allied to ministerial intervention, public management reforms have created an "anarchy of aggressive competitive accountability" that undercuts performance (Behn 2001, 216).

3.6   Holding Networks to Account

To the ambiguity of management reforms, we can also add the institutional complexity of networks, which obscures who is accountable to whom for what. For many governments, outside police, defense, and social security, there are few policy areas where the centre has hands-on control and where a command operating code might work. Governments work with and through many other agencies; they manage networks, commonly referred to nowadays as partnerships. As Mulgan (2003, 211–14) argues, buck-passing is much more likely in networks because responsibility is divided and the reach of political leaders is much reduced. Agencies and special purpose bodies have multiple constituencies, each seeking to hold them to account, and there is no system, just disparate, overlapping demands. As Peters (1998, 302) argues, "strong vertical linkages between social groups and public organizations makes effective coordination and horizontal linkages within government more difficult." Once agreement is reached in the network, "the latitude for negotiation by public organizations at the top of the network is limited." The brute fact is that multiple accountabilities weaken central control (Mulgan 2003, 225).

So, if we focus on ministerial responsibility, we have a seriously lopsided view of accountability in parliamentary government. Rather, we need to think about webs of accountabilities; about sets of organizations, not the individual minister; and about legal, professional, and managerial accountability as well as political.

4 Policy Advice and Policy Capacity

Over the past quarter of a century there has been a major restructuring of the state in Western Europe. Whether conceptualized as the hollowing out of the state or the shift from bureaucracy to markets to networks, a recurrent concern in the changes has been the capacity of the core executive. Some argue the core executive is "overloaded;" that is, the demands on the core executive exceed its capacities. For others, and especially prime ministers and ministers, the concern has been to get more and better advice. The public service was found wanting and replaced with a plurality of advisers. Finally, because of government reform, critics charge there has been a politicization of advice.

4.1 Government Overload

Although the phrase "government overload" is associated with the neoliberal critique of big government (see for example Brittan 1975), it also has a specific if related meaning, referring to the excessive workloads of ministers and prime ministers. Peter Hennessy (1995, 174–5) turns to psychiatry and occupational health to argue that "institutional overload" and "personal overstretch" undermine both health and the quality of decision-making. Ministers and prime ministers are all too keenly aware of the pressures. There are endless suggestions for strengthening "central capability," as it is known, to combat such pressures (see Lee, Jones, and Burnham 1988). For example, Hennessy (2000, 539–41) seeks to distance No. 10 from a frenetic everyday life by developing both a plurality of analytical capacities and a greater capacity to provide risk and strategic assessments. He wants a "small-but-smart model" of No. 10 in which the prime minister is "the guardian of the government's overall strategy" backed by a risk assessment unit with a wide remit: "all those areas and activities where setbacks, catastrophes or unforeseen developments can (rightly or wrongly) be laid at a PM's door."

The problem and solutions are not peculiarly British. Peters, Rhodes, and Wright (2000) cover trends and reforms in the administrative support for core executives in twelve countries. They identify a battery of shared pressures on core executives, including the media and the personalization of executive politics, international affairs, especially security and defense post-9/11, and the pressure for domestic policy coordination. As a result, most countries have developed and continue to develop support structures so their core executive can cope.

4.2   Plurality of Advice

In Westminster systems, the civil service had a monopoly of advice and this advice was collated and coordinated by the cabinet through its ministerial and official committees and the Cabinet Office. Campbell and Wilson (1995, 59–61, 294–6) argue for the death of the Westminster approach insisting the civil service monopoly of advice to ministers has been broken. We now have competing centers of advice and coordination, with the civil service putting together packages of advice from many sources, insisting not on their monopoly but on staying "in the loop." Prime ministers have their own sources of advice, whether from advisers, management consultants, or think-tanks. For example, total staff employed by the British prime minister rose from 71 in 1970 to over 200 under Blair (Kavanagh and Seldon 1999, 300), creating "the department that-will-not-speak-its-name" (Hennessy 2002, 20). It is important to keep this increase in perspective. For example, in Britain, the total number of political and policy advisers remains small compared with the 3,429 members of the senior civil service. Most ministers have only one or two advisers.

The growth of advisers has been and remains controversial. For example, in Australia, there has been much criticism of their role in protecting the minister—for creating firewalls that protect them not only from outside criticism but also from his or her department, from unpleasant and unwelcome information, and from parliament (see Marr and Wilkinson 2003). The problems are endemic. In both Australia and Britain, there has been much debate about their numbers, cost, expertise, conduct, roles and responsibilities, and relationship to civil servants. The British government introduced a code of conduct (see Blick 2004). The Australian government denied there was a problem. Clearly we have plural sources of advice, ministerial advisers who are here to stay, and problems that will not go away. It is less clear there will be effective management of their roles or accountability for their actions, irrespective of whether there is a code of conduct.

4.3   Politicization

During Margaret Thatcher's premiership fears were expressed that the civil service would be politicized. They have not subsided since. The Royal Institute of Public Administration (1987, 43) concluded, "the appointment process has become more personalised" but "we do not believe that these appointments and promotions are based on the candidate's support for or commitment to particular ideologies or objectives." Some found it more difficult to hold the sanguine view that it was "personalisation not politicisation" (Plowden 1994, 100–9).

In Australia, since Labor's 1972–5 term of office, fears have been expressed about a "creeping politicization" (Weller 1989, 369). By the late 1990s, it had escalated to the point where many charged ministers were no longer receiving "frank and fearless" advice. Others saw the shift as civil servants becoming more responsive to their political masters (Weller 2001). There may have been no overt party politicization of the public service in either country but it has lost its "institutional scepticism" (Hugo Young cited in Plowden 1994, 104). Rhodes and Weller (2001, 238) conclude from their six-country survey that top civil servants "are selected and kept in part because of their style and approach, in part because of their policy preferences, and in part because ministers are comfortable with them." They also note that for most changes Australia and New Zealand were the exceptions. For most of the reforms, they had gone further, faster than any other country.

Peters, Rhodes, and Wright (2000, x) argue that three conclusions stand out from their country studies of the policy advice and policy capacity of core executives. First, there are the increasing pressures for centralization as core executives confront the differentiation and pluralization of government. Second, the staffs of executive leaders have grown in size and have common tasks, but the weight attached to each task varies from country to country. Finally, despite common domestic and international pressures, national distinctiveness, rather than convergence, characterizes the institutional response of the several countries. The interplay of constitutional, political, and institutional factors, and above all the governmental tradition in which actors construct their own interpretation of the pressures and trends, shape the core executive's response.

5   So What? The Consequences of Institutional Differences

If prime ministerial power is the defining debate in the literature about Westminster systems, then the debate about the effects of consensus government typifies the literature on West European systems.[3] The Westminster approach is not only

---

[3] On the comparative analysis of executives in West European parliamentary systems see: Blondel and Müller-Rommell 1993*b*, 1997; Jones 1991; Poguntke and Webb 2005*c*; Strøm, Müller, and Bergman 2003.

descriptive but also normative. All too often, it displays both a preference for strong leadership and a belief that majority party systems deliver more effective government.

The most wide-ranging attempt to measure, rather than assert, the differences between majoritarian and consensual parliamentary governments is Lijphart (1999 [1984]). Lijphart (1999, chs. 15 and 16) asks whether consensus democracy makes a difference. He challenges the conventional wisdom on the trade-off between quality and effectiveness in which proportional representation and consensus government provide better representation whereas plurality elections and majority government provide more effective policy-making. He concludes that consensus democracies do outperform majoritarian democracies but, because the statistical results are "relatively weak and mixed," he phrases his conclusion as a negative: "majoritarian democracies are clearly *not* superior to consensus democracies in managing the economy and in maintaining civil peace" (Lijphart 1999, 274; emphasis in original). However, consensus democracies combine, on the one hand, better women's representation, great political equality, and higher participation in elections, with "gentler qualities," such as persuasion, consultation, and "more generous policies" on, for example, the environment. So the good news is there is no trade-off between effectiveness and democracy. The bad news is that "institutional and cultural traditions may present strong resistance to consensus democracy" (Lijphart 1999, 305). Also, as Peters (1999, 81–2) argues, the advantage of majoritarian government is that the executive can act as it wants—a prime minister can shape policy more effectively. The fact they are less effective could well be a function of poor policy choices not of institutional differences—in a phrase, "leaders do not know best." In turn, this criticism begs the question of whether policy choices would be better if they were the product of persuasion and consultation rather than of adversary politics (on how "leaders knowing best" can lead to policy disaster see Butler, Adonis, and Travers 1994).

And so it goes on, but the key point is there can be no easy assumption about the effects of differing institutional arrangements. The effortless superiority enshrined in the conventional wisdom that attributes decisiveness and effectiveness to the Westminster approach flounders on the sheer variety of political practice within and between regime types (see also Blondel and Müller-Rommell 1993*b*; Weaver and Rockman 1993, 445–6, 454; Strøm, Müller, and Bergman 2003).

6   COMPARATIVE ANALYSIS

In part, the complexity we seek to understand is compounded by confusions about "what are we comparing?" It may seem straightforward to ask this question but the answer reveals some odd features in the comparative analysis of cabinets and prime ministers.

First, much of the published work on Westminster systems is not strictly speaking comparative, but compilations of country studies (see Weller, Bakviss, and Rhodes 1997, 7–11 for citations). Nothing wrong with that, but it is not comparative analysis (cf. Weller 1985). Second, the modernist-empiricist project can take such labels as "cabinet" at face value and compare apples and oranges. Switching cabinets for (say) ministers will not solve the problem (see Blondel and Thiébault 1991). Third, most comparative research is between regime types, not on variations within one regime type (see Shugart, Chapter 18). Finally, and potentially the most misleading of all, there are the comparisons of American presidents with UK prime minsters. Rose (2001, 237–44) identifies one similarity—the impact of the mass medias in personalizing chief executives and election campaigns—and many differences, including different recruitment and career paths, direct popular election of the president, fixed term of office, constitutional checks and balances, and limited control of the legislature and, therefore, domestic policy. It might seem an overly simple-minded conclusion but the comparative analysis of prime ministers and cabinets needs to compare like with like. It is simply not revealing to be told there are big differences in the powers of prime ministers, there are big differences in the powers of presidents, and there are big differences between prime ministers and presidents.

There are two fruitful lines of analysis: rational choice institutionalism (see Strøm, Müller, and Bergman 2003) and core executive models (see Elgie 1997, 1998). I have provided already a brief summary of Strøm's principal–agent theory (above, p. 326). Alternatively, Elgie suggests we use the six models of core executive operations to analyse prime ministerial and semi-presidential systems:

1. *Monocratic government*—personal leadership by prime minister or president.
2. *Collective government*—small, face-to-face groups decide with no single member controlling.
3. *Ministerial government*—the political heads of major departments decide policy.
4. *Bureaucratic government*—non-elected officials in government departments and agencies decide policy.
5. *Shared government*—two or three individuals have joint and equal responsibility for policy-making.
6. *Segmented government*—a sectoral division of labour among executive actors with little or no cross-sectoral coordination.

The advantage of this formulation is that it gets away from bald assertions about the fixed nature of executive politics. While only one model may operate at any one time, there can still be a fluid pattern as one model succeeds another. It also concentrates the mind on the questions of which model of executive politics prevails, when, how, and why did it change. Focusing on the power of prime minister and cabinet is limiting, whereas these questions open the possibility of explaining similarities and differences in executive politics (Elgie 1997, 231 and citations). Whatever the preferred analytical approach, the key point is that the comparative analysis of executives must not, as in the case of Westminster systems, become inward looking and oblivious to developments elsewhere in comparative politics.

7 Conclusions—Whither the Study of Executives?

Any commentator who underestimates the longevity of and commitment to modernist-empiricism does so at his or her peril. There is a lifetime's work for any number of political scientists in documenting and comparing trends in parliamentary government in the Commonwealth and Western Europe. All the topics covered earlier were and remain challenges.

For those modernist-empiricists with even greater aspirations, rational choice institutionalism offers a thoroughgoing redefinition of the field. Tsebelis's (2002) analysis of veto-players is the key contribution. His general theory of institutions posits that governments, in order to change policies, must get individual actors or veto-players to agree. Institutional veto-players are specified by the constitution and partisan veto-players are specified by the party system. Each country has a set of veto-players, with specific ideological distance between them, and a degree of cohesion. This configuration is the status quo. When there are many veto-players, significant change in the status quo is impossible, giving policy stability. Variations in the institutional framework cease to be significant. Rather, countries differ in "the number, ideological distances, and cohesions of the corresponding veto-players." So, he reverses the usual meaning of presidential and parliamentary government: "agenda control most frequently belongs to governments in parliamentary systems and parliaments in presidential ones" (Tsebelis 2002, 67).

Such propositions are nothing if not challenging, so debate ensues. For example, Strøm, Müller, and Bergman (2003, chs. 3 and 23) argue veto-players differ by type and specific authority. They distinguish between a dictator whose consent is both necessary and sufficient, a veto-player whose consent is necessary, a decisive player whose consent is sufficient, and a powerful player who can credibly threaten to take action. Such disagreements matter not in this context. The key point is, as Elgie (2004, 327–8) argues, that the veto-players approach makes the study of specific regimes part of the wider debate about how we study political institutions and renders such notions as "semi-presidentialism" and cabinet government irrelevant.

That is one agenda. There is another agenda that focuses on the analysis of traditions, and on a political anthropology of executive politics. A governmental tradition is a set of inherited beliefs about the institutions and history of government. For Western Europe it is conventional to distinguish between the Anglo-Saxon (no state) tradition; the Germanic Rechtsstaat tradition; the French (Napoleonic) tradition; and the Scandinavian tradition which mixes the Anglo-Saxon and Germanic. There is already a growing body of work on the impact of such traditions. Bevir, Rhodes, and Weller (2003, 202) comment that Westminster systems share a tradition of strong executive government that can force through reform in response to economic pressures whereas, in the Netherlands, reform hinged on coalition governments operating in a tradition of consensual corporatism. France provides another contrast. The combination of departmental fragmentation at the centre, coupled with the grand corps tradition and its beliefs about a strong state, meant that reform rested on the consent of those about to be reformed, and it was not forthcoming. As Helms (2005, 261) argues convincingly, that an historical and comparative perspective is the best way to explore core executives and the variety of political practice within and between regime types: that is, the analysis of traditions by another name (as is the analysis of path dependencies in Pierson 2004).

Why does the study of executive government and politics matter? We care because the decisions of the great and the good affect all our lives for good or ill. So, we want to know what prime ministers and ministers do, why, how, and with what consequences. In other words, we are interested in their reasons, their actions, and the effects of both. To understand their reasons we need a political anthropology of executive politics. We need to observe prime ministers, ministers, and cabinets "in action."

The obvious objection is that the secrecy surrounding executive politics limits the opportunities for such work (but see Shore 2000). The point has force but we must take care to avoid saying "no" for the powerful. We can learn from biography and journalism. Biographers probe the reasons. Journalists with their exposé tradition probe actions to show that "all is not as it seems." Each has their answer to the question of why study executive government. Both observe people in action. If we want to know this world, then we must tell stories that enable listeners to see executive governance afresh. A political anthropology of executive politics may be a daunting prospect but it behoves us to try.

Whichever agenda prevails, the study of executives in parliamentary government must not become yet one more of the multiplying sub-fields of political science.

Vim and vigour lies not in microspecialization but in engaging with the bigger debates in comparative politics and political science. Even that ossified variant of formal-legalism known as the Westminster approach can be reinvented by engaging with the interpretive turn; by analysing the written constitutional documents and their associated beliefs and practices; and by drawing on history and philosophy—the founding constituent disciplines of political science—to explore the historical evolution of political institutions.

References

AUCOIN, P. 1995. *The New Public Management: Canada in Comparative Perspective.* Quebec: Institute for Research on Public Policy.

AULICH, C. and WETTENHALL, R. (eds.) 2005. *Howard's Second and Third Governments.* Sydney: UNSW Press.

BAGEHOT, W. 1963 [1867]. *The English Constitution,* intro. R. H. S. Crossman. London: Fontana.

BAKVIS, H. 2000. Prime minister and cabinet in Canada: an autocracy in need of reform? *Journal of Canadian Studies,* 35 (4): 60–79.

BEHN, R. D. 2001. *Rethinking Democratic Accountability.* Washington, DC: Brookings Institution.

BEVIR, M. and RHODES, R. A. W. 2006. *Governance Stories.* London: Routledge.

—— —— and WELLER, P. 2003. Comparative governance: prospects and lessons. *Public Administration,* 81 (1): 191–210.

BLICK, A. 2004. *People Who Live in the Dark: The Special Adviser in British Politics.* London: Politico's.

BLONDEL, J. 1980. *World Leaders: Heads of Government in the Postwar Period.* London: Sage.

—— and MÜLLER ROMMELL, F. 1993a. Introduction. Pp. 1–19 in *Governing Together: The Extent and Limits of Joint Decision-making in Western European Cabinets,* ed. J. Blondel and F. Müller-Rommell. Houndmills: Macmillan.

—— —— (eds.) 1993b. *Governing Together: The Extent and Limits of Joint Decision-making in Western European Cabinets.* Houndmills: Macmillan.

—— —— (eds.) 1997 [1988]. *Cabinets in Western Europe,* 2nd edn. London: Macmillan.

—— and THIÉBAULT, J.-L. (eds.) 1991. *The Profession of Government Minister in Western Europe.* Houndmills: Macmillan.

BOGDANOR, V. 1999. Comparative politics. Pp. 147–79 in *The British Study of Politics in the Twentieth Century,* ed. J. Hayward, B. Barry, and A. Brown. Oxford: Oxford University Press for the British Academy.

BRITTAN, S. 1975. The economic contradictions of democracy. *British Journal of Political Science,* 5: 129–59.

BUTLER, D., ADONIS, A., and TRAVERS, T. 1994. *Failure in British Government: The Politics of the Poll Tax.* Oxford: Oxford University Press.

CABINET OFFICE 1994. *Next Steps: Moving On* (The Trosa Report). London: Cabinet Office.

CAMPBELL, C. 1998. *The US Presidency in Crisis: A Comparative Perspective*. New York: Oxford University Press.

—— and WILSON, G. 1995. *The End of Whitehall: Death of a Paradigm?* Oxford: Blackwell.

COATES, D. and LAWLER, P. (eds.) 2000. *New Labour in Power*. Manchester: Manchester University Press.

COX, G. W. 1987. *The Efficient Secret: The Cabinet and the Development of Political Parties in Victorian England*. Cambridge: Cambridge University Press.

CROSSMAN, R. H. S. (ed.) 1963. Introduction. Pp. 1–57 in *The English Constitution*, ed. W. Bagehot. London: Fontana.

DOGAN, M. and PELASSY, D. 1990. *How to Compare Nations: Strategies in Comparative Politics*, 2nd edn. Chatham, NJ: Chatham House.

DOWDING, K. 1995. *The Civil Service*. London: Routledge.

DUNLEAVY, P. and RHODES, R. A. W. 1990. Core executive studies in Britain. *Public Administration*, 68 (1): 3–28.

ELGIE, R. 1995. *Political Leadership in Liberal Democracies*. Houndmills: Macmillan.

—— 1997. Models of executive politics: a framework for the study of executive power relations in parliamentary and semi-presidential regimes. *Political Studies*, 45 (2): 217–31.

—— 1998. The classification of democratic regime types: conceptual ambiguity and contestable assumptions. *European Journal of Political Research*, 33: 219–38.

—— 2004. Semi-presidentialism: concepts, consequences and contesting explanations. *Political Studies Review*, 2 (3): 314–30.

FOLEY, M. 2000. *The British Presidency*. Manchester: Manchester University Press.

GAMBLE, A. 1990. Theories of British politics. *Political Studies*, 38: 404–20.

GREEN, D. P. and SHAPIRO, I. 1994. *Pathologies of Rational Choice*. New Haven, Conn.: Yale University Press.

HARGROVE, E. C. 2001. Presidency and prime ministers as institutions: an American perspective. *British Journal of Politics and International Relations*, 3 (1): 49–70.

HAY, C. 2004. Theory, stylised heuristic or self-fulfilling prophecy? The status of rational choice theory in public administration. *Public Administration*, 82 (1): 39–62.

HELMS, L. 2005. *Presidents, Prime Ministers and Chancellors*. Houndmills: Macmillan.

HENNESSY, P. 1995. *The Hidden Wiring: Unearthing the British Constitution*. London: Gollancz.

—— 2000. *The Prime Ministers*. London: Allen Lane/The Penguin Press.

—— 2002. The Blair government in historical perspective: an analysis of the power relationships within New Labour. *History Today*, 52 (1): 21–3.

JONES, G. W. (ed.) 1991. *West European Prime Ministers*. London: Frank Cass.

KAVANAGH, D. and SELDON, A. 1999. *The Powers Behind the Prime Minister: The Hidden Influence of Number Ten*. London: HarperCollins.

KING, A. 1969. *The British Prime Ministers*. London: Macmillan.

—— 1985. *The British Prime Ministers*, 2nd edn. London: Macmillan.

KIPLING, R. 1990. *The Complete Verse*. London: Kyle Cathie.

LAVER, M. and SHEPSLE, K. 1996. *Making and Breaking Governments: Cabinets and Legislatures in Parliamentary Democracies*. Cambridge: Cambridge University Press.

LEE, J. M., JONES, G. W., and BURNHAM, J. 1988. *At the Centre of Whitehall*. Basingstoke: Macmillan.

LIJPHART, A. 1999 [1984]. *Patterns of Democracy: Government Forms and Performance in Thirty-six Countries*, 2nd edn. New Haven, Conn.: Yale University Press.

MAC (Management Advisory Committee) 2004. *Connecting Government: Whole of Government Response to Australia's Priority Challenges.* Canberra: Australian Public Service Commission.

Mackintosh, J. 1968. *The British Cabinet,* 2nd edn. London: Stevens.

Marinetto, M. 2003. Governing beyond the centre: a critique of the Anglo-Governance School. *Political Studies,* 51: 592–608.

Marr, D. and Wilkinson, M. 2003. *Dark Victory.* Crows Nest: Allen and Unwin.

Marshall, G. 1986. *Constitutional Conventions: The Rules and Forms of Political Accountability.* Oxford: Clarendon Press.

Mughan, A. 2000. *Media and the Presidentialisation of Parliamentary Elections.* Houndmills: Macmillan.

—— and Patterson, S. C. (eds.) 1992. *Political Leadership in Democratic Societies.* Chicago: Nelson-Hall.

Mulgan, R. 2003. *Holding Power to Account: Accountability in Modern Democracies.* Houndmills: Palgrave-Macmillan.

Pattapan, H., Wanna, J., and Weller, P. (eds.) 2005. *Westminster Legacies: Democracy and Responsible Government in Asia, Australasia and the Pacific.* Sydney: University of New South Wales Press.

Peters, B. G. 1998. Managing horizontal government: the politics of coordination. *Public Administration,* 76: 295–311.

—— 1999. *Institutional Theory in Political Science: The "New Institutionalism."* London: Pinter.

—— Rhodes, R. A. W., and Wright, V. (eds.) 2000. *Administering the Summit: Administration of the Core Executive in Developed Countries.* Houndmills: Macmillan.

Pierson, P. 2004. *Politics in Time: History, Institutions, and Social Analysis.* Princeton, NJ: Princeton University Press.

Plowden, W. 1994. *Ministers and Mandarins.* London: Institute for Public Policy Research.

Poguntke, T. and Webb, P. 2005a. The presidentialization of politics in democratic societies: a framework for analysis. Pp. 1–25 in *The Presidentialization of Politics: A Comparative Study of Modern Democracies,* ed. T. Poguntke and P. Webb. Oxford: Oxford University Press.

—— —— 2005b. The presidentialization of contemporary democratic politics: Evidence, causes, consequences. Pp. 336–56 in *The Presidentialization of Politics: A Comparative Study of Modern Democracies,* ed. T. Poguntke and P. Webb. Oxford: Oxford University Press.

—— —— (eds.) 2005c. *The Presidentialization of Politics: A Comparative Study of Modern Democracies.* Oxford: Oxford University Press.

Pollitt, C. and Bouckaert, G. 2000. *Public Management Reform: A Comparative Analysis.* Oxford: Oxford University Press.

Punnett, R. M. 1977. *The Prime Minister in Canadian Government and Politics.* Toronto: Macmillan of Canada.

Pryce, S. 1997. *Presidentializing the Premiership.* New York: St. Martin's Press.

Rhodes, R. A. W. 1995. From prime ministerial power to core executive. Pp. 11–37 in *Prime Minister, Cabinet and Core Executive,* ed. R. A. W. Rhodes and P. Dunleavy. London: Macmillan.

—— and Dunleavy, P. (eds.) 1995. *Prime Minister, Cabinet and Core Executive.* London: Macmillan.

—— and WELLER, P. (eds.) 2001. *The Changing World of Top Officials: Mandarins or Valets?* Buckingham: Open University Press.

RIPA (ROYAL INSTITUTE OF PUBLIC ADMINISTRATION) 1987. *Top Jobs in Whitehall: Appointments and Promotions in the Senior Civil Service.* London: RIPA.

ROSE, R. 2001. *The Prime Minister in a Shrinking World.* Cambridge: Polity.

SAVOIE, D. 1999. *Governing from the Centre.* Toronto: Toronto University Press.

SEIDMAN, H. 1975. *Politics, Position and Power,* 2nd edn. Oxford: Oxford University Press.

SELDON, A. 2004. *Blair.* London: Free Press.

SEYMOUR-URE, C. 2003. *Prime Ministers and the Media: Issues of Power and Control.* Oxford: Blackwell.

SHORE, C. 2000. *Building Europe: The Cultural Politics of European Integration.* London: Routledge.

SMITH, M. J. 1999. *The Core Executive in Britain.* London: Macmillan.

STRØM, K., MÜLLER, W. C., and BERGMAN, T. 2003. *Delegation and Accountability in Parliamentary Democracies.* Oxford: Oxford University Press.

THOMPSON, E. and TILLOTSEN, G. 1999. Caught in the act: the smoking gun view of ministerial responsibility. *Australian Journal of Public Administration,* 58 (1): 48–57.

TSEBELIS, G. 2002. *Veto Players: How Political Institutions Work.* Princeton, NJ: Princeton University Press and Russell Sage Foundation.

WEAVER, R. K. and ROCKMAN, B. A. 1993. When and how do institutions matter? Pp. 445–61 in *Do Institutions Matter? Government Capabilities in the United States and Abroad,* ed. R. K. Weaver and B. A. Rockman. Washington, DC: Brookings Institution.

WELLER, P. 1985. *First Among Equals: Prime Ministers in Westminster Systems.* Sydney: Allen and Unwin.

—— 1989. Politicization and the Australian public service. *Australian Journal of Public Administration,* 48 (4): 369–81.

—— (ed.) 1993. *Menzies to Keating: The Development of the Australian Prime Ministership.* London: Hurst.

—— 2001. *Australia's Mandarins: The Frank and the Fearless?* Crows Nest: Allen and Unwin.

—— 2003. Cabinet government: an elusive ideal? *Public Administration,* 81 (4): 701–22.

—— BAKVISS, H., and RHODES R. A. W. (eds.) 1997. *The Hollow Crown: Countervailing Trends in Core Executives.* London: Macmillan.

WILSON, R. 1999. The civil service in the new millennium. Speech delivered at City University, London, 5 May.

WOODHOUSE, D. 2003. Ministerial responsibility. Pp. 281–332 in *The British Constitution in the Twentieth Century,* ed. V. Bogdanor. Oxford: Oxford University Press for the British Academy.

—— 2004. UK ministerial responsibility in 2002: the tale of two resignations. *Public Administration,* 82 (1): 1–19.

WRIGHT, V. and HAYWARD, J. 2000. Governing from the centre: policy coordination in six European core executives. Pp. 27–46 in *Transforming British Government, Volume 2: Changing Roles and Relationships,* ed. R. A. W. Rhodes. London: Macmillan.

CHAPTER 18

··

COMPARATIVE EXECUTIVE–LEGISLATIVE RELATIONS

··

MATTHEW SØBERG SHUGART

The great expansion of constitution writing, especially after the fall of European and then Soviet Communism after 1989, has generated a profusion of scholarship about the effects of different constitutional systems of executive–legislative relations. The purpose of this chapter is to consider how the two basic democratic regime types—parliamentary and presidential—differ fundamentally through how they structure the relations of the executive to the legislative branch in either a *hierarchical* or a *transactional* fashion. In a hierarchy, one institution derives its authority from another institution, whereas in a transaction, two (or more) institutions derive their authority independently of one another.

The distinction between hierarchies and transactions is critical, because in a democracy, by definition, the legislative power (or at least the most important part of it) is popularly elected. Where parliamentary and presidential systems differ is in how executive power is constituted: Either subordinated to the legislative assembly,

* I acknowledge the research assistance and advice of Royce Carroll and Mónica Pachón-Buitrago.

which may thus terminate its authority (parliamentary democracy), or else itself elected and thus separated from the authority of the assembly (presidential democracy). All forms of democratic constitutional design must trade off these two competing conceptions of hierarchy vs. transaction in the relations of the executive to the legislative assembly. As we shall see, there are numerous hybrid forms—*semi-presidential* and other. What makes them hybrids is precisely that they combine some structural elements that emphasize hierarchical subordination of the executive to the assembly with other elements that emphasize transaction between the executive and legislative powers.

1   EARLY THEORETICAL CONSIDERATIONS AND THEIR MODERN APPLICATION

An important early justification for the "separation of powers" between executive and legislative (and judicial) authority is to be found in Montesquieu's *The Spirit of the Laws*, which argued for the importance of separating the various functions of government as a safeguard against tyranny. This notion strongly influenced the founders of the US Constitution, James Madison, Alexander Hamilton, and John Jay, who collectively expounded a theory of executive–legislative relations in several chapters of their *Federalist Papers*. Written to explain and defend their choices in the then-proposed US Constitution, the Federalists' essays provide a blueprint for the transactional executive–legislative relations that typify presidentialism. On the other hand, modern parliamentary government does not derive from a single set of advocacy essays. Rather than prescribed, parliamentarism was famously described in Walter Bagehot's classic, *The English Constitution*. Bagehot noted that the cabinet, hierarchically accountable to parliament, had replaced the English monarchy as the "efficient" portion of government, whereas parliament itself had essentially become an "electoral college" that chose the government, but did little else. Bagehot explicitly contrasted the English system of "Cabinet Government" with the American system, where:

... the President is elected from the people by one process, and the House of Representatives by another. The independence of the legislative and executive powers is the specific quality of the Presidential Government, just as the fusion and combination is the precise principle of Cabinet Government. (Bagehot 1867/1963, 14)

With this passage, then, Bagehot captures the essence of the distinction between parliamentarism and presidentialism. It was indeed the American presidential model that most caught the eye of early proponents of alternatives to the

British model, especially as South American countries gained independence in the nineteenth century. Nonetheless, British and continental European contemporaries of Bagehot were already arguing for elections via proportional representation, a fundamental political reform that would generate multiparty cabinets (Droop 1869; Mill 1862) and thus transform executive–legislative relations in a more transactional direction (as explained below) while retaining the parliamentary framework. As a result of the spread of proportional representation across the European continent, in the decades after Bagehot, Droop, and Mill, the practice of most parliamentary systems had diverged from the English model. Yet, as concerns constitutional structure, even parliamentarism with multiparty cabinets remains hierarchical because the executive must maintain the "confidence" of the legislative majority—in sharp distinction to the presidential model in which the legislature and executive are separate from and independent of one another.

Although the terminology is somewhat different, the conceptual perspective of hierarchy versus transaction has its roots in the *Federalist Papers*, and specifically the essays therein by Madison. The basic theoretical underpinning of the Federalists is that the extent to which government ensures liberty or gives way to tyranny is directly related to the manner in which it channels political ambition. Like contemporary rational-choice approaches, Madison took it as axiomatic that political actors are motivated by personal gain. He accepted selfish motivation as inevitable and sought to harness it for the greater good. Doing so, he argued, entailed establishing a system of institutions that structures and checks that ambition. Thus, Madison wrote in *Federalist* 51, the design of government "consists in giving to those who administer each department [i.e. branch] the necessary constitutional means and personal motives to resist encroachments of the others" (Hamilton, Madison, Jay, and Fairfield 1787/1937, 337).

Ambition is checked, in Madison's vision, through the creation of distinct branches with separate "agency" (i.e. delegated authority) that must compete with one another, because neither is subordinated in a hierarchy to the other. Systems of executive–legislative relations may be viewed in this framework as different means of defining the hierarchical or transactional relationship of the executive to the legislature. The two pure types of institutional design— parliamentary and presidential—are thus almost perfectly opposed to one another. A parliamentary system makes the executive an agent of the assembly majority, hierarchically inferior to it because the majority in parliament creates and may terminate the authority of the executive. A presidential system, on the other hand, features an assembly and executive that are elected independently for fixed terms, and thus have incentives to transact, or bargain, with one another, in order to produce legislation and to govern.

The most basic and stylized comparison, then, is what is shown in Fig. 18.1. The political process of the parliamentary system is depicted as having a hierarchical chain of delegation, and no transactional relations. Voters select (delegate to) a

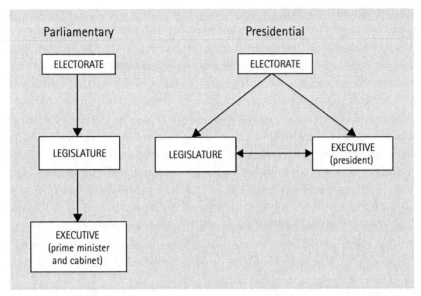

Figure 18.1. Basic hierarchical and transactional forms of executive–legislative relations

legislature, and the legislature selects (delegates to) the executive. The political process of the presidential system is depicted with two delegation links from the electorate to both the legislature and the popularly elected executive; additionally, there is a transactional relationship between the executive and the legislature, which are located at the same level, rather than with one subordinate to the other. They then engage in a horizontally depicted process of interbranch transactions.

As has been noted frequently in the literature, at least since Bagehot and right up to recent works (Moe and Caldwell 1994; Palmer 1995), the Westminster democracy of Great Britain and the presidential system of the United States offer the closest approximations to these ideal types. The parliamentary system with a single-party majority government generates a highly hierarchical form of democratic delegation. By contrast, the public bargaining and institutionalized conflict between the American presidency and Congress represent a virtually ideal manifestation of transactional executive–legislative relations.

Pure as examples the British and American models may be, neither system is typical of experience in the rest of the world. Most parliamentary systems do not have single-party majorities like Britain. In the absence of such majorities, the key features of politics in the system are transactional, because the assembly to which the executive is accountable is not itself controlled by a single hierarchical organization. Rather, authority is shared by two or more parties. Similarly, most presidential systems feature less prominently the interbranch policy transactions that so typify the US. The reasons lie in an often unstated condition for the pitting of ambition against ambition in the Federalists' conception: that the assembly be sufficiently organized with its own *internal hierarchy* that it can bargain as an independent collective actor vis-à-vis the executive (Cox and McCubbins 1993). As we shall see below, the literature on presidential systems outside the United States suggests that the conditions for an internal legislative hierarchy that is independent of the executive, may not be common. In their absence, presidential systems may take on aspects of informal hierarchy, or even a relatively anarchic pattern. Thus the actual behavior of institutions and political actors in the two "pure" types of systems contains mixes of hierarchical and transactional relations. It is important to recognize, however, that these mixes are occurring within a constitutional structure that remains either hierarchical (parliamentary) or transactional (presidential). What leads to the mixing of elements is the nature of the organization of the assembly itself (principally whether controlled by a single party or not) as well as informal relations between executives and the parties. Before exploring each main type further, it will be useful to develop precise definitions of the types, as well as of hybrid forms of constitutional structure.

2 Forms of Constitutional Structure: Defining Presidential, Parliamentary, and Hybrid Systems

In order to put the analysis of constitutional design into practice, we need simple and mutually exclusive definitions of regime types. A "pure" parliamentary democracy is defined by the following two basic features:

1. executive authority, consisting of a prime minister and cabinet, arises out of the legislative assembly;
2. the executive is at all times subject to potential dismissal via a vote of "no confidence" by a majority of the legislative assembly.

These two criteria express the hierarchical relationship of executive to legislative authority in the way that is depicted in Fig. 18.1: The executive arises from and is responsible to the assembly majority. Presidential democracy, on the other hand, is defined by the following three basic features:

1. the executive is headed by a popularly elected president who serves as the "chief executive;"
2. the terms of the chief executive and the legislative assembly are fixed, and not subject to mutual confidence;

3. the president names and directs the cabinet and has some constitutionally granted law-making authority.

The defining characteristics of parliamentary and presidential democracy, then, speak first to the question of the *origin* and *survival* of executive and legislative authority. In a parliamentary system, executive authority originates from the assembly. The precise institutional rules for determining who shall form a cabinet vary across parliamentary systems, but in all of them the process of forming a government falls to the majority party, if there is one. If there is not, the government emerges from bargaining among those politicians who received their mandate at the most recent assembly elections. Once formed, the government survives in office only so long as it maintains the "confidence" of the majority in the assembly. Again, the precise rules for determining when a government has lost this confidence vary, but always the executive is subject to the ongoing confidence of parliament.

In a presidential system, on the other hand, the origin and survival of executive and legislative authority are separate. The first criterion of the definition of presidentialism contrasts starkly with that for parliamentarism, in that it denotes the existence of a chief executive whose authority originates with the electorate. The second criterion specifies that, unlike in a parliamentary system, the chief executive is not subject to dismissal by a legislative majority. Furthermore, neither is the assembly subject to early dissolution by the president. Both branches thus survive in office independent of one another. The addition of the third criterion, regarding the president's authority, is important for establishing the independence of the president not only in terms of origin and survival, but also in the executive function, for it sets out that the cabinet derives its authority from the president and not from parliament. It further stipulates that the president has some legislative authority, and thus is not "merely" the executive. It is the absence of interbranch hierarchy combined with shared law-making powers that generates the incentive for interbranch transactions, providing two independent agents of the electorate that must cooperate in order to accomplish any legislative change.

If we think of parliamentary and presidential government as Weberian ideal types, we must acknowledge that there are numerous regimes that contain elements of each, and are thus hybrids. By far the most common hybrid form is *semi-presidential* government. Adapted from Duverger's (1980) original and influential definition, semi-presidentialism may be defined by three features:

1. a president who is popularly elected;
2. the president has considerable constitutional authority;
3. there exists also a prime minister and cabinet, subject to the confidence of the assembly majority.

These features define a dual executive (Blondel 1984), in that the elected president is not merely a head of state who lacks political authority, but also is not clearly the chief executive, as there is also a prime minister with a relationship to the assembly that resembles that of a parliamentary democracy. The precise relationship of the president to the prime minister and cabinet, and of the latter to the parliament, vary widely across regimes that fit the basic definition of semi-presidential. It is precisely this variance that has made delimiting regime types controversial, or at least confusing, in the literature. For the sake of conceptual continuity and clarity, it would be advisable to reserve the term, *semi-presidential*, for only those regimes that fit the three Duvergerian criteria. Other hybrid forms are feasible—most notably the Swiss case of an assembly-selected executive that sits for a fixed term, and the brief Israeli experience of a directly elected chief executive who remained subject to parliamentary confidence. These hybrids are neither parliamentary nor presidential, but they also are not semi-presidential in the Duvergerian sense (Shugart 2005).

The geographical distribution of these types can be seen in Table 18.1. At a glance it is readily apparent that geography is virtually destiny as far as concerns a country's constitutional structure. Parliamentary systems dominate Europe, defined as EU members (new and old) and the non-EU countries of Western Europe and the Mediterranean region. To a lesser extent semi-presidential systems are common in the EU region, and they dominate the post-Communist region. On the other hand, presidentialism dominates the Americas, aside from the Common-wealth countries. Indeed, Bagehot (1867, 14) referred to the proliferation of presi-dential regimes in the then newly independent Latin American countries, decrying the possibility that parliamentarism might be overtaken by "its great competitor, which seems likely, unless care be taken, to outstrip it in the progress of the world." In the remaining regions, however, we find examples of all three main types. It is noteworthy that almost all of the parliamentary systems outside of Europe are former British colonies, while the former French and Portuguese colonies in Africa are generally semi-presidential (as are France and Portugal).

In the most of the remainder of this chapter, I turn to discussing each consti-tutional format in turn, and how understanding the juxtaposition of hierarchical and transactional relationships in each can elucidate the incentives and likely behavior of actors in democracies.

3   PARLIAMENTARY SYSTEMS

In a parliamentary system, the extent of hierarchical or transactional relationships between executive and legislative institutions depends in practice on whether

Table 18.1 Constitutional forms of executive–legislative relations among democracies and semi-democracies, 2006

Region	Parliamentary	Presidential	Semi-presidential	Other hybrid
European Union/ Western Europe & Mediterranean	Belgium, Czech Republic, Denmark, Estonia, Finland,* Germany, Greece, Hungary, Ireland,* Israel, Italy, Latvia, Netherlands, Norway, Slovenia,* Spain, Sweden, Turkey, United Kingdom	Cyprus	Austria, France, Lithuania, Poland, Portugal, Slovakia	Switzerland
Post-Communist (but not EU)	Albania, Moldova		Armenia, Belarus, Bosnia–Hercegovina,** Bulgaria, Croatia, Georgia, Macedonia, Mongolia, Romania, Russia, Serbia and Montenegro,*** Ukraine	
Americas	Canada, Jamaica, Trinidad and Tobago	Argentina, Brazil, Chile, Colombia, Costa Rica, Dominican Republic, Ecuador, El Salvador, Guatemala, Honduras, Mexico, Nicaragua, Panama, Paraguay, United States, Uruguay, Venezuela	Peru	Bolivia, Guyana
East and South Asia/Pacific	Australia, Bangladesh, Fiji, India, Japan, Malaysia, Nepal, New Zealand, Papua New Guinea, Thailand	Indonesia, Philippines, South Korea	Sri Lanka, Taiwan	

(Continued)

Table 18.1 (*continued*)

Region	Parliamentary	Presidential	Semi-presidential	Other hybrid
Africa	Botswana, Lesotho, Mauritius, South Africa	Benin, Ghana, Malawi, Nigeria	Burkina Faso, Madagascar, Mali, Mozambique, Namibia, Niger, Senegal	

Notes: Includes countries of at least 500,000 population with Freedom House political rights score of 4 or better, averaged throughout the period 1990–1 to 2004, or for each year since 2000. Belarus and Bosnia–Hercegovina do not meet these conditions, but are included so as to cover all Europe. Malaysia is also included for having consistently held semi-competitive elections.

*Indicates presence of elected president lacking any significant constitutional powers (government formation, dissolution, or veto).

** Collegial (three-person) presidency.

*** Each autonomous republic retains an elected presidency, although the federal presidency is no longer elected.

Source: Author's coding of constitutions from http://confinder.richmond.edu/, except Niger (http://droit.francophonie.org/doc/html/ne/con/fr/1999/1999dfneco1.html), and Taiwan (Noble 1999); Freedom House website (http://www.freedomhouse.org) for level of (semi-)democracy.

single-party majorities result or not. Majoritarian systems preserve the hierarchy in its purest form, whereas multiparty systems tend towards a more transactional form of parliamentarism.

3.1 Majoritarian Parliamentarism

When a single party obtains a majority of seats, a parliamentary system is every bit as hierarchical as it is portrayed in Fig. 18.1. The hierarchical accountability of the cabinet to parliament is what generates the "fusion of powers" described famously by Bagehot (1867/1963). Post-Bagehot, scholars increasingly recognized that effective power is concentrated in the leadership of the majority party, rather than within parliament (e.g. McKenzie 1912). As party leaders in the cabinet gained greater autonomy over their own backbench members (Cox 1987), the fusion of executive and legislative powers was essentially extended to a fusion of party and executive. Commenting on the greater importance in the British model of relations between the cabinet and the backbenchers in both government and opposition, King (1976, 26) went so far as to say that there is hardly such a thing in Britain as "the relationship between the executive and the legislature." Rehabilitating the language of executive–legislative relations to describe majoritarianism, Lijphart (1984, 1999) has noted that the result of Westminster's concentration of authority is "executive dominance" over the legislature. What this means in practice is that so long as the majority party remains united, the executive is unassailable, because it enjoys the confidence of the parliamentary majority.

Majoritarian parliamentarism thus contains the potential for extreme concentration of power, tempered only by the possibility that internal party disagreements might come into the open and by the fear of alienating sufficient voters as to lose the next election. In this system there is no room for transaction; however, the opposition within parliament provides an indirect check, in the form of being the electorate's monitor over the government (Palmer 1995).

3.2 Transactional Parliamentarism

In the absence of a majority party, a parliamentary executive may be held by a *coalition* that jointly controls the assembly majority, in which case the cabinet survives as long as this majority remains together. Alternatively, a *minority government* may form, in which case the cabinet remains in place as long as the opposition does not combine forces against it. These non-majoritarian variants of parliamentarism remain hierarchical in terms of the formal relation of the executive to the legislature. However, they are transactional in terms of the relationship of parties to one another, because a bargain between two or more parties is necessary for a government to originate and then survive in office.

The transactions between parties and how coalitions form has been the focus of an extensive literature (reviewed in Laver 1998; Martin and Stevenson 2001), as has the duration of coalition governments and the causes of their termination (reviewed in Grofman and Van Roozendaal 1997; Laver 2003). Like King's (1975) observation about Britain, this literature also is not concerned primarily with executive–legislative relations per se. Rather it focuses squarely on the bargaining that occurs within the shadow of the hierarchical subordination of the cabinet to the assembly. Some scholars have focused their attention more directly on the law-making process, noting variations across systems in the agenda power and procedural advantages enjoyed by the cabinet (Döring 1995a, 1995b; Huber 1996; Heller 2001). The presence of multiple parties to a cabinet transaction, each with an interest in ongoing monitoring of the government, often results in a legislative committee system that gives backbenchers a notably greater role in scrutinizing and amending government bills than their counterparts in majoritarian systems (King 1975; Strom 1990; Huber and Powell 1994; Mattson and Strom 1995; Haller-berg 2000). The more influence the opposition has over policy-making, the more a parliamentary system has what Lijphart (1984) referred to as an "informal separation of powers," as distinct from the fusion of powers we see in majoritarian systems, and also in contrast to the formal separation of powers of presidential systems, to which we now turn.

4   PRESIDENTIAL SYSTEMS

In presidential systems, as was depicted in Fig. 18.1, there are two distinct delegations from voters to political agents: one to the assembly and the other to the chief executive. Owing to their separate origins in the electorate and their fixed terms (separate survival), there is no formal hierarchy between legislative and executive authority. Interbranch transactions are thus necessary because the independent branches need each other to accomplish any policy goals that require the passage of legislation that may be sought by their respective electorates.

The extent of executive–legislative divergence over policy preferences depends on how constituent interests are translated through the electoral process. In the unlikely event that the two branches share identical preferences, executive–legislative relations resemble total presidential dominance, as no disagreements are observed. In that case, the system would resemble a hierarchy with no interbranch transactions.[1] More typically, given their separate election, the executive and legislature are likely to disagree, often in public, in a process that informs the electorate of issues and controversies (Strøm 2000).

In cases of very extreme divergence of preferences between the branches, it is also possible for the interbranch transactions of the ideal type depicted in Fig. 18.1 to break down, and for executive–legislative relations to be characterized by near anarchy, as opposed to either hierarchy or transactions. In such a scenario the president may govern without much regard for any collective preferences of the legislative branch, using decree and appointment powers to circumvent the legislature. These presidents may bargain on an ad hoc basis, perhaps providing patronage to specific legislators or legislative factions, but never forming a stable relationship—either hierarchical or transactional—with congress as an institution. This latter scenario approximates the so-called "perils of presidentialism" that Juan Linz (1994) warned against in a seminal work on the relationship between regime type and the sustainability of democracy. Linz suggested that presidents in newly democratizing countries with weakly institutionalized legislatures may be able to exercise de facto powers well beyond those granted in the constitution, threatening democracy itself.

Notwithstanding the Linzian concern with concentration of executive authority, Mainwaring noted that the experience of democratic presidentialism had resulted in presidents so checked by congress and other actors that "most Latin American presidents have had trouble accomplishing their agendas" (Mainwaring 1990, 162). In fact, much of the experience of presidentialism in Latin America has consisted of presidents' struggling not to circumvent the legislature, but to find a way to generate a workable relationship with it. Given that presidents have to bargain with the legislature to accomplish any agenda, they may be willing to trade off their formal control over the composition of their cabinets in order to develop a more stable interbranch relationship. That is, presidents may have an incentive to bargain over the formation of cabinets even where they have no formal requirement to do so (Cheibub, Przeworski, and Saiegh 2004).

The reason for interbranch transactions over cabinets in presidential systems lies in the need of the president to transact with the legislative branch in order to implement policy—a definitional aspect of presidentialism. Where the assembly is organized by a majority party (whether that of the president or not) it has the institutional capacity to bargain with the president over legislation of interest to

---

[1] For example, Mexican presidents, by virtue of being the head of a highly disciplined hegemonic party, dominated the legislature over many decades (Weldon 1997).

that majority. In such a context, the president may not need a cabinet that is itself reflective of interbranch transactions. Both institutions may prefer the clarity of position that comes from their own control over the composition of their respective institution, given that they are "bargaining before an audience" (Groseclose and McCarty 2000; see also Strøm 2000). Thus in the USA, presidents do not bargain with Congress in shaping their cabinet (despite the requirement that individual cabinet members be confirmed by the Senate), and opposition participation in the cabinet is only sporadic even when the opposition party controls Congress.

On the other hand, where the assembly is highly fragmented and the president has little partisan support therein, the president may prefer not to have a cabinet reflective of interbranch transactions, because coming to an agreement would restrict his ability to use his decree powers (if provided or claimed) and to transact with individual legislators (offering patronage for votes, for example). This is the "anarchic" pattern. It is thus in the intermediate contexts of no legislative majority, but substantial partisan support for the president in congress, that presidents may both need and want an interbranch cabinet transaction in order to link the two branches together and facilitate legislative bargaining.

To the extent that interparty bargaining in a presidential system permits the president to control the agenda of the assembly, a coalition cabinet introduces an element of interbranch hierarchy. A transactional relationship between the president—acting simultaneously as both the elected head of government and the head of his own party—and other parties in congress may even generate a "cartel" that in turn dominates congress (Amorim Neto, Cox, and McCubbins 2003). Thus, just as the transactional relationship between separate parties in multiparty parliamentary systems generates an "informal separation of powers" (Lijphart 1984), the transactions of a multiparty presidential system may generate an "informal fusion of powers" that binds the formally separate executive and legislative branches together for the duration of the coalition. It is important not to forget, however, that in presidential systems the chief executive always maintains the option of appointing a single-party or non-party cabinet. Presidents make strategic choices regarding the value for their legislative goals of having a coalition or not (Amorim Neto 2002; Geddes 1994). It is this heterogeneity of presidential strategies, resulting from the president's relative freedom of maneuver over the cabinet, that presumably generates the observed higher turnover rates seen in the ministries of presidential systems compared to parliamentary systems (Blondel 1985; Stepan and Skach 1993). Thus, while in most presidential systems only the process of making laws is formally in the domain of executive–legislative relations, that process is so central to the entire edifice of presidentialism that it may, under some circumstances, induce the president to bargain over cabinets as well.

5 SEMI-PRESIDENTIAL SYSTEMS

Recently there has been a proliferation of semi-presidential systems, especially with democratization in the former Communist bloc and Africa. The juxtaposition of an elected president with a cabinet responsible to parliament was an innovation of the German Weimar constitution, designed on the advice of eminent social scientists Hugo Preuss, Robert Redslob, and Max Weber (Mommsen 1984; Stirk 2002). Weber (1917/1978, 1452–3) mistrusted parties and believed that the "plebiscitary" selection of the president would force parties "to submit more or less unconditionally to leaders who held the confidence of the masses." Redslob (1918), on the other hand, was an advocate of what he called "authentic parliamentarism" on the British model, with a parliamentary opposition capable of assuming the government. Preuss, as summarized by Stirk (2002, 514), justified Weimar's synthesis as providing for a president and parliament, each with "an autonomous source of legitimacy," thus echoing Madison's separation of powers, yet retaining government responsibility to parliament. Given the subsequent collapse of the Weimar Republic, its designers' justifications for what would later be called semi-presidentialism became discredited. Today semi-presidentialism is more closely identified with France and with Charles de Gaulle's call, in his Bayeux Manifesto of 1946, for a "chief of state, placed above the parties,"[2] yet as I shall show, the neo-Madisonian logic of Preuss and his colleagues continues in all the regimes that can be meaningfully classified as semi-presidential.

The practice of semi-presidentialism has been quite diverse, as Duverger (1980) noted, both in formal constitutional powers and in actual behavior. Some presidents that appear quite powerful on paper are actually observed to exercise few powers (e.g. Austria), while others seemingly have limited formal powers, yet are dominant political players (e.g. France). Under the rubric of semi-presidentialism, there is much variation in formal powers, leading Shugart and Carey (1992) to propose a further subdivision of the concept into *premier-presidential* and *president-parliamentary* subtypes. Under premier-presidentialism, the prime minister and cabinet are *exclusively* accountable to the parliamentary majority, while under president-parliamentarism, the prime minister and cabinet are *dually* accountable to the president and the parliamentary majority. This distinction has not always been appreciated in the literature, and has been criticized on various terms by Sartori (1994a) and Siaroff (2003). Nonetheless, structurally, these are potentially important differences that shape the behavior of actors in a system (Shugart 2005).

---

[2] Nonetheless, De Gaulle at the time favored a president "elected by a body which includes the parliament but which is much larger" (excerpted in Lijphart 1992, 140–1), rather than by universal suffrage.

In a premier-presidential system, only the assembly majority may dismiss cabinets, which makes them quite close to being "parliamentary systems." However, they have "presidential" characteristics as well, in that the president has constitutional authority to act independently of the assembly, either in the process of forming governments or in law-making. Technically speaking, the power to dissolve parliament, which is common in premier-presidential systems, is not a "presidential" feature, because dissolution breaks the independence of the president and assembly that typifies presidentialism. However, any semi-presidential system already deviates from presidentialism owing to the possibility that the head of government (i.e. the prime minister) might be voted out of office by the assembly. In that context, presidential power of dissolution provides a counterweight to this enhanced authority of the assembly. Presidential authority as a check on the assembly is thus a feature that separates all presidential and semi-presidential systems from parliamentary systems.

In president-parliamentary systems, the president enjoys stronger constitutional powers over the composition of cabinets than is the case under premier-presidentialism. The German Weimar Republic was a prototype with serious design flaws, in that both the president and the assembly retained authority to postpone a resolution of political conflict by exercising unilateral powers. More recent president-parliamentary systems, including in the successor states to the former Soviet Union and in Africa, have incorporated several institutional innovations that promote interbranch cooperation (on Russia see Morgan-Jones and Schleiter 2004).

In some president-parliamentary systems, the president's authority over the process of government formation is limited because the nominee for prime minister (or the entire government) must be confirmed by the assembly majority. Provisions for investiture or confirmation—found in the contemporary cases of Armenia, Georgia, Russia, and Ukraine—obviously give the president the incentive to bargain over government composition. In fact, some cases (e.g. Russia and Taiwan) require a series of contingencies before either branch may threaten the survival of the other—even restricting the assembly's right to bring a no confidence vote—and hence generate incentives for the executive and assembly to transact that resemble pure presidential systems more than the premier-presidential variant of semi-presidentialism, as well as more than the Weimar model. Despite these incentives for interbranch transaction, all the president-parliamentary systems maintain the dual accountability of the prime minister and cabinet to the president and the assembly, putting the president in a stronger position than is the case in premier-presidential systems (e.g. France) to upend an existing cabinet transaction and start the process anew. Thus both variants of semi-presidentialism force the assembly majority to transact with a president, but the president has fewer formal tools at his disposal under a premier-presidential design than under president-parliamentarism.

6   SO, WHAT DIFFERENCE DOES IT MAKE?

The subtitle of Linz's (1994) now-famous essay on presidential vs. parliamentary government, was "Does it make a difference?" This chapter has already identified several ways in which regime type matters for proximate political consequences such as how executive authority is constituted and how law-making proceeds. Any system with a politically powerful elected presidency creates an agent of the electorate with whom legislators must transact. Linz, and many who have followed, call our attention to more distal effects of constitutional design, specifically, in Linz's case, for the survival of democracy itself. Linz argued that political crises in presidential systems were more likely to be "crises of regime" that could lead to breakdown, whereas in parliamentary systems they tended to be "crises of govern-ment" that can be resolved via recourse to a new cabinet transaction or early elections. Stepan and Skach (1993), and Przeworski, Alvarez, Cheibub, and Limongi (1996) are among those whose empirical studies generally have concurred with Linz. Mainwaring (1993) suggested that it was multiparty presidentialism that was specifically prone to breakdown. Yet Power and Gasiorowski (1994) found that neither presidentialism nor its combination with multipartism had a statistically significant relationship to democratic breakdown in developing countries. A fun-damental problem that remains with attempts to settle this question is the absence of parliamentarism in Latin America or presidentialism in Europe—the two regions with the greatest experience with democracy, stable or otherwise. The regional distribution of regime types (see Table 18.1) makes it difficult to determine whether constitutional forms are directly related to democratic "consolidation" or whether they are proxies for other conditions that affect the prospects for stable democracy.

Other variables besides formal constitutional design likewise complicate efforts to uncover effects on policy performance. Given the challenges of multivariate analysis, perhaps it is not surprising that the literature on policy performance remains inconclusive, with sometimes conflicting conclusions. For instance, Persson and Tabellini (2003) argue that presidential democracy reduces corruption, while Gerring and Thacker (2004) find the opposite. Yet, Persson, Roland, and Tabellini (2000) found more targeted spending in presidential systems in contrast to greater spending on public goods in parliamentary systems. A greater tendency for targeted spending could be generalized as a result of party organizational weakness. In turn, party weakness has been indicated as likely to result from the absence of formal hierarchy between the executive and legislature (Epstein 1967; Sartori 1994a, 1994b). The weakening of parties is likewise one of the features Gerring and Thacker (2004) say results in more corruption.

Most likely, these policy-output variables are related to interactions between the executive–legislative structure and the party system. In fact, as noted throughout this review, patterns of party competition are crucial to the extent to which the formal hierarchy of parliamentary interbranch relations is tempered with interparty transactions. Similarly, the formal interbranch transactions of presidentialism may give way to elements of informal hierarchy if the president is the head of a majority party or a coalition that controls the congressional agenda. In other cases, presidents may eschew coalitions altogether, resulting in a nearly anarchic pattern of inerbranch relations. The British model of parliamentarism and the US model of presidentialism are among the few systems that retain in practice the nearly pure form of, respectively, hierarchical and transactional relations inherent in the formal constitutional structure. In this context, it may be more meaningful for cross-national studies to look inside the regime type and consider what the locus of accountability in a system is, for accountability is closely related to patterns of policy output and to corruption (Samuels and Shugart 2003; Samuels 2004).

The statistical regression techniques that are most suited to uncovering cross-national variation in output and performance necessarily require collapsing complex reality into a small number of key values. This exigency makes it all the more critical that, in generating variables suitable for large-N analysis, the analyst ensures that the values chosen reflect the theoretically relevant variation across systems. As this chapter has argued, collapsing the notion of executive–legislative relations into two categories, presidential vs. parliamentary, possibly with a residual "hybrid" category, assumes away much of what is essential to understanding how the chain of democratic delegation and accountability is characterized by degrees of hierarchy and transaction. With the ongoing enterprise of cross-national statistical analysis of institutional variables, it may one day be possible to identify clusters of institutional variables that have clear effects on performance variables.

7 CONCLUSION

The study of constitutional structure is by now one of the most active sub-fields of comparative politics. Using a framework that has its roots in the *Federalist Papers*, we have seen that any system with an elected presidency creates an agent of the electorate with which the legislative assembly must transact, provided the constitution or political practice endows the presidency with bargaining leverage. This is a fundamentally different model of constitutional design from the parliamentary system, in which executive authority rests upon the consent of the legislative majority. This chapter has been an attempt to synthesize some of what we know about comparative executive–legislative relations, but before concluding, we should consider some of the high-priority areas in which we do not know much. Without attempting to be exhaustive, I would list the following as high-priority areas for near-term research agendas.

7.1 Origins of Systems of Executive–Legislative Relations

In Table 18.1, above, we saw that there is a marked geographic clustering of system types, with parliamentarism (and to a lesser extent, semi-presidentialism) dominating Western Europe, presidentialism the Americas, and semi-presidentialism the post-Communist countries. Nonetheless, beyond this simple fact, we know little about why this is the case, or what consequences it might have for these countries' policy-making processes and prospects for longer-term stable democracy. Historical trajectories and cultural affinities clearly play a role in constitutional choices, but how? And how do such deeper potential determinants of regime type complicate our ability to understand more precisely the interrelationships between institutional and performance variables?

Consider the following possibility. Systems of exclusive executive accountability to the assembly (including premier-presidentialism) may be adopted precisely where the conditions for well-organized parties of national scope already exist. If so, then systems that create greater separation of the executive from the legislature (including president-parliamentarism) may be more likely to be adopted precisely where those conditions are absent. See Shugart (1999), who further suggests that parliamentary cabinet accountability may be more conducive to public goods provision (as Persson, Roland, and Tabellini 2000 found), *except* where the party system is underdeveloped. With underdeveloped parties, Shugart (1999) suggests, the national accountability of presidents may increase public goods compared to a parliamentary (or premier-presidential) system in a similar context. These more complex notions of the relations among constitutional design, party systems, and policy provision remain untested in the cross-national statistical literature.

7.2 Variants of Semi-presidentialism

Above, I attempted to make the case for maintaining the distinction within the broader semi-presidential category between premier-presidential and president-parliamentary systems. Quite apart from the typological exercise, is the distinction meaningful? Does it capture something fundamental about the way different systems operate? Or is the broader category, semi-presidential, more useful? Or, would it make more sense to collapse the premier-presidential systems into the parliamentary category and the president-parliamentary within the broader category of presidential systems? These are ultimately empirical questions, but we need much richer case studies and comparative analyses of how presidents, prime ministers, and legislators relate to one another under different constitutional and other contexts before we can settle these questions. With the profusion of semi-presidential systems and the increasing accumulation of years of democracy under them, answering such questions is becoming more feasible.

7.3   Bureaucratic Oversight

There is now a vast literature on the American case that takes as its point of departure the challenges legislators have in attempting to ensure the faithful application of laws that must be implemented by executive agencies that they cannot directly control. Hardly any such literature exists for other presidential and semi-presidential systems. What are the implications of different constitutional authorities for the executive and of different party systems and forms of internal legislative organization for how (or if) bureaucracies are controlled? This is a high priority for future research.

The foregoing list of future questions is only a beginning. As reviewed in this chapter, there is now a vibrant sub-field of comparative executive–legislative relations and a rich empirical laboratory in which it can ply its trade. It is likely that the twenty-first century will see rapid progress in understanding this important aspect of democratic institutional design.

REFERENCES

AMORIM NETO, O. 2002. Presidential cabinets, electoral cycles, and coalition discipline in Brazil. In *Legislative Politics in Latin America*, ed. S. Morgenstern and B. Nacif. New York: Cambridge University Press.

—— Cox, G. W., and McCUBBINS, M. D. 2003. Agenda power in Brazil's Câmara dos Deputados, 1989 to 1998. *World Politics*, 55: 550–78.

BAGEHOT, W. 1867/1963. *The English Constitution.* London: Chapman and Hall.

BLONDEL, J. 1984. Dual leadership in the contemporary world: a step towards regime stability? In *Comparative Government and Politics: Essays in Honor of S.E. Finer*, ed. D. Kavanagh and G. Peele. Boulder, Colo.: Westview Press.

—— 1985. *Government Ministers in the Contemporary World.* London: Sage.

CHEIBUB, J. A., PRZEWORSKI, A. and SAIEGH, S. 2004. Government coalitions and legislative success under presidentialism and parliamentarism. *British Journal of Political Science*, 34 (4): 565–87.

Cox, G. W. 1987. *The Efficient Secret: The Cabinet and the Development of Political Parties in Victorian England.* Cambridge: Cambridge University Press.

—— and McCUBBINS, M. D. 1993. *Legislative Leviathan: Party Government in the House*, California Series on Social Choice and Political Economy, 23. Berkeley: University of California Press.

DÖRING, H. 1995a. Institutions and policies: why we need cross-national analysis. In *Parliaments and Majority Rule in Western Europe*, ed. H. Döring. Frankfurt: St. Martin's Press.

—— 1995b. Time as a scarce resource: government control of the agenda. In *Parliaments and Majority Rule in Western Europe*, ed. H. Döring. Frankfurt: St. Martin's Press.

DROOP, H. R. 1869. On the political and social effects of different methods of electing representatives. *Pamphlets on the History of England in the 19th Century*, 50: 1–39.

DUVERGER, M. 1980. A new political-system model: semi-presidential government. *European Journal of Political Research*, 8 (2): 165–87.

EPSTEIN, L. D. 1967. *Political Parties in Western Democracies.* New York: Praeger.

GEDDES, B. 1994. *Politician's Dilemma: Building State Capacity in Latin America.* Berkeley: University of California Press.

GERRING, J. and THACKER, S. 2004. Political institutions and corruption: the role of unitarism and parliamentarism. *British Journal of Political Science*, 34 (2): 295–330.

GROFMAN, B. and VAN ROOZENDAAL, P. 1997. Modeling cabinet durability and termination. *British Journal of Political Science*, 27: 419–51.

GROSECLOSE, T. and McCARTY, N. 2000. The politics of blame: bargaining before an audience. *American Journal of Political Science*, 45 (1): 100–19.

HALLERBERG, M. 2000. The role of parliamentary committees in the budgetary process within Europe. In *Institutions, Politics and Fiscal Policy*, ed. R. Strauch and J. Von Hagen. Dordrecht: Kluwer.

HAMILTON, A., MADISON, J., JAY, J., and FAIRFIELD, R. P. 1787/1937. *The Federalist Papers: A collection of essays written in support of the Constitution of the United States: from the original text of Alexander Hamilton, James Madison, John Jay.* New York: Random House.

HELLER, W. B. 2001. Making policy stick: why the government gets what it wants in multiparty parliaments. *American Journal of Political Science*, 45 (4): 780–98.

HUBER, J. D. 1996. The vote of confidence in parliamentary democracies. *American Political Science Review*, 90 (2): 269–82.

—— and POWELL, G. B., JR. 1994. Congruence between citizens and policymakers. *World Politics*, 46: 291–326.

KING, A. 1976. Models of executive–legislative relations: Great Britain, France, and West Germany. *Legislative Studies Quarterly*, 1 (1): 11–36.

LAVER, M. 1998. Models of government formation. *Annual Review of Political Science*, 1: 1–25.

—— 2003. Government termination. *Annual Review of Political Science*, 6: 23–40.

LIJPHART, A. 1984. *Democracies: Patterns of Majoritarian and Consensus Government in Twenty-one Countries.* New Haven, Conn.: Yale University Press.

—— (ed.) 1992. *Parliamentary versus Presidential Government.* Oxford: Oxford University Press.

364 MATTHEW SØBERG SHUGART

LIJPHART, A. 1999. *Patterns of Democracy: Government Forms and Performance in Thirty-six Countries.* New Haven, Conn.: Yale University Press.

LINZ, J. J. 1994. Presidential or parliamentary government: does it make a difference? In *The Failure of Presidential Democracy, Vol. 1: Comparative Perspectives,* ed. J. J. Linz and A. Valenzuela. Baltimore: Johns Hopkins University Press.

MCKENZIE, W. S. 1912. *The New Democracy and the Constitution.* London: John Murray.

MAINWARING, S. 1990. Presidentialism in Latin America. *Latin American Research Review,* 25: 157–79.

—— 1993. Presidentialism, multipartism, and democracy: the difficult combination. *Comparative Political Studies,* 26 (2): 198–228.

MARTIN, L. W. and STEVENSON, R. T. 2001. Government formation in parliamentary democracies. *American Journal of Political Science,* 45: 33–50.

MATTSON, I. and STRØM, K. 1995. Parliamentary committees. In *Parliaments and Majority Rule in Western Europe,* ed. H. Döring. Frankfurt: St Martin's Press.

MILL, J. S. 1862. *Considerations on Representative Government.* New York: Harper.

MOE, T. M. and CALDWELL, M. 1994. The institutional foundations of democratic government: a comparison of presidential and parliamentary systems. *Journal of Institutional and Theoretical Economics,* 150 (1): 171–95.

MOMMSEN, W. J. 1984. *Max Weber and German politics, 1890–1920,* trans. M. S. Steinberg. Chicago: University of Chicago Press.

MONTESQUIEU, C. DE SECONDAT 1768. *The Spirit of Laws,* 4th edn. 2 vols. Edinburgh: A. Donaldson.

MORGAN-JONES, E. and SCHLEITER, P. 2004. Governmental change in a president-parliamentary regime: the case of Russia 1994–2003. *Post-Soviet Affairs,* 20 (2): 132–63.

MÜLLER, W. C. 1999. Austria. In *Semi-Presidentialism in Europe,* ed. R. Elgie. Oxford: Oxford University Press.

NOBLE, G. W. 1999. Opportunity lost: partisan incentives and the 1997 constitutional revisions in Taiwan. *China Journal,* 41: 89–114.

PALMER, M. S. 1995. Toward an economics of comparative political organization: examining ministerial responsibility. *Journal of Law, Economics and Organization,* 11 (1): 164–88.

PERSSON, T., ROLAND, G., and TABELLINI, G. 2000. Comparative politics and public finance. *Journal of Political Economy,* 108: 1121–61.

—— and TABELLINI, G. 2003. *The Economic Effects of Constitutions.* Cambridge, Mass.: MIT Press.

POWELL, G. B. 1982. *Contemporary Democracies: Participation, Stability, and Violence.* Cambridge, Mass.: Harvard University Press.

—— 2000. *Elections as Instruments of Democracy: Majoritarian and Proportional Visions.* London: Yale University Press.

POWER, T. J., and GASIOROWSKI, M. J. 1994. Institutional and democratic consolidation in the Third World. *Comparative Political Studies,* 30 (2): 123–55.

PRZEWORSKI, A., ALVAREZ, M., CHEIBUB, J. A., and LIMONGI, F. 1996. What makes democracies endure? *Journal of Democracy,* 7 (1): 39–55.

REDSLOB, R. 1918. *Die parlamentarische Regierung in ihrer wahren und unechten Form: Eine vergleichende Studie über die Verfassungen von England, Belgien, Ungarn, Schweden und Frankreich* [The parliamentary government in its true and its false form—A comparative study on the constitutions of England, Belgium, France, Hungary, Sweden and France]. Tübingen: J. C. B. Mohr.

SAMUELS, D. 2004. Presidentialism and accountability for the economy in comparative perspective. *American Political Science Review*, 98: 425–36.

—— and SHUGART, M. S. 2003. Presidentialism, elections, and representation. *Journal of Theoretical Politics*, 15: 33–60.

SARTORI, G. 1994a. *Comparative Constitutional Engineering: An Inquiry into Structures, Incentives and Outcomes*. Basingstoke: Macmillan.

—— 1994b. Neither presidentialism nor parliamentarism. In *The Failure of Presidential Democracy, Vol. 1: Comparative Perspectives*, ed. J. J. Linz and A. Valenzuela. Baltimore: Johns Hopkins University Press.

SHUGART, M. S. 1996. Executive–legislative relations in post-Communist Europe. *Transition*, 13: 6–11.

—— 1999. Presidentialism, parliamentarism and the provision of collective goods in less-developed countries. *Constitutional Political Economy*, 10 (1): 53–88.

—— 2005. Semi-presidentialism: dual executive and mixed authority patterns. *French Politics*, 3 (3): 323–51.

—— and CAREY, J. M. 1992. *Presidents and Assemblies: Constitutional Design and Electoral Dynamics*. Cambridge: Cambridge University Press.

—— and HAGGARD, S. 2001. Institutions and public policy in presidential systems. In *Structure and Policy in Presidential Democracies*, ed. M. D. McCubbins and S. Haggard. New York: Cambridge University Press.

SIAROFF, A. 2003. Comparative presidencies: the inadequacy of the presidential, semi-presidential and parliamentary distinction. *European Journal of Political Research*, 42 (3): 287–312.

STEPAN, A. and SKACH, C. 1993. Constitutional frameworks and democratic consolidation: parliamentarianism vs. presidentialism. *World Politics*, 46 (1): 1–22.

STIRK, P. 2002. Hugo Preuss, German political thought and the Weimar Constitution. *History of Political Thought*, 23: 497–516.

STRØM, K. 1990. *Minority Government and Majority Rule*. Cambridge: Cambridge University Press.

—— 2000. Delegation and accountability in parliamentary democracies. *European Journal of Political Research*, 37: 261–89.

—— and SWINDLE, S. M. 2002. Strategic parliamentary dissolution. *American Political Science Review*, 96: 575–91.

WEBER, M. 1917/1978. Parliament and government in a reconstructed Germany. In *Economy and Society: An Outline of Interpretive Sociology*, vol. 3, ed. R. Guenther and C. Wittich. Berkeley: University of California Press.

WELDON, J. 1997. Political sources of presidencialismo in Mexico. In *Presidentialism and Democracy in Latin America*, ed. S. Mainwaring and M. S. Shugart. New York: Cambridge University Press.

CHAPTER 19

PUBLIC BUREAUCRACIES

DONALD F. KETTL

Although government's other institutions frame basic public policy, its bureaucracies have always been responsible for carrying it out. In fact, bureaucracy predates most of the institutions of modern democratic government. When Moses organized the tribes of Israel for their departure from Pharaoh's rule, he organized them into a simple bureaucracy as he sought to build them into a new nation. Millennia later, the Romans institutionalized a fighting force that terrified their enemies. The centurion commanded eighty men, which gathered into legions, and which led to the conquest of most of the known world. The locus of government action has long been in public bureaucracies. It is one thing for government officials to make decisions. It is quite another for them to carry out them out. Stalin famously mocked the Pope, sarcastically asking, "How many divisions does he have?" Government power is bureaucratic power, whether the bureaucracy is the military or another agency.

The term "bureaucracy" has deep roots. Its origin lies in the French word, *bureau*, at least as far back as the 1300s. The king's administrators brought their financial records to a special room, the Chamber of Accounts, and laid them out on brown woolen cloth, know as *la bure*. In time, they came to call the room the "bureau," and "bureaucracy" was born. Since then, bureaucracy has acquired a wide variety of meanings, some highly negative ("that's just so bureaucratic!"). More generally, however, "bureaucracy" refers to the complex organizations assigned to perform specific tasks. Its historical roots and most common usage apply to public bureaucracies. Bureaucracy, however, is a generic term, and private companies typically have bureaucracies as well. Understanding the reasons for bureaucracy's enduring use, the reasons why it sometimes has an unsavory reputation, and what steps reformers have taken to solve those problems provides a rich guide to government's inner workings.

The key lies in understanding three puzzles. First, bureaucratic actions are the locus of governmental power. What are the characteristics of bureaucracy that have made it an instrument so widely respected (and sometimes feared)? Second, much of the work of bureaucracy occurs through the coordination of complex activities. How does that coordination occur? Third, such power is important for democratic government, both to protect it from forces that seek to destroy it and to empower it to do what the people want done. But how can the bureaucracy be strong enough to do its work without becoming so strong that it threatens the very system it is supposed to support? Government, let alone modern twenty-first century government, is impossible without bureaucracies, but its very existence poses a fundamental dilemma that lies at the very heart of democracy.

1   POWER

The power of the state is only as strong as its ability to translate its ideas into actions. Most decisions, after all, are not self-executing. God might have said, "Let there be light," but no leader since has been able to make anything complicated happen simply by speaking it. Medieval kings knew they could not rule without armies to back them up. Without sufficient power, their serfs and vassals could rise up, their neighbors could invade, and their reigns would end. The first need of a state is security; security demands, at a minimum, defensive force; and such a force embodies power.

The power of the state, of course, stretches far beyond the military. Rulers must pay for the military, which demands that government have a system of taxes. People who are secure then aspire for more. They demand better roads, improved transportation, safe water, and protection from threats like crime and fire. They want richer lives through education and libraries. They seek a cleaner environment, good health care, and security in old age. They try to do good things for others, like providing safe homes for orphans and strategies for helping the poor escape poverty. Each of these ambitions, in turn, requires its own bureaucracy, from transportation and police departments to welfare and social security agencies. And those bureaucracies further increase government's power.

"Bureaucracy" often conveys a negative connotation; "bureaucratic" is a pejorative condemnation. All too often, the clumsy or unresponsive actions of bureaucracies give grounds for just such a negative image. But two things are important. First, throughout thousands of years, governments have yet to discover any better instrument that empowers them to do what they need to do. Government without powerful bureaucracies is no government at all (Goodsell 2004). Second, the pathologies of bureaucracy, of which there are many, are not solely the province of public bureaucracies. They apply to private bureaucracies as well, from large corporations to small-scale operations. They are inherent in the effort to organize groups of people to do hard, complex things.

Bureaucratic power is not simply a matter of the power of bureaucracies. It is also a matter of power within bureaucracies. In any complex job, the leader at the top cannot possibly prescribe the actions of everyone responsible for carrying it out. No military commander can possibly hope to dictate the actions of each fighting man and, in fact, any effort to do so would make it impossible for the commander to command with any sense of strategy. In a large organization, despite the vast potential of snooping technology like systems that track the keystrokes workers make on their keyboards, top officials can never control the actions of every worker in every cubicle. In many government organizations, like schools and police departments, front-line bureaucrats often work alone, without direct supervision. These "street-level bureaucrats," as Michael Lipsky (1980) has called them, exercise enormous power, because they carry the authority of the state but the state cannot directly oversee how they use that power.

The flow of power in a bureaucracy involves two related notions. First, because top decision-makers cannot possibly oversee everything, they must delegate power to lower-level officials. It is a paradox of bureaucratic power that top officials can acquire it only by giving it up, but attacking any complex problem demands that top-level officials trust those at lower-levels with the details. Second, in deciding how to deal with those details, individual bureaucrats have power because they have discretion in how they do their jobs. Police officers can choose whether or not to pull over a driver going 62 miles per hour in a 55 mph zone. Teachers can decide whether or not to send a child to the principal's office. Firefighters can decide whether they need to break windows or pull down walls to fight a blaze, and prison guards can determine if an inmate needs discipline for an offense behind bars. A major issue for managing bureaucracies, therefore, is ensuring compliance, with bureaucrats exercising their discretion in ways that are consistent with the organization's mission (Etzioni 1961; Gouldner 1967).

Public bureaucracies have power because they are the instruments of the policies of the state. Individual bureaucrats have power because they decide how those instruments are used. Indeed, the real meaning of "policy" comes only through bureaucratic action. Regardless of what top officials decide, their decisions have meaning only in how bureaucrats administer. Most drivers assume that they can safely violate the officially posted speed limit because they know that police officers are highly unlikely to stop them for driving slightly faster than the official limit. The "real" speed limit is determined by the enforcement decisions of the police.

Thus, to a powerful degree, bureaucratic power depends on decisions. Indeed, Herbert Simon (1976, 1; compare Barnard 1938) contended that "a theory of administration should be concerned with the processes of decision as well as with the processes of action." Simon argued:

The task of "deciding" pervades the entire administrative organization quite as much as does the task of "doing"—indeed, it is integrally tied up with the latter. A general theory of organization that will insure correct decision-making must include principles of organization that will include correct decision-making, just as it must include principles that will insure effective action.

Understanding—and controlling—those decisions depends on information. But that, in turn, helps identify bureaucratic pathologies. Formal theorists from within economics agreed that information is essential and that information asymmetries plague relationships within bureaucracies. They imagined bureaucracy as a series of contracts between principals (the higher-level official charged with responsibility for a policy) and agents (the lower-level official charged with carrying it out). Principals hire agents to do the bureaucracy's job; agents agree to do it in return for compensation. Such relationships cascade through bureaucracies, from top to bottom. They tend to produce two pathologies. First, principals need to pick good agents, but they can never know enough about the agent to make sure they have made the right choices. Theorists call this "adverse selection," and poorly chosen agents might not have the ability—or the inclination—to carry out a policy as the principal wants. Second, principals can never know enough about what the agent does to ensure that the agent carries out the terms of the contract. Theorists call this "moral hazard," and the problem makes it hard to provide adequate supervision: to detect and correct problems in getting the bureaucracy's work done (Coase 1937; Williamson 1975; Wood and Waterman 1991).

The task of making decisions, however, depends heavily on the bureaucrat's position within the bureaucracy.[1] As former US federal administrator Rufus Miles (1978) famously put it, "Where you stand depends on where you sit." Indeed, Michel Crozier's powerful analysis, *The Bureaucratic Phenomenon* (1964), concludes that bureaucratic institutions must be understood in terms of the cultural context within which they work. Within bureaucracies, officials at different

---

[1] More generally, there is a rich tradition within political science of treating "bureaucracy" as a political actor, and as an institution composed of political actors. In addition to Wilson 1989, see Allison 1969, 1971; Derthick 1972; Halperin 1974; Pressman and Wildavsky 1974; Bardach 1977; and Hogwood and Peters 1985. There is also an emerging tradition that traces the roots of bureaucratic behavior to its historical development. See, in particular, Skowronek 1982; Carpenter 2001; and Orren and Skowronek 2004.

levels tend to have different cultures: they think differently, they process information differently, they decide differently. At top levels, James Q. Wilson found (1989), operators work at the front lines on the organization's basic tasks. Managers work in the middle to organize resources, while executives manage the organization's external relations, including political support. The fact that officials at different levels of the organization focus on different kinds of problems also means that some information gets filtered out as it moves up the chain of command. Investigators of the space shuttle Challenger accident in 1986, for example, found that warnings about the risk of launching the shuttle in cold weather, which prevented rubber seals from containing the flow of super-hot gases, were blocked by managers and never reached the programme's executives. That information pathology led to the destruction of the shuttle and a searching examination of the flaws in NASA's culture, which helped lead to the accident (see Vaughn 1997; Khademian 2002).[2] Bureaucracies thus need to be understood as collections of individual workers; as groups of people with shared identity; and as collective actors that, in turn, interact with other organizations (Blau and Scott 1962).

Thus, public bureaucracies have power because they are the instruments of state power. Individual bureaucrats have power because they have discretion over how to exercise those instruments of power. Bureaucracy can therefore be understood as a system of cascading decisions, plagued by problems of information. Empowering and controlling bureaucracies is a problem of managing those decisions and the information about them.

2   COORDINATION

Performing complex jobs requires a high degree of coordination—the ability to link related tasks efficiently and effectively into concerted action. In the silent film era, the "Keystone Cops" popularized a vision of what coordination does not look like—uniformed officers dizzily scurrying in all directions, getting in each other's way and providing more comedy than action. On the other hand, the work of firefighters when they arrive on the scene of a blaze is a carefully choreographed ballet, with each firefighter assigned a specific task, from searching for possible victims to coupling hoses. Coordination is a twin-headed task: making sure that what needs to get done is done (that no problem slips through the cracks) and

---

[2] For a more general and comparative approach to bureaucratic culture, see Hofstede 1997.

ensuring that this is done efficiently (that the bureaucracy does not waste resources in having different people doing the same thing).

There are several approaches to coordination within organizations, as sociologist Max Weber pointed out (Gerth and Mills 1958; Weber 1964). Charismatic leaders can inspire their followers to act, but that works only as long as does the charismatic leader and it works poorly for complex problems. Indeed, the New Testament records that the disciples of Jesus, soon after he ascended into heaven, faced the dilemma of how to carry on the work. Without the charismatic leadership of Jesus, they decided they needed a more formal structure. A second option is tradition, but tradition works poorly in incorporating new people into the organization (since new members need to learn the age-old rules of the game) and for new problems (since old ways often fail to solve new puzzles). A third option is bureaucracy. Though it has legions of detractors, no better lasting alternative has ever emerged.

Bureaucracies, Weber explains, tend to have basic characteristics, which he calls the "ideal types" (not in the sense of "best" but, rather, "typical"):

- A mission defined by top officials.
- Fixed jurisdictions within the organization, with the scope of work defined by rules.
- Authority graded from top to bottom, with higher-level officials having more authority than those at the bottom.
- Management by written documents, which create an institutional record of work.
- Management by career experts, who embody the organization's capacity to do work.
- Management by rules, which govern the discretion exercised by administrators.

At the core, bureaucracies tend to be characterized by layers of workers structured hierarchically, with supervision through authority. The structure follows the tasks to be completed. Top officials decide how to allocate the work down the chain of command (hence the term "command structure"). Higher-level officials supervise lower-level workers. Work is understood as a contract: the worker's agreement to accept the higher-level official's authority and director over work in exchange for compensation.

This approach to hierarchical authority promotes coordination. Supervisors can assess the work to be done. They can organize the bureaucracy according to the work, fill each position with individuals best trained for each task, and issue orders as needed to ensure the work is done. Bureaucracies exist to perform complex tasks; hierarchical authority makes that possible by providing the mechanism for coordination. Bureaucracies can be "tall," with many layers, or "flat," with relatively little distance from top to bottom. Officials can supervise a relatively large number of workers (what is called the "span of control") or relatively few. They can use their authority like an iron fist or grant subordinates wide discretion. There is nothing in the nature of bureaucracy itself that dictates these things. It is, quite simply, a method that seeks to organize people efficiently, to perform complex actions in a coordinated way.

Public bureaucracies have these characteristics, plus several others (Seidman 1998). Indeed, Wallace Sayre (1958, 245) once commented that "business and public administration are alike only in all unimportant respects." First, unlike private bureaucracies, in which top officials can define their own missions (which cars to build, for example, or which movies to make), top officials in public bureaucracies have their missions defined by elected policy-makers. Second, not only must public administrators do what the law says; they can do only what the law says. For example, public administrators cannot spend money in any way not specified in appropriations or provide any service not authorized in law. That is why the federal government faces periodic shutdown crises: if the authority to spend money expires, all but essential government employees must turn out the lights and go home. Third, public administrators tend to work under civil service rules, which grew out of an effort in the late nineteenth century to eliminate political patronage in the hiring of public employees. By law, public administrators are supposed to demonstrate neutral competence: efficient administration of the law, without regard to political favoritism. Finally, public administrators must pay great attention to the standards by which they do their work. Laws require equal treatment and forbid discrimination. There are standards for financial record keeping and due process.

Not all coordination is formal or hierarchical, as Charles E. Lindblom contended (1959, 1977; Dahl and Lindblom 1953). In his famous argument about incrementalism, Lindblom contended that partisan mutual adjustment, a bargaining process among players in a system, can produce efficient outcomes without subjecting the system to the high costs and difficulty of trying to align everyone's behavior through central direction. Just as pluralism was becoming the dominant model for understanding how competing political forces bargain out their differences, Lindblom applied the same approach to decision-making within organizations and, in the process, introduced an important challenge to orthodox bureaucracy. Instead of an approach in which authority and formal structure dominated, Lindblom explained how bargaining and informal relationships could edge out orthodoxy and, he claimed, produce decisions that were both more efficient and more responsive to the wishes of the public.

All of these issues, of course, go to the heart of the role of bureaucracy in a democracy. But they also help reinforce the sometime sense of "bureaucracy" as a dirty word. The bureaucratic form of organization carries with it several well-known pathologies. Organizational rules can create powerful incentives to follow them for their own sake—a phenomenon that became known as "red tape" after the red ribbons once used to tie up the box of official papers presented to the king (Kaufman 1977). (In the United States, similar red ribbons were used to tie up the records of Civil War veterans, and "cutting the red tape" was an effort to shortcut the rules in making required payments to them.) An emphasis on procedures can limit an organization's responsiveness to those it is supposed to serve. The exercise of authority can make it difficult for workers to use their professional judgment in dealing with problems that might not fit the standard rubric. Once set, organizational structure can be hard to change.

All in all, bureaucratic pathologies are numerous and serious. And they echo Winston Churchill's famous comment, "Democracy is the worst form of government except for all those others that have been tried." For thousands of years, people have chafed under the burdens of "bureaucracy," and for thousands of years, reformers have sought alternatives. The bureaucratic form of organization has endured because society has yet to discover anything that works better in coordinating complex action.

As both the ambitions and the tools of government became more complex, government came to rely more on networks of service providers, involving both different levels of government and partners outside government, in non-governmental organizations and private contractors (Goldsmith and Eggers 2004). In the United Kingdom, the government embraced the "joined-up government" initiative, focused on improving the coordination of services across government agencies. Australia adopted a "whole-of-government" approach, while some American governments pursued a "no-wrong-door" strategy (in which managers used information technology to help people solve their problems, however they entered government's domain, instead of sending them to a series of offices by claiming that other agencies were responsible for solving the problem) (see 6, P. et al. 2002). Coordination rose to a puzzle of far greater importance, as fewer government agencies could fully control the organizational resources they needed to meet their mission—and as the search for effective administration demanded stronger, more effective partnerships for service delivery. Indeed, one of the most important budding challenges of twenty-first-century bureaucracy is adapting traditional hierarchical bureaucracy to manage such multiorganizational networks.

3   Accountability

Bureaucracy is a generic form of organization, not one limited to the public sector. (Public utilities and cellular phone companies are typically private organizations, and grievances about their bureaucracies rival the worst complaints about public organizations.) Public bureaucracies must solve an additional problem. Their task is not only to perform the work for which they were created. In a democracy, they must do so in a way that is accountable to elected policy-makers and, ultimately, to the people who elect them. The challenge is empowering them enough to do their jobs while restraining their power to prevent abuse (Albrow 1970; Behn 2001).

There are several approaches to accountability. One is based on Weber's rational-legal approach to bureaucratic power. Elected officials delegate power to bureaucrats. Bureaucrats have only the power delegated to them, through the chain of command. Thus, the nature of the law and the structure of the bureaucracy shape bureaucratic accountability.

A second approach views democracy and efficiency as conflicting values (Okun 1975). Governments often seek broad discussion and debate to frame policy. They seek streamlined and efficient administration of that policy. The steps taken to maximize participation can often hinder efficiency, and vice versa. In this approach, accountability is a problem of balancing the two important but conflicting goals.

A third approach pursues a market-based strategy, built on the principal–agent model described above. Administrators have important resources that policy-makers need, including information about their programs and the capacity to act. Policy-makers have resources, including authority, money, and support, that administrators need if they are to do their job. Accountability, in this approach, is seen as an exchange relationship, in which each side bargains its needs and resources with the other.

These multiple approaches underline an important feature of accountability. Everyone wants it, and everyone thinks they know what they want. Getting agreement on what accountability is and how it ought to work, however, is often deceptively difficult. The fragmentation of bureaucracy tends to aggravate this problem, moreover. "Bureaucracy," after all, is not just one entity but many, each with its own and often conflicting jurisdictions and missions. There are multiple layers within each bureaucracy and external control agencies, including budget and personnel offices, exercise leverage over elements of bureaucratic action. The central imperative of public bureaucracy is that its substantial power must remain under the control of policy-makers. Determining how best to do so, however, is fraught with complexity and contradiction.

4   Challenges

That frames the fundamental dilemma of public bureaucracies: being powerful enough to do the job (for who would want to waste money on a bureaucracy that did not perform?) yet not so powerful as to threaten the sovereignty of elected officials (for who in a democracy would want to surrender their autonomy to overbearing bureaucrats?). This is certainly not a new problem, of course. Medieval serfs put up with overbearing nobles because they protected them when marauders raided, and the Roman Emperor Caligula was killed by his own Praetorian guard because they did not like where he was taking the empire. As government has grown larger and more complex, keeping powerful bureaucracy at heel has become even more important—and difficult.

For modern public bureaucracies, however, new challenges have grown atop the traditional ones. Bureaucracies tend to be best at routine matters, such as dispatching emergency workers to accident scenes and processing tax returns. After all, the building blocks of bureaucracy are building capacity and devising standard routines to manage complex but predictable problems. They tend to be far less effective on problems that fall outside of the normal routine, and modern society offers a host of such issues, from homeland security to environmental management. Bureaucracies remain the core of government action. They are the repositories of expertise, but equipping them to deal flexibly with new and rapidly evolving policy problems is a major issue.

So, too, is the challenge of managing the complex collection of organizations— public, private, and nonprofit—on which government increasingly relies for implementing public services. Much public administration occurs through contracts with for-profit and nonprofit organizations, grants to other governments and nonprofit organizations, regulations, special tax preferences, loan programs, and other indirect tools of government action (Salamon with Elliott, 2002). Managing these tools sometimes is harder than managing directly administered government programs but, more important, managing them is different. Government cannot rely on authority and hierarchy to manage programs outside the bureaucracy. Instead, public administrators must rely on a host of other tools, from negotiated contracts to incentives. This in turn offers skills that are often in short supply, as NASA discovered in managing its space shuttle program and the US Department of Defense found in many weapons procurement projects. As a result, programs administered through such indirect tools have often developed serious problems.

These puzzles have, in turn, led to a new approach to bureaucracy, founded on interorganizational networks instead of hierarchies. It is an approach that focuses primarily on the relationships between organizations instead of within them. As Stephen Goldsmith and William D. Eggers (2004, 7) argue:

The traditional hierarchical model of government simply does not meet the demands of this complex, rapidly changing age. Rigid bureaucratic systems that operate with command-and-control procedures, narrow work restrictions, and inward-looking cultures and operational models are particularly ill-suited to addressing problems that often transcend organizational boundaries.

Instead, as Lester Salamon puts it, "a dense mosaic" of policy approaches, full of "complex, interdependent relationships with a host of third-party providers," increasingly characterizes much government action (Salamon 2002, 3). In fact, the federal government spends very little of its money on programs its bureaucrats directly administer. Federal administrators manage air traffic control, airline security, and the national parks, and they pay out entitlements. For most government programs that remain, contracts, grants, and other programs account for most activity. Networked forms of action account for a great deal of state and local government administration as well. The administration of a substantial part of government activity therefore requires finding leverage over government's network of partners instead of directly managing the programs. That, in turn, increasingly requires the development of new capacity for network management.

At the same time, however, public bureaucracy has keenly felt citizen pressure for a smaller, more responsive, higher-performing government. As the locus for much of government's action, and as the center for most government employment, the taxpayer revolts that have rolled through government since the late 1970s have put public bureaucracy under increasing pressure. "Doing more with less" has been the watchword, often with substantially fewer government employees and fewer rewards (like pay increases) with which to reward good performance. Indeed, the impulse for government reform has often focused squarely on bureaucratic behavior.

5   THE IMPULSE FOR REFORM

Americans had periodically reformed their bureaucracies for more than a century, in a series of changes that Paul Light (1997) has called the "tides of reform." By the 1980s and 1990s, reform had become a truly global phenomenon. Governments everywhere, of widely different sizes, faced remarkably similar complaints from their citizens about government's size and ineffectiveness, and those complaints launched a global revolution in public management reform (Kettl 2005). The puzzle: how to make government smaller, more effective, and more responsive. The diagnosis centered on the pathologies of bureaucracy. The solutions varied widely.

5.1   The New Public Management

The major initiative was a movement, first launched in New Zealand and quickly followed in the United Kingdom, called "the new public management." Reformers complained that the traditional bureaucratic approach rendered public organizations unresponsive to citizens and wasteful of public money. The problem, they contended, was that these bureaucracies became locked into their own internal games and had no incentive to improve. In contrast, markets created strong incentives for efficiency and responsiveness. Organizations that successfully competed in the market grew and prospered; those that did not failed and folded. The reformers drew heavily on the path-breaking article by Ronald Coase (1937), writings by Oliver Williamson (1975), and the theories developed by the Chicago School of economics. (Their reliance on that work was clear and direct—public officials in New Zealand's capital, Wellington, could be heard quoting from the writings of relatively abstract economists.) That work argued that the relationships between principals and agents structured the key relationships in public bureaucracies, that government bureaucracies tended to stumble into the worst pathologies affecting the principal–agent relationship, and that by inserting market-like incentives into that relationship government could vastly improve its performance.

They began by arguing government should shed as many functions as it could to the private sector. New Zealand and the United Kingdom sold off large state-owned enterprises, including telephone, oil, insurance, post office, and airline companies. In New Zealand, the government sold off more than twenty state-owned companies. More fundamentally, the government came to view all activities as market transactions. It owned the service, and its goal was to provide the maximum return for taxpayers.

To do so, the New Zealanders aggressively pursued several reforms. One was strategic planning. The government defined its basic goals and constructed its budget to finance them. In addition, New Zealand was the world's first nation to adopt accrual accounting, which required the government to account for the full cost of a program when it was created. (In the American system—and in the system of most governments—the budget accounts for the annual cost of the program. That often creates a strong incentive for making short-term investments now that carry large long-term—but unbudgeted—costs that cause serious problems in future budgets.)

Another feature was transparency, based on a separation of the purchase and production functions. The government set policy by deciding what ought to be done. It would then rely on whoever could do the job most effectively and cheaply, whether within the government or on the outside. Unlike the American privatization movement, there was no presumption that private production was better. The goal was to give the job to whoever could do it best. For government-produced services, the government hired chief executives with fixed-term contracts and performance incentives. They had broad authority and flexibility in producing the programs. The government then negotiated production contracts with the suppliers, including with government agencies and their chief executives. The contracts specified outputs—from the miles of roadway to be built or the number of individuals to receive job training—and held the chief executive responsible for delivering those outputs.

In short, the reformers tried to draw a sharp line between policy-making and policy administration. Elected officials remained responsible for policy-making; the reformers sought to replace traditional authority-driven government bureaucracy with market-driven competition. Their goal was to shrink the size of government and improve the way it worked. The ultimate measure of accountability became results.

The New Zealand reforms sparked a global revolution that swept through the United Kingdom, Australia, Canada, and other nations to a lesser degree. It generated an enormous and wide-ranging debate (Aucoin 1996; Barzelay 2001; Boston, Martin, Pallot, and Walsh 1996; Hood 1984, 1998; Kettl 2005). Reformers around the world hailed the approach as an imaginative and innovative strategy to improve the performance of government and to excise the pathologies of government bureaucracy. The strategy had dual power, in part because of the long intellectual tradition from which it grew and in part because it offered commonsense solutions to the problems of bureaucracy that nagged many governments. The reforms predictably did not solve all of bureaucracy's problems. Creating and sustaining markets proved difficult. So was measuring outputs. Moreover, output measures—the activity surrounding government programs—did not address the more important political issue—what impact these programs had. Over time, the reforms moved more toward the assessment of impacts, but the deeper they got into these issues, the more difficult the problems became (Schick 1996).

Finally, the reforms could not resolve the core political issues that inevitably surround the delivery of services. The effort to separate policy from administration could not remove the political implications from administrative acts. Government bureaucracies inevitably deal with issues that are intricately interconnected with the politics of government. Nevertheless, the reforms—especially their strong emphasis on measuring results—had an enormous impact on government bureaucracies around the world (Pollitt 1990; Pollitt and Bouckaert 2000).

5.2 American Reform

The United States launched its own government reform movement, but the movement came fifteen years later than in New Zealand and it followed a very different strategy. Americans, of course, had long had a strong instinct for reform. But in 1993, following Bill Clinton's narrow victory over the senior George Bush, the Clinton administration launched a broad reform effort. Clearly worried by the strong third-party candidacy of H. Ross Perot, who won 19 percent of the electoral vote by arguing big deficits and poor performance were plaguing American government, Clinton decided to launch a broad initiative to address Perot's critique—and to reduce the chances Perot's effort might grow and undermine Clinton's campaign for a second term. He seized on a strategy outlined by David Osborne and Ted Gaebler (1992), an author and a city manager, to "reinvent government." He then put Vice President Al Gore in charge of the project and Gore, in turn, put hundreds of federal employees to work on a six-month effort to develop money-saving ideas throughout government. Their report listed 384 recommendations, promised $108 billion in savings, and pledged to shrink the federal workforce by 12 percent within five years. Gore promised (1993) nothing less than "creating a government that works better and costs less" (compare Kettl 1998).

On the "works better" side, Gore developed tactics for sweeping away barriers that, he said, prevented government employees from doing their jobs effectively. He made the case for eliminating obsolete structures, ancient processes, and poor leadership, while replacing them with employees empowered with the authority to do their jobs as their experience told them was the best approach. The plan was to replace top-down, rule-driven government with a bottom-up, customer-driven approach to service delivery. On the "costs less" side, Gore proposed to eliminate obsolete programs, trim extra layers of management and make the bureaucracy flatter, and reduce the number of government employees.

The reinventing government effort, however, quickly ran afoul of the Republicans own effort, the "Contract with America," which sought a far smaller and more privatized government. Gore quickly had to push back the "works better" initiatives to concentrate on the "costs less" side, especially the reduction in government employment, which the administration ratcheted up to 273,000 employees. There was little strategic thinking behind the downsizing. The reductions left some agencies with a serious mismatch between the skills of employees and the requirements of agency missions. But although the downsizing was haphazard, the administration did indeed hit its target, through an aggressive program of early retirement bonuses.

Gore became closely identified with the effort, but he got little political credit for it. He barely mentioned "reinventing government" during his failed 2000 presidential campaign. Nevertheless, the Clinton administration did indeed leave behind a smaller government, at least when measured by the number of government employees, as well as significant improvements in electronic government and procurement. Despite its political roots, however, the reinvention campaign produced little political impact.

Soon after he became president, however, George W. Bush launched his own five-point management improvement initiative. He sought to improve the strategic management of human capital, the capacity of government employees to do their jobs; to increase the contracting out of public services; to improve financial management; to expand electronic government; and to integrate performance measures for government programs into budget decisions. Like the New Zealand reforms, the effort had a heavy results-based flavor and sought to couple the measurement of results with budgetary decisions. But Bush pushed the USA past the New Zealand reforms by focusing squarely on outcomes, the impact that government programs had. On one level, these were the questions that drove politics. If teachers teach, do children learn? If job training programs educate workers, do they acquire useful long-term skills that help them get and keep good jobs? Of course, measuring outcomes proved extraordinarily difficult. Getting policy-makers to pay attention to the measures was a challenge as well. But introducing the measurement of results into the process proved a significant accomplishment of the Bush administration. And it underlined the broader theme of government reform around the world: the central role that measurement of results has come to play in the effort to improve the functioning of public bureaucracies.

6   CONCLUSION

Public bureaucracy is thus the focus of enduring paradoxes. "Bureaucratic" suggests behavior everyone hates, yet bureaucracy is an inescapable part of government. Without it, little of what we value in government would be possible. Bureaucracy is thus a major center of government power, but critics constantly seek to restrain that power. Bureaucracy is structured to maximize its ability to perform routine tasks, yet more of its work occurs through indirect tools and networks that challenge bureaucracy's basic function and structure. No part of government has seen as much fundamental reform over the last generation, yet despite all the changes the core features of bureaucracy have proved surprisingly enduring.

Some of this is because of bureaucracy's central position in government. As both symbol and instrument of government power, the fundamental conflicts over what government is and what it ought to do become stuck to it. Some of this is because what citizens expect from government—and how much they are willing to pay to get it—is in the midst of a fundamental reassessment, and bureaucracy is caught in the crossfire. Bureaucracy is an enduring part of government because there can be no effective government without it. Its place within democratic government is inevitably full of contradictions because of the way citizens view government.

On one hand, bureaucracy is one element of government that, it can be said with certainty, will endure through the ages, just as it always has. On the other hand, efforts to change and reform bureaucracy will endure, just as certainly, because of the inherent conflicts it embodies. Thus, the paradox of permanence and change is the defining reality of public bureaucracy.

The paradox revolves around bureaucracy's central questions: empowering bureaucracy enough to be effective without making bureaucracy so powerful as to threaten democratic rule; using hierarchy to coordinate programs without making bureaucracy inflexible; and securing accountability of bureaucracy to elected officials (and ultimately to the public) without rendering it incapable of effective action. The long tradition of theory about public bureaucracies has sought to manage these paradoxes by drawing boundaries: boundaries that constrain power, promote coordination, and seek accountability. But the inescapable reality of twenty-first-century government is that the very boundaries that have been created over time to manage the paradoxes have, in turn, often crippled government in addressing the most important public policy issues. For example, in addressing the tough puzzles surrounding the 2001 anthrax attacks in the United States, the Centers for Disease Control's Julie Gerberding found that her bureaucracy hindered, not helped her effort to devise an effective response. In case after case, from the outbreak of anthrax to SARS to monkey pox, Gerberding discovered that she needed to devise new organizational strategies to deal with inescapable problems. Indeed, she found a "global-to-local and local-to-global connectivity" that "truly exemplifies the 'small world',", one where the old boundaries often did not fit (2005, 2).

For both international organizations and developing countries, these issues are especially sharp. Developing countries are struggling to accelerate their pace of economic transformation, so they can satisfy the aspirations of their citizens. Doing so, however, requires the creation of strong private markets and robust public bureaucracies to regulate and control them. Trying to fuel development without first building adequate public institutions, or trying to wring out corruption without creating the preconditions for effective administrative performance, can lead to enormous problems, Allen Schick (1998) persuasively argues. For international organizations like the World Bank and International Monetary Fund, which are seeking to support the growth of developing nations, the challenge is doubled. They not only have to find ways of solving this dilemma, but they also have to reform their own operations to meet the challenges of a rapidly evolving world economy. Otherwise, they risk increasing the already large gap between the world's richer and poorer nations.

The management of public programs increasingly spills beyond public bureaucracies, a phenomenon that students of bureaucracy have come to call "governance" (Pierre and Peters 2000; Peters 2001; Kettl 2002). As was the case with Gerberding's puzzles, many of the most important problems that government faces—and, indeed, many of the strategies government follows in attacking many programs—spill over the boundaries of the government bureaucracies created to manage them. Where the problems strain the boundaries, they also strain the theories created to guide the hands of bureaucrats. Network approaches to government have arisen to manage these tough, boundary-spanning problems. But these approaches have grown faster than the theories to guide them. The theories of government bureaucracy find themselves challenged to devise new arguments to guide and control bureaucracy. Problems ranging from terrorism to health care demand government's best efforts. Governments are struggling with empowering bureaucracies enough to attack these tough problems while avoiding the trap of making them so powerful as to challenge democratic rule.

Moreover, as the reform movements that have bubbled constantly since the 1980s have shown, both practitioners and theorists of bureaucracy have struggled to devise new approaches to governance. Some, like the "new public management," have been top-down. Others, like "reinventing government," have been bottom-up. None have proven to be fully satisfactory, but that has only fueled the reformers' inventiveness. The rich tradition of hierarchical bureaucracy provides a strong foundation for governance. However, the problems facing governments increasingly strain its precepts. That leaves practitioners and theorists alike with the twin task of safeguarding its basic principles while experimenting with new approaches, which might perhaps better fit society's tough problems but which pose new challenges to the ageless puzzles of bureaucratic power, coordination, and accountability.

REFERENCES

6, P. LEAT, D., SELTZER, K., and STOKER, G. 2002. *Toward Holistic Government: The New Reform Agenda*. Houndmills: Palgrave.

ALBROW, M. 1970. *Bureaucracy*. New York: Praeger.

ALLISON, G. T. 1969. Conceptual models and the Cuban missile crisis. *American Political Science Review*, 63: 689–718.

—— 1971. *Essence of Decision: Explaining the Cuban Missile Crisis*. Boston: Little, Brown.

AUCOIN, P. 1996. *The New Public Management: Canada in Comparative Perspective*. Montreal: Institute for Research on Public Policy.

BARDACH, E. 1977. *The Implementation Game*. Cambridge, Mass.: MIT Press.

BARNARD, C. I. 1938. *The Functions of the Executive*. Cambridge, Mass.: Harvard University Press.

BARZELAY, M. 2001. *The New Public Management*. Berkeley: University of California Press.

BEHN, R. D. 2001. *Rethinking Democratic Accountability*. Washington, DC: Brookings Institution Press.

BLAU, P. M. and SCOTT, W. R. 1962. *Formal Organizations: A Comparative Approach*. San Francisco: Chandler.

BOSTON, J., MARTIN, J., PALLOT, J., WALSH, P. 1996. *Public Management: The New Zealand Model*. Auckland: Oxford University Press.

CARPENTER, D. P. 2001. *The Forging of Bureaucratic Autonomy: Reputations, Networks, and Policy Innovation in Executive Agencies, 1862–1928*. Princeton, NJ: Princeton University Press.

COASE, R. H. 1937. The nature of the firm. *Economica*, 4: 386–405.

CROZIER, M. 1964. *The Bureaucratic Phenomenon*. Chicago: University of Chicago Press.

DAHL, R. A. and LINDBLOM, C. E. 1953. *Politics, Economics, and Welfare: Planning and Politico-Economic Systems Resolved into Basic Social Processes*. New York: Harper.

DERTHICK, M. 1972. *New Towns In-Town*. Washington, DC: Urban Institute.

ETZIONI, A. 1961. *A Comparative Analysis of Complex Organizations*. Glencoe, Ill.: Free Press.

GERBERDING, J. 2005. *Protecting the Public's Health with Small World Connections: The 2004 James E. Webb Lecture*. Washington, DC: National Academy of Public Administration.

GERTH, H. W. and MILLS, C. W. (trans. and eds.) 1958. *From Max Weber: Essays in Sociology*. New York: Oxford University Press.

GOLDSMITH, S. and EGGERS, W. E. 2004. *Governing by Network: The New Shape of the Public Sector*. Washington, DC: Brookings Institution Press.

GOODSELL, C. T. 2004. *The Case for Bureaucracy: A Public Administration Polemic*, 4th edn. Washington, DC: CQ Press.

GORE, A. 1993. *From Red Tape to Results: Creating a Government that Works Better and Costs Less*. Washington, DC: GPO.

GOULDNER, A. W. 1967. Cosmopolitan locals: toward an analysis of latent social roles. *Administrative Science Quarterly*, 2: 281–306.

HALPERIN, M. H. 1974. *Bureaucratic and Foreign Policy*. Washington: Brookings Institution Press.

HOFSTEDE, G. H. 1997. *Cultures and Organizations: Software of the Mind*. New York: McGraw-Hill.

HOGWOOD, B. W. and PETERS, B. G. 1985. *The Pathology of Public Policy*. Oxford: Clarendon Press.

HOOD, C. 1984. *The Tools of Government*. Chatham, NJ: Chatham House.

—— 1998. *The Art of the State: Culture, Rhetoric, and Public Management*. Oxford: Clarendon Press.

KAUFMAN, H. 1977. *Red Tape: Its Origins, Uses, and Abuses*. Washington, DC: Brookings Institution.

KETTL, D. F. 1998. *Reinventing Government: A Fifth Year Report Card*. Washington, DC: Brookings Institution.

—— 2002. *The Transformation of Governance: Public Administration for the 21st Century*. Baltimore: Johns Hopkins University Press.

—— 2005. *The Global Public Management Revolution*, 2nd edn. Washington, DC: Brookings Institution Press.

KHADEMIAN, A. M. 1997. *Working with Culture: How the Job Gets Done in Public Programs*. Washington, DC: CQ Press.

LIGHT, P. C. 1997. *Tides of Reform: Making Government Work, 1945–1995*. New Haven, Conn.: Yale University Press.

LINDBLOM, C. E. 1959. The science of "muddling through." *Public Administration Review*, 19: 79–88.

LIPSKY, M. 1980. *Street-Level Bureaucrats: Dilemmas of the Individual in Public Services*. New York: Russell Sage Foundation.

MILES, R. E. 1978. The origin and meaning of Miles' law. *Public Administration Review*, 38: 399–403.

OKUN, A. 1974. *Equality and Efficiency: The Big Tradeoff.* Washington, DC: Brookings Institution.

ORREN, K. and SKOWRONEK, S. 2004. *The Search for American Political Development.* New York: Cambridge University Press.

OSBORNE, D. and GAEBLER, T. 1992. *Reinventing Government: How the Entrepreneurial Spirit is Transforming the Public Sector.* Reading, Mass.: Addison-Wesley.

PETERS, B. G. 2001. *The Future of Governing*, 2nd edn. Lawrence: University Press of Kansas.

PIERRE, J. and PETERS, B. G. 2000. *Governance, Politics, and the State.* New York: St. Martin's Press.

POLLITT, C. 1990. *Managerialism in the Public Sector.* Oxford: Basil Blackwell.

—— and BOUCKAERT, G. 2000. *Public Management Reform: A Comparative Analysis.* Oxford: Oxford University Press.

PRESSMAN, J. L. and WILDAVSKY, A. 1973. *Implementation.* Berkeley: University of California Press.

SALAMON, L. M. with O. V. ELLIOTT (eds.) 2002. *The Tools of Government: A Guide to the New Governance.* New York: Oxford University Press.

SAYRE, W. 1958. The unhappy bureaucrats: views ironic, helpful, indignant. *Public Administration Review*, 10: 239–45.

SCHICK, A. 1996. *The Spirit of Reform: Managing the New Zealand State Sector in a Time of Change.* Wellington: New Zealand State Services Commission and the Treasury.

—— 1998. Why most developing countries should not try New Zealand reforms. *World Bank Research Observer*, 13: 123–31.

SEIDMAN, H. 1998. *Politics, Position, and Power: The Dynamics of Federal Organization*, 5th edn. New York: Oxford University Press.

SIMON, H. A. 1976. *Administrative Behavior: A Study of Decision-Making Processes in Administrative Organization*, 3rd edn. New York: Free Press.

SKOWRONEK, S. 1982. *Building a New American State: The Expansion of National Administrative Capacities, 1877–1920.* New York: Cambridge University Press.

VAUGHN, D. 1997. *The Challenger Launch Decision: Risky Technology, Culture, and Deviance at NASA.* Chicago: University of Chicago Press.

WILLIAMSON, O. E. 1975. *Markets and Hierarchies: Analysis and Antitrust Implications.* New York: Free Press.

WILSON, J. Q. 1989. *Bureaucracy: What Government Agencies Do and Why They Do It.* New York: Basic Books.

WOOD, B. D. and WATERMAN, R. W. 1991. The dynamics of political control of the bureaucracy. *American Political Science Review*, 85: 801–28.

CHAPTER 20

THE WELFARE STATE

JACOB S. HACKER

In the last two decades, students of public affairs have taken an increasingly keen interest in the welfare state—the complex of policies that, in one form or other, all rich democracies have adopted to ameliorate destitution and provide valued social goods and services. Leading scholarly journals are awash with analyses of social welfare policy, and a number of books and articles on the topic now stand as modern classics (notably, Cameron 1978; Esping-Andersen 1990; Heclo 1974; Skocpol 1992). Contemplating this non-stop rush of academic commentary, one prominent social policy expert (Taylor-Gooby 1991, xi) invoked the lament of Ecclesiastes: "Of making many books there is no end; and much study is a weariness of the flesh."

As natural as this state of affairs has come to seen, it was not always so. In 1974, in one of the first political analyses of social policy, Hugh Heclo observed that "for anyone interested in the human terms of politics, perhaps the most fundamental change that is taken for granted is the growth of modern social policy" (Heclo 1974, 1). Indeed, what is striking in retrospect—not to mention, in light of the huge share of the economy that social spending consumes—is precisely how *few* scholars concerned themselves with the welfare state in the years before Heclo's words were penned.

What happened? The simple answer is that the welfare state leapt into the headlines. Once protected by a real, if uneasy, postwar consensus, the welfare state came under increasing political and economic strain in the post-1970s period, making it a subject of debate as it had not been for decades. Ironically, while the two to three decades after the Second World War featured dramatic welfare state expansion, it was only when the welfare state was less "taken for granted," in Heclo's words, that scholars really started wondering what drove its development and evolution.

Still, the growing debate might not have attracted scholarly attention were it not for changes within the academic world that made the welfare state more attractive as an object of research. Particularly important was the rise of institutional analysis within political science. The goal of many institutionalists was to highlight enduring structural features of modern polities, "bringing the state back in" to political analysis (Evans, Skocpol, and Rueschemeyer 1985). That meant, it turned out, bringing the *welfare state* back in as well, for a major share of what modern states do falls within the bounds of social policy. What is more, the welfare state is not simply a major institution of the state; it is also, scholars soon discovered, profoundly shaped by the basic structure of a nation's political institutions, providing one of the most concrete examples of how the rules of political decision-making shape what government does.

The upshot of these two streams of development—political change and scholarly innovation—was that social scientists woke up to a fact so obvious it had been frequently overlooked: The welfare state is a central institutional feature of modern politics. The seminal trigger for this awakening was Gøsta Esping-Andersen's landmark 1990 study, *The Three Worlds of Welfare Capitalism*. Esping-Andersen replaced the common unilinear view of welfare state development with a hugely influential threefold typology that contrasted the "social-democratic" welfare states of Scandinavia with the "conservative" model of Continental Europe and the "liberal" model found in Britain and the United States. Much as John Rawls' *A Theory of Justice* revitalized first-order political theory, Esping-Andersen's *Three Worlds of Welfare Capitalism* provided a major impetus for criticism, praise, and refinement of arguments about the welfare state both old and new.

And yet a curious thing has happened to the welfare state on its way from the periphery to the center of scholarly concern. Political analysts are now writing about the welfare state, but they are not really all that concerned with the welfare state as such. For most, instead, the welfare state has become a convenient window into some larger system of power or politics. Nor, indeed, are most scholars really writing about *the* welfare state. Some concern themselves with public assistance for the poor; others with social insurance programs like unemployment insurance; still others with labor policies, such as rules governing unions. An increasing number, in fact, are interested in policies well *beyond* the typical conception of the welfare state, such as tax policies and workplace benefits. In short, the near-perfect silence on the welfare state that once reigned has given way not to a single or harmonious tune, but to a cacophony of sometimes discordant notes that occasionally threatens to drown out the very subject of the melody.

This should not be surprising. The very breadth and complexity of the welfare state guarantee that scholars will pursue myriad research avenues. The question is whether these diverse inquiries are also leading to a more general picture, or simply making more complex and foreboding the topography that has to be traversed. The premise of this chapter is that while work on the welfare state has dramatically improved our knowledge and understanding, there is a risk that the stories that emerge will read like "one damn thing after another"—study piled upon study, fact upon fact, without adequate integration, explanation, or advancement. One way of avoiding this fate, this chapter argues, is for students of the welfare state to think more seriously of welfare states as distributive institutions whose socioeconomic effects and patterns of evolution are both systematic and systematically interrelated. Three questions should be central: What effect does the welfare state have on the lives of citizens, is that effect changing, and how can we explain the adaptation (or failure of adaptation) of the welfare state to the shifting realities around it?

The positive judgment, however, is the one to emphasize up front: Studies of the welfare state have revolutionized our understanding of comparative politics and policy—and, indeed, have a good claim to represent the strongest area in institutional analysis more generally. The chapter begins, therefore, with a review of the rich and fertile avenues of inquiry that students of the welfare state have pursued in recent years. Collectively as well as individually, these recent works testify to the tremendous progress that has taken place. Given how much of value has been written, in fact, any review will of necessity be highly selective. This chapter places special emphasis on writings on the American welfare state, which has provoked some of the most lively scholarly debates of the past decade—looking in particular at five areas of recent debate: race and the welfare state, gender and social policy, the role of business, the interplay of public and private benefits, and the politics of welfare state reform.

1 RACE AND SOLIDARITY

Students of the welfare state have long recognized that racial and ethnic cleavages pose distinctive dilemmas for social policy. The welfare state rests on a foundation of social solidarity (Baldwin 1990), a sense of kinship among those it protects. Deep cleavages can erode this social glue and, with it, the foundations on which the welfare state rests.

While this observation is long-standing, recent scholarship has started to map out exactly *how* race and ethnicity affect social policy. We learn that racial and ethnic stereotypes—and the exclusionary impulses to which they give rise—informed the original design of many social programs and continue to shape public perceptions of them, particularly in the United States (Brown 1999; Faye Williams 2003; Gilens 1999; Lieberman 1998). Moreover, because racial disadvantage is embedded in the larger political economy that these programs seek to influence, race enters into social policy even when it is not on the minds of citizens or elites. Not only, then, do perceptions of racial difference undermine the social solidarity that is the cement of the welfare state; equally important, many features of the world that social policies seek to change are "race-laden," in the words of political scientist Robert Lieberman (1998), and hence ostensibly race-neutral policies may have deeply racialized effects.

Recently, this new work has extended into the realm of comparative political economy. Two recent analyses by respected political economists take up the question of how the United States' distinctively conflicted history of race relations affects popular support for social programs. Alberto Alesina, Edward Glaeser, and Bruce Sacerdote (2001, 247) look across nations, arguing that US public social spending is lower than that of other nations in large part "because the majority of Americans believe that redistribution favors racial minorities." Woojin Lee and John Roemer (2004) instead look at the United States over time, tracing out the independent effect of two race-related factors on popular support for redistribution. The first factor is the now-familiar solidarity effect, in which perceptions of group difference undermine the sense of kinship that motivates social provision. The second, and more neglected factor that Lee and Roemer highlight is what they call the "policy-bundle" effect. Candidates in their model can choose to appeal to voters on the basis of their economic self-interest or on the basis of their racial perceptions. If candidates opposed to broader social provision appeal to downscale voters on the basis of racism, this further undercuts the constituency for redistribution.

The new scholarship on race has made major contributions to our understanding of social welfare politics. Yet when it comes to placing race in the context of other forces shaping social policy, it tends to falter. Few scholars, of course, are so bold as to claim that race is the motor force of welfare state development. But in their emphases and their arguments, they generally suggest that citizens inevitably judge social provision through blinders heavily shaped by racial, ethnic, and religious prejudice. Martin Gilens, in his (1991) account of Why Americans Hate Welfare, argues, for example, that distrust of antipoverty relief in the United States reflects the twin beliefs of white Americans that "most people who receive welfare are black" and that "blacks are less committed to the work ethic than are other Americans." While Gilens's point is restricted to antipoverty benefits, the general tenor of the new work on race and social policy is that such benefits are the leading case for a basic relationship: the welfare state and debates about it are explicable first and foremost through the lens of racial analysis.

In pointing toward this more ambitious claim, the new scholarship on race risks running aground on two opposed shoals. On the one hand, relatively straightforward arguments about how racist beliefs inform the formation and evolution of social programs are clear in their mechanisms and in their implications about what supportive evidence should look like. Yet they are also limited in their reach, for many areas of the welfare state do not appear racialized in the sense of being motivated by explicitly racist intentions. On the other hand, the claim that social policies are "race-laden" because they intersect with larger features of society marked by racial hierarchy has considerable—indeed near-total—reach, but the political mechanisms it highlights are diffuse, and quite problematic as subjects of empirical inquiry. Ironically, in fact, the broadest of such claims are quite similar in their observational implications to the arguments of dissenting scholars who have argued that what is notable about social policy development is the general *absence* of explicit attention to race (an argument made with regard to the debate over US social policies by Davies and Derthick 1997). If race is everything—hidden, all-encompassing, unchanging—then it risks being nothing, too.

2   GENDER AND SOCIAL POLICY

While race has long been a central theme in the study of the welfare state, gender has not. This despite the fact that women represent chief beneficiaries of the major family assistance programs of the welfare state, and despite the fact that female reform leaders have played a large role in the development of social policy in many nations. No doubt a good deal of this neglect can be chalked up to the biases of traditionally male-dominated and -oriented research. Yet this explanation is incomplete. Long after gender was a major focus of work in the social sciences, the welfare state was mostly viewed through the lens of male wage-earners and their struggle for expanded social protection.

To understand this, it helps to recognize that the major theoretical current in welfare state scholarship—up to and including today—draws from Marx in emphasizing class struggle as the root cause of welfare state building. Social policies, on this view, are primarily a means of "decommodification" (Esping-Anderson 1990), a way of freeing workers from wage dependence by providing them with income when they are unable to engage in well-paid labor. Traditionally if women entered into such analyses at all, they were subsumed within the larger category of "worker"—a move that ignored the extent to which women's relationship to the labor market differed from men's and the degree to which ostensibly self-supporting male workers were supported by female domestic work.

This blinkered perspective is no longer tenable. In welfare state research, "feminist" scholarship has had a major impact over the last decade or so. As with research on race, a good deal of this work has concerned the American experience. Emblematic is Skocpol's (1992) *Protecting Soldiers and Mothers*—which, while controversial within feminist circles, details the role played by women's groups and reformers at the turn of the last century in promoting what she calls a "maternalist" vision of the welfare state oriented around state protection for women and children. Against Skocpol's interpretation, other scholars have emphasized the repressive elements of the maternalist vision in the United States, while a growing body of writing has reinterpreted the development of the welfare state in light of the taken-for-granted subordinate position of women. Recent work has emphasized, for example, that many social insurance and employment programs initially excluded female workers, focused on risks and needs distinctive to men, and were built on the assumption that women would remain home to support male breadwinners.[1]

In comparative research, in particular, gender has become a central frame of reference (see especially Orloff 1993; Stetson and Mazur 1995). Welfare states do not merely "decommodify," this new comparative work argues. They can also "defamilialize," lessening the extent to which women are required to remain home and care for children by providing public day care and structuring policies in gender-neutral ways. Put simply, welfare states not only affect citizens place and power in the economy; they also affect their place and power in the household—and, indeed, it is at the nexus of these two realms that women's distinctive role, and dilemmas, lie.

The success of feminist scholarship in reorienting existing theories and suggesting new historical interpretations cannot be gainsaid. Nonetheless, this work has also suffered from a number of common weakness, many of which it shares with recent scholarship on race. The first is that the singular emphasis on gender, like the singular emphasis on race, tends to occlude other forces that shape policy and politics, and to limit analysis to certain corners of the social welfare field—in this case, again, overwhelmingly poverty relief. As with work on race, feminist scholars are also often less than clear whether they are talking about sexist beliefs held by citizens and elites, or about the impact of ostensibly gender-neutral policies in a world marked by vast gender inequalities, or both. Indeed, far more than recent research on race, feminist scholars face the challenge of interpreting *absence*, for what is striking in many early social policy debates is precisely how little was said distinguishing women and men. This contrasts with the clear, repeated, and often breathtakingly crude references to race in many of the same political debates.

---

[1] Notable works include Gordon 1994; Mink 1995; Mettler 1999; Kessler-Harris 2001; and the essays in Gordon 1990.

3   BUSINESS AND THE WELFARE STATE

Work on gender challenges the laborist perspective for its alleged sins of omission. New writings on the role of business, by contrast, tackle it for its alleged sins of commission. The essence of these works' critique is that previous scholarship has overstated the antinomy of interests between capitalists and labor and, in doing so, missed the strong capitalist bases of support for domestic social reform (see, in particular, Gordon 1994, 2003; Jacoby 1997; Mares 2003; Martin 2000; Swenson 2002).

An important spur for much of this work is an emerging literature on "varieties of capitalism" (Hall and Soskice 2001). This work argues that capitalism comes in at least two alternative forms. It may be oriented around the short-term, hyper-competitive, and based on arms-length contracts (the American, or "liberal market economy," model). Or it may be long-term, consensual, and based on interlocking financial and social ties (the continental European, "coordinated market econ-omy," model). And while social welfare policies that strengthen workers' autonomy and power might interfere with the normal competitive market in the first model, they may be highly market-enhancing in the latter. For example, in an economy based on high skills and wages, protecting workers against the risk of occupational displacement encourages them to invest in skills that are highly specific to an industry or firm—skills they would otherwise fear investing in, because of their lack of transferability from job to job (Iversen and Soskice 2001).

While the "varieties of capitalism" framework suggests strong commonalities of interests between business and labor, it does not rest on the claim that business is a prime mover in the development of the welfare state. After all, the fact that some social policies are economically beneficial is no guarantee that business will support them. Many policies that are good for economic growth have *no* organized defenders. And even if it can be shown that business supports certain social policies, that still leaves open the critical question of whether capitalists were behind their creation. The powerful, distinctive, and controversial claim of the new literature on business power is that capitalists have a strong preference for key social programs *before* they are enacted.

This argument has two main variants, which are not mutually exclusive. One says that businesses want social programs to impose costs on competitors—for example, by requiring that all firms pay for benefits they already provide (Swenson 2002). The other says that businesses want social programs to offload their costs onto the public fisc—for example, by socializing risks to which they are particularly susceptible (Mares 2003). Both variants argue, however, that some (but, crucially, not all) businesses want generous social programs. To be sure, organized labor demands social programs, too. But their success hinges on the emergence of "cross-class alliances" with capitalists (Swenson 2002). Only when the bourgeoisie are on board does the proletariat get what it wants.

The recent sweeping work of Peter Swenson, *Capitalists Against Markets* (2002)—which compares the fate of social reforms in the United States during the 1930s and in Sweden immediately after the Second World War—exemplifies, while deepening, the new business power thesis. Swenson argues that in the United States during the Depression a significant segment of the American business community (large employers that paid generous wages and benefits) was at least latently supportive of new social insurance programs that would cripple their low-wage, low-price competitors. Meanwhile, in Sweden, according to Swenson, business support for social programs emerged only after the Second World War, during a period of acute upward pressure on wages, which Swedish employer associations hoped to compress by socializing non-wage labor costs. The original turn in Swenson's argument is not so much his identification of a capitalist interest in reform, but his attempt to tease out the bases of capitalist influence. Swenson argues that neither the so-called instrumental power of business (its lobbying prowess and resources) nor its "structural" power (its control over investment and jobs, about which politicians care regardless of whether business organizes to press for policy change) were crucial.[2] Rather, it was politicians' anticipation of long-term capitalist support for—and fear of long-term capitalist opposition to—domestic reforms that, Swenson argues, represents the primary means by which the largely unexpressed pro-reform sentiments of the business community shaped the making of social policy (Swenson 2002).

As this brief summary indicates, there is more than a whiff of the New Left to Swenson's provocative thesis. Yet unlike earlier New Left scholars who argued that seemingly progressive social reforms were essentially conservative creatures of business interests (e.g. Kolko 1977), Swenson and those who make related claims do not believe that the leftist ambitions of social reformers were hijacked by corporate America. They want to argue instead that underlying business interests were largely consistent with what reformers wanted. This, of course, raises the issue of how one demonstrates *influence*. If reformers want what business wants, that could evidence influence, or simply preference congruence. And indeed, in much of the recent literature, Swenson's contribution included, surprisingly scant and circumstantial evidence is offered that reformers actually responded to actual or anticipated business power in crafting their proposals.

No less serious, for all the close attention to historical detail that characterizes recent business power accounts, these works are often, at their core, notably ahistorical. Swenson, for example, uses large employers' eventual acceptance of the US Social Security Act as an important piece of evidence in favor of his thesis that the Act was initially consistent with their interests. But, of course, the eventual business response to new social programs is hardly an accurate gauge of initial

---

[2] On the distinction between structural and instrumental power, see Hacker and Pierson 2002; Lindblom 1982.

interests. Once legislation is in place, after all, employers may simply believe they cannot realistically overturn it, or the policy may in fact change what employers want by altering market conditions, reshaping the population of employers, or encouraging new conceptions of business interests.

Similarly, many works that stress employers' influence tend to begin the story when reform gets on the agenda, then trace the direct interventions of business on specific policy choices. But this "snapshot" approach makes it nearly impossible to judge the true power of employers, because it leaves unanswered the profound question of whether the policy terrain on which business operates at any particular moment is tilted toward or against it (Hacker and Pierson 2002). Nonetheless, the renewed emphasis on business' role does powerfully call into question the traditional assumption that capitalists are merely recalcitrant stumbling blocks on the road to social reform.

4   THE "HIDDEN" WELFARE STATE

In at least one respect, however, new work on business emulates older theories of the welfare state—and that is in its emphasis on public spending programs like government old-age pensions and public health insurance. In this, the business power literature is of a piece with nearly everything that has been written on the welfare state. While scholars often note the importance of taxation and policy tools besides direct social spending, studies of the welfare state are, almost without exception, studies of social spending, with little attention paid either to tax policy (including the actual provision of benefits through the tax code) or to the wide range of "publicly subsidized and regulated private social benefits" (Hacker 2002), such as private, employment-based health insurance, that tax policy usually helps underwrite.

On one level, this conflation of social policy and public spending is understandable. Much of what welfare states do, after all, is spend—as much as two-fifths of GDP in some Nordic countries. But on another level, it is unexpected, for taxation and the role of the private sector have probably been the most consistently explosive issues in welfare state development. It is also surprising because one of the most influential writings on the welfare state—Richard Titmuss's (1976) famous *Essays on the "Welfare State"*—placed tax policy (which he termed "fiscal welfare") and private social benefits (which he called "occupational welfare") on a par with spending as a means of achieving social welfare ends. Yet Titmuss's insights on this point, unlike many of his other contributions, have produced relatively little follow-up analysis.

That has started to change, but not nearly as quickly or as fully as in the other areas we have reviewed. Much of the credit for the shift must go to Christopher Howard's (1997) *The Hidden Welfare State*, which examines the use of tax breaks with social welfare aims, such as the Earned Income Tax Credit (EITC) for the working poor. Howard argues that US federal social spending is perhaps 150 percent as large as official spending figures indicate when tax breaks with social welfare aims are included in the tally. In making this crucial claim, Howard stresses a point that policy-makers know well, but which welfare state scholars have generally overlooked: Governments have alternative instruments for achieving their ends (see Hood 1983). The welfare state literature has, not implausibly, identified spending as the key instrument of social policy. Yet in the process, it has missed other means by which policy-makers could achieve their goals—from regulation to tax breaks to judicial empowerment to the use of government credit and insurance.

But while Howard and others have examined the tools at policy-makers' disposal, they have had relatively little to say about the vast private-sector field of social welfare, including employer-sponsored benefits, that these tools were often designed to shape. Recent scholarship, however, has started to highlight this even more "hidden" realm of social policy. Interestingly, much of this work has come from historians, rather than political scientists (Gordon 2003; Jacoby 1997; Katz 2001; Klein 2003). Political scientists have been slower to move into the field, perhaps because there is so little secondary historical work to build on. But recent work by political scientists (Brown 1999; Gottschalk 2000; Stevens 1990; Hacker 2002, 2004) indicates a growing interest in incorporating the role of private benefits into theories of the welfare state.

In the process, this new scholarship has fundamentally challenged at least one prevailing verdict in the comparative policy field—that the American welfare state is much smaller that its European counterparts. In fact, properly measured, American social welfare spending is at or above the average for comparable advanced industrial democracies (Hacker 2002). "Properly measured," in this case, means adjusting for relative tax burdens and including private employer-provided benefits that are substantially regulated or subsidized by government. Because US tax levels are comparatively low and its private social welfare sector is far and away the largest in the world, these two simple adjustments raise US social spending from approximately 17 percent of GDP to nearly 25 percent. In short, "what is distinctive about US social spending is not the *level* of spending, but the *source*" (Hacker 2002, 7).

This does not mean, however, that the distribution of social benefits in the United States is the same as it is in other advanced industrial democracies. The United States may spend as much as many European governments when private social benefits and tax policy are taken into account, but the distribution of benefits up and down the income ladder is almost certainly much less favorable toward lower-income citizens. Employment-based benefits are much more prevalent and generous at higher ends of the wage scale, and tax subsidies, because they forgive tax that would otherwise be owed, are generally worth the most to taxpayers in the highest tax brackets. Overall, only about two-thirds of workers receive health insurance through employment, and fewer than that have a pension plan, much less contribute to it (Hacker 2002)

All of which raises a deeper questions: By what standard are we to call indirect policy tools and government-supported private benefits part of that body of state activity conveniently, if often imprecisely, termed the "welfare state?" The scholarship just reviewed makes a strong case for thinking that these tools and benefits should, indeed must, be analyzed in studies of social policy. But despite frequent use of the evocative (and highly contestable) term "private welfare state" to describe workplace benefits, much of this recent work has surprisingly little to say about why these benefits and tax breaks are on a par with the public programs that students of the welfare state usually study. To the extent, moreover, that it is simply assumed that the concept of the welfare state can be "stretched" to include all these diverse instruments and policies, then it is not immediately clear why it could not or should not stretch even further—to include almost anything that government does to affect social welfare. Certainly, once the rubric of the welfare states opens up, it cannot be assumed that the generalizations about welfare state development advanced to explain public programs hold equally well in explaining other realms of social provision. Yet why and how indirect policies and private benefits differ from traditional programs—enough that they require new theories and histories, but not so much that they fall outside the bounds of social welfare policy—are questions scholars have only started to explore.

5   WHITHER THE WELFARE STATE?

The literature on indirect policy tools takes on particular significance in the context of current struggles over the welfare state. In a number of nations, leaders have issued impassioned calls for the "privatization" of social duties once handled primarily by government. Many of the proposals that travel under this controversial label envision shifting from direct state spending toward less direct forms of social provision, such as the subsidization of private social benefits. But even in nations where such reforms have not been on the table, citizens have witnessed major debates over the restructuring and trimming of social programs that were once considered politically sacrosanct. Not surprisingly, then, the progress and consequences of welfare state "retrenchment" have become leading topics in contemporary scholarship on the welfare state.

The beginning of the recent wave of interest in retrenchment can be conveniently dated to Pierson's groundbreaking book on welfare state retrenchment in Britain and the United States, *Dismantling the Welfare State?* (1994). By "retrenchment," Pierson means "policy changes that either cut social expenditure, restructure welfare state programs to conform more closely to the residual welfare state model, or alter the political environment in ways that enhance the probability of such outcomes in the future" (1994, 17). On the basis of this definition, Pierson concludes that "the fundamental structure of social policy [in Britain and the United States] remains comparatively stable" (1994, 182). The reasons for this resilience, according to Pierson, are multiple: Cutting programs entails imposing losses rather than the more electorally attractive activity of distributing benefits. The possible benefits of restructuring in the form of lower debt-spending or stronger economic growth are diffuse, while the costs are highly concentrated on specific populations. Political institutions that give governments centralized power to cut popular benefits also create clear lines of political accountability that make it difficult for them to do so without risking electoral defeat. Above all, social programs are popular, and they have created powerful constituencies well positioned to fight retrenchment. In short, the prospects for retrenchment are—to use a phrase Pierson deploys in more recent writings—highly "path dependent" (Pierson 2000). Past social policy choices create strong vested interests and expectations, which are extremely difficult to undo even in the present era.

A wave of subsequent research, relying on both large-scale statistical modeling and detailed historical analysis, has largely ratified Pierson's evaluation (see, e.g., Bonoli, George, and Taylor-Gooby 2000; Esping-Andersen 1999; Huber and Stephens 2001; Pierson 1994, 2001; Weaver 1998). In this now-conventional view, welfare states are under strain, cuts have occurred, but social policy frameworks remain secure, anchored by their enduring popularity, their powerful constituencies, and their centrality within the postwar order.

This research has produced major gains in understanding. Yet it has some significant limits. The first and simplest is its emphasis on authoritative changes in existing social welfare programs. Although this may seem an obvious focus, it excludes from consideration a host of "subterranean" (Hacker 2002, 43) means of policy adjustment that can occur without large-scale policy change: from "bureaucratic disentitlement" (Lipsky 1984) caused by the decisions of front-line administrators to decentralized cutbacks in social welfare benefits caused by the actions of nongovernmental benefit sponsors and providers. Almost all this scholarship, moreover, leaves out of consideration the "hidden" policy tools just discussed. It thus misses not only the restructuring of employer-provided benefits (which, in many nations, has been profound), but also the creation of new indirect policies that encourage highly individualized private benefits, such as 401(k) retirement plans in the United States.

Perhaps most important, in emphasizing affirmative decisions, the retrenchment literature also excludes from consideration a wide range of agenda-setting and -blocking activities that may well be quite crucial in shaping the welfare state's long-term evolution. Like the pluralists of the 1950s and 1960s (Dahl 1961), retrenchment scholars have assessed power mainly by tracing observable decisions. The influential critique made against pluralism (Bachrach and Baratz 1970; Lukes 1974) thus carries weight here too: By looking only at affirmative choices on predefined issues, retrenchment analyses tend to downplay the important ways in which actors may shape and restrict the agenda of debate and prevent some kinds of collective decisions altogether.

Most critical in this regard are deliberate attempts to prevent the updating of policies to reflect changing circumstance. In the United States in the early 1990s, for example, President Bill Clinton embarked on an ambitious campaign to counteract the declining reach of private health benefits and provide universal health insurance—something the United States, almost alone among rich democracies, lacks (Hacker 1997; Skocpol 1996). His efforts ultimately fell victim to a concerted counter-mobilization among affected interests and political conservatives, who denied that government should step in to deal with the increasing hardships caused by skyrocketing costs and dwindling protections. This defeat has enormous implications for the scope of US social policy, as well as for judgments about the relative influence of pro- and anti-welfare-state forces in American politics. Yet from the standpoint of the conventional approach to retrenchment, the failure of health reform in the United States is a non-event.

This example only hints at the broad range of policy processes and outcomes occluded by a single-minded focus on formal policy change. Historically, welfare states have been directed not just toward ensuring protection against medical costs, but also toward providing security against a number of major life risks: unemployment, death of a spouse, retirement, disability, childbirth, poverty. Yet the incidence and extent of many of these risks have changed dramatically in recent decades, leading to potentially significant transformations in the consequences of policy interventions, even without formal changes in public programs. As Esping-Andersen (1999, 5) puts it, "The real 'crisis' of contemporary welfare regimes lies in the disjuncture between the existing institutional configuration and exogenous change. Contemporary welfare states ... have their origins in, and mirror, a society that no longer obtains."

To be sure, we should not assume that the welfare state should naturally adjust to deal with changing risk profiles, or that gaps between risks and benefits are always deliberate. And yet, we cannot ignore these disjunctures either. Welfare states, after all, constitute institutionalized aims as well as an arsenal of policy means for achieving them, and their development over time must be assessed in that dual light.

In this respect, the literature on retrenchment runs into a problem that all of the scholarship we have reviewed so far faces: how at once to do justice to the complexities of social welfare policy *and* provide relatively simplified accounts that add to our common knowledge. It is fair to say that this is a problem that work on retrenchment faces acutely. But difficulty advancing general claims that can unify disparate research agendas is a notable characteristic of nearly all the scholarship taken up thus far. The closing portion of this chapter discusses two particularly salient examples of this difficulty: The typically underdeveloped understanding of the link between politics and policy in welfare state research, and the general failure of welfare state analysts to develop broader arguments about institutional change.

6   RISK, REDISTRIBUTION, AND THE WELFARE STATE

Perhaps the most striking feature of discussions of social policy is the extent to which, until recently at least, they have proceeded without much hard evidence on policy *outcomes* of any kind. Traditionally, work on the welfare state took public spending as the measure of program generosity (Wilensky 1975). Even after the conflation of spending levels and program generosity were subject to withering critique (e.g. Esping-Andersen 1990), many scholars continued to use public spending as a convenient proxy for program effects. Government spending was easy to measure and widely available, and there were few, if any, competing metrics that scholars could utilize.

As a consequence, well into the 1990s informed works had to piece together scattered evidence to come to even a preliminary judgment about how welfare states affected income and well-being among citizens (e.g. Goodin and Le Grand 1987). As Frances Castles noted in 1993, "The centrality of the welfare state in the comparative public policy literature has until now drawn its rationale from plausible inferences concerning the impact of government intervention on distributional outcomes.... However, in the absence of any independent measure of outcomes, both aggregate expenditures and types of instruments necessarily became proxies for distributional consequences, making any serious distinction between means and ends impossible" (Castles and Mitchell 1993).

We now know far more about the income effects of social policies, thanks in large part to the development of the Luxembourg Income Study (LIS)—a cross-national analysis of income and demographics that began in 1983 and now encompasses twenty-five nations, with data in some cases spanning three decades.

The LIS assembles and harmonizes data from cross-sectional surveys of house-holds, which include fairly comprehensive measures of household and personal income and expenditures. This allows the LIS data to be used to construct intuitive measures of the effect of government taxes and transfers on inequality. The LIS data show that inequality before taxes and transfers rose sharply in most nations in the 1980s. What they also show, however, is that taxes and transfers have done much more to offset this rise in market income inequality in some nations than in others, with the United States and the United Kingdom standing out as distinctly unresponsive.

The LIS data represent a huge advance in the study of the welfare state. For one, they provide an essential reminder that the formal rules written into social policies are not always obediently followed by administrators or consistently responded to by citizens. For another, they allow much firmer conclusions about the *interaction* of social policies with broader changes in the economy and society. Yet the LIS data also have notable weaknesses. Perhaps the most glaring is that they rely on cross-sectional surveys, which provide only point-in-time estimates of the distribution of income in any given year. In other words, these data can tell us how much of the population is poor or rich in any given year, but not whether the same people are poor or rich from year to year. Similarly, they can tell us how much redistribution transfers and taxes create at a specific time, but not how much redistribution occurs over the life cycle or across risk classes or between those experiencing an adverse event and those not experiencing it.

Responding to these shortcomings, a handful of scholars have started to turn to an alternative source of evidence: panel studies of income dynamics. These are studies that repeatedly interview the same families and individuals over many years—in the case of the longest such study, the US Panel Study of Income Dynamics (PSID), over more than thirty years. To date, however, only a small handful of studies attempt to use panel income data to analyze the effects of welfare states. Because most of these studies are cross-national in focus, they are limited by the availability of panel data comparable to the PSID, the gold standard in the field. Only two other long-term panel studies of comparable scope and consistency exist: the German and Dutch socioeconomic panel surveys. Because neither is available before 1984, researchers interested in longer-term patterns have essentially found themselves forced to focus their cross-national analyses on the period between the mid-1980s and mid-1990s—all years that postdate the major shocks to the welfare state and economy of the 1970s and early 1980s.

Nonetheless, these studies have already contributed important insights. The most basic is that there is, in fact, a great deal of variability in family income from year to year. For this reason, point-in-time estimates of the redistribution effected by public programs almost certainly overstate the extent to which welfare state policies take from the rich and give to the poor. Over time, the population at the lower and higher ends of the income scale change considerably. One year's benefactor may be next year's beneficiary. Moreover, recent research suggests that the effect of the welfare state on these income dynamics differs significantly across nations. For example, although per capita GDP is higher in the United States than in Europe, household income is considerably less stable in the United States than in Germany and the Netherlands. According to comparative panel research, this is partly because Americans are subject to greater labor- and family-related income shocks and partly because the US social insurance system is less extensive (DiPrete and McManus 2000; Goodin, Headey, Muffels, and Dirven 1999).

Nonetheless, our tools for linking family income dynamics to concrete policy changes within the welfare state—much less to the political processes that produce those changes—remain quite blunt. Put simply, our knowledge of policy effects is improving, but our ability to link those policy effects back to theories of the welfare state has not kept pace. Nothing better illustrates this gap than the general absence of careful theorizing by welfare state scholars about the ways in which politics and policy remake each other over long stretches of time.

7   WELFARE STATE CHANGE AS INSTITUTIONAL CHANGE

Perhaps the most common theme of recent works on the political development of social policy is that contemporary debates have their roots in the past. Yet *why* the past is so important, and its effects so enduring, is much less clear. In some cases, the argument appears to be merely that past conflicts created present policies. In others, it seems deeper: that past policies have given rise to self-reinforcing dynamics that push the welfare state down highly resilient historical tracks. This does not, of course, exhaust the possibilities. In some cases, the claim is not about endurance but fragility—for example, the relative political *weakness* of antipoverty programs in many nations since the 1970s. But what is at stake in all these claims is the place of time, if you will, in studies of social policy. Why must we take the long view in analyses of the welfare state? Why are some policies resilient, while others are not? What explains continuity and change within specific policies? And how do policies reshape political life after they are enacted?

The deepest shortcoming of social welfare scholarship to date is its inability or unwillingness to engage with these critical issues. This shortcoming is all the more glaring because, in the last decade, mainly because of the pathbreaking scholarship of political scientists Paul Pierson (1993, 1994, 1997, 2004) and Theda Skocpol

(Pierson and Skocpol 2000; Skocpol 1992), there has emerged a relatively powerful set of generalizations about the effect of public policies, once implemented, on political dynamics going forward. This notion of "policy feedback" has built upon and furthered a related theoretical enterprise in the social sciences: the exploration of processes of "path dependence" in which early developments structure later ones by giving rise to institutions and dynamics that are inherently difficult to reverse. For the most part, however, welfare state scholars have not engaged with these theoretical currents, and in the rare cases when they are invoked, they are usually treated quite superficially.

Happily, greater engagement appears to be the direction in which institutionally minded political scientists are heading. Pierson, for example, has written a new book, *Politics in Time* (2004), that lays out his own arguments about how path dependence creates change as well as continuity. Kathleen Thelen (2003) and Eric Schickler (2001), in quite different ways, have pushed forward the study of institutional development by tracing the evolution of German labor-market institutions and the US Congress, respectively. In a recent article (Hacker 2004), I have built on these authors' to present a fourfold model of policy change. In this model, once policies with strong support coalitions are in place, "big bangs" of policy reform or replacement are rare, requiring as they do a consolidation of political power that most nations' political institutions make difficult. Nonetheless, even without epochal transformations, social policies may change markedly through three less studied processes. The first is what Thelen calls "conversion"—the internal transformation of policies without formal change. In programs run by private organizations or front-line agents, there are numerous opportunities to reorient programs without going through the legislative process, and many of the most consequential changes in US social policy over the past two decades—such as cutbacks in antipoverty benefits and the decline and restructuring of tax-subsidized workplace benefits—have occurred through such conversion processes.

The second process of change that occurs without formal transformation of the existing program is what Schickler terms "layering," the creation of new policies that can alter the operation of older policies. "Layering" requires legislative action, but it does not require dismantling older programs—a far more difficult prospect. Thus, for example, conservative critics of social security in the United States have been consistently rebuffed in their effort to scale back the program significantly, but they have succeeded handsomely at capitalizing on periods of conservative ascendance to enact new policies encouraging highly individualized tax-subsidized retirement accounts, like 401(k) pension plans.

The third process of change is perhaps the least recognized, and often the most important—what might be called "drift" within the bounds of formally stable policies. Drift occurs when changes in the environment of policies make them less capable of achieving their initial goals, but the policies are not updated, either because the gap between goals and reality is not recognized or, more interesting still, is recognized but there is active opposition to the updating of policies.[3] In the past three decades, the employment market and structure of families have changed dramatically. Yet most of the welfare state has not. The result is a growing gulf between the new social risks that citizens face and the existing framework of social benefits on which they depend. This gulf is no accident: Opponents of the welfare state have faced great difficulties in cutting it back. But they have proved extremely capable of blocking the updating of social policies to reflect changing social realities—as they did, for example, when they decisively defeated President Clinton's ill-fated 1993 health plan in the United States.

The observation that welfare states may fail to respond to changing social risks turns on its head the traditional institutionalist argument about welfare state retrenchment—and in so doing, suggests how important a longer-term historical perspective can be. Early institutional research on the welfare state showed conclusively that political institutions that created a large number of "veto-points" or "veto-players" retarded the creation of large and generous social programs. Based on this important finding, it was often argued that in the era of retrenchment, it was (ironically) precisely those countries with the most veto-point-ridden political structures whose welfare states were most secure. Yet, as the foregoing discussion makes clear, this claim was only half the story. Institutionally induced stalemate makes direct retrenchment of the welfare state more difficult, but it also makes it more difficult for advocates of welfare state adaptation to reorient welfare states to accommodate new and newly intensified social risks. A longer-term perspective shows that in the present era institutional obstacles to policy change are a double-edged sword, blocking full-scale retrenchment but also stymieing necessary adaptation.

Although issues of institutional development are rightly moving to center of debate and analysis in political science, it is certainly premature to declare that robust generalizations about processes of institutional change are destined to shift into studies of social policy, much less that generating arguments of this sort will become a primary concern of social welfare scholars. Nonetheless, for analysts of the welfare state to ignore these emerging issues would be to pass up a tremendous opportunity for the development of a set of explanatory tools that could create greater cohesion and clarity in a field that, for all its richness and depth, would benefit from both.

In all this, however, the ultimate goal should be to understand not merely the details of social policies, but what they do—to and for citizens and to and for polities and societies. The welfare state expresses, at root, a sense of solidarity, a belief in a shared fate. At a moment when the fates of citizens often seem to be

---

[3] Of course, drift can and does run in the opposite direction—that is, toward expansion. The proliferating use of disability insurance as a means of early retirement in Europe is a powerful contemporary example.

shared more in fear than in hope, the link between policies and the collective commitments they reflect and nurture is as vital a subject for political leaders as it is for political analysts.

REFERENCES

ALESINA, A., GLAESER, E., and SACERDOTE, B. 2001. Why doesn't the United States have a European-style welfare state? In *Brookings Papers on Economic Activity*, 2: 187–277.

BACHRACH, P. and BARATZ, M. S. 1970. *Power and Poverty: Theory and Practice*. New York: Oxford University Press.

BAKER, T. and SIMON, J. (eds.) 2002. *Embracing Risk: The Changing Culture of Insurance and Responsibility*. Chicago: University of Chicago Press.

BALDWIN, P. 1990. *The Politics of Social Solidarity*. Cambridge: Cambridge University Press.

BARR, N. 1998. *The Economics of the Welfare State*, 3rd edn. Oxford: Oxford University Press.

BECK, U. 1992. *Risk Society: Towards a New Modernity*. London: Sage.

BONOLI, G., GEORGE, V., and TAYLOR-GOOBY, P. 2000. *European Welfare Futures*. Cambridge: Polity Press.

BRADLEY, D., HUBER, E., MOLLER, S., NIELSEN, F., and STEPHENS, J. D. 2003. Distribution and redistribution in post-industrial democracies. *World Politics*, 55 (2): 193–228.

BRANDES, S. D. 1976. *American Welfare State Capitalism, 1880–1940*. Chicago: University of Chicago Press.

BROWN, M. K. 1999. *Race, Money, and the American Welfare State*. Ithaca, NY: Cornell University Press.

CAMERON, D. 1978. The expansion of the public economy: a comparative analysis. *American Political Science Review*, 72 (4): 1243–60.

CAMPBELL, A. L. 2003. *How Policies Make Citizens: Senior Political Activism and the American Welfare State*. Princeton, NJ: Princeton University Press.

CASTLES, F. G. and MITCHELL, D. 1993. Worlds of welfare and families of nations. In *Families of Nations: Patterns of Public Policy in Western Democracies*, ed. F. G. Castles. Sydney: Dartmouth.

DAHL, R. 1961. *Who Governs? Democracy and Power in an American City*. New Haven, Conn.: Yale University Press.

DAVIES, G. and M. DERTHICK. 1997. Race and social welfare policy: the Social Security Act of 1935. *Political Science Quarterly*, 112 (2): 217–35.

DiPRETE, T. A. and McMANUS, P. A. 2000. Family change, employment transitions, and the welfare state: household income dynamics in the United States and Germany. *American Sociological Review*, 65 (3): 343–70.

ESPING-ANDERSEN, G. 1990. *The Three Worlds of Welfare Capitalism*. Princeton, NJ: Princeton University Press.

—— 1999. *Social Foundations of Postindustrial Economies*. New York: Oxford University Press.

EVANS, P., SKOCPOL, T., and RUESCHEMEYER, D. (eds.) 1985. *Bringing the State Back In*. New York: Cambridge University Press.

FAYE WILLIAMS, L. 2003. *The Constraint of Race: Legacies of White Skin Privilege in America*. University Park: Pennsylvania State University Press.

GILENS, M. 1999. *Why Americans Hate Welfare: Race, Media, and the Politics of Antipoverty Policy.* Chicago: University of Chicago Press.

GOODIN, R. E. and LE GRAND, J. 1987. Not only the poor. In *Not Only the Poor: The Middle Classes and the Welfare State,* ed. R. E. Goodin and J. Le Grand. London: Allen and Unwin.

—— HEADEY, B., MUFFELS, R., and DIRVEN, H.-J. 1999. *The Real Worlds of Welfare Capitalism.* Cambridge: Press Syndicate of the Cambridge University Press.

—— and et al. 2000. *The Real Worlds of Welfare Capitalism.* Cambridge: Cambridge University Press.

GORDON, C. 1994. *New Deals: Business, Labor, and Politics in America, 1920–1935.* Cambridge: Cambridge University Press.

—— 2003. *Dead on Arrival: The Politics of Health Care in Twentieth-Century America.* Princeton, NJ: Princeton University Press.

GORDON, L. (ed.) 1990. *Women, the State, and Welfare.* Madison: University of Wisconsin Press.

GOTTSCHALK, M. 2000. *The Shadow Welfare State: Labor, Business, and the Politics of Health Care in the United States.* Ithaca, NY: Cornell University Press.

GRAETZ, M. J. and MASHAW, J. L. 1999. *True Security: Rethinking American Social Insurance.* New Haven, Conn.: Yale University Press.

HACKER, J. S. 1997. *The Road to Nowhere: The Genesis of President Clinton's Plan for Health Security.* Princeton, NJ: Princeton University Press.

—— 2002. *The Divided Welfare State: The Battle over Public and Private Social Benefits in the United States.* Cambridge: Cambridge University Press.

—— 2004. Privatizing risk without privatizing the welfare state: the hidden politics of social policy retrenchment in the United States. *American Political Science Review,* 98 (2): 243–59.

—— 2006. *The Great Risk Shift.* New York: Oxford University Press.

—— and PIERSON, P. 2002. Business power and social policy: employers and the formation of the American welfare state. *Politics and Society,* 30 (2): 277–325.

HALL, P. A. and SOSKICE, D. (eds.) 2001. *Varieties of Capitalism.* New York: Oxford University Press.

HECLO, H. 1974. *Modern Social Politics in Britain and Sweden.* New Haven, Conn.: Yale University Press.

HOOD, C. C. 1983. *The Tools of Government.* Chatham, NJ: Chatham House.

HOWARD, C. 2003. Is the American welfare state unusually small? *PS: Political Science and Politics,* 36 (3): 411–16.

HUBER, E. and STEPHENS, J. D. 2001. *Development and Crisis of the Welfare State.* Chicago: University of Chicago Press.

IVERSEN, T. and SOSKICE, D. 2001. An asset theory of social policy preferences. *American Political Science Review,* 95 (4): 875–93.

JACOBY, S. M. 1997. *Modern Manors: Welfare Capitalism Since the New Deal.* Princeton, NJ: Princeton University Press.

KATZ, M. B. 2001. *The Price of Citizenship: Redefining the American Welfare State.* New York: Metropolitan.

KESSLER-HARRIS, A. 2001. *In Pursuit of Equity: Women, Men and the Quest for Economic Citizenship in 20th-Century America.* New York: Oxford University Press.

KLEIN, J. L. 2003. *For All These Rights: Business, Labor, and the Shaping of America's Public–Private Welfare State.* Princeton, NJ: Princeton University Press.

KOLKO, G. 1977. *The Triumph of Conservatism.* New York: Free Press.

LI, W. and ROEMER, J. 2004. *Racism and Redistribution in the United States: A Solution to the Problem of American Exceptionalism.* New Haven, Conn.: Yale University Press.

LIEBERMAN, R. 1998. *Shifting the Color Line.* Cambridge, Mass.: Harvard University Press.

LINDBLOM, C. E. 1982. The market as prison. *Journal of Politics*, 44 (2): 324–36.

LIPSKY, M. 1984. Bureaucratic disentitlement in social welfare programs. *Social Service Review*, 58: 3–27.

LUKES, S. 1974. *Power: A Radical View.* New York: Macmillan.

MARES, I. 2003. *The Politics of Social Risk: Business and the Politics of Welfare State Development.* New York: Cambridge University Press.

MARTIN, C. J. 2000. *Stuck in Neutral: Business and the Politics of Human Capital Investment Policy.* Princeton, NJ: Princeton University Press.

METTLER, S. B. 1998. *Dividing Citizens: Gender and Federalism in New Deal Public Policy.* Ithaca, NY: Cornell University Press.

MINK, G. 1995. *The Wages of Motherhood: Inequality in the Welfare State, 1917–1942.* Ithaca, NY: Cornell University Press.

MOENE, K. O. and WALLERSTEIN, M. 2001. Inequality, social insurance, and redistribution. *American Political Science Review*, 95 (4): 859–74.

MOSS, D. A. 2002. *When All Else Fails: Government as the Ultimate Risk Manager.* Cambridge, Mass.: Harvard University Press.

ORLOFF, A. S. 1993. Gender and the social rights citizenship: the comparative analysis of gender relations and welfare states. *American Sociological Review*, 58: 303–28.

PIERSON, P. 1993. When effect becomes cause: policy feedback and political change. *World Politics*, 45 (4): 595–628.

—— 1994. *Dismantling the Welfare State? Reagan, Thatcher, and the Politics of Retrenchment.* New York: Cambridge University Press.

—— 1997. Increasing returns, path dependence and the study of politics. Jean Monnet Visiting Professor Lecture, April, European University Institute.

—— 2000. Increasing returns, path dependence, and the study of politics. *American Political Science Review*, 94 (2): 251–67.

—— (ed.) 2001. *The New Politics of the Welfare State.* Oxford: Oxford University Press.

—— 2004. *Politics in Time: History, Institutions, and Social Analysis.* Princeton, NJ: Princeton University Press.

—— and SKOCPOL, T. 2000. Historical institutionalism in contemporary political science. Paper read at American Political Science Association, August 30–September 2, Washington, DC.

SCHICKLER, E. 2001. *Disjointed Pluralism: Institutional Innovation in the U.S. Congress.* Princeton, NJ: Princeton University Press.

SKOCPOL, T. 1992. *Protecting Soldiers and Mothers: The Political Origins of Social Policy in the United States.* Cambridge, Mass.: Belknap Press of Harvard University Press.

—— 1996. *Boomerang: Clinton's Health Security Effort and the Turn against Government in U.S. Politics.* New York: W. W. Norton.

SOSS, J. 2000. *Unwanted Claims: The Politics of Participation in the U.S. Welfare System.* Ann Arbor: University of Michigan Press.

STETSON, D. M. and MAZUR, A. G. (eds.) 1995. *Comparative State Feminism.* Thousand Oaks, Calif.: Sage.

STEVENS, B. 1990. Labor unions, employee benefits, and the privatization of the American welfare state. *Journal of Policy History*, 2 (3): 233–60.

SWENSON, P. 2002. *Capitalists Against Markets: The Making of Labor Markets and Welfare States in the United States and Sweden.* New York: Oxford University Press.

TAYLOR-GOOBY, P. 1991. *Social Change, Social Welfare, and Social Science.* Toronto: University of Toronto Press.

THELEN, K. 2003. How institutions evolve: insights from comparative-historical analysis. In *Comparative Historical Analysis in the Social Sciences*, ed. J. Mahoney and D. Rueschemeyer. Cambridge: Cambridge University Press.

TITMUSS, R. M. 1976. *Essays on "The Welfare State,"* 3rd edn. London: Allen and Unwin.

WEAVER, R. K. 1998. The politics of pensions: Lessons from abroad. In *Framing the Social Security Debate*, ed. R. D. Arnold. Washington, DC: Brookings Institution Press.

—— 2000. *Ending Welfare As We Know It.* Washington, DC: Brookings Institution.

WILENSKY, H. L. 1975. *The Welfare State and Equality: Structural and Ideological Roots of Public Expenditures.* Berkeley, Calif.: University of California Press.

CHAPTER 21

THE REGULATORY STATE?

JOHN BRAITHWAITE

1 REGULATION AND GOVERNANCE

States can be thought of as providing, distributing, and regulating. They bake cakes, slice them, and proffer pieces as inducements to steer events. Regulation is conceived as that large subset of governance that is about steering the flow of events, as opposed to providing and distributing. Of course when regulators regulate, they often steer the providing and distributing that regulated actors supply. Governance is a wider set of control activities than government. Students of the state noticed that government has shifted from "government of a unitary state to governance in and by networks" (Bevir and Rhodes 2003, 1; Rhodes 1997). But because the informal authority of networks in civil society not only supplements but also supplants the formal authority of government, Bevir, Rhodes, and others in the networked governance tradition (notably Castells 1996) see it as important to study networked governance for its own sake, rather than as simply a supplement to government. This chapter proceeds from the assumption that there has been a rise of networked governance and builds on Jacint Jordana and David Levi-Faur's (2003, 2004) systematic evidence that, since 1980, states have become rather more

* My thanks to Rod Rhodes, Peter Grabosky, Jennifer Wood, Susanne Karstedt, Clifford Shearing, Christine Parker, and Peter Drahos for helpful comments on drafts of this chapter.

preoccupied with the regulation part of governance and less with providing. Yet non-state regulation has grown even more rapidly, so it is not best to conceive of the era in which we live as one of the regulatory state, but of regulatory capitalism (Levi-Faur 2005).

The chapter sketches historical forces that have produced regulatory capitalism as a police economy that evolved from various feudal economies, the supplanting of police with an unregulable nineteenth-century liberal economy, then the state provider economy (rather than the "welfare state") that gives way to regulatory capitalism. In this era, more of the governance that shapes the daily lives of most citizens is corporate governance than state governance. The corporatization of the world is both a product of regulation and the key driver of regulatory growth, indeed of state growth more generally. The major conclusion of the chapter is that the reciprocal relationship between corporatization and regulation creates a world in which there is more governance of all kinds. 1984 did arrive. The interesting normative question then becomes whether this growth in hybrid governance contracts freedom, or expands positive liberty through an architecture of separated powers that check and balance state and corporate dominations. While that is the quandary of our time the chapter sets up, it does not answer it.

2   THE RISE OF REGULATORY STUDIES

In the 1970s and 1980s the Chicago School could lay claim to an extraordinary swag of Nobel Prize winners such as Milton Freidman and George Stigler (1988), and preeminent law and economics scholars such as Richard Posner, who made regulation a central topic in economics. The Keynesian orthodoxies of statist remedies to market failure were supplanted by what became a Chicago orthodoxy that state failure meant the cure was worse than the disease of market failure. While from within a Chicago framework this is an odd thing to say, it is nevertheless accurate that the Chicago School studied markets as the preeminent regulatory tool. Private property rights and the price mechanism would solve problems like excessive exploitation of resources. If something like pollution was a market externality, then the most efficient way to regulate it would be to create a market in tradable pollution rights. While the Chicago intellectual dominance of these decades crowded out regulation as a topic in political science, notions of regulatory capture by the regulated industry (Bernstein 1955), carved out by political scientists decades earlier, became central to the Chicago discourse.

The Chicago School captured the political imaginations of the Carter and Reagan administrations in the USA, the Thatcher government in the UK, and beyond from the late 1970s. But over time policy-makers became cynical that if whales were endangered, either the rising price of whale meat, or property rights in whales, or creating markets in whale killing rights, were smart or dependable solutions to the problem. By the 1990s, the Chicago School ascendancy had ended and the domination of regulatory studies by economics with it. Many political scientists, including Eugene Bardach and Robert Kagan (1982), John Scholz (1991), Margaret Levi (1988), James Q. Wilson (1980), Joseph Rees (1994), Michael Moran (2003), Christopher Hood (Hood et al. 1999), Giandomenico Majone (1994), Jacint Jordana and David Levi-Faur (2004), and Peter Grabosky (1994) became leading figures in an interdisciplinary field more or less equally populated also by sociologists, criminologists, economists, accountants, and lawyers with also some interest from other disciplines, with interdisciplinary chairs in regulatory studies becoming popular recently, especially in the UK and Australia.

Regulatory studies grew with the realization that neoliberal politics had not produced privatization and deregulation, but privatization and regulatory growth. The most dominant style of research became the study of the politics of particular state regulators and self-regulators, such as those of the nuclear industry (Rees 1994), in ways that revealed the connections among private and public governance networks. In Rees' (1994) case, it is revealed how the players in this governance network were "hostages of each other;" they feared another Three Mile Island, another Chernobyl, might bring them all down.

3   THE RISE OF THE REGULATORY STATE?

In the first two years of the Reagan presidency there was genuine deregulatory zealotry. But by the end of the first Reagan term, business regulatory agencies had resumed the long-run growth in the size of their budgets, the numbers of their staff, the toughness of their enforcement, and the numbers of pages of regulatory laws foisted upon business (Ayres and Braithwaite 1992, 7–12). Later in the Reagan administration financial deregulation came unstuck with a Savings and Loans debacle that cost American taxpayers over $200 billion (Rosoff, Pontell, and Tillman 2002, 255). In this domain, the Reagan and Thatcher governments actually reversed direction globally as well as nationally. The Federal Reserve (US) and Bank of England led the world down to financial deregulation in the early 1980s, then led global prudential standards back up through the G-10 after the banking crises of the mid-1980s for fear of the knock-on effects foreign bank collapses could have on American business (Braithwaite and Drahos 2000, 4). The current Republican administration has presided over a 42 percent increase in regulatory staffing levels since 2001, to 242,473 full-time equivalents by 2005. Admittedly 56,000 of the increase were airport screening agents in the Transportation Security Agency (Dudley and Warren 2005, 1).

In Britain, privatization proliferated in a way that created a need for new regulatory agencies. When British telecommunications was deregulated in 1984, Oftel was created to regulate it (now Ofcom); Ofgas was born for the regulation of a privatized gas industry in 1986, OFFER for electricity in 1989 (now combined in Ofgem), OfWat for water in 1990, and the Office of the Rail Regulator (mercifully not Ofrails!) appeared in 1993 (Baldwin, Scott, and Hood 1998, 14–21). Privatization combined with new regulatory institutions is the classic instantiation of Osborne and Gaebler's (1992) prescription for reinventing government to steer rather than row. Jordana and Levi-Faur (2003, 2004) show that the tendency for state regulation to grow with privatization is a global one. As privatization spreads, they find new regulatory agencies spread even faster, and they show how the diffusion of regulatory agencies moved from the West to take off in Latin America in the 1990s.

I used to describe the key transition as one from the liberal nightwatchman state, to the Keynesian welfare state, to the new regulatory state (after 1980) and a regulatory society (see also Majone 1994; Loughlin and Scott 1997; Parker 1999; Jayasuriya 2001; Midwinter and McGarvey 2001; Muller 2002; Moran 2003). The nub of the regulatory state idea is that power is deployed "through a regulatory framework, rather than through the monopolization of violence or the provision of welfare" (Walby 1999, 123). Now I prefer Levi-Faur's (2005) adaptation of the regulatory state idea into regulatory capitalism. According to Levi-Faur, we have seen since 1980 not only what Vogel (1996) found empirically to be *Freer Markets, More Rules*, but also "more capitalism, more regulation". Privatization is part of Levi-Faur's characterization of regulatory capitalism. But it sits alongside a proliferation of new technologies of regulation and meta-regulation (Parker 2002), or control of control (Power 1997), increased delegation to business and professional self-regulation and to civil society, to intra- and international networks of regulatory experts, and increased regulation of the state by the state, much of it regulation through and for competition (Hood et al. 1999). The regulatory capitalism framework theorizes the New Public Management post-1980 as a conscious separation of provider and regulator functions within the state, where sometimes the provider functions were privatized and regulated, and sometimes they were not privatized but nevertheless subjugated to the "audit society" and government by (audited) contract (Power 1997).

The Keynesian welfare state now seems a poor description of the institutional package that dominated until 1980. One reason is that Keynes is alive and well in his influence on policy processes. Second, it is not really true that states have hollowed out; they have continued to grow as regulators as they have contracted as providers. Nor has the welfare state atrophied. Welfare state spending by rich nations has not declined (Castles 2004). Finally, the state provider economy was not just about providing welfare; it was about states providing transport, industrial infrastructure, utilities, and much more beyond welfare, a deal of which was privatized in the transition to regulatory capitalism.

Even the idea of the nightwatchman state of the nineteenth century needs qualification. The prehistory of the institutional change summarized in this paper could be described as a transition from various feudalisms to a police economy. The sequence I will describe is a transition then from that police economy to the unregulable economy tending to laissez-faire after the collapse of police, to the "state provider economy" (rather than the "welfare state") to "regulatory capitalism" (rather than the "regulatory state").

4   THE POLICE ECONOMY

What does Tomlins (1993, 37–8) mean when he says that writing a history of the American state without a reference to the genealogy of "police" is "akin to writing a history of the American economy without discussing capitalism?" In white settler societies it is easier to see with clarity the police economy because it did not have to struggle to supplant the old economy of monopolies granted by the king to guilds, market towns, and trading companies like the Hudson Bay Company (even as the New World was partly constituted by the latter). That economy of monopoly domination granted by the king was not only an earlier development in the transition from feudalism to capitalism that was subsequently (de)regulated by police, it was also a development largely restricted to cities which were significant nodes of manufactures and long-distance trade.[1] Tiny agricultural communities that did not have a guild or a chartered corporation had a constable. The early modern idea of police differs from the contemporary notion of an organization devoted to fighting crime (Garland 2001). Police from the sixteenth to the nineteenth century in continental Europe meant institutions for the creation of an orderly environment, especially for trade and commerce. The historical origins of the term through German back to French is derived from the Greek notion of "policy" or "politics" in Aristotle (Smith 1978, 486; Neocleous 1998). It referred to all the institutions and processes of ordering that gave rise to prosperity, progress, and happiness, most notably the constitution of markets. Actually it referred to that subset of governance herein conceived as regulation.

---

[1] France was an exception that made guilds state organs and spread their regulatory authority out from towns across the entire countryside (Polanyi 1957, 66).

Police certainly included the regulation of theft and violence, preventive security, regulation of labor, vagrancy, and the poor, but also of weights and measures and other forms of consumer protection, liquor licencing, health and safety, building, fire safety, road and traffic regulation, and early forms of environmental regulation. The institution was rather privatized, subject to considerable local control, relying mostly on volunteer constables and watches for implementation, heavily oriented to self-regulation, and infrequent (even if sometimes draconian) in its recourse to punishment. The *lieutenant de police* (a post established in Paris in 1667) came to have jurisdiction over the stock exchange, food supplies and standards, the regulation of prostitutes, and other markets in vice and virtue. Police and the "science of police" that in eighteenth-century German universities prefigured contemporary regulatory studies sought to establish a new source of order to replace the foundation laid by the estates in the feudal order that had broken down.

English country parishes and small market towns, as on the Continent, had constables and local watches under a Tudor system that for centuries beyond the Tudors regulated the post-feudal economic and social order. Yet there was an English aversion to conceptualizing this as police in the French, German, and Russian fashion. The office of the constable had initially been implanted into British common law and institutions by the Norman invasion of 1066. The office was in turn transplanted by the British to New England, with some New England communities then even requiring Native American villages to appoint constables. Eighteenth-century English, but not American, political instincts were to view Continental political theory of police as a threat to liberty and to seek a more confined role for the constable. Admittedly, Blackstone in his fourth volume of *Commentaries on the Laws of England* (1769 [1966]) adopts the Continental conception of police, and Adam Smith applauds it in his *Lectures on Jurisprudence* (1762–4 [1978]). But Neocleous (1998, 444) detects a shift from the Smith of the *Lectures* to the *Wealth of Nations*, both of which discuss police and the pin factory. The shift is from seeing:

police power contributing to the wealth-producing capacities of a *politically constituted* social order to being a site of autonomous social relations—the independent factory employing independent wage-labourers within a *laissez faire* economy.

Polanyi (1957, 66) quotes Montesquieu as sharing the early Smithian view of English police as constitutive of capitalism, when he says in the *Spirit of Laws* that "The English constrain the merchant, but it is in favor of commerce." Even as institutions of eighteenth-century police are to a considerable degree in place in the nations that become the cutting edge of capitalism (this is also true of the extremely effective policing of the Dutch Republic (Israel 1995, 677–84)), the leading interpreters of capitalism's success move from an interpretation of markets constituted by police to laissez-faire markets.

Peel's creation of the Metropolitan Police in London in 1829 and the subsequent creation of an even more internationally influential colonial model in Dublin were watersheds.

Uniformed paramilitary police, preoccupied with the punitive regulation of the poor to the almost total exclusion of any interest in the constitution of markets and the just regulation of commerce, became one of the most universal of globalized regulatory models. So what happened to the business regulation? From the mid-nineteenth century, factories inspectorates, mines inspectorates, liquor licensing boards, weights and measures inspectorates, health and sanitation, food inspectorates, and countless others were created to begin to fill the vacuum left by constables now concentrating only on crime. Business regulation became variegated into many different specialist regulatory branches. The nineteenth-century regulatory growth is more in the number of branches than in their size and power. Laissez-faire ideology underpinned this regulatory weakness. The regulators' feeble resourcing compared to the paramilitary police, and the comparative wealth of those they were regulating, made the early business regulators even more vulnerable to capture and corruption than the police, as we see with poorly resourced business regulators in developing economies today.

5   THE UNREGULABLE LIBERAL ECONOMY

Where problems were concentrated in space, nineteenth-century regulation secured some major successes. Coal mines became much safer workplaces from the latter years of the nineteenth century, as did large factories in cities (Braithwaite 1985), regulatory transitions that are yet to occur in China that today accounts for 80 percent of the world's coal mine fatalities. Rail travel was causing thousands of deaths annually in the USA late in the nineteenth century (McCraw 1984, 26); by the twentieth century it had become a very safe way to travel (Bradbury 2002). Regulation rendered ships safer and more humane transporters of exploited labor (slaves, convicts, indentured labor, refugees from the Irish famine) to corners of the empire suffering labor shortages (MacDonagh 1961). The paramilitary police were also successful in assisting cities like London, Stockholm, and Sydney to become much safer from crimes against persons and property for a century and a half from 1820 (Gurr, Grabosky, and Hula 1977). But it was only problems like these that were spatially concentrated where nineteenth-century regulation worked. In most domains it worked rather less effectively than eighteenth-century police. This was acceptable to political elites, who were mainly concerned to make protective regulation work where the dangerous classes might congregate to threaten the social order—in cities, convict ships, factories.

In addition to the general under-resourcing of nineteenth-century regulatory inspectorates, the failure to reach beyond large cities, the capture and corruption, there was the fact that the inspectorates were only beginning to invent their regulatory technologies for the first time. They were still learning. The final and largest limitation that made their challenge impossible was that in the nineteenth century almost all commerce was small business. It is harder for an inspector to check ten workplaces employing six people than one with sixty workers. This remains true today. We will see that the regulatory reach of contemporary capitalism would be impossible without the lumpiness of a commerce populated by big businesses that can be enrolled to regulate smaller businesses. Prior to the nineteenth century, it was possible to lever the self-regulatory capabilities of guilds in ways not dissimilar to twentieth-century capabilities to enrol industry associations and big business to regulate small business. But the well-ordered world of guilds had been one of the very things destroyed by the chaotic emergence of laissez-faire capitalism outside the control of such premodern institutions. Where guilds did retain control, capitalism did not flourish, because the guilds restricted competition.

While the nineteenth-century state was therefore mostly a laissez-faire state with limited reach in its capacity to regulate, it was a state learning to regulate. While the early nineteenth-century tension was between the decentralized police economy and laissez-faire liberalism, the late-century tension was between laissez-faire and the growth of an administrative state of office blocks in large cities.

6 THE UNREGULABLE LIBERAL ECONOMY CREATES THE PROVIDER STATE

A simple solution to the problem of private rail companies charging monopoly prices, bypassing poorer towns, failing to serve strategic national development objectives, and flouting safety standards, was to nationalize them. A remedy to unsanitary private hospitals was a public hospital system that would make it unnecessary for patients to resort to unsafe private providers. The challenge of coordinating national regulation of mail services with international regulation through the Universal Postal Union (established in 1863) rendered a state postal monopoly the simplest solution to the coordination that was otherwise beyond the unregulable nineteenth-century liberal economy. The spread of socialist ideas during the nineteenth century gave an ideological impetus to the provider state solution. Progressively, until the beginning of the second half of the twentieth century, the provider state model proliferated, especially in Europe, with airlines, steel, coal, nuclear power, urban public transport, electricity, water, gas, health insurance, retirement insurance, maternal and child welfare, firefighting, sewerage, and countless other things being provided by state monopolies.

Bismarck consciously pursued welfare state provision as a strategy for thwarting the growing popularity of the idea of a socialist revolution to replace capitalism entirely with a state that provided everything. Lloyd-George was impressed by Bismarck's diagnosis and the British Liberal Party also embraced the development of the welfare state, only to be supplanted by a Labour Party that outbid the Liberals with the state provision it was willing to provide to workers who now had votes and political organization.

While many of these state takeovers also occurred in the United States during the century and a half that preceded the arrival of regulatory capitalism, the scope of what was nationalized was narrower there. One reason was that trade unions and the parties and ideologies they spawned were weaker in the USA during the twentieth century. There were periods up to the first decade of the twentieth century when trade unions in the United States were actually numerically and politically stronger than in Europe. The big businesses that grew earlier in the United States used their legal and political capabilities to crush American unionism in the late nineteenth and early twentieth century, frequently through the murder of union officials and threats of violence (Braithwaite and Drahos 2000, 229). American big business could simply organize more effectively against the growth of trade unions and the provider state ideologies they sponsored than against the smaller family firms that predominated in Europe.

A paradox of the fact that American business culture moderated the growth of the provider state was that the regulatory state grew more vigorously in the USA, especially during the progressive era (1890–1913) (which saw the creation of the Federal Trade Commission, Food and Drug Administration, and Interstate Commerce Commission, among other agencies) and the New Deal (1930s) (which saw the creation of the Securities and Exchange Commission, the National Recovery Administration, the Federal Communications Commission, the Civil Aeronautics Board, among others) (McCraw 1984). Building paradox upon paradox, the growth in the sophistication of regulatory technologies in the USA showed that there were credible alternatives to the problems the provider state set out to solve. The New Deal also supplied an economic management rationale to an expansive state. Keynes' general theory was partly about increasing public spending to stimulate an economy when it was in recession, as it was at the time of the New Deal.

7   REGULATION CREATES BIG BUSINESS

Braithwaite and Drahos (2000) have described the corporatization and securitization of the world as among its most fundamental transformations of the last three centuries. I will summarize here how this was enabled by regulation, but then how corporatization in turn enabled regulatory capitalism to replace the provider state economy. Corporations existed for more than a millennium before securities. For our purposes, a security is a transferable instrument evidencing ownership or creditorship, as a stock or bond. The legal invention of the security in the seventeenth century was the most transformative movement in the history of corporations. It enabled the replacement of family firms with very large corporations based on pooled contributions of capital from thousands of shareholders and bondholders. These in turn enabled the great technological projects of eighteenth- and nineteenth-century capitalism—the railroads, the canals, the mines.

When it was first invented, however, the historical importance of the security had nothing to do with the corporatization of the world. Rather, it transformed state finances through bonds that created long-term national debts. While the idea of dividing the national debt into bonds was invented in Naples in the seventeenth century, it was England that managed by the eighteenth century to use the idea in a financial revolution that helped it gain an upper hand over its principal rival, France (Dickson 1993). England became an early provider state in a particularly strategic way by seizing full national control of public finance: formerly private tax and customs collecting were nationalized in the seventeenth century, a Treasury Board was established in the eighteenth, and finally the Bank of England was given national regulatory functions. The Treasury Board realized that the national debt could be made, in effect, self-liquidating and long-term, protecting the realm from extortionate interest rates at times of war and the kind of vulnerability that had brought the Spanish empire down when short-term loans had to be fully repaid after protracted war. Instead of making England hostage to Continental bankers, the national debt was divided into thousands of bonds, with new bond issues placed on the market to pay for old bonds that were due to be paid.

Securitization paid for the warships that allowed Britannia to rule the waves, to trade and colonize—to be a state provider of imperial administration and national as opposed to feudal security on a scale not imagined before. Today, of course, national debts can no longer be used to rule the world because they are regulated by other states through the Paris Club and the IMF (International Monetary Fund). The key thing here is that the early providers of state control of public finance in the process also induced a private bond market. This created the profession of stockbroking and the institution of the stock exchange. For most of the period when Amsterdam and London were the leading stock exchanges in the world, they were predominantly trading securities in the debts of nations. Gradually this created a market in private stocks and bonds. These enabled the English to create the Massachusetts Bay Company, the Hudson Bay Company, the British South Africa Company, the East India Company, and others that conquered the world, and the Dutch to create an even more powerful East India Company and the United New Netherland Company that built a New Amsterdam which was to succeed London as the next capital of the world.

State creation of a London market in the broking of securities fomented other kinds of securities exchanges as well, the most important of which was Lloyd's of London. Britannia's merchant fleet ruled the waves once an efficient market in spreading the lumpy risk of ships sinking with valuable cargos was created from a base in Lloyd's Coffee Shop. Lloyd's in turn became an important inventor of regulatory technologies that made regulatory capitalism possible in advance of the supplanting of the provider state with regulatory capitalism. For example, in building a global reinsurance market, it invented the plimsoll line that allowed insurers to check by simple observation at ports whether ships arrived overloaded.

But by far the most important impact of securitization was that it began a process, that only took off quite late in the nineteenth century, of replacing a capitalism of family firms with one of professional managers of securities put in their trust by thousands of shareholders. Even in New York, where the corporatization of the world was most advanced, it was not until the third decade of the twentieth century that the majority of litigants in appellate courts were corporations rather than individual persons and the majority of actors described on the front page of the *New York Times* were corporate rather than individual actors (Coleman 1982, 11).

8   ANTITRUST GLOBALIZES AMERICAN MEGA-CORPORATE CAPITALISM

In the 1880s, predominantly agrarian America became deeply troubled by the new threat to what they saw as their Jeffersonian agrarian republic from concentrations of corporate power that they called trusts. Farmers were especially concerned about the "robber barons" of railroads that transported their produce across the continent. But oil, steel, and other corporate concentrations of power in the northeast were also of concern. Because Jeffersonian republicanism also feared concentrations of state power in the northeast, the American solution was not to nationalize rail, oil, and steel. It was to break up the trusts. By 1890 at least ten US states had passed antitrust laws, at which point the Sherman Act was passed by a virtually unanimous vote of the US Congress.

The effect of enforcement of the Sherman Act by American courts was not exactly as intended by the progressive era social movement against the railroad, oil, steel, and tobacco trusts. Alfred Chandler (1977, 333–4) noted that "after 1899 lawyers were advising their corporate clients to abandon all agreements or alliances carried out through cartels or trade associations and to consolidate into single, legally defined enterprises." US antitrust laws thus actually encouraged mergers instead of inhibiting them, because they "tolerated that path to monopoly power while they more effectively outlawed the alternative pathway via cartels and restrictive practices" (Hannah 1991, 8). The Americans found that there were organizational efficiencies in managerially centralized, big corporations that made what Chandler (1990, 8) called a "three-pronged investment:" (1) "an investment in production facilities large enough to exploit a technology's potential economies of scale or scope;" (2) "an investment in a national and international marketing and distribution network, so that the volume of sales might keep pace with the new volume of production;" and (3) "to benefit fully from these two kinds of investment the entrepreneurs also had to invest in management."

According to Freyer's (1992) study in the Chandler tradition, the turn-of-the-century merger wave fostered by the Sherman Act thrust US long-term organization for economic efficiency ahead of Britain's for the next half-century, until Britain acquired its Monopolies Act 1948 and Restrictive Trade Practices Act 1956. Until the 1960s, the British economy continued to be dominated by family companies that did not mobilize Chandler's three-pronged investment. Non-existent antitrust enforcement in Britain for the first half of the twentieth century also left new small business entrepreneurs more at the mercy of the restrictive business practices of old money than in the USA. British commitment to freedom of contract was an inferior industrial policy to both the visible hand of American lawmakers' rule of reason and the administrative guidance of the German Cartel Courts. For the era of managerial capitalism, liberal deregulation of state monopolies formerly granted to Indies Companies and guilds was not enough. Simple-minded Smithean invocation of laissez-faire missed the point. A special kind of regulation for the deregulation of restrictive business practices was needed which tolerated bigness.

Ultimately, Braithwaite and Drahos (2000) show that this American model of competitive mega-corporate capitalism globalized under four influences:

1. Extension of the model throughout Europe after the Second World War under the leadership of the German anti-cartel authority, the *Bundeskartelamt*, a creation of the American occupation.
2. Cycles of Mergers and Acquisitions (M&A) mania in Europe catalyzed in part by M&A missionaries from American law firms.

3. Extension of the model to the dynamic Asian economies in the 1980s and 1990s, partly under pressure from bilateral trade negotiations with the USA and Europe (who demanded breaking the restrictive practices of Korean *chaebol*, for example).

4. Extension of the model to developing countries with technical assistance from organizations such as UNCTAD (United Nations Conference on Trade and Development), prodded by the IMF good governance agenda.

This history of a regulatory capitalism that promotes competition among large corporations dates from the 1880s for the US but is very recent for other states. Most of the world's competition regulators have been created since 1990. There were barely twenty in the 1980s; today there are approximately 100.

9   MEGA-CORPORATE CAPITALISM CREATES REGULATORY CAPITALISM

The regulatory state creates mega-corporations, but large corporations also enable regulatory states. We have seen that antitrust regulation is the primary driver of the first side of this reciprocal relationship. But other forms of regulation also prove impossible for small business to satisfy. In many industry sectors, regulation drives small firms that cannot meet regulatory demands into bankruptcy, enabling large corporates to take over their customers (see, for example, Braithwaite's (1994) account of how tougher regulation drove the "mom and pops" out of the US nursing home industry in favor of corporate chains). For this reason, large corporations often use their political clout to lobby for regulations they know they will easily satisfy but that small competitors will not be able to manage. They also lobby for ratcheting up regulation that benefits them directly (e.g. longer patent monopolies) but that are mainly a cost for small business (Braithwaite and Drahos 2000, 56–87).

To understand the second side of this reciprocal relationship more clearly— mega-corporates create regulatory capitalism—consider the minor example of the regulation of the prison industry (Harding 1997). It is minor because most countries have not taken the path of privatizing prisons, though in the USA, where prisons house more than two million inmates and employ about the same number, it is not such a minor business. In the 1990s many private prisons were created in Australia, a number of them owned by the largest American prison corporations. A question that immediately arose was how was the state to ensure that American corporations met Australia's national and international human rights obligations. When the state was the monopoly provider of prison places, it simply, if ineffectively, told its civil servants that they would lose their jobs if they did not fulfill their duty in respect of such standards. This requirement was put into contracts with the private prisons. But then the state has little choice but to invest in a new regulatory agency to monitor contract compliance.

As soon as it puts this in place, prisoner rights' advocates point out that in some respects the old state-run prisons are more abusive than the new private providers, so the prison inspectorate should monitor the public prisons. Moreover, it should make public its reports on the public prisons so that transparency is as real there as with private prisons (Harding 1997). Of course, the private corporations lobby for this as well to create a "level playing field" in their competition with the state. Hence, the corporatization of the prison industry creates not only a demand for the independent, publicly transparent regulation of the corporates, it also creates a potent political demand for regulation of the state itself. This is central to understanding why the regulatory state is not the correct descriptor of contemporary transformations; regulatory capitalism involves heightened regulation of the state as well as growth in regulation by the state (Hood et al. 1999). We have seen this in many other domains including the privatization of British nursing home provision described earlier which led to the inspection of public nursing homes.

Security generally has been a major domain of privatization. Most developed economies today have a ratio of more than three private police to one public police officer (Johnston and Shearing 2003). Under provider capitalism it was public police officers who would provide security at football stadiums, shopping complexes, universities, and airports. But today, as we move from airport to shops to leisure activity to work, we move from one bubble of private security to another (Shearing and Wood 2003; Johnston and Shearing 2003). If our purse is stolen at the shopping mall, it is a private security officer who will come to our aid, or who will detain us if we are caught shoplifting. The public police will only cover us as we move in the public spaces between bubbles of private security. As with prisons, public demand for regulation of the private security industry arises when high profile incidents occur, such as the recent death of one of Australia's most talented cricketers after a bouncer's punch outside a nightclub.

International security has also been privatized. Some of those allegedly leading the abuses at Abu-Grahib in Iraq were private security contractors. Many of these contractors carry automatic weapons, dress like soldiers, and are killed as soldiers by insurgents. In developing countries, particularly in Africa, military corporations have been hired to be the strike infantry against adversaries in civil wars. An estimated 70 per cent of the former KGB found employment in this industry (Singer 2002). This has led the British government to produce a White Paper on the need to regulate private military organizations and to the quip that the regulator be dubbed OfKill!

So the accumulation of political power into the hands of large private corpor-ations creates public demand for regulation. Moreover, we have seen that the largest corporations often demand this themselves. In addition, the regulatory processes and (partly resultant) competitive imperatives that increase the scope and scale of corporations make what was unregulable in the nineteenth century, regulable in the twentieth. The chemicals/pharmaceuticals industry, for example, creates a huge public demand for regulation. Incidents like Bhopal with the manufacture of agricultural chemicals and thalidomide with pharmaceuticals, that kill thousands, galvanize mass concern. The nineteenth-century regulatory state could only respond to public outrage by scapegoating someone in the chemical firm and throwing them in prison. It was incapable of putting a regula-tory regime in place that might prevent a recurrence by addressing the root causes of disasters. There were too many little chemical producers for state inspectors to monitor and it was impossible for them to keep up with technological change that constantly created new risks.

After the Bhopal disaster, which ultimately caused the demise of Union Carbide, the remaining large chemical producers put in place a global self-regulatory regime called "Responsible Care," with the objective of averting another such disaster that might cause a multinational to go under leaving a stain on the reputation of the entire industry (Moffet, Bregha, and Middelkoop 2004). That's all very well, the regulatory cynic notes, but it still remains the case today that most chemical risks are posed by small, local firms with poor self-regulatory standards, not by the multinationals. Yet the fact of mega-corporate capitalism that has evolved over the past century is that almost all small chemical firms are linked upstream or downstream to one multinational or another. They buy or sell chemical ingredients to or from the large corporates. This fact creates a mass tort risk for the multi-nationals. The multinationals are the ones with the deep pockets, the high public profile, and brand reputation; so they are more vulnerable to the irresponsibility of small chemical firms linked to them than are those firms themselves. So Respon-sible Care requires large firms to sustain a chain of stewardship for their chemicals upsteam and downstream. This has the effect of making large corporations the principal regulators of small chemical firms, not the state. This is especially so in developing countries where the temptations of state laissez-faire can make the headquarters' risks potentially most catastrophic.

State regulation and private regulation through tort creates larger chemical corporations. We see this especially in pharmaceuticals where the costs of testing new drugs now run to hundreds of millions of dollars. Global scandals that lead to demand for still tougher regulation creates a community of shared fate among large firms in the industry (note Rees's (1994) study of how the Three Mile Island disaster created a community of fate in the nuclear industry, a belief that another Three Mile Island could cripple the entire industry). Big business responds to finding itself in a community of fate in a risk society (Beck 1992) by industry-wide risk management. This implies managing upstream and downstream risks. Again we see that regulatory capitalism is not only about the regulatory state, though this is a big part of the chemicals, pharmaceuticals, and nuclear stories. It is also about regulation by industry associations of their large members and regulation of small producers by large producers who share the same chain of stewardship for a risk. At the end of the day, it is not only states (with technical assistance from international organizations like the World Health Organization and the OECD (Organization for Economic Co-operation and Development)) doing the regulating; it is global and national industry associations and large multinational firms. Not only does this ease some of the logistical burdens upon the regulatory state in monitoring a galaxy of small firms, it also eases some of the information problems that made chemicals unregulable in the nineteenth century. As partners in regulatory capitalism, state regulators can lean on Responsible Care, the OECD, and large multinationals that may know more than them about where new chemical risks are emerging. Of course there is debate about how well these private–public partnerships of regulatory capitalism work (Gunningham and Grabosky 1998).

Braithwaite and Drahos (2000) revealed the importance of yet other actors who are as important as non-state regulators. Ratings agencies like Moody's and Standards and Poors, having witnessed the bankrupting of imprudent chemical producers, downgrade the credit rating of firms with a record of sloppy risk management. This makes money more expensive for them to borrow. Reinsurers like Lloyd's also make their risks more expensive to reinsure. The cost and availability of lending and insurance also regulates small firms. Care homes (including nursing homes) frequently go bankrupt in the UK; these bankruptcies are often connected to the delivery of poor quality care. Reports of British government care home inspections are on the Internet. When homes approach banks for loans, it is good banking practice today to do an Internet check to see if the home has any looming quality of care problems. If it does, banks sometimes refuse loans until these problems are addressed. Banks have thence become important regulators of little and large British care home firms.

9.1   Corporatization, Tax, and the Constitution of Provider and Regulatory Capitalism

One effect of the corporatization of capitalism in the twentieth century was that it made it easier for the state to collect tax. This revenue made it possible to fund both the provider state and the regulatory state. State provision of things like welfare and transport, and state regulation are expensive activities. So taxpaying becoming regulable was decisive to the subsequent emergence of the provider state and regulatory capitalism. In most developing societies taxpaying remains unregulable and this has closed the door on credible state provision and state regulation.

Of course it is more cost-effective to collect tax from one large corporation than ten small ones and most corporate tax is collected from the largest 1 percent of corporations in wealthy nations. But this is not the main reason that corporatization created a wealthy state. More fundamentally, corporatization assisted the collectability of other taxes (see Braithwaite and Drahos 2000, ch. 9). As retailing organizations became larger corporates, as opposed to family-owned corner stores, the collection of indirect tax became more cost-effective. When most of the Australian working class was rural, itinerantly shearing sheep for graziers, cutting cane, or picking fruit, collecting taxes from them was difficult and costly. But as the working class became progressively more urban—in the employ of city-based corporations—income tax collections from workers became a goldmine, especially after the innovation of Pay As You Earn (withholding of tax from pay packets by employers, which started in Australia in 1944). The final contribution of mega-corporatization was financial institutions becoming more concentrated and computerized, making withholding on interest and dividends feasible. So tax on salary income, corporate tax, sales taxes, and tax on income from interest and dividends all became more collectable. The result was that, contrary to the fairytale of neoliberalism, the state grew and grew into a regulatory capitalism where the state both retained many of its provider functions and added many new regulatory ones.

Pay As You Earn was an innovative regulatory technology of wider relevance. PAYE taxpayers cannot cheat because it is not them, but their employers, who hand over the money. Theoretically of course the employer can cheat. But they have no incentive to do so, since only their employee benefits from the cheating, and the cheating is visible in the accounts. The regulatory strategy of general import here is to impose regulatory obligations on keepers of a gate that controls the flow of the regulated activity, where the gatekeepers do not benefit personally from opening and closing the gate. This not only separates the power from the incentive to cheat, it also economizes on surveillance. It is not necessary to monitor all the regulated actors at all times. The regulator must only monitor the gatekeeper at those points when gates can be unlocked.

10   THE REGULATED STATE

For 90 percent of the world's states there are large numbers of corporations with annual sales that exceed the state's GDP. The CEOs of the largest corporations typically are better networked into other fonts of power than the presidents of medium-sized states. Consequently large corporations do a lot of regulating of states. There are also some smaller global corporations like Moody's and Standard and Poors that have specialized regulatory functions over states—setting their credit ratings. More generally, finance capital holds sway over states. This is exercised through capital movements, but also through lobbying global institutions such as the IMF, the Basle Committee, World Trade Organization Panels, and the World Bank, who might have more direct control over a specific sphere of state activity. The most formidable regulator of debtor states is the IMF, as a result of its frequently used power to impose regulatory conditions upon debt repayment.

While states have formidable regulatory leverage over airlines, for example, airlines can enrol the International Civil Aviation Organization to regulate landing rights to and from states that fail to meet their obligations to the orderly conduct of international transport. While states regulate telecoms, they must submit to regulation by the ITU (International Telecommunication Union) if they want inter-connectivity with telecoms in other states, and powerful corporations invest heavily in lobbying the ITU and in having their executives chair its technical committees.

Many states simply forfeit domains of regulation to global corporations that have superior technical capability and greater numbers of technically competent people on the ground. For example, in many developing nations the Big Four accounting firms effectively set national accounting standards. States are also regulated by international organizations (and bilaterally) to comply with legal obligations under treaties they have signed. Sanctions range from armed force to air and sea blockades, suspension of voting rights on international organizations, trade sanctions, and "smart sanctions" such as seizure of foreign assets and denial of visas to members of the regime and their families. Regional organizations such as the EU (European Union) and the African Union, of course, also have a degree of regulatory leverage over member states. Leverage tends to be greatest when states are applying for membership of an international club such as the World Trade Organization or EU from which they believe they would benefit.

One of the defining features of regulatory capitalism is that parts of states are set up with independent capacities to regulate other parts of the state. Since 1980 the globalization of the institution of the Ombudsman and the proliferation of audit offices has reached the point where some describe what Levi-Faur calls regulatory capitalism as *The Audit Society* (Power 1997). Finally, there is the development of independent inspectors of privatized industries moving their oversight back to public provision.

Of course the idea of a separation of powers where one branch of governance regulates another so that neither executive, judiciary, nor legislature can dominate governance is an old one, dating at least from the Spartan constitution and Montesquieu (Braithwaite 1997). But practice has become more variegated, especially in Asian constitutions such as those of Thailand and Taiwan that conceive of themselves as having more than three branches of governance, with branches such as the Election Commission, Ombudsman, Human Rights Commission, Counter Corruption Commission, and Audit and Examination Offices enjoying constitutionally separated powers from the legislative, executive, and judicial branches. The theory as well as the practice of the doctrine of separation of powers under regulatory capitalism has also moved forward on how innovative separations of powers can deter abuse of power (see Braithwaite 1997). To the extent that there are richer, more plural separations within and between private and public powers in a polity, there is a prospect of moving toward a polity where no one power can dominate all the others and each power can exercise its regulatory functions semi-autonomously even against the most powerful branch of state or corporate power. As Durkheim began to see, the art of government "consists largely in coordinating the functions of the various self-regulating bodies in different spheres of the economy" (Schepel 2005, ch. 1; see also Cotterrell 1999; Durkheim 1930, preface).

11   CONCLUSION

The transitions since feudal structures of governance fell to incipient capitalist institutions have been from a police economy, to an unregulable nineteenth-century liberal economy that oscillated between laissez-faire, dismantling the decentralized police economy, and laying the bricks and mortar of an initially weak urban administrative state, to the provider state economy, to regulatory capitalism. Across all of these transitions, markets in fits and starts have tended to become progressively more vigorous, as has investment in the regulation of market externalities. Not only have markets, states, and state regulation become more formidable, so has non-state regulation by civil society, business, business associations, professions, and international organizations. Separations of powers within polities have become more variegated, with more private–public hybridity. This means political science conceived narrowly as a discipline specialized in the study of public governance to the exclusion of corporate governance, NGO governance, and the governance of transnational networks makes less sense than it once did. If we have entered an era of regulatory capitalism, regulation may be, in contrast, a fruitful topic around which to build intellectual communities and social science theory.

Interesting agendas implied by this perspective are empirical studies of how networked regulators like the Forest and Marine Stewardship Councils, Social

Accountability International, and the Sustainable Agriculture Network (Courville 2003) operate, research on devolved regulatory technologies that harness local knowledge (Shearing and Wood 2003), Levi Faur's (2006) agenda of documenting and comparatively dissecting the *Varieties of Regulatory Capitalism*, the Hall and Soskice (2001), Stiglitz (2002), and Rodrik (2004) agendas of diagnosing the institutional mixes that make capitalism buzz and collapse in the context of specific states, the Dorf and Sabel (1998) agenda of evidence-based "democratic experimentalism," the Campbell Collaboration, and behavioral economics agendas for real policy experiments on the impacts of regulatory interventions. Important among these are experiments on meta-regulation—regulated self-regulation—as a form of social control that seems paradigmatic of regulatory capitalism (Parker 2002; Braithwaite 2005).

In seeing the separations among the periods posited in this chapter, it is also important to grasp the posited continuities. Both markets and the state become stronger, enlarged in scope and transaction density, at every stage. Elements of eighteenth-century police are retained in the creation of nineteenth-century paramilitary police and other specialized regulators. Post-1980 regulatory capitalism learns from and builds upon the weaknesses (and the strengths) of nineteenth- and early twentieth-century regulation—from twenty-first-century private security corporations learning from Peel's Metropolitan Police and the KGB, to state shipping regulators and the International Maritime Organization learning from regulatory technologies crafted in Lloyd's Coffee Shop. While many problems solved by state provision prior to 1980 are thence solved by privatization into contested, regulated markets, most of the state provision of the era of the provider state persists under regulatory capitalism. Even some renationalization of poorly conceived privatization has begun.

A contribution of this chapter has been to suggest that regulation, particularly antitrust and securitization of national debt, enabled the growth of both provider and regulatory states. Regulation did this through pushing the spread of large corporations that made Chandler's (1977, 1990) three-pronged investment. The corporatization of the world increased the efficacy of tax enforcement, funding provider and regulatory state growth. The corporatization of the world drove a globalization in which transnational networks, industry associations, professions, international organizations, NGOs, NGO/retailer hybrids like the Forest Stewardship Council, and most importantly corporations themselves (especially, but not limited to, stock exchanges, ratings agencies, the Big Four accounting firms, multinationals that specialize in doing states' regulation for them like Société Général de Surveillance,[2] and large corporates that regulate small upstream and

---

[2] This is a large Swiss multinational that provides all manner of regulatory services for states from environmental inspection to collecting nations' customs duties for them in innovative ways (Braithwaite and Drahos 2000, 492–3).

downstream firms in the same industry) became important national, regional, and global regulators. This was a very different capitalism and a very different world of governance than existed in the early twentieth-century industrial capitalism of family firms. Hence the power of Levi-Faur's conceptualization of regulatory capitalism. While states are "decentred" under regulatory capitalism, the wealth it generates means that states have more capacity both to provide and to regulate than ever before.

References

Ayres, I. and Braithwaite, J. 1992. *Responsive Regulation: Transcending the Deregulation Debate.* New York: Oxford University Press.

Baldwin, R., Scott, C., and Hood, C. 1998. *A Reader on Regulation.* Oxford: Oxford University Press.

Bardach, E. and Kagan, R. A. 1982. *Going by the Book: The Problem of Regulatory Unreasonableness.* Philadelphia: Temple University Press.

Beck, U. 1992. *Risk Society: Towards a New Modernity.* Beverly Hills, Calif.: Sage.

Bernstein, M. 1955. *Regulating Business by Independent Commission.* Princeton, NJ: Princeton University Press.

Bevir, M. and Rhodes, R. 2003. *Interpreting British Governance.* London: Routledge.

Blackstone, W. 1966. *Commentaries on the Laws of England, Vol 4.* London: Dawsons.

Bradbury, N. 2002. Face the facts on transport safety. *Railwatch,* November: 6–7.

Braithwaite, J. 1985. *To Punish or Persuade: Enforcement of Coal Mine Safety.* Albany: State University of New York Press.

—— 1994. The nursing home industry. Pp. 11–54 in *Beyond the Law: Crime in Complex Organizations, Crime and Justice: A Review of Research,* ed. M. Tonny and A. J. Reiss. Chicago.: University of Chicago Press.

—— 1997. On speaking softly and carrying sticks: neglected dimensions of republican separation of powers. *University of Toronto Law Journal,* 47: 1–57.

—— 2005. *Markets in Vice, Markets in Virtue.* Oxford: Federation Press.

—— and Drahos, P. 2000. *Global Business Regulation.* Melbourne: Cambridge University Press.

Castells, M. 1996. *The Information Age: Economy, Society and Culture, Volume 1: The Rise of the Network Society.* Oxford: Blackwell.

Castles, F. G. 2004. *The Future of the Welfare State: Crisis Myths and Crisis Realities.* Cambridge: Cambridge University Press.

Chandler, A. D., Jr. 1977. *The Visible Hand: The Managerial Revolution in American Business.* Cambridge, Mass.: Belknap Press.

—— 1990. *Scale and Scope: The Dynamics of Industrial Capitalism.* Cambridge, Mass.: Belknap Press.

Coleman, J. S. 1982. *The Asymmetric Society.* Syracuse, NY: Syracuse University Press.

Cotterrell, R. 1999. *Emile Durkheim: Law in a Moral Domain.* Palo Alto, Calif.: Stanford University Press.

COURVILLE, S. 2003. Social accountability audits: challenging or defending democratic governance? *Law and Policy*, 25 (3): 267–97.

DICKSON, P. G. M. 1993 *The Financial Revolution in England: A Study in the Development of Public Credit, 1688–1756*. Brookfield, Vt.: Gregg Revivals.

DORF, M. and SABEL, C. 1998. A constitution of democratic experimentalism. *Columbia Law Review*, 98: 267–473.

DUDLEY, S. and WARREN, M. 2005. *Regulators' Budget Continues to Rise: An Analysis of the U.S. Budget for Fiscal Years 2004 and 2005*. St. Louis: Weidenbaum Center, Washington University.

DURKHEIM, E. 1930. *De la Division du Travail Social*, 2nd edn. Paris: PUF.

FREYER, T. 1992. *Regulating Big Business Antitrust in Great Britain and America, 1880–1990*. Cambridge: Cambridge University Press.

GARLAND, D. 2001. *The Culture of Control: Crime and Social Order in Contemporary Society*. Oxford: Oxford University Press.

GRABOSKY, P. N. 1994. Green markets: environmental regulation by the private sector. *Law and Policy*, 16: 419–48.

GUNNINGHAM, N. and GRABOSKY, P. 1998. *Smart Regulation: Designing Environmental Policy*. Oxford: Clarendon Press.

GURR, T. R., GRABOSKY, P. N., and HULA, R. C. 1977. *The Politics of Crime and Conflict*. Beverly Hills, Calif.: Sage.

HALL, P. A. and SOSKICE, D. (eds.) 2001. *Varieties of Capitalism: The Institutional Foundations of Comparative Advantage*. Oxford: Oxford University Press.

HANNAH, L. 1991. Mergers, cartels and concentration: legal factors in the US and European experience. Pp. 3–13 in *Antitrust and Regulation*, ed. G. H. Burgess, Jr. Aldershot: Edward Elgar.

HARDING, R. W. 1997. *Private Prisons and Public Accountability*. Buckingham: Open University Press.

HOOD, C., SCOTT, C., JAMES, O., JONES, G. W., and TRAVERS, A. J. 1999. *Regulation Inside Government: Waste-Watchers, Quality Police, and Sleaze-Busters*. Oxford: Oxford University Press.

ISRAEL, J. 1995. *The Dutch Republic: Its Rise, Greatness and Fall, 1477–1806*. Oxford: Clarendon Press.

JAYASURIYA, K. 2001. Globalization and the changing architecture of the state: the politics of the regulatory state and the politics of negative co-ordination. *Journal of European Public Policy*, 8 (1): 101–23.

JOHNSTON, L. and SHEARING, C. 2003. *Governing Security: Explorations in Policing and Justice*. London: Routledge.

JORDANA, J. and LEVI-FAUR, D. 2003. The rise of the regulatory state in Latin America: a study of the diffusion of regulatory reforms across countries and sectors. Paper to the Annual Meeting of the American Political Science Association, 28 August.

——— ——— (eds.) 2004. *The Politics of Regulation: Examining Regulatory Institutions and Instruments in the Governance Age*. Cheltenham: Edward Elgar.

LEVI, M. 1988. *Of Rule and Revenue*. Berkeley: University of California Press.

LEVI-FAUR, D. 2005. The global diffusion of regulatory capitalism. *Annals of the American Academy of Political and Social Science*, 598: 12–32.

——— (ed.) 2006. Varieties of regulatory capitalism. From David Levi-Faur's homepage: My special issue on "Varieties of Regulatory Capitalism," published by *Governance*, May 2006.

LOUGHLIN, M. and SCOTT, C. 1997. The regulatory state. Pp. 205–19 in *Developments in British Politics 5*, ed. P. Dunleavy, I. Holliday, and G. Peele. London: Macmillan.

McCRAW, T. K. 1984. *Prophets of Regulation*. Cambridge, Mass.: Harvard University Press.

MACDONAGH, O. 1961. *A Pattern of Government Growth: The Passenger Acts and Their Enforcement*. London: Macgibbon and Kee.

MAJONE, G. 1994. The rise of the regulatory state in Europe. *West European Politics*, 17: 77–101.

MIDWINTER, A. and McGARVEY, N. 2001. In search of the regulatory state: evidence from Scotland. *Public Administration*, 79 (4): 825–49.

MOFFET, J., BREGHA, F., and MIDDELKOOP, M. J. 2004. Responsible care: a case study of a voluntary environmental initiative. Pp. 177–208 in *Voluntary Codes: Private Governance, the Public Interest and Innovation*, ed. K. Webb. Carleton: Carleton Research Unit on Innovation, Science and Environment.

MONTESQUIEU, C. DE SECONDAT 1989. *The Spirit of the Laws*, trans. and ed. A. M. Cohler and B. C. Miller. Cambridge: Cambridge University Press.

MORAN, M. 2003. *The British Regulatory State: High Modernism and Hyper-Innovation*. Oxford: Oxford University Press.

MULLER, M. M. 2002. *The New Regulatory State in Germany*. Birmingham: Birmingham University Press.

NEOCLEOUS, M. 1998. Policing and pin-making: Adam Smith, police and the state of prosperity. *Policing and Society*, 8: 425–49.

OSBORNE, D. and T. GAEBLER. 1992. *Reinventing Government: How the Entrepreneurial Spirit is Transforming the Public Sector*. Reading, Mass.: Addison-Wesley.

PARKER, C. 1999. *Just Lawyers*. Oxford: Oxford University Press.

—— 2002. *The Open Corporation*. Melbourne: Cambridge University Press.

POLANYI, K. 1957. *The Great Transformation*. Boston: Beacon Press.

POWER, M. 1997. *The Audit Society: Rituals of Verification*. Oxford: Oxford University Press.

REES, J. 1994. *Hostages of Each Other: The Transformation of Nuclear Safety Since Three Mile Island*. Chicago: University of Chicago Press.

RHODES, R. A. W. 1997. *Understanding Governance*. Buckingham: Open University Press.

RODRIK, D. 2004. *Rethinking Growth Policies in the Developing World*. Cambridge, Mass.: Harvard University Press.

ROSOFF, S. E., PONTELL, H. N., and TILLMAN, R. H. 2002. *Profit Without Honor: White-Collar Crime and the Looting of America*. Upper Saddle River, NJ: Prentice Hall.

SCHEPEL, H. 2005. *The Constitution of Private Governance*. Oxford: Hart.

SCHOLZ, J. T. 1991. Coperative regulatory enforcement and the politics of administrative effectiveness. *American Political Science Review*, 85: 115–36.

SHEARING, C. and WOOD, J. 2003. Nodal governance, democracy and the new "denizens." *Journal of Law and Society*, 30 (3): 400–19.

SINGER, P. W. 2002. Corporate warriors: the rise and ramifications of the privatised military industry. *International Security*, 26 (3): 186–220.

SMITH, A. 1978. *Lectures on Jurisprudence*, ed. R. L. Meek, D. D. Raphael, and P. G. Stein. Oxford: Clarendon Press.

—— 1979. *Inquiry into the Nature and Causes of the Wealth of Nations*, ed. R. H. Campbell, A. S. Skinner, and W. B. Todd. Indianapolis: Liberty Fund.

STIGLER, G. J. (ed.) 1988. *Chicago Studies in Political Economy.* Chicago: University of Chicago Press.

STIGLITZ, J. E. 2002. *Globalization and its Discontents.* New York: W. W. Norton.

TOMLINS, C. L. 1993. *Law, Labor, and Ideology in the Early American Republic.* New York: Cambridge University Press.

VOGEL, S. K. 1996. *Freer Markets, More Rules: Regulatory Reform in Advanced Industrial Societies.* London: Cornell University Press.

WALBY, S. 1999. The new regulatory state: the social powers of the European Union. *British Journal of Sociology,* 50 (1): 118–38.

WILSON J. Q. 1980. *The Politics of Regulation.* New York: Basic Books.

CHAPTER 22

LEGISLATIVE ORGANIZATION

JOHN M. CAREY

1 INTRODUCTION

Legislatures are, at least according to the formal rules set out by constitutions, the principle policy-making institutions in modern democracies. The most fundamental policy decisions—budgets, treaties and trade agreements, economic, environmental, and social regulation, elaboration of individual and collective rights—all must be approved by legislatures. In light of this, what is expected from legislatures in a democracy? To put it another way, how are legislatures to go about meeting this formidable array of responsibilities? I suggest that the following jobs top the list:

- representing diversity;
- deliberation;
- cultivating information and expertise;
- decisiveness;
- checking majority and executive power.

If these are the goals at which democratic legislatures aim, then it is worth asking what research on comparative legislatures tells us about whether they are realized. This chapter examines each of the normative goals in turn, beginning with a brief description of each, and then drawing on current research that reflects on how legislative organization reaches these ideals and the manners in which it frequently falls short.

1.1 Representation

Legislatures are plural bodies with larger membership than executives, and so offer the possibility both to represent more accurately the range of diversity in the polity, and to foster closer connections between representatives and voters. The diversity represented in legislatures may be defined along collective lines; that is, representation operates through groups of politicians who are selected in "teams" to represent some set of interests. The rules by which collective representatives are selected, in turn, must identify some set of principles defining interests, such as geographical location, partisanship, race, ethnicity, gender, language, religion, etc. Alternatively, legislatures may include representatives who simply draw strong individual-level support from sub-groups of voters who self-identify by their choice of which candidates to support. Most legislatures have elements of both sorts of representation, but individualism and collectivism entail trade-offs and cannot be maximized simultaneously.

1.2 Deliberation

Legislatures are forums for debate and reasoned consideration of the diverse viewpoints they embrace. Their internal workings are supposed to be subject to monitoring from outside actors. By forcing debate into an open setting, legislatures may limit admissible arguments on behalf of interests or policy positions to those that can be defended in public. Furthermore, by virtue of their transparency, legislatures open the possibility that representatives can be held accountable for their actions by those they represent. In practice, however, the extent to which legislative deliberation and decision-making is transparent to those outside the institutions varies considerably, which in turn affects the extent to which legislatures can serve as vehicles for transparency and accountability.

1.3 Information

The size of legislatures also allows for specialization and the development of expertise among members. Legislatures are frequently organized so as to encourage this information building function, with committee systems that break down policy-making responsibilities according to distinct jurisdictions. The extent to which legislatures become repositories of policy expertise, however, varies enormously.

1.4 Decisiveness

The size and diversity of legislatures also reflects a specific challenge. The number of policy options available in any political environment is generally vast. Well-known theoretical problems of collective decision-making among multiple actors over large choice sets include indeterminacy and the potential for cycling among alternatives. Remedies to these problems can involve distributing procedural rights among legislators, providing some with special authorities to block proposals, to make privileged proposals, or some combination of these. These remedies, in turn, can become sources of contentiousness, especially to the extent that they generate inequalities among legislators in their ability to influence collective decisions. At any rate, legislatures are supposed to boil down the potentially infinite number of policy options available to a manageable and coherent set of alternatives, among which a meaningful collective decision can be reached.

1.5 Checks

Notwithstanding the privileged place of majorities in almost all democracies, unrestrained majority rule is widely mistrusted as subject to excesses and abuse of minority rights. Opposition groups may use the legislature as a forum to oppose, and perhaps to obstruct, actions by majority coalitions. Moreover, legislatures everywhere are embedded in broader institutional environments in which policy-making decisions depend on multiple actors. Legislatures may challenge the actions of executives who act, to varying degrees, independently. The capacity for checking majority action within legislatures depends on the distribution of procedural rights among members; and the capacity for checking external actors depends on the distribution of policy-making authorities across branches and across legislative chambers in bicameral systems. In all cases, however, the desirability of legislative checks rests on much the same foundation as the normative properties of legislatures discussed previously. Checks should reveal information about policies and about the motivations of their advocates that might not have been disclosed otherwise. In doing so, checks should encourage deliberation and foster accountability. Finally, checks may undermine decisiveness in the short run by delaying agreement, but by making it more difficult to alter the status quo, they should encourage policy stability in the long run, and thereby make legislative decisions stick once they are taken.

2   REPRESENTATION

In 2005, as this chapter is being drafted, debate among both policy-makers and academics is ongoing over how to craft mechanisms to represent diversity in two particularly challenging legislative environments: Afghanistan and Iraq.[1] In both cases, US-led invasions in 2001 and 2003, respectively, produced governments commissioned to craft new constitutions, and to hold elections to fill the political offices so founded. In both cases, there is widespread acknowledgment that plural societies warrant representation of broad diversity within the legislature. The fundamental stumbling block in both cases is to identify what sort of diversity ought to be privileged in legislative representation. Various dimensions of representation—including geography, ethnicity, religion, and gender—have been prominently on the table in each case. Less-widely noted is that the Afghan and Iraqi cases, and the associated debates surrounding how best to move toward electoral democracy, embody the fundamental trade-off between collective and individualistic representation in a context relatively unbounded by existing precedent.

2.1   Iraq and Afghanistan

The Iraqi election of January 2005, which chose a dual-purpose constituent assembly and parliament, embodies the extreme collectivist end of this trade-off. The electoral law handed down by the outgoing, US-led Coalition Provisional Authority, the regulatory details of which were filled in with UN assistance, stipulated that the entire country encompassed a single electoral district with 275 seats, the implications of which were far-reaching, however, for the types of legislative representation possible in Iraq.[2] First, the high district magnitude effectively

---

[1] The brief discussion that follows here of Iraq and Afghanistan at a particular moment in time—2005—is not meant to serve as a thorough review of legislative electoral rules, much less as a comprehensive analysis of the politics of these countries. The former is provided in an impressive literature on comparative electoral systems (Duverger 1954; Taagepera and Shugart 1989; Lijphart 1994; Cox 1997; Monroe 2005), and the latter is well beyond my capacity.

[2] One compelling motivation for this choice had to do simply with logistics of electoral administration: Iraq lacked a reliable census by which legislative seats might be apportioned across districts according to population.

mandated that elections would be based on closed lists, and that voters would not have the option of casting preference votes for individual candidates. Second, high magnitude made it possible to award legislative seats to lists that won relatively small vote shares overall, thus allowing for a high degree of proportionality. Third, the nationwide list system is technically agnostic among many competing conceptions of representation—for example geographical, ethnic, religious— and simply rewards lists that can mobilize the most voters. However, because the composition of the assembly is determined as much by the selection of candidates as by the popular vote, closed lists also open up the possibility of tipping legislative representation toward categories of candidates who might not survive in a more individualistic electoral marketplace. Specifically, in the Iraqi case, gender quotas for candidates mandated that every third candidate must be a woman.

The January 2005 election in Iraq produced an assembly in which twelve separate lists won representation, with an effective number of seat-winning parties of 3.14 (Laakso and Taagepera 1979), a close correspondence between votes cast and seats awarded to each list, with a Gallagher Index of less than 3 percent (Gallagher 1991) and substantial representation of ethnic groups previously marginalized in Iraqi politics (Burns and Ives 2005). The guaranteed placement of women at regular intervals on closed lists translated into an assembly with 29 percent women overall—about twice the worldwide average (Inter-Parliamentary Union 2005). In sum, the Iraqi system made it feasible to realize many of the normative goals associated with the representation of diversity at the collective level.

The Afghan experience with establishing a national assembly has been substantially different. An indirectly elected assembly drafted a new Afghan Constitution that was ratified in early 2004 and stipulated the popular election of both a presidency and a bicameral legislature later that year. The presidential election was carried off, on close to the original schedule, in October 2004, but legislative elections have been twice postponed in part due to the logistical challenges of conducting elections that simultaneously honor the determination of the Afghan government to:

- guarantee an element of regional representation via geographical districts;
- avoid a winner-take-all system of elections in which only the top party or candidate in a district wins representation;
- ensure voter choice over individual legislative candidates; and
- guarantee the representation of women.

The electoral system that has remained at the center of debate in Afghanistan is the single non-transferable vote (SNTV), currently used only in Taiwan, Jordan, and Vanuatu, and most familiar mainly for its long use in Japanese elections, from 1958–94. SNTV is plurality rule in multimember districts. Each voter casts a ballot for her or his first-choice candidate, and the candidates with the most votes are elected in each district, up to the number of seats available. SNTV is attractive in its simplicity, and for its potential to allow minority groups to secure representation while simultaneously holding out the promise of a bond of direct personal accountability between voters and their representatives.

SNTV, however, is subject to at least two severe drawbacks that undermine its potential to provide viable representation in the Afghan context. First, SNTV presents any collective political actor—a party, for example—with a formidable coordination problem in translating electoral support into legislative representation. The problem is a fundamental conflict of interests between the party and its individual politicians.[3] Parties seek to win as many seats as possible. Individual politicians may prefer to be members of strong parties, but their first priority is to win office. Under SNTV, candidates who seek to minimize the risk of individual defeat have incentives to draw votes away from co-partisans, undermining the collective goal of translating votes to legislative representation efficiently. By privileging electoral individualism, SNTV presents formidable challenges to parties' ability to foster internal cooperation among politicians, and so to provide collective representation (McCubbins and Rosenbluth 1995; Cox and Thies 1998).

An even more immediate challenge to the feasibility of SNTV in Afghanistan is the incompatibility between individualistic legislative representation and the representation of women. The Afghan Constitution requires that at least two lower-house legislators from each of the country's thirty-four provinces be female (Article 83). SNTV provides no alternative basis than individual vote totals for awarding legislative seats, so unless at least two of the top candidates in each province are women, the Afghan legislature will be confronted with the prospect of bypassing male candidates with more votes in order to seat female candidates with fewer votes. In a society where gender-based inequalities in personal resources, as well as gender bias among voters, may constrain the viability of female candidates, this prospect appears inevitable, and may undermine public acceptance of the elections generally.

2.2 The Collectivism vs. Individualism Trade-off

The fundamental contrast in the Iraqi and Afghan choices over electoral rules, at this point, is between privileging collective versus individualistic representation. For myriad reasons, the system chosen for Iraq's January 2005 election leans toward the former. This facilitated the initial, descriptive representation of various collective identities—most notably by party alliance, ethnicity, religion,

---

[3] The problem is also increasingly severe as district magnitude increases. Magnitudes in Japanese SNTV elections ranged from three to five. In Afghanistan, the average district magnitude for parliamentary elections would be around seven, and some districts would be considerably larger (Constitution of Afghanistan, Art. 82).

and gender. Afghan rules—as outlined initially—lean toward privileging connections between voters and individual candidates, but try simultaneously to guarantee minority representation and representation according to at least one prominent form of collective identity: gender. Reconciling individualistic and collective representation in a set of workable electoral rules has proven difficult in the Afghan context.

With respect to legislative representation more generally, these cases suggest that the individualistic vs. collective representation distinction may be as important as the principle characteristic by which electoral systems are more frequently distinguished—whether elections are winner-take-all in single-member districts (SMD), or proportional (PR). The characteristics and relative merits of SMD vs. PR are central to a long-standing literature on legislative elections, the predominant conclusion from which has been that PR is normatively superior to SMD elections (Sartori 1976; Lijphart 1994; Huber and Powell 1994; Colomer 2001). This conclusion rests on some key assumptions however: that political parties are fundamental units of legislative representation, and that a left–right spectrum meaningfully describes the ideological arena of party competition. In the industrialized, long-standing democracies, where most studies of legislative representation have been conducted, there is solid empirical evidence for these assumptions (Powell and Vanberg 2000). They are open to greater skepticism in other environments, however, particularly where party systems are more volatile or party reputations less stable.

The point here is that the foundation on which the conventional SMD vs. PR debate has been conducted is weak in many political environments where the most critical choices about how to organize legislative representation remain open. The complete absence of established party systems in the Iraqi and Afghan cases are extreme examples, but it is worth noting that SMD versus PR was not central to debate in either context; winner-take-all rules gained traction in neither case. Rather, the critical distinction in these cases is over whether electoral rules ought to prioritize collective vs. individualistic representation. This theme has been central to debates over reforming legislative representation much more widely during recent decades, particularly with respect to mixed-member electoral systems that combine SMD with list PR elections within the same legislative chamber, variants of which were adopted in the 1990s by over twenty countries (Shugart and Wattenberg 2001; International Institute for Democracy and Electoral Assistance 1997; Culver and Ferrufino 2000; Carey 2003).

To sum up, legislatures offer the promise of representing the diversity of the polity, but electoral rules affect the dimensions along which diversity can be translated into representation. Although the differences between SMD and PR elections have traditionally been essential to the study of comparative legislatures, this distinction is growing less central relative to that between individualistic and collective representation, which is quite a different matter, both theoretically and empirically (Carey and Shugart 1995). Whereas the literature on comparative legislative representation tends to favor PR over SMD, there is less academic consensus on the relative merits of individualistic vs. collective representation (Golden and Chang 2001; Persson and Tabellini 2003). This is an area that ought to attract substantial attention among scholars of comparative legislatures.

3   DELIBERATION

Once representatives, of whatever type, are selected, they must establish procedures to consider alternative policy proposals. In this instance, legislative process is very much a part of the product; democratic legislatures are *public* forums of debate and deliberation. What is the relevance of *public*-ness? Adherents of deliberative democracy contend that public debate is characterized by norms that limit admissible arguments on behalf of proposals in ways that contribute to the public good.

3.1   Elevating the Debate

Imagine there are two types of policy available, those that serve the general public good, and those that serve the good of some actors at the expense of others. In a closed decision process I might pursue—via my proposals, my coalition-building efforts, my vote, etc.—either type of outcome. The deliberative democracy claim is that public debate constrains me from pursuing the latter type (Goodin 1986). As David Miller (1993) puts it, "To be seen to be engaged in political debate we must argue in terms that any other participant could potentially accept, and 'It's good for me' is not such an argument." The central implication is that, by placing decisions over public policy in a public forum, legislatures elevate the public goods character of the set of policies that can be supported, thereby improving policy outcomes.

How might this elevation come about? First, per the deliberative democracy claim, it may be that only public-serving proposals can be defended in public. A less demanding scenario would divide policy proposals into those that serve only politicians and those that serve some segment of the general public. Even if norms of public debate are less constraining than the deliberative democracy position would have it, fear of electoral or other punishment by citizens may still make politicians unwilling to support public policies that serve *only* themselves. Thus, whether norms of debate or punishment by citizens are the key mechanism, the public-ness of legislative decision-making would appear to be a public good.

3.2   Accountability through Transparency

In light of this, it is worth considering the extent to which legislatures do, in practice, serve as public forums of decision-making. That is, to what extent are the essential components of legislative decisions visible to outside observers? As a common currency of decisions across legislatures, I suggest floor votes. Legislators may provide actual public justifications for their votes in speeches and debates in committee or on the floor, but the amount of attention and energy required to monitor such activities systematically is well beyond what can be reasonably expected from citizens. Instead, the bottom line of each legislator's support for any policy proposal is her or his floor vote. Floor votes are where statutes, budgets, treaties, veto overrides, and constitutional amendments are ultimately approved or rejected, and the availability of vote records indicates how much hard information citizens have about the most consequential actions of their representatives (Smith 1989). The vast bulk of legislative floor voting is, technically, public, insofar as votes cast by secret ballot are rare, but in many legislatures the votes of individual representatives are, effectively, not public because no records beyond aggregate outcomes (e.g. 200 aye, 100 nay) are published.

Table 22.1 presents data on the mean annual number of floor votes for which the position (aye, nay, abstain, non-vote, absent) of each representative is recorded and published for twenty-four legislative chambers across sixteen presidential democracies in the Americas during the 1990s and/or early 2000s. The overall variance in the amount of information about legislative voting available to those outside the chambers, however, is striking, particularly in contrast to the United States, where full disclosure of floor voting records is an essential part of legislative politics, of campaign discourse, and of academic studies of Congress and (increasingly) the state legislatures. Although systematic data on recorded votes from parts of the world beyond the Americas are not yet available, it is clear that availability is spotty. Variability in transparency exists across parliamentary as well as presidential systems, and information about votes is plentiful in some environments and absent in others (Noury 2005; Vote World 2005).

In every case, members may request recorded votes. The procedural barriers to such requests vary. In Table 22.1, the cases are grouped according to the procedural barriers to recording—whether recording is the default procedure or must be requested, and whether an electronic voting system is used. The connection between the procedural obstacles to recording votes and the amount of such information available is not surprising, but it is striking nonetheless. The experiences of individual countries that have adopted electronic voting suggest that once systems are in place, demands grow to alter rules of procedure to facilitate recorded voting, and where these demands are successful, the numbers of recorded votes skyrocket (Carey 2005b). The bottom line here is that what time-series information is available supports the clear pattern in the cross-national data: electronic voting and

Table 22.1 Mean number of recorded votes per year across twenty-four legislatures in the Americas

Procedure: Record by...	Technology	Votes	Legislatures (chamber, if bicameral)
Default	Electronic	459	Chile (both), Nicaragua, Peru
	Manual	350	US (upper)
Request	Electronic	154	Argentina (lower), Brazil (both), Mexico (both), US (lower), Venezuela
	Manual	4	Argentina (upper), Bolivia (both), Colombia (both), Costa Rica, Ecuador, El Salvador, Guatemala, Panama, Uruguay (both)

minimizing procedural barriers to recorded voting boost the amount of information available to those outside the legislature about legislative decision-making.

Party leaders and the members of dominant coalitions sometimes prefer not to make voting records public even when they are kept, and not to use electronic voting systems even when they are in place. By virtue of their physical location and resources, party and coalition leaders are institutionally advantaged in their ability to monitor voting, even when formal records are not systematically produced and published. Non-public voting thus produces an asymmetry of information between legislative insiders and citizens, that insiders can exploit in pressuring legislators on votes. Public voting, by contrast, empowers citizens to monitor their representatives, and empowers many legislators themselves to resist pressure to approve policies that might attract public opprobrium (Brennan and Pettit 1990; Snyder and Ting 2003). With remarkable frequency, however, the basic conditions necessary for votes to be public—recording and publication—are not met. Further study of both the causes and effects of legislative transparency will help clarify the conditions under which legislatures realize their potential as public forums of deliberation.

4 INFORMATION

The policy decisions legislators are called upon to make are frequently complex. They may depend on technical information that can be marshaled and deciphered only by experts, or entail trade-offs among competing demands that interact in non-obvious ways. Where politics is sufficiently professionalized that representatives can make a career out of legislative service alone, as in most national-level assemblies, representatives are effectively policy-making specialists in that they devote their professional energies to this task (or at least whatever energies are left over from the scramble to attain and maintain office, or seek the next). But legislatures also hold informational potential beyond the sum of the individual efforts of their members through the division and specialization of analytical labor.

4.1 Specialization

Legislatures are often set up to encourage division and specialization through a set of committees with policy-specific jurisdictions. These committees are charged with supporting the development and review of policy proposals in their domains, and drawing on the expertise of their members and staff to make recommendations to the full assembly. An organizational diagram of just about any national legislature would exhibit precisely such a set-up, with committees assigned policy jurisdictions over economics, foreign affairs, security, agriculture, labor, and so forth. There is relatively little variation at the level of flow charts, but considerably more in the extent to which legislatures realize their potential as information-producing institutions.

Londregan (2001) characterizes the expertise produced by well-informed policy-makers as a public good insofar as it can generate high-valence policies, which improve the lot of all citizens. Information can also be a political good, however, insofar as those who can make legislative proposals can secure concessions from their ideological opponents in exchange for delivering policy valence. In Londregan's study of Chilean politics, the president is vested with extensive constitutional powers to control the legislative agenda, and the executive branch is also far better endowed than the legislature with the institutional resources—primarily staff—to collect information. Thus the Chilean executive, and the legislative coalition that supports it, are the primary ideological beneficiaries of a combination of agenda powers and information asymmetry (Londregan 2001).

Londregan's account captures a key element of executive–legislative relations in many polities—that executive branches are better endowed with policy expertise than are legislatures—but raises the questions why this asymmetry exists, and how stark is it? Chile is unusual in the extent to which the executive is exogenously endowed with control over the legislative agenda (Baldez and Carey 1999; Siavelis 2000). In environments where legislatures are not similarly constrained, the question is why some organize themselves to produce information and to be able to develop high-valence policy proposals whereas others do not? We lack comparative analyses of legislative staffing levels or other factors that measure systematically how much informational value legislatures produce and provide to their members (Cox 2006).

Gilligan and Krehbiel (1990) develop the best-known formal model of information specialization among legislators. By this account, individual legislators are motivated to collect information on policies that improve outcomes for all in exchange for policy concessions on the margin that can be translated into personal electoral support. Committees serve as the seed beds both of policy expertise and, via their control over the legislative agenda, of opportunities for their members to secure advantageous policies on the margin. The informational model provides a compelling account of the committee system in the US Congress (Krehbiel 1992). The question for comparative legislative studies is to what extent committees play this role elsewhere.

4.2 Tenure

The quantity and quality of information are difficult to measure, but time is a necessary condition for the development of policy expertise in legislatures. Studies of the effects of legislative term limits, for example, suggest that reelection is necessary for legislators to develop expertise, and that short tenure weakens legislatures relative to executives in shaping policy outcomes (Carey 1996; Carey, Niemi, and Powell 2000; Kousser 2005). Comparative politics scholars have begun to take an interest in reelection rates across legislatures. Reelection rates tend to be substantially lower than in the United States, although longer legislative terms (than those of the US House, at any rate) in most other assemblies mean that differences in overall rates of tenure are somewhat less dramatic (Morgenstern and Nacif 2002).

Samuels (2000) and de Luca, Jones, and Tula (2002) document low reelection rates in Brazil and Argentina, respectively. Both are federal systems in which parties and political careers are primarily organized at the sub-national level. Samuels (2000) shows evidence that state-level offices attract many of the strongest politicians away from the national congress. De Luca, Jones, and Tula (2002), meanwhile, argue that state-level party bosses who control candidate nominations in most Argentine states systematically rotate up-and-coming legislators off party lists, and so out of Congress, before they can harness the institutional resources there to challenge the primacy of state-level machines. In both these cases, explanations for high legislative turnover hang partly on characteristics of federalism— the lure of state-level office in Brazil, and turf guarding by party bosses in Argentina. The US example demonstrates that long tenure is not impossible under federalism, of course, but the comparative evidence suggests it may be worth testing systematically whether institutional factors such as the availability of sub-national offices and the decentralization of nomination procedures systematically affect legislative reelection rates.

Beyond reelection rates and the overall level of legislative tenure, patterns of committee appointments should also be indicative of the extent to which legislatures cultivate information. Again, this terrain is well mapped in the US case (Shepsle 1978; Smith and Deering 1984; Kiewiet and McCubbins 1991; Cox and McCubbins 1993), but largely uncharted elsewhere. The studies we have of committee membership suggest substantial variance in rates of committee tenure. In Costa Rica, committee membership rotates annually, and most members hold distinct assignments for each year of their four-year terms (Carey 1996). In Chile, by contrast, where reelection rates are higher, there is also greater stability in committee assignments from year to year and from term to term. Moreover, there is a correlation between the jurisdictional salience of a committee and tenure rates, with committees that handle higher-profile policy issues also exhibiting the most stable membership, as in the US Congress (Carey 2002). In general, however, our knowledge of committee tenure across legislatures, particularly in new dem-ocracies, is limited. Excellent studies of legislative institutions in post-Soviet Russia, for example, provide data on the distribution of committee seats across parties and factions, but not on the stability of membership at the individual level (Remington 2001; Smith and Remington 2001).

Finally, although studies of legislative staffing are scarce, committees' procedural resources are potential indicators of their centrality to the legislative process and, indirectly, of their ability to generate information and expertise. The most prom-inent studies here have been motivated by a desire to understand minority gov-ernments in parliamentary systems and suggest that the frequency of minority governments prompts legislators to construct stronger committee systems (Strom 1990; Powell 2000). I return to this topic below, in Section 6.

Legislatures can potentially serve as hothouses of information and expertise about policy. The extent to which they play this role can affect both their ability to bargain over policy on equal footing with executives as well as the overall quality— or valence—of the policies produced. Prevalent patterns of formal legislative or-ganization indicate that committees are the most promising mechanism by which legislatures might cultivate expertise. The conditions that would allow legislative committee systems to play this role appear to vary widely across national legisla-tures, but our empirical knowledge in this area is relatively underdeveloped. Legis-lative tenure and reelection rates vary considerably as, it appears, does the composition of committees. Committee resources similarly vary, but there is evidence from parliamentary systems that partisan opposition between the branches triggers the development of strong, informative committees. Testing this hypothesis more widely seems a promising avenue for future comparative research.

5   DECISIVENESS

Collecting information and deliberating over alternatives are merely precursors to deciding on which policies to adopt. Legislatures are called upon to reach decisions on policy and to make those decisions stick, and criticisms of legislatures frequently focus on failures along these lines. In this section, I suggest that the strength of political parties in organizing legislative agendas is critical to whether, and what type of decisiveness problems they confront.

5.1   Bottlenecks and Cycling

In his overview of legislative organization, Cox (2006) posits a "legislative state of nature" in which all members have equal rights to make proposals and plenary time is unregulated. The latter assumption is taken to imply unlimited filibuster (i.e. that no proposal can be brought to a vote over the objection of any member), which in turn implies that the decision rule is effectively unanimity. Such a state of nature implies a strong egalitarian norm that privileges the ability of members to block assembly action over the ability to trigger action, and it follows that instability of legislative decisions should not be a problem, whereas inaction should be (Colomer 2001; Tsebelis 1995, 1999). From this point of departure, Cox (2006) proceeds to note that legislatures everywhere resolve the bottleneck problem with internal organization that redistributes agenda powers unequally, and that in modern legislatures, political parties consistently control access to the privileged agenda-setting positions.

Whether or not one assumes that the legislative state of nature necessarily implies unlimited filibuster, there is reason to believe that parties are critical to legislative decisiveness. Formally, as least, most assemblies rely on simple majority rule for most decisions. Well-known theoretical characteristics of majority rule decisions over multiple alternatives suggest that failures of decisiveness would be characterized by a general instability of legislative decisions—that is, by cycling, rather than inaction (Condorcet 1785; McKelvey 1976; Riker 1982). Yet, even accounts of legislative politics that take the instability problem as a point of departure frequently point to political parties as the key factors that bring order to the potential chaos of majority rule (Laver and Shepsle 1996; Cox and McCubbins 1993).

In either account—bottleneck-based or cycling-based—parties are credited with providing decisiveness by establishing privileged agenda setters who determine which proposals are debated and voted on, and in which order, and in doing so make it possible for legislators to realize gains unrealizable in unorganized, state-of-nature assemblies. The relative balance of agenda control residing in legislative committees, directory boards, and presiding offices varies across legislatures. In parliamentary systems, these powers are generally vested in cabinet ministries— technically part of the executive branch, but which themselves are filled from among members of the legislature, and are dependent on its confidence for survival. The key point is that, in almost all democratic systems, parties are the gatekeepers of the formal offices that control the legislative agenda. Moreover, Carroll, Cox, and Pachon (2004) demonstrate that, as democracies mature, parties expand their control over the offices that determine the legislative agenda, and the distribution of these offices among parties grows increasingly regular. In short, as party systems stabilize, so do the key partisan elements of legislative organization.

5.2 Parties and the Legislative Agenda

How does partisan agenda control provide decisiveness? Diverse accounts of legislative politics converge around the idea that parties reduce the potentially infinite number of policy options to a limited set, primarily by establishing platforms or manifestos that advertise party positions to voters, and then by disciplining legislators to constrain their voting in line with these party positions (Aldrich 1995). Comparative studies of roll call voting suggest that legislative agendas are strongly limited in ways consistent with the idea that parties produce procedural order. Cox, Masuyama, and McCubbins (2000) demonstrate that the long-dominant LDP in Japan used its control over the parliamentary agenda to prevent proposals that might divide its governing coalition from coming to the floor. Amorim Neto, Cox, and McCubbins (2003) provide evidence that multiparty legislative coalitions in Brazil acted similarly, as cartels that limit legislative proposals to protect the policy interests of member parties. In both cases, the point is that parties—sometimes as partners in coalitions—both limit the policy alternatives among which legislatures formally choose, preventing cycling, and ensure that some alternatives enjoy procedural advantages that prevent bottlenecks.

Other empirical evidence also highlights the relative orderliness of voting in legislatures, in contrast to the theoretical prospect of majority rule cycles. The most widely used method for estimating legislator ideal points suggests that agendas across a wide range of legislatures show remarkably limited dimensionality (Poole and Rosenthal 2001; Rosenthal and Voeten 2004). That is, across various legislatures in quite different political systems, and in the US Congress throughout most of its history, legislators' voting patterns can be accurately mapped using only a single dimension of a potentially N-dimensional spatial model. Legislators' estimated ideal points, moreover, tend to be extremely stable over time (Poole 1998). Because parties so consistently dominate legislative organization, it is difficult to test the extent to which they account for the orderliness of voting patterns. In a pair of ingenious studies, however, Jenkins (1999, 2000) compares voting in the Confederate Congress of 1861–5 with that in the US Congress during the same era. The legislatures were similar in formal structure, in membership (many legislators served in both chambers), and even in the issues on which they voted, but the Confederate Congress was not organized along party lines, and the voting patterns of Confederate legislators were far less stable in important ways. First, spatial models correctly classify fewer votes in the Confederate than the US Congress (Jenkins 1999). Second, Confederate legislators, operating in a party-less environment, are less stable in their ideological positions over time (Jenkins 2000). Overall, the results suggest that political parties impose order on voting in ways that make legislative decisions predictable and stable.

Political parties may play this role in general, but even casual observers will note that not all parties are equivalent. Comparative legislative scholarship has long made much of the difference between strong and weak political parties in controlling legislative outcomes. Scholarship on the US Congress has been largely occupied for over a decade with the extent to which the levels of party voting we observe are due to like-mindedness among co-partisans (cohesiveness) or pressure from party leaders (discipline) (Krehbiel 1998; Cox and Poole 2004). Much of the rest of the legislative world, however, has yet to be mapped at all in terms of party unity in voting. Factors that may account for relative levels of party unity can be divided between those that operate at the system level, and are constant across all parties within an assembly (e.g. regime type, federalism, electoral system, regime age), and those that vary across parties within assemblies (e.g. government vs. opposition, seat share, ideological composition, party age). Hix (2004) takes advantage of the European Parliament's multinational structure to gain analytical leverage on the effect of the electoral system—normally constant within a given legislature—showing higher voting unity in parties with centralized control over legislators' election (and reelection) prospects than in those where legislators cultivate personal support among voters to secure election. Carey (2005a) draws on voting data from eighteen legislatures to confirm the conventional distinction between highly unified parties in parliamentary systems and less unified ones in presidential regimes, and shows that governing parties are more unified than opposition parties in the former regime type, but indistinguishable in terms of unity in the latter. Cross-national analyses of legislative voting remain relatively rare, and mostly limited in their scope (Morgenstern 2003; Noury 2005). Recent efforts by comparative legislative scholars to archive voting data from across many legislatures in a standard format will facilitate cross-national research, however, and can be expected to enhance our understanding of what accounts for the relative strength of legislative parties (Vote World 2005).[4]

6   CHECKS

The last category of expectations regarding legislatures identified at the outset of this chapter is checks, which include oversight and limitations on the ability of policy-makers to take action. Demand for a checking function rests in part on a pervasive distrust of authority, and frequently a specific distrust of majority rule, a term one often sees prefaced with qualifiers such as "unrestrained," "plebiscitary," or "intemperate."[5] It is also based in part on the expectation that checks contribute to the other legislative ideals discussed thus far, ensuring balanced public debate so legislatures may fulfill their deliberative role; and reveal information about policy options and about the motivations of their champions, enhancing the informational role. To the extent this is the case, legislative checks may in turn guarantee that the policies ultimately enshrined in statute are durable, thus affecting decisiveness.

Given the weight of expectations placed on legislative checks, it is worth being quite clear about what mechanisms fall under this label. By checks, I mean the constitutional requirement for legislative approval before governments may act in areas such as:

- passing statutes that change policy, authorize spending, levy taxes, etc.;
- amending constitutions, thus altering the structure of government or the distribution of power among its officers;
- ratifying treaties, declarations of war, or states of emergency initiated by executives;
- approving appointments of high officials to executive, judicial, or independent offices.

Approval most often takes the form of a majority vote, but may also require a supermajority in some cases, in which case checks—withholding approval

---

[4] It is worth noting that the search for factors that account for legislative party strength does not imply a normative judgment that stronger is always better. Indeed, legislative parties that exhibit iron-clad discipline regularly attract criticism and popular demand for reform (Coppedge 1994; Carey 2003).

[5] Madison's argument in *Federalist 63* for the necessity of a Senate to temper the "passions" of House majorities (which, in *Federalist 57*, he had just contended would actually be quite judicious) may be the most famous along these lines, at least to American audiences, but the theme is widespread.

for government action—may be exercised by minorities. Closely related to withholding approval, and sequentially prior to it in practice, is legislative oversight—monitoring policy-makers to verify that their actions are consistent with the intent of current law and do not exceed the reach of their formal authorities. Oversight is the revelation of information, which is particularly valued to the extent that those who exercise government authority are inclined to misuse it (Persson and Tabellini 2003).

We might think of checks as either internal or external, with the former referring to those exercised within a given assembly, generally by opposition representatives or parties against the majority; and the latter referring to those exercised either between chambers, in the case of bicameral systems, or between branches.[6] Procedural rights reserved for minorities to stall progress on proposals, and sometimes even to scuttle them as with filibusters in the US Senate, constitute an internal check, and are frequently defended on the grounds that they guarantee careful study and consideration of initiatives, contributing to outcomes that improve the overall quality of legislation. Dion (2001) counters that, in practice, minority rights are treated less as social welfare enhancing than as resources at stake in a non-cooperative battle between majorities and legislative opposition. His historical study of the US Congress, the British Commons, and the Austrian parliament suggests that rule changes to curtail minority rights are most likely precisely when majorities are least secure. One implication is that legislative checks internal to a chamber should be least effective precisely when the electoral mandate of the majority coalition is weakest.

In a different vein, Strom (1990) identifies parliamentary committees as potential sources of opposition party power, particularly in systems where committee chairs are distributed proportionally rather than monopolized by government parties. He notes that procedural rights for minorities in European parliamentary systems are greater where majorities are least secure, particularly where majority coalitions cannot form, and minority governments wield executive power. Powell (2000) reaches a similar conclusion, suggesting that internal legislative checks are, in fact, strongest when the majority coalition's claim to authority is most tenuous. Whether Dion's non-cooperative story or Strom's more cooperative one better accounts for the level of internal checks we observe across legislatures more generally warrants further research attention.

---

[6] Tsebelis's (1995) veto-players model disregards this distinction on the grounds that all political actors, whether a party within a majority coalition, or an opposition-party president, who can block legislative action by disapproval are equivalent in terms of the stickiness of the status quo. I retain the distinction, however, on the grounds that legislative coalitions, whether composed of partisan or other actors, are potentially fluid, insofar as any recalcitrant actor can be substituted with any other agreeable actor carrying as many seats; whereas constitutionally-endowed veto-players (e.g. courts, executives, other chambers) are irreplaceable.

Martin and Vanberg (2005) take an important step in this direction, expanding into the study of legislative checks on external (executive) actors in their study of legislative review in Germany and the Netherlands. In multiparty parliamentary systems, control of any government ministry by a particular party generates the potential for policy disputes among parties within the governing coalition over legislative proposals in that policy area. Martin and Vanberg demonstrate that the greater the scope of policy disagreement between coalition partners, the greater are the revisions made by parliaments to government proposals. This form of check on the executive appears to be greatest precisely where alternative legislative coalitions to the government—for example government parties apart from the one control-ling the ministry of jurisdiction, plus opposition parties—are most viable. Martin and Vanberg's account is consistent with Thies (2001), who documents internal checks within coalitions in the form of split party control over ministerial and junior ministerial portfolios.

Finally, there has been a boom in the past decade, fueled largely by transitions to democracy in presidential and hybrid constitutional systems, in the study of legislative checks on presidents. Linz (1994) identified presidential systems as problematic in part on the grounds that partisan incompatibility between legisla-tures and executives could produce intransigence in bargaining, which in turn could induce executives to pursue non-constitutional means in pursuing their agendas. Carey and Shugart (1998) examine a specific vehicle frequently associated with abuse of presidential power, executive decree authority, and argue that its use frequently follows patterns consistent with legislative delegation rather than executive usurpation. Figuereido and Limongi (2000) argue that the centralization of authority over the legislative agenda in the Brazilian presidency is potentially consistent with the interests of legislative majorities in maximizing decisiveness. There is little in their account to suggest potential for checks on the executive, but Amorim Neto, Cox, and McCubbins (2003) demonstrate that the conditions required to centralize agenda control are actually contingent—present when stable legislative majority coalitions support the president, absent otherwise—thus re-viving the prospect that even legislatures with relatively high partisan fragmenta-tion might impose effective checks on presidents. The extent to which this prospect is realized, and the specific conditions that encourage or discourage it, ought to be central to academic research on comparative legislatures in presidential systems (Cox and Morgenstern 2001).

Focusing specifically on separation of powers between legislative chambers, Tsebelis and Money (1997) make the case that bicameralism does more than encour-age policy stability by making it more difficult to change the status quo (although it does this, too). It also focuses policy debate and deliberation on the dimension of conflict that separates the collective preferences of the two chambers. If this dimen-sion happens not to reflect an important political cleavage in the electorate—say, because on the most salient issues the chamber majorities are quite close, whereas they differ on matters unimportant to most voters—then bicameralism will channel legislative debate and bargaining toward inessential issues, perhaps marginalizing the legislature. If, on the other hand, differences in preferences across chambers span a cleavage highly salient to citizens, then legislative bargaining will focus on finding compromise along that dimension of conflict. This insight suggests a qualification of the claim often advanced by advocates of deliberative democracy that open debate is, in itself, a public good. It may be, if it is aimed at achieving mutually acceptable outcomes on salient issues, but otherwise it may trivialize the deliberative forum. With respect to institutional design, moreover, the nature of incongruence between chambers in a bicameral system—that is, how differences in the composition of the two chambers map onto conflicts in the electorate—may help explain whether legislative checks are politically productive, or even relevant.

7   CONCLUSION

The purpose of this chapter has been both to outline what we know, and to organize some ideas about comparative legislative organization so as to direct attention to specific things we do not yet know, or that we do not know with sufficient certainty and empirical authority, but that would help us understand the extent to which legislatures fulfill their normative potential within democratic systems. In identifying five broad sets of expectations to which legislatures are subject, I am suggesting a normative case for strong legislatures. Assemblies that meet these expectations are heavyweights in their respective policy-making environments.

The claim that strong legislatures are desirable rests on the potential to exploit their plural nature in areas where it implies a comparative advantage relative to other types of institutions—in representing diversity, providing transparent debate, dividing labor, and profiting from specialization, generating and revealing information—and to strike a workable balance between deliberateness and decisiveness. This chapter reviews scholarship that sheds light on the conditions that affect whether legislatures realize these expectations, and highlights some promising avenues for future research. Specifically, I suggest that studies of legislative electoral systems should recognize the trade-off between collectivist and individualistic representation as distinct from, and frequently more important than, that between proportional and single-winner systems. I suggest that in order to understand legislative accountability, we need to pay closer attention to the transparency of deliberation—who can monitor legislative actions and who has the incentive to do so. I encourage cross-national research into the conditions that allow for legislatures to develop policy expertise, such as tenure and reelection rates, committee resources, and reassignment rates. I also promote cross-national analysis of roll call voting to map and model the legislative universe of party and coalition unity, the essential components of decisiveness. Finally, I encourage empirical studies of legislative–executive bargaining to determine with greater precision the conditions under which one branch or the other is better able to secure the policy outcomes it prefers. This is a large agenda, but the immense progress in the field of comparative legislative studies achieved in recent years—only a sample of which is reviewed in detail here—suggests it is well within reach.

References

ALDRICH, J. H. 1995. *Why Parties? The Origin and Transformation of Political Parties in America.* Chicago: University of Chicago Press.

AMORIM NETO, O., COX, G. W., and McCUBBINS, M. D. 2003. Agenda power in Brazil's Camara dos Deputados, 1989–98. *World Politics,* 55 (4): 550–78.

BALDEZ, L. A. and CAREY, J. M. 1999. Presidential agenda control and spending policy: lessons from General Pinochet's constitution. *American Journal of Political Science,* 43 (1): 29–55.

BRENNAN, G. and PETTIT, P. 1990. Unveiling the vote. *British Journal of Political Science,* 20 (3): 311–33.

BURNS, J. F. and IVES, N. February 13: 2005. Shiites win most votes in Iraq, election results show. *New York Times International,* February 13: 1–22.

CAREY, J. M. 1996. *Term Limits and Legislative Representation.* New York: Cambridge University Press.

—— 2002. Parties, coalitions, and the Chilean Congress in the 1990s. In *Legislative Politics in Latin America,* ed. S. Morgenstern and B. Nacif. New York: Cambridge University Press.

—— 2003. Discipline, accountability, and legislative voting in Latin America. *Comparative Politics,* 35 (2): 191–211.

—— 2005a. Political institutions, competing principals, and party unity in legislative voting. University of California, Institute of Governmental Studies, Paper WP2005-8. Available at: http://repositories.cdlib.org/igs/WP2005-8.

—— 2005b. Visible votes: recorded voting and legislative accountability in Latin America. Working paper. Available at: http://www.dartmouth.edu/~jcovey/publications.htm.

—— and SHUGART, M. S. 1995. Incentives to cultivate a personal vote: a rank ordering of electoral formulas. *Electoral Studies,* 14 (4): 417–39.

—— —— (eds.) 1998. *Executive Decree Authority.* New York: Cambridge University Press.

—— NIEMI, R. G., and POWELL, L. W. 2000. *Term Limits in the State Legislatures.* Ann Arbor: University of Michigan Press.

CARROLL, R., COX, G. W., and PACHÓN, M. 2004. How political parties create democracy. Prepared for delivery at the annual meeting of the American Political Science Association, Chicago, 2–5 September.

COLOMER, J. M. 2001. *Political Institutions: Democracy and Social Choice.* New York: Oxford University Press.

CONDORCET, MARQUIS DE 1785. *Essay on the Application of Analysis to the Probability of Majority Decisions (Essai sur l'application de l'analyse a la probabilté des decisions rendues a la pluralité des voix).* Paris: De L'Imprimerie royale.

COPPEDGE, M. J. 1994. *Strong Parties and Lame Ducks: Presidentialism, Partyarchy, and Factionalism in Venezuela.* Stanford, Calif.: Stanford University Press.

COX, G. W. 1997. *Making Votes Count: Strategic Coordination in the World's Electoral Systems.* Cambridge: Cambridge University Press.

—— 2006. The organization of democratic legislatures. In *The Oxford Handbook of Political Economy,* ed. B. Weingast and D. Wittman. New York: Oxford University Press.

—— and McCUBBINS, M. D. 1993. *Legislative Leviathan: Party Government in the House.* Berkeley: University of California Press.

—— and MORGENSTERN, S. 2001. Latin America's reactive assemblies and proactive presidents. *Comparative Politics,* 33 (2): 171–90.

—— and POOLE, K. T. 2004. On measuring partisanship in roll-call voting: the US House of Representatives, 1877–1999. *American Journal of Political Science,* 46 (3): 477–89.

—— and THIES, M. F. 1998. The cost of intraparty competition: the single, nontransferable vote and money politics in Japan. *Comparative Political Studies,* 31 (3): 267–91.

—— MASUYAMA, M., and McCUBBINS, M. D. 2000. Agenda power in the Japanese House of Representatives. *Japanese Journal of Political Science,* 1 (1): 1–12.

CULVER, W. W. and FERRUFINO, A. 2000. Diputados uninominales: la participacion politica en Bolivia. *Contribuciones,* 1: 1–28.

DEERING, C. J. and SMITH, S. S. 1990. *Committees in Congress,* 2nd edn. Boulder, Colo.: Westview Press.

DE LUCA, M., JONES, M. P., and TULA, M. I. 2002. Back rooms or ballot boxes? Candidate nomination in Argentina. *Comparative Political Studies,* 35 (4): 413–36.

DION, D. 2001. *Turning the Legislative Thumbscrew: Minority Rights and Procedural Change in Legislative Politics.* Ann Arbor: University of Michigan Press.

DUVERGER, M. 1954. *Political Parties.* New York: John Wiley.

FIGUEIREDO, A. C. and LIMONGI, F. 2000. Presidential power, legislative organization, and party behavior in Brazil. *Comparative Politics,* 32 (2): 151–70.

GALLAGHER, M. 1991. Proportionality, disproportionality and electoral systems. *Electoral Studies,* 10: 33–51.

GILLIGAN, T. W. and KREHBIEL, K. 1990. The organization of informative committees by a rational legislature. *American Journal of Political Science,* 34 (2): 531–64.

GOLDEN, M. A. and CHANG, E. C. C. 2001. Competitive corruption: factional conflict and political malfeasance in postwar Italian Christian democracy. *World Politics,* 53 (4): 588–622.

GOODIN, R. 1986. Laundering preferences. In *Foundations of Social Choice Theory,* ed. J. Elster and A. Hylland. New York: Cambridge University Press.

HIX, S. 2004. Electoral institutions and legislative behavior—explaining voting defection in the European Parliament. *World Politics,* 56 (2): 194–223.

HUBER, J. D. and POWELL, G. B. 1994. Congruence between citizens and policymakers in two visions of liberal democracy. *World Politics,* 46: 291–326.

INTERNATIONAL INSTITUTE FOR DEMOCRACY AND ELECTORAL ASSISTANCE 1997. *Handbook of Electoral Systems*. Stockholm: IDEA.

INTER-PARLIAMENTARY UNION 2005. Women in national parliaments. Available at: http://www.ipu.org/wmn-e/world.htm.

JENKINS, J. A. 1999. Examining the bonding effects of party: a comparative analysis of roll-call voting in the US and confederate houses. *American Journal of Political Science*, 43 (4): 1144–65.

—— 2000. Examining the robustness of ideological voting: evidence from the confederate house of representatives. *American Journal of Political Science*, 44 (4): 811–22.

KIEWIET, D. R. and MCCUBBINS, M. D. 1991. *The Logic of Delegation: Congressional Parties and the Appropriations Process*. Chicago: University of Chicago Press.

KOUSSER, T. 2005. *Term Limits and the Dismantling of State Legislative Professionalism*. New York: Cambridge University Press.

KREHBIEL, K. 1992. *Information and Legislative Organization*. Ann Arbor: University of Michigan Press.

—— 1998. *Pivotal Politics: A Theory of U.S. Lawmaking*. Chicago: University of Chicago Press.

LAAKSO, M. and TAAGEPERA, R. 1979. Effective number of parties: a measure with application to West Europe. *Comparative Political Studies*, 12: 3–27.

LAVER, M. and SHEPSLE, K. 1996. *Making and Breaking Governments: Cabinets and Legislatures in Parliamentary Democracies*. New York: Cambridge University Press.

LIJPHART, A. 1994. *Electoral Systems and Party Systems: A Study of 27 Democracies, 1945–1990*. New York: Oxford University Press.

LINZ, J. J. 1994. Presidentialism or parliamentarism: does it make a difference? In *The Failure of Presidential Democracy*, ed. J. J. Linz and A. Valenzuela. Baltimore: Johns Hopkins University Press.

LONDREGAN, J. 2001. *Legislative Institutions and Ideology in Chile*. New York: Cambridge University Press.

MCCUBBINS, M. D. and ROSENBLUTH, F. M. 1995. Party provision for personal politics: dividing the vote in Japan. In *Structure and Policy in Japan and the United States*, ed. P. F. Cowhey and M. D. McCubbins. New York: Cambridge University Press.

MCKELVEY, R. 1976. Intransitivities in multidimensional voting models: some implications for agenda control. *Journal of Economic Theory*, 12: 472–82.

MARTIN, L. W. and VANBERG, G. 2005. Coalition policymaking and legislative review. *American Political Science Review*, 99 (1): 93–106.

MILLER, D. 1993. Deliberative democracy and social choice. In *Prospects for Democracy*, ed. D. Held. Stanford, Calif.: Stanford University Press.

MONROE, B. L. 2006. *Electoral Systems in Theory and Electoral Systems in Practice*. Ann Arbor: University of Michigan Press.

MORGENSTERN, S. 2003. *Patterns of Legislative Politics: Roll Call Voting in Latin America and the United States*. New York: Cambridge University Press.

—— and NACIF, B. (eds.) 2002. *Legislative Politics in Latin America*. New York: Cambridge University Press.

NOURY, A. and MIELCOVA, E. 2005. Electoral performance and voting behavior. Institute of Governmental Studies, Paper WP2005-14. Available at: http://repositories.cdlib.org/igs/WP2005-14.

PERSSON, T. and TABELLINI, G. 2003. *The Economic Effects of Constitutions*. Cambridge, Mass.: MIT Press.

POOLE, K. T. 1998. Recovering a basic space from a set of issue scales. *American Journal of Political Science*, 42 (3): 954–93.

—— and ROSENTHAL, H. 2001. D-Nominate after 10 years: a comparative update to "Congress: A political-economic history of roll-call voting." *Legislative Studies Quarterly*, 26 (1): 5–30.

POWELL, G. B. 2000. *Elections as Instruments of Democracy: Majoritarian and Proportional Visions*. New Haven, Conn.: Yale University Press.

—— and VANBERG, G. 2000. Election laws, disproportionality and median correspondence: implications for two visions of democracy. *British Journal of Political Science*, 30 (3): 383–411.

REMINGTON, T. F. 2001. *The Russian Parliament: Institutional Evolution in a Transitional Regime, 1989–1999*. New Haven, Conn.: Yale University Press.

RIKER, W. H. 1982. *Liberalism Against Populism*. Prospect Heights, Ill.: Waveland Press.

ROSENTHAL, H. and VOETEN, E. 2004. Analyzing roll calls with perfect spatial voting: France 1946–1958. *American Journal of Political Science*, 48 (3): 620–32.

RUBIN, B. R. 2005. The wrong voting system. *International Herald Tribune International*, 16 March: 9.

SAMUELS, D. 2000. Ambition and competition: explaining legislative turnover in Brazil. *Legislative Studies Quarterly*, 25 (3): 481–97.

SARTORI, G. 1976. *Parties and Party Systems: A Framework for Analysis*. New York: Cambridge University Press.

SHEPSLE, K. A. 1978. *The Giant Jigsaw Puzzle: Democratic Committee Assignments in the Modern House*. Chicago: University of Chicago Press.

SHUGART, M. S. and WATTENBERG, M. P. (eds.) 2001. *Mixed-member Electoral Systems: The Best of Both Worlds?* New York: Oxford University Press.

SIAVELIS, P. 2000. *The President and Congress in Postauthoritarian Chile: Institutional Constraints to Democratic Consolidation*. University Park: Pennsylvania State University Press.

SMITH, S. S. 1989. *Call to Order: Floor Politics in the House and Senate*. Washington, DC: Brookings Institution Press.

—— and DEERING, C. J. 1984. *Committees in Congress*. Washington, DC: Congressional Quarterly Press.

—— and REMINGTON, T. F. 2001. *The Politics of Institutional Choice: The Formation of the Russian State Duma*. Princeton, NJ: Princeton University Press.

SNYDER, J. M. and TING, M. M. 2003. Why roll calls? A model of position taking in legislative voting and elections. Unpublished paper.

STROM, K. 1990. *Minority Government and Majority Rule*. New York: Cambridge University Press.

TAAGEPERA, R. and SHUGART, M. S. 1989. *Seats and Votes: The Effects and Determinants of Electoral Systems*. New Haven, Conn.: Yale University Press.

TSEBELIS, G. 1995. Decision making in political systems: veto players in presidentialism, parliamentarism, multicameralism and multipartyism. *British Journal of Poltical Science*, 25: 289–325.

—— 1999. Veto players and law production in parliamentary democracies: an empirical analysis. *American Political Science Review*, 93 (3): 591–608.

THIES, M. F. 2001. Keeping tabs on partners: the logic of delegation in coalition governments. *American Journal of Political Science*, 45 (3): 580–98.

—— and MONEY, J. 1997. *Bicameralism*. New York: Cambridge University Press.

VOTE WORLD 2005. International legislative roll-call voting website. Available at: http://voteworld.berkeley.edu.

CHAPTER 23

COMPARATIVE LEGISLATIVE BEHAVIOR

ERIC M. USLANER
THOMAS ZITTEL

Parliamentary legislative systems are orderly. Congressional legislative systems are disorderly. This claim may seem a bit odd when we think about the loudness, sometimes even the rowdiness, of debate in parliaments compared to the more flowery and civil language on the floor of the United States House of Representative and especially the Senate. The orderliness of parliamentary systems (and the disorderliness of congressional systems) refers not to language or style, but rather to how conflict is structured.

Parliamentary procedure is all about the power of political parties. Parliaments are the embodiment of collective responsibility of the prime minister and his/her governing party. In congressional systems, political parties play a much more limited—some would say a subsidiary—role. Individual members answer to their constituencies, their consciences, and especially their committees more than they do to their party leaders. Congressional procedure is disorderly because there is no centralized authority and no sense of collective responsiblity. Woodrow Wilson, the first modern student of Congress (1967, 59), argued in 1885: "It is this

* Eric M. Uslaner is grateful to the General Research Board, University of Maryland, College Park, for support on this and other projects.

multiplicity of [committee] leaders, this many-headed leadership, which makes the organization of the House too complex to afford uninformed people and unskilled observers any easy clue to its methods of rule....There is no thought of acting in concert."

The standard explanation for these differences is institutional. Parliaments are majoritarian, centralizing power in party leaders who have the power to punish members who might dare to take an independent course. Congressional systems have weak parties and strong committees and leaders lack the power to discipline legislators who respond more to their constituents than to their parties. These explanations take us far, but in recent years we see growing power for congressional parties and weaker parties in parliametary systems—even as institutional structure remains constant. The critical changes seem to be behavioral—as legislators in the United States represent increasingly homogenous constituencies in polarized parties. Legislators in parliamentary systems have fought to become more independent of party leaders.

We now speak of increasing polarization and heightened partisanship in the United States Congress, where party leaders control the agenda with iron fists (at least in the House) and where voters in congressional elections are more likely than at any time in the past 100 years to divide along party lines. We also speak of greater attention to constituency demands in parliamentary systems. We focus on the changing role of political parties in legislative institutions, both parliamentary and congressional, in this chapter—and examine the structural and behavioral roots of legislative behavior. We examine the impact of different institutions, varying informal rules of the game, and the varying relations between legislators and constituents.

1   INSTITUTIONAL INFLUENCES ON PARTISANSHIP IN LEGISLATURES

A. Lawrence Lowell (1901, 332, 346), who pioneered the study of how legislators vote (in England and the United States), argued: "The parliamentary system is...the natural outgrowth and a rational expression of the division of the ruling chamber into two parties...since the ministry may be overturned at any moment, its life depends upon an unintermittent warfare and it must strive to keep its followers constantly in hand.... In America...the machinery of party has...been created outside of the regular organs of government and, hence, it is less effective and more irregular in its action." Almost three quarters of a century later, David R. Mayhew

(1974, 27) wrote: "no theoretical treatment of the United States Congress that posits parties as analytic units will go very far." Philip Norton observed that for European parliamentary systems, "Political parties have served to ... constrain the freedom of individual action by members of legislatures" (Norton 1990, 5).

The collective responsiblity of parliamentary systems binds legislators to their parties. If the government loses on a major bill, it will fall and there will be new elections. The parliamentary party can deny renomination to members who vote against the party. Constitutents vote overwhelmingly along party lines—members of parliament do not establish independent identities to gain "personal votes" as members of Congress do. Within the legislature, the only path to power is through the party organization. None of these factors hold within congressional systems. Members are independent entrepreneurs who serve on legislative committees that have been independent of party pressure—and often at odds with party goals. Members run for reelection with no fear that the national party can deny them renomination—or even cost them another term.

Even though roll calls are not frequent in many European parliaments, party cohesion in European national parliaments is very high. Beer (1969, 350) remarked about the British House of Commons by the end of the 1960s, that cohesion was so close to 100 percent that there was no longer any point in measuring it.

Parties were weaker in the United States. Yet, Lowell (1901, 336) noted at the turn of the twentieth century: "The amount of party voting varies much from one Congress, and even from one session, to another, and does not follow closely any fixed law of evolution." Later scholars would invest considerable effort in finding the patterns that eluded Lowell and in comparing the relative power of parties, committees, and constituencies across the House and the Senate. The larger House of Representatives with two-year terms was much more conducive to partisanship than the smaller Senate, where members served six-year terms and were not initially publicly elected.

Saalfeld's studies (1990, 1995) of the German Bundestag between 1949 and 1987 find strong levels of party voting for each of the three major parties. This finding is supported by other single-country studies for other European parliaments (Cowley and Norton 1999; Müller and Jenny 2000; Norton 1980).

The likelihood of defection is affected by the nature of an issue and the factor that moral as well as local issues are most likely to trigger the defection of single MPs from their party line (Skjaeveland 2001). Particularly in countries with a strong local tradition, such as Norway and Denmark, party leadership is reportedly understanding towards members dissenting for matters of local concern (Damgaard 1997). Other authors suggested that electoral factors such as a "mixed member voting system" (Burkett 1985) or the marginality of a seat (Norton 2002) might explain defections form the party line.

Power in parliamentary systems is centralized in the party leadership. In the German Bundestag party cohesion is the result of lobbying and arm twisting on the part of the party leadership (Saalfeld 1995). Similar conclusions have been reached for other European legislatures such as the Austrian Nationalrat (Müller and Jenny 2000). In the United States Congress, power has been decentralized to committees, which are often autonomous of the party leadership. Parliamentary parties' organizational clout can be measured in terms of budget, people, and rules. In most European legislatures, individual MPs have little staff support and budget resources to forge a strong link to their constituents and to establish a knowledge and information basis to participate effectively in the parliamentary process. In contrast to this, parliamentary party groups are well equipped in this respect with their own budgets and a sizeable staff. Party groups in European parliaments have developed a multitude of status positions that oversee and manage the decision process within the group.

The scope of party cohesion in European parliaments has been documented on the basis of measures that go beyond floor voting. Andeweg (1997, 118) found that 44 percent of Dutch MPs in 1990 reported asking for prior permission for a written question from the parliamentary party chairperson, even though this is a constitutional right of individual MPs.

Parliamentary parties also enjoy a preeminent legal status. In the German Bundestag, standing orders require that only groups comprising 5 percent of the whole—also the threshhold for a formal caucus—may introduce legislation. Individual members of parliament have few rights to participate such as introducing amendments on the floor or asking questions on the floor. In congressional systems, the individual has far more power.

In Europe and elsewhere, parliament possesses the power to make and break governments. These functions integrate particular groups of members of parliament (MPs) in the process of government formation and government breakdown. It defines MPs in the voters' perception and thus establishes collective responsibility. Parliamentary systems provide executives with resources such as ministerial appointments that can be used by party leaderships to induce MPs to go along with the policies of the government (Depauw 1999).

Beyond the simple dichtomy of parliamentary versus congressional systems other institutional features of the US Congress should lead to weaker partisanship as well. The president and members of each house of Congress run for election at different times and may not share a common fate, whereas a prime minister *comes from parliament and is responsible to it*. There is the possibility of divided control of the legislative and executive branches in the United States—and this makes assigning responsibility for legislation problematic. Senators serve six-year terms to insulate them from the whims of public opinion. Senators were initially appointed by state legislatures rather than elected. The upper chamber was designed, in George Washington's words, to "cool" the passions of the lower house. The House has long had procedures similar to those in parliamentary systems, where the majority, if it willed, could work its will.

The Senate's procedures have always been less majoritarian: In 1806, Senators eliminated a rule that allowed a majority to proceed to a vote and it was not until 1917 that the Senate had *any* procedure for calling the question. Unlimited debate, the filibuster, is a cherished tradition—now it takes sixty Senators to cut off debate. And most of the time, neither major party has sixty seats (or even when it does, sixty reliable votes). Krehbiel (1998) has argued that the potential for a filibuster means that legislative productivity in Congress does not simply reflect a "median voter" model. Instead, the capacity for enacting legislation depends upon where the "filibuster pivot" is—the positions of the member whose vote can break a filibuster in the Senate. The potential for gridlock (stalemate) is large and ordinarily it takes large majorities to enact major policy changes in the Senate (Krehbiel 1998, 47)—even more so under divided government. The existence of larger districts (states) of the Senate means that constituencies are more heterogeneous—so that it is more difficult for Senators to please their electorates than it is for members of the House. It also means that Senators' own ideologies will be more diverse, with more liberal Republicans and conservative Democrats than we find in the House. Party is not the common bond for ideology in the Senate as it is in the House—Senators from the same party and the same state are rivals for leadership and often try to distinguish themselves from each other ideologically to bolster claims to power (Schiller 2000). Finally, the Senate has a long tradition of strong bonds among members (what White 1956 called the "Inner Club"), which puts a premium on getting along rather than emphasizing party differences.

Parties have not always been weak in the USA: under Czar rule in 1890–1911, party leaders had extraordinary power: Speaker Thomas Reed (R, ME) chaired the powerful House Rules Committee, made all committee assignments himself, and had complete control over the House floor and the right of recognition. Members were regularly reassigned from one committee to another when they fell out of favor with the Speaker. A division within the Republican party—as Progressives became a more important force—led to the fall of Reed's successor, Clarence Cannon, on an obscure procedural vote in 1911 (when Progressives aligned with Democrats)—and to a decline in the role of parties in the US Congress.

The constitutional structure of the United States clearly shapes the lesser power of parties compared to parliamentary systems, especially in Europe. Yet students of Congress, from Woodrow Wilson to contemporary formal theorists, have focused more on an institutional feature of Congress that is extra-constitutional: the congressional committee system. The end of Czar rule led to the growth of a committee system that was independent of party pressures and that gave positions of authority to members based upon seniority (longevity on the committee) rather than party loyalty. Legislators seek committee assignments based upon the interests of their constituents and upon their own expertise. Once appointed to a committee, membership becomes a "property right" that cannot be abrogated (a reform enacted following the downfall of Czar rule).

Fenno (1973) stressed committee autonomy from the 1950s to the 1970s and emphasized how committees responded differently to their clienteles and their environments, rather than to a single master such as party leadership. Since conservative Southern Democrats were the most electorally secure, they dominated committee chair positions in both the House and the Senate and often blocked the agenda of the liberals who dominated the party's legislative contingent through the 1970s.

The new institutionalist perspective of Shepsle and Weingast (1994) focuses on committees as "preference outliers" from others in the chamber and argue that distributive policy-making stems from implicit logrolling among outlier committees (see also Wilson 1967, 121). These logrolls can occur *because committees are monopoly agenda setters—they operate under closed rules that prohibit others in the legislature from offering amendments.* Committees, then, have an extraordinary degree of power in these models.

An alternative institutionalist perspective focuses on committees as information providers (Krehbiel 1991). This informational power gives committees even greater power over legislation. They may not have monopoly agenda-setting power, but their greater knowledge of policy consequences implies that they can generally get their way within the legislature. Committees are *not* autonomous in this model— they must respond to the majority position within the legislature (regardless of party). But committees themselves are representative of the full chambers, not preference outliers. While these "new institutionalist" perspectives are at direct variance with each other, *both* downplay the role of parties in Congress.

Strong committees, under any account, lead to a policy-making arena that is very different from the party-dominated legislative process found in parliamentary systems. Parties in parliamentary systems promote policies *in order to get them adopted.* In European parliaments, parties control committee assignments and procedures (Damgaard 1995). In the United States, committees are designed to protect constituency interests and this often means *blocking rather than passing legislation.* The committee system is often seen as a "legislative graveyard" since only about 6 percent of bills introduced by members become law.

The institutional structure of the congressional system is thus insufficient to explain why bills get passed. Legislators rely upon *informal institutions (or norms)* to build cross-party coalitions. These norms—courtesy, reciprocity, legislative work, specialization, apprenticeship (members traditionally worked their way up from minor committees to more important ones), and institutional patriotism (respecting the rules and prerogatives of each chamber)—were key factors in securing bipartisan majorities for legislation (Matthews 1960). The norms waned during the period of heightened partisanship that took hold in the 1980s (Uslaner 1993). Since parliamentary systems do not depend upon the cooperation of the majority with the minority, a strong set of norms of collegiality never took hold.

2   THE BEHAVIORAL FOUNDATIONS OF PARTISANSHIP

The institutional structure of Congress laid the foundation for strong ties between legislators and their constituents. Members of the House faced election frequently and both House and Senate elections occurred in years when the president was not on the ballot. The weak parties meant that legislators were free to pay attention to the people who elected them—and committees were devoted to protection of constituency interests, even at the expense of party programs. Speaker of the House Thomas P. O'Neill (1977–1986) had a famous line that he told to junior members contemplating whether to support their party or their constituency: "All politics is local."

A large literature, developed mostly during the period of weak parties, posited that members of Congress were torn between serving two masters: their parties and their constituents. In the eighteenth century, British MP (and political philosopher) Edmund Burke told his electors in his Bristol constituency that he did not feel bound to abide by their views—that he would follow his own conscience and would accept the verdict of the voters as to whether they believed he was correct (they turned him out of office).

Burke's speech became the basis for *role theory* in the study of legislatures where legislators chose between the roles of *delegates*, who followed constituency opinion, or *trustees*, who followed their own conscience or their parties. Wahlke, Eulau, Buchanan, and Ferguson (1962) found, perhaps surprisingly, that most American state legislators in the five states they examined in the 1950s considered themselves trustees—with figures ranging from 55 percent in California to 81 percent in Tennessee. Only between 6 and 20 percent took on the pure "delegate" role, with the rest in between as "politicos." A decade later Davidson (1969) found similar results for members of the US Congress.

The Burkean distinction has been used in the European context as well (Barnes 1977; Converse and Pierce 1986; Searing 1994). Only a small minority of European MPs would consider themselves delegates. In the late 1970s only 3 percent of the members of the German Bundestag regarded themselves as instructed delegates (Farah 1980, 238). Compared to their American colleagues, many European MPs spend less time communicating with constituents. An analysis of the time budget of members of the German Bundestag found that about one quarter of an average member's time is devoted to "information and contact activities," a summary category which also includes time spent with constituency communication (Herzog et al. 1990, 83–92).

Searing (1994) interviewed 521 British MPs to distinguish between four preference roles (policy advocate, ministerial aspirant, constituency member, parliament man) and four position roles (parliamentary private secretary, whip, junior minister, minister). Searing found many policy advocates and few parliament men among the backbenchers he interviewed. While parliament men resemble the classical concept of an amateur who enjoys being a Member of Parliament and who is absorbed by the conduct of parliamentary business, policy advocates aim at influencing government policy and develop carrying degrees of issue familiarity and expertise.

Patzelt's (1997) interviews with German MPs from 1989 to 1992 demonstrated that MPs aim to reconcile and to synthesize the roles of trustee and delegate. European MPs are characterized by complex role sets that cannot be reduced to any single role type and that, at the same time, incorporate the notion of a partisan as a strong and predominant element within this role set (Müller and Saalfeld 1997).

In Europe, constituency has always taken a back seat to party. For the United States from the 1890s until 1911, partisanship reigned supreme and there was no conflict between party and constituency for legislators. Czar rule came to an end because of growing factionalism within the Republican Party, leading the Progressives in the House to side with the minority party (the Democrats) to defeat a routine procedural motion—marking the end of the strong Speaker. With the downfall of strong party leadership, members of Congress established committees with tenure not touchable by party leaders, and legislative authority of their own. Members looked more and more to their constituencies rather than to parties. Legislators were torn between which to support on the floor, as we saw as early as the 1920s, as shown by Julius Turner (later revised by Edward Schneier in Turner and Schneier 1970).

The parliamentary model of solidarity with one's party fell by the wayside in the United States: Some issues (states rights, legislative–executive relations, patronage) showing high levels of party conflict and others (foreign policy, business, agriculture, social welfare) dividing the parties less frequently. Clausen showed for the House (and Sinclair 1982 for both houses) that levels of voting along party lines depended heavily on the nature of the issue. Economic issues were the most heavily partisan and foreign policy and social issues were the least partisan.

Many of the least loyal Democrats were from the South and the least loyal Republicans were from the East. Southern Democrats often voted more frequently with Republicans than with Northern Democrats, forming an informal "conservative coalition." Yet, the very diversity of the Democratic Party may have been the key to the party's long-term electoral dominance.

Mayhew (1966) argued that House Democrats were the party of "inclusive compromise." The Republicans, with a much narrower ideological base, were the party of "exclusive compromise," destined to maintain minority status.

Miller and Stokes (1963) earlier showed that the connections between legislators' votes and constituency attitudes were frequently weak because members of Congress often misperceived public opinion. Most studies reported at best moderate correlations between legislators' votes and public opinion. Achen (1975) corrected the Miller–Stokes constituency opinions for measurement error and found much stronger correlations with legislators' votes.

Fenno (1978) argued that legislators focus not on just one constituency (the entire district), but have multiple masters. Of particular importance is the reelection constituency—mostly comprised of fellow partisans. Using data on public opinion derived from statewide exit polls in the states (Erikson, Wright, and McIver 1993) for both the full constituency (the state) and the reelection constituency (fellow state partisans), Uslaner (1999) showed that Senators respond primarily to their fellow partisans—and that there is generally a close correspondence between their own ideology and that of their reelection constituencies. His findings mirror Kingdon's (1973) analysis of House members' explanations for their voting behavior: the "field of forces" members face on roll calls—constituency opinion, interest group pressure, leadership mobilization, the administration, fellow members, their staff, and their own values—mostly have the bare minimum of conflict. This strikes a key blow at both the notion that legislators "shirk" their constituents in favor of their party or their own ideology—or that members must adopt either a delegate or a trustee role.

Yet, there remains tension between party and constituency demands. Members of Congress expanded their electoral base beyond their own partisans in the 1960s and 1970s by developing a strong "personal vote" apart from party identification. They attracted support across party lines through a combination of bringing back projects to the district, personal attention to constituents and their problems, and the ability to raise large amounts of money for their campaigns (Fiorina 1977; Jacobson and Kernell 1983). During the period of weak partisanship, the two major parties' constituencies were not ideologically polarized. However, even as the party coalitions began to diverge more sharply in presidential politics in the 1970s, the rise in candidate-centered (as opposed to party-centered) campaigns shielded congressional incumbents from national tides favoring one party or another (Brady and Hahn 2004).

Members of Congress focused on developing "home styles" to convince constituents that they were "one of them." Members use these "home styles" to broaden their bases of support—and they generally treat issues gingerly because ideological appeals may repel some constituents. Legislators do claim that they have power in Washington, but they are hardly above tearing down the institution to make themselves look good (Fenno 1978, 245–6). Much as Wilson feared a century earlier, "running for Congress by running against Congress" leads to a lack of concern for the collective good of the institution.

Members care more about their own electoral fates than about how well their party does—the reelection rates for the House now approach 100 percent while Senators fare less well but still prevail in about 85 percent of their races. Even in the Democratic debacle of 1994, when the party lost control of both houses (losing the

House for the first time since 1954), 84 percent of Democratic Representatives seeking an additional term won (Jacobson 2004, 23). By developing home styles that focus on members' character and service to the district, incumbents have largely insulated themselves against national political tides—and even congressional performance. The level of gridlock (or stalemate) in Congress, Binder (2003, 110) reports, has little effect on the reelection prospects of incumbents.

3   THE RISE AND FALL IN PARTISANSHIP: INSTITUTIONAL AND BEHAVIORAL EXPLANATIONS

Cox and McCubbins (1993) argue that other "new institutionalists" have underestimated the impact of parties in Congress. Even during periods of strong committees, parties played a key role in shaping committee membership—and party leaders rarely lost votes on the floor when pitted against recalcitrant committee leaders. Poole and Rosenthal (1997) also argue that legislative voting has always been unidimensional. This single dimension encompasses both ideology and partisanship (Poole and Rosenthal 1997, 6)—so models focusing on ideology and models focusing on party are actually examining the same thing using different terms.

Most analysts still stand by the argument that American legislative parties were weak for much of the twentieth century, even as Brady and Hahn (2004) argue that American political life has normally been highly partisan and that the weak party era was exceptional rather than the norm. There is also general agreement that partisanship in the 1960s and especially the 1970s was much lower than normal. Beginning in 1981 with the inauguration of the Reagan administration, partisanship increased more dramatically and has continued to grow almost unabated (Rohde 1991, 51). Partisanship has now reached levels not seen in the Congress since the era of Czar rule (marked by an all-powerful Speaker) in the House at the turn of the century.

The major institutional explanations focus on structural reforms in the House of Representatives in the 1970s. The "Subcommittee Bill of Rights" transferred power from full committees to subcommittees. The initiation of electronic voting increased amending activity sharply. Party leaders also gained power at the expense of committees: the Speaker was given greater control over assigning members to committees and over referring bills to committees. There was also an expanded

leadership system in the House that gave the Speaker and his aides more information. These reforms weakened most norms, especially courtesy, reciprocity,
and institutional patriotism (Sinclair 1989; Smith 1989)—and placed greater
power in the hands of both the party leaders and junior members. Three Southern
committee chairs were removed from their positions in 1975 by the House Democratic caucus, one of the first steps in the move toward stronger parties. An even
bigger boost in partisanship occcured in 1995, when the Republicans took control
of Congress. Committees became much less independent of party leadership—the
Speaker and his allies now control the committee appointment process, committee
chairs are limited to three terms, and party renegades have found themselves
relegated to minor committees and unable to advance within the party (Evans
and Oleszek 1997). Recalcitrant committees faced the prospect that the leadership
would take favored legislation out of their jurisdictions to be handled by special
"task forces" appointed by the Speaker.

Strong party institutions and weaker committees, these institutional accounts
argue, provide the foundation for greater partisanship on the part of the rank and
file. Members of Congress will be more likely to toe the party line when parties are
stronger. Demonstrating the effects of strong leadership on legislative voting is not
so simple. Krehbiel (1993) argues that party influence in legislative voting is a
mirage. Partisanship in legislative voting is simply a proxy for members' own
ideologies—Democrats are more liberal, Republicans are more conservative.
As each party becomes more homogenous, partisan polarization in the legislature
increases. Finding an *independent effect for leadership mobilization* is elusive. On
precisely those issues that are most important to the parties, the leaders make the
greatest efforts to mobilize their bases. What appears to be strong mobilization by
leaders is really little more than homogenous preferences among followers—real
party pressure would involve voting for a bill favored by the leadership *even when
the member does not agree with it*. Without information about members' "true
preferences," there is no way to verify this claim.

There have been a few studies that attempt to get past this conondrum: Sinclair
(2001) examines the selection of procedural rules in the House of Representatives
from 1987 to 1996. She finds that majority party members are more likely to vote for
the rule than for the bill—especially when the rule restricts the freedom of the
minority. Ansolabehere, Snyder, and Stewart (2001) use surveys of candidate
attitudes to obtain independent measures of policy preferences and show that the
legislators' party shapes voting on roll calls even beyond the effect of member
attitudes. Neither of these studies, however, measure leadership effects directly.
Perhaps the only studies that get directly at leadership effects are Kingdon (1973)
and Burden and Frisby (2004). Kingdon asked members of the House what factors
shaped their roll call voting right after the legislators cast their ballots.
He conducted his study in the weak party era (1969), so it is no surprise that
he reported (Kingdon 1973, 121): "the sanctions [of party leaders] are not very

effective, simply because many congressmen care more about voting as they see fit, either for ideological or political reasons, than about the risk of negative party sanctions. Members repeatedly voiced perfect willingness to defy the leadership and take whaetever consequences might come." Burden and Frisby examine previously private Democratic whip counts in 1971–2 (also the weak party era) to see if party pressure can switch votes. These data have preferences before party efforts and on the votes on the House floor. Only a small share of votes were changed. Consistent with Krehbiel's (1993) argument, there was general agreement within the Democratic Party (even during this period of relatively low cohesion) on the sixteen bills analyzed.

One key problem with these institutional approaches beyond the difficulty in establishing party leader effects is that the structural reforms that many posit as key to the rise in partisanship and polarization were restricted to the House of Representatives. Polarization increased *in both the House and the Senate* (Binder 2003; Brady and Hahn 2004; Poole and Rosenthal 1997; Uslaner 1993). The Senate was not the subject for widespread structural change at any point during the past fifty years—yet the trends in party polarization almost exactly mirror those of the House. This should not be so surprising: About 120 years ago Wilson (1967, 152–3) wrote (even as the Senate was still not directly elected): "there is a 'latent unity' between the Senate and the House, which makes continued antagonism between them next to impossible.... The Senate and the House are of different origins, but virtually of the same nature."

A more behavioral approach focuses on changes *outside the legislature—mostly in the electorate.* Cohesive floor voting as well as party driven role conceptions and institutional choices are seen as the result of common ideologies and shared values that become manifest in strong party structures at the social level. This, in turn, is seen as the result of historical and antecedent cultural factors such as the strength of localism in society or the pattern of cleavages underlying the party system.

Cooper and Brady (1981) argue that partisanship in the United States varies over time in a cylical fashion. When partisan and constituency ties overlap (as under Czar rule and from the 1980s to the present), parties will be strong. When they do not (as in the 1940s through the 1960s), parties will be weak. Rohde (1991) argues that the Voting Rights Act (VRA) of 1965 was the turning point leading to stronger parties in the United States. By enfranchising African-Americans in the South, the VRA pushed white Southern conservatives into the Republican Party (where they now predominate) and made the Southern Democratic Party largely African-American (and liberal). As the Republican Party moved right, the Democrats became dominant in formerly Republican areas such as the northeast and the parties polarized. Rohde's (1991, 35–6) argument, following upon Cooper and Brady, is called "conditional party government:" "instead of strong party leaders being the cause of high party cohesion, cohesive parties are the main precondition for strong leadership."

While American congressmen seem to move toward the European pattern of legislative behavior, there are signs that their European colleagues are focusing less on parties and more on individual member initiative. European legislatures have reallocated resources to the benefit of individual MPs. Personal staff has increased in many legislatures since the late 1960s. In 1969, the German Bundestag bestowed German members of parliament with a moderate budget that can be used to employ staff or to pay for office expenses. Since then the figure has increased substantially. When the number of districts in Germany was reduced from 328 to 298 prior to the 2002 election, parts of the savings were used to increase the budget of individual MPs (Saalfeld 2002, 59). Similar reallocations of resources have also been reported regarding other European legislatures (Gladdish 1990).

European MPs take constituency communication and constituency services more seriously. Cain, Ferejohn, and Fiorina (1984) showed over two decades ago that paying attention to constituencies through weekly surgeries (among other things) did have a payoff in a "personal vote" for British MPs. Norton reports more recently that newly elected British MPs increasingly took up residence in their constituencies and spent more time there compared to their older colleagues (Norton 2002, 25).

Carey and Shugart (1995) and Norris (2004, ch. 10), pinpoint the ballot structure as the most important incentive to cultivate a personal vote and to stress constituency rather than party. Some European countries such as the Netherlands and Sweden apply flexible list systems which provide incentives to forge a closer link between constituents and MPs. This ballot form allows voters to move candidates up the list and to ignore the rank order as determined by party elites. However, factors such as a large district size counter-balance the initial effect of the ballot structure towards personalization.

The UK has a single member district with plurality elections system that is similar to the one in the United States. It should act as an incentive to cultivate a direct bond between MPs and constituents, since there is greater accountability than in a multimember proportional representation system. This works regarding service responsiveness to some respect but it obviously does not affect party discipline in the House of Commons and the predominance of party structures in this parliament. One might assume that the British parliamentary system as well as the social environment counter-balances the effects of the electoral system. Bogdanor (1985, 193) sees this districting system as an empty vessel because it does not allow voters choices between different party candidates like in flexible list systems. An extra device is needed, such as the primary, if they are to provide for the choice of a candidate.

There are other signs of greater independence for legislators in parliamentary systems as well: European national parliaments have experienced increases in individual member initiatives such as questions to the government (Gladdish 1990). Patzelt (1997) argues that European MPs are no longer simply torn between party and constituency. Instead, they are increasingly using their new resources to assert their own influence within the party—and with independent policy networks. Legislators are now increasingly becoming policy specialists (Searing 1994).

4   Consequences of Changes in Partisanship

We see two trends moving in opposite directions: stronger partisanship with a closer linkage between party and constituency in the United States; and declining partisanship and a weakening of historically strong bonds between parties and their followers in many other places, especially in Europe.

The polarization of constituents along partisan lines in the United States, together with the decline in competitive congressional districts, has heightened the level of partisan conflict in Congress. Even though voters began to sort themselves out ideologically (and by party) as early as the 1960s, it was not until the 1980s that voters' partisanship and ideological identification began to correlate strongly with their votes for Congress (Jacobson 2004, 248–52; Brady and Hahn 2004). As older members who were out of step with their constituents (especially Southern Democrats) retired, their replacements were much more ideologically in tune—and relied less on a "personal" than an ideological (party) vote to get reelected.

Wilson argued that the weakness of the American party system, especially in comparison to stronger parties in Europe, meant less governmental responsibility and a reduced capacity for informed policy-making. The stronger partisanship, measured by both roll call voting and the strength of congressional party leadership (especially at the expense of committee leaders), would have led a "resuscitated" Wilson to rejoice. He would see a political system that has a stronger capacity for policy-making.

Yet, there remain institutional obstacles to legislative productivity, even as congressional parties behave in the manner of their majoritarian counterparts in congressional systems. An institutional factor that observers from Wilson onward have long believed to hinder the enactment of legislation is divided government. Even as the electorate has become more polarized since the 1980s, it has also shown a tendency to give both parties at least some share of the legislative and executive branches. From 1981 to 2006, there has been divided control of government 77 percent of the time. *With high levels of polarization, this should be a recipe for legislative stalemate.* Yet, Mayhew (1991) argues that divided government does *not* affect the number of major laws passed in Congress. Binder (2003, ch. 4), however, argues that Mayhew's simple count of major laws does not take into account the size of the congressional agenda—and her measure of gridlock, which is the share of legislation on the nation's agenda (as determined by daily editorials in the *New York Times*) that does not pass, is strongly shaped by divided control of the legislative and executive branches. Conley (2003) provides a more nuanced view of structural factors: In the era of weak parties, divided government had no significant effect on the president's success in getting his agenda enacted by Congress. Only since party polarization has increased does divided government matter. As the level of partisanship has increased, the capacity for policy-making has *decreased.* Legislative stalemate became more frequent as party polarization rose (Binder 2003, 80). This polarization, among both elites and the public, has led to the waning of the norms that helped promote legislative policy-making in Congress (Uslaner 1993).

In European parliamentary systems, party voting remains as high as ever. The European Parliament is a different story: Members of the European Parliament (MEPs) overwhelmingly stick with their national parties, but are more likely to defect from their European party group. Even though this defection level is not high (about 13 percent from July 1999 to June 2000), voting contrary to one's European party was greatest when: (1) the electoral system for an MEP is candidate-centered and decentralized; and (2) there is policy conflict between European and the national party (Hix 2004).

Increased citizen demands for more responsiveness stimulated MPs to provide more opportunities for direct communication and interaction (Saalfeld 2002; Norton 2002, 180). Changes in technological opportunity structures decrease the costs of constituency communication and also remove practical obstacles in linking MPs and their constituents, bypassing political parties (Zittel 2003). Last but not least, the weakness of political parties themselves, their loss of membership, and the erosion of their social roots raises serious questions regarding the future of party government in European democracies.

Ironically, even though norms of cooperation have not been a major focus of parliamentary systems, there is at least anecdotal evidence (from British Labour MP Tony Colman to the senior author) that incivility has become a problem. In a chamber where booing and hissing have long been part of the legislative show, it is ironic that Europe and the United States are both experiencing more hostile legislative chambers, even as one becomes more partisan and the other less ruled by parties.

We know much about what American legislators do outside of Congress and what members in parliamentary systems (especially in Europe) do inside the legislature. Future research should help us understand what we don't know. In parliamentary systems, we should shift our emphasis away from roll calls toward behavior such as campaign strategies, constituency service, and constituency communication, or the use of parliamentary privileges such as asking questions to ministers. These are less visible and less consequential activities that will help us understand the weakening of parliamentary parties. In the United States, the key puzzle is over the "real" power of party leaders. Can leaders change members' votes in more than a handful of cases? These questions, mixing quantitative research with the more intensive qualitative designs of Fenno (1973) and Kingdon (1973)—and perhaps also a greater focus on state legislatures—will help us understand why congressional parties are growing stronger and parliamentary parties are becoming weaker.

REFERENCES

ACHEN, C. 1975. Mass political attitudes and the survey response, *American Political Science Review*, 69: 1218–31.

ANDEWEG, R. B. 1997. Role specialisation or role switching? Dutch MPs between electorate and executive. Pp. 110–27 in *Members of Parliament in Western Europe: Roles and Behavior*, ed. W. C. Müller and T. Saalfeld. Portland, Oreg.: Frank Cass.

ANSOLABEHERE, S., SNYDER, J. M., JR., and STEWART, C., III 2001. The effect of party and preferences on Congressional roll-call voting, *Legislative Studies Quarterly*, 26: 815–31.

BARNES, S. 1977. *Representation in Italy: Institutionalized Tradition and Electoral Choice*. Chicago: University of Chicago Press.

BEER, S. H. 1969. *British Politics*. London: Faber.

BENDINER, R. 1964. *Obstacle Course on Capitol Hill*. New York: McGraw-Hill.

BINDER, S. 2003. *Stalemate*. Washington, DC: Brookings Institution.

BOGDANOR, V. 1985. Conclusion. Pp. 1–12 in *Representatives of the People? Parliamentarians and Constituents in Western Democracies*, ed. V. Bogdanor. Aldershot: Gower.

BRADY, D. W. and HAHN, H. 2004. An extended historical view of Congressional party polarization. Unpublished paper, Stanford University.

BURDEN, B. C. and FRISBY, T. M. 2004. Preferences, partisanship, and whip activity in the U.S. House of Representatives. *Legislative Studies Quarterly*, 29: 569–91.

BURKETT, T. 1985. The West German Deputy. Pp. 117–31 in *Representatives of the People? Parliamentarians and Constituents in Western Democracies*, ed. V. Bogdanor. Aldershot: Gower.

CAIN, B., FEREJOHN, J., and FIORINA, M. 1984. *The Personal Vote*. Cambridge, Mass.: Harvard University Press.

CAREY, J. M. and SHUGART, M. 1995. Incentives to cultivate a personal vote: a rank ordering of electoral formulas. *Electoral Studies*, 14: 417–39.

CLAUSEN, A. R. 1973. *How Congressmen Decide: A Policy Focus*. New York: St. Martin's Press.

CONLEY, R. S. 2003. *The President, Congress, and Divided Government*. College Station: Texas A&M University Press.

CONVERSE, P. E. and PIERCE, R. 1986. *Political Representation in France*. Cambridge, Mass.: Cambridge University Press.

COOPER, J. and BRADY, D. W. 1981. Institutional context and leadership style. *American Political Science Review*, 75: 411–25.

COWLEY, P. and NORTON, P. 1999. Rebels and rebellions: Conservative MPs in the 1992 parliament. *British Journal of Politics and International Relations*, 1: 81–105.

COX, G. W. and McCUBBINS, M. D. 1993. *Legislative Leviathan*. Berkeley: University of California Press.

DAMGAARD, E. 1995. How parties control committee members. Pp. 308–25 in *Parliaments and Majority Rule in Western Europe*, ed. H. Döring. Frankfurt: Campus Verlag.

—— 1997. The political roles of Danish MPs. Pp. 79–90 in *Members of Parliament in Western Europe: Roles and Behavior*, ed. W. C. Müller and T. Saalfeld. London: Frank Cass.

DAVIDSON, R. 1969. *The Role of the Congressman*. New York: Pegasus.

DEPAUW, S. 1999. Parliamentary party cohesion and the scarcity of sanctions in the Belgian Chamber of Representatives (1991–1995). *Res Publica*, 41: 15–39.

ERIKSON, R. S. 1978. Constituency opinion and Congressional behavior: a reexamination of the Miller–Stokes representation data. *American Journal of Political Science*, 22: 511–35.

—— WRIGHT, G. C., and MacIVER, J. P. 1993. *Statehouse Democracy*. New York: Cambridge University Press.

EVANS, C. L. and OLESZEK, W. 1997. *Congress Under Fire*. Boston: Houghton Mifflin.

FARAH, B. G. 1980. Political representation in West Germany. Ph.D. dissertation, University of Michigan.

FENNO, R. F., JR. 1973. *Congressmen in Committees*. Boston: Little, Brown.

—— 1978. *Home Style*. Boston: Little, Brown.

FIORINA, M. P. 1977. *Congress: Keystone of the Washington Establishment*. New Haven, Conn.: Yale University Press.

GLADDISH, K. 1990. Parliamentary activism and legitimacy in the Netherlands. Pp. 103–19 in *Parliaments in Western Europe*, ed. P. Norton. Portland, Oreg.: Frank Cass.

HEIDAR, K. 1997. Rules, structures and behavior: Norwegian parlamentarians in the nineties. Pp. 91–109 in *Members of Parliament in Western Europe: Roles and Behavior*, ed. W. C. Müller and T. Saalfeld. Portland, Oreg.: Frank Cass.

HERZOG, D., REBENSTORF, H., and WEßELS, B. 1990, *Abgeordnete und Büvger*. Opladen: Westdeutscher Verlago.

HIX, S. 2004. Electoral institutions and legislative behavior: explaining voting defection in the European Parliament. *World Politics*, 56: 194–223.

JACOBSON, G. C. 2004. *The Politics of Congressional Elections*, 6th edn. New York: Longman.

—— and KERNELL, S. 1983. *Strategy and Choice in Congressional Elections*, 2nd edn. New Haven, Conn.: Yale University Press.

KINGDON, J. W. 1973. *Congressmen's Voting Decisions*. New York: Harper and Row.

KREHBIEL, K. 1991. *Information and Legislative Organization*. Ann Arbor: University of Michigan Press.

—— 1993. Where's the party? *British Journal of Political Science*, 23: 235–66.

—— 1998. *Pivotal Politics*. Princeton, NJ: Princeton University Press.

LOWELL, A. L. 1901. The influence of party upon legislation in England and America. *Annual Report of the American Historical Association for 1901*, 1: 319–542.

MATTHEWS, D. R. 1960. *U.S. Senators and Their World*. Chapel Hill: University of North Carolina Press.

MAYHEW, D. R. 1966. *Party Loyalty Among Congressmen*. Cambridge, Mass.: Harvard University Press.

—— 1974. *Congress: The Electoral Connection*. New Haven, Conn.: Yale University Press.

—— 1991. *Divided We Govern*. New Haven, Conn.: Yale University Press.

MÜLLER, W. C. and JENNY, M. 2000. Abgeordnete, parteien und koalitionspolitik: individuelle präferenzen und politisches handeln im Nationalrat. *Österreichische Zeitschrift für Politikwissenschaft*, 29: 137–56.

—— and SAALFELD, T. (eds.) 1997. *Members of Parliament in Western Europe: Roles and Behavior*. Portland, Oreg.: Frank Cass.

NORRIS, P. 2004. *Electoral Engineering: Voting Rules and Political Behavior*. Cambridge: Cambridge University Press.

NORTON, P. 1980. *Dissension in the House of Commons 1974–1979*. Oxford: Clarendon Press.

—— (ed.) 1990. *Parliaments in Western Europe*. Portland, Oreg.: Frank Cass.

—— 2002. Introduction. Pp. 1–18 in *Parliaments and Citizens in Western Europe*, ed. P. Norton. London: Frank Cass.

PATZELT, W. J. 1997. German MPs and their role. Pp. 55–78 in *Members of Parliament in Western Europe: Roles and Behavior*, ed. W. C. Müller and T. Saalfeld. London: Frank Cass.

POOLE, K. T. and ROSENTHAL, H. 1997. *Congress: A Political-Economic History of Roll Call Voting*. New York: Oxford University Press.

ROHDE, D. W. 1991. *Parties and Leaders in the Postreform House*. Chicago: University of Chicago Press.

SAALFELD, T. 1990. The West German Bundestag after 40 years: the role of parliament in a "party democracy." Pp. 43–65 in *Parliaments in Western Europe*, ed. P. Norton. Portland, Oreg.: Frank Cass.

—— 1995. *Parteisoldaten und Rebellen: Eine Untersuchung zur Geschlossenheit der Fraktionen im Deutschen Bundestag (1949–1990)*. Opladen: Leske u. Budrich.

—— 2002. Parliament and citizens in Germany: reconciling conflicting pressures. In *Parliaments and Citizens in Western Europe*, ed. P. Norton. London: Frank Cass.

SCHILLER, W. J. 2000. *Partners and Rivals*. Princeton, NJ: Princeton University Press.

SEARING, D. D. 1994. *Westminster's World: Understanding Political Roles*. Cambridge, Mass.: Cambridge University Press.

SHEPSLE, K. and WEINGAST, B. 1994. Positive theories of congressional institutions. *Legislative Studies Quarterly*, 19: 149–80.

SINCLAIR, B. 1982. *Congressional Realignment, 1925–1978*. Austin: University of Texas Press.

—— 1989. The transformation of the U.S. Senate. Baltimore: Johns Hopkins University Press.

—— 2001. Do parties matter? Pp. 36–63 in *Party, Process, and Political Change: New Perspectives on the History of Congress*, ed. D. Brady and M. McCubbins. Stanford, Calif.: Stanford University Press.

SKJAEVELAND, A. 2001. Party cohesion in the Danish parliament. *Journal of Legislative Studies*, 7: 35–56.

SMITH, S. S. 1989. *Call to Order: Floor Politics in the House and Senate*. Washington, DC: Brookings Institution.

TURNER, J. and SCHNEIER, E. V., JR. 1970. *Party and Constituency*, rev. edn. Baltimore: Johns Hopkins University Press.

USLANER, E. M. 1993. *The Decline of Comity in Congress*. Ann Arbor: University of Michigan Press.

—— 1999. *The Movers and the Shirkers*. Ann Arbor: University of Michigan Press.

WAHLKE, J., EULAU, H., BUCHANAN, W., and FERGUSON, L. 1962. *The Legislative System*. New York: John Wiley.

WHITE, W. S. 1956. *The Citadel*. New York: Harper and Brothers.

WILSON, W. 1967. *Congressional Government*. Cleveland, Ohio: Meridian; orig. pub. 1885.

ZITTEL, T. 2003. Political representation in the networked society: the Americanisation of European systems of responsible party government? *Journal of Legislative Studies*, 9: 32–53.

CHAPTER 24

BICAMERALISM

JOHN UHR

The term "bicameralism" refers to legislative institutions with two chambers sharing legislative powers. In bicameral assemblies, both first and second (or lower and upper) chambers play a role in consenting to proposed laws, although not necessarily equally. First chambers in parliamentary systems tend to have primary legislative responsibility, particularly for taxation and government budgeting, but also in relation to votes of confidence in the political executive (Diermeier and Feddersen 1998). Of course, there are interesting exceptions; for every rule of bicameral relationships, there are important qualifications, and plenty of debates over the qualities of bicameral institutions. Bicameralism has a very long history, leading many commentators to treat it not simply as predemocratic but as anti-democratic—on the evidence that upper houses have traditionally represented "upper classes" of privileged minority interests. Interestingly, many modern upper houses have taken their name from the anti-democratic Roman Senate (Patterson and Mughan 1999). Yet many political institutions with origins in the distant past can be adapted to take on new tasks. Bicameralism provides interesting examples of such institutional makeovers.

There is no one model of bicameralism in political practice and so there is unlikely to be one political theory of bicameralism. As a topic in contemporary political science, bicameralism is surprisingly under-researched and is quite under-theorized. Bicameralism has rightly been called "a concept in search of a

* My thanks to the editors for helpful criticism of earlier drafts and also to Stanley Bach, Mike Pepperday, Kevin Tuffin, and John Wanna.

theory" (Smith 2003, 3). A useful preliminary step is to recognize the two families of bicameralism exemplified in the existing literature by the contrasting models of the British Westminster system and the US congressional system (Lijphart 1999, 200–15). Bicameralism is about more than the presence or absence of upper houses. Bicameralism is about power-sharing relationships within political assemblies and the various balances of political representation in parliamentary and presidential regimes.

In this chapter, I review current research on bicameralism, arguing that there is no one model of bicameralism and no one explanatory theory. Instead, contemporary bicameral systems blend "inheritance" and "innovation" to form distinctive legislative arrangements of political representation. Inheritance here refers to the continuity of past institutional arrangements, such as the traditional representation of hereditary peers in the British House of Lords. Innovation here refers to the design of new institutional arrangements, such as the 1999 reforms under the Blair government drastically to reduce the representation of hereditary peers by allowing peers themselves to elect ninety-two of their own representatives to be retained in the House of Lords. As this example suggests, the nature of upper house representation in a bicameral system can change in quite fundamental ways, preserving elements of inherited practices blended in with new elements that alter the overall mix with untested and in many cases unpredictable consequences. This example also suggests that even the most enduring of bicameral systems are subject to change, as for example the Belgian system in 1995 when moving towards federalism, just as new unicameral systems, such as Indonesia today, can begin transformation towards a bicameral system. Hence, one should be wary of sweeping generalizations about the current state of bicameralism given that the powers and practices of bicameral legislatures are often under review and renovation.

Although bicameralism is often overlooked in scholarly literature, it is of considerable policy importance with recent critics arguing that "bicameralism is an effective institution to strengthen liberal market forces" (Vatter 2005, 209; cf. Castles and Uhr 2005). My analysis begins with some defining issues, clarifying the two main types of bicameralism as they appear in parliamentary and presidential political systems. I then locate the common theoretical justification for both forms of bicameralism by reference to "redundancy theory." The bulk of the chapter then investigates the consequences for political systems of the presence of bicameralism, investigating three contrasting accounts of "balance" attributed to bicameralism. First, a brief mention of the historical account of "balance" derived from premodern theories of the mixed regime which capture some of the institutional dynamics of non-elective representation found in many older upper houses. Second, a review of liberal constitutional accounts of bicameralism illustrating two complementary tendencies or institutional norms. The first tendency has bicameralism play negative roles by restraining the vices of majoritarianism ("tyranny of the majority") and restraining political activists ("factions") threatening vulnerable interests. The second tendency has bicameralism promote more robust democratic public deliberation through political participation by interested groups in civil society. Most contemporary systems of bicameralism display both tendencies or norms, resulting in degrees of institutional uncertainty about the ongoing balance of negative and positive expectations. Third, examination of political science accounts of strong and weak bicameralism, using contemporary data to help identify the institutional characteristics of both of these ideal types of bicameralism. Once again, many contemporary systems of bicameralism exist comfortably within these notional extremes and are strong in some limited respects and weak in other limited respects. My aim is not to provide an organizational chart of contemporary bicameral assemblies but to help explain reasons for the remarkable diversity of achievements across the family of bicameral systems.

1   THE RISE AND FALL OF BICAMERALISM

As Philip Norton reports, there are more bicameral legislatures than we might believe (Norton 2004). Around a third of the world's legislatures are bicameral, and around two-thirds of the world's advanced democracies have bicameral legislatures. The larger the democratic state, the greater the chance of bicameralism; and the more federal the polity, the greater the likelihood of bicameralism. Eighteen of the world's twenty-two federal countries (all except the very smallest) have bicameral legislatures where the second house represents regions, provinces, or states, and the first house represents overall population. Non-federal or unitary countries are fairly evenly divided between bicameral and single chamber (or unicameral) legislatures (Lijphart 1999, 202–3). In addition to unicameral and bicameral legislatures, there are rare additional types with more than two chambers. Historically, three or four chambers are not unknown, each representing a distinct class or social "estate." There are also examples of parliaments, such as that of Norway, which are elected as one body (the Storting) but subsequently reconvene as two chambers (the smaller Lagting and the larger Odelsting) when conducting legislative business.

But bicameralism is far from universal. Whatever its theoretical virtues, many nations have turned their backs on it as a practical guide to everyday politics; and many policy analysts have argued that bicameralism is an obstacle to social democracy and "a significant brake on government intervention and on the expansion of the welfare state" (Vatter 2005, 209). Examples of nations which have rejected bicameral systems in favour of unicameral systems include: New Zealand in 1950, Denmark in 1953, Sweden in 1970, Iceland in 1991, Peru in

1993, and Scotland in 1999. Many of these are examples of "two into one" stories, where the discarded upper houses were typically less democratic than their lower houses: often with restricted franchises and narrower qualifications for membership, usually with considerable powers over legislation, and sometimes selected by appointment rather than election (Longley and Olson 1991). Much like the traditional House of Lords in the UK, many European upper houses survived, in J. S. Mill's words, simply to provide those with "conventional rank and individual riches" the opportunity to "overawe the democracy" arising below them (Mill 1984, 356). In the famous language of French revolutionary activist Abbe Sieyes, where upper houses agree they are superfluous and where they disagree they are mischievous—primarily because they paralyze the will of the people as represented in the more democratic lower house (quoted in Russell 2000, 79).

Also relevant is the slow but steady rejection of bicameralism at the sub-national level in such advanced liberal democracies as Canada, which saw its last provincial upper house abolished in 1968, and whose national senate is formally very powerful but of uncertain public legitimacy because members are appointed rather than elected (Marriott 1910, 131–52; Smith 2003, 3). Democratic constitutions, like the revised Belgium constitution of 1995, typically restrict the powers of upper houses over financial bills, and this widespread restriction reflects the primacy of lower houses as "the people's chamber" and the preferred site of government and home of the political executive (Wheare 1968, 140–1; Lijphart 1999, 205–6). There are very few examples over the last fifty years of nations with unicameral systems adopting bicameralism (Lijphart 1999, 201–3). Unicameralism deserves its own distinctive theory of the model legislature. Nebraska is the only US state to have rejected bicameralism and it did so because "experience has shown that the check exerted by a second chamber is often only nominal, seldom results in good, and is occasionally detrimental to the public welfare" (Johnson 1938, 93; cf. Binder 2003, 127).

Yet despite this history, bicameral legislatures remain a prominent feature of the international political scene. Although approximately one-third of the legislatures of the world are bicameral, around two-thirds of *democratic* national legislatures are bicameral. Federalism suggests one reason: the second chamber acting as a states house or representative of the regions. But even half of the *unitary* democratic states have bicameral legislatures, and further, many sub-national democratic legislatures are bicameral (Lijphart 1999, 201–3). Although it is notable that many small nations have unicameral legislatures, the adoption of bicameralism cannot be explained solely by reference to federalism: only around a third of bicameral assemblies are located in federal systems (Patterson and Mughan 1999, 10). No special representative function such as regional representation is necessarily required: instead, bicameralism "can be justified as a protection against electoral excesses," with the upper house serving a "protective role" much like "all genuine insurance facilities" (Brennan and Lomasky 1993, 214–15; Patterson and Mughan 1999, 3).

2   DEFINING ISSUES

Studies of bicameralism typically focus on the role of second or upper chambers and on institutional relationships between the two chambers. The convention in parliamentary studies is to regard the upper chamber as "secondary" compared to the first or lower chamber, on the basis that the first chamber is "lower" in the sense of closer to the people, with a scheme of representation credited with being more democratic because it reflects the population at large rather than geographical regions or social minorities. Within particular national settings, two houses might have similar legislative powers but, even in these rare situations of similar legal powers, the two houses will rarely have similar schemes of representation. Italy is one important exception, with both parliamentary houses arranged to represent similar interests and even sharing similar powers—this unusual duplication of interests and powers helps explain the comparative weakness of what on paper appears a very strong upper house (Lijphart 1999, 205–11; Russell 2000, 29, 50, 82). The practical power of an upper house depends less on the forms of legislative power available to it and more on the substance of public support for its role in the national legislative system, reflecting the wider political and public legitimacy attached to its distinctive scheme of representation. Even unelected or indirectly elected second chambers with limited legislative powers can exercise great policy power. This situation has been termed "Cicero's puzzle," referring to the power able to be deployed by upper houses in the face of constitutional pre-eminence of lower houses (Tsebelis and Money 1995, 126).

The convention about the "secondary-ness" of second houses does not hold for legislative studies across the board: many upper houses in non-parliamentary or presidential systems (e.g. the US Senate and upper houses in the US states) are rarely if ever regarded as secondary. This goes well beyond the sphere of US politics because the US provides "the model on which Latin American constitutions have been based" (Llanos and Nolte 2003, 55). Upper houses in presidential systems share many of the attributes of upper houses in parliamentary systems— typically smaller than lower houses (the House of Lords is a rare exception), with constitutional restrictions on powers over public finance, but with longer terms than lower house members, often arranged through a staggered election cycle. These differences in schemes of representation do not necessarily render non-parliamentary (or congressional) upper houses "secondary." Thus, not all forms of bicameralism are alike; indeed, not even all forms of parliamentary or congressional bicameralism are alike. Bicameralism is a term of convenience covering a great variety of types of legislatures comprising two chambers, with the powers of upper chambers and their relationships to lower chambers varying across and within parliamentary and presidential systems. Then there are the crossovers: the so-called "semi-presidential" systems (Lijphart 1999, 121–4).

French bicameralism, for example, combines elements of both parliamentary and presidential systems, with the upper house representing the regions and potentially a third force under circumstances of "cohabitation" when the presidency and the lower house are under opposing political parties—and very powerful when, for instance in the late 1970s, supporting president Giscard against mutual opponents in the lower house (Tsebelis and Money 1995, 124–5; Russell 2000, 87–9).

Most of the early political science studies of bicameralism focused solely on the formal constitutional role served by upper houses (e.g. Marriott 1910; Bryce 1921). The most important theme of this early wave of research is the recognition that the public value claimed for bicameralism derives from differences between the two houses' schemes of political representation. At the foundation of modern studies of bicameralism is the claim that bicameralism implies that the two legislative bodies embody *diversity* rather than *duplication* of political representation. Germany provides one example, with the lower house elected by the people and the upper house appointed by state governments (Konig 2001). An older example is the difference in rules over representation for members of the two houses of the US legislature. Federalism explains some of these differences in the architecture of representation (e.g. equality of state representation regardless of population size), but many other differences reflect a deeper commitment to structural diversity in the logics of representation embodied by each house: for example, the US Constitution provides that the Senate will be considerably smaller than the House of Representatives, stipulates a higher minimum age for senators (followed in different ways by Canada, India, Mexico, France, Italy, among others), grants senators longer terms (three times that of House members), and puts them on a staggered election cycle, with a third being elected each House election. Structural differences in representation between two houses are a common feature of the institutional logic of bicameralism (Russell 2000, 25–33).

By contrast, recent studies of bicameralism tend to take a different perspective, turning away from the public law dimension of constitutional norms to examine public decision-making dimensions of constitutional practice. Although this new perspective is not confined to rational choice analysis, many of the most influential contributions have used techniques of formal modeling drawn from game-theoretic analysis and mathematical models of politics (see generally Tsebelis 1995; Tsebelis and Money 1997; Diermeier and Feddersen 1998; Tsebelis 2002). Skimming over many subtle variations in emphasis in this new generation of bicameral studies, I want to note one important common element—which is the inclusion of the institutional interests of the political executive in the current analysis of bicameralism. Analysts of bicameralism frequently chart the many ways that bicameralism can affect the strategy of policy choice open to political executives. This is a fresh contribution to an old story about the institutional design of the separation of powers in modern representative government. Where many traditional studies confined themselves to examinations of two institutions managing legislative power, contemporary studies of bicameralism reach out to include the institutional management of legislative–executive relationships. The turn to formal modeling in bicameral studies is not necessarily an alternative to more traditional public law approaches. But instead of sorting through the many variations in bicameralism in order to identify desirable constitutional norms of intercameral comity, a game-theoretic analysis subjects bicameralism to a considerably more demanding examination of institutional logic framing the political executive's political management of those wielding legislative power. Formal modeling brings the promise of greater political realism by dealing-in the single political actor with the greatest public power: the chief political executive (Bottom, Eavey, Miller, and Victor 2000; Ansolabehere, Snyder, and Ting 2003).

What does bicameralism begin to look like when the analysis turns from a preoccupation with constitutional norms to a focus on executive management of legislative power? To anticipate: bicameralism emerges as a cluster of veto points allowing political representatives to restructure the legislative process and to reframe the options open to political executives. This systematic analysis of executive–legislative relations can reveal many of the very practical consequences posed by bicameralism, including many unintended consequences (Binder 2003, 12–33). Formal modeling of bicameralism drew initially on case studies from presidential (or congressional) systems of government (see e.g. Hammond and Miller 1987; Miller, Hammond, and Kile 1996; but see also Tsebelis and Rasch 1995; Konig 2001). Although many presidential systems have bicameral legislatures, one promising way to explain bicameral relationships *within* the legislature is to begin with the fact that executive power is separated from the legislature. Executive power is held by a president supported by a public mandate independent of the legislature. By comparison, many parliamentary systems with bicameral legislatures place executive power in the hands of the leader of the political party or grouping able to command the political support and formal confidence of parliament—or at least of its lower house, given that the "first chamber is always the most important one" (Lijphart 1999, 201). The division of legislatures according to two broad types of political regime (parliamentary and presidential) means that bicameralism divides into two broad types, illustrating two different families of relationships between bicameral legislatures and political executives. Parliamentary systems display tugs of war between the chamber housing the political executive (the lower house) and the upper house. Presidential systems display a different set of institutional dynamics. There is still a struggle between the two legislative houses but it tends to deal more openly with disputes over the use and abuse of *legislative* powers—rather than disputes over the use and abuse of *executive* powers as displayed in parliamentary systems. Both systems display bicameral policy bickering, but in presidential systems the legislative bickering is over each chamber's policy priorities, whereas in parliamentary systems the legislative bickering is over each chamber's view of the appropriateness of the policy priorities of the political executive, which initiates the vast bulk of parliamentary legislation (Diermeier and Feddersen 1998).

With some exceptions (e.g. Tsebelis and Rasch 1995; Tsebelis and Money 1995), studies of parliamentary bicameralism have been less forthright about the place of the political executive in defining the scope of bicameralism. This is not surprising given the prevailing if polite fiction that these political systems are examples of parliamentary rather than prime-ministerial government. Unlike presidential systems, parliamentary systems are traditionally ruled by a shared or collegial political executive under a system known as "cabinet government" (Lijphart 1999, 118). But in the wake of the steady rise of executive power concentrated in chief ministers, a debate has arisen about the "presidentialization" of the role of parliamentary heads of government. This debate is covered in Chapter 17 in this volume and its relevance here is limited to the changing terms in debates over parliamentary forms of bicameralism. Before the rise of debates over parliamentary presidencies, political debates over parliamentary bicameralism were about intercameral roles and responsibilities in sharing legislative power. But increasingly, with the growth of prime-ministerial control over executive powers, public debate over bicameralism has changed in important ways from one primarily about the roles of upper houses in managing *legislative* power to include debate about the role of upper houses in managing *executive* power. This change reflects increasing awareness of the political executive as the driving force in the parliamentary process. As chief political executives take greater control over the parliamentary process, public debates over the value of upper houses turn from traditional preoccupations about their legislative capacities to new preoccupations about their capacities to balance growing executive power with new forms of parliamentary and public accountability.

Finally, in this review of basic defining issues in the study of bicameralism, I note that concepts of *tricameralism* and even *multicameralism* have emerged as ways of explaining the influence of the political executive over legislatures (see, e.g., Levmore 1992; Tsebilis 2002, 141–5). An example of de facto tricameralism arises from the legislative power exercised by the US president authorized by the constitutional veto over bills passed by Congress: Legislation thus requires the consent of three potential "veto-players," if we include in this definition of tricameralism the House, the Senate, and the president. Analysts of tricameralism are advocates of realism: in the context of presidential studies, they are widening the focus to include all holders of legislative power, including presidents with constitutional power to veto legislation emerging from the institutional struggle between the two houses of the legislature. The realist call for a tricameral approach has also begun to arise in studies of parliamentary bicameralism, acknowledging the institutional struggle between those wielding executive and legislative power. But again we see interesting differences between parliamentary and presidential studies. Analysts of presidential systems note the power of the executive to negate legislative outcomes, whereas analysts of parliamentary systems note the power of the executive to initiate and control parliamentary outcomes—and the power of upper houses to use their legislative power to try to negate or modify executive schemes. An example of the acknowledgment of tricameralism in a parliamentary context is Reid and Forrest's "trinitarian" framework (political executive, lower house, upper house) for investigating the institutional relationships embedded in the Australian constitutional setting (Reid and Forrest 1989). Reid's analysis makes good sense of Australia's famous 1975 constitutional crisis when the opposition-controlled Senate refused to pass the budget of the Whitlam Labor government, provoking the governor-general to dismiss the government (despite its majority in the lower house) and install the opposition as caretaker government, pending a general election for all members of both houses (a so-called "double dissolution" election), which the opposition comfortably won (Bach 2003, 83–119).

3   BICAMERALISM AS REDUNDANCY

Before we examine the consequences of bicameralism for democratic politics, we should pay some attention to the causes or drivers of bicameralism. The intellectual and institutional history of bicameralism has generated "one of the classic debates in the history of political theory" (Vatter 2005, 194; see also Shell 2001). My focus here is on the currents of political theory that have kept bicameralism alive, as a matter for constitutional reflection as well as a political institution, and not on the historical sources that brought it life in the first place. The favorite model for contemporary thinking about bicameralism is "redundancy theory" which helps identify the institutional design considerations appropriate to the various forms of bicameralism (Riker 1955; Landau 1969; Patterson and Mughan 1999). In theories of institutional design, as in many parts of engineering, redundancy is highly valued as a reinforcement mechanism, or safeguard, in the event that systems fail to operate as planned. For example, automobiles have front and rear brakes and hand as well as foot-operated brake levers. While not all are strictly necessary for ordinary motoring, the duplication and overlap can be positively beneficial when, as can happen, there is a system failure in one set of brakes or one set of brake operators.

The benefits of redundancy only come into play when the braking system is designed as two or more parallel subsystems, allowing the second or apparently superfluous subsystem to perform independently of any malfunction in other subsystems. What might at first sight appear as over-engineering can then appear as a prudent design because of the security it provides against malfunction in one of two or more parallel systems. Federalism is a case in point where two or more levels of government either duplicate services or, more likely, duplicate demand for services and thereby strengthen the political accountability facing those responsible for providing public services. Of course, there are many limits to constructive redundancy. As federalism so often shows, accountability can go missing when each level of government blames the other for preventing success-ful delivery of public services. So too in bicameralism: the parties dominating each chamber can also play the blame game, trying to avoid public accountability for their decisions or even their non-decisions. Landau's challenge still stands: "the task remains to learn to distinguish between inefficient redundancies and those that are constructive and reinforcing" (Landau 1969, 356).

Over recent years, rational choice analysts have taken up the cause of bicam-eralism (see, e.g., Hammond and Miller 1987; Brennan and Hamlin 2000, 234–54). One valuable contribution that this school provides to redundancy theory is a richer explanation of how bicameral *diversity* of political representation differs from situations with *duplicated* representation. Bicameral diversity can overcome the policy instability associated with the cycling of alternative preferences often found in systems of majority rule, with no stable core of majority preferences. Bicameralism provides considerable evidence of the relevance of "the core" as "a basic concept in social science theory and cooperative game theory" (Tsebelis and Rasch 1995, 379). Thus, one of the primary consequences of bicameralism is said to be relatively greater stability in legislative decision-making, with final decisions hard to arrive at, but also very hard to overturn. The effects are held to be important to democratic government: In the language of Buchanan and Tulloch, bicameralism is an important "stopping mechanism" able to diminish "external costs" imposed by well-organized factions (Levmore 1992, 145–7). In this view, minorities are less capable of hijacking government decisions when governments are forced to muster majorities across two sites of legislative decision-making, provided that the two sites are differently constituted and that each site of law-making power can exercise a veto power over proposals initiated by those controlling the other house or the initiating government. By examining the nature of "the bargaining game" between two houses, analysts can reveal the public benefits of dispersed political power with, in effect, requirements for supramajority voting in order to mobilize political support across the two houses or sites.

The most detailed case studies of legislative redundancy tend to come from presidential rather than parliamentary systems, and they identify many of the ways that redundancy differs from duplication. Redundancy in political representation can involve two complementary systems of representation, with each legislative house drawing on a particular range of representative interests. "In general, the different chambers represent different 'principals' or 'legitimacies,' that is, different parts of the electorate or ways to represent the electorate" (Tsebelis 1995, 310). An example comes from Binder's study of "stalemate" in the US Congress, often wrongly attributed to episodes of "divided government"— referring to the division of policy priorities that occurs when the political executive is of one party and the legislature is dominated by another party (Binder 2003, 34–56). Institutional stalemate within Congress occurs even when the legislative and executive branches are in the hands of the same political party. The root cause is in the institutional design of the bicameral legislature as it has developed historically, revealing its potential for persistent discord arising from structural division in forms, even styles, of political representation between the House and the Senate. The public policy preferences of each house reflect or at least grow out of the differently-structured routines of representation, as exemplified by the House's short election cycle dominating the careers of all members in the one large chamber, and the Senate's longer and staggered election cycle reinforcing a less frenzied culture of electoral responsiveness in the smaller chamber.

The fundamental point arising from Binder's analysis of US "stalemate" is that the formal constitutional provisions for bicameralism have given rise to contrasting sets of rules of the game of institutional politics. Whatever the original intentions, the effect is that bicameralism has encouraged two sets of procedural rules promoting two contrasting types of legislative processes, resulting more often than not in deep-seated policy disagreements between the two houses. Even political executives with party majorities in both legislative houses have to reconcile themselves to this burden of bicameralism (Binder 2003, 97–105). We can see that one likely consequence of bicameralism is policy stability: Although the policy process includes a complicated legislative procedure, once policy has been translated into law opponents of that policy face formidable obstacles when they attempt to bring in alternative policies (Bottom, Eavey, Miller, and Victor 2000; Konig 2001; Tsebelis 2002, 143–9). In the language of formal political analysis, bicameralism has "stability-inducing properties" which protect "the core" of majority rule (i.e. "the set of un-dominated alternatives") from the many instabilities found in unqualified forms of majority rule (Hammond and Miller 1987; Miller, Hammond, and Kile 1996). But another possible consequence is higher government debts, because governments have to include benefits for a wider range of political interests when negotiating under bicameral circumstances and, consistent with the previous point about stability, benefits once given can rarely be retracted, even by incoming governments from opposed parties (Heller 1997).

4   BICAMERALISM AS BALANCE

Historically, the standard model for the stability attributed to bicameralism was *balanced* government, implying that two chambers could bring desirable balance to legislative decision-making. But what does "balance" mean in this context? This question gets us into the heart of many of the most hotly contested disputes in the theory and practice of bicameralism. Bicameral studies include many debates over the claims of particular systems to meet tests of "balance," but remarkably few accounts of the benchmarks appropriate to sound judgments of balance in legislative institutions. A traditional model of this approach to bicameral balance emerged in classical theories of the mixed regime, with its idea of mixing or blending different classes and interests through distinct political institutions, each with a role in policy-making and legislation. Bicameralism originally emerged from this traditional interest in the balance of competing claims to rule exercised by antagonistic groups. Aristotle's "polity" provides students of bicameralism with an influential model of a mixed regime with an institutional design blending democracy and oligarchy in an arrangement of "dual deliberation" (Tsebelis and Money 1997, 17–21). This classical model of bicameralism lacks liberalism's constitutional norms of popular sovereignty and limited government. The ancient model resembles modern bicameralism in bringing together diverse political interests, but it differs by not testing the legitimacy of each legislative house by reference to the one source of sovereignty in "the people." Referring to ideal types, classical bicameralism mixed competing sources of political authority; modern bicameralism blends different but complementary expressions of popular sovereignty: for example, the people as "one people" and the people as state residents.

The distinctive character of "balance" arising out of liberal or modern bicameralism can be seen in the constitutional doctrine justified in the *Federalist Papers*. I will highlight two contrasting tendencies within the liberal doctrine of bicameralism: one designed to restrain government and another designed to energize government. Even the most systematic of game-theoretic approaches examine the institutional design of liberal constitutionalists like the authors of the *Federalist Papers* (see, e.g., Riker 1955, 452–5; Hammond and Miller 1987, 1157–8, 1169–70; Miller, Hammond, and Kile 1996, 98; Tsebelis 2002, 140–1). This broad doctrine defends bicameralism in two often contrasting ways: negatively, in terms of weakening the tendency to abuse of power by political executives; and positively, in terms of energizing and strengthening the deliberative process within the political assembly. At their broadest, liberal doctrines of bicameralism deal with both tendencies as a pair of supplementary measures for effective representative government.

Of course, the practice of most bicameral assemblies tends to show the greater influence of one or other of these two approaches. It is not uncommon for bicameral systems to remain in the negative mode of clamping down on executive abuse of power, usually by using the second chamber as an accountability mechanism to curb executive excesses, including excessive executive control over the independence of the lower chamber. But there are examples of bicameral systems moving over, at least from time to time, to the positive mode to promote strengthened deliberative processes in the legislative assembly. Just as most practical bicameral systems combine elements from both negative and positive modes, so too liberal theories of bicameralism also combine both justifications. The balance of justification varies across theorists, but for present purposes I can round out the negative mode as exemplified in the influential eighteenth-century constitutional doctrine of the *Federalist Papers*, and the positive mode in the equally influential nineteenth-century liberal theory of John Stuart Mill. Both articulations converge in favor of bicameralism and my present contrast is not completely faithful to the rich detail both versions contain. Suitably warned then about the provisional nature of this contrast, we can begin with the negative mode so characteristic of eighteenth-century liberal constitutionalism (Mahoney 1986).

It is notable that the phrase "legislative balances and checks" appears early in the *Federalist Papers* as an example of the modern science of politics unknown to "the ancients" who, as we have seen, pursued a different concept of institutional balance (*Fed 9*; Tsebelis and Money 1997, 27–9). For Madison, the legislature is the deliberative assembly and the Senate, as the controversial second chamber in the proposed US legislature, is justified in terms of the balance it brings to political deliberation. Madison explains the merits of this second chamber by reference to the limited deliberative capacity of the first chamber. In *Federalist 51*, Madison argues that in modern political regimes, legislative authority will tend to overpower the authority of the other two branches of government (the political executive and the judiciary). This overpowering tendency meant that the legislature itself should be divided further into two sub-branches based on "different modes of election and different principles of action," with each sub-branch "as little connected with each other" as possible in one branch of government. Madison's liberal convictions are apparent in *Federalist 62* where he notes that this bicameral structure is a useful precaution against "the facility and excess of law-making" which are "the diseases to which our governments are most liable." For Madison, the problem was that too much concentrated power in one political assembly would generate too much law making and too much government. This liberal model of representative government is one of limited government: government limited in scope to liberal causes of civil liberty and limited in process to the rule of law. The attraction of bicameral solutions is that they allow constitutional designers to graft complementary models of political representation on to the core stock of popular representation. In the US case, this meant that Madison and his fellow framers could accept the legitimacy of a system of relatively popular representation with larger numbers of locally elected members in the lower house, in the knowledge that this popular model would in practice be modified by the presence of another model of representation in the upper house.

Using contemporary language, we can say that this early version of bicameralism was designed to modify the potential for populism through two contrasting versions of democratic legitimacy in the two chambers of Congress. This is not the only approach to modern bicameralism, but it is a very influential one reflecting a commitment to federalism, where the polity arises through a federation of states with equal representation in the second house. There are many variations of federally-organized legislative chambers, and it is useful at the outset to note that the US framers did not expect their federal chamber to restrict itself to act solely as a "states house," protecting only state interests. Federalism helps explain the composition of a second chamber but it alone does not explain the construction or purpose of the second chamber. One only has to see the near-universal existence of bicameralism at state-level legislatures in the USA to begin to appreciate the wider policy purposes associated with US bicameralism. The distinctive competence of the second house of the national legislature goes far beyond its federalist composition, illustrating the broader institutional logic of bicameralism. Describing the Senate as "a second branch of the legislative assembly distinct from and dividing the power of the first," Madison defends this as a "salutary check on government." Factious rulers will require "the concurrence of two distinct bodies in schemes of usurpation or perfidy:" the concurrence of "separate and dissimilar bodies" (*Fed. 63*). Of importance here is Madison's emphasis in *Federalist 62* on "the dissimilarity in the genius of the two bodies," with the Senate having considerably fewer members, each with a considerably longer tenure than members in the House of Representatives, arranged to promote "stability" through a rotation re-election system where a third of its members face re-election every two years. The intended policy goal is a greater sense of *public responsibility* in the Senate when compared to the necessary but insufficient *public responsiveness* expected of the more openly democratic House of Representatives.

A step from Madison to British philosopher J. S. Mill and his account of second chambers in his *Considerations of Representative Government* brings us closer to the second strain of liberal bicameralism (Mill 1984, 352–9). Mill accepted the value of the negative mode of bicameralism with its anti-corruption potential, but his version reaches beyond that to promote the positive values of public deliberation. Acknowledging "the corrupting influence of undivided power," Mill clearly defends the negative dimension of bicameralism. But his deeper justification is in terms of the positive mode of wider public deliberation. Democracy requires important political virtues, of which none is more necessary than what he calls "conciliation: a readiness to compromise; a willingness to concede something to opponents, and to shape good measures so as to be as little offensive as possible to persons of opposite views" (Mill 1984, 353). The context for Mill's analysis of conciliatory conduct is bicameralism which, in his view, lent itself to structured public discussion of antagonistic political viewpoints.

A critical friend of democracy, Mill feared the tyranny of the majority over liberal minorities. His ideal preference was for unicameralism, with a fully representative single chamber using proportional representation to promote the parliamentary representation of neglected "minoritites." But in the absence of that idealized single chamber, Mill saw merit in a second chamber representing interests not adequately represented in the first chamber able to "oppose itself to the class interests of the majority" and protest "their errors and weaknesses." Such a "wisely conservative body" might even be modeled on the Roman Senate, comprising persons of "special training and skill" brought together "to moderate and regulate democratic ascendancy." This mode of positive support for more representative public deliberation carries through to later British defences of bicameralism. James Bryce is perhaps the most influential of this school. Bryce pioneered the comparative science of modern democracy. His *Modern Democracies* is the first classic investigation of democratic institutions in empirical political science (Bryce 1921, II, 437–57). The chapter on upper houses is a core part of Bryce's anatomy of bicameralism, which reflected his personal political activism in the cause of House of Lords reform and his political influence on many subsequent Westminster institutional developments in modernizing upper houses. Bryce thus provides the most influential twentieth-century account of the positive mode of bicameralism as a device for sounder public deliberation (Patterson and Mughan 1999, 11, 13, 204).

5   Contrasting Strong and Weak Bicameralism

If bicameralism is about balance, what happens when one of the two houses outbalances the other? If the weight is overwhelmingly in favor of the lower house, the result is unicameralism in substance, if not in form. But what if the weight is in favor of the upper house: is this too a form of unicameralism? This issue is not simply academic. It is politically alive in the Westminster democracies: for example the United Kingdom, Canada, and also Australia—a country that has had "more experience with bicameralism than any other parliamentary democracy" (Smith 2003, 6, 22–30). Some Australian state upper houses still reflect traditional class interests or at least attract reform movements proclaiming the need to "democratize" them (Stone 2002, 2005). This call for reform demands that traditional restrictions on upper house franchise, membership qualifications, and electorate weightings be repealed. But is the model of a democratic upper house one with identical qualifications for franchise and membership with the lower house, and with the same tolerance for minimal variation in electorate enrollments? Tempted as we might be to reply "yes," we might be even more demanding of democratic standards and explore other options that allow upper houses to get ahead of their lower house institutions, and achieve even fairer forms of democratic representation. To stay with an Australian example: The Australian Senate was overhauled in 1948 when proportional representation was first adopted, with each state acting as one large multimember electorate. Nothing was done to the formal legislative powers of the Senate but this one electoral change brought about a significant lift in the public legitimacy of the Senate, which many analysts began to describe as "more democratic" than the lower house with its conventional single-member system biased against the return of minor party candidates (Uhr 1998, 113–15; Russell 2000, 55–6, 82–4).

This example of change to the rules of representation for upper houses shows how existing bicameral systems can be strengthened with minimal alteration of the formal constitutional powers of either house. More generally, we can see that the institutional strength of a bicameral system is closely related to its scheme of representation: Those systems with institutions capable of widening the scope of parties represented are more likely to develop capacities for what analysts term "cleavage management." In this context, "cleavage" means political division based on entrenched social identities, such as class, religion, ethnicity, or even regional geography. Effective political management occurs where groups separated by such entrenched divisions are brought together, or their preferred party representatives are brought together, in institutional circumstances conducive to intergroup agreement on "a way ahead." Thus, for these purposes, strong bicameralism describes an institutional environment for multiparty political deliberation capable of generating negotiated policy outcomes acceptable to the representatives involved.

This is only one version of the strong bicameralism literature. A simpler version equates "strong" with two houses sharing equal institutional power, whether or not this results in effective cleavage management. This simpler version really measures the strength of the upper house's resistance to initiatives derived from the lower house—measured in terms of everyday institutional conventions rather than the often misleading legal provisions when divorced from prevailing political conventions, such as those associated with the norms of Westminster responsible parliamentary government. Thus, evaluating the strength of any particular bicameral system is no easy matter, given that we must approach each national political assembly as comprising "at least outwardly, unique aggregations, each with its own history, its special traditions and customs, its time-honoured norms and practices, its constitutional status, and its impact on the laws of the land" (Patterson and Mughan 1999, 9). While it is difficult to rate or measure the operational dynamics of each and every bicameral system, there is agreement that we can identify some of the institutional qualities found in the two extreme ends of the range of strong–weak possibilities. With suitable cautions, I draw on Lijphart's influential framework of contrasts between ideals of a strong and weak bicameral system (Lijphart 1999, 201–11; cf. Bryce 1921, 441; Druckman and Thies 2002, 767–9; Llanos and Nolte 2003, 57–60).

Strong bicameral systems comprise what Lijphart terms an arrangement of symmetrical but incongruent chambers: With both chambers *converging* through a symmetry of fairly evenly balanced legal powers but *diverging* through their incongruent cultures of representation. As noted earlier, the impact of bicameralism depends greatly on the presence of "two differently constituted chambers:" If bicameralism is to act as a "truly strong and meaningful institution," then it needs to combine two chambers equal or nearly equal in formal powers but different in the political and policy viewpoints represented. One other quality is required: public legitimacy, which tends to attach to elected rather than appointed legislative houses (Lijphart 1999, 200, 205). When push comes to shove, none of the alignments of symmetry or congruence will make much difference to the real institutional strength of a bicameral system if the system lacks public legitimacy. That is, strength is a measure of public confidence in the value of the constitutional system. Of course, it is doubtful that strong public confidence in a bicameral system would arise in the absence of Lijphart's other two qualities: a convergence of power and a divergence of representation (Russell 2000, 250–4).

Which national systems display strong bicameralism? Lijphart locates Britain down the rankings, somewhere between medium and weak; other analysts put Britain into the weak category, some even calling the UK and Italy effectively unicameral (Lijphart 1999, 212; see also Tsebelis 1995, 316). This nicely indicates the degree of difficulty of rating and ranking bicameral systems, and the great value of Lijphart's two tests of bicameral strength. Some of Lijphart's "medium-strength" systems meet the symmetry test but fail the congruence test: for example Italy, Colombia, the Netherlands, Belgium, and Japan. Other "medium-strength" systems meet the congruence test but fail the symmetry test: for example, Canada, France, and Spain. Many systems meet the tests of "weak bicameralism," with asymmetry of powers and congruence of representation: for example Austria and Ireland. Only a few bicameral systems meet both tests of "strong bicameralism:" for example the USA, Germany, Switzerland, and Australia (Lijphart 1999, 205–13; see also Konig 2001; Llanos and Nolte 2003, 64–75).

6   CONCLUSION

Caution is advisable when speaking of the weaker forms of bicameralism. As Lijphart records, there is no such institutional creature as "insignificant bicameralism:" Where bicameralism exists, it always matters—even if only as an institution to be domesticated by political executives whenever they can render it weak (Lijphart 1999, 211). The existing literature on bicameralism has done much to deepen our understanding of the political significance of bicameralism. The main focus of this literature has been on the resolution of conflict arising from different forms of political representation in two legislative houses. My argument in this chapter has been that the range of functions performed by contemporary bicameralism are best explained in terms of changing blends of inheritance and innovation in political representation. Even stable democratic constitutions permit remarkable institutional change in the workings of legislative institutions. How can theoretical research keep up with such fascinating practical changes in the workings of bicameralism? I suggest a focus on three priority research areas. A first priority is a richer analytical history of bicameralism. The intellectual history of bicameralism has received some recent attention (see, e.g., Shell 2001) but there are very few institutional histories of the many different examples of bicameralism explaining distinctive national blends of inheritance and innovation. Even within national settings, bicameralism evolves, often in unintended but significant ways (Binder 2003). We know relatively little about the institutional histories of the leading models of bicameralism. Further, we know very little about the process of policy transfer across the families of bicameralism, just as we know very little about the history of cross-adaptation between parliamentary and presidential forms of bicameralism. These histories of inheritance and innovation await their analysts.

A second priority is more detailed mapping of the constitutional settings for the many varieties of contemporary bicameralism. Parliamentary and presidential regimes each come in many varieties, with important differences in the institutional design of legislative powers. We need to know more about how those legislative powers have been affected by the architecture and deployment of executive and judicial powers, and about how bicameralism evolves in different constitutional settings—as a product but also as an agent of change. Bicameralism can contain threatened change or it can preserve past changes; and over time, any one bicameral system can perform both functions under different political circumstances (Vatter 2005; Castles and Uhr 2005). The possibilities for institutional variation among democracies are increasing as democracy spreads across cultures. Frameworks of strong and weak systems highlight the main poles of performance, but there remains much to do to revise and update conventional accounts of the many constitutional forms that bicameralism has begun to take, and to explain how some blends of inheritance and innovation work better than others.

A third priority deals with the elusive concept of "balance" in bicameral relationships. We now know quite a lot about the institutional battles over balances of power internal to bicameral legislatures; but we know much less about the external balances between bicameral legislatures and the wider political community. We know something about how political parties manage bicameral legislatures but we know less about how bicameral processes contribute, if at all, to public debate and participation in the democratic public sphere. Public opinion data would help, but there are many larger issues about relationships and balances between democratic legislatures and democratic public deliberation that are shaping up as research priorities. We also need better explanations of the balance of deliberative capacities within bicameral legislatures. Traditional studies of bicameralism often restricted themselves to the investigation of "the second chamber problem," documenting the procedural profiles of different houses of review. The priority now is to explain the distinctive institutional behaviors noted, and sometimes grudgingly admired, by many analysts of second chambers in both parliamentary and presidential systems. Contrary to the skeptics, empirical researchers like Russell note the "independence of mind, stability of character, and a capacity for high quality and detailed legislative work" she finds characteristic of second chambers at their best, as well as their "reputation for more detailed scrutiny," their "higher degree of consensus," and their "less adversarial atmosphere" (Russell 2000, 102, 131–2; cf. Vatter 2005). Lijphart also notes the "more informal and relaxed manner" typical of the procedural life of second chambers (Lijphart 1999, 205). Of course, the study of bicameralism is about systemic relationships between two legislative houses, and not simply the virtues or vices of either house. Each of these three research priorities highlights systemic issues of bicameralism which, when properly investigated, can help to explain better many other institutional dynamics of democratic governance.

References

Ansolabehere, S., Snyder, J., and Ting, M. 2003. Bargaining in bicameral legislatures. *American Political Science Review,* 97 (3): 471–81.

Bach, S. 2003. *Platypus and Parliament: The Australian Senate in Theory and Practice.* Canberra: Department of the Senate.

Binder, S. 2003. *Stalemate: Causes and Consequences of Legislative Gridlock.* Washington, DC: Brookings Institution Press.

Bottom, W., Eavey, C., Miller, G., and Victor, J. 2000. The institutional effect of majority rule instability. *American Journal of Political Science,* 44 (3): 523–40.

Brennan, G. and Hamlin, A. 2000. *Democratic Devices and Desires.* Cambridge: Cambridge University Press.

—— and LOMASKY, L. 1993. *Democracy and Decision*. Cambridge: Cambridge University Press.

BRYCE, J. 1921. *Modern Democracies*, 2 vols. London: Macmillan.

CASTLES, F. G. and UHR, J. 2005. Australia: federal constraints and institutional innovations. Pp. 51–88 in *Federalism and the Welfare State*, ed. H. Obinger, S. Leibfried, and F. G. Castles. Cambridge: Cambridge University Press.

DIERMEIER, D. and FEDDERSEN, T. 1998. Cohesion in legislatures and the vote of confidence procedure. *American Political Science Review*, 92 (3): 611–21.

DRUCKMAN, J. and THIES, M. 2002. The importance of concurrence. *American Journal of Political Science*, 46 (4): 760–71.

HAMMOND, T. and MILLER, G. 1987. The core of the constitution. *American Political Science Review*, 81 (4): 1155–74.

HELLER, W. 1997. Bicameralism and budget deficits. *Legislative Studies Quarterly*, 22 (4): 485–516.

JOHNSON, A. 1938. *The Unicameral Legislature*. Minneapolis: University of Minnesota Press.

KONIG, T. 2001. Bicameralism and party politics in Germany. *Political Studies*, 49: 411–37.

LANDAU, M. 1969. Redundancy, rationality and the problem of duplication and overlap. *Public Administration Review*, 29 (4): 346–58.

LEVMORE, S. 1992. Bicameralism: when are two decisions better than one? *International Review of Law and Economics*, 12: 145–62.

LIJPHART, A. 1999. *Patterns of Democracy*. New Haven, Conn.: Yale University Press.

LLANOS, M. and NOLTE, D. 2003. Bicameralism in the Americas. *Journal of Legislative Studies*, 9 (3): 54–86.

LONGLEY, L. D. and OLSON, D. M. (eds.) 1991. *Two Into One: The Politics and Processes of National Legislative Cameral Change*. Boulder, Colo.: Westview Press.

MAHONEY, D. J. 1986. Bicameralism. Pp. 109–11 in *Encyclopedia of the American Constitution*, ed. L. W. Levy. New York: Macmillan.

MARRIOTT, J. 1910. *Second Chambers*. Oxford: Oxford University Press.

MILL, J. S. 1984. *Utilitarianism, On Liberty and Considerations on Representative Government*. London: Dent.

MILLER, G., HAMMOND, T., and KILE, C. 1996. Bicameralism and the core. *Legislative Studies Quarterly*, 21 (1): 83–103.

NORTON, P. 2004. How many bicameral legislatures are there? *Journal of Legislative Studies*, 10 (4): 1–9.

PALMER, G. and PALMER, M. 2004. *Bridled Power: New Zealand's Constitution and Government*. Oxford: Oxford University Press.

PATTERSON, S. and MUGHAN, A. 1999. *Senates: Bicameralism in the Contemporary World*. Columbus: Ohio State University Press.

REID, G. and FORREST, M. 1989. *Australia's Commonwealth Parliament*. Carlton: Melbourne University Press.

RIKER, W. 1955. The Senate and American federalism. *American Political Science Review*, 49 (2): 452–69.

RUSSELL, M. 2000. *Reforming the House of Lords: Lessons from Overseas*. Oxford: Oxford University Press.

SHELL, D. 2001. The history of bicameralism. *Journal of Legislative Studies*, 7 (1): 5–18.

SMITH, D. E. 2003. *The Canadian Senate in Bicameral Perspective*. Toronto: University of Toronto Press.

STONE, B. 2002. Bicameralism and democracy. *Australian Journal of Political Science*, 37 (2): 267–81.

—— 2005. Changing roles, changing rules: procedural development and difference in Australian state upper house. *Australian Journal of Political Science*, 40 (1): 33–50.

SWENDEN, W. 2004. *Federalism and Second Chambers: Regional Representation in Parliamentary Federations*. Brussels: P.I.E.-Peter Lang.

TSEBELIS, G. 1995. Decision making in political systems. *American Political Science Review*, 94 (4): 837–58.

—— 2002. *Veto Players: How Political Institutions Work*. Princeton, NJ: Princeton University Press.

—— and MONEY, J. 1995. Bicameral negotiations. *British Journal of Political Science*, 25 (1): 101–29.

—— —— 1997. *Bicameralism*. Cambridge: Cambridge University Press.

—— and RASCH, B. E. 1995. Patterns of bicameralism. Pp. 365–90, in *Parliaments and Majority Rule in Western Europe*, ed. H. Doring. New York: St Martin's Press.

UHR, J. 1998. *Deliberative Democracy in Australia: The Changing Place of Parliament*. Cambridge: Cambridge University Press.

VATTER, A. 2005. Bicameralism and policy performance. *Journal of Legislative Studies*, 11 (2): 194–215.

WHEARE, K. C. 1968. *Legislatures*, 2nd edn. Oxford: Oxford University Press.

CHAPTER 25

COMPARATIVE LOCAL GOVERNANCE

GERRY STOKER

The study of comparative local governance is an area that cannot be accused of following the path of mainstream political science. As a result, the study of local governance is regarded by many as a rather disappointing backwater, outshone and left behind by the more dynamic areas of investigation. On the other hand, comparative local governance never made the mistake addressed throughout this volume of overlooking the importance of institutions. Both old and new institutionalism are alive and well in the field of study, although considerable scope for further development exists. This chapter will argue that the main difficulties are created by the challenge of comparative analysis and that lesser problems surround the understanding of institutional factors and forces.

Institutions in the "old" sense of formal organizations that set the rules and create the context for collective decision-making have been and remain central to the comparative study of local governance. The chapter opens by examining the literature in the field that offers a more traditional institutional perspective. The development of that literature can be divided into three phases. A group of studies that looked to establish some of the basic differences between local government systems across the world; a second phase where more emphasis was placed on explaining the differences between local government systems; and a third phase that has focused on shared trends in reform that has led to a focus on complex systems of governance rather than formal institutions of government. Each of these literatures offers some valuable insights but all struggle to meet the challenge of a comparative politics where the number of democracies has increased dramatically in the last quarter of the twentieth century. The formal study of the institutions of local governance needs to become more global in its reach and less focused on Europe and North America.

The second half of the chapter shows how the study of comparative local governance has taken on the "new" institutional slant and examines how systems of governance are constructed through a complex interplay between formal and informal institutional forces. The key area of investigation in comparative local governance has been the study of regimes—ways of organizing power in complex societies in order to ensure outcomes in tune with particular interests. The institutions of local governance from this perspective are seen as less handed down by history, legislation, or constitutional framing and more made by actors creating informal networks through which direction over formal institutions, resources, and capacities are then exercised. The informal networks are institutions in the sense that they are sustained over time and are driven by a set of rules. The second half of the chapter explores work on urban regimes as an exemplar of a more "new" institutionalist understanding of comparative local governance. Again the main difficulties surround comparative rather than institutional understanding.

The concluding section explores the idea that comparative institutional analysis may be prone to a particular set of problems. Our understanding of formal institutions is dogged by the complexity of institutional arrangements and a focus on more informal arrangements is constrained by their embeddedness in particular settings. Both these factors make the establishment of frameworks for effective comparison very problematic. Future directions for the institutional investigation of comparative local governance are identified.

1   THE CHALLENGE OF CLASSIFICATION

A starting point for exploring comparative local government is to describe the variety of different arrangements adequately. This section of the chapter looks first at the challenge of classification before moving on to what have been the substantive questions addressed by the institutional analysis of comparative local governance, namely why systems are different and whether any shared reform trends can be identified.

The comparative study of local governance institutions is dominated by a concern to comprehend the range of local government systems and as a result we certainly know more now than fifty years ago about how the position of local government varies between states. Lidstrom (1999, 98) refers to Samuel Humes and Eileen Martin as the "post-war giants in the field" which might be somewhat of an exaggeration but their book (Humes and Martin 1969), which offers a comparative study of local government in eighty-one countries, does show an impressive range of knowledge of systems. Other work that has not quite got the encyclopedic quality of Humes and Martin, but nevertheless has added to the richness of our descriptive understanding of local government in various parts of the world, includes the very impressive overviews provided by Hesse (1991) and Norton (1994). Further insights can be gleaned from the work of Bennett (1989, 1993), Chandler (1993), and Batley and Stoker (1991), all of which track practices in several countries and make a number of comparative observations.

These overviews have commonly been criticized on two grounds (Lidstrom 1999). The descriptions contained within them can inevitably lack a certain depth and any capacity to examine the underlying more informal practices going on beneath the surface. Second, because they are mainly descriptive studies, they often offer little in the way of explanatory theory. When they do attempt to explain why differences might exist they do so in a relatively unsystematic way, with references to history or some dramatic event in the countries under comparison.

Both these criticisms are accurate but they reflect in many respects the sheer challenge of the study of comparative local governance. Even within one country it is possible to spend a lot of time and effort in describing internal differences in institutional form and practice. Nation-state comparison is tough enough but at least in terms of democracies there are only 121 of them (Diamond 2003). Within any one country there might be several different tiers or levels of local government and the form of each might vary according to local choice or local circumstances.

To illustrate the challenge just think of the case of France (Borraz and Le Galès 2005). There are 36,565 municipalities, almost 98 percent of which have populations of less than 10,000. The differences between local government in the big cities and the surrounding rural areas in terms of access to technical capacity and style of politics are considerable. And so too is the layered institutional complexity. Because of the need to develop cooperation between many small municipalities, there are a little over 20,000 ad hoc associations of municipalities. In addition there are several meso level institutions with 100 departments and twenty-two regions plus four overseas regions. The complexity is further compounded by a range of other organizations that operate in a vast world of quasi-autonomous governance. There are publicly owned associations of service providers. There are the mixed sector agencies that are privately owned but with a majority of public sector shareholders. Some organizations managing public housing are public and some running planning, transport, and other services are private. The result is "a diversity of organisations, many of which do not have genuine public status (even though they may well operate on public funding) and whose integration is highly problematic" (Borraz and Le Galès 2005, 14).

The truth is that the complexity of local governance institutional arrangements often belies understanding within countries and makes the task of comparative study very taxing. The French case may be an extreme one but there is a substantial element of institutional complexity built into virtually every system in the world. In order to begin to address the issue of explaining differences the literature has had to engage in some simplifications and has tended to focus on the formal elected institutions of local government rather than the vast array of quasi-governmental institutions that tend to surround it. While such a procedure makes sense, it does leave you wondering if important elements of an understanding of the way systems work are being left aside.

If you discount these concerns about capturing the complexity of different systems, the next problem is that there is clearly no consensus in the literature on the basis for any institutional demarcations. In an overview of the main classification options that have been tried, Lidstrom (1999, 100–6) identifies a range of criteria that have been applied.

The first choice is whether to focus on historical or present-day criteria. Historical heritage might lead in one direction in terms of the distinctions drawn, while a concern with present-day realities might lead in another. The former option could lead to the overlooking of recent developments. So again, taking the example of France once more, since the decentralization legislation of the early 1980s, a system that before might have been described as having the classic Napoleonic heritage of centralized control and strong oversight has given way to a much more autonomous system with far more political clout and technical capacity being held at the level of local municipalities. As Borraz and Le Galès (2005, 12) exclaim, "France is no longer the Jacobin centralist state it used to be."

On the other hand, if you take a current position as the basis of your classification, much depends on what you choose to focus on. If you take the overall scale and capacity of a local government system, the size, budgets, and staff available to municipalities, then the UK along with Ireland, Sweden, the Netherlands, and Denmark emerge as the strongest local authorities (Bours 1993). Using a criteria of formal local government autonomy and freedom from central control, however, neither Ireland, the UK, nor the Netherlands would reach the top table of European local government. Indeed a standard lament of British commentators is that the UK has the weakest local government system among Western democracies (see Chandler 1993). Buried in this difference in categorization is a distinction between positive and negative freedom. UK local government may have only limited freedom from central control but it has, because of its capacity and size, consid-erable freedom to do things and undertake initiatives. Indeed one of the great conundrums of local governance comparison is that you get some local authorities that have seized an agenda and run with it and done much to transform their locality and others who have failed to make any impact. Looking at formal structural differences only reveals part of the picture; there has also to be a focus on how practices are put into place.

Given a concern with informal practice as well as formal structure, the most fruitful search for a criterion to distinguish systems of local government would appear to involve a focus on present-day characteristics rather than historical legacies. The next issue that needs to be confronted is whether to focus on a single factor or multiple factors in drawing up divisions. Single criteria do not seem completely convincing and are more prone to shifts in patterns of behavior; that is, to deterioration over time as effective criteria. Thus, for example, some studies have looked at how local governments in different countries responded to fiscal crises (Pickvance and Pretceceille 1991) and produced useful insights, but, as time and financial circumstances have changed, the distinctions are not sustainable. Goldsmith (1990, 1992) suggests that you could focus on the underlying ethos of local government systems. Thus it could be that local government is understood as part of a clientelistic or patronage system in which local leaders are seen as defenders of their localities. Such a model might apply to southern Europe. Alternatively local government might see itself as a promoter of economic devel-opment and such an ethos is strongest in the United States, Canada, and Australia. Finally local government might see itself as a welfare provider, and the British, German, and Nordic systems would all follow that ethos. The trouble is that, although there is some value in such a classification, it is difficult to sustain given the breakdown of the more clientelistic model in southern Europe and the mixing of welfare and economic development foci in other countries.

The most dominant form of classification in comparative local governance looks at local government systems as a whole and links together a range of factors. According to Lidstrom (1999, 103), "the most widely accepted and frequently cited" is that provided by Hesse and Sharpe (1991). There are three main groups according to this categorization: A Franco group that would include many of the countries of southern Europe, an Anglo group based around the UK and Ireland and to some extent the United States and New Zealand, and finally a north and middle European variant including the Nordic countries, Germany, and the Netherlands. But it is difficult to be entirely convinced by this classification since there are such big differences within each of the groups.

Page and Goldsmith (1987) and John (2001), where the focus is more narrowly on Europe, adopt a similar classification with a strong division between northern and southern countries. Denters and Rose (2005, 10–11), with a wider world focus, adapt the Hesse and Sharpe model but distinguish between local governments embedded in unitary and federal systems. Norton (1994, 13–14), in what is claimed to be a classification of "world systems of local government," does add a Japan group and splits the United States and Canada away to a separate North America group.

The major problem with all of these classifications is their narrow, Western focus. They are concerned almost entirely with mature rather than new wave democracies. In the 1970s less than a third of the countries in the world could be classified as democratic. But a drive to democracy dominated the last quarter of the twentieth century and, as a result, by the start of the twenty-first century nearly two-thirds of all countries were democratic (Diamond 2003).

All of the countries identified above have the minimum requirement that they hold regular, free, fair, and competitive elections to fill positions in their governments. These democracies all have a secret ballot, fair access to a range of media, and basic rights to organize, campaign, and solicit votes. Not all would count as full liberal democracies and many still suffer from significant human rights abuses, corruption, and a weak rule of law. But crucially, from the perspective of this chapter, local democratic governance has become a more significant part of their systems. For the new wave of democracies, having a strong system of local government has often been one of the main reform options promoted by international organizations and consultants. As the twenty-first century unfolds, the new challenge for the classification is to provide for coverage of both mature and new democracies. Comparative local governance needs to be more global.

There are some pioneering studies that provide a number of useful insights. McCarney and Stern (2003), for example, offer some valuable reflections on the development of local governance in cities across the south of the globe (from the Philippines, through South Africa, to Mexico). In addition to the scale and rapid progress of urbanization, they note that reform measures have generally seen local governments in these countries gain substantially more power. A study sponsored by the United Nations looks at local government in Asia and the Pacific (Sproats 2002). This study focuses a lot of attention on the problems confronted by newly established local government systems in having the capacity in finances, human resources, and political sophistication to manage complex and substantial social and economic challenges. Coulson (1995) looks at progress in Eastern Europe in countries in the initial phases of reform. Swianiewicz's (2005) interesting case study of Poland shows there has been a significant flowering of local government since the fall of the Communist regime at the end of 1980s. These studies hint at a need for a more far-reaching and cross-cutting analysis in order to classify and better understand world systems of local governance. The task is beyond this chapter, but it urgently needs to be addressed.

2   EXPLAINING DIFFERENCE AND IDENTIFYING REFORM TRENDS

Beyond classification, the focus in the institutional analysis of comparative local governance has been on trying to explain differences and identifying new trends. The former approach tends to draw on the continuity and historical embeddedness of institutional arrangements. The latter looks at the other side of coin and is focused on how organizations are changing, and changing in similar directions. In the previous section it emerged that we are in the foothills when it comes to classification. The conclusion in this section is that we are only just about walking on the level when it comes to two of the central issues of comparative institutional analysis: why institutions are set up as they are and how they are changing.

Page (1991) and Page and Goldsmith (1987) offer a systematic explanation of differences in local government systems even if it is within the more contained framework of European local government. Broadly, there is a distinction drawn between the functions or responsibilities taken up by local government systems, the extent of discretion that is provided to them in decision-making, and finally their access to central government. Some systems such as those of northern Europe score high on the first set of criteria but low on the last one. Other systems—primarily those of southern Europe—score low on the first two criteria but higher on the last one. As to why the systems evolved in this way, the institutional starting point for Page's analysis is, as Lidstrom (1999) points out, a focus on path dependency and institutional inertia. History entrenched a certain response in different countries. Northern European systems developed more formal and extensive welfare-based local government, while southern European systems were more community focused, with limited responsibilities but a fruitful clientelistic relationship with central authorities.

The problem is that it appears that systems are not so path dependent as the analysis would imply. The French (Borraz and Le Galès 2005) and Italian systems (Bobbio 2005) over the last two decades have undoubtedly gained considerably in terms of formal responsibilities, technical capacity, and autonomy from central government. Northern systems, such as that of Britain, have slipped back in terms of responsibilities and formal autonomy although perhaps gained increased access to central government, especially under New Labour since 1997, without positive benefit. In short the broad framework provided by Page and Goldsmith is insightful and helpful in providing a focus on key defining factors in judging the state of comparative local government systems. It is less advantageous because of its focus on issues of path dependency and institutional continuity rather than the issue of institutional change.

When it comes to the forces of institutional change, the work of Peter John (2001) has blazed a trail, although again the focus is specific to Western Europe.

The topic of his main study is the shift from local government to local governance. Across public administration much of the new focus in governance is on forms of politics and managements that go beyond top-down, hierarchical options through the greater use of contracts or partnerships (see Stoker 1998).

With respect to local government John (2001) argues that formal, enclosed styles of decision-making are changing across Europe in response to the internationalization of economies, the Europeanization of decision-making, new policy challenges, and the move to more flexible, less bureaucratic forms of delivery. In a broad sense John concludes that there has been a shift from government to governance:

Across Western Europe there have been many changes in institutional structures, attempts at coalition formation, stronger leadership styles, a more visible executive structures, new management ideas and more of a focus on European liaison. (2001, 168)

In short, in response to new governing conditions, different country systems have tried to develop a similar mix of institutional changes and options. The commitment to a similar range of reforms is far from even with some countries in the lead on innovation and others lagging behind. But the pattern of change does not follow the north–south divide identified in earlier institutional studies of comparative local governance. Spain, the UK, Germany, and the Netherlands led the reform charge in the 1990s according to John (2001, 174).

Other studies have been broadly supportive of the argument that the pattern of change in local politics has been one from government to governance. Le Galès (2002) is the most skeptical and emphasizes differences in the trajectory of European cities as well some similarities. In particular he argues that the neoliberal turn in UK local government that started under the Thatcher governments of the 1980s has taken it closer to the US model and that other parts of Europe are not signed up to that model. He views the UK and Ireland as special cases in Europe but nevertheless concedes that reforms favoring business partnerships and new public management can be observed in many European cities. Moreover he notes that reform trends "are rather tending to blur" the north–south divide favored in the comparative local government literature on Europe (Le Galès 2001, 262).

Denters and Rose (2005), taking in a wider sweep of Western democracies than those in Europe alone, confirm that a broad shift towards governance has occurred. They note that three major changes can be observed. The first is the widespread use of New Public management techniques and public–private partnerships. There is much more use of performance targets, internal and external contracting, and the involvement of the private sector in the development and management of public service programs and services. The second change is the bringing in of a wider network of local associations, business groups, and private actors into the local decision-making process. The third is the introduction of new forms of citizen involvement. The first trend is virtually universal across Western democracies, although in some cases the adoption of changes appears more symbolic than substantial. The second and third trends are less universally observable but again, in the judgment of Denters and Rose (2005, 261), the differences that do emerge do not follow any clear north–south divide, in Europe at least. Studies of local leadership in particular confirm a pattern of enhanced focus on political leadership and an increased emphasis on using the office of leadership to bolster the democratic legitimacy and effectiveness of local government (Borraz and John 2004; Mouritzen and Svara 2002).

The central questions addressed in the formal study of comparative local governance institutions can be related to those identified by Bo Rothstein (1996, 134) in the study of political institutions in general: What explains the variety of institutional arrangements? What difference do different institutional arrangements make to the behavior and practice of local politics? Finally, and explicitly from a normative perspective, what arrangements are best for good governance or effective local democracy? The greatest (but still modest) progress has been made in answering the first question. The second question has received some considerable attention in a few specific areas of institutional reform. The third question remains the most problematic and an area where it would be difficult to highlight much, if any, progress. It remains uncertain whether the drift from government to governance is an enhancement of local democracy, or whether greater effectiveness in governing has been achieved, and if so whether it has been at the cost of a loss of meaningful accountability. What is clear is that many systems are now so complex and opaque in the way they make decisions that insiders find it difficult enough to fathom what is going on let alone the relatively disengaged voting citizen. Comparativists are not alone in being tripped up by the complexity of the systems of local governance that we are in the process of creating.

3   LOCAL GOVERNANCE AS INSTITUTIONAL REGIME BUILDING

The formal institutional literature has tended to conclude that local governance over the last two decades has become more complex and at the same time more informal. This understanding has opened the door to more "new" institutionalist understandings that are concerned to address the informal construction and maintenance of institutions. These newer ways of working are not assembled in some ad hoc manner; they follow patterns and can in their construction have a determining influence on access to power. The "new" institutional concern with the ways in which institutions are made and the way that those institutions in turn influence actors and their decision-making has, as a result, become a major focus for the literature on comparative local governance. Most debate has been around the concept of urban regime, a framework for analysis developed in the United States (Stone 1989; Stoker 1995) but then applied in a considerable range of studies outside North America (Mossberger and Stoker 2001). This part of the chapter lays out the basic ideas of regime analysis before exploring the comparative material related to it. The world of urban political theory is much broader than regime analysis (see Judge, Stoker, and Wolman 1995) but it is the regime concept that is the most widely travelled from a comparative local governance perspective.

According to Stone, regimes are "the informal arrangements by which public bodies and private interests function together in order to be able to make and carry out governing decisions" (Stone 1989, 6). Effective urban governance is achieved through building civic cooperation across institutional boundaries.[1] The making and sustaining of interorganizational relationships are central to Stone's understanding of local politics. A regime constitutes "a relatively stable group *with access to institutional resources* that enable it to have a sustained role in making governing decisions" (emphasis in original) (Stone 1989, 4). Informal modes of coordination are explained using what is called the social production model of power. The previous more formal understanding of power as the exercise of detailed influence or control over decision-making gives way to a more informal understanding that power is about giving direction and then mobilizing the resources necessary to ensure that the vision is fulfilled:

If the conventional model of urban politics is one of social control . . . then the one proposed here might be called "the social-production model". It is based on the question of how, in a world of limited and dispersed authority, actors work together across institutional lines to produce a capacity to govern and to bring about publicly significant results. (Stone 1989, 8–9)

In a complex, fragmented urban world, the paradigmatic form of power is that which enables certain interests to blend their capacities to achieve common purposes. The power sought by regimes is the "power to" or the capacity to act, rather than "power over" others or social control (Stone 1989, 229). Regime analysis directs attention to the conditions under which such effective long-term coalitions emerge in order to accomplish public purposes (Stoker 1995).

The social production model is about the exercise of pre-emptive power and the spreading of influence. There are two different types of relationship between actors. The first is the relationship between the organizations at the *core* of a

---

[1] The discussion in this section draws on joint work with Graham Smith, of Southampton University.

regime. These actors with access to institutional resources in their own right blend their capacities in order to establish a hegemonic control over the policy agenda in a locality. In the US literature it is typically the local municipality and key private corporations who blend their capacities and resources to occupy such a strategic position.

The second important relationship in understanding regimes is between the core of the regime and other actors it draws into the governing coalition. Having created the conditions to exercise pre-emptive power, regimes are then able to secure the participation of other actors through the distribution of selective incentives, such as contracts, jobs, community facilities, and other small-scale benefits. Thus an effective regime requires a core set of actors to occupy the strategic position in a city and have the capacity to exercise pre-emptive power through a combination of blending their own resources and offering selective incentives to ensure the cooperation and participation of more peripheral actors.

A regime then emerges as a bridging institutional construct that draws together actors, with those who have access to institutional resources at its core. Having access to institutional resources is vital because actors in that position can enter the game in terms of setting the vision for a locality and combining their resources with others to ensure that the vision is delivered. Control over institutional resources is also necessary in order to bargain for the support of more peripheral interests so that they are encouraged to stay as part of the partnership.

4   REGIMES IN COMPARATIVE PERSPECTIVE

The North American literature on regimes is substantial (for a review see Mossberger and Stoker 2001; Davies 2001). The key starting point remains, however, Clarence Stone's study of Atlanta. That study focuses on a development regime that dominated Atlanta for much of the postwar period. Stone shows, with careful historical analysis, how the regime maintained a steady focus on the regeneration and expansion of the city. He shows how the business community came to an accommodation with the African-American political leadership of the city and how, through various selective incentives and deals, key community leaders were also bought into the project. Against the odds in many ways, and certainly in a manner not achieved to the same degree elsewhere, Atlanta was able to build for itself a growth dynamic that culminated after the conclusion of Stone's study in the staging of the Olympics in 1996.

A number of other studies of regimes in American cities have been undertaken (see, e.g., DeLeon 1992; Whelan, Young, and Lauria 1994). In most American studies business is a key participant in governing coalitions because of the resources it controls. However, the relative strength of business, the composition of particular businesses engaged in the coalition, and the presence of other interests, such as neighborhood groups or environmental groups, will vary from place to place, and may change over time (Mossberger and Stoker 2001).

Outside of the USA, the regime concept has been picked up, especially in studies of the urban regeneration practices of European cites in the 1980s and 1990s (for a review see John 2001, ch. 3). What these studies found (see Mossberger and Stoker 2001) is that economic development partnerships in Europe are more likely to be led by the public sector, with less participation from local businesses, and with less policy autonomy from national government. Some European scholars have also pointed out that the economic development partnerships they have observed do not have the pre-emptive capacity that Stone's work suggests is characteristic of an urban regime. Consumption and service issues are still predominant in local politics, in comparison to economic development (Harding 1997). In short, while coalitions of business and city leaders were found in European cites, no business-dominated regimes similar to those established in some US cities have operated.

The regime literature offers a way of studying the institutional capacity to set an agenda and get things done. It has provided an opportunity for researchers on both sides of the Atlantic to break from a narrow focus on formal institutions to a broader concern about how actors from various sectors and organizations can use their access to institutional resources to build a capacity to act. But the discussion of regimes has at times been confused. The problems relate to general challenges faced in making comparisons. As Mossberger and Stoker (2001) argue, regime studies have fallen into each of the four traps identified by Sartori (1991): parochialism, misclassification, degreeism, and concept stretching.

Parochialism refers to the tendency for comparativists continually to invent new terms or to use existing ones in an unintended way. The case that is under investigation by the researcher is considered so unique or different that it deserves a new or additional label, all of its own. Many regime studies seek to qualify the term regime by putting a descriptive label in front of it. Dowding et al. (1999) approach the issue of business participation by making this an optional criterion for regimes. They define eight criteria for what they call "policy regimes" or "urban policy regimes" (1999, 516). Why these regimes are called policy regimes is not really explained. The exclusion of business as a necessary element from a regime undermines a crucial factor in the original regime concept. As Mossberger and Stoker comment:

If regimes are simply coalitions that bring together actors in a complex policy environment, but where the division between market and state is not a factor, then how do urban regimes differ from networks? This alternative concept is flexible, and has many forms, without specifying that it bridges the divide between popular control of government and private control of the economy. (Mossberger and Stoker 2001, 824)

What is lost by this adaptation of the regime term is its political economy focus. Network is an excellent generic term for partnerships between sectors, but urban regime is driven by an understanding of what operating in a capitalist society implies for governing as well as an appreciation of the institutional dynamic that can also condition and direct that process of governing. It may be true that in London, and in Europe more generally, business participation in regimes is less central than in the United States but partnerships that exclude business cannot be accurately included within the original concept of urban regime. Putting a new label such as policy in front of the term in the end hampers the effort to aggregate research and to test and refine existing theories.

Misclassification consists of ignoring important differences and clustering together unlike phenomena. The problem stems from a misunderstanding of regime theory and in particular the mistaken view that all cities must have regimes. But as a careful reading of Stone's work makes clear, the establishment and maintenance of a regime over an extended period of time is an unusual occurrence. As Mossberger and Stoker argue:

The privileged position of business fosters the conditions for the development of regimes at the local level in all capitalist countries, although local job creation may be more of a concern in some countries, and local tax revenues in others. Despite this, it is clear... urban regimes are intentional partnerships, and are difficult to maintain because participants have divergent as well as overlapping interests. Regimes, with their varied agendas, represent political choice. Whether or not a regime exists in a particular place is an empirical question, and it entails a specific set of relationships, including the ability to build public–private cooperation around a chosen agenda. (Mossberger and Stoker 2001, 815)

The problem comes when all coalitions are claimed to be regimes. Kantor, Savitch, and Haddock (1997) in their cross-national comparative study, for example, characterize Liverpool during the 1980s as a "radical regime" (1997, 358), although it clearly lacked the prerequisites of public–private cooperation in pursuit of a common agenda. In Liverpool, the Militant Tendency of the Labour Party was more interested in resisting central government and business interests than in building collaboration with local business. Indeed it did not develop partnership with voluntary and community sector organizations either. It had a rather narrow focus on power held within the local state. Whatever else the Militant Tendency was doing, they were not building an urban regime. The problem lies in the typology presented by Kantor, Savitch, and Haddock (1997) that approaches comparison by describing a number of factors that influence the economic, intergovernmental, and political contexts of cities, and uses these in various combinations to generate eight regime types *as a starting point*. Their framework as a descriptive device may be useful and the empirical material is certainly valuable but it is not about regimes as cross-sectoral institutional pacts for the making of governance capacity, as presented in Stone's regime theory.

Degreeism refers to abuse of continua to represent all differences as merely quantitative rather than qualitative—a matter of degree (see, for discussion, Mossberger and Stoker 2001). The potential for this problem to arise in urban regime theory is considerable because there is no clear demarcation within the theory for operationalizing a "sufficient" degree of cooperation, stability, or coherence. It could be asked whether descriptions of "emerging" regimes in the cross-national literature (DiGaetano and Klemanski 1999; Bassett 1996; DiGaetano and Lawless 1999; John and Cole 1998) constitute degreeism. The authors cited here described certain European cities as having coalitions that were more limited or fragile. They were, however, careful to depict some ability to cooperate as a condition for regimes. The ambiguity about when a regime has "enough" to be a regime is problematic in the American literature as well, because consensus is achieved over time, and certain regimes, like progressive regimes, are assumed to be less stable, with more potential for conflict. The problem here is the inadequate formulation of the original concept. It emerged out of a case study in one setting and has struggled to identify or specify a full-blown theoretical statement stripped of that baggage.

Concept stretching consists of removing aspects of the original meaning of the concept so that it can accommodate more cases. As with the other mistakes in comparative conceptualization, the problem is that if we never know when something ceases to apply, the variation that may help to explain and predict it is therefore obscured by definitional sloppiness. The difference between concept stretching and misclassification is that in concept stretching there is some recognition of differences in the phenomena being observed, and that some of the properties of the original concept do not apply. But rather than "rising on a ladder of abstraction" (Sartori 1991, 254), and developing a more general, umbrella concept (for example, mammals to describe cats and dogs), concept stretching simply states that not all cats have the same properties in order to include dogs. The better strategy in this case is to rise to a higher level of abstraction, to stay within the parameters of the regime concept but to find a way of being more systematic about the differences that do exist between regime types.

Drawing on the United States context, Stone has defined four different regime types: maintenance or caretaker regimes, which focus on routine service delivery and low taxes; development regimes that are concerned with changing land use to promote growth; middle-class progressive regimes which include aims such as environmental protection, historic preservation, affordable housing, and linkage funds; and lower-class opportunity expansion regimes that emphasize human investment policy and widened access to employment and ownership. The latter two are the most difficult to achieve, in part because they entail a measure of coercion or regulation of businesses rather than voluntary cooperation, but Stone's discussion makes it clear that the participation of businesses is still an ingredient in the regime (see Stone 1993, 19–22).

The Stoker and Mossberger (1994) typology constructed for purposes of cross-national comparison adapts the typology of maintenance, development, and progressive regimes by including them in the broader categories of organic, instru-mental, and symbolic regimes. For example, the more specific case of "caretaker regimes" becomes a subtype of a more general "organic regime" that is based on tradition and local cohesion, and maintenance of the status quo. The maintenance of the status quo may not be maintenance of low tax rates, as found in the prototypical caretaker regimes, but could include maintenance of traditional elites or racial or class exclusion. The instrumental regime is similar to Stone's development regime (i.e. Atlanta) and reflects the importance of selective incentives and tangible results in coalition maintenance. Symbolic regimes include Stone's progressive regimes and also revitalizing cities bent on changing their image. The main purpose of the regime is redirection of the ideology or image. Selective incentives are less important in symbolic regimes or organic regimes. These regimes are more tenuous, and may be transitional, especially in the case of revitalizing regimes.

Does this revised typology constitute an example of concept stretching? The case for the prosecution is strongest when it comes to the discussion of symbolic regimes since the ephemeral and non-dominant nature of that regime type may make it impossible for it to claim pre-emptive power over the agenda of a city, a key quality of a regime. The case for the defence is that all the regimes identified are cross-sectoral, although the partners and the incentives used to bind them together vary. In short the analysis seeks to "cleanse regime theory of its ethnocentric preoccupations and to apply a set of criteria that enables scholars to identify different sorts of governance" (John 2001, 49).

The idea of a regime aimed at expanding the opportunities for lower-class citizens—the fourth element in Stone's original typology—has not been entirely neglected and has become central to Stone's work with colleagues on education reform in the United States. In the Civic Capacity and Urban Education Project (Henig, Mula, Orr, and Pedescleaux 1999; Stone 1998a) the insights of urban regime theory have been used to investigate a specific policy other than economic devel-opment. Although human capital issues have been discussed in the context of urban regimes before (Orr and Stoker 1994), this newer work represents a focus on a specific policy area with a different array of actors. The concept of "civic capacity," or "the mobilization of various stakeholders in support of a community-wide cause" (Stone 1998*b*, 15), is used to explain coalition building in urban education. The conclusions drawn by Stone are in some respects depressing but consistent with his earlier analysis. Coalitions had been assembled crossing sectors. Several cities had seen some small-scale successes in school improvement but there remained a problem in getting these neighborhood initiatives to play out more successfully on a wider stage. And even in those cites where regimes had in the past strongly delivered on an economic agenda, capacity in the education field has eluded them. As complex institutional constructions, regimes that give a real capacity to deliver policy change are not easy to construct.

In both North America and Europe the regime concept has helped to encourage the shift away from a narrow focus on the formal institutions of elected government to to concern with how cross-sectoral institutional capacity is built in localities in order to get things done. Given the shift from government to governance noted in the earlier section, this literature has opened up a way of exploring the way in which the capacity for governance is established and maintained.

5   CONCLUSIONS

From an institutional perspective the big positive in the study of comparative local governance is that institutions remain central to the field. There has been a lot of valuable research conducted, and through that work we know more about the operation of local institutions both formally and informally. There is now at least a base for comparative analysis from which to build.

The field provides scope for a more traditional institutionalism focused on the study of local government systems. So far it has produced some powerful insights into the differences that exist in mature democracies and their shared trends of reform. What the field lacks and has yet to deliver is a genuine global take on comparative local governance. The arrival of a new wave of democracies and developments in the mature democracies make a compelling case for a sustained intellectual effort in this area. The scope of the task is considerable given the complex institutional structure of local government in each country. Because local government is about delivering certain services and programs as well as about deliberating and deciding over policy issues, the challenge of understanding the institutional architecture in any one country often requires extensive knowledge of the different forms of government and also of a myriad of surrounding delivery institutions and agencies. However, with appropriate conceptualization, the task has been undertaken within several countries, but the challenge remains to provide a global comparative framework in which these studies can be fitted.

What might that more global take reveal? The first thing it would do is complete the orientation away from formal focus on the powers of different local government systems to a more substantive focus on their capacity to get things done. Studying local government in developmental states such as South Korea, newly developed states such as India, and developing states in Africa, Asia, and Latin America brings strongly into focus the financial and human resources as well as the blending regime power that is available to local government rather than what is written in the constitution. These considerations also apply to the former Communist regimes. The second area that is brought into focus is the quality of the democracy that is established at a local level and the nature of the relationship between local politicians and citizens. Too often in the cosy world of Western local government it is assumed that local government is good government and one that automatically engages the citizen. That assumption is invalid in mature Western democracies and certainly does not apply in the new democracies.

Comparative local governance faces further difficulties when trying to address the more new institutionalist concern with the way in which rules of the game and bridging institutional frameworks are established in order to move formal institutional resources into direction and practice on the ground. The interest in regime literature signals the concern of scholars in a variety of settings with these issues and again valuable insights and understandings have emerged, especially in the analysis of more mature democracies. There are some problems with the conceptualization of regimes. We need a better understanding of what constitutes a regime (how solid and how long living does it need to be?). We require a better framework for identifying regime types. We need to understand what binds regimes together and what might lead them to break up. But the greatest difficulties lie, thus far, in the inadequate way in which comparative studies in the field have developed. A range of faults common to comparative analysis have certainly been in evidence in some of the comparative debate about regimes. These faults can be corrected and with improved conceptualization there is hope for development in this new institutionalist element of the field as well.

References

Bassett, K. 1996. Partnerships, business elites and urban politics: new forms of governance in an English city? *Urban Studies*, 33: 539–55.

Batley, R. and Stoker, G. 1991. *Local Government in Europe*. London: Macmillan.

Bennett, R. J. (ed.) 1989. *Territory and Administration in Europe*. London: Pinter.

—— 1993. *Local Government in the New Europe*. London: Belhaven.

Bobbio, L. 2005. Italy: after the storm. Pp. 29–46 in *Comparing Local Governance*, ed. B. Denters and L. Rose. Basingstoke: Palgrave Macmillan.

Borraz, O. and John, P. (eds.) 2004. Symposium on the transformation of leadership in Western Europe. *International Journal of Urban and Regional Research*, 28 (1): 107–200.

—— and Le Galès, P. 2005. France: the intermunicipal revolution. In *Comparing Local Governance*, ed. B. Denters and L. Rose. Basingstoke: Palgrave Macmillan.

Bours, A. 1993. Management, tiers, size and amalgamations of local government. In *Local Government in the New Europe*, ed. R. J. Bennett. London: Belhaven.

Chandler, J. (ed.) 1993. *Local Government in Liberal Democracies: An Introductory Survey*. London: Routledge.

Coulson, A. (ed.) 1995. *Local Government in Eastern Europe*. Aldershot: Edward Elgar.

Davies, J. 2001. *Partnerships and Regimes*. Aldershot: Ashgate.

deLeon, R. E. 1992. The urban antiregime: progressive politics in San Francisco. *Urban Affairs Quarterly*, 27: 555–79.

Denters, B. and Rose, L. (eds.) 2005. *Comparing Local Governance*. Basingstoke: Palgrave Macmillan.

Diamond, L. 2003. Universal democracy? *Policy Review*, Jun.–Jul.: 119.

Diatano, A. and Klemanski, J. S. 1999. *Power and City Governance: Comparative Perspectives on Urban Development*. Minneapolis: University of Minnesota Press.

—— and Lawless, P. 1999. Urban governance and industrial decline: governing structures and policy agendas in Birmingham and Sheffield, England, and Detroit, Michigan, 1980–1997. *Urban Affairs Review*, 34: 546–77.

Dowding, K., Dunleavy, P., King, D., Margetts. H., and Rydin, R. 1999. Regime politics in London local government. *Urban Affairs Review*, 34: 515–45.

Goldsmith, M. 1990. Local autonomy: theory and practice. In *Challenges to Local Government*, ed. D. King and J. Pierre. London: Sage.

—— 1992. Local government. *Urban Studies*, 29: 393–410.

Harding, A. 1997. Urban regimes in a Europe of the cities? *European Urban and Regional Studies*, 4: 291–314.

Henig, J. R., Hula, R. C., Orr, M., and Pedescleaux, D. S. 1999. *The Color of School Reform: Race, Politics, and the Challenge of Urban Education*. Princeton, NJ: Princeton University Press.

Hesse, J. J. (ed.) 1991. *Local Government and Urban Affairs in International Perspective*. Baden-Baden: Nomos Verlagsgesellschaft.

—— and Sharpe, L. J. 1991. Local government in international perspective: some comparative observations. In *Local Government and Urban Affairs in International Perspective*, ed. J. J. Hesse. Baden-Baden: Nomos Verlagsgesellschaft.

Humes, S. and Martin, E. M. 1969. *The Structure of Local Government: A Comparative Survey of 81 Countries*. The Hague: International Union of Local Authorities.

John, P. 2001. *Local Governance in Western Europe*. London: Sage.

—— and Cole, A. 1998. Urban regimes and local governance in Britain and France: policy adoption and coordination in Leeds and Lille. *Urban Affairs Review*, 33: 382–404.

Judge, D., Stoker, G., and Wolman, H. (eds.) 1995. *Theories of Urban Politics*. Thousand Oaks, Calif.: Sage.

Kantor, P., Savitch, H. V., and Haddock, S. 1997. The political economy of urban regimes: a comparative perspective. *Urban Affairs Review*, 32: 348–77.

Le Galès, P. 2002. *European Cities*. Oxford: Oxford University Press.

LIDSTROM, A. 1999. The comparative study of local government: a research agenda. *Journal of Comparative Policy Analysis*, 1: 95–115.

McCARNEY, P. L. and STERN, R. E. (eds.) 2003. *Governance on the Ground: Innovations and Discontinuities in Cities of the Developing World*. Baltimore: John Hopkins University Press.

MOSSBERGER, K. and STOKER, G. 2001. The evolution of urban change theory. *Urban Affairs Review*, 36: 6.

MOURITIZEN, P. and SVARA, J. 2002. *Leadership at the Apex*. Pittsburgh: University of Pittsburgh Press.

NORTON, A. 1994. *International Handbook of Local and Regional Government*. Aldershot: Edward Elgar.

ORR, M. and STOKER, G. 1994. Urban regimes and leadership in Detroit. *Urban Affairs Quarterly*, 30: 48–73.

PAGE, E. 1991. *Localism and Centralism in Europe*. Oxford: Oxford University Press.

—— and GOLDSMITH, M. (eds.) 1987. *Central and Local Relations*. London: Sage.

PICKVANCE, C. and PRETECEILLE, E. 1991. *State Restructuring and Local Power*. London: Pinter.

ROTHSTEIN, B. 1996. Political institutions: an overview. In *A New Handbook of Political Science*, ed. R. Goodin and H.-D. Klingemann. Oxford: Oxford University Press.

SARTORI, G. 1991. Comparing and miscomparing. *Journal of Theoretical Politics*, 3: 243–57.

SPROATS, K. 2002. *Local Government in Asia and the Pacific: A Comparative Analysis*. Bangkok: United Nations Economic and Social commission for Asia and the Pacific. Available at: www.unescap.org.

STOKER, G. 1995. Regime theory and urban politics. Pp. 54–71 in *Theories of Urban Politics*, ed. D. Judge, G. Stoker, and H. Wolman. Thousand Oaks, Calif.: Sage.

—— 1998. Governance as theory: five propositions. *International Social Science Journal*, 155: 17–28.

—— and MOSSBERGER, K. 1994. Urban regime theory in comparative perspective. *Environment and Planning C: Government and Policy*, 12: 195–212.

STONE, C. N. 1989. *Regime politics: Governing Atlanta, 1946–1988*, Lawrence: University Press of Kansas.

—— 1993. Urban regimes and the capacity to govern: a political economy approach. *Journal of Urban Affairs*, 15: 1–28.

—— (ed.) 1998a. *Changing Urban Education*. Lawrence: University Press of Kansas.

—— 1998b. Introduction: urban education in political context. Pp. 1–20 in *Changing Urban Education*, ed. C. N. Stone. Lawrence: University Press of Kansas.

SWIANIEWICZ, P. 2005. Poland: a time in transition. Pp. 100–18 in *Comparing Local Governance*, ed. B. Denters and L. Rose. Basingstoke: Palgrave Macmillan.

WHELAN, R. K., YOUNG, A. H., and LAURIA, M. 1994. Urban regimes and racial politics in New Orleans. *Journal of Urban Affairs*, 16: 1–21.

CHAPTER 26

....

JUDICIAL
INSTITUTIONS

....

JAMES L. GIBSON

Legal institutions throughout the world have become increasingly powerful. Tate and Vallinder (1995) refer to this as the "judicialization of politics" while also recognizing and acknowledging the "politicization of judiciaries."—by judicialization they mean the transfer of political disputes from the political arena to courts and legal institutions. Because courts in every corner of the world are being asked to decide explosive issues of politics and law, these institutions have achieved a prominence—and a level of controversy—perhaps never before seen.

The stunning role of the judiciary in the 2004 Ukrainian presidential election is just one example of the influence of courts in politics. On Friday, December 3, 2004, the Ukrainian Supreme Court nullified the second presidential election of November 21 which had resulted in an apparent victory for Viktor Vanukovych. Calling for a new presidential vote, the Court concluded that the November election violated a number of articles of the constitution governing the electoral process. To the surprise of almost everyone, Ukrainian politicians accepted the Supreme Court decision and new elections were launched. As a result Vicktor Yushenko now governs as the president of Ukraine. That a court in a fledgling democracy would succeed with this level of political stakes, in a country not noted for its obdurate commitment to the rule of law, is a breathtaking development.

* I gratefully acknowledge the useful research assistance of Marc Hendershot and Briana Morgan on this chapter.

Other examples are easy to find: Gibson, Caldeira, and Baird (1998) observed that in 1996, the Irish Supreme Court accepted an appeal challenging the recent referendum approving a constitutional amendment to permit divorce. Prior to the appeal, the Court had ordered the government to stop spending money to run advertisements in favor of the referendum (Parkin 1996). Both actions had the effect of delaying a majority intent on liberalizing divorce.

The Supreme Court of the Russian Federation found in 1996 in favor of Greenpeace and overturned President Yeltsin's decree permitting the importation of nuclear waste into Russia. Yeltsin's government had hoped to use funds earned from the processing of imported nuclear waste to finance the completion of a plant in Krasnoyarsk (Gurushina 1996). The Supreme Court of Poland upheld the presidential election of November 1995 and declared Kwasniewski the winner, despite his having violated electoral law by giving false information about his educational background. The justices unanimously agreed on the violation, but disagreed on whether it had made any difference to the outcome of the elections (Karpinski 1995).

And of course no list of politically significant court rulings could ignore *Bush* vs. *Gore*, the decision by the US Supreme Court in 2001 that effectively awarded the presidency to George W. Bush.

In sum, then, the decisions of high courts throughout the world have made a difference for both the leaders and the led in society, affecting matters of high policy, the details of everyday life, as well as the "leadership of the free world." As Alexis de Tocqueville (1945, vol. 1, 280) said long ago, "Scarcely any political question arises in the United States that is not resolved, sooner or later, into a judicial question." How right he has become, not just in the USA, but throughout the world!

The purpose of this chapter is therefore to consider the state of the literature on courts and the judicial process. With the massive proliferation of research on judiciaries throughout the world, I cannot hope to provide an exhaustive consideration of all interesting and relevant research. The scholarship (like the discipline of political science itself) is diverse, and therefore difficult to organize. One cannot ignore, however, the vast research on the processes by which judges make decisions; nor the impressive scholarship on the essential and distinctive political capital of courts— institutional legitimacy. In addition, the emerging literature on judicial independence and accountability is highlighted in this review. Throughout, I will attempt to identify important research questions to which the field must attend.

1 JUDICIAL DECISION-MAKING

The heart of research on courts has been and continues to be the study of judicial decision-making. In 1983, I asserted, "In a nutshell, judges decisions are a function of what they prefer to do, tempered by what they think they ought to do, but constrained by what they perceive is feasible to do" (Gibson 1983, 9). This pithy summary still provides a useful means of organizing the literature on judicial decision-making. What judges prefer to do is the central focus of the Attitudinal Model, most closely associated with the research of Jeffrey Segal and Harold Spaeth. What judges ought to do is a concern of the Legal Model, and especially of role theorists, while feasibility lies within the province of Strategic Models (where I also locate the interactions between courts and their various constituents). I begin my consideration of judicial decision-making with the Attitudinal Model.

2   Attitudes as Determinants of Judges' Decisions

Without any doubt whatsoever, the most important theory of judicial decision-making is that of Segal and Spaeth, and it is not hyperbole to assert that this work has an extremely strong claim to being the most important contribution to our understanding of courts and judges in the last two to three decades.[1] The Attitudinal Model begins with the hypothesis that Supreme Court justices decide "disputes in light of the facts of the case vis-à-vis [their] ideological attitudes and values" (Segal and Spaeth 2002, 86). Thus, the model is fairly simple: liberals decide cases liberally; conservatives, conservatively. The model is slightly complicated by the reference to case facts, but is still fairly simple: liberal judges see and weight facts in particular ways, and their perceptions of facts cause them to make liberal decisions. Judges' decisions, according to this theory, reflect their ideological preferences, tempered by case facts.

In some respects, the Attitudinal Model is not a general model of judicial decision-making; instead, it is closely tailored to the circumstances of the United States Supreme Court. "Attitudinalists argue that because legal rules governing decision-making (e.g. precedent, plain meaning) in the cases that come to the Court do not limit discretion; because the justices need not respond to public opinion, Congress, or the President; and because the Supreme Court is the court of last resort, the justices, unlike their lower court colleagues, may freely implement personal policy preferences" in their rulings (Segal and Spaeth 2002, 111). Presumably, in courts in which these characteristics do not apply, the

---

[1] Although Segal and Spaeth have published widely in academic journals, their two books (1993, 2002) include most of the theory and much of the data on which the Attitudinal Model is based.

Attitudinal Model is of lesser importance. In general, however, little progress has been made in determining the relative importance of the various institutional attributes characterizing decision-making on the United States Supreme Court.

The Attitudinal Model relies heavily on the ability to measure the attitudes of judges apart from their decisions. In a highly original approach to this problem, Segal and Cover (1989) used newspaper editorials to derive a measure of the justices' values at the time of their appointment (see also Segal and Spaeth 2002, 322, for an updated set of attitude scores for the justices). Since 1953, the most conservative justice to serve on the United States Supreme Court is Justice Scalia (followed closely by Justice Rehnquist); the most liberal are Justices Brennan, Fortas, and Marshall (all tied).

The Attitudinal Model has been used to predict the decisions of the justices of the US Supreme Court. In an interesting investigation of the model, two political scientists pitted their predictive skills against legal experts. The experts were relying upon their knowledge of law, cases, and justices, whereas the political scientists used a simple predictive algorithm grounded in the Attitudinal Model. The objective was to predict each individual vote cast in the 2002–3 term of the United States Supreme Court. As it turns out, the political scientists were able to predict 75 percent of the case outcomes; the legal experts did somewhat worse at 59.1 percent (Martin, Quinn, Ruger, and Kim 2004). In terms of predicting the individual votes of the justices, both approaches did equally well (67.9 percent vs. 66.7 percent, for the experts and political scientists, respectively). What is perhaps most interesting is that the statistical model is so simple, and that by relying on such non-legal factors as the circuit of origin, the type of the petitioner and respondent, etc., the model produced such a high level of predictive success. This is likely a function of unexplored correlations between the factual elements of the cases and the attitudinal predispositions of the justices (just as the expert predictions undoubtedly built in implicit judgments about the ideologies of the justices). That three-fourths of the decisions of the Court can be predicted without knowing anything at all about legal doctrine, precedents, and constitutional law is impressive indeed.

Thus, it seems highly probable that judges rely upon their own ideological predilections in making their decisions. This is undoubtedly true of the rarified atmosphere of decision-making by the Supreme Court (e.g. no accountability, no review of decisions), but may also be true of lower court judges who often work with laws delegating enormous discretion (e.g. sentencing laws) and without fear of review by a higher court (because appeals are so rare).[2] And few judges would disavow the intention to do justice by their decisions. What is less well

---

[2] For an example of research based at least in part on the Attitudinal Model in Courts of Appeal see Klein 2002. At the level of the federal district courts, the Attitudinal Model plays an extremely prominent role (e.g. Rowland and Carp 1996), even if attitudes are typically inferred, rather than directly measured, from attributes such as the party of the president who appointed the judge. On the Attitudinal Model and state supreme courts see Langer 2002; Brace and Hall 1997; and Brace, Langer, and Hall 2000.

acknowledged is the intimate connection between one's sense of justice in an instant case and one's general ideological predispositions.

An attitude is a predisposition, and a relatively fixed one at that (but see Martin and Quinn 2002). Behavior, on the other hand, is characterized by a distribution of discrete decisions. Attitudes, if they are useful, should predict the central tendency in such distributions, and they do. However, it would be unreasonable to expect attitudes to predict every single individual decision. It may be, for instance, that the votes of voters with Democratic attitudes are well predicted by the attitudes in general, even if a specific voting decision may deviate from the attitudes (e.g. "Reagan Democrats"). We know that in general attitudes are moderate to strong predictors of behavior (e.g. Kraus 1995), but also that attitudes never provide a complete explanation of actual behaviors. What must be added to our analyses is an understanding of the factors that might deflect a decision away from the predisposition of the decision-maker. Thus, our models of decision-making require an additional layer of complexity.

3   NORMATIVE CONSTRAINTS ON DECISION-MAKING: WHAT JUDGES THINK THEY OUGHT TO DO

Attitudinalists are often challenged by those who assert that judges are frequently strongly constrained by *stare decisis* and precedent. The argument has more plausibility at the trial court level, where judges are often faced with routine decisions requiring the application of existing law to instant disputes. At the appellate court level it appears that law rarely dictates outcomes. Segal and Spaeth (1996), for instance, show that most justices of the US Supreme Court do not put aside their policy preferences in order to defer to existing precedents. Others disagree, however (e.g. Knight and Epstein 1996; Spriggs and Hansford 2001), so this is an issue requiring further inquiry.

Undoubtedly, the answer is that laws (constitutions, statutes, and precedents) vary in the degree to which discretion is afforded to judges. And since fact patterns rarely reproduce themselves precisely, some discretion is virtually always available to judges to determine what body of law is relevant to an instant case.[3] Perhaps all

---

[3] When a new policy is set, it changes the relative weights assigned to the fact-based aspects of the cases. For example, Richards and Kritzer (2002) show that the factors related to decisions in free

judges believe that similar cases ought to be treated similarly, but determining to which body of law an individual case belongs is no easy or mechanical task (especially at the appellant level, where one side of the case has already prevailed with the court below, and the other side of the case believes its argument sufficiently strong to risk the high cost of appeal). To the extent that judges are free to pick which precedents they "follow," then it is difficult to assign much causal influence to the prior court decisions. Moreover, many of the decisions of judges are in areas where vast discretion is granted by law and precedent is of little guidance or meaning (e.g. sentencing decisions).

In discussing the role of precedent in judicial decision-making, Epstein and Knight (2004, 186) assert: "judges have a preferred rule that they would like to establish in the case before them, but they strategically modify their position to take account of a normative constraint—a norm favoring precedent—in order to produce a decision as close as is possible to their preferred outcome." What Epstein and Knight are acknowledging is that judges are subject to expectations about how they ought to behave. Not all decisional options can be exercised by judges without repercussions. Moreover, judges hold their own views about how they *ought to* behave. Many judges take, for instance, an oath to obey the law, and obeying the law to many means following precedent whenever possible. And even if judges do not themselves accept a particular model of good judging, they may be subject to norms and expectations that constrain their behavior. Perhaps the most important conclusion here is that judging is different from other forms of decision-making by public officials. Courts are not simply mini-legislatures. Because judging is different, and specifically because impartiality is an expected behavior of all judges, normative models of decision-making have uncommon influence. Moreover, the legitimacy of judicial decisions is to some degree influenced by the procedures judges use in making decisions (Tyler and Mitchell 1994), and, importantly, judges know that.

Judges differ in whether they believe their primary obligation is to justice or to strict legality. Some judges value the orderliness and predictability of law more highly than justice in individual cases. Other judges are more strongly committed to achieving justice in their decisions than maintaining strict legal consistency. These judges cite as part of the obligation of a judge in a Common Law System the need to ensure that law keeps up with changing social values and norms, and they attribute the legitimacy of courts to their ability to make decisions commonly regarded as just.

Gibson (1978) has shown that judges' perceptions of what they ought to do as judges do in fact influence their decision-making behavior. This is not simply a matter of "activist" judges making liberal decisions, and "restraintist" judges

expression cases change as a result of a new "jurisprudential regime" announced and implemented in *Chicago Police Department* vs. *Mosley* and *Grayned* vs. *Rockford*.

making conservative decisions. Instead, these orientations influence styles of decision-making. "Activist" judges, for instance, are more likely to be concerned with the social consequences of their decisions, since activists are seeking to maximize "justice" (be it a conservative or liberal version of justice). Restraintists seek to maximize "legality" (and the law is sometimes liberal, just as it is sometimes conservative), to the extent possible. Thus, judicial activism is not correlated with the ideological thrust of decisions, but instead is a description of the types of variables upon which judges are likely to base their decisions.

Although role theory is rarely referenced in contemporary research on judicial decision-making, one can readily find instances in which the theory is implicitly implicated. For instance, consider again the competition between political scientists and legal experts in predicting Supreme Court decisions. One commentator on the contest observed that, "The more conservative the justice, the larger the role played by ideology and the more accurate the model's attitudinalist prediction." However, "Legalism, not attitudinalism, is a better way to predict the votes of the four liberals because they place more emphasis on law than politics" (Sherry 2004, 771). In essence, Sherry is making the observation Gibson (1977) made long ago: Judicial activists need not be (nor are they usually) liberals; conservative activism is quite common; and role orientations determine styles of decision-making.

Norms influence many aspects of judicial behavior, as, for instance, the important influence of the norm of consensus (a further example of implicit role theory). This norm—which grants or denies legitimacy to the public expression of dissent by judges—has changed over time in the US Supreme Court (Caldeira and Zorn 1998), and these norms have clearly shaped the behavior of judges. Strong norms against dissent still seem to govern in many state supreme courts (Brace and Hall 2005), and these norms directly influence the behavior of judges. Judges are not free to adopt with impunity any particular decision-making style; instead, they are constrained by normative expectations.

There is a rich but unfinished empirical literature on judges' beliefs about what constitutes proper judicial behavior, and there are some important lessons from that research. First, judges vary. Any analyst who treats judges as a homogeneous group when it comes to conceptions of judging is making a serious mistake. Thus, micro-level analysis of individual differences is essential. Second, what one believes one should do is not always what one can do. A judge who believes strongly in strictly following precedent will inevitably be confronted with cases for which no precedent exists. Perhaps more important, the feasibility of following precedent may be undermined by other conflicting objectives (e.g. maintaining the legitimacy of the court itself), forcing judges to choose between competing cherished values. Finally, simplistic and symbolic (and politically valuable) descriptions of methods of decision-making often obscure very real differences among judges. When judges are asked for instance whether judges should follow precedent, they overwhelmingly reply, yes. But when asked whether they agree or disagree with the statement that "it is just as legitimate to make a decision and then find the precedent as it is to find the precedent and then make the decision," then substantial dissensus emerges. Now if a judge can choose which precedents to follow, or if a decision legitimately precedes the precedent, what sort of logic compels us to understand the precedent as having *caused* the decision? Finally, the empirical question of how these beliefs about proper behavior influence actual decision-making can only be resolved through careful empirical analysis, based mainly on positivist methods.

Many debates exist among scholars of judicial behavior in part because judges and others are often disingenuous in describing how they go about making decisions, and in part due to concerns about judicial legitimacy. This then raises the more general issue of whether strategic factors play a role in judicial processes.

4 STRATEGIC CONSIDERATIONS

Epstein and Knight (2000, 625) have documented well the rise of rational choice approaches to judicial decision-making, and in particular models of strategic choices by judges. They define the strategic model as: "(1) social actors make choices in order to achieve certain goals; (2) social actors act strategically in the sense that their choices depend on their expectations about the choices of other actors; and (3) these choices are structured by the institutional setting in which they are made" (2000, 626). Of course, at this level of abstraction, no one could disagree with the application of this model to judicial decision-making. Judges have policy preferences they try to implement, but they cannot act as entirely free agents. Instead, they must take into account the preferences of their constituents (broadly defined), as well as formal and informal institutional rules, prescriptions, and proscriptions.

Theories of constrained choice often fall within the Separation of Powers (SoP) approach (e.g. Segal 1999). This is a body of research examining the degree to which judges factor into their decision-making their beliefs and perceptions about the reactions of the other branches of government to their policies. As such, it has much in common with theories of legitimacy (see below) that argue that judicial institutions are dependent upon others for the successful implementation of their decisions.

Assuming that judges are single-minded, with policy goals entirely dominant, few would argue with the view that no institution can be effective without acting strategically in this sense. Neustadt long ago taught us that even the US president is severely constrained by others when he documented that the power of the president is the power to persuade, not to command. Undoubtedly, judges do not judge in a vacuum.

But it is likely that judges, like all humans, attempt to maximize many different objectives by their actions on the bench, and there is no clear evidence that affecting the implementation of their policies is the overriding goal of most justices. For instance, the single-minded pursuit of policy goals may on occasion threaten the legitimacy of a court, and therefore judges will act to protect the institution rather than maximize policy preferences. Consequently, it is not surprising that evidence in support of the strategic hypothesis is decidedly mixed. Even though Epstein and Knight (2000, 640) provide a list of twenty-nine citations that provide "empirical support for the plausibility of the assumption of strategic interaction," it is unlikely that this body of research actually tests the strategic hypothesis within a fully specified model—that is, in the context of controlling for plausible rival hypotheses. Moreover, the strategic hypothesis seems to be nothing more than that judges consider more than their own policy preferences in making decisions. Consequently, research on the effect of elections on court decision-making, a voluminous and long-standing concern of judicial scholars, scores as support for the strategic hypothesis. From this perspective, strategic behavior seems to be any behavior taking into account anything other than one's own personal policy preferences. Moreover, it seems likely that some justices consider it improper to engage in anything but sincere decision-making, that others view the reactions of others to be too unpredictable to warrant much consideration, that some justices simply mispredict the reactions of others, and that which goal comes to dominate any particular decision depends mightily upon a series of contextual variables. Thus, it is probably not surprising that the empirical evidence for this form of strategic behavior is so contested.

It is also unclear how strategic behavior fits within normative theories of how judges ought to behave. One factor the strategic literature rarely considers is that many judge strategic behavior as normatively inappropriate. A synonym for "strategic" is "insincere." Many expect judges to act sincerely, directly and only considering matters of legality, justice, and right and wrong. Strategic action makes good sense for consumers in economic marketplaces; one buying a home from another often acts insincerely and in a manipulative fashion without a great deal of ethical opprobrium. But law and judging are not economics. It is easy to imagine that the colleagues and constituents of strategic judges come to disapprove of such behavior, and ultimately to distrust and dismiss such judges. In its inattention to most normative considerations, rational choice models of human behavior are typically incomplete accounts of how decision-makers in public political roles make decisions.

4.1 Neoinstitutionalism

Strategic theories are certainly correct that judges are often constrained by the institutions within which they work, and "neoinstitutionalism" has become quite fashionable among students of judicial behavior (see Clayton and Gillman 1999 for a fine collection of essays on neoinstitutionalism). The neoinstitutional hypothesis is simple: Institutions matter. As collections of formal and informal norms, institutions prescribe and proscribe behaviors. Institutions are certainly human creations, and far from invariant, but few would argue with the basic contention that Robinson Crusoe used a decision-making process quite unlike that employed by actors within institutional settings.

But it is unlikely that institutions have uniform effects on all institutional decision-makers. "Mavericks" obviously exist—is it possible to be more "maverick" than William O. Douglas? More generally, individuals vary in the degree to which they respond to institutional incentives, in the degree to which they internalize institutional norms. To treat unthinkingly the institution as the most useful unit of analysis seems unwise. Courts do not make decisions; judges do, even if they are much influenced by their courts. Developing useful cross-level theories of *individuals in institutions* has received insufficient attention in contemporary studies of courts.

A crucial and obvious attribute of many judicial institutions is the requirement of popular accountability: The occupant of the judicial role must seek reelection. It seems certain, therefore, that the goal of re-election or reappointment is influential for many judicial actors. For example, Hall (1995) discovered that state supreme court judges are more inclined to uphold challenges to the death penalty when they are approaching the time for their re-election. Huber and Gordon (2004) produce similar evidence on the sentencing behavior of trial judges, claiming to be able to "attribute more than two thousand years of additional incarceration to this dynamic" among Pennsylvania trial judges (2004, 261). That judges are rarely voted out of office seems to be of little consequence (just as it is inconsequential that members of Congress are rarely voted out; see Hall 2001).

Furthermore, the influence of interest groups in shaping the agenda of the US Supreme Court should be counted as a constraint on justices' decisions. Research in this area has become increasingly sophisticated, as in studies that actually survey organizations, rather than just tending to formally filed *amicus* briefs (e.g. Hansford 2004). Undoubtedly, some sort of interaction exists between the decisions of courts and the political calculus of interest groups.

Perhaps the most outstanding investigation of the strategic hypothesis can be found in Langer's (2002) study of state supreme courts. What I find most compelling about her research is that it investigates multiple causes of judges' decisions, and argues that the degree to which judges engage in strategic behavior varies across contexts. Specifically, her research "demonstrates that the likelihood of strategic behavior by judges varies by preference distributions, divided party control of state governments, constitutional amendment procedures, judicial retention practices, length of judicial terms, and the degree of saliency associated with the area of law" (2002, 123). Put more simply: "these analyses demonstrate that state supreme court justices vote sincerely when [they] feel they can and strategically when they feel they must." The finding of conditionality is surely correct, and should not be lost on future research.

In the final analysis, the strategic hypothesis has certainly contributed to our understanding of the factors influencing judicial decision-making, and the adherents of the theory are quite correct to criticize those who adopt simple (and simplistic) models of decision-making that ignore the institutional, political, and social contexts of judging. Whether this contribution is revolutionary is doubtful, for two reasons. First, the strategic hypothesis is closely connected to long-standing thinking about the dependence of courts on their environments, and second, with few exceptions, the hypothesis has only been stated and tested in its most crude form, ignoring, for instance, a host of conditional variables, ranging from individual psychology to institutional structure. Most important, the assumption of single-mindedness ignores the vast complexity that arises when decision-makers seek to maximize many desiderata simultaneously. Finally, it is entirely unclear at this point that the rational choice approach is the only framework within which the strategic hypothesis can be tested.

An important element of the strategic hypothesis is that courts are dependent upon their environments. As Epstein and Knight (2004, 186) note, "To the extent that judges are concerned with establishing rules that will engender the compliance of the community, they will take account of the fact that they must establish rules that are legitimate in the eyes of that community." Thus, an important and obvious connection exists between strategic considerations and theories of institutional legitimacy.

5   THE LEGITIMACY OF JUDICIAL INSTITUTIONS

All institutions need political capital in order to be effective, to get their decisions accepted by others and be successfully implemented. Since courts are typically thought to be weak institutions—having neither the power of the "purse" (control of the treasury) nor the "sword" (control over agents of state coercion)—their political capital must be found in resources other than finances and force. For courts, their principal political capital is institutional legitimacy.

Legitimacy Theory is one of the most important frameworks we have for understanding the effectiveness of courts in democratic societies (e.g. Gibson 2004a). Fortunately, considerable agreement exists among social scientists and legal scholars on the major contours of the theory. For instance, most agree that legitimacy is a normative concept, having something to do with the right (moral and legal) to make decisions. "Authority" is sometimes used as a synonym for legitimacy. Institutions perceived to be legitimate are those with a widely accepted mandate to render judgments for a political community. "Basically, when people say that laws are 'legitimate,' they mean that there is something rightful about the way the laws came about . . . the legitimacy of law rests on the way it comes to be: if that is legitimate, then so are the results, at least most of the time" (Friedman 1998, 256).

In the scholarly literature, legitimacy is most often equated with "diffuse support." Diffuse support refers to "a reservoir of favorable attitudes or good will that helps members to accept or tolerate outputs to which they are opposed or the effects of which they see as damaging to their wants" (Easton 1965, 273). Diffuse support is *loyalty* to an institution; it is support that is *not* contingent upon satisfaction with the immediate outputs of the institution. Easton's apt phrase "a reservoir of good will" captures well the idea that people have confidence in institutions to make, in the long-run, desirable public policy. Institutions without a reservoir of goodwill may be limited in their ability to go against the preferences of the majority.[4]

Legitimacy becomes vital when people disagree about public policy. When a court, for instance, makes a decision pleasing to all, discussions of legitimacy are rarely heard. When there is conflict over policy, then some may ask whether the institution has the authority, the "right," to make the decision. Legitimate institutions are those recognized as appropriate decision-making bodies *even when* one disagrees with the outputs of the institution.[5] Thus, legitimacy takes on its primary importance in the presence of an *objection precondition*. Institutions such as courts need the leeway to be able to go against public opinion (as for instance in protecting unpopular political minorities). Scholars sometimes refer to this leeway in the context of the Rule of Law. Legitimacy provides the political capital enabling courts to rule according to the dictates of legal principles, rather than according to

---

[4] Comparativists (e.g. Tsebelis 2000) often focus on courts as "veto-players" and have acknowledged that legitimacy is a necessary resource if courts are to play this role.

[5] No better example of this can be found than in the reactions to *Bush* vs. *Gore* (e.g. Gibson, Caldeira, and Spence 2003; Yates and Whitford 2002; and Kritzer 2001). Legitimacy may be thought of as an element of the "informal institutions" that are so important to the functioning of courts (see Helmke and Levitsky 2004).

the demands of their constituents (for an elaboration of this idea, see Gibson 2004b). Thus, a crucial attribute of political institutions is the degree to which they enjoy the loyalty of their constituents; when courts enjoy legitimacy, they can count on compliance with (or at least acquiescence to) decisions running contrary to the preferences of their constituents.

According to the research of Gibson, Caldeira, and Baird (1998), the United States Supreme Court is an extremely legitimate institution, even if other constitutional courts (e.g. the German Federal Constitutional Court—see Baird 2001) have vast stores of goodwill as well. Indeed, because the Court's legitimacy is so widespread, it had the political capital necessary for having its decision in *Bush* vs. *Gore* respected. The Court worries about its legitimacy (e.g. *Planned Parenthood of Southeastern Pennsylvania* vs. *Casey)* but at present no issues (with the possible exception of abortion) seem poised to threaten it.

Legitimacy Theory asserts that courts are especially dependent upon legitimacy for their effectiveness. But legitimacy is fragile, and its origins are poorly understood; to date, no comprehensive theory of how legitimacy for law and courts emerges has been produced. There are, however, several extremely fecund facts arising from the literature that can serve as the building blocks of such theory:

1. Long ago, Casey (1974) demonstrated that the more one knows about law and courts, the *less* realistic are perceptions of judicial decision (i.e. the more one is likely to believe in the theory of mechanical jurisprudence). Something about being exposed to information about courts contributes to people embracing this traditional mythology of judicial decision-making (see also Scheb and Lyons 2000, who refer to this as the "myth of legality").

2. More recently, Hibbing and Theiss-Morse (1995) have shown that greater awareness of the Supreme Court leads to *more* support for it, whereas greater awareness of Congress is associated with *less* support for that institution. Kritzer and Voelker (1998) make a similar argument. Again, something about being exposed to the institution increases support for it, and there is apparently something unique about exposure to judicial institutions.

3. Caldeira and Gibson (1995) have shown in several contexts that greater awareness of judicial institutions is related to a greater willingness to extend legitimacy to courts. Gibson, Caldeira, and Baird (1998) have confirmed this finding in research in roughly twenty countries.

4. Caldeira and Gibson (1995) have suggested that the legitimacy of courts is *not* undermined by the disagreeable opinions issued by the institution. This is in part related to the ability to shirk responsibility for decisions by reference to the dictates of precedent and *stare decisis.* If more knowledgeable people are more likely to be predisposed toward the theory of mechanical jurisprudence, just as they are more likely to be attentive to courts, then it follows that they are

also more likely to be persuaded by the justices' denial of responsibility for the decision.

5. Gibson, Caldeira, and Spence (2003) have posited a mechanism by which these findings can be integrated. They suggest a "positivity bias," which means that exposure to courts is typically associated with exposure to the legitimizing symbols of courts (robes, decorum, media deference, etc.), thereby contributing to legitimacy. Even when the initial stimulus for paying attention to courts is negative (as *Bush* vs. *Gore* was for many), judicial symbols enhance legitimacy, which shields the institution from attack based on disagreement with its decision. The 2000 US presidential election provides a powerful and compelling example of this process (see also Yates and Whitford 2002; Kritzer 2001). Thus, ironically, even disagreement with court decisions may increase exposure to legitimizing judicial symbols, which in turn enhances the perceived legitimacy of the court.

6. At this point, more speculation is required about how this process evolves. I begin by positing that citizens do not naturally differentiate between the judiciary and the other branches of government. That courts are special and different is something that must be learned. Thus, those most ignorant about politics are likely to hold views of courts and other political institutions that are quite similar—courts are not seen as special and unique.[6]

Exposure to legitimizing judicial symbols reinforces the process of distinguishing courts from other political institutions. The message of these powerful symbols is that "courts are different," and owing to these differences, courts are worthy of more respect, deference, and obedience—in short, legitimacy.

Three important developments in contemporary American politics may very well undermine the degree to which attention to courts is associated with exposure to legitimizing symbols. First, in 2002, the United States Supreme Court ruled that, owing to the First Amendment to the Constitution, judges could no longer be prohibited from expressing policy positions during electoral campaigns for state judicial offices (*Republican Party of Minnesota* vs. *White* 536 U.S. 765 (2002)). The majority based its opinion in part on the view that speech about the qualifications of candidates for public office is essential to electoral processes in democratic politics. Although such candidates are not now permitted *every* type of speech (promises about how one would judge specific cases are legitimately proscribed, at least at the moment), this Supreme Court decision has opened the door for freewheeling discussions of legal policy issues by both incumbents and challengers for judicial offices. As a consequence, judicial elections now focus on judges' ideologies and judicial policy-making far more than in the past.

---

[6] This conjecture is certainly true of many countries other than the United States, as in the former East Germany, for instance (see Markovits 1995).

At the same time, interest groups and legal activists have become increasingly desirous of influencing the outcomes of state judicial elections. This stems partly from the relative inactivity of the US Supreme Court (which now issues fewer than 100 full opinions per year), and partly from the realization that state judicial policies can have enormous economic, political, and social consequences (as in so-called tort reform; see for example Baum 2003). As a consequence, the USA has witnessed in the last few years an unprecedented injection of money into state judicial elections (e.g. the activism of the US Chamber of Commerce and the Trial Lawyers Associations; see for example Echeverria 2001), with campaign spending reaching all-time highs.[7] The confluence of broadened freedom for judges to speak out on issues, the increasing importance of state judicial policies, and the infusion of money into judicial campaigns has produced what may be described as the "Perfect Storm" of judicial elections. This storm has fundamentally reshaped the atmosphere of state judicial elections.

Undoubtedly one of the most important research questions for future inquiry has to do with the consequences of this intense politicization of the American state courts (and federal court as well, for that matter). To the extent that campaigning takes on the characteristics of "normal" political elections, courts will be seen as *not* special and different, with the consequence that their legitimacy may be undermined.

6   JUDICIAL INDEPENDENCE VS. DEMOCRATIC ACCOUNTABILITY

Controversies over how to select and retain judges inevitably implicate theories of judicial independence and accountability. Unfortunately, independence and accountability are locked in zero-sum tension with each other (e.g. Hall 2001; Baum 2003); the American people, however, seem to want both independence and accountability from their courts.

Baum (2003, 14) defines judicial independence as "a condition in which judges are entirely free from negative consequences for their decisions on the bench. The degree of judicial independence is the degree of such freedom." Conventional wisdom holds

---

[7] No better illustration of this phenomenon can be found than in the judicial elections of 2004. According to the Brennan Center at NYU Law School, an all-time high of $21 million dollars was spent on advertising in state supreme court elections in 2004, an increase of almost 20% as compared to 2000 (Brennan Center, Press Release 2004). A total of 181 ads was produced, with 42,096 airings in fifteen states. Over 10,000 airings were shown in each of four states: Ohio, Alabama, West Virginia, and Illinois.

that judicial independence is among the most valuable institutional resources of courts. For courts to fulfill their role as impartial arbiters of disputes—and as veto-players—they must be insulated to some degree from ordinary political pressures. When judiciaries lose their independence, they may lose their effectiveness.[8]

A brittle tension exists between judicial independence and democratic accountability. In democratic societies, policy-making institutions are typically held accountable through the political process.[9] To the extent that courts are recognized as policy-makers, then expectations of accountability naturally emerge. Where few mechanisms exist to hold judges accountable (as in the federal courts in the United States, where all judges hold lifetime appointments), courts are vulnerable to the loss of legitimacy when their opinions clash with those of the majority.

One difficulty of assessing accountability and independence is that formal institutional structures (i.e. formal selection systems) often do not perform as they are intended. On the basis of systematic empirical inquiry, Hall (2001, 326), for instance, asserts: "Court reformers underestimate the extent to which partisan elections have a tangible substantive component and overestimate the extent to which nonpartisan and retention races are insulated from partisan politics and other contextual forces." And clearly nonpartisan and retention elections are unsuccessful at removing politics from the selection of state judges.

Many crucial unanswered problems in research on judicial selection systems require additional investigation. For instance (as already mentioned above), what is the effect of the new-style of judicial elections on judges and courts? In addition, we know too little about how lawyers decide to become judges (which often entails significant financial sacrifice) and how institutions establish incentives to recruit systematically certain types of individuals. To what degree are courts drawing on a pool of talent similar or dissimilar to that relied upon by other political institutions? How and why do judges decide to leave the bench; are strategic considerations at play; to what degree do judges work in concert with executives (e.g. governors) to time and coordinate their departure from the bench?

Institutional change is also quite interesting: How do interest groups mobilize to attempt to change judicial selection systems; what groups are involved and with what degree of coordination; and how successful are they? We know that citizens rarely want to give up their role in selecting judges; by what means are they persuaded to rate independence more highly than accountability?

---

[8] An interesting example of the obverse of this statement (as courts become more independent, they become more effective) is the finding of Giles and Lancaster (1989) that willingness to use the courts in Spain (litigiousness) increased rather dramatically after the fall of the Franco regime. Lancaster and Giles attribute this to the growing legitimacy of the courts which emerged from the perception that the courts are independent and impartial.

[9] For an excellent account of the efforts of constitutional courts in Central and Eastern Europe to achieve judicial independence, see Schwartz 2000.

Finally, we know very little about voters in judicial elections. The conventional view is that law and courts are practically invisible to ordinary people, most of whom are uninformed about judicial contests (e.g. Griffen and Horan 1979; Baum 1988–89, 2003). As Morin (1989) notes, more Americans can name the judge on the television show *The People's Court* (Judge Wapner) than can name a member of the US Supreme Court (an oft-cited finding that has become part of the conventional wisdom about courts and their publics).[10] Are voters uninformed dolts? Can judicial elections capture the attention of voters, and, if so, with what consequences? Some evidence exists to the effect that knowledge of law and courts is remarkably high in the United States, if the correct questions are asked on surveys. For instance, Gibson, Caldeira, and Spence (2001) report that fully 73 percent of a representative sample of the American people know that US Supreme Court justices are appointed to their position. Two-thirds realize that Supreme Court justices serve for a life term, and 61 percent are aware that the Court has the "last say" on the Constitution. Furthermore, roughly two-thirds of the American people know that the Court has made rulings on the right to have abortions and on the rights of black Americans. Nearly 80 percent know that there is an African-American on the Court, and 88 percent of those can identify Clarence Thomas as the justice. Similar numbers know that the Court has a woman on the bench, with 77 percent of those respondents able to identify Sandra Day O'Connor as a female Supreme Court justice. It is certainly true that most Americans cannot name a single member of the US Supreme Court when asked to do so in an open-ended question (i.e. the respondent is entirely responsible for generating the name, as in the American National Election Study), but difficult questions such as these vastly underestimate the level of information people hold about their legal system. Americans apparently know far more about their courts than most scholars realize (and this may be in part due to the advent of descriptive representation on the courts). The old saw that the constituents of courts know nothing about judging needs to be subjected to much more comprehensive investigation.

7   CONCLUDING COMMENTS

Perhaps few areas of research in political science are as vibrant as the sub-field of law and courts. While this chapter has focused on institutions, a vast amount of

---

[10] Kritzer and Voelker note that court systems in a number of states have commissioned public opinion polls "with an eye toward finding ways to improve the quality of service delivery and public support" (1998, 59). So obviously the court systems themselves believe that the views of their constituents are important and not entirely void of content.

interesting research is being conducted in the sub-field on culture (legal and otherwise), justice (distributive, procedural, retributive, and restorative), and institutions other than courts (e.g. juries, interest groups), to name just a few. Research in the sub-field is as narrow as studies of opinion-assignment behavior on the United States Supreme Court and as broad as trying to understand the conditions under which law can bring about social change. Methodological eclecticism characterizes the field, although there is a growing recognition among most scholars that theory without data is of limited value, just as are data (and databases) without theory. Although the United States Supreme Court continues to be (and will always be) the focus of a great deal of research effort, comparative research on law and courts is becoming commonplace. And one of the most exciting opportunities can be found in the reinvigorated research on state law and courts. The states do indeed provide a laboratory for research of this sort, in particular through their enormous institutional variability (both in structure and in function).

And finally, theoretical innovation in the sub-field, though perhaps not keeping up completely with available data, is impressive. The growth of rational choice is noteworthy, as is the growing tendency to subject such models to rigorous empirical investigation. Noteworthy as well is the tendency to adopt larger perspectives on the processes we study, as in research investigating the influence of interest groups on courts, from the interest group, not the court, perspective. All of these trends and tendencies speak to the vibrancy of the field. Law and courts are not marginal to politics; they are central, and this is increasingly being understood by the entire discipline of political science.

Nonetheless, important lacunae and unanswered questions exist for the sub-field. Perhaps the most glaring is that research on US courts continues to dominate the study of courts. With the exception of studies of judicial legitimacy—where research on a couple of dozen national high courts has been reported, as well research on the European Court of Justice—little is known about non-US courts. Fortunately, scholars have recognized this and a variety of new research is currently being conducted on courts throughout the world (e.g. Haynie 2003). Perhaps the next time a review such as this is written, it will be clear that the study of courts is a truly international enterprise.

REFERENCES

BAIRD, V. A. 2001. Building institutional legitimacy: the role of procedural justice. *Political Research Quarterly*, 54 (2): 333–54.

BAUM, L. 1988–89. Voters' information in judicial contests: the 1986 contests for the Ohio Supreme Court. *Kentucky Law Journal*, 77: 645–70.

—— 2003. Judicial elections and judicial independence: the voter's perspective. *Ohio State Law Journal*, 64: 13–41.

BRACE, P. R. and HALL, M. G. 1997. The interplay of preferences, case facts, context, and rules in the politics of judicial choice. *Journal of Politics,* 59 (4): 1206–31.

—— —— 2005. Is judicial federalism essential to democracy? State courts in the federal system. Unpublished manuscript.

—— LANGER, L., and HALL, M. G. 2000. Measuring the preferences of state supreme court judges. *Journal of Politics,* 62 (2): 387–413.

BRENNAN CENTER, PRESS RELEASE 2004. Buying Time 2004: Total Amount Spent on Judicial Advertising Peaks at $21 Million. Available at: http://www.brennancenter.org/presscenter/releases_2004/pressrelease_2004_1118.html [accessed December 22, 2004].

CALDEIRA, G. A. and GIBSON, J. L. 1995. The legitimacy of the Court of Justice in the European Union: models of institutional support. *American Political Science Review,* 89 (2): 356–76.

—— and ZORN, C. J. W. 1998. Of time and consensual norms in the Supreme Court. *American Journal of Political Science,* 42 (3): 874–902.

CASEY, G. 1974. The Supreme Court and myth: an empirical investigation. *Law and Society Review,* 8: 385–419.

CLAYTON, C. W. and GILLMAN, H. (eds.) 1999. *Supreme Court Decision-Making: New Institutionalist Approaches.* Chicago: University of Chicago Press.

EASTON, D. 1965. *A Systems Analysis of Political Life.* New York: John Wiley.

ECHEVERRIA, J. D. 2001. Changing the rules by changing the players: The environmental issue in state judicial elections. *New York University Environmental Law Journal,* 9: 217–303.

EPSTEIN, L. and KNIGHT, J. 1998. *The Choices Justices Make.* Washington, DC: CQ Press.

—— —— 2000. Toward a strategic revolution in judicial politics: A look back, a look ahead. *Political Research Quarterly,* 53 (3): 625–61.

—— —— 2004. Courts and judges. Pp. 170–94 in *The Blackwell Companion to Law and Society,* ed. A. Sarat. Malden, Mass.: Blackwell.

FRIEDMAN, L. M. 1998. *American Law: An Introduction,* rev. edn. New York: W. W. Norton.

GIBSON, J. L. 1977. Discriminant functions, role orientations, and judicial behavior: theoretical and methodological linkages. *Journal of Politics,* 39 (4): 984–1007.

—— 1978. Judges' role orientations, attitudes and decisions: an interactive model. *American Political Science Review,* 72 (3): 911–24.

—— 1983. From simplicity to complexity: the development of theory in the study of judicial behavior. *Political Behavior,* 5 (1): 7–49.

—— 2004a. *Overcoming Apartheid: Can Truth Reconcile a Divided Nation?* New York: Russell Sage Foundation.

—— 2004b. Truth, reconciliation, and the creation of a human rights culture in South Africa. *Law and Society Review,* 38 (1): 5–40.

—— CALDEIRA, G. A., and BAIRD, V. 1998. On the legitimacy of national high courts. *American Political Science Review,* 92 (2): 343–58.

—— —— and SPENCE, L. K. 2001. Public knowledge of the United States Supreme Court, 2001. Available at: http://www.artsci.wustl.edu/~legit/Courtknowledge.pdf [accessed December 20, 2004].

—— —— —— 2003. The Supreme Court and the U.S. presidential election of 2000: wounds, self-inflicted or otherwise? *British Journal of Political Science,* 33: (4): 535–56.

GILES, M. W. and LANCASTER, T. D. 1989. Political transition, social development, and legal mobilization in Spain. *American Political Science Review*, 83 (3): 817–33.

GRIFFEN, K. N. and HORAN, M. J. 1979. Merit retention elections: what influences the voters? *Judicature*, 63: 78–88.

GURUSHINA, N. 1996. Supreme Court overturns Yeltin's Decree on Nuclear Waste Disposal. *OMRI Daily Digest*, April 5.

HALL, M. G. 1995. Justices as representatives: elections and judicial politics in the American states. *American Politics Quarterly*, 23 (4): 485–503.

—— 2001. State supreme courts in American democracy: probing the myths of judicial reform. *American Political Science Review*, 95 (2): 315–30.

HANSFORD, T. G. 2004. Information provision, organizational constraints, and the decision to submit an Amicus Curiae brief in a U.S. Supreme Court case. *Political Research Quarterly*, 57 (2): 219–30.

HAYNIE, S. L. 2003. *Judging in Black & White: Decision Making in the South African Appellate Division, 1950–1990*. New York: Peter Lang.

HELMKE, G. 2002. The logic of strategic defection: court–executive relations in Argentina under dictatorship and democracy. *American Political Science Review*, 96 (2): 291–303.

—— and LEVITSKY, T. 2004. Informal institutions and comparative politics: a research agenda. *Perspectives on Politics*, 2 (4): 725–40.

HIBBING, J. R. and THEISS-MORSE, E. 1995. *Congress as Public Enemy: Public Attitudes Toward American Political Institutions*. Cambridge: Cambridge University Press.

HUBER, G. A. and GORDON, S. C. 2004. Accountability and coercion: is justice blind when it runs for office? *American Journal of Political Science*, 48 (2): 247–63.

KARPINSKI, J. 1995. Polish Supreme Court validates presidential elections. *OMRI Daily Digest*, December 11.

KLEIN, D. E. 2002. *Making Law in the United States Courts of Appeals*. New York: Cambridge University Press.

KNIGHT, J. and EPSTEIN, L. 1996. The norm of stare decisis. *American Journal of Political Science*, 40: 1018–35.

KRAUS, S. J. 1995. Attitudes and the prediction of behavior: a meta-analysis of the empirical literature. *Personality and Social Psychology Bulletin*, 21: 58–75.

KRITZER, H. M. 2001. The impact of *Bush v. Gore* on public perceptions and knowledge of the Supreme Court. *Judicature*, 85 (1): 32–8.

—— and VOELKER, J. 1998. Familiarity breeds respect: how Wisconsin citizens view their courts. *Judicature*, 82: 58–64.

LANGER, L. 2002. *Judicial Review in State Supreme Courts: A Comparative Study*. Albany: State University of New York Press.

MALTZMAN, F., SPRIGGS, J. F., II, and WAHLBECK, P. J. 2000. *Crafting Law on the Supreme Court: The Collegial Game*. New York: Cambridge University Press.

MARKOVITS, I. 1995. *Imperfect Justice: An East–West German Diary*. New York: Oxford University Press.

MARTIN, A. D. and QUINN, K. M. 2002. Dynamic ideal point estimation via Markov Chain Monte Carlo for the U.S. Supreme Court, 1953–1999. *Political Analysis*, 10 (2): 134–53.

—— —— RUGER, T. W., and KIM, P. T. 2004. Competing approaches to predicting Supreme Court decision making. *Perspectives on Politics*, 2 (4): 761–7.

MORIN, R. 1989. Wapner v. Rehnquist: no contest; TV judge vastly outpolls justices in test of public recognition. *Washington Post*, June 23: A21.

PARKIN, C. 1996. Irish divorce change delayed. *United Press International*, February 8.

RICHARDS, M. J. and KRITZER, H. M. 2002. Jurisprudential regimes in Supreme Court decision making. *American Political Science Review*, 96 (2): 305–20.

ROWLAND, C. K. and CARP, R. A. 1996. *Politics and Judgment in Federal District Courts*. Lawrence: University Press of Kansas.

SCHEB, J. M., II, and LYONS, W. 2000. The myth of legality and public evaluation of the Supreme Court. *Social Science Quarterly*, 81 (4): 928–40.

SCHWARTZ, H. 2000. *The Struggle for Constitutional Justice in Post-Communist Europe*. Chicago: University of Chicago Press.

SEGAL, J. A. 1999. Supreme Court deference to Congress: an examination of the Marxist model. Pp. 237–53 in *Supreme Court Decision-Making: New Institutionalist Approaches*, ed. C. W. Clayton and H. Gillman. Chicago: University of Chicago Press.

—— and COVER, A. D. 1989. Ideological values and the votes of U.S. Supreme Court justices. *American Political Science Review*, 83 (2): 557–65.

—— and SPAETH, H. J. 1993. *The Supreme Court and the Attitudinal Model*. New York: Cambridge University Press.

—— —— 1996. The influence of Stare Decisis on the vote of United States Supreme Court justices. *American Journal of Political Science*, 40: 971–1003.

—— —— 2002. *The Supreme Court and the Attitudinal Model Revisited*. New York: Cambridge University Press.

SHERRY, S. 2004. What's law got to do with it? *Perspectives on Politics*, 2 (4): 769–75.

SOLOMON, P. H., JR. and FOGLESONG, T. S. 2000. *Courts and Transition in Russia: The Challenge of Judicial Reform*. Boulder, Colo.: Westview Press.

SPRIGGS, J. F., II and HANSFORD, T. G. 2001. Explaining the overruling of U. S. Supreme Court precedent. *Journal of Politics*, 63 (4): 1091–111.

TATE, C. N. and VALLINDER, T. 1995. *The Global Expansion of Judicial Power*. New York: New York University Press.

DE TOCQUEVILLE, A. 1945. *Democracy in America*. New York: Vintage; repr. 1990.

TSEBELIS, G. 2000. Veto players and institutional analysis. *Governance*, 13 (4): 441–74.

TYLER, T. R. and MITCHELL, G. 1994. Legitimacy and the empowerment of discretionary legal authority: the United States Supreme Court and abortion rights. *Duke Law Journal*, 43: 703–815.

YATES, J. L., and WHITFORD, A. B. 2002. The presidency and the Supreme Court after *Bush v. Gore*: implications for legitimacy and effectiveness. *Stanford Law and Policy Review*, 13 (1): 101–18.

Cases Cited

Bush vs. *Gore* [2000] 531 U.S. 98

Chicago Police Department vs. *Mosley* [1971] 408 U.S. 92

Grayned vs. *Rockford* [1972] 408 U.S. 104.

Planned Parenthood of Southeastern Pennsylvania vs. *Casey* [1992] 533 U.S. 833.

Republican Party of Minnesota vs. *White* [2002] 536 U.S. 765

CHAPTER 27

THE JUDICIAL PROCESS AND PUBLIC POLICY

KEVIN T. MCGUIRE

Courts are curious institutions. Unlike elected bodies that regard governing as their explicit responsibility, members of the judiciary are often less certain about their function within the polity. To be sure, legislative and executive officials frequently disagree about the types of policies that should be enacted. Questions such as "To what degree should the state regulate economic and social affairs?" and "What should be the government's priorities in foreign affairs?" are some of the basic issues with which representatives must come to terms. Regardless of the role they believe that government should play, however, elected representatives scarcely doubt that it is their obligation to establish the rules that order relations in society.

Judges, by contrast, must ask themselves not only what policies are appropriate but also whether they should be making them in the first place. For some, courts are major decision-makers that function as principals on a par with legislators and executives in developing, monitoring, and adapting public policies. Others take quite the opposite view, envisioning courts as more modest institutions whose functions involve arbitrating public and private disputes by doing little more than faithfully interpreting existing law. And it is not merely judges who have this ambivalence. These divisions about the role of courts exist among other policy-makers as well as businesses, organizations, and the mass public.

Such disagreements about whether judges should lead or follow in the process of governing presuppose that courts actually have the capacity to effect policy change—the ability to bring about meaningful reform—and that the work that courts do has major consequences for the various constituencies that are touched by the decisions of judges. It is not at all clear, though, that courts possess the policy-making capacity necessary to bring about such change. Nor is it obvious that the policies of courts bring about the reforms that are intended.

Just how well suited are courts to making policy? Are judges capable of actually producing changes within society? In this chapter, I consider a number of issues related to the judicial process with an eye towards illuminating the policy capacities that courts possess and the impact of their decisions. Specifically, I discuss the conditions that must be met in order for courts to make effective policy and then describe how several of the basic features of the judicial process undermine realizing those conditions. To illustrate, I will draw on several different strands of research that underscore various problems that are endemic to judges serving as policy-makers. Since the bulk of scholarly research on judicial policy-making examines the United States, most of my illustrations involve American courts. Still, political scientists are increasingly interested in courts outside the USA, and I rely upon this growing body of research as well. My purpose is not to suggest that courts in the USA or elsewhere are ineffective policy-makers. Rather, I try to temper the expectations about what courts can do by describing how judges, like any set of governmental actors, face certain institutional constraints that limit their policy ambitions.

1   CONDITIONS FOR EFFECTIVE POLICY-MAKING

For quite some time, lawyers, judges, and scholars took it on faith that the policies handed down by courts were just as significant as the enactments of legislatures, indeed in some cases even more so. After all, beginning in the 1950s, the Supreme Court of the United States entered the fray over some of the most visible issues within society, crafting major legal reforms in such policy areas as the freedoms of speech, press, and religion, the rights of the criminally accused, and racial discrimination. As a result, the American courts now address such issues as abortion, the right to die, the death penalty, gender discrimination, affirmative action, regulation of the Internet, legislative apportionment, and property rights, as well as questions of legislative, executive, and state power. The Court's decisions in these areas are regarded as particularly consequential; since many involve interpretation of the US Constitution, there is effectively no recourse—save the unlikely route of amending the Constitution—for elected officials who might seek to modify or undo judicial policies that they find disagreeable.

Over the past fifteen years, however, researchers have begun to look closely at the actual consequences of judicial policy-making and have found the results to be far more variable than had been assumed. In light of these findings, scholars have reassessed the subject of judicial capacity, thinking with greater care about the conditions that must be met in order for the decisions of judges to produce significant policy change. That courts announce significant policies does not necessarily mean that those policies are followed or have pronounced effects for society.

One of the most important assessments of the impact of courts can be found in Gerald Rosenberg's (1991) analysis of several of the Supreme Court's most prominent policy domains. His work delineates both the institutional constraints that courts face and the several "conditions for efficacy," that is, the circumstances that must obtain if courts are to be truly effective policy-makers (1991, 10–36). In particular, he argues that the legal system requires courts to operate within the traditions and language of the law; thus, judges who are inclined to create major policy innovations must still be able to trace those policies to a widely shared understanding of the Constitution and its laws. Moreover, whatever the policy ambitions of judges, they are inevitably constrained by the courts' lack of an enforcement power and consequently their reliance upon popular support for their decisions.

In light of these considerations, courts must lay the legal groundwork for change by institutionalizing a series of precedents upon which to build their policies. Once those policies are established, there must be a reasonable amount of acceptance by both the public and elected officials. To the extent that there is resistance to judicial policy, government officials must be willing to offer rewards or punishments to bring about implementation.

In short, because courts lack the ability to put their rulings into effect, they must depend upon the goodwill of others to act on their behalf. The greater care courts take in establishing the legitimacy of their rulings, the more likely they are to be supported by those who can create the conditions necessary for implementors to carry out the courts' will.

2   CHARACTERISTICS OF COURTS

Are courts well situated to meet these conditions? Judges have both formal and informal characteristics that facilitate their policy-making; they possess the authoritative power to resolve legal disputes, and in doing so they are generally accepted as legitimate, enjoying the esteem of both the public and other government officials. At the same time, there are a number of distinctive characteristics of the judicial process that complicate the ability of courts to bring about effective policy change.

2.1 Judicial Selection

Both across and within countries, judges vary a good deal in the mechanisms by which they are chosen, and different methods of selection create various incentives for judges, which do not necessarily enhance independent policy-making. In England, for example, lower court judges are selected by the Lord Chancellor, in consultation with local advisory boards, while appellate judges are chosen (at least nominally) by the prime minister, who receives advice from the Lord Chancellor and a committee for judicial appointments (Kritzer 1996). For quite some time, selection was largely a function of political patronage, thus making it attractive for judges to bring political considerations to bear in their decisions (Drewry 1993). In its modern manifestation, however, it is a system that tends to place greater emphasis on the qualifications of judges (Griffith 1991; Kritzer 1996).

In the United States, by contrast, the vast majority of the judiciary is elected. Most American judges are creatures of state government, and most states opt for some form of election for their judicial officials. As a result, there is little guarantee that the people most competent to serve as judges will be selected. Indeed, voters know precious little about candidates for judicial office (Klein and Baum 2001). Much has been made of this apparent weakness, and since judging requires fidelity to the law, not politics, reformers often argue that members of the bench should be selected by some form of independent commission that can evaluate the objective qualifications of potential jurists. This, it turns out, is not as serious a limitation as critics charge, since the same types of individuals who are disposed to be judges have fairly consistent professional backgrounds; thus, the same sorts of people end up being chosen, regardless of the method of selection (Glick and Emmert 1987). In terms of their qualifications, those who are elected resemble very closely those who are appointed.

The same cannot be said, however, about their voting behavior. For those judges who are elected, the very incentives that guide the actions of popular policy-makers often end up motivating their decisions as well. Thus, for example, judges who are about to stand for re-election engage in strategic behavior, frequently voting in ways that will not alienate the electorate (Hall 1992). Judges are (theoretically, at least) obligated to make decisions in light of what the rule of law dictates, and in practice, of course, they may not be able to realize that goal. But, when elected judges are guided by a desire to satisfy constituents, they forgo the pursuit of it.

Under such conditions, it will be difficult for judges to take the lead as policy-makers. Inasmuch as they are tethered to public opinion, elected judges will be inhibited from innovating and looking for ways to produce legal change.

Appointed judges are no less prone to be attentive to the public. Political scientists have long recognized that even life-tenured judges may be constrained by the law-making majority. They too evince a reluctance to challenge sitting elected officials (Dahl 1957; Murphy 1964), and a good deal of scholarship shows that, despite life tenure and no supervising authority, the members of the Supreme Court are often mindful of the preferences of their coordinate branches and the public as well (see, e.g., McGuire and Stimson 2004; Mishler and Sheehan 1996; Segal 1988).

For appointed judges whose goals may be to craft policies that have genuine efficacy, the lack of enforcement power requires a reliance upon an acceptance of their decisions. Those who stray too far from the tolerance limits of the political system do so at the risk of their legitimacy. Thus, the institutions that govern how judicial pronouncements are translated into public policies provide some obvious limits on the judiciary. If judges seek to chart new ground with their legal policies, they must consider the extent to which their policies will be accepted.

2.2   The Process of Decision-making

Perhaps more significant for an understanding of judicial policy-making is an appreciation of the mechanics of the judicial process. At first glance, one might be inclined to overlook the actual procedures by which judges render their decisions and focus on the substance of those decisions. Judging strictly by the broad array of topics to which courts address themselves—medical malpractice, employment discrimination, rights of the handicapped, labor disputes, voting rights, privacy, commercial regulation, punitive damages, just to name a few—courts are surely taking a leading role in the development of social and economic policies.

Given that courts touch virtually all aspects of public and private life, it is easy to imagine that their policy purview is on a par with the elected branches. Nevertheless, courts face a number of important limitations that are endemic to the judicial process. The very nature of adjudication—the set of institutions that govern how courts make decisions—serves as a serious limitation on the extent to which courts can generate meaningful legal change. These constraints are not immediately obvious, but they consistently conspire to moderate the impact of judicial outcomes.[1]

---

[1] The following is adapted from Horowtiz (1977, 33–56).

One characteristic of the judicial process that is distinctive from the work done by legislative and executive officials is that adjudication tends to focus on a limited range of policy alternatives. In any given case, two litigants are pitted against one another, each asking for some specific remedy. All else being equal, judges regard it as their responsibility to decide cases as narrowly as possible and develop limited, not expansive rulings.

As Justice Louis Brandeis famously explained in *Ashwander* vs. *Tennessee Valley Authority* (1936), courts should not actively seek to challenge the decisions of their coordinate branches but rather must wait until such a question has been presented by the litigants. Moreover, when litigants do call into question the constitutionality of a legislative act, judges must first look for some alternative grounds for resolving the case and, barring that, attempt to construe the statute in such a way as to avoid having to strike it down. Of course, judges can and do violate these guidelines. Even so, judges take these admonitions seriously and generally do not actively seek to strike down laws unless asked to do so (Howard and Segal 2004).

As a result of this orientation, judges often look for the most limited ways of solving legal problems and consider only such solutions as are channeled to them through the litigants. By contrast, legislators are not bound by such norms and are free to consider what policies they regard as most sensible, even if those policies constitute major departures from the status quo.

Perhaps not surprisingly, courts tend to make policies only on a step-by-step basis. By limiting themselves to the specific contours of a case, judges select solutions that are short-term in nature. Rulings are established to fit individual cases, and whatever uncertainty remains must be clarified by later litigation. To take one example, the warnings that police are obligated to convey to criminal suspects were articulated quite clearly in *Miranda* vs. *Arizona* (1966). Among other things, those warnings specify that individuals do not have to respond to police questioning once they are taken into custody.

Despite the clarity of that ruling, however, the Supreme Court left undefined what constituted "questioning" and "custody" for the purposes of the *Miranda* decision. Because the *Miranda* Court limited itself purely to the warnings required by the Fifth Amendment, not addressing the definition of their terms, those issues had to be resolved in subsequent cases. Of course, the definition of such terms is a common legislative practice; it reduces ambiguity and allows for a common understanding of the meaning of policy enactments. Surely, judges can foresee the need for clarifying the meaning of a ruling, but the judicial process dictates that those questions be addressed on an individual basis in later cases.

The reason courts tend not to act preemptively is that policy-making through adjudication requires that judges be presented with a genuine legal controversy that plainly presents the issues that judges wish to address. Stated differently, courts do not speak until spoken to. Thus, judges who might have particular policy goals must await an appropriate case in which to craft their policies. A judge who has designs in the area of, say, commercial law or environmental protection, will be unable to advance his or her goals if the cases that judge must decide involve primarily child custody or criminal prosecutions.

Appellate courts can offer greater opportunities in this regard, especially those that have the ability to set their own agenda. Even among judges who can pick and choose their cases, however, some members may be disposed to allow lower courts the chance to find sensible solutions before intervening (Perry 1991). Elected officials, by contrast, need nothing beyond their own initiative to stimulate policy change. They may promote reform whenever they see fit.

Even when a court is presented with a specific case, there is no guarantee that the court will be able to act. Whether a court is capable of providing genuinely meaningful relief in a case—the requirement that a case be "justiciable"—is a serious limit on the actions of courts. A number of different legal threads weave together to make a case justiciable. Concepts such as adverseness, mootness, and standing may sound esoteric to the outsider, but they are critical constraints on what courts can do.

To take one example, in the spring of 2004 many Americans anxiously awaited the Supreme Court's decision as to whether the words "under God" in the Pledge of Allegiance when recited by public schoolchildren constituted a violation of the First Amendment's prohibition against government establishing religion. When the Court's decision was announced, observers learned that the Court did not address this issue at all. Rather, the justices declined to address the merits of this salient legal question. They concluded that, since the father of the girl involved in the legal challenge did not have legal custody of his daughter—her parents had been divorced, and her mother had received custody—the father did not have the legal standing to challenge the Pledge on her behalf.[2] Thus, even when asked, courts cannot be counted upon to answer.

To many, this limitation seems perverse; shouldn't the Court simply go ahead and issue a ruling on the Pledge, especially after having gone to the trouble of having the case argued? To others, it is an important feature of the adjudicatory process that serves to ensure that policy-making is primarily in the hands of elected officials. However it is conceived, a requirement that a court refrain from making a decision until a case is properly presented surely inhibits the capacity of courts to promote policy innovations.

Quite apart from the passive nature of courts, adjudication tends to generate only limited amounts of information upon which to base decisions. When Congress seeks to develop new policies in telecommunications or agriculture or foreign policy, it gathers information, conducts committee hearings, and considers testimony for various affected interests. In fact, this informing function is

---

[2] See *Elkgrove Unified School District* vs. *Newdow* [2004] 542 U.S. 1.

considered to be an implicit part of the legislative power. Judges, though, resolve cases with an eye towards crafting legal solutions that are consistent with their notions of what the law permits or requires. Courts are not supposed to assess the wisdom of policy, only its validity.

Nevertheless, judges are inevitably drawn into considering how their interpretations of the law will affect different segments of society, whether their resolution of a dispute will make sense as a matter of public policy for those who are consumers of their decisions. Although cases are ostensibly disputes between two individual litigants, those litigants, as often as not, are drawn from larger populations that stand to win or lose by a case's outcome. Thus, a decision in a case in which a single corporation is a party may affect an entire industry. A case in which a state is a party may be one which many other states watch with interest, since they are apt to feel the effects of the decision. And so on.

Unlike legislators, however, courts have little capacity to summon additional information to inform their decisions. They must rely instead upon the abstract arguments of law presented by the parties to a case. In some courts, affected interests have the opportunity to inform judges through their participation as *amici curiae* (that is, as "friends of the court"). Again, however, judges have little control over the source or quality of this information. In this respect, they are at a distinct disadvantage relative to elected officials who, as a routine matter, seek to gather as much information and analysis as they deem useful on the impact of various policy alternatives.

Finally, courts differ from other decision-makers in that the judicial process does not provide for regular monitoring and oversight of the policies crafted by judges. Naturally, judges can adjust policies through subsequent litigation, but there is no formal mechanism by which judges can examine the ongoing impact of their policies. That adjudication does not provide such mechanisms means that courts will not learn in a timely way—if indeed they learn at all—that the policies they have put into place may be failing to realize their objectives.

These limitations notwithstanding, judges on both trial and appellate courts are generally quite competent in discharging their responsibilities, and many of their policies clearly produce important, substantive change for various segments of society. A great deal of scholarly work, in fact, demonstrates that courts can be the source of significant innovations in the policy priorities of government (see, e.g., Glick 1991; Rowland and Carp 1996).

For their part, legislative and executive officials are by no means immune from suffering the fate of ineffective or ill-considered policy. Any governmental institution is limited by various handicaps that hamper what they may achieve. As a comparative matter, there are a number of important factors that differentiate legal from political policy-makers, and these factors serve to place somewhat greater limits on the members of the judiciary than they do officials who are popularly chosen.

3   ACTORS IN THE JUDICIAL PROCESS

Judges are the central players in the business of judicial policy-making. They weigh alternatives and craft authoritative rules that affected constituencies are obliged to respect. Because the development of those rules is so contingent upon decisions made by others (decisions about when to go to court, what arguments to present, and the like) any attempt to understand the links between the judicial process and judicial policy-making requires that one consider with special care the role of other actors in the legal system.

Foremost among those are the litigants themselves. Courts, as I have noted, are passive institutions that require genuine legal controversies within which to develop policies. For that reason, the decision to go to court is crucial for creating the opportunities necessary for judges to advance their legal policy goals.

On the one hand, the sheer size of court caseloads at both the federal and state levels suggest that judges are not lacking for legal vehicles in which to develop policy. On the other hand, the evidence also suggests that most potential conflicts tend not to make it before judges. Instead, cases are either settled or never initiated in the first place. In criminal cases, prosecutors and defense attorneys frequently opt to plea bargain (Heumann 1978; Mather 1979), and consequently many of the cases that might otherwise be brought before a judge are resolved by a defendant agreeing to accept a guilty plea in exchange for some form of consideration from the prosecutor.

In the case of civil disputes, much has been made of the tendency for individuals to avail themselves of courts at the slightest provocation. Objective assessments of the flow of litigation, though, suggest that the notion of a litigation crisis is vastly oversold (Galanter 1983; Miller and Sarat 1980–81). The media are largely culpable for stimulating such perceptions; by placing unwarranted reliance upon sensational and unrepresentative cases, the media present a largely perverted picture of the legal system and the courts' policy role in resolving private disputes (Haltom and McCann 2004).

Such perceptions have implications for the policy-making capacity of courts. One of the conditions for effective legal change is that courts enjoy support and acceptance from the public and other governmental officials. So, to the extent that the legal system is perceived as irrational or inefficient, this will impede the implementation of judicial rulings (Canon and Johnson 1999, 33–43; Edwards 1980).

Such distortions aside, many citizens do regard litigation as a kind of right, and as a result they often turn to the courts as a forum for solving their interpersonal conflicts, even as judges are reluctant to consider them (Merry 1990). For the most part, though, the vast majority of individuals who suffer some form of wrong opt not to go to court. Many simply capitulate and accept their losses; far fewer actually complain. Among those who do complain, only a limited number take steps to consult a lawyer, and increasingly there are non-lawyers who work as representatives in some alternative form of dispute resolution (Kritzer 1998). For those who do seek legal counsel, relief is often secured without proceeding to actual litigation. When lawyers (or their functional equivalents) are unable to secure a settlement, it is only then that individuals actually turn to the courts (Miller and Sarat 1980–81). Thus, however large the number of individuals who go to court may be, it is inevitably only a small fraction of the number that could turn to the judicial system.

Knowing which litigants ultimately enter the process of litigation is important, because it is their substantive claims which, taken together, constitute the range of possible policies to which courts can address themselves. As passive policy-makers, judges can speak only to those concerns that are brought to the courthouse door.

If a representative sample of potential legal claims makes its way onto the courts' dockets, then judges will have as broad a set of issues as possible within which to articulate policy. If, on the other hand, there are systematic differences between those who *could* go to court and those who, in fact, *do* go to court, then those differences necessarily limit the available policy options.

Do actual litigants differ from potential litigants? In fact, scholars have known for some time that those who choose to go to court are quite different from those who do not. The universe of would-be litigants consists principally of two groups: large, aggregated interests, such as corporations and governments, that have greater resources, expertise, and access to legal representation, and smaller, more particularized interests, such as individuals and small businesses, that possess fewer resources and less sophistication and experience with the judicial system (Galanter 1974). Because the former are regular participants in the judicial process, they are commonly known as "repeat players." The latter group—the "one-shotters"—are distinctive for their more limited use of litigation.

Although there is obviously variation across courts, the use of the judicial system is favored by larger, wealthier interests. Because of their resources and expertise, the repeat players litigate more often—and win more often—than the one-shotters. This finding seems to hold at different levels of the judicial system (Farole 1999; Songer, Sheehan, and Haire 1999) as well as across different countries. (Dotan 1999; Flemming 2005). To some extent, however, the bias in favor of the repeat player is mediated by the participation of interest groups in the judicial process. Because organized interests constitute one variety of repeat player, the sheer diversity of interests that use litigation ensures that voices from across the socioeconomic spectrum will enjoy the benefits of sophisticated and experienced representation in the courts (Caldeira and Wright 1990). Across a range of countries, organized interests provide these advantages (Brodie 2002; Epp 1998).

This differentiation among litigants is vital to an understanding of judicial policy-making, since lawyers and organized interests provide an important framing function for the disputes that judges consider. Courts serve as a venue for transforming various social, economic, and political problems into broader questions of public policy. This transformation of disputes from limited and bifurcated conflicts into general questions of public policy is a basic function of the courts (Mather and Yngvesson 1981). "Thus, when litigants and lawyers file legal claims and present arguments, they are defining problems and formulating policy alternatives" (Mather 1991, 148).

Given that lawyers and organized interests have a major hand in defining the terms of legal contention, their decisions to go to court mean that legal policy is guided to a substantial degree by larger sets of interests, such as governments, big business, trade and professional associations, and the like. It is these types of litigants who choose to go to court, who lay the foundation for the policies they seek, and trade on their expertise and experience to help shift judicial policy in their direction.

4   LEGAL FOUNDATIONS FOR POLICY

One of the essential conditions for courts to succeed in effecting legal reform is that judges construct an intellectual infrastructure upon which to rest their policy goals, a kind of a network of supporting precedents that will support their ultimate aims. The idea that judge-made law be derived from established principles is a venerated tradition (Cardozo 1921; Levi 1948). If the policy innovations of judges are to succeed, they must be seen as legitimate. Establishing a legal basis in advance of those innovations serves to smooth the way to acceptance and reduce the likelihood of those policies being rejected.

Legal decision-making often relies heavily upon the tradition of the common law, where judges derive legal principles in the absence of promulgated law and apply those principles in later cases. This approach is a critical component for a great deal of judicial policy. To take one example, the supreme courts of the individual American states are under no obligation to follow one another's decisions, at least as far as issues of state law are concerned. Nevertheless, it is clear that appellate judges look to other state supreme courts, especially those that carry the highest reputations for professionalism, for precedents that can be employed to underwrite their own opinions (Caldeira 1985). Likewise, appellate courts at the national level take considerable pains to rely upon the decisions of the US Supreme Court (Songer, Segal, and Cameron 1994). Transnationally, courts likewise look outside their own borders for the guidance and experience of other tribunals.

There seems little doubt that judges use these established principles to help gain acceptance of their policy designs. For that reason, for example, the National Association for the Advancement of Colored People's legal fight against state-imposed segregation took place through a series of small steps over several decades, rather than an all-or-nothing proposition that would have almost certainly failed to produce legal reform (Tushnet 2005). Inevitably, when judges seek to innovate without first laying the intellectual cornerstones for their decisions, their policies will be met with resistance. There are ample illustrations of courts provoking resistance by exceeding their respective legal traditions. In the United States, the Supreme Court accelerated the outbreak of the Civil War by declaring in *Dred Scott* vs. *Sandford* (1857) that slave-ownership was a right over which Congress exercised no authority (Fehrenbacher 2001). In the early twentieth century, rulings that developed and upheld a constitutional liberty of contract, such as *Lochner* vs. *New York* (1905), were considered an affront by many states that had enacted various commercial regulations to protect the health, safety, and welfare of their citizens (Kens 1998). Likewise, the modern conflict over abortion rights is, at least in part, attributable to the Supreme Court making policy in an area (i.e. privacy) whose legal foundations were not well established at the time of the decision in *Roe* vs. *Wade* (1973) (Hull and Hoffer 2001).[3]

5   Systemic Support

As should be evident by now, courts require considerable cooperation and support from other actors as a condition for effective policy-making. Without enforcement power, judges must rely upon actors outside the judicial arena to give force to the edicts emanating from the bench. When courts cultivate the support of outsiders, those who control resources and opportunities can, in turn, offer rewards or impose punishments as a means of bringing about the courts' expected changes. This is a basic condition for effective judicial policy (Rosenberg 1991).

A strong test of this assumption would be to examine the extent of implementation of any salient policy decision on an issue in which the courts are seen as having assumed a major leadership role. No doubt one of the best cases to fit this

---

[3] Time also seems to be a necessary correlate in this process. Taken by itself, simply having a pretense of legal justification can scarcely be sufficient. Indeed, citation to precedent is the most frequently employed method of legal reasoning, regardless of which side of a case an opinion writer happens to support (see, e.g., Gates and Phelps 1996).

category is the elimination of racially segregated public schools in the United States. In 1954, the Supreme Court decided that separating schoolchildren on the basis of race violated the constitutional guarantee of equal protection of the laws. The decision in *Brown* vs. *Board of Education* ought to have produced major shifts in educational practices, especially in the South, where segregation of African-American children was so widely used.

This decision proved to be enormously unpopular among those most affected by it, producing vocal protests and, in the extreme, calls for the removal of Earl Warren, the chief justice under whom the decision was issued. Local officials in these areas were generally unsupportive and resisted, quite strenuously, any suggestion that their public schools should be integrated. Especially affected were the federal judges in the South—judges who lived and worked in close proximity to the longstanding practice of segregation—who were charged with overseeing the process of desegregation; those whose courts were located in the school districts they supervised were quite lax in bringing about implementation (Giles and Walker 1975).

The resistance from these officials was emblematic of a more general opposition. With little support—and no means by which to compel compliance—the Supreme Court faced widespread and sustained refusal to put its policy into effect. Segregation simply continued. "Statistics from the Southern states are truly amazing," writes Gerald Rosenberg. "For ten years, 1954–64, virtually nothing happened. Ten years after *Brown* only 1.2 percent of black schoolchildren in the South attended school with whites" (Rosenberg 1991, 52).

Beginning in 1964, however, compliance with the Court suddenly began to take place at a stunning rate. What had to be satisfied was one of the conditions for judicial efficacy; Congress, opting for the stick rather than the carrot, enacted the Civil Rights Act of 1964, which withdrew federal educational funds from school districts that discriminated on the basis of race. Faced with the loss of substantial moneys, public schools in the South quickly fell into line. Thus, the Court required the coordinated efforts of both Congress and the president to provide the support necessary to produce the policy changes that the Court demanded.

In the absence of the sword or the purse—that is, the absence of support from elsewhere within the political system—change will likely not occur if that change generates widely shared opposition. Research on reactions to the Supreme Court's early rulings outlawing devotional activities and Bible readings in public schools were widely disobeyed in the American South (Dolbeare and Hammond 1971; Way 1968). More recent analysis shows that a variety of outlawed religious practices still remain within Southern schools, often at surprisingly high levels (McGuire 2005).

Just as legislative bodies can oppose judicially-mandated change, so too can executive officials. Law enforcement in the United States has long sought to circumvent the Supreme Court's *Miranda* decision, which requires police to inform suspects who are in custody that they do not have to incriminate themselves. While adhering to the letter of the Court's ruling, police have found creative mechanisms for convincing suspects to disregard their Fifth Amendment privilege, and judges sympathetic to the goals of law enforcement have, for their part, likewise sought to undercut the policy's effectiveness (White 2003). In the absence of other institutions to give force to the warnings requirement, police have been successful in muting the influence of judicial policy.

Of course, when judicial policy is directed at those institutions to whom courts must typically turn for support, it is not surprising that they encounter resistance. Coordinate branches of government have interests of their own, and when adjudication arises over the extent of their powers, the political branches can balk at the prospect of judicial encroachment on their authority.

Under such conditions, one option for the political branches is simply to refuse to recognize that they are bound by judicial policy. For example, the decision of the US Supreme Court to invalidate the legislative veto demonstrates how such policy can fail to be effective. The case of *Immigration and Naturalization Service* vs. *Chadha* (1983)—a seemingly innocuous issue of deportation of an alien whose visa had expired—tested the ability of Congress to monitor and override the implementation of the law by the executive branch. The Supreme Court held that this mechanism violated the separation of powers by permitting Congress to make policy (i.e. to legislate) without presenting that policy to the president for approval.

The decision was regarded as sweeping in its scope, inasmuch as it called into question more federal laws than the combined total of all previously invalidated congressional enactments. Because the legislative veto was so useful a tool by which Congress could monitor the implementation of its policies, however, it was greeted largely with indifference by legislators. Indeed, Congress continued to incorporate this device into a great deal of subsequent legislation (Korn 1996). Any challenge to the prerogatives of those upon whom judges rely for implementation support is prone to be ineffective.

Of course, judges no doubt anticipate such reactions and often trim their sails accordingly. Some of this strategic behavior is conditioned by institutional factors; in England, to take one illustration, the tradition of parliamentary supremacy has limited the independence of British judges (Stevens 2001). Other institutional factors relate to the substantive powers with which different branches are entrusted. In the area of foreign affairs, for example, courts are typically loathe to question the decisions of elected officials, even when those actions might be constitutionally questionable (see, e.g., Fisher 2004). In other instances, courts recognize that their policies will likely be challenged—at the extreme, reversed by new legislation—and they opt strategically for preserving their legitimacy over imposing ineffective policy (Ferejohn and Weingast 1992). High national courts in various countries, such as Germany and Argentina, are also forward-looking and thus will often opt for something other than their preferred policies as a means of preserving or strengthening their authority over the long term (Helmke 2002; Vanberg 2001).

Similarly, judges in young Asian democracies have also had to come to terms with elected officials. One interesting case occurred in Malaysia in the mid-1980s, where, after a series of decisions that questioned various powers of elected officials, the government sought to remove a number of judges who were regarded as threats to its authority. Knowing that challenging the actions of elected representatives might result in removal from office, "the Malaysian judiciary is a more cautious institution" (Ginsburg 2003, 80).

In the United States, as well, decisions that conflict with the preferences of lawmakers and outside interests will generate efforts to undo the rulings of the Supreme Court (Meernik and Ignagni 1997). Accordingly, the justices have sought to avoid congressional overrides of their interpretations of statutes by taking such considerations into account when formulating their policies (Eskridge 1991). Alternatively, when the Court concludes that it is constrained by existing law to make decisions that will provoke public displeasure, it will often openly invite lawmakers to overturn their policies (Hausegger and Baum 1999).

Examples such as these illustrate the courts' acute awareness of the need for systemic support. Knowing that their policies demand acceptance and support, judges will strive to produce policy that will, in the long run, help to guarantee their effectiveness by sacrificing short-term gains. Stated differently, courts trade what they expect will be largely symbolic policies for a sustained level of efficacy.

6   Conclusions

Like any set of institutions, courts have a limited degree of policy-making capacity. The political system provides a variety of restrictions that circumscribe their authority. As agents of the legal system, however, courts encounter unique forces that intervene to curb their influence. Among other things, bifurcated disputes tend to limit the terms of policy debate as well as the range of options that judges may consider. Moreover, these options are typically not presented by a representative sample of interests but rather are skewed in favor of advantaged social, economic, and political interests. In addition, because judges make policy within the context of legal conflicts, the various technical criteria that govern how cases may be brought, when, and by whom insert an additional layer of complexity into the process of judicial policy-making.

All this makes judges highly dependent upon other institutions to put their decisions into effect. The various conditions for policy efficacy combine with the absence of enforcement power to require judges to rely in a special way upon other governmental actors to carry out their wishes. In order to cultivate their support, judges must take care to develop a solid legal foundation for any serious form of legal change, lest they lose the valuable political capital upon which they rely for their legitimacy.

There seems little doubt that these constraints genuinely operate on the courts. The limited effectiveness of legal reform that is frequently seen can be traced, in one way or another, to a failure to meet the problematic conditions for efficacy. Across different courts, different countries, and different policy domains, judges discover that they frequently face disregard for their judgments.

It is tempting to interpret such resistance as a sign of judicial impotence. One must bear in mind, however, that to a great degree interinstitutional resistance is endemic to any system of divided authority. Governments that adhere more strongly to notions of separation of powers, however, are more likely to generate friction between the branches. Courts may, perhaps, enjoy less effectiveness in their policy-making, but this is really a difference of degree rather than kind. After all, presidents, prime ministers, and other executives are unable to guarantee consistent support for their agendas. Likewise, legislative decision-makers routinely demonstrate greater attentiveness to the needs of advantaged interests whose resources have always helped to ensure greater access. The limitations of policy-making are scarcely unique to the judiciary.

In addition, the limitations that judges face as they make decisions should not be overstated. Despite their constraints, courts can still monitor the development of the law over a series of cases; they often have access to a good deal of policy information; and even policies that produce discord inside and outside of government can enjoy a high degree of respect. Indeed, recent evidence suggest that the role of courts around the world is actually expanding, with judges assuming an ever increasing scope of influence (see, e.g., Stone Sweet 2000; Tate and Vallinder 1995).

The future holds remarkable promise for our understanding of judges and judicial policy-making. As courts continue to expand their influence in individual countries, scholars will need to focus more attention on law and courts. Moreover, the increased importance of the expanding European Union will necessarily mean that transnational courts, such as the European Court of Justice and the European Court of Human Rights, will become increasingly involved in managing the domestic and foreign policies of member nations. At the same time, students of the courts will need to think with particular care about the best methods for studying judicial policy-making. For courts that have only recently begun to take on greater visibility, quantitatively-oriented scholars may be hampered by a relatively small number of observations. More traditional scholars will face difficulties in defining important concepts, such as judicial independence, that

will make sense across a range of countries with different institutional arrangements. Where courts are relatively recent political players, it will also take some
time before we can speak with confidence about the long-term impact of courts.

Whatever their level of effectiveness, courts will always bear careful scrutiny
because they are both political and legal institutions. The substance of their
policies—which so often resemble the issues taken up by elected officials—may
shade this fact. Still, understanding the rules and norms that uniquely govern the
judicial process is essential if one is to make sense of what courts can and cannot
reasonably accomplish.

REFERENCES

BOND, J. R. and JOHNSON, C. A. 1982. Implementing a permissive policy: hospital abortion
services after Roe v. Wade. *American Journal of Political Science,* 26: 1–24.

BRODIE, I. 2002. *Friends of the Court: The Privileging of Interest Group Litigants in Canada.*
Albany: State University of New York Press.

CALDEIRA, G. A. 1985. The transmission of legal precedent: a study of state supreme courts.
American Political Science Review, 79: 178–93.

—— and WRIGHT, J. R. 1990. Amici Curiae before the Supreme Court: who participates,
when, and how much? *Journal of Politics,* 52: 782–806.

CANON, B. C. and JOHNSON, C. A. 1999. *Judicial Policies: Implementation and Impact.*
Washington, DC: Congressional Quarterly.

CARDOZO, B. N. 1921. *The Nature of the Judicial Process.* New Haven, Conn.: Yale University
Press.

DAHL, R. A. 1957. Decision-making in a democracy: the Supreme Court as a national policy-
maker. *Journal of Public Law,* 6: 279–95.

DOLBEARE, K. M., and HAMMOND, P. E. 1971. *The School Prayer Decisions: From Court Policy
to Local Practice.* Chicago: University of Chicago Press.

DOTAN, Y. 1999. Do the "Haves" still come out ahead? Resource inequalities in ideological
courts: the case of the Israeli High Court of Justice. *Law and Society Review,* 33: 1059–80.

DREWRY, G. 1993. Judicial politics in Britain: patrolling the boundaries. In *Judicial Politics
and Policy-Making in Western Europe,* ed. M. L. Volcansek. London: Frank Cass.

EDWARDS, G. C. 1980. *Implementing Public Policy.* Washington, DC: Congressional Quarterly.

EPP, C. R. 1998. *The Rights Revolution: Lawyers, Activists, and Supreme Courts in Comparative Perspective.* Chicago: University of Chicago Press.

ESKRIDGE, W. N., JR. 1991. Reneging on history? Playing the Court/Congress/President civil
rights game. *California Law Review,* 79: 613–84.

FAROLE, D. J., JR. 1999. Reexamining litigant success in state supreme courts. *Law & Society
Review,* 33: 1043–58.

FEHRENBACHER, D. E. 2001. *Dred Scott Case: Its Significance in American Law and Politics.*
New York: Oxford University Press.

FEREJOHN, J. and WEINGAST, B. 1992. A positive theory of statutory interpretation.
International Review of Law and Economics, 12: 263–79.

FISHER, L. 2004. *Presidential War Power*, 2nd edn. Lawrence: University Press of Kansas.

FLEMMING, R. B. 2005. *Tournament of Appeals: Granting Judicial Review in Canada*. Vancouver: University of British Columbia Press.

GALANTER, M. 1974. Why the "Haves" come out ahead: speculations on the limits of legal change. *Law & Society Review*, 9: 95–160.

—— 1983. Reading the landscape of disputes: what we know and don't know (and think we know) about our allegedly contentious and litigious society. *UCLA Law Review*, 31: 4–72.

GATES, J. B. and PHELPS, G. A. 1996. Intentionalism in constitutional opinions. *Political Research Quarterly*, 49: 245–62.

GILES, M. W. and WALKER, T. G. 1975. Judicial policy-making and Southern school segregation. *Journal of Politics*, 37: 917–36.

GINSBURG, T. 2003. *Judicial Review in New Democracies: Constitutional Courts in Asian Cases*. Cambridge: Cambridge University Press.

GLICK, H. R. 1991. Policy making in state supreme courts. In *The American Courts: A Critical Assessment*, ed. J. B. Gates and C. A. Johnson. Washington, DC: Congressional Quarterly.

—— and EMMERT, C. F. 1987. Selection systems and judicial characteristics. *Judicature*, 70: 228–35.

GRIFFITH, J. A. G. 1991. *The Politics of the Judiciary*, 4th edn. London: Fontana.

HALL, M. G. 1992. Electoral politics and strategic voting in state supreme courts. *Journal of Politics*, 54: 427–46.

HALTOM, W. and MCCANN, M. 2004. *Distorting the Law: Politics, Media, and the Litigation Crisis*. Chicago: University of Chicago Press.

HAUSEGGER, L. and BAUM, L. 1999. Inviting congressional action: a study of Supreme Court motivations in statutory interpretation. *American Journal of Political Science*, 43: 162–85.

HELMKE, G. 2002. The logic of strategic defection: court–executive relations in Argentina under dictatorship and democracy. *American Political Science Review*, 96: 291–303.

HEUMANN, M. 1978. *Plea Bargaining: The Experiences of Prosecutors, Judges, and Defense Attorneys*. Chicago: University of Chicago Press.

HOROWITZ, D. L. 1977. *The Courts and Social Policy*. Washington, DC: Brookings Institution.

HOWARD, R. M. and SEGAL, J. A. 2004. A preference for deference? The Supreme Court and judicial review. *Political Research Quarterly*, 57: 131–43.

HULL, N. E. H. and HOFFER, P. C. 2001. *Roe v. Wade: The Abortion Rights Controversy in American History*. Lawrence: University Press of Kansas.

KENS, P. 1998. *Lochner v. New York: Economic Regulation on Trial*. Lawrence: University Press of Kansas.

KLEIN, D. and BAUM, L. 2001. Ballot information and voting decisions in judicial elections. *Political Research Quarterly*, 54: 709–28.

KORN, J. 1996. *The Power of Separation: American Constitutionalism and the Myth of the Legislative Veto*. Princeton, NJ: Princeton University Press.

KRITZER, H. M. 1996. Courts, justice, and politics in England. In *Courts, Law & Politics in Comparative Perspective*, ed. H. Jacob, E. Blankenburg, H. M. Kritzer, D. M. Provine, and J. Sanders. New Haven, Conn.: Yale University Press.

—— 1998. *Legal Advocacy: Lawyers and Nonlawyers at Work*. Ann Arbor: University of Michigan Press.

Levi, E. H. 1948. *An Introduction to Legal Reasoning.* Chicago: University of Chicago Press.

McGuire, K. T. 2005. Schools, religious establishments, and the U.S. Supreme Court: an examination of policy compliance. Paper presented at the Annual Meeting of the Midwest Political Science Association.

—— and Stimson, J. A. 2004. The least dangerous branch revisited: new evidence on Supreme Court responsiveness to public preferences. *Journal of Politics,* 66: 1018–35.

Mather, L. 1979. *Plea Bargaining or Trial? The Process of Criminal-Case Disposition.* Lexington, Mass.: Lexington Books.

—— 1991. Policy making in state trial courts. In *American Courts: A Critical Assesment,* ed. J. B. Gates and C. A. Johnson. Washington, DC: Congressional Quarterly.

—— and Yngvesson, B. 1981. Language, audience, and the transformation of disputes. *Law & Society Review,* 15: 775–821.

Meernik, J. and Ignagni, J. 1997. Judicial review and coordinate construction of the constitution. *American Journal of Political Science,* 41: 447–67.

Merry, S. E. 1990. *Getting Justice and Getting Even: Legal Consciousness among Working-Class Americans.* Chicago: University of Chicago Press.

Miller, R. E. and Sarat, A. 1980–81. Grievances, claims, and disputes: assessing the adversary culture. *Law & Society Review,* 15: 525–65.

Mishler, W. and Sheehan, R. S. 1996. Public opinion, the attitudinal model, and Supreme Court decision making: a micro-analytic perspective. *Journal of Politics,* 58 (1): 169–200.

Murphy, W. F. 1964. *Elements of Judicial Strategy.* Chicago: University of Chicago Press.

Perry, H. W., Jr. 1991. *Deciding to Decide: Agenda Setting on the United States Supreme Court.* Cambridge, Mass.: Harvard University Press.

Rowland, C. K., and R. A. Carp. 1996. *Politics and Judgment in Federal District Courts.* Lawrence: University Press of Kansas.

Rosenberg, G. N. 1991. *The Hollow Hope: Can Courts Bring About Social Change?* Chicago: University of Chicago Press.

Segal, J. A. 1988. Amicus Curiae briefs by the solicitor general during the Warren and Burger Courts. *Western Political Quarterly,* 41: 135–44.

Songer, D. R., Segal, J., A., and Cameron, C. M. 1994. The hierarchy of justice: testing a principal–agent model of Supreme Court–circuit court interactions. *American Journal of Political Science,* 38: 673–96.

—— Sheehan, R. S., and Haire, S. B. 1999. Do the "haves" come out ahead over time? Applying Galanter's framework to the decisions of the U.S. Courts of Appeals, 1925–1988. *Law & Society Review,* 33: 811–32.

Stevens, R. 2001. Judicial independence in England: a loss of innocence. In *Judicial Independence in the Age of Democracy,* ed. P. H. Russell and D. M. O'Brien. Charlottesville: University Press of Virginia.

Stone Sweet, A. 1994. Constitutional politics in France and Germany. In *On Law, Politics, and Judicialization,* ed. M. Shapiro and A. Stone Sweet. New York: Oxford University Press.

—— 2000. *Governing with Judges.* New York: Oxford University Press.

Tate, C. N. and Vallinder, T. 1995. *The Global Expansion of Judicial Power.* New York: New York University Press.

TUSHNET, M. V. 2005. *NAACP's Legal Strategy against Segregated Education, 1925–1950.* Chapel Hill: University of North Carolina Press.

VANBERG, G. 2001. Legislative–judicial relations: a game-theoretic approach to constitutional review. *American Journal of Political Science,* 45: 346–61.

WAY, H. F., JR. 1968. Research on judicial decisions: the prayer and Bible reading cases. *Western Political Quarterly,* 21: 189–205.

WHITE, W. S. 2003. *Miranda's Waning Protections: Police Interrogation Practices after Dickerson.* Ann Arbor: University of Michigan Press.

Cases

Ashwander vs. *Tennessee Valley Authority* [1936]. 297 U.S. 288.

Brown vs. *Board of Education* [1954]. 347 U.S. 483.

Dred Scott vs. *Sandford* [1857]. 19 How. 393.

Elkgrove Unified School District vs. *Newdow* [2004]. 542 U.S. 1.

Immigration and Naturalization Service vs. *Chadha* [1983]. 462 U.S. 919.

Lochner vs. *New York* [1905]. 198 U.S. 45.

Miranda vs. *Arizona* [1966]. 384 U.S. 436.

POLITICAL PARTIES IN AND OUT OF LEGISLATURES

JOHN H. ALDRICH

Richard Fenno explained his career-long devotion to the study of the US Congress by saying that Congress is where democracy happens (pers. comm.). It is, metaphorically, the crossroads of democracy, where the public and politician, the lobbyist and petitioner meet. If legislatures are where democracy most visibly happens, political parties are the institutions that let us see *how* it happens. It may not be true that parties are literally necessary conditions for democracy to exist as Schattschneider (1942) famously wrote, but their ubiquity suggests that they are virtually, if not actually, a necessity for a democracy to be viable.

Political parties—in and out of legislatures—are the subjects of this chapter. As the chapter title suggests, we are to look at parties specifically here, but we cannot fully decouple parties from electoral systems (nor from other aspects of political institutions), and in particular from the virtually co-companion of electoral systems, party systems, nor can we decouple that from the study of parties as institutions. But we shall cover those extraordinarily rich literatures only to aid our focus on the specific questions considered here: how political parties mediate and integrate the goals and aspirations of the citizens with the often quite different goals and aspirations of politicians, and how these together shape policies adopted by government.

1   POLITICAL PARTIES AS INSTITUTIONS

The greatest scholar of twentieth-century American politics, V. O. Key Jr. (1964), led us to understand the American political party as organized around its three core activities. The party-in-the-electorate was the party of the campaign, the creation of the party's image and reputation in the public's mind, and the way the public used those sources as informational short-cuts and decision-making devices or aides. One of these "informational shortcuts" stands out as particularly important, creating a special role for political parties. Durable political parties develop long-term reputations that the personalities of particular politicians or variable agendas of policy concerns are generally unable to provide. While many things can go into these long-term reputations, the most important are the policy-based performances that create a partisan reputation and ideology. The party-in-government is the party that organizes the legislature and coordinates actions across the various institutions of national government, horizontally, and, for systems with vertical divisions of power, across the federal structures (Hofstadter 1969; Cox and McCubbins 1993; Haggard and McCubbins 2000). The party-as-organization is the party of its activists, resources, and campaign specialists; that is, those who negotiate between the public and government, sometimes rather invisibly, sometimes quite visibly, sometimes autonomously from the party-in-government, but often times as its external extension (Cotter, Gibson, Bibby, and Huckshorn 1984; Herrnson 1988; Kitschelt 1989, 1999). This three-part structure applies to and certainly helps structure our thinking about political parties in all democracies, even if Key primarily writes about American politics.

Second, political parties differ from many other political institutions covered in this volume by virtue of being created, most often, external to the constitutional and, in some cases, developed largely external even to the legal order, per se. It is, for example, commonplace to note that the first parties, those in late eighteenth-century America (Hofstadter 1969; or early nineteenth-century America, depending upon one's point of view (e.g. Formisano 1981)), arose in spite of the wishes of their very founders and were unanticipated in writing the Constitution and early laws. Instead, political parties are organizations that are created by political actors themselves, whether emanating from the public (as, for instance in social movements that turn to electoral politics, such as social democratic parties: Lipset and Rokkan 1987; Przeworksi and Spraque 1986; and green parties, e.g. Kitschelt 1989) or, quite commonly, from the actions of current or hopeful political elites. The key point here is that, relative to most political institutions, political parties are shaped as institutions by political actors, often in the same timeframe and by the actions of the same figures who are shaping legislation or other political outcomes. They are, that is, unusually "endogenous" institutions, and we therefore must keep in mind that the party institutions (or at least organizations) can be changed with greater rapidity and ease than virtually any other political organization (Riker 1980; Aldrich 1995). To pick one simple example of the power of thinking about endogenous parties, consider the case of third parties in America. To be sure, there are the Duvergerian forces at work (1954; Cox 1997). But that explanation is only why two parties persist, not why the Democrat and Republican parties persist. The answer to the latter question is that they act in duopoly fashion so as to write rules that make entry and persistence by any contender to replace one or the other as a major party all but untenable (e.g. Rosenstone, Behr, and Lazarus 1996). Thus, the makeup of the party system is endogenously determined by the actors already in it. Indeed, the creation of the majority electoral system itself was the consequence of endogenous choice by partisan politicians in the USA (see Aldrich 1995).

2   PARTY SYSTEMS

Most of this chapter looks at the makeup of and/or actions taken in the name of the political party. It is, in that sense, a microscopic look inside the typical party. No democracy, however, has only one party. When there are two or more parties in competition over the same things—control over offices, over legislation, or over whatever—we should expect that each party will be shaped in part by its relationship to the other parties. How these parties form a system will not be assessed here, but we cannot look at the party in and out of the legislature without at least addressing two points.

The first is that a political system is not truly democratic unless its elections are genuinely competitive. Competition, in turn, does not exist without at least two parties with reasonable chances of electoral success. It is often thought that a fledgling democracy has not completed its transformation until there has been a free and competitive election that has peacefully replaced the incumbent party with one (or more) other parties. This happened, for example, in both Mexico and Taiwan in 2000, when erstwhile authoritarian one-party states transformed themselves into competitive democracies, and, in their respective elections, the erstwhile authoritarian party was voted out of office and peacefully surrendered power. Note that in Mexico, the long-reigning PRI had allowed the PAN to compete earlier, but did not allow free and open elections by virtue of restricting opposition-party access to the media before the 2000 election. This changed in 2000 and the PAN candidate, Vicente Fox, was elected president, marking the full democratic transition (see Aldrich, Magaloni, and Zechmeister 2005; Magaloni 2006).

Second, it could fairly be said that the central means of political representation is the political party. To be sure, individuals can be agents of representation as well, whether the chief executive or the individual legislator. But it is the political party that most systematically and durably represents the public in government. But representation is a relative thing, and as such it is a property of the party system, even more than it is a property of an individual or a single party. Thus, the question voters ask is not "how well does this party represent me, absolutely?" It is only relative both to the agenda that comes before the assembly and relative to the alternative or alternatives offered. Thus, it is rather more helpful to think of whether a member of party A voted (acted, spoke, etc.) more like any given constituent than did a member of party B, C, and so on.

The US Congress is often seen as exceptional. It is special by virtue of the nearly unique concatenation of having a two-party system with single-member districts and no formal party discipline. A two-party system exaggerates the limited range of feasible representation, compared to the more numerous choices faced in multiparty systems. Of all the myriad combinations of policy choices (let alone other matters of representation), the voters really have but two in front of them, and they grow accustomed to trying to decide which is the better choice—or, often, which is the "lesser of two evils." This is shared with most other Anglo-American democracies, among others (Lijphart 1984, 1999; Chhibber and Kollman 2004). Still, the range of choices is limited even in a multiparty system, and voters must decide which of this range is the best available, rather than search for the absolute best imaginable choice. The lack of formal party discipline means, on the one hand, that a party chosen to be representative may be sufficiently ineffective as to be able to enact its platform. On the other hand, the individual representative is often best understood, in the words of Gary Jacobson (2004), as responsive to the wishes of their constituents, but not responsible for outcomes. Limited choice and limited accountability tends to weaken if not undermine representation, perhaps uniquely in the USA.

Two-party parliaments with high party discipline can be more accountable. They are, however, just as limited to two effective options to present to the public. In some senses, the ability of the individual member of Congress to differentiate herself from her party provides the voters with a stronger sense of the range of feasible options in the USA than tends to be articulated in, say, England. But even there, there is growing attenuation of party discipline, and to that limited degree, two-party parliaments are at least slightly more like the USA—showing a marginal increase in the range of policy options coupled with a marginal decline in accountability.

Multiparty parliaments are often seen as much more representative bodies, especially so as the electoral rules are increasingly close approximations to purely proportional, and the resulting relatively high number of effective parties provides a closer approximation to representation of the various interests in society. That is, these systems are better at re-presenting the voices and preferences of the public inside the legislature. But this contrast between the two- and multiparty system should not be pushed too far, for two reasons.

First, while there may be many parties, their distribution of seats is often quite asymmetric (Laver and Budge 1992). Take Israel, for example (see, e.g., Aldrich, Blais, Indridiason, and Levine 2005; Blais, Aldrich, Indridiasan, and Levine forthcoming). As one of the more nearly proportional party systems (a single, nationwide district with low threshold for representation of 1.5 percent of the vote, soon to increase to 2 percent), it generally offers many choices to its voters, with a good fraction of them holding seats after the election. Thus, they are particularly strong in representing a relatively large fraction of the electoral views within the Knesset. Still, until Prime Minister Sharon broke with Likud while actually in office, Labor and Likud were invariably the two largest parties. One or both still is invariably in the government, meeting that their voice is heard where policy is really made (for theoretical views, see Laver and Shepsle 1996; Laver and Schofield 1990). And, of course, the strongest voice of all, the prime minister, always comes only from a major party, which in Israel's case was one of these two until very recently. Thus, "voice" and influence/power are quite differently distributed. Israel is far from unique in this regard. Governments are very far from random samples of members of the legislature, and prime ministers are not drawn as a simple random sample from the names of all legislators. This asymmetry in voice is in some sense parallel to the asymmetry in majoritarian electoral systems that results from the disproportionate translation of votes into seats in the two-party cases.

If there is asymmetry of one kind or another in both types of electoral systems, there is also a sort of accountability problem in multiparty systems, perhaps a stronger accountability problem than found in two-party systems. Take the case of Israel, again. In their election of 2003, everyone knew who would "win" the election (and where everyone understands that "winning the election" is quite different from merely winning a seat and thus a voice even in a multiparty parliament). It was clear from the outset that Likud would win and that their leader, Ariel Sharon, would become the prime minister. What was a mystery was what sort of government he would be able to form. Public discussion of alternative governments was commonplace in that campaign. Voters could—and some did—have preferences among the various coalitions that might form, and could—and some did—even condition their vote on those preferences over coalition governments rather than parties (Blais, Aldrich, Indridiason, and Levine forthcoming). But, the break in accountability is that there is little Sharon could do to bind himself to any promise about what sort of government would form and thus the range of policies he would make as prime minister. Therefore, voters could not really hold Likud or anyone else accountable on those grounds. In the event, the most popular coalition in the public view was rejected by Labor, and Sharon successfully formed a governing coalition consisting of an entirely different coalition than the ones considered in the campaign. There are no data about public preferences on this coalition, because no survey researcher imagined including it as a possible coalition, but it is reasonable to assume that it probably would have proved unpopular had it been considered in and by the public. The central lesson of this example is that accountability suffers dramatically. Post-election circumstances might, at least on occasion, force the selection of someone to be prime minister who deviates sharply from public opinion and perhaps even from the basis of voters' decisions. Even more commonly, negotiations over coalition governments might well force the outcome to be a government—and consequent set of policies—that differs sharply from the choices and preferences of the public.

In sum, both two- and multiparty systems generate problems over representation. This is true in terms of representation in two senses. It is true in interest articulation. That is, even the purest PR systems fail to create legislatures that mirror the preferences of the public, and this bias is systematic rather than random. It is also true in terms of accountability. Voters who wanted a Labor–Likud coalition in national unity could hardly hold Sharon and Likud, as winners of the election, accountable for Labor's refusal (announced during the campaign) to agree to enter any such coalition. And as it happens, they could not easily hold them accountable for the failure of his first coalition government, since it was replaced early in the electoral cycle. If there is going to be any voting on the basis of accountability (a.k.a. retrospective voting), it presumably will be based in the next election on the second, the lasting, and the more recent coalition.

In both two-party and multiparty coalition cases, then, the question is who or what can be held responsible? In the extreme US case, voters can basically hold their representatives accountable for failures to be responsive to their wishes, but not for failure to be responsible for the outcomes. In other two-party systems, voters can hold the majority party accountable, but typically only for failure to achieve a set of policies that the voters might have thought was not very close to their views in the first place. In the general multiparty case, one might hold a Sharon and Likud responsible (and if so, perhaps realistically, could turn to Labor as, in this case, the only responsible alternative), but who or what else? The party you voted for? The parties in the government?

In sum, the study of political parties necessarily entails two central aspects of the national party system, regardless of how focused one may be on the internal workings of a particular political party. First, the famous Schattschneiderian position on partisan necessity for democracy does not mean that it is this or that party that is necessary. Rather, it means that there must be a system of parties, and that every party forming or being in the government has to be at reasonable risk of electoral defeat in the next election. And for that to be true, there has to be a system of two or more parties. Second, it is equally true that representation requires not just a desirable option in the election for any particular citizen to choose. Rather, representation requires comparison between or among options, and thus also requires there to be a party system. Further, representation entails not only choices for the citizens as to how best to articulate their desires in government; it also requires the ability of the citizenry to hold the successful parties accountable for their actions in the government. The argument here is that both aspects of representation, first, require a party system, and, second, are not as different across the various types of party systems, two- or multiparty systems with greater or lesser degrees of party discipline, as often assumed. Indeed, in some ways, the account-ability problem—how the public can try to ensure that their preferred choices really do represent them in government and in policy-making and not just on the campaign trail and in the manner needed to win votes—is greater in multiparty than in two-party systems.

3   THE PARTY OUTSIDE THE LEGISLATURE

In this and the following section, we consider the two major arenas of action for the political party. In this section, we look at the party as it is perceived by the public and as it thus helps the public negotiate the political process, make electorally relevant assessments, and take actions, particularly with respect to the turnout and vote decisions. In the next section, we examine the party as it operates in the legislative arena.

As was true above, so it is true here that a good place to start is with V. O. Key, Jr. In his magisterial account of *Southern Politics in State and Nation* (1949), he made the relevant comparison. Imagine the workings of a democracy with an established party system in comparison to the workings of a democracy without such a system. In this he was aided by the unique "natural experiment" of the embedding of a putative democracy in the American South, but one that had no party system throughout the sixty years of the "Jim Crow" system that Key was studying (that is the laws and practices that excluded blacks and poor whites from politics). The Jim Crow South was, however, also set within a functioning democracy with an established, durable two-party system at the national level. While this "natural experiment" happened to be found in the USA, he offers no reason, nor can I think of one fifty years later (Aldrich 2000), that makes his contrast less than fully general. The result of the experiment was clear, clean, and simple to convey. Politics was a perfectly reasonable real-world approximation of democracy as imagined in theory when found within an established and durable party system. Politics was extraordinarily undemocratic in the South, that is, it was undemocratic when not embedded in a competitive and durable party system, and Key was scathing in his description of the choices, such as they were, confronting voters.

The question of this section, then, is what role does the party play in furthering electoral democracy? Of the myriad aspects of parties-in-the-electorate, the core questions are "What does the party mean to potential and actual voters?" and "How does that meaning help shape their political decisions?" Here, I therefore address that core pair of questions.

The first question opens an apparent case of American exceptionalism, in that the theoretical understandings of party identification developed in the context of American survey research, are distinct and possibly theoretically unique to the USA. I suggest here that such a conclusion may be premature. The claim is that, if we can parse out the contemporaneous context of *voting* for, rather than assessing of, political parties, we may find beliefs akin to American party identification.

Campbell, Converse, Miller, and Stokes' classic accounts (1960, 1966) conceived party identification as an early-formed, durable, affectively-based loyalty to a political party. Their data showed that this conception was consistent with the beliefs and attitudes of a substantial majority in the American electorate, both in the 1950s and 1960s as they developed their theory, and again in recent years, as the (actually rather modest) attenuation of partisanship in the 1970s resurged to roughly the earlier levels (Bartels 2000). The key point was that this notion of partisan identification was relevant for understanding how ordinary citizens, with typically marginal interest in politics, were able to negotiate the complicated political world. This affect-centered view held that most people began with a bias in favor of their favored party (childhood socialization), they tend to hear things in a way biased toward their party (selective perception), and they are likely to further that bias even more by consuming information from sources that are themselves in favor of the citizen's preferred party (selective attention). Thus reinforced, partisan loyalty means that it is hard to change the minds of supporters of the opposing party, more so than it is to win over independents and apolitical citizens. In turn, it is harder to woo the uncommitted than to cement those already predisposed in one's favor.

An alternative view is due to Downs (1957), Key (1966), and Fiorina (1981). This view is of a more cognitively-based assessment. It assumes that voting and the partisanship that underlies those vote choices are based on assessments of outcomes, looking at past performance by partisan office holders to understand choices between partisan leaders for offices in the current election. The cognitive component to partisanship assesses how well or poorly politically induced outcomes—especially over economic and foreign affairs—have been under the management of one party compared to the other(s). Thus, unlike the affective account, partisanship is responsive to political events.

One might expect that these two contrasting views would be relatively easily distinguishable. Fiorina (1981) and Achen (1992) demonstrate, however, that both produce very similar empirical predictions. As a result, debate over these two understandings remains an active part of the contemporaneous research agenda within American politics (see especially Erikson, MacKuen, and Stimson 2002; Green, Palmquist, and Schickler 2002).

And, while the above two theories are often characterized as social-psychological vs. economic-rational views of politics, there is a third stream of research that looks at one large class of the uses to which partisanship (of whichever stripe) is put. While implicit in Campbell, Converse, Miller, and Stokes' (1960) account, it was Key (1966) again who first developed the notion of partisanship as a "standing decision." More recently, drawing from the "cognitive miser" approach in social psychology, scholars argued for the ability of extant partisanship to function as an aid in decision-making, reducing the costs of information processing and making of assessments in a complex world, and thus to serve variously as a schema, heuristic, or other decision-making short-cut. In the more economic and rational choice camps, scholars argued for, well, what is essentially the same thing. Popkin (1994) popularized this view for rationally negotiating the political world in general in what he called "gut-level rationality" (see Lupia and McCubbins 1998, for more formal development). Hinich and Munger (1994) put the idea of partisanship on ideological grounds, especially by looking at ideology as an informational short-cut, and developing scaling and related technologies to measure how partisan stances on ideology can operate much like the heuristics of the social-cognitive psychologist. In this, they were developing the ideas presented by Downs (1957) in which he argued that the political party was important by virtue of being consistent over time and therefore in aiding voters who are motivated to acquire information only incidentally. As a result, parties had incentives induced by voters to be consistent and moderately divergent on major dimensions of choice. Hinich and Munger (1994) developed the technology to make all of that estimable and to incorporate ideology into the account as the dimensions of divisions between parties and as the basis of choice by voters.

The important characteristic of all three of these conceptions is that partisanship is a property of the voters. That is, all view the political parties as they are perceived and employed by the voters, seeing parties as external objects to the electorate and as helping them negotiate the political process, especially the electoral system.

Parties are objects about which beliefs and loyalties, preferences and assessments, are formed and used. They help lead the voters in making choices rather than being the objects of choice themselves. And, all of these are particularly American conceptions.

The authors of the Michigan model, to be sure, sought to develop the comparative extension of their ideas from the beginning. Perhaps the most extensive example is by Butler and Stokes (1974), in which they sought to use the ideas of *The American Voter* (Campbell, Converse, Miller, and Stokes 1960), including partisanship, to understand British politics. This was, of course, the obvious natural extension, given its similar continuity of an essentially two-party system with comparable continuity in stances of the major parties. Of course, the problem was that Britain differed from America in being a unitary parliamentary government with strict party loyalty, so that voters decided which party to vote for, rather than which nominee of a major party to support in their riding. To put it otherwise, voters typically said they voted for the party and not the person, the exact reverse of the claims of the American voter.

The great theorist of partisanship, Phil Converse, made a strong case for the general, comparative utility of partisanship, perhaps especially in his classic article, "Of Time and Partisan Stability" (1969). There, he demonstrated that the conception of partisanship was helpful for understanding major properties of party systems, and one might infer back that partisanship in the electorate is a function of the party system and not "just" of the properties of the parties themselves. He and Dupeux (1962) saw a surrogate identification to partisanship, what they called an ideologically based "tendence" in the then current French system with its diverse and highly variable cast of political parties contending for votes (see Converse and Pierce 1986 for a more modern view of French partisanship and voting). This "stand in" for partisanship suggested that voters thrived when they could find ways to hold matters sufficiently constant to provide structure to their conception of politics. Retrospective voting, for its part, is one of the most migratory of American-originated conceptions for understanding electoral politics. Fiorina's notion of party identification as a running tally has been applied metaphorically, although rarely in precise ways. The result, often, is a use of the term party identification or partisanship in comparative contexts, which lack precise and theoretical specification. Finally, it seems evident that if voters in stable two-party systems need heuristics to guide them through electoral decision-making, voters in less stable and/or in multiparty systems would be in far greater need of such informational short-cuts.

And yet, the concept of party identification did not travel particularly well as, say, retrospective voting did. The question for here is why? The answer I propose is not that there is no general value in these ideas. Rather, it is that the American electoral landscape has a unique configuration of attributes that highlights "parties-as-assessments," while in virtually all other systems, political parties are objects of actual *choices*, not just the basis for making assessments. Thus, the continuity of parties combined with a lack of rigorous party discipline in the legislature means that *choices* are and must be over candidates and not over parties. This is narrowly so, as in many systems votes are cast for political parties and not individual candidates, but it is also true more metaphorically. In Britain or other Anglo-American two-party systems, votes can (often *must*) be cast for individual candidates, but high party discipline dilutes the personal name-brand value any candidate may have, something of high value in the USA, and accentuates the value of the name brand of the party. As a result, vote decisions made in the name of a party naturally trump assessments of individual candidates, and that is reflected in responses to party-identification-like questions on an election survey. It does not follow from a concept being hard to measure that the concept is not relevant in those systems. It only follows that the concept is obscured—explaining, perhaps, why Converse could find the very abstract patterns so striking in the very same political systems where the micro-measures were difficult to observe.

The above is inferential. Historical evidence in America seems consistent with this set of claims. Voting in eighteenth century America was highly partisan, indeed as strongly so as in contemporary parliamentary systems. Historians of American elections naturally and correctly point to the form of ballot—non-secret voting, ballots made by the separate parties, etc.—and their interaction with institutions, notably partisan machines, to explain highly partisan elections (e.g. Hays 1980). While the move from open to secret balloting and other technical features of the voting process are important parts of the explanation of the decline of partisan elections in the USA, it is by now well understood that intervening between ballot reform and candidate-centered elections was the development of the individual office seeking motivation that these reforms and others made possible (Katz and Sala 1996; Price 1975). Thus, it was the increasingly candidate-centered campaigns of the late nineteenth and early twentieth centuries that generated the first level of decline in partisan elections, followed by the new technology of mid- to late-twentieth century politics that finalized the candidate-centered campaign as all but fully replacing the party-centered contests of the earlier era (Aldrich 1995). In short, the voters were responding to the possibilities of the electoral setting and especially to the nature of the campaigns they observed in generating first highly partisan and then highly candidate centered voting. Perhaps were party identification questions asked in nineteenth-century America, they would have been understood as asking vote intention.

In a comparative context, the above argument is also inferential. Several empirical observations might test the notion. For example, as party discipline is tending to erode in many nations' parliaments, those with single-member districts combined with durable parties dominating the system, or other systems (e.g. Japan) where candidate names have some value, the importance of party-as-assessment should be increasing, while as party discipline increases in the USA, party-as-choice should be more commonplace. Other convergences may be exploitable to examine whether party-as-assessment is, in fact, valuable for citizens in many nations as they seek to negotiate a complex political world. Indeed the Comparative Study of Electoral Systems (CSES) are making such explorations and convergences increasingly possible. Note, interestingly, that the question wording for "party identification" questions in the CSES (and, of course, that means as generated from comparative scholars from their own research traditions) are about how *close* one feels toward the various parties. Such a format leaves open the question of whether respondents mean they feel close to a party in the sense of identifying with it, or being close to what they *stand for*, and thus having a higher ideological proximity.

Partisanship, however defined and understood in the literature, focuses on the individual citizen. But the questions as to meaning have turned out to depend upon how they observe politicians and the parties they belong to. Thus, as Key taught us long ago, we can spend a good deal of time looking at, say, the party-in-the-electorate, but we cannot, in the final analysis, really understand it in isolation from the party-in-government or the party-as-organization. Our questions about what the party means to the voter have taken us to the party-in-government.

4   THE PARTY INSIDE THE LEGISLATURE

In this section we again ask two core questions, the two that emerged above. It should not be surprising that the core questions about the value of the political party for citizens and for politicians are closely related. That was Key's point. The questions are when and why do politicians support their party in the legislature—how united are parties—and when and why do parties align with, or oppose, one another? These questions have tended to be the focus of the literature on American parties and Congress, on the one hand, and on comparative parties and legislatures, on the other hand, and it is fair to say that the two party-and-legislature literatures are often close to dominated by their respective questions. Increasingly, new questions and new data are emerging especially within comparative politics, but we will only briefly touch on them. The core questions form the end points of a continuum, with the US two-party system candidate-centered elections at one end to a multiparty system with party-centered elections at the other.

Let us begin at the American exemplar end of the continuum. What forces shape the roll call vote? There has been considerable variation in the level of support the members gives their party. The post-Second World War era was particularly low, and the contemporary period (as in the nineteenth century) is considerably higher. Even at lowest ebb, however, party had by far the largest effect on the casting of the roll call vote (Weisberg 1978). He put the scholarly challenge to be to take party voting as the base line, with the theory tested by seeing how much it improved on party-line voting. This was at a point when the Democratic majority was divided, with nearly as many votes being cast with a "conservative coalition" (a majority of northern Democrats opposed by a majority of Southern Democrats and a majority of Republicans) as were being cast along party lines. To be sure, claiming a vote is a "party vote," when a simple majority of one opposes a simple majority of the other party, set a modest standard, even though the effect of party on the individual vote was stronger than that aggregate pattern suggested. Still, if congressional voting was primarily "party plus," it was nonetheless the case that party was much less consequential in shaping legislative choice than in virtually all other legislatures.

The above reflect, in effect, a parallelism between citizens' and legislators' voting choices. In both cases, party served as a strong base line, but there was more. In both cases, the role of party reached a low point at about 1970, climbing back to a more historically precedented high level more recently.

Congressional theory sought to explain the variation in levels of party voting and, at least indirectly, answering the question of why the US Congress lagged its European counterpart, even at its contemporary higher levels of party voting. The theoretical literature poses three explanations (for reviews see, e.g., Aldrich and Rohde 2000; Cox and McCubbins 2005). One is that the observed levels of party voting revealed very little to do with the role of party in Congress. Championed most vigorously by Krehbiel (1991, 1993), his argument is that the pattern of party voting in Congress mirroring that of party voting in the public is no coincidence. Legislators' votes reflect the wishes of the public as filtered through the goal of reelection. To be sure, legislators do not simply vote the views of their constituency, but the role of the party organization and leadership in Congress is, at best, marginal. And this makes a sharp contrast with their European brethren.

Cox and McCubbins take a different view (1993, 2005). In their view, party is the primary organizing device of Congress. Congress is thus organized to fulfill the collective interests of the majority party, and one important aspect of that is to ensure that the majority party structures Congress so that it does not put the reelection chances of the duly elected members of the majority at risk. The party thus shapes the agenda so that members can vote for what the majority party's members want without voting against their constituents' wishes often or on important matters. Thus, the majority party is pleased to have its members on committees that serve their constituents' concerns and can reward their constituents with distributive benefits. But while it provides room for its members to serve their constituents, it also provides room for its members to act on their collectively shared interests, all in the name of assisting their members' reelection chances.

Circumstances dictate the kinds of power the majority will wield. When there were fewer collective interests to serve, the party was consequently less important to citizens, and it was better to be discrete in its use of power, typically by the use of negative agenda control. As polarization has led to more common interests and the party has thus become more important to the public, then it is increasingly satisfactory to exert more positive control over the agenda, to pass majority-preferred policies.

The third view is what Aldrich and Rohde call "conditional party government" (1997–98, 2000). If, they assert, there is variation in the influence of party in Congress, then we should investigate conditions under which it is at a higher and at a lower level. They argue that it is at a higher level when the electorate has selected members of the majority party with more homogenous preferences than at other times, and with preferences that are more clearly differentiated from the (typically also more homogenously distributed) preferences of the minority party. There is more for the majority party to win by acting together. And, when party preferences are more homogenous, there is less risk for the individual member of ceding authority to the party leadership than when their party is more heterogeneous. This view differs from that of, say, Krehbiel by virtue of its conditionality. That is, they agree that the electorate is the driving force. They differ in the role of the party in Congress. According to Krehbiel, it is epiphenomenal. In conditional party government, it magnifies the effect of the constituency at high levels, but not at low levels. It differs from the "party cartel" argument of Cox and McCubbins, if at all, by virtue of the latter's emphasis on the importance of negative agenda control (that is, blocking legislation from coming to a vote) when the majority party is heterogeneous, and emphasis on positive agenda control (that is seeking to pass legislation favored by the majority) otherwise. The conditional party government argument is simply that, instead of negative agenda control, a divided majority party exerts little control at all.

All three accounts argue that the driving force for explaining the observation of variation in levels of party voting in Congress are due to changes in the preferences of the electorate. Missing from all three accounts is an explanation of how and why those preferences change. Erikson, MacKuen, and Stimson (2002) argue that there is a thermostatic relationship or feedback between what the government does and how the electorate's partisan preferences and voting choices react. In particular, they find that the majority party tends to overshoot what the public wants, the Democratic Party acts too liberally, and a Republican Party too conservatively when in the majority. As a result, the public shifts back in the direction favored by the minority party, helping them work toward achieving majority status. Like a pendulum, parties in Congress sweep left and right farther than voters prefer and the public serves as counterweight, pulling the overly extreme policy choices back toward what the public as a whole desires. These propositions are new and still only lightly tested but seem both plausibly descriptive and enticing. The question then is why reelection minded officeholders would overshoot in this "macro polity." Two likely possibilities are that the politicians are personally more extreme in their policy beliefs than the public or that these politicians need resources from relative extreme partisan and interests groups for renomination and reelection. Of course, since many politicians were themselves once policy activists, both might be true. Further the public, in the aggregate, is generally moderate (indeed may literally be the definition of moderate) and so these activists may be only modestly "extreme." But, to answer the question of why party resources come from relative extremists is to ask a question about the party organization, a subject we will touch on in the conclusion. For now, note that findings that party activists are more extreme than the partisan identifiers in the electorate is not unique to the USA. It holds in many nations, and is one basis to begin to develop that general account that places the USA at one end and multiparty parliaments at the other end of the same continuum.

Whereas the traditional question asked of American legislative parties is whether they are ever united, the archetypical multiparty parliament finds the political party almost invariably united. Indeed, parties are often the unit of analysis, in virtual atom-as-billiard-ball fashion, rather than the American counterpart of party as atom-as-mostly-empty-space. In this tradition, the primary question is how parties form, maintain, or disband coalition governments, with the government and its ministers choosing policies for the parliament to ratify with strict party line voting. As Diermeier and Feddersen demonstrate (1998), the power of the no-confidence vote forces at least the parties in government into unity. It is only recently that the atom has been broken open, as it were, and non-lock-step unanimous behavior of party politicians considered.

The multiparty parliament inserts the extra step of government formation in the democratic crossroads of going from citizen preferences to policy (even when one party, majority or minority, see Strom, 1990, ends up forming the government). Technically, this is true in the US House, too, as its first action is to select from its own internal government by choosing a Speaker and a committee structure. All but invariably, that vote is also a strictly party-line vote, just as in, say, Britain. Perhaps the lack of a no-confidence vote in the Speaker undermines primarily party-line voting.

A substantial literature has sought to understand coalition formation in multiparty parliaments based on policy preferences. Thus, one beginning point would be with applications of Riker's (1962) minimal winning coalition hypothesis, with quite mixed empirical results. Axelrod (1970) added policy considerations per se by modifying minimal winning to "minimal winning connected coalition," and by "connected" he meant stand close or adjacent to each other on policy/ideology. The empirical findings were improved but still mixed. Then, Laver and Schofield (1990; see also Laver and Budge 1992) and Laver and Shepsle (1994, 1996) applied insights from social choice theory. In the first, Schofield developed a multi-dimensional analogue to the centrality of policy in the one-dimensional, median voter, and he and Laver applied this notion successfully in a number of empirical cases. Laver and Shepsle took a model that Shepsle (1979) had originally developed for the US Congress to describe how particular parties would form specific coalitions based on policy positions, even when there was no dominant majority outcome. Essentially, the coalition process strikes bargains in which party A is given control over policy x, party B over policy y, etc. It would be a different coalition with different policy outcome if party A controlled policy y and B policy x. They and others applied their model extensively to explain governments that formed (Laver and Shepsle 1994).

If the first question was which government formed, the second was how long would it last. Again, this literature moved toward alignment between theory and substance, but in this case, the literature unfolded in close dialogue between the two. A short version of this is that Browne, Frerdreis, and Gleiber (1986) developed a sophisticated statistical model of government duration that essentially showed how governments could handle exogenous shocks (or collapse in the face of them). King, Alt, Laver, and Burns (1990) developed this approach further. Lupia and Strom (1995) then began to develop a theoretical model that endogenized these events, followed by an increasingly sophisticated series of game theoretic models by Diermeier and associates (Diermeier and van Roozendaal 1998; Diermeier and Stevenson 1999) that moved toward testable implications to pit against and eventually extend the original statistical modeling of Browne, Frendreis, and Gleiber.

All of this increasingly precise, sophisticated, and empirically extensive research treats the parliamentary party as the unit of analysis. Two developments have moved towards treating the member of parliament as the unit of analysis. One thrust was due to the study of new democracies and therefore the study of the formation of parliaments and their practices, especially in Latin American (Morganstern and Nacif 2001) and former Soviet Union and Warsaw Pact nations. Smyth (2006), for example, examines early Russian Duma elections to study conditions under which candidates in their mixed system would choose to ally with a political party and when to run as an individual. Remington (2001) and Remington and Smith (2001) examine the formation of the Duma in the new era, looking at many of these same questions, while Andrews (2002) examines the policy formation process (or its failure!) in the early years of the post-Soviet Duma, finding precisely the kind of theoretical instability and policy chaos that underlies much of the theoretical work noted above. This study shows that the apparent stability of policy choices of most established legislatures, including the US Congress and the archetypal European multiparty parliament, needs to be derived—apparently from an established party system—rather than be assumed. Party instability occurs even in established parliaments, however. Heller and Mershon (2005) have examined the fluidity in MP partisan attachments after the reforms of the Italian parliamentary system. Here, unlike the Russian case, there seems to be reasonable policy stability within a great deal of partisan instability.

The second line of research inside the "black box" of the parliamentary party is to examine behavior in addition to roll call voting by which MPs can exert influence within and some degree of autonomy from their party. Martin and Vanberg (2004, 2005), for instance, examine means by which parliamentary committees and other devices can provide non-governing legislatures with influence over policy choices. As can be seen, "opening up" the black box of parliamentary parties is in its infancy, but these results imply that there is a good deal more legislative party politics of the kind ordinarily associated with American parties in their Congress to be found in multiparty parliaments. It may prove to be simply that the vote of confidence and electoral mechanisms that create party and government discipline have made it difficult to observe what Americans have thrust in front of them in much more public fashion.

5 CONCLUSION

There are a vast number of important themes that could direct a study of political parties in the legislature, out of the legislature, or both. This has focused on a small number of them. They were chosen because they have a common thread. That thread is one-half of the democratic process, looking at the role of political parties in shaping the beliefs and values of citizens and shaping their electoral decisions. Their choices, in turn, determined which parties and their candidates won legislative office. In some cases, a single party formed a majority, in others it required multiple parties to do so. In either case, the final step was how that majority governed, in terms of realizing (or deflecting) the wishes of the public who elected them.

This is but half the story, because the policies thus enacted shape the preferences and concerns of citizens going into the next election, repeating the process. This lacuna in coverage reflects the lacuna in analysis. However, ambitious politicians hoping to remain in office pick policies at least in part with an eye towards their best guess about public reaction, and so we, like they, anticipate voting for the next election, imperfectly embedding that anticipation into the policies chosen. As I hope this chapter made clear, there has been a great deal of scholarly progress on this Schattschneiderian role of the political party in shaping democratic politics in recent years, in the theoretical literature, in the substantive literature, and even more in their combination.

Examining how government actions might shape public preferences is one way to approach the problem of endogenous parties. A second is to consider seriously the relationship between the party system and the set of parties that make up that system. One theme has been the importance of a party system for the effective functioning of democracy. In general we define "party system" practically by the (effective) number of parties. The effective number tells us something about the case such as Israel, but perhaps better is to add to the effective number consideration of parties that serve as generators of prime ministerial candidates, or candidates for the major portfolios. In either case, the example above implies a sort of path dependency on the particular parties that make up the party system and on the height of barriers to entry to new parties and perhaps to achieving major party status.

Key's party-in-three-parts organized this chapter, but the reader may note that the third part, the party-as-organization, appeared on stage only briefly. Here it is appropriate to observe that one of the major components of the party organization, the activists and the resources in time, money, and effort that they control, is a critical component for synchronizing the party in the public's mind and the party in the legislature (see especially Aldrich 1995; Kitschelt 1989, 1999). There is an important regularity about party activists that cuts across the various types of party systems. In majoritarian and proportional, in two- and multiparty systems, in the US and European archetypical cases of this chapter, activists have turned out to be more extreme than the electoral members of their parties. Recently, Kedar (2005) has developed and tested a theory of this process, arguing that voters support parties with activists more extreme than they are, so that actual policy will be able to be moved in the direction of the activists, but, through the inertia created by the rest of the political system, almost assuredly less far than the activists would desire. The result is a change in policy much like the more-moderate voter actually desires. Aldrich and McGinnis (1989) offer a different but complementary story based on the US parties. Party activists can induce candidates and officeholders to move policy in their direction, but not as far in their direction (in this instance balancing their need for extremity to gather resources from activists to win votes and their need for moderation to retain support in the electorate). In either case, relatively more extreme activists are motivated to connect public and politician, pushing both to affect policy changes more to the activists' liking. Whatever the details, the activists are central party organization members for aggregating and articulating public desires and tying politicians to policy outcome. And, if Erikson, MacKuen, and Stimson (2002) have the dynamics right, they are the source of the swing of the policy pendulum.

Let me close with a fourth area which appears ripe for research breakthroughs. This chapter pointed towards a fully comparative political parties project. Instead of distinguishing between American political parties and the political parties of other (advanced, industrial, and postindustrial) democracies, we are beginning to see more clearly that political parties are common to all democracies, and they are so because democracy is, indeed, unthinkable save through the agency of the party. And it is through the theoretical unification of the party in and out of the legislature (perhaps accomplished through the party organization) that we can understand just how parties are necessary components of democracies. In this, American parties are not different, theoretically, from their European counterparts. We can explain apparent American exceptionalism as simply based on an unusual combination of empirical conditions, explainable through a common set of factors, and thus there is closer to a singular set of explanations of the party in and out of the legislature across at least the established democratic world.

REFERENCES

ACHEN, C. H. 1992. Breaking the iron triangle: social psychology, demographic variables and linear regression in voting research. *Political Behavior*, 14 (3): 195–211.

ALDRICH, J. H. 1995. *Why Parties? The Origin and Transformation of Political Parties in the United States*. Chicago: University of Chicago Press.

—— 2000. Southern parties in state and nation. *Journal of Politics*, 62: 643–70.

—— and MCGINNIS, M. D. 1989. A model of party constraints on optimal candidate positions. *Mathematical and Computer Modeling*, 12 (4–5): 437–50.

—— and ROHDE, D. W. 1997–98. Theories of party in the legislature and the transition to Republican rule in the House. *Political Science Quarterly*, 112 (4): 541–67.

—— —— 2000. The consequences of party organization in the House: the role of the majority and minority parties in conditional party government. Pp. 31–72 in *Polarized Politics: Congress and the President in a Partisan Era*, ed. J. R. Bond and R. Fleisher. Washington, DC: CQ Press.

—— BLAIS, A., INDRIDIASON, I. H., and LEVINE, R. 2005. Coalition considerations and the vote. Pp. 143–66 in *The Elections in Israel—2003*, ed. A. Arian and M. Shamir. New Brunswick, NJ: Transaction.

—— MAGALONI, B., and ZECHMEISTER, E. 2005. When hegemonic parties lose: the 2000 elections in Mexico and Taiwan. Unpublished.

ANDREWS, J. T. 2002. *When Majorities Fail: The Russian Parliament, 1990–1993*. Cambridge: Cambridge University Press.

AUSTIN-SMITH, D. and BANKS, J. 1988. Elections, coalitions, and legislative outcomes. *American Political Science Review*, 82 (2): 405–22.

AXELROD, R. M. 1970. *Conflict of Interest: A Theory of Divergent Goals with Application to Politics*. Chicago: Markham.

BARTELS, L. M. 2000. Partisanship and voting behavior, 1952–1996. *American Journal of Political Science*, 44: 35–50.

BLAIS, A., ALDRICH, J., INDRIDIASON, I., and LEVINE, R. forthcoming. Voting for a coalition. *Party Politics*.

BROWNE, E., FRENDREIS, J., and GLEIBER, D. 1986. The process of cabinet dissolution: an exponential model of duration and stability in western democracies. *American Journal of Political Science*, 30: 628–50.

Butler, D. and Stokes, D. 1974 [1969]. *Political Change in Britain: The Evolution of Electoral Choice*, 2nd edn. New York: St. Martins Press.

Campbell, A., Converse, P. E., Miller, W. E., and Stokes, D. E. 1960. *The American Voter.* New York: John Wiley.

—— —— —— —— 1966. *Elections and the Political Order.* New York: John Wiley.

Chhibber, P. K. and Kollman, K. 2004. *The Formation of National Party Systems: Federalism and Party Competition in Canada, Great Britain, India, and the United States.* Princeton, NJ: Princeton University Press.

Converse, P. E. 1969. Of time and partisan stability. *Comparative Political Studies*, 2: 139–71.

—— and Dupuex, G. 1962. Politicization of the electorate in France and the United States. *Public Opinion Quarterly*, 26 (1): 1–23.

—— and Pierce, R. 1986. *Political Representation in France.* Cambridge, Mass.: Belknap Press of Harvard University Press.

Cotter, C. P., Gibson, J. L., Bibby, J. F., and Huckshorn, R. J. 1984. *Party Organizations in American Politics.* New York: Praeger.

Cox, G. W. 1997. *Making Votes Count.* Cambridge: Cambridge University Press.

—— and McCubbins, M. D. 1993. *Legislative Leviathan: Party Government in the House.* Berkeley: University of California Press.

—— —— 2005. *Setting the Agenda: Responsible Party Government in the US House of Representatives.* Cambridge: Cambridge University Press.

Diermeier, D. and Feddersen, T. J. 1998. Cohesion in legislatures and the vote of confidence procedure. *American Political Science Review*, 92 (3): 611–21.

—— and Stevenson, R. 1999. Cabinet terminations and critical events. *American Political Science Review*, 94: 627–40.

—— and Roozendaal, P. van 1998. The duration of cabinet formation processes in western multi-party democracies. *British Journal of Political Science*, 28 (4): 609–26.

Downs, A. 1957. *An Economic Theory of Democracy.* New York: Harper and Row.

Duverger, M. 1954. *Political Parties: Their Organization and Activities in the Modern State.* London: Methuen.

Erikson, R. S., MacKuen, M. B., and Stimson, J. A. 2002. *The Macro Polity.* Cambridge: Cambridge University Press.

Fiorina, M. P. 1976. The voting decision: instumental and expressive aspects. *Journal of Politics*, 38 (2): 390–415.

—— 1980. The decline in collective responsibility in American politics. *Daedalus*, 109 (3): 25–45.

—— 1981. *Retrospective Voting in American National Elections.* New Haven, Conn.: Yale University Press.

—— 1990. An era of divided government. Pp. 195–232 in *Developments in American Politics*, ed. B. Cain and G. Peele. London: Macmillan.

—— 1991. Divided governments in the states. Harvard University Center for American Political Studies Occasional Papers, January.

—— 1992. *Divided Government.* New York: Macmillan.

Formisano, R. P. 1981. Federalists and Republicans: parties, yes—system, no. Pp. 33–76 in *The Evolution of American Electoral Systems*, ed. P. Kleppner, W. D. Burnham, R. P. Formisano, S. P. Hays, R. Jensen, and W. G. Shade. Westport, Conn.: Greenwood Press.

Green, D., Palmquist, B., and Schickler, E. 2002. *Partisan Hearts and Minds: Political Parties and the Social Identities of Voters.* New Haven, Conn.: Yale University Press.

HAGGARD, S. and McCUBBINS, M. D. (eds.) 2000. *Presidents, Parliaments, and Policy.* Cambridge: Cambridge University Press.

HAYS, S. 1980. *American Political History as Social Analysis.* Knoxville: University of Tennessee Press.

HELLER, W. B. and MERSHON, C. 2005. Party switching in the Italian Chamber of Deputies, 1996–2001. *Journal of Politics*, 67: 536–59.

HERRNSON, P. S. 1988. *Party Campaigning in the 1980s.* Cambridge, Mass.: Harvard University Press.

HINICH, M. J. and MUNGER, M. C. 1994. *Ideology and the Theory of Political Choice.* Ann Arbor: University of Michigan Press.

HOFSTADTER, R. 1969. *The Idea of a Party System: The Rise of Legitimate Opposition in the United States, 1780–1840.* Berkeley: University of California Press.

JACOBSON, G. C. 2004. *The Politics of Congressional Elections*, 6th edn. New York: Pearson Longman.

KATZ, J. N. and SALA, B. R. 1996. Careerism, committee assignments, and the electoral connection. *American Political Science Review*, 90 (1): 21–33.

KEDAR, O. 2005. When moderate voters prefer extreme parties: policy balancing in parliamentary elections. *American Political Science Review*, 99 (2): 185–99.

KEY, JR., V. O. 1949. *Southern Politics in States and Nation.* New York: Knopf.

—— 1964. *Politics, Parties, and Pressure Groups*, 5th edn. New York: Crowell.

—— 1966. *The Responsible Electorate: Rationality in Presidental Voting, 1936–1960.* Cambridge, Mass.: Harvard University Press.

KING, G., ALT, J., LAVER, M., and BURNS, N. 1990. A unified model of cabinet dissolution in parliamentary democracies. *American Journal of Political Science*, 34: 846–71.

KITSCHELT, H. 1989. *The Logics of Party Formation: Ecological Politics in Belgium and West Germany.* Ithaca, NY: Cornell University Press.

—— 1999. *Post-Communist Party Systems.* Cambridge: Cambridge University Press.

KREHBIEL, K. 1991. *Information and Legislative Organization.* Ann Arbor: University of Michigan Press.

—— 1993. Where's the party? *British Journal of Political Science*, 23: 235–66.

LAVER, M. J., and BUDGE, I. (eds.) 1992. *Party Policy and Government Coalitions.* New York: St Martin's Press.

—— and SCHOFIELD, N. 1990. *Multiparty Government: The Politics of Coalition in Europe.* Oxford: Oxford University Press.

—— and SHEPSLE, K. A. (eds.) 1994. *Cabinet Ministers and Parliamentary Government.* Cambridge: Cambridge University Press.

—— —— 1996. *Making and Breaking Governments: Cabinets and Legislatures in Parliamentary Democracies.* Cambridge: Cambridge University Press.

LIJPHART, A. 1984. *Democracies: Patterns of Majoritarian and Consensus Government in Twenty-one Countries.* New Haven, Conn.: Yale University Press.

—— 1999. *Patterns of Democracy: Government Forms and Performance in Thrty-six Countries.* New Haven, Conn.: Yale University Press.

LIPSET, S. M. and ROKKAN, S. (eds.) 1987. *Party Systems and Voter Alignments: Cross-National Perspectives.* New York: Free Press.

LUPIA, A. M. and McCUBBINS, M. D. 1998. *The Democratic Dilemma: Can Citizens Learn What They Need to Know?* Cambridge: Cambridge University Press.

LUPIA, A. M. and STROM, K. 1995. Coalition termination and the strategic timing of parliamentary elections. *American Political Science Review*, 89: 648–65.

McCORMICK, R. P. 1982. *The Presidental Game: Origins of American Politics*. New York: Oxford University Press.

MAGALONI, B. 2006. *Voting for Autocracy: Hegemonic Party Survival and its Demise in Mexico*. Cambridge: Cambridge University Press.

MARTIN, L. and VANBERG, G. 2004. Policing the bargain: coalition government and parliamentary scrutiny. *American Journal of Political Science*, 48: 13–27.

—— —— 2005. Coalition policymaking and legislative review. *American Political Science Review*, 99: 93–106.

MORGENSTERN, S. and NACIF, B. (eds.) 2001. *Legislatures in Latin America*. Cambridge: Cambridge University Press.

PAGE, B. I. 1978. *Choices and Echoes in Presidential Elections: Rational Man and Electoral Democracy*. Chicago: University of Chicago Press.

POPKIN, S. L. 1994. *The Reasoning Voter: Communication and Persuasion in Presidential Campaigns*, 2nd edn. Chicago: University of Chicago Press.

PRICE, H. D. 1975. Congress and the evolution of legilsative "professionalism." Pp. 2–23 in *Congress in Change*, ed. N. J. Ornstein. New York: Praeger.

PRZEWORSKI, A. and SPRAGUE, J. 1986. *Paper Stones: A History of Electoral Socialism*. Chicago: University of Chicago Press.

REMINGTON, T. F. 2001. *The Russian Parliament: Institutional Evolution in a Transitional Regime, 1989–1999*. New Haven, Conn.: Yale University Press.

—— and SMITH, S. S. 2001. *The Politics of Institutional Choice: Formation of the Russian State Duma*. Princeton, NJ: Princeton University Press.

RIKER, W. H. 1962. *The Theory of Political Coalitions*. New Haven, Conn.: Yale University Press.

—— 1980. Implications from the disequilibrium of majority rule for the study of institutions. *American Political Science Review*, 74 (2): 432–46.

—— 1982a. *Liberalism Against Populism: A Confrontation Between the Theory of Democracy and the Theory of Social Choice*. San Francisco: W. H. Freeman.

—— 1982b. The two-party system and Duverger's Law: An essay on the history of political science. *American Political Science Review*, 76 (4): 753–66.

ROSENSTONE, S. J., BEHR, R. L., and LAZARUS, E. H. 1996. *Third Parties in America*, 2nd edn. Princeton, NJ: Princeton University Press.

SCHATTSCHNEIDER, E. E. 1942. *Party Government*. New York: Rinehart.

SHEPSLE, K. A. 1979. Institutional arrangements and equilibrium in multidimensional voting models. *American Journal of Political Science*, 23 (1): 27–59.

SMYTH, R. 2006. *Candidate Strategies and Electoral Competition in the Russian Federation: Democracy without Foundation*. Cambridge: Cambridge University Press.

STROM, K. 1990. *Minority Government and Majority Rule*. Cambridge: Cambridge University Press.

WARWICK, P. 1992. Rising hazards: an underlying dynamic of parliamentary government. *American Journal of Political Science*, 36: 857–76.

WEISBERG, H. F. 1978. Evaluating theories of congressional roll-call voting. *American Journal of Political Science*, 22 (3): 554–77.

CHAPTER 29

ELECTORAL SYSTEMS

SHAUN BOWLER

This chapter looks at electoral systems and electoral system change from an institutional perspective. As we will see, it is a perspective that lends itself to a rational actor framework that emphasizes the strategic choices made by voters and political elites. A central organizing theme of this chapter is the way in which Duverger's Law can be taken to be the canonical statement of what electoral systems as institutions do and why the choice of electoral institutions matters so much. Discussions of electoral system effects and consequences can be seen as a generalization of Duverger's insight as it applied to single member simple plurality (SMSP) electoral systems. In subsequent sections we discuss changes in electoral systems or, more accurately, the remarkable lack of changes in electoral systems worldwide. Despite many opportunities for change, and a theoretical expectation which suggests parties and candidates are constantly seeking to change the rules to their advantage, electoral systems rarely, if ever, change. In some ways, explaining the absence of change is harder than explaining change itself. We begin, however, by placing electoral systems in the broader theoretical context of political institutions.

1 ELECTORAL SYSTEMS AS POLITICAL INSTITUTIONS

"At the most basic level, electoral systems translate the votes cast in [an election] into seats won by parties and candidates [in the legislature]" (IDEA 2002, 7).

Duverger's Law remains the canonical statement of the political consequence of electoral systems, and one that informs the topic of electoral system change in general.

Duverger's Law notes that single-member simple plurality electoral systems are associated with far fewer parties than are systems such as list PR (list proportional representation) and offers a causal explanation of why this is the case (see Cox 1999 for details and also Riker 1982). This statement of the relationship between electoral system and number of parties has meant that an important agenda for electoral systems research has been identifying who wins and who loses under the huge variety of electoral rules (see, e.g., Rae 1971; Farrell 2001). Duverger is credited with identifying one of the more prominent, if not the most prominent, effects and subsequent scholarship has searched for and established other such effects in other countries or with other systems, and with greater precision and detail. The electoral systems literature is one of the more advanced within political science and a large part of that advance has been due to ever better elaboration and generalization of the kinds of effects noted by Duverger.

In a practical political sense, because electoral systems make winners and losers, the question of which electoral system is chosen to be used is an important one. It did not take Duverger to realize that point. Electoral changes in Victorian Britain make it plain that at least some politicians of the time understood the point. But Duverger's Law is an especially clear and focal statement of the argument.

Taken together, these two points mean that the study of electoral systems is one that is closely allied to the study of institutions more generally and, in some sense, represent an idealized type of what Tsebelis calls "distributional" institutions. Tsebelis categorizes institutions as either "distributional" or "efficient" (Tsebelis 1990, 104–15). Efficient institutions are ones in which all or almost all people are made better off. Examples of these kinds of institutions might be the rules of the road in which the rule is to stop at red traffic lights and go on green, or the decision to drive on one side of the road rather than other. Others might range from the adoption of a standardized system of weights and measures through (more arguably) to a rule of law. This kind of institutional arrangement benefits all or most people. Distributional institutions, however, divide people into winners and losers. Knight argues that all institutions have, at their base, some distributional element. Even seemingly innocuous ones (say whether to use imperial or metric systems of measurement) that make almost everyone better off may make some people better off still, in which case there is scope for conflict among those many who get better over who gets best off (Knight 1997). It may be more accurate then to talk of a continuum of institutions whose end points are defined by idealized types that are never fully realized in the real world.

But even with a more nuanced categorization of institutions, electoral systems remain one of the clearest examples of distributional institutions. Not only do electoral systems make winners and losers, this fact is common knowledge among all actors involved. In the "real world," political fights and disagreements ensue and, in the academic world, analysis of electoral systems establishes who wins and who loses under various systems. In a general sense the winners from any electoral system are political parties as organizations. As Schattschneider wrote, "the political parties created democracy and modern democracy is unthinkable save in terms of the political parties" (Schattschneider 1942, 1). What helps makes parties so prominent is that they have to fight elections. The functionality of parties and party-like organizations as vehicles for fighting elections means that, in general, political parties are encouraged by elections and voting. Even non-partisan elections in US local governments see party-like organizations devoted to getting out the vote and endorsing candidates. Of course the more pointed question becomes which parties win and which lose under various electoral systems. Over and above that, electoral systems shape the internal cohesion and discipline of parties. Some systems—such as the single transferable vote (STV)—encourage factionalism and intraparty competition, while others—list PR—reinforce party discipline. Electoral systems, too, shape the relationship between voters and representatives: some systems, especially those that allow voters to cast a ballot for individual candidates, encourage constituency service and the cultivation of a "personal" vote. Other systems do not encourage such a relationship and so shift the incentives of candidates to focus more upon party than upon individual voter concerns (Bowler and Farrell 1993; Carey and Shugart 1995).

But the main focus of electoral systems research has been upon which kinds of parties win and which lose under various schemes. Studies of electoral systems show repeatedly that different electoral arrangements privilege or discriminate against different kinds of parties or candidates (Lakeman 1954; Rae 1971; Grofman and Lijphart 1986; Taagepera and Shugart 1989; Lijphart 1990, 1994; Farrell 2001).[1] With few exceptions, discussion of electoral system effects have considered the question of which parties benefit largely without reference to the ideological or programmatic component of parties and the discussion within this literature has tended to consider how many parties are produced under various systems.

2 DUVERGER'S LAW

Duverger's Law occupies pride of place in this series of studies as one of the major statements in electoral studies research and the canonical statement of the role of

---

[1] Farrell 2001 is an excellent and accessible overview of the electoral systems literature.

electoral systems in general. The major insight remains that electoral systems are not merely neutral systems for totting up votes and producing an outcome but instead systematically privilege some parties over others: specifically, single member simple plurality (SMSP) pushes party systems towards having two big parties, more proportional electoral systems produce greater numbers of smaller parties.

There are a series of amendments, elaborations, and caveats made in relation to that statement. Some proportional systems, for example, are more proportional than others (Gallagher 1991). In addition there are a number of empirical studies on the failure of Duverger ("non-Duvergerian equilibria"). Duverger's Law may work well enough within particular districts to produce two parties but that is not necessarily the same as working nationwide to produce the same two parties. In varying degrees Canada, India, and the UK do not conform neatly to the model and explanations for this have been advanced that relate to social diversity and federalism (see Chhibber and Kollman 2004; Riker 1982). But the basic argument of Duverger remains. Cox (1997) provides the seminal discussion of a precise statement of Duverger's Law and the number of expected parties, anchoring his interpretation in the kinds of coordination problems elections bring to the fore: parties have to coordinate on which candidate(s) to put forward while voters have to coordinate on which candidate(s) to vote for.

One reading of Duverger is that it remains a fairly simple statement about the number of parties in a political system and the role of the electoral system in shaping that number. But it is possible to give Duverger a broader reading by noting the wider consequences of the number and ideological range of parties for several features of politics. Some of those consequences concern governability or, more accurately, the ungovernability that may be associated with multipartyism while others relate to underlying normative ideas of representation and accountability.

The examples of Weimar Germany, the French Fourth Republic, (most of) postwar Italy, and Israel are often held to have pathologies of ungovernability and the consequent encouragement of extremism that stem directly from multipartyism. In that sense, the tendency of electoral systems to reduce the number of parties helps simplify coalition building which in turn helps put in place governments that last longer (see Laver and Schofield 1998). There are, it can be argued, further payoffs in accountability for reducing the number of choices at election time. The multiparty governments that tend to result from proportional systems do not make for the easiest system of accountability since voters may be confused over which governmental party to reward or blame. Coalitions may also be formed in a way that can thwart voter attempts at reward and punishment if parties which lose votes end up gaining a place in government (Anderson 1995; Powell 2000). Accountability, then, is tied to the number of parties in government which is in turn tied back to the number of parties successful at election time and, in its turn, tied back to the operation of Duverger's Law.

Other implications of the consequences of Duverger focus on the issues associated with proportionality and representation. To the extent that proportionality provides more parties then this provides both more choice to voters and, in principle, a party voice for a wider range of interests than may be expressed by just two parties. The wider range of views is especially important to those who are concerned with minority rights and descriptive representation (see Amy 2000 and Birch 1971 for general discussion). The concern is not simply a concern for opinion minorities but for demographic—and most especially racial and ethnic—minorities. The empirical example here is that of South Africa's choice of PR in a racially divided society. A less successful example might be the use of a single transferable vote system of proportional representation (STV-PR) in Northern Ireland in the face of sectarianism there. Others, especially those who favor systems that allow voters to choose individual candidates, stress "substantive" representation and the activities of the representative on behalf of his/her voters regardless of whether voter and representative share demographic traits. These kinds of concerns tend to focus on giving voters the ability to reward and punish representatives but also to allow voters not just to act *ex post* but also to select candidates *ex ante* on some desirable behavioral attribute. Just how realistic it is to expect voters to perform these functions is a matter of some concern (see Fearon 1999 for theoretical discussion; Cain, Ferejohn, and Fiorina 1987 for empirical evidence). Nevertheless, different electoral systems imply different mixes of the normative components of representation. One implication buried within Duverger's Law is that representation of interests between different interests or groups in society will be conducted and brokered within a small number of large parties rather than between parties who must form coalitions in order to govern.

The implications in terms both of governability and also of representation are related to the bias of the electoral system in favor of or against particular parties. For the cases of SMSP, especially when compared to list proportional representation, the bias towards bigger parties and against smaller ones seems especially pronounced.

Within the class of proportional systems we can see similar, though much more muted affects, depending on the particular counting rule involved. Exact proportionality is hard to achieve. It is arithmetically easier to achieve with larger district magnitudes and large elected assemblies but even with a district magnitude (the number of seats to be elected) of 100 it is hard to achieve exact proportionality. There are always fractions of vote shares that cumulate to remainders. How these fractions and leftovers are distributed can shade the outcome towards larger or smaller parties, too. In the end the effects are much less pronounced than those implied by Duverger's Law but at the margin the choice of "largest remainder" or "highest average" may well change the results by one or two seats (see Farrell 2001, 71–9 for an especially clear discussion). This may sound small potatoes but it does shift who wins and who loses.

A more obvious method than this, having electoral thresholds—such as Germany's 5 percent threshold—places hurdles in front of smaller parties that they may find hard to overcome. In fact it is, in part, the intent of these thresholds to stifle smaller (and often more extreme) political parties, parties that can make coalition bargaining even more difficult.

In general terms, then, the electoral system shapes the number of parties but, like a pebble thrown into a pond, the effects of the number of parties ripples through the political system. Often these effects are of great consequence to our normative understanding of representation, of accountability, and of governability. Changing an electoral system is not something to be done lightly. However, when either analysts or politicians consider changes to the electoral system it seems that the main topics of debate really focus on the distributional effects of the system. That is, even though changing the electoral system does involve many changes on ideas of representation or accountability, a lot of the discussion focuses on who wins and who loses (see, e.g., Benoit 2004 and Bawn 1993 for discussion of postwar Germany).

In effect, this means that many of the studies of change in electoral systems focus on the central point of who is doing the choosing. Colomer has an especially thorough statement of the way in which parties themselves may or may not choose to invoke the effects of Duverger's Law. His insight is to note that parties choose electoral systems and not—as a mechanical reading of Duverger suggests—vice versa (Colomer 2005; Blais, Dodrzynska, and Indridasan 2005). Electoral system choice is, as Colomer notes, made by parties and so, to a large extent, Duverger's effects are endogenous to the initial choice of institutions, a fact that actors in early post-cold war Eastern Europe knew well. The choice of electoral systems in the newly democratic Europe was neither easy, straightforward, nor without controversy precisely because actors recognized that electoral systems do have effects on political parties (Colomer 2005; Birch, Millard, and Williams 2003). So for these authors Duverger may have it the wrong way round to some extent: a party system with a few big parties will choose an electoral system that favors keeping a few big parties and not want to change that. Similarly, a party system with lots of small parties is likely to want to keep a system such as list PR that favors small parties.

3   CHANGING ELECTORAL SYSTEMS?

Clear-cut points of choice of electoral systems are fairly rare, although in principle countries can consider reforming their current system at any time. Electoral institutions change relatively infrequently and the major changes of recent years—in Italy, New Zealand, and Japan—attracted a great deal of attention as special cases. Colomer (2004) presents an encyclopedic study of electoral system change. In general there are not many examples of change. Colomer gives a total of eighty-two changes from the nineteenth century. Of these, just fourteen are considered to have taken place in the present democratic period (Colomer 2004, 57). Given the (increasing) number of democracies and the number of years involved, examples of change are few and far between. It is hard to come up with satisfactory priors of how often we might reasonably expect to see electoral systems change or how often the opportunity for change would come up. With, say, twenty to thirty democracies over a thirty- to fifty-year time period this would seem to give somewhere between 60 and 150 opportunities to change electoral systems if we are willing to assume that each country has a chance to change its electoral system every decade (i.e. every two electoral cycles). If a more reasonable timeframe is once every generation (thirty years) then the figures drop to between twenty and fifty opportunities to change. But the figures presented above are lower by far than these numbers or, at the least, suggest that most attempts at change fail.

One of the main patterns to explain, then, is the striking absence of change in electoral systems. Andrews and Jackman (2005) note the importance of uncertainty as a deterrent to change (Colomer 2004, 6; Shvetsova 2003). They identify three kinds of uncertainty at work in electoral reforms.

3.1 Uncertainty over the Number of Political Parties

At moments of constitutional choice—in the wave of democratizations in Eastern Europe in the 1990s—it was far from clear who the players were going to be. Parties other than the Communist party typically did not exist in any recognizable or organized form and so the identity, party programme, and size of successor parties was not known to electoral engineers. Instability in party systems and blocs in the early post-Wall years did little to help this uncertainty settle down and so allow accurate gaming. Explanations of electoral choice in early stages of democratization can easily assume that parties and players are more unified and cohesive than might actually be the case. In fact, the early electoral arrangements pretty much determine which parties exist to play the game of institutional choice in the next round. But even in established democracies it may not be entirely clear what the impact of a shift in electoral system will bring about by way of new entrants into the system. New Zealand's change from single-member simple plurality to a mixed-member propor-tional system (MMP) provides a good and remarkably well-documented "real world" example of this point and the following one (Vowles 1995; Vowles et al. 2002; Boston, Levine, Mcheay, and Roberts 1997; Remington and Smith 1996 for a Russian example; Bawn 1993 for a German example).

3.2   Uncertainty over the Preferences of Voters

A decision to change electoral systems can involve decision-makers trying to predict how voters will respond both to the system and to the party alternatives on offer. It is not always clear how voters will jump under different electoral rules. Again this was especially true for Eastern Europe in the 1990s. At an extreme, when an electoral regime is put in place as a country moves from dictatorship to democracy, decision-makers may have little idea what voters want and the kinds of parties that are going to develop to cater to those wants. But even in established democracies it may be the case that, say, a move to proportionality may well produce some uncertain shifts among voters towards, say, more extreme or single interest parties.

3.3   Uncertainty over the Impact of Electoral Systems

While the general principle of electoral systems shaping winners and losers is well known and also the broader lesson of Duverger's Law is quite quickly learned, more specific effects are often unknown. Again, this is more likely to be the case at times of innovation of new electoral institutions. As Birch, Millard, and Williams note in their discussion of changes in Eastern Europe, "actors had some understanding of the *general* consequences of electoral systems vis-à-vis party development. Yet they were often mistaken when it came to the specifics of how laws would affect individual political groups and this hampered their ability to craft electoral institutions to suit their immediate political ends" (Birch, Millard, and Williams 2003, 170; emphasis in original). Indeed electoral architects were often surprised by events such as the success of the ultranationalists in Russia (Birch, Millard, and Williams 2003, 170).

Even players within established electoral regimes may experience uncertainty. As Andrews and Jackman (2005) argue, uncertainty about the consequences of electoral system change were important in Britain when it considered a move to proportional representation around the end of the First World War. It is important to underscore that when we move away from the well-established electoral systems such as single-member simple plurality (SMSP)[2] and list proportional representation (list PR)[3] uncertainty increases. The effects of systems such as the single transferable vote (STV)[4] are much less studied and understood than the "bigger"

---

[2] The system used in Britain, the USA, Canada, and India.

[3] List PR is widely used in Scandinavia but there are important variations in this system in terms of how many seats are to be elected (district magnitude) and whether voters have the chance or not to vote for individual candidates (open vs. closed list).

[4] The system used in Ireland and Malta to elect their parliaments. It is also used to elect the Australian Senate and has been used in local elections in the USA and UK (Barber 1995).

or at least more common systems, in part because their effects much more contingent (Bowler 1996; Bowler, Donovan, and Brockington 2004).

Cox argues that coordination problems lie at the heart of any electoral system—even SMSP. Some electoral systems tend to raise more problems of coordination than others and so demand more of both voters and parties. Outcomes under such systems are therefore much more highly contingent under some systems than others and are especially chronic under multicandidate systems that allow voters to choose over candidates. For example, under both SMSP and also list PR some thought may go into what kinds of candidates to nominate but little thought has to go into the number of candidates to nominate. Some disagreement may take place (and hence some coordination be required) over which candidates to nominate—which local notables or party stalwarts—but almost none over the number. Under systems such as STV or cumulative voting (CV)[5] the eventual outcome depends in part on the number of candidates each party nominates. These systems have multiseat districts (district magnitude > 1) and also allow voters to express an intensity of preference over several candidates. Under STV, voters are allowed to rank order candidates; under CV, voters are allowed to cast as many votes as there are seats and either give one vote to each preferred candidate or cumulate those votes on one or two candidates. These features permit a much greater deal of strategic leeway on the part of both voters and candidates and so outcomes under these systems are contingent on the abilities of the players to play the game as well as upon the rules themselves. Under STV and CV, for example, parties can do either better or worse than a purely proportional outcome depending on their ability to strategize and be disciplined (Bowler 1996; Bowler, Donovan, and Brockington 2004).

Some systems, then, would seem to produce outcomes that are less dependent on how players play the game than others: perhaps because, following Cox's interpretation, they simply require fewer coordination problems to be solved. The fact that commonly used electoral systems such as list PR and SMSP produce clear outcomes in addition to our well-developed understanding of proportionality (Gallagher 1991; Lijphart 1985; Blais 1988; Farrell 2001) can lead to a false sense of confidence in our ability to engage in electoral engineering. While we can say small or large parties will benefit under various regimes, we cannot predict with any precision the question of interest to most politicians: which large party and which small party?

Uncertainty about electoral system effects seemed especially prevalent in "big bang" changes where democracy is introduced. After a while this uncertainty—at least the first two forms of uncertainty—may well be reduced but electoral systems nevertheless seem to remain relatively stable, despite the seemingly ever-present incentive to jockey for or shore up an advantage, through the electoral process. The

---

[5] Used in local elections in the modern USA and Victorian Britain and many corporate settings (Bowler, Donovan, and Brockington 2004).

third kind of uncertainty—over the specifics of electoral system effects—may well deter change but it may not be the only factor at work in shaping the decision to change system or not in established democracies.

One of the biggest roadblocks to change is surely that it requires winners under the current system to consider altering a system under which they have won. Benoit (2003) argues that we can expect to see electoral system change when the people who have the power to do so see a way to improve their seat share under alternative electoral arrangements. The obvious point is that change in an electoral system— especially if its effects are uncertain—essentially asks current winners to run the risk of losing. Parties and candidates are typically reluctant to do that to themselves and so uncertainty will impact whether or not players think they can win more seats. In the meantime, the current incumbents are doing just fine out of the current system.

Self-interest, then, provides a major obstacle to change not least because reformers may be tempted to renege. Reform promises, for example, were long a part of the platform of the Parti Quebecois (PQ) in Quebec. After winning only a handful seats in the provincial legislature, despite winning 24 and 30 percent of the vote in the 1970 and 1973 elections respectively, the PQ promised to incorporate PR into Quebec's electoral system. When the PQ won power in 1976, premier Levesque set up a Ministry for Parliamentary and Electoral Reform whose mandate included consideration of alternate voting systems for Quebec, but proposals were shelved. Milner's explanation for this failure of reform refers in part to the uncertainty of members of the PQ over the effects of any change and also the belief of many PQ parliamentarians that they, themselves, were safe from electoral loss because of the strength of their standing within their own districts even though the party itself was low in the polls (Milner 1994). Similarly, while the UK Labour Party's commitment to electoral reform was put into practice for European elections, city elections, and elections to the assemblies in Wales and Scotland, they were not put in place for general elections to the national parliament—the elections that matter.

In addition to demonstrating the infrequency of electoral change, Colomer's figures also show a trend towards "increasingly inclusive, less risk formulas ... [from majority systems to] mixed systems and to proportional representation" (Colomer 2005, 4). Proportionality should make change even less likely by giving more parties a stake in the current system. Under majoritarian systems losing is both definitive ("winner takes all" after all) and likely to affect relatively large numbers of candidates and parties—the main actors—in the system. Under proportional systems, however, not only are more players likely to be included in government but also a wider variety of opinions and parties are much more likely to be elected to some role in the system to begin with (Powell 2000). That is, proportionality may well create a broad enough group of winners or stakeholders to make subsequent change harder. Once systems drift towards proportionality it may be hard to move back away from it.

4   REASONS FOR CHANGE

Still, change does occur and explanations may be grouped into several kinds of categories: the role of values, the role of popular pressure, and the working of self-interest.

As noted above, elections carry with them implications for governability, representation, and accountability. Since elections do not just involve winners and losers but also have symbolic and even ritual importance, discussions of electoral reform can easily invoke those underlying values. Discussion of elections is often cast in terms of their contribution to a normative definition of a way a good society should be governed. Electoral reform may therefore also realize certain normative objectives as well as practical political ones. Britain's Liberal Democrats justify their support for a shift towards proportional representation as a process concern:

Governments likely to result from the introduction of proportional representation would be more reliant on persuasion and debate, rather than sheer weight of numbers, to guide through legislation. (Liberal Democrats 2000, 16)

Or consider the California Green Party's justification:

Our goal is direct, participatory, grassroots democracy centered around deeply democratic community assemblies and bioregional confederations. To accomplish this goal, our current focus is on proportional representation. It will give voters more choice, allow more voters to vote for winners, and break up the two-party monopoly, which discourages participation. (GPCA Platform 2004)

In both these cases prized normative democratic virtues (deliberation and participation) are to be accomplished through proportional representation. As a happy coincidence this shift not only helps realize democratic virtue; it would also likely give more seats to the Liberal Democrats and California Greens. Such happy coincidences muddy the waters when we try to distinguish between self-interested motivations and other kinds of concerns in electoral system reform. However, rather than see this as a rhetorical device disguising true intentions we could, equally, see the comments of California's Greens and Britain's Liberal Democrats as sincere statements of principle. Birch, Millard, and Williams' (2003, 185) discussion of reform in Eastern Europe, for example, notes the relevance of such factors as a concern for legitimacy or, where voters were involved, the reduction of corruption and an increase in the responsiveness of politicians (Sakamoto 1999).

Different electoral systems emphasize different aspects of the normative conception of representation. Descriptive representation in both the legislature and government is typically best fostered by proportional or semi-proportional systems (Powell 2000). These systems are also associated with higher levels of voter turnout (Blais and Dobryznska 1998). On the other hand, responsiveness may well be better achieved under majoritarian systems (Powell 2000). The choice of electoral system is not simply a choice over who wins and who loses but is also a choice between different—and possibly contradictory—normative values.

Appeals to the underlying values of democracy may well resonate especially strongly when voters are involved. Popular pressure may help change and may come through voters in established democracies. Voter discontent at key aspects of political performance—the corruption of the system and the lack of responsiveness of politicians—was instrumental in pushing changes in Italy and New Zealand (Sakamoto 1999; Vowles 1995). Similarly, debates over Canadian reform involved heavy citizen engagement. At the local level in the USA considerable experimentation with electoral systems takes place. Individual cities may well decide to experiment with electoral reform as a consequence of grass roots lobbying, an important example being San Francisco's move to Instant Runoff voting.[6]

As Sakamoto notes, however, it is easy to overstate the importance of popular pressure in electoral reform. In part this is because there are examples of reform efforts—such as Japan's but also many of the Eastern European changes—that simply do not involve a popular voice. In part, too, it is because most political systems just do not allow for voter choice over electoral institutions. Devices such as the initiative process are simply too rare to give voters a direct say in many places. Even the much more limited Italian version of direct democracy, while central to the story of reform in that country, is hardly more common. But even when political systems are listening or a least being exposed to popular discontent, it is far from clear that the solution to popular disaffection is to change the electoral system. There are other, less dramatic and possibly more consequential, changes that could be put in place. Electoral reform may well present a temporary fix but it is not clear that—even after an electoral reform—voters become re-enamored with the political system.

Nevertheless many electoral reform efforts are anchored in terms of the narrow self-interest of political parties. During 2004–5 Canada began a series of debates about electoral reform closely involving popular participation and opinion, most notably in British Columbia's "Citizens Assembly." This reform process began in Premier Campbell's 2001 election promise to change the system. This promise had its roots in the previous election (1996) when the New Democratic Party won a majority government, even though Campbell's Liberals polled more votes. Not surprisingly, the NDP did not feel the need to legislate any kind of electoral reform—until it was reduced to a two-member caucus in the 2001 election. Sakamoto's account of reform in Japan, for example, refers to the self-interest of factions within the LDP as a motor for change. A subtler version of self-interest and

---

[6] Instant Runoff (or, as the Australians call it, the Alternative Vote) is a single-member district in which voters rank order the candidates.

electoral change is found in Boix (1999) who sees electoral change by ruling parties being introduced in part to fend off worse results under majoritarian systems. A modern recent example may well be the French decision to abandon districts in favor of PR for the 1986 elections because the socialists worried about seat loss. Boix's interpretation has come under criticism from scholars who tend to see electoral change driven more by straightforward concerns over seat maximization of the kind outlined by Benoit in his model of electoral system change (Andrews and Jackman 2005; Blais, Dobrzynska, and Indridason 2005). But this disagreement turns more on a difference in the kind and definition of self-interest at stake rather than the self-interested motivations. Perhaps as exemplified in the decision of the French socialists to move back to districted systems after the 1986 election.[7] As Colomer notes, there are persistent patterns in the demand for change, smaller parties tend to push towards proportionality, larger parties are much more reluctant:

In general it can be postulated that *the large will prefer the small and the small will prefer the large.* A few large parties will prefer small assemblies, small district magnitudes (the smallest being one) and small quotas of votes for allocating seats (the smallest being simple plurality, which does not require any specific threshold), in order to exclude others from competition. Likewise, multiple small parties will prefer large assemblies, large district magnitudes and large quotas (like those of proportional representation) able to include them within. (Colomer 2005, 2)

The story of wholesale change in an electoral system is a complex one. The default is that no change takes place and it is easy to see why. It seems we need a more fully specified model of self-interest than the ones we have to date: self-interest seems to provide ample motive for winners to keep the system as is. But something must happen—either exogenous shocks or new calculations—to make the system change and we do not, yet, have a good sense of what those factors are.

5   OTHER THINGS DO CHANGE ... A LITTLE

One way of approaching the question of change is to look not so much at the system but at the supporting body of electoral laws. Most scholarly attention has focused—quite rightly—on the relationship between seats and votes and the

---

[7] Benoit himself uses the example of the first switch, not the switch back.

question of proportionality and "fairness" of a system. These are the main building blocks of an electoral system. But electoral laws have many more components than the system itself. Rules on ballot access, political advertising, or the financing of parties all affect, or at least we think they may affect, the performance of parties in elections. And the list of laws and rules governing features of elections is much longer than these three examples (Massicotte, Blais, and Yoshinaka 2004). The kinds of effects pointed out by Duverger may well explain what happens within a district but these broader kinds of supporting laws may regulate both the kinds of coordination that may occur across districts or, more simply, shape the playing field for parties in different ways. Laws on elections, then, may have similar, albeit milder, effects as electoral systems.

More importantly perhaps, they may be easier to change than electoral systems. A fairly simple model of electoral system change in which self-interested politicians jockey for advantage would—absent uncertainty and any costs to change at least— have us suppose that electoral systems are in a constant state of flux. This is, as the evidence of Colomer shows, most definitely not the case. Models of institutional change driven by rational actor models would probably need to build in compon- ents of uncertainty and costliness as a means of slowing down the changes. On the other hand, changes in electoral laws may well be easier to change and confer the same kinds of advantages as electoral manipulation, if on a smaller and more modest scale.

Some evidence of changes in laws does seem to support that pattern, as Birch shows for the Eastern European cases: the gradual inching up of some thresholds, some tightening of nomination procedures, and/or the introduction of a "deposit" for candidates tended to benefit bigger parties (with more resources) but, more importantly, raised the barriers to entry for newcomers (Birch, Millard, and Williams 2003, 189–91). But these tendencies were not seen everywhere. Some countries did not increase the vote threshold and in some places nomination requirements were relaxed.

One question is whether we see evidence of this attempt to keep out new entrants and protect current players in more established democracies as would be consistent with models grounded in rational self-interest. The available evidence on that is decidedly mixed. If anything, changes in some of the supporting electoral laws have seen a relaxation of barriers that could favour new entrants or at least smaller parties (Bowler, Carter, and Farrell 2001).

Even these kinds of changes have their own uncertainties and their own costs. It may not be worth changing entire electoral systems or even laws for the sake of one or two seats, notwithstanding the fact that politicians are motivated by seat maximization. Furthermore, too blatant a manipulation of electoral rules of any kind could well discredit the result from any new set of laws or rules in the eyes of voters or even some politicians. The choice of electoral rules may thus not be entirely unconstrained.

6   CONCLUSION: SUMMARY AND FUTURE DIRECTIONS

The study of electoral systems is one of the best developed in political science. It is a literature that has allowed us to arrive at a clear understanding both of the general properties of electoral systems and some specific features. In some ways, however, and despite the very real progress in our understanding of electoral systems, much remains to be done. After all, there seems to be far more stability, and far less scope for relatively simple rational self-interested explanations of electoral system change, than might be first thought. Given that our understanding of electoral systems is driven by the insight that systems shape outcomes and will, therefore, be subject to repeated attempts at manipulation for short-term gain, the appearance of stability is a little surprising. There seems to be lot less manipulation than we expect to see and would seem to require models of change that pay more attention to questions of uncertainty and cost.

One implication of this surprising pattern of stability is that we may, perhaps, be a little too confident of our understanding of elections. Scholars of electoral systems tend to be quite close to debates over electoral system reform and are often involved as expert witnesses (Jenkins Commission 1998). The flourishing of democracy over the past generation has been paralleled by attempts at electoral engineering with academic experts often acting as engineer or assistant engineer. Within the literature on electoral systems, scholars such as Taagepera (1998) are not hesitant to make recommendations and believe there is a role for electoral engineering. Farrell notes that scholars such as Taagepera are not alone and that the "bulk" of political scientists advocate for specific systems (Farrell 2001, 181). But some scholars are more circumspect. Katz in *Democracy and Elections* is among the most cautious in thinking that the best system for a country depends "who you are, where you are, and where you want to go" (Katz 1997, 208). None of these questions necessarily have straightforward answers. And outside the well-traveled path of proportionality and the broader brush strokes of Duverger's Law, the consequences of electoral laws are not entirely clear. Like the politicians in post-cold war Eastern Europe, the academic literature may have a general understanding of electoral systems but, despite the richness of the literature, we still need to know more.

Future directions of electoral studies research will move beyond the question of proportionality—which is by now pretty much settled—and into newer areas. One area is in the effects of the electoral system on governance. Electoral systems typically involve trade-offs among different properties and Lijphart and Powell have begun to move the literature forward in examining the trade-offs that are, or are not, possible. For Powell, for example, there are distinct trade-offs between policy responsiveness on the one hand and representation on the other (Powell 2000).

For some this means that mixed systems—systems that combine elements of both plurality and proportionality—are the answer (Shugart and Wattenberg 2003).[8] However, our understanding of the working of these systems seems to be both more restricted and also more dependent on specific cases than our understanding of other systems. But we also need more work examining the trade-offs implied by different electoral systems, an area that has received relatively little attention to date.

Finally, democracy has spread to a new range of countries. We have already seen work re-examining the old findings in new contexts to see, for example, if what held for Germany will hold, say, for Poland or Hungary. But the countries of Eastern Europe neighbor rich and democratic Western Europe and, in many cases, had brief experiences of democracy prior to Communist rule. Their—largely successful—experience with elections may not be so readily copied in countries such as Afghanistan and Iraq. Perhaps one of the bigger trends in electoral studies, then, will follow one of the bigger trends in world politics: The spread of elections to the Middle East and Asia. One of the biggest possibilities of this move of elections to "the East" is not so much what these regions will learn but what the rest of us will learn about electoral systems from those regions.

REFERENCES

AMY, D. J. 2002. *Real Choices/New Voices: How Proportional Representation Elections Could Revitalize American Democracy* New York: Columbia University Press.

ANDERSON, C. 1995. *Blaming the Government: Citizens and the Economy in Five European Democracies.* New York: M. E. Sharpe.

ANDREWS, J. and JACKMAN, R. 2005. Strategic fools: electoral choice under extreme uncertainty. *Electoral Studies,* 24 (1): 65–84.

BARBER, K. 1995. *Proportional Representation and Election Reform in Ohio.* Columbus: Ohio State University Press.

BAWN, K. 1993. The logic of institutional preferences: German electoral law as a social choice outcome. *American Journal of Political Science,* 37: 965–89.

BENOIT, K. 2004. Models of electoral system change. *Electoral Studies,* 23: 363–89

BIRCH, A. H. 1971. *Representation.* London: Pall Mall Press.

BIRCH, F., MILLARD, M., and WILLIAMS, K. 2003. *Embodying Democracy: Electoral System Design in Post-Communist Europe.* London: Palgrave-Macmillan.

BLAIS, A. 1988. The classification of electoral systems. *Electoral Studies,* 16: 99–110.

—— and DOBRZYNSKA, A. 1998. Turnout in electoral democracies. *European Journal of Political Research,* 33: 239–61.

—— —— and INDRIDASON, I. 2005. To adopt or not to adopt proportional representation: the politics of institutional choice. *British Journal of Political Science,* 35 (1): 182–90.

BOIX, C. 1999. Setting the rules of the game: the choice of electoral systems in advanced democracies. *American Political Science Review,* 93 (3): 609–24.

[8] Examples of these systems are found in Germany, New Zealand, Russia, and Mexico.

Boston, J., Levine, S., McLeay, E., and Roberts, N. (eds.) 1997. *From Campaign to Coalition: The 1996 MMP Election*. Wellington: Dunmore Press.

Bowler, S. 1996. Reasoning voters, voter behaviour and institutions. In *British Elections and Parties Yearbook*, ed. D. Farrell, D. Broughton, D. Denver, and J. Fisher. London: Frank Cass.

—— and Farrell, D. 1993. Legislators shirking and voter monitoring: impacts of European Parliament electoral systems on legislator–voter relationships. *Journal of Common Market Studies*, 31: 45–69.

—— Carter, E., and Farrell, D. M. 2003. Studying electoral institutions and their consequences. Pp. 81–114 in *Democracy Transformed?* ed. B. E. Cain, R. J. Dalton, and S. E. Scarrow. Oxford: Oxford University Press.

—— Donovan, T., and Brockington, D. 2004. *Electoral Reform and Minority Representation: Local Experiments with Alternative Elections*. Columbus: Ohio State University Press.

Cain, B. E., Ferejohn, J., and Fiorina, M. 1987. *The Personal Vote: Constituency Service and Electoral Independence*. Cambridge, Mass.: Harvard University Press,

Carey, J. and Shugart, M. 1995. Incentives to cultivate a personal vote: a rank ordering of electoral formulas. *Electoral Studies*, 14 (4): 417–39.

Chhibber, P. and Kollman, K. 2004. *The Formation of National Party Systems*. Princeton, NJ: Princeton University Press.

Colomer, J. 2004. *Handbook of Electoral System Choice*. London: Palgrave Macmillan.

—— 2005. It's parties that choose electoral systems (or Duverger's laws upside down). *Political Studies*, 53 (1): 1–21.

Cox, G. 1997. *Making Votes Count*. Cambridge: Cambridge University Press.

Farrell, D. M. 2001. *Electoral Systems: A Comparative Introduction*. London: Palgrave.

Fearon, J. 1999. Electoral accountability and the control of politicians: selecting good types versus sanctioning poor performance. In *Democracy, Accountability, and Representation*, ed. B. Manin, A. Przeworski, and S. Stokes. Cambridge: Cambridge University Press.

Gallagher, M. 1991. Proportionality, disproportionality and electoral systems. *Electoral Studies*, 10 (1): 33–51.

Grofman, B. and Lijphart, A. 1986. *Electoral Laws and their Political Consequences*. New York: Agathon Press.

International Institute for Democracy and Electoral Assistance (IDEA) 2002. *The International IDEA Handbook of Electoral System Design*. Stockholm: Sweden.

Jenkins Commission 1998. *Independent Commission On Electoral Reform*. London: HMSO.

Katz, R. 1997. *Democracy and Elections* Oxford: Oxford University Press.

Knight, J. 1992. *Institutions and Social Conflict*. Cambridge: Cambridge University Press.

Lakeman, E. 1954. *How Democracies Vote*. London: Faber and Faber.

Laver, M. and Schofield, N. 1998. *Multiparty Government: The Politics of Coalition in Europe*. Ann Arbor: University of Michigan Press

Lijphart, A. 1990. The political consequences of electoral laws. *American Political Science Review*, 84: 481–96.

—— 1994. *Electoral Systems and Party Systems: A Study of Twenty-Seven Democracies 1945–1990*. Oxford: Oxford University Press.

Massicotte, L., Blais, A., and Yoshinaka, A. 2004. *Establishing the Rules of the Game: Election Laws in Democracies*. Toronto: University of Toronto Press.

Milner, H. 1994. Obstacles to electoral reform in Canada. *American Review of Canadian Studies* 24 (1): 39–55.

Powell, G. B., Jr. 2000. *Elections as Instruments of Democracy: Majoritarian and Proportional Visions*. New Haven, Conn.: Yale University Press.

Rae, D. 1971. *The Political Consequences of Electoral Laws*. New Haven, Conn.: Yale University Press.

Remington, T. F. and Smith, S. S., 1996. Political goals, institutional context, and the choice of an electoral system: the Russian parliamentary election law. *American Journal of Political Science*, 40: 1253–79.

Riker, W. H. 1982. The two-party system and Duverger's law: an essay on the history of political science. *American Political Science Review*, 76: 753–66.

Sakamoto, T. 1999. Explaining electoral reform: Japan versus Italy and New Zealand. *Party Politics*, 5 (4): 419–38.

Schattschneider, E. E. 1942. *Party Government*. Westport, Conn.: Greenwood Press; repr. 1977.

Shugart, M. S. and Wattenberg, P. (eds.) 2003. *Mixed-Member Electoral Systems: The Best of Both Worlds?* Oxford: Oxford University Press.

Shvetsova, O. 2003. Endogenous selection of institutions and their exogenous effects. *Constitutional Political Economy*, 14: 191–212.

Taagepera, R. 1997. The Tailor of Marrakesh: Western electoral systems advice to emerging democracies. In *Electoral Systems for Emerging Democracies*, ed. J. Elklit. Copenhagen: Danish Ministry of Foreign Affairs.

—— and Shugart, M. 1989. *Seats and Votes: The Effects and Determinants of Electoral Systems*. New Haven, Conn.: Yale University Press.

Tsebelis, G. 1999. *Nested Game: Rational Choice and Comparative Politics*. Berkeley: University of California Press.

Vowles, J. 1995. The politics of electoral reform in New Zealand. *International Political Science Review*, 16: 95–115.

—— Aimer, P., Karp, J., Banducci, S., Miller, R., and Sullivan, A. 2002. *Proportional Representation on Trial: The 1999 Election in New Zealand and the Fate of MMP*. Aotearoa: Auckland University Press.

CHAPTER 30

DIRECT DEMOCRACY

IAN BUDGE

1 DEMOCRACY AND DIRECT DEMOCRACY

Most scholars agree broadly with the definition of democracy (Saward 1998, 51) as a "necessary correspondence between acts of governance and the equally weighted felt interests of citizens with respect to these acts." A key element is *necessary* correspondence. It is included to answer a stock criticism: Would not a benevolent despot do as well for citizens' felt interests as a democracy?—or, in terms of our discussion below: Would not autonomous and benevolent representatives serve citizens' interests as well as or better than direct majoritarian democracy? The answer, in either form of the question, holds that a simple correspondence of interests and policy is not enough. What distinguishes democracy is an institutional mechanism for *ensuring* the correspondence. This mechanism is the democratic election. The centrality of elections to democracy stems from the fact that they provide a recurring opportunity for citizens to express and empower their interests.[1]

---

[1] The literature on direct democracy is highly fragmented, straddling normative and empirical aspects, comparative analyses and single country case studies, technical studies of the effects of new technology on direct debate, and discussion and mathematical analyses of voting procedures. The most comprehensive synthesis remains Budge 1996. The equivalent for the actual practices of direct democracy is Le Duc 2003—the most up-to-date general review of this field. Indispensable earlier compilations were Butler and Ranney 1994, now however a little dated by the explosion of new research, and Gallagher and Uleri 1996. The most recent and relevant is Mendelsohn and Parkin 2001.

From this point of view, there is also a scholarly consensus that direct voting by all citizens on individual policies *is* the most direct way of ensuring that their preferences are necessarily reflected in policy (e.g. Mill 1861/1910, 217–18). This has led to measures for extending direct democracy being placed among the key demands of most radical and progressive groups, and accounts for its growing popularity and use in the late twentieth century (Budge 1996; Mendelsohn and Parkin 2001; Le Duc 2003).

At this point, however, the scholarly consensus veers the other way, seeing long-term disadvantages and many short-term threats to democratic stability and order associated with direct democracy. The major criticisms can be summarized as follows:

1. General elections already let citizens choose between alternative governments and programs.
2. It is impossible to have direct debate and voting on policies in modern democracies owing to the impossibility of getting all citizens together for the requisite time.
3. Ordinary citizens do not have the education, interest, time, expertise, and other qualities required to make good political decisions.
4. Good decisions are most likely to be produced where popular participation is balanced by expert judgment.
5. Those who vote against a particular decision do not give their consent to it, particularly if the same people are always in the minority.
6. No procedure for democratic collective decision-making can be guaranteed not to produce arbitrary and unwanted outcomes (cf. Arrow 1951).
7. Without intermediary institutions (parties, legislatures, governments) no coherent, stable, or informed policies will be made. Direct democracy undermines intermediary institutions including parties and opens the way to the tyranny of a shifting majority.

With few exceptions, classical political theorists from the eighteenth to the twentieth centuries have viewed direct democracy in these critical terms, the most influential perhaps being the authors of the *Federalist Papers* (Madison 1787–8/ 1911) with their distrust of popular majorities and emphasis on representation, balance of powers, and institutional constraints. The great exception has been Rousseau (1762/1973) with *his* focus on untrammeled popular sovereignty. Most critics have taken this as the only form in which direct democracy could express itself. But there are others described below.

Modern empirical research (Butler and Ranney 1994; Gallagher and Uleri 1996; Mendelsohn and Parkin 2001; Le Duc 2003; Kriesi 2005) has set out to investigate these claims with evidence from actual policy votes (referendums and initiatives) which are now held in a surprising number of countries. It is fair to say that their conclusions tell against the more extreme criticisms of popular involvement in decision-making. In particular, recent research provides quite positive responses to many of the criticisms listed above:

1. Many issues are not discussed at general elections so, if the people are to decide, they need to vote on them directly
2. Even postal ballots and the print media let alone two-way communication devices allow interactive debate and voting among physically separated citizens.
3. Politicians do not necessarily show expertise and interest. Participation expands citizen capacities. Citizens currently spend a lot of time informing themselves about politics through TV and radio.
4. Expertise is important but not infallible. In any case it can inform popular decisions. Modern representative (party) democracies are heavily imbalanced against popular participation.
5. Those who vote against decisions do not consent to them. But this problem is general and not confined to direct democracy. Voting on issues one by one gives minorities more voice.
6. Arbitrary decisions may emerge from cyclic voting. But such problems are generic to all democratic voting procedures. Voting on dichotomous questions one by one (the usual procedure in popular policy consultations) eliminates cyclical voting and guarantees a majority.
7. Direct democracy does not *have* to be unmediated. Parties and governments could play the same role as in representative (party) democracies today.

The last point, of those listed above, is perhaps the most relevant today since modern democracy *is* largely party democracy. Curiously, the debate on the merits of direct vs. representative democracy has generally ignored the major political innovation of the last century, the development of the mass political party. Direct policy voting by all citizens through referendums and initiatives has been contrasted with classic early nineteenth-century election of individual representatives on their own merits, rather than on the basis of common party programs. It is assumed that representatives will use their own judgment in deciding on policy, exposing themselves to popular opinion only when they come up for re-election.

However, parties now mainly compete by offering ideologically differentiated policy programs to the electorate. "Representative democracy" in its modern form thus adds up to direct policy voting. But in contrast to "direct democracy," as classically and currently conceived, this is voting on a package of policies rather than on each individual policy within the package. This could make a difference. Voting on policies individually, one by one, cannot be absolutely guaranteed to produce the same outcome as voting on a policy package as a whole—though of course it generally may (Budge 1996, 143, for an illustration).

However, one thing is clear—all democracies these days and all forms of democracy, involve elections based on policy choices. Any idea that parties or elected individuals can proceed exclusively, or even largely, on their own judgment simply ignores reality. The real debate is whether package voting of policy under "representative" democracy is more or less democratic than individual votes on policy, or vice versa.

The similarities between all modern forms of democracy are further reinforced by the presence of parties in all of them. Direct policy voting and particularly initiatives (where voting can be initiated by any group of citizens with sufficient support) are often advocated as a way of avoiding, or even undermining, parties. In practice however parties find their way back in—using these devices to publicize and organize themselves, bargain to their own advantage, force through proposals blocked in parliament, or avoid internal splits by "agreeing to disagree" on potentially damaging issues (Mendelsohn and Parkin 2001). It has been convincingly argued that parties are just as essential for organizing the vote and informing citizens of the real issues involved in individual policy votes as in general elections (Lupia 1994)[2].

If modern "representative democracy" and "direct democracy" are only different forms of "party democracy," many of the contrasts traditionally drawn between them dramatically disappear. A telling criticism of direct democracy which increasingly appears in modern discussions is, therefore, that it dispenses with or undermines intermediary institutions like parties, legislatures, and governments. This certainly seems a valid criticism of the unmediated direct democracy many radicals yearn for—a direct and undiluted expression of the popular will uncontaminated by wheeling-and-dealing and party fixes. To assess the force of the criticism we have to ask if this unmediated form is the only one direct individual/policy voting can take? In practice parties often intervene in referendums or sponsor initiatives for their own ideological or office seeking purposes. In the next section we ask whether this is a valid expression of direct democracy or a perversion of it, and whether therefore the criticism of unanchored majority tyranny applies to direct democracy as such or simply to particular manifestations of it.

2   Varieties of Direct Democracy

Many criticisms of direct policy voting are based on the idea that it dispenses with mediating institutions such as parties and with the rules and procedures which, for example, guide legislative debate. This removes the constraints which produce

---

[2] Political systems which have incorporated direct democracy into their processes for a long time have been much studied for its long-term effects. Switzerland is the obvious case, with excellent books by Linder 1994 and Kriesi 2005. Italy has a special chapter in most compilations, particularly Gallagher and Uleri 1996. The US states are the subject of two thorough and excellent studies by Magleby 1984 and Cronin 1989—the latter quoting conclusions to the effect that there is little discernable difference in policy outcomes between states with direct legislation and those without. The post-Communist countries of Central and Eastern Europe mostly incorporate provisions for popular legislation into their constitutions, so it is interesting to see how and how often they were used in their first decade (Auer and Bützer 2001).

compromise and stability and overstrains the capacity of citizens to make good decisions by effectively placing them in a vacuum. In turn this promotes instability by favoring the emergence of a new majority concerned to correct the mistakes or counter the imbalances produced by the previous one.

Certainly the idea of unmediated voting which "lets the people speak" is one that has inspired many supporters of direct democracy. Equally clearly their ideal opens itself to many of the criticisms made above. In most countries and popular consultations, however, voting is not unmediated: parties and other groups participate and courts, governments, and legislatures may all decide the wording of questions, lay down rules for the conduct of the campaign, and even take sides.

All this underlines the point that direct democracy is as synonymous with party and other mediation as with a lack of it. Rules and procedural constraints may be more or less present in referendums and initiatives but are never entirely absent. Insofar, therefore, as criticisms are focused on unmediated direct democracy they are possibly valid—but for that form only, not for direct democracy as such.

Conceptually the same point may be made by considering the base definition of direct democracy—which has surely to be the electorate voting on questions which, in traditional representative democracy, parliament votes on. How the vote is held clearly affects the concrete form which direct democracy takes. But it is clear that both mediated and unmediated forms fall under the definition. The only requirement of direct democracy is that the people vote on individual policies. How they organize themselves to vote does not affect the fact that this is direct democracy.

Looking at the extent of party mediation under various forms of direct democracy cautions us against identifying it exclusively with an unmediated form. Even in ancient Athens, crude party organizations were present in the form of political clubs (Bonner 1967, 45, 61): they were the most effective way for statesmen like Pericles and Demosthenes to ensure their majority in the Assembly and thus maintain stability and continuity in public policy—the functions of the political party in all ages.

This contrasts with the idealized Rousseauesque account (Rousseau 1762/1973) where the popular will has to be unmediated to be pure. California is the modern example which approaches closest to unmediated direct policy voting but even there, parties and party-affiliated groups intervene. Lupia and Johnson (2001, 191–210) argue that this is necessary for "competent voting" and point out that even in California voters are pretty adept at spotting which groups support which side and making inferences from this about the political import of proposals. Other American states see greater party intervention on important proposals (Magleby 1994, 88, 94), a tendency which becomes the norm in countries like Italy and Switzerland.

All this is to make the obvious point that procedural rules are necessary for votes, even popular votes, to be held. We would not expect a representative democracy to function without a constitution (written or unwritten), presiding officers, rules of procedure, and debate. No more should we expect a direct democracy to do so. Just as representative democracies may have more or less regulation of these matters, so may direct democracies. To California we can contrast Quebec with a whole branch of law devoted to the few referendums that have been held.

Most of the criticisms made in Section 1 apply particularly or exclusively to unmediated and relatively unregulated forms of popular policy voting. As such they may have a high degree of validity. However, the solution under direct democracy as under representative democracy is not to abandon it but to strengthen procedures in order to deal with these dangers, and to encourage mediation rather than discourage it. This may put off many advocates of participatory or discursive democracy who wish to let the people speak unmediated. But if direct democracy consists in deciding individual policy through popular votes, mediation is quite consistent with it (Budge 2000).

3   DOES DIRECT DEMOCRACY WEAKEN POLITICAL PARTIES?

In popular votes in the contemporary world many bodies play an important mediating role: courts, governments, and legislatures may all decide on the exact question to be put to voters, when the vote will be held, what the consequences will be—as well even as advocating what option to vote for. As we have argued above, this does not disqualify such voting as expressions of direct democracy. Mediated forms are as valid within this context as unmediated.

Of the groups intervening in votes, by far the most important are political parties, for the reasons already given. They formulate the questions to be put, inform electors what is at stake, and put the issue in a broader context. They generally finance and organize the campaign.

One objection to direct democracy, however, is that it may itself undermine and subvert political parties, by corroding their organizations, electoral loyalty, control of government, agenda setting, internal discipline, and ideological coherence. Clearly if that did happen it would mean that direct democracy necessarily weakens mediation and thus give renewed force to the criticisms summarized above.

No conclusive case has been put forward for such effects existing however (Budge 1996, 105–32; Mendelsohn and Parkin 2001, 7–8). The United States is often cited as a country where parties weakened considerably in the last third of the twentieth century (e.g. Wattenburg 1990). As organizations they have often been seen as "hollowed out" by candidates like Carter and Kerry who fought their way through primary elections with their own personal organization and finances, using the formal party apparatus only as an adjunct in the later campaign. The growing impact of third party candidates like Wallace, Perot, and Nader also seemed to testify to the eclipse of traditional parties. California, with its plethora of largely unmediated policy votes and weak parties, was at the forefront of all these developments. Accordingly the weakening of parties was associated with the growth of initiatives and primaries which took decisions out of the traditional smoke-filled rooms and into the hands of untutored electors. In the light of these trends, American scholars saw popular voting weakening parties elsewhere (Kobach 1994, 132), ignoring their 150-year survival or even flourishing coexistence with referendums and initiatives (Switzerland) or long history of institutionalized factionalism *before* popular policy voting (Italy).

These critiques overlook the possibility that parties can change without necessarily weakening or declining. The resurgence of intense party competition in the 2004 presidential election, the massive organizational efforts of both parties, and unprecedented turnout of that year indicate that the preceding thirty years may only have been a phase in the USA. In any case this was the period when the Republicans built themselves up for their takeover of power at federal and state level—partly by exploiting referendums and initiatives where they were available. The point is that the same trends occurred in states with and without popular policy voting so can hardly be attributed to it in any causal sense (Budge 2001, 81–2).

An emphasis on the ability of autonomous legislators to produce compromise also reflects an idealized picture of US politics before they became ideological. Where is the room for compromise in the confrontational clashes of government and opposition under the "elective dictatorship" of the Westminster model? The *immobilisme* of the French and Italian legislatures was only made tolerable by social and constitutional reforms passed in referendums.

As for control of the political agenda passing out of the hands of political parties, this simply ignores the ability of parties to pursue their objectives by other than parliamentary means when they are blocked at that level. The efforts of Australian parties to promote constitutional reforms in their own interest (Mendelsohn and Parkin 2001, 114–19) have mostly been blocked by lack of support. But they keep on trying. In Italy the new and excluded parties (radicals, greens, and communists) saw in the peculiar constitutional form of the "referendum abroga-tivo,"[3] the opportunity to promote popular initiatives by collecting signatures and organizing a nationwide vote on policy. This unblocked the parliamentary process

---

[3] Constitutionally in Italy popular votes can only repeal a particular piece of legislation which parliament can then decide to replace. In practice the alternative law to be enacted forms part of the popular campaign and parliament has almost always voted in line with popular opinion.

and thus kept the existing system in being until the 1990s. It also strengthened the position of these parties in both organizational and popular terms.

This use of referendums and initiatives by new and opposition parties to publicize themselves and sometimes to threaten governments was historically used in Switzerland, first by the Catholic party at the end of the nineteenth century and then by the socialists in the interwar period to force themselves into the governing coalition (Linder 1994, 19–21, 29–31). From the 1970s onwards the Republicans have used this technique to transform themselves from the subordinate to the dominant party in southern and western US states, and are now starting to do the same in California. One should avoid equating the decline of previously dominant parties like the Democrats as evidence for a weakening of parties as such. All these cases demonstrate that as one party goes down the others go up. It could even be argued that direct democracy strengthens "the forces restoring party competition" (Stokes and Iverson 1962).

In a careful comparative analysis based on both case studies and statistical evidence, Mendelsohn and Parkin (2001, 7–8 and passim) conclude there is simply no evidence for direct democracy weakening parties. On the contrary, as argued above, it adds to their repertoire—while of course allowing for more interventions by other groups and by electors themselves. We turn in the next section to an examination of how the concrete forms and procedures of direct democracy give relative advantages to the various participants—again with a primary focus on political parties, given that modern direct democracy like modern representative democracy is above all party democracy.

4   PROCEDURES OF DIRECT DEMOCRACY— REFERENDUM AND INITIATIVE

The two forms which individual policy voting takes in the modern world are the referendum and the initiative. In general the referendum is called by some political body, most often the (party-controlled) government, while the initiative is instituted by petition from a sufficient number of citizens. The rules governing initiation of the process obviously give greater or lesser scope to various political actors to influence voting. If voting is at the government's discretion they can call a referendum only when they hope to win (or "agree to disagree" to avoid damaging internal splits). This gives them considerable tactical advantages as well as diminishing the efficacy of the popular vote. On the other hand, where initiatives can be organized independently of government wishes, greater scope exists for excluded and new parties to achieve some policy objectives, as well as publicizing themselves. This procedure also allows other groups and indeed spontaneous organizations of electors themselves to exert influence[4].

However, we should avoid making too sharp a contrast between referendums and initiatives, since there are important distinctions to be made within both categories (cf. Bowler and Donovan 2001, 128–9). Referendums mandated by the constitution—especially when this provision is interpreted by the courts—fall outwith the control of government and may occur at very inconvenient times from their point of view. Some initiatives on the other hand are not conclusive—like the Italian "referendum abrogativo" (see footnote 3)—and the final decision has to be made by parliament (even if it broadly conforms to majority preferences).

There is thus considerable variation in terms of government control over voting. The ability to set the date of a referendum favors governing parties. Usually this implies also that they have full control of the wording of the question to be put to the vote and may also slant this to favor their side, as well as campaigning vociferously for it. Referendums of this nature are most common under the "Westminster model" where constitutions commonly do not have any provision for popular consultations other than general elections, so that the referendum takes the form of a special dispensation by the government to allow a popular vote.

Where the constitution makes explicit reference to the need for a referendum on certain policy matters (often constitutional change itself) the process can be initiated by the government—in which case it is still largely in its discretion whether it wants to pursue the question or not. Where however the process is triggered automatically by constitutional provisions (usually in this case supervised by courts) voting may occur at an awkward time for government parties and their control is diminished. Again this is particularly true in Switzerland where practically all matters of foreign policy have to be put to a vote: Swiss cantons and certain US states also have wide provisions forcing votes on fiscal or revenue matters.

Such effects are of course intensified where popular votes can be prompted by popular petition. While this is inconvenient for governing parties in whatever form it exists, it may be particularly so where by convention or rule the process can be started by parties. Opposition parties generally use this opportunity to embarrass governments while new parties use it to promote their own causes and themselves. In any case the issues are likely either to be off the government agenda or to call into question established policy.

[4] Most empirical research is spurred by a general concern to find out whether the postulated negative effects of direct democracy actually appear when it is practiced. Generally they do not seem to, though researchers have hedged this conclusion around with qualifications about what might occur in the long term. They have also discerned some problematic effects for established political parties. The theoretical consequences of destructured forms of voting are covered in Arrow 1951, McKelvey 1979, McLean 1989, and—from the opposed point of view that structure is rarely absent—in Niemi 1969. Grofman and Feld 1988 provide a fascinating account of a mathematical theorem which might lead us to the belief that unstructured popular majority voting on policy produces the best results.

This is also true where the process of organizing an initiative is outside the control of any party, established or opposition (even though new parties, as yet barely distinguishable from interest groups or social movements, may still benefit from a free-for-all). In the long run, however, such a situation approaches unmediated direct democracy and can be expected to have some of the negative effects on all parties, particularly in terms of agenda setting, as spelled out above.

The form in which electors are asked to vote in both referendums and initiatives is generally to approve or disapprove a specific proposal such as joining the EU (e.g. in many of the Eastern European candidate members in 2004). Majority disapproval means that the situation remains unchanged. In other words, the alternative to the proposed change is usually the status quo. Voters tend to favor no change as a safe alternative when they are confused or unclear about the effects a new proposal will have. This happens quite often. Insofar as popular voting undermines the agenda of established parties, this tendency favors them.

The status quo, and the government position, are also reinforced in federal systems such as Switzerland and Australia where not only is a national majority required for a measure to pass, but also majorities in a majority of states (e.g. in Australia in four out of six). This puts considerable blocking power in the hands of states with small populations which may even form the majority of federal units. Federal as well as democratic values are being protected here and territorial minorities may be effectively safeguarded from a steamrolling popular majority if they predominate within some of the units. Similar effects flow from provisions that a popular vote is valid only if total voting passes a stipulated threshold (commonly, 50 percent of electors or voters in the previous general election). In several recent Italian votes, opponents have urged abstention. This effectively lines up the apathetic and uninterested on your side under a stipulated turnout rule and has been very successful in defeating new proposals.

Phrasing the policy question as a yes or no choice—an almost universal practice—helps to simplify decisions for voters and avoids the kind of Condorcet voting cycles which might arise from rank-ordering a set of alternatives (Arrow 1951). Where the maneuver is permitted, opponents of the measure may, however, also seek to dilute its effects by putting a series of modified alternative proposals on the same ballot (often involving little change to the existing situation). Even if the original proposal also gets a majority, the composite policy which emerges as the final outcome will dilute the effects of change fairly effectively. Tactics of this kind are common in the unregulated situations typical of California, and have been used in Switzerland. In more regulated situations, such tactics are prohibited and courts stipulate that only one proposal may be put in each policy area (Mendelsohn and Parkin 2001; Le Duc 2003).

All this reinforces the general point that parties are better served by extensive regulation of direct policy votes than by an absence of them. Quebec, where a whole codification of the process has been passed into law, can be contrasted with

California, where very few regulations exist about the actual conduct of campaigns. Thus, in Quebec, groups on each side of the debate must register the nature of their interest with an umbrella "No" or "Yes" committee, spending is minutely regulated for each group, and broadcasting is allocated proportionately. Advertising is also regulated. Contrast this with California where groups can campaign as Democrats for Life even though the party itself supports abortion.

Extensive regulation of referendums and initiatives is likely to favor established parties, at least insofar as it imposes barriers to the uninhibited tactics of new parties. But even the latter are favored by some regulation: spending limits for example mean that opponents cannot simply drown out competition with their spending and advertising. Lack of regulation leaves the field open for all sorts of organizations to campaign, often financed covertly by those who benefit directly (going back to earlier points made about unmediated direct democracy).

5 Policy Areas Covered by Popular Voting

Popular policy votes tend to be held disproportionately in five areas of policy: changes in the constitution; territorial questions covering secessions or extensions of the national territory, devolution, and autonomy; foreign policy; moral matters such as divorce, abortion, and homosexuality; and ecology and environment (including local campaigns for protection of particular features, or in opposition to the siting of a power plant). In Swiss cantons and American states, fiscal matters are increasingly voted on, usually involving tax limitation and restrictions on the size of government. (For up to date surveys of content-matter see Le Duc 2003.)

It can be seen from this that policy voting tends to take place either on issues of a certain level of generality—constitutions or foreign policy measures like trade liberalization that will have a long-term effect—or in areas which fit uneasily into the left–right division of party politics and which might indeed provoke internal splits, like moral and ecological matters. The closest policy votes come to influencing the current political agenda is on fiscal matters. Even tax limitation has a long-term rather than an immediate effect however. Almost never is a vote held to "prioritize unemployment now," "stop inflation," "end the war," "reduce prison population," and so on.

Several factors contribute to this pattern of policy consultation. First, and perhaps most importantly, governments do not want to put their central policies to referendum. So where they have control, voting will not cover issues central to left–right conflicts—only to off-issues which might split the party. New and opposition parties have generally also mobilized to put such issues on the agenda and not to refight continuing party battles.

A party-based explanation is only one part of the answer, however, since the same pattern occurs also in fairly unregulated initiatives where parties have less control. It is probable that electors themselves and even self-interested groups see no point in taking up matters that have already been part of the general election debate, putting into office parties which are pursuing them as part of a mandate. As we stressed at the outset, so called representative elections are heavily focused around medium-term policy plans, so it is natural that they should be left to get on with them at least in their first years in office (and it often takes time to organize a referendum or initiative).

In this way a certain division of labor seems to be emerging spontaneously between general, programmatic, elections and direct policy voting on individual issues. Where issues are linked together and form an integral part of the activity of governments, usually within the traditional left–right framework, the parties in power are left to get on with them. Where individual issues have long-term implications and do not fit so easily into a unifying framework, they tend disproportionately to be the subject of special popular votes. This overall mix does not seem to be a bad way of trying to translate popular preferences into public policy and in fact approaches that advocated by Budge (1996, 183–6) as a way in which contemporary democracies could evolve into (mediated) direct ones.

6 SETTING PARAMETERS FOR A REALISTIC DEBATE ABOUT DIRECT DEMOCRACY

A final conclusion about individual issue voting is that it is on the increase. In the latest, survey Le Duc (2003, 21–2, 152) estimates that its use increased from around 250 times in the period 1961–80 to nearly 350 in the period 1981–2000 over the countries of the world, excluding Switzerland. In both the American states and Switzerland policy votes doubled in the last twenty years compared to the preceding period. In many jurisdictions such as the German Länder, the UK, and New Zealand individual policy votes have now been introduced for the first time.

There is probably little to surprise us in this trend. In a world where the majority of citizens are better-educated, better off, and increasingly self-confident, it is natural that they should take the promise of democracy seriously and seek to get their preferences directly enacted into public policy. The ability of democracy to make a "necessary connection" between the two through elections is as we have seen its core characteristic. This is what gives direct democracy its driving force and wide appeal in the modern world: there is no better way of enforcing the link than by voting directly on each policy.

Of course, the groups pressing for direct voting often have other motivations too. They feel their causes—whether to reduce taxes or protect the environment—are so obviously correct that they will get majority support if they can only get them on the ballot and sweep self-serving parties away. So far analysts have failed to find any clear evidence that direct policy voting favors particular outcomes, in terms of either direct votes or indirect influence on legislatures from the threat of an initiative. There is some evidence, however, that its presence does bring policy closer to median (majority) voter preferences—which vary of course over time and between jurisdictions (Gerber and Hug 2001, 106). This is a matter which clearly merits further research.

As critics have pointed out, sweeping away parties and other mediating institutions brings many undesirable consequences which may lead in the end to popular majorities voting against their own preferences and interests. This may result from a lack of the essential if minimal information about wider implications which party endorsements provide, or from shifting majorities voting against taxes in one consultation and for public services in another.

Despite the aspirations of many of its advocates, however, direct democracy does not generally take on an anti-party or non-partisan form. It can be argued that even in the US states established parties fought back successfully against policy proposals which threatened their central interests, as with tax cuts (Cronin 1989, 205–6). The minority Republicans also built up to their present dominance by exploiting popular initiatives, among other tactics. Elsewhere established parties dominate referendums, and opposition and emergent parties exploit policy votes to embarrass the government and force their own recognition. Of course, the best way to fight parties is to form an anti-party party, which many proponents of extended participation and popular voting do (e.g. the German Greens and Danish Progress Party).

In terms of actual practice, therefore, direct democracy tends towards either strongly mediated or moderately mediated rather than unmediated forms. This is hardly surprising as it tends to take place in party-run representative democracies with a plethora of institutions—governments, parliaments, bureaucracy, and courts—overseeing its processes and codifying them along the lines of fair play embodied in general elections. The American experience should not be allowed to dominate discussion, especially since weak regulation of representative as well as direct elections is the norm there.

Convergence between specific policy consultations and general election practice should not be surprising since they are both about policy. An essential starting point for informed debate should be that so-called representative democracy is actually about putting policy packages to electors and following through on them in government. By making the party supported by the median voter the median party in parliament, its program is empowered even under coalition governments (McDonald and Budge 2005).

Our choice between direct democracy and representative democracy should not therefore continue to base itself on outdated contrasts between popular policy decision and representative deliberation. Rather it should characterize itself as being between individual policy voting and package policy voting. Put this way it seems much less apocalyptic than it has been portrayed. The two procedures cannot be 100 percent guaranteed against producing different outcomes but this is far from saying that they will generally do so.

In any case, decisions on the issues involved are probably best arrived at using the different procedures. Where issues are linked to each other, generally through forming part of left–right divisions, decisions on one may well have consequences for the others and so are best voted on as a package to be effected over four or five years. Where issues are more discrete and have less mutual interactive effects they are probably best voted on separately, especially when they do not "fit" in left–right terms and get ignored or totally excluded in a general election debate.

Happily this division of labor seems to be evolving in actual democratic practice. In this sense the modern extension of individual policy voting enhances and extends the "necessary democratic connection" between popular preferences and public policy, much rather than threatening and undermining it.

References

ADAMS, J. F. and ADAMS, E. F. 2000. The geometry of voting cycles. *Theoretical Politics*, 12: 131–54.

ARROW, K. 1951. *Social Choice and Individual Values*. New York: Wiley.

AUER, A. and BÜTZER, M. (eds.) 2001. *Direct Democracy: The Eastern and Central European Experience*. Burlington, Vt.: Ashgate.

BONNER, R. J. 1967. *Aspects of Athenian Democracy*. New York: Russell and Russell.

BUDGE, I. 1996. *The New Challenge of Direct Democracy*. Cambridge: Polity.

—— 2000. Deliberative democracy versus direct democracy. Pp. 195–212 in *Democratic Innovation: Deliberation, Representation and Association*, ed. M. Saward. London: Routledge.

—— KLINGEMANN, H.-D., VOLKENS, A., BARA, J., and TANENBAUM, E. 2001. *Mapping Policy Preferences: Estimates for Parties, Electorates and Governments 1945–1998*. Oxford: Oxford University Press.

BURKE, E. 1790/1955. *Reflections on the Revolution in France*, ed. T. H. D. Mahoney. New York: Liberal Arts Press.

BUTLER, D. and RANNEY, A. (eds.) 1994. *Referendums Around the World*. London: Macmillan.

CRONIN, T. E. 1989. *Direct Democracy: The Politics of Initiative, Referendum and Recall*. Cambridge, Mass.: Harvard University Press.

GALLAGHER, M. and ULERI, P. V. (eds.) 1996. *The Referendum Experience in Europe*. London: Macmillan.

GERBER, E. R. and HUG, S. 2001. Legislative response to direct legislation. Pp. 88–108 in *Referendum Democracy: Citizens, Elites and Deliberation*, ed. M. Mendelsohn and A. Parkin. London: Palgrave.

GROFMAN, B. and FELD, S. L. 1988. Rousseau's General Will: a Condorcetian perspective. *American Political Science Review*, 82: 568–76.

KOBACH, K. W. 1994. Switzerland. Pp. 98–152 in *Referendums Around the World*, ed. D. Butler and A. Ranney. London: Macmillan.

KRIESI, H. P. 2005. *Direct Democratic Choice: The Swiss Experience*. Lanham, Md.: Lexington.

LAVER, M. J. and BUDGE, I. 1992. *Party Policy and Coalition Government*. London: Macmillan.

LE DUC, L. 2003. *The Politics of Direct Democracy: Referendums in Global Perspective*. Peterborough: Broadview.

LINDER, W. 1994. *Swiss Democracy*. New York: St Martin's Press.

LUPIA, A. 1994. Shortcuts vs encyclopedias: information and voting in California insurance reform elections. *American Political Science Review*, 88: 63–76.

McDONALD, M. and BUDGE, I. 2005. *Elections, Parties, Democracy: Conferring the Median Mandate*. Oxford: Oxford University Press.

McKELVEY, R. D. 1979. General conditions for global intransitivities in formal voting models. *Econometrica*, 47: 1085–111.

—— 1991. Rational choice and politics. *Political Studies*, 39: 496–512.

McLEAN, I. S. 1989. *Democracy and New Technology*. Cambridge: Polity.

MADISON, J. with HAMILTON, A. and JAY, J. 1787–8/1911. *The Federalist Papers*. London: Dent.

MAGLEBY, D. B. 1984. *Direct Legislation: Voting on Ballot Propositions in the United States*. Baltimore: Johns Hopkins University Press.

—— 1994. Direct legislation in the American states. Pp. 218–54 in *Referendums Around the World*, ed. D. Butler and A. Ranney. London: Macmillan.

MENDELSOHN, M. and PARKIN, A. (eds.) 2001. *Referendum Democracy: Citizens, Elites and Deliberation in Referendum Campaigns*. London: Palgrave. Chapters by Budge, 67–87; Gerber and Hug, 88–108; Bowler and Donovan, 125–146; Lupia and Johnson, 191–230 cited in text.

MILL, J. S. 1861/1910. *Utilitarianism, Liberty, Representative Government*, ed. H. B. Acton. London: Dent.

MILLER, W., PIERCE, R., THOMASSEN, J., HERRERA, R., HOLMBERG, S., ESSAIASSON, P., and WESSELS, B. 1999. *Policy Representation in Western Democracies*. Oxford: Oxford University Press.

NIEMI, R. 1969. Majority decision-making with partial unidimensionality. *American Political Science Review*, 63: 488–97.

RIKER, W. 1982. *Liberalism against Populism*. San Francisco: Freeman.

ROUSSEAU, J. J. 1762/1973. *The Social Contract and Discourses*, trans. G. D. H. Cole, J. Brumfitt, and P. J. C. Hall. London: Dent.

SAWARD, M. 1998. *The Terms of Democracy*. Cambridge: Polity.

—— (ed.) 2000. *Democratic Innovation: Deliberation, Representation and Association.* London: Routledge.

STOKES, D. E. and IVERSON, G. R. 1962. On the existence of forces restoring party competition. *Public Opinion Quarterly,* 26: 159–71.

WATTENBERG, M. P. 1990. *The Decline of American Political Parties.* Cambridge, Mass.: Harvard University Press.

INTERNATIONAL POLITICAL INSTITUTIONS

RICHARD HIGGOTT

1 INTRODUCTION

The study of international organization in international relations now has a strong intellectual tradition (see Katzenstein, Keohane, and Krasner 1998; Simmons and Martin 2002; Kratochwil and Mansfield 2005). When we talk about organizations in international relations we are invariably talking about institutions. As Robert Keohane (1989, 3) notes, institutions define limits and set choices on actor behavior in both formal and informal ways. They do so in economic, political, and social settings. Thus one way to think of organizations is as bodies that advance certain norms and rules. All organizations are institutions, but not all institutions are organizations. Institutions can lack organizational form, while some organizations may have multiple institutional roles. This chapter, therefore, sees "institutions" and "organizations" in international relations as two inseparable sides of one coin.

In this *Handbook*, the editors have chosen to make the distinction between international economic, political, and security organizations, with the provision of separate chapters on each. This might make organizational sense, but for analytical-cum-theoretical purposes in the study of international organization(s) this distinction is difficult to apply. The major international organizations do not lend themselves to discrete issue-area segmentation. International organizations can exhibit behavior driven by all three issue-areas and some international organizations see themselves as operating in all three domains. Under conditions of globalization, economics, security, and politics become increasingly blurred analytical categories.

Thus, this chapter uses theoretical lenses that span all three issue-areas. But, it eschews empirical discussion of the international economic institutions (IEIs) even though the WTO, IMF, and WBG are political organizations in terms of their agendas and in the manner of their decision-making. The relationship between economics and security or economic growth and political stability and economics and democracy promotion are, for example, inextricably interlinked (especially in the new global security environment post-9/11). Similarly, this chapter eschews discussions of security treaties and alliances such as NATO. More useful is to have a general conceptual understanding of the concept of an international organization and international institutional behavior as part of a wider process of global governance.

Contemporary understandings of global governance extend beyond the role of governments, and intergovernmental organizations and the late twentieth century saw the role of private international regimes and non-state actors from within the wider reaches of the corporate world and civil society grow dramatically (see Cutler, Haufleur, and Porter, 1999; Higgott, Underhill, and Bieler 2000). Yet it is international institutions such as the UN and the EU—notwithstanding that their role in world politics is at a crossroads greater than at any time since 1945—that remain the major sites of global governance.

The discussion is in three sections. Section 2 offers some historical and theoretical insights into the understanding of international organization. Section 3 looks at the UN, the EU, and several other regional actors as exemplars of contemporary international organization noting that *regional* organizations are becoming increasingly important. It is in both international and *regional* settings that we find modern international organizations. Section 4 looks at the different ways in which international organizations have been studied by scholars of international relations.

There are two seemingly contradictory threads running throughout this chapter. On the one hand it demonstrates the manner in which states, all states, use international organizations as vehicles for cooperation. At the same time, however, the relationship between states and international organization is shown to be one of tension. States often exhibit distrust in their relations with international organizations. At the very least states grow weary of the cost of formal organization and suspicious of international bureaucracies. Thus Section 3 and the conclusion suggest that we are at an important theoretical juncture in not only the practice of international organization in the early years of the twenty-first century but by extension how we study them. As we shall see when we look at the UN and the EU, theoretical analysis and practical institutional reform are two sides of the same coin.

2 INTERNATIONAL ORGANIZATION: SOME HISTORICAL AND THEORETICAL INSIGHTS

2.1 Historical Context

International organization is about rules agreed amongst independent political communities. To a greater or lesser extent these rules help determine the shape of world order. Historically they were developed to overcome the limits of bilateral state-to-state diplomacy. Technical institutions, limited in scope and aspiration, emerged prior to organizations with more sweeping economic and sociopolitical agendas, especially during the "first wave of globalization" at the end of the nineteenth century (Hirst and Thompson 1999). The International Telegraph Union (founded in 1865) is often thought of as the first intergovernmental organization. Between 1900 and 2000 the number of IGOs grew from 37 to well over 400 (Krieger 1993, 451; Schiavone 2001). Key institutions that developed in the second half of the nineteenth century included the Universal Postal Union and the Concert of Europe.

The Concert of Europe, while acknowledged as an IO geared to consultation between the European Great Powers as a way of pre-empting the use of force, was never imbued with the substantive executive capabilities that we now assume of international organizations. But, it gave birth to a number of norms concerning the conduct and status of states and the development of international conference diplomacy as an important stage in the evolution of international organizations as actors in international politics (Armstrong 2004, 4). The period between the Congress of Vienna (1815) and the outbreak of the First World War was the "era of preparation for international organization" (Claude 1971, 41). The Hague conferences of 1899 and 1907 through to the Paris Peace Conference, that saw the creation of the League of Nations, experimented with the tools of collective intergovernmental conflict resolution (mediation, arbitration, commissions of inquiry, and the like.)

Notwithstanding the failure of the League, the growth of international organization, especially since the end of the Second World War, has been the quintessential characteristic of the international politics (and economics) of the twentieth century, especially through the birth of the Bretton Woods system (1944) and the creation of the United Nations in 1945 and its ancillary organizations (such as the Food and Agricultural Organization, International Atomic Energy Agency, the World Health Organization, UNESCO, and the Economic Commissions for Africa, Latin America, and Asia Pacific, between 1947 and 1974. This organizational growth reflected the attempt to manage respect for the *principle of sovereignty* while at the same time recognizing the growing practical need for states to engage in collective action problem solving in a range of complex issue-areas. Even as international organization, as both principle and practice, has come under increasing challenge in the late twentieth and early twenty-first century, this has been no deterrent to the transformation of existing organizations or the emergence of new ones (especially at the regional level).

Examples of transformation are the birth of the WTO out of GATT in 1995 and the African Union from the OAU in 2002. Dramatic developments at a regional level are to be found in East Asia in the early years of the twenty-first century. Even older organizations that, to all intents and purposes, have outlived their remits continue to exist. Notable here are the (former British) Commonwealth and its weaker facsimile *la Francophonie*. In addition, NATO still functions vigorously in a range of areas long after its initial rationale of resisting Soviet expansion in Europe has passed. Such organizations survive by a process of reinvention. NATO has moved to a broader definition of security in keeping with the evolution of the twenty-first-century war on global terrorism. The Commonwealth reaffirmed its value in the 1991 Harare declaration by adopting a stronger "development" oriented mission enhancing best practice in the pursuit of good governance.

2.2 Classification

Organizations can be transnational and/or cross-regional; they can be explicitly built around the provisions to be found in Chapters VI, VII, and IX of the UN charter; some are simply *sui generis*.[1] Many international organizations have overlapping agendas and competencies. Scholarly analysis has tended to make general judgments based on membership and the degree of integration of an organization, functional purpose and policy area, and by structure and legal status.

2.2.1 *Scope of Membership and Degree of Integration*

Here we can identify: (a) global multilateral organizations—with three or more members—notably the UN but also the major IEIs and (b) regional multilateral organizations—again with three or more members but within specific geographical containers: bodies such as the EU, Association of Southeast Asian Nations (ASEAN), the African Union (AU), and Mercosur. A difference between these groupings is the degree of integration they have achieved. The EU, in contrast to others, has the ability to take decisions and make policy that can be binding not only on its member states and but also directly on sub-state public and

---

[1] This chapter is not a catalog of international organizations. A comprehensive survey is to be found in the *Yearbook of International Organisations* published annually by the Union of International Associations found at www.uia.org. See also Archer 2001 and Schiavone 2001.

private enterprises and persons within states. The other, less integrated organizations only have jurisdiction over such sub-state actors through the member states themselves.

2.2.2 *Function or Policy Area*

The function or policy area are where IOs become agents for a particular course of action. Some—like the UN and the EU—are multifunctional in nature. Others—for example the World Health Organisation or the ILO—are purpose specific. Yet others—the ILO, WHO, and UNCTAD—exercise promotional functions. Some, such as the Bretton Woods institutions, are agents for the delivery of public goods although, along with the WTO, they also play regulatory roles.

Some organizations are purely consultative and/or confidence building in nature, for example the Non Aligned Movement (NAM) that attempted to secure a common developing world position on a range of foreign policy issues during the cold war era or, more recently, the ASEAN Regional Forum that advances a confidence building cooperative dialogue on regional security issues between the states of Southeast Asia and the major Asia-Pacific powers. The largely ritualistic and aspirational nature of such bodies does not mean that they are without the potential to engender meaning and identity as important precursors of deeper organizational cooperation, as seen in Europe (Rosamond 2000) and even, some argue, in Southeast Asia (Acharya 2000.)

2.2.3 *By Structure and Formal Legal Powers*

Two ways to distinguish international organizations from the more general notion of international institutions is by their legal standing and by the degree of centralization and independence they possess. International organizations, reflecting the notional sovereign equality of states, are institutionalized by treaties. But, in practice, many IOs have little more than discursive power with no facility for legal, as opposed to moral, sanction. The evolution of international law invites only limited comparison with the development of national legal systems. The development of international organization is a reflection of the practical limitations on the emergence of a pattern of systematized rules at the international level.

But it is the presence of formal structures of administration (a bureaucracy and all that is implied by its presence) that distinguishes an international organization from the general understanding of an institution. Established organizations usually have a degree of managerial autonomy from their constituent membership; even if only of a technical nature pertaining to policy implementation. Notwithstanding that member states zealously guard their dominion over policy-making and policy ratification, the powers possessed by IOs are not as insignificant as might be assumed. To a greater or lesser extent, the power to mold understandings, articulate organizational norms, and act as mediators in disputes between members can give organizations considerable operational autonomy (see Abbot and Snidal 2001, 15–23).

Notable among those bodies that do have instruments of formal legal suasion over (some) member states in the "political domain," is the UN with the provisions for taking collective security action under Chapter VII of the Charter. The WTO, with its dispute settlement mechanism, also falls into this category. To date, only the EU has supranational legal power over citizens of member states. The impact of organizations, however, is determined less by formal legal rules than the internal politics of a given organization and especially the role of the major actors within it. In this regard, the *theory* of international organization is important to understanding their role in *practice*.

2.3 Theorizing International Organization

By way of initial clarification we should note that for scholars of "international politics," "international" usually means interstate relations while "global politics" embraces the activities of all international actors be they states, or non-state actors. Similarly, "global governance" has become a hosting metaphor for all political and economic actors, including international organizations that practice politics and administration beyond the boundaries of the modern state. By way of further complication, "international" is also often transposed with "multilateral," as in the way bodies such as the UN or the IMF are called either international institutions or multilateral institutions.

It is, therefore, worth recalling the standard definition of multilalteralism as the management of transnational problems with three or more parties making policy on the basis of a series of acceptable "generalized principles of conduct" (Ruggie 1993, 11). The key principles identified by Ruggie are indivisibility, non-discrimination, and diffuse reciprocity. It was expected that over time, decision-making underwritten by these principles would lead to collective trust amongst players within an institution. A key element in the development of trust would come from the willingness of the institutional hegemon—that is, the strongest member of the institution—to agree to be bound by these principles. That is, to accept the principle of "self-binding" (Martin 2003).

Within this context, the principal way of thinking about the theory and practice of international organization in the last quarter of the twentieth century was through institutionalist and regime theory literature. The lesson drawn from this literature is a recognition of the importance of IOs as vehicles for maximizing information sharing, generating transparency in decision-making and advancing the institutional ability to generate credible collective action problem solving in a given issue area, eventually (in some if not all instances) leading to the development of enforcement/compliance mechanisms and dispute resolution procedures. International organizations/institutions are transaction cost reducers (see Keohane 1984, 1989).

But it is not sufficient simply to describe organizational processes. We must also understand the degree to which these processes deliver outcomes; the prominence of an international organization does not always correlate with a high rate of success in problem solving in a given area of international relations. Ambitious organizations might try to structure rules and behavior in some of the key policy areas of contemporary global politics but often to little avail.

Unlike the role of IEIs in economic transactions, many of the world's political transactions are not conducted through international organizations. They remain primarily the affairs of states. In its search for generalization, the hallmark of scientific theorizing, this distinction between the economic and the political was often unaddressed in the theoretical literature, leading to the conflation of institutions, regimes, and international organizations with a generic definition as "principles, norms and decision-making processes around which the expectations of actors converge" (Krasner 1983) and with the implication that informal actions, underwritten by these principles, could be as, if not more, important than the role of formal organizations. Indeed, Simmons and Martin (2002) argue that it was the decreasing salience of IOs in the late 1970s to the early 1980s that led a focus on regimes, rules, and norms.

There was an important insight here; but the regime approach on its own failed to illuminate the internal dynamics and interstate political contests that take place within IOs (see Strange 1983). Theoretical lenses, other than those of rationalist and neoliberal institutionalist theories of cooperation, through which to observe IOs, especially the EU and smaller regional bodies, emerged. Scholarly insight moved beyond institutionalist regime literature to take more account of history, culture, and identity. In addition, explanations of the intersubjective sociolegal context for interstate behavior were extended to the study of international organization (see Kratochwil and Ruggie 1986; Hurrell 1993).

These approaches, finding fullest expression in the constructivist theorizing of the late twentieth century (see Wendt 1992, 2000) focused less on the role of IOs as actors and more on the role of institutions as norm brokers (see Finnemore 1996). States not only use international organizations to reduce uncertainty and transaction costs. They also use them "*to create* information, ideas, norms and expectations ... [and] ... to legitimate or delegitimate particular ideas and practices" (Abbott and Snidal 2001, 15; emphasis added). IOs are thus more than arbiters, and trustees, they are also norm brokers and "enforcers."

Other approaches to international organization, drawing on the empirical experience of the EU, focus instead on questions pertaining to the "degree" of integration. In the theory and practice of international organization the EU is an interesting case. The EU, throughout the closing decades of the twentieth century, has become increasingly difficult to categorize simply as an IO. A stronger tendency has been to see it rather as a more complex system of multilevel governance (see *inter alia*: Wallace and Wallace 1996, 3–37; Rosamond 2000; Hooghe and Marks 2001). Notwithstanding the failure of some states to ratify the constitution in 2005, the EU has undergone a greater process of sovereignty pooling than any other actor that started life as an IO.

Straddling, or perhaps mediating, institutionalist and integrationist approaches is what we might call the intergovernmentalist insight into enhanced and efficient interstate bargaining (Moravcsik 1994, 1998). Again, notwithstanding setbacks, or more specifically what we might describe as a two steps forward one step back approach to closer integration, the EU confirms (in part at least) the normative aspirations of idealist integration theorists in ways that qualify narrower realist certainties about the limited utility of enhanced institutional cooperation over time. One final take on the changing role of international organizations should be noted. During the closing years of the twentieth century it became increasingly fashionable to look at international organizations through theoretical perspectives on "global governance," seeing institutions as players in a growing regulatory network of actors in global politics that also diminishes the traditional realist understanding of the more or less exclusive role of states in the global decision-making process.

Thus IOs are seen as increasingly important actors in the provision of global public goods (see Kaul, Grunberg, and Stern 1999). Through these lenses, the key issue for international organizations is the degree to which they can combine the effective and efficient provision of public goods through collective action problem solving on the one hand at the same time as they satisfy the increasing global demand for representation and accountability under conditions of globalization on the other. The tension between these two understandings of governance remains unresolved. It is addressed in the Conclusion.

3 CONTEMPORARY INTERNATIONAL ORGANIZATION: THE UN, THE EU, AND THE REGIONAL REGULATORY FRAMEWORK

The early twenty-first century sees feverish discussion of the continued salience of the UN after the Iraq war on the one hand and the future prospects of the EU in the wake of the crisis in the ratification of the constitution on the other. It is also a time when other regions of the world are experimenting with international organization at the regional level. In assessing contemporary events, it is all too easy to get caught up in the immediate. This section locates these principle institutions in a longer-term context at the same time that it takes account of the very real challenges facing IOs in the contemporary era.

3.1 The United Nations

A detailed history of the UN is not possible here. Rather, we need to tease out the salience of its evolution, contemporary standing, and prospects for a more generalized understanding of the role of international organizations in global politics. Perhaps the key element in its origins is the degree to which it claimed not to repeat the structure of the failed League of Nations, but to which, with hindsight, it has a greater resemblance and salience for the future of the organization than the founders might care to admit.

Although established in a much more professional manner than the League, the UN as a collective security system, with its Secretariat, General Assembly, and Security Council and underwritten by the principle of the sovereign equality of states, resembled the earlier failed institution (see Armstrong, Lloyd, and Redmand 2004: 37ff). The key difference was, of course, the veto of the permanent members (P5) in the Security Council. But there was more to the UN system than that. There was also the creation of UN agencies dealing with issues ranging from atomic energy (IAEA), children (UNICEF), civil aviation (ICAO), development (UNDP and UNCTAD), education, science, culture, research and training (UNESCO, UNITAR, and UNU), food and agriculture (FAO), human rights, narcotics, and drugs (ECOSOC), through to intellectual property (WIPO), and this list is by no means exhaustive.

While these agencies have never worked other than sub-optimally, the end of the cold war saw a renewed optimism that the UN might at long last fulfil those roles which many had originally conceived for it—as the only "universal, general purpose" IO (Diehl 2001, 6) charged with generating global public goods to mitigate conflict and guarantee peace, security, and well-being. In order to understand why this has not happened to date it is important to note that the world in 2005 is not the world into which the UN was born sixty years previously and that reform poses major difficulties given changes in world order. The key inhibitor of the UN's core business is, as UN Secretary General Kofi Annan (2000, 6) has frequently noted, "globalization" or more precisely the inability of the UN to mitigate the negative elements of globalization such as global poverty or enhance global security in the face of the major change in war-fighting—the shift from interstate war to non-state (terrorist) war-fighting.

If accession to the UN was for many states the *sine qua non* of sovereignty, then the spread of economic globalization on the one hand and non-state violence on the other are perhaps the major challenges to that sovereignty in the early twenty-first century. The challenges faced by the UN in the early twenty-first century are in many ways a product of its historical privileging of an insistence on sovereign equality; or more precisely, the challenges posed by the practical denial of this theoretical state as international politics, lead by the USA and it principle allies, drifts into an era of non-UN sanctioned humanitarian intervention in places like Bosnia and pre-emptive security in Iraq.

The attitude of the vast majority of members of the UN to these proactive policies in the security domain is deeply conditioned by what they see as the failure on the other hand of the global community, and the UN as the principle IO, to deal with the exacerbating issue of poverty and global inequality. These twin trials for the UN, and especially the attitude of the USA towards it and its goals, seem to be undoing the earlier progress that the organization had made by the identification of the importance of providing collective action problem solving in socioeconomic, developmental, and ecological policy areas. The UN's historical progress as a vehicle for peace building and generating socioeconomic well-being has not been trivial, but the fundamental contemporary problem is that UN's potential remains inhibited by "the pretence of state governments that they have 'sovereignty' over a multitude of problems in public policy that now flow across borders" (Alger 2001, 493).

This chapter cannot review the "UN reform industry" that has been in full swing since the turn of the century (but see Heinbecker and Goff 2005). But even under optimistic scenarios it will be a problematic endeavor. It in part explains the concerns of states in international relations to preserve their sovereignty yet at the same time enhance collective action decision-making in "trans-sovereign" policy areas (see Cusimano 2000). It also sees states make greater recourse to regional organization. The final problem facing the UN is one that faces many IOs, namely a legitimacy deficit in the relationship between the dominant actors and the weaker players in the organization on the one hand and in the relationship between the institution and the people it purports to serve on the other. Both issues, as real world policy issues and as key factors for scholarly analysis, receive consideration in the Conclusion.

3.2 Regional Organization as International Organization

It is at the regional level that the growth in international organization has been most dramatic. This does not occur in isolation from wider traditions and concerns. Indeed, the UN spells out the possible mandates that "regional arrangements," and "regional and other inter-governmental agencies" under the UN Charter (chapters VI, VII, VIII, and IX) might have, and the operational partnerships of the United Nations with its regional agencies.

Early scholarly debates about regionalism emerged from two sources: (a) normative questions about the sustainability of the nation state as a vehicle for effective and peaceful human governance and an interest in functional and technocratic imperatives for new forms of authority beyond the state; and (b) the appearance of actual regional integration schemes in Western Europe from the late 1950s (the European Coal and Steel Community, the abortive European Defence Community, and the eventual European Economic Community) that became the intellectual laboratory for the study of regional organizations. Early neofunctionalists (cf. Haas 1958; Schmitter 1971) used the European experience to generalize about the prospects for regional integration elsewhere but this optimism proved short-lived as analogous projects such as the Latin American Free Trade Area and the East African Common Market failed.

This earlier work often saw regionalism as a defensive mechanism to reduce dependence on the international economy. But more recently, scholars of the new regionalism (see Gamble and Payne 1996) see it in a more proactive manner as a means of greater access to global markets under conditions of globalization. It is no longer about securing regional autarchy. States now engage in any number of overlapping regional endeavors without sensing that there may be contradictions in such a process. It is also a more inclusive process of regionalization than the UN had in mind in its relations with its various regional agencies. The new regionalism is a sociopolitical project as well as an economic one. The process of regionalization also has structural consequences beyond the particular region in which it takes place. Transregionalism is an increasingly important dimension of international relations as institutions and organizations play larger mediating roles between regions (see Hettne 1999).

It is at the meso regional level, between globalization and the nation state, that increasing effort has been applied to the management of transterritorial or multiterritorial collective action problem solving. To date, moves toward regionally integrated problem solving have been more active in Europe than in other parts of the world. But this is not only a European project. Elsewhere, the growing linkages between different regional integration schemes are evident.

3.2.1 *The European Union*

The EU is the most developed example of a hybrid, multiperspectival, multi-issue international organization to date. Its evolution was analysed largely through the lens of neoclassical trade theory as it developed—from a free trade area, to a common market, to an economic union—in classic terms (see Belassa 1961). But in so doing, it made the separation of economics from the politics impossible. The EU is an economic actor (especially in world trade), a political actor in global politics (even when members cannot agree amongst themselves), and a security actor (even without as effective a military capability as its major transatlantic partner would wish it to possess). This is its unique characteristic.

While regionalization processes can be observed throughout the world, there is no single model of regionalization. But there is a desire for collective action by societies, through forms of regional cooperation to counter the adverse effects of globalization on the one hand, and to maximize the benefits to be gained from globalization on the other. But, global governance structures are not monolithic and regional governance systems display great differences in both scope and capacity to maintain order as countries make choices that reflect their own needs and political commitments.

The EU has developed sophisticated regulatory frameworks through its institutional architecture and the crystallization of common policies in areas such as trade and investment. Other regions are developing different regulatory and governance frameworks. While all, in their own ways, are aiming towards regional governance systems that can be considered not only effective but also democratic, legitimate, and inclusive, the EU remains the major exercise in intergovernmental decision-making to date. We can say this for several reasons:

- Although contested, Europe does have an integrated governance system, linking institutional structures, policies, and legal instruments that bring together the national and supranational levels of decision-making and policy implementation.
- European approaches to governance have developed flexible and multidimensional concepts of sovereignty in the international system. These ideas of sovereignty contrast with the bounded, state-based/intergovernmental characterizations of sovereignty and international relations to be found in most non-European practice and analysis.
- In individual policy areas (for example, trade) Europe has a regulatory framework unequaled at the global level. Only Europe, of all regional actors, negotiates within the WTO as a single actor.
- Europe is already engaged in a web of transregional and interregional cooperative relations with other groupings, based upon either formal, institutional dialogue or more informal agreements. Interinstitutional cooperation has increased. Although often misunderstood, the Asia–Europe (ASEM) process, EU–Mexico, EU–Mercosur, and the Cotonou Agreements with the African, Caribbean, and Pacific States reflect aspirations of regional groups to build a density of relations and foster trust fundamental to a global governance framework.
- The EU governance model relies heavily on the rule of law. The role of the European Court of Justice (ECJ) is crucial in ensuring a system that is both effective and fair. The ECJ is thus a political actor, as much as a legal one. It is

accessibility to the legal system that makes the EU distinctive from other international governance models. Contrast it with the WTO, where only states can make a complaint to the Dispute Settlement Body.

In short, the EU, for all its shortcomings, is a community of sovereign states that has proved that cooperation can be learned and that cooperation need not be a zero-sum game. In essence, cooperation within the context of an international governance system produces results where the participants can in many, if not all, circumstances perceive cooperative action as a public good. But cooperation among sovereign states or between states and non-state actors in the establishment of a governance system is neither automatic nor easy. Successful cooperation to date has depended on a public sector push, an emerging supranational structure and the willingness of the member states to pool sovereignty in key areas, to delegate decision-making and to accept authority in matters over which they would otherwise have national autonomy. The EU has proceeded further than any other regional grouping in the establishment of a governance system based upon the principle of pooled sovereignty.

But the EU's major problem, a problem for most international organizations, is that it has only achieved a limited degree of democratic legitimacy. While the proposed European Constitution may have reflected a desire to ensure democratic governance, there was a clear imbalance between the supranational and the national democratic structures. Finding legitimacy among its citizens and in public discourse within the EU on the one hand, and among the actors and institutions of global governance on the other, has proved difficult. There is a "sovereignty trap" in the European project. While states have done much to develop democracy and social justice in the advanced economies, the limits of national governance, and of the concepts on which it is based, appear less clear in regional and global integration processes.

This has implications for the role of international organizations as vehicles for global governance. There are examples from EU experience, including the intro-duction of the single currency, which provide us with a practical example of the "division" of sovereignty. But for international organizations to deliver better global governance, it is necessary to escape from a bounded notion of sovereignty and narrow definitions of security and state interest in international relations. Central to overcoming these limitations, as normative scholarship suggests, must be the recognition that sovereignty can be disaggregated and redistributed across institutional levels from the local to the global (Held 2004).

3.2.2 *International Organization and the Rise of Regulatory Regionalism in the Developing World*

While it clearly differs from the "European project," international organization in the developing world has proliferated from the last quarter of the twentieth century. Noting the major initiatives only, we can identify organizations such as the Economic Community of West African States (ECOWAS) and the Southern African Development Co-ordination Conference (SADCC) in Africa; the Organisation of Black Sea Economic Cooperation (BSEC) in Central and Eastern Europe; Mercosur in Latin America; and a range of initiatives in East Asia commencing with the development of ASEAN in the 1970s, the growth of APEC from the early 1990s, and initiatives to establish an East Asian Community (initially via the "ASEAN Plus 3" format) in the early twenty-first century.

But the approach to international organization in the developing world is different to what (too) many scholars think of as the "European template" (Breslin and Higgott 2000). What has been important in parts of the world such as Latin America and East Asia is the recognition of the importance of "the region" as a meso level at which to make policy under conditions of globalization. This chapter can only provide a sample illustration of this emerging non-EU template. It does so using the most advanced case—the growth of regional organizational initiatives in East Asia, especially since the financial crises of the second half of the 1990s.

ASEAN may have started out as a security organization in the context of the cold war but it, like most regional organizations in the South, has taken on a different character since then.[2] The search for state competitiveness in an era of economic globalization is now as salient as was the search for state security in the context of the cold war. The essence of the new institutional regionalism is an endeavor to create organizational structures that advance regional competitiveness in the global economy and provide a venue for policy discourse on key regional issues whilst at the same time preserving state sovereignty. It is this process that has come to be known as "regulatory regionalism" since the East Asian financial crises of the late twentieth century (Jayasuriya 2004).

What the Asian crises told regional policy elites was that there was no consensus on how to manage international capitalism in the closing stages of the twentieth century. But the economic crises also provided a positive learning experience at the multilateral organizational level. The crises demonstrated that for economic globalization to continue to develop in an orderly manner requires necessary institutional capability to provide for prudential economic regulation. While most regional policy analysts continue to recognize that such institutional regulation is best pursued at the global level, regional level organizational initiatives have become increasingly important. Thus, strong structural impediments to integration notwithstanding, East Asia has become more interdependent and even more formally institutionalized (see Higgott 2005).

But this is not the kind of regional cooperation that has its antecedents in Europe. Rather it is a regulatory regionalism that links national and global understandings of regulation via intermediary regional level organizations. Effectively,

---

[2] A history of regional organization in East Asia is not possible here. See Acharya 2000.

regional organizations become transmission belts for global disciplines to the national level through the depoliticizing and softening process of the region in which regional policy coordination has become the "meso" link between the national and the global. Regulatory regionalism sees regional organizations acting as vehicles for regional policy coordination to mitigate risk while not undermining national sovereignty. Indeed, there is a strong relationship between state form, the global economic and political orders, and the nature of regional organization emerging at the meso level in many regions of the world.

This institutional compromise is inevitable if the continuing tension between nationalism and regionalism in East Asia (and other regions) is not to jeopardize cooperation. The meshing of multilevel processes of regulation to reinforce the connections between the international institutions (e.g. IMF and World Bank) and regional institutions—for example between the Asian Development Bank and the emerging instruments of regional monetary regulation in East Asia—have developed strongly in the early twenty-first century. Similarly, regional organizations pass down internationally agreed global market standards. In discursive terms, "regional regulation" carries fewer negative connotations for sovereignty and regime autonomy than "regional institution building" which, throughout the pre-crisis days in East Asia, carried with it negative, European style, implications of sovereignty pooling.

4 International Organization and the Limits to Global Governance

International organizations exhibit a characteristic shared by many other kinds of organizational structures. They tend to be extremely durable over time even to the extent of having outlived their usefulness in some instances. There are reasons for durability specific to each individual organization. But there are also more generalized explanations. In addition to the obvious effects of inertia, the development of an internal bureaucratic dynamic and an organizational instinct for self-preservation are worth noting. Notably, in an era of globalization, problem solving becomes increasingly complex and less amenable to state-based resolution.

Policy problems are increasingly defined as global, or trans-sovereign, problems, especially in the domains of trade, finance, environment, and also security given the changing nature of threat, human rights, and development. Governments, especially in the second half of the twentieth century, developed a habit of seeking international organizational responses to problems not amenable to state level resolution. This is at one level the same for all states, including the USA, although international organizations are usually more important to smaller than larger players, even though it is larger players rather than the smaller players that get to set and steer the agenda of the organizations.

The principal question about the role of international organizations as vehicles of global governance (economic and political) pertains to the quantity and quality of this governance in an era where we have an overdeveloped global economy and an underdeveloped global polity. There is a strong disconnect between governance seen as effective and efficient collective action problem solving in a given issue area on the one hand and governance as a system of accountability and representation within international organization on the other. It is this that leads to the debate about the "legitimacy deficits" in major international organizations.

The UN and EU, and international organizations in general, share this problem. The UN has problems of effectiveness and efficiency in the delivery of global public policy and of legitimacy. The EU has less of a problem with delivery but it also has a major legitimacy problem within European civil society (Bellamy 2005). The disjuncture between securing legitimation from the bottom up and effective and efficient administration from the top down in international organizations is captured in the distinction between input legitimacy and output legitimacy (Keohane 2004; Grant and Keohane 2005). This challenges the all too easy assumption that multilateral international organizations will inevitably remain key actors in global governance in the twenty-first century. We tend to forget that multilateralism as a foreign policy tool was always a modest endeavor and, as Keohane notes, "a social construction of the twentieth century" that holds less sway at the beginning of the twenty-first. This is a key issue for international organization. Without this balance the rational, stable, and harmonious development of an accountable and acceptable system of regulation at the global level will not be possible.

5 Conclusion

So where do we stand? In the early twenty-first century the theory and practice of international organization is subsumed within wider scholarship on international institutions and regimes seen as sets of international rules and norms principally, but not exclusively, for states. An intellectual contest exists between those who see international cooperation as rationalist and rational, but limited, and those who have a more sociological, constitutive understanding of international institution-alism. Esoteric as this might seem, it casts long policy shadows.

If, within a sociological context, we see international organization as institu-tionalized international relations, then we might conclude by saying that there appears not to be a strong correlation between the volume of international organizational activity and its ability to deal effectively and efficiently with the large issues in international relations. The strong still operate outside the borders of organizational norms when it suits them. This is especially the case with regards to war and military conflict (such as the US-led invasion of Iraq). To this extent, if realist theory is principally about the interests of the powerful it seems difficult to brook its assertions about the irrelevance of international institutions (Mearshei-mer 1994–5). But as Simmons and Martin ask (2002, 195), if realism was the sole form of reasoning in international relations then it would not explain why the United States spent so much of the second half of the twentieth century underwriting the principles of international organization. Even for realists—policy-makers more than theorists it needs to be added—IOs still fulfill important functions. Even realists cooperate.

We do not have to accept the "end of globalism" literature (Ralston Saul 2005) to recognize the manner in which a range of events have curtailed enthusiasm for international organization in major quarters. It is not an axiomatic assumption at the beginning of the twenty-first century that an expanded role for international organization in this era is assured. The crisis in the role of the UN Security Council in the wake of the invasion of Iraq, the failure of the USA to ratify the Kyoto Protocol and to sign on to the International Criminal Court, are testament to the need to be context specific and time specific in our judgments of the salience of IOs. Constraints on the further development of the EU in the wake of the abortive constitution also bear witness to the limitations of regional projects to advance beyond certain stages. These judgments give rise to the question, "where now in the theory and practice of international organization?"

Research on international organization in the early twenty-first century will axiomatically be embedded within the wider study of global governance and particularly the degree to which international organizations can bridge the gap between their abilities to provide effective and efficient decision-making underwritten by the best technical expertise on the one hand and the ability of international organizations to legitimate their actions on the other. The key issues in any future research agenda therefore will revolve around issues of institutional reform, great power commitment, and questions of organizational/institutional legitimacy. Empirically, the focus of research will stay on the major organizations—the UN, the EU, and important emerging regional actors.

It is difficult to disaggregate theory from practice in any future research agenda. In the UN context, for example, no one denies the need for reform nor the key elements of an institutional reform agenda—from adjusting the Security Council to fit the contemporary global realities of power rather than those of 1945 through to securing the Millennium Development Goals. The interesting question, for scholar and practitioner alike, is less "what reform?" than "how to get there?" (Maxwell 2005, 1). The "what" questions are set out in the 2005 report of the Secretary General (http://www.un.org/largerfreedom). For the scholar of international organization the "how" question is a "cooperation" and "collective action" question that requires theoretical tools such as game theory but used in a manner sensitive to the political dynamics of the organization and international politics.

At this early stage in the twenty-first century, the principal political dynamic in practical terms revolves around how the rest of the members of the UN deal with the United States. How do you keep the hegemonic actor wedded to multilateralism and the international organizations through which it functions when the hegemon is convinced that other states see international organization as a way to constrain it (Beeson and Higgott 2005)? This has created an atmosphere of mutual distrust that is not only inhibiting the institutional reform process but also the ability to embed important new international norms such as the "Responsibility to Protect" (see CIGI 2005, 1–12).

Like the UN, the EU too exhibits serious contemporary problems. But scholars of the EU tackle these problems in a different way to researchers working on UN reform. If enhancing institutional performance is the independent reform variable and greater representation is the dependent variable when looking at the UN, then this situation is reversed in current research on the EU. Because the EU is at an advanced legal and institutionalized state of development (see Stone Sweet 2004) it is the politics of the legitimacy deficit rather than the institutional performance deficit to which scholars turn their attention. Performance and legitimacy are related, but they can work against each other (see Bellamy 2005).

Scholars of political theory are battling to identify a balance in the relationship that allows for efficient decision-making that is both legitimate and accountable. To date, there is no definitive answer how this might be achieved given the deficiencies in institutional arrangements on the one hand and the absence of a European demos on the other. This debate currently turns on different readings of the degree to which efficiency in the provision of public goods is enhanced or inhibited by too little (or too much) democratic input. As this chapter shows, transparency and information sharing, central to the efficient operation of international organization, is not the same as democratic accountability (see Keohane 2004; Eriksen and Fossum 2004; Moravcsik 2004).

In sum, multilateralism as a principal (and principled) element of global governance in both the economic and the security domains in the early years of the twenty-first century—and with it, the standing of many international organizations—is strained at the global level and at a crossroads at the regional level. Public goods for a "just" global era—economic regulation, environmental security, the containment of organized crime and terrorism, the enhancement of welfare—cannot be provided by states alone. They must be provided collectively, be it at global or at regional levels. Notwithstanding the increasing importance of non-state actors, interstate cooperation, primarily via international organizations, is still at the heart of successful global policy-making and it is still driven by the *domestic actor preferences* of powerful countries (Milner 1997) whether it be the US in the international organizations or major state actors at critical junctures in regional projects. Despite persuasive normative arguments in favor of collective action problem solving, prospects for enhanced successful multilateral cooperation, via international organizations, should not be exaggerated. For multilateralism to work, and major international organizations to function, rules must (self-)bind the hegemon, as well as the smaller players. "Without the self-binding of the hegemon, multilateral organizations become empty shells" (Martin 2003, 14).

References

Abbot, K. W. and Sridal, D. 2001. Why states act through formal organisations. In *The Politics of Global Governance: International Organisations in an Interdependent World*, ed. P. F. Diehl. Boulder, Colo.: Lynne Rienner.

Acharya, A. 2000. *The Quest for Identity: The International Relations of Southeast Asia.* Singapore: Oxford University Press.

Alger, C. 2001. Thinking about the future of the UN system. In *The Politics of Global Governance: International Organizations in an Interdependent World*, ed. P. F. Diehl. Boulder, Colo.: Lynn Rienner.

Annan, K. 2000. "*We the People:*" The Role of the United Nations in the 21st Century. New York: United Nations.

Archer, C. 2001. *International Organizations*, 3rd edn. London: Routledge.

Armstrong, D., Lloyd, L., and Redmond, J. 2004. *International Organisation in World Politics.* London: Palgrave.

Beeson, M. and Higgott, R. 2005. Hegemony, institutionalism and US foreign policy: theory and practice in comparative historical perspective. *Third World Quarterly*, 26 (7): 1173–88.

Belassa, B. 1961. *Theory of Economic Integration.* Holmwood, Ill.: Richard Urwin.

Bellamy, R. 2005. Still in deficit: rights, regulation and democracy in the EU. For the Democracy Task Force of the EU 6th Framework Integrated Project on New Modes of Governance, np. nd. 1–31.

Breslin, S. and Higgott, R. 2000. Studying regions: learning from the old, constructing the new. *New Political Economy*, 5 (3): 333–52.

CIGI 2005. *The UN: Adapting to the 21st Century.* Waterloo: Centre for International Governance Innovation.

CLAUDE, I. 1971. *Swords into Ploughshares: The Problem and Progress of International Organisation.* New York: Random House.

CUSIMANO, M. 2000. Beyond sovereignty. the rise of trans-sovereign problems. In *Beyond Sovereignty: Issues for a Global Agenda,* ed. M. Cusimano. Boston: St Martin's.

CUTLER, C., HAUFLEUR, V., and PORTER, T. (eds.) 1999. *Private Authority and International Affairs.* New York: SUNY Press.

DIEHL, P. F. (ed.) 2001. *The Politics of Global Governance: International Organizations in an Interdependent World.* Boulder, Colo.: Lynne Rienner.

ERIKSEN, E. O. and FOSSUM, J. E. 2004. Europe in search of legitimacy: strategies of legitimation assessed. *International Political Science Review,* 25 (4): 439–41.

FINNEMORE, M. 1996. Norms, culture and world politics: insights from sociology's institutionalism. *International Organisation,* 50 (2): 887–918.

GAMBLE, A. and PAYNE, A. J. (eds.) 1996. *Regionalism and World Order.* London: Macmillan.

GRANT, R. W. and KEOHANE, R. O. 2005. Accountability and the abuses of power in world politics. *American Political Science Review,* 99 (1): 17–28.

HAAS, E. 1958. *The Uniting of Europe: Political Social and Economic Forces, 1950–57.* Stanford, Calif.: Stanford University Press.

HEINBECKER, P. and GOFF, P. 2005. *Irrelevant or Indispensable: The United Nations in the 21st Century.* Waterloo: Wilfrid Laurier University Press.

HELD, D. 2004. *Global Covenant: The Social Democratic Alternative to the Washington Consensus.* Cambridge: Polity.

HETTNE, B. 1999. Globlisation and the New Regionalism: the second great transformation. In *Globalisation and the New Regionalism,* ed. B. Hettne, A. Inotai, and O. Sunkel. Basingstoke: Macmillan.

HIGGOTT, R. 2001. Economic globalization and global governance: towards a post Washington consensus? In *Global Governance and the United Nations System,* ed. V. Rittberge. Tokyo: United Nations University Press.

—— 2005. Economic regionalism in East Asia: consolidation with centrifugal tendencies. In *Political Economy and the Changing Global Order,* ed. R. Stubbs and G. Underhill. Oxford: Oxford University Press.

—— UNDERHILL, G., and BIELER, A. (eds.) 2000. *Non State Actors and Authority in the Global System.* London: Routledge.

HIRST, P. and THOMPSON, G. 1999. *Globalization in Question,* 2nd edn. London: Polity.

HOOGHE, L. and MARKS, G. 2001. *Multi-Level Governance and European Integration.* Boulder, Colo.: Rowman and Littlefield.

HURRELL, A. 1993. International society and the study of regimes: a reflective approach. In *Regime Theory and International Relations,* ed. V. Rittberge. Oxford: Clarendon Press.

JAYASURIYA, K. (ed.) 2004. *Asian Regional Governance: Crisis and Change.* London: Routledge.

KATZENSTEIN, P., KEOHANE, R., and KRASNER, S. (eds.) 1998. International organisation at fifty: exploration and contestation in the study of world politics. *International Organisation,* 52 (4): 646–1061.

KAUL, I., GRUNBERG, I., and STERN, M. (eds.) 1999. *Global Public Goods: International Cooperation in the 21st Century.* New York: Oxford University Press for the UNDP.

KEOHANE, R. 1984. *After Hegemony: Cooperation and Discord in the World Political Economy.* Princeton, NJ: Princeton University Press.

—— 1989. *International Institutions and State Power: Essay in International Relations Theory.* Boulder, Colo.: Westview Press.

—— 2004. Global governance and democratic accountability. In *Taming Globalization: Frontiers of Governance,* ed. D. Held and M. K. Archibugi. Cambridge: Polity Press.

KRASNER, S. (ed.) 1983. *International Regimes.* Ithaca, NY: Cornell University Press.

KRATOCHWIL, F. and RUGGIE, J. 1986. The state of the art on an art of the state. *International Organisation,* 40 (4): 753–75.

—— and MANSFIELD, E. (eds.) 2005. *International Organisation: A Reader.* New York: Longman.

KREIGER, J. (ed.) 1993. *The Oxford Companion to World Politics.* Oxford: Oxford University Press.

LINDBERG, L. 1966. *The Political Dynamics of European Economic Integration.* Stanford, Calif.: Stanford University Press.

MARTIN, L. 2003. *Multilateral Organisations after the US–Iraq War of 2003.* Harvard University, Weatherhead Centre for International Affairs, August.

MAXWELL, S. 2005. *UN Reform: How?* London: Overseas Development Institute, mimeo.

MEARSHEIMER, J. 1994–5. The false promise of international institutions. *International Security,* 19 (3): 5–49.

MILNER, H. 1997. *Interests, Institutions and Information: Domestic Politics and International Relations.* Princeton, NJ: Princeton University Press.

MORAVCSIK, A. 1994. Preferences and power in the European Community: a liberal intergovernmental approach. In *Economic and Political Integration in Europe,* ed. S. Bulmer and A. Scott. Oxford: Blackwell.

—— 1998. *The Choice for Europe: Social Purpose and State Power From Messina to Maastricht.* Ithaca, NY: Cornell University Press.

—— 2004. Is there a "democratic deficit" in world politics? A Framework for analysis. *Government and Opposition,* 39 (3): 344–6.

NYE, J. 1971. *Peace in Parts: Integration and Conflict in International Organisations.* Boston: Little, Brown.

RALSTON SAUL, J. 2005. *The Collapse of Globalism.* London: Atlantic.

ROSAMOND, B. 2000. *Theories of European Integration.* Basingstoke: Macmillan.

RUGGIE, J. G. (ed.) 1993. Multilateralism: the anatomy of an institution. In *Multilateralism Matters: The Theory and Praxis of an Institutional Form,* ed. J. G. Ruggie. New York: Columbia University Press.

SCHIAVONE, G. 2001. *International Organizations: A Dictionary and a Directory,* 5th edn. Basingstoke: Palgrave.

SCHMITTER, P. 1971. A revised theory of European integration. In *Regional Integration: Theory and Research,* ed. L. Lindberg and S. Scheingold. Cambridge, Mass.: Harvard University Press.

SIMMONS, B. and MARTIN, L. 2002. International organisations and institutions. In *The Handbook of International Relations,* ed. W. Carlsnaes, T. Risse, and B. Simmons. London: Sage.

SMOUTS, M. C. 1993. Some thoughts on international organisations and theories of regulation. *International Social Science Journal,* 45 (4): 443–51.

STONE SWEET, A. 2004. *The Judicial Construction of Europe.* Oxford: Oxford University Press.

STRANGE, S. 1983. Cave! Hic Dragones: a critique of regime analysis. *International Organisation,* 36 (2): 479–97; repr. in Krasner, 1983.

WALLACE, H. and WALLACE, W. (eds.) 1996. *Policy Making in the European Union,* 3rd edn. Oxford: Oxford University Press.

WENDT, A. 1992. Anarchy is what states make of it: the social construction of power politics. *International Organisation,* 46 (3): 391–425.

—— 2000. *Social Theory of International Politics.* Cambridge: Cambridge University Press.

CHAPTER 32

INTERNATIONAL SECURITY INSTITUTIONS: RULES, TOOLS, SCHOOLS, OR FOOLS?

JOHN S. DUFFIELD

1 INTRODUCTION

Just as international security is one of the central sub-fields of international politics, international security institutions (ISIs) constitute an important subset of international institutions and political institutions more generally. Both despite and because of that fact, however, any attempt to write a chapter on ISIs must overcome two significant hurdles. First, scholars have written very little about ISIs per se. A thriving academic literature exists on the more general topic of international institutions. But with only a few exceptions (Jervis 1983; Müller 1993; Duffield 1994; Wallander 1999; Haftendorn, Keohane, and Wallander 1999), theoretical writings on the subject either draw their examples primarily from other realms, such as the international political economy (e.g. Keohane 1984) and international environmental cooperation (e.g. Young 1999), or make no effort to distinguish among international institutions in different issue areas.

One reason for this relative neglect may be that, as discussed more fully below, security affairs is the arena in which international institutions have been expected, on theoretical grounds, to be least consequential. Of course, this expectation, however well grounded, is at variance with the large numbers of ISIs that have in fact existed. Indeed, the ubiquity and diversity of ISIs is the source of the second obstacle. Scholars have produced numerous works on specific types of ISIs, such as laws of war, alliances, arms control agreements, and collective security systems, and countless analyses of particular institutions, such as the United Nations (UN), the North Atlantic Treaty Organization (NATO), the nuclear non-proliferation regime, and others. Arguably, the relevant literatures are too vast to summarize in a single chapter.

Thus the dual challenge is to say something distinct about ISIs as a whole that nevertheless does justice to them in all their variety. With that goal in mind, this chapter will focus on two issues. The first concerns those features that distinguish ISIs from international institutions in other issue areas. I argue that ISIs may be usefully differentiated on the basis of two fundamental analytical distinctions that are especially relevant, if not unique, to security affairs. The second focus is on the significance of ISIs. The chapter examines four leading theoretical perspectives that offer varying, and often conflicting, assessments of the degree to—and ways in—which international institutions matter.

2 Definitions: What Are ISIs?

Like many other topics in international politics, the terms "international security" and "international institutions" have multiple meanings. Security has long been a contested concept. Not only the nature of the sources of insecurity (e.g. military, economic, social, environmental, etc.) but also the appropriate units of concern (e.g. individuals, national groups, states, global society, etc.) have been the subjects of considerable debate (e.g. Wolfers 1962; Buzan 1983; Ullman 1983). And with the end of the cold war and the existential threat of mutual assured destruction, the question of what should be the proper ambit of "security studies" assumed even greater prominence (e.g. Haftendorn 1991; Walt 1991; Kolodziej 1992).

In hopes of placing some reasonable limits on the discussion, however, this chapter will employ a relatively narrow and traditional definition of security. For our purposes, international security concerns intentional, politically-motivated acts of physical violence directed by one political actor against another, typically—but not exclusively—states, that cross international boundaries. Thus ISIs are those that seek to address or regulate:

1. the threat and use for political purposes of instruments (weapons) designed to cause injury or death to humans and damage or destruction to physical objects, and responses to such threats and uses by other actors;

2. the production, possession, exchange, and transfer of weapons of various types; and
3. the peacetime deployment and activities of military forces armed with such weapons.

It should nevertheless be noted that many ISIs also address concerns that extend beyond these issues.

Unfortunately, the task of defining international institutions is no less problematic. Over the years, scholars have employed multiple conceptions and definitions. One important distinction is that between institutions that are consciously constructed by states and other actors, such as specific treaties and agreements, and those that evolve in a more spontaneous and less intentional fashion, such as sovereignty and many laws of war (Young 1989). A closely related distinction is that between institutions made up of formal rules and procedures and those that consist largely of intersubjective norms. Again, in order to bound the problem, this chapter will focus on relatively formal and consciously constructed "sets of rules meant to govern international behavior" (Simmons and Martin 2002, 194), especially those that are negotiated and endorsed by states.

This conception raises in turn the question of the relationship between international institutions and international organizations. Prominent international relations scholars have offered opposing views on the issue. Robert Keohane includes formal organizations in his influential definition of international institutions (1989, 3–4), while Oran Young explicitly distinguishes between institutions and organizations, which he defines as "material entities possessing physical locations (or seats), offices, personnel, equipment, and budgets" (1989, 32). Certainly, it is important to recognize the material and agentic qualities of international organizations, which can become important international actors in their own right (e.g. Barnett and Finnemore 2004). Nevertheless, most international organizations have a strong basis in rules that define their roles, functions, authority, and capabilities. For example, the UN Security Council and its procedures are established in the UN Charter. Whether it is more fruitful to regard an international organization as an institution or as an actor will depend upon the precise question that one seeks to answer. But as a practical matter, it may be difficult to distinguish between their agentic and institutional characteristics.

3 FORMS OF ISIs

Now that ISIs have been defined, we may begin to differentiate among basic types. As suggested above, ISIs can assume a perhaps bewildering array of forms:

international laws, treaties, agreements, organizations, regimes, and perhaps others. How can we make sense out of—and impose meaningful order on—this diversity?

3.1 Inclusive vs. Exclusive ISIs

As a first cut, we might seek to categorize them according to their spatial or functional scope (e.g. Young 1989, 13; Buzan 2004). Alternatively, we might distinguish between different degrees of formality or explicitness (e.g. Keohane 1989, 3–4). Despite the usefulness of these and other conceptualizations, however, they offer no unique insights with regard to ISIs.

Nevertheless, ISIs can be differentiated on the basis of two other fundamental analytical distinctions that are particularly relevant, and perhaps even unique, to security affairs. The first and more familiar distinction is that between inclusive and exclusive ISIs, which reflect fundamentally different goal orientations (e.g. Duffield 1994; Wallander and Keohane 1999). Inclusive or internally-oriented ISIs are primarily intended to enhance the security of their participants with respect to one another by reducing the likelihood of military conflict among them. They include collective security systems, prohibitions on the use of force, arms control agreements, and other possible arrangements between actual or potential adversaries. In contrast, exclusive or externally-oriented ISIs serve principally to provide security to their participants with respect to non-members that are regarded as posing actual or potential physical threats. Their ultimate objective is to influence the behavior, intentions, and/or capabilities of such non-members, although the achievement of this goal often requires influencing the behavior, intentions, and/or capabilities of participants as well. Into this category fall alliances and arrangements for restricting the export of armaments or goods and technologies with military applications to third parties.

3.2 Operative vs. Contingent Rules

A second and much less noted distinction applies to the types of substantive rules that lie at the core of an ISI. These may be grouped into two basic categories: operative rules and contingent rules. Operative rules concern the ongoing activities of states. In principle, a state can be said to be in compliance or not with an operative rule at any given time. Most ISIs based on operative rules can be subsumed in three categories: arms control agreements, prohibitions on the use of force, and export control arrangements. The first two are inclusive while the latter are exclusive.

Arms control agreements are perhaps the most common form of operative rule-based ISIs. Some actively restrict the numbers, types, or deployment of the military forces that adherents may acquire and maintain, as have the ABM, SALT,

INF, and CFE treaties. Others place limits on peacetime military activities, such as training, military exercises, and other measures intended to prepare forces for combat and to enhance their readiness, as have the Stockholm and Vienna agreements on confidence-building measures (CBMs) and the US–Soviet Incidents at Sea Agreement.

Other familiar ISIs based on operative rules are those that proscribe the use of force. The UN Charter, for example, prohibits the initiation of all military hostilities. Others ban the use of certain types of weapons, such as chemical weapons, or restrict the purposes for which weapons can be employed, such as attacks upon civilians, in conflict.

Finally, export control arrangements place constraints on their participants' assistance to or cooperation with third parties that are regarded as actual or potential military threats. Prominent examples are the Coordinating Committee for Multilateral Export Controls (COCOM), the Australia Group, and the Missile Technology Control Regime (MTCR), which have restricted the transfer of armaments and technologies with military applications to certain non-members. Their purpose is to limit the military capabilities of potential adversaries, thereby minimizing or even preventing the emergence of external threats and thus enhancing the security of their participants.

Contingent rules, in contrast, concern the activities of states in hypothetical circumstances that may never obtain. They are generally prescriptive, indicating what actions participants should take if the triggering conditions were to materialize. In fact, the purpose of contingent rules is typically to prevent the indicated circumstances from arising in the first place. Put differently, the principal issue involved is not whether states will comply with the rules when called upon to do so but whether the behavior of other states will be sufficiently altered by the prospect of compliance with the rules so as to obviate the need to invoke them.

ISIs based on contingent rules come in two basic varieties: inclusive collective security systems (CSS) and exclusive alliances (Claude 1962, 144–9; Wolfers 1962). The institutional character of alliances has often been overlooked in studies of the subject, yet it can be quite pronounced. At the core of an alliance is the positive injunction to provide assistance to a member if it is attacked by a non-member. This rule is often formalized in a treaty of alliance, although it need not be. It is the existence of such a rule, however, that distinguishes alliances from uninstitutionalized alignments between states based on common or complementary interests (Snyder 1997). Nevertheless, alliances may also contain numerous operative rules concerning the peacetime military activities and preparations of their members, but such rules are derivative and supportive of the contingent rules regarding wartime assistance on which an alliance is based.

The characterization of CSSs as contingent-rule based ISIs may be disputed. CSSs contain core rules prescribing the actions that participants should take in the event that aggression occurs (Claude 1962; Kupchan and Kupchan 1991). At the same time, they are typically predicated on the existence of more or less explicit operative rules proscribing the use of force or other harmful actions by participants against one another. Thus it may be tempting to view CSSs simply as auxiliary sanctions regimes. Nevertheless, the operative rules prohibiting aggressive acts and the contingent rules prescribing responses to them need not be formally related and may in practice develop independently. For example, a regional CSS could be based on universal principles of international law.

The distinctions between inclusive and exclusive ISIs, on the one hand, and operative and contingent rules, on the other, suggest a fourfold typology of ISIs, which can be represented by a two-by-two matrix (see Table 32.1)

It should be stressed that each of these categories is an ideal type. Actual ISIs may fall into two or more of them. For example, nominal alliances may simultaneously be CSSs if they also require their members to defend one another against attacks by other members. Alternately, alliances and CSSs may be accompanied by export control arrangements or arms control agreements.

4 The Significance of ISIs

The most important question to be asked of ISIs is whether they make any difference in international politics. After all, if an affirmative answer cannot be offered, there would seem to be little point in discussing the nature and determinants of ISIs, let alone the mechanisms through which they may work their effects.

To be sure, the large numbers of ISIs that have existed as well as the demonstrated willingness of states to invest considerable time, energy, and resources in them constitute prima facie evidence of the important of ISIs. Yet the presence of

Table 32.1 A typology of ISIs

	Inclusive ISIs	Exclusive ISIs
Operative rules	Arms control agreements (e.g. ABM, SALT, NPT, CBMs)	Export controls arrangements (e.g. COCOM, Nuclear Suppliers Group)
	Use of force prohibitions (e.g. UN Charter)	
Contingent rules	Collective security systems (e.g. League of Nations, UN)	Alliances (e.g. NATO, WEU)

these phenomena is usually not regarded as sufficient even by those who believe that ISIs are consequential. Instead, we must look at the theoretical arguments— pro and con—that have been advanced regarding the influence of ISIs and the empirical evidence that has been offered in support of those arguments.

Unfortunately, there is as yet no distinct body of theory regarding the effects of ISIs. Rather, we must turn to the more general theoretical literature on the significance of international institutions, identifying where possible the distinct ways in which ISIs might (or might not) make a difference. That said, international security may provide an especially valuable arena for adjudicating among the competing claims of different theories insofar as it is the area where theorists of all stripes have expected international institutions to be least consequential (e.g. Lipson 1984; Keohane 1984, 6–7; Grieco 1988, 504; 1990, 11–14; Mearsheimer 1994–5). This chapter will review and evaluate four of the most influential theoretical approaches, laying out their principal arguments and providing empirical illustrations from the universe of ISIs.

Of course, institutions can have effects only where they exist. Yet potentially influential ISIs have not always been created in situations where they could in theory have mattered. In this regard, there may be a close connection between the causes and consequences of international institutions. Given space constraints, however, this chapter will not be able to address the important issues of whether and when ISIs are actually created and the forms they may take.

4.1 The Neorealist Baseline: Institutions (or Institutionalists) as Fools

The principal theoretical source of the null hypothesis that ISIs do not matter is neorealism. This approach emphasizes the potential for conflict inherent in the ability of states to use force against one another, the anarchic nature of the international system, and the presence of a substantial degree of uncertainty about other states' intentions, capabilities, and actions. Neorealist scholars hold a highly skeptical view about the significance of international institutions in general and ISIs in particular. In short, institutions, or at least those who believe in their importance, are fools.

Neorealists argue that international institutions exert minimal influence over state behavior and international outcomes on several grounds (e.g. Grieco 1988; Mearsheimer 1994–5). First, they maintain that states will be reluctant both to create institutions in the first place and to observe the rules of any institutions that they do establish. One reason is the fear that other states will cheat on their obligations, leaving any states that do comply at a disadvantage. Given uncertainty about others' intentions, states can never be sure that their partners will abide by agreements and not seek to exploit them.

A more fundamental concern is that even when fears of cheating are absent and all states enjoy absolute benefits, some states may gain more than others and thus be able to increase their relative capabilities. Concerns about the distribution of gains are likely to be especially acute in security affairs, since states may be able to use any advantage they obtain in military power to coerce or conquer their adversaries (Grieco 1988; Wallander 1999, 15). As evidence of the salience of relative gains concerns, scholars have offered examples of unwillingness even among allies to strike deals on economic issues that would make all better off (Grieco 1990; Mastanduno 1991). In the security realm, one might also point to the hard bargaining that typically proceeds—and sometimes prevents—the achievement of mutually beneficial arms control accords.

Another leading neorealist argument is that international institutions are epiphenomena. Even if states do choose to create international institutions, the latter merely reflect the calculations of self-interest of the most powerful states (Krasner 1983b; Strange 1983; Krasner 1991; Mearsheimer 1994–5). Thus powerful states are free to disregard institutional obligations whenever compliance is no longer viewed as convenient, and institutions are subject to restructuring or abandonment with each shift in the distribution of state power and interests. As examples of this dynamic, one might cite NATO's continuing dependence on US sufferance, the unilateral abrogation of the ABM Treaty by the United States, and the latter's highly controversial decision to invade Iraq without the explicit authorization of the UN Security Council.

A related rational-choice argument is that international institutions typically require states to make at most marginal changes of behavior. Deeper cooperation involving greater departures from the status quo is avoided because the utility of cheating rises faster than the utility of compliance and participating states are unwilling or unable to pay the higher costs of enforcement. Thus US–Soviet arms control treaties rarely required either side to alter its planned military programs substantially, and perhaps the most ambitious arms control agreement ever formulated, the 1923 Washington Naval Treaty, was marked by a high degree of non-compliance (Downs, Rocke, and Barsoom 1996).

Other scholars, however, have cast doubt on each of these claims, thereby creating theoretical space within which ISIs might exert independent effects. Most easily dispensed with is the argument about fears of cheating. Uncertainty about the behavior of other states as well as their capabilities and intentions is a variable, not a constant (Wallander 1999, 24). Thus rather than simply assume the worst, states have an incentive to reduce uncertainty by obtaining more information. To this end, they may take unilateral measures, such as spy satellites, but they can also make use of international institutions.

Likewise, neorealists have exaggerated both the prevalence and the magnitude of relative gains concerns. Such worries are not always present in security affairs, and when they are present, they may not be sufficient to inhibit cooperation. Consequently, the potential of ISIs to shape state behavior and international outcomes is much greater than neorealists have acknowledged. First, as the distinction between inclusive and exclusive ISIs suggests, concerns about relative gains are likely to be less prominent in relations among allies than in relations between adversaries. Notwithstanding the truism that today's ally may be tomorrow's enemy, alignments may be highly stable under some configurations of power and interest. In those cases, states will not fear that their partners might soon turn on them. And even where relative gains concerns are not insignificant, they may be overridden by the imperative to work together in the face of a hostile common enemy.

In relations among adversaries, moreover, concerns about relative gains may not exist because institutions have no distributional consequences. Some ISIs may increase the security of all participants without affecting their relative power. For example, confidence-building measures that place constraints on peacetime military activities can lower the risk of an unintended conflict due to mistrust or misperception without affecting military capabilities.

And even where institutions do have distributional consequences, a state may have little or no opportunity to exploit relative gains. Thus in relations among nuclear-armed states, an agreement that enables one party to gain or maintain a numerical advantage in nuclear weapons will do little to diminish the security of other parties if they already possess invulnerable second-strike capabilities (Weber 1991). Likewise, in a world of conventionally-armed states, the distribution of gains will have little impact if defense is easy and offense is difficult (Glaser 1994–5, 79).

As for the argument that institutions are epiphenomena of power and interests, even the most powerful states may have incentives to comply with the rules of established institutions when doing so is inconvenient, and sometimes these incentives will outweigh those favoring non-compliance. Certainly, it is rational for no less a country than the United States to weigh the benefits to be gained from circumventing the UN Security Council against the possible costs before choosing a course of action. In addition, even if institutions exhibit little autonomy and robustness, they may still be "essential mediators" between the distribution of state power and interests, on the one hand, and the precise forms that behavior may take, on the other (Hasenclever, Mayer, and Rittberger 1997, 108). The importance of this fact is reinforced by the indeterminacy of structural factors. A range of particular institutional forms may be compatible with a given constellation of power and interests.

Going further, international institutions may in fact exhibit considerable resilience in the face of structural changes (Krasner 1983a; Keohane 1984, 100–3; Duffield 1992; Wallander 2000). One reason is uncertainty about whether the institution will be required—or at least of use—in the future, especially if states are risk averse. Another is the fact that institutions embody sunk costs and are thus usually easier to maintain than to construct anew. A third may be that an existing institution's "assets" can be adapted for new purposes (Wallander 2000). Indeed, the existence of fungible institutional capabilities may lead states to discover new applications to which they might be put (March and Olson 1998, 966–8), as illustrated by the development of UN peacekeeping and NATO's post-cold war interventions in the Balkans. A fourth reason is what March and Olson (1998) term the "competency trap:" actors will tend to buy into a particular institution by virtue of developing familiarity with the rules and capabilities for using them. Whatever the reasons, as March and Olson observe, "institutions are relatively robust against environmental change or deliberate reform...the character of current institutions depends not only on current conditions but also on the historical path of institutional development" (1998, 959). Certainly, one can point to a number of examples of ISIs—the UN Security Council, the Nuclear Non-proliferation Treaty, the Conventional Forces in Europe Treaty, and NATO, to name but a few—that have outlived their original circumstances and endured in the face of major structural changes.

4.2 Neoinstitutionalism: Institutions as Rules

In sum, strong theoretical grounds exist for concluding that ISIs may have important independent consequences. Through what mechanisms, then, can they work their influence?

The most well-developed school of thought on the impact of international institutions is neoliberal institutionalism or, more simply, neoinstitutionalism. This approach shares many assumptions with neorealism: that states are the primary actors in international politics, that they are rational egoists concerned only about their own interests, and that they interact in an anarchic setting with no higher authority to protect them from each other and enforce agreements. Despite these commonalities, neoinstitutionalists nevertheless employ a functionalist logic to argue that states will create sets of more or less formal rules where they expect such rules to serve their interests. These institutions can do so by increasing the options available to states and by altering the incentives to select one course of action or another, thereby producing different behaviors and outcomes than would have obtained in their absence.

Neoinstitutionalists have identified at least four specific mechanisms through which institutional rule sets can make a difference (Keohane 1984; Martin 1992b). First, and most simply, they can provide or serve as focal points that help states solve coordination problems. In many situations, more than one potentially beneficial and stable cooperative outcome (equilibrium) exists. Although different states may prefer different outcomes, once a particular solution is chosen, they all have an interest in complying with it. Any departure, such as choosing to drive on the left-hand side of the road (in North America, anyway), is likely to make the violator worse off, at least in the short term. Examples from security affairs include cold war spheres of influence (Duffield 1994), the US–Soviet Incidents at Sea Agreement (Lynn-Jones 1985), and common NATO standards for military forces and doctrines.

In other situations, such as those represented by the Prisoner's Dilemma, states may benefit from mutual adjustments in their behavior but still have incentives to return to the status quo. Adversaries may attempt to gain a temporary military advantage in peacetime or war, and allies may seek to free-ride on the efforts of their partners. In these so-called collaboration problems with unstable equilibria, institutional rules may serve as well-defined standards of behavior that reinforce the incentives to cooperate. Not only does one state's non-compliance risk the loss of the benefits generated by other states' cooperation and perhaps even the immediate imposition of additional sanctions, but it may also have significant reputational costs. Other states may be less inclined to cooperate with a recognized rule violator on other potentially beneficial issues (Hasenclever, Mayer, and Rittberger 1997, 35).

Such standards of behavior lie at the heart of many ISIs based on operative rules. These include arms control agreements that place limits on the numbers and types of weapons states may field, NATO conventional force goals during the cold war (Duffield 1992), and laws of war that prohibit certain military practices. ISIs based on contingent rules of behavior may perform a similar function. By entering into an alliance or a collective security system, a state can signal or clarify its intentions to both potential adversaries and allies that it will resist aggression against and provide assistance to those attacked. Although subsequent non-compliance may be subject to fewer immediate costs and cannot be ruled out, it may still have important reputational consequences. Thus by signing the North Atlantic Treaty, the United States engaged its reputation and raised the stakes associated with possible future choices.

A third important way in which institutions can have an impact is by reducing uncertainty (Keohane 1984; Martin 1992b). Where states have agreed to clear standards of behavior, they may be unsure that others are observing their commitments and thus experience additional incentives not to comply themselves. And even in situations where no party can improve its situation by defecting, so-called assurance problems, states may nevertheless be uncertain of others' intentions and thus fear that others may seek to exploit them. In both cases, institutions can promote cooperation by helping fearful states obtain greater certainty about others' behavior, capabilities, and interests and, conversely, by allowing states to reassure others that they are in compliance or have only benign intentions. To achieve these goals, international institutions may include rules requiring states to provide each other with certain forms of information or allowing others to carry out various types of inspections.

Such transparency provisions sometimes form the central elements of ISIs, as in the case of confidence building measures. At other times, such as the increasingly elaborate monitoring provisions of arms control agreements like the INF Treaty, they supplement more fundamental behavioral standards. A third example is NATO's force planning process, which involves the sharing of detailed information about each member's military capabilities and plans and has played a central role in allaying concerns about free riding as well as of potential intra-alliance threats (Tuschhoff 1999)

Finally, international institutions can provide negotiating opportunities for their participants (Keohane 1984; Hasenclever, Mayer, and Rittberger 1997, 34). By reducing transaction costs, standing decision-making procedures make it easier for states to resolve disputes over existing rules and distributional conflicts, to devise new rules as needed, and to react in an effective manner to whatever instances of non-compliance that may occur. This is a central function of the UN Security Council, which interprets and organizes responses to violations of rules contained in the UN Charter. It has also been prominently on display over the years in NATO, whose members have made repeated decisions about peacetime military preparations and activities and, more recently, foreign deployments and military interventions.

4.3 Institutions as Organizational Tools

As the examples suggest, decision-making procedures are typically associated with international organizations, although they need not be (Young 1989). Thus a third theoretical approach emphasizes the organizational characteristics of many international institutions. From this perspective, international institutions become tools with a physical or material dimension that states can use to pursue their individual or collective interests. It is useful nevertheless to distinguish here between two general organizational forms: as collective actors and as autonomous actors.

Many international organizations take the form of rule-bound structures in which the representatives of member states interact and make collective choices. In the security realm, these include the UN Security Council, the North Atlantic Council, the US–Soviet Standing Consultative Commission, the Board of Governors of the International Atomic Energy Agency (IAEA), and others. As such, international organizations can perform several functions—beyond simply reducing transaction costs—more effectively than ad hoc groupings of states.

First, they allow the members to speak, should they choose to do so, with a single voice. In particular, they are able to dispense politically significant approval and disapproval of the claims, policies, and actions of states (Claude 1966). This collective legitimation function in turn facilitates the mobilization of international support on behalf of or in opposition to particular behaviors. Traditionally, it has been the prerogative of the Security Council, as exemplified by its response to Iraq's invasion of Kuwait in 1990. But when the Council has been deadlocked, other organizations have occasionally been employed, such as the General Assembly under the 1950 Uniting for Peace Resolution and NATO during the 1999 Kosovo crisis.

A second important function of international organizations as collective actors is the centralization of members' activities and resources (Abbott and Snidal 1998). At a minimum, such pooling may result in greater efficiencies, as when it allows— or requires—participants to specialize in particular activities. It may provide less capable members with resources that they could not obtain on their own. And it may even result in the generation of capabilities on a scale that no single member alone could produce.

Perhaps the best example in the security realm has been NATO's force planning process and integrated military planning and command structure. These organizational structures have discouraged the unnecessary duplication of military capabilities. They have provided the smaller members with access to intelligence about potential external threats and other assets that they would otherwise have lacked. And as a side benefit, they have placed constraints on the ability of many members to use their forces for purely national purposes (Duffield 1994; Tuschhoff 1999).

Third, international organizations of this type facilitate the use of issue linkage, especially where their mandates comprehend multiple issue areas. States can attempt to link issues outside of formal organizational frameworks. But the influence that organizational decision rules confer upon members can be a powerful source of leverage. Thus Britain was able to use its position in the European Community to obtain continued support for economic sanctions on Argentina by its reluctant partners during the 1982 Falklands Islands conflict (Martin 1992a).

Whether international institutions take the form of sets of rules or collective organizational actors, even some leading neoinstitutionalists have questioned just how significant their independent effects actually are (Keohane and Martin 2003). If states form institutions in response to the structural conditions they face, is it not those conditions that best explain the outcomes associated with the institutions? One further response to this "endogeneity" problem is to recognize that international organizations can also assume the form of autonomous actors. States often create bodies to perform various executive functions, such as the UN Secretariat, the NATO International Staff, and others (Abbott and Snidal 1998).

These supranational bodies are typically endowed with responsibilities, resources, such as technical expertise and information, and a certain degree of discretion that enable them to act independently to an important extent, or what has been termed "agency slack" (Keohane and Martin 2003, 102–3; Barnett and Finnemore 2004).

Although such organizations are not typically able to act in ways that directly contravene the interests of the states that create them, especially the more powerful ones, their autonomy allows them to perform certain functions more effectively than individual or even groups of states. As relatively neutral actors, international organizations may be able to serve as monitors or arbiters in politically charged situations where others may be refused access. Even if they are working on behalf of member states, their seemingly non-partisan nature will often make their activities more acceptable (Abbott and Snidal 1998).

In the security realm, the secretaries general of both the UN and NATO or their representatives have often been called upon to serve as mediators. Within NATO, the perceived impartiality of its high-level military commanders has enabled them to resolve conflicts and gain national concessions on disputed issues (Tuschhoff 1999). IAEA inspectors are more likely to gain access to the nuclear facilities of the organization's members than would representatives of some individual countries. Perhaps the most prominent example is the practice of UN peacekeeping, which has allowed powerful states to support conflict resolution without becoming directly involved (Abbott and Snidal 1998, 19).

4.4 Social Constructivism: Institutions as Schools

A second escape from the endogeneity trap lies in the recognition that international institutions can sometimes alter the basic structural variables that give rise to them in the first place through a variety of feedback mechanisms (Krasner 1983a). Such a process is implicit in the problem of relative gains, whereby states' compliance with international institutions can result in shifts in the distribution of power. Of particular interest here, however, are situations in which a state's participation in international institutions can alter its effective policy preferences.

Preference change can come about in several general ways. One approach focuses on the internal distributional consequences of international institutions, which can promote the formation and strengthening of domestic and transnational actors with an interest in compliance and weaken those that are opposed (Milner 1988; Haas 1990). Another approach emphasizes the internalization of institutional rules, which can be translated into domestic legislation, organizational routines, and standard operating procedures (Müller 1993; Young 1999).

Perhaps the most developed and influential approach is social constructivism, which starts from the premise that (international) actors and social structures are mutually constituted. In contrast to rationalist approaches, social constructivism holds that the nature of actors is malleable and subject to modification through processes of interaction (e.g. Adler 1997; Ruggie 1998; Wendt 1999). In particular, for the purposes of this discussion, a state's involvement with or participation in an ISI can bring about changes in its interests and even its very identity, which in turn can have long-term behavior implications. From this perspective, then, international institutions are effectively schools in which actors learn or are taught new understandings and meanings.

Beyond these broad shared parameters, social constructivist work varies on a number of dimensions. One is the unit of analysis. Social constructivists have focused on individuals, elites, central decision-makers, governmental organizations, social groups, and society as a whole. With few exceptions, however, they agree that meaningful analysis requires abandoning the state-centric ontology of neorealism and neoinstitutionalism and considering various domestic actors. Another source of variation is the particular ideational change that is of interest. Although social constructivism is usually framed in terms of interests/goals and identities/loyalties, it can also comprehend world-views or definitions of the situation, including images of other actors; beliefs about how most effectively to achieve one's goals; and values.

In addition, social constructivists have identified and explored several mechanisms through which ideational change might occur in international institutional contexts. One is learning. Here, exposure via direct experience, such as personal contacts and interaction, or more goal-directed study may lead to emulation or imitation (Nye 1987; Checkel 1997). A second mechanism is teaching, whereby an organizational actor actively seeks to instruct state members via conferences, training programs, on-site consulting, and other means (Finnemore 1993). Teaching models typically presuppose some asymmetry in authority or technical expertise. Finally, actors may seek to persuade one another, using international institutions and especially organizations as discourse arenas that facilitate argumentative processes (Risse 2000; Checkel 2001; Johnston 2001).

Whether and how much ideational change will occur within ISIs as a result of such processes may depend on a number of institutional characteristics, not to mention other factors. One is the extent of exposure or density of interactions, which would seem to favor ISIs with well-developed organizational components. A second is the informality of intrainstitutional interactions, which may facilitate argumentative processes. A third is the degree of hierarchy inherent in the institutional setting, which can both facilitate and hinder the transfer of ideas depending on the other characteristics of the actors involved.

Thus far, related empirical work has not focused particularly on the effects of ISIs. Nevertheless, a number of relevant examples of social constructivist dynamics at work in the security realm can be found. Perhaps the first to be noted concerned US–Soviet security relations, where interactions in a variety of institutional forums were seen as contributing to changing Soviet elite views about nuclear weapons and of the United States (Nye 1987; Müller 1993). Within NATO, scholars have also found evidence of institutionally-driven ideational change. Individuals working within the organization have developed more complex loyalties (Tuschhoff 1999), and the alliance allegedly played a role in reshaping post-unification German attitudes about the legitimacy of outside military interventions (Harnisch and Maull 2001). More recently, Chinese participation in the dialogue process of the ASEAN Regional Forum (ARF) has changed the beliefs of Chinese officials in charge of ARF policy about their country's interests with regard to regional security institutions and issues (Johnston 1999, 291).

5 By Way of Conclusion: The Importance of ISIs in a Neohegemonic Era

What can we conclude about the significance of ISIs? The empirical record indicates that they have had noteworthy effects of different types through a variety of causal mechanisms. These effects range from modifications of state behavior induced by the presence of institutional rules to the autonomous activities of international organizations to changes in the internal characteristics of states through their involvement in ISIs.

Although one can offer a number of illustrations of such effects, however, existing scholarship leaves a number of important questions unanswered. It is not yet possible to say much about (a) when or how often particular effects will occur; (b) how significant particular effects are with regard to the overall nature, behavior, and security of affected states; (c) how the different types of effects and the mechanisms through which they occur may vary across the basic types of ISIs; and (d) how they may or may not differ between ISIs and international institutions in other issue areas. Clearly, there is room for much more theory-guided, comparative empirical research on the subject.

Another important area for future research concerns ISIs as dependent variables. Again, one can find a substantial number of theoretical works on the determinants of international institutions more generally and the forms they may take (e.g. Krasner 1983b; Snidal 1985; Martin 1992b; Richards 1999; Gruber 2000;

Koremenos, Lipson, and Snidal 2001). Indeed, this literature is better developed than that on institutional effects (Martin and Simmons 1998). But it has not paid particular attention to ISIs and the ways in which they may differ both among themselves and from international institutions in other issue areas. Perhaps the choice between inclusive and exclusive ISIs and between operative and contingent rules might best be understood in terms of the basic security challenges faced by states. But few actual ISIs fall neatly into just one of these categories, and considerable additional variation in their formation, persistence, and characteristics would remain to be explained.

Even as scholars continue to develop new theories and to examine the historical record, it is also important for them to draw on the insights so far obtained in order to shed light on current problems and to inform policy choices. Indeed, the present era would seem to pose a particularly useful test for theories bearing on the significance of ISIs. On the one hand, the international system is characterized by the presence of a number of well-developed ISIs. On the other hand, with the end of the cold war and the disintegration of the Soviet Union, the structural conditions that gave rise to many of these ISIs have been profoundly altered. In particular, the United States has emerged as an unrivaled and unprecedented superpower (Ikenberry 2003). And in more recent years, the international security agenda has come to be dominated, at least for some important states, by a concern—international terrorism—that was not foreseen when most of the existing ISIs were founded. Consequently, it is well worth asking just how useful these ISIs can and will prove to be and how much influence they may be expected to exert. Scholars associated with the various approaches discussed above are unlikely to be of one mind on the issue, but it is nevertheless instructive to explore the implications of their theoretical arguments.

Current conditions would seem to be especially propitious for the realization of neorealist expectations. A hegemonic power should be uniquely free to disregard its pre-existing institutional obligations and even to reshape them to suit its interests. This dynamic should be particularly pronounced in the novel circumstances attending the war on terrorism. ISIs should significantly affect the behavior of only relatively weak states, which the hegemon may alternatively force or induce to comply.

Recent years have offered a wealth of evidence that can be interpreted as supporting this perspective. Even before the terrorist attacks of September 2001, the United States had rejected several recently negotiated security arrangements that enjoyed broad international support, including the International Criminal Court, and it was moving to withdraw from the long-standing ABM Treaty. The immediate US response to the attacks in Afghanistan took place largely outside existing institutional frameworks such as the UN and NATO, and it subsequently invaded Iraq without the endorsement of the Security Council. More generally, the United States under the Bush administration has attempted to loosen traditional international restrictions regarding the use of force.

At the same time, however, other perspectives suggest reasons not to expect the postwar institutional security architecture to be abandoned and, beyond that, for existing ISIs to continue to enjoy significant influence, even with the United States. One is the enduring relevance of more traditional security concerns, such as interstate conflict and nuclear non-proliferation, for which the institutions were devised.

Another reason is the practical limits on the ability of the United States to address by itself the full range of threats, both new and traditional, that it faces. As the war in Iraq has shown, the United States may be able single-handedly to overthrow an unfriendly regime, but not to provide security and stability in the aftermath. Likewise, without the cooperation of other states, the United States is less likely to be able to prevent the further proliferation of technologies and materials useful for the construction of nuclear weapons. More generally, even hegemonic powers have incentives to build and maintain rule-based international orders that place some constraints on their behavior as a means of preserving their power and securing the acquiescence of others (Ikenberry 2003).

Third, only institutions can provide one resource that even powerful states find helpful—and sometimes essential—for achieving their goals: international legitimacy. With institutionally-conferred legitimacy comes the possibility of greater cooperation and less opposition by other states (Ikenberry 2003). Just how important this is has been evidenced by the difficulties experienced by the United States in obtaining international support for post-conflict operations in Iraq. It is also suggested by the lengths to which the Bush administration went to work through the UN Security Council before ultimately deciding to invade without authorization.

Finally, some existing ISIs are characterized by a considerable degree of adaptability, which renders them potentially useful under a wide range of circumstances. One important example is the development and continued broadening of UN-sponsored peacekeeping operations. Another is the post-cold war use of NATO to intervene militarily and mount post-conflict peace operations in the Balkans and even distant Afghanistan. Just how adaptable any particular ISI might be will depend on the fungibility of its assets (Wallander 2000), but it would seem to be far too early to write off many as irrelevant to today's security challenges.

REFERENCES

ABBOTT, K. W. and SNIDAL, D. 1998. Why states act through formal international organizations. *Journal of Conflict Resolution*, 42 (1): 3–32.

ADLER, E. 1997. Seizing the middle ground: constructivism in world politics. *European Journal of International Relations*, 3 (3): 291–318.

BARNETT, M. N. and FINNEMORE, M. 2004. *Rules for the World: International Organizations in Global Politics*. Ithaca, NY: Cornell University Press.

BUZAN, B. 1983. *People, States, and Fear: The National Security Problem in International Relations*. Chapel Hill: University of North Carolina Press.

—— 2004. *From International to World Society? English School Theory and the Social Structure of Globalisation*. Cambridge: Cambridge University Press.

CHECKEL, J. T. 1997. International norms and domestic politics: bridging the rationalist–constructivist divide. *European Journal of International Relations*, 3(4): 473–95.

—— 2001. Why comply? Social learning and European identity change. *International Organization*, 55 (3): 553–88.

CLAUDE, I. L. 1962. *Power and International Relations*. New York: Random House.

—— 1966. Collective legitimation as a political function of the UN. *International Organization*, 20 (2): 267–79.

DOWNS, G. W., ROCKE, D. M., and BARSOOM, P. 1996. Is the good news about compliance good news about cooperation? *International Organization*, 50 (3): 379–406.

DUFFIELD, J. S. 1992. International regimes and alliance behavior: explaining NATO conventional force levels. *International Organization*, 46 (4): 819–55.

—— 1994. Explaining the long peace in Europe: the contributions of regional security regimes. *Review of International Studies*, 20: 369–88.

FINNEMORE, M. 1993. International organizations as teachers of norms: the United Nations Educational, Scientific, and Cutural Organization and science policy. *International Organization*, 47 (4): 565–97.

GLASER, C. L. 1994–5. Realists as optimists: cooperation as self-help. *International Security*, 19 (3): 50–90.

GRIECO, J. M. 1988. Anarchy and the limits of cooperation: a realist critique of the newest liberal institutionalism. *International Organization*, 42: 485–507.

—— 1990. *Cooperation among Nations: Europe, America, and Non-tariff Barriers to Trade*. Ithaca, NY: Cornell University Press.

GRUBER, L. G. 2000. *Ruling the World: Power Politics and the Rise of Supranational Institutions*. Princeton, NJ: Princeton University Press.

HAAS, P. M. 1990. *Saving the Mediterranean: The Politics of International Environmental Cooperation*. New York: Columbia University Press.

HAFTENDORN, H. 1991. The security puzzle: theory-building and discipline-building in international security. *International Studies Quarterly*, 35 (1): 3–17.

—— KEOHANE, R. O., and WALLANDER, C. A. 1999. *Imperfect Unions: Security Institutions over Time and Space*. Oxford: Oxford University Press.

HARNISCH, S. and MAULL, H. W. 2001. Conclusion: "Learned Its Lesson Well?" Germany as a civilian power ten years after unification. Pp. 128–56 in *Germany as a Civilian Power? The Foreign Policy of the Berlin Republic*, ed. S. Harnisch and H. W. Maull. Manchester: Manchester University Press.

HASENCLEVER, A., MAYER, P., and RITTBERGER, V. 1997. *Theories of International Regimes*. Cambridge: Cambridge University Press.

IKENBERRY, G. J. 2003. Is American multilateralism dead? *Perspectives on Politics*, 1 (3): 533–50.

JERVIS, R. 1983. Security regimes. Pp. 173–94 in *International Regimes*, ed. S. Krasner. Ithaca, NY: Cornell University Press.

JOHNSTON, A. I. 1999. The myth of the ASEAN way? Explaining the evolution of the ASEAN regional forum. Pp. 287–324 in *Imperfect Unions: Security Institutions over Space and Time*, ed. H. Haftendorn, R. O. Keohane, and C. A. Wallander. Oxford: Oxford University Press.

—— 2001. Treating international institutions as social environments. *International Studies Quarterly*, 45 (4): 487–515.

KEOHANE, R. O. 1984. *After Hegemony: Cooperation and Discord in the World Political Economy*. Princeton, NJ: Princeton University Press.

—— 1989. *International Institutions and State Power: Essays in International Relations Theory*. Boulder, Colo.: Westview Press.

—— and MARTIN, L. L. 2003. Institutional theory as a research paradigm. Pp. 71–107 in *Progress in International Relations: Appraising the Field*, ed. C. Elman and M. F. Elman. Cambridge, Mass.: MIT Press.

KOLODZIEJ, E. A. 1992. Renaissance in security studies? *Caveat lector! International Studies Quarterly*, 36 (4): 421–38.

KOREMENOS, B., LIPSON, C., and SNIDAL, D. (eds.) 2001. *The Rational Design of International Institutions*. Special issue of *International Organization*, 55 (4).

KRASNER, S. D. 1983a. Regimes and the limits of realism: regimes as autonomous variables. Pp. 355–68 in *International Regimes*, ed. S. D. Krasner. Ithaca, NY: Cornell University Press.

—— 1983b. Structural causes and regime consequences: regimes as intervening variables. Pp. 1–21 in *International Regimes*, ed. S. D. Krasner. Ithaca, NY: Cornell University Press.

—— 1991. Global communications and national power: life on the Pareto frontier. *World Politics*, 43 (3): 336–66.

KUPCHAN, C. A. and KUPCHAN, C. A. 1991. Concerts, collective security, and the future of Europe. *International Security*, 16 (1): 114–61.

LIPSON, C. 1984. International cooperation in economic and security affairs. *World Politics*, 36: 1–23.

LYNN-JONES, S. M. 1985. A quiet success for arms control: preventing incidents at sea. *International Security*, 9 (4): 154–84.

MARCH, J. G. and OLSON, J. P. 1998. The institutional dynamics of international political orders. *International Organization*, 52 (4): 943–69.

MARTIN, L. L. 1992a. Institutions and cooperation: sanctions during the Falkland Islands conflict. *International Security*, 16 (4): 143–78.

—— 1992b. Interests, power, and multilateralism. *International Organization*, 46 (4): 765–92.

—— and SIMMONS, B. 1998. Theories and empirical studies of international institutions. *International Organization*, 52 (4): 729–57.

MASTANDUNO, M. 1991. Do relative gains matter? America's response to Japanese industrial policy. *International Security*, 16 (1): 73–113.

MEARSHEIMER, J. J. 1994–5. The false promise of international institutions. *International Security*, 19: 5–49.

MILNER, H. V. 1988. *Resisting Protectionism: Global Industries and the Politics of International Trade*. Princeton, NJ: Princeton University Press.

MÜLLER, H. 1993. The internalization of principles, norms, and rules by governments: the case of security regimes. Pp. 361–88 in *Regime Theory and International Relations*, ed. V. Rittberger. Oxford: Oxford University Press.

NYE, J. S. 1987. Nuclear learning and U.S.–Soviet security regimes. *International Organization*, 41 (3): 371–402.

RICHARDS, J. E. 1999. Toward a positive theory of international institutions: regulating international aviation markets. *International Organization*, 53 (1): 1–37.

RISSE, T. 2000. "Let's argue!" Communicative action in world politics. *International Organization*, 54 (1): 1–39.

RUGGIE, J. G. 1998. What makes the world hang together? Neo-utilitarianism and the social constructivist challenge. *International Organization*, 52 (4): 855–85.

SIMMONS, B. A. and MARTIN, L. L. 2002. International organizations and institutions. Pp. 192–211 in *Handbook of International Relations*, ed. W. Carlsnaes, T. Risse, and B. A. Simmons. London: Sage.

SNIDAL, D. 1985. Coordination versus prisoners' dilemma: implications for international cooperation and regimes. *American Political Science Review*, 79 (4): 923–42.

SNYDER, G. H. 1997. *Alliance Politics*. Ithaca, NY: Cornell University Press.

STRANGE, S. 1983. *Cave! Hic dragones*: a critique of regime analysis. Pp. 337–54 in *International Regimes*, ed. S. D. Krasner. Ithaca, NY: Cornell University Press.

TUSCHHOFF, C. 1999. Alliance cohesion and peaceful change in NATO. Pp. 140–61 in *Imperfect Unions: Security Institutions over Space and Time*, ed. H. Haftendorn, R. O. Keohane, and C. A. Wallander. Oxford: Oxford University Press.

ULLMAN, R. H. 1983. Redefining security. *International Security*, 8 (1): 129–53.

WALLANDER, C. A. 1999. *Mortal Friends, Best Enemies: German–Russian Cooperation after the Cold War*. Ithaca, NY: Cornell University Press.

—— 2000. Institutional assets and adaptability: NATO after the Cold War. *International Organization*, 54 (4): 705–35.

—— and KEOHANE, R. O. 1999. Risk, threat, and security institutions. Pp. 21–47 in *Imperfect Unions: Security Institutions over Space and Time*, ed. H. Haftendorn, R. O. Keohane, and C. A. Wallander. Oxford: Oxford University Press.

WALT, S. M. 1991. The renaissance of security studies. *International Studies Quarterly*, 35 (2): 211–39.

WEBER, S. 1991. *Cooperation and Discord in U.S.–Soviet Arms Control*. Princeton, NJ: Princeton University Press.

WENDT, A. 1999. *Social Theory of International Politics*. Cambridge: Cambridge University Press.

WOLFERS, A. 1962. *Discord and Collaboration: Essays on International Politics*. Baltimore: Johns Hopkins Press.

YOUNG, O. R. 1989. *International Cooperation: Building Regimes for Natural Resources and the Environment*. Ithaca, NY: Cornell University Press.

—— 1999. *Governance in World Affairs*. Ithaca, NY: Cornell University Press.

INTERNATIONAL ECONOMIC INSTITUTIONS

LISA L. MARTIN

Many of the world's international economic transactions today are organized by international economic institutions (IEIs). The international political economic environment is highly institutionalized, and international economic organizations play an important role in the international distribution of wealth. As such, these organizations have become subject to intense public scrutiny, some supportive and some hostile.[1] IEIs have also increasingly been the subject of rigorous scholarly study. These political institutions are particularly studied by political scientists, using the same intellectual frameworks used to study international organizations more generally.

This chapter considers the frameworks used to study IEIs and highlights issues that should prompt future research agendas on this topic. I focus on the following themes: First, an understanding of the causes and consequences of IEIs requires that we begin by specifying the fundamental strategic problems that IEIs address.

---

[1] There is a valid distinction between institutions and organizations, as other chapters in this *Handbook* make clear. In the international relations literature, the term "institutions" is used to refer more generally to sets of rules and norms. "Organizations" embody these norms and are empowered to take actions. However, in this case, the distinction does not hold any great analytical consequences. Most institutions also have substantial organizational structure. One exception, perhaps, is the GATT. The GATT began as a series of bargained agreements, and had barely any organizational structure, not even a mailing address. However, the GATT gained such structure over time, and now as the WTO its organizational status is firmly established.

In the realm of international trade, states face large potential gains from reducing barriers to exchange, but also constant political pressures to renege on liberalizing agreements. Thus, IEIs confront dilemmas at the bargaining, monitoring, and enforcement stages. In the international financial institutions (IFIs), the basic problem is to encourage beneficial flows of capital while avoiding moral hazard problems that would result from unfettered access to external resources. As a result, these organizations constantly balance political and economic interests, and much research has treated the IFIs as principals of their state agents. A second major theme, running through all of the above issues, is the balance between rule-based interaction and the unconstrained exercise of economic and political power.

As the number of IEIs is vast, I have to be selective about the organizations on which I concentrate. Generally, I will focus on institutions that structure trade and financial relationships. In particular, I will consider the GATT/WTO (the General Agreement on Tariffs and Trade, now called the World Trade Organization) and regional trade organizations, and the Bretton Woods institutions in the financial area (the World Bank and International Monetary Fund (IMF)). This is not to say that other organizations are unimportant. The Organization for Economic Cooperation and Development (OECD) is a vital grouping of developed economies that collects and exchanges substantial economic information, for example. A wide range of organizations facilitates more specific forms of economic exchange, such as tourism or trade in particular commodities. Regional development banks play an increasingly important role in development, and regulatory accords (such as the Basle Accord) have at times had profound effects. Nevertheless, concentrating on the major trade and financial institutions has advantages. The scholarly work on these organizations is richer and deeper than that on other IEIs. In addition, the general analytical questions addressed in studies of these organizations should provide substantial insight into other types of IEIs.

I begin by providing some background on the study of institutions generally in international relations (IR). This discussion shows how the study of institutions moved from being purely descriptive or normative to developing strong analytical foundations. The modern study of IEIs is firmly grounded in this more general IR tradition. Then I turn to focus on trade organizations, then the IFIs. I conclude by summarizing where the study of IEIs now stands, and what the most promising directions for future research might be.

1 INTELLECTUAL BACKGROUND

Our understanding of the functioning and effects of IEIs has its roots in the modern scholarly study of international institutions and international organizations (IOs) generally, which began in the early 1980s. Prior to this time, the study of IOs was quite policy-oriented and descriptive, lacking an overarching analytical framework (Martin and Simmons 1998). This lack of a theoretical foundation meant that, although individual studies generated strong insights, they did not cumulate to create a coherent picture of or debate about the role of IOs in the world economy. This situation changed with the publication of an edited volume called *International Regimes* (Krasner 1983) and of Robert Keohane's book *After Hegemony* (Keohane 1984). These books cast international institutions in a new light and suggested a novel explanatory framework for studying them. The puzzle that motivated this research began with two observations: That international economic cooperation in the 1970s was stable in spite of substantial shifts in the distribution of international economic power, and that organizations such as the Bretton Woods institutions and the GATT were prominent features of the economic landscape. Keohane and others argued that these two observations were connected to one another, and that the existence of institutions and IOs explained the persistence of economic cooperation.

The fundamental logic of this line of work is summarized in Keohane (1982). In order for states to cooperate, they must overcome a range of collective-action problems. No external enforcement exists in the international economy, so any agreements must be self-enforcing. This means that states must find ways to avoid temptations to cheat, for example by reneging on agreements to encourage trade by erecting protectionist barriers. Avoiding such temptations requires high-quality information about the actions and preferences of other states, and about the likely consequences of cheating on agreements. In addition, states must coordinate their actions, for example agreeing on common technological and public-health standards. IOs provide forums in which states can mitigate collective-action problems that threaten stable patterns of cooperation. IOs can perform monitoring functions, providing assurance that others are living up to the terms of their commitments. They are forums for negotiating to resolve coordination problems, and to learn about the preferences and constraints facing other governments. They create structures for enforcement and dispute resolution, although actual enforcement powers typically remain in the hands of member states.

Through these functions, IOs become a valuable foundation for cooperation and for the global economy. Thus patterns of cooperation can be more resilient in the face of underlying shifts in economic power and interests. The initial work applying this "contractual" view of institutions concentrated on international regimes, defined as sets of principles, norms, rules, and decision-making procedures (Krasner 1982). One advantage of examining regimes, as compared to the earlier focus on individual IOs, is that this shift allowed researchers to consider informal institutions as well as formalized bodies. While in more recent years much attention has shifted back to formal IOs, the understanding that informal bodies of norms sustain cooperation in the global economy underlies even work on individual organizations today.

While research on international regimes represented a major step forward in the analysis of international institutions, it was subject to criticism from a number of perspectives. Friedrich Kratochwil and John Ruggie (1986) recognized the contributions of regime analysis, but worried that it was moving too far from the analysis of specific IOs, thus missing some important internal organizational dynamics. Stephan Haggard and Beth Simmons (1987) surveyed a number of weaknesses of regime analysis from the perspective of those undertaking positive empirical research on regimes. Because the concept of regimes was broadly defined and regimes difficult to observe independent of their effects, much effort went into determining whether or not regimes actually existed in various issue-areas, and whether changes in patterns of behavior reflected changes *within* regimes or *of* regimes. It is not clear that these descriptive debates added a great deal to our understanding of the causes and consequences of institutions in the international environment.

Other major weaknesses of the literature included its state-centric focus and neglect of domestic politics. Giulio Gallarotti (1991) argued that IOs systematically failed in their attempts to manage difficult problems in international relations. The inability of IOs to resolve serious conflict, in his analysis, reflected not just random mistakes, but a systematic pattern of failure. IOs could even have perverse effects, exacerbating conflict rather than mitigating it. For these reasons, Gallarotti argued against relying too heavily on formal IOs to manage international relations. Oran Young (1991) criticized the regimes literature for neglecting the role of political leadership. Many of these criticisms have been echoed in recent years in the analysis of IEIs.

One of the most telling critiques of the regimes literature came, perhaps paradoxically, from the editor of the *Regimes* volume, Stephen Krasner (1991). He charged that the work on regimes was too focused on market failures: Instances where all could potentially benefit from mutual cooperation, but where collective-action problems such as high transaction costs prohibited states from reaching the "Pareto frontier." In his survey of efforts to cooperate in the field of communication, he found that states had little trouble reaching the Pareto frontier. It was relatively easy for them to identify the set of bargains from which it would be impossible to make all better off. Instead, they found themselves trapped by distributional conflict, having to choose among bargains that benefited some while harming others. Thus the most significant problem plaguing efforts at international cooperation was not providing a good contractual environment to overcome transaction-costs problems such as informational limitations, but a coordination problem in which states disagreed over which of multiple Pareto-efficient equilibria they preferred. Krasner's insight has led to a revision of early work on regimes, which claimed that coordination problems would be relatively easy to solve (Stein 1982). A new focus on how institutions might aid in resolving coordination problems has added depth to our understanding of IOs' functions (Morrow 1994; Oatley and Nabors 1998).

In the 1990s, the theory of international institutions became deeper and richer. Ruggie and Keohane brought the concept of multilateralism back into the study of institutions. Keohane (1990) defined multilateralism simply, as cooperation among three or more states, while Ruggie (1992) conceptualized multilateralism as a set of norms that prescribed certain patterns of behavior, such as non-discrimination. Both served to redirect attention to variation among types of institutions, a highly productive move for the field. Another debate arose regarding the problem of compliance with the rules of IOs and with international agreements more generally. A managerial school, representing primarily the views of legal scholars, argued that states generally wanted to comply with international rules, and that variation in compliance was therefore not a compelling puzzle (Chayes and Chayes 1993). Political scientists responded by noting that the managerial argument was plagued by selection bias: if states almost always complied with the rules, it was likely because they would only accept rules that demanded minimal changes in their patterns of behavior. The appropriate question, therefore, was not so much compliance as how different structures of rules would promote far-reaching changes in behavior that left states open to exploitation, or "deep cooperation" (Downs, Rocke, and Barsoom 1996). Interestingly, both the managerial and contractual schools agreed on the conclusion that variation in patterns of compliance was not a terribly important or interesting question, although they came to this conclusion by different paths. The managerial school argued that little variation in compliance could be observed because states are obliged to comply. The formal analysis of compliance argued that minimal observed variation in compliance simply reflected the fact that states are unlikely to make commitments on which they intend to renege. Nevertheless, empirical research on variation in compliance has continued, leading to some intriguing findings (Brown Weiss and Jacobson 1998; Simmons 2000).

Other theoretical developments focus on the form and design of IOs. One body of work asks why IOs are becoming more "legalized:" They more often incorporate legalistic features such as third-party dispute settlement (Goldstein, Kahler, Keohane, and Slaughter 2000). Researchers have begun to explore the advantages and possible disadvantages of legalization for promoting international cooperation. Another body of work focuses on design principles for IOs. Starting from the assumption that IOs are designed to resolve collective-action problems, analysts have derived a number of hypotheses about the form of IOs (Koremenos, Lipson, and Snidal 2001). For example, if states design an IO to reduce the transaction costs of monitoring members' behavior, we would expect the organization to have relatively centralized monitoring capacities. Using logic like this, dimensions of IOs such as their central-ization and autonomy from member states can be explained. David Lake (1996) broadens our theoretical perspective on institutions by noting that the typical IO constitutes only one point on a wide spectrum of forms of international organization, ranging from complete anarchy to hierarchical organization, as in empires. Kenneth Abbott and Duncan Snidal (1998) returned to one of the initial questions posed by the regimes literature, about why sometimes states cooperate informally, while at other times they choose to create formal IOs. Coming from a contractual perspective, Abbott and Snidal argue that transaction costs and trade-offs between autonomy and the benefits of commitment explain patterns of formalization.

Overall, these developments in the study of international institutions provide a firm foundation for more specialized studies of IEIs. They suggest that one of the first questions to be asked when studying a particular organization is to ask about the problems it was designed to address. An understanding of these issues then leads to predictions about the form and functioning of the organization, and about its effects on economic flows and conditions. Two areas where this style of analysis has been applied most extensively are trade institutions and the IFIs. I turn first to analysis of the GATT/WTO and regional trade agreements, then to the Bretton Woods institutions.

2   Trade Institutions

Much recent work in IEIs has turned to rigorous empirical analysis, applying the kinds of models and analytical frameworks described above. Most international trade is now regulated by structures of rules and formal organizations, most notably the GATT/WTO on the global level. In addition, a number of powerful regional trade agreements such as the North American Free Trade Agreement (NAFTA) have developed. Understanding the functioning of these global and regional organizations, their form and effects, is crucial for an understanding of international trade more generally, and has implications for the broader analysis of international political institutions. In general terms, the story of the institutionalization of international trade can be described as a continuing struggle between attempts to negotiate and enforce consistent norms and rules, and the desire of powerful states to exert their influence over outcomes. Whether we consider the process of bargaining, of dispute resolution, or the use of institutional loopholes, we see this struggle defining the terms of political and scholarly debate. As the works discussed in this section suggest, while there are large potential benefits to be gained from consistently enforced rules, the evidence suggests that most international trade outcomes continue to be heavily influenced by power politics.

As the general framework described above suggests, the first step in analyzing a trade organization is to identify the fundamental problems it needs to address. International trade presents a classic strategic problem, often modeled as a Prisoners' Dilemma. Impediments to trade are costly, decreasing the aggregate welfare of states by increasing costs to consumers, depriving exporters of markets, and generally distorting the allocation of economic resources. Thus, decreasing impediments to trade offers aggregate welfare benefits for states. Jointly moving away from a situation of high levels of protection for domestic producers is a Pareto-improving move for states as aggregate entities. However, this does not mean that every individual within these states will benefit from freer trade. In particular, domestic producers who will be forced into increased competition from imports will not benefit from trade liberalization, and will lobby the government for continued protection (Grossman and Helpman 1994). Thus, governments face continual pressure to renege on the terms of trade agreements, providing protection for injured domestic actors.

International trade institutions thus have to face two fundamental problems. First is to structure and facilitate international bargaining to move toward reduction of trade barriers. While small states—those who cannot influence world prices because of the small size of their economies—exercise little bargaining power and can do best by unilaterally removing trade barriers, large states bargain hard to gain advantages for their exporters in exchange for reducing their own levels of protection. In fact, "empowered" exporters are typically the most important force driving negotiation of reduced levels of protection (Gilligan 1997). By creating a framework in which negotiators can agree on which trade barriers to reduce and by how much, trade institutions can do much to enhance international flows of goods and services. The second major problem, however, is to set up mechanisms to encourage states to live up to the terms of these agreements. Because of the constant political pressure to deviate from the terms of liberalized trade, governments are tempted to impose new barriers or simply fail fully to implement the liberalization measures agreed on. As the framework described above suggests, we are unlikely to see trade institutions directly empowered to enforce agreements in order to overcome these temptations. However, they can nevertheless play a substantial role in facilitating decentralized enforcement. We see trade institutions developing strong monitoring and dispute-resolution mechanisms, and standards for punishment of those who defect from agreements, in response to these challenges.

Consider first the bargaining problems associated with international trade. Kyle Bagwell and Robert Staiger (1999) offer a general economic theory of the structure of the GATT/WTO based on an analysis of the bargaining problem. They begin from the observation that the only feasible and self-enforcing bargains on international trade are those that preserve the existing terms of trade: if deals change the terms of trade, at least one of the parties to the bargain will refuse to live up to its terms.[2] The structure of GATT/WTO is thus designed to promote liberalization—reduction in barriers to exchange—while maintaining existing terms of trade. This principle explains why norms such as non-discrimination and reciprocity are so important in trade institutions, and why they go hand-in-hand. Reciprocity assures that any agreements reached will maintain existing terms of trade, as reduced protection in one state must be matched by similar "concessions" by others. Non-discrimination means that any liberalizing measures need to be extended to all trading partners, most famously through the "most-favored-nation" principle. Reciprocity without non-discrimination would lead to an extremely complex set of bilateral deals and allow opportunities to undermine agreements' intent through shifting the location of production and other mechanisms. The GATT/WTO also structures bargaining so that the major producers and consumers for various goods are given a primary role in reaching deals. While this somewhat exclusionary process is often protested by smaller states, without it the necessary deals that preserve terms of trade could never be reached.

Another aspect of the bargaining process is how it can be structured so as to encourage liberalization. One element of this process is to assure that the process encourages exporters—the most immediate beneficiaries of liberal trade—to mobilize and exert pressure on governments to reach deals. The GATT/WTO structure assures that exporters have incentives to mobilize, by making clear the benefits that will accrue to them; again, the norm of reciprocity plays a large role here (Gilligan 1997). In addition, the fact that negotiators reach complex "package deals" that are subject to an up-or-down vote back home allows them to put together sets of measures that will meet with political approval. One important question is how transparent negotiations should be. They are often carried out behind closed doors, although with sufficient information available that affected exporters recognize the potential benefits on the table. However, Goldstein and Martin (2000) point out that too much transparency in the bargaining process could be detrimental to the process of liberalization, as it could increase the certainty that particular import-competitors would lose from deals, leading them to mobilize more extensively.

From an institutional perspective, a major question about bargaining is whether the institutional structure itself influences the outcomes. Compared to unstructured, ad hoc bargaining, does the GATT/WTO structure lead to outcomes that protect the interests of smaller states, for example? Does it encourage greater liberalization? Both could well be true. Although the "principal suppliers" norm

---

[2] The terms of trade are the relative price of imports to exports. A country improves its terms of trade by increasing the price it gets for its exports, or by paying less for its imports. Obviously, a shift in these terms will benefit one side while hurting the other. Thus, as long as trade agreements must be approved by all parties, they must hold the terms of trade constant, otherwise one side will veto the agreement.

means that interests of large states, those that can affect world prices, continue to be powerful in bargaining within the GATT/WTO, the fact that small states are engaged in various ways in each negotiating round, and have to approve the final agreement, could give rise to more respect for their interests. On the question of liberalization, one advantage of multilateral, structured negotiations is that they enhance the scope for mutually-beneficial deals, compared to bilateral bargaining.

These institutionalist hypotheses have been subjected to empirical investigation. On the outcomes of bargaining, Richard Steinberg (2002) finds that the GATT/WTO structure has not demonstrably promoted the interests of developing countries. He argues that each bargaining round begins with a law-based process designed to give account to all participants' interests. However, the conclusion of a round involves tough deal-cutting, and has generally been dominated by powerful states. Thus, the United States and European Union (EU) have dominated the agenda, in spite of the attempt to use rules to craft a more equitable consensus. In contrast, Christina Davis (2003) finds substantial support for the proposition that multilateral bargaining leads to greater liberalization than a bilateral setting. Concentrating on one of the toughest trade issues, agriculture, she demonstrates that trade conflict between the United States and EU or Japan is resolved in a manner that promotes liberalization when bargaining takes place in a multilateral setting. Davis attributes this outcome to the potential for issue-linkage as well as legal framing and reputation.

The other major problem to be resolved by a global trade organization is to assure that states will uphold the agreements they reach. On the one hand, information must be widely available about whether states are living up to the terms of their commitments. Here, institutions face a relatively easy challenge, because many private (and public) actors are highly motivated to monitor what other governments are doing. If an exporter is finding it more difficult than expected to sell to a particular country or is losing market share, this actor has high incentives to discover any violations of international agreements by competitors. In addition, the structure of punishment procedures creates incentives for producers for the domestic market to uncover violations as well. If another country is found to have violated a commitment, the type of punishment approved by the WTO is to impose some kind of countervailing duty; that is, to increase tariffs on imports from that country in retaliation. Since domestic producers will benefit from such retaliation, they have an interest in monitoring other states' compliance with trade accords. Thus, the rather ingenious but simple punishment scheme typically used in trade agreements facilitates "fire-alarm" monitoring mechanisms; little direct oversight by the organization itself would appear necessary (McCubbins and Schwartz 1984). However, governments have become adept at non-obvious forms of protection, such as obscure product-standard regulations. Not surprisingly, we see that as the GATT/WTO has developed over time, it has gained enhanced monitoring capacities, now undertaking regular systematic reviews of members' practices. Nevertheless, nearly all enforcement cases at the WTO come from interested parties, not from the WTO's own efforts.

Both economists and political scientists have focused on the WTO's dispute resolution mechanism. Economists, like lawyers, typically ask whether it is optimal from the perspective of promoting trade (Bütler and Hauser 2000; Hudec 1993; Jackson 1998). They also ask whether, as structured, it is effective in reaching this goal. These studies generally find that, while the WTO mechanisms are not fully optimal, over time the development of these mechanisms has been moving in the right direction. Rules that allowed the blatant exercise of state power, such as the ability to veto panel decisions, have been phased out. It has become easier for states without extensive legal and administrative capacities to initiate the dispute process. Overall, as the system has become more institutionalized and legalized, in normative terms it has come closer to meeting the demands of economic efficiency. However, the evidence on whether these new rules are in fact operating as intended remains quite mixed.

Political scientists, in contrast to the normative focus of economists, tend to focus on the distributional effects of the dispute settlement mechanism, for example whether it tends to favor larger or smaller states. This leads them to consider questions such as which states bring complaints more often and against whom. They also focus on the patterns of settlement, asking which cases are resolved early and which go through the full process, and attempt to make judgments about which states most often prevail in these disputes. Marc Busch (2000) has focused on the formation of dispute settlement panels, asking which cases actually escalate to the panel stage as opposed to being settled at an earlier stage. This question is fundamental, because the evidence shows that the threat of future legal proceedings tends to generate larger levels of concessions if disputes are settled early; states are threatened as much by the process itself as by the actual decision (Reinhardt 2001). However, Busch finds that changes in procedures have not substantially altered paneling outcomes. Busch and Reinhardt (2003) similarly find that improved WTO procedures have not, in fact, allowed poor countries to achieve better outcomes. Instead, wealthier countries have tended to do better, suggesting that the capacity to litigate is an important component of success. Overall, the theoretical and empirical studies of the GATT/WTO suggest that the demands of politics and power continue strongly to influence international trade outcomes, in spite of higher levels of institutionalization over time.

Beyond the WTO, another notable development in the institutionalization of trade has been the proliferation and strengthening of regional trade organizations. Dispute settlement is a prominent feature of regional trade organizations, as it is of the WTO. James McCall Smith (2000) asks about variation in the legalization of dispute resolution mechanisms, and finds that it is largely explained by asymmetry in the powers of states that belong to the organizations. Small states prefer legalized mechanisms that bind powerful ones, while powerful states prefer to avoid legal constraints so that they can exercise their bargaining power. Frederick Abbott (2000) also examines a regional organization, NAFTA, from the perspective of legalization. While Abbott finds legalization an important strategy in the Americas, in Asia it has gained little foothold for a variety of reasons surveyed by Miles Kahler (2000). A number of hypotheses exist for explaining variation in legalization and formalization across regions and issue-areas, but systematic empirical exploration of these hypotheses is one of the significant remaining challenges for scholars of IEIs.

The impact of domestic economic interests on regional trading arrangements, and the relationship between the WTO and such arrangements, have also received rigorous empirical scrutiny. Again, the balance between rule-based constraints and the exercise of bargaining power informs these studies. Mansfield and Reinhardt (2003) argue that the growth of regional preferential trading arrangements (PTAs) has in fact been driven by the dynamics of bargaining within the WTO. As each round of WTO bargaining commences, states look to enhance their bargaining power. Entering or establishing PTAs, which improve the "exit options" for their members should WTO bargaining fail, is a mechanism by which states enhance their leverage within the WTO. Kerry Chase (2003), focusing more on the domestic level, instead finds that the primary forces driving the creation of a major PTA, NAFTA, were the demands of firms with large economies of scale. These were the firms that would benefit the most from the creation of a PTA, and drove US policy toward NAFTA through intense lobbying. Of course, this argument requires that the economies of scale these firms face exist on a regional rather than global level; otherwise, the same dynamic would lead these firms to push for more intense WTO lobbying instead.

Issues of institutional design and its effects have dominated studies of bargaining and dispute resolution in international trade. One specific issue of institutional design, across both global and regional institutions, is the conditions under which states can "legally" evade trade rules, at least on a temporary basis. Downs, Rocke, and Barsoom (1996) developed a general model of international cooperation in the face of domestic political uncertainty that provides great insight into this problem. When governments negotiate trade agreements, they know that they will face political pressure to renege on these agreements. However, they do not know with certainty how intense these pressures will be or from which sectors they will come, because these pressures are subject to exogenous economic shocks and shifting patterns of political mobilization. If unexpectedly intense demands to renege emerge, governments may find that they are better off acceding to these demands and withdrawing entirely from trade deals. However, if they were instead allowed the option of temporarily backing out of their commitments in the face of unusually high political pressures, the trade regime could survive and make all better off than if these "pressure valves" did not exist. Thus, the authors argue that a certain level of "optimal imperfection" should be observed in agreements that have this political structure, including trade agreements.

From an institutional perspective, this analysis suggests that the design of escape clauses and related loopholes in trade institutions is of vital importance to the success of these organizations. Scholars have picked up on this idea and developed fairly precise arguments about the appropriate design of such loopholes. Rosendorff and Milner (2001) show that escape clauses enhance the durability and stability of trade institutions in the face of domestic political uncertainty. However, to prevent the abuse of these clauses, states must bear a cost for using them. This "self-enforcing penalty" appears to be reflected in various dimensions of the WTO, for example, requiring offsetting concessions for the use of escape clauses. Barbara Koremenos (2001) considers the flexibility built into agreements in more general terms. She sees the fundamental problem as one of assuring a certain distribution of gains across states, rather than a response to unexpected domestic pressures. This sort of uncertainty explains the incidence of renegotiation provisions in many agreements.

Of course, all of this discussion of institutional bargaining, dispute resolution, and design begs the question of the overall effect of trade institutions on patterns of international trade. Have trade flows responded to the creation of global and regional institutions? This is a complex issue, involving many counterfactuals, that has barely begun to be explored. However, one influential study of the GATT/WTO argues that it has, in fact, made little difference in patterns of trade (Rose 2004). Controlling for other factors that determine trade flows, there is little evidence that GATT membership per se has increased observed levels of trade. However, Rose does find that developing countries that participated in the Generalized System of Preferences under the GATT (a major deviation from the general norm of non-discrimination) did experience increased trade. It is also possible that the great powers, which were able to dominate the terms of debate, derived the greatest benefits. Clearly, further work on this issue is required. For example, to determine accurately the effects of trade institutions studies will have to deal adequately with the challenge of selection bias: Controlling for the factors that determine which states join liberalizing institutions in the first place.

Overall, research on global and regional trade institutions nicely bears out the major themes of this chapter. In many ways, the design and functioning of these institutions reflects the basic strategic dilemmas of international trade. Promoting beneficial exchanges requires that institutions structure bargaining, monitor compliance with commitments, and provide enforcement mechanisms. We also see that the ongoing struggle between rule-based interaction and the exercise of power plays out continually in these trade regimes. While rules attempt to constrain the processes of bargaining and dispute resolution, the best empirical studies confirm that the actual functioning of these institutions reflect continuing realities of power politics. I next turn from trade to finance, to consider the functioning of the IFIs.

3   INTERNATIONAL FINANCIAL INSTITUTIONS

The other type of economic IO that has drawn extensive attention from political scientists is the IFI. IFIs such as the IMF and the World Bank play a major role in the world of international finance and money, and we are just beginning to understand how the interaction of politics and economics works in these institutions. In order to understand what IFIs do, we need to begin with some insight into the fundamental strategic problems that they confront. These problems have led many analysts to use a principal–agent framework to study the IFIs, asking about the relative freedom of maneuver available to these organizations, given patterns of state interests. As in the case of trade, this problem is played out in an ongoing battle between rules that attempt to constrain state behavior and the continual exercise of state power. And, again as in the case of trade, the empirical evidence shows both that rules matter and that they have not succeeded in fully defeating power politics. While the theoretically-informed study of IFIs is newer, and therefore not as deep, as that of trade institutions, some intriguing insights are emerging.

The IMF and World Bank are known as the Bretton Woods institutions, as they were created at the end of the Second World War at the Bretton Woods conference. Initially, the main purpose of the IMF was to oversee the functioning of a fixed exchange rate regime. In order to make this regime work, the IMF was to organize short-term support for members that were facing balance-of-payments crises. Over time, the exchange rate regime fell apart. However, by then the IMF had proven itself valuable at providing relief for states facing financial crises, and has continued to play the central role in these situations. The World Bank was initially intended to provide funding for development efforts, particularly for states too poor reliably to access the private international capital market. Thus, the Bank funded longer-term development projects, such as the construction of dams and roads. Over time the specific types of programs funded by the IMF and Bank have tended to converge, but some distinction remains.

In any financial transaction, institutions need to walk a fine line between encouraging the provision of funding that will be beneficial for both the borrower and the lender and encouraging moral hazard. Moral hazard is a serious concern in these transactions. Consider the typical case addressed by the IMF. A country has fallen into a financial crisis, either through poor policy or exogenous shocks. The government finds itself unable to make good on its commitments to make payments on its outstanding debt, and the value of its currency is collapsing. If the roots of the crisis will pass, the provision of temporary financing will benefit both the country that receives the financing and lenders, who will be likely to recover more of their assets once the crisis has passed. However, a government that knows that it will be bailed out of such crises is likely to behave more recklessly, adopting inappropriate policies and overborrowing. This is the moral hazard dilemma.

The IMF has addressed the moral hazard problem by imposing conditions on the lending programs that it offers, attempting to force states to adopt more responsible fiscal policies. While initially some IMF members opposed the use of such conditionality, arguing that the organization's role was to provide funding as needed, the major creditors (especially the United States) have insisted on imposing conditions. The number and types of conditions has expanded substantially over the years. Governments wishing to conclude a program with the IMF must typically commit to reduce public spending, increase collection of taxes, liberalize their international economic relations, and even improve other areas of governance. Of course, such conditions are not popular for the governments that must accept them. Even if they are economically justified (a point that some would dispute), there are occasions on which the major creditor states would prefer looser conditions for purely political reasons. For example, it is widely understood that the United States opposed the imposition of tough conditions on Russia in the early 1990s, wishing to assure Russia's political stability. In addition, states that are home to private creditors with substantial exposure in the crisis country are likely to prefer looser conditions and flows of capital.

This basic strategic problem—potential benefits from capital flows, but a moral hazard problem—has led many scholars to use a principal–agent framework to study the IMF and, less extensively, the World Bank. In this framework, the members of the IFIs, especially the major creditors, are treated as the principals that use the IFI to implement their preferred policies. IFIs, as agents, have their own interests, usually understood as technocratic economic interests. The question is then the extent to which the IFIs can pursue their own agenda vs. responding to the specific demands of their principals. As such, the ongoing tug-of-war between rules and power describes the dynamics of the IFIs.

Some analysts, such as Strom Thacker, demonstrate that the IMF's patterns of lending respond to the geopolitical interests of the United States, its dominant member (Thacker 1999). The "public choice" school has studied the IMF as a self-interested organization attempting to assert itself in the face of constant political demands from its powerful member states. This work, like Thacker's, illustrates that these states are often able to exert substantial influence over the IMF's activities. Thus, while the IMF is an agent with some autonomy, it has a hard time escaping its political confines. Dreher and Vaubel (2004) apply this analysis to examine the evolution of conditionality over time, asking about the content and number of conditions imposed. They demonstrate that the IMF can usefully be studied as a bureaucracy with its own internal rules and interests. In this sense, they posit that it has more autonomy than others have recognized. They reason that an autonomous IMF should impose stringent conditionality on states that have a poor record of living up to past commitments, and find evidence to support this argument. Overall, the evidence suggests that the IMF is an agent constrained by the political interests of its principals, but one that is able to exert autonomy under certain conditions.

Others scholars, working within the same general principal–agent framework, focus on the delegation of authority to IFIs. They ask why states would choose to allow them what appears to be a substantial degree of autonomy. Some analysts find that delegation has not undermined the interests of the most powerful member states, as delegation is itself a strategy for promoting these interests. For example, Daniel Nielson and Michael Tierney (2003) demonstrate that the World Bank's environmental policies correlate highly with measures of the environmental interests of the United States. Ngaire Woods (1998) has also argued that the United States exerts very a substantial impact on World Bank and IMF programs. On the other hand, Erica Gould (2003) is more skeptical about the ability of member states to maintain control over IFI actions once they delegate authority. She argues that the IMF, in its use of conditionality, often responds to private financial actors rather than state interests.

Thus, the institutionalist perspective has given rise to insights about the design of the IFIs, particularly focusing on issues of delegation and influence. Some have begun to critique this view of the IFIs, arguing that it underestimates the autonomy of the staff of IFIs. Through the exercise of authority that is perceived as legitimate, especially because it has the veneer of science, the IFIs may in fact be able to pursue agendas that have little relationship to the interests of either major donors or borrowers (Barnett and Finnemore 2004). This line of analysis presents a potentially strong threat to the entire contractual framework, as it conceives of a very different relationship between states and institutions. For example, it suggests that we should spend much more time analyzing processes of socialization within institutions (see Johnston 2001). Another perspective suggests that we need to draw on alternative theories of accountability to make sense of the role of IEIs (Grant and Keohane 2005). While this perspective does not directly challenge the contractual one, it does suggest that the contractual approach and its emphasis on principal–agent relationships is too narrow a prism through which to study IEIs. Issues of accountability have long been a concern both within the World Bank and among those who study it, leading for example to the creation of an Inspection Panel in 1993 to investigate complaints about the Bank's activities (Bradlow 1996; Shihata 1994; see also Pauly 1997).

The other major set of questions, of course, regards the impact of the IFIs on the economies of the states where they are active. A literature is emerging around this topic, and space prevents me from doing justice to it here. However, it is safe to say that the evidence on the IMF, in particular, suggests that it has not been terribly effective in bringing countries high levels of growth (Easterly 2001). Countries that enter IMF programs, rather than relying on them temporarily and then resuming a "normal" growth pattern, tend to remain under IMF tutelage for long periods of time. IMF programs may increase income inequality even while failing to promote aggregate growth (Vreeland 2003). Scholars have debated the causes of this apparent lack of efficacy. Some argue that it is precisely the autonomy of the

IMF, which wishes to loan large amounts of money, that causes conditions not to be enforced and undermines programs (Vaubel 1986). Randall Stone (2004), however, has recently presented persuasive evidence that the fundamental problem is the reverse: that the Fund's principals frequently intervene to promote leniency toward favored states. This persistent influence of political pressures means that the conditions the IMF so painstakingly negotiates are rarely imposed with any consistency or credibility. Thus, the problem with IMF programs is not that they are poorly designed or based on an inappropriate economic ideology. It is that even well-designed programs are not enforced. Thus, just as in the case of trade, we find that the struggle between political influence and rule-based behavior defines the impact of the IFIs on the world economy.

4   CONCLUSION

The new global economy is highly institutionalized. Understanding this phenomenon has led to the development of a vibrant field of political science centered on the study of international institutions and IOs. This field continues to hold to a primarily contractual view that sees institutions as solutions to collective action problems. Thus, the study of IEIs begins by identifying the underlying strategic problems that IEIs address. In the case of trade institutions, these problems involve overcoming obstacles to bargaining, monitoring compliance with commitments, and enforcing agreements. In the IFIs, the fundamental problem is to provide flows of needed capital while avoiding moral hazard problems. This tension sets up the IFIs as agents of their state principals who frequently have conflicting interests. Thus, the contractual approach with its emphasis on principals and agents has been a powerful tool for studying IEIs. New perspectives are beginning to emerge, as noted in this chapter, with a focus on socialization, legitimacy, and accountability. However, they are not yet developed to the degree that they present a fundamental challenge to the contractual approach.

The study of the IEIs consistently shows that their dynamics, design, and effects reflect an ongoing struggle between the exercise of power and the rule of law. While some authors find more evidence for the weight of one side in this battle than the other, careful empirical research reveals that neither side triumphs. The IEIs will continue to have a major influence on the global creation and distribution of wealth. Those studying them need to push further to understand the sources of their specific design features and to move toward more conditional, precise statements of their effects. However, the analytical frameworks so far developed have proven insightful and appear to provide a strong foundation for this research agenda.

REFERENCES

ABBOTT, F. M. 2000. NAFTA and the legalization of world politics: a case study. *International Organization*, 54: 519–48.

ABBOTT, K. and SNIDAL, D. 1998. Why states act through formal international organizations. *Journal of Conflict Resolution*, 42: 3–32.

BAGWELL, K. and STAIGER, R. 1999. An economic theory of GATT. *American Economic Review*, 49: 215–48.

BARNETT, M. and FINNEMORE, M. 2004. *Rules for the World: International Organizations in Global Politics*. Ithaca, NY: Cornell University Press.

BRADLOW, D. D. 1996. A test case for the World Bank. *American University Journal of International Law and Policy*, 11: 247–94.

BROWN WEISS, E. and JACOBSON, H. K. 1998. *Engaging Countries: Strengthening Compliance with International Accords*. Cambridge, Mass.: MIT Press.

BUSCH, M. L. 2000. Democracy, consultation, and the paneling of disputes under GATT. *Journal of Conflict Resolution*, 44: 425–46.

—— and REINHARDT, E. 2003. Developing countries and General Agreement on Tariffs and Trade/World Trade Organization dispute settlement. *Journal of World Trade*, 37: 719–35.

BÜTLER, M. and HAUSER, H. 2000. The WTO dispute settlement system: a first assessment from an economic perspective. *Journal of Law, Economics, and Organization*, 16: 503–33.

CHASE, K. 2003. Economic interests and regional trading arrangements: the case of NAFTA. *International Organization*, 57: 137–74.

CHAYES, A. and CHAYES, A. H. 1993. On compliance. *International Organization*, 47: 175–205.

DAVIS, C. 2003. *Food Fights Over Free Trade: How International Institutions Promote Agricultural Trade Liberalization*. Princeton, NJ: Princeton University Press.

DOWNS, G. and ROCKE, D. M. 1995. *Optimal Imperfection? Domestic Uncertainty and Institutions in International Relations*. Princeton, NJ: Princeton University Press.

—— —— and BARSOOM, P. N. 1996. Is the good news about compliance good news about cooperation? *International Organization*, 50: 379–406.

DREHER, A. and VAUBEL, R. 2004. The causes and consequences of IMF conditionality. *Emerging Markets Finance and Trade*, 40: 26–54.

EASTERLY, W. 2001. *The Elusive Quest for Growth: Economists' Adventures and Misadventures in the Tropics*. Cambridge, Mass.: MIT Press.

GALLAROTTI, G. M. 1991. The limits of international organization: systematic failure in the management of international relations. *International Organization*, 45: 183–220.

GILLIGAN, M. J. 1997. *Empowering Exporters: Reciprocity, Delegation, and Collective Action in American Trade Policy*. Ann Arbor: University of Michigan Press.

GOLDSTEIN, J., KAHLER, M., KEOHANE, R. O., and SLAUGHTER, A.-M. 2000. Legalization and world politics: introduction. *International Organization*, 54: 385–99.

GOLDSTEIN, J. and MARTIN, L. L. 2000. Legalization, trade liberalization, and domestic politics: a cautionary note. *International Organization*, 53: 603–32.

GOULD, E. R. 2003. Money talks: supplementary financiers and international monetary fund conditionality. *International Organization*, 57: 551–86.

GRANT, R. W. and KEOHANE, R. O. 2005. Accountability and abuses of power in world politics. *American Political Science Review*, 99: 29–43.

GROSSMAN, G. M. and HELPMAN, E. 1994. Protection for sale. *American Economic Review,* 84: 833–50.

HAGGARD, S. and SIMMONS, B. A. 1987. Theories of international regimes. *International Organization,* 41: 491–517.

HUDEC, R. E. 1993. *Enforcing International Trade Law: The Evolution of the Modern GATT Legal System.* Salem, NH: Butterworth.

JACKSON, J. H. 1998. *The World Trade Organization: Constitution and Jurisprudence.* London: Royal Institute for International Affairs.

JOHNSTON, A. I. 2001. Treating international institutions as social environments. *International Studies Quarterly,* 45: 487–515.

KAHLER, M. 2000. Legalization as strategy: the Asia-Pacific case. *International Organization,* 54: 549–71.

KEOHANE, R. O. 1982. The demand for international regimes. *International Organization,* 36: 325–55.

—— 1984. *After Hegemony: Cooperation and Discord in the World Political Economy.* Princeton, NJ.: Princeton University Press.

—— 1990. Multilateralism: an agenda for research. *International Journal,* 65: 731–64.

KOREMENOS, B. 2001. Loosening the ties that bind: a learning model of agreement flexibility. *International Organization,* 55: 289–325.

—— LIPSON, C., and SNIDAL, D. 2001. The rational design of international institutions. *International Organization,* 55: 761–99.

KRASNER, S. D. 1982. Structural causes and regime consequences: regimes as intervening variables. *International Organization,* 36: 185–205.

—— 1983. *International Regimes.* Ithaca, NY: Cornell University Press.

—— 1991. Global communications and national power: life on the Pareto frontier. *World Politics,* 43: 336–56.

KRATOCHWIL, F. and RUGGIE, J. G. 1986. International organization: a state of the art or an art of the state. *International Organization,* 40: 753–75.

LAKE, D. A. 1996. Anarchy, hierarchy, and the variety of international relations. *International Organization,* 50: 593–627.

McCUBBINS, M. D. and SCHWARTZ, T. 1984. Congressional oversight overlooked: police patrols versus fire alarms. *American Journal of Political Science,* 28: 165–79.

MANSFIELD, E. and REINHARDT, E. 2003. Multilateral determinants of regionalism: the effects of GATT/WTO on the formation of regional trading arrangements. *International Organization,* 57: 829–62.

MARTIN, L. L. and SIMMONS, B. 1998. Theories and empirical studies of international institutions. *International Organization,* 52: 729–57.

MORROW, J. 1994. The forms of international cooperation. *International Organization,* 48: 387–423.

NIELSON, D. L. and TIERNEY, M. J. 2003. Delegation to international organizations: agency theory and World Bank environmental reform. *International Organization,* 57: 241–76.

OATLEY, T. and NABORS, R. 1998. Redistributive cooperation: market failure, wealth transfers, and the Basle Accord. *International Organization,* 52: 35–54.

PAULY, L. W. 1997. *Who Elected the Bankers? Surveillance and Control in the World Economy.* Ithaca, NY: Cornell University Press.

REINHARDT, E. 2001. Adjudication without enforcement in GATT disputes. *Journal of Conflict Resolution,* 45: 174–95.

Rose, A. 2004. Do we really know that the WTO increases trade? *American Economic Review*, 94: 98–114.

Rosendorff, B. P. and Milner, H. V. 2001. The optimal design of international trade institutions: uncertainty and escape. *International Organization*, 55: 829–58.

Ruggie, J. G. 1992. Multilateralism: the anatomy of an institution. *International Organization*, 46: 561–98.

Shihata, I. F. I. (ed.) 1994. *The World Bank Inspection Panel*. New York: Oxford University Press.

Simmons, B. A. 2000. International law and state behavior: commitment and compliance in international monetary affairs. *American Political Science Review*, 94: 819–35.

Smith, J. M. 2000. The politics of dispute settlement design: explaining legalism in regional trade pacts. *International Organization*, 54: 137–80.

Stein, A. A. 1982. Coordination and collaboration: regimes in an anarchic world. *International Organization*, 36: 299–324.

Steinberg, R. H. 2002. In the shadow of law or power? Consensus-based bargaining and outcomes in GATT/WTO. *International Organization*, 56: 339–74.

Stone, R. W. 2004. The political economy of IMF lending in Africa. *American Political Science Review*, 98: 577–91.

Thacker, S. C. 1999. The high politics of IMF lending. *World Politics*, 52: 38–75.

Vaubel, R. 1986. A public choice approach to international organization. *Public Choice*, 51: 39–57.

Vreeland, J. R. 2003. *The IMF and Economic Development*. Cambridge: Cambridge University Press.

Woods, N. 1998. Governance in international organizations: the case for reform in the Bretton Woods institutions. *International Monetary and Financial Issues for the 1990s*, 9: 81–106.

Young, O. R. 1991. Political leadership and regime formation: on the development of institutions in international society. *International Organization*, 45: 281–308.

CHAPTER 34

INTERNATIONAL NGOS

ANN FLORINI

1 INTRODUCTION

From tanks in the streets of Seattle in 1999 to untold millions of anti-war protestors thronging cities throughout the world in 2003, a new type of political institution has captured widespread attention, both popular and scholarly. After the 2003 protests, the *New York Times* referred to the rise of a "second superpower" in world affairs in the form of mobilized citizens able and willing to work together across borders in a common cause. A growing literature has examined in detail many such cases, from the international campaign to ban landmines to the misnamed "anti-globalization" movement to such visible organizations as Greenpeace and Amnesty International.

But this new type of political institution is hard to define and to describe. Governments are legally constituted entities, and their natures, mandates, and sources of legitimacy are the subject of a rich theoretical literature. The parts of the private sector that are politically influential tend to be legally defined businesses, whose management and rights and responsibilities are likewise covered in a substantial literature. Social movements, non-governmental organizations (NGOs), and other citizens' groups constitute a much more amorphous set of politically influential institutions, identified more by what they are not—governments or profit-seeking entities—than by what they are.

As this amorphous "third sector" and its thickening web of cross-border ties rose to international prominence in the 1990s and thereafter, a scholarly literature began to tackle theoretical and empirical questions entailed by these growing roles. This chapter provides a broad overview of that literature. Section 2 gives a historical overview of the rise of INGOs and other non-governmental cross-border ties. Section 3 reviews the definitional debates. Section 4 discusses the research on whether, when, and why these non-governmental bodies increasingly matter to the conduct of global affairs, in what ways, and under what conditions. The chapter concludes with a discussion of possible research agendas.

2   HISTORICAL OVERVIEW

Although much of the literature dates from the 1990s, INGOs and other border-crossing elements of civil society have played a role in global affairs for much longer than scholars have written about them (Florini 2000). Rudolph (1997) points out that "Religious communities are among the oldest of the transnational: Sufi orders, Catholic missionaries, Buddhist monks carried work and praxis across vast spaces before those places became nation states or even states." Religious organizations provided the impetus behind some of the first formal cross-border ties among NGOs in the nineteenth-century campaign to end slavery. NGOs dedicated to ending the slave trade date to 1775, with the establishment of the Pennsylvania Society for Promoting the Abolition of Slavery, followed a decade later by the British Society for Effecting the Abolition of the Slave Trade and the French Société des Amis des Noirs (Charnovitz 1997). The links among the movements solidified in 1839 with the establishment of the British and Foreign Anti-Slavery Society, "the first transnational moral entrepreneur—religious movements aside—to play a significant role in world politics."[1]

Civil society has existed in something approaching its current form since the rise of the nation-state system more than three centuries ago. The term was used during the Scottish Enlightenment, conceived as "a realm of solidarity held together by the force of moral sentiments and natural affections" strong enough to root individuals in a community of natural sympathy and collective action (Seligman 1992, 33). Over time, the focus of political philosophy shifted from "civil society" to "citizenship," and the term "civil society" faded away.

But while the term fell out of use, the reality continued to grow. As states grew stronger, they required an industrial base, a legal infrastructure, and a citizenry

---

[1] Betty Fladeland, *Men and Brothers: Anglo-American Antislavery Cooperation* (1972), p. 258, cited in Charnovitz 1997, 192.

"with the skills necessary to staff the armies, pay the taxes, and turn the wheels of industry" (Tarrow 1994, 66). The communications and transportation infrastructure created by the emerging states made it easier for geographically separated individuals and groups to recognize common interests and join together to carry out collective action independently of the state. And increasing state penetration of society gave groups something to mobilize against. Much state-building consisted of raising taxes and conscripting soldiers, both unpopular extensions of state authority.

2.1 The Rediscovery of "Civil Society"

Over the course of the twentieth century, in some cases the state became so dominant and coercive that no political space was left within which alternative societal groups could persist. Such was the case in the Soviet Union and, to a lesser extent, some of its satellites. When the Soviet bloc began to disintegrate in the late 1980s, the citizens and new governments of the former Warsaw Pact countries were forced to rethink how modern democratic countries deal with the plethora of collective action problems that face all modern societies. Thanks in part to the urgings of Western, and particularly American, funding agencies, the creation of a vigorous civil society was assumed to be a large part of the answer. Substantial international aid soon flowed to new NGOs throughout the region in an effort to create rapidly a new non-governmental sector (Ottaway and Carothers 2000), and the term "civil society" returned to the limelight.

At the same time, non-governmental actors in disparate parts of the world began to develop increasingly strong ties with their counterparts elsewhere. Some literature has attempted to explain how and why those ties developed. Florini (2000), for example, argues that global economic integration gave groups in disparate parts of the world a common stake in common issues, at the same time that the sharply dropping costs of transportation and communication made it possible for groups to meet and work together, ties that often originated or were cemented at the enormous global conferences organized by the United Nations in the 1980s and 1990s.

Just as a great deal of economic activity takes place in the "grey" informal sector, much important citizen sector activity takes place outside of formal NGO and INGO auspices. But while grey economic activity tends to remain local, the non-formal citizen sector sometimes cumulates into transnational movements. INGOs are just a piece of a larger phenomenon: the cross-border ties among groups that are neither governmental bodies nor primarily profit-seeking businesses. Some are amorphous networks, able to mobilize thousands or millions of citizens to take to the streets in various "mobilizations," as in the various "anti-globalization" protests or the massive anti-war demonstrations of early 2003. Some, like the various "social forums" including the annual World Social Forum that began in Brazil in 2001, explicitly have no purpose beyond dialogue (Kaldor, Anheier, and Glasius 2003*a*).

3   DEFINITIONS

" 'NGOs: They're everywhere, but what are they?' " Thus begins one of the many edited volumes on the subject to appear in the 1990s, citing a question posed by a reporter in a public forum (Smith, Chatfield, and Pagnucco 1997, xiii). One of the harder tasks facing scholars in this area is defining the subject. Another edited volume lists a litany of terms in current usage, with overlapping and competing definitions: " 'nongovernmental organization'... independent sector, volunteer sector, civic society, grassroots organizations, private voluntary organizations, transnational society movement organizations, grassroots social change organizations, and non-state actors" (Gordenker and Weiss 1996, 18). To this list could be added civil society organization, third sector, citizen sector, transnational civil society, and an ever-growing list of alternatives.

One important distinction among the various terms and meanings is the one between formal organizations and informal associations. Although the terms tend to be used interchangeably, NGOs and civil society are not the same thing. NGOs are the formally constituted, legally recognized entities that pursue public purposes. International NGOs, or INGOs, are NGOs with members in more than one country.

Civil society is a much broader term that includes NGOs but can also include a wide array of other types of associations. Its definition is much contested. American usage tends to define "civil society" as a "third sector," the large and amorphous realm of non-governmental associations among people beyond the level of the family that are not primarily motivated by profit-seeking; and that is the definition adopted in this chapter. It is important to know, however, that elsewhere in the world, particularly in continental Europe, "civil society" can refer to all nongovernmental associations, including for-profit enterprises. This chapter uses the American definition, focusing on the literature that addresses the unique characteristics and roles of politically active entities motivated by goals other than financial profit.

In a book that makes a major contribution to untangling the very confused debate over the meaning and therefore the roles of civil society, Michael Edwards (2004) laid out three different ways the term "civil society" is used:

1. Analytically, with "civil society" constituting the world of voluntary associations à la Toqueville. This definition of civil society looks at voluntary

associations as the gene carriers of the good society, within which citizens develop democratic skills and norms. Edwards argues that this perspective is not empirically valid—democratic skills and norms are also shaped in families, schools, and other institutions. And many voluntary associations do not foster democratic attitudes and values. Moreover, voluntary associations can rarely if ever enforce or develop a broad societal consensus.

2. Normatively, with "civil society" constituting the ideal society citizens strive to create, à la Aristotle to Hobbes. This definition largely disappeared after the Enlightenment, but has the advantage that it mitigates against the tendency to privilege one sector over another.

3. Most recently, "civil society" as the public sphere in which citizens argue and debate with one another. When politics are polarized, polities cannot resolve problems. Thus there is a need to create new publics across the usual lines of division.

Edwards argued that the three meanings of "civil society" are all relevant and need to be integrated into a coherent whole. The second is the ultimate goal that all citizens should strive for—the good society—with the first and third providing important mechanisms to achieve that goal. Some works have developed detailed scenarios of how this could happen at the global level in practice (Florini 2003; Hammond 1998).

As Edwards noted, however, the first definition makes clear that those mechanisms do not necessarily lead humanity toward anything that most people would accept as an ideal society. Other authors similarly have stressed the importance of recognizing the "dark side" of these largely self-constituted, often unregulated, and in some ways unaccountable political institutions. Precisely because of their amorphous nature, they can serve a wide variety of purposes. Although the people who come together in civil society organizations are ostensibly motivated by some notion of collective good, that "collective" may be a self-serving group interest or a very warped notion of what is good for humanity as a whole. Al Qaeda can serve as an example of a civil society organization from the dark side: It is a collectivity that is not primarily motivated by profits, is not a government, and seems to think it is working to achieve a version of the public good. The literature on NGOs in particular has developed a lexicon of terms, often unflattering, for various types of NGOs. There is the ever-popular term QUANGOs—quasi-NGOs—which is used to refer broadly to NGOs whose independence is questionable, including NGOs that are service providers rather than advocacy organizations and that sometimes are little more than government subcontractors. Another term is DONGOs, or donor-organized NGOs, referring to groups that arise in response to the availability of funding and that may serve the goals of funders over those of the communities where the NGOs operate. Similarly, GONGOs are government-organized NGOs, that serve as fronts for governments to carry out activities for which governments are unwilling to accept direct responsibility (Weiss and Gordenker 1996, 21). BONGOs are business-organized NGOs that may appear similar to public-interest advocacy groups but in reality are funded by and advance the interests of specific businesses. Moreover, civil society groups are made up of individuals, whose interests may differ from those of the group and who may use group structures to advance individual rather than group goals.

Kaldor (2003) parsed the definitional landscape differently, identifying two traditional and three contemporary usages of the terms. The two traditional meanings are:

1. the *societas civilis*, the oldest of the meanings, referring to a society character-ized by rule of law, where legitimate violence has become the monopoly of the state;
2. the bourgeois society as defined by Hegel and Marx, the arena of ethical life between the state and the family, produced by capitalism which created individuals who came together in arenas outside the state.

Kaldor's three contemporary meanings overlapped with Edwards', but with the crucial distinction that she explicitly considered how those meanings would apply at the international level. At the national level, the voluntary associations covered in Edwards' first definition can serve as essential intermediaries between citizens and the state. At the global level, that intermediation role is much murkier, as there is neither a global state nor a recognized, well-defined global citizenry. Kaldor (2003, 7) argues that the emerging framework of international law, notable in the development of human rights and humanitarian law, the establishment of the International Criminal Court and other international tribunals, and the expansion of international peacekeeping, constitute a framework for global governance that may fill in to some extent for the absence of a global state.

1. The activist version: referring to active citizenship and self-organization. Kaldor argued that what occurred in the latter twentieth century was the development of a global public sphere: "inhabited by transnational advocacy networks like Greenpeace or Amnesty International, global social movements like the protestors in Seattle, Prague and Genoa, international media through which their campaign can be brought to global attention, new global 'civil religions' like human rights or environmentalism" (Kaldor 2003, 8).
2. The neoliberal version: similar to Edwards' first definition, civil society as associational life via a non-profit, voluntary "third sector."
3. The postmodern version: civil society as an arena of pluralism and contest-ation, including nationalists and fundamentalists.

The definitional problems give rise to data problems as well. It is very difficult to measure something whose parameters are not agreed on. Nonetheless, several sources attempt to give a sense of the size of the sector and trends in its development. One such source is the Union of International Associations, which since 1950 has published an annual *Yearbook* providing data on the number of formally constituted INGOs whose members, funding, and officers comes from at least three countries. For lack of alternatives, UIA numbers are widely used by authors tracking the development of "transnational civil society," "global civil society," "transnational society movements," and other variants. But as Sikkink and Smith (2002) point out, there are significant problems with using the UIA data as the basis for analyzing transnational civil society as a political institution. The data omit the informal but politically significant connections that tie groups and individuals together across borders, meaning that at best the data capture a subset of the sector. Second, the UIA does not distinguish among the many types and purposes of INGOs, conflating advocacy groups that have a direct impact on global politics and social change with professional associations, service providers, research organizations, and religious groups that may or may not play a part in efforts to bring about social change. However, by carefully mining the data to select the subset of INGOs relevant to a discussion of political institutions, Sikkink and Smith (2002) were able to show a significant trend: a nearly sixfold increase in the number of social-change INGOs from 1953 to 1993, with a particular jump in the last decade of that period. They argue that such a trend is indicative of the broader development of transnational civil society, even if the data do not allow scholars to document the overall size of the phenomenon.

4 WHETHER AND WHEN THEY MATTER

In the 1970s, the international relations field saw a major debate on "transnational relations"—that is, regular interactions across borders involving non-state actors (Keohane and Nye 1972; Keohane and Nye 1977; Rosenau 1980). Some of the literature, particularly the contributions from Keohane and Nye, posed useful questions about the (significant but not dominant) roles of non-state actors in what was still assumed to be a strongly state-based system. They cited examples from multinational business, NGOs, revolutionary movements, trade unions, scientific networks, and international cartels to argue that while states remained central, such factors as growing interdependence among nation states, the rise of economic and environmental issues alongside military topics on the global agenda, and advances in transportation and communication technology, had made it possible for a wide array of non-governmental entities to play an increasingly direct role in global policy-making. Others argued more strongly for a society-based alternative to state-based thinking. That debate withered away as state-centric approaches to international relations thinking came to dominate. But as Thomas Risse-Kappen put it in his edited volume on *Bringing Transnational Relations Back In*[2] (1995, xi), "The end of the Cold War and the dissatisfaction with prevailing approaches to international relations have opened new space for theorizing about world politics."

Thus, the 1990s saw an explosion in the number of scholarly works examining the causes and consequences of the rapid rise of transnational citizen-group ties. Because the dominant strands of theory in international relations simply assume that non-state actors play little if any role in the world, much of this early literature was aimed at proving those theories wrong, or at least incomplete (Boli and Thomas 1999; Florini 2000; Keck and Sikkink 1998; Risse-Kappen 1995; Smith, Chatfield, and Pagnucco 1997).

The scholarly literature frequently used in-depth case studies in a theoretical framework aimed at understanding whether, how, and when NGOs mattered in international politics. The Risse-Kappen volume, for example, set out to ask "under what domestic and international circumstances do transnational coalitions and actors who attempt to change policy outcomes in a specific issue-area succeed or fail to achieve their goals?" (Risse-Kappen 1995; see also Edwards and Gaventa 2001). The volume incorporated cases ranging across disparate issue-areas, including international economics, environment, security, and human rights. The actors examined included not only formal international NGOs but also multinational corporations, transgovernmental ties, and loosely connected social groups. The theoretical bases of the volume brought together insights from theories focused on domestic structures within polities and from theories looking at degrees of international institutionalization, such as regime theory.

Other works have drawn on theoretical traditions in sociology that address broad social movements. Boli and Thomas (1999), for example, interpreted the history of INGOs through the framework of a sociological theory known as world-polity institutionalism. This edited volume used eight case studies, four on social movements (environment, women, Esperanto, and the International Red Cross) and four examining technical, scientific, and development sectors. The volume concluded with an analysis of a core theoretical problems—how can INGOs exercise influence given their lack of resources and coercive enforcement capabilities?—arguing that the authority of INGOs is legitimated by their structures, their procedures, their purposes, and the credential and charisma of their members.

Some scholars have crossed disciplinary boundaries to combine the insights of sociology with theories taken from the international relations field to examine

---

[2] This title was a reference to the influential edited volume by P. B. Evans, D. Rueschmeyer, and T. Skocpol, *Bringing the State Back In* (Cambridge University Press, 1985).

social movements that cross national borders. Smith, Chatfield, and Pagnucco (1997), for example, drew on both sociological theory and international relations theory to address international NGOs and the broader social movements of which they are part in nine case studies. Khagram, Riker, and Sikkink (2002) aimed to bridge the literature on transnationalism, regimes, and norms in the international relations sub-field of political science with sociology's literature on domestic social movements. Their volume identified three different forms by which non-governmental groups could work across borders: Transnational advocacy networks, which are usually informally and loosely linked sets of actors that exchange information; transnational coalitions that coordinate strategies and/or tactics in concerted international campaigns; and transnational social movements that "have the capacity to generate coordinated and sustained social mobilization in more than one country to publicly influence social change" (Khagram, Riker, and Sikklink 2002, 8). Although the three types operate differently, they are all "forms of transnational collective action involving non-governmental organizations interacting with international norms to restructure world politics" (2002, 3).

In the late 1990s, a more policy-oriented literature also emerged, exemplified by articles in two top journals that focused on the impacts of formally organized NGOs on world affairs. In *Foreign Affairs,* Mathews (1997) focused on broad normative questions: If NGOs are having a major influence on world affairs, is that good or bad? She argued that non-state actors in general and NGOs in particular have been able to influence the decisions of the most powerful governments (such as the United States during the NAFTA negotiations) while compelling weaker states to modify their behavior significantly (such as Mexico during the Chiapas rebellion). This shift of power from state to non-state actors may enhance the ability of the international community to address pressing needs. But it may also raise problems. First, NGOs' limited capacity prevents them from undertaking large-scale endeavors. Second, in trying to expand their financial base, NGOs may compromise their operational independence. Finally, given that NGOs are by definition usually special-interest groups whose sole purpose is to further their narrowly defined objectives, if such organizations begin to replace state governments, the result could be a fragmented and paralyzed society.

Mathews' fears that NGOs could create a fragmented, paralyzed global society echo older arguments by Mancur Olson (1982) on democratic sclerosis. He contended that as self-interested groups multiply and lobby to increase their share of the distributional pie, the outcome of interest group competition is political gridlock and policy incoherence.

But the evidence from the national level in rich and poor countries alike fails to support this prediction. If the hypothesis were true, the United States, with its vibrant citizen sector, should be frozen into immobility by its vast array of competing interest groups, associations, think tanks, and NGOs. The hypothesis also suggests that more authoritarian governments that strictly limit the activities of NGOs should adopt more coherent and effective policies. The evidence for that proposition is, to put it mildly, mixed at best.

Much of the literature on transnational civil society begins from a different starting point that disagrees with the basic premise of Olson's argument and Mathews' fears. Not only are independent groups not necessarily bad for policy, they can be downright good for both policy-making and society. The creation of "social capital"—relations within and among civic groups—promotes both economic growth and political stability (Putnam 2000).

In *Foreign Policy*, Simmons (1998) pointed out the multiple ways NGOs influence national governments, multilateral institutions, international corporations, and societies. They influence agendas—forcing leaders, policy-makers, and publics to pay greater attention to various topics. They help to negotiate outcomes, designing treaties and facilities agreements. They confer legitimacy, promoting or restricting public support for issues and institutions. They can help to implement solutions and push governments and other actors to abide by their commitments. But the result of NGO involvement is not foreordained. NGOs can sometimes improve domestic and international governance by drawing on their expertise and resources, grassroots connections, sense of purpose, and freedom from bureaucratic constraints. But they can also distort public opinion with false or inaccurate information, lose their sense of purpose by growing larger and more bureaucratic, or lose their organizational autonomy by increasingly relying on state funding.

Florini (2000) drew on the scholarly literature to aim at a policy-making and activist audience, taking a largely empirical approach to address three questions: "How powerful is transnational civil society? How sustainable is its influence? How desirable is that influence?" The book drew together six case studies written by authors, mostly scholars, who had actively participated in the networks they were describing and thus could bring detailed inside knowledge to bear. Some of its authors are among the long list of authors of book-length case studies that have detailed how the growing phenomenon of transnational ties among citizens' groups work in practice with regard to specific issues (Khagram 2004; Clark 2001; Evangelista 1999; Risse, Ropp, and Sikkink 1999; Lipschutz 1996; Wapner 1996).

This literature argued strongly that the answer to the most fundamental question—do INGOs and other types of transnational civil society connections matter to the conduct of international affairs—was a resounding "yes." Some went on to consider the conditions under which they matter. The best known of such works is Keck and Sikkink (1998), which focused on international advocacy networks and argued that they are most likely to emerge around issues when channels of communication between governments and peoples are blocked, activists believe that networking will help them get better results more quickly, and various forms of international contact facilitate the creation and strengthening of networks.

Politically significant INGOs and other transnational civil society groups do not operate in a sphere constituted by civil society alone. Civil society groups rarely control economic or military resources that give them direct power as it is usually understood. The political effectiveness of such groups depends on their ability to persuade others—state actors, the general public, corporations, or inter-governmental organizations—to alter their policies or behavior. Most of the literature described above focused on the efforts of transnational civil society to influence states. But another strand of the literature has focused on the interactions between civil society groups and other actors. Doh and Teegen (2003), for example, provide insights into the growing range of interactions directly between NGOs and the business community. A substantial literature has addressed the formal organs of global governance: Intergovernmental organizations such as the World Bank, the International Monetary Fund, and the United Nations. Such interactions are at least as much in need of scholarly investigation as are the influences of civil society groups directly on governments, as intergovernmental organizations are established by states explicitly to serve the interests of states. Why, to what extent, and under what conditions do such organizations find themselves influenced by non-governmental actors?

Nelson (1995) constituted the first overall assessment of the role of NGOs in influencing the World Bank. He found that the World Bank's claims to have successfully incorporated NGOs into project design and implementation obscured a more mixed picture. His data, collected between 1973 and 1990, revealed that of the 304 joint projects between the World Bank and the NGO community, only 54 involved NGOs in project design. In most cases, NGOs played either a minor role or were involved solely in the implementation phases of projects, having no influence on determining what the Bank was trying to accomplish.

Weiss and Gordenker's (1996) edited volume took on the subject of the United Nations and its interactions with NGOs as a vantage point from which to analyze the roles of NGOs in global governance. They noted that the United Nations Charter contains specific language in Article 71 authorizing the Economic and Social Council (ECOSOC) to "make suitable arrangements for consultation with non-governmental organizations which are concerned with matters within its competence," a notable formalization of what had been only informal ties between the UN's predecessor, the League of Nations, and NGOs. Over time, as the scope of the UN's activities broadened and as other parts of the UN developed mechanisms for dealing directly with NGOs, the impact of NGO participation become more and more significant, particularly after the end of the cold war. The volume has a particularly useful theoretical framework (Gordenker and Weiss 1996).

Willetts' (1996) edited volume of the same year took more of a policy approach to the question of NGO relations with various intergovernmental organizations, including the United Nations and the World Bank. After several chapters describing how interactions between the two sectors have led to some extraordinary accomplishments in human rights, environmental protection, and humanitarian assistance, the book argues that IGOs could and should do more to involve NGOs in their activities. That may require revising the IGO's state-centric constitutions and charters to allow NGOs of all types—national and international, northern and southern—greater access.

But as Florini (2000, 215–16) points out, the evolution of NGO–IGO interactions has been anything but smooth. After NGOs demonstrated their growing prominence through their active participation in and around the large UN conference of the 1980s and 1990s, and as post-cold war euphoria set in, ECOSOC opened intergovernmental negotiations in 1993 on expanding NGO access at the United Nations. But many governments remained deeply uneasy about allowing a stronger NGO role. Those that had been the targets of NGO campaigns on human rights abuses were less than eager to reward such groups with a place at the intergovernmental table. And many governments, especially those that were still struggling to build effective state institutions, saw little value in encouraging non-governmental actors that might threaten their monopoly on decision-making. By the mid-1990s, as the General Assembly was considering the question of broader NGO access throughout the UN system, a backlash had arisen.

The interactions of specific NGOs with specific intergovernmental institutions are part of a much larger phenomenon: The loose agglomeration of activists who for a period around the turn of the millennium came to be known as the "anti-globalization movement." The term was always a misnomer. Few are actually opposed to global integration per se. Most participants in the movement are more accurately referred to as "globalization's critics"—people who have specific objections to the consequences of certain types of economic integration, or to the political processes by which globalization is being governed, or both. Globalization's critics may have come together in a loose-knit "movement," but it is far from a single coherent group. Indeed, it is so broad that many of its participants, rejecting the "anti-globalization" label but unable to come up with an accurate replacement, simply call it "the movement."

Toward the turn of the millennium, and particularly after the highly visible protests at the ministerial meeting of the World Trade Organization in Seattle in 1999, analysts began to focus on this broad phenomenon. Scholte and Schnabel (2002) brought together an unusual mixture of activists, officials, and researchers to examine in depth the role of civil society in global finance.

O'Brien, Williams, Goetz, and Scholte (2000) examined "the relationship between multilateral economic institutions (MEIs) and global social movements (GSMs) as one aspect of a much wider global politics . . . and governance structure" (2000, 2). They argued that this relationship has transformed global economic governance, moving it away from an exclusively state-centric system and leading to significant institutional modification (though rather less change in policy substance). The book examined four cases: The World Bank and women's movements; the World Trade Organization and labor; the World Bank, the WTO, and the environmental social movement; and the International Monetary Fund and social movements.

A key new source of information and analysis is the *Yearbook on Global Civil Society* (2001, 2002, 2003, 2004), put out by the London School of Economics. The *Yearbooks* analyze and describe a variety of forms of individual action by which people outside the governmental and corporate sectors aim to influence global issues and institutions. The first *Yearbook* (2001) laid out a normative conception of civil society as an emerging arena for global civic action that connects people across borders. Its conceptual frameworks lay out alternative ways of thinking about the world in the era of globalization, in opposition to the "methodological national-ism" that has dominated the social sciences and made it difficult for policy analysts and scholars to understand the role of individual agency in global affairs (Kaldor, Anheier and Glasius 2003*b*; Shaw 2003; Beck 2003). Its chapters cover everything from broad conceptual topics to specific issues such as civil society's role in global policies on trade, weapons of mass destruction, or violence against women, to questions related to the nature and infrastructure of global civil society. It also provides a useful chronology and other data on global civil society.

Increasingly, writing on civil society's global roles is woven into larger works concerned with global governance and authority in the international system (Higgott, Underhill, and Bieler 2000). While it is not possible in the confines of one chapter to cite, much less review, the vast literature on globalization, a few examples are useful. The works of David Held and his colleagues (Held and McGrew 2002; Held and McGrew 2003*a*; Held and Archibugi 2003; Held and McGrew 2003*b* provides a useful short summary), for example, broadly examined the emergence of a global political sphere in response to the rapid increase in global public goods and bads. Florini (2003) examined transnational civil society within the broader context of global governance and the need to develop more democratic processes for decision-making on how to address global issues. Scholte (2005) raised questions about the value of relying on civil society involvement as a means of democratizing globalization given the relatively small scale of such participating to date.

Most of the literature referenced above casts what is meant to be a disinterested, objective eye on a political phenomenon of increasing interest. Others, however, took a more negative perspective, arguing that the growing influence of INGOs and other elements of transnational civil society is largely pernicious. The American Enterprise Institute and the Federalist Society briefly sponsored an "NGOWatch" project whose website (which has since been taken down) argued that "The extraordinary growth of advocacy NGOs in liberal democracies has the potential to undermine the sovereignty of constitutional democracies." Manheim (2000) analyzed campaigns directly by what he called the new anti-corporate left against businesses. Anderson and Rieff (2004) provided cautionary words in one edition of the LSE *Yearbook*.

5   EMERGING DIRECTIONS OF RESEARCH

In the immediate aftermath of 9/11, speculation abounded that now that the "interwar" period (between the end of the cold war and the emergence of the next great military conflict) had drawn to an end, the conditions that allowed civil society participation in global affairs to flourish would prove to have been only a passing stage in a world still heavily dominated by nation-state decision-makers. And it is true that the more spectacular manifestations of global civil society—the massive demonstrations that had surrounded meetings of the WTO, the World Bank and IMF, and the G-8—did die down. But it appears that the more fundamental trends that drove the rise of transnational civil society in the 1980s and 1990s still exist: The reality of border-crossing problems that national governments are not adequately addressing; the relative ease of cross-border communication among ordinary people in the information age; the availability of sufficient (if limited) human and financial resources. As the LSE *Yearbooks* and other recent publications demonstrate, the empirical evidence continues to show that transnational civil society continues to matter in global politics.

But that one answer—that transnational civil society does matter to outcomes in global politics—leaves open three enormously important questions that future research should continue to address. The first is to further elucidate how and when transnational civil society matters. As Price (2003) pointed out, the literature has raised numerous hypotheses about the interaction between domestic political norms and structures and the successes and failures of transnational campaigns, but only occasionally have scholars rigorously vetted their empirical cases against other possible theoretical explanations.

Second, until very recently, the literature focused almost entirely on the interactions between transnational civil society and states, or state-created intergovernmental organizations, and tended to explore the adversarial side of those interactions. Given that much of what motivated the civil society actors was opposition to what states and IGOs were doing, this was a natural and appropriate focus. But the pattern of civil society's global interactions is shifting. Increasingly, actors from the public, profit-seeking, and citizen sectors are working out partnerships, sometimes explicit, sometimes tacit. In some cases, civil society actors have been included in the delegations of governments involved in official intergovernmental negotiations, a phenomenon that has received little scholarly attention. And the sectoral divides, never perfectly sharp, are blurring. Some of global problem-solving is being tackled by "social entrepreneurs" who use business models to develop profitable, and hence sustainable, mechanisms for solving public goods problems (World Economic Forum 2005). Future research needs to consider carefully the shifting boundaries of, and patterns of relations among, the public, profit-seeking, and citizen sectors.

Third, as Sikkink (2002, 301) has pointed out, as "transnational social movements and networks are increasingly permanent features of international life, scholars and activists need to grapple more thoughtfully with the dilemmas that the presence and power of these nontraditional actors pose:" dilemmas of representation, democracy, deliberation, and accountability. The power of INGOs and other manifestations of transnational civil society is a soft, diffuse power, one that shapes norms and ideas in crucial ways but that is often not reflected in formal power structures. Thus, traditional political mechanisms, such as electoral politics, that have evolved over the centuries to apply a modicum of democracy and accountability to political power do not easily apply here.

But some such mechanisms may be needed if transnational civil society is to find a long-term place as a legitimate participant in global politics. One problem is the enormous asymmetries within the world of civil society, with citizens of rich countries far more likely to be able to use civil society channels to participate in global decision-making than citizens of poor ones. Decisions about which networks and campaigns to fund, and thus which part of the many possible global agendas are likely to see progress, are often made by foundations based in wealthy countries. Progress is being made toward greater equity. NGOs have proliferated throughout the developing world (Fisher 1993), and northerners involved in transnational campaigns have become more aware of the need to work with, rather than on behalf of, counterparts in the south. Yet often these groups find themselves in competition for available resources.

Moreover, the claim of these groups to a place in international decision-making rests on claims that their expertise, representativeness of a group legitimately entitled to a say, and/or processes of deliberation meets a standard that entitles them to influence or even make decisions that have consequences for other people. No scholar surveyed in this chapter would argue that transnational NGOs and networks measure up to ideals of representation, democracy, deliberation, accountability, or autonomy (Sikkink 2002, 315). Nonetheless, public opinion surveys in many parts of the world find that NGOs routinely outrank governments and businesses in assessments of trustworthiness and credibility. Little research has yet been done on why that is true in some parts of the world but not others, or what such groups need to do if they wish to create or sustain high levels of credibility.

In short, during the 1990s and in the early years of the new millennium, scholarship on INGOs and other forms of transnational civil society contributed greatly to the understanding of this amorphous, fluid, yet increasingly significant type of political actor on the international scene. That research has convincingly demonstrated that transnational civil society has a significant impact, and has begun to make inroads on questions concerning why that impact varies across issues and political structures. The broader, more normative questions, however, have just begun to receive attention. In the absence of a world government to channel the activities of non-governmental actors, what are the appropriate roles for civil society? And who decides?

REFERENCES

ANDERSON, K. and RIEFF, D. 2004. Global civil society: a sceptical view. Pp. 26–39 in *Global Civil Society 2004*, ed. H. Anheier, M. Glasius, and M. Kaldor. London: Centre for the Study of Global Governance.

BECK, U. 2003. The analysis of global inequality: from national to cosmopolitan perspective. Pp. 45–55 in *Global Civil Society 2003*, ed. M. Kaldor, H. Anheier, and M. Glasius. London: Centre for the Study of Global Governance.

BOLI, J. and THOMAS, G. 1999. *Constructing World Culture: International Nongovernmental Organizations Since 1875*. Stanford, Calif.: Stanford University Press.

CHARNOVITZ, S. 1997. Two centuries of participation: NGOs and international governance. *Michigan Journal of International Law*, 18 (2): 183–286.

CLARK, A. M. 2001. *Diplomacy of Conscience: Amnesty International and Changing Human Rights Norms*. Princeton, NJ: Princeton University Press.

DOH, J. P. and TEEGEN, H. (eds.) 2003. *Globalization and NGOs: Transforming Business, Government, and Society*. Westport, Conn.: Praeger.

EDWARDS, M. and GAVENTA, J. (eds.) 2001. *Global Citizen Action*. Boulder, Colo.: Lynne Rienner.

—— 2004 *Civil Society*. Oxford: Blackwell.

EVANGELISTA, M. 1999. *Unarmed Forces: The Transnational Movement to End the Cold War*. Ithaca, NY: Cornell University Press.

FISHER, J. 1993. *The Road From Rio: Sustainable Development and the Nongovernmental Movement in the Third World*. Westport, Conn.: Prager.

FLORINI, A. M. (ed.) 2000. *The Third Force: The Rise of Transnational Civil Society*. Washington, DC: Carnegie Endowment for International Peace and Japan Center for International Exchange.

—— 2003. *The Coming Democracy: New Rules for Running a New World*. Washington, DC: Island Press; 2005 edn. Brookings Press.

GORDENKER, L. and WEISS, T. G. 1996. Pluralizing global governance: analytical approaches and dimensions. Pp. 17–50 in *NGOs, the UN, and Global Governance*, ed. T. G. Weiss and L. Gordenker. Boulder, Colo.: Lynne Rienner.

HAMMOND, A. 1998. *Which World? Scenarios for the 21st Century*. Washington, DC: Island Press.

HELD, D. and KOENIG-ARCHIBUGI, M. (eds.) 2003. *Taming Globalization: Frontiers of Governance*. Cambridge: Polity Press.

—— and MCGREW, A. (eds.) 2002. *Governing Globalization: Power, Authority, and Global Governance*. Cambridge: Polity Press.

—— —— 2003a. Political globalization: trends and choices. Pp. 185–99 in *Providing Global Public Goods: Managing Globalization*, ed. I. Kaul, P. Conceicao, K. Le Goulven, and R. U. Mendoza. Oxford: Oxford University Press, for the United Nations Development Programme.

—— —— 2003b. *The Global Transformations Reader: An Introduction to the Globalization Debate*. Cambridge: Polity Press.

HIGGOTT, R. A., UNDERHILL, G. R. D., and BIELER, A. (eds.) 2000. *Non-State Actors and Authority in the Global System*. New York: Routledge.

KALDOR, M. 2003. *Global Civil Society: An Answer to War*. Cambridge: Polity Press.

—— Anheier, H., and Glasius, M. (eds.) 2003a. *Global Civil Society 2003.* London: Centre for the Study of Global Governance.

—— —— 2003b. Global civil society in an era of regressive globalisation. In *Global Civil Society 2003,* ed. M. Kaldor, H. Anheier, and M. Glasius. London: Centre for the Study of Global Governance.

Keck, M. and Sikkink, K. 1998. *Activists Beyond Borders: Advocacy Networks in International Politics.* Ithaca, NY: Cornell University Press.

Keohane, R. and Nye, J. S., Jr. (eds.) 1972. *Transnational Relations and World Politics.* Cambridge, Mass.: Harvard University Press.

—— —— 1977. *Power and Interdependence.* Boston: Little, Brown.

Khagram, S. 2004. *Dams and Development: Transnational Struggles for Water and Power.* Ithaca, NY: Cornell University Press.

—— Riker, J. V., and Sikkink, K. (eds.) 2002. *Restructuring World Politics: Transnational Social Movements, Networks, and Norms.* Minneapolis: University of Minnesota Press.

Lipschutz, R. 1996. *Global Civil Society and Global Environmental Governance.* Albany: State University of New York Press.

Manheim, J. 2000. *The Death of a Thousand Cuts: Corporate Campaigns and the Attack on the Corporation.* London: Lawrence Erlbaum Associates.

Mathews, J. 1997. Power shift. *Foreign Affairs Magazine,* 76 (1): 50–71.

Nelson, P. J. 1995. *The World Bank and Non-Governmental Organizations: The Limits of Apolitical Development.* London: Macmillan.

Newell, P. 2000. *Climate for Change: Non-State Actors and the Global Politics of the Greenhouse.* Cambridge: Cambridge University Press.

O'Brien, R., Williams, M., Goetz, A. M., and Scholte, J. A. 2000. *Contesting Global Governance: Multilateral Economic Institutions and Global Social Movements.* New York: Cambridge University Press.

Olson, M. 1982. *The Rise and Decline of Nations: Economic Growth, Stagflation, and Social Rigidities.* New Haven, Conn.: Yale University Press.

Ottaway, M. and Carothers, T. (eds.) 2000. *Funding Virtue: Civil Society Aid and Democracy Promotion.* Washington, DC: Carnegie Endowment for International Peace.

Price, R. 2003. Transnational civil society and advocacy in world politics. *World Politics,* 55: 579–606.

Putnam, R. 2000. *Bowling Alone: The Collapse and Revival of American Community.* New York: Simon and Schuster.

Risse, T., Ropp, S. C., and Sikkink, K. (eds.) 1999. *The Power of Human Rights: International Norms and Domestic Change.* New York: Cambridge University Press.

Risse-Kappen, T. (ed.) 1995. *Bringing Transnational Relations Back In: Non-State Actors, Domestic Structures and International Institutions.* Cambridge: Cambridge University Press.

Rosenau, J. N. 1980. *The Study of Global Interdependence: Essays on the Transnationalization of World Affairs.* London: Frances Pinter.

Rudolph, S. H. 1997. Introduction: religion, states, and TCS. Pp. 1–24 in *Transnational Religion and Failing States,* ed. S. H. Rudolph and J. Piscatori. Boulder, Colo.: Westview Press.

Scholte, J. A. (ed.), with Schnabel, A. 2002. *Civil Society and Global Finance.* London: Routledge.

—— 2005. *Globalization: A Critical Introduction.* London: Macmillan.

Seligman, A. 1992. *The Idea of Civil Society.* New York: Macmillan.

SHAW, M. 2003. The global transformation of the social sciences. In *Global Civil Society 2003*, ed. M. Kaldor, H. Anheier, and M. Glasius. London: Sage.

SIKKINK, K. and SMITH, J. 2002. Infrastructures for change: transnational organizations, 1953–1993. Pp. 26–44 in *Restructuring World Politics: Transnational Social Movements, Networks, and Norms*, ed. S. Khagram, J. V. Riker, and K. Sikkink. Minneapolis: University of Minnesota Press.

SIMMONS, P. J. 1998. Learning to live with NGOs. *Foreign Policy*, 112: 82–96.

SMITH, J., CHATFIELD, C., and PAGNUCCO, R. (eds.) 1997. *Transnational Social Movements and Global Politics: Solidarity Beyond the State*. Syracuse, NY: Syracuse University Press.

TARROW, S. 1994. *Power in Movement: Social Movements, Collective Action, and Politics*. Cambridge: Cambridge University Press.

WAPNER, P. 1996. *Environmental Activism and World Civic Politics*. Albany: State University of New York Press.

WEISS, T. G. and GORDENKER, L. (eds.) 1996. *NGOs, the UN, and Global Governance*. Boulder, Colo.: Lynne Rienner.

WILLETTS, P. (ed.) 1996. *"The Conscience of the World:" The Influence of Non-Governmental Organizations in the UN System*. Washington, DC: Brookings Press.

WORLD ECONOMIC FORUM 2005. *Global Governance Annual Report 2005*. Geneva: World Economic Forum.

PART IV

OLD AND NEW

CHAPTER 35

....

ENCOUNTERS WITH MODERNITY

....

SAMUEL H. BEER

1 WHY POLITICAL SCIENCE?

....

I have been asked to write a personal commentary on the role of institutions in political science. This is a welcome opportunity to look into a question that has been nagging at my thoughts in recent years. "Why did I take up the study of politics? How did I go about it? And what have I learned from it?" I have sometimes characterized my work in British and American politics as the study of ideas and institutions and for many years I gave an interdisciplinary course titled Western Thought and Institutions in which I used the classics of political thought to interpret and analyze political history. This present assignment gives me the chance to emphasize the role of institutions, while giving an account of my ventures in the comparative study of the politics of Britain and the USA.

The main cause of that initiative was the intellectual shock of communism and fascism. This two-edged totalitarian threat forced my generation to rethink the meaning of freedom. At the University of Michigan, although avoiding political science courses as boring and undemanding, I was greatly attracted to the study of history and philosophy and managed to do well enough to win a Rhodes Scholarship. While living and traveling in Europe in the years 1932–5, direct contact with fascism and communism as movements and as governments forced me to come to terms with what was going on in the world, ultimately with such relevance as to make me a political scientist instead of a medieval historian with a penchant for philosophy of history, as I had intended.

1.1   The Liberalism of Modernity

Those medieval studies from which I had turned away, however, continued to orient my effort to find a way through the intellectual chaos of current politics. Thanks to them I can call this commentary *Encounters with Modernity*. They gave me the perspective to perceive the onset of modernity as that profound turning point in the development of the Western mind which produced the free society I found under such dire assault. The freedom of that society is modern freedom, so distinctive as to be the defining characteristic of the age we call modernity and of the process of modernization which transformed and continues to transform the civilization of the West and of the other great cultural areas of the world. This historical contrast brings out the basic traits of the political institutions of the new age.

To be sure, freedom in one or another form has been a concern of Western thought since ancient times. Plato's myth of the cave is an allegory of liberation, rendered even more illuminating by his vision in *The Symposium* of the soul rising through levels of being toward identification with the Absolute. In the Middle Ages a similar version of "the great chain of being" was embodied in conceptions of government which made liberty their organizing principle. The plural is a more accurate rendering of the idea, as seen in a classic expression, *Magna Carta Libertatum* (1215). In this document a variety of freedoms were guaranteed respectively to the several ranks of a structure, ranging down from the *ecclesia anglicana* to the *villanus* at the bottom of the legal and political hierarchy. This structure foreshadowed the "polity of estates" (Weber's *mittelaelterliche Staendestaat*) which emerged later in the thirteenth century, as a mature expression of the hierarchic and corporatist ideals of the high Middle Ages.

For 2,000 years or more the leading minds of the West championed a doctrine of hierarchic inequality. Classical philosophy had taught the rule of the wise; Christian theology the rule of the holy. Medieval thinkers had combined the two imperatives, vesting authority in a hierarchy of natural virtue and divine grace. They differed in the relation of secular and sacerdotal power. They did not doubt that the few should rule the many; that the ruler, whether prince or prelate, knew what was good for the ruled and, therefore, had the right, indeed the duty, to direct them toward that good.

In this society the exercise of freedom of thought and expression could be a grievous offense. "Heresy", wrote Thomas Aquinas, "merits not only excommunication, but death, for it is worse to corrupt the faith, which is the life of the soul, than to issue counterfeit coins, which administer to the secular life. Since counterfeiters are justly killed by princes as enemies to the common good, so also heretics deserve the same fate."

Modernity turned things upside down. Freedom of thought, which in the Thomistic world pointed the way to excommunication and death, became the first freedom of the modern political order. A term is needed to mark the great divide between premodern and modern freedom. In the scholarly taxonomy of political ideas that term is "liberalism." This usage may well raise the hackles of those students of politics who think of themselves as conservatives in contrast with and opposition to liberals. My understanding of the term copes with that criticism. I recognize and indeed emphasize that as a value system pervading the politics of modern times, liberalism in the broad sense has been expressed in a variety of different and sometimes conflicting ways, ranging from laissez-faire to the welfare state to democratic socialism. In this big ideological tent of modern liberalism, I find right-wing Republicans and left-wing Democrats, Tory democrats and Labour socialists, and, in general, the mainstream political tendencies of modern Western democracies.

At the American founding Thomas Jefferson reasserted the first principle of liberalism in the curt, explosive manifesto with which he led off his argument for independence: "all men are created equal." This assertion of equality is a powerful message of liberation. To say that all are equal is to deny that any have authority over others. The egalitarian denial of authority to the few, moreover, follows from a positive faith in the capacities of the many. The claim of "equal rights" for each would be empty and unconvincing absent this premise which affirms the capacity of the many for self-government, individually and collectively. That capacity is no small power. The attack on hierarchy did more than assert the rights of self-government. It liberated not only what people do, but what they think. The liberation proclaimed in the rights of self-government presumes the liberation embodied in the capacity claimed for the human mind. According to liberal doctrine, the reason men should be free to govern themselves is that they can think for themselves. They ought to be free outwardly because they are free inwardly. Thanks to that capacity—James Madison called it "a gift of nature"— their first freedom is freedom of thought and expression, appropriately enshrined in the First Amendment. "I have sworn eternal hostility", said Jefferson, "to every form of tyranny over the human mind."

The prospect is boundless. The break out of the old closed society toward a new world which was opened up and driven on by the liberated mind led to achievements on a grand scale. Democratic politics, capitalistic wealth, and scientific progress in their different ways expressed the independent, inquiring, inventive force of modernity. No less richly diverse, literature and the arts reflected a powerful burst of the imagination. But although the promise and the achievements have been grand, the risks and the disasters have been apocalyptic. On the one hand, such triumphs of the free mind as the increase of the wealth of nations, the spread of civil liberties, and the victories of medicine over infectious disease; on the other hand, such disasters as the social injustice of industrialization, the rise of communism and fascism, the outburst of total war, and the invention of weapons of mass destruction. The present nuclear threat to human life on this planet is a product of modernity. The consequences, intended and unintended, of the process of modernization set in motion by liberalism have been tragically ambivalent.

In the liberal order, therefore, the task of those humanly devised incentives and restraints on human action which we call political institutions is to release the power of the free mind while reducing the risks of its exercise.

1.2   The City of Reason

By the time I came to Harvard in the fall of 1938, I was a fierce anti-communist, a fervent New Dealer, a devotee of Emerson, and ready to try to put it all together. Finding a bit to my surprise that I was expected to write a dissertation for a Ph.D., I launched myself, with the audacity known only to graduate students, on a defense of liberalism against the totalitarian threat. The dissertation, completed in 1943, was not published until after the war in 1949 under the title, *The City of Reason.* In essence the book was a restatement of the political theory of philosophical idealism, descending from Hegel and set out by the British and American idealists such as T. H. Green and Josiah Royce. To say a word along these lines was woefully old-fashioned and academically incorrect at that time, when logical positivism with its view of science as the only kind of truth dominated philosophical thinking. On this score I was put at ease by the fact that the two current thinkers on whom I mainly depended, Alfred North Whitehead and John Dewey, were in no sense hostile to science. Whitehead, the more systematic of the two, presented what he called "a philosophy of organism." It had two themes: on the one hand, a theory of "creative advance," postulating the autonomy of the human mind, and, on the other hand, a theory of "social union," asserting the "real togetherness" possible for individuals. Hunches and hypotheses derived from the work of these two authors will appear in the account of my empirical study of the institutions of free government. At a very abstract level, the two themes of creative advance and social union state the philosophical background of the following two sections of this chapter, "Liberal Democracy" and "Liberal Nationalism."

There is, however, a metaphysical problem which needs first to be briefly dealt with, since it has serious implications for political behavior. A doctrine of creative advance and social union, if not put in a larger context, is just too good to be true. It surely does not fit the twentieth-century's record of human finitude and fallibility, of limited minds and evil intentions. The perils of modernization, in short, confirm a current of skepticism which has washed against the foundations of Western thought since ancient times. This tradition of pessimistic doubt has both Greek and Biblical sources. Plato, needless to say, directed the Western mind toward magnificent vistas of aspiration. Yet it must be the rare student who, on first opening Plato's dialogues, has not felt the enormous force of the doubts raised by Socrates. Despite the happy resolutions Socrates extracts from his compliant respondents, the reader must wonder if the master has not done more to make the case for appearance than for reality. To the student of politics, for instance, *The Statesman* is the classic celebration of the rule of law and constitutionalism. Yet the reader can hardly be blamed if he doubts that the affirmative case can stand against the forceful exposition and clear-eyed perception of the inevitability of personal rule in a world where "all is flux." On a still grander scale, that same Heraclitan hypothesis inspires probing inquiries into the relativity of knowledge and morality which severely shake the cosmic architecture in which the dialogues seek to shelter human rationality. In modern times skepticism has forceful advocates in Hobbes, Nietzsche, and the contemporary postmodernists and deconstructionists. Not so many years ago, during a conversation with Isaiah Berlin, while he was attacking the belief in a philosophy of history, which he incorrectly attributed to me, he exclaimed, "Sometimes I agree with A. J. P. Taylor that history is just one damned thing after another!"

The encounter with the skeptical proposition that all is flux is not just a contretemps of the intellectual life. Once its meaning for individual and human effort dawns, a paralyzing pessimism may set in. What is the use of trying to control history, when consequences are so unpredictable? Why seek justice when you know that any conceivable version will be controverted? Into this intellectual and emotional void the totalitarian temptation may well enter with its promise of power and faith, if only reason, the source of doubt and uncertainty, is surrendered. The brilliant negativism of the cultural life of pre-Hitler Germany is a cautionary example.

Whitehead's idea of the interconnectedness of things makes it possible to conceive a cosmos in which the flux is overcome in a "saving order" which creates and preserves the partial orders of the temporal world. In his severe barebones intellectualism, F. H. Bradley summarized this conclusion: "We have no knowledge of plural diversity, nor can we attach any sense to it, if we do not have it somehow as one." Emerson is more relaxed and closer to ordinary experience when he says, "We grant that human life is mean, but how did we find out that it is mean?... What is this universal sense of want and ignorance, but the fine innuendo by which the great soul makes its enormous claim?" I like Miloscz' concise summary:

For me, therefore, everything has a double existence,
    Both in time and when time shall be no more.

This cosmology makes sense of human purpose. The whole cannot exist without the parts. Infinitesimal as they are in that cosmic scheme, human efforts to make the temporal world less imperfect are not lost. Followed to its affirmation of such a saving order, the doctrine is robustly affirmative. Immunized against pessimism and despair by its critique of reason, it affirms the value of human aspiration regardless of any temporal disaster and fortifies the will to understand and advance human freedom. So I was ready to go to work as political activist and political scientist.

2   Liberal Democracy

By the early postwar years, thanks to academic study and personal experience, I had got a pretty good hold on the rudiments of a liberal philosophy of politics. Its major premise was the autonomy of the mind and its principal working hypothesis was the powerful influence of ideas on political behavior. It lacked a developed view of the interaction between ideas and behavior, in other words, an empirically grounded view of political institutions. Working toward an institutional approach took me through a struggle with the way some of my colleagues looked at the process of government. Comparison of the process of government in Britain and the United States helped me with that task.

2.1   Escape from Group Theory

At Harvard, as generally in American political science in these years, group theory—later known as interest group pluralism—dominated the discipline, inspiring splendid empirical research in American politics as displayed in the work of Pendleton Herring, Peter Odegard, and David Truman. When, however, the perspectives of the leading work of theory, Arthur Bentley's *Process of*

Government (1908), were turned on British politics the results were puzzling. While pressure groups were seen, to the dismay of many, to flourish in American politics, they were commonly believed to be negligible in Great Britain. It is, therefore, understandable that in 1956 the *American Political Science Review* should give page one billing to a paper of mine asserting that "if we had a way of measuring power we should probably find that pressure groups are more powerful in Britain than in the United States... numerous, massive, well-organized, and highly effective."

Some of my colleagues have said that I discovered British pressure groups. That is not quite correct. But it is true that I was the first to show where and how they operated. This revelation resulted from the commonsense hypothesis once put into words by V. O. Key: "Where power is, there the pressure will be applied." In Britain this did not mean the legislature, since there that body is substantially under the control of the executive. It was, therefore, in the corridors of Whitehall in the daily contacts of ministers and civil servants that one found the representatives of the great economic and social interests of the nation.... As I worked out the structure of the postwar British polity, these interconnections appeared so well developed as to constitute a veritable institution of functional representation, serving as an effective instrument of the government's management of the economy. Something more than group pressure was at work.

Nor was group theory adequate when applied to certain basic features of American politics. I recall the attempt of some of us young instructors to make it work as an explanation of familiar nationwide traits. "Shall we say then," sarcastically asked our authority on constitutional law, "that the general hostility to homicide means that alongside the farmers, workers and capitalists, there is simply another group, the big anti-murder interest group?" We were avoiding the use of terms such as "the national interest" or "the common good" as moralistic and non-operational. Our thinking was still clouded by Charles Beard's ridicule of "abstract ideas" as a political force.

The British comparison helped us see the larger context in which pluralism operated. The Brits had their interest groups and they exercised "pressure," if by that you meant "influence." There was, however, in contrast with American manners, an easy acceptance of group representation in government and quite different expectations of how groups and government should interact. And how did I find this out? Often conversations with someone I knew socially—the old-boy network—were the most revealing source. I enjoy recalling, for instance, the annual dinner in 1958 of the Chamber of Shipping, the trade association of the great shipping companies. I attended thanks to a contact I had made at Harvard with a Commonwealth Fellow who had also gone to Balliol and who was now the assistant secretary in the appropriate department of the civil service.

I sat with him as his minister, Lord Mancroft, gave an after dinner talk on the government's relations with the industry. This speech, I then and there learned, had been composed, except for its whimsy, by my friend and his opposite number in the trade association. They would nod and make remarks *sotto voce* as they followed their copies of the minister's rendition of their joint composition.

The facts were clear but I needed some construct that would pull together these observations of attitude and expectation into a tool for systematic comparative analysis. I found it in the concept of "culture" which Talcott Parsons had deployed in his *Theory of Social Action* (1951), drawing largely on the work of Max Weber. In my 1956 discussion of British pressure politics, a central theme was "the cultural context," consisting of certain general ideas which determined not only the process of group representation, but also in a degree the very substance of these interests.

2.2   From Culture to Institutions

In this use of the concept of culture as a tool of analysis, social scientists were reflecting the modern liberal belief in the autonomy of the mind as a basic force in the social and political process. We had groped for a term to express this point of methodology. "Ideology" (Karl Mannheim) overemphasized the limiting function of ideas. "The role of ideas in history" (Crane Brinton) was too intellectual. "Operative ideals" (A. D. Lindsay) asserted that ideas can have consequences, but focused narrowly on the normative aspect. "Culture," however, has the necessary breadth by embracing the normative, the cognitive, and the affectual aspects of "the ordered set of symbols" (Parsons) by which the members of a group sharing them similarly see and sense the situation, physical and social, constituting their environment. Its further use in political study was greatly advanced by a brilliant paper presented by Gabriel Almond at a conference in 1955—the same meeting, incidentally, at which I presented my paper on British pressure groups and parties. His term "political culture" has continued to be used in the profession and in everyday speech.

The concept of political culture supplied the missing link between political philosophy and political behavior. In a political culture ideas drawn from political philosophy are embodied in the motivations of political actors, dictating what ought and ought not to be done and what can and cannot be done. Such a body of incentives and restraints on behavior is a political institution. The political culture is not itself an institution. The political culture is the body of dos and don'ts, cans and can'ts which is embodied in various institutions, the actual patterns of intended behavior.

2.3   The Liberal Constitution

But how well do the institutions of a country perform? Do they meet the liberal commitment to evoke the powers of the free mind, while also guarding against its risks? The institution charged with this comprehensive task is commonly called a constitution. You might say that any government has a constitution, insofar as it displays some regularity in how it exercises power and what for. And so the term is sometimes used merely to refer to a frame of government, a pattern of government, a political system. But constitutionalism means more than that. It also means that this regularity in behavior is intentional, conforming to a body of rules which regulate and authorize the rules embodied in the various subordinate institutions of the political system—in short, an institution of institutions.

The primary task of the liberal constitution is to foster creative advance. Encourage that pluralism. Put the First Amendment to work in all spheres. Cultivate incentives for the assertion of a variety of ideas and interests. Yet this basic commitment of liberalism has its inherent dangers. They are twofold. First, that very pluralism may be self-defeating. This consequence, however unintended, has been denounced by the champions of hierarchy as the inevitable penalty of democracy and analyzed by modern game theorists as "the multi-persons' prisoners dilemma." The vice lies not in the ill-will of the actors, whether individuals or groups, but in the structure of the situation which, because of its dispersion of decision-making among so large a number, virtually compels participants to act against their common long-run interest. The incoherence and immobilism of so overly responsive a democracy frustrates creative advance. The liberal constitution averts this risk by its provision for coordination. This function dominated my study of British and American institutions from the mid-1940s to the mid-1960s, the main focus being on political parties and party systems as the institutions which aggregated the pluralistic plenty of the free mind.

The liberal constitution may open the way to a far greater evil than the incoherence and immobilism of pluralistic stagnation. My generation experienced this possibility when the chaos of the Great Depression brought on the totalitarian response. The ideologies of fascism and communism which lay siege to the political culture of modern freedom were themselves the product of that freedom. What this attempt of self-destruction intended, and in some places achieved, was a coercive unity based on race or class, not the social union which fulfills creative advance in liberal nationalism. That positive achievement was the main concern of my work from the mid-1960s to the mid-1990s.

2.4   Constitutions for Deliberative Democracy

How does the liberal constitution cope with self-defeating pluralism? What does the British/American comparison tell us? In Britain the collectivist polity which emerged in the postwar years was a marked economic and political success. Building on prewar foundations, successive governments created a welfare state and managed economy which provided proximate solutions to some of the worst problems of industrial capitalism. Although marred by miscalculation and misfortune, the overall economic record was, in the words of Professor James E. Meade, "an outstanding success story for a quarter of a century." The political success was that the radical program initiated by the Attlee government, although originally enacted by a partisan majority, was substantially accepted and developed by the opposition, signifying that this great program of reform had won the assent of the British nation as a whole. Majoritarianism had been transformed into convergence. I do not say "consensus" as that might well be taken to mean that the contending public philosophies of the two main parties, Labour and Conservative, had become identical. That did not happen. Differences in values, revolving around questions of equality vs. inequality and public choice vs. market choice, persisted, but, so to speak, in the background, capable of forcing their way into strong, open electoral and parliamentary conflict at a later date. In the meantime, however, party preferences on both sides had been sufficiently transformed to produce a convergence in policy which led to a mid-century period of relative party peace.

Convergence is no small achievement. Although majority rule must be accepted in order to get decisions in elections and legislation, majoritarianism can be tyrannical. Even if by chance some sort of rotation in office gives each minority the power for a time to rule in its interest, one can hope for a more comprehensive and stable outcome. In postwar Britain both parties went through phases of revisionism moving them toward acceptance of the welfare state and a managed economy. Labour had to give up its old socialist pursuit of equality through common ownership (read: nationalization) in favor of the redistributive spending of their massive new social programs, which would now be nourished by an admittedly capitalistic system embracing private property and moved by self-interest. For the Conservatives, who inherited their party's prewar reassertion of state control, including the first steps in nationalization, the great and fateful concession was the further step of accepting the huge budgetary burdens of the Keynesian and Beveridgean commitments. That difficulty was eased when "Mr Butskell" appeared, his presence being noted in the *Economist* of February 13, 1954. The new fiscal methodology facilitated not only the revisionist egalitarianism of Labour, but also the revival of the graded paternalism of the

Conservatives. "Toryism," as Harold Macmillan once said, "has always been a form of paternal socialism."

The outcome was a coherent and effective program of government action. Competititon for power moved the parties to adapt to the realities of governing and winning office. How each saw these realities was conditioned by its public philosophy. The outcome, however, was not some inevitable result of group formation and cultural context. Essential to its achievement was also that process of revisionism in each party and between them. Here a kind of collective thinking took place, exhibiting once again that basic feature of modern liberalism, the truth generating capacity of uncensored debate. I followed, wrote about, and in a very modest way took part in the prolonged "rethinking" occasioned by revisionism in Britain. General descriptions fail to convey the vitality and passionate nature of the process. I can reproduce one inside moment of Labour revisionism which was evoked by the publication of *The New Fabian Essays* in 1952. We Harvard liberals sympathized with the programs of social services and economic mangement being pioneered in Britain. But we were disappointed by the confusion and sense of drift in the *Essays* and expressed our opinions in some highly critical reviews, as well as in private conversations with the socialist dons and journalists with whom we exchanged visits. One Sunday afternoon in the American Cambridge, following the rural walk which was obligatory when our visitors were British, we got into a long wrangle over public ownership. Finally, Arthur Schlesinger Jr. exploded, "Do you really think that everything should be nationalized, even newspapers, magazines, book publishing? How could you maintain freedom of the press under these conditions?" Needless to say that was a powerful argument among a bunch of aspiring authors. Thus, we social liberals dropped our grain of common sense into the process of deliberative democracy by which policy preferences were transformed as revisionism triumphed.

2.5 Party Government in Britain and America

In admiring American eyes, the key to the political success of postwar Britain was "party government." In 1957, noting that party cohesion had been increasing markedly for some time, I sketched the Westminster model. Two-party competititon, unity among partisans in the legislature and executive, a government program based on a distinctive public philosophy. Moreover, the Westminster model presumed that the two-party system would conform to a similar duality in the preferences of the voters. And as it happened, during the glory days of the collectivist polity British voters did tend to think and act in terms of two classes, the working class and the middle class, their party preferences strongly correlating with class. Given this dualism in the electorate, the party system did afford the voters an effective choice, while also producing governments with cohesive majorities carrying out coherent programs.

The American attraction to party government had a history going back to Woodrow Wilson's *Congressional Government* in 1885. Inspired by contrast with the glowing portrait of the British system in Bagehot's *English Constitution* (1867), Wilson gave a depressing report of the disorderly regime of a weak presidency and a fragmented Congress, which he saw in the years after the Civil War. In 1950 the same logic inspired the plea for party government in a celebrated report, entitled *Toward A More Responsible Two Party System* and sponsored by the American Political Science Association. Its argument was that a concentration of power similar to that enjoyed by British governments could be democratically achieved by reforms of party organization in the legislature and in the country. The reforms would include such organizational devices as mass dues-paying memberships, cooperation with class based organizations, issue oriented party conventions, and platforms binding on nominees for executive and legislative office. Many American observers, politicians as well as professors, thought that in this way we could remedy the incoherence and gridlock which we felt often issued from our interest group pluralism.

As it happened, the new pattern of government inaugurated by the Roosevelt administration made our hopes plausible. Beginning as a huge, short-lived venture into corporatist planning, the real and lasting New Deal took shape in a series of separate reforms amounting to a constitutional and economic revolution. Government power was sharply centralized within the federal system toward Washington and in Washington toward the presidency. Among the voters, moreover, the political base of this power became more national as FDR taught them to look to him and to Washington for solutions to their economic and social problems and the old, rustic, and sectional constituencies gave way to a more urban and class-based formation.

New Deal rhetoric, however, was not framed in class terms, in contrast with Britain and other industrialized countries where the economic collapse brought into prominence socialist parties explicitly identified with the working class. The New Deal had a coherent public philosophy, but its inspiring principle had been proclaimed by FDR when, during his 1932 campaign, he identified the Democrats as "the party of liberalism—militant liberalism." Needless to say, this was not the libertarian creed which at this time Herbert Hoover also championed as liberalism. It was rather the social liberalism introduced by Lloyd George during the great reforming Government of Asquith of 1908–16, which, I remember as a lowly speech-writer among the New Dealers, was a model among American reformers. After Roosevelt the New Deal programs were defended by Truman and, to the surprise of reactionaries, accepted by Eisenhower in an American example of convergence in a two-party system. American administrations, however, were never able to command reliable partisan legislative majorities in the British fashion.

Presidents normally needed and enjoyed some support from the opposing party for their majorities in Congress. The coordinating institution, then as now, was presidential leadership, not party government.

2.6   Constitutions Make a Difference

The key to this difference is constitutional. Party organization and class structure were contributing causes, but the heart of the matter was the American separation of powers in contrast with the fusion of powers in Britain. Under the British constitution, the cabinet exercised not only the executive power of directing the various departments of the state, but also the legislative power of deciding what laws would be passed and what taxes levied. Therefore, when the Queen read the prime minister's annual announcement of what laws his government proposed to adopt, you knew that would happen. Compare those virtual certainties with the mere probabilities of what a president proposes in his State of the Union address. To be sure, in Britain as in the USA, bills become laws only if passed by the legislature. That enactment required the assent of the monarch, still expressed in the old Anglo-Norman imperative, *la reine le veult*, which has not been refused since Queen Anne's days. The monarch had the legal right to refuse consent, but by long-established convention her consent, in effect, was a power of the cabinet.

What the parliament may enact, moreover, had no legal limit. The Crown in Parliament was still legally as sovereign as proclaimed in the celebrated declarations of Coke and Blackstone. Thanks, however, to the fusion of powers in the cabinet, which included what laws would be made, it was in that body that this great power of ultimate legal sovereignty actually resided.

To be sure, the House of Commons could dismiss the cabinet by withdrawing its confidence. In this manner the House could deprive one cabinet of the power to govern, but only in order to install another in its place. The House decided who governs, but it did not itself govern. The legislature could change one monopolist of power for another, thereby effecting the wishes of the democratic electorate, but it did not itself resume that power by turning over the business of law-making to individuals or committees, except, you might wish to say, for that dominant committee, which thereby became the executive.

This plural executive, the cabinet, was bound to act as a unit by the constitutional convention of collective responsibility. This meant that every member of the cabinet must comply with and, if necessary, defend in public the decisions of the cabinet, even if he disliked them and had opposed them in cabinet discussions. The cabinet, however, could not satisfy this norm independently of the prime minister. He determined the agenda for cabinet discussion and his summations gave the government machine its principal marching orders. He appointed and dismissed its members, moved them from one post to another, and decided if and when the cabinet would resign or go to the country in a general election.

These norms of cabinet government are not laws enforceable by courts like imperatives of the American constitution, but conventions whose effectiveness as restraints and incentives are hardly less, as illustrated by their survival over generations and in some respects centuries. The fusion of powers itself dates back to the premodern monarchy. Criticizing Bagehot's view that the cabinet is a committee of the House of Commons, Leo Amery argued that the two elements of the constitution "today as when William I was king" are, on the one hand, a central energizing, initiating, directing element, which exercises both executive and legislative power—formerly the monarch and today the cabinet; and, on the other hand, a peripheral element, which complains, criticizes, and consents, but does not itself govern—formerly the baronage and today the House of Commons, especially the opposition. A Tory inellectual, Amery neglected a fact which fundamentally qualifies his assertion, while also confirming it. From the great reform act of 1832 to the current representation of the people acts, statutes have given Britain a vigorously democratic constitution, which, however, is expressed through institutions inheriting the concentrated governing powers of the old monarchic regime.

This transfer of authority from monarch to cabinet was a remarkable and inherently implausible piece of constitutional history. One might well suppose that as the liberalizing forces of modernity shifted power from the monarchic toward a democratic regime, the old concentration of power would be dispersed among representative groups in the legislature as individuals and committees reflected the pluralism of the empowered electorate. For a new pluralism in the electorate and a heightened individualism in the legislature did emerge. On the contrary, however, a new convention arose which vested the old fusion of powers in the cabinet so long as, and only so long as, it had the confidence of the House of Commons. The classic formulation was framed by the leader of the opposition in 1841 in a motion of no confidence, which led to the defeat of the government, a dissolution, and election of a new government. By this link, democratization was fitted into the institutional norms of the old concentration. The same rigidity survived as the constitution also continued to display its flexibility in the further development of cabinet government and prime ministerial authority.

So elaborated, this paradoxical constitution of "elective dictatorship"—to use Lord Hailsham's perceptive exaggeration—based on a coherent framework of convention and statute, was an indispensable condition for the rise of party government. The dominant political formations of the collectivist age, the Conservative and the Labour parties, both complied with its imperatives. Both accepted the fusion of powers, whether exercising them as the government, or as the opposition, holding the government accountable for their exercise and aspiring to have it for themselves.

While both parties also accepted and complied with the requirement of democratic consent, they differed radically over how they understood that the flow of influence should move within their ranks and within the electorate, from the top down or from the bottom up. "Tory democracy" still bore strong traces of premodern *noblesse oblige* and deference. Labour's sense of working class solidarity was strengthened by traditions of an organic society which harmonized with trade union dominance.

So the British constitution, as constitutions must be if they are to perform their coordinating function, was accepted by all participants despite their conflicting partisan perspectives. And indeed, thanks to its ancient authorization of the dualism of government vs. opposition, the constitution so framed perceptions and preferences as to favor a two-party system. As the changing political culture reshaped the institutions of party and group behavior, the constitution, that institution of institutions, fitted them to its enduring contours.

In the American case the democratic thrust of the constitution was dominant, the preamble of its legal text declaring it to be ordained by that ultimate sovereign, the People of the United States. Although its norms cannot compete with the British in antiquity, they display rigidities with notable powers of endurance. There is that 1787 text of explicit rules of law establishing and empowering our institutions of government. To be sure, in the course of constitutional development, this body of law has been changed by amendment, as in the case of the first ten, the Bill of Rights, and the three massive amendments occasioned by the Civil War. Few in number, however, the amendments have done little to offset the popular impression, often confirmed by the rhetoric of editorial writers and even judges, that we enjoy a wise and unchanging code bequeathed to the ages by our Founding Fathers.

Actually and, on balance, fortunately, that amended text is being continually transformed by its reinterpretation by the Supreme Court exercising its power of judicial review. The constitution's "ambiguous libertarian generalities," to use Justice Frankfurter's phrase, such as "due process of law" and "equal protection of the laws," have been something of a palimpsest for profound rewriting of the verbal texts. In performing this function, the Court, it has been said, follows the election returns, sometimes, however, lagging far behind, sometimes forging far ahead. For instance, the words that were held to justify racial segregation in 1896 were not held to prohibit it until 1954. In those postwar years, the Warren–Burger Court served as the most active agency of American government in pressing forward the liberalizing of public policy. Given the ambiguity of the general language of the constitutional text, the Court cannot help being a law-making rather than a mere law applying institution.

Our constitutional norms, however, depend not only on the amended text and judicial interpretation, but also, in the British manner, on conventions, old or new. By convention the two-term rule on the presidency prevailed from the administration of George Washington until, having been broken by FDR, it was enacted by constitutional amendment in 1951. It is still only by convention that presidential electors are bound to vote in accordance with the popular vote in their state. The greatest change in the course of our constitutional development has surely been the immense increase in the powers of the presidency. The words of the text would seem to make him merely the executor of the decisions in peace and war by the Congress and the Court. Yet that massive economic and constitutional revolution in domestic and foreign affairs achieved by Franklin Roosevelt was accomplished without formal amendment and in the teeth of judicial resistance. The latter barrier was overcome when FDR's plan to pack the Court failed, but was a sufficient threat to cause the Court to discover in the legal text of the constitution the broader powers of federal legislation Roosevelt sought for the New Deal. Under Roosevelt and his successors the "imperial presidency" in peace and war has been achieved step by step, each incident of increase serving to authorize the next, making the overall advance a matter of convention rather than judicial interpretation or constitutional amendment.

Yet despite all these shifts in power within the executive, legislative, and judicial branches of our constitutional system, its commitment to a separation of these powers, though not explicitly stated in the legal text, has endured, a convention as fundamental to our system as its opposite, the fusion of powers, has proved to be to the British. Despite the best efforts of reformers, whether politicians or political scientists, the response of the American polity to the new demands of peace and war, therefore, was not party government, but presidential leadership.

On both sides of the Atlantic, as the 1960s dawned the mood was euphoric. In 1959 Macmillan won reelection on slogans that have not inaccurately been summarized as "You never had it so good!" At the same time the cheerful data for the civic culture study of Almond and Verba was being gathered, showing British trust in their government and politics at a peak among nations. In a book on postwar Britain published in 1965 and titled *British Politics in the Collectivist Age*, I could conclude, "Happy the country in which consensus and conflict are ordered in a dialectic that makes of the political arena at once a market of interests and a forum for the debate of fundamental moral concerns." In these years the United States discovered its affluence, reported its own high pride in its government, and, despite the menace of the cold war and the trauma of Kennedy's assassination, acclaimed the reforms of Johnson's Great Society. "For," as our foremost authority on presidential elections, Theodore White, proclaimed in 1965, "Americans live today on the threshold of the greatest hope in the whole history of the human race."

3   LIBERAL NATIONALISM

In neither country did this happy continuum last. In Britain and in the United States the success story of postwar collectivism was disrupted by a series of government failures which, beginning in the 1960s, persisted into the following decade. Although reaching deeper levels of change in Britain, cause and effect were similar. The coordinating power, party government in Britain and presidential leadership in the USA, succumbed in classic illustrations of self-defeating pluralism, or as I called it in the subtitle of *Britain Against Itself* (1982), "the political contradictions of collectivism."

This loss of control over fiscal and economic policy contributed massively to burgeoning budget deficits and raging price and wage inflation, as exemplified in the last days of the Great Society and the "winter of discontent" of the Callaghan government. Experimenting with models of rational choice theory, I thought at first that the source of the troubles was democratic collectivism itself, the inclusion of so many decision-makers as to make collective decisions virtually impossible. Yet these failures of collectivism also had a further source. As anyone who lived through the 1960s and 1970s will recall, the government failures were overshadowed and indeed precipitated by an immense cultural upheaval. The attack on authority and order struck every sphere: dress, music, manners, education, sex, marriage, work, religion, race relations, and, perhaps most sharply, politics and government. Indirectly this attack on the old solidarities opened the way for the free market advance in public policy initiated by Reagan and Thatcher and the subsequent economic recovery. In the political culture of both countries, a shift from the collectivist attitudes of the postwar period to more individualist attitudes eased the movement of policy from public choice toward market choice. Accordingly, when the left-of-center opposition took over, both Clinton and Blair accepted the new outlook, acclaiming in their identical rhetoric "the end of big government." Still, both also sought to add a radical modification which they termed the Third Way.

In Britain, reflecting this reorientation of political culture, Thatcher's eradication of Tory paternalism from the Conservative program was complemented by Blair's no less radical purge of socialism from New Labour. One outcome was a marked Americanization of British political institutions and public policy. One cannot fail to note the contrast with the strong Anglophile tendencies of American politics during the immediate postwar years.

In broad outline, the institutions of the welfare state and managed economy created in the postwar years had still framed the outlook of Gaitskell and Macmillan. Leading the attack on this bureaucratic, corporatistic, interventionist regime, Thatcher abolished the nationalized industries, privatized public housing, and demolished the privileged position of organized labor. No less surprising, this radical and comprehensive divergence in public policy was wholly accepted by Tony Blair, thereby bringing about a new convergence between the parties. I christened it "Blatcherism" in order to recall the similar somersault thirty years before when the Conservatives adopted the major reforms of the Attlee government, thereby earning the nickname "Butskellism." In quite serious ways, however, Blair's Third Way was an advance from Blatcherism.

3.1   The Nation's Constitution

What did these events teach me about political institutions? The main lesson was that the liberal constitution performs the function of not only coordination, but also integration. The collective thinking of deliberative democracy can reconcile the diverse preferences of interest group pluralism. But who or what does this? To say that "the people" rule does not say who the people are. One could take them to include all mankind, as some Enlightenment radicals presumed. This utopian hope is not to be disdained. It could be entertained as an operative ideal recognizing and welcoming the possibility that existing units of self-government can be expanded in ever wider regimes. The various peoples of the present European Union of nation states may someday become sufficiently integrated to act as the European People who ordain a European Republic. In any case, it remains true that the definition of the manner of government does not identify the unit of government. Fierce conflicts sometimes rage between advocates who agree on the manner of government, the democracy question, but disagree on who is to be included, the nationality question. Under the American constitution, government by the people is also expected to be government for the people. It is in our nationhood that we find our sense of identity and purpose, telling us who we are and what we are trying to make of ourselves. The legal text declares that "We, The People" seek "a more perfect union."

3.2   Three Models of Liberal Nationalism

There are various kinds of bonding by which a number of individuals may be connected sufficiently to form a self-governing unit. One is the simple libertarian contract not to harm one another, and therefore to form and to support a government that protects this right for all. Closer to reality the communitarian model identifies the national bond as a common culture which unites its members by similarities of behavior and feelings of sympathy and belonging. Given its intrinsic intolerance of diversity, the communitarian democracy threatens creative advance by individuals or groups. A third variation which I have called social liberalism combines the merits of a common culture and a commitment to diversity. In this model of nationhood the integration of persons is achieved because they are diverse, but complementary; that is, the various members differ in such ways that they fit together as a more inclusive whole. The favorite analogy is with a living body; hence the designation "organic nationalism" for this idea of a free, egalitarian, democratic, and passionate form of social union. The point to stress is that the interaction of its citizens is not merely external and instrumental, but inward and constitutive, so transforming one another as to make the aggregate a unified whole and a fulfillment of creative advance.

To be members of such a nation is to be joined together not only by ideas, but also by what Edmund Burke called "public affections"—the whole range: fear, joy, pride, shame, anger, devotion, and revulsion. Not that all members will at all times react to events in the same way, as they did in grief over JFK's assassination and the shattering events of 9/11. At times some Americans will feel shame for what others take pride in, as happened during our bitter divisions over war in Vietnam and Iraq. But both the shame and the pride spring from a common sense of nationhood. You cannot be ashamed of your country unless you love it.

3.3   Blair's New Nationalism

"I like to think of myself," Thatcher once said, "as a Liberal in the nineteenth-century sense—like Gladstone." Her repudiation of Tory paternalism fits her libertarian mold. Tony Blair's repudiation of socialism, although not explicit, was no less thorough. Does that make him a liberal too? If so, it would be as a fellow traveler not with Gladstone, but with David Lloyd-George. His was a liberalism heartily committed to capitalism, but, as he showed in word and deed, a capitalism modified by far-reaching reform. This social liberalism advances Blair beyond Blatcherism, distinguishing him from libertarians as well as socialists.

The socialist favors equality of condition, in accord with the ancient admonition, "From each according to his ability, to each according to his needs." Even after having served as prime minister, Attlee assured me that he still thought that, as he had written before the war, the ultimate goal basically should be equal incomes for all. Some on the Labour left today may still share this faith. In sharp contrast, the libertarians, with whom it is not unfair to class Reagan and Thatcher, defend the right of each person to pursue his or her own idea of the good life and, therefore, find government intervention sufficient if it ensures all equal protection against harm by any. Recognizing that beyond this negative right the individual may well need positive assistance, if he is to pursue his better possibilities, social liberalism offers equality of opportunity, but with the crucial proviso that the offer of opportunity entails the duty of its responsible use.

Welfare policy, declared Blair at the party conference of 1997 in a vivid oxymoron, should be governed by "compassion with a hard edge." He accordingly warned the unemployed, especially the young, not to lapse into dependency on welfare entitlements, but seriously and persistently to look for work. I was reminded of how, as a youthful ghost-writer for the New Deal, I had learned, when justifying aid to the unemployed, to add "through no fault of their own." These were exactly the same words which had often been used by Lloyd-George in a similar context. Precisely this rationale of encouraging self-reliance by empowerment rather than entitlement informed the workfare provisions of the welfare reform act which President Clinton signed in 1996 and which served as a precedent for the measure adopted by Tony Blair, similar even to the extent of using the term "new deal" for certain provisions. In a significant way the social liberal shares the libertarian belief in and hope for individual autonomy.

The individual freely makes his choice, but with social assistance and for a further purpose, as Blair concluded in his 1997 conference address, to make Britain, if no longer "the mightiest," now and in the future, "the best place to lead a fulfilled life." Earnestly as he supported, on the one hand, devolution in the UK and, on the other hand, a leading role in the European Union, to his way of thinking, the British nation state was alive and well and on its way to becoming "a beacon for good at home and abroad." In what he had said and done I found enough such emphasis to speak of Blair's "New Nationalism."

The ground for this new hope was a new fact. While public policy was institutionalizing greater individual freedom and greater individual responsibility, at the same time and for the same reason the ancient class system was dissolving. This "collapse of deference," as I with some exaggeration called it in *Britain Against Itself* (1982), had the positive effect of facilitating the advance of social liberalism. The ancient cultural premises of British politics had been hammered home on me by my tutor in medieval history at Balliol, the renown Vivian Hunter Galbraith. "Beer," he said to me, "you will never understand England until you understand her middle ages." And then as if in logical sequence, he continued, "In England the upper classes do not hold the lower classes down, the lower classes hold the upper classes up." That penetrating observation of core values of Toryism and socialism was finally losing its relevance.

3.4   Integrating the American Nation

In the USA the most prominent, though not the only illustration of a new nationalism, was the constitutional revolution brought about by the civil rights movement. Its purpose was to eliminate the deeply held racism—legal, political, economic, and social—of the American people. That negation had the positive purpose of "making the nation more of a nation," to cite the theme of my book, *To Make A Nation* (1993). Some black spokesmen, on the contrary, likewise demanded an equalization of rights, but so designed as to enable blacks to develop and enjoy their own way of life separately from whites. Against these separatists the mainstream of the civil rights movement, however, steadfastly favored integration on a nationwide scale, as Walter White had successfully contended against W. E. B. Dubois in the 1930s, as Thurgood Marshall had insisted against Stokely Carmichael and Rap Brown in the 1950s, and as Martin Luther King Jr. had foreseen before an audience of a quarter of a million in front of the Lincoln Memorial on August 28, 1963 dreaming of a future when "the sons of former slaves and the sons of former slaveowners will sit together at the table of brotherhood." That famous metaphor had a literal meaning: lunch counters had been among the first arenas of integration in the South. As a metaphor, it envisioned American civilization nourished by the free and uncoerced communion of both races.

What actually happens? There is an interchange in which individuals come to appreciate and to emulate one another's virtues. Ideally, in this American *paideia*, the individuality of separate persons is enhanced and our union as a nation is made less imperfect. These gifts of American pluralism are not skills or techniques, but the human capacities that enable individuals to acquire and exercise skill and knowledge. These capacities may properly be called "virtues" in the original meaning of the term, *arête*, real powers of human achievement. As such they are the gifts of individuality. But as elements in a social division of labor, they are also complementary. They not only empower those who possess them; as items of social interchange they also empower others. This process of social interchange is not like economic exchange, in which what one gives one no longer has and what one receives the other no longer has, leaving the parties as separate as before. In social interchange, what the parties give one another they also keep. They do not have something more; they have become something else. Therein their connection becomes stronger and richer and more beautiful, in Whitman's words, making "the united states...the greatest poem."

It is vital to sense what actually happens in the integrating process if the institutions of social liberalism, such as affirmative action, are to be properly designed. These legal and moral institutions of civil rights reform provide the opportunity and incentives for assimilation. But if assimilation is to continue as an inward and constitutive integration of persons, that culminating step from equal rights to fraternal communion must be voluntary.

It was a moment of great promise. If the task of liberal institutions is to release the creative powers of the free mind, while also guarding against its risks, social liberalism is a sensible third way between the libertarians and the socialists. So it was this name, the Third Way, that Clinton and Blair gave to their distinctive public philosophy. New Democrat and New Labour seemed to be in the process of establishing a complex of institutions which would repeat the success of welfare reform in new programs in such fields as education, health care, the environment, fiscal policy, and law and order. The Third Way also had a global aspect as a model for other free countries. In its glory days from 1998 through 2000, these proposals were seen as promising to strengthen the liberal nation state against "rogue states" and "terrorists" and won the approval of a series of summits of left-of-center governments in the West. Perhaps the most grandiose was the Berlin meeting on June 1, 2000 when thirteen heads of governments signed a joint communiqué praising the Third Way and advocating a comprehensive global program of reforms as "a new international social compact." In the individual states, however, the institutional demand proved hard, sometimes too hard, to meet and after 9/11 American leadership succumbed to the more immediate needs of national security. As recently as the dedication of his Presidential Library on November 19, 2004, however, Clinton could still hail the Third Way and repeat his mantra of Community, Opportunity, and Responsibility.

4   A Good Word for Institutionalism

Institutionalism is a big tent. This review of my work has helped me see how the concept I have chosen gets at the role of ideas in history. My basic working hypothesis is that the free mind is and ought to be the ethical premise of modernity and the governing force in modernization. Switching from Jeffersonian rhetoric to modern social science, I say in the words of Clifford Geertz, "the autonomous process of symbol formulation" enables man to be "the agent of his own realization" who through "the construction of schematic images of social order... makes himself for better or worse a political animal." Liberalism in the very broadest sense is the word for this primary norm and fact. The politics of the free mind that follows from this liberal premise promises achievement on a grand scale, but also threatens self-inflicted failure and disaster. The need for some means to realize the promise and avert the perils points toward an institutional approach.

By an institution I mean a pattern of motivation imposing restraints and incentives on behavior. Its source is the free mind's ceaseless revelation of possibility. The political culture so created is embodied in a set of incentives and restraints on political behavior. The political culture is not itself an institution, nor is political behavior in itself. The institution is the behavior with the meaning given it as the product of these incentives and restraints.

This concept of an institution directs attention to the nature and function of a liberal constitution. In any liberal polity, its inherent pluralism will create a complex of institutions in wider or narrower arenas of behavior, thereby creating a need for an institution that orders the complex as a whole. The institution charged with such a comprehensive task of coordination is appropriately called a constitution. Proposals of constitutional reform need such an overall perspective. A few years ago, for example, it seemed to me that Charter 88's admirable concern to relax Britain's over-centralized system had become so one-sided that their program, if enacted as a whole, would have quite destroyed the power of coherent governance. The task of the liberal constitution, moreover, is not only coordination, but also integration. Incentives and restraints to facilitate and coordinate liberal democracy are obviously needed. No less a constitutional imperative is the integration that makes the nation more of a nation. The process of creative advance, we may hope, is in constant motion; likewise its fulfillment in a more perfect social union.

ABOUT INSTITUTIONS, MAINLY, BUT NOT EXCLUSIVELY, POLITICAL

JEAN BLONDEL

If institutions are regarded as central in a social science discipline, it is in political science. This has been the case during the long process of maturation of the subject from its very early beginnings to the increasingly rapid pace of its development up to the Second World War. After an interlude of at most two decades during which, under the impact of the "behavioral revolution," they seemed to be receding in importance, political institutions saw their crucial position once more restated as a result of the "new institutionalism" wave started in the 1980s by March and Olsen: political institutions have flourished ever since, in particular in the rational choice context. Indeed, even the temporary "decline" in prestige of institutions in the 1960s and 1970s must not be exaggerated. Not only did such "institutions" as parties, legislatures, or governments constitute the framework within which single country and even comparative studies tended typically to be analyzed, but the prevailing "grand model" of the period, structural-functionalism, gave a central position to "structures," a term which was felt more neutral than the word institution, but covering at least in large part the same reality.

Institutions may have thus prevailed in political science, but what might be termed "clarification" endeavors with respect to the concept were rare. There is indeed more interest in the determination of what institutions are in economics or sociology than in political science: moreover, bizarrely, there appears to have been no concern in political science for the vagueness, to say the least, of what should come under the umbrella of the concept. It was as if the meaning of that concept was self-evident and we should immediately recognize an institution when we saw one. This is strange since, outside political science, definitions are complex, for instance those given by sociologists. Talcott Parsons thus said that institutions are "those patterns which define the essentials of the legitimately expected behaviour of persons insofar as they perform structurally important roles in the social system" (1954, 239). W. R. Scott, almost half a century later, was only a little more concrete: "institutions consist of cognitive, normative and regulative structures and activities that provide stability and meaning to social behavior" (1995, 33). These definitions suggest that major problems need to be clarified: in the case of the second one, for instance, alongside "cognitive, normative and, regulative" structures, we have also to consider "activities." If applied to politics, what this definition would exclude would be small and indeed debatable.

Yet, in the political context at least, the definition problem is not the only one in need of "clarification:" "institutionalization" raises difficulties as well, although the expression has been in great use since the Second World War. In his 1968 *Political Order in Changing Societies*, Huntington gave a broad definition as well when he said that institutionalization is "the process by which organisations and procedures acquire value and stability" (1968, 12) and that four characteristics affected it: "adaptability, complexity, autonomy and coherence." The scope of the concept is somewhat narrowed, since the reference here is to "procedures" and not to "activities," but the question of the development of institutions over time now arises. Time itself becomes a variable, although other reasons why institutionalization has to "develop" are added, which means that institutions can also decay (Huntington 1968, 13–14). Institutions are not regarded as automatically efficient; their efficiency seems ostensibly to depend, not just on *internal* characteristics, as on the way the actors use them, but on *external* aspects, as on the way the broader society reacts to them: The strength of institutions, at any rate in the political realm, appears linked in part to the support these may enjoy outside their "borders." The institutionalization process thus needs to be explored alongside the concept of institution: It provides a key to understanding why and how new institutions might have to be "designed" to cope with problems hitherto not handled satisfactorily. These problems are only beginning to be considered and are in great need of systematic examination.

A chapter such as this can explore these matters only generally. What can be done, under the guidance of the literature, is, first, to come closer to a satisfactory definition of the concept of institution by looking at its components and, second, to examine the way in which institutionalization can increase (or decrease). The first section of this chapter thus considers the place to be given to organizations and to procedures in the definition of institutions: Major differences across the social sciences and in particular in the political, social, and economic fields emerge in this context. The second section is concerned with institutionalization: Marked differences are found among the social sciences in this respect as well.

1   INSTITUTIONS IN THE POLITICAL CONTEXT IN CONTRAST TO THE ECONOMIC AND SOCIAL CONTEXT

1.1   The Non-problematic Character of Institutions in Political Science up to the 1990s

The indifference which political scientists displayed traditionally with respect to what constitutes political institutions is remarkable: Indeed, at any rate up to the emergence of the behavioral movement, the empirical study of politics seemed to be viewed as coextensive with the study of political institutions. Thus a department in a university could be labeled "Department of Political Institutions" to indicate that it was concerned with empirical politics, not political philosophy. Thus studies undertaken in the early post-Second World War period did not even need to mention institutions in their index nor did Finer's three-volume *History of Government* published in 1993 do so. Despite the "concept clarification" aims of that work, Sartori's *Social Science Concepts*, published in 1980, does not refer to institutions at all, in the index or elsewhere, as if the concept was "non-problematic" and "self-evident."

Discussion, though not controversy, had begun to arise on the subject, however, as the study of politics, even before behaviorism emerged, went beyond (or below) classical "political institutions" and into the social realm in particular by studying groups. In his *Governmental Process*, published in 1962, Truman stated: "The word [institution] does not have a meaning sufficiently precise to enable one to state with confidence that one group is an institution whereas another is not" (1962, 26). Some questions were being raised as to whether bodies such as groups were institutions in the same way as parties or legislatures; but the matter was mentioned indirectly, casually even. In their introduction to their volume on *The Politics of the Developing Areas* (1960), Almond and Coleman drew a distinction, in the context of the "Interest Articulation" function, between "(1) institutional interest groups" and three other types of groups (non-associational, anomic, and associational) (1960, 33), but no attempt was made to define these "institutional interest groups." More generally, they said they had "in mind phenomena occurring within such organisations as legislatures, political executives, armies, bureaucracies, churches *and the like*" (Almond and Coleman 1960, 33; emphasis added). Very early in the book, they had simply said that "instead of 'institutions,' which again directs us towards formal norms, [we prefer] structures" (1960, 4). A few years later, in 1966, in their *Comparative Politics*, Almond and Powell referred in a similarly casual manner to "*formal and institutional* channels of access which exist in a modern political system. The mass media constitute one such access channel" (1966, 84–5; emphasis in original). Parties, legislatures, bureaucracies, and cabinets are then mentioned as being also formal and institutional channels.

Despite what has been frequently said about the attitude of "behaviorists" vis-à-vis institutions, there is therefore not so much a negative approach to these elements of political life as a "taken-for-granted" standpoint. Easton, in the index to his *Political System* (1953), lists a number of points at which institutions are mentioned (he does not do so at all in his subsequent *A Systems Analysis of Political Life* (1965)), but in the body of the text, as when he discusses the works of Bagehot or Bryce, the word institution is not even mentioned: he appears to assume that the kinds of bodies which these authors referred to are "institutions."

Thus behaviorists did not deny that institutions had a role, but, by introducing the "broader" notion of structure, Almond (and indeed, by introducing the notion of system, Easton and Almond) brought about a distinction which was bound one day to lead to questions about possible differences between these concepts. The notion of institution was rendered controversial by the sheer fact that a second notion was introduced without abandoning the first, but, in the 1960s and 1970s, the point had not been reached when one could say, as Rothstein did in his contribution to the *New Handbook of Political Science* of R. E. Goodin and H.-D. Klingemann (1996), "Political Institutions: an Overview:" "whichever story political scientists want to tell, it will be a story about institutions. A central puzzle in political science is that what we see in the real world is an enormous variation, over time and place, in the specifics of these institutions" (1996, 134–5). Possibly the first text which truly raised the issue was that of Lawson, *The Human Polity*, published in 1985, where it is stated under the subtitle of institutions: "An *institution* is a structure with established, important functions to perform; with well-specified rules for carrying out these functions; and with a clear set of rules governing the relationships between the people who occupy those roles" (1985, 29).

The nature of the debate was of course transformed by March and Olsen's work, *Rediscovering Institutions*, published in 1989, after the article entitled "The New Institutionalism" was published in the *American Political Science Review* in 1984. The influence of the volume has been extraordinarily large, but the text is also extraordinarily laconic, not to say more than laconic, about what institutions are. The first sentence echoes the phraseology of Almond and Coleman, a generation earlier, the words "such as" being used as substitutes for a definition: "In most contemporary theories of politics, traditional political institutions, such as the legislature, the legal system and the state, as well as traditional economic institutions, such as the firm, have receded in importance from the position they held in earlier theories" (March and Olsen 1989, 1). The first chapter is thus devoted to what are described as "Institutional Perspectives on Politics," but nowhere is the chapter concerned with the definitional problem. In the last section of that chapter, entitled "The role of institutions in politics," the authors state: "In the remainder of the present book we wish to explore some ways in which the institutions of politics, particularly administrative institutions, provide order and influence change in politics" (1989, 16). Thus March and Olsen are not apparently more conscious than their predecessors of the fact that a problem of definition arises with respect to institutions and that a distinction has to be made between institutions and other "elements" which play a part in politics.

The question of the meaning of the concept of "institution" came to be raised only a few years later, in the mid-1990's; yet this was done at first somewhat marginally by Goodin who noticed the different part which institutions play in the various social science disciplines (1996, 1–24). Probably the first full confrontation with the problem was in Lane and Ersson's volume on *The New Institutional Politics* (2000). This was something of a "volte-face" by these authors, as they still adopted, in the fourth edition of their *Politics and Society in Western Europe*, published in 1999, the kind of "unproblematic" language of March and Olsen. No attempt was then made, for instance, in the section of the introductory chapter entitled "Social Structure versus Political Institutions," to define these expressions. The authors had stated, without any further concern, that "[t]he focus on the variation between institutions of political democracy and their sources in civil society as well as their consequences for political outcomes creates a certain logical structure for the contents of the volume" (Lane and Ersson 1999, 14). Yet, one year later, they devoted a whole chapter to the question "What is an institution" (2000, 23–37) in which they referred, among other problems, to the "ambiguity of institution" (24–7) and proceeded to discuss a distinction which they made between what they described as "holistic" or "sociological institutionalism" and "rational-choice institutionalism" (29–36). This was real progress, but Lane and Ersson do not appear to consider that institutions have a particular "resonance," so to speak, in the political science context. To find out why there is such a "resonance," we need first to turn to a general examination of the differences among the various disciplines on the subject.

1.2   What Institutions are for Economists and Sociologists and why Political Scientists have to Differ

In *The Theory of Institutional Design*, edited by R. E. Goodin (1996), the question of different kinds of "institutionalisms" is evoked, possibly for the first time, at least in such a clear-cut manner: "Each of the several disciplines that collectively constitute the social sciences contained an older institutionalist tradition. In each case that tradition has recently been resurrected with some new twist....The new institutionalism mean [sic] something rather different in each of these alternative disciplinary settings" (Goodin 1996, 2). The characteristic meaning of institutions in each discipline is then examined, and the author continues: "There is wide diversity within and across disciplines in what they construe as 'institutions' and why. That diversity derives, in large measure, from the inclination within each tradition to look for definitions that are somehow 'internal' to the practices they describe" (1996, 20). A "central defining feature" is then attempted: having adopted what he refers to as an "external" account of what institutions are and what they do, the author states that "a social institution is...nothing more than a 'stable, valued, recurring pattern of behaviour' " (1996, 21), the formula being that of Huntington.

Yet it is probably more fruitful to look at differences among the social sciences in this respect and in particular at what is suggested by economists and sociologists alongside political scientists. There appears to be a dimension, with economics and political science at the two extremes and sociology somewhere in the middle. As was noted early in this chapter, W. R. Scott, a sociologist, stated that institutions covered both organizations and activities: this is indeed the middle position characterizing sociological analysis with respect to institutions. What was said earlier suggests that in politics the traditional stress—including that which both Lawson and Lane and Ersson indicated—was that institutions were first and foremost organizations. In economics, on the contrary, the emphasis is exclusively on procedures. "Institutions are the rules of the game in a society or, more formally, are the humanly devised constraints that shape human interaction:" this is how D. C. North begins his book on *Institutions, Institutional Change and Economic Performance* (1990, 3). No reference whatsoever is made to organizations in this description.

Whether it is worth trying to reconcile the points of view of the disciplines about institutions is debatable: it is unquestionably valuable to note that major differences exist about the meaning of the concept. These exist because the three disciplines are concerned with different sets of problems. As Goodin points out, economists are primarily concerned with solving the problem of *individual* choice (1996, 11) and are therefore concerned with rules. The individuals are the agents of the economic "machine" (whether as physical individuals or in association with each other in firms): Individuals cannot be expected to achieve their goals unless there are rules which determine how they are to relate to each other.

The situation is different in the society at large: Individuals congregate to form associations, unless they find themselves in bodies which have existed for generations, whether in traditional societies (tribes) or in modern societies (from families to churches). These bodies constrain individuals. Institutions cannot just be based on rules; they have to include the way collective arrangements, in groups, affect the behavior of individuals. As Offe states in the *Encyclopedia of Democratic Thought*, edited by P. B. Barry and J. Foweraker, in a rubric entitled, not institutions, but "institutional design:" "The rules and behavioural routines that make up the institutions are not just contractually agreed upon between the actual participants, but recognised, validated and expected by third parties and observers. Some of the more important institutions come with elaborate normative theories, 'charters', 'animating ideas'" (2001, 363). Social analysis has to be based both on the choice of individuals and on what might be regarded as the "pressure" of the groups to which these individuals belong. Hence the emphasis of W. R. Scott (1995) on both organizations and procedures.

The case of politics is different. Politics is a process of decision-making—and in that it resembles economics—but a process of decision-making taking place not between individuals but in communities (in "systems") and applicable to those who belong to these communities, whether they participated or not in the decisions or indeed even agreed to them. This is why, as Easton pointed out in *The Political System*, politics has to be an "authoritative" process of decision-making (1953, 135–41). Two key consequences follow. First, choice in politics is rarely individual, except if someone leaves the community to which he or she belongs, a move which is easily doable in the case of the membership of an association ("exit"), but is appreciably more difficult, in practice, with respect to the state. Second, much of politics concerns people not involved in the decisions taken. This is not equally the case in (conventional) economics or even in much of what sociologists are concerned with. The point is critical: It leads to the distinction between the way economists and sociologists, on the one hand, and political scientists, on the other, understand the meaning of institutions. Strangely enough, Rothstein does not point out that difference, although he distinguishes between the approaches of economists and sociologists (in Goodin and Klingemann 1996, 144–9).

2   INSTITUTIONS AND POLITICS: A CASE OF ORGANIZATIONS AND OF PROCEDURES, BUT WITHIN ORGANIZATIONS

One can therefore see why in politics the emphasis has been almost automatically placed on organizations rather than on procedures or rules when the question of the definition of institutions has arisen. Rules count: They are part of the institutional process; but rules and procedures become applicable, in politics, through organizations only, as they have to be applicable to large numbers who have not participated (because they do not have the right to do so, in most cases) in the process of decision-making. Thus only if rules and procedures are "legitimized," so to speak, by an organization whose "authority" the individual is prepared to recognize can they be also recognized. Economics does indeed need such a blessing by an authority: This is why economists declare that the state has to impose the rules which economics needs, but they do so sometimes with a degree of superior nonchalance as if "politics simply had to do its job." D. C. North is more "generous:" he notes that "[b]roadly speaking, political rules in place lead to economic rules, though the causality runs both ways" (1990, 48). The same occurs in the social field, but not always: Many social organizations are very small and can operate, at least ostensibly and so long as there is no major conflict, without having to call on the "authority" of the state. Only in politics is the recourse to authority continuous and universal; only in politics are organizations always on the front line: Rules and procedures, however important, have to be defended and supported by organizations.

In the political context, institutions are therefore primarily organizations. This is so whether these organizations are "fully" political, so to speak, as legislatures or parties, or "intermittently" political, as groups. Behaviorists were right to introduce these social bodies in the political process, but being intermittently in politics, these share the characteristics of both political and social organizations. This is indeed also the case of such economic organizations as, for instance, large companies and in particular multinational corporations.

A definition of institutions cannot therefore be applicable uniformly to all social sciences, as it then becomes a common denominator without much real significance. In the political science context, the search for a definition has to be around the concept of bodies able to take authoritative decisions, these bodies being in a position to develop practices—that is to say, procedures and rules—which those who recognize these bodies have to accept as being, so to speak, the "arms and legs" of these organizations. Much further research is needed in this context: But only in this direction can one expect to solve the key puzzle of political institutions. The puzzle is that institutions have been perceived as clear and distinct for generations, but there are uncertainties about what these cover in terms of both the organizations concerned and the manner in which organizations express the decisions which they take.

3 Institutionalization and its Great Role in Politics

Do political, social, or economic "arrangements" come to be institutions automatically and immediately? Or do they become institutions after time passes? Is there, in this case, an "institutionalization" period with the consequence that some arrangements are "more" (or "less") institutional than others or that the same arrangements become "more" (or "less") institutional?

3.1 Institutionalization in Political Science, Economics, and Sociology

The question of institutionalization has concerned political scientists more than other social scientists, Huntington being perhaps the political scientist who reflected most on the problem. From his view that, as we noted, institutions are "organisations and procedures which acquire value and stability" (1968, 12), it can be inferred that the process takes place over time. Institutions do not have "value and stability" automatically from the moment they are set up. Indeed, an often-cited (1962) Polsby article in the *American Political Science Review* had given an empirical basis to such a standpoint: It showed in great detail the way in which the districts of the House had become more competitive in the course of the development of the American republic. What Huntington stated six years later seemed to be a general and theoretical statement of the viewpoint that institutionalization takes time.

In this, as with respect to the nature of institutions, political science differs from economics and sociology, a point which does not appear to have been noted. In these last two disciplines, arrangements seem to become institutions immediately. D. C. North notes that there is institutional change, but nowhere does he mention institutionalization. He refers to the fact that "institutions change incrementally" (1990, 6), but merely to state that these changes take place incrementally "rather than in a discontinuous fashion" (North 1990, 6). What is being considered is how property rights have come to be altered in different societies, but not how, in the specific economic case, these "rules" have "acquire[d] value and stability." An economist interested in institutions and their role, such as North, is not concerned with how institutions (i.e. rules) *develop*, but (merely) how new rules replace older ones.

Given that economists view institutions exclusively as rules, it is perhaps not surprising that their approach to these rules should not be "evolutionary." It is more surprising that this should be the case for sociologists, since they are concerned with organizations as well as with rules. It might indeed seem that sociological theory should be "evolutionary" about institutions. W. R. Scott uses the concept of institutionalization, which is listed in the index (but not in North's text). However, in Scott's text, the role of time is wholly different from—and indeed much less important than—the one which it has in political science. Referring to a work by Selznick, Scott says that "[o]rganisations with more precisely defined or with better developed technologies are less subject to institutionalization than those with diffuse goals and weak technologies" (1995, 19). He then notes the difference between "official" and "real" goals of organizations and the part played by power. Quoting Stinchcombe, who stated that institutions are "structures in which powerful people are committed to some value or interest" (1968, 107), he emphasizes that "values are preserved and interests are protected if those holding them retain power" (Scott 1995, 19). Referring to experiments conducted by Zucker (1977), Scott states that "to create higher levels of institutionalization, the subject [of the experiment] was told that she and her co-worker were both participants in an organization and the co-worker (the confederate) was given the title of 'light operator'" (Scott 1995, 83). Institutionalization is "manipulable," so to speak. It is not a state acquired over time, but a state which an institution has when certain conditions are fulfilled, conditions which may or may not, more or less at will, be introduced.

Why is it the case with the kind of social organizations which Scott examines, and apparently not the case in politics? The point is that Scott is concerned with what occurs among the members of an organization and not with the effect which the organization may have on persons outside the organization. Such a point of view is justified from the point of a sociologist, particularly of a sociologist who focuses on relatively small organizations or on firms which do not have to ensure that their decisions are applied outside the organization. For those in the organization, the organization *is* indeed institutionalized: Employees have to abide by the rules, not merely because if they do not, they are likely to be dismissed, but because they cannot relate to other employees unless there is some agreement, that is to say unless some rules are institutionalized.

The case is different in politics, as was pointed out earlier, as it is different in "social" organizations which attempt to impose their views on non-employees, for instance trade unions, employers' organizations, or many NGOs. When what can be described as an "external constituency" plays a part in the life of an organization, it cannot be taken for granted that people will abide by the rules and therefore that institutionalization will be "automatic" and "instantaneous:" It has to be built. The fact that institutionalization has to be built (and, conversely, can be "unbuilt") explains why institutionalization is such a central concept in the analysis of political scientists. Yet, although it is central for political scientists—and somehow perceived as central—it is surprising that the basis for the development of institutionalization has not been systematically explored.

4   THE ROLE OF "EXTERNAL"
CONSIDERATIONS IN THE
INSTITUTIONALIZATION OF
POLITICAL INSTITUTIONS

Unlike economists and sociologists, political scientists have placed considerable emphasis on institutionalization. There is no absence of interest in this case, as in the definition of institutions, but the origins of the institutionalization process and the forms it takes need a comprehensive examination. Admittedly, Huntington is concerned with the ways in which and to an extent with the reasons for which institutionalization develops, but as the sociologists tend to do, merely "internally." He notes that time is crucial for the four key characteristics of institutionalization, adaptability, complexity, autonomy, and coherence, to mature but the process is presented in a rather mechanical manner. Time is viewed as being by itself one of the "causes," so to speak, of institutionalization (Huntington 1968, 13): Yet it is simply not the case that "the longer an organisation or procedure has been in existence, the higher the level of institutionalisation" (1968, 13–14). The process is not only unlikely to be linear; it can also be reversed, as is shown by examples of decline and collapse of well-established regimes. Huntington himself does indeed point out that when "a function is no longer needed, the organization faces a major crisis: It either finds a new function or reconciles itself to a lingering death" (1968, 15). However, the analysis is concerned only with the extent to which, within the institution, there is more adaptability, complexity, autonomy, or coherence, as a sociologist such as Scott does when he refers to Parsons: "A system of action was said [by Parsons] to be 'institutionalised' to the extent that actors in an ongoing relation oriented their actions to a common set of normative standards and value patterns" (Scott 1995, 12). What is not taken into account is how the institution relates to the rest of the society, although this matter is crucial in the case of political institutions, since, as we noted, these institutions exist essentially in order to affect the polity as a whole.

Huntington is not the only author to consider institutionalization merely from the point of view of the internal problems of the institution. Goodin and his collaborators, thirty years later, in *The Theory of Institutional Design* (1996), analyze the problem from the same standpoint. In the introductory chapter to the volume, Goodin suggests that institutional change emerges in three ways, by accident, by evolution, or by intention or design (1996, 24 ff). In this third case, the analysis of the development of institutions is exclusively devoted to the various ways in which "agents" develop their designs, which can be on "policy," on "mechanisms," and on "system" (1996, 31–3). These distinctions may well correspond to different ways in which institutions can overcome problems of "de-institutionalization" arising when the institution does not fulfill the functions it should fulfill: But the question arises as to why this is the case and specifically why, having fulfilled that function in the past, it no longer does so.

The absence of any part played by "the polity at large" is even clearer in Offe's analysis, in the same volume, under the title of "Designing institutions in East European transitions" (Goodin 1996, 199–226). In a section entitled "Challenges, breakdowns and survival responses," that author suggests that "breakdowns of institutions can occur in response to any of three challenges. First, they [the institutions] may fail to inculcate the *norms and preferences* that condition the loyalty of members ... Second, institutions may decay because *alternatives* emerge which allow for the satisfaction of those needs and the fulfilment of those functions over which the institution used to hold a monopoly.... Third, institutions may break down because of their manifest failure in performing the functions with which they are charged" (Goodin 1996, 219–20; emphasis in original). All three points refer exclusively to internal problems although in all three cases the breakdown is most likely to occur because those outside the institution, who for some reason depend on the institution (on the government, for instance), may have ceased to have confidence in the institution and its agents. The notion that institutions "fail to inculcate norms and preferences" clearly shows that the analysis is undertaken from the point of view of the institution and of its agents: That the members of the polity at large may not or no longer feel comfortable with the institution is simply not considered.

Such a state of affairs is strange. *Support* is central to political science and has indeed concerned political philosophers as well as empiricists for generations: Yet the point does not appear to be recognized as being at all relevant in the context of the setting up, life, and death of political institutions, whether these institutions are organizations or procedures. Probably no political scientist would deny that some support at least is necessary for regimes to be maintained; probably no political scientist would deny that this support is subject to fluctuations. Why should a notion of this kind not have permeated into the analysis of the political institutionalization process and by extension into the analysis of political institutions?

It is not suggested that the "external" elements of the problem are more important than the "internal" elements in the process of institutionalization and of "de-institutionalization" of political institutions. What is pointed out is that political institutions (as well as a few social institutions which are "intermittently" political) are peculiar, as they take decisions going well beyond the boundaries of the institution itself. For that reason, those who are the objects of these decisions affect the extent to which the institution achieves what its leaders may wish it to do. Thus, to a degree at least and indeed to a varying degree depending on the regime, the political culture, and the circumstances, the extent of support for the institution needs to be taken into account alongside its structure.

It is because support cannot fail but to play a part in the context of political institutions that institutionalization has a peculiar and indeed a peculiarly important character in the political context. Yet, while the introduction of support in the equation renders the analysis of institutionalization in politics more realistic, it seems to complicate further the question of a definition of institutions in the political context: This is because the question arises as to whether political institutions can be examined independently from the support which they might enjoy. Is a political organization or procedure still an institution even if it does not have support or has only very little support? Are political institutions conditional on them enjoying support?

It seems prima facie unrealistic to tie the very existence of political institutions to the support which they might have: Institutions are organizations or procedures, as we saw, characterized by "stable, valued, recurring patterns of behaviour" (Goodin 1996, 21). Support seems extraneous to these characteristics: The way an institutional arrangement is shaped does not seem to depend on the support for that arrangement. Moreover, if support is brought into the picture, since support is never "total," the question arises as to what is the threshold below which the extent of support would be too small for the arrangement to be an institution. The difficulties are such that one is tempted to conclude that what makes an arrangement an institution, in politics as elsewhere, is merely whether that arrangement is a "stable, valued and recurring pattern of behavior."

It does seem prima facie reasonable to claim that governments, legislatures, parties, indeed constitutions, exist as institutions even with very few followers and need coercion to remain in being; But it is also doubtful as to whether, in the extreme case of the near-complete collapse of such bodies, one can still refer to them as "institutions," unless one comes to the conclusion that one must distinguish between institutions and institutionalization. The government of a regime on the verge of collapse is clearly "de-institutionalized:" Such a government seems therefore to be no more than a "pseudo-institution." The point needs to be registered somewhere in the description of the organization or procedure under consideration. Perhaps this is the reason why, deep down, political scientists have found it difficult to define what an institution is and why they have in some ways felt more at home with the concept of institutionalization than with the concept of institution.

Much work manifestly needs to be done before a coherent conception can be expected to be found of what institutions consist of. Given the major differences among the social sciences as to what institutions appear to be, however, it is probably more realistic to undertake disciplinary efforts before an overall social science view of institutions is elaborated. There is no doubt that the notion refers to highly distinct realities in economics, sociology, and politics. True to their traditions, economists are able to simplify the concept and reduce it to what seems a homogeneous viewpoint. True to their traditions, too, political scientists are confronted with "big rocks in the landscape," such as governments, legislatures, parties: They cannot deny the importance of these bodies nor can they reduce these "rocks," despite valiant efforts made by some, to sets of homogeneous arrangements. Sociologists are somewhere between these two extremes, depending on whether they focus on a huge number of relatively small bodies or on a relatively small number of large ones. The differences in the character of institutions are directly connected to differences in the nature of the institutionalization process, thus further complicating the picture and making it even more difficult, if not wholly unrealistic, to look for an overall picture. What difficulties and differences suggest is that the dearth of studies on the nature of institutions, except until very recently, is not just a puzzle needing a solution, but a serious gap in our understanding of social life, as studies of institutions and institutionalization are likely to provide major clues about key variations in approach among the social sciences.

References

Almond, G. A. and Coleman, J. S. 1960. *The Politics of the Developing Areas*. Princeton, NJ: Princeton University Press.

—— and Powell, G. B. 1966. *Comparative Politics*. Boston: Little, Brown.

Barry, P. B. and Foweraker, J. (eds.) 2001. *Encyclopedia of Democratic Thought*. London: Routledge.

Easton, D. 1953. *The Political System*. New York: Knopf.

—— 1965. *A Systems Analysis of Political Life*. New York: Wiley.

Finer, S. E. 1993. *A History of Government*, 3 vols. Oxford: Oxford University Press.

Goodin, R. E. (ed.) 1996. *The Theory of Institutional Design*. Cambridge: Cambridge University Press.

—— and Klingemann, H.-D. 1996. (eds.) *A New Handbook of Political Science*. Oxford: Oxford University Press.

Huntington, S. P. 1968. *Political Order in Changing Societies*. New Haven, Conn.: Yale University Press.

Lane, J. E. and Ersson, S. 1999. *Politics and Society in Western Europe*, 4th edn. Los Angeles: Sage.

—— —— 2000. *The New Institutional Politics*. London: Routledge.

Lawson, K. 1985. *The Human Polity*. Boston: Houghton Mifflin.

March, J. G. and Olsen, J. P. 1984. The new institutionalism. *American Political Science Review*, 78: 734–49.

—— —— 1989. *Rediscovering Institutions*. New York: Free Press.

North, D. C. 1990. *Institutions, Institutional Change and Economic Performance*. Cambridge: Cambridge University Press.

Parsons, T. 1954. *Essays in Sociological Theory*, rev. edn. Glencoe, Ill.: Free Press.

Polsby, N. W. 1962. The institutionalisation of the House of Representatives. *American Political Science Review*, 62: 144–68.

SARTORI, G. (ed.) 1980. *Social Science Concepts.* London: Sage.

SCOTT, W. R. 1995. *Institutions and Organisations,* London: Sage.

STINCHCOMBE, A. L. 1968. *Constructing Social Interests.* Chicago: University of Chicago Press.

TRUMAN, D. B. 1962. *The Governmental Process.* New York: Knopf.

ZUCKER, L. G. 1977. The role of institutionalisation in cultural perspective. *American Sociological Review,* 42 (5): 726–43.

....

CHAPTER 37

THINKING
INSTITUTIONALLY

....

HUGH HECLO

By the mid-twentieth century, intellectual and cultural currents were taking an increasingly dim view of institutions.

My first introduction to this fact came courtesy of Yale University's splendid graduate department of political science in the mid-1960s. Sitting at the head of our seminar tables were leading lights in political science's version of the "behavioral revolution:" Robert Dahl, Karl Deutsch, Robert Lane, Charles Lindblom, David Danelski, James Barber, and even the aged Harold Laswell. There we dutifully read Truman, Key, Schattsneider, all of whom we learned were drawing on the much earlier insights of the mysterious Arthur Bentley. Government was the process of adjustment among groups. With that insight, institutions faded into the background and process came to the fore. Corwin on the presidency's powers was out; Neustadt on presidential power was in. At best, the formal legal framework represented by institutions offered an insufficient picture of reality. A more accurate understanding of an institution's reality had to be built up from observation of the interactions of people participating in it. One gets "nowhere" by taking an institution for what it purports to be. The norms of official behavior had the quality of myth, of values that were professed but not necessarily practiced (Truman 1963, 263, 351). From here, our impatient young minds nimbly jumped to the conclusion that professed values were of no value.

I soon learned that behind the social science of the time lay much deeper cultural currents. As the various liberation movements of the 1960s swept through Yale (unknown to me, undergraduates George W. Bush and John Kerry were down the street prepping for the later culture wars) the view of institutions became even dimmer. Critical theory taught us that we were living amidst the "colonization of the lifeworld by the system" (Habermas 1984, 988). The duty seemed to be to rebel against the system—another name for the Establishment, power structure, or just plain institutions. Whether or not you let your hair grow long, any thinking person knew that institutions represented the blighted life of mid-twentieth-century "organization man"—the people "who have left home, spiritually as well as physically, to take the vows of organization life, and it is they who are the mind and soul of our great self-perpetuating institutions" (Whyte 1956, 3). Institutions were purely instruments of social control, end of story. Even before the arrival of the immense modern power structures of industrial production, consumption, transportation, the state, and media, the Romantics we studied in political theory class had gotten it right. Institutions were about chains. The liberation mentality of the 1960s had already been given voice in Rousseau's *Emile*:

Civil man is born, lives, and dies in slavery. At his birth he is sewed in swaddling clothes; at this death he is nailed in a coffin. So long as he keeps his human shape, he is enchained by our institutions. (Rousseau 1979, 43)

Needless to say, I was only vaguely aware of the paradox in all this. I was learning, on one hand, to be dismissive of institutions as mere formalities of textbook description, and on the other hand to be afraid of institutions as oppressive structures of overweening power. Some very smart people, the 1960s' descendents of the Romantic movement, were telling me to "raise my consciousness" and see institutions as vehicles for "institutionalized" racism, sexism, consumerism, militarism, and the like. Other very smart people, descendents of the Enlightenment, were telling me that institutions were merely social techniques we invented and reformed at will to meet our goals. In short, institutions were both the icing on the cake of behavioral reality and the iron cages of social control.

The 1980s saw the arrival of a "new institutionalism" in the social sciences (March and Olson 1984; Cammack 1992). Political scientists talked about "bringing the state back in," which seemed a good thing for political scientists to do (Evans, Rueschemeyer, and Skocpol 1985). Sociologists found that organizational theories needed to consider institutions, and that too seemed a very good thing (Zucker 1987). Economists pondered anew the fact that economic actions might be embedded in structured social relations (Granovetter 1985) and then pondered if the "new institutional economics" was really much better than the "old institutional economics" of John R. Commons (Andersen and Bregn 1992). Some left the fraternity altogether and started calling their field socioeconomics (Stern 1993).

It seems to me that all of these ways of talking about institutions represent a worthy endeavor occupying the minds of very erudite people. But if that is all scholars are doing, it also seems to me that something important is missing. It is missing not simply in an intellectual sense, but in a human sense of what it is we need to pass on to younger people to help them get their bearings. What is missing is the understanding that comes from working from the inside out. Very intelligent academics have much to say about institutions from the outside, but what it is it like to be on the inside, to be thinking institutionally?

To think about science is not the same thing as thinking with a scientific mind. To think about marriage is not necessarily to think like a married person, and similarly, to think about Christianity is not equivalent to having, as Paul put it, the mind of Christ Jesus "in you" (Philippians 2:5). So too, thinking about institutions is not the same thing as thinking institutionally. "Thinking about" does not tell us what it is like for a person to go around with presuppositions of things institutional in his or her head. In fact, "thinking about" may actually diminish capacities for thinking institutionally. It has the effect of confining a person to a subject/object relationship, never telling you what it means to inhabit mentally the world presented by institutions. This outside-in vs. inside-out distinction matters because, while thinking about institutions is an academic's intellectual project, thinking institutionally is something that people do or do not do in the real world—at the office, in their family relations, at the polls, in talking about the news at the local diner. Whatever academics may say about institutions, an institutional way of thinking—and its absence—has consequences.

Thus, my self-appointed task here is to describe a way of thought that comes with being inside an institutional frame of mind and looking out. This mental interiority amounts to an "appreciative system" (Vickers 1965). The term appreciation does not necessarily mean an attitude of gratitude (though as we shall see there is that at work). It means a coherent, sensitive awareness in making judgments. I may not "appreciate" your singing but I can "appreciate" that it is a song we both know that you are trying to sing. Such an interpretive approach trains its attention on what institutions, actions, images, and so on mean to those whose institutions, actions, images they are (Geertz 1983).

To make this appreciative system more attractive to modern sensibilities, it is very tempting to tone down the ostensibly alien quality of institutional thinking. I hope to resist that temptation. By seeing the elements of institutional thinking in their starkest form, we may really begin to get the idea of the thing. Unminced words may even spark the thought that perhaps it is non-institutional rather than institutional thinking that is quite strange. Institutional thinking is undramatic, unassuming, and unfashionable. That helps explain why we hear so little about it.

1   WHAT IS IT TO THINK INSTITUTIONALLY?

Just as human speech is always a matter of speaking some specific language, so institutional thinking always occurs in the context of some particular institution.

Neglecting this particularity, there is only so much that reasonably can be said on the subject. But some things can be said, and the task here is to try and distil elements in the common essence of institutional thinking. The institution in question may be an organized social structure (such as the family, court system, or church) or a social practice (such as marriage, rules of legal procedure, or religious ritual). Here we are trying to sketch the coherence and significance of mental life inside any and all such institutions. The four points are obviously overlapping; they probably have to do so in order to constitute a system for appreciating the world.[1]

1.1   What Institutional Thinking is Not

We might begin by observing what institutional thinking is not. It is not critical thinking, as intellectuals use that term today. In other words, the central impulse is not to question rigorously and challenge everything presented. It does not have the "critical" agenda to unmask, demystify, and expose the real from the apparent. Against all modern trends, institutional thinking is not focused on a "hermeneutics of suspicion" (Stewart 1989). On the contrary, institutional thinking offers some good reasons to be rather suspicious of unremitting suspicion.

By beginning this way, one risks burning bridges to any well-schooled reader. The widespread assumption and teaching throughout academia is that the only kind of real thinker is the critical thinker. A constantly questioning, skeptical awareness is taken to be the very hallmark of intelligence. However, the truth is that modern intellectuals, who are the sort of people who write about institutions, are a peculiar social type with a particular outlook. They champion the idea of self-consciously thinking about and questioning everything we are doing, while—just like the rest of us—most of their lives are filled with doing things from habit. Since there is much about thinking institutionally that is not focused on thinking critically about what you are doing, the conventional intellectual perspective subtly but consistently devalues institutions. It does so by missing or holding in low esteem one of their central operations, which is internalizing norms to the point of habitual practice. As one of the more exceptional intellectuals put it almost a century ago:

It is a profoundly erroneous truism, repeated by all copybooks and by eminent people when they are making speeches, that we should cultivate the habit of thinking of what we are doing. The precise opposite is the case. Civilization advances by extending the number of important operations which we can perform without thinking about them. (Whitehead 1911, 61)

---

[1] Here I leave aside the question of whether or how institutions themselves might "think." See Douglas 1986.

If we leave it at this, institutional thinking risks quickly degenerating into simple conformity either to what someone else tells you to do or what everyone else is doing. That is the sort of conformity which some see in the modern decline of culture, and it is precisely against such a loss of "will to meaning" that institutions stand guard (Frankl 1993). Modern prejudices to the contrary, thinking institutionally is still thinking. Rather than being mindless, it means being mindful in certain ways. It means exercising a particular form of attentiveness to the world.

1.2   Institutional Thinking as Faithful Reception

As a basic stance toward life, institutional thinking understands itself to be in a position of receiving rather than of inventing or creating. The emphasis is not on thinking up things for yourself, but on faithfully taking delivery of and using what has been handed down to you. Because the known ways are valued, there is no special premium given to novelty, newness, or originality for its own sake.

Here too, modern minds can find this emphasis on receiving to be quite strange, to say the least. When some issue arises, we expect to consult different opinions, consider alternatives, and come up with a working solution, preferably something new and innovative. From the institutionalist perspective, things are different. What has been received from those who preceded carries authority. It is precisely the authority of what has been given to us that makes it an institution that is at work in our minds/lives, rather than some passing arrangement or mood of convenience.

This does not mean closing off thought or any form of innovation. Quite the contrary. Precisely because it regards itself as a legatee of something of great value, institutional thinking eagerly seeks to understand what has been received in light of new circumstances that are always intruding. To be submissive to what has been received is a distinctly unfashionable idea, but it does not mean being servile. Because some things are regarded as fixed (such as the essential mission of a business, the ritual of a church, or in a politician like Lincoln's case, the ideal of the Union), there is something against which to be adaptable.

1.3   Institutional Thinking as Infusions of Value

It has been famously observed that to institutionalize something is to "infuse with value beyond the technical requirements of the task at hand" (Selznick 1957, 17). This is a helpful view because it points toward the distinction between strictly instrumental attachments needed to get a particular job done and the deeper commitments that express one's enduring loyalty to some group or process. However, institutional thinking requires us to go a good deal farther down this path.

That becomes clear if we ask where the infusion of value is coming from. If it is simply the individual actor at work, then we are implicitly relegating institutions to objects of psychological purchase that people choose to make based on some sort of pleasure/pain criteria. For example, the devout baseball fan may infuse the game with value, "getting a kick out of it" over and beyond any particular game his team is playing. Yet, it is also clear that the fanatical team fan may have little interest in and may actually behave in ways harmful to baseball as an institution. In other words, institutional thinking is about value diffusion as well as infusion. Institutions diffuse values beyond the personal preferences for the task at hand. They make claims on one's thinking to acknowledge, and then through choices and conduct to realize, a normative order.

Institutions embody what Charles Taylor has termed "strong evaluations." As he puts it, these "involve discriminations of right or wrong, better or worse, higher or lower, which are not rendered valid by our own desires, inclinations or choices, but rather stand independent of these and offer standards by which they can be judged" (Taylor 1989, 4). These intrinsic (rather than extrinsic) values imply relations of obligation, not convenience. They demand that primary attention be given what is appropriate rather than what is expedient. From inside the institutional world-view one not only thinks about but is moved by a central fact—that there is something estimable that is larger than yourself and your immediate interests. In approaching a situation the question is not, how can I get what I want? It is the more duty-laden question of, what expectations and conduct are appropriate to my position? Of what am I to be an example?

A prominent example in modern times has been the development of professions and formal professional standards. To invoke claims of professionalism is to appeal to standards for guiding and judging conduct that lie beyond our individual preferences. In recent years many people have tended think of a profession as a group monopolizing a body of knowledge or practicing specialized techniques. However, if this is all a profession means, it lacks the institutional quality we are discussing here. The institutional thinking embodied in any true profession is the remnant of much older ideas having to do with "office" and "vocation." It is the attitude of responding to a call from beyond yourself. More than simply acquiring a body of knowledge or techniques, one enters into a professional lore such that applying this or that technique fits into a normative scheme of things.

Of course, it is common these days to hear complaints about the behavior of lawyers, doctors, teachers, and others. However, even the most cynical lawyer or doctor jokes are, in a backhanded way, affirming strong evaluations that should be guiding the delinquent practitioners of modern professions. Likewise, when one hears complaints about higher education or a news organization losing its soul to economic market forces, the assumption is that there really is a soul to lose. However obliquely, all such criticisms are pointing to a belief that in talking about the university, or lawyering, or news journalism at its "truest and best," one is talking about something real (Kirp 2005; Cuban 2004; Linowitz 1999). Even the churchy hypocrite, by not being himself on Sunday, is indirectly testifying to the standard of a higher and truer self.

1.4 Institutional Thinking as Lengthened Time Horizons

It follows from earlier points that institutional thinking also involves being mindful about time in a particular way. To think institutionally is to stretch the time horizon backward and forward. One senses the shadows of both past and future lengthening into the present. This outlook is typically expressed by being attentive to precedent. Unfortunately, to modern ears that term evokes the image of being controlled by the "dead hand of the past."

A more adequate view of institutional thinking understands precedent as a form of solidarity. Choices made in the present serve to strengthen or erode solidarity among an "us" that is peopled by the living, the dead, and the yet unborn. Because there are attachments through time, institutional thinking means living an implicated life, always both receiving and bequeathing. Decisions made in the present are under the obligations of usufruct, the sense that one is enjoying the fruits of something belonging to predecessors and successors. Therefore, while change is inevitable, it is embedded in a strong appreciation for what has gone on before and what will go on after you are gone. Inheritance keeps finding fresh work. To put it another way, institutional thinking restrains conduct by making it beholden to its own past history and to the history it is creating. The present is never only the present. It is one moment in a going concern.

Thus institutional thinking values continuity and long-term over short-term calculations. Even within the realm of economics, it understands the world in terms of ongoing customer markets not pointillistic auction markets (Okun 1981). The focus in institutional thinking is on enduring relationships rather than point-in-time transactions. This idea is illustrated by the story of three major highways donated to the development program in Nepal by American, Indian, and Chinese governments. The Americans imported an immense fleet of heavy equipment, quickly pushed the road through to completion, and departed, leaving most of the machinery behind with no skilled operators to use it. With the Indians came a large labor force. This labor force was organized into construction camps, which moved along the highway until they reached the road's destination and left. The Chinese brought in foremen who recruited and trained village workers for each section of the highway. These checkerboard sections were worked on in relays, leaving behind experienced straw bosses and workers in each locale. Each of the three highways was completed as planned, but only one had any prospects for sustained maintenance (Montgomery 1983, 99).

2   WHY MIGHT ANY OF THIS MATTER

Without institutional thinking to make them real, institutions truly are little more than unpopulated, empty formalities. No one really lives there. The firm, the political body, the university, the marriage—all so-called institutions become sites for transient, interpersonal transactions with no deeper, more enduring meanings. Institutions have been described as solutions grown by cultural evolution, often seeming to take shape planlessly like coral reefs (Sait 1938). If this is even partially true, then it would be imprudent, to put it mildly, to regard institutional thinking as something archaic and unimportant.

At the societal level, there is the basic matter of sustainability and survival. We began by considering the most elemental form of institutional thinking, the habit of not critically thinking about what you are doing but simply carrying on with your job in the unexamined larger scheme of things. The steady habits (not the same thing as addictive behavior) have immense survival value for society at large. Institutional thinking habits are implicit testimony to and support for the value of the going concern of the social order. The multitude of nameless people "just doing my job" amounts to a sheet anchor sustaining civilized life together, something we are never likely to notice until disaster strikes.

The scale of such sustaining work ranges from the most personal home life to the massive social structures of civilization itself. To grab for the family photo album when the house catches fire is an elemental act of this mentality. At the other extreme, history offers compelling examples of societies surviving through devastating cataclysms by virtue of ordinary people simply carrying on with appointed duties. One historian has noted the similar grounds of social survival in the atomic bombing of Japan and the Black Death in fourteenth-century Europe: "In the worst years of the mortality, Europeans witness horrors comparable to Hiroshima and Nagasaki, but even when death was everywhere and only a fool would dare to hope, the thin fabric of civilization held.... Enough notaries, municipal and church authorities, physicians and merchants stepped forward to keep governments and courts and churches and financial houses running—albeit at a much reduced level" (Kelly 2004, 16).

In ordinary times as well, institutional thinking has great value in the political councils of society as a going concern. It tends to interject several kinds of reality checks into any decision-making. The first is a voice independent of the claims of personal power. This voice may be inside the leader's head or it may be standing in front of him. The former is illustrated by President Lincoln's determination to hold the scheduled 1864 election as scheduled, despite being in the midst of a deteriorating civil war and the strong likelihood of his own defeat. Lincoln understood that regardless of his personal political fate, the cause of constitutional government under the Union would already be defeated if the election were cancelled or postponed. The latter embodiment of institutional thinking in a staff person is illustrated by an incident from FDR's presidency. Rudolph Forster had been in the White House since the McKinley administration and as Executive Clerk had seen presidents come and go. When, in October 1944, FDR left on one of his last campaign trips, Foster, with a guilty air, shook the president's hand warmly and wished him good luck. As Foster waved goodbye to the departing car, Roosevelt told his companion, with pride and real emotion in his voice, "That's practically the first time in all these years that Rudolph has ever stepped out of character and spoken to me as if I were a human being instead of just another President" (Sherwood 1950, 209). Roosevelt, who had had special legislation passed to allow Foster to stay on indefinitely past the legal retirement age, understood that with at least some people around you who are thinking institutionally, there is a greater chance of being told what you need to hear rather than simply what you want to hear.

A second reality check is institutional thinking's protection against the willful ignorance called presentism, the arrogant belief in the privileged entitlements and moral superiority attached to one's own little moment in time. Institutional thinking transforms the past into memory, which is a way of keeping alive what is meaningful about people's deepest hopes and fears. "As such, memory is another evidence that we have a flexible and creative relation to time, the guiding principle being not the clock but the qualitative significance of our experiences" (May 1953, 258). Likewise, institutional thinking transforms the future into a present voice by a concern for passing on what has been received. Memory and anticipation speak together in the present tense.

One could go on listing various advantages of institutional thinking in politics and society at large. Because it is attentive to rule-following rather than personal strategies to achieve personal ends, thinking institutionally enhances predictability in conduct. Predictability in turn can enhance trust, which can enhance reciprocating loyalty, which can facilitate bargaining, compromise, and fiduciary relationships. Because institutional thinking goes beyond merely contingent, instrumental attachments, it takes daily life into something deeper than a passing parade of personal moods and feelings.

In the end, the advantages of institutional thinking come down to what is distinctly human. The point is not that it is wrong to see institutions as cages of human oppression, but that this is a dangerously incomplete half-truth.

Institutions can also be the instruments for human liberation and enriched, flourishing lives. As several authors have put it, "we live through institutions" (Bellah 1991, ch. 1). For example, without institutions upholding private property, even the most liberated individual will soon find his or her freedom an empty slogan. But it goes beyond that. By its nature, institutional thinking tends to cultivate belonging and a common life. It leads to collective action that not only controls but also expands and liberates individual action. Humans flourish as creatures of attachments, not unencumbered selves. Growing up detached from the authoritative communities that social institutions are, children exhibit signs of deteriorating mental and behavioral health (Commission on Children at Risk 2003). Without a similar deep connectedness, individuals also age and die poorly by the standards of human dignity. What Rousseau depicted as enchaining were in fact signs of human nurturing. The swaddling clothes and coffin testify that humans are something more than beasts dropped in the field or left dead by the roadside.

Works of modern fiction routinely portray rebellion against institutions as courageous adventures of liberation. The promise is perfect freedom. The truth found in any reliable work of non-fiction—whether it is history, biography, or current events—is that a life without institutions becomes a perfect hell. A life without institutional thinking tends toward self-destructive excesses, at the center of which is the ultimate excess, the overweening Self-Life. Without authority for freedom to play against, the adventure itself is extinguished into existential nothingness.

Obviously, I have emphasized only the positive aspects of institutional thinking. There is, of course, another side. For example, in terms of criminal activity, the Mafia is an outstanding example of institutional thinking across the generations. Depending on the overall goals and the operative conduct of people in a particular institution, the implications for human flourishing may be positive, negative, or indifferent. To live in a world of nothing but institutional thinking would be a monstrosity. By the same token, to live in a world where institutional thinking is absent, or so heavily discounted as to fade into insignificance, would also be a monstrosity.

To me at least, the evidence from the current scene is clear. The great danger is not too much but too little institutional thinking. To test that proposition, one might consider the common lamentations about any given realm of contemporary life—the scandals in accounting firms and news organizations; the sports figures and businessmen who put short-term gain ahead of the sport and the business; the loss of stature and trust in legal, medical, and teaching professions; the marriages deinstitutionalized into contracts of mere mutual convenience; the politicians who blithely mortgage the future, and the citizens who let them. Amid all the particular complaints, we do not seem to perceive the larger fact that we are living amid the rubble produced by an indifference and even aversion to thinking institutionally about our affairs. In one realm after another, modern minds find it much easier and more tempting to shun institutional commitments. Here we might adopt the pragmatic test espoused by critical thinkers and ask ourselves: how is that working?

Trying to think institutionally, I believe that a good question for the leader of any major public or private enterprise to put to himself or herself is this: Would I want to be my own successor in this office? An equally good question for each generation to ask itself is: Are we producing a world we would want to inherit? If the answers are no, it is time to think, and then act, differently.

References

ANDERSEN, O. and BREGN, K. 1992. New institutional economics: what does it have to offer? *Review of Political Economy,* 4: 484–97.

BELLAH, R., MADSEN, RICHARD, MADSEN, ROBERT, and TIPTON, S. 1991. *The Good Society,* New York: Knopf.

CAMMACK, P. 1992. The new institutionalism. *Economy and Society,* 21: 397–429.

COMMISSION ON CHILDREN AT RISK 2003. *Hardwired to Connect: The New Scientific Case for Authoritative Communities.* New York: Institute for American Values.

CUBAN, L. 2004. *The Blackboard and the Bottom Line: Why Schools Can't Be Businesses.* Cambridge, Mass.: Harvard University Press.

DOUGLAS, M. 1986. *How Institutions Think.* Syracuse, NY: Syracuse University Press.

EVANS, P., RUESCHEMEYER, D., and SKOCPOL, T. (eds.) 1985. *Bringing the State Back In.* New York: Cambridge University Press.

FRANKL, V. 1993. *Man's Search for Meaning.* New York: Pocket Books; orig. pub. 1963.

GEERTZ, C. 1983. *Local Knowledge.* New York: Basic Books.

GRANOVETTER, M. 1985. Economic action and social structure. *American Journal of Sociology,* 91: 481–510.

HABERMAS, J. 1984. *The Theory of Communicative Action.* Boston: Beacon Press.

KELLY, J. 2004. *The Great Mortality.* New York: HarperCollins.

KIRP, D. L. 2005. *Shakespeare, Einstein, and the Bottom Line: The Marketing of Higher Education.* Cambridge, Mass.: Harvard University Press.

LINOWITZ, S. M. 1999. *The Betrayed Profession: Lawyering at the End of the Twentieth Century.* New York: Scribners.

MARCH, J. and OLSEN, J. 1984. The new institutionalism. *American Political Science Review,* 78: 734–49.

MAY, R. 1953. *Man's Search for Himself.* New York: Norton.

MONTGOMERY, J. D. 1983. When local participation helps. *Journal of Policy Analysis and Management,* 3: 90–105.

OKUN, A. 1981. *Prices and Quantities.* Washington, DC: Brookings.

ROUSSEAU, J. J. 1979. *Emile: Or on Education.* New York: Basic Books; orig. pub. 1762.

SAIT, E. 1938. *Political Institutions.* New York: Appleton.

SELZNICK, P. 1957. *Leadership in Administration*. Berkeley: University of California Press.

SHERWOOD, R. E. 1950. *Roosevelt and Hopkins*. New York: Harper and Brothers.

STERN, P. 1993. The socio-economic perspective and its institutional prospects. *Journal of Socio-Economics*, 22: 1–11.

STEWART, D. 1989. The hermeneutics of suspicion. *Journal of Literature and Theology*, 3: 296–307.

TAYLOR, C. 1989. *Sources of the Self*. Cambridge, Mass.: Harvard University Press.

TRUMAN, D. 1963. *The Governmental Process*. New York: Knopf.

VICKERS, SIR G. 1965. *The Art of Judgment*. New York: Basic Books.

WHITEHEAD, A. N. 1911. *An Introduction to Mathematics*. New York: Holt.

WHYTE, W. H., JR. 1956. *The Organization Man*. New York: Simon and Schuster.

ZUCKER, L. G. 1987. Institutional theories of organization. *Annual Review of Sociology*, 13: 443–64.

CHAPTER 38

POLITICAL INSTITUTIONS—OLD AND NEW

KLAUS VON BEYME

"Political institutions—old and new" as a topic has two dimensions: The evolution of old and new institutions and the reflection of these developments in political theory. There is, however, an asymmetry of these dimensions.

1 FROM OLD TO NEW INSTITUTIONS

Few really "new institutions" developed in the three waves of democratization after 1789. The three major branches of public life existed not only in Montesquieu's theory, but their weight had shifted, especially in tune with the decline of *monarchical power*. The first old institution which spread all over the world—with the exception of the United Kingdom—was the "*constitution*," mostly considered as an emanation of the popular will, and since 1918 frequently submitted for ratification by a popular referendum. The revolutionary constitutions in France (since 1792) and in the United States (in 1787) did not completely break with the institutions of the pre-revolutionary regime, but adapted them to the needs of representative—and later when universal suffrage was accepted—democratic government. Constitutions by the conservatives of the early nineteenth century were considered as "revolutionary institutions." But under the threat of revolution various forms of adaptation of this institution by the existing monarchies took place. Constitutions were either imposed by monarchs (*octroi*), as the Piedmontese "Statuto Albertino" of 1849 which was to become the constitution of the kingdom of Italy, or negotiated by legislatures and monarchs (France 1792, Spain 1810, and in many European territories after 1815). Even dictatorships normally adapted some kind of constitution, including a bill of rights which the regime rarely respected.

Old assemblies of "estates" were transformed into *modern parliaments*, sometimes as late as 1866 in Sweden. Various forms of advisers to the crown developed into a *modern cabinet* with a *"prime minister."* Important institutional changes were grounded not so much in the internal change of institutions, but in their mutual relationship within the system. The major institutional innovation was the development of dependence of cabinets on the confidence of parliamentary majorities over almost one century. It happened in systems with continuity of former estate systems (Britain, final conflict 1832, Netherlands 1868, Sweden 1917). New institutions were created by new revolutionary systems which established *parliamentary responsibility of governments* (France and Belgium 1831). Parliamentarization of neoabsolutist regimes was normally late—with the exception of Italy (1860). The latest latecomers in this group were Germany and Austria (1918). Parliamentarization did not evolve in harmony with the extension of voting rights. *Suffrage* in the first parliamentary systems on the continent was hardly above 1–2 percent. Germany introduced universal suffrage as early as 1871, but full parliamentary responsibility of governments followed only in 1918 (von Beyme 2000, 28).

Most regimes in the nineteenth century were dualistic constitutional monarchies. Revolutions which led to a republican system—as in France in 1848, in Germany and Finland in 1918—tried to find a republican equivalent for a system with a president elected by popular vote and not depending on parliamentary majorities. Only in the Fifth French Republic was this type of government dubbed a *"semi-presidential regime."* Frequently it evolved in a constitution making process with extensive debates on the virtues of the American "presidential system." Finally a European compromise led to a hybrid of parliamentary systems in which the prime minister and the cabinet depended on parliamentary votes and the president was equipped with the right to dissolve parliament as a counterweight against permanently hostile legislative majorities (von Beyme 1987, 33ff).

Two major institutions had existed already in Ancient Rome but developed into powerful organizations which penetrated the whole life of society: bureaucracy and parties. *Bureaucracy* for Max Weber was the dominant institution of modernization. *Parties*—frequently discriminated as unpleasant extra-constitutional and anomic institutions under the label of "factions"—only in modern times became the basic element which coordinated all the institutions of the state.

An exception to the "nothing-new-under-the-sun approach" to institutions was the success story of *constitutional courts*. This institution was new only if we exclude the functional equivalent of the American Supreme Court which developed— not completely in tune with the ideas of most founding fathers of the constitution —judicial review of legislative acts from its seminal decision *Marbury* vs. *Madison* in 1803. In the light of former colonial history, the USA did not accept special courts because the American states were afraid of a continuation of the "Star chamber proceedings" of the British Crown. Not even a special constitutional court was feasible. Therefore the drafters of the American constitution deliberately did not accept "abstract judicial review." The Supreme Court was the least democratic decision-making body and it was meant by the Federalists to serve—like the Senate—as another check on volatile democratic decisions in an elitist deliberating institution with no direct access for the people.

It is an exaggeration that judicial review after 1945 was accepted "at the point of a gun" (Martin Shapiro). Only Japan followed the American model. In Europe the "Austrian model" was accepted, developed by Hans Kelsen in 1920–1. Kelsen (1922, 55) was inspired by the "Imperial Court" of the "German Confederation" and its revolutionary constitution of 1849 which envisaged already the "constitutional complaint" (§ 126 f, g). This type of judicial review became prominent in the European model, which largely followed the German example. A variation of a constitutional court sprang up even in political cultures such as France in the "conseil constitutionnel"—a country which originally was hostile to the very idea of "judicial review" against laws and acts of "the state" because it contradicted the French republican tradition of popular sovereignty.

Some institutions spread from one area to others, such as the *ombudsman*. This office was not really new. Ombudsmen were even remainders of pre-democratic enlightened absolute rule as a safety valve for individual complaints. New institutions such as *planning authorities* were developed in an era of a rational optimism that society can be shaped by the state. But they withered away in the wave of neoliberalism, which followed the collapse of Communist systems and the high days of the welfare state. New institutions with a political impact were also developed to guarantee a balance between the economic institutions. A *national bank* and *committees for the control over monopolies* gained influence. The market system no longer looked for democratic socialist institutional schemes but tried indirectly to steer the economy by independent institutions.

Institutional theories always developed in cycles after revolutions (1789, 1830, 1848, 1871, 1918, 1945). Never did so many regimes break down at one time as in 1989. Never were so many regimes transformed from one fairly uniform Communist institutional type to another fairly uniform type of Western democracy.

Special national roads of development to democracy were no longer hailed, as in the period after the First World War. At no time did so many countries launch an institutional debate as in the "new democracies." "*Constitutional engineering*" became the highly misleading basic term of the new branch of "transitology" in the third wave of democratization (Sartori 1994). Grandpa's institutionalist political science was again in vogue. Old-fashioned debates on the preference of semi-presidentialism vs. parliamentary systems were revitalized. Old institutions such as the one-party monopoly, the collective presidium of the legislature as an equivalent to Western presidents, planning offices, the wide range of competences of a "*prokuratura*" which was more than a prosecuting attorney, and the gigantic bureaucracies of state security had to disappear. The new institutions, however, were the old ones—mostly institutions from Western countries. The most influential institutions proved to be the French semi-presidential system and the German Constitutional Court. Many details of institutions were copied from a 5 percent threshold for parties during elections to electoral laws, votes of constructive non-confidence, and abstract judicial review (von Beyme 1996, 98f).

2   THE EVOLUTION OF THEORIES OF INSTITUTIONS

2.1   Theories and Methodological Approaches to Institutions

Theories tended to be changing more quickly than the institutions they had pretended to analyze. Quite frequently theories of institutions lagged behind the real functioning of a system, such as Montesquieu's doctrine which ignored the institutions of parties and adhered to a schematic view of the British system. Some older theories of politics started from the assumption that political science as a whole works with an institutional approach, whereas sociology emphasizes the aspect of stratification (Allardt 1969, 17). This assumption was never correct. Even older approaches combined "elite"—a more important notion in American social sciences than "class"—predominant in European sociology with institutional studies. This concept neglected the necessary differentiation between theory and method. Elites or stratification are basic notions of social theory. The institutional approach, on the other hand, belongs to the methods of political science. A theory can be falsified. Methods, however, survive even if certain theories which have been applied with the help of certain methods proved to be wrong. The institutional approach is not obsolete when the old institutional paradigm of a "separation of powers" was no longer applicable to modern parliamentary systems. Older institutional theories amalgamated elements of new theories such as the theory of pluralism and methods which went beyond the old-fashioned juridical normative approach to institutions. Theoretical concepts like "pluralism" or "federalism" can be put into empirical operation with institutionalist, behavioralist, or rational choice methods.

Political science initially tried to legitimize itself with a revival of the Aristotelian concept of politics. It tended to favor the institutional approach—compared to eschatological theories of politics from St Augustine to Marx. The virtue of the classical institutional approach was that it started from the assumption that the political process is "open" in principle, and full citizens are basically "equal." No ontological essentialist differences between princes and the people, enlightened elites and humble subjects, or proletarian avant-gardes and the masses were accepted.

Classical institutionalists from Montesquieu to de Tocqueville were never naive ontological analysts but described institutions in comprehensive social settings of a system. Each institution was linked to a special promoting social group. Only rarely were deistic or mechanistic metaphors of a clockwork applied in a formalistic way to political institutions. The "mechanics" of institutions included contradictory elements, such as in inter- and intrainstitutional conflicts in two-chamber systems of parliaments and the difference of government and opposition. Most institutional theories favored a procedural concept of politics. For Max Weber the typical occidental development—deviating from the rest of the world—can be explained by institutional differentiation of religious and secular power. The most interesting institution for Max Weber was the constitution of "cities" which were not mere agglomerations around a power center and which deviated from the pattern of patrimonial and feudal systems of rule ("*Herrschaft*"). From Max Weber to Stein Rokkan "modernization" in politics was basically understood as a process of institution building. Contrary to economic modernization theories, institutions such as bureaucracies or the military were seen as the momentum of modernization. Weberian concepts were influential: bureaucracies were superior to parochial or feudal elites. Beyond Weber some analysts preferred bureaucratized party politics to bureaucratic rule.

A social concept of institutions gradually differed from merely normative legal and political theories. In Britain, Barker (1961, 166) suspected even after 1945 that most institutionalists hailed their preferred institution as a disguise for a cult around a social group. In French legal theory, Maurice Hauriou (1906) tried to avoid this danger of the old institutionalism by the differentiation of "*institution-chose*" having objective dignity and the "*institution-groupe*" suspected of being only disguised selfish group interest. Group theories of institutions were mostly unable to agree on the relative weight of certain institutions. The continental Roman law tradition suggested that "*the state*" was the most important institution, whereas a leftist British tradition from guild-socialism to Harold Laski insisted that the state was just another "collective group". Anglo-Saxon theories—with the exception of some Hegelians in Britain from Thomas H. Green to Bernard Bosanquet—nourished a deep distrust of the notion of the state and rather preferred "*government*" as the central notion for institutional analysis.

The development of institutional theory after 1945 proved to be oscillating between waves of neglect and rediscovery of institutions. The attempt to make political science finally scientific stood against the accepting institutional analysis as the centre of research. The "*new science of politics*" in the USA used the term "institution" in the vague sense of neighboring social sciences, such as sociology or anthropology, as "a pattern composed of culture traits specialized to the shaping and distribution of a particular value (or set of values)" (Lasswell and Kaplan 1950, 47). The "*behavioral revolt*" was directed against the old institutionalism, but did not avoid institutions altogether. Heinz Eulau (1969, 1, 158), a pioneer of the "behavioral persuasion," developed a synthesis of "behavioral-institutional research," mainly concentrated in legislative and judicial studies. Whereas Eulau critically worked on a theory of micro–macro-relations—in spite of the basic individualism of this approach—later behavioralists frequently uncritically generalized the findings on the micro level in the macropolitics of institutions. The "epitaph of a successful protest" which Robert Dahl proclaimed in 1969 was premature in the eyes of later analysts. John C. Wahlke (1979) in his presidential address for the American Political Science Association ten years later was more skeptical. After a quantitative analysis of review articles and research notes in the *American Political Science Review,* he came to the conclusion that old-fashioned institutional studies prevailed even in this journal which was considered to be the "battle organ" of the victorious behavioral revolt.

Behavioralism was accused of lacking theory-building. *Systems theory* hoped to heal this shortcoming. Systems theories in America had the virtue to develop—for the first time since Weber—a generalized theory of institution, overcoming the shortcomings of ad hoc theories in Europe. For Talcott Parsons (1959), deeply influenced by Weber, institutional patterns, perceived in a demystified way, were the backbone of social systems. Only in later variations of the theory of systems did "structures" become more important than institutions. They had, however, no predetermined role. Similar functions within the system were completed by very different structures. The early Luhmann (1965, 13), originally Parsons' devoted disciple but soon a defector who created his own autopoietic version of a theory of systems, still used institutions and structures as synonyma: "Institutions are behavioural expectations generalized in temporal and social dimensions, and thus create the structure of social systems." Systems theory created a new methodological terminology, but on the descriptive level it classified the traditional powers, such as the executive and parliament, adding bureaucracy and parties. They got, however, more scientific names such as "rule-setting," "rule applying," "rule adjudicating," and "rule-enforcing" institutions.

Institutions in the new approaches like behavioralism and functionalism were no longer independent entities and were dealt with—according to research questions as "independent or dependent variables"—just like other elements of analysis. In "*structural functionalism*" the systemic needs of the social system tended to produce political institutions needed to solve the basic problems of any society (Eisenstadt 1965). Thus the analysis ended in a global justification of all the institutions developed in various societies. "*Historical institutionalism*" was closest to treating institutions, such as "the state," as the independent variable. The impact of institutions was studied over time—from the way political groups defined their interests to policy outcomes under various regimes (Steinmo and Longstreth 1992). The old generalization of modernization theories was overcome. Researchers discovered the dependence of policy outcomes on historical institutions and decisions which could not easily be changed by political actors. Policy results proved to be "path dependent." A variety of models—particularly in the field of welfare policies—was discovered (Esping-Andersen 1990). The new institutionalism can better account for the paths that political actors will follow in order to arrive at the prescribed equilibria.

Behavioralism and functionalism were the major foes of the old institutional school represented by Carl J. Friedrich and Herman Finer. The old institutionalism paradoxically got theoretical support from radical political thinkers who opposed the institutions of the existing Western democracies. *Neo-Marxism* and *radical post*-behavioralist approaches brought the "State back in" even in American discussions. But political institutions were always the dependent variable; the independent variable was the economic subsystem of society. Systems theory reacted in a hostile way to the new debate on the state. David Easton (1981, 322), a pioneer in substituting the "political system" to old-fashioned theories of "the state," was afraid that the neoradical wave in political theory from Miliband to Poulantzas might end up in a "romantic backlash" and that the state would start to besiege the political system. Easton's misgivings were exaggerated. Neither neo-Marxism nor neoconservatism elaborated a new metaphysical concept of the state. But since these new approaches concentrated on the economic aspects of the relationship between state and society, they failed to develop a differentiated theory of institutions. At the end of the neoradical movement which had influenced the development of political theories, the holistic theories of the 1960s were approaching each other.

The new wave of the *policy approach* in the 1970s ended in a merger of systems theory and neo-Marxist state theories. A central actor was needed and though many empirical scholars no longer called it "the state," a great variety of actors and their institutions were introduced in order to demonstrate the genesis of a decision—or of a "non-decision." *Network approaches* discovered so many veto-players to avoid the impression that one actor, such as "the state," was still considered as an ontological entity as in some older institutionalist theories (Tsebelis 2002).

The *rational choice school* offered another approach which rediscovered the institutions. The bias of this school was that theory perceived social systems as consisting of only utility-maximizing rational individuals. They engage in strategic interactions which stabilize an equilibrium. This approach was highly quantifiable but its predictive capacities were rather limited because apparently non-rational collective and ideological motives distorted the "necessary outcome" of the prognosis. Political institutions—such as parliamentary groups and their leaders—had to explain why the "normal behavior" within larger institutions, such as parliaments, did not function in the utility-maximizing way the strict individualism of the theory had envisaged. The rational choice approach had the virtue of making cooperation in institutions plausible as far as norms of cooperation were internalized. These norms, however, hardly rise with one institution. They are pre-existing to most institutions, and only historical political culture studies can enlighten us about their genesis. Social institutions apparently determined policy outcome and even the economic performance of systems. *Organizational theory* discovered these institutions in many fields—from legislation to industrial relations (Streeck 1992).

2.2   National Traditions and Transnational Diffusion of Institutions and Theories about Institutions

Institutional theories developed in tune with national traditions of institutions. Continental "statism" has always differed from Anglo-Saxon concepts which did not accept a dogmatic typology of "state and society"—the expression of a historical compromise between monarchy and the legislative powers of "estates"— from Hegel to Lorenz von Stein. In spite of many typologies of the role of institutions in various political cultures, the dynamics of institutional theories were never strictly limited to national traditions. The more radical-minded constitution makers and political theorists worked in their countries, the stronger was the influence of *foreign models*. After 1789 and after 1848 the French model had some impact on the Continent. The French model of a so-called "unauthentic parliamentarianism" later was less attractive than the British model for liberals in Europe. France, moreover, was constitutionally unstable. According to a famous anecdote a British traveler who asked in Paris for the French constitution got the ironical answer from the book dealer: "Sorry, we don't carry periodical literature." The opposite example was the American revolution, frequently admired for its sheer institutional stability over time. For certain parties in Europe the American model was hailed because the American revolution was considered as being only "political"—not aiming at a complete change of social powers in the society as did the French revolutionary model from Hannah Arendt to Dolf Sternberger.

The theory of institutions was strong in American anthropology and developed some impact on the neighboring social sciences. A long debate was launched between "*diffusionists*" who thought that social institutions developed from one center to other areas (Thor Heyerdal even tried to demonstrate the possibility of diffusion of institutions by imitating boat trips from Polynesia to South America) and "*functionalists*"—prevailing in America—who considered the development of social institutions rather as the result of social needs which led to functional equivalents of rather similar institutions. The political debate in the North Atlantic world was, however, more diffusionist than in the realm of cultures preserving only oral traditions. "*Institutional engineering*" in political systems relied on a huge bulk of constitutional models and political theories which shaped them. Conscious adaptations of foreign institutions merged with national traditions since the belief that national institutions "grow" out of national traditions—widely accepted by conservative parties in the nineteenth century—was withering away.

The USA never shared the cult of the state as a major institution. Nevertheless the citizens were more proud of their institutions than in other countries. The study by Almond and Verba (1963, 102) found that 85 percent of Americans were proud of their institutions, but only 46 percent of British, 7 percent of Germans, and 3 percent of Italians. Already one of the first European evaluations of the American system, by Lord Bryce (1888/1959, vol. 1, 1) was puzzled by a typical American question, "What do you think of our institutions?" which he never heard in Britain. American preference for institutions was explained by the lack of a cult of personality and monarchical symbolism.

2.3   Institutional Crises and the Para-theories of Institutions

Later theories had to cope with the fact that attitudes towards institutions are not permanent features of some kind of "national character." Periodical crises of national institutions inspired less the creation of new institutions than the development of new theories on institutions. Most of them hardly deserved the term "theory" and were *ad hoc generalizations* which did not survive in long-term developments. Crisis-mongering leads to much discussed bestsellers in the intellectual sphere which contributed at best para-theories. Cycles of corruption and unlawful practices can undermine basic confidence in the institutions.

Huntington (1981, 4) found a general gap between ideal and institutions—the so-called IvI gap—as "a peculiarly American form of cognitive dissonance." The message was not without hope in post-Watergate America. Ideals of the American creed periodically purify and revitalize American institutions. In other countries another crisis of institutions was criticized. The scenarios were frequently even more pessimistic. New institutions seemed to undermine the old constitutionally guaranteed institutions. The "new social movements" caused fear and misgivings. They may have been centered in Berkeley, Paris, or Berlin, but they spread all over the world and formed loose revolutionary networks.

After the students' riots in the Western world, combined with protests against the Vietnam war, a new wave of crisis-of-institutions theories swept over Western democracies. In Germany sociologists, such as Schelsky (1973, 21), suspected that a "revolutionary march through the institutions" might undermine the system. No systems change happened. The only long-term consequence was that former student rebels in 1998 entered the federal government. Germany, as a country of conservative institutional immobilism, all of a sudden became the "Mecca" for a new institution, the ecological "Green Party."

In France the sociologist Michel Crozier (1970) came to rather far-reaching conclusions with his fear that a society is in danger where institutions block each other and lead to non-decision. Under the temporary pressure of the students' rebellion in 1968, the historical fear sprang up again: that French systems proved to be unable to reform their institutions. The traumatic inspiration from French history which dooms the country to develop by periodical revolutionary systems changes led to a premature prognosis. The French Fifth Republic survived, though de Gaulle withdrew earlier than expected, whereas the Italian system collapsed, but at a time in the early 1990s when the storms of para-revolutionary unrest had calmed down. There was a lot of theory building on a second Italian Republic, but the changes of the system hardly justified speaking of an institutional revolution. The party system was the only institution which was substantially affected by the institutional crisis of the system. The "new Republic" proved to be the "old Republic." The syndicalist enthusiasm for new social movements without bureaucratic structures which endangered established institutions from 1968 was met by new institutional arrangements of the old institutions. "*Neocorporatism*" in northern Europe had to explain why regimes did not collapse in a crisis of institutions. From 1985 to about 1995 no book on the relationship between state and society was successful unless it contained the catchphrase "neocorporatism." Ten years later no book could be sold if it still stuck to this paradigm. Neocorporatism has withered away under the glare of neoliberalism. Together with the term "ungovernability" for which it was meant by Schmitter to serve as a remedy, neocorporatism showed again how short-lived theoretical fashions are— especially in the realm of institutions which invite, more than other subjects, simplistic everyday evidence in the style of theorizing.

3   CONCLUSION

Institutions develop less quickly than theories on institutions. "Historical institutionalism" has demonstrated that institutional traditions are not easy to change. Institutions which have lost their former justification, such as certain ministries or state agencies, adapt new purposes and continue to exist. Even oddities like the electoral college in the USA or an "executive second chamber" in Germany from Bismarck to Adenauer have not been changed in spite of numerous reform initiatives. Even the occupation forces in Germany after 1945 failed in trying to impose on West Germany different systems of a federal chamber, different forms of industrial relations, or a unified social security system. The cold war soon promoted other priorities than the overhauling of traditional institutions.

Organizational theory has developed many strategies for the reform of political institutions. They were more successful in the revived "new institutional economics" in the context of enterprises and industrial relations (Richter 1994, 3). The "new institutionalism" in political science, however, has to live with the fact of the persistence of many forms of organizational routines and structures. Most institutional reform proved to be ad hoc activity (March and Olsen 1989, 69ff).

There is a permanent division in political science between the "hard" type of analysis aiming at universal laws—as in behavioralism and rational choice—and the "soft" historically oriented analysis of political events and lines of cultural development. The hope remains that both camps engage in a fruitful exchange (Rothstein 1996, 156). The *new institutionalism* was a major step in the direction of this synthesis. March and Olsen (1984, 747) hoped for a "gentle confrontation between the wise and the smart" which characterizes innovations in intellectual history. Many movements and theories have called themselves "new." As in other fields—such as art—they quickly ended in "post-"movements. In the best case this lead to a development "from post- to neo." Is neoinstitutionalism really new? (a) It differs from the older institutionalism in the attempt to work theory-oriented. (b) It contains the achievements of former revolts—such as the behavioral and rational choice revolts—to differentiate between dependent and independent variables, though some authors blur this difference and treat their institutions simultaneously as dependent and independent (Pedersen 1991, 131f). Neoinstitutional approaches observe actual behavior instead of legal and formal aspects of political behavior which prevailed in older theories. (c) The main virtue is that concepts have been developed which make new institutionalism more comparative than the older juxtapositions of regimes in early institutionalism (Peters 1996, 206).

Comparative studies on institutions in Europe developed between European traditions and American innovations. The first foreign influences on my own thinking took place in France in the late 1950s. As a student in France, Duverger and Aron exercised considerable influence. My book on *Political Parties in Western Democracies* (1985) has sometimes been dubbed as an "updated version" of Duverger's study. This perception hardly did justice to my own intentions: comparative studies of institutions according to my interests had to get rid of three vices of the older institutionalism in France: (a) The preoccupation with a unilinear causality between electoral laws and parties in the school of André Siegfried and Duverger; (b) The benign neglect for foreign languages besides

French and the lacking interest in "Smaller European Democracies." The project under this title, developed by Stein Rokkan and Hans Daalder, was seminal for my own studies on parliaments, parties, interest groups, and trade unions; (c) The study of institutions without reference to policy outcomes.

My own academic socialization in political science was affected by American theoretical developments in two waves. As a "true disciple" of an old institutionalist, Carl J. Friedrich, I carefully followed the lectures at Harvard University of Friedrich, V. O. Key, W. Y. Elliott, and McCloskey. The new developments, however, took place in the sociology department. Two German students in 1961–2 went to the courses of Talcott Parsons: Niklas Luhmann and myself. Only the former became a true disciple of Parsons. Institutionalists like myself rather felt a subversive joy of pilgrimage to MIT in order to study with Lasswell (teaching as a visiting professor) and Karl W. Deutsch. The second personal involvement took place when I was a visiting professor at Stanford University and underwent the influences of my colleagues, Gabriel Almond, Seymour Martin Lipset, and Heinz Eulau. My work was shaped by a moderate deviation from "paleo-institutionalism" in a turn to sociological views in the tradition of Karl Deutsch and Martin Lipset.

In Germany "the state" was no longer a subject for political scientists like Dolf Sternberger and Carl J. Friedrich who ran the Heidelberg Institute. The state after Nazi rule was considered as the incarnation of misled nationalism. Institutions were kept free from "identity politics" which only in the age of postmodernity became a new concern of political science. Identity building was promoted in a rational way, via "constitutional patriotism" in German theories from Sternberger to Habermas. "The state" of the older German "Staatslehre" was no longer a concern. The problem with state institutions was rather an almost silly anglophile bias in studies of parliamentary systems and electoral laws, initiated by F. A. Hermens, D. Sternberger, and others. Institutional theory was frequently dependent on political reforms. There was a period when the "Grand Coalition" in Germany (1966–9)—with advice from many political scientists and jurists—seriously planned to introduce the British relative majority electoral law, in the hope that only a two-party system would survive. But even early political culture studies had a certain bias in favor of the "Anglo-Saxon" model. With Almond's neglect of the consociational democracies which he lumped into one category of hybrids between the British and the "continental" model, consisting of the Benelux countries and Scandinavia, the younger generation had to take issue. Arend Lijphart and Gerhard Lehmbruch—with whom I worked in an institute at Tübingen—have enlightened me more than the traditional state-orientation of the "nestor" of German political science, Theodor Eschenburg, then my colleague at Tübingen (cf. Daalder 1997, 227ff). The younger generation on the continent discovered the traditions of "consociationalism," which diverges from British winner-takes-all concepts.

My own work differed increasingly from Carl Friedrich's in two respects. The impact of American political sociology directed my interest to elites, interest groups, and trade unions (1980) which were undeveloped in European comparative studies. In studies on Communism, Carl Friedrich emphasized totalitarianism with a static bias. The neglect of interest groups was also detrimental to studies on Eastern Europe. No internal conflict and development was possible. Even Friedrich's co-author, Z. Brzezinski, was no longer able to follow Friedrich and did not participate in the second revised edition of *Totalitarian Dictatorship and Autocracy* (1965). I came into a conflict of loyalty with my teacher because I was not willing to substitute for Brzezinski. Since my studies in Moscow (1959–60) I was more able than the older generation of Sovietologists and theoreticians of totalitarianism to discover modest steps towards liberalization and the erosion of dictatorship. Moreover, in comparative studies in both East and West, I was not interested in institutions per se, but in combination with their impact on policies (1982). In that respect I was a "neoinstitutionalist" before the label has been invented.

The most interesting institution for older institutionalists, like Friedrich, was federalism. Especially when they worked on the institutions of the budding European Community they started from the normative assumption that federalism was "progressive" per se. Doubts from the rational choice school in the work of William Riker (1964) who calculated the costs of federalism by reluctant veto groups in the decision-making process and especially in the implementation of decisions at the national level, were widely ignored in Europe. In recent studies on federalism I turned rather to comparisons of federalist and decentralized unitary states. Only in the 1990s did scholars from smaller European countries, like Switzerland, Sweden, or the Netherlands (D. Braun, H. Keman), discover that decentralized non-federal states in many respects had better performances than federalist systems. The institutional economy studies discovered in addition that the American model of a "competitive federalism"—instead of a "federalism of joint decision-making"—does not prosper in federations with many small units and that corruption spoils the decision-making process of federal institutions.

The new wave of institutional studies in economics proved to be fertile in political science, enlarging the range of institutions to many quasi-governmental institutions from the national banks to units which administer unemployment or protection of environment. Comparative politics as a study of institutions will certainly continue to develop in the direction of policy studies and include a greater number of actors and veto groups than recognized in the older schools of institutionalism, still largely thinking in terms of a global "checks-and-balances" theory. Neoinstitutionalism will never develop back into the old institutionalism. Even specialists of institutions who are inclined to accept the organization they have chosen as an independent variable, can no longer prevent that non-institutionalist approaches accept institutions only as one dependent variable among others. Even a blatant nostalgia for the older institutionalism can lead only to half a comparative analysis when it excludes the other half of the individual behavior of actors. Neoinstitutionalism cannot substitute for the behavioral and the rational choice revolts, but can only correct their theoretical and methodological exaggerations.

REFERENCES

ALLARDT, E. 1969. Political science and sociology. *Scandinavian Political Studie*, 4: 11–21.

ALMOND, G. and VERBA, S. 1963. *The Civic Culture*. Princeton, NJ: Princeton University Press.

BARKER, E. 1961. *Principles of Social and Political Theory*. Oxford: Oxford University Press.

VON BEYME, K. 1980. *Challenge to Power: Trade Unions and Industrial Relations in Capitalist Countries*. London: Sage.

—— 1982. *Economics and Politics within Socialist Systems: A Comparative and Developmental Approach*. New York: Praeger.

—— 1985. *Political Parties in Western Democracies*. New York: St Martin's Press.

—— 1987. *America as a Model: The Impact of American Democracy in the World*. New York: St. Martin's Press.

—— 1996. *Transition to Democracy in Eastern Europe*. New York: St. Martin's Press.

—— 2000. *Parliamentary Democracy: Democratization, Destabilization, Reconsolidation, 1789–1999*. Houndmills: Macmillan.

BICCHIERI, C. 1993. *Rationality and Coordination*. Cambridge: Cambridge University Press.

BRYCE, J. 1888/1959. *The American Commonwealth*, 2 vols. New York: Putnam.

CROZIER, M. 1970. *La société bloquée*. Paris: Seuil.

DAALDER, H. (ed.) 1997. *Comparative European Politics: The Story of a Profession*. London: Pinter.

DAHL, R. 1969. The behavioral approach in political science. Epitaph for a monument to a successful protest. Pp. 118–36 in *Contemporary Political Thought*, ed. J. A. Gould and V. Thursby. New York: Holt, Rinehart and Winston.

DOGAN, M. and PAHRE, R. 1990. *Creative Marginality: Innovations at the Intersections of Social Sciences*. Boulder, Colo.: Westview.

EASTON, D. 1981. The political system besieged by the state. *Political Theory*, 9: 303–25.

EISENSTADT, S. N. 1965. *Essays on Comparative Institutions*. New York: Wiley.

ESPING-ANDERSEN, G. 1990. *Three Worlds of Welfare Capitalism*. Oxford: Polity Press.

EULAU, H. 1969. *Micro–Macro Political Analysis*. Chicago: Aldine.

GÖHLER, G. (ed.) 1987. *Grundfragen der Theorie politischer Institutionen*. Opladen: Westdeutscher Verlag.

HAURIOU, M. 1906. *L'institution et le droit statuaire*. Paris: Sirey.

HUNTINGTON, S. P. 1981. *American Politics: The Promise of Disharmony*. Cambridge, Mass.: Belknap.

KELSEN, H. 1922. *Die Verfassungsgesetze der Republik Österreich, Part V*. Vienna: Deuticke.

LASSWELL, H. and KAPLAN, A. 1950. *Power and Society: A Framework for Political Inquiry*. New Haven, Conn.: Yale University Press.

MARCH, J. G. and OLSEN, J. P. 1984. The new institutionalism: organizational factors in political life. *American Political Science Review*, 78 (2): 734–49.

———— ———— 1989. *Rediscovering Institutions: The Organizational Basis of Politics.* New York: Free Press.

OSTROM, E. 1995. New horizons in institutional analysis. *American Political Science Review,* 89: 174–8.

PARSONS, T. 1954. *Essays in Sociological Theory.* Glencoe, Ill.: Free Press.

PEDERSEN, O. K. 1991. Nine questions to a neo-institutional theory in political science. *Scandinavian Political Studies,* 14: 125–48.

PETERS, B. G. 1996. Political institutions, old and new. Pp. 205–20 in *A New Handbook of Political Science,* ed. R. E. Goodin and H.-D. Klingemann. Oxford: Oxford University Press.

RICHTER, R. 1994. *Institutionen ökonomisch analysiert.* Tübingen: Mohr.

RIKER, W. H. 1964. *Federalism: Origin, Operation, Significance.* Boston: Little, Brown

ROTHSTEIN, B. 1996. Political institutions: an overview. Pp. 133–66 in *A New Handbook of Political Science,* ed. R. E. Goodin and H.-D. Klingemann. Oxford: Oxford University Press.

SARTORI, G. 1994. *Comparative Constitutional Engineering.* Basingstoke: Macmillian.

SCHELSKY, H. 1973. *Systemüberwindung, Demokratisierung, Gewaltenteilung.* München: Beck.

SHEPSLE, K. A. 1989. Studying institutions: some lessons from a rational choice approach. *Journal of Theoretical Politics,* 1: 131–47.

STEINMO, S. and LONGSTRETH, F. (eds.) 1992. *Structuring Politics: Historical Institutionalism in a Comparative Perspective.* Cambridge: Cambridge University Press.

STREECK, W. 1992. *Social Institutions and Economic Performance.* Beverly Hills, Calif.: Sage.

TSEBELIS, G. 2002. *Veto Players: How Political Institutions Work.* Princeton, NJ: Princeton University Press.

WAHLKE, J. C. 1979. Pre-behavioralism in political science. *American Political Science Review,* 73: 9–31.

NAME INDEX

Subject Index